T0190167

Lecture Notes in Computer Science   13787

More information about this series at https://link.springer.com/bookseries/558

Xingliang Yuan · Guangdong Bai ·
Cristina Alcaraz · Suryadipta Majumdar (Eds.)

Network and System Security

16th International Conference, NSS 2022
Denarau Island, Fiji, December 9–12, 2022
Proceedings

 Springer

Editors
Xingliang Yuan (iD)
Monash University
Clayton, VIC, Australia

Guangdong Bai
The University of Queensland
Queensland, QLD, Australia

Cristina Alcaraz
University of Malaga
Málaga, Spain

Suryadipta Majumdar (iD)
Concordia University
Montreal, QC, Canada

ISSN 0302-9743   ISSN 1611-3349 (electronic)
Lecture Notes in Computer Science
ISBN 978-3-031-23019-6   ISBN 978-3-031-23020-2 (eBook)
https://doi.org/10.1007/978-3-031-23020-2

This Springer imprint is published by the registered company Springer Nature Switzerland AG
The registered company address is: Gewerbestrasse 11, 6330 Cham, Switzerland

Preface

This volume contains the papers selected for and presented at the 16th International Conference on Network and System Security (NSS 2022) held in Denarau Island, Fiji, during December 9–12, 2022.

The mission of NSS is to provide a forum for presenting novel contributions related to all theoretical and practical aspects related to network and system security, such as authentication, access control, availability, integrity, privacy, confidentiality, dependability, and sustainability of computer networks and systems. NSS provides a leading-edge forum to foster interaction between researchers and developers within the network and system security communities, and gives attendees an opportunity to interact with experts in academia, industry, and government.

There were 83 submissions for NSS 2022. Each submission was reviewed by at least 3, and on average 3.1, Program Committee members. The evaluation process was based on significance, novelty, and technical quality of the submissions. After a rigorous double-blind review process and thorough discussion of each submission, the Program Committee selected 23 full papers and 18 short papers to be presented during NSS 2022 and published in the LNCS volume 13787 proceedings. The submission and review processes were conducted using the EasyChair system.

The selected papers are devoted to topics such as secure operating system architectures, applications programming and security testing, intrusion and attack detection, cybersecurity intelligence, access control, cryptographic techniques, cryptocurrencies, ransomware, anonymity, trust, and recommendation systems, as well machine learning problems.

In addition to the contributed papers, NSS 2022 included invited keynote talks by Robert Deng, Willy Susilo, Joseph Liu, Cong Wang, Raymond Choo, and Surya Nepal.

We would like to thank our general and local co-chairs Shawkat Ali and Kim-Kwang Raymond Choo; our publication chair Shangqi Lai; our publicity co-chairs Weizhi Meng, Guanquan Xu, and Ruitao Feng; our special issues co-chairs Yanjun Zhang, Chao Chen, and Wei Zhou; the local organization team; and all the Program Committee members for their support to this conference.

Finally, we also thank The University of Fiji, for their full support in organizing NSS 2022.

October 2022

Xingliang Yuan
Guangdong Bai
Cristina Alcaraz
Suryadipta Majumdar

Organization

General and Local Co-chairs

Shawkat Ali · The University of Fiji, Fiji
Kim-Kwang Raymond Choo · University of Texas at San Antonio, USA

Program Co-chairs

Cristina Alcaraz · University of Malaga, Spain
Guangdong Bai · The University of Queensland, Australia
Suryadipta Majumdar · Concordia University, Canada
Xingliang Yuan · Monash University, Australia

Publication Chair

Shangqi Lai · Monash University, Australia

Publicity Co-chairs

Weizhi Meng · Technical University of Denmark, Denmark
Guanquan Xu · Tianjin University, China
Ruitao Feng · Nanyang Technological University, Singapore

Special Issues Co-chairs

Yanjun Zhang · The University of Queensland, Australia
Chao Chen · RMIT University, Australia
Wei Zhou · Swinburne University of Technology, Australia

Registration Chair

Kunal Kumar · The University of Fiji, Fiji

Online Conference Infrastructure Co-chairs

Viet Vo · Monash University, Australia
Lei Xu · Nanjing University of Science and Technology, China

Web Chair

Minfeng Qi   Swinburne University of Technology, Australia

Program Committee

Alban Gabillon	Université de la Polynésie Française, France
Arcangelo Castiglione	University of Salerno, Italy
Cheng-Kang Chu	Institute of Infocomm Research, Singapore
Chunhua Su	Osaka University, Japan
Chunpeng Ge	Nanjing University of Aeronautics and Astronautics, China
Derek Wang	CSIRO's Data61, Australia
Ding Wang	Peking University, China
Fatemeh Rezaeibagha	Murdoch University, Australia
Guido Schmitz	Royal Holloway, University of London, UK
Guomin Yang	University of Wollongong, Australia
Haibo Zhang	University of Otago, New Zealand
Haoyu Wang	Huazhong University of Science and Technology, China
Hagen Lauer	Fraunhofer SIT, Germany
Helei Cui	Northwestern Polytechnical University, China
Hongxin Hu	University at Buffalo, SUNY, USA
Hung-Min Sun	National Tsing Hua University, Taiwan
Jianfeng Wang	Xidian University, China
Jiangshan Yu	Monash University, Australia
Jin Hong	University of Western Australia, Australia
Joonsang Baek	University of Wollongong, Australia
Jose Morales	Carnegie Mellon University, USA
Kailong Wang	National University of Singapore, Singapore
Kouichi Sakurai	Kyushu University, Japan
Kun Sun	George Mason University, USA
Kwok Yan Lam	Nanyang Technological University, Singapore
Lei Xue	The Hong Kong Polytechnic University, China
Leo Yu Zhang	Deakin University, Australia
Luca Caviglione	CNR - IMATI, Italy
Maurantonio Caprolu	Hamad Bin Khalifa University, Qatar
Mauro Conti	University of Padua, Italy
Meisam Mohammady	CSIRO's Data61, Australia
Mengyuan Zhang	The Hong Kong Polytechnic University, China
Nora Cuppens-Boulahia	Polytechnique Montréal, Canada
Panayiotis Kotzanikolaou	University of Piraeus, Greece
Paria Shirani	Ryerson University, Canada
Pino Caballero-Gil	University of La Laguna, Spain

Contents

Privacy-Preserving Machine Learning Protocols and Systems

Privacy-Preserving Networked Systems and Protocols

Blockchain Security

Blockchain-Powered Systems

Attacks

Cryptographic Algorithms and Protocols

AI for Network Security

Vulnerability Detection Using Deep Learning Based Function Classification

Huihui Gong[1,2(✉)] ⓘ, Siqi Ma[3] ⓘ, Seyit Camtepe[2] ⓘ, Surya Nepal[2] ⓘ, and Chang Xu[1] ⓘ

[1] The University of Sydney, Sydney, NSW 2008, Australia
hgon9611@uni.sydney.edu.au, c.xu@sydney.edu.au
[2] Data61, CSIRO, Sydney, NSW 1466, Australia
{sayit.camtepe,surya.nepal}@data61.csiro.au
[3] University of New South Wales Canberra, Canberra, ACT 2612, Australia
siqi.ma@adfa.edu.au

Abstract. Software vulnerabilities are becoming increasingly severe problems, which can pose great risks of information leakage, denial of service, or even system crashes. However, their detection is still formidable, due to the diverse forms of software development and the diverse programming styles of software developers. In this paper, we propose a vulnerability detection tool to explore security issues in source code using deep learning-based function classification. Specifically, we first extract and parse function prototypes in the source code. Then, with the help of the pre-built corpus, we split the function prototypes into segmentations with semantic meanings. By utilizing deep learning-based classifiers, the segmentations are further classified into seven categories. Finally, we use static scanning analyzers to separately detect vulnerabilities of different types of functions. Additionally, the experimental results show that the proposed method can effectively and efficiently distinguish vulnerabilities in the benchmark source code (5 of 7 memory corruptions, 13 of 18 cryptography vulnerabilities, 5 of 6 data processing errors, and 13 of 18 random number issues).

Keywords: Vulnerability detection · Deep learning · Text classification · Static analysis

1 Introduction

Software is commonly designed and implemented by following specific principles and rules proposed by security researchers or vendors. In order to assist developers in implementation, standard libraries are supported when implementing certain functionalities and protecting against attacks. Unfortunately, these standard libraries are limited to fit the implementation varieties. To improve its scalability, developers usually customize their own functions or invoke encapsulated APIs supported by third-party libraries. Nonetheless, most developers including the

ⓒ The Author(s), under exclusive license to Springer Nature Switzerland AG 2022
X. Yuan et al. (Eds.): NSS 2022, LNCS 13787, pp. 3–22, 2022.
https://doi.org/10.1007/978-3-031-23020-2_1

third-party vendors are not security experts, the customized functions (functions that are defined by programmers instead of standard libraries) and encapsulated APIs are error-prone and might be vulnerable to attacks [8,37,43,45].

To exploit these vulnerabilities, most existing research works [6,14,21,22,49] rely on abstracted patterns to identify one or two specific types of vulnerabilities. Unfortunately, with thousands of vulnerabilities being reported daily, analysis through pattern abstraction and matching is time-consuming and unscalable, which is unable to reduce the vulnerability propagation. Static analysis is proposed as a promising approach to explore vulnerabilities from source code timely, through which developers can sweep out the signs of vulnerabilities during the design and implementation stages. Therefore, many efforts have been made in this direction, such as pattern-based methods and code similarity-based methods. Pattern-based analyses [6,31,48,49] require relevant experts to define the vulnerability patterns to represent the features of vulnerabilities, which are error-prone and burdensome. Code similarity-based analyses [14,21] can check vulnerabilities that are caused by code cloning. When vulnerabilities are not incurred by code cloning, such methods will have high false-negative rates shown in [22]. Therefore, a feasible and ideal detection method should not only effectively detect various vulnerabilities but also require little manual effort. Deep learning is good at reducing manual work, thus becoming a great candidate to meet the above requirements.

Since its brilliant performance in the ImageNet LSVRC-2010 contest [16], deep learning has attracted more and more attention. Deep learning models, including convolutional neural networks (CNNs), recurrent neural networks (RNNs) and deep belief networks (DBNs), have achieved impressive performance in the task of image classification [9,16,39,54], video scene parsing [17,25,34,51], natural language processing (NLP) [7,32,42] and so on. Thus, it is attractive to use deep learning models to help detect software vulnerabilities. In recent years, some deep learning-based methods have been proposed for detecting software vulnerabilities. Russell et al. [35] used CNNs and random forest classifier to learn the deep representation of source code and detect vulnerabilities with labeled vulnerability datasets. Li et al. [22] presented a deep learning-based vulnerability detection system, dubbed VulDeePecker, to detect vulnerabilities at the slice level. However, these methods need much manual effort to define the representation of the source code. Besides, these methods can only detect one type of vulnerability.

Motivated by the superior performance of deep learning classifiers and the idea of separate detection of different types of vulnerabilities, we propose a new vulnerability detection method using deep learning classifiers in source code, which will only focus on the function prototypes instead of the specific implementation of the functions. Firstly, we process and segment the function prototypes in the target source code, obtaining semantic texts. Then, we use labeled data of the Linux Kernel source code and some functions obtained online to train seven deep classifiers, and these classifiers are fused into an integrated classifier. The integrated classifier is used to classify the semantic texts of the target source code into seven pre-defined categories. At last, we utilize static scanning analyzers to separately detect vulnerabilities or misuses of functions from each category. Instead of analyzing all the source code, our method only scans a few partial codes to detect vulnerabilities. Moreover, our method can detect different kinds of vulnerabilities.

In order to evaluate our method, we used the OpenHarmony OS source code as our target source code. We analyzed all the code to find all the vulnerabilities as benchmarks. And we used our method to analyze functions from four different categories to detect vulnerabilities. Results show that our method detected 5 of 7 memory corruptions, 13 of 18 cryptography vulnerabilities, 5 of 6 data processing errors, and 13 of 18 random number issues with less time cost.

Contributions. The main contributions of this paper are listed as follows.

- We proposed a new deep learning-based function classification method for detecting software vulnerabilities, which only analyzes a small fraction of the source code.
- We established a function prototype classification dataset and used it to train an integrated classifier to effectively classify the function prototypes in the target source code.
- We separately detected vulnerabilities of functions of different categories, which facilitates the detection efficiency. For example, we detected memory corruptions in memory operation functions and detected cryptography vulnerabilities in cryptography functions, respectively.

Organization. The rest of this paper is organized into five sections. In Sect. 2, we present our motivation as well as some challenges of detecting software vulnerabilities in source code and offer corresponding perceptions to settle down these challenges. Section 3 displays the proposed deep learning-based vulnerability detection method. Moreover, experimental results are shown in Sect. 4. Section 5 reviews some related works. Finally, Sect. 6 concludes this paper.

2   Background

In this section, we introduce the security flaws that are analyzed and further discuss the challenges of detecting these security flaws in an efficient way. Referring to each challenge, we propose a solution to address it.

2.1   Vulnerability Categories

Referring to the vulnerabilities introduced on *CWE* [30], we showed several common vulnerabilities, listed below.

- **Vulnerability 1: Use of uninitialized memory or variable.** Some programmers forget to initialize variables and then directly use them in the subsequent operations, which may cause program errors or unexpected running results. An example is shown below. In the definition of Class Foo, programmers forgot initializing the private variable num_value_. Therefore, when someone creates a new object of this class without initializing the variable num_value_, the function cFoo.GetValue() (Line 16) returns a meaningless value, thus the two branches of the if statement may be executed. This will cause unexpected running results.

```
1  class Foo{
2  private:
3      int num_value_ ;
4  public:
5      Foo();
6      int GetValue() { return num_value_ ; }
7  };
8
9  Foo::Foo()
10 {
11 // forget to initialize the variable ''num_value_''
12 }
13
14 int main(){
15     Foo cFoo;
16     if (cFoo.GetValue() > 0){
17     ...  // do something
18     }else{
19     ...  // do something else
20     }
21 }
```

- **Vulnerability 2: Comparison of incompatible types.** This vulnerability often occurs when one compares two different types of data, e.g., string and int. The example below displays this vulnerability. The extracted number num_in_str from the string s still has the data type of *String*. Thus, when comparing it with the *int* type constant in Line 7, the error of comparison of incompatible types occurs.

```
1  #define SOME_CONSTANT 1024
2
3  int main(){
4      string num_in_str, s = "textContent_1024";
5      num_in_str = s.substr(s.length()-4,s.length()-1);
6      ...
7      if (SOME_CONSTANT==num_in_str){
8          ...
9      }
10     ...
11 }
```

- **Vulnerability 3: Use of a predictable random mode to generate random numbers.** Similar to Vulnerability 8, this vulnerability may the random function to return a predictable sequence of numbers. The codes below show such vulnerability. Even though one feeds different seeds into the customized random function, an attacker can "guess" the returned random sequences due to the constant random mode in Lines 8–9.

```
1  static uint64_t seed;
2
3  void srand(unsigned s){
4      seed = s-1;
5  }
6
7  int rand(void){
8      seed = 6364136223846793005ULL*seed + 1;
9      return seed>>33;
10 }
```

– **Vulnerability 4: Use of not secure encryption algorithms to encrypt.**
Using some not secure encryption algorithms to encrypt gives experimented attackers a chance to crack these algorithms. The following example displays this vulnerability. *DES* encryption algorithm (`EVP_des_cbc` in Line 3) only supports a 56–bit keysize, which is too small for given today's computers. Thus, it is recommended to use a different patent-free encryption algorithm with a larger keysize, such as *3DES* or *AES*.

```
1      ...
2      case CRYPTO_CIPHER_ALG_DES:
3          cipher = EVP_des_cbc();
4          break;
5      ...
```

2.2 Challenges

Unlike the standard functions, it is difficult to identify vulnerabilities through simple program analysis because customized functions are named and implemented variously. Due to the implementation weaknesses, it is essential to recognize the customized functions and analyze whether these functions are correctly implemented. In order to recognize the customized functions, the following challenges need to be addressed.

Challenge I: Diverse Naming. To identify a kind of function, it is the common approach to search for concrete keywords. For instance, we may locate the keyword `random` to find out random number functions. Nevertheless, different programmers may use diverse abbreviations and irregular words to name function prototypes, it is formidable to effectively extract the semantic information of function prototypes with the keyword searching approach. Take the function name `gen_rand_uuid` as an example, the abbreviation `gen_rand_uuid` means "generate random universally unique identifier". With the keyword searching approach, it is difficult to understand the semantic meaning of `gen_rand_uuid`.

Challenge II: Equivocal Name Expressions. It might not be able to understand the semantic meaning of a function by only analyzing the meaning of every single word. For some function names, they might indicate different functionalities even though the same words are adopted. For example, `bdi_init` and `bdi_debug_init` are two functions in the dataset. The first function is to initialize the bdi (backing device info), while the other is to debug the bdi initializer. Although the two functions both contain the word *init*, their semantic meanings of them are entirely different. In the function `bdi_init`, *init* denotes the operation of initialization, while in the function `bdi_debug_init`, *init* represents the state of initialization. Therefore, apart from extracting the semantic meanings of function prototypes, we also need to analyze the format of the function prototypes.

Challenge III: Complex Vulnerability Types. The complexity of the different types of vulnerabilities makes it more challenging to detect vulnerabilities effectively. For example, memory corruptions are mainly about memory operations; while data processing errors are related to parameter handling, data compression/decompression, and data comparison. Most existing vulnerability detection methods [37,38,43,50] only aim at one type of vulnerability. Thus, it is contributive to develop a method to detect different types of vulnerabilities.

2.3 Perceptions

Referring to the challenges introduced in Sect. 2.2, we propose several perceptions to address them.

Perception I: Comprehensive Lexical Segmentation. The most common approach for word segmentation is to use a natural language corpus. However, a such corpus is insufficient and error-prone for word segmentation in a computer programming language, because programmers would like to use "programming language" in their programs for simplifying natural language. Thus, we consider both natural language corpus and programming language corpus to solve the problem in **Challenge I**. The comprehensive corpus includes common natural language in programming (e.g., generate, random) and programming words (e.g., gen, rand).

Perception II: Deep Representation Learning. Although function prototypes are named variously, they generally follow certain patterns. For example, although programmers do not follow natural language grammar when naming a function, they are likely to use synonyms (e.g., free, release, deallocate) to represent the same semantics. It is inefficient and imprecise to summarize such patterns manually, deep learning is good at dealing with massive patterns. Thus, we train a deep learning model to learn features and patterns of function prototypes to settle down **Challenge II**. For example, if we "tell" deep models that `bdi_malloc` is to allocate memory for the bdi, `bdi_debug_malloc` is to debug the stat of the bdi allocator; `bdi_deinit` is to deinitialize the bdi, `bdi_debug_deinit` is to debug the stat of the bdi deinitializer; then, the deep

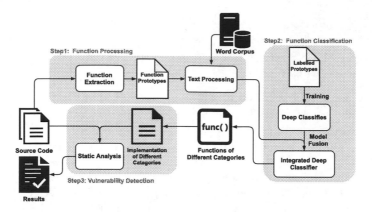

Fig. 1. Overview of our proposed method.

models can learn that `bdi_init` is to initialize the bdi, `bdi_debug_init` is to debug the bdi initializer. Given massive data, deep models can resolve the problem of **Challenge II** well.

Perception III: Separate Detection of Different Vulnerabilities. In order to detect vulnerabilities precisely, we first recognize the function types by using the trained classification model. Knowing the function types, we separately detect the relevant vulnerabilities of each category to address **Challenge III**.

3   Method

We propose a semantic-based analyzer, FUNDL, to infer the functionalities through the function prototypes and further analyze whether the corresponding implementations are secure. The overview of FUNDL is demonstrated in Fig. 1, which includes three components, *Function Processing*, *Function Classification*, and *Vulnerability Detection*.

3.1   Function Processing

To learn the semantic meaning of each function, FUNDL analyzes the function prototype instead of analyzing the entire code snippet of the function. FUNDL first conducts *function extraction* to extract function prototypes from source code and deletes the invalid information that might affect the semantic study. It further adopts *text processing* to obtain semantic texts.

Function Extraction. To extract functions from the target source code, we build FUNDL on top of *Clang Static Analyzer* [1], which offers a finding declarations plugin [41,53] to identify function prototypes. FUNDL stores the extracted function prototypes in the dictionary format, e.g., {"fuction":"main"}.

Text Processing. By taking function prototypes as inputs, FUNDL regards the function prototypes as text and proceeds a classifier of deep text classification to identify the semantic meaning of each function. However, function prototypes are generally different from natural language texts, which impairs the performance of the deep text classifiers to some extent. Therefore, we preprocess function prototypes in two steps:

- **Step 1. Invalid information removal.** FUNDL removes the invalid information that is useless while training the classifier such as the namespace and special symbols (e.g., '~' and '_').
- **Step 2. Text Segmentation.** FUNDL further segments the string referring to the word weight-based segmentation algorithm [11,36]. To construct a word corpus that is suitable for segmenting programming language, we include the natural language corpus, Google Web Trillion Word corpus [5], and the programming corpus, Windows API sets [29] as well as Microsoft API reference library [27] (**Perception I**). The natural language corpus is adopted to understand the semantic meanings of the commonly used words. FUNDL relies on the programming corpus to identify the abbreviations and informal words.

  For an n-letter prototype, there are 2^{n-1} possible segmentation. FUNDL computes the frequency of each segmentation by comparing it with the integrated corpus:

$$F_{\text{seg}} = \prod_{i=1}^{|W|} f(w_i), \tag{1}$$

  where F_{seg} is the frequency of each segmentation; $|W|$ is the number of words in the segmentation; $f(w_i)$ is the frequency of each word w_i appeared in the integrated corpus. We finally segment the function prototypes in the form with the highest frequency F_{seg}.

  Consider an example in Fig. 2, FUNDL first extracts the function prototype `uint32_t TypedText::GetUTF8CharacterSi- ze(...)` and stores the prototype as a dictionary. Then, FUNDL removes the invalid information of the prototype and gets a text string `GetUTF8CharacterSize` that needs to be segmented. Finally FUNDL segments the text string and calculates the frequency of each segmentation, such as `G etUTF8Charactersize`, `Ge tUTF8CharacterSize`, etc. In total, 2^{19} segmentation could be applied to the function name. By calculating the frequency, the segmentation result `Get UTF8 Character Size` has the highest frequency value, and it would become the segmentation output.

As there are a large number of functions in each program, we refer to the weakness ranking and select the five types of functions that commonly caused weaknesses:

1. **Memory operation functions (*Mem*).** The standard and customized functions that conduct memory operations are defined as memory operation functions.
2. **Cryptography functions (*Crypto*).** We define the encryption/decryption functions and the integrated cryptographic algorithm functions (e.g., `md5`, `sha256`, `ripemd128`) as cryptography function category.

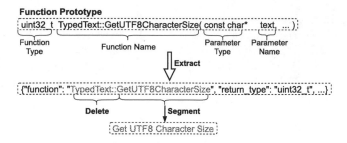

Fig. 2. A example of function prototype and its processing.

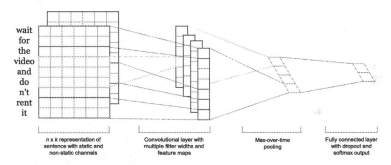

Fig. 3. Architecture of the text classifier for a text example.

3. **Data processing functions (*DataProc*).** Functions that handle values, parameters, elements, regular expressions, data compression/decompression and data comparison are defined as data processing function.
4. **Random number generation functions (*Random*).** The standard and customized functions, whose goal is generating PRNs, are defined as random number generation functions.
5. **Plain functions (*Plain*).** All the other functions are considered plain functions, including authentication functions (process authentication requests or response authentication requests), file handling functions (handle temporary files, input/output files, and cope with the file paths), and other functions.

3.2   Function Classification

After segmenting the function names, FUNDL refers to the semantic meaning of each word in the segmentation to classify the functions into different categories. Since different deep learning models have different expressive abilities while processing data, FUNDL combines the advantages of different classifiers to obtain an integrated classifier with the benefits of all these classifiers. In this work, we focus on seven deep text classifiers with the training set and fuse these classifiers into an integrated classifier for better classification performance.

Deep Classifiers. FUNDL consists of the following seven deep text classifiers: *TextCNN* [15], *TextRCNN* [19], *TextRNN* [24], *TextRNN* with Attention (*TextRNN_Att*) [55], *FastText* [13], *DPCNN* [12], *Transformer* [42].

TextCNN applies the convolutional neural networks to the task of text classification and utilizes many kernels of different sizes to extract the key information from the input sentences. Three parts are included:

- **Word embedding:** Because deep learning models are good at handling vectors but not good at handling texts, texts should be converted to vectors (embeddings). Specifically, FUNDL randomly maps the training texts to vectors as initialization and updates the vectors throughout the training process.
- **Representation learning:** Multiple kernels with different sizes are used to extract the features of the embedded vectors in the convolutional layers. Besides, key features are selected in the max-polling layer.
- **Classifcation:** The selected feature inputs to the fully connected layer and softmax layer, outputting the probability of each category.

The summary of the classifier architecture is shown in Fig. 3 (extracted from [15]). Generally, the other six classifiers are similar to *TextCNN*: converting texts to vectors, using different deep learning architectures (e.g. convolutional neural networks and recurrent neural networks) to learn features and classify them, so the details of the other six classifiers are omitted. Interested readers can refer to the listed references [12, 13, 19, 24, 42, 55].

Training Deep Classifiers and Model Fusion. Given the classifier, we provide labelled function segmentation to train the deep text classifiers separately. To achieve a better classification performance, the trained classifiers are fused into an integrated classifier. Referring to model fusion strategies, FUNDL adopts hard voting [33]. While predicting the category of an input segmentation, FUNDL gets seven outputs from the seven classifiers and calculates the classification results. The input will be determined to belong to a specific category if most classifiers vote the input to be a member of that category. For example, if the input is labelled as Category *Mem* by four classifiers and is labelled as the other categories by the other classifier, FUNDL will regard the input as belonging to Category *Mem*. Note that when two or more categories have the same vote, FUNDL randomly assigns a category to the input.

3.3   Vulnerability Detection

After identifying the category of each function, FUNDL further conducts scanning analyzers to detect vulnerabilities for functions that are classified into different categories, respectively.

For functions of Category *Mem*, we use static scanning analyzers to detect memory corruptions, like null pointer dereference, buffer overflow and memory leak. For functions of Category *Crypto*, we mainly detect the CWE–327 vulnerability (use of a broken or risky cryptographic algorithm), which is an unnecessary risk that may result in the exposure of sensitive information. For functions of Category **DataProc**, we mainly detect the CWE–19 vulnerability (data processing errors) and some specific data processing vulnerabilities, such as improper handling of elements, case sensitivity, values, parameters, data types and so on. For functions of Category **Random**, we focus on the CWE–1213 vulnerability (random number issues) and some specific random number vulnerabilities, like small space of random values and use of a predictable algorithm in random number generator.

4   Experiments and Results

We evaluate the effectiveness and efficiency of FUNDL in recognizing semantic meanings of functions by answering two research questions:

- **RQ1: Function Classification.** How effective is FUNDL to classify the function prototypes?
- **RQ2: Vulnerability Detection.** How effective is FUNDL to improve the performance of the existing vulnerability detectors?
- **RQ3: Runtime Cost.** How efficient is FUNDL to improve the runtime cost of vulnerability detection?

4.1   Experiment Setup

Datasets. To train the deep learning classifiers, we chose the Linux Kernel source code (LKSC) [3] as our training set, which contains 33,745 functions. As LKSC includes various types of functions, it is fit to train the deep classifiers. However, the number of functions in some categories, e.g., Categories **Crypto** and **Random**, are insufficient. In order to ensure the performance of the integrated classifier, we further expanded the training set. Specifically, we inserted 763 C/C++ functions of these categories collected from GitHub [28] and Stack Overflow [2]. Eventually, a training set of 34,508 data was involved, named as *LKSC+*. To test the performance of FUNDL, we adopted *OpenHarmony* OS source code as our test set, which contains 14,268 functions after deleting the meaningless and reduplicative functions.

Because there lack of labeled functions of different categories, we created our benchmarks (cf., Table 1). Specifically, we asked two experienced programmers to independently label the datasets and then checked the results together. If there were some disagreements on some function labels, they would discuss an agreement about these functions. Such a manual effort is a one-time effort. The final results demonstrated in Table 1.

Experiment Setup. In order to train an effective classifier, we divided the training set into two subsets, the training subset, and the development subset. We randomly selected 85% data from the training set to construct a training subset and the rest 15% data to form a development subset. FUNDL leveraged the training subset to train the deep text classifiers and used the development subset to guide the adjusting hyper-parameters of classifiers. The parameter setting was similar to [47]. Considering runtime costs and effectiveness of FUNDL, it finished training the seven deep classifiers when there was no improvement within 1,000 epochs.

Table 1. Number of functions of each category and number of total functions in the two data sets.

	LKSC+	OpenHarmony
Mem	4,866	1,171
Crypto	1,163	710
DataProc	821	1,297
Random	92	97
Plain	27,566	10,993
Total	34,508	14,268

Table 2. $F1$-score of each classifier, the average of the seven classifiers and the integrated classifier for each category, where DP denotes *DataProc*; Rd denotes *Random*.

	Mem	*Crypto*	*DP*	*Rd*	*Plain*
TextCNN	0.8806	0.7772	0.4124	0.9524	0.8467
TextRNN	0.8478	0.7771	0.4122	0.7593	0.8495
FastText	0.7470	0.5986	0.3844	0.8040	0.8532
TextRCNN	0.9315	0.8108	0.4403	0.9189	0.8639
TextRNN_Att	0.8989	0.7918	0.4113	0.8768	0.8395
DPCNN	0.9069	0.7926	0.4338	0.9158	0.8619
Transformer	0.6385	0.4482	0.3291	0.6457	0.7785
Integrated	0.9036	0.7902	0.4388	0.9412	0.8628

4.2   RQ 1: Function Classification

The results of function classification is shown in Table 2. Among the seven classifiers, *TextCNN* achieved the best classification performance of Category **Random**; *TextRCNN* obtained the best classification results of Categories **Mem**, **Crypto**, **DataProc** and **Plain**. By manually inspecting **DataProc** whose $F1$-score is much lower than the other categories, we found that the functions involved for training are quite different from the functions used for testing, which decreases the classification performance in this category. The integrated classifier, performance almost achieved the best performance for every single classifier, which is good for avoiding the shortcomings of a single model.

4.3   RQ2: Vulnerability Detection

To detect vulnerabilities, we used two static analyzers, *TscanCode* [40] for detecting vulnerabilities related to **Mem** and **DataProc**, and *Flawfinder* [46] to detect vulnerabilities related to **Crypto** and **Random**. To set up the benchmarks, we executed each analyzer to detect vulnerabilities in the whole *OpenHarmony* source code. Then, we run analyzers in the found functions of different categories. Besides, we asked the two experienced programmers to help us confirm the detected vulnerabilities. The vulnerability detection and confirmation results are illustrated in Table 3.

By manually checking the results of vulnerability detection, the vulnerability detection accuracy rates of FUNDL of analyzing the four categories are 71.4%, 72.2%, 83.3% and 72.2%, while the corresponding accuracy rates of analyzing the whole source code are 61.5%, 63.0%, 52.9%, 55.6%. Specifically, FUNDL successfully detected 5 out of 7 memory corruption vulnerabilities, 13 out of 18 cryptographic misuses, 5 out of 6 data processing errors, and 13 out of 18 pseudo-random number issues. It indicates that FUNDL effectively improves the performance of the existing vulnerability analyzers.

Table 3. Vulnerability detection results.

	Detected	Confirmed		Detected	Confirmed
Mem	7	5	*Crypto*	18	13
Benchmarks	13	8	Benchmarks	27	17
DataProc	6	5	*Random*	18	13
Benchmarks	17	9	Benchmarks	27	15

By further analyzing the detection results, we observed that some function prototypes in *OpenHarmony* are informal (e.g., `addrmap_set_entry`, `get_frag_time`), FUNDL is unable to recognize these function prototypes into **Mem**. While processing the complicated function prototypes such as `ddr_training_cfg_set_dmc` and `drv_otp_read_product_pv`, FUNDL mistakenly labelled these functions as **Random**. More data can improve semantic feature learning.

4.4   RQ 3: Runtime Cost

We assessed the overall runtime for FUNDL to classify function prototypes. Note that we did not consider the time of classifier training because the training step is only a one-time effort. The results are shown in Table 4, which displays that for every type of vulnerability, the efficiency of FUNDL improves by about 50 percent.

Table 4. Runtime of our method and the benchmarks

	FUNDL	Benchmarks
Mem	1,747 s	2,952 s
Crypto	162 s	365 s
DataProc	1,339 s	2,952 s
Random	238 s	365 s

4.5   Case Study

In this subsection, we discuss four representative vulnerability examples in the OpenHarmony dataset.

A buffer overflow example is shown in Listing 1.1 (in the file *sys_eeprom.c*). The function `do_mac` is declared to allocate memories. It calls the standard library function `memcpy` (Lines 6 and 9), whose standard declaration is `void *memcpy(void *str1, const void *str2, size_t n)` with the purpose of copying n chars in memory block `str2` to memory block `str1`. If the allocated memory size of memory block `e.id` is less than the memory block "NXID" or "CCID", an information leak or buffer overflow will be triggered.

```
1  int do_mac(cmd_tbl_t *cmdtp, int flag, int argc, char *
       const argv[])
2  {
3      ...
4  #ifdef CONFIG_SYS_I2C_EEPROM_NXID
5      memcpy(e.id, "NXID", sizeof(e.id));
6      e.version = cpu_to_be32(NXID_VERSION);
7  #else
8      memcpy(e.id, "CCID", sizeof(e.id));
9  #endif
10     ...
11 }
```

Listing 1.1. A buffer overflow example in OpenHarmony.

One cryptography vulnerability example is presented in Listing 1.2 (in the file *tls_openssl.c*). The function `tls_init` used the encryption function `EVP_rc2_40_cbc` (Line 8) to generate cipher. However, the key size of the generated cipher is only 40-bit, which is too small for today's computers. It is easy for hackers to "guess" (crack) the cipher and encryption algorithms with a larger key size are recommended.

```
 1  void * tls_init(const struct tls_config *conf)
 2  {
 3      struct tls_data *data;
 4      SSL_CTX *ssl;
 5      struct tls_context *context;
 6      const char *ciphers;
 7      ...
 8      EVP_add_cipher(EVP_rc2_40_cbc());
 9      ...
10  }
```

Listing 1.2. A cryptographic vulnerability example that uses a risky cryptographic algorithm in OpenHarmony.

Due to space limit, more cases are shown in Appendix A.

4.6 Limitations

The proposed method can effectively and efficiently detect some software vulnerabilities. Nevertheless, it has several limitations.

1. Our method cannot cope with the function prototypes that have no semantic information. For example, if a memory operation function is named as abcd, our method will classify it into Category **Plain** and will not detect whether it has memory corruptions, thus causing detection failure.
2. The training set can be further expanded to train a better integrated classifier.
3. Our experiments only use static analyzers to detect vulnerabilities. Future work should investigate the effectiveness of other useful analyzers.
4. We concentrate on detecting vulnerabilities in C/C++ program source code, which means that the method may need to be adapted to deal with code written in other programming languages.

5   Related Work

There are many prior studies that analyze or scan source code to identify vulnerabilities. Here, we introduce four kinds of them that relate to our work: 1) data-flow based analyzers [4,18,26]; 2) pointer information based analyzers [38,50]; 3) code similarity based analyzers [14,21]; 4) deep learning based analyzers [10,20,22,23,35,44,52,56].

Data Flow-Based Analyzers. Some tools detect vulnerabilities by comparing data flows with some pre-defined rules or violations. The C bounded model checker of CBMC [18] checks the safety of the assertions under a given bound. It translates assertions and loops into formulas. If the formulas meet any pre-defined violations, then a violated assertion will be recognized. Besides, data flow-based analyzers are also utilized in the Linux Kernel: Dr. Checker [26] and K-Miner [4], which are developed to analyze a large amount of code in Linux Kernel more effectively and more efficiently. Dr. Checker leverages a soundy method with program analysis, which is capable of performing large-scale analysis and detecting numerous categories of bugs in Linux Kernel drivers. K-Miner sets up a virtual kernel environment and processing syscalls separately for vulnerability discovery.

Pointer Information-Based Analyzers. Similar to data flow-based analyzers, some scanners utilize pointer information to detect bugs in source code. CRED [50] detects use-after-free vulnerabilities in source code of C programs, which uses a path-sensitive demand-driven method to extract pointer information. Besides, to decrease false-positive, it applies the spatio-temporal context reduction technique to establish use-after-free pairs precisely. However, the obvious weakness of CRED is time-consuming, because every path in the source code is required to be analyzed and memorized. Without analyzing the whole source code, Pinpoint [38] proposes sparse value-flow analysis to distinguish vulnerabilities in C programs, such as double-free and use-after-free. Specifically, Pinpoint first analyzes local data dependence and then performs symbolic execution to memorize the non-local data dependency and path conditions, which reduces the cost of data dependency analysis.

Code Similarity-Based Analyzers. Other methods just analyze part of the source code instead of the entire program. These methods detect vulnerabilities based on the code similarity [14,21]. VulPecker [21] develops a vulnerability dataset via diff hunk features collected from each vulnerable code and its corresponding patch code. VUDDY [14] regards every vulnerable function as a unit, and then abstracts and normalizes these functions to achieve the goal that they are able to detect cloned code even with modifications. However, code similarity-based approaches need plenty of data and when vulnerabilities are not caused by code cloning, such methods will have high false-negative rates.

Deep Learning-Based Analyzers. With the wide application of deep learning in various fields, cybersecurity researchers have tried to use deep learning models to detect vulnerabilities in source code. Three popular deep learning architectures are convolutional neural networks (CNNs), recurrent neural networks (RNNs), and Deep Belief Networks (DBNs). All these three models have been used for software vulnerability detection: [10,20,35] use CNNs for vulnerability detection; [22,23,56] utilize RNNs for vulnerability detection; [44,52] apply DBNs for vulnerability detection. Different from these methods, we used deep learning models to classify function prototypes in source code and use static scanning tools to detect vulnerabilities. Our method takes less time because we only need to learn the features of function prototypes instead of function implementation or code slices. However, deep learning-based vulnerability detection is a promising research direction that is far from mature. There are many other deep learning technologies that can be used to improve the effectiveness and efficiency in the field of vulnerability detection.

6   Conclusion and Future Work

In this paper, we proposed a vulnerability detection approach that leverages a deep learning-based function classification. Based on the dataset of function prototypes that we collected and labeled, we learned an integrated classifier that can predict the category of a given function prototype. Then, we used static analysis tools to detect vulnerabilities of different categories. The novelty of our proposed method is that we search the function semantics with a little information, i.e., function prototypes. Besides, we borrow the idea of model fusion to obtain an integrated classifier that classifies functions with better performance. Instead of scanning all the source code, our method only scans a small partial code to detect vulnerabilities more effectively and more efficiently. In the future, with more available labeled data, we plan to extend our method to detect more types of vulnerabilities and further adapt it to other programming languages.

Acknowledgement. This work was supported in part by the Australian Research Council under Project DP210101859 and the University of Sydney Research Accelerator (SOAR) Prize.

Appendices

A   Additional Vulnerability Cases

An example with a data processing error is shown in Listing 1.3 (in the file *ddr_training_impl.c*). In the **if** condition of Line 5, if the type of PHY_DRAMCFG_TYPE_LPDDR4 is different from that of cfg->phy[0].dram_type, the CWE–1024 vulnerability (comparison of incompatible types, e.g., comparison of **string** data and **int** data) will be incurred. Furthermore, if the **struct** cfg is NULL, the codes within the **if** condition will not be executed, which may cause other unexpected vulnerabilities.

```
1  void ddr_training_cfg_set_dmc(struct ddr_cfg_st *cfg)
2  {
3      unsigned int ddrt_pattern;
4      if (PHY_DRAMCFG_TYPE_LPDDR4 == cfg->phy[0].dram_type) {
5          ...
6      }
7      ...
8  }
```

Listing 1.3. A data processing error example in OpenHarmony.

For random number issues, Listing 1.4 (in the file *rand.c*) presents an example with the CWE–1241 vulnerability, which is about using a predictable algorithm in random number generation. The random number function rand (Lines 12–15) calls the function rand_r (Lines 3–10), which uses a constant value 1U (Line 1) as the random number seed and an invariable algorithm (Lines 5–7) to generate random numbers, which is predictable/non-random and vulnerable.

```
 1  static unsigned int y = 1U;
 2  unsigned int rand_r(unsigned int *seedp)
 3  {
 4    *seedp ^= (*seedp << 13);
 5    *seedp ^= (*seedp >> 17);
 6    *seedp ^= (*seedp << 5);
 7    return *seedp;
 8  }
 9  unsigned int rand(void)
10  {
11    return rand_r(&y);
12  }
```

Listing 1.4. A random number issue example in OpenHarmony.

References

1. Apple: Clang Static Analyzer. https://clang-analyzer.llvm.org/
2. Atwood, J., Spolsky, J.: Stack overflow. https://stackoverflow.com/
3. Corporation, C.P.B.: The Linux Kernel Archives. https://www.kernel.org/
4. Gens, D., Schmitt, S., Davi, L., Sadeghi, A.R.: K-Miner: Uncovering memory corruption in Linux. In: Network and Distributed System Security Symposium (2018)
5. Google: Google Web Trillion Word Corpus. https://ai.googleblog.com/2006/08/all-our-n-gram-are-belong-to-you.html
6. Grieco, G., Grinblat, G.L., Uzal, L.C., Rawat, S., Feist, J., Mounier, L.: Toward large-scale vulnerability discovery using machine learning. In: ACM Conference on Data and Application Security and Privacy (2016)
7. Gu, Y., et al.: Domain-specific language model pretraining for biomedical natural language processing. arXiv preprint arXiv:2007.15779 (2020)
8. Gu, Z., Wu, J., Li, C., Zhou, M., Gu, M.: SSLDoc: automatically diagnosing incorrect SSL API Usages in C Programs. In: International Conference on Software Engineering and Knowledge Engineering (2019)
9. He, K., Zhang, X., Ren, S., Sun, J.: Deep residual learning for image recognition. arXiv preprint arXiv:1512.03385 (2015)
10. Huo, X., Li, M., Zhou, Z.: Learning unified features from natural and programming languages for locating buggy source code. In: International Joint Conference on Artificial Intelligence (2016)
11. Jenks, G.: Python word segmentation. https://pypi.org/project/wordsegment/
12. Johnson, R., Zhang, T.: Deep pyramid convolutional neural networks for text categorization. In: Annual Meeting of the Association for Computational Linguistics (2017)
13. Joulin, A., Grave, E., Bojanowski, P., Mikolov, T.: Bag of tricks for efficient text classification. In: Conference of the European Chapter of the Association for Computational Linguistics (2017)
14. Kim, S., Woo, S., Lee, H., Oh, H.: VUDDY: a scalable approach for vulnerable code clone discovery. In: IEEE Symposium on Security and Privacy (2017)
15. Kim, Y.: Convolutional neural networks for sentence classification. In: Conference on Empirical Methods in Natural Language Processing (2014)
16. Krizhevsky, A., Sutskever, I., Hinton, G.E.: ImageNet classification with deep convolutional neural networks. In: International Conference on Neural Information Processing Systems (2012)

17. Kroeger, T., Timofte, R., Dai, D., Van Gool, L.: Fast Optical flow using dense inverse search. In: Leibe, B., Matas, J., Sebe, N., Welling, M. (eds.) ECCV 2016. LNCS, vol. 9908, pp. 471–488. Springer, Cham (2016). https://doi.org/10.1007/978-3-319-46493-0_29
18. Kroening, D., Tautschnig, M.: CBMC-C bounded model checker. In: International Conference on Tools and Algorithms for the Construction and Analysis of Systems (2014)
19. Lai, S., Xu, L., Liu, K., Zhao, J.: Recurrent convolutional neural networks for text classification. In: AAAI Conference on Artificial Intelligence (2015)
20. Li, J., He, P., Zhu, J., Lyu, M.R.: Software defect prediction via convolutional neural network. In: IEEE International Conference on Software Quality, Reliability and Security (2017)
21. Li, Z., Zou, D., Xu, S., Jin, H., Qi, H., Hu, J.: VulPecker: an automated vulnerability detection system based on code similarity analysis. In: Annual Conference on Computer Security Applications (2016)
22. Li, Z., et al.: VulDeePecker: a deep learning-based system for vulnerability detection. In: Annual Network and Distributed System Security Symposium (2018)
23. Lin, G., Zhang, J., Luo, W., Pan, L., Xiang, Y.: POSTER: vulnerability discovery with function representation learning from unlabeled projects. In: ACM SIGSAC Conference on Computer and Communications Security (2017)
24. Liu, P., Qiu, X., Huang, X.: Recurrent neural network for text classification with multi-task learning. In: International Joint Conference on Artificial Intelligence (2016)
25. Long, J., Shelhamer, E., Darrell, T.: Fully convolutional networks for semantic segmentation. In: IEEE Computer Society Conference on Computer Vision and Pattern Recognition (2015)
26. Machiry, A., Spensky, C., Corina, J., Stephens, N., Kruegel, C., Vigna, G.: Dr.Checker: a soundy analysis for Linux Kernel drivers. In: USENIX Security Symposium USENIX Security (2017)
27. Microsoft: API reference docs for Windows Driver Kit (WDK). https://docs.microsoft.com/en-us/windows-hardware/drivers/ddi/
28. Microsoft: GitHub. https://github.com/
29. Microsoft: Windows API sets. https://docs.microsoft.com/en-us/windows/win32/apiindex/windows-apisets
30. MITRE: Common Weakness Enumeration. https://cwe.mitre.org/data/index.html
31. Neuhaus, S., Zimmermann, T., Holler, C., Zeller, A.: Predicting vulnerable software components. In: ACM Conference on Computer and Communications Security (2007)
32. Neumann, M., King, D., Beltagy, I., Ammar, W.: Scispacy: fast and robust models for biomedical natural language processing. arXiv preprint arXiv:1902.07669 (2019)
33. Qiu, S., Chang, G.H., Panagia, M., Gopal, D.M., Au, R., Kolachalama, V.B.: Fusion of deep learning models of MRI scans, mini-mental state examination, and logical memory test enhances diagnosis of mild cognitive impairment. Diag. Assess. Prog. **10**, 737–749 (2018)
34. Qiu, Z., Yao, T., Mei, T.: Learning deep spatio-temporal dependence for semantic video segmentation. IEEE Trans. Multim. **20**, 939–949 (2018)
35. Russell, R.L., et al.: Automated vulnerability detection in source code using deep representation learning. In: IEEE International Conference on Machine Learning and Applications (2018)
36. Segaran, T., Hammerbacher, J.: Beautiful Data: The Stories Behind Elegant Data Solutions. O'Reilly Media, Inc. Beijing (2009)

37. Shar, L.K., Tan, H.B.K., Briand, L.C.: Mining SQL injection and cross site scripting vulnerabilities using hybrid program analysis. In: International Conference on Software Engineering (2013)
38. Shi, Q., Xiao, X., Wu, R., Zhou, J., Fan, G., Zhang, C.: Pinpoint: fast and precise sparse value flow analysis for million lines of code. In: ACM SIGPLAN Conference on Programming Language Design and Implementation (2018)
39. Simonyan, K., Zisserman, A.: Very deep convolutional networks for large-scale image recognition. arXiv preprint arXiv:1409.1556 (2014)
40. Tencent: TscanCode. https://github.com/Tencent/TscanCode
41. Tutorial, C.: Finding Declarations. https://xinhuang.github.io/posts/2014-10-19-clang-tutorial-finding-declarations.html
42. Vaswani, A., et al.: Attention is all you need. In: Conference on Neural Information Processing Systems. In: 36th Proceedings of the Conference on Advances in Neural Information Processing Systems (NIPS 2017) (2017)
43. Wang, J., et al.: NLP-EYE: detecting memory corruptions via semantic-aware memory operation function identification. In: International Symposium on Research in Attacks, Intrusions and Defenses (2019)
44. Wang, S., Liu, T., Tan, L.: Automatically learning semantic features for defect prediction. In: International Conference on Software Engineering (2016)
45. Wei, X., Wolf, M.: A survey on HTTPS implementation by Android Apps: Issues and countermeasures. Appl. Comput. Inform. **13**, 101–117 (2017)
46. Wheeler, D.A.: Flawfinder. https://dwheeler.com/flawfinder/
47. Xing, H.: Chinese-Text-Classification-Pytorch. https://github.com/649453932/Chinese-Text-Classification-Pytorch (2020)
48. Yamaguchi, F., Lottmann, M., Rieck, K.: Generalized vulnerability extrapolation using abstract syntax trees. In: Annual Computer Security Applications Conference (2012)
49. Yamaguchi, F., Wressnegger, C., Gascon, H., Rieck, K.: Chucky: exposing missing checks in source code for vulnerability discovery. In: ACM SIGSAC Conference on Computer and Communications Security (2013)
50. Yan, H., Sui, Y., Chen, S., Xue, J.: Spatio-temporal context reduction: a pointer-analysis-based static approach for detecting use-after-free vulnerabilities. In: IEEE/ACM International Conference on Software Engineering (2018)
51. Yan, X., et al.: Video scene parsing: An overview of deep learning methods and datasets. Comput. Vis. Image Underst. **201**, 103077(2020)
52. Yang, X., Lo, D., Xia, X., Zhang, Y., Sun, J.: Deep learning for just-in-time defect prediction. In: IEEE International Conference on Software Quality, Reliability and Security (2015)
53. Yunlongs: Clang-function-prototype. https://github.com/Yunlongs/clang-function-prototype
54. Zagoruyko, S., Komodakis, N.: Wide residual networks. arXiv preprint arXiv:1605.07146 (2016)
55. Zhou, P., et al.: Attention-based bidirectional long short-term memory networks for relation classification. In: Annual Meeting of the Association for Computational Linguistics (2016)
56. Zou, D., Wang, S., Xu, S., Li, Z., Jin, H.: μVulDeePecker: a deep learning-based system for multiclass vulnerability detection. IEEE Trans. Depend. Sec. Comput. **18** (2019)

RAIDER: Reinforcement-Aided Spear Phishing Detector

Keelan Evans[1,3], Alsharif Abuadbba[2,3(✉)] ⓘ, Tingmin Wu[2] ⓘ,
Kristen Moore[2] ⓘ, Mohiuddin Ahmed[1] ⓘ, Ganna Pogrebna[4,5,6] ⓘ,
Surya Nepal[2,3] ⓘ, and Mike Johnstone[1] ⓘ

[1] Edith Cowan University, Joondalup, Australia
[2] CSIROs Data61, Canberra, Australia
sharif.abuadbba@data61.csiro.au
[3] Cybersecurity Cooperative Research Centre, Joondalup, Australia
[4] Charles Sturt University, Sydney, Australia
[5] The University of Sydney, Sydney, Australia
[6] The Alan Turing Institute, Sydney, Australia

Abstract. Spear Phishing is one of the most difficult to detect cyber attacks facing businesses and individuals worldwide. In recent years, considerable research has been conducted into the use of Machine Learning (ML) techniques for spear-phishing detection. ML-based solutions are vulnerable to zero-day attacks, as when the algorithms do not have access to the relevant historical data, they cannot be reliably trained. Furthermore, email address spoofing is a low-effort yet widely applied forgery technique in spear phishing which the standard email protocol SMTP fails to detect without the use of extensions. Detecting this type of spear threat requires (i) a close investigation of each sender within the mailbox; and (ii) a thorough exploration of the similarity of its characteristics to the spoofed email. This raises scalability challenges due to the growing number of features relevant for investigation and comparison, which is *proportional to the number of the senders within a particular mailbox*. This differs from traditional phishing attacks, which typically look at email bodies and are generally limited to a binary classification between *'phishing'* and *'benign'* emails.

We offer a possible solution to these problems, which we label RAIDER: Reinforcement AIded Spear Phishing DEtectoR. A reinforcement-learning based feature evaluation system that can automatically find the optimum features for detecting different types of attacks. By leveraging a reward and penalty system, RAIDER allows for autonomous features selection. RAIDER also keeps the number of features to a minimum by selecting only the significant features to represent phishing emails and detect spear phishing attacks. After extensive evaluation of RAIDER on over 11,000 emails and across 3 attack scenarios, our results suggest that using reinforcement learning to automatically identify the significant features could reduce the dimensions of the required features by 55% in comparison to existing ML-based systems. It also increases the accuracy of detecting spoofing attacks by 4%, from 90% to 94%. Furthermore, RAIDER demonstrates reasonable detection accuracy against a sophisticated attack named "Known Sender", in which

X. Yuan et al. (Eds.): NSS 2022, LNCS 13787, pp. 23–50, 2022.
https://doi.org/10.1007/978-3-031-23020-2_2

spear phishing emails greatly resemble those of the impersonated sender. By evaluating and updating the feature set, RAIDER is able to increase accuracy by close to 15%, from 49% to 62% when detecting Known Sender attacks.

Keywords: Spear phishing · Zero-day attack · Reinforcement learning

1   Introduction

Phishing is a type of cyber attack in which the adversary uses social engineering techniques to either convince a user to do something they should not do or motivate them to abstain from doing something they are supposed to do. In other words, adversaries attempt to disguise themselves as trusted individuals to elicit sensitive information from a target, or get them to perform some specific task like installing malware on their computer or transferring money to the attacker. Spear Phishing, a variant of phishing attacks, targets a specific individual with an attack crafted based on prior information about the target and their relationship with the impersonated sender [1]. This differs from traditional phishing attacks which blindly target a large number of people with a generic attack, and results in a more effective disguise, making it difficult in a lot of cases to discern between what is a spear phishing attack and what is a legitimate email. It is estimated that over 80% of organisations in the US alone have experienced a spear phishing attack, and that they account for billions of dollars in losses annually [2]. While spear phishing attacks are effective on their own, they may also be used to gain a foothold into a network as a part of a more extensive attack [3,4]. Spear phishing attacks are conducted across many forms of Internet communication but are most commonly delivered by means of an email [5].

There are a variety of different spear phishing techniques used by attackers to masquerade themselves as another (trusted) sender. Effective spear phishing attacks are two-pronged attacks which involve both **(1)** manipulating the headers of an email to forge certain fields to more closely resemble an email of the sender they are trying to impersonate, and **(2)** psychologically manipulating the recipient of the email (e.g., by mentioning a third party or an individual a potential victim trusts, enticing a sense of urgency, using common knowledge facts, etc.). Email address spoofing is one of the most common forgery techniques, requiring low effort on the part of an adversary. This technique involves manipulating the header of an email to make the email appear to be from a different sender than the individual or entity who actually sent the email. Email address spoofing in itself is not a spear phishing attack, but it is a commonly used tool in spear phishing helping the attacker to masquerade as another sender they are impersonating. Considering that email address spoofing techniques are commonly used in spear phishing emails [6], observing spoofing could be considered a reliable indicator of a spear phishing attack in progress.

Existing defences against spear phishing include both (a) "patching with people" techniques - i.e., educating end-users to identify spear phishing attacks; as well as (b) "patching with tech" (which is a focus of this paper) - i.e., building detection algorithms for reliable spear phishing identification [7,8] and development of software solutions to scan emails and predict whether they are spear phishing or benign. Software solutions can make use of blacklists of IP addresses and URLs associated with phishing attacks [9–11], as well as Machine-Learning (ML) based solutions [12–15].

While general phishing and spear phishing are somewhat related, the design of ML based detection models for them differs significantly. Unlike general phishing where ML detection is a binary classification problem with emails either being 'phishing' or 'benign' [16], spear phishing ML detection is a more complex multi-class classification problem in which each class corresponds to a sender. To create the spear phishing detection model, one, therefore, needs to look at the metadata and extract features from each class (sender) within every mailbox. Then, once a new email is received, features would be extracted from that email's metadata and the model would measure how close those features align to all possible senders to detect discrepancies between the features of the email and the features of the alleged sender. The existence of these discrepancies is an indication of a potential spear attack.

So while on the surface the problem may seem like only a 2-class binary classification problem in which an email is being classified as either 'spear phishing' or 'benign', in actuality, there are two phases to the classification of spear phishing. The first phase is a multi-class classification problem where an incoming email is being classified as one of the existing sender classes, and the second phase is to determine whether an email is spear phishing or not based on the result of the first classification problem. Therefore the spear phishing problem is a lot more complex than the binary classification problem of general phishing attacks, with the complexity of the multi-class classification problem being variable and dependent on the number of senders within a mailbox/organisation/etc.

Despite the efficacy of ML as a defence against spear phishing, we have identified several challenges that limit the practical implementation of these solutions. Existing implementations produce large feature vectors for each individual sender within a mailbox [12]. This limits scalability, as each new email in a mailbox will produce another large vector, which consumes significant amounts of memory and is impractical beyond small-scale implementations; that is *as the number of senders increases, so does the number of classes and dimensions of the feature vectors*. Current research also neglects changes within the dataset. Zero day attacks can cause a performance reduction in classifiers as they can differ significantly from the initial training data. To the best of our knowledge, no prior research has attempted to evaluate nor update features in response to emerging threats within spear phishing.

This motivates us to address the following research question:

How can a spear phishing detection system operate efficiently as well as effectively over time while keeping feature vector dimensions low and continuously detecting new attacks?

To answer this question, we explored the possibility of automated feature engineering using Reinforcement Learning (RL) [17]. RL is the training of ML models to make an autonomous optimum sequence of decisions in uncertain situations using rewards and penalty strategies. RL has been used in various domains such as games [18], car racing simulators [19], robotic simulator [20], and virtual reality [21]. In this work, we aim to leverage the autonomous RL ability to select the optimum number of features required to achieve a reasonable balance between accuracy and low feature dimensions to detect spear phishing.

Our key contributions are summarized as follows:

- **(Existing Limitations)** We explore previous spear phishing classifiers and identify the key challenges facing their practical implementation. After exploring with 32,000 reported phishing emails over 5 years (2016–2020), we find that the dimension of feature vectors is considerably high (>8000) dimensions when features are extracted manually using existing techniques [12], and that the importance of features and their contribution to the efficacy of the classifier is obscured. We identify that spear phishing attacks are intentionally modified over time in order to avoid detection, and that because of the nature of static learning, classifiers misinterpret previously unseen attacks.
- **(RAIDER)** We develop a novel RL-based feature selection model, called RAIDER[1]. To the best of our knowledge, RAIDER is the first spear phishing detector that can account for changing data over time by generating new feature subsets for specific types of attacks. This is achieved by employing a reward/penalty system that determines how much influence a feature has over prediction accuracy. RAIDER automatically chooses only the key features that allow it to best predict a variety of different spear phishing attacks.
- **(Lightweight and Effective)** We perform an extensive evaluation of RAIDER over 11,000 emails across 3 attack scenarios: Blind spoofing, Known domain, and Known sender. Our results suggest that using RL to automatically identify the significant features could reduce the required feature dimensions by 55% compared to manual feature extraction, while eliminating the time and effort required for manual feature extraction. It also allows us to achieve an accuracy improvement in spoofing attack detection by 4% (an increase from 90% to 94%).

2   Background

In this section, we provide the prior knowledge for K Nearest Neighbours and Reinforcement Learning.

2.1   K Nearest Neighbours (KNN)

KNN is a classification algorithm that groups training samples into classes and then predicts what class the incoming data belongs to [22]. To find which class

---

[1] Code and artifacts will be released upon publication or reviewers request.

a new data point belongs to, KNN finds the k most similar training samples to that data point and then facilitates a 'voting' selection procedure to determine the predicted class of the data. An example is shown in Fig. 1, $k = 3$ means that the 3 data points nearest to the incoming data will be counted in the vote. Each data point 'votes' on behalf of its class. Two of the three data points belong to the '*spear phishing*' class (in blue), and the rest represents '*benign*' (in red). The new data point (in green) will be classified as '*spear phishing*'. The value of k and the specific algorithm used to calculate the distance between points is dependent on the type of data that KNN is working with, and therefore varies between use cases.

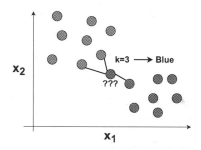

Fig. 1. KNN makes predictions based on a vote between the k nearest data points. (Color figure online)

RAIDER uses KNN to predict whether an email is spear phishing or not. It is used to determine the effect each feature has on accuracy during the RL phase, as well as to make predictions using the automatically generated feature subset. KNN has been chosen because it calculates the distances between data points when predictions are being made, not during the training phase. So while adding new data requires the KNN model to be retrained from scratch, the distances between data points do not need to be recalculated, since this is all done when making predictions. Specific uses of KNN are explained in more detail in Sect. 4.3.

2.2   Reinforcement Learning (RL)

RL is a subsection of ML that uses a penalty and reward system to train an agent to perform specific tasks in response to certain circumstances [17]. The reinforcement agent is given an environment in which it can perform actions and learn their impact. The specific situation the agent is in within the environment is called a state. The agent selects an action based on its interpretation of the state it is in at that time. Rewards and penalties are given to the agent based on the action it performs. By associating the combination of state and action with the resulting reward/penalty, the reinforcement agent learns what actions are the best to perform in each scenario. The mapping of states to particular actions is called a policy, and it defines how a reinforcement agent acts in any given situation.

For RAIDER, we propose an RL algorithm based on Fard et al.'s Average of Rewards (AOR) policy from their RL-based feature selection model [23]. In particular, they propose an approach to select the best subset of features to use in a classification model. We adapt their approach to select the best feature collection to detect email spear phishing. Each feature has an AOR, which is defined to be the average increase/decrease in accuracy incurred by using that feature. We choose the features based on exploring the action space and its impact on the bottom line accuracy by randomly selecting a new subset of features at a time. When a feature is chosen 2 times within subsets, the increase/decrease in accuracy for each of these actions will be summed and divided by 2. The formula for AOR is as follows:

$$(AOR_f)_{New} = [(k-1)(AOR_f)_{Old} + V(F)]/k \tag{1}$$

where f is the selected feature, $(AOR_f)_{Old}$ is the current feature value in the table and $(AOR_f)_{New}$ is the updated value. $V(F)$ is the assessment value of the current state F and k is the number of times the feature f has been used during RL training.

While, to the best of our knowledge, there have been no previous applications of RL to the detection of spear phishing emails, RL has been successfully applied to the detection of generic phishing emails. Smadi et al. [24] used RL to dynamically update a neural network-based general phishing detection system over time in response to changes in the environment. The detection of generic phishing attacks is a binary classification problem, whereas spear phishing is commonly implemented as a large multi-class classification problem in which each class corresponds to a sender. Therefore, re-applying binary classification from generic phishing detection, such as in [24], is not sufficient for detecting spear phishing attacks. Also, due to the growing size of classes (senders), auto-learning neural network approaches are not suitable. Hence, a new RL design is required for auto-feature selection in the multi-class classification spear phishing problem.

3   Key Insights: Analysis of Spear Phishing Emails

We build on the previous work by Gascon et al. [12] as their research offers very promising results for ML-based detection of spear phishing emails (these results appear to outperform many competitive models). We first reproduce Gascon et al. results by implementing a KNN-based system as reported in their paper, making use of a subset of their 46 features. Our experimental approach also utilizes the attack methods Gascon et al. used to test and evaluate their security ecosystem. By reproducing this state-of-the-art spear phishing detection mechanism, we are able to gain two insights into the challenges that are faced by traditional feature engineering in the detection of spear phishing emails: the first insight is related to the feature vector stability and the second insight to the feature importance.

Insight (1): Feature Vector Stability. We found that the features produced by manual feature engineering are unstable, sparse and high-dimensional. This causes high memory consumption and is not a scalable solution. As more classes are added to the initial classifier (through the addition of new senders' characteristics to the model), the number of feature vectors will also grow. This can quickly become impractical and difficult to manage as there will be a significant number of high dimensional feature vectors. Figure 2 visualises the features generated by the state-of-the-art manual feature engineering over time in a 2D space using the PCA (Principal Component Analysis). The distribution of the data points illustrates that the feature vectors have different spreads, which are unstable and sparse over the years.

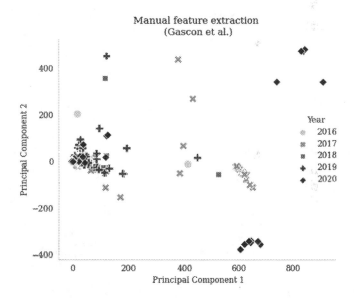

Fig. 2. The visualisation of traditional feature extraction of phishing emails as in [12] over five years (2016–2020) using the PCA (Principal Component Analysis). Here PCA projects the data points into a new 2D space while the axes do not have physical meaning. The new values on the x-axis and y-axis (Principal Component 1 and 2) contribute most to the variation through a transformation.

Insight (2): Feature Importance. Current uses of traditional feature engineering within the field of spear phishing detection do not allow for the understanding of the importance of individual features. Manually extracted features also cannot be adjusted or improved over time without manual intervention. This is a significant problem when considering previously unseen attacks not present in the classifier's training data. It has been demonstrated that spear phishing attacks change over time, and that phishing campaigns are modified throughout their life span in order to evade detection. Heijden et al. [25] recently demonstrated how over the period of a phishing campaign, there were intentional attempts to modify and alter spear phishing emails in order to avoid detection. It is therefore important to have a method for autonomously evaluating the efficacy of features for detecting spear phishing attacks, and updating these features in response to changes within the data and the emergence of new threats.

This problem presents the question of *how can we determine the most important features for detecting spear phishing emails while ensuring the efficiency and practicality of our solution by reducing the size of our feature vectors as much as possible?*

4 RAIDER System Design

In this section, we provide the RAIDER model design. We first define the threat models that we focused on in this paper. We then provide an overview of the proposed RAIDER detection system followed by an in-depth explanation (Fig. 3).

4.1 Threat Model

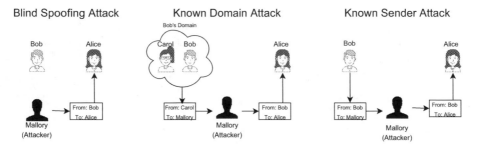

Fig. 3. The three simulated attack methods borrowed from Gascon et al. [12]. In Blind Spoofing the attacker crafts a spear phishing email without any external information about the structure of the emails of the impersonated sender or their email domain. In Known Domain the attacker has access to emails from other individuals from within the impersonated sender's email domain and uses this information to forge spear phishing attacks with traits unique to this domain. In Known Sender the attacker has access to previous emails from the impersonated sender and this information to forge spear phishing attacks with traits unique to the impersonated sender.

We target three attacks scenarios similar to [12]. These are (i) *Blind Spoofing*, (ii) *Known Domain*, and (iii) *Known Sender*. These attacks represent different scenarios in which the attacker has different levels of information about the impersonated sender. **(i)** The simplest of these attacks, *Blind Spoofing*, attempts to simulate a scenario in which the attacker has very little information about the sender they are claiming to be. In this scenario we simply take a legitimate email and forge the sender address to that of a different sender. This aims to simulate a scenario in which the attacker doesn't have any information about the sender they are trying to impersonate beyond the sender's email. While blind spoofing is a common technique deployed in other email-based attacks and not unique to spear phishing, it is used here because it is a crucial component of a large amount of spear phishing attacks and has shown to be capable of bypassing various security protocols and authentication methods [6].

(ii) The second, more sophisticated attack, is a *Known domain* attack. In this scenario, the attacker has access to emails that belong to different senders within the same domain as the sender they are trying to impersonate. Therefore, the attacker will be able to forge transport features that are common between senders within the same domain. To simulate this attack, we take legitimate emails and change the sender address to a different address within the same domain. The reasoning behind this is that the emails of two different senders from within the same domain will have composition and transportation features that are the same but will still have behavioural features that are unique to the two senders. So by simply changing the email address to a different sender within the same domain, we can simulate a scenario where the domain-specific features that could have been used to successfully detect blind-spoofing attacks are no longer adequate for detecting this more advanced spear phishing attack. Essentially we limit the avenues that the classifier can take to identify spear phishing attacks and see how they perform when there are less clues to work with.

(iii) The final attack method, which is the hardest to detect, is *the Known sender*. In this scenario the attacker has access to emails from the sender they are impersonating, allowing them to incorporate the sender's features into their crafted emails and accurately impersonate the sender. This is replicated by taking an email from the sender to be impersonated, and changing the intended recipient. This is done under the assumption that with access to prior emails sent by the impersonated sender, the attacker would be able to forge all previous domain-specific features as well as the behavioural features that are unique to the sender with very little difference between the crafted spear phishing email and a legitimate email from the impersonated sender. As such this kind of attack is very difficult to detect and is intended to push the classifiers to their limits.

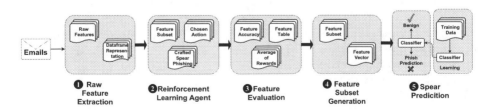

Fig. 4. Overview of RAIDER. Emails are taken as input. From here a feature subset is generated based on what features get the highest accuracy when detecting spear phishing attacks. From here the final feature subset is used for future predictions.

4.2   Overview of RAIDER

We developed RAIDER, a system that automatically selects the best features for detecting spear phishing emails, and predicts whether an email is a spear phishing attack or a benign email. Figure 4 depicts the workflow of RAIDER. In the following, we explain the steps in detail. A detailed overview of the reinforcement learning process is presented in Fig. 5. This figure walks through a single step within the reinforcement learning process and shows how the reward for an action & state pair is calculated. It also shows how these values are stored in and retrieved from RAIDER's AOR table.

4.3   RAIDER in Detail

❶ **Raw Feature Extraction.** The first phase in RAIDER is the feature subset generation. In this phase, each field within an email is extracted and considered a 'raw' feature. The raw features are then evaluated for their importance in detecting spear phishing attacks using our RL-based system. The features most useful for detecting spear phising attacks are those that can uniquely identify the behaviour of individual senders. Composition and transportation features that are unique to different email domains and email clients can also help flag incoming emails are spear phising attacks. While RAIDER does not directly interact with the body of the email, and therefore does not directly interact with email attachments, by using information and metadata from the header it can learn sender behavioural characteristics and detect spear-phishing attacks from non-text based features.

When a representation of the email dataset is produced, the features are organized in a vector form according to the bag-of-words model[2], where each email is represented as a matrix of integers, each integer denoting the frequency at which a specific word from within the dataset appears within that email. The matrix contains integers for every word within the dataset. The bag-of-words approach is used simply as a way to represent the header data of an email and determine the existence of certain traits within the header. This results in the aforementioned array which represents the existence and frequency of certain traits within an email.

❷ **RL Agent.** Choosing the specific feature to evaluate is decided by our RL agent. The RL agent chooses an action either by getting the best possible action from the feature table, or by randomly choosing an action from the action space. This process of selecting a feature, adding it to the feature subset, determining the feature effect, and updating the feature table represents a single step within the RL environment. After a step is performed, the resulting state is returned to the agent. In RAIDER the state is the current feature subset and corresponding accuracy. After a specified number of steps, the round finishes. After each round, the feature subset up to that point is discarded and the RL agent starts

---

[2] https://artsandculture.google.com/entity/bag-of-words-model.

from scratch; allowing us to evaluate the importance of features within a variety of circumstances. A feature may only result in favorable/unfavorable accuracy changes when paired with other features. Therefore, it is important to evaluate features within a variety of circumstances to get a better understanding of the importance of each feature independently. The feature table is not reset and continues to be updated throughout the rounds.

❸ **Feature Evaluation.** RL is used to evaluate feature importance adapting Average of Rewards (AOR) approach introduced in [23]. The RL agent's action space consists of adding different possible features. The state in the environment consists of the current feature subset and the corresponding accuracy of the selected subset. Given a state the agent attempts to add features that will result in the highest possible accuracy increase. *The agent determines the importance of each feature by creating a variety of feature subsets, testing these subsets with KNN, and determining how much of the increase in accuracy each feature is responsible for.*

In RAIDER, the Feature importance is determined by the AOR and the times a feature was added. This latter value is incremented each time a feature is chosen during the RL phase. It is used to calculate the AOR and when generating the feature subset after the RL phase has ended. The action space for the agent is as follows: the agent can choose to add any one of the raw features to the existing subset. The specific feature is chosen by either exploiting the feature table by choosing the feature with the highest AOR, or by exploring the action space by randomly selecting a feature.

The accuracy increase/decrease for a feature is calculated by making predictions with KNN using the current feature subset. After the RL agent has chosen a feature, new training and testing datasets are generated using the new feature subset to make predictions. The training dataset contains benign emails only and the sender's email address serves as the label for each data sample. In this way, KNN is learning what values and patterns in the data represent what senders. This is also to be consistent with the assumptions in [12] which 'sender profiles' are generated for each sender. The testing dataset is a set of emails, 50% of these are benign, whereas the remaining 50% are spear phishing emails that we have crafted according to the different attack methods previously outlined. KNN, using the learnt sender profiles, attempts to predict what sender sent the email in question. If the predicted sender address is different from the address on the email, we assume that this is a spear-phishing attack-*someone masquerading as the sender rather than the sender themselves.* The predictions are then compared to the real status of the test emails and an accuracy is calculated for that feature subset. Any changes in accuracy between steps are calculated and using this information the feature table is updated with the new AOR (assuming there was some change in accuracy generated by adding the feature.)

❹ **Feature Subset Generation.** After a specified number of rounds, a final feature subset is created based on the values in the feature table. Any features that produced a positive increase in accuracy will be added to the final feature subset, whereas any features that resulted in a decrease, or no change, in accuracy will be removed. Any features that were not called during the RL phase will also be removed. This process allows us to generate a set of features to identify spear phishing attacks without any manual feature engineering. The process is fully automated by simply determining how each feature affects accuracy. This method also allows us to generate the features best suited for different attacks, and can adapt to zero-day attacks. A new feature subset can simply be generated as new threats emerge without the need for manual feature evaluation and engineering.

❺ Spear Prediction. After the RL process is complete and a feature subset has been generated, RAIDER can then make predictions on incoming emails. At this point the algorithm is no longer being trained, and simply makes predictions on whether an incoming email is spear phishing or not. These emails are represented according to the feature subset. So for every incoming email a feature vector is generated that represents each email using only the features specified during the RL phase. RAIDER can be retrained and new features produced automatically if there are changes within the incoming data and the initial model can no longer adequately detect spear phishing emails.

Table 1. Datasets used in the evaluation of RAIDER. During training sender profiles were built using emails in these datasets, with the exception of the CSIRO dataset where it is independently used as a measure for feature dimensions analysis. During testing spear phishing emails were crafted based on information obtained from these emails.

Dataset	Description	Emails #
Enron Corpus	Collection of emails of Enron Corporation	4,279
Uni. Buffalo Dataset	Bread Secured program from University at Buffalo	75
SpamAssassin easy ham	Legit emails from Apache's SpamAssasin	2,551
SpamAssassin hard ham	Legit emails from Apache's SpamAssasin	250
IWSPA-AP	Emails from IWSPA 2018	4,082
CSIRO Dataset	Phishing emails(2016 to 2020) from CSIRO	32,959

5   Evaluation

This section describes the experimental setup and performance evaluation for RAIDER.

5.1   Experimental Setup

We introduce our datasets, two phases of experimental settings (Reinforcement Learning and Zero-Day Simulation), and evaluation metrics below.

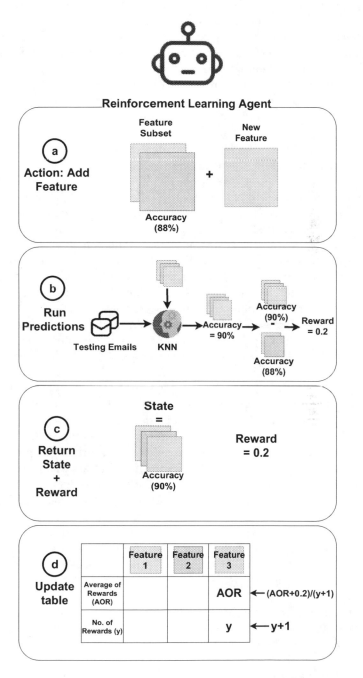

Fig. 5. Overview of RAIDER's reinforcement learning process that is used to evaluate raw features and generate feature subsets.

Datasets. For our experiments we used a combination of publicly available email datasets (Table 1). These datasets were chosen in order to have a diverse selection of emails to test our algorithm on. In order to avoid bias and over-fitting our system to any one dataset or email type we sourced a variety of different emails from different sources. The datasets used are as follows: The Enron Corpus, a collection of emails from the Enron Corporation prior to the company's collapse in 2001 [26], University at Buffalo's Bread Secured dataset [27], Apache's SpamAssasin 'easy ham' and 'hard ham' datasets [28], and a dataset of political emails from the International Workshop on Security and Privacy Analytics (IWSPA-AP) 2018 [29]. All of these email datasets are assumed to be comprised solely of benign emails sent from legitimate senders.

As previously mentioned, the spear phishing emails that we used for our experiments were crafted by us and used publicly available benign emails as a source of information when imitating senders. Spear phishing emails of varying sophistication were crafted according to the attack methods in Sect. 4.1. The sender address of the emails as well as domain and sender-specific traits were all taken from these benign datasets. Every feature is extracted from the email header and sensitive information such as the body of the email is left untouched. Our reasoning behind this approach is that the headers of emails contain not only information that is unique to each sender, but also information unique to email domains. We operate under the assumption that (1) the majority of spear phishing attacks are not at the level of complexity and sophistication where all uniquely identifying fields can be accurately forged, and (2) that even in sophisticated attacks where the attacker has access to significant information to create their deception, it is still possible for holes to exist within an attacker's masquerade and for certain uniquely identifying fields to be left unaltered. Therefore we use RAIDER to attempt to identify which fields within an email's header provide the highest level of reliability in uniquely identifying different senders and detecting different attacks. In the three different attack scenarios, the spear phishing emails are crafted according to the level of information the attacker is assumed to have about the sender. The more information the sender has, the more closely the spear phishing email resembles a benign email of the same impersonated sender.

Essentially we attempted to impersonate the senders in these public datasets with our crafted spear phishing emails. The crafted spear phishing emails are consistent with [12]. We incorporate email forgery techniques and take into account different scenarios based on how much information the attacker has on their target.

When training KNN, whether it be within an iteration of the reinforcement learning process or for our prediction experiments, 7518 benign emails are used to train KNN and learn the sender classes. We imposed the rule that there must be at least two emails belonging to each sender within the training data. This is because one email isn't enough to identify traits common to emails sent by the same user. Ultimately this reduces the final number of benign emails to 8719 and results in 987 unique senders. During the testing phase 1201 benign emails and 1201 crafted spear phishing emails are used for making predictions, therefore giving the testing dataset a 50/50 split between benign and spear phishing emails. These 1201 benign emails are different from those used during training and are used to see whether the algorithm can correctly identify benign emails it hasn't seen before. Therefore of the total 8719 benign emails, 80% of these are used for training and the remaining 20% are used for testing. The 1201 spear phishing emails are crafted according to the attack method being used for the experiment and are used to see whether the algorithm can correctly identify spear phishing attacks.

Experimental Settings. RAIDER utilises an off-policy algorithm in which the behaviour policy is the Epsilon-Greedy policy. The behaviour policy is followed by the agent while the target policy is improved. This allows us to sufficiently explore all of our large numbers of features. Exploiting previous values too much would result in our agent neglecting the yet unexplored features.

To simulate a zero-day attack, the RL algorithm is trained on one attack type and then during the testing phase one of the other previously unseen attack types is introduced. We compared accuracy between static training in which the feature subset is never updated, and online learning in which the subset is generated in response to new attacks.

Evaluation Metrics. To evaluate the results of our experiments the primary metric we make use of is accuracy. Accuracy in regards to Spear Phishing classification refers to the proportion of emails that were correctly predicted as either spear phishing or benign. Accuracy is defined as:

$$Accuracy = (TP + TN)/(TP + FP + FN + TN) \qquad (2)$$

where P/N (Positives/Negatives) refers to predicted outcome and T/F (True/False) refers to the actual outcome. For instance, TP (True Positives) refers to the proportion of emails predicted by the classifier to be spear-phishing that have been correctly identified.

5.2 Results of RAIDER

Effectiveness of RAIDER

Table 2 shows that by using automatically generated features RAIDER is able to detect spear phishing emails with slightly better or comparable accuracy to the state of the art [12]. Obtaining equal (and in the case of blind spoofing, superior) results while eliminating the need to manually engineer features results in considerable time and effort saved. Data preparation such as cleaning data and engineering features accounts for 80% of the work for data scientists and 76% of data scientists view this as the least enjoyable part of their work [30]. It has also been demonstrated that different classifiers produce different results with the same set of features [31], so in order to maximise the efficacy of a classifier, features will have to be engineered specially for that classifier and not reused. Therefore, being able to automatically generate features saves a lot of

Table 2. Comparison of accuracy results for RAIDER and KNN with manually engineered features across a variety of attacks. Percentages represent the number of emails RAIDER correctly predicts as either spear phishing or benign.

Attack scenario	RAIDER (Automatic feature subset)	KNN (Manually engineered features)
Blind spoofing	94%	90%
Known domain	83%	83%
Known sender	62%	62%

time and effort when engineering lots of features. Manually engineering features also limit the transferability of the feature set as features are built according to the problem being solved and can not be applied to other use cases.

We compared the true positive rate and false positive rate of RAIDER with Gascon et al.'s [12] KNN implementation when detecting spear phishing emails. This is depicted in Fig. 6, where the True and False Positive (TP/FP) rates of both systems are presented alongside one another. It is obvious that RAIDER performs better in detecting TP. RAIDER also has less FP in the two more realistic threat models named *Blind Spoofing* and *Known Domain*, but performs worse than the state of art when it comes to the hardest yet rare threat model named *Known Sender*.

Figure 7 shows that RAIDER and the manual KNN implementation obtain comparable precision and recall, with the manually extracted features just beating the automatically extracted features. Across all three attacks the manually-extracted features slightly beat the automated feature extraction when it comes to precision. I.e. of all the emails labeled as spear phishing more of these classifications were correct when using the manually extracted features than automatic. The recall shows that for all three attacks a higher percentage of the total spear phishing attacks were detected using the manually extracted features with the exception of the known sender attack. For the known sender attack, more than half of the spear phishing emails were correctly identified by RAIDER's automatically extracted features, whereas less than 20% were correctly identified by KNN using the manually-engineered features. While the overall accuracy is about equal between the two systems, this suggests that RAIDER's automatically generated features are better identifying known sender spear phishing attacks whereas the manually engineered features more commonly identify spear phishing emails as benign.

Figure 8 shows the ROC curve for RAIDER's automatically generated features and the manual KNN implementation against the three different attack types. The results suggest that there is very little difference in the performance of the two feature sets with RAIDER performing slightly better in two of the three attacks.

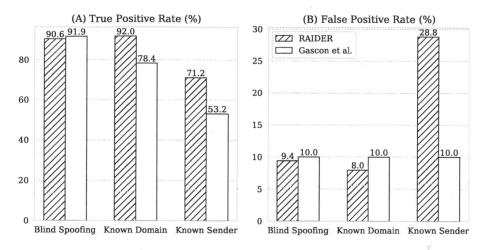

Fig. 6. Comparison of (A) TP rate and (B) FP rate of RAIDER with [12].

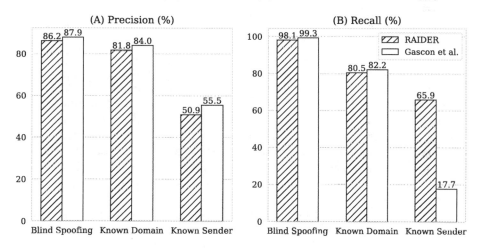

Fig. 7. Comparison of (A) Precision (B) Recall of RAIDER with [12].

The evaluation metrics performed suggest that the two feature subsets have comparable performance in terms of accurately classifying spear phishing emails. This shows that we are able to obtain classification accuracy comparable with state-of-the-art systems while automatically extracting features and eliminating the need for the manual feature engineering process. This not only saves time, but allows us to eliminate possible manual errors.

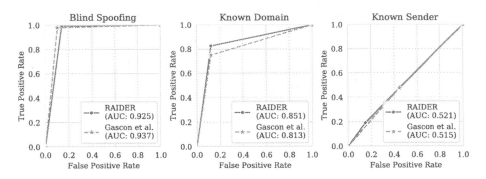

Fig. 8. ROC curve of RAIDER and Gascon et al. [12].

Robustness of RAIDER

Figure 9 indicates that for any given attack method (with the exception of known domain attack), the feature subset that was generated using attacks of the same type always returns the highest level of accuracy. This trend is most significant in the case of blind spoofing and known domain attacks. The 'Updating features' column shows an implementation of RAIDER where a new feature subset is generated every time a new attack type is encountered. So if the system was originally trained using blind spoofing attacks, when known domain attacks appear RAIDER will retrain using known domain attacks and produce a new feature subset. The 3 other columns train using only one type of attack and never update regardless of what attacks they encounter. The updating features column consistently obtains the highest accuracy whereas the systems that don't retrain experience lower accuracy when detecting attacks they have not previously seen.

The blind spoofing subset returned an accuracy rate of 94% when predicting blind spoofing spear phishing emails, while the known sender subset returned a rate of 78% and known domain returned 77% -A difference of 16% and 17% respectively. Testing known sender attacks with the known sender subset returned an accuracy rate of 62%, an increase of 14% over the known domain subset, and 13% over the blind spoofing subset. We believe this demonstrates our system's ability to adapt to different attack methods and previously unseen threats by generating a new feature subset in response to changes within the data. In this scenario, the subset from one kind of attack being applied to another kind of attack represents a prediction system that has been previously trained statically at one point in time and is now encountering previously unseen data. Therefore, we believe that by leveraging RAIDER's ability to automatically generate feature subsets, the system can be updated to better detect new types of attacks. Although it is also worth noting that while this method provides higher accuracy than statically trained models, there is still a decrease in accuracy between attack types, regardless of whether the feature subset is generated or not. This is expected as each attack has a varying level of sophistication and complexity.

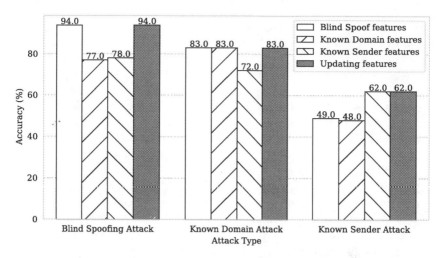

Fig. 9. Accuracy of the different feature vectors over time. Feature subsets are generated based on one kind of attack, then are tested with crafted spear phishing emails from all the different attack types. Graph shows how the accuracy of predictions changes when new attacks are introduced. Accuracy refers to the percentage of emails that are correctly identified as either benign or spear phishing. The x axis describes the attack type used for the testing of RAIDER, with the accuracy on the y axis showing the accuracy of each variation of RAIDER against the type of attack on the x axis. Each bar represents a different variation of raider where the independent variable is the type of training data used. Training data can either be blind spoofing attacks, known domain, known sender, or updating features. For any of the first 3 the features were derived using only spear phishing emails using that type of attack. So for blind spoofing, a feature subset was generated using only blind spoofing spear phishing emails. For updating features, the feature subset is updated every time a new type of attack occurs. So when known domain attacks are introduced to RAIDER, it then retrains using known domain attacks and produces a new feature subset. This attempts to simulate a scenario where RAIDER updates the feature subset in response to new attacks.

Our experiments thus far have simply compared the prediction abilities of a statically-trained implementation of RAIDER to that of a dynamic one that updates the feature set to adjust to new attacks. To comprehensively demonstrate RAIDER's zero-day capabilities further testing may need to be done to compare state-of-the-art statically trained systems to RAIDER, to see how accuracy is affected by the emergence of new threats. However, the detailed 3 attack methods we picked are not suitable for testing the ability of Gascon et al's system [12] to detect zero-day attacks, as all of their manually engineered features are intended to be used across all 3 of these attack types. Therefore, to sufficiently test the state-of-the-art manual feature engineering system, we would need to craft a variety of different attacks that the current feature set is not based around which we found to be very challenging to achieve in practice.

Feature Stability. We then conducted Principal Component Analysis (PCA) on our automated feature extraction process, as well as the manual process based on Gascon et al.'s work [12]. We did this using CSIRO's phishing email dataset which contains over 32,000 emails from 2016 to 2020. As shown in Fig. 10, we reduce the dimension and visualise the features into a new 2D space. The features generated by our automated process shows stronger stability and less dimensionality over the years compared to [12].

RAIDER is able to gain this comparable accuracy with feature vectors of significantly smaller dimensions than those of state-of-the-art spear phishing feature extraction. Figures 10 and 11 show that excluding a few outliers, emails extracted using RAIDER remain clustered with low dimensionality, whereas those extracted using Gascon et al.'s features are spread out more, meaning that their feature vectors are more volatile and more frequently reach higher dimensions. This means that our system manages to achieve comparable, and in certain cases superior, accuracy to state-of-the-art spear phishing detection systems while maintaining smaller feature vectors. Looking at Fig. 10 shows that our feature vectors are more tightly concentrated while also have a smaller upperbound than state-of-the-art feature extraction.

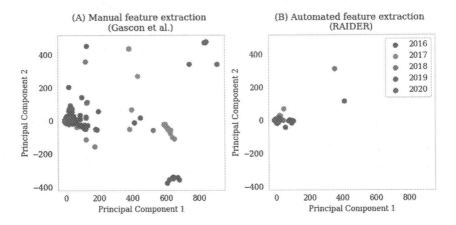

Fig. 10. Principal Component Analysis (PCA) scatterplot of the two feature engineering methods. Here PCA projects the data points into a new 2D space while the axes do not have physical meaning. The new values on x-axis and y-axis (Principal Component 1 and 2) contribute most to the variation through a transformation.

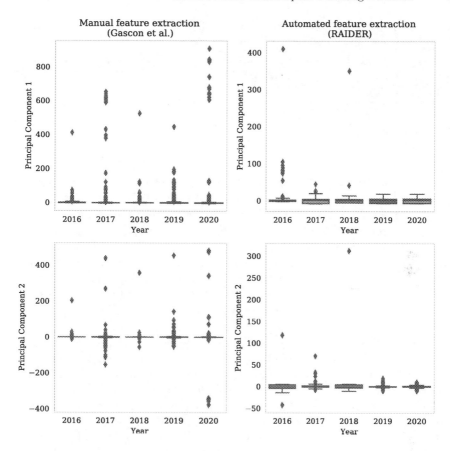

Fig. 11. Boxplot representation of PCA.

6   Discussion and Future Work

6.1   Complexity and Time Overhead

The runtime cost was recorded for making predictions with our manual feature extraction process as well as RAIDER's automated feature extraction. For both methods, we recorded the time it takes to pre-process and prepare the datasets, as well as the time taken to train and perform predictions using KNN. Additionally, we also recorded the time taken by RAIDER to evaluate and extract features using the reinforcement learning process. Due to the difficulty of quantifying the time requirements of the manual feature engineering process, it is difficult to make a meaningful comparison between manual and automated feature engineering. The automated feature extraction process is more computationally demanding and results in a longer runtime but circumvents the prolonged real-world time and labour requirements of manual feature engineering. It also alleviates the risk of human error.

Table 3. The runtimes for both the system using manually engineered features and the system using automated feature extraction. All times are in seconds.

	KNN (Manual features)	RAIDER (Automated feature extraction)
Dataset preprocessing time	136.84	317.8
Reinforcement learning time	n/a	1489.81
Prediction time	23.93	20.65
Total (Seconds)	**160.77**	**1828.26**

The results in Table 3 show that RAIDER's automated feature extraction process is more computationally complex and results in a longer run-time than using the manually engineered features. This is due to two reasons. The first is that the pre-processing and representing of the dataset takes longer at 317.8 s for the automated feature extraction process and 136.84 for manually extracted features. This is due to the fact that because RAIDER initially extracts every field within the email header before the reinforcement learning phase it is working with significantly more features than the 32 manually extracted features. The second reason being that the reinforcement learning process takes considerable time (1489.91 s) to accurately determine the importance of each feature. Ultimately in a real-world scenario, the reinforcement learning process would not be executed very frequently and while there is more computational overhead associated with automated feature extraction, there is considerable time and human labour costs avoided by eliminating the need for manual feature engineering. The automated feature extraction process can also adapt to new attacks and evolve whereas the system that uses manually engineered features cannot.

In addition, after the initial deployment and fitting of the algorithms, the actual time cost of classifying emails is slightly better for automated features. Using the manual features resulted in a prediction time of 23.93 s for all 2402 testing emails, or 0.009962531 s/email whereas using the automated features resulted in 20.65 s overall or 0.008597002 s/email.

6.2 Contextual Analysis Limitations

In its current implementation RAIDER analysis and classifies each unique email independently. This means that if an email being analysed by RAIDER is a part of a conversation in which previous emails have already been sent between the sender and the victim, RAIDER would neglect the previous correspondence and make predictions using only the single email that is currently being analysed. I.e. it would attempt to classify the email based only on that email's similarity to the training data, and would not take into consideration its context within the ongoing conversation between the sender and the victim.

This could potentially limit the efficacy of RAIDER as the existence of a spear phishing attack may only be apparent using information sourced from multiple emails. It is also possible that if an attacker sends multiple emails, some of these may be flagged as spear phishing while others avoid detection. Obviously, if one email within a chain is a spear phishing email, the legitimacy of the other emails sent by this sender should be called into question and the sender be considered untrustworthy.

This could also improve the accuracy at which the more sophisticated known sender attacks are detected. By taking into consideration entire conversations rather than just individual emails it may be more difficult for attackers to disguise themselves as a legitimate entity as they would require more information. Scenarios in which the attacker has access to a single email from the sender (Known sender attacks) may no longer deal such a critical blow to RAIDER, as behavioural characteristics that only become apparent across conversations may be difficult to replicate with limited information, thus increasing the information required by the attacker to create a deception possible of fooling RAIDER.

Possible further work for RAIDER involves expanding on this functionality and seeing how the efficacy of RAIDER is affected by a more contextually aware classification algorithm. At the very least a system to flag senders who have previously sent phishing attacks as untrustworthy could help prevent false negatives.

6.3   Crafted vs Real Spear Phishing Emails

As previously mentioned, due to the targeted nature of spear phishing attacks, spear phishing emails based on publicly available benign emails were crafted for these experiments. This was due to a lack of availability of spear phishing datasets suitable for this research. Because the algorithms work by constructing sender profiles for each sender within a mailbox, if genuine spear phishing emails were to be used, multiple legitimate emails for a sender would be needed (both for training and testing), as well as genuine spear phishing attacks targeted towards that sender (for testing.) This kind of data is not readily available in large enough quantities for it to adequately test the systems used.

The three different attack types are crafted based on real spear phishing techniques which have been proven to be frequently used in genuine spear phishing emails [14,32,33]. Despite their basis in real spear phishing attacks, they are still emails crafted for the purpose of testing spear phishing classifiers, and may fall short of fully replicating real-world spear phishing attacks and the phenomena of attacks evolving over time. As such, to fully understand the applicability of RAIDER, it may require real-world testing in which it can encounter genuine spear phishing emails. While we believe the research we have done addresses the computational requirements of existing spear phishing detection systems and proposes a time-proof system that can detect zero-day attacks, we acknowledge that there is still more research to be done to fully quantify the strength and weaknesses of our system and that while the data so far is promising, we can not categorically assume that the exact same results will be replicable in a real-world scenario.

Ultimately the aim of RAIDER was to demonstrate the efficacy and practicality of using automatically generated features as opposed to manually engineered features. We believe we have achieved this and that the work we've done shows the transferability of RAIDER's framework to different attack types. Therefore, in the way that RAIDER can be applied to our multiple different attacks we believe that it will also be applicable to real-world spear phishing attacks. RAIDER's use in a real-world environment is outside the scope of this research but to us is the next logical step in evaluating its capabilities.

7   Related Work

Current literature regarding the identification of spear phishing utilises technical controls and software solutions such as email authentication [34], black-listing IP addresses [35], and ML techniques [36]. ML-based approaches have proved an effective method of detecting spear phishing attacks, but as far as we are aware there has been no previous work on detecting zero-day attacks with these systems. The current landscape of ML-based spear phishing detection is summarised based on the information that different implementations make use of to make predictions.

Stylometric Features. Stylometric or linguistic analysis involves generating features that represent a sender's style of writing. The idea here is that, an email sent by an attacker will have subtle differences in their style of writing than the sender they are impersonating, and that the presence of these differences suggests a spear phishing attack. Dewan et al. [13] and Stringhini and Thonnard [37] implement systems that analyse the linguistic style and behavioural patterns of emails such as the number of paragraphs a sender typically uses or whether they use a space after punctuation. [14] performed similar research into using stylometric features from the subject and body of an email to detect spear phishing attacks. Their solution also considers different deployment options such as having a remote trusted server that users can query when they receive an incoming email.

Email Header Metadata. Previous research has also been done into analysing email header metadata to detect spear phishing attacks. Gascon et al. [12] leveraged a variety of email headers as means to identify spear phishing attacks. They found that composition features such as the encoding of an email and transportation features such as the timezone path an email takes to reach its destination provide a means of validating an email when other fields have been spoofed. Bhadane and Mane [38] made use of email metadata within an organisational setting, looking at scenarios where a spear phishing attack is being launched from a compromised legitimate account within a network. They made use of information such as IP addresses and an email's travel route to detect spear phishing attacks within a real-world scenario. Samad and Gani [15] used the metadata of email attachments to detect spear phishing emails.

Misc. In addition to extracting information from the email in order to predict spear phishing attacks, there also exist studies that make use of external information sources when evaluating incoming emails. In addition to stylometric features, Dewan et al. [13] also made use of information sourced from senders'

LinkedIn profiles to determine if an email was spear phishing or not. Although they found that using these social features did not provide any benefit to prediction accuracy. Other studies [38–40] queried *WHOIS* and *FQDN* information based on data retrieved from the email headers-usually combining these with stylometric and metadata features.

The work of Gascon et al. [12] can be considered the best state-of-the-art work due to their balancing of high true positive rates with low false positives rates, and their privacy-friendly feature extraction method. As far as we are aware there has been no previous spear phishing detection approach that (a) selects significant features autonomously in response to emerging threats, and (b) considers the scalability of the solution based on the existing required large feature vectors. Therefore, the aim of our work is to address those two challenges to produce smaller feature vectors that autonomously change in response to emerging threats.

Feature Selection. We identified the shortcomings of contemporary spear phishing detection systems as a result of the lack of optimization in the feature selection process. While to the best of our knowledge there has been no previous application of feature selection optimization within the realm of spear phishing, there has been considerable research into optimized feature selection. Stochastic optimization algorithms have been demonstrated as an effective way to find meaningful features within data with an extremely large number of possible variables [41]. Dai & Guo proposed a Beta Distribution-based Cross-Entropy framework capable of effectively selecting features across a variety of high-dimensional datasets [42]. Yamada et al. applied stochastic gates to non-linear classification and regression functions using a variety of real and artificial datasets [43]. While stochastic algorithms have proven to be an effective method of optimizing the feature selection process, there have been no prior studies as to their effectiveness within the sphere of detecting spear phishing attacks. Although as the above works show certain stochastic frameworks have proven to be agnostic and transferable to different data types.

8   Conclusion

In this paper, we have explored the possibility of using reinforcement learning to detect zero-day spear phishing attacks. We have devised a spear phishing email detection system (RAIDER) which uses reinforcement learning to automatically evaluate and select important features, while using KNN to make predictions on incoming emails. By simulating different spear phishing attack techniques of varying sophistication, we have demonstrated how our classifier responds when trained with different datasets. We have shown that our automatically generated feature sets (based on a reinforcement-learning algorithm) are of equal or better accuracy than systems, which use manually engineered features. We have also provided evidence that RAIDER saves time and effort in spear phishing identification tasks. The process of generating features takes, on average, 24.83 min and allows for a prediction accuracy of 94% for blind spoofing attacks, which is one of the most widespread techniques employed by adversaries. We have also found that by automatically generating a feature subset, we can potentially detect previously unseen attacks and maintain a more consistent level of accuracy across different attack specimens than statically-trained alternatives. Our results show that by utilising the RAIDER's automatic feature generator, we can avoid accuracy drops of up to 14% when encountering new (previously unseen) attacks.

References

1. Benenson, Z., Gassmann, F., Landwirth, R.: Unpacking spear phishing susceptibility. In: Brenne, M., et al. (eds.) FC 2017. LNCS, vol. 10323, pp. 610–627. Springer, Cham (2017). https://doi.org/10.1007/978-3-319-70278-0_39
2. Thomas, J.E.: Individual cyber security: empowering employees to resist spear phishing to prevent identity theft and ransomware attacks. Int. J. Bus. Manag. **12**(3), 1–23 (2018)
3. O'Gorman, B., et al.: Internet security threat report volume 24 — February 2019, April 2019
4. Ho, G., et al.: Detecting and characterizing lateral phishing at scale. In 28th {USENIX} Security Symposium ({USENIX} Security 19), pp. 1273–1290 (2019)
5. Kim, B., Abuadbba, S., Kim, H.: DeepCapture: image spam detection using deep learning and data augmentation. In: Liu, J.K., Cui, H. (eds.) ACISP 2020. LNCS, vol. 12248, pp. 461–475. Springer, Cham (2020). https://doi.org/10.1007/978-3-030-55304-3_24
6. Shen, K., et al.: Weak links in authentication chains: a large-scale analysis of email sender spoofing attacks. In 30th {USENIX} Security Symposium ({USENIX} Security 21) (2021)
7. Caputo, D.D., Pfleeger, S.L., Freeman, J.D., Johnson, M.E.: Going spear phishing: exploring embedded training and awareness. IEEE Sec. Privacy **12**(1), 28–38 (2013)
8. Canova, G., Volkamer, M., Bergmann, C., Borza, R.: NoPhish: an anti-phishing education app. In: Mauw, S., Jensen, C.D. (eds.) STM 2014. LNCS, vol. 8743, pp. 188–192. Springer, Cham (2014). https://doi.org/10.1007/978-3-319-11851-2_14
9. Ghafir, I., Prenosil, V.: Advanced persistent threat and spear phishing emails. In: Proceedings of the International Conference Distance Learning, Simulation and Communication (DLSC), pp. 34–41 (2015)
10. Ramachandran, A., Feamster, N., Vempala, S.: Filtering spam with behavioral blacklisting. In: Proceedings of the 14th ACM Conference on Computer and Communications Security, pp. 342–351 (2007)
11. Parmar, B.: Protecting against spear-phishing. Comput. Fraud Sec. **2012**(1), 8–11 (2012)
12. Gascon, H., Ullrich, S., Stritter, B., Rieck, K.: Reading between the lines: content-agnostic detection of spear-phishing emails. In: Bailey, M., Holz, T., Stamatogiannakis, M., Ioannidis, S. (eds.) RAID 2018. LNCS, vol. 11050, pp. 69–91. Springer, Cham (2018). https://doi.org/10.1007/978-3-030-00470-5_4
13. Dewan, P., Kashyap, A., Kumaraguru. P.: Analyzing social and stylometric features to identify spear phishing emails. In 2014 APWG Symposium on Electronic Crime Research (Ecrime), pp. 1–13. IEEE (2014)

14. Duman, S., Kalkan-Cakmakci, K., Egele, M., Robertson, W., Kirda, E.: Email-profiler: Spearphishing filtering with header and stylometric features of emails. In: 2016 IEEE 40th Annual Computer Software and Applications Conference (COMPSAC), vol. 1, pp. 408–416. IEEE (2016)
15. Samad, D., Gani, G.A.: Analyzing and predicting spear-phishing using machine learning methods. Multidiszciplináris Tudományok **10**(4), 262–273 (2020)
16. Thapa, C., et al.: Performance measurement of privacy-friendly phishing detection enabled by federated learning. arXiv preprint arXiv:2007.13300 (2020)
17. Sutton, R.S., Barto, A.G.: Reinforcement Learning: An Introduction. MIT Press, London (2018)
18. Machado, M.C., Bellemare, M.G., Talvitie, E., Veness, J., Hausknecht, M., Bowling, M.: Evaluation protocols and open problems for general agents: revisiting the arcade learning environment. J. Artif. Intell. Res **61**, 523–562 (2018)
19. Chou, P.-W., Maturana, D., Scherer, S.: Improving stochastic policy gradients in continuous control with deep reinforcement learning using the beta distribution. In: International Conference on Machine Learning, pp. 834–843, PMLR (2017)
20. Lowrey, K., Kolev, S., Dao, J., Rajeswaran, A., Todorov, E.: Reinforcement learning for non-prehensile manipulation: transfer from simulation to physical system. In: 2018 IEEE International Conference on Simulation, Modeling, and Programming for Autonomous Robots (SIMPAR), pp. 35–42. IEEE (2018)
21. Zhu, Y., et al.: Target-driven visual navigation in indoor scenes using deep reinforcement learning. In: 2017 IEEE International Conference on Robotics and Automation (ICRA), pp. 3357–3364. IEEE (2017)
22. Cunningham, P., Delany, S.J.: k-nearest neighbour classifiers-. arXiv preprint arXiv:2004.04523 (2020)
23. Fard, S.M.H., Hamzeh, A., Hashemi, S.: Using reinforcement learning to find an optimal set of features. Comput. Math. Appl. **66**(10), 1892–1904 (2013)
24. Smadi, S., Aslam, N., Zhang, L.: Detection of online phishing email using dynamic evolving neural network based on reinforcement learning. Decis. Support Syst. **107**, 88–102 (2018)
25. Van Der Heijden, A., Allodi, L.: Cognitive triaging of phishing attacks. In: 28th {USENIX} Security Symposium ({USENIX} Security 2019), pp. 1309–1326 (2019)
26. Ocampoh, D.: diegoocampoh/machinelearningphishing, November 2017
27. Batra, S., Chowdhury, M.: Bread secured. And the Quality is Good (2018)
28. The Apache Software Foundation. Index of /old/publiccorpus, June 2004
29. Ganesh, B., Balakrishnan, H.: Barathiganesh-hb/iswpa-ap, April 2018
30. Foebes: Cleaning Big Data: Most time-Consuming, Least Enjoyable Data Science Task, Survey Says. Gil Press, March 2016
31. Heaton, J.: An empirical analysis of feature engineering for predictive modeling. In: SoutheastCon 2016, pp. 1–6. IEEE (2016)
32. Hu, H., Wang, G.: End-to-end measurements of email spoofing attacks. In: 27th {USENIX} Security Symposium ({USENIX} Security 2018), pp. 1095–1112 (2018)
33. Gori Mohamed, J., Visumathi, J.: WITHDRAWN: predictive model of machine learning against phishing attacks and effective defense mechanisms. In: Materials Today: Proceedings (2020)
34. Xiujuan, W., Chenxi, Z., Kangfeng, Z., Haoyang, T., Yuanrui, T.: Detecting spear-phishing emails based on authentication. In 2019 IEEE 4th International Conference on Computer and Communication Systems (ICCCS), pp. 450–456, IEEE (2019)
35. Ecclesie Agazzi, A.: Phishing and spear phishing: examples in cyber espionage and techniques to protect against them. arXiv preprint arXiv:2006.00577 (2020)

36. Han, Y., Shen, Y.: Accurate spear phishing campaign attribution and early detection. In: Proceedings of the 31st Annual ACM Symposium on Applied Computing, pp. 2079–2086 (2016)
37. Stringhini, G., Thonnard, O.: That ain't you: blocking Spearphishing through behavioral modelling. In: Almgren, M., Gulisano, V., Maggi, F. (eds.) DIMVA 2015. LNCS, vol. 9148, pp. 78–97. Springer, Cham (2015). https://doi.org/10.1007/978-3-319-20550-2_5
38. Bhadane, A., Mane, S.B.: Detecting lateral spear phishing attacks in organisations. IET Inf. Sec. **13**(2), 133–140 (2018)
39. Das, A., Baki, S., El Aassal, A., Verma, R., Dunbar, A.: SoK: a comprehensive reexamination of phishing research from the security perspective. IEEE Commun. Surv. Tutor. **22**(1), 671–708 (2019)
40. Ho, G., Sharma, A., Javed, M., Paxson, V., Wagner, V.: Detecting credential spearphishing in enterprise settings. In: 26th {USENIX} Security Symposium ({USENIX} Security 2017), pp. 469–485 (2017)
41. Gadat, S., Younes, L.: A stochastic algorithm for feature selection in pattern recognition. J. Mach. Learn. Res. **8**, 509–547 (2007)
42. Dai, W., Guo, D.: Beta distribution-based cross-entropy for feature selection. Entropy **21**(8), 769 (2019)
43. Yamada, Y., Lindenbaum, O., Negahban, S., Kluger, Y.: Feature selection using stochastic gates. In: International Conference on Machine Learning, pp. 10648–10659. PMLR (2020)

Network Intrusion Detection Adversarial Attacks for LEO Constellation Networks Based on Deep Learning

Yunhao Li[1], Weichuan Mo[1], Cong Li[1], Haiyang Wang[1], Jianwei He[2], Shanshan Hao[2], and Hongyang Yan[1(✉)]

[1] Guangzhou University, Guangzhou, Guangdong, People's Republic of China
`hyang_yan@gzhu.edu.cn`
[2] CASIC Space Engineering Development Co., Ltd., Hubei 430416, People's Republic of China

Abstract. Low-Earth orbit satellite networks have received attention from academia and industry for their advantages in terms of wide coverage and low latency. Meantime deep learning can provide more accurate traffic anomaly detection and has become an important class of methods for LEO satellite network security. However, deep learning is susceptible to adversarial sample attacks, and the LEO satellite network system has not been investigated to find a framework for adversarial sample attacks and defence systems, which poses a potential risk to network communication security. In this paper, we design a framework to generate and defend against adversarial samples in real time. By capturing traffic from LEO satellites, it can generate traffic adversarial samples to detect whether malicious traffic classification models are vulnerable to attacks, and defense against adversarial sample attacks in real time. In this paper, a simple LEO satellite simulation platform is built to generate traffic adversarial samples using four classical adversarial sample generation methods, and a two-classification deep learning model is trained to determine the effectiveness of the attack and defence. Experiments show that the framework proposed in the paper can crawl traffic and perform self-attack and defence tests.

Keywords: LEO · Traffic classification · Adversarial attack

1 Introduction

Satellites are receiving increasing attention as a new type of broadband Internet access. The biggest difference between LEO communication satellites compared to conventional communication satellites is their altitude from the ground and the complexity of their systems. Indeed, satellite communication has been used for decades in television, telephone, radio, internet and military applications [2].

Support by the Key Research and Development Program of Guangzhou (No. 202103050003).

X. Yuan et al. (Eds.): NSS 2022, LNCS 13787, pp. 51–65, 2022.
https://doi.org/10.1007/978-3-031-23020-2_3

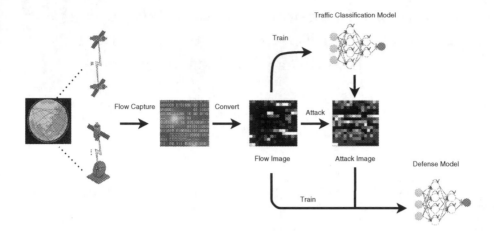

Fig. 1. Architecture

To make LEO satellite communication secure, scientists have been working deeply [1] in the field of spaceflight. However, even if the integrity of the content can be guaranteed during transmission, the satellite's ability to identify and defend against abnormal traffic has been neglected.

Currently, deep learning-based methods for detecting and countering attacks and defences against malicious traffic are not widely used in this area of LEO satellites. From the point of view of defense, a deep learning model to detect whether a perturbation has been added to a data sample can cause an attacker to delay or cancel the attack.

A framework for counteracting perturbation generation and a unified defence framework against attacks based on LEO satellite systems, on the other hand, still requires in-depth research in this area. In this paper, we propose a counter-attack defence framework for LEO satellite Internet by crawling traffic data in LEO satellites and train deep learning models to classify LEO satellite traffic, as well as using a generic counter-attack perturbation generation framework by applying FGSM [7], I-FGSM [11], MI-FGSM [3], PGD [13], four typical perturbation generation methods to achieve the efficient generation of adversarial samples. And study the unified defence framework for adversarial samples to achieve efficient detection of adversarial samples through deep learning models.

The overall structure of the thesis is shown in Fig. 1. We crawl different types of communication traffic in LEO satellites, classify the traffic and train a traffic classification model. Train a traffic defence model to defend against network traffic attacks.

In this paper, we propose a countermeasure framework against LEO satellite internet attacks based on the LEO satellite simulation platform. We apply these techniques in the field of LEO satellite communication, to guarantee the security and robustness of data communication of LEO satellite by identifying traffic, classifying it correctly, thus avoiding attacks on malicious traffic, qualifying the anomalous behavior of attacks through traffic, and taking counteracting sample-based deceptive attacks that can better simulate the traffic of LEO satellites.

The rest of this paper is organized as follows. In Sect. 2, we describe the necessity of the LEO simulation platform and our related work on the simulation platform, the generation of malicious traffic data set, and introduce five kinds of attacks. But also introduces the ResNet-18 model we apply, the adversarial sample, and its four types of adversarial sample generation. In Sect. 3, we describe the process of the traffic adversarial sample generate algorithm and the defense algorithm for adversarial samples, and the method of the flow image pre-processing. We conclude the paper in Sect. 4.

2   Related Work

2.1   Low Earth Orbit Satellite Traffic Simulation Platform

LEO satellite networks are able to break geographical limitations and achieve global wireless coverage [17]. Therefore, it is of great practical importance to study LEO satellites. In order to ensure the work of LEO satellites in specific communication, its reliability and security are particularly prominent. If there are design flaws in the software and hardware design of a satellite and the faults are not discovered until the satellite is sent into actual operation in space, then all previous efforts may be wasted and the satellite may become space junk [5] or even interfere with the work of other satellites and disrupt space [16]. Simulation of LEO satellite satellites allows problems in the design process of LEO satellites to be exposed early and corrected in time, thus achieving maximum cost savings; it also helps one to evaluate whether the space planning is feasible, whether the overall objectives are met, and whether the constraints are satisfied, etc. The satellite simulation constructed by Roberto et al. [14] platform models satellite networks for broadband Internet service access, which generates different types of traffic, interferes with them, classifies the traffic, and assigns different levels of priority to them.

2.2   Malicious Traffic Collection

The training data used in the LEO satellite traffic classification model and the adversarial sample-based traffic classification defense model constructed in this paper all come from our LEO satellite simulation platform. The traffic capture module is deployed in each simulated satellite of the platform to listen to and capture the traffic packets sent by satellite and collected by the simulation system.

2.3   Launch Attack

Distributed Denial of Service (DDoS) [22] can expose many computers to attack at the same time, rendering the target hosts under attack unable to use properly

[10]. This attack can spoof the source IP address, making it difficult to detect when such an attack is generated, and it is also very difficult to detect the attack, making it a very difficult attack to prevent [22].

SSH and FTP Brute Force Attacks (BFA) [19] are attacks in which an attacker attempts to obtain user credentials via the SSH and FTP protocol. The attack attempts to exhaust different combinations of usernames and passwords until they succeed by finding valid credentials or terminating when all expected possibilities have been tried [4]. Brute-force attacks can be easily automated, and an attacker can launch an aggressive attack on the target host with a small amount of attack information and intervention.

Port Scan refers to the hacker's attempt to invade a computer by sending a series of port scanning information, so as to understand and obtain the network service types provided by the computer, thus obtaining the key information of the attacked host [18].

Web Directory Scan uses word lists to perform brute-force attacks on directories and files on web and application servers [9]. If the backend of a website is discovered through this method, security tests such as storming libraries, SQL injection, and even gaining access to the website can be attempted.

2.4   Traffic Classification Model

Traffic classification is the first step to help identify the different applications and protocols present in the network. Segmentation operations such as monitoring and optimization can be performed on the identified traffic to improve network performance. Gao et al. [6] introduce an intrusion detection system using machine learning methods and define a set of attributes in their proposed method and use different thresholds to obtain better classification accuracy. Shafiq et al. [15] used different types of packet sizes to extract information and employed various machine learning based cross-identification methods to test and identify the packets that can be used to obtain traffic identification and classification stages through various tests to compare different datasets to obtain better performance of the system.

CNN. Convolutional neural network (CNN) is a deep learning model. And residual neural network is part of the CNN architecture, which consists of jump connections to overcome the gradient problem.

Wang et al. [20] proposed a CNN-based traffic classification model that treats traffic data as images for representation learning. They identified the best traffic features in other layers through various experiments. Martin et al. [12] proposed a statistical feature-based traffic classification model based on CNN. The results show that the model does not require any engineering features and can provide better performance than other methods. Wang et al. [21] proposed a real-time traffic classification method based on a parallel CNN model. They applied using the Spark platform, and the Spark Streaming framework to simulate the requirements of real-time classification of network traffic.

In subsequent experiments, we chose ResNet-18 as the traffic picture classification model. Compared to a normal CNN network, the residual neural network is more expressive and it is easier to stack the model layers for better accuracy when performing the classification task.

2.5   Adversarial Examples

The computation and generation of the adversarial perturbation is the key to generating the adversarial interference. In the field of computer vision, the generated perturbations must be at a level that is invisible to the human eye and capable of spoofing the model. Currently, adversarial sample generation techniques based on deep neural network classification models are only used for conventional network traffic, but no relevant research on adversarial samples for LEO satellite network traffic has been seen.

FGSM. FGSM was proposed by Goodfellow et al. [7] and is one of the basic methods for generating adversarial samples. It is based on the principle of gradient descent by adding increments in the direction of the gradient so that the deep learning model misclassifies. The perturbation is calculated as Eq. 1

$$P = \varepsilon sign(\nabla \mathfrak{I}(\theta, x, y)) \tag{1}$$

where ε is the constraint limiting the perturbation to be too large, $||P|| <$ *varepsilon* (different parametrizations generate perturbations with different effects). $\nabla \mathfrak{I}(\theta, x, y)$ is the loss function used in training the neural network, θ is the parameter of the classification model, x is the input to the model, and y is the correct label corresponding to the model input. $sign(\nabla \mathfrak{I}(\theta, x, y))$ is the direction of the gradient of the loss function at the point x, and ε can be seen as the offset of the generated perturbation in that direction.

I-FGSM. The FGSM contains only one gradient update, and sometimes one update is not enough to enable the attack to succeed, so Kurakin et al. [11] propose an iterative FGSM based on the FGSM, namely the I-FGSM, whose perturbation is calculated as Eq. 2

$$
\begin{aligned}
\boldsymbol{X}_0^{adv} &= \boldsymbol{X}, \\
\boldsymbol{X}_{N+1}^{adv} &= \text{Clip}_{X,\epsilon} \left\{ \boldsymbol{X}_N^{adv} - \alpha \, \text{sign} \left(\nabla_X J \left(\boldsymbol{X}_N^{adv}, y_{LL} \right) \right) \right\}
\end{aligned}
\tag{2}
$$

So with a constant noise amplitude e, you can set the α and N parameters directly with $\alpha = \frac{e}{N}$. The *Clip* in the formula means that the overflowing values are replaced with boundary values. This is because in iterative updates, as the number of iterations increases, some of the pixel values may overflow, and it is then necessary to replace these values with zeros or ones. Y_{LL} is the class with the lowest classification probability in the classification model for the original input image, which can be calculated by the formula 3

$$y_{LL} = \arg \min_{y} \{p(y \mid \boldsymbol{X})\} \tag{3}$$

Apply this formula multiple times in smaller steps and crop the pixel values of the intermediate results after each step to ensure they lie in the value domain of the original image.

MI-FGSM. FGSM is a linear assumption that applies the sign of the gradient to a practical example by determining the decision boundary near the data point, thus producing an adversarial sample. However, when large distortions are produced, the linearity assumption of the method does not hold and therefore the adversarial sample produced by FGSM does not fit the model well, thus limiting the power of the FGSM attack. Conversely, during each iteration, I-FGSM causes the adversarial samples to move greedily along the gradient direction. Therefore, the adversarial samples can easily fall into local optima and produce overfitting, which is unlikely to transfer between models. In contrast, Yinpeng Dong [3] et al. proposed a method based on momentum iteration to enhance adversarial attacks. The momentum method is a technique to speed up the gradient descent algorithm by accumulating velocity vectors in the direction of the gradient of the loss function during the iterative process, which eliminates the defect of local maxima by combining the momentum term with the attack iteration process to make the update direction stable. Thereby producing more transferable adversarial samples. Its perturbation is calculated as Eq. 4

$$\boldsymbol{g}_{t+1} = \mu \cdot \boldsymbol{g}_t + \frac{\nabla_{\boldsymbol{x}} J\left(\boldsymbol{x}_t^*, y\right)}{\left\| \nabla_{\boldsymbol{x}} J\left(\boldsymbol{x}_t^*, y\right) \right\|_1} \tag{4}$$

g_t collects the gradients of the previous t iterations using the decay factor μ defined in Eq. 4. If $\mu = 0$, the MI-FGSM degenerates to I-FGSM. At each iteration, the current gradient $\nabla_{\boldsymbol{x}} J\left(\boldsymbol{x}_t^*, y\right)$ is normalized by its own L_1 distance.

PGD. The PGD (Project Gradient Descent) attack is an iterative attack, an iteration-based attack method proposed by Aleksander et al. [13]. FGSM requires only one iteration to take a large step in the direction of the gradient, whereas PGD requires multiple iterations repeatedly, taking only one small step at a time, with each iteration will perturb *clip* to a prescribed range, so PGD is a generic attack method among first-order methods.

$$x_{t+1} = \prod_{x+S} \left(x_t + \alpha \cdot \text{sign} \left(\nabla_{\boldsymbol{x}} J\left(x_t, y\right) \right) \right) \tag{5}$$

In the process of PGD, first find the adversarial sample by calculating the loss gradient of the original image, subtracting the adversarial sample from the original image to obtain the perturbation value and restrict the perturbation to the sphere, and then combine the original image with the perturbation value to form the final adversarial sample.

3 Methods

3.1 LEO Traffic Simulation System

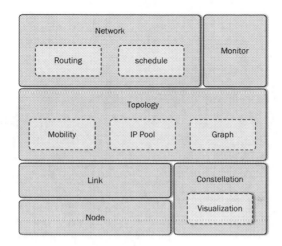

Fig. 2. Architecture of LEO Traffic Simulation system

This paper we designs a real-time, complete simulation framework for LEO satellite constellation network, which is simple to operate and fully functional compared to other simulation platforms. Shown in Fig. 2. The system generates and crawls network traffic, classifies it in real-time, and adds perturbations to normal traffic to generate adversarial samples for spoofing attacks, in addition to designing a detection system for adversarial sample-based attacks.

3.2 Traffic Adversarial Sample Generate Algorithm

The overall algorithm flow of this paper is shown in Algorithm 1, we will crawl the satellite network traffic and convert the traffic into images, attack the traffic images to determine whether the attacked category matches the original category, if it matches the original category, the attack is successful.

Based on the deep learning and the perturbation generation algorithm, this paper designs a spoofed traffic countermeasure sample generation algorithm. The algorithm first requires traffic crawling and format conversion of the LEO satellite traffic, and numerical normalization of each feature in the traffic data to facilitate subsequent training of the traffic classification model. Traffic visualization is then performed, treating the stream of traffic as a grey-scale value of the image.

Next, a convolutional neural network is constructed and trained so that it can classify the visualized flow data and test the correctness of the model. A

Algorithm 1. Traffic adversarial sample generate algorithm

1: Capture and convert from LEO traffic to numerical traffic
2: Normalising numerical flows
3: Converting normalised traffic to images
4: Constructing a CNN model
5: Training the model
6: correct rate: $R1 \leftarrow$ Classifying the test set using normal traffic images
7: The structure and parameters of the trained CNN model are used as known conditions to generate the respective perturbations
8: Overlaying perturbations with real traffic to form spoofed traffic images
9: correct rate: $R2 \leftarrow$ Classifying the spoofed traffic images
10: **if** $R1 \neq R2$ **then**
11:     Return Attack successful
12: **else**
13:     Return Attack failed
14: **end if**

---

perturbation generation method is also chosen to generate the structure and parameters of the trained convolutional neural network model as known conditions to generate the respective perturbations, superimpose them with the real traffic to form the spoofed traffic, and compare the difference between the spoofed and real traffic in a visualized manner. Finally, the resulting spoofed traffic is tested for classification using the trained convolutional neural network, and the test results are compared with the accuracy of classification of real traffic.

3.3 Datasets

The dataset used in this paper is a self-built dataset, the traffic characteristics of LEO satellites may not be the same as normal traffic, we use the LEO satellite simulation platform to simulate LEO satellite traffic, capture traffic from it and manually classify the traffic into one of the six application categories.

Flow Image Pre-processing. Based on the traffic grab packets within the LEO satellite system, the grab packet data was extracted and serialised into images by the method proposed by Wang et al. [20] for converting traffic packets into images. In order to make the deep learning model have a larger perceptual field and facilitate model classification, an image size of 224×224 is used in this paper. The final construction of the LEO satellite traffic dataset has 22,363 normal traffic, 32,239 DDos traffic, 17,471 FTP bursts, 11,381 port scans, 24,882 SSH bursts, and 18,183 Web directory scans. The traffic images are shown in the following Table 1. In the experiments of this paper, 80% were used as the training set and 20% as the validation set.

Table 1. Flow image dataset

Label	Number	Example	Example	Label	Number	Example	Example
Normal	22363			DDos	32239		
FTP brust	17471			Port Scan	11381		
SSH brust	24882			Web scan	18183		

3.4   Traffic Classification Model

The traffic image classification model used in this paper is the ResNet-18 [8] model, which consists of an input layer, a convolutional layer, a pooling layer, and a fully connected layer. In this paper, we improve the ResNet-18 model by designing the input layer as a 224×224 matrix, which corresponds to the visualized traffic, and the output layer as six neurons, which corresponds to the classification results.

In the process of designing the model input layer, we fully consider the LEO satellite traffic characteristics. When converting LEO satellite traffic into pictures, considering the continuity and continuity of traffic characteristics, a model input of 224×224 is used. The model can sense 50176 bits of traffic information in one picture, which helps the model to fully learn the attack traffic characteristics of LEO satellites and improve the accuracy of the model.

We eventually trained a traffic picture classification model with an accuracy of 99.838%, which basically meets the requirements of LEO satellite traffic classification.

3.5   Adversarial Sample Defense Algorithm

The defender identifies the adversarial samples of traffic generated in LEO satellites based on the adversarial sample defense model, determines whether the traffic picture samples are adversarial or not, and achieves efficient detection of the adversarial samples.

In training the adversarial sample defense model, the traffic adversarial sample dataset is generated by the adversarial sample generation algorithm described in this paper, which is combined with the original traffic dataset to form the adversarial sample defense dataset. The dataset contains two categories, adversarial samples, and non-adversarial samples. The defense detection model has the same structure as the traffic classification model so that the defense model can obtain a better fit with the traffic classification model.

Table 2. Adversarial attack dataset

Based on the above traffic picture and the traffic picture adversarial sample, it is possible to construct the LEO satellite traffic classification defence dataset. The dataset is divided into two categories, one for normal LEO satellite traffic and one for LEO satellite traffic adversarial samples. The traffic defence dataset is shown in Table 2.

The adversarial sample defence model used in this paper is the ResNet-18 model, which has the same structure as the traffic picture classification model, so as to obtain a better similarity with the picture classification model, and also to facilitate training and validation. In the end, our trained adversarial sample defence model achieves an accuracy of 99%. Almost all traffic adversarial samples in the LEO satellite system can be identified by the defence model, achieving efficient detection of adversarial samples.

4 Experiment

The attack and defence scenarios built in this paper are divided into four parts: traffic sending, attack perturbation, traffic identification and counter sample defence. The traffic sending side sends normal traffic, SSH burst traffic, FTP burst traffic, WEB directory scan traffic, port scan traffic and DDos traffic. On the attack scrambling side, the PGD [13], FGSM [7], I-FGSM [11], MI-FGSM [3] methods are used to add scrambling to the traffic on the traffic sending side. On the traffic identification side, a deep learning based classification model is used to classify the traffic, and different perturbations are added to the traffic sender so that the traffic is misclassified for spoofing purposes. On the counter-sample defence side, it determines whether a perturbation has been added to the traffic picture.

Table 3. Distribution of single class deception rate and classification for different methods

Type	Deception rate		Classification distribution					
	Method	Rate	Normal	DDoS	FTP-Burst	SSH-Burst	PortScan	WebScan
Normal	PGD	98.273%	1.726%	0.008%	5.652%	42.382%	49.572%	0.657%
	FGSM	92.344%	7.655%	7.320%	26.239%	10.740%	34.507%	13.535%
	I-FGSM	92.872%	7.127%	7.722%	26.342%	10.906%	34.507%	13.392%
	MI-FGSM	92.706%	7.293%	7.610%	25.882%	10.799%	34.825%	13.589%
DDoS	PGD	73.200%	0.058%	26.799%	15.459%	5.276%	51.232%	1.172%
	FGSM	92.149%	4.820%	7.850%	25.891%	1.367%	45.175%	14.895%
	I-FGSM	92.205%	4.959%	7.794%	25.832%	1.256%	45.358%	14.798%
	MI-FGSM	92.133%	4.928%	7.866%	25.993%	1.336%	45.268%	14.606%
FTP burst	PGD	52.303%	0.000%	0.000%	47.696%	0.000%	52.303%	0.000%
	FGSM	70.213%	4.264%	3.863%	29.786%	0.927%	43.546%	17.612%
	I-FGSM	70.459%	4.292%	3.823%	29.540%	0.766%	43.769%	17.806%
	MI-FGSM	70.390%	4.304%	3.857%	29.609%	0.887%	43.718%	17.623%
SSH burst	PGD	99.454%	0.008%	0.000%	9.090%	0.546%	90.330%	0.024%
	FGSM	77.288%	5.055%	1.000%	18.957%	22.711%	35.652%	16.622%
	I-FGSM	77.382%	5.132%	0.856%	18.965%	22.618%	35.547%	16.879%
	MI-FGSM	77.370%	5.148%	0.924%	18.957%	22.630%	35.322%	17.016%
Port scan	PGD	49.970%	42.948%	0.123%	4.788%	1.783%	50.030%	0.325%
	FGSM	62.192%	8.751%	4.173%	28.424%	3.488%	37.808%	17.353%
	I-FGSM	62.236%	9.146%	3.751%	28.327%	3.620%	37.764%	17.388%
	MI-FGSM	62.209%	9.366%	3.804%	28.486%	3.470%	37.791%	17.081%
Web scan	PGD	59.215%	0.000%	0.236%	5.169%	5.120%	48.688%	40.785%
	FGSM	84.381%	2.419%	1.765%	33.866%	0.318%	46.010%	15.618%
	I-FGSM	84.683%	2.348%	1.847%	34.218%	0.280%	45.988%	15.316%
	MI-FGSM	84.551%	2.502%	1.814%	34.042%	0.296%	45.894%	15.448%

In this paper, we build a deep learning model based on PyTorch. Based on PyTorch 1.11.0 and Ubuntu 18.04 to build the simulation system, and we use the LEOCN for the LEO satellite simulation platform to simulate the attack.

Table 4. Attack examples

Method	Success rate
PGD	58%
FGSM	82%
I-FGSM	83%
MI-FGSM	80%

Of these, the specific experimental parameters for the generation of perturbation methods in 4 are:

- **PGD**: Number of iterations 15, bias 0.2, sample clip range 0 to 1
- **FGSM**: bias 0.2, sample clip range 0 to 1
- **I-FGSM**: Number of iterations 10, bias 0.2, sample clip range 0 to 1
- **MI-FGSM**: Number of iterations 10, bias 0.2, sample clip range 0 to 1, Decay factor μ 0.1.

Table 4 shows the visual difference between the spoofed traffic after adding perturbations and the original real traffic, and the most obvious perturbations and the highest success rate of perturbation attacks using I-FGSM generated samples. Table 4 shows the visual difference between the spoofed traffic after adding perturbations and the original real traffic, and the most obvious perturbations and the highest success rate of perturbation attacks using I-FGSM generated samples.

4.1   Defense Model

Based on the above traffic picture and the traffic picture adversarial sample, it is possible to construct the LEO satellite traffic classification defence dataset. The dataset is divided into two categories, one for normal LEO satellite traffic and one for LEO satellite traffic adversarial samples. The traffic defence dataset is shown in Table 2.

The adversarial sample defence model used in this paper is the ResNet-18 model, which has the same structure as the traffic picture classification model, so as to obtain a better similarity with the picture classification model, and also to facilitate training and validation. In the end, our trained adversarial sample defence model achieves an accuracy of 99%. Almost all traffic adversarial samples in the LEO satellite system can be identified by the defence model, achieving efficient detection of adversarial samples.

4.2   Experimental Results

The evaluation metrics of the experimental results include classification spoofing rate, general spoofing rate (GFR, general fooling rate) and single classification spoofing rate (SCFR, single classificatin fooling). The relevant equations are shown in Eq. 6 and Eq. 7.

$$SCFR_i = 1 - Acc_i$$
$$Acc_i = \frac{TP_i}{TP_i + FN_i} \tag{6}$$

$$GFR = 1 - GAcc$$
$$GAcc = \frac{\sum_{i=1}^{m} TP_i}{\sum_{i=1}^{m} (TP_i + FN_i)} \tag{7}$$

where Acc_i is the classification accuracy of the ith class of samples, $GAcc$ is the overall classification accuracy of the test samples, TP_i is the number of samples of actual type i that are predicted normally by the classification model, FN_i is the number of samples of actual type i that are misclassified as other classes by the classification model, and $m = 6$ indicates that there are six classes in total. The overall deception rate is shown in Table 4.

The accuracy of the attacker's classification of the real network using the traffic classification model before the spoofed traffic was generated was 99.83%. The corresponding spoofing rates for the four different perturbation generation methods are shown in Table 4. It can be seen that after the implementation of the perturbation, the probability of the type of traffic being misclassified is greatly increased regardless of which perturbation generation method is used, taking the FGSM method as an example, the attacker uses the ResNet traffic picture classification model to classify the traffic The error rate reached 82% when using the FGSM method.

According to the formula 7, the statistical single-class spoofing rate corresponding to the four perturbation generation methods and the post-spoofing classification distribution are shown in Table 3.

In Table 3, the distribution of raw traffic being classified as different traffic is depicted in the classification distribution. For normal traffic, for example, when using the PGD attack method, 0.008% is misclassified as DDoS class, 5.652% is misclassified as FTP-Burst class, 42.382% is misclassified as SSH-Burst, 49.572% were misclassified as PortScan, 0.657% were misclassified as WebScan, and for normal traffic, they were mainly misclassified as PortScan.

Using the FGSM method as an example, the highest spoofing rate among the six traffic applications was 92.344% for normal traffic and the lowest rate was 62.192% for PortScan.

The following conclusions can be drawn from the above experimental results.

- For the ResNet convolutional neural network model, the different perturbation generation methods chosen all have good spoofing effects, with I-FGSM having the best spoofing effect and PGD having the worst spoofing effect
- for the overall deception rate of the dataset, the FGSM series methods show high adversarial properties, mainly because the FGSM series are generated for non-target specific adversarial samples, while the PGD methods are slightly worse in terms of overall deception rate compared to the other three methods
- Comparing the different perturbation generation methods, the sample perturbations generated using the FGSM series are significantly more than those generated by PGD, illustrating the subtlety of the perturbations generated by PGD
- In terms of the single-class spoofing rate for traffic, although the spoofing effects of the four methods differ, the four methods have roughly the same tendency to misclassify traffic types, for example, traffic has a higher probability of being misclassified to PortScan, followed by a higher probability of not misclassifying to FTP-Burst, all of which reflect some similarity in the timing of traffic types.

5   Conclusion

In this work, we study a real-time LEO satellite traffic classification system and then proposes a spoofing traffic generation method based on four adversarial attack methods. A unified defence framework for adversarial attack samples is also studied, enabling efficient detection of adversarial attack samples through deep learning models.

These techniques are applied to the field of LEO satellite communication, thus guaranteeing the security and robustness of LEO satellite data communication and avoiding malicious traffic attacks.

Experiments have verified the feasibility of the proposed approach for LEO satellite platforms, and in future work, this paper will address the following areas for further research.

- Using more adversarial attack sample generation methods for adversarial attacks on LEO satellite platforms to generate spoofing traffic samples with higher spoofing rates against more complex deep neural networks
- Study spoofing traffic generation methods for LEO satellites, taking into account the characteristics of LEO satellite traffic
- Verify the migration of spoofing traffic countermeasures against different models, and discover the stability of different deep neural networks against spoofing traffic countermeasures

References

1. RAKS: robust authentication and key agreement scheme for satellite infrastructure | SpringerLink. https://link.springer.com/article/10.1007/s11235-022-00923-0#citeas
2. Darwish, T., Kurt, G.K., Yanikomeroglu, H., Lamontagne, G., Bellemare, M.: Location management in internet protocol-based future Leo satellite networks: a review. IEEE Open J. Commun. Soc. **3**, 1035–1062 (2022). https://doi.org/10.1109/OJCOMS.2022.3185097
3. Dong, Y., et al.: Boosting adversarial attacks with momentum (2017). https://doi.org/10.48550/ARXIV.1710.06081, https://arxiv.org/abs/1710.06081
4. Fahrnberger, G.: Realtime risk monitoring of SSH brute force attacks. In: Phillipson, F., Eichler, G., Erfurth, C., Fahrnberger, G. (eds.) I4CS 2022. CCIS, vol. 1585, pp. 75–95. Springer, Cham (2022). https://doi.org/10.1007/978-3-031-06668-9_8
5. Fung, T.Y., Roy, S.S., Shi, Q., DeLaurentis, D.A.: Space junk aggregation, neutralization, in-situ transformation, and orbital recycling. In: 2022 17th Annual System of Systems Engineering Conference (SOSE), pp. 239–245 (2022). https://doi.org/10.1109/SOSE55472.2022.9812659
6. Gao, J., Senchun, C., Zhang, B., Xia, Y.: Research on network intrusion detection based on incremental extreme learning machine and adaptive principal component analysis. Energies (2019)
7. Goodfellow, I.J., Shlens, J., Szegedy, C.: Explaining and harnessing adversarial examples (2014). https://doi.org/10.48550/ARXIV.1412.6572, https://arxiv.org/abs/1412.6572

8. He, K., Zhang, X., Ren, S., Sun, J.: Deep residual learning for image recognition. In: Proceedings of the IEEE Conference on Computer Vision and Pattern Recognition, pp. 770–778 (2016)
9. Huizinga, T.: Using machine learning in network traffic analysis for penetration testing auditability (2019)
10. Mohmand, M.I., et al.: A machine learning-based classification and prediction technique for DDoS attacks. IEEE Access **10**, 21443–21454 (2022). https://doi.org/10.1109/ACCESS.2022.3152577
11. Kurakin, A., Goodfellow, I., Bengio, S.: Adversarial examples in the physical world (2016). https://doi.org/10.48550/ARXIV.1607.02533, https://arxiv.org/abs/1607.02533
12. Lopez-Martin, M., Carro, B., Sánchez-Esguevillas, A., Lloret, J.: Network traffic classifier with convolutional and recurrent neural networks for internet of things. IEEE Access (2017)
13. Madry, A., Makelov, A., Schmidt, L., Tsipras, D., Vladu, A.: Towards deep learning models resistant to adversarial attacks (2017). https://doi.org/10.48550/ARXIV.1706.06083, https://arxiv.org/abs/1706.06083
14. Puddu, R., Popescu, V., Murroni, M.: An open source satellite network simulator for quality based multimedia broadband traffic management. In: 2022 IEEE International Symposium on Broadband Multimedia Systems and Broadcasting (BMSB), pp. 01–07 (2022). https://doi.org/10.1109/BMSB55706.2022.9828566
15. Shafiq, M., Yu, X.: Effective packet number for 5g im WeChat application at early stage traffic classification. Mob. Inf. Syst. (2017)
16. Singh, S., Purbey, S.: Space debris - it's effect on the earth. Int. J. Recent Adv. Multidiscipl. Top. **3**(6), 13–16 (2022). https://www.journals.resaim.com/ijramt/article/view/2135
17. Tang, Q., Fei, Z., Li, B., Han, Z.: Computation offloading in Leo satellite networks with hybrid cloud and edge computing. IEEE Internet Things J. **8**(11), 9164–9176 (2021). https://doi.org/10.1109/JIOT.2021.3056569
18. Tundis, A., Mazurczyk, W., Mühlhäuser, M.: A review of network vulnerabilities scanning tools: types, capabilities and functioning. In: Proceedings of the 13th International Conference on Availability, Reliability and Security. ARES 2018. Association for Computing Machinery, New York (2018). https://doi.org/10.1145/3230833.3233287
19. Vykopal, J., Drašar, M., Winter, P.: Flow-based brute-force attack detection. Department of Mathematics & Computer Science (2013)
20. Wang, W., Zhu, M., Zeng, X., Ye, X., Sheng, Y.: Malware traffic classification using convolutional neural network for representation learning. In: International Conference on Information Networking (2017)
21. Wang, X., Liu, Y., Su, W.: Real-time classification method of network traffic based on parallelized CNN. In: 2019 IEEE International Conference on Power, Intelligent Computing and Systems (ICPICS) (2019)
22. Zargar, S.T., Joshi, J., Tipper, D.: A survey of defense mechanisms against distributed denial of service (DDoa) flooding attacks. IEEE Commun. Surv. Tutor. **15**(4), 2046–2069 (2013). https://doi.org/10.1109/SURV.2013.031413.00127

A Proof of Concept Implementation of Explainable Artificial Intelligence (XAI) in Digital Forensics

Stuart W. Hall[✉], Amin Sakzad, and Sepehr Minagar

Faculty of Information Technology, Monash University, Melbourne, Australia
swhal3@student.monash.edu, {amin.sakzad,sepehr.minagar}@monash.edu

Abstract. Explainable Artificial Intelligence (XAI) has been a subject of much research related to its potential to have a transformative impact on industries where AI implementations require a high degree of trust. Digital Forensics is one such field, with practitioners dealing with an ever-increasing volume of data and a variety of devices. This research first examines the concept of XAI and what it could accomplish in the Digital Forensics field. Using of series of 23 manufactured virtual hard disk (VHD) images, AI models were trained to make predictions on image and video file content and file system metadata. The manufactured VHD images can be of independent interest for educational purposes as well. The predictions were then processed using the Local Interpretable Model-Agnostic Explanations (LIME) toolkit. These results were then used as the basis for a discussion on the future of XAI in the digital forensics industry and potential areas for further research.

Keywords: XAI · Digital forensics · LIME

1 Introduction

The field of IT forensics faces significant challenges related to increases in data sources and volume, data access, data sophistication, data standardization, the implementation of standardized processes and associated practitioner certifications, and the legitimacy of digital evidence production and processes [3,5,10,14]. Increases in the volume and sources of data have severely impacted the time required for IT forensic service delivery [20,21]. In response to these challenges, IT Forensic software developers have integrated proprietary Artificial Intelligence (AI) functions into their products to assist investigators in identifying evidentiary data of interest faster. These AI models, while useful, do not provide explanations for their predictions [12]. In response to trust issues posed by 'blackbox' AI implementations, Explainable Artificial Intelligence (XAI) research has become an area of significant academic interest. The creation of reasoned and justifiable explanations for predictions made on IT forensic data could be transformative for the industry and the wider justice system.

© The Author(s), under exclusive license to Springer Nature Switzerland AG 2022
X. Yuan et al. (Eds.): NSS 2022, LNCS 13787, pp. 66–85, 2022.
https://doi.org/10.1007/978-3-031-23020-2_4

Investigators, researchers, and IT forensics practitioners have long sought ways to reduce the impact of confronting material on individuals without compromising processing speed, accuracy and the quality of reporting [23, p. 132]. XAI in IT Forensics could have a massive impact on how investigations and prosecutions proceed in relation to Child Sexual Abuse Material (CSAM). For example, consider a case where DF investigators locate suspected CSAM files on a device belonging to a specific suspect. However, the images and video files located are not deemed sufficient grounds to prosecute based on issues with the CSAM depictions. In the image and video files, the age of the victims cannot be readily determined without thorough examination or victim identification. The prosecution is unlikely to proceed with ambiguously aged and unidentified victims. Investigators in this case process the images through an AI model that returns two float values, i and l, where $0 \leq i, l \leq 1$ and $i + l = 1$, for whether the file is illegal or legal, respectively. The prediction with the higher value is considered the overall prediction. Even if such a model were trained to have $\approx$ 99% accuracy, recall and precision when scoring a file as illicit with a score >0.8, prosecutors and the general judiciary would be right to be wary of its predictions. Questions would remain around how the model made the prediction and whether the identified features should be used as grounds for such a prediction. One could expect an illicit file's predicted score to be produced based on physical features related to the victim present in the file, such as the size and build of the victim or the presence of first and secondary sex characteristics (genital development, the presence of pubic hair, etc.). Poorly trained AI models can make predictions based on unintended characteristics of the training data set, e.g. if a significant number of illicit CSAM images used in the training data set had blue wallpaper, then blue wallpaper's presence in an image could weight its prediction as an illicit file.

By implementing the same model using existing XAI technologies or using model-agnostic methods to approximate the predictions of the model, it is possible to create explanations based on specific aspects of a data feature to justify specific predictions. This allows for more efficient validation of the predicted label, as well model performance in predictive tasks [22]. This approach allows flaws within the training dataset (like the presence of blue wallpaper) to be properly identified and countered. It is possible a trained XAI's predictions could be used for expert evidence in the courts in the future. A 'truly explainable' AI may one day be considered a better expert witness than an IT Forensic practitioner since its performance and interpretations of empirical evidence could be readily measured and evaluated [12,17].

XAI can also help DF investigators in the automation of the entire investigation process. Hall et al. [12] identified how XAI implementations could potentially transform the IT forensics industry, greatly assisting investigators to more quickly progress investigations and identify key data of interest. The authors of [12] also conceptualized the XAI for DF model, through which aspects of IT forensic report generation could be automated. This model requires the processing of extracted forensic data from all relevant evidence items related to the case through an AI model (or models) working with XAI technologies. After enriching this data with secondary sources (such as an organization's intelligence holdings), the XAI should then output a set of reasoned assertions based on temporal and geographic data points observed (e.g. Suspect A was at Location B on dates C, D, E, and undertook browsing activity F, G, and sent messages H, I, etc.). Assertions and their associated explanations would be based on contextual elements of the case (e.g. date of offence, known parties and locations of interest and their relationships, etc.), which would assist in highlighting the most significant attributes that could significantly impact an investigation. These examples raise the following important questions:

How could XAI be integrated into a DF workflow? What would be the impact of such integration in the context of DF investigations?

1.1   Our Contributions

This paper first sets aspirations for the integration of XAI technology in addressing challenges extant in the IT Forensics industry. In particular, we provide a proof of concept for the implementation of XAI in IT forensics. We also demonstrate how Local Interpretable Model-Agnostic Explanations (LIME), a widely used XAI technology, can enhance the performance and investigative capabilities of AI's implemented to assist DF forensic practitioners. The tests developed use manufactured IT forensic data to evaluate how XAI tools can be applied to image, video and file metadata classification tasks in the context of IT forensic investigations. The results of these tests are then used as the basis for a discussion of XAI and its impacts on the IT forensic industry. The manufactured IT forensics data, which can be of independent interest for educational purposes, and AI models trained as part of this project use open-source and non-proprietary technologies that could one day be used as evidence in a court following further developments in legislation and policy.[1]

1.2   AI in Digital Forensics: The Current State

To assist IT Forensic Investigators, forensic software developers like Cellebrite, Magnet Forensics and Griffeye Technologies have integrated proprietary, opaque AI-based predictive models into their software to assist in the identification of potentially evidentiary data [12, p. 4]. Data identified by these models require manual validation by an IT Forensic examiner and (as of the time of publication) does not provide any form of explanation to assist investigators in determining how such a prediction was made. The authors of [23] conducted a survey of IT Forensic practitioners examining their use of different forensic tools, methodologies and software capabilities in assisting in the investigation of offences involving CSAM. 28% of the respondents identified issues related to tools and technology as the most significant workflow limitation when undertaking investigations.

---

[1] Please see https://github.com/swhal3/Proof-Of-Concept-Explainable-AI-in-DF-Research-Paper.git.

More recently, [24] provided a series of recommendations for overcoming the trust threshold for AI in DF, specifically by insuring that AI tools are contextualized to the scenario; that intrinsically explainable AI tools (e.g. Decision Trees) are used were possible, especially for well-structured forensic data; that interpretable models be used as necessary for unstructured data tasks (e.g. image/video/audio examination), but be selected based on their capacity to be explained; and that AI tools in DF must be modular in nature and data type specific.

2   Background, Dataset, and Models

2.1   What Is XAI?

An XAI is an artificial intelligence that 'produces details or reasons to make its function clear or easy to understand' to a given audience [2, p. 2]. In practice, different user roles require different levels of explainability for a given AI model to have utility. Explainability can relate to specific aspects of the AI's functioning, such as its algorithmic transparency, or can be indicative of a model's ability to produce explainers along with predictions that make understanding input data features' relative impacts more feasible. As AI's use has increased, so has the importance of ensuring that AI models can be relied upon to make accurate decisions explainable to end-users. An XAI implementation helps users assess a predictive model's 'impartiality in decision-making'; identify features that reverse predictions or have an undue impact on their level of significance, and help identify unknown biases in training or testing datasets. Identifying and countering these features makes a better predictive model [2, p. 2], [13]. In making a case for XAI, Ribeiro, Singh, and Guestrin [22] identify trust, specifically the capacity of a user to trust a model's rationality and predictions, as a key factor impacting whether the tool will have long term use. XAI is key to increasing trust in AI models by providing developers with tools through which to evaluate and improve the performance of their models and to provide justifications to end-users for specific predictive labels.

2.2   The Datasets

A sample of 23 virtual hard disk (.vhd) files, each approximately 2 GB in size, formed the basis for this study's sample. These images were produced for the assessment of students studying IT forensics in a university-level course. Real-world data was not available for this research, a key challenge of which was access to appropriate training and testing data. As such, the images were limited in scope by design to not overwhelm students. The images contained a simplified Windows system partition with a New Technology File System (NTFS) and a single user account. To create the unique features of each image, the user account profile folder was changed to a directory within the virtual hard disk to capture files created by Microsoft Windows per user activity. The user then would perform certain actions for a short period of time, such as visiting several web-sites, including a suspicious website under the creators' control, searching some keywords, downloading text files and editing the files etc. Four main Windows Registry files were exported and copied to the virtual disk for each image. Students were challenged to recover key forensic information about the system and user activity within the image through examination of the files and filesystem, metadata and the Windows Registry hives for the image assigned to them. The analysis of the Windows Registry, however, is outside the scope of this research.

In addition to the above educational cases and the use in this research, we see the creation of manufactured IT forensic data of great potential as it can be considered as a way to train AI without requiring ethics or going through the steps of getting real data. We also note that these sample images could be greatly expanded for further creation of data. For example, the number of images can increase easily, the variety of implanted artifacts can change, and similar techniques can be adapted to expand this to Mobile and/or Memory Forensics.

2.3 Data Models

Project Video Image Classification Standard (VIC). Images and videos were exported from the VHD files in the Project VIC Video Image Classification Standard (VICS) - an internationally accepted approach used by law enforcement for sharing data between forensic tools [19]. Project VIC has been implemented in major forensic software suites, including Cellebrite Physical Analyzer, Magnet Axiom, Griffeye Analyze, Forensic Explorer, AccessData FTK and open text EnCase Forensic, and is available for law enforcement as a plug-in for the open-source forensic software Autopsy. The VIC 2.0 standard was used to create the datasets used for training and testing the AI models. CSAM data and official VICS formatted intelligence were not used in the preparation of this research paper. The Project VIC data model was available to one of the authors as a digital forensic practitioner in law enforcement.

TensorFlow and the Keras API. TensorFlow is an open-source software platform developed by Google for machine learning and AI [1]. Working in unison with Keras, a 'minimalist, high-level neural networks library with a focus on enabling easy and fast prototyping and experimentation' through the Keras functional API, TensorFlow can be used to quickly and efficiently train, produce, save and query machine learning models for data prediction and analysis [25][26, p. 227]. As the emphasis in this research is not necessarily on producing models that make sufficiently accurate predictions but on demonstrating how XAI tools can be used to improve the quality of AI predictive models in IT forensics, these implementations were deemed fit for purpose.

Local Interpretable Model-Agnostic Explanations (LIME). LIME is a type of local surrogate model. Local surrogate models 'are interpretable models that are used to explain individual predictions of black box machine learning models' [16]. LIME takes a model and specific predictions and provides explanations for those predictions. It does not directly alter the prediction or model's performance. Specifically, LIME was designed 'to identify an interpretable model over the interpretable representation that is locally faithful to the classifier' [22, p. 3]. Local faithfulness means features impacting individual predictions can be determined based on predictions that fall in their local area within the prediction space, but not across all predictions. LIME generates perturbations of a local instance in the vicinity of a prediction, which is then classified and used as training data for an interpretable model. Each data point is weighted based on its distance from the original predictor. For images, LIME can be used to highlight the super-pixels (small regions of pixels within an image that share common characteristics) that are most influential in a model making a specific prediction [9, p. 1][22, p. 3]. For classifying text, LIME can identify the significance of individual words when assigning a predictive label but does not account for feature interactions (e.g. combinations of words) [6]. LIME's model-agnostic nature makes it an excellent solution for XAI implementations in IT forensics. Evidentiary forensic artefacts indicating specific user behaviours can come from file content and metadata (both file system created/modified/access dates and e.g. Embedded Exchangeable Image File Format (EXIF) data). XAI solutions for IT forensics must therefore have the flexibility to deal with multiple file formats, aggregate overall data, and make meaningful and explained predictions. Another advantage of LIME was its implementation in Python and integration with TensorFlow and Keras, allowing for easier data analysis and visualization when paired with powerful Python modules like matplotlib, pandas, and numpy.

3   Forensic Processing

Figure 1 depicts an overview of the processing undertaken to facilitate the creation of the forensic datasets, the testing and training of the AI models, and the generation of the LIME explanations.

3.1   Target Files

Each VHD file contained target files that needed to be successfully identified and analyzed by students. These target images had EXIF data that students also needed to recover and record to receive full marks. For image files within the Virtual Hard Disk, the target file of interest was denoted with a white square and 16-character hexadecimal code. Similarly, the target video files contained a 16-character hexadecimal code appearing during the video for a few seconds.

The VHD files were initially processed using the Autopsy Command Line Interface [4]. The created Autopsy cases were used for result validation and confirmation of data structures. The Project VIC media export dataset was created using GetData Forensic Explorer, which has inbuilt functionality for exporting hashed files in the Project VIC 1.3 and 2.0 formats [11]. All VHD files were added

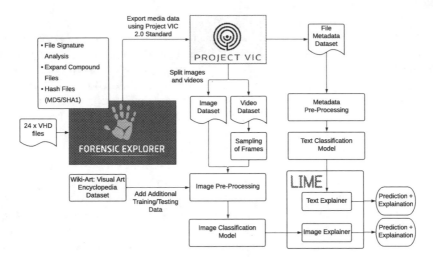

Fig. 1. An Overview Diagram of the processing undertaken to the Forensic Data to train and test the AI models and produce LIME explanations.

to the same Forensic Explorer Case with the same import configuration, which expanded compound files (e.g. archives, thumbnails caches, open office XML files, etc.), conducted file signature analysis, hashed files using MD5 and SHA-1 algorithms and cached image and video thumbnails for more efficient review. Once pre-processing was complete, all hashed files available to be exported by the software were used to create the VIC 2.0 dataset.

3.2   Parsing Media Data

The AI models created were designed to use the VIC 2.0 dataset as the basis for data ingest, replicating a key method for how media data is shared between various tools by IT forensic practitioners. First, a vics_media class in python was defined. The class's main object holds all the metadata for an individual file stored in a VIC 2.0 export and uses a class-specific method to load media files. Additional processing splits the media files by file type. Information stored in this parsed object also allowed for interaction with the exported dataset.

3.3   File Pre-processing

There was a total of 14,112 media files exported into the VIC 2.0 dataset from the VHD files, of which 5,728 were unique. This includes 99.bmp, 143.db (Thumbnail cache), 5,152.jpeg, 53.mp4, 253.png, and 28.webm files.

Images. Images were first divided into "target" and "ignorable" images. The target images were images with the 16-digit hexadecimal flag visible in the files' content. The ignorable images were all other images without said tag. Due to the nature of the source dataset, there were only 23 target image files across the 23 VHD files from which the media files were exported. The first attempts at training a model with such a small target dataset were unsuccessful, with all testing files classified as ignorable. To assist in strengthening the significance of the tag feature within image files, an additional 2,559 target image files were produced. Python Image and Random libraries were used to generate a tag and add it to randomly sampled images from the Wiki-Art Visual Art Encyclopedia dataset [15]. Some of these images were also processed as additional test data ran against the developed model. All image files were then resized to 256 × 256 pixels to enable their ingest as training data into a TensorFlow Keras Sequential model.

Videos. It was decided that video files would also be processed through the same predictive model as the image files. To facilitate this, each video from the VIC 2.0 dataset was processed using the CV2 python library to sample every 25 frames. These frames were then resized and ran against the predictive model. A video was deemed to be a target or ignorable based on the modal prediction for all its sampled frames. As with images, videos were deemed to be target videos if the hexadecimal tag was visible in any of their frames' content.

File System Metadata. Different files' file system and embedded metadata can form the basis for compelling digital forensic evidence. Often specific forensic artefacts are created, updated or modified without the user's knowledge when specific activities take place. Being able to correctly interpret the significance and meaning of specific features is a key aspect of IT forensic analysis. The Project VIC metadata was processed into usable training and testing datasets for this research. Features with homogeneous values were removed to streamline processing. Half of the exported Project VIC dataset was randomly assigned for use as training data. To inflate target training data scores beyond files identified by the hexadecimal tag extant in the original dataset, a set of arbitrary rules was devised to approximate a training set of roughly half target and half ignorable data. The following target features were selected:

- The files had a Created Date (NTFS Created Date/time - 'Created' feature in the VIC 2.0 dataset) between 00:00:00 hrs on the 4th of September 2021 and 12:00:00 hrs on the 4th of September 2021, and;
- The files were from images 4, 5, 6, 15, 16, 17 or 18, and;
- The files did not contain 'OneDrive' in any field (only present in FilePath and FileName parameters)

All other files in the training dataset were classified as ignorable.

3.4 Implementing AI and Explainability

As previously stated, the predictive models for this research were implemented using TensorFlow's Keras API. For image classification, an image of a standardized size (256 × 256 pixels) is first loaded using the Python Image Library (PIL) and converted into a numpy.ndarray. This array is then provided to the model, which in turn returns a numpy array of the shape (1,2)(e.g. [[0.4,0.6]]) containing ignorable and target scores in the first and second positions, respectively. The label for the prediction is then determined by using the np.argmax function to return the index of the higher of the two predicted scores, which is the same index as the class label for that score in a python list. The TensorFlow softmax method was then used to generate the softmax activations for each category (thus expressing an image's scores as an np.array [[i,t]] where $0 \leq i, t \leq 1$ and $i + t = 1$.). This ensured that the dominant label and the strength of the prediction could be easily recognized.

For the classification of file system metadata, a TensorFlow Keras Basic Text Multi-class classification model was trained. By handling metadata as a string processed through a text classification model, unique features of the 'FilePath' Feature (containing the NTFS File Path information) were able to be individually assessed to measure their impact on the prediction. Similar to the image classification model, the text classification model returned a numpy.ndarray of shape (1,2) containing ignorable and target probabilities in the first and second positions, respectively, with these scores adding to a total of one.

Using LIME to Implement Explainability. Following the creation of the results (as an np.array object of shape (1,2)), the input data was provided to a LIME Explainer instance (a LimeImageExplainer object from the lime_image library or LimeTextExplainer object from the lime_text library for image or text data respectively) with the TensorFlow model predict method used to generate the results. For the image classification problem, the top five fields indicative of an image being a target, and those of the image being ignorable were identified using LIME. The overall top six features indicative of either label were identified for each file metadata record.

4   Results

To assess the models' performance in their tests, the testing data was used to generate predicted labels, which were then compared to the expected result. The results of these tests were collated into a confusion matrix, a table that displays the totals of correctly classified data for the positive and negative predictions, as well the totals of false positive and false negative predictions [8, p. 234]. The following key metrics were also calculated for the purpose of evaluating the two models' performance across their tests:

- Precision: 'Denotes the proportion of predicted positive cases that are correctly real positives', thus allowing for the evaluation of how well a model correctly finds the target data [18, p. 38].
- Recall: 'The proportion of real positive cases that are correctly Predicted Positive', used for evaluating the likelihood of target data being misclassified [18, p. 38].

– Accuracy: The total proportion of correct predictions out of all predictions made, used for evaluating basic model performance.

4.1   Image Classification Results

Table 1. Table of results for image, video and metadata cassification tasks.

	Images		Videos		Metadata	
	Positive	Negative	Positive	Negative	Positive	Negative
True	3,932	2,220	9	38	1,716	5,186
False	399	925	15	14	154	0

Totals	7,476	76	7,056

Precision	0.907873	0.3750	0.9176

Recall	0.809553	0.3913	1

Accuracy	6,152/7,476 (82.29%)	47/76 (61.8%)	6,902/7,056 (97.8%)

Image classification models in IT forensics are often used to increase the efficiency with which significant data can be identified. Beyond the general identification and tagging of target data, LIME presents a unique tool through which further analysis can be undertaken on individual files to determine how different features influence a prediction. The trained image classification model was produced using 2,566 ignorable files from the original dataset, and 2,506 target files of which 10 were sourced as original target files and the rest were created for the purpose of training the model. The testing dataset consisted of 7,476 image files, containing both files extant in the VIC 2.0 dataset and those created from the 'Wiki-Art: Visual Art Encyclopedia' dataset. Table 1 shows the confusion matrix and key performance metrics for image classification testing. Of the tested files, 50 from each of the True Positive (TP), True Negative (TN), False Positive (FP) and False Negative (FN) datasets were randomly selected for processing by LIME and additional examination. As LIME is a local surrogate model, its outputs are best for interpreting the quality of individual predictions. From these predictions, inferences about trends within the entire model can be made with additional analysis of results [7]. The evaluation of LIME results have been used to make inferences about how XAI can impact the IT forensic industry.

Examination of the 50 TP results from LIME indicated that in 35 of the 50 images, the target label was not identified as one of the top five segments indicative of the image being a target. All of the sampled images were files created for this project and did not originate from the VHD files. All files classified were therefore images depicting works of art. Segments incorporating the hexadecimal tag were only highlighted in 15 of the images examined in LIME. Each of these images shared a similar colour palette but varied in style, shape and structure. In the remaining images, the prediction of a target was based on segments external to the tag. These performance statistics show that the AI model has not been sufficiently trained to recognize the hexadecimal tag as the significant target feature in every image.

To measure the degree of impact the data tag had on predicted labels, additional analysis was undertaken on the 50 TN results processed through LIME. This sample contained no images depicting artwork. Four images were Windows OS system icons, two images were of movie posters and 46 were of photos sourced from the original VHD files. In manufacturing additional target files using the 'Wiki-Art: Visual Art Encyclopedia' dataset, the model appeared to have been trained to recognize unquantifiable features of artwork (e.g. brushwork patterns, blocks of colours, etc.) as features indicative of an image being a target. These fifty files were reprocessed with a data tag attached, and the differences between their ignorable and target probabilities were measured. This showed that, on average, adding a data tag to an image shifted both the predicted probabilities of an image being ignorable and it being a target .26 towards being a target. Fifteen of the fifty images changed prediction from ignorable to target after the tag was added, thus proving its presence could affect predicted scores.

4.2   Video Classification

The performance of the video classification model in the tests are summarised in Table 1. As was previously stated, video classification was undertaken by sampling frames from the video files from the VIC 2.0 dataset and processing these through the Image Classification Model. There was a total of 76 video files within the dataset. Predictions were derived by taking the modal prediction for all a video's sampled frames. This approach is reflected in the predictive models poorer performance at this classification task than the image classification task. In most cases within the testing sample, the hexadecimal data tag was only present for eight to ten sampled frames of footage. As the video files examined varied in length, the proportion of target frames to the overall number of frames also varied widely across the dataset. The ability of the Image Classification model to identify the data tag's presence or absence is therefore not well represented in the statistical performance of the model. This may not be a major problem for standard feature identification in IT forensic datasets, where video classification implementation may simply look for the presence of specific objects (as data features) in ranges of frames, but does undermine the ability to successfully evaluate the model's performance when examining binary categorical features like 'target' and 'ignorable' in this case. Frames returning the highest and lowest target and ignorable scores were processed through LIME to identify the top five segments influencing a target and ignorable prediction.

Video f5b2e69d36cc668bbe352e4919bfe331 was classified as a target, and had 49 frames sampled, over which ten frames were target frames containing the data tag (frames 350 to 575 inclusive with sampling occurring every 25 frames). Figure 2 graphs changes in the predicted score for target and ignorable throughout the sampled frames. A green line denotes the range in probability scores in range $y \in [t, i]$ where t is the target probability and i is the ignorable probability where $0 \leq t, i \leq 1$ and $t + i = 1$. If more of this line falls above zero, then the predicted label for that specific frame was a target. If more of the line falls below zero, then that frame was labelled ignorable. In this video, the change in score when the data tag appears in the video can clearly be seen. There is marked increase in the target score, coupled with a decrease in the ignorable score. This video was correctly labelled as a target. Despite the poor overall performance of the model as shown by the accuracy, precision and recall, these results are further indication that the model was trained on relevant features. Video fdcdd12198760a0599319e8407cb85c8 was classified as ignorable, and had 85 frames sampled, over which 10 frames were target frames containing the data tag (frames 400 to 600 inclusive with sampling occurring every 25 frames). Figure 3 graphs the changes in the predicted score for target and ignorable throughout the sampled frames. The significance in this video is that the depicted scene in the video changes while the tag is visible (between frame 500 & 525), which triggers a shift in the predictions. Examination in LIME shows that for Frame 600, the 'most target' frame sampled, the data tag is one of the significant features indicative of frame being a target. Frame 500 was also processed through LIME to review results. Frame 500 and 600 and their corresponding LIME outputs are shown in Fig. 4. The LIME results show that changes to the composition of the frame significantly changed the interpretation of the tag as an ignorable or target data feature such that changes in framing shot equate to significant changes in the predicted outcomes. To have confidence in the quality of the predictive model, adequate training data should be used to eliminate the effects of these variances in ignorable data features when undertaking predictions.

4.3   File Metadata Classification

There were 7,056 randomly sampled metadata records used for testing the Text Classification model, all of which came from the VIC 2.0 Export. Of these, 5,340 were ignorable records and 1,716 were target records. The remaining 7,056 records from the dataset were used for training the model.

Overall, the Text Classification model performed very well, with high accuracy and recall, as shown in Table 1. This was made easier by the homogenous nature of the dataset and the arbitrary rules employed for the creation of target data. When processing these records through LIME, it was therefore expected that these arbitrary rules would be displayed in the LIME output data. To measure the most influential words (and therefore features) of an ignorable or target prediction, all instances of the testing data were processed via the LIME

Text Explainer, and their six most influential features recorded, along with their impact on the overall prediction expressed as a decimal between zero and one.

From the results, the Text Classification Model performed better at identifying key features influencing a record being ignorable than it did it being a target. The 20 top features indicative of a record being classified as ignorable are shown in Table 2. The presence of the volume names of ignorable volumes 0, 1, 3, 7, 8, 9, 10, 11, 12, 13, 19, 20, 22, and 23 all averaged between .25 and .31 in their

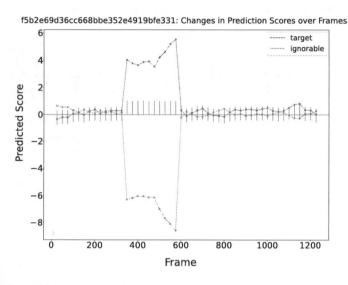

Fig. 2. The graphed results of video f5b2e69d36cc668bbe352e4919bfe331

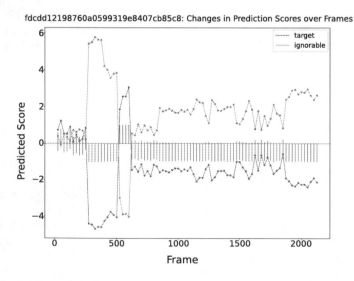

Fig. 3. The graphed results of video fdcdd12198760a0599319e8407cb85c8

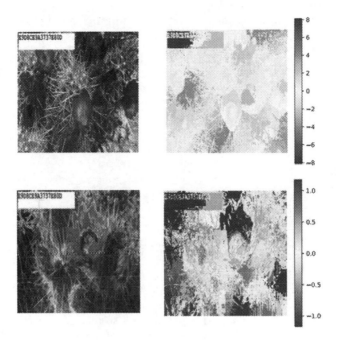

Fig. 4. Results for segments indicating a target label for frames 500 and 600 from video fdcdd12198760a0599319e8407cb85c8. NOTE: Heatmap scales are not the same

average impact, making their presence a very strong indicator of an ignorable label. Interestingly, the LIME Text Explainer did not determine the presence of 'OneDrive' in 'FileName' or 'FilePath' as being a significant feature indicative of an ignorable label. The presence of 'OneDrive' not being indicative of a record being ignorable is also reflected in FP results. Of the 154 FP predictions, only one did not contain 'OneDrive' in the file path. All the FP records originated from VHD files containing volumes from which the target data was selected, further indicating the strength of the volume name as a predictive feature.

The most indicative target labels were unexpected but provided insights into dataset that had previously not been identified. These results are shown in Table 3. The first feature, the presence of '37014' and '7894' in records being indicative of a target label, came from the media_size field. Both sizes are standard sizes of files stored in Application Icon Caches for Windows Apps. Reviewing 1,061 records where '37014' was a predictor and the 375 records where '7894' was a predictor showed that all these files were from the AppIconCache directory and had either '37014' or '7894' as their file size. As expected, the volume labels for the VHD files used to create the target datasets (images 4, 5, 6, 16, 17, and 18) were all also identified as features indicative of a record being a target.

Table 2. The Top 20 Features present in testing data that were indicative of a record having the ignorable label, and their average impact on the overall prediction.

Prediction labels	Occurrences	Avg. of predictive impact
image12	418	0.3139
image20	419	0.3097
image10	379	0.3043
image13	355	0.3027
image22	367	0.3024
image1	314	0.2998
image23	308	0.2994
image8	327	0.2941
image19	310	0.2935
image11	279	0.2923
image7	287	0.2921
image0	294	0.2875
image9	297	0.2865
Partition	5,160	0.2846
vhd	5,160	0.2844
image3	175	0.2653
3824	23	0.2157
8a25b51a25a79e1fb9a57c3301aafaa2	23	0.2135
2c7a9e323a69409f4b13b1c3244074c4	27	0.1960
1642	26	0.1949

Table 3. The Top 20 Features present in testing data that were indicative of a record having the target label, and their average impact on the overall prediction.

Prediction labels	Count of occurrences	Average of predictive impact
37014	1,061	0.0603
7894	375	0.0515
24	234	0.0412
image4	193	0.0397
image17	201	0.0359
image16	333	0.0353
vhd	1,889	0.0345
Partition	1,881	0.0341
image5	282	0.0341
image6	205	0.0339
image18	377	0.0325
image15	297	0.0324
1048576	32	0.0173
Cache	561	0.0121
Default	562	0.0118
Data	594	0.0117

5   Discussion on Results, Limitations, and Future Work

This paper provides a framework for creating explanations for individual files from a forensic dataset. It also takes the first steps toward introducing explainability into IT forensic implementations of AI. Our work presents a method for interacting and moving media data in a forensically sound manner and using open-source XAI tools to explain predictions made from models trained on forensic data.

The results of image classification testing show individual instances can be used and further permutated to undertake an additional evaluation of biases inherent in the classification model and thus used to improve its performance. In the context of CSAM, for example, training models that identify not just whether an image depicts offensive material but an illicit image's content and specific features would significantly assist investigators, potentially eliminating unnecessary review of ignorable parts of the material. Further, with authorized and ethical access to appropriately labelled training data, additional models could be run to assist in other aspects of CSAM investigation, such as victim identification (e.g. through age estimation, tagging and labelling of identifying or indicative features of the locale of production) and therefore facilitate the levelling of additional charges.

The utility of LIME is its capacity to explain features identified by an AI in specific parts of a video file that may interest the investigator. To automate this process, an investigator could provide a series of videos (e.g. surveillance footage) to a DF investigator, who would then run the footage against a predictive model, looking for features of interest (weapons, drugs, etc.). When predictions for specific frames reach a certain threshold, this triggers the XAI tool to undertake analysis, regardless of whether the video is predicted to be of interest or ignorable overall. It then shows a DF investigator the parts of the footage it believes to be of interest and the features of the keyframes that led to this prediction. In this way, a DF investigator could still find a false negative such as video fdcdd12198760a0599319e8407cb85c8 based on an examination of its strongest counterfactual prediction, which may otherwise be overlooked.

The LIME Text Explainer was unable to identify and distinguish between dates within the testing dataset. Each date was perceived to be a single word and as such, could only be used for training if files were created, accessed or written (modified) at the same time as one another down to the nearest second. The LIME Text Explainer could, in future, be used as feed predictions to a LIME Tabular Explainer, which could potentially make more informative explanations out of associated metadata that cannot be easily parsed by a Text Classification Model. Features like date/times should be treated as date/time data to improve prediction quality. In this case, splitting the date entries into dates and times could have positively impacted detecting the date rule used to identify target data. As all target data was created on 4 September 2021, splitting a target date into two separate words, one for date and one for time, would likely have led to '2021-09-04' being a strong predictive feature for a target label. However, LIME does not detect feature interaction and as such, would struggle to identify the date feature as '2021-09-04' and a time feature between '00:00:00' and '12:00:00' as together being indicative of a target label when parsed via the Lime Text Explainer [6]. Integrating and better handling diverse datatypes present in IT Forensic metadata is an area for future research.

5.1   Limitations

A key challenge of this research was gaining access to appropriate forensic data to use for testing and training of AI models and XAI tools. The dataset selected was identified as the best available for the proof of concept but is limited in its applicability to real forensic data. Firstly, the dataset is very limited in size and scope. IT forensic practitioners often analyze data that vary in the source (e.g. smartphones, PCs, portable storage devices, cloud data, etc.) and quality (e.g. a rudimentary 'advance logical' smartphone extraction targeting key user data versus a full file system extraction). The simplified Windows OS presented in the datasets is not representative of the practical challenges extant in IT forensic analysis. When analysing forensic data, not all data from a device may be available for forensic examination. Also, practitioners often encounter a variety of devices and operating systems requiring varied forensic techniques to facilitate data access.

Another limitation of the dataset is that though it is homogeneous, it is not linked by narrative, content, or metadata. This significantly limits the dataset's use for creating a production-ready AI model on which to test XAI tools. Models developed with our dataset could not be trained to identify relationships between devices, users, and other identifiers that could be indicative of device interaction, file knowledge, and patterns of behaviour, etc. Case information based on DF artifacts that contain geospatial and temporal metadata is key in using forensic analysis for investigative or judicial purposes. This metadata is used to inform aspects of the investigation in the real world, such as a specific device's (and, therefore a suspect's) location during the offence period. Images and videos present in these datasets have file system metadata reporting creation, modification and access dates over three days between the 4th and 7th of September 2021. In a real case, this temporal metadata could span years before and after an offence date. Developing an AI which can process narrative features such as date of offence and suspects is outside the scope of this proof of concept but should be an aspiration of future research.

For this research, the limited diversity of features made contextualising analysis to the case circumstances and type of offence impossible. This was identified by Hall, Sakzad, and Choo [12] as a key requirement for the implementation of justified and reasoned explanations in relation to case specifics in the form of profiling user and device activities. Even if this is not feasible, future research in this area should attempt to make use of more appropriate training data for the creation of AI models and associated XAI testing, recognizing, of course, that accessing data related to the investigation of criminal offences (including surveillance footage or CSAM) has its own legal and ethical requirements. This training data should also be appropriately tagged and labelled, meaning that data already being processed and reported on for IT forensic investigations would likely make for the highest quality training dataset.

5.2   Avenues for Further Research

Another avenue for expansion of this research is the inclusion of additional forensic artefact types from both Windows systems and other types of devices. Forensic data of interest can be found in a plethora of locations across the Windows
OS. This research, for example, does not examine the integration of artefacts
from the Windows Registry, which is often thoroughly examined by IT forensic
investigators to determine OS configurations and profile user behaviour. Another
area where XAI may be of assistance is in the processing of web data. Some of
the VIC 2.0 datasets used for Image and Video Classification were files exported
from the Internet Explorer Cache, but information such as web and file access history stored in the WebcacheV01.dat Extensible Storage Engine (ESE) database
can also be crucial in understanding user activities in the context of criminal or
civil IT forensic investigations. Other modern browsers, such as Microsoft Edge,
Google Chrome and Mozilla Firefox, as well as most smartphone applications on
the iOS and Android platforms, store user data in SQLite databases. Using XAI
tools to intelligently join and highlight specific records within these databases
with reasoned justifications as to their significance to an investigation could
greatly assist IT forensic investigators and potentially help identify significant
user data from less known applications that may not be automatically parsed
by IT forensic tools and/or manually examined by investigators. Other significant artefacts recording information about users and applications on smartphone
devices are often stored in Property Lists (.plist files, widely used in Apple OS
environments like MacOS and iOS/iPadOS) or in JSON and Extensible Markup
Language (.xml) files, both widely used in the Android OS. These file types could
also be parsed by future AI/XAI tools. This approach could even be expanded
to include other data types beyond media file types to collate and analyze an
entire filesystem. Each of these differing artefact types would likely need specific
models to be trained to recognize and locate specific data for specific investigative types. Given the diversity of data types and devices that are now subjected
to IT forensic investigation, integration or interaction with IT Forensic software
suites that already successfully parse diverse data sources could form part of an
XAI data processing pipeline.

    With such diversity in the data sources and data types for processing, there
is also a need for the aggregation and comparison of the significance of results
from across varied, processed data sources. Indeed, adding AI and XAI processing into the standard IT forensics workflow without some kind of data reduction and prioritisation mechanism in place would only exacerbate, rather than
resolve, industry challenges related to data volume and processing time [21].
Implementations of AI and XAI in IT forensics need to be developed to meet
differing requirements for granularity, depending on the analysis activities being
undertaken (e.g. triage or a more thorough examination). To facilitate this, AI
predictive model results and their associated explanations (such as LIME output) could be used as input data for additional AI aggregate models with implemented XAI capabilities. The arrangement of AI models and XAI tools would
feed results from specialized models built for analyzing specific data types at

a more granular level to aggregation models that attempt to summarize what occurred in a case's provided context. These aggregation models may require the use of XAI methods capable of better measuring feature interaction to assist in the aggregation process. Ultimately, these models should attempt to replicate the aggregation and summary activities undertaken by IT forensic practitioners when summarizing findings for reporting or presentation of evidence, thus realizing rationalized and justified explanations using AI within the IT forensic field.

References

1. Abadi, M., et al.: TensorFlow: Large-scale machine learning on heterogeneous systems. arXiv preprint arXiv:1603.04467 (2015)
2. Arrieta, A.B., et al.: Explainable Artificial Intelligence (XAI): concepts, taxonomies, opportunities and challenges toward responsible AI. Inf. Fusion **58**, 82–115 (2020)
3. Belshaw, S., Nodeland, B. (2021). Digital evidence experts in the law enforcement community: understanding the use of forensics examiners by police agencies. Security Journal, 1–15
4. Carrier, B.: Autopsy (2022). https://www.sleuthkit.org/autosy/. Accessed 27 Oct 2022
5. Casey, E.: The chequered past and risky future of digital forensics. Aust. J. Forensic Sci. **51**(6), 649–664 (2019)
6. Chen, H., Zheng, G., Ji, Y.: Generating hierarchical explanations on text classification via feature interaction detection. arXiv preprint arXiv:2004.02015 (2020)
7. Dieber, J., Kirrane, S.: Why model why? Assessing the strengths and limitations of LIME. arXiv preprint arXiv:2012.00093(2020)
8. Ertel, W.: Introduction to Artificial Intelligence, 1st edn. Springer, Cham (2011). https://doi.org/10.1007/978-3-319-58487-4
9. Liu, H., Qu, Y., Wu, Y., Wang, H.: Class-specified segmentation with multi-scale Superpixels. In: Park, J.-I., Kim, J. (eds.) ACCV 2012. LNCS, vol. 7728, pp. 158–169. Springer, Heidelberg (2013). https://doi.org/10.1007/978-3-642-37410-4_14
10. Forensic Capability Network, Transforming Forensics, National Police Chiefs' Council, Association of Police and Crime Commissioners. (2020). Digital Forensic Science Strategy. https://www.npcc.police.uk/Digital%20Forensic%20Science%20Strategy%202020.pdf.. Accessed 27 Apr 2022
11. GetData Forensics: Forensic Explorer (FEX)'. https://getdataforensics.com/product/forensic-explorer-fex/.. Accessed 27 Oct 2022
12. Hall, S., Sakzad, A., Choo, K.K.R.: Explainable artificial intelligence for digital forensics. WIREs Forensic Sci. **4**(2), e1434 (2022)
13. Islam, S.R., Eberle, W., Ghafoor, S.K., Ahmed, M.: Explainable artificial intelligence approaches: a survey. arXiv preprint arXiv:2101.09429(2021)
14. Jarrett, A., Choo, K.K.R.: The impact of automation and artificial intelligence on digital forensics. WIREs Forensic Sci. **3**, e1418 (2021)
15. Innat, M.: Wiki-Art: visual Art Encyclopedia, 1, 2020, September. https://www.kaggle.com/datasets/ipythonx/wikiart-gangogh-creating-art-gan. Accessed 3 Jan 2022
16. Molnar, C.: terpretable Machine Learning: A Guide for Making Black Box Models Explainable, 2nd ed. (2022). https://christophm.github.io/interpretable-ml-book/

17. National District Attorneys Association. Forensic Science in the Criminal Courts: Ensuring scientific validity of feature-comparison methods. https://obamawhitehouse.archives.gov/sites/default/files/microsites/ostp/PCAST/pcast_forensic_science_report_final.pdf. Accessed 20 Apr 2022

18. Powers, D.M.: Evaluation: from precision, recall and F-measure to ROC, informedness, markedness and correlation. arXiv preprint arXiv:2010.16061 (2020)

19. Project VIC International: Project VIC "VICS" Data Model (2021). https://www.projectvic.org/vics-data-model.. Accessed 27 Apr 2022

20. Quick, D., Choo, K.K.R.: Impacts of increasing volume of digital forensic data: a survey and future research challenges. Digit. Investig. **11**(4), 273–294 (2014). https://doi.org/10.1016/j.diin.2014.09.002

21. Quick, D., Choo, K.-K.R.: Big forensic data reduction: digital forensic images and electronic evidence. Clust. Comput. **19**(2), 723–740 (2016). https://doi.org/10.1007/s10586-016-0553-1

22. Ribeiro, M.T., Singh, S., Guestrin, C.: Why should I trust you?" Explaining the predictions of any classifier. In: Proceedings of the 22nd ACM SIGKDD International Conference on Knowledge Discovery and Data Mining, pp. 1135–1144 (2016)

23. Sanchez, L., Grajeda, C., Baggili, I., Hall, C.: A practitioner survey exploring the value of forensic tools, AI, filtering, & safer presentation for investigating child sexual abuse material (CSAM). Digit. Investig. **29**, S124–S142 (2019)

24. Solanke, A.A.: Explainable Digital Forensics AI: Towards Mitigating Distrust in AI-Based Digital Forensic Analysis with Interpretable Models. Forensic Science International: digital Investigationd. **422**, 301403 (2022)

25. TensorFlow: Why Tensorflow (2022). https://www.tensorflow.org/about. Accessed 27 Apr 2022

26. Zaccone, G., Karim, M. R., Menshawy, A.: Deep Learning with TensorFlow. Packt Publishing Ltd., Birmingham (2017)

Graph Intelligence Enhanced Bi-Channel Insider Threat Detection

Wei Hong[1] , Jiao Yin[2](✉) , Mingshan You[2] , Hua Wang[2] , Jinli Cao[3] ,
Jianxin Li[4] , and Ming Liu[4]

[1] School of Artificial Intelligence, Chongqing University of Arts and Sciences,
Chongqing 402160, China
hongwei.auto@outlook.com
[2] Institute for Sustainable Industries and Liveable Cities, Victoria University,
Melbourne, VIC 3011, Australia
{jiao.yin,mingshan.you,hua.wang}@vu.edu.au
[3] Department of Computer Science and Information Technology,
La Trobe University, Melbourne, VIC 3086, Australia
j.cao@latrobe.edu.au
[4] School of Information Technology, Deakin University, Melbourne, VIC 3125,
Australia
{jianxin.li,m.liu}@deakin.edu.au

Abstract. For an organization, insider intrusion generally poses far
more detrimental threats than outsider intrusion. Traditionally, insider
threat is detected by analyzing logged user behaviours and then establishing a binary classifier to distinguish malicious ones. However, most
approaches consider user behaviour in an isolated manner, inevitably
missing the background information from organizational connections
such as a shared supervisor or e-mail interactions. Consequently, the performance of those existing works still has the potential to be enhanced. In
this paper, we propose a bi-channel insider threat detection (B-CITD)
framework enhanced by graph intelligence to improve the overall performance of existing methods. Firstly, We extract behavioural features
from a series of log files as the inner-user channel features. Secondly,
we construct an organizational connection graph and extract topological
features through a graph neural networks (GNN) model as the inter-user
channel features. In the end, the features from inner-user and inter-user
channels are combined together to perform an insider threat detection
task through a binary classification model. Experimental results on an
open-sourced CERT 4.2 dataset show that B-CITD can enhance the performance of insider threat detection by a large margin, compared with
using features only from inner-user or inter-user channels. We published
our code on GitHub: https://github.com/Wayne-on-the-road/B-CITD.

Keywords: Insider threat · Graph neural networks · Topological
feature · Supervised learning

X. Yuan et al. (Eds.): NSS 2022, LNCS 13787, pp. 86–102, 2022.
https://doi.org/10.1007/978-3-031-23020-2_5

1 Introduction

In recent years, cyber-security has been gaining attention from time to time with data breach incidents or system sabotage events that affected users worldwide [19,41]. With covid-19 plaguing the world unprecedentedly, cybercrime seems to see a rise-up due to an abrupt shifting to remote work. According to Accenture's recent report for 2021 [1], each responding company experienced 270 attacks on average in this year, an increase of 31% compared with 2020.

Among those cyber attacks, a survey from PwC shows that 68% respondents consider inadvertent actions of insiders is the greatest threat to the organisation's information security [18]. Another early survey also shows nearly 30% respondents think insider attacks were more costly than outsider attacks, and nearly one-third of participants experienced an insider incident [15].

Generally speaking, malicious insider refers to current or former personnel who has or had authorised access to an organisation's network, system, or data and has intentionally used that access to affect the confidentiality, integrity, availability, or physical well-being of the organisation's information and information systems [27,40].

Access control methods are fundamental technology for data privacy and security protection [12,24,31,33]. It has been applied in various areas such as healthcare system and data publications [25,26,30,32]. With authorised access, however, insider threat normally can not be blocked out by traditional security measures [23,34]. Therefore, detecting those malicious behaviours from inside is the key to preventing or recovering loss in time. Common approaches consider this a classification problem if labelled data are available [16,20]. User behaviour logs are first engineered in various ways to extract the most valuable features [10, 22]. Then machine learning algorithms such as support vector machine (SVM), gaussian naive bayes (GNB), linear regression (LR) and random forest (RF), or deep learning models such as long short-term memory (LSTM) or convolutional neural networks (CNN) are introduced to perform the classification task [37,39, 42].

However, when doing feature engineering, most approaches only consider user behaviour to be isolated ones, missing the fact that users in a similar organisational structure (e.g. shared supervisor, same department, working relationship) may behave similarly. Therefore, we argue that incorporating organisational structure information into feature engineering will help boost traditional classification algorithm performance.

In contrast with the traditional data representation method, which facilitates characteristic analysis of individual actors, graph representations are more powerful in exploiting relationships between actors [2,38]. Popular GNN models for node and graph embedding include graph convolutional networks (GCN) [11], GraphSAGE [7], graph attention networks (GAT) [29], EdgeGCN [35] and GINGCN [36].

In recent years, graph-based techniques are gaining popularity in many fields. Inspired by these works, we propose a bi-channel insider threat detection (B-CITD) framework to investigate the influence of GNN-based graph intelligence on the performance of insider threat detection. On the one hand, we extract inner-user channel features from user behavioural log files. On the other hand, we also build an organisational graph and use a supervised GNN model to extract node embeddings containing topological information as the inter-user channel features. In the end, we concatenate features from two channels to perform insider threat detection via a binary classifier.

Briefly speaking, our work makes contributions in the following ways:

- We proposed a bi-channel insider threat detection (B-CITD) framework combining isolated behavioural inner-user features and latent topological inter-user features to boost insider threat detection performance. B-CITD is algorithm independent, which means it can be implemented with any GNN models to extract node embeddings and with any binary classifiers to detect malicious users.
- We designed a behavioural feature extraction method for isolated users, a graph construction method and an organisational feature extraction method, which are essential for inner-user channel and inter-user channel feature extraction.
- Experimental results on an open-sourced CERT 4.2 dataset show that B-CITD and the corresponding bi-channel feature extraction methods are effective in improving insider threat detection. Specifically, B-CITD is tested effective on four traditional classifiers, namely, CNN, GNB, SVM, and LR, improving their F1 score on insider threat detection by 1.61%, 1.41%, 1.31% and 1.11% respectively, compared with using only inner-user channel features.
- We investigated the power of different GNN models on extracting inter-user features and on boosting the performance of insider threat detection within the proposed B-CITD framework. Experimental results show that GCN, GAT and GraphSAGE achieved the equivalent boosting power, even though the performance of different GNN models varies when only using inter-user features.

The rest of the paper is organised as follows: Sect. 2 presents related works on malicious insider detection and the applications of graph-based techniques in insider threat detection. Section 3 introduces the scope of researched question and elaborates the proposed framework and methodology in detail. Section 4 presents a use case implementation with detailed processes of user-day behavioural feature extraction and GNN-enhanced inter-user connection feature extraction. Section 5 describes the experimental results and offers an in-depth analysis of experimental results followed by discussions. A conclusion with limitation analysis and future work is given in Sect. 6.

2 Related Works

2.1 Insider Threat Detection

Previous works on insider threat detection have contributed in two directions: conceptual and operational. Conceptual works focus on how to detect and assess insider threat theoretically, while operational works go further to give practical solutions on specific datasets [8].

In those operational works, insider threat detection is mostly considered an anomaly-based detection task. In the early stage, Schonlau, M. et al. [21] introduced Unix/Linux command history based dataset SEA, which mixed commands from authorised users with commands randomly injected from other users, and six statistical methods are used on this dataset. Further on this dataset, Maxion, R.A. and Townsend, T.N. [14] used a Naive Bayes classifier with an updating scheme, achieving significant improvement in performance. Garg, A. et al. [4] expanded the insider detection task from just command lines to a graphical user interface (GUI) based system, using the SVM method to analyse user's operations on a mouse, and achieved detection rates of up to 96% with few false positives.

Earlier works often focus on a specific domain of user behaviour, and the adopted detection methods are also limited. With the emergence of richer datasets involving more user activities [6], more machine learning approaches are increasingly introduced for insider threat detection. Gavai, G. et al. [5] used a modified version of the isolation forest algorithm to perform supervised and unsupervised learning on a real-world dataset with artificially injected insider threat events, which contains rich enterprise social and online activity data. Tuor, A. et al. [28] developed a real-time online framework to detect insiders from system logs with supervised deep recurrent neural networks. To exploit the sequential behaviour pattern of the same user in one day, Yuan, F. et al. [42] designed a methodology to extract fixed-size feature representation using LSTM and then utilized a CNN classifier to detect insiders. Those works mainly focused on exploiting individual user behaviour to the most, inevitably omitting connections between different personnel inside an organization.

2.2   Graph-Based Insider Threat Detection

Several graph-based works have been introduced in insider threat detection in recent years. Gamachchi, A. and Boztas, S. [3] constructed a hierarchy graph for an organisation and then used attributed graph clustering techniques to rank outliers. However, information used in this work is common graph statistical information, such as node degree and betweenness centrality, which are not representative enough. Another later work also took the community detection approach [17], but combined it with an LSTM auto-encoder to compare individual behaviour patterns with community patterns. Though LSTM is commonly used for sequential pattern extraction, graph neural networks based approaches are more suitable for topological feature extractions.

Liu, F. et al. [13] proposed a novel heterogeneous graph embedding method for user behaviours log mining, which converts log entries into a heterogeneous graph, and then designed an improved embedding method and detection algorithm to find insiders. Jiang, J. et al. [9] developed a similarity function to calculate the similarity of different organisational users and used this information to construct a weighted graph. Based on this graph, this paper adopted

GCN to do classification task and achieved satisfactory performance. Those two works demonstrated that the popular graph neural network approaches have the potential to handle insider threat detection problems.

However, to the best of our knowledge, no previous work has investigated and compared the influence and effect of different GNN models on an insider threat detection task with exactly the same setting.

3   Methodology

In this section, we illustrate the whole process of the proposed bi-channel insider threat detection framework. The detailed inner-user and inter-user feature extraction, including organisational graph construction, will be presented in Sect. 4, taking the CERT 4.2 dataset as a use case implementation.

Previously, different works defined insider threat detection in different granularity. In our paper, considering that users' behaviours are evolving and a malicious user can act harmless on most days and only act abnormally in a few days, we follow the common practice of examining user behaviours on a daily basis. Therefore, insider threat detection in this paper aims to detect malicious user-days.

Malicious users can act in different patterns compared with benign users. These patterns are hidden in users' daily behaviours, such as the log-on frequency and times, the domain of websites they visited, the email contacts, and the connection of removable devices. Therefore, we first extract inner-user features from user behavioural log files to perform effective insider threat detection. The detailed behavioural feature extraction method is given in Subsect. 4.2. As shown in Fig. 1, the inner-user feature matrix, denoted as X_b, is extracted from daily behaviours of isolated user-days, where $X_b \in \mathbb{R}^{m \times n_b}$, m is the total number of user-days and n_b is the dimension of extracted inner-user features. For a single user-day, the extracted feature vector can be denoted as $x_{b,i} \in \mathbb{R}^{n_b}$ ($i \in \{1, 2, \cdots, m\}$).

To extract the inter-user features, we first construct a graph $G = \{\mathcal{V}, A, X_b\}$, where $\mathcal{V}$ is the vertex set of the graph, A is the adjacency matrix indicating the organizational connections between different user-days and X_b is the behavioural user-day feature matrix. The total number of nodes in G equals the total number of user-days, which is to say, $|\mathcal{V}| = m$. A single user-day, denoted as a node $v \in \mathcal{V}$ and the node attribute is $x_{b,i} \in X_B$ ($i \in \{1, 2, \cdots, m\}$).

As shown in Fig. 1, after constructing graph G, we employ a GNN model as a graph feature extractor. The process of extracting latent organizational connection features can be described in Eq. (1).

$$H_c = f_{GNN}(G, \Theta_g), \tag{1}$$

where $H_c \in \mathbb{R}^{m \times n_c}$ denotes the extracted latent inter-user feature matrix, n_c is the dimension of inter-user features, $f_{GNN}(\cdot)$ is the mapping function from the original node attribute feature space to the latent graph node embedding feature space, and Θ_g is the trainable parameters of the GNN model. For a

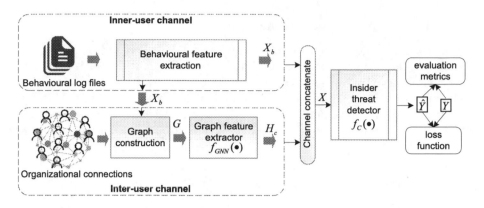

Fig. 1. Visualized schema of bi-channel insider threat detection framework

single user-day node $v \in \mathcal{V}$, the extracted inter-user feature can be denoted as $h_{c,v} \in \mathbb{R}^{n_c}$. The exact forms of $f_{GNN}(\cdot)$ and Θ_g are determined by the structure of the selected GNN model, and we will test GCN, GAT and GraphSAGE as the selected GNN models in Sect. 5. The detailed graph construction and GCN feature extractor on inter-user feature extraction is given in Subsect. 4.3.

Features extracted from two channels are concatenated as the final feature matrix, as shown in Eq. (2).

$$X = concatenate(X_b, H_c), \tag{2}$$

where $X \in \mathbb{R}^{m \times (n_b + n_c)}$ is the final user-day feature matrix for insider threat detection, and the dimension of the final feature equals $n_b + n_c$.

Finally, we choose a binary classifier as the insider threat detector. The predicted values of the detector can be calculated as Eq. (3).

$$\hat{Y} = f_c(X, \Theta_c), \tag{3}$$

where $\hat{Y} \in \mathbb{R}^m$ is the predicted results on whether a user-day is malicious or not, f_c is the mapping function of the chosen classifier, and Θ_c is the trainable parameters of the classifier. The parameters Θ_c can be optimised on the training set by comparing the predicted results $\hat{Y}$ with the true labels, $Y \in \mathbb{R}^m$, and minimising the loss function. Finally, the performance of the B-CITD architecture can be evaluated on the test set, as shown in Fig. 1.

4 A Use Case Implementation

To give a use case implementation of B-CITD, we constructed a sample dataset from an open-sourced dataset, CERT4.2, which is a synthetic dataset for insider threat research in the context of corporate environment [6]. This section presents details on dataset pre-processing, inner-user channel feature extraction and inter-user channel feature extraction.

4.1   Dataset and Pre-processing

CERT 4.2 is considered the richest dataset, with 70 insiders out of 1000 users, among all available versions of the CERT dataset. The raw dataset is organised according to activity category, namely file, logon, device, email, and http, with each type of activity stored in a separate CSV file. Beyond that, LDAP files indicating organisational information such as supervisor and department are also provided. Table 1 shows a detailed description on file information provided in the CERT 4.2 dataset.

Table 1. File information description of CERT 4.2 dataset

File Name	Description	Attributes
LDAP File	Monthly updated csv file, containing organizational structure of the enterprise	Employee_Name, User_Id, Email, Role, Business_Unit, Functional_Unit, Department, Team, Supervisor
device.csv	Record of USB device usage information	Date, User, PC, Activity (Connect/Disconnect)
email.csv	Record of all email activity information	Date, User, PC, To, Cc, Bcc, From, Size, Attachments, Content
file.csv	Record of file usage information on each PC	Date, User, PC, Filename, Content
http.csv	Record of website browsing information from each PC	Date, User, PC, Url, Content
logon.csv	Record of PC logon/logoff information for all users	Date, User, PC, Activity (Logon/Logoff)
psychometric.csv	Personality evaluation for each employee using big five OCEAN model	Employee_Name, User_Id,O,C,E,A,N

Since the original data set is extremely imbalanced, while our goal is to investigate the power of latent graph information, we first reconstructed a smaller balanced dataset by downsampling the normal users. Then the dataset is split into 70% for training and 30% for testing.

4.2   Inner-User Channel Feature Extraction

In the paper, we utilise two activity files(device.csv and logon.csv) to extract five behavioural features from users' daily routines. As for the data label, if one user committed at least one malicious activity for a certain user-day, that user-day is labelled as an insider threat incident.

Specifically, for each user-day sample, the five inner-user behavioural features are listed below:

- First logon time: extracted from the logon.csv file by mapping the timestamp of the first login activity to the range of [0, 1] according to a 24 h basis;
- Last logoff time: extracted from the logon.csv file by mapping the timestamp of the last logoff activity to the range of [0, 1] according to a 24 h basis;

- First device activity time: extracted from the device.csv file by mapping the timestamp of the first device activity (connect or disconnect) to the range of [0, 1] according to a 24 h basis;
- Last device activity time: extracted from the device.csv file by mapping the timestamp of the last device activity (connect or disconnect) to the range of [0, 1] according to a 24 h basis;
- Number of off-hour device activities: extracted from the device.csv file by counting the number of the device activities (connect or disconnect) during off-hour time (18:00 pm - 8:00 am).

Those five features work as, on the one hand, the inner-user channel features and, on the other hand, the original node attributes in the constructed organizational graph.

4.3   Inter-User Channel Feature Extraction

Organizational Graph Construction. To extract inter-user channel features between different user-days, we first design a connected organisational graph following certain rules. The organisational graph construction involves generating nodes, assigning nodes attributes and adding edges between nodes. Each user-day is set as a node for the insider threat detection problem, and the five extracted inner-user channel features are set as the original node attributes. Then, we add edges between nodes following the three rules below, based on the organisational structures provided in the LDAP.csv file.

- Rule 1: If user A is supervised by user B, then add undirected edges between user A's user-days and user B's user-days.
- Rule 2: If user A and user B share the same supervisor, then add undirected edges between user A's user-days and user B's user-days.
- Rule 3: If two user-days belong to the same user, add an undirected edge between them.

The basic statistical information of the constructed graph is shown in Table 2. Specifically, the label of a node is the same as the label of the corresponding user-day. Therefore, the label cardinality equals 2, indicating whether a node is malicious or not.

Table 2. Statistics of constructed organisational graph

Category	Value	Category	Value
Number of Nodes	1908	*Number of Edges*	103788
Node attribute dimension	5	*Input matrix ($m \times n_b$)*	1908×5
Number of training node	1336	*Adjacency matrix ($m \times m$)*	1908×1908
Number of testing node	572	*Label cardinality*	2

GNN-Based Inter-User Feature Extraction. After constructing a connected graph G, the inter-user channel features can be extracted based on GNN models through supervised GNN model training and trained GNN model application processes.

Specifically, in the supervised GNN model training process, a GNN model takes the training set split from the constructed graph $G = \{\mathcal{V}, A, X_b\}$ as input. Through the message passing mechanism, the initial attributes of nodes in $\mathcal{V}$ are combined with aggregated messages passed through their neighbouring nodes and then propagated through the GNN model. The trainable parameters of the adopted GNN model are optimised by conducting supervised training on the training set. Subsequently, in the trained GNN model application process, the trained GNN model is used for inter-user feature extraction. Following the proposed B-CITD framework illustrated in Fig. 1, and feeding the graph $G = \{\mathcal{V}, A, X_b\}$ into the trained GNN model, the inter-user channel features can be calculated by Eq. (1).

After that, features from the inner-user and inter-user channels can be concatenated to conduct the insider threat detection task. The detailed experimental setting and results are reported in Sect. 5.

5   Experiments

To investigate the effectiveness of the proposed B-CITD framework, we conducted comparative experiments between B-CITD and inner-user channel in Sect. 5.1, and then between B-CITD and inter-user channel in Sect. 5.2, respectively. An in-depth analysis of the experimental findings is listed in Sect. 5.3.

All experiments are implemented in Python programming language. The package PyTorch Geometric[1] is used to implement GNN models, PyTorch[2] is used to implement CNN model and scikit-learn[3] is for binary classifier implementation. We adopt default parameter settings for all CNN, GNN and classifiers unless otherwise specified.

5.1   Comparison Between B-CITD and Inner-User Channel

Since B-CITD is classifier independent, we applied four commonly used classifiers in binary classification, namely, CNN, GNB, SVM and LR, to investigate the improvement achieved by graph intelligence, compared with using inner-user features only. Specifically, the CNN model consists of two convolutional layers with kernel size = 3, in and out channel sizes equal to 16 and 32, respectively. The learning rate for the CNN model is set to 0.01. In this section, we apply a two-layer GCN model for inter-user feature extraction, which has 16 hidden channels, and the output dimension is 2. The comparison results on insider threat detection between B-CITD and inner-user channel are presented in Table 3.

---

[1] https://pytorch-geometric.readthedocs.io/en/latest/.

[2] https://pytorch.org/docs/stable/index.html.

[3] https://scikit-learn.org/stable/.

Table 3. Performance between inner-user channel and bi-channel for different classifiers (%)

Classifier	Channel	Acc	Pre	Rec	F1	ΔAcc	ΔPre	ΔRec	ΔF1
CNN	inner-user	90.42	86.92	93.65	90.16	↑1.71	↑3.04	0.00	↑1.61
	bi-channel	92.13	89.96	93.65	91.77				
GNB	inner-user	90.38	86.85	93.66	90.13	↑1.58	↑3.37	↓0.75	↑1.41
	bi-channel	91.96	90.22	92.91	91.54				
SVM	inner-user	90.21	86.55	93.66	89.96	↑1.40	↑2.46	0.00	↑1.31
	bi-channel	91.61	89.01	93.66	91.27				
LR	inner-user	90.03	86.51	93.28	89.77	↑1.23	↑2.42	↓0.37	↑1.11
	bi-channel	91.26	88.93	92.91	90.88				

Results in Table 3 show that for each tested classifier, the performance achieved by bi-channel features is significantly improved compared with using inner-user channel features only. Specifically, accuracy has increased by 1.71%, 1.58%, 1.40%, 1.23%, precision also increased 3.04%, 3.37%, 2.46%, 2.42% respectively for CNN, GNB, SVM, and LR classifier. Although GNB and LR suffered a slight drop in Recall score, the F1 scores on all classifiers are improved by at least 1.11%.

Since F1-score combines the precision and recall of a classifier into a single metric by taking their harmonic mean, it can reflect the overall performance more clearly than other metrics listed in Table 3. We highlighted the F1 score comparison in Fig. 2, which shows general improvement in F1 score across all classifiers.

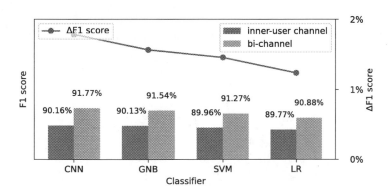

Fig. 2. F1 score comparison between inner-user channel and bi-channel for different classifiers

The CNN classifier performs better than other classifiers in terms of the general performance across different metrics. At the same time, the CNN classifier also generally gained more benefit (improvement) from our bi-channel frame-work. The LR classifier comes in the last place either in terms of standalone performance or gained improvement from bi-channel features.

We draw the receiver operating characteristic (ROC) curves for all classifiers in Fig. 3, showing that bi-channel features are superior to inner-user channel features. The area under the ROC Curve (AUC) values are listed in Fig. 3. Taking CNN as an example, the AUC is improved from 0.9101 to 0.9488 when using B-CITD.

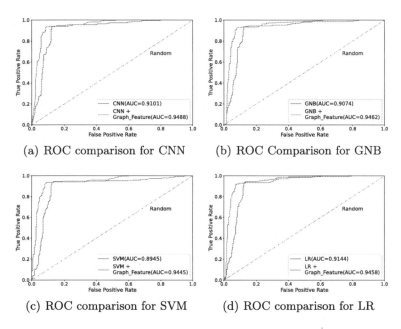

(a) ROC comparison for CNN   (b) ROC Comparison for GNB

(c) ROC comparison for SVM   (d) ROC comparison for LR

Fig. 3. ROC comparison between inner-user channel and bi-channel for different classifiers

5.2   Comparison Between B-CITD and Inter-user Channel

The GCN model shows positive effect in extracting inter-user features in B-CITD, as shown in Fig. 2, Fig. 3 and Table 3. We further conducted experiments to investigate whether different GNN models will have different capabilities to extract inter-user features. Three popular GNN models, namely, GCN, GAT, and GraphSAGE, are selected to cooperate with the CNN classifier to compare the performance of the inter-user channel and bi-channel.

Table 4 shows the comparison results of using inter-user channel and bi-channel features on the accuracy, precision, recall and F1 score. Bi-channel features achieve performance improvement over inter-user features on all three GNN models. This further verifies our hypothesis that the proposed B-CITD framework could improve the insider detection performance by cooperating features from both inner-user and inter-user channels. Taking Δ F1 score as an example, the improvements in F1 scores are 16.20%, 17.70% and 0.97%, corresponding to GCN, GAT and GraphSAGE models, which are also demonstrated by the blue line in Fig. 4.

Table 4. Performance comparison between inter-user channel and bi-channel for different GNN models (%)

GNN model	Channel	Acc	Pre	Rec	F1	ΔAcc	ΔPre	ΔRecall	ΔF1
GCN	inter-user	70.45	61.93	95.90	75.26	↑21.35	↑27.43	↓2.24	↑16.20
	bi-channel	91.80	89.36	93.66	91.46				
GAT	inter-user	68.50	60.30	95.89	74.04	↑23.60	↑29.60	↓2.23	↑17.70
	bi-channel	92.10	89.90	93.66	91.74				
GraphSAGE	inter-user	90.58	87.18	93.65	90.30	↑1.03	↑1.83	0.00	↑0.97
	bi-channel	91.61	89.01	93.65	91.27				

Figure 4 and Fig. 5 show the highlighted F1 score and ROC curve comparison. They both show the same trend with Table 4, demonstrating the effectiveness of bi-channel features in improving insider threat detection performance compared with inter-user channel features.

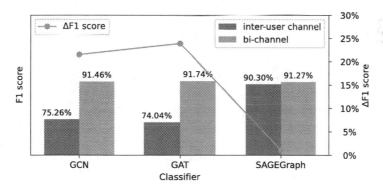

Fig. 4. F1 score comparison between inter-user channel and bi-channel for different GNN models

5.3   Discussion

This section gives further discussion and analysis on the experimental results shown in Sects. 5.1 and 5.2.

The comparison between inner-user channel and bi-channel features presented in Sect. 5.1 confirms our hypothesis that behavioral connections probably do exist both between user-days and users. This connection information is

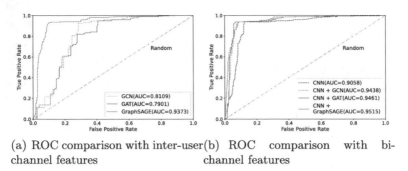

(a) ROC comparison with inter-user channel features
(b) ROC comparison with bi-channel features

Fig. 5. ROC comparison between inter-user channel and bi-channel for different GNN models

effective in enhancing the performance of insider threat detection. Traditional approaches only take individual user behaviour into analysis, failing to place it in the context of a connected organisational graph. For example, workers who share the same supervisor may have a similar workload on a specific day. Therefore, they are more likely to show a similar behavioural pattern. Features extracted from the inter-user channel by GNN models can characterize that connected pattern. The proposed B-CITD integrates both inner-user behavioural and inter-user topological features, offering the classifier new graph-based information to improve detection performance.

Table 4 clearly shows that GraphSAGE achieves far better performance than GCN and GAT when using inter-user features only. For example, the accuracy achieved by GraphSAGE is 90.58%, compared with 70.45% by GCN and 68.50% by GAT. At the same time, the performance of GCN and GAT are also different from each other. For example, the F1 score achieved by GCN is 75.26 % and by GAT is 74.04 %. The significant performance differences between GCN, GAT and GraphSAGE when using inter-user features are also reflected by the blue bars in Fig. 4 and the ROC curves in Fig. 5 (a). One explanation is that when only using GNN models to do inter-user channel feature extraction, the message passing mechanism will cause the degeneration of node features(inner-user features) to different extents for different GNN models. According to the results, GAT has the largest degeneration, getting the worst performance. By contrast, GraphSAGE has minor node feature degeneration and achieves the best results.

Interestingly, the detection performance is almost the same when feeding bi-channel features extracted by different GNN models to the same CNN classifier using the B-CITD framework, as reflected in Table 4 and Fig. 4. Also, Only slightly difference can be observed in ROC curves and AUC values in Fig. 5 (b). Our speculation is that these GNN models can extract equivalent topological information from the connected graph, and when adopted in B-CITD framework, they can achieve the equivalent performance with the same inter-user features and the same graph setting. In other words, B-CITD provides the same inner-user channel features, concatenated with the inter-user channel features to compensate inner-user feature degeneration caused by the massage passing mechanism of GNN models. As long as the GNN models can extract the same level of inter-user features, B-CITD framework will have the potential to achieve the equivalent performance.

6   Conclusion

We proposed a B-CITD framework to incorporate inner-user behavioural and inter-user topological features for better insider threat detection performance. Experimental results on the open-accessed CERT 4.2 dataset show that the proposed B-CITD outperforms algorithms using features from either the inner-user or inter-user channels. Especially by comparing the performance of using bi-channel features and each single channel features, we demonstrated the enhancement effect from graph intelligence introduced by our B-CITD framework. We further investigated the power of different GNN models in extracting inter-user features and interestingly found that different GNN models could extract equivalent topological information to contribute nearly the same improvement for the downstream insider threat detection task.

The B-CITD is dedicatedly designed to investigate the performance enhancement provided by graph intelligence on the insider threat detection problem, and it is just a starting point. Several limitations can be improved further in future work. Firstly, we only extracted five behavioural features from the device and logon files. We believe the performance of B-CITD can be further improved with more behavioural features from the inner-user channel, such as the email content and attachment, file usage, personality evaluation and website browsing information. Secondly, we only considered three rules when constructing the organisational graph for inter-user channel feature extraction. In future work, we could further consider the email correspondence and website browsing overlapping to build a more comprehensive graph. Last but not least, in real-world scenarios, insider threat detection is an imbalanced learning problem since most user-days are benign. However, this paper builds a balanced dataset to conduct the experimental evaluation by randomly downsampling the majority class. In future work, specific strategies can be developed to handle real-world data imbalance problems.

References

1. Accenture: State of cybersecurity resilience 2021. Accenture Official Website, 03 November 2021. https://www.accenture.com/us-en/insights/security/invest-cyber-resilience
2. Coffman, T., Greenblatt, S., Marcus, S.: Graph-based technologies for intelligence analysis. Commun. ACM **47**(3), 45–47 (2004)
3. Gamachchi, A., Boztas, S.: Insider threat detection through attributed graph clustering. In: 2017 IEEE Trustcom/BigDataSE/ICESS, pp. 112–119. IEEE (2017)

4. Garg, A., Rahalkar, R., Upadhyaya, S., Kwiat, K.: Profiling users in GUI based systems for masquerade detection. In: Proceedings of the 2006 IEEE Workshop on Information Assurance, vol. 2006, pp. 48–54 (2006)
5. Gavai, G., Sricharan, K., Gunning, D., Rolleston, R., Hanley, J., Singhal, M.: Detecting insider threat from enterprise social and online activity data. In: Proceedings of the 7th ACM CCS International Workshop on Managing Insider Security Threats, pp. 13–20 (2015)
6. Glasser, J., Lindauer, B.: Bridging the gap: A pragmatic approach to generating insider threat data. In: 2013 IEEE Security and Privacy Workshops. pp. 98–104. IEEE (2013)
7. Hamilton, W.L., Ying, R., Leskovec, J.: Inductive representation learning on large graphs. In: Proceedings of the 31st International Conference on Neural Information Processing Systems, pp. 1025–1035 (2017)
8. Homoliak, I., Toffalini, F., Guarnizo, J., Elovici, Y., Ochoa, M.: Insight into insiders and it: a survey of insider threat taxonomies, analysis, modeling, and countermeasures. ACM Comput. Surv. (CSUR) $52(2)$, 1–40 (2019)
9. Jiang, J., et al.: Anomaly detection with graph convolutional networks for insider threat and fraud detection. In: MILCOM 2019–2019 IEEE Military Communications Conference (MILCOM), pp. 109–114. IEEE (2019)
10. Kabir, M.E., Mahmood, A.N., Wang, H., Mustafa, A.K.: Microaggregation sorting framework for k-anonymity statistical disclosure control in cloud computing. IEEE Trans. Cloud Comput. $8(2)$, 408–417 (2015)
11. Kipf, T.N., Welling, M.: Semi-supervised classification with graph convolutional networks. arXiv preprint arXiv:1609.02907 (2016)
12. Li, M., Sun, X., Wang, H., Zhang, Y.: Multi-level delegations with trust management in access control systems. J. Intell. Inf. Syst. $39(3)$, 611–626 (2012)
13. Liu, F., Wen, Y., Zhang, D., Jiang, X., Xing, X., Meng, D.: Log2vec: a heterogeneous graph embedding based approach for detecting cyber threats within enterprise. In: Proceedings of the 2019 ACM SIGSAC Conference on Computer and Communications Security, pp. 1777–1794 (2019)
14. Maxion, R.A., Townsend, T.N.: Masquerade detection using truncated command lines. In: Proceedings International Conference on Dependable Systems and Networks, pp. 219–228. IEEE (2002)
15. Miller, S.: 2017 u.s. state of cybercrime highlights. Carnegie Mellon University's Software Engineering Institute Blog, 17 January 2018. http://insights.sei.cmu.edu/blog/2017-us-state-of-cybercrime-highlights/
16. Pandey, D., Wang, H., Yin, X., Wang, K., Zhang, Y., Shen, J.: Automatic breast lesion segmentation in phase preserved dce-mris. Health Inf. Sci. Syst. 10 (2022). https://doi.org/10.1007/s13755-022-00176-w
17. Paul, S., Mishra, S.: Lac: LSTM autoencoder with community for insider threat detection. In: 2020 the 4th International Conference on Big Data Research (ICBDR 2020), pp. 71–77 (2020)
18. PwC: Cybercrime survey 2020. PwC Official Website, 28 August 2021. https://www.pwc.dk/da/publikationer/2021/cybercrime-survey-2020-en.html
19. Rasool, R., Ahmed, K., Anwar, Z., Wang, H., Ashraf, U., Rafiq, W.: Cyberpulse++: A machine learning based security framework for detecting link flooding attacks in software defined networks. International Journal of Intelligent Systems 2021, 1–28 (04 2021). https://doi.org/10.1002/int.22442
20. Sarki, R., Ahmed, K., Wang, H., Zhang, Y., Wang, K.: Convolutional neural network for multi-class classification of diabetic eye disease. EAI Endorsed Trans. Scalable Inf. Syst. $9(4)$ (2021). https://doi.org/10.4108/eai.16-12-2021.172436

21. Schonlau, M., DuMouchel, W., Ju, W.H., Karr, A.F., Theus, M., Vardi, Y.: Computer intrusion: detecting masquerades. Stat. Sci. **16**, 58–74 (2001)
22. Singh, R., Zhang, Y., Wang, H., Miao, Y., Ahmed, K.: Investigation of social behaviour patterns using location-based data - a melbourne case study. ICST Trans. Scalable Inf. Syst. **8**, 166767 (2020). https://doi.org/10.4108/eai.26-10-2020.166767
23. Sun, L., Ma, J., Wang, H., Zhang, Y., Yong, J.: Cloud service description model: an extension of USDL for cloud services. IEEE Trans. Serv. Comput. **11**(2), 354–368 (2015)
24. Sun, X., Li, M., Wang, H., Plank, A.: An efficient hash-based algorithm for minimal k-anonymity. In: Conferences in Research and Practice in Information Technology (CRPIT), vol. 74, pp. 101–107. Australian Computer Society Inc. (2008)
25. Sun, X., Wang, H., Li, J.: Satisfying privacy requirements: one step before anonymization. In: Zaki, M.J., Yu, J.X., Ravindran, B., Pudi, V. (eds.) PAKDD 2010. LNCS (LNAI), vol. 6118, pp. 181–188. Springer, Heidelberg (2010). https://doi.org/10.1007/978-3-642-13657-3_21
26. Sun, X., Wang, H., Li, J., Pei, J.: Publishing anonymous survey rating data. Data Min. Knowl. Disc. **23**(3), 379–406 (2011)
27. Theis, M., et al.: Common sense guide to mitigating insider threats (2019)
28. Tuor, A., Kaplan, S., Hutchinson, B., Nichols, N., Robinson, S.: Deep learning for unsupervised insider threat detection in structured cybersecurity data streams. arXiv preprint arXiv:1710.00811 (2017)
29. Veličković, P., Cucurull, G., Casanova, A., Romero, A., Lio, P., Bengio, Y.: Graph attention networks. arXiv preprint arXiv:1710.10903 (2017)
30. Vimalachandran, P., Liu, H., Lin, Y., Ji, K., Wang, H., Zhang, Y.: Improving accessibility of the Australian my health records while preserving privacy and security of the system. Health Inf. Sci. Syst. **8**(1), 1–9 (2020)
31. Wang, H., Cao, J., Zhang, Y.: A flexible payment scheme and its role-based access control. IEEE Trans. Knowl. Data Eng. **17**(3), 425–436 (2005)
32. Wang, H., Zhang, Y., Cao, J.: Effective collaboration with information sharing in virtual universities. IEEE Trans. Knowl. Data Eng. **21**(6), 840–853 (2008)
33. Wang, H., Zhang, Y., Cao, J., Varadharajan, V.: Achieving secure and flexible m-services through tickets. IEEE Trans. Syst. Man Cybern.-Part A: Syst. Hum. **33**(6), 697–708 (2003)
34. Wang, Y., Shen, Y., Wang, H., Cao, J., Jiang, X.: MTMR: ensuring mapreduce computation integrity with Merkle tree-based verifications. IEEE Trans. Big Data **4**(3), 418–431 (2016)
35. Wang, Y., Sun, Y., Liu, Z., Sarma, S.E., Bronstein, M.M., Solomon, J.M.: Dynamic graph CNN for learning on point clouds. ACM Trans. Graphics (tog) **38**(5), 1–12 (2019)
36. Xu, K., Hu, W., Leskovec, J., Jegelka, S.: How powerful are graph neural networks? arXiv preprint arXiv:1810.00826 (2018)
37. Yin, J., Tang, M., Cao, J., Wang, H., You, M.: A real-time dynamic concept adaptive learning algorithm for exploitability prediction. Neurocomputing **472**, 252–265 (2022)
38. Yin, J., Tang, M., Cao, J., You, M., Wang, H., Alazab, M.: Knowledge-driven cybersecurity intelligence: software vulnerability co-exploitation behaviour discovery. IEEE Trans. Ind. Inform. (2022)

39. Yin, J., You, M., Cao, J., Wang, H., Tang, M.J., Ge, Y.-F.: Data-driven hierarchical neural network modeling for high-pressure feedwater heater group. In: Borovica-Gajic, R., Qi, J., Wang, W. (eds.) ADC 2020. LNCS, vol. 12008, pp. 225–233. Springer, Cham (2020). https://doi.org/10.1007/978-3-030-39469-1_19
40. You, M., Yin, J., Wang, H., Cao, J., Miao, Y.: A minority class boosted framework for adaptive access control decision-making. In: Zhang, W., Zou, L., Maamar, Z., Chen, L. (eds.) WISE 2021. LNCS, vol. 13080, pp. 143–157. Springer, Cham (2021). https://doi.org/10.1007/978-3-030-90888-1_12
41. You, M., et al.: A knowledge graph empowered online learning framework for access control decision-making. World Wide Web, pp. 1–22 (2022)
42. Yuan, F., Cao, Y., Shang, Y., Liu, Y., Tan, J., Fang, B.: Insider threat detection with deep neural network. In: Shi, Y., et al. (eds.) ICCS 2018. LNCS, vol. 10860, pp. 43–54. Springer, Cham (2018). https://doi.org/10.1007/978-3-319-93698-7_4

Network Security

Exploiting Redundancy in Network Flow Information for Efficient Security Attack Detection

Siqi Xia[1]([⊠])(iD), Sutharshan Rajasegarar[1](iD), Christopher Leckie[2](iD),
Sarah M. Erfani[2](iD), and Jeffrey Chan[3](iD)

[1] Deakin University, Geelong, Australia
{xiasiq,sutharshan.rajasegarar}@deakin.edu.au
[2] The University of Melbourne, Melbourne, Australia
{caleckie,sarah.erfani}@unimelb.edu.au
[3] RMIT University, Melbourne, Australia
jeffrey.chan@rmit.edu.au

Abstract. Securing communication networks has become increasingly important due to the growth in cybersecurity attacks, such as ransomware and denial of service attacks. In order to better observe, detect and track attacks in large networks, accurate and efficient anomaly detection algorithms are needed. In this paper, we address how the redundancy of the normal and attack traffic information available from network flow data can be exploited to develop a computationally efficient method for security attack detection. In this work, several sampling strategies are integrated with two graph neural network frameworks that have been employed to detect network attacks with reduced computational overhead, while achieving high detection accuracy. Using network flow data from several types of networks, such as Internet of Things data, the trade-off between model accuracy and computational efficiency for different attacks has been evaluated.

Keywords: Security · Anomaly detection · Graph neural network

1 Introduction

Anomaly detection plays an increasingly important role in network security management, in terms of detecting the occurrence of new types of network attacks. Traditional anomaly detection methods involve analysing a fixed vector of features of network traffic. However, there is growing interest in the use of graph neural networks (GNN) that can exploit the topological properties of the traffic flows in a network to improve anomaly detection accuracy. A key challenge in this context is how to improve the scalability of training GNNs so that large networks can be monitored in an efficient manner. The aims of this paper are to propose several approaches for using sampling in GNNs for network traffic analysis, and to empirically analyse the effectiveness of these sampling strategies to improve the scalability of GNNs for anomaly detection on realistic network traffic data.

© The Author(s), under exclusive license to Springer Nature Switzerland AG 2022
X. Yuan et al. (Eds.): NSS 2022, LNCS 13787, pp. 105–119, 2022.
https://doi.org/10.1007/978-3-031-23020-2_6

The convolutional operations used in GNN include spectral and spatial methods. Spectral methods define operations for signal processing that remove noise from graph signals, whereas, spatial based methods define convolutions by information propagation [14]. Graph Convolutional Neural Networks (GCN) [7] bridge the gap between the spectral and spatial based GNN.

Training a GCN with a large graph can generate computational problems in time and memory [9]. Sampling methods can be leveraged to deal with this limitation. The embedding of a node in a GCN involves aggregating information from all its neighbours. Therefore, it is advantageous to use sampling of nodes that are in the neighborhood of a particular node during the training process to improve efficiency. The sampling method constructs a mini-batch in comparison to the full-batch. Hence, using a mini-batch for aggregation can significantly reduce computation without affecting accuracy. Sampling can thus ensure the efficiency and scalability of GCN training [9]. Sampling methods can also be applied to GCN auto-encoders for unsupervised learning.

The aim of this paper is to propose methodologies that exploit the redundancy of the normal and attack traffic information available from the network flow data to develop a computationally efficient method for security attack detection. In particular, we investigate how different sampling methods can be integrated with a variety of GNN architectures to improve the overall efficiency of training GNNs on large datasets. Further, we investigate the trade-off between efficiency and accuracy for different sampling approaches. The contributions of this paper include:

- Developing a graph-based unsupervised machine learning intrusion detection system using auto-encoder based GCN. A sampling based GCN auto-encoder framework for intrusion detection is also developed. The sampling process can be embedded in the GCN auto-encoder at either the preprocessing stage or the training stage.
- Comparing different sampling methods intergrated with the graph-based auto-encoder model to assess the influence on accuracy for anomaly detection on network flow data. Further, we assess the trade-off between training efficiency and detection results.
- Finding the minimum number of nodes required for training in order to achieve a certain level of accuracy for detecting attacks. In particular, we exploit the redundancy of normal (non-attack) data to minimise the computational and memory requirements to achieve the highest possible accuracy for detecting attacks from network flow data using our sampling based GCN scheme.

2   Literature Review

Intrusion detection system (IDS) can analyse and identify abnormal behaviours in networks. Two major detection categories exist, namely anomaly detection and signature detection [1] depending on whether known patterns exist for training or not. Anomaly detection is important and widely used in IDS especially when there is no prior information, which is common for attacks or intrusions in networks. Accordingly, anomaly detection can be used to detect new types of intrusions in a network [12]. Anomaly detection methods can be categorised into different classes like statistical based, rule based or machine learning based [2].

Network flow data in the real world can contain millions or billions of records to be analysed, where the data can have significantly high dimensions and large scale. The graph is a type of data structure that models both the objects and their interactions. It allows us to mathematically represent and analyse the relations for the objects and can be used to represent the network flow data. With the significance of the data scale, machine learning methods can also be utilised with graph data representations to build Graph Neural Network (GNN) models to solve network flow data related problems.

Graph Convolutional Neural Networks (GCNs) [7] make several approximations and simplifications for the eigendecomposition of the Laplacian matrix in the spectral GNN [15]. Among the GNN structures, the auto-encoder framework has attracted growing attention because it can be used to represent the deep latent factors of the graph geometrical structure [8]. Graph Auto-encoders (GAEs) are deep neural architectures that embed the nodes into a latent feature space followed by decoding the graph information from these feature spaces. Recent graph auto-encoder techniques for anomaly detection includes DOMI-NANT [5] and GALA [11].

With the large scale data usually used for graph deep learning, the computational cost in storage and time for GCN can be significantly high. Thus, sampling methods are good ways to increase efficiency without harming the performance substantially. The sampling methods applied to a GCN with their processing and time evaluation are analysed and summarised in [9]. However, there is no existing work to investigate the influence of GCN sampling methods applied to anomaly detection. This is the main focus of this paper in later discussions.

3   Methodology

3.1   Background Techniques

Graph Definitions.

Definition 1 (Plain Graph) A static plain graph is denoted $G = \{V, E\}$ comprising nodes $V = \{v_i\}_1^n$ and edges $E = \{e_{i,j}\}$, where n denotes the number of nodes and $e_{i,j} = (v_i, v_j)$ represents an edge between nodes v_i and v_j [15]. The adjacency matrix $A = [a_{i,j}]_{n \times n}$ defines the graph structure, where $a_{i,j} = 1$ if an edge is present between the nodes v_i and v_j, otherwise $a_{i,j} = 0$.

Definition 2 (Attributed Graph). A static attributed graph $G = \{V, E, X\}$ comprises a node set V, an edge set E and an attribute set X. In an attributed graph, the graph structure follows Definition 1. The attribute matrix $X = [x_i]_{n \times d}$ comprises the nodes' attribute vectors, where x_i is the attribute vector associated with node v_i and d is the dimension of the vector. The node attributes are in $X \in \mathbb{R}^{n \times d}$, where the ith row vector $x_i \in \mathbb{R}^d (i = 1, ..., n)$ is the attribute information for the ith node [15].

GCN. The definition of a GCN starts with the spectral convolution GNN [15]. A spectral convolution on a graph [14] is obtained by the multiplication of an input signal $x \in \mathbb{R}^n$ with a spectral filter $g_\theta = diag(\theta)$ parameterized by the vector of Fourier coefficients $\theta \in \mathbb{R}^n$. The forward-path of the GCN can be expressed by

$$H^{(m+1)} = \xi(\tilde{D}^{\frac{1}{2}} \tilde{A} \tilde{D}^{\frac{1}{2}} H^{(m)} \Theta^{(m)}), \tag{1}$$

where $H^{(m)}$ is the activation matrix in the mth layer and $H^{(0)}$ is the feature matrix X of the input nodes, $\xi(\cdot)$ is a nonlinear activation function like $ReLU(\cdot) = max(0, \cdot)$, and $\Theta^{(m)}$ is a trainable weight matrix. The GCN presents a computationally efficient convolutional process (given the assumption that A is sparse) and achieves improved accuracy over state-of-the-art methods in semi-supervised node classification tasks by simultaneously using the features of nodes and the geometric structure of the graph.

Auto-encoder GCN. There are two auto-encoder techniques that have been applied in this method. Both auto-encoders are used for graph representation and possess different architectures for encoding and decoding, especially in the adjacency matrix. Moreover, the auto-encoders can be applied for anomaly detection, by leveraging the learnt representations from the encoder to reconstruct the original data.

DOMINANT Auto-encoder. The first type of auto-encoder embeds nodes in the graph structure as well as the attributes of the nodes based on a GCN called DOMINANT [5]. The model structure is built on the base of a deep auto-encoder. It comprises three parts: (i) attributed network encoder - attributed graph representation learning with GCN to transfer the attributed nodes structure into an embedding, (ii) structure reconstruction decoder - reconstructs the nodal structure based on the graph representations, (iii) attribute reconstruction decoder - reconstructs the attributes for nodes in the reconstructed graph from the encoded embedding.

The reconstruction of the network structure and attributes are from the latent embedding representation Z. Let $\hat{A}$ be the reconstructed adjacency matrix from the intermediate layers. The reconstruction error is defined as $R_s = \hat{A} - \tilde{A}$. The reconstruction errors can be considered as the anomaly scores. The threshold is then calculated as $\mu + 2\sigma$. The reconstruction errors above this threshold are regarded as anomalies. The link prediction layer can be trained from the encoded Z as:

$$\hat{A} = sigmoid(ZZ^T) \tag{2}$$

In addition, the reconstruction for the attribute matrix is derived from the latent representation Z as well as the nodal structure giving:

$$\hat{X} = f_{Relu}(Z, A|W^{(l+1)}) \tag{3}$$

Symmetric Auto-encoder (GALA). The second type is the symmetric graph convolutional auto-encoder for graph embedding, called GALA [11]. In contrast to the previous auto-encoder architecture, this method has a complete symmetric auto-encoder form for both the encoder and decoder [11]. GALA comprises two parts: (i) attributed network encoder - which uses the Laplacian smoothing method to encode the inputs as the weighted average from both the node itself and its neighbours, and (ii) symmetric network decoder - which performs Laplacian sharpening, reconstructing the feature of each node farther away from the centroid of its neighbours.

Laplacian smoothing, the general form of GCN, is used to calculate a new representation of the inputs. With the affinity matrix defined as $\tilde{A} = A + I_n$ and the degree matrix defined as $\tilde{D} = D + I_n$, Laplacian smoothing can be defined as:

$$x_i^{(m+1)} = (1 - \gamma)x_i^{(m)} + \gamma \sum_j \frac{\tilde{A}_{ij}}{\tilde{D}_{ii}} x_j^{(m)} \tag{4}$$

where $x_i^{(m+1)}$ is the new representation of $x_i^{(m)}$ and γ is a regularisation parameter that determines the significance between itself and its neighbours. This can be shown in an equation as:

$$X^{(m+1)} = X^{(m)} - \gamma \tilde{L}_{rw} X^{(m)} \tag{5}$$

where $\tilde{L}_{rw}$ can be replaced with $\tilde{L}$ if $\gamma = 1$. The representations can also be defined as

$$X^{(m+1)} = \tilde{D}^{(-1/2)} \tilde{A} \tilde{D}^{(-1/2)} X^{(m)} \tag{6}$$

Laplacian sharpening is the process of reconstructing the attribute matrix from the representations, and is used to build the decoder in the auto-encoder model. The Laplacian sharpening equation can be written as:

$$x_i^{(m+1)} = (1 + \gamma)x_i^{(m)} - \gamma \sum_j \frac{\tilde{A}_{ij}}{\tilde{D}_{ii}} x_j^{(m)} \tag{7}$$

and this also can be rewritten as:

$$X^{(m+1)} = X^{(m)} + \gamma \tilde{L}_{rw} X^{(m)} \tag{8}$$

from which the reconstructed attribute matrix can be obtained as the output from the auto-encoder, which can be used for anomaly detection.

GCN Sampling Methods. GCN sampling methods can be divided into two main types, namely pre-training sampling and sampling in the latent layers during training.

GRAIN. GRAIN is a method for selecting significant nodes before training [16]. The outputs from GRAIN can be leveraged as the initial inputs for the auto-encoder model. In GRAIN, we measure the sensitivity of nodes by computing how it has been aggregated through feature propagation. We then maximise the influence of the selected nodes (i.e., seed nodes) to increase the involvement of non-selected nodes in the downstream model training. The method can select the most significant nodes and can be used as the initial values for the auto-encoder training. GRAIN includes information for both graph structure and aggregated features. The magnitude and diversity components are further used to calculate the diversified influence, which can be regarded as a score for the data selection.

LADIES. Layer-dependent importance sampling (LADIES) is a technique used for node-wise sampling based on the latent layers of the encoder, during the process of auto-encoder training [17]. LADIES selects the neighbourhood nodes based on nodes from the upper layers and constructs a sub-graph in the latent space according to the significance probability of the neighbourhood nodes. LADIES is a layer-dependent importance sampling method that applies neighbour-dependent sampling to utilise the dependency between layers, which leads to a dense computational graph. The sampled nodes at the lth layer (S_t) are generated depending on the sampled nodes that have been generated in all the upper layers. Note that for each node, we only need to aggregate the embeddings from neighbouring nodes in the previous layer. Thus, at a particular layer, we only need to generate samples from the union of neighbours of the nodes that we have sampled in the upper layer, as defined by:

$$V^{(l-1)} = \cup_{v_i \in S_t} N(v_i) \tag{9}$$

The nodes are sorted using an importance sampling scheme that relies only on the matrix $Q^{(l)}$ and P. The importance probability is defined as:

$$p_i^{(l-1)} = \frac{||Q^{(l)}P_{*,i}||_2^2}{||Q^{(l)}P||_F^2} \tag{10}$$

The Laplacian matrix is defined as $\tilde{P}^{(l-1)} = Q(l)PS^{(l-1)}Q^{(l-1)T}$. In the sampling mechanism, we have $\mathbb{E}[S^{(l-1)}] = L^{(l-1)}$, where $L^{(l-1)}$ is defined as the diagonal matrix with:

$$L_{s,s}^{(l-1)} = \begin{cases} 1, & \text{if } s \in V^{(l-1)} \\ 0, & \text{otherwise.} \end{cases} \tag{11}$$

Reorder. Our third sampling approach is a reordering method, which is applied to vertices based on a reordering for nodes [13]. It is used in conjunction with LADIES. During the sampling of each layer using LADIES, 10% additional nodes will be sampled, and then all nodes will be reordered based on their vertices. The reorder method aims to further select the more informative nodes based on LADIES.

3.2   Sampling Based Frameworks

Based on these background techniques, we now describe how these are combined in our traffic analysis framework.

GCN Sampling on Network Flow Data. First, we analyse the effect of the different GCN sampling methods on detecting various security attacks from the network flow data. The sampling methods used to build the anomaly detection system are node-wise, layer-wise and subgraph sampling methods. The model is built based on GCN. For node-wise sampling, we use the GraphSAGE [6] method. For layer-wise sampling, we use LADIES [17], and for subgraph sampling, we use Cluster-GCN sampling [3]. This analysis focuses on finding the most suitable sampling methods for supervised learning.

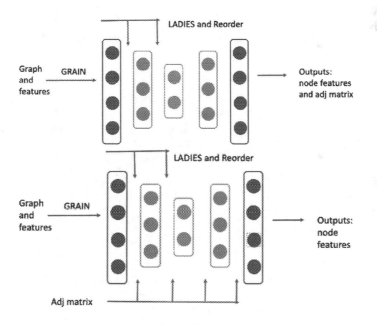

Fig. 1. Auto-encoder with sampling for the upper: DOMINANT and lower: GALA model

GCN Auto-encoder Sampling Combination on Network Flow Data. Here we analyse the influence of sampling techniques on the GCN auto-encoder model when unsupervised learning is used. Two different auto-encoder structures, DOMINANT [5] and GALA [11] have been chosen to build the sampling model. Both auto-encoders include the encoder and decoder parts, and the sampling process is integrated before and during the encoder operation.

Two types of sampling techniques have been applied to the GCN auto-encoder to build the sampling models. First is GRAIN [16], which chooses nodes with the most significant information based on the graph structures. Before training the GCN auto-encoder, the GRAIN node selection is performed, hence it is regarded as a preprocessing method. The second approach is to sample during the GCN auto-encoder training process, both using layer-wise sampling and reordering methods. These techniques are applied to every layer during the encoder training session.

The general workflow of the sampling method is as follows:

- Original graph data are input to the GRAIN model for data selection.
- The selected data is then used as the initial data for the training process. The input nodes are selected at each layer during the training process based on the LADIES and reorder mechanisms.
- With the LADIES mechanism, nodes are selected based on their importance. Then, the reordering process further selects the nodes from the nodes selected by LADIES. Finally, the selected nodes are forwarded to the next latent layer for training.

An overview of the process for both of the auto-encoder structures are shown in Fig. 1.

The training and testing process for the auto-encoders are the same as their original definition. The training process is based on the loss function defined for the auto-encoders according to their model structure.

For the DOMINANT model, the loss function is defined as:

$$L = (1 - \alpha)||A - \tilde{A}||_F^2 + \alpha||X - \tilde{X}||_F^2 \tag{12}$$

For the GALA model, the loss function is defined as:

$$L = ||X - \tilde{X}||_F^2 \tag{13}$$

The auto-encoder model with sampling is trained via backpropagation of the loss function. The outputs of the auto-encoders are the original node features and the graph structure based on the adjacent matrix. The dissimilarity between the estimated results and the original inputs can be evaluated based on the scores of the auto-encoders, which are determined according to the loss function as follows.

For DOMINANT, the loss function is defined as:

$$s(v_i) = (1 - \alpha)||a_i - \tilde{a}_i||^2 + \alpha||x_i - \tilde{x}_i||^2 \tag{14}$$

For GALA, the loss function is defined as:

$$s(v_i) = ||x_i - \tilde{x}_i||^2 \tag{15}$$

To perform anomaly detection, we need to define a threshold on the reconstruction loss to determine whether the node samples are anomalous or normal.

This threshold can be determined through statistical criteria such as $\mu + 2\sigma$, where μ and σ represent mean and standard deviation of the anomaly scores respectively. Also, we can use a ranking of the specific number of node scores to define the threshold. In our later experiments, $\mu + 2\sigma$ is the criterion used as the threshold.

4   Experiments

4.1   General Experiment Settings

Datasets. Two published network flow datasets have been used to evaluate the performance of the GCN and GCN auto-encoder with sampling. Both datasets contain network records, features for the flow records and labels (anomalous/benign) along with the associated class of attack. The datasets included are UNSW-NB15 [10] and LitNet [4], both of which have proprietary formats and feature sets and have been widely used to evaluate machine learning based network intrusion detection systems. A brief overview of these datasets is provided in the following.

- **UNSW-NB15:** UNSW-NB15 dataset was created by Moustafa et al. [10] using IXIA tools to generate a detailed network traffic dataset in a complex network environment including nine main attack types. The Argus Bro-IDS network-monitoring tool has been used to analyse and generate 49 traffic features.
- **LitNet:** LitNet-2020 is a new network benchmark dataset obtained from a real-life academic network [4]. The dataset includes normal and anomalous records for real-life network traffic. The dataset contains 85 network flow features and 12 types of attacks.

4.2   Results and Analysis

GCN Sampling Comparison on Network Flow Data

GCN Sampling Method Comparison. The first experiment is conducted based on the UNSW-NB15 dataset with selected nodes. In total, 5784 nodes for training and 869 for testing have been selected with a 9.6% anomaly ratio. This is a subset of the original dataset extracted using stratified sampling for experimental use. The experiment is conducted by sampling varying proportions of nodes using different sampling methods and analysing how these methods perform with the increasing proportion of sampling nodes. The experiments are run based on five trials, with the mean results presented based on different graph selections. The sampling percentage represents each layer's sampling proportion, i.e., the number of nodes in the mini-batch size compared to the full-batch.

In Table 1 it can be seen that layer-wise GCN provides better performance generally, and layer-wise GCN achieves a more steady accuracy level from a

Table 1. Accuracy (%) Comparison for GCN Sampling Methods

Sampling proportion	20%	40%	60%	80%	100%
Node-wise GCN	49.59	60.73	75.56	83.77	92.15
Layer-wise GCN	55.75	74.56	80.78	86.15	94.35
Cluster-GCN	43.98	56.49	77.64	81.56	90.34

lower proportion of sampling through nodes. Thus in these three comparisons, layer-wise GCN provides the best performance on the dataset.

Table 2 shows how sampling can influence the nodes, especially the abnormal node proportions. We can define the nodes sampled as the non-redundant nodes and in later studies, we will further discuss how sampling can influence the anomaly detection results. According to the results, 60% and larger proportions of sampling can have less influence on the anomaly ratio, and thus is defined as non-redundant data and is safer to use for better results in anomaly detection.

Table 2. Anomaly ratio (%) comparison for GCN sampling methods

Sampling proportion	20%	40%	60%	80%	100%
Node-wise GCN	3.4	5.5	8.4	8.7	9.6
Layer-wise GCN	4.2	6.3	8.8	8.9	9.6
Cluster-GCN	3.8	4.9	7.4	8.6	9.6

GCN Sampling for Attack Types. The second experiment assesses the influence of sampling on different attacks. In each experiment trial, 2000 nodes were selected with an anomaly ratio of 10%, with each trial only including one specific attack type. The results are given in Table 3 for three attack types that involve large traffic volumes.

Table 3. Accuracy(%) Comparison for Layer-wise GCN Sampling Method With Various Attack Types

Samp. proportion	20%	40%	60%	80%	100%
General	53.24	65.17	79.97	83.6	90.83
Generic	55.85	68.54	79.54	87.15	93.94
Fuzzer	53.33	66.3	77.96	85.33	91.59
Exploits	46.52	53.64	69.77	82.96	88.48

We observe that there is considerable variation in the effect of sampling for different attack types. Taking the layer-wise sampling method as an example, it is shown that the Generic and Fuzzer attacks perform similarly to the general scenario, while the Exploits attacks have lower accuracy, especially for low sampling ratios. It can be seen that the different attacks have different sensitivity to the sampling proportion, especially at lower levels, and react differently depending on the sampling method.

GCN Auto-encoder Sampling Combination on Network Flow Data. Experiments for GCN auto-encoder sampling were conducted on both the UNSW-NB15 and LitNet dataset. For UNSW-NB15, 28k nodes are selected with an anomaly ratio of 11%, while for LitNet, 2.1k nodes are selected. The accuracy of detection is composed for sampling using a combination of LADIES, LADIES and GRAIN, and LADIES with GRAIN and reordering. The execution time is compared for sampling using LADIES with GRAIN, and LADIES with GRAIN and reordering. The GRAIN process has not been included in the time calculation as it is applied in pre-processing. One hundred twenty-eight nodes have been selected as the input and used for training GRAIN. The sampling percentage represents each layer's sampling proportion, which corresponds to the mini-batch size compared to the full-batch in terms of the number of nodes.

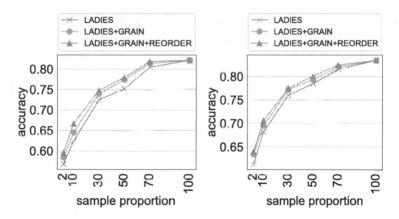

Fig. 2. Accuracy comparison for different sampling combination and the sampling proportion for UNSW-NB15. The left graph is using DOMINANT and the right one is using GALA auto-encoder.

Accuracy Comparison for Sampling Combinations. The performance comparison with different combinations of sampling techniques is presented in Fig. 2 and Fig. 3. The two different auto-encoders react similarly to the sampling methods. The trend in the figures show that the two auto-encoders are more sensitive to sampling with less than 30% of nodes layer-wise. These results reveal that it can be used in fields when accuracy requirements are more tolerant with fewer nodes included in the training process while not sacrificing accuracy too much.

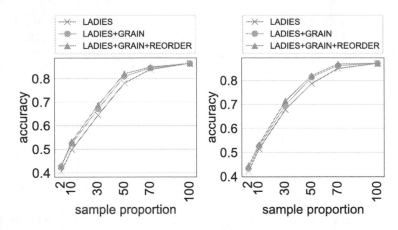

Fig. 3. Accuracy comparison for different sampling combination and the sampling proportion for LitNet. The left graph is using DOMINANT and the right one is using GALA auto-encoder.

Comparing different combinations of sampling methods, LADIES and GRAIN with Reorder has the highest accuracy, while the performance improvement over LADIES with GRAIN may not be that significant. In comparison, there is a more noticeable drop in performance when LADIES alone is used, indicating that GRAIN plays an important role in the sampling during training. Comparing the performance differences between the datasets, LitNet is more sensitive to the effects of sampling, especially at low sampling proportions.

Time-Consumption Comparison. One of the key advantages of introducing sampling in training is that it improves the running time. To analyse the influence of the sampling schemes, the time consumption for the experiments has also been compared.

In Fig. 4 and Fig. 5, we compare the time consumption of different combinations of sampling methods. The 100% value represents the time used for the full-sized dataset as a baseline for comparison. Overall, it is clear that the sampling methods can significantly reduce the time required for training.

In comparing different sampling method combinations, using the reorder sampling method increased computation time. It requires computation of the node degrees and sorting to find the most significant samples. When comparing the results from different datasets, the UNSW-NB15 dataset shows a steady increase with the sampling proportion. For LitNet, the time increases more sharply after 50% for the $LADIES+GRAIN+REORDER$ method, and the reorder method incurs more time for larger proportions of sampling for LitNet.

Comparing the results from different datasets, the different data structures and different numbers of features used for the two datasets can bring different levels of time consumed for the sampling process.

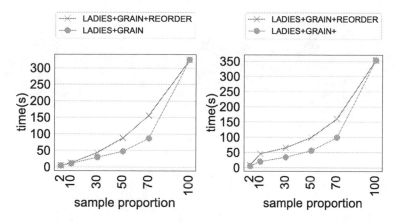

Fig. 4. Time comparison for different sampling combinations and sampling proportion for UNSW-NB15. The left graph is using DOMINANT and right one is using GALA auto-encoder.

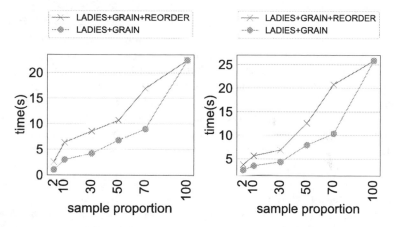

Fig. 5. Time comparison for different sampling combinations and sampling proportion for LitNet. The left graph is using DOMINANT and right one is using GALA auto-encoder.

Sensitivity of Different Attack Types Towards Sampling. The aim of this experiment is to further interpret the potential reasons why different attacks react differently toward sampling. T-SNE plots have been generated for embeddings from the penultimate layer of the GCN model. This is motivated by the result in Table 3. The experimental data includes normal data and different attacks. We investigate the embedding distributions for normal and attack data under different sampling proportions. Sampling is generated with LADIES. From Fig. 6, it can be seen that for some attack types, such as Exploits, sampling leads to mixing of the attack data and normal data, which explains why this specific attack type is more sensitive to sampling.

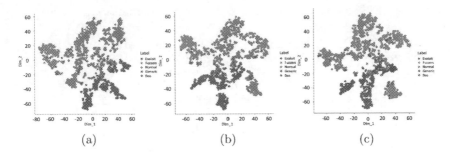

(a)   (b)   (c)

Fig. 6. -SNE plot for the GCN penultimate layer embeddings under (a) 100%, (b) 50% and (c) 30% sampling proportions.

5   Conclusion

Timely detection of security attacks in a communication network is important for providing reliable and safe information flow as well as preventing loss and damage to the system. In this work, we investigated how redundant information in the data can be removed by sampling to reduce computation time while ensuring accurate detection of attacks. Different sampling strategies for graph based deep learning frameworks are analysed for the detection of attacks in a computationally efficient manner. Using network flow data, the efficiency of detecting attacks using different sampling methods in terms of accuracy, as well as the sensitivity for different types of attacks, has been analysed. The results reveal that certain types of attacks are more sensitive to the choice of sampling method. Moreover, for a majority of the attack types, significant savings can be achieved in terms of computational overhead, by removing the redundancy in the network flow data. In light of this study, in the future, we aim to propose a novel loss function that exploits this redundancy information to guide the graph auto-encoder based deep anomaly detection process to improve detection accuracy and computational overhead.

References

1. Axelsson, S.: Intrusion detection systems: a survey and taxonomy. Technical report, Citeseer (2000)
2. Butun, I., Morgera, S.D., Sankar, R.: A survey of intrusion detection systems in wireless sensor networks. IEEE Commun. Surv. Tutor. **16**(1), 266–282 (2013)
3. Chiang, W.L., Liu, X., Si, S., Li, Y., Bengio, S., Hsieh, C.J.: Cluster-GCN: an efficient algorithm for training deep and large graph convolutional networks. In: Proceedings of the 25th ACM SIGKDD International Conference on Knowledge Discovery & Data Mining, pp. 257–266 (2019)
4. Damasevicius, R., et al.: Litnet-2020: an annotated real-world network flow dataset for network intrusion detection. Electronics **9**(5), 800 (2020)
5. Ding, K., Li, J., Bhanushali, R., Liu, H.: Deep anomaly detection on attributed networks. In: Proceedings of the 2019 SIAM International Conference on Data Mining, pp. 594–602. SIAM (2019)

6. Hamilton, W.L., Ying, R., Leskovec, J.: Inductive representation learning on large graphs. In: Proceedings of the 31st International Conference on Neural Information Processing System, pp. 1025–1035 (2017)
7. Kipf, T.N., Welling, M.: Semi-supervised classification with graph convolutional networks. arXiv preprint arXiv:1609.02907 (2016)
8. Kipf, T.N., Welling, M.: Variational graph auto-encoders. arXiv preprint arXiv:1611.07308 (2016)
9. Liu, X., Yan, M., Deng, L., Li, G., Ye, X., Fan, D.: Sampling methods for efficient training of graph convolutional networks: a survey. arXiv preprint arXiv:2103.05872 (2021)
10. Moustafa, N., Slay, J.: Unsw-nb15: a comprehensive data set for network intrusion detection systems (unsw-nb15 network data set). In: Proceeding of the 2015 Military Communications and Information Systems Conference (MilCIS), pp. 1–6. IEEE (2015)
11. Park, J., Lee, M., Chang, H.J., Lee, K., Choi, J.Y.: Symmetric graph convolutional autoencoder for unsupervised graph representation learning. In: Proceedings of the IEEE/CVF International Conference on Computer Vision, pp. 6519–6528 (2019)
12. Rajasegarar, S., Leckie, C., Palaniswami, M.: Anomaly detection in wireless sensor networks. IEEE Wirel. Commun. 15(4), 34–40 (2008)
13. Rashidi, L., et al.: Node re-ordering as a means of anomaly detection in time-evolving graphs. In: Frasconi, P., Landwehr, N., Manco, G., Vreeken, J. (eds.) ECML PKDD 2016. LNCS (LNAI), vol. 9852, pp. 162–178. Springer, Cham (2016). https://doi.org/10.1007/978-3-319-46227-1_11
14. Shuman, D.I., Narang, S.K., Frossard, P., Ortega, A., Vandergheynst, P.: The emerging field of signal processing on graphs: extending high-dimensional data analysis to networks and other irregular domains. IEEE Signal Process. Mag. 30(3), 83–98 (2013)
15. Wu, Z., Pan, S., Chen, F., Long, G., Zhang, C., Philip, S.Y.: A comprehensive survey on graph neural networks. IEEE Trans. Neural Networks Learn. Syst. 32(1), 4–24 (2020)
16. Zhang, W., et al.: Grain: improving data efficiency of graph neural networks via diversified influence maximization. arXiv preprint arXiv:2108.00219 (2021)
17. Zou, D., Hu, Z., Wang, Y., Jiang, S., Sun, Y., Gu, Q.: Layer-dependent importance sampling for training deep and large graph convolutional networks. arXiv preprint arXiv:1911.07323 (2019)

A Learning Methodology for Line-Rate Ransomware Mitigation with P4 Switches

Kurt Friday[1]([✉]), Elias Bou-Harb[1], and Jorge Crichigno[2]

[1] The Cyber Center for Security and Analytics, The University of Texas at San Antonio, San Antonio, USA
{kurt.friday,elias.bouharb}@utsa.edu
[2] Integrated Information Technology, The University of South Carolina, Columbia, USA
jcrichigno@cec.sc.edu

Abstract. Ransomware is currently the leading malware threat propagating throughout today's networks and is the preeminent attack vector for adversaries aiming to extort a broad array of targets for financial gain. The de facto strategies for combating such maliciousness have long been host-based; however, these strategies are often inconsistently deployed and are typically not supported by devices with more modest computational capacity, such as the Internet of Things (IoT) domain. As a result, host-based techniques often do not scale well. Alternatively, network Intrusion Detection and Prevention Systems (IDSs/IPSs) mitigate this issue to some extent by offering a degree of network-level protection, but they too ultimately suffer the same scalability pitfall, as their performance degrades substantially amid higher traffic rates. Moreover, IDSs and IPSs are heavily reliant upon deep packet inspection, which adversaries easily circumvent with encryption. In response to such issues, we present a novel in-network methodology for integrating Random Forests (RFs) into programmable switches for traffic classification tasks, which we leverage to perform line-rate ransomware detection and mitigation. In turn, the Tbps packet processing capability of programmable switches seamlessly allows the proposed methodology to scale to even the busiest networks. Our methodology functions solely on network traffic features that are invariant to encryption. Additionally, our network-based approach can also be instrumented as a secondary defense strategy to host-based approaches that lack full network coverage. The proposed methodology was implemented on an Intel Tofino hardware switch and was shown to fit comfortably within the device's resource bounds, with room to spare for other essential switch-based applications. In addition, the methodology was empirically evaluated using a number of the most prominent ransomware strains, demonstrating that it is capable of performing both binary or multiclass ransomware traffic classification with a precision and recall of over 0.99. Furthermore, this performance was obtained with as little as three packets from a compromised source. Indeed, such prompt detection can enable the mitigation of both ransomware propagation and the encryption of a victim's files.

© The Author(s), under exclusive license to Springer Nature Switzerland AG 2022
X. Yuan et al. (Eds.): NSS 2022, LNCS 13787, pp. 120–139, 2022.
https://doi.org/10.1007/978-3-031-23020-2_7

Keywords: Ransomware · Machine learning · Random forests · Network traffic classification · Programmable switches · P4

1   Introduction

The advent of the programmable data plane technology has enabled a plethora of advancements in network traffic classification tasks. Simultaneously, Machine Learning (ML) has cemented itself as capable of carrying out any number of pattern identification activities in a manner vastly superior to other more traditional techniques and even humans. However, how best to integrate such pattern recognition capabilities into programmable switches to further advance the performance of current network traffic classification schemes is still an open research question [22, 24].

Among the most needed traffic classification tasks is a method for countering mounting ransomware threat. Since the WannaCry attack of May 2017, the frequency of ransomware attacks and magnitude of their damages has been increasing at alarming rates, on a global scale [5]. For instance, in 2021, the occurrence of attacks rose by 48% around the world, with the U.K. and the U.S. observing an uptick of 233% and 127%, respectively, with an average of 9.7 attempted attacks being recorded on a daily basis per organization [50]. Moreover, recent ransomware variants have extend WannaCry's worm-like capabilities in order to self-propagate to other machines [20, 29, 32, 41, 48].

To address the aforementioned challenges, we propose a novel methodology for interleaving the ability of RF classifiers to fingerprint a number of network traffic classification tasks into the pipeline of programmable switches, and we utilize this methodology to detect and mitigate ransomware in real-time. Our methodology relies only on unidirectional traffic to allow for flexibility amid asymmetric routing [19, 24] and is based upon network and transport layer headers to accurately classify ransomware amid encrypted traffic. In addition to classifying offending source IP addresses from only a small amount of the packets that they transmit, the proposed methodology operates solely in the data plane in order to circumvent the detection latency and network overhead associated with communicating traffic artifacts to a centralized controller and awaiting classification results [23, 24]. This combination of detection speed enhancements enables the proposed methodology to mitigate ransomware propagation, the encryption of a victim's files, and even thwart such encryption altogether, as the asymmetric key exchanges can be halted.

Our approach was written in P4 [8] and compiled on an Intel Tofino hardware switch, showing that our P4 program fits conservatively within the switch's resource bounds. We also generated a training and testing dataset in a Triage sandbox environment [47] from a number of the most prominent ransomware variants and demonstrated that such variants can be quickly fingerprinted with both high precision and recall. Indeed, with Intel Tofino switches now capable of processing throughput of up to 25.6 Tbps [28], our methodology's network-based approach note only can compliment existing host-based defenses to protect devices logged into networks that are incapable of defending themselves (e.g., connected IoT and mobile devices that are now being targeted [26,55,56]) but also mitigate the ransomware epidemic at scale within high-speed networks, such as science DMZs, campuses, critical infrastructure [9], medical services, and numerous others [39], as well as the backbones that serve them. Finally, the proposed methodology has been fully automated to facilitate ease of implementation. All source code, datasets, and analytics scripts have been made available to the public at large [40] to facilitate advancements in programmable switch-based learning and ransomware mitigation.

This work's contributions are summarized as follows:

– We present a novel methodology for extracting network traffic features for RF classification entirely within a programmable switch for line-rate network traffic classification tasks. The methodology leverages several optimizations in order to implement full-size RF models in such devices, including the parallelization of feature processing to minimize expensive sequential operations and performing a number of Ternary Content-Addressable Memory (TCAM) consumption reduction steps. Our methodology was implemented on an Intel Tofino switch, demonstrating that it conserves the switch's limited resources.
– We showcase our methodology's ability to mitigate the ransomware threat at scale. A comprehensive evaluation was performed, showing that the proposed methodology can reliably fingerprint a host infected with a number of the most prominent ransomware strains from only a small number of packets. Moreover, the methodology is capable of performing multiclass classification in order to reveal the ransomware family responsible for the infection. Additionally, we interleaved varying rates of benign packets in between the malicious transmissions of an infected host to emulate the varying degrees of additional legitimate processes that may be running on that host despite being compromised that may be observed in the wild. The proposed approach's performance experienced negligible degradation amid such interleaving, which further demonstrates the approach's ability to safeguard machines regardless of their legitimate network activity.
– We implemented a number of measures to promote the proposed approach's adoption in practice. In particular, flexible deployment options are supported by our approach's compatibility with asymmetric routing and its independence from the controller. Furthermore, the methodology is fully converted to generic Behavioral Model version 2 (BMv2) [1] code and entirely automated to facilitate its application by practitioners on a variety of switch hardware targets, regardless of their background. Additionally, we make all source code, datasets, and analytics scripts publicly available [40] to promote future advancements in this domain.

The remainder of the paper is organized as follows. We begin by reviewing the related literature. Subsequently, Sect. 3 elaborates upon the ransomware threat model for this work. In Sect. 4, we present the proposed methodology and highlight its various intricacies. We then comprehensively evaluate our methodology to verify its effectiveness and practicality in Sect. 5. Finally, we conclude this work and summarize its findings in Sect. 6.

2   Related Work

Switch-Based RF Classification. The enhanced classification speed that can be acquired by pairing ML with the processing capabilities of programmable switches has began garnering attention from researchers in recent years. In terms of RF development, the notable contribution of Xiong and Zilberman [54] first brought attention to such possibilities by demonstrating how Decision Trees (DTs) could theoretically be sequentially (i.e., traversing the root node down to a leaf) encoded into the switch's pipeline. Subsequently, Busse-Grawitz et al. [16], Lee and Singh [36], and Zheng and Zilberman [57] extended this functionality by combining noteworthy variations of sequential DT processing to ultimately realize RFs in the data plane. As such sequential processing limits the size of in-network RF models that can be developed and leaves little-to-no resources on the switch for storing and processing features, as well as essential forwarding and telemetry applications, we endeavor to build upon the advancements of the aforementioned authors by diverging from more of an `if-else` sequential programmatic approach to leveraging `ternary` key Match-Action Tables (MATs) to assess the ranges of the RF's features in parallel in order to preserve the switch pipeline's stages. In general, consecutive stages are consumed whenever dependencies between statements in a P4 program are present. Moreover, we take a number of additional measures to conserve TCAM utilization, thereby enabling us to fit a larger RF comfortably within the switch's pipeline. Lastly, we take the next step in switch-based ML development by also incorporating feature extraction, processing, and storage into the P4 program to arrive at a full-fledged ransomware traffic classification scheme on an Intel Tofino switch.

Ransomware Detection. Given the urgency for effective network-based ransomware protection is dire, such development has began taking place in Software Defined Networking (SDN) environments. Cusak et al. [21] and Cabaj et al. [17] led the charge by utilizing the data plane to prompt server-based classification via an RF and Deep Packet Inspection (DPI), respectively. Subsequent works [2,3,46] took an approach similar to Cusak et al. by instructing the SDN switch to forward all relevant traffic to server-based analysis mechanisms to perform DPI and other techniques in order to detect ransomware. Building upon the aforementioned authors' momentum, we extend ransomware detection and mitigation to programmable data planes. However, rather than forwarding a wealth of traffic data to the controller and other server-based analysis mechanisms, which can lead to flooding in busy networks and result in detection delays [23], we fingerprint ransomware solely on the programmable switch. Indeed, such controller independence coupled with the proposed approach's strategy of only analyzing unidirectional traffic allows it to support any number placement strategies within a given network topology. Further, while previous efforts were specifically designed to defend against one or so variants and frequently rely on unencrypted traffic to perform DPI, we bridge this gap by performing both binary and multiclass classification on a number of variants of the most prominent ransomware strains, regardless if the traffic is encrypted.

3   Ransomware Threat Model

In this section, we elaborate upon the threat model for which the proposed RF learning methodology was applied.

Behavior. In general, we do not make any assumptions about the behavior of ransomware families, and we aspire to fingerprint each promptly and with high accuracy. To support this notion, we incorporated a variety of the most prominent crypto ransomware families into the methodology's evaluation, ranging from samples that transmit both encrypted and non-encrypted traffic, to those that can self-propagate. Crypto ransomware families were selected for the evaluation (as opposed to the older locker variants) since they are almost always employed by adversaries nowadays.

Network Communications. Being that the proposed classification methodology is network-based, it requires that a given ransomware sample initiate some form of network communication before it can be fingerprinted. This is a reasonable requirement, considering that a host infected with crypto ransomware will typically request an encryption key from the (Command and Control) C&C server through multiple layers of proxies before encryption takes place [21]. Additionally, self-propagating ransomware variants have also become the norm, which scan for vulnerable systems and thereby produce probing traffic [10–15,43]. Such network transmissions not only allow these variants to be detected on the network but also enables their spreading to other vulnerable machines and the encryption of a victim's files to be mitigated, provided the variants are detected swiftly. Indeed, it is this innate network behavior of modern ransomware families that the proposed methodology herein aims to use against them for detection purposes.

4   Proposed Methodology

In this section, we present the proposed methodology for detecting and mitigating ransomware attacks, as summarized in Fig. 1. Moreover, such a methodology provides a blueprint for the development of other RF-based traffic classification tasks on programmable switches. To that extent, we kindly refer interested readers to our publicly available source and data analysis code [40] for additional implementation details.

4.1   Overview and Intuition

When contemporary ransomware infects a target, the ransomware will often emit traffic pertaining to either (1) C&C-related communications or (2) probing for additional targets. Note that (1) may include both locating the C&C server and the exchange of data once a C&C connection has been established. Based off these two types of malicious transmissions, there are three primary ways that the proposed methodology aspires to mitigate ransomware.

In terms of the first way, quickly eradicating C&C-related communications has shown to be effective for circumventing the encryption of a victim's files for variants that preemptively exchange a public encryption key [17,18,52]. However, in situations where such a public key is embedded within the malicious executable, other C&C-related communications can be leveraged to identify the ransomware promptly. As recent ransomware research has demonstrated that the median time of a number of ransomware variants to encrypt 53.93 GB of data is 42 min and 52 s [34], quickly fingerprinting the presence of ransomware via other C&C-related communications can dramatically mitigate damages.

The second way is to halt the ransomware's propagation, which mitigates any further spread of the malware within the network or to adjacent networks. Indeed, in the age of network shares and cloud storage that we currently reside in, this mitigation step is crucial as such storage mechanisms are often targeted by modern ransomware variants. Moreover, there has been a recent shift from ransomware targeting individual users to entire enterprises. In general, the aim of attackers for extorting enterprises is to sufficiently disrupt business operations in order to obtain the ransom, which was apparent in attacks such as that on the Colonial Pipeline [45] and Hollywood Presbyterian Medical Center [37]. To that end, the primary modus operandi of such attacks against enterprises is to infect a large numbers of machines within a target network in order to obtain a larger ransom, which necessitates lateral movement and rapidly infecting machines inside the network. This trend was first observed by Cisco's Talos team in 2016 [35] and has continued its increase in the years to follow [31].

Lastly and more broadly, the third way that the proposed methodology mitigates ransomware is by alerting administrators to its presence and by isolating the infected machines. This is a critical step, as measures such as powering down infected machines and removing them from the network must be immediately taken to mitigate propagation and any possible drive corruption that has already taken place [30]. Our proposed network-based detection and mitigation methodology is particularly beneficial in cases such as this [4], particularly because of its capacity to block traffic on the switch [33] (i.e., to promptly prevent infected machines from communicating on the network) and to alert the control plane. Additionally, while ransomware that reaches its target may lie dormant for an extended period of time before it attacks, the aforementioned malicious traffic types (1) and (2) will typically be transmitted well in advance to the attack being executed [52]. In turn, the proposed methodology has the capability to fingerprint dormant infections on the deploying networks that bypassed any host-based defenses.

In light of this information, the speed of detection is paramount to successfully executing the aforesaid three mitigation tactics, in addition to performing such detection in the network itself. To this extent, the proposed methodology aims to fingerprint an infected machine from a small portion of consecutive packets that it transmits. We refer to this portion of consecutive packets from a particular machine as p_{thresh} herein, and we aim to minimize p_{thresh} such that a desirable ransomware classification can still be obtained. Further, given the growing reliance upon encryption in today's Internet, the proposed approach only utilizes packet timing and layer three and four headers to fingerprint ransomware, which are characteristics that have proven to be reliable for performing detection amid encrypted traffic [25, 49]. Additionally, the unidirectional traffic analysis that our approach employs not only enhances deployment flexibility amid networks that employ asymmetric routing but also eliminates additional variables associated with the response traffic that may degrade detection performance [24]. For instance, the complex features associated with the behavior of the C&C server or legitimate services that have been contacted that can entail any number of characteristics are effectively eliminated from consideration.

An overview of the proposed methodology's flow of operations and how p_{thresh} is applied is shown in Fig. 1. In particular, Fig. 1 portrays the interactions between the controller and programmable switch. The principle function of the controller in our methodology is to initialize the switch's data structures. As demonstrated in Fig. 1, such initialization begins with generating a CSV from a combination of benign traffic packet captures and captures from ransomware variants, for a chosen p_{thresh} value. The resultant CSV file is then used by the controller to train an RF classifier. During such training, the controller aims to select a reduced set of features from a number of default features that were applied when generating the CSV, as reducing these features can not only enhance the performance of the RF but also decreases the switch's resource consumption [24]. Once the RF has been trained, the controller performs several optimizations before populating the switch-based RF data structure in order to reduce TCAM utilization.

Upon the switch-based RF being initialized, it will begin aggregating features on the switch for every source IP address IP_{source} that it observes over p_{thresh} packets. This aggregation procedure is depicted in Fig. 1, where an incoming IP_{source} is first hashed, which results in an index that maps to where each of the features pertaining to such IP_{source} are stored. Once a given IP_{source} has sent p_{thresh} packets, the aggregated features are then passed through the switch-based RF. The switch-based RF is composed of a novel transformation of an RF classifier to P4 MATs, which are tasked with determining if the features of an IP_{source} indicate that it is infected with ransomware. If a ransomware infection has been attributed to an IP_{source}, subsequent packets from this IP_{source} will be blocked and a notification will be pushed to the controller. Note that more customized mitigation actions can also be taken at the network operator's discretion. In addition, note that we have observed that a first generation Intel Tofino hardware switch [27] performs the aforementioned switch-based operations in around 350 ns per pass of a packet. In fact, this measurement will remain relatively fixed regardless of any P4 program's algorithmic complexities, given the program compiles on the hardware switch and does not utilize recirculations. Thus, we perform the aforementioned operations for every packet traversing the switch, even amid Tbps traffic rates, without any performance penalties or throughput degradation on the switch.

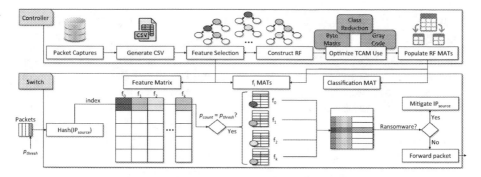

Fig. 1. Overview of the proposed methodology's flow of operations.

4.2   Data Processing

Training Data Generation. As shown in Fig. 1, the first step of the methodology is to place all packet capture datasets on the controller to produce the training data, which encompasses a broad array of features that can seamlessly be extracted by the switch (i.e., header-based computations using simple arithmetic). Given the prevalence of encrypted traffic in the datasets, only timestamps and network and transport layer headers were used as a the basis for the features, which are also ideal for maintaining line-rate processing on programmable switches [24]. Features were processed for a sliding window of p_{thresh} consecutive packets from an individual source IP address, for $p_{thresh} \leq 50$ packets. Formally, each feature f_i is defined as $\sum_{j=1}^{p_{thresh}} f_{i,j}$. Note that we omit headers such as source and destination IP addresses, as they would not produce a generalizable model [42]. Further, while we found header summations to be sufficient for ransomware detection, any number of other possibilities for computing features exist, given they can be calculated within the hardware switch target's strict computational and stage constraints. Ultimately, the end result is a CSV of data samples that appear exactly as they would on the switch when processing traffic in real-time.

Recursive Feature Selection. From the broad array of features in the CSV file, the next task shown in Fig. 1 is to reduce them to a feature set F that will enable accurate ransomware detection yet is small enough that their storage and processing on the switch will only consume a small amount of resources. To arrive at such an F, the controller first uses all features in the CSV file to train a software-based RF (via Python). This training procedure is repeated for each sliding window $p_{thresh} \leq 50$. Next, the mean `feature importance` score over all p_{thresh} is taken based on Gini impurity for each feature in the CSV file. Once the controller has recorded the RF's performance for the given F, the feature with the lowest `feature importance` is then omitted from consideration, and the process is repeated until one feature is left. Indeed, this procedure is beneficial for identifying the ideal trade-off between minimal $|F|$ and desirable classification performance. Ultimately, five features were arrived at via this technique and are displayed in Table 1, along with their corresponding `feature importance` values.

Switch-Based Feature Processing. Following Fig. 1, when a packet arrives at the switch, the resultant selected F that could indicate the presence of ransomware are processed. Each $f \in F$ is stored in an Static Random-Access Memory (SRAM) matrix of size N by $|F|$, where N is the number of source IPs that the switch will be tasked with analyzing concurrently. In contrast to bucket-based estimations such as count-min sketch, note that each of the N IP_{source} values are evaluated for ransomware individually to provide the necessary feature granularity to promote accurate detection [6]. The index of a row $n \in N$ allocated to a specific IP_{source} is determined by its hash, and we circumvent collisions entirely by adding another column to the matrix for storing the non-hashed IP_{source} currently holding each $n \in N$ to verify that no collision has occurred prior to the feature processing. Subsequently, the each of the features f from the ingress packet are integrated with the corresponding column f_i in row n using simple mathematical operations (e.g., addition) that the switch can easily perform.

Table 1. Selected ransomware traffic features.

Feature	Importance
duration	0.2963
tcp_flag_sum	0.2397
icmp_type_sum	0.1669
udp_length_sum	0.1635
ip_total_length_sum	0.1335

4.3 RF Implementation

The last column in the SRAM matrix holds the packet count p_{count}, which signals the RF to consume the aforementioned F when $p_{count} = p_{thresh}$, as portrayed in Fig. 1. Given that traversing the Decision Trees (DTs) of the RF sequentially to arrive at their leaves for classification consumed a number of extra stages of the switch in past works, we alternatively evaluate *all* of the DTs' nodes within the RF in parallel. A simplified view of how we perform this technique with an RF with three features f_1, f_2, and f_3, and two classes, is portrayed in Fig. 2. As shown, the RF-to-MAT conversion procedure can be summarized in three primary steps. First, the controller generates the RF, and extracts every path amid the DTs that arrives at a malicious classification. Such paths are denoted in Fig. 2 with numbered boxes that are shaded in gray next to each malicious class label 1. Note the decision boundaries d for every intermediary node in the DTs has subscripts of the format DT number, feature number, and the numbered occurrence of that feature within the given DT. Subsequently, the ranges for each f_i are extracted from the malicious paths, sorted, and split so that each split portion of each of the ranges for a given f_i map to a unique integer. Lastly, the combinations of return integers for each f_i that map to the aforementioned numbered malicious paths are placed in Classification MAT, utilizing `exact` `match` keys. Additionally, note that the benign DT paths were not extracted in the first step, as we default anything not malicious to a benign classification of 0 in the classification MAT.

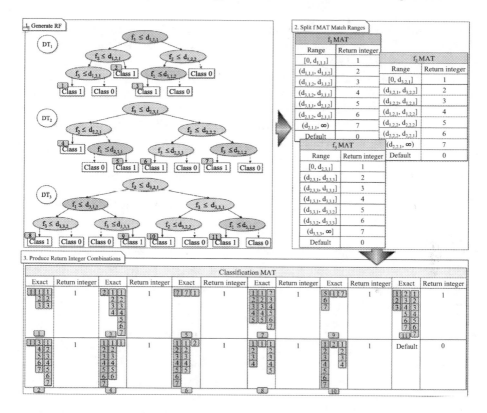

Fig. 2. Visualization of the proposed methodology's RF-to-MAT conversion.

Reducing f_i TCAM Utilization. While the controller is identifying such `ternary` entries for the f_i MATs, it also takes three steps to minimize the number of these entries to reduce TCAM utilization. Full-scale RF models many contain many DTs, which consequently may result in a large number of d. This is because each of the MAT's ternary ranges $[d_{i,j,k}, d_{i,j,k+1}]$ must be unique to ensure that each of the DT's classifications are respected, as shown in the split step of Fig. 2. For example, if a given f_i MAT contains the ranges [5, 15] and [10, 20] from two DTs that result in two different classifications, respectively, a the controller will perform a split to get the ranges [5, 9], [10, 15], and [16, 20], where ranges [5, 9] or [10, 15] can result in the first classification and either [10, 15] or [16, 20] can result in the second (when coupled with ranges of other features).

The first reduction step is to omit entries based on the final classification they result in. Once the controller breaks down the RF into the aforementioned ranges, it generates an N row CSV, where the rows correspond to all malicious paths in each of the DTs. Subsequently, the controller generates a random integer $x \in [d_{i,j,k}, d_{i,j,k+1}]$ for every f_i in row $n \in N$ to be classified by the software-based RF. As an RF is a voting ensemble of all its encompassed DTs, the controller then omits any row that leads to a `benign` classification. When applying the proposed methodology to other traffic classification tasks, the majority class can be substituted for `benign` in this ransomware classification scenario in order to conserve the switch's resources.

The next reduction step is based on the intuition that, given a sequence of bytes $b_0, b_1, ..., b_k$ from higher-order to lower-order that make up an integer, if b_i is incremented j times, b_{i+1} is guaranteed to cycle through all 256 values at least $j - 1$ times. Thus, a 00000000 mask can be applied to b_{i+1} a minimum of $j - 1$ times in such instances, which thereby reduces the number of `ternary` entries for the given MAT by at least $256(j - 1)$. This is because the initial j_0 value of b_i and its final increment j_n may only partially cycle though the 256 values for b_{i+1}.

For the final reduction step, we perform a variation of a Gray Code (GC) [7] conversion of the feature values on the switch, prior to applying them to the f_i MATs in Fig. 1. This conversion entails the binary encoding of integers in a contiguous range in a manner such that the codes of any two consecutive integers differ only by a single bit. Such a single-bit difference can promote the seamless masking of integers to identify ranges. An example of a 4-bit GC conversion and the masking it facilitates is shown in Fig. 3, which can be extended to 8 bits and beyond. Note that the single bit difference property of GC encoding is enabled by reflecting a given sequence of bits once they have cycled through all possible values. For instance, observe that the bits corresponding to integers [0, 3] in Fig. 3 are then reflected in integers [4, 7]. Due to such reflection, we cannot necessarily deterministically convert a given b_i of a particular feature in a MAT, as the GC for b_i may not be the same for different integers. Alternatively, our variation of a GC conversion is performed efficiently on the switch by using P4$_{16}$ bit slicing to divide a feature's binary representation into its individual bytes $b_0, b_1, ..., b_k$, from higher-order to lower-order. Next, the controller populates a separate GC_i MAT that is applied for each b_i to perform deterministic byte-level GC conversions, which only requires 256 P4 `exact` match keys. Subsequently, the resultant GC conversions are applied to the aforementioned f_i MATs in Fig. 1.

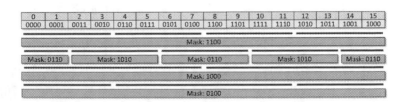

Fig. 3. The TCAM masking strategy derived from GC. The bold horizontal black lines indicate ranges that can be distinguished via applying the mask underneath.

Classification MAT TCAM. The final idea of the proposed methodology is to use the combination of unique integers returned by the f_i MATs to arrive at a classification. However, while the RF-to-MAT conversion procedure highlighted in Fig. 2 will operated efficiently for a single DT instance or an RF of a small amount of DTs with limited depth (e.g., a depth of five), a full-scale RF may result in many `exact` match combinations in the Classification MAT, which could exhaust a great deal of the switch's. To offer an alternative for larger RFs, we perform `ternary` matching on the unique integers returned by each f_i, rather than the portrayed `exact` matching strategy in Fig. 2. Thus, this alternative approach aims to identify the range of unique integers shown for each malicious path in Fig. 2. To minimize the amount of `ternary` entries needed to cover such ranges, we utilize the aforementioned GC strategy shown in Fig. 3; however, in this case, no GC conversion takes place on the switch, as the unique integers returned by the f_i MATs are already formatted in GC by the controller during the RF initialization process.

5 Evaluation

In this section, we extensively evaluate the proposed methodology to asses its viability and practicality as an in-network traffic classification technique that is capable of thwarting ransomware. The datasets used in this evaluation are listed in Table 2. Such datasets include a multitude of variants associated with eight prominent ransomware families,

Table 2. Datasets utilized.

Source	Class	Instances	Encrypted	Self-propagating
Ryuk	ransomware	5 variants	✓	✓
Lockbit	ransomware	4 variants	✓	✓
Teslacrypt	ransomware	10 variants	✓	✗
Virlock	ransomware	11 variants	✓	✗
Cryptowall	ransomware	8 variants	✗	✗
Cerber	ransomware	5 variants	✗	✗
Wannacry	ransomware	3 variants	✓	✓
Locky	ransomware	3 variants	✗	✗
Stratosphere Laboratory [51]	benign	6 captures	✓	NA
P2P [44]	benign	6 captures	✓	NA

including those that utilize encrypted traffic and self-propagate. To arrive at the ransomware family datasets, we captured the traffic from the machines they infected in a Triage sandbox environment, which we made publicly available for download [40]. Note that leveraging such a sandbox allows us to assess precisely which packets originating from an infected host are of malicious intent for labeling purposes, regardless if the traffic is encrypted. Additionally, we included a variety of notable benign traffic datasets in our experiments from the Stratosphere Laboratory [51] that encompass DNS and P2P traffic, as well as HTTPS connections to Alexa top 1k domains. Since P2P traffic often entails a source IP contacting several destination IPs, it can prove challenging for probing and C&C detection techniques. To this extent, we included another P2P dataset [44] for good measure. In our experiments, we consider an IP_{source} that is correctly and incorrectly classified as ransomware to be a True Positive (TP) and False Positive (FP), respectively, and such IPs that are correctly and incorrectly classified as benign as True Negatives (TNs) and False Negatives (FNs), respectively. Given the class imbalance in our datasets, we use $precision = TP/(TP+FP)$ and $recall = TP/TP+FN$ as our evaluation metrics.

Environmental Setup. The environment setup consisted of a client-server approach utilizing an Intel Tofino switch connected to four clients via Linux network namespaces for transmitting the packet capture traffic with `tcpreplay`. The aforementioned clients were run on two Intel Xeon Silver 4114 machines functioning off 4-core CPUs at 2.20 GHz, underneath Debian GNU/Linux 9. After applying a grid search to the RF training with the five features previously discussed in Sect. 4, we found that an RF of 32 DT classifiers having a maximum depth of 15 gave optimal results. A 70–30% training-test split was applied to the final dataset in our experiments, where 10-fold cross validation was performed to verify that no overfitting was occurring [53]. Additionally, we set the size of the feature matrix rows $N = 16,384$, as such N provided an appreciable trade-off between minimizing SRAM consumption and row collisions in the matrix. Recall that our low p_{thresh} facilitates the use of smaller N, as it enables our methodology to quickly recycle each IP_{source} out of the matrix.

Interleaving Benign Traffic. Along with incorporating a wealth of benign datasets into our experiments, we took another step to create a realistic evaluation environment that puts the methodology's ability to circumvent FPs to the test. In particular, a compromised host will still have varying degrees of legitimate processes running and will thus be transmitting their associated traffic [24]. While the sandbox environment executes such legitimate processes, some hosts residing on the networks in which our methodology is deployed may employ more. To this end, we interleaved different ranges of benign traffic rates with the ransomware traffic to observe how our methodology's detection performance was impacted.

To achieve this aim without compromising the integrity of the ransomware traffic or the interleaved benign packet captures, samples from each of the benign packet captures mentioned in Table 2 were first grouped by IP_{source}. The motivation for such grouping is to interleave the traffic of one benign IP_{source} with one ransomware IP_{source}, as opposed to pairing the traffic of different benign machines with one ransomware IP_{source}. This technique ensured that our strategy is realistic, since it would be unclear which legitimate process traffic from multiple hosts would actually be observed in-the-wild as originating from a single IP_{source}, given that essential information pertaining to the processes running on the hosts in the benign datasets was not given and the majority of the traffic is encrypted (i.e., such information cannot be reliably extracted). Subsets of 50 consecutive packets were then extracted from the entirety of the grouping of each benign IP_{source}, and the mean interarrival time of such groupings were individually calculated. An amount of 50 was selected because it covers the largest p_{thresh} that we were evaluating yet it is small enough to assert that our calculated interarrival time ranges for source IPs are accurate. For instance, 50K packets from a particular source IP might have a mean interarrival time of 1.5K μs, but the portion of its traffic that is interleaved with our ransomware sample for a p_{thresh} of, say, 50, may have a mean interarrival time of 150K μs.

Empirical preliminary analysis of the common benign interarrival times present in our datasets revealed that, over $p_{thresh} = 50$, such times were relatively uniformly distributed over the four ranges of $[0.0, 0.55)$, $[0.55, 1.0)$, $[1.0, 5.5)$, and $[5.5, 10.0)$ ms. In turn, we aggregated the aforementioned IP_{source} groupings of $p_{thresh} = 50$ samples into buckets of these ranges. Once the interleaving was completed for each benign-ransomware IP_{source} pair, the IP_{source} of the benign packets were spoofed to that of the host compromised with ransomware. This procedure was repeated for every ransomware IP_{source} in the experiment. scapy was then used to transmit the aforementioned interleaved traffic through the Intel Tofino switch as the ransomware class, while simultaneously transmitting the entirety of the benign datasets via tcpreplay as the benign class.

Ransomware Classification. The first experiment that we conducted was to measure the effectiveness of the proposed methodology for performing the binary classification of benign hosts and those possessing ransomware. Additionally, we executed this test over varying p_{thresh}, namely, 1, 2, 3, 5, 10, 15, 20, 30, 40, and 50, as lower p_{thresh} directly translates to faster detection and mitigation times. This experiment was also performed for each of the aforementioned interleaved benign interarrival time ranges. Per the results visualized in Fig. 4, it can be observed that the proposed methodology obtained high precision and recall for $p_{thresh} \geq 3$. Moreover, the interleaved benign traffic had little impact on ransomware classification. Some subtle performance degradation can be observed for higher rates of benign traffic interleaved with greater p_{thresh}, but that is expected as the prominence of ransomware indicators present in the features will be smoothed out to a degree over such p_{thresh}. For example, attempting to attribute ransomware with a $p_{thresh} = 50$ from only three actual malicious packets among the 47 benign will likely result in some misclassifications.

In a similar manner, we performed the multiclass classification of each ransomware family listed in Table 2, with all benign datasets given a benign classification. Indeed, effective multiclass classification offers more granularity that

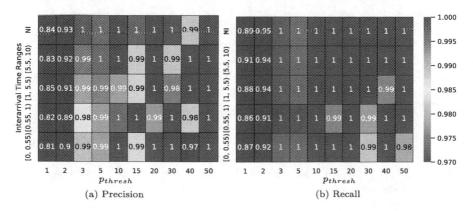

(a) Precision   (b) Recall

Fig. 4. Binary classification performance with varying p_{thresh} amid different interarrival times. The topmost rows are denoted at No Interleaving (NI), as the ransomware traffic for those instances applied as extracted from the sandbox environment.

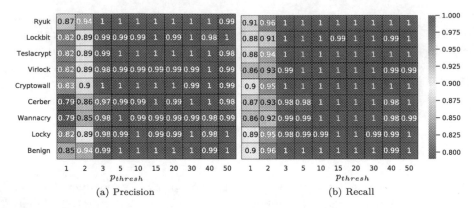

Fig. 5. Multiclass classification performance over varying p_{thresh} with an interleaved benign traffic rate range of [0.55, 1.0) ms.

can facilitate a number of network provisioning and system hardening, as well as offer additional useful cyber intelligence. The results of the ransomware multiclass classification evaluation are portrayed in Fig. 5. Note that we applied the [0.55, 1.0) interleaved benign traffic rate range to the ransomware data, since it largely gave the median performance for binary classification. Nevertheless, the results shown in Fig. 5 showcase the proposed methodology's ability to not only promptly detect ransomware from only a small number of packets but also attribute the offending family.

State-of-the-Art Performance Assessment. In terms of the related network-based ransomware detection works that paved the way for our innovations, their detection performance cannot be directly compared to that of the proposed approach on the same datasets due to limitations associated with dataset availability, implementation-specific hardware such as SDN OpenFlow [38] switches, lack of source code, and so forth. As an alternative, we mention the detection performance arrived at by the authors for the ransomware families that match that of the ransomware samples that we were able to obtain. In particular, Cusack et al. [21] detected Cerber ransomware with an F1-score, false positive rate, and false negative rate of 0.94, 12.5%, and 0.0%, respectively, using a controller-based RF comprised of 40 DTs with depth 15. Additionally, Cabaj et al. [17] utilized centroid analysis on the controller to detect CryptoWall with true positive and false positive rates of 98% and 1.2%, respectively, and Locky with true positive and false positive rates of 97% and 2.2%, respectively. Indeed, while the proposed approach slightly improves upon the aforementioned authors' commendable detection performances of Cerber, Cryptowall, and Locky, more notably, we do so entirely within the switch from a limited number of packets (regardless of encryption) to dramatically reduce detection speeds, and we extended such detection performance to a multitude of other prominent ransomware variants.

Hardware Resource Utilization. To examine the resource consumption of the proposed methodology, we first observed the percent of MAT entry reduction that can be obtained by utilizing the GC conversions for the ternary range matching strategies. In particular, we compiled RFs consisting of 1 through 36 DTs, with each of the DTs possessing a depth of 15, which was the maximum depth used in our experiments. The results portrayed in Fig. 6 show the trends of the f MAT (Stage 1) and Classification MAT (Stage 2) GC implementations, along with the overall percent reduction in MAT entries throughout the entirety of our methodology. While all percent reductions are high, a downward trend can be observed pertaining to the Stage 1 entries, which is due to more splits occurring in the f MAT ranges as the number of DTs in the RF are increased. Conversely, the Stage 2% reduction quickly approached 100% because our methodology averages about one entry in the Classification MAT per malicious classification path in the RF, whereas the combinations of the f MATs' return integers for each Classification MAT malicious path entry grow exponentially. Ultimately, the maximum size of RFs tested of 36 DTs at depth 15 gave 21,073 and 2,629 f MAT and Classification MAT entries, respectively. This RF resulted in 33.33%, 5.00, 10.00%, 6.25%, 12.98% and 10.94% of available TCAM, stage, arithmetic-logic unit, hash bit, and gateway resources being consumed, respectively. Indeed, examining the MAT entry reduction with respect to the number of DTs demonstrates the proposed learning methodology's ability to counteract the substantial amount of TCAM that would otherwise be required to support larger switch-based RF models.

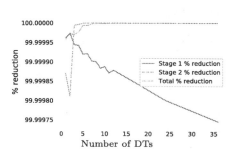

Fig. 6. The percent of table entry reduction offered by the GC encoding scheme.

6   Concluding Remarks and Future Directions

The extent to which ransomware has been plaguing our networks has never been greater. Moreover, contemporary ransomware strains are now commonly employing self-propagation techniques to infiltrate other hosts and network shares, as well as targeting devices that cannot defend themselves. To address this threat at scale, we proposed a novel methodology for embedding a learning-based defense, namely, a large RF, within programmable switches. After instrumenting an Intel Tofino switch with our methodology, we showed that it can both detect compromised hosts and even attribute the ransomware family they are currently housing with high precision and recall. Moreover, we show that the proposed methodology is resource conservative and scalable to a variety of networks that may observe differing rates of traffic. Finally, we make all source and analysis code along with the ransomware datasets we generated for this research effort publicly available to promote future advancements in this domain. Future work will entail extending our multiclass detection strategy to encompass more ransomware families, and the proposed approach will be deployed in the wild to further substantiate its ability to classify ransomware traffic amid real-world settings.

Acknowledgements. This material is based on research funded by the National Science Foundation (NSF) grant #2104273.

References

1. p4lang/behavioral-model, November 2019. https://github.com/p4lang/behavioral-model
2. Akbanov, M., Vassilakis, V.G., Logothetis, M.D.: Ransomware detection and mitigation using software-defined networking: the case of wannacry. Comput. Electr. Eng. **76**, 111–121 (2019)
3. Alotaibi, F.M., Vassilakis, V.G.: Sdn-based detection of self-propagating ransomware: the case of badrabbit. IEEE Access **9**, 28039–28058 (2021)
4. AlSabeh, A., Khoury, J., Kfoury, E., Crichigno, J., Bou-Harb, E.: A survey on security applications of p4 programmable switches and a stride-based vulnerability assessment. Comput. Netw. **207**, 108800 (2022)
5. AlSabeh, A., Safa, H., Bou-Harb, E., Crichigno, J.: Exploiting ransomware paranoia for execution prevention. In: ICC 2020–2020 IEEE International Conference on Communications (ICC), pp. 1–6. IEEE (2020)
6. Barradas, D., Santos, N., Rodrigues, L., Signorello, S., Ramos, F.M., Madeira, A.: Flowlens: enabling efficient flow classification for ML-based network security applications. In: Proceedings of the 28th Network and Distributed System Security Symposium, San Diego, CA, USA (2021)
7. Bitner, J.R., Ehrlich, G., Reingold, E.M.: Efficient generation of the binary reflected gray code and its applications. Commun. ACM **19**(9), 517–521 (1976)
8. Bosshart, P., et al.: P4: programming protocol-independent packet processors. ACM SIGCOMM Comput. Commun. Rev. **44**(3), 87–95 (2014)
9. Bou-Harb, E.: A brief survey of security approaches for cyber-physical systems. In: 2016 8th IFIP International Conference on New Technologies, Mobility and Security (NTMS), pp. 1–5. IEEE (2016)
10. Bou-Harb, E., Debbabi, M., Assi, C.: A statistical approach for fingerprinting probing activities. In: 2013 International Conference on Availability, Reliability and Security, pp. 21–30. IEEE (2013)
11. Bou-Harb, E., Debbabi, M., Assi, C.: A systematic approach for detecting and clustering distributed cyber scanning. Comput. Netw. **57**(18), 3826–3839 (2013)
12. Bou-Harb, E., Debbabi, M., Assi, C.: Behavioral analytics for inferring large-scale orchestrated probing events. In: 2014 IEEE Conference on Computer Communications Workshops (INFOCOM WKSHPS), pp. 506–511. IEEE (2014)
13. Bou-Harb, E., Debbabi, M., Assi, C.: Big data behavioral analytics meet graph theory: on effective botnet takedowns. IEEE Network **31**(1), 18–26 (2016)
14. Bou-Harb, E., Debbabi, M., Assi, C.: A novel cyber security capability: inferring internet-scale infections by correlating malware and probing activities. Comput. Netw. **94**, 327–343 (2016)

15. Bou-Harb, E., Lakhdari, N.E., Binsalleeh, H., Debbabi, M.: Multidimensional investigation of source port 0 probing. Digit. Investig. **11**, S114–S123 (2014)
16. Busse-Grawitz, C., Meier, R., Dietmüller, A., Bühler, T., Vanbever, L.: pforest: In-network inference with random forests. arXiv preprint arXiv:1909.05680 (2019)
17. Cabaj, K., Gregorczyk, M., Mazurczyk, W.: Software-defined networking-based crypto ransomware detection using http traffic characteristics. Comput. Electr. Eng. **66**, 353–368 (2018)
18. Cabaj, K., Mazurczyk, W.: Using software-defined networking for ransomware mitigation: the case of cryptowall. IEEE Network **30**(6), 14–20 (2016)
19. Chen, X., Kim, H., Aman, J.M., Chang, W., Lee, M., Rexford, J.: Measuring TCP round-trip time in the data plane. In: Proceedings of the Workshop on Secure Programmable Network Infrastructure, pp. 35–41 (2020)
20. Chernikova, A., et al.: Cyber network resilience against self-propagating malware attacks. In: Atluri, V., Di Pietro, R., Jensen, C.D., Meng, W. (eds) ESORICS 2022. LNCS, vol. 13554, pp. 531–550. Springer, Cham (2022). https://doi.org/10.1007/978-3-031-17140-6_26
21. Cusack, G., Michel, O., Keller, E.: Machine learning-based detection of ransomware using SDN. In: Proceedings of the 2018 ACM International Workshop on Security in Software Defined Networks & Network Function Virtualization, pp. 1–6 (2018)
22. Friday, K., Bou-Harb, E., Crichigno, J., Scanlon, M., Beebe, N.: On offloading network forensic analytics to programmable data plane switches. Book Series: World Scientific Series in Digital Forensics and Cybersecurity (2021)
23. Friday, K., Kfoury, E., Bou-Harb, E., Crichigno, J.: Towards a unified in-network DDoS detection and mitigation strategy. In: 2020 6th IEEE Conference on Network Softwarization (NetSoft), pp. 218–226. IEEE (2020)
24. Friday, K., Kfoury, E., Bou-Harb, E., Crichigno, J.: Inc: In-network classification of botnet propagation at line rate. In: Atluri, V., Di Pietro, R., Jensen, C.D., Meng, W. (eds.) ESORICS 2022. LNCE, vol. 13554, pp. 551–569. Springer, Cham (2022). https://doi.org/10.1007/978-3-031-17140-6_27
25. Gutterman, C., et al.: Requet: real-time QOE detection for encrypted YouTube traffic. In: Proceedings of the 10th ACM Multimedia Systems Conference, pp. 48–59 (2019)
26. Humayun, M., Jhanjhi, N., Alsayat, A., Ponnusamy, V.: Internet of things and ransomware: evolution, mitigation and prevention. Egyptian Inform. J. **22**(1), 105–117 (2021)
27. Intel: Intel Tofin Series Programmable Ethernet Switch ASIC. https://www.intel.com/content/www/us/en/products/network-io/programmable-ethernet-switch/tofino-series/tofino.html
28. Intel: Intel tofino 3 intelligent fabric processor brief. https://www.intel.com/content/www/us/en/products/network-io/programmable-ethernet-switch/tofino-3-brief.html
29. Jareth: How ransomware spreads: 9 most common infection methods and how to stop them, December 2019. https://blog.emsisoft.com/en/35083/how-ransomware-spreads-9-most-common-infection-methods-and-how-to-stop-them/
30. of Justice, T.U.S.D.: How to protect your networks from ransomware, March 2022. https://www.justice.gov/criminal-ccips/file/872771/download
31. Kapoor, A., Gupta, A., Gupta, R., Tanwar, S., Sharma, G., Davidson, I.E.: Ransomware detection, avoidance, and mitigation scheme: a review and future directions. Sustainability **14**(1), 8 (2021)

32. Keshet, Y.: Prevent automated propagation of ransomware attacks, June 2021. https://www.silverfort.com/blog/prevent-automated-propagation-of-ransomware-attacks/

33. Kfoury, E.F., Crichigno, J., Bou-Harb, E.: An exhaustive survey on p4 programmable data plane switches: taxonomy, applications, challenges, and future trends. IEEE Access **9**, 87094–87155 (2021)

34. Kovar, R.: Ransomware encrypts nearly 100,000 files in under 45 minutes, March 2022. https://www.splunk.com/en_us/blog/security/ransomware-encrypts-nearly-100-000-files-in-under-45-minutes.html

35. Largent, W.: Ransomware: Past, present, and future, September 2022. https://blog.talosintelligence.com/ransomware-history-past-prologue/

36. Lee, J.H., Singh, K.: Switchtree: in-network computing and traffic analyses with random forests. Neural Comput. Appl. 1–12 (2020)

37. Maurya, A., Kumar, N., Agrawal, A., Khan, R.: Ransomware: evolution, target and safety measures. Int. J. Comput. Sci. Eng. **6**(1), 80–85 (2018)

38. McKeown, N., Anderson, T., Balakrishnan, H., Parulkar, G., Peterson, L., Rexford, J., Shenker, S., Turner, J.: Openflow: enabling innovation in campus networks. ACM SIGCOMM Comput. Commun. Rev. **38**(2), 69–74 (2008)

39. Moreira, C.M., Kaddoum, G., Bou-Harb, E.: Cross-layer authentication protocol design for ultra-dense 5g hetnets. In: 2018 IEEE International Conference on Communications (ICC), pp. 1–7. IEEE (2018)

40. NetSecResearch, June 2022. https://github.com/NetSecResearch/InNetworkRansomwareDetection

41. Paganini, P.: Self-propagating ransomware spreading in the wild, May 2016. https://securityaffairs.co/wordpress/47890/malware/self-propagating-ransomware.html

42. Pour, M.S., et al.: On data-driven curation, learning, and analysis for inferring evolving internet-of-things (IoT) botnets in the wild. Comput. Secur. **91**, 101707 (2020)

43. Pour, M.S., et al.: Data-driven curation, learning and analysis for inferring evolving IoT botnets in the wild. In: Proceedings of the 14th International Conference on Availability, Reliability and Security, pp. 1–10 (2019)

44. Rahbarinia, B., Perdisci, R., Lanzi, A., Li, K.: Peerrush: mining for unwanted p2p traffic. J. Inf. Secur. Appl. **19**(3), 194–208 (2014)

45. Robertson, J., Turton, W.: Colonial hackers stole data thursday ahead of shutdown, May 2021. https://www.bloomberg.com/news/articles/2021-05-09/colonial-hackers-stole-data-thursday-ahead-of-pipeline-shutdown

46. Rouka, E., Birkinshaw, C., Vassilakis, V.G.: SDN-based malware detection and mitigation: The case of expetr ransomware. In: 2020 IEEE International Conference on Informatics, IoT, and Enabling Technologies (ICIoT), pp. 150–155. IEEE (2020)

47. Sandbox, T., January 2022. https://hatching.io/triage/

48. Seals, T.: Ryuk ransomware: now with worming self-propagation, March 2021. https://threatpost.com/ryuk-ransomware-worming-self-propagation/164412/

49. Shen, M., Liu, Y., Zhu, L., Xu, K., Du, X., Guizani, N.: Optimizing feature selection for efficient encrypted traffic classification: a systematic approach. IEEE Network **34**(4), 20–27 (2020)

50. SonicWall, October 2021. https://www.sonicwall.com/news/sonicwall-the-year-of-ransomware-continues-with-unprecedented-late-summer-surge/

51. Stratosphere: Stratosphere laboratory datasets (2015). https://www.stratosphereips.org/datasets-overview. Accessed 13 Mar 2020

52. Tandon, A., Nayyar, A.: A comprehensive survey on ransomware attack: a growing havoc cyberthreat. Data Management, Analytics and Innovation, pp. 403–420 (2019)
53. Wheelus, C., Bou-Harb, E., Zhu, X.: Tackling class imbalance in cyber security datasets. In: 2018 IEEE International Conference on Information Reuse and Integration (IRI), pp. 229–232. IEEE (2018)
54. Xiong, Z., Zilberman, N.: Do switches dream of machine learning? toward in-network classification. In: Proceedings of the 18th ACM Workshop on Hot Topics in Networks, pp. 25–33 (2019)
55. Yaqoob, I., et al.: The rise of ransomware and emerging security challenges in the internet of things. Comput. Networks **129**, 444–458 (2017)
56. Zahra, S.R., Chishti, M.A.: Ransomware and internet of things: a new security nightmare. In: 2019 9th International Conference on Cloud Computing, Data Science & Engineering (confluence), pp. 551–555. IEEE (2019)
57. Zheng, C., Zilberman, N.: Planter: seeding trees within switches. In: Proceedings of the SIGCOMM 2021 Poster and Demo Sessions, pp. 12–14 (2021)

Reducing Intrusion Alert Trees to Aid Visualization

Eric Ficke[1]([⊠]) (iD), Raymond M. Bateman[2] (iD), and Shouhuai Xu[3] (iD)

[1] The University of Texas at San Antonio, San Antonio, USA
eric.ficke@utsa.edu
[2] U.S. Army Research Laboratory South - Cyber, San Antonio, USA
[3] University of Colorado Colorado Springs, Colorado Springs, USA

Abstract. Cyber defense tools, such as intrusion detection systems, often produce huge amounts of alerts which must be parsed for defensive purposes, particularly cyber triage. In this paper, we utilize the notion of *alert trees* to represent the collection of routes that may have been used by a cyber attacker to compromise a set of computers. Although alert trees can be visualized to aid analysis, their usefulness in practice is often discounted by the fact that they can become unmanageable in size. This makes it difficult for cyber defenders to identify patterns or pinpoint network hotspots in order to prioritize defensive maneuvers, raising the need to reduce strain on defenders by minimizing the presence of non-critical information. To address this problem, we propose several methods, as well as a novel data structure, for modifying alert trees in order to reduce visual strain on defenders. We evaluate our methods using a real-world dataset, which demonstrates that our methods are effective at reducing redundancy while limiting collateral information loss.

Keywords: Alert tree · Cyber triage · Visualization · Hypotree · Information loss · Intrusion detection · Network security

1 Introduction

Real-world cyber defense tools often produce a huge number of alerts on a daily basis. It is an important problem to leverage these alerts for defense purposes because they are often the first opportunity for the defender to detect attacks. A common approach for this problem is to use graph-based visualization. However, large graphs can be difficult to analyze manually. It is important to enable this process because human defenders may be able to detect attacks or make sense of alerts that automated tools cannot. Nevertheless, the practice of maintaining "human in the loop" decision-making is often overlooked.

Alert trees have been proposed as an alternative to arbitrary network graphs (or multigraphs). Intuitively, alert trees offer several advantages over graphs: The first advantage is their *planarity*, under which no edges overlap [14]. This is important because planarity makes it easier to visually distinguish edges.

© The Author(s), under exclusive license to Springer Nature Switzerland AG 2022
X. Yuan et al. (Eds.): NSS 2022, LNCS 13787, pp. 140–154, 2022.
https://doi.org/10.1007/978-3-031-23020-2_8

The second advantage is that alert trees show the *temporal relationships* among alerts. Graphs prioritize spatial relationships, and can only model temporal relationships by either adding dynamic animations, which take time to observe, or annotating edges with timestamps, which require the effort of granular inspection and interpretation.

Alert trees themselves exhibit some limitations, such as: (i) trees can be prohibitively large; and (ii) trees may present redundant information, which can confuse defenders. Thus it is not trivial to use alert trees to represent the temporal relationships between alerts. This motivates the present study.

1.1   Our Contributions

In order to aid the visualization of alert trees, we hereby contribute a data structure, three algorithms, two metrics and a case study. First, we introduce the concept of *hypotree*, which is useful in the set of reductions that follow by identifying repeated attack patterns across particular links. Second, we propose several novel algorithms for reducing the size of alert trees. One algorithm for *merging sibling leaves*: this eliminates redundancy while preserving significant threats. One algorithm for *merging sibling branches*: this eliminates redundancy while preserving the underlying structure. One algorithm for *truncating hypotrees*, the aforementioned novel data structure: this reduces redundancy by grouping subsequent co-located alerts. Third, we propose methods and metrics for evaluating the usefulness of the above algorithms. Specifically, we consider the effects of the algorithms on *tree size* and *information retention*. These act as trade-offs, representing the sensitive conflict between not enough and too much information. This trade-off poses as a new challenge because information loss has not been studied in the present context, despite research in other contexts (e.g., data anonymization [18] and data perturbation [19]). Fourth, we demonstrate the usefulness of the proposed approach by applying these three algorithms to a well-known dataset. We measure the reduction in visual strain (i.e., tree size) and compare it to the trade-off in lost information.

1.2   Related Work

Since our study is centered at visualizing alerts to help defenders, we divide the relevant prior studies into the following three categories.

Alert and Attack Trees. There have been studies on leveraging alerts to help defenders, such as: correlating alerts to construct attack scenarios or enable collaborative defense [7,20,28], leveraging alerts to learn attack strategies [21], and alert fusion and reasoning [12]. These approaches are useful for modeling various attack patterns. However, these patterns are often not reliable enough to incorporate into a fully automated system, which could damage systems if deployed too aggressively. In light of this, it remains important for alert-based systems to present models that are intuitive to human defenders.

Alert trees [9] are conceptually related to attack trees [1,5,22]. Attack trees are often used to describe the preconditions that allow attackers to achieve their goals. Because of this, attack trees are often used to guide the hardening of a network, and constitute preventive measures. By contrast, alert trees are meant to make sense of the alerts produced by cyber defense tools as attacks enter the network. This means that alert trees are more appropriate than attack trees for the sake of cyber triage, which measures the scope of various attacks against a network. Alert trees are detective measures. Because the semantics of alert trees differ from attack trees and arbitrary network graphs, the patterns exhibited by alert trees are likely unique. This motivates us to tailor our approach to the specific case of alert trees. To our knowledge, no other works have targeted the problem of reducing redundancy for alert trees in particular.

Alert Aggregation. While the notion of an alert tree does not necessarily demand alert reduction in general, it may be useful during alert tree construction. In this regard, alert reduction is related to the notion of alert aggregation (see, e.g., [17,23,24]), which aims to reduce alert cardinality in order to improve efficiency. The present work contrasts this by managing redundancies after the trees have been constructed, rather than before or during construction. This difference means that any potential data loss is delayed until further down the processing line and should be easier to recover if necessary.

Graph Visualization. Network visualization has been used to present data to defenders for the purposes of cyber triage [16,26]. These visualizations are primarily targeted at identifying individual attacks or aggregating similar attacks, rather than tracking consecutive attacks in a spatiotemporal context. Other works have used graphs in which nodes represent computers, while arcs represent security events, such as attacks or remote access [11,13]. These works focus on detecting anomalies, rather than tracking attacks deterministically and over time. As mentioned above, planarity is guaranteed in alert trees but not alert graphs. Metrics used to rank and color graphs vary, as alert trees contain multiple types of data such as the type and number of attacks observed, vertex connectedness, and number of paths [1,15]. Some libraries used for graph visualization include Tulip [2], Graphviz [8], and Pajek [3].

1.3 Paper Outline

The rest of the paper is organized as follows. Section 2 introduces the research problem and defines important terms. Section 3 details the methods used. Section 4 presents a case study. Section 5 discusses strengths and weaknesses of the work. Section 6 concludes the present paper with future research directions.

2 Problem Formalization

This section introduces the concepts and terms used throughout the paper and describes the context for their use. It also discusses the research questions we hope to answer.

2.1   Setting and Terminology

We investigate the problem of intuitive and efficient cyber triage. We use the context of an enterprise network, which consists of computers, networking devices, and security devices, is managed by a cyber *defender*, and is targeted by a cyber *attacker* who resides inside or outside the enterprise network. Once the attacker establishes a foothold in the network (through exploits, social engineering attacks, or other means), they conduct lateral movement to compromise additional computers. These attacks leave footprints that can be detected by security devices in order to form *alert paths*. The first computer in an alert path is known as the *origin* and all other computers are considered *victims*. The final computer may also be called the path's *target*.

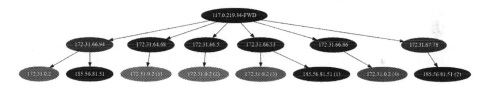

Fig. 1. A forward alert tree, where vertices represent computers (labeled by IP address), arcs represent sets of attacks between computers (according to alerts from security devices), and node colors indicate the threat score of the incoming set of attacks (i.e., the arc from the parent), with red being the highest score. A given computer may appear multiple times, indicating that multiple alert paths exist from the root to that computer. (Color figure online)

When multiple paths branch out from a single origin, these can be formulated into an *alert tree*. Computers in an alert tree are represented by vertices, and arcs between them denote sets of alerts. Alert trees may be forward-looking or backward-looking, such that the root of the tree belongs to all of the tree's paths as either the origin or target, respectively.

The concept of alert trees is important because they serve a critical role in facilitating incident response. Specifically, alert trees help defenders intuitively understand the scope of an attack in terms of the breadth of network impact and focal points thereof.

The visualization of alert trees has presented some significant limitations. Firstly, alert trees have been shown to be particularly large, with some cases resulting in over 5000 nodes, in under a week of attacks [9]. This size of tree is prohibitive to analyze as a whole, but simply removing parts may introduce errors. Thus, the focus of this paper is *reducing visual strain while minimizing information loss*.

2.2 Intuitive Problem Statement

The above discussion naturally leads to several intuitive needs regarding alert tree visualization. Specifically: (i) trees must be reasonably sized for visualization and viewing by defenders, (ii) trees must accommodate or preserve valuable information, and (iii) relevant information on trees must stand out. These problems highlight some of the limitations in the related literature, which offers visualization techniques but does not analyze them for robustness. This inspires us to design and implement the methods here proposed. In what follows we first introduce the concepts used in this paper using formal definitions.

2.3 Data Structures

The core of this work is the reduction operations on alert paths and trees. These concepts are used throughout the paper.

Alert Path. Intuitively, an *alert path* describes a series of attacks traversing one or more network connections, which may have been used by an attacker to conduct a multi-step attack.

Definition 1 (Alert Path). *Given a graph $G = (V, E)$, define an alert path $p = (nodes, edges)$; where $p.nodes = (v_1, v_2, \ldots, v_\ell) \subseteq V$, such that $\forall v_i, v_j \in p.nodes$, $v = v \rightarrow i = j$; and $p.edges = ((v_1, v_2), (v_2, v_3), \ldots, (v_{\ell-1}, v_\ell))$, such that $e \in p.edges \rightarrow e \in E$.*

Alert Tree. An alert tree represents a set of alert paths with a common origin or target and is composed of nodes with corresponding parent/child relationships.

Each node has a name and a color that represents some metric used to show the importance of a node. For this work, we will use the threat score (TS) metric as defined in [9], although the model is metric agnostic. Threat score is used to describe the severity of attacks against a given target. For alert trees, we isolate threat score with respect to a given attacker as well (the node's parent, as described below). It is sufficient to note that node colors range from red to black (i.e., in hexadecimal notation: 0xFF0000 to 0x000000), where red indicates a higher value of the relevant metric, denoting a higher importance. This is demonstrated in Fig. 1, and will be elaborated further in Sect. 3. These nodes are used to construct an alert tree based on the following definition.

Definition 2 (Alert Tree). *An alert tree t is an arborescence (i.e., a rooted directed acyclic graph (DAG) where each node is accessible from the root by a unique sequence of ancestors), rooted at a particular node t.root, and for which each node n is annotated by name (denoted n.name) and color (denoted n.color). Nodes may not share names with any of their siblings or ancestors.*

Alert trees come in two logical forms: forward and backward. For any node n_f in a forward tree, an arc $(n_f.parent, n_f)$ indicates an attack from $n_f.parent$ to n_f. Conversely, for any node n_b in a backward alert tree, an edge $(n_b.parent, n_b)$

indicates an attack from n_b to $n_b.parent$. These are formulated respectively to show the scope of victims that a particular attacker may have targeted, and the scope of attackers that may have targeted a particular victim.

It is also worth noting that alert paths can be reconstructed from an alert tree by extracting a node's ancestors. Note that in the case of backward alert trees, the ancestors must be reversed to retrieve the proper alert path.

Hypotree. Intuitively, a *hypotree* is a tree which resembles a portion of another tree (i.e., its *hypertree*), where the two trees have identical roots. This relationship is distinct from the concept of a subtree, which constitutes a branch of its supertree. By contrast, a hypotree may be missing individual nodes or branches relative to its hypertree.

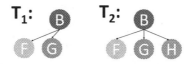

Fig. 2. Example hypotree, where $T_1 \lhd T_2$. Color coding shows analogous nodes in the hypertree. (Color figure online)

Remark 1 ("Hypotree" Usage). The term *hypotree* has been used to refer to an altered subtree structure in [10], but is otherwise absent from the literature. Our usage is not inconsistent with this one. However, this usage may seem to imply that its inverse is a *hypertree*, which has been used to denote an unrelated concept [4,25]. For our purposes, it is sufficient to exclusively use the one-way relationship of hypotree.

Based on the naming restrictions given in the definition of *alert tree*, we can see that for any given alert tree, each node has a single ancestry which is unique in the tree. With this in mind, we define hypotree in Definition 3.

Definition 3 (Hypotree). *A tree T_{hypo} is a hypotree relative to a tree T_{hyper} if $\forall n \in T_{hypo}, \exists n' \in T_{hyper} : n'.ancestors = n.ancestors$*

Denote "T_{hypo} is a hypotree of T_{hyper}" as $T_{hypo} \lhd\!\!\!\!\lhd T_{hyper}$. Similarly, we derive hypertree ($\rhd\!\!\!\!\rhd$); proper hypertee ($\rhd$), a hypertree that is not also a hypotree; and proper hypotree ($\lhd$), a hypotree that is not also a hypertree. Recall that "hypertree" is an existing concept in other contexts, so "hypotree" is preferred where possible. Where necessary, the symbol ($\rhd\!\!\!\!\rhd$) can be used to avoid confusion, as this is specific to the current usage.

An example hypotree is given in Fig. 2. If these were each members of the same alert tree, it would indicate that the T_1 attacks occurred after the T_2 attacks, since consecutive links in an alert path follow a happens-before relationship. In other words, the attacks (B, F) and (B, G) must have come after the attack (B, H). This means that if the two trees were produced by different attackers and only node H was compromised, we can conclude it was done by the attacker that produced T_2.

2.4   Formalizing Intuitive Problems as Research Questions

Equipped with the preceding formalisms, we can now translate the intuitive problems into rigorous Research Questions (RQs) as follows. Computers may appear multiple times in an alert tree, and thus represent redundant data. Removing this redundant data can improve usability of alert trees. This motivates RQ1 and RQ2.

- **RQ1:** How much can we reduce alert tree size by merging similar nodes?
- **RQ2:** How much can we reduce alert tree size by removing duplicate nodes?

While modifying an alert graph, the removal and merging of nodes can reduce the amount of information available to the defender. Specifically, when merging nodes, we want to maximize the ratio of size reduction to information loss. Similarly, when removing duplicate nodes, we want to preserve to location information of the nodes that were removed. This motivates RQ3.

- **RQ3:** How can we preserve information lost in the solutions to RQ1 and RQ2?

Salient information can represent a wide variety data, such as threat score, asset value, etc. One way to represent such data is to color-code the relevant graph elements. This motivates RQ4.

- **RQ4:** How can we highlight salient information in an alert graph without increasing visual strain on the user?

3   Methods

In this section, we propose several methods for reducing an alert trees. Specifically, we propose merging sibling leaves, merging sibling branches, and truncating hypotrees, as highlighted in Fig. 3.

Each of the three base functions can be used on its own to reduce a given alert tree. These represent reduction schedules one, three and five, respectively. However, because the nodes they merge or remove may overlap, it is unsafe to apply more than one reduction at a time. The only exception is the *merge sibling leaves* reduction, which may be applied after (but not before) either of the other two base reductions because it does not create conflicts with them. This forms reduction schedules two and four.

The model requires alert trees as inputs, as defined in Sect. 2. Once the trees are imported, it annotates them to facilitate the reduction algorithms and sends them to the appropriate functions. The remainder of this section describes the base reductions.

AVR

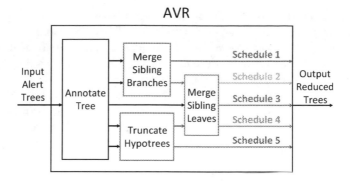

Fig. 3. Reductions overview. The colored boxes represent reductions, while colored arrows represent reduction schedules. Reduction schedules 1,3, and 5 utilize only a single reduction, while 2 and 4 apply two reductions in sequence. (Color figure online)

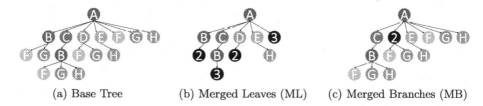

(a) Base Tree   (b) Merged Leaves (ML)   (c) Merged Branches (MB)

Fig. 4. Example tree with reduction schedules 3 and 1 applied. Colors show unique nodes. Black denotes merges along with number of nodes merged. (Color figure online)

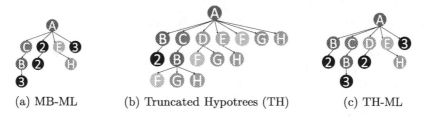

(a) MB-ML   (b) Truncated Hypotrees (TH)   (c) TH-ML

Fig. 5. Example reduction schedules 2, 5 and 4. Colors shows unique nodes. Black denotes merges or truncations along with the number of nodes reduced. (Color figure online)

3.1   Merging Sibling Leaves

Intuitively, high volume and low yield information can be reduced by merging sibling leaves, preserving information about the severity of attacks against the merged leaves according to the TS of the merged leaves. In attack trees, this is done by adopting the color of the node with the highest TS among those merged.

The approach is as follows. We use a breadth-first traversal to iterate over the tree, parsing the list of each internal node's children. For each set of children, we check each node to determine if it is a leaf node and document the highest TS within the set of those leaves. We then replace the leaves with a single node, showing the number of leaves merged and color coded according to the TS selected above. Figure 4b shows the result of merging leaves on the example tree from Fig. 4a.

3.2   Merging Sibling Branches

We can reduce the amount of duplicate information presented to the viewer by merging identical branches. This allows the viewer to more quickly identify common patterns within the tree.

The approach is as follows. In order to find identical branches, we conduct a breadth-first traversal of the tree, recursively comparing the branches of each set of siblings. When we identify two siblings with identical subtrees, we combine the siblings into a single node, preserving the shared form of the subtree. We label the new node with the number of siblings that were merged, applying the same color from the sibling with the highest ETS. Node data for the merge is archived in case it needs to be retrieved later.

Branches are compared using a hash function, which produces a tuple $H(root) = (root, (H(node) : node \in root.children))$, which incidentally produces $H(leaf) = (leaf, ())$ for leaf nodes. Figures 4c and 5a show examples of the *merge branches* reduction.

3.3   Truncating Hypotrees

Because all nodes in hypotrees are duplicated in their respective hypertrees, they are redundant. For this reason, we choose to truncate hypotrees in order to reduce visual strain on the viewer. This preserves the most amount of information since all edges are preserved (in the corresponding hypertree), even if their location and number are lost.

The basic idea of the algorithm is described as follows. We parse the tree using a breadth-first traversal, marking all nodes that share the same address. We then compare the hypotrees of each set of identical nodes, preserving trees which have no proper hypertrees and truncating the rest. In the case of two equivalent hypotrees (i.e., $A \trianglelefteq B \wedge B \trianglelefteq A$), we preserve only the one appearing first in the traversal. Truncated trees contain annotations to refer viewers to the corresponding hypertree. Archives save information about removed hypotrees so they can be reconstructed if needed. The method for truncating hypotrees is given in Algorithm 1. Figures 4b and 4c show an example usage of the algorithm.

Algorithm 1. Truncate Hypotrees

Input: *Root*

Output: *Root, Archives*

1: $Candidates \leftarrow \emptyset$
2: $Unique\_Names \leftarrow \emptyset$
3: **for each** $Node \in Root.descendants$ **do**
4:     **if** $\exists Name\_List \in Unique\_Names : Name\_List_1 = Node.name$ **then**
5:         $Name\_List \leftarrow Name\_List \cup (Node)$
6:         $Candidates \leftarrow Candidates \cup \{Node.name\}$ ▷ Nodes sharing a name
    become candidates
7:     **else**
8:         $Unique\_Names \leftarrow Unique\_Names \cup \{(Node.name, Node)\}$
9:                      ▷ Here elements 2 onward are nodes with the same name
10:     **end if**
11: **end for**
12: $Trunks \leftarrow (\emptyset^{|Unique\_Nodes|})$
13: $Colors \leftarrow (()^{|Unique\_Nodes|})$
14: **for each** $n \in [1, 2, \ldots, |Unique\_Names|]$ **do**
15:     **if** $Unique\_Names_n \in Candidates$ **then**
16:         **for each** $i, j \in [2, 3, \ldots, n), i < j]$ **do**   ▷ Compare pairs of candidates
17:             **if** $Unique\_Names_{n,i} \lhd Unique\_Names_{n,j}$ **then**
18:                 **if** $|Unique\_Names_{n,i}.descendants| > 1$ **then**
19:                     $Trunks_n \leftarrow Trunks_n \cup (Unique\_Names_{n,i})$ ▷ Mark i for
    truncation
20:                     $Colors_n \leftarrow Colors_n \cup (\max_{d \in Unique\_Names_{n,i}\ descendants}(d.color))$
21:                 **end if**
22:             **else**
23:                 **if** $|Unique\_Names_{n,j}.descendants| > 1$ **then**
24:                     $Trunks_n \leftarrow Trunks_n \cup (Unique\_Names_{n,j})$ ▷ Mark j for
    truncation
25:                     $Colors_n \leftarrow Colors_n \cup (\max_{d \in Unique\_Names_{n,j}.descendants}(d.color))$
26:                 **end if**
27:             **end if**
28:         **end for**
29:     **end if**
30: **end for**
31: $Archives \leftarrow \emptyset$
32: **for** $i \in [1, \ldots, |Trunks|]$ **do**
33:     **for** $j \in [1, \ldots, |Trunks_i|]$ **do**   ▷ Truncate and archive
34:         $trunk\_archive \leftarrow \mathsf{copy}(Trunks_{i,j}.parent)$
35:         $trunk\_archive.parent \leftarrow \emptyset$
36:         $new\_trunk \leftarrow \mathsf{copy}(Trunks_{i,j})$
37:         $new\_trunk.color \leftarrow Colors_{i,j}$
38:         $Trunk_{i,j}.parent \leftarrow trunk\_archive$
39:         $Archives \leftarrow Archives \cup \{trunk\_archive\}$
40:     **end for**
41: **end for**
42: **return** $Root, Archives$

---

4   Case Study

For the case study, we used CSE-CIC-IDS2018 [27], a well-known dataset collected from a testbed with both injected and wild attacks. From the network traffic, Snort [6] produced 3.3M alerts. These were assembled into trees using APIN [9]. Nodes were ranked according to threat score, calculated as the geometric mean of the volume and diversity of alerts incident to the node. Trees were ranked according to the threat score of their root node.

From the resulting trees, we selected 15 for AVR to reduce: 5 each from the top ranked, bottom ranked, and randomly selected trees. Statistics for the selected trees are as follows. The top 5 set had on average 9.8 vertices, 7.6 unique vertices and 8.8 unique arcs. Next, the bottom 5 set had on average 15 vertices, 10.6 unique vertices and 14 unique arcs. Finally, the random 5 set had on average 1999 vertices, 234.4 unique vertices and 825.6 unique arcs.

4.1   Evaluation Metrics

In order to evaluate the effectiveness of our methods, we utilize a total of 4 metrics, including three atomic metrics and one aggregate metric. The atomic metrics are visual strain reduction (VSR), node retention (NR) and threat score retention (TSR). The latter two are derived from the notion of *information loss*, as its additive inverse (i.e., $1 - loss$). These three metrics are also combined to create a *reduction index*.

For the first metric, we measure VSR as the number of nodes in the reduced tree relative to the full tree. VSR has a range of [0,1], where 100% is ideal.

For the following two metrics, we measure *information retention* as the number of unique nodes or threat score values from the full tree that remain after the reduction. For unique nodes, recall that a given computer may appear multiple times in an alert tree because there may be multiple paths that an attacker may have taken to reach it. If the unique node remains in the tree after the reduction, it is considered retained. For threat score values, recall that threat score describes the severity of a set of attacks between two nodes. Thus, if the corresponding color (for the node representing the target of those attacks) remains in the tree, the corresponding TS is considered retained. Both NR and TSR have a range of [0,1], where 100% is ideal.

Note that NR is not necessarily $1 - $ VSR, since some reductions add supplemental nodes after pruning. These new nodes increase visual strain but not node retention, since they do not belong to the full tree. However, they may increase TSR, since some of the supplemental nodes inherit color codes (i.e., threat score) from the node(s) they replaced.

To ensure a balance between size reduction and information retention, we combine the three metrics into a *reduction index* using their harmonic mean.

4.2   Results

Results of the experiments are given in Table 1. Of the basic reductions, the *truncate hypotrees* performed the worst in most cases, with its RI trailing by margins of 0.373 and 0.354 for the random 5 and bottom 5 categories, respectively. In the top 5 category, however, it outperformed both other algorithms by at least 0.131.

Table 1. Results evaluated on alert trees sampled according to threat score. VSR is average visual strain reduction, NR is average node retention, TSR is average threat score retention, and RI is reduction index as the harmonic mean of VSR, NR and TSR.

Algorithm	VSR	NR	TSR	RI
1. Merge branches (top 5)	0	1	1	0
1. Merge branches (rand 5)	.448	.533	.254	.373
1. Merge branches (bot 5)	.567	.493	.360	**.457**
2. MB-ML (top 5)	.977	.008	.010	.013
2. MB-ML (rand 5)	.561	.357	.929	**.530**
2. MB-ML (bot 5)	.761	.205	.120	.206
3. Merge leaves (top 5)	.977	.008	.010	.013
3. Merge leaves (rand 5)	.118	.824	.799	.274
3. Merge leaves (bot 5)	.209	.255	.270	.242
4. TH-ML (top 5)	.981	.008	.010	.013
4. TH-ML (rand 5)	.118	.824	.201	.204
4. TH-ML (bot 5)	.239	.743	.713	.433
5. Trunc hypotrees (top 5)	.053	1	1	**.144**
5. Trunc hypotrees (rand 5)	0	1	1	0
5. Trunc hypotrees (bot 5)	.037	1	.983	.103

Overall, reduction schedule 2 performed the best in the random 5 category, and schedule 4 performed the best in the bottom 5 category. This suggests that merging branches then leaves is the best general-purpose strategy, while truncating hypotrees then merging leaves then is the best strategy for reducing relatively small trees.

With respect to any one particular metric, results varied across reduction schedules and sample sets. This means it may be difficult to predict which schedule one should use when trying to optimize for any particular metric.

4.3   Answering Research Questions

Answering RQ 1: How much can one reduce alert tree size by merging similar nodes? By merging leaves, tree size can be reduced by as much 98%, and by merging branches tree size can be reduced by as much as 57%.

Answering RQ 2: How much can one reduce alert tree size by removing duplicate nodes? By truncating hypotrees, tree size can be reduced by as much as 5.3%.

Answering RQ 3: How can one preserve the information lost in the solutions to RQ1 and RQ2? The best way to preserve information is to truncate hypotrees, which contain almost exclusively redundant information. Otherwise, results from the other algorithms have variable results depending on the sample used.

Answering RQ 4: How can one highlight salient information in an alert graph without increasing visual strain on the user? Color-coding salient information allows the tree to highlight important data such as network hotspots and threat activity. Color can be used for both nodes and edges, so NR and TSR are the metrics to look at when one needs information salience.

The novel reductions had a broad range of performance, with each one having a different strength. Since user needs will vary, it will be important to consider these differences when choosing how to handle alert trees. Meanwhile, these results are only preliminary and warrant further study.

5   Discussion

Limitations of the Methodology. The methods used in this study have the following limitations. First, the reductions for merging branches and truncating hypotrees have overlapping domains under composition. This means running them in sequence may give different results depending on the order used. This results in only five valid reduction schedules.

Additionally, alert paths do not necessarily give a precise account of an attacker's activity. This is for the following reasons: (i) attacks may fail, producing alerts that do not indicate compromise; (ii) attacker addresses may be spoofed or reflected, such that the source of the connection is not visible to network monitors; (iii) security devices may have false positives or negatives; and (iv) some attacks may use client-side exploits, resulting in arcs that are inverted (i.e., the compromised computer may be the source of an attack rather than its destination). These phenomena can induce errors in the experimental results.

Limitations of the Case Study. The dataset in the case study utilizes threat score to rank edges and paths. This metric has not been robustly studied and may not produce the best scores relative to a particular attack. However, the methods proposed in the present study need not use threat score, but could easily be adapted to rank nodes according to monetary value, vulnerability score, or other related risk metrics.

6   Conclusion

This work introduced several methods for reducing the size of alert trees while retaining as much information as possible. The three core functions can be used independently or combined in a total of five reduction schedules. One of the reductions involves the use of a novel data structure, the hypotree. These reductions were applied to alert trees from a research testbed dataset, and were evaluated for information retention and visual strain reduction. Results show that the reductions have varied performance relative to each other for different types of trees. This finding warrants more research into how the application of the reductions may be optimized.

Acknowledgments. This work was supported in part by NSF Grants #1736209, #2122631 and #2115134, and by Colorado State Bill 18-086.

References

1. Angelini, M., Prigent, N., Santucci, G.: PERCIVAL: proactive and reactive attack and response assessment for cyber incidents using visual analytics. In: 2015 IEEE Symposium on Visualization for Cyber Security (VizSec), pp. 1–8. IEEE (2015)
2. Auber, D.: Tulip—a huge graph visualization framework. In: Jünger, M., Mutzel, P. (eds.) Graph Drawing Software. Mathematics and Visualization, pp. 105–126. Springer, Heidelberg (2004). https://doi.org/10.1007/978-3-642-18638-7_5
3. Batagelj, V., Mrvar, A.: Pajek-program for large network analysis. Connections **21**(2), 47–57 (1998)
4. Brandstädt, A., Chepoi, V.D., Dragan, F.F.: The algorithmic use of hypertree structure and maximum neighbourhood orderings. Discret. Appl. Math. **82**(1–3), 43–77 (1998)
5. Chen, Y., Boehm, B., Sheppard, L.: Value driven security threat modeling based on attack path analysis. In: 2007 40th Annual Hawaii International Conference on System Sciences (HICSS 2007), pp. 280a–280a. IEEE (2007)
6. Cisco: Snort - network intrusion detection & prevention system, March 2018. http://www.snort.org/downloads
7. Cuppens, F., Miège, A.: Alert correlation in a cooperative intrusion detection framework. In: Proceedings of the 2002 IEEE Symposium on Security and Privacy, SP 2002, p. 202 (2002)
8. Ellson, J., Gansner, E., Koutsofios, L., North, S.C., Woodhull, G.: Graphviz—open source graph drawing tools. In: Mutzel, P., Jünger, M., Leipert, S. (eds.) GD 2001. LNCS, vol. 2265, pp. 483–484. Springer, Heidelberg (2002). https://doi.org/10.1007/3-540-45848-4_57
9. Ficke, E., Xu, S.: APIN: automatic attack path identification in computer networks. In: IEEE ISI 2020 (2020)
10. Gerbessiotis, A.V.: An architecture independent study of parallel segment trees. J. Discrete Algorithms **4**(1), 1–24 (2006)
11. Goodall, J.R., et al.: Situ: identifying and explaining suspicious behavior in networks. IEEE Trans. Vis. Comput. Graph. **25**(1), 204–214 (2019)
12. Gu, G., Cárdenas, A., Lee, W.: Principled reasoning and practical applications of alert fusion in intrusion detection systems. In: Proceedings of ACM Symposium on Information, Computer and Communications Security (ASIACCS 2008), pp. 136–147 (2008)

13. Harshaw, C.R., Bridges, R.A., Iannacone, M.D., Reed, J.W., Goodall, J.R.: Graph-Prints: towards a graph analytic method for network anomaly detection. In: Proceedings of the 11th Annual Cyber and Information Security Research Conference, CISRC 2016, pp. 15:1–15:4. ACM, New York (2016). https://doi.org/10.1145/2897795.2897806

14. Herman, I., Melançon, G., Marshall, M.S.: Graph visualization and navigation in information visualization: a survey. IEEE Trans. Visual Comput. Graphics **6**(1), 24–43 (2000)

15. Kerzner, E., et al.: Graffinity: visualizing connectivity in large graphs. In: Computer Graphics Forum, vol. 36, pp. 251–260. Wiley Online Library (2017)

16. Lohfink, A.P., Anton, S.D.D., Schotten, H.D., Leitte, H., Garth, C.: Security in process: visually supported triage analysis in industrial process data. IEEE Trans. Visual Comput. Graphics **26**(4), 1638–1649 (2020)

17. Nadeem, A., Verwer, S., Yang, S.J.: SAGE: intrusion alert-driven attack graph extractor. In: 2021 IEEE Symposium on Visualization for Cyber Security (VizSec), pp. 36–41. IEEE (2021)

18. Nettleton, D.F.: Information loss evaluation based on fuzzy and crisp clustering of graph statistics. In: 2012 IEEE International Conference on Fuzzy Systems, pp. 1–8. IEEE (2012)

19. Nettleton, D.F., Torra, V., Dries, A.: The effect of constraints on information loss and risk for clustering and modification based graph anonymization methods. arXiv preprint arXiv:1401.0458 (2014)

20. Ning, P., Cui, Y., Reeves, D.S.: Constructing attack scenarios through correlation of intrusion alerts. In: Proceedings of the 9th ACM Conference on Computer and Communications Security, CCS 2002, pp. 245–254 (2002)

21. Ning, P., Xu, D.: Learning attack strategies from intrusion alerts. In: Proceedings of the 10th ACM Conference on Computer and Communications Security, CCS 2003, pp. 200–209 (2003)

22. Ray, I., Poolsapassit, N.: Using attack trees to identify malicious attacks from authorized insiders. In: di Vimercati, S.C., Syverson, P., Gollmann, D. (eds.) ESORICS 2005. LNCS, vol. 3679, pp. 231–246. Springer, Heidelberg (2005). https://doi.org/10.1007/11555827_14

23. Sadoddin, R., Ghorbani, A.: Alert correlation survey: framework and techniques. In: Proceedings of the 2006 International Conference on Privacy, Security and Trust: Bridge the Gap Between PST Technologies and Business Services, pp. 1–10 (2006)

24. Salah, S., Maciá-Fernández, G., Díaz-Verdejo, J.E.: A model-based survey of alert correlation techniques. Comput. Netw. **57**(5), 1289–1317 (2013)

25. Schidler, A., Szeider, S.: Computing optimal hypertree decompositions. In: 2020 Proceedings of the Twenty-Second Workshop on Algorithm Engineering and Experiments (ALENEX), pp. 1–11. SIAM (2020)

26. Sethi, A., Wills, G.: Expert-interviews led analysis of EEVi-a model for effective visualization in cyber-security. In: 2017 IEEE Symposium on Visualization for Cyber Security (VizSec), pp. 1–8. IEEE (2017)

27. Sharafaldin, I., Lashkari, A.H., Ghorbani, A.A.: Toward generating a new intrusion detection dataset and intrusion traffic characterization. In: ICISSP, pp. 108–116 (2018)

28. Valeur, F., Vigna, G., Kruegel, C., Kemmerer, R.A.: A comprehensive approach to intrusion detection alert correlation. IEEE Trans. Dependable Secur. Comput. **1**(3), 146–169 (2004)

Attacker Attribution via Characteristics Inference Using Honeypot Data

Pierre Crochelet$^{(\boxtimes)}$, Christopher Neal, Nora Boulahia Cuppens,
and Frédéric Cuppens

Polytechnique Montreal, Montreal, Canada
{pierre.crochelet,christopher.neal,nora.boulahia-cuppens,
frederic.cuppens}@polymtl.ca

Abstract. Increasingly, the computer networks supporting the operations of organizations face a higher quantity and sophistication of cyber-incidents. Due to the evolving complexity of these attacks, detection alone is not enough and there is a need for automatic attacker attribution. This task is currently done by network administrators, making it slow, costly and prone to human error. Previous works in the field mostly profile attackers based on external tools or lists of rules that need to be updated regularly. Some tackle this problem through particular methodologies that cannot be easily generalized to any data source. We focus on using a self-sufficient technique that allows us to characterize attackers through motivation, resourcefulness, stealth, intention and originality. Furthermore, we show that this technique can easily be used on several protocols by applying it to a dataset consisting of real attacks performed on several honeypots. We show that more than 90% of the recorded data is relatively harmless and only a limited number of attackers are alarming. This process enables network administrators to readily discard benign traffic and focus their attention towards high-priority attacks.

Keywords: Attacker attribution · Information security · Honeypot data · Intelligent data analysis

1 Introduction

In today's world, cybersecurity has an increasing importance as cyberattacks are more and more frequent [1]. Initially, many researchers focused on the detection of these incidents through the use of Intrusion Detection System (IDS) platforms that attempt to capture the essence of the attack itself [7,14]. However, with continual advances in technology, new forms of attacks appear every day, creating a need to regularly update an IDS. Therefore, detection alone is no longer sufficient and an IDS must consider the attribution problem as well [18]. Attribution, sometimes referred to as "attacker profiling", is the process of characterizing the attacker instead of the attack. Currently, attribution tasks are mostly done by network administrators, thus the quality of attribution will vary. There is a great need to automate, at least some, part of this process with an unbiased tool to increase the reliability and speed of this task.

© The Author(s), under exclusive license to Springer Nature Switzerland AG 2022
X. Yuan et al. (Eds.): NSS 2022, LNCS 13787, pp. 155–169, 2022.
https://doi.org/10.1007/978-3-031-23020-2_9

Fraunholz et al. [11] propose attributes to perform attacker profiling through the use of logs collected from a honeypot. Honeypots are specific decoy servers on a network that aim to lure attackers and record their attacks [16]. As honeypots do not have any production functionality, we know that all recorded traffic on honeypots is malicious or at least suspicious. The process proposed by Fraunholz et al. is an important step in the field of attacker profiling, however, it lacks a generalization as it focuses on only one type of log from one specific honeypot.

We propose a novel method to characterize attackers from logs of various services collected by a series of low-interaction honeypots and a way to identify the actual threats from harmless attackers. As such, we define new attributes that can be induced for multiple protocols through features found in many of them. We also show that this method works not only for Information Technology (IT) protocols but also for Operational Technology (OT) ones as well. The contributions of this work are summarized as follows:

1. Validate Fraunholz et al.'s approach on a new dataset.
2. Add a time constraint when considering attacks to reflect the dynamic assignment of IP addresses.
3. Expand and improve Fraunholz et al.'s approach to consider other IT and OT protocols.
4. Propose another way to analyse the results through clustering.

The remainder of this work is organized as follows. In Sect. 2, we discuss recent developments in attacker attribution. Section 3 introduces the methodology in [11] and presents our proposed generalized methodology. In Sect. 4 we apply both of these methodologies to logs of real attacks from multiple honeypots. Finally, Sect. 5 discusses the results and the limitations of our approach.

2   Background and Related Work

When considering the attribution problem, two challenges arise. First, attackers often use deceptive techniques to avoid detection [12]. Second, there is a lack of suitable datasets to research the relationship between an attacker's actions and the required characteristics to build a profile. However, to circumvent this second problem, Doynikova et al. [9] propose, amongst other things, to collect real attacker data through the use of honeypots, which is the focus of our work.

Nevertheless, different ways to gain intelligence about attackers have been proposed. Indeed, Bar et al. [6] use Hidden Markov Models (HMMs) to study attacker propagation in a network of honeypots. They construct communities within the network, where the majority of attacks are within the communities, and do not cross the borders of those communities. However, they do not explicitly use attacker models to identify the profiles of attackers and therefore do not outline which attackers require a deeper analysis.

Mallikarjunan et al. [15] introduce a way to build attacker profiles from IDS alerts through fuzzy rules. First, low-level alerts are grouped to generate a meta-alert for each intruder. Then, fuzzy rules are proposed to find the broad category of an attacker, which is later refined into an exact attacker profile through other specific rules. Finally, a database of attacker profiles is searched to find a match for this attacker profile. This methodology is very dependent on the set of IDS alerts generated and therefore requires an up-to-date tool to be effective. Regardless, it will not be possible to consider attackers using zero-day exploits. Similarly, Karafili et al. [13] use argumentation-based reasoning to help forensic analysts with attribution tasks. On the one hand, they use a set of rules described as *background knowledge* that needs to be updated regularly. On the other hand, they use a set of core rules that aims to mimic the analysts' reasoning during the attribution tasks. Ultimately, these two methodologies are not self-sufficient since they require human-based assistance or a high-performing tool to generate interesting results.

Deshmukh et al. [8] use real attack logs gathered from the Cowrie honeypot as a basis for attribution [2]. The authors identify the need for unsupervised or semi-supervised learning methods and propose Fusion Hidden Markov Models (FHMMs) that fall in the latter category. FHMMs are more resistant to noise and profit from all the advantages associated with ensemble learning. However, for the FHMMs, they define 19 states in terms of data specific to the Cowrie logs, making their technique hard to generalize to other types of honeypot logs.

Similarly, Fraunholz et al. [10] introduce an attacker model, GAMfIS, to characterize attackers in four attributes: Motivation (M), Skill (S), Intention (I) and Resources (R). Using those attributes, they define a Threat Rating (TR) as M+I, a Capability Rating (CR) as S+R, and finally a Total Threat Score as TR+CR. Then in [11], the authors apply their attacker model to a series of logs collected from a Cowrie Honeypot. They conclude that most attacks are coming from botnet traffic that can be mapped to rather harmless attackers. However, [11] only use logs from a Cowrie Honeypot that implements the SSH and Telnet protocols and focuses on a statistical analysis of their results. To do this, they use features that are specific to this honeypot. Our method builds on the work of [11] but focuses on features that can be extracted from various honeypots and services. Furthermore, after the statistical analysis, our method introduces a clustering analysis to differentiate harmless and malicious attacks.

3   Methodology

3.1   Data Collection and Processing

Our data has been collected for more than a year, starting in December 2020, through a series of honeypots. In total, we have more than two million log entries. The distribution of these logs is the following; Redis 44.9%, SSH 34.4%, Telnet 5.1%, Modbus 5.0%, HTTP 4.5%, HTTP-proxy 3.7%, DNP3 1.4%, FTP 0.9%, and BACnet 0.1%. All of these logs resemble the ones obtained from a Cowrie Honeypot. They are in a "NDJSON" format and contain information about the attacker, such as the source Internet Protocol (IP) address and port, as well as about the attack, such as the protocol, the command typed, and when it was executed. From these logs, we extract several features to classify each attacker.

We include all protocols but focus on the 6 that we can easily interpret and for which we have interesting data, namely: SSH, Telnet, Redis, FTP, Modbus, and HTTP. The extracted features are shown in Table 1.

Table 1. Extracted features for each protocol

	SSH/Telnet	Redis	FTP	Modbus	HTTP	Other protocols
Number of logs	**Yes**	**Yes**	**Yes**	**Yes**	**Yes**	**Yes**
List of methods	**Yes**	**Yes**	**Yes**	**Yes**	**Yes**	No
Number of scans	No	**Yes**	**Yes**	**Yes**	No	No
Number of sessions initiated	**Yes**	No	**Yes**	No	No	No
Number of malware files	**Yes**	No	No	No	No	No
Frequently used entries	**Yes**	No	No	No	No	No

3.2 Basic Methodology

Fraunholz et al. [11] perform the attribution on the attacks, defined as all attack sessions sharing the same IP address. In practice, this means that they group together all logs that share the same source IP, not considering the time. Then, for each attack, they propose characterizing them with:

– **Motivation:** the amount of effort the attacker puts into the attack,
– **Skill:** the degree of expertise of the attacker,
– **Resources:** the degree of automation the attacker has access to, and
– **Intention:** the attacker's goals and severity of the attack.

All these attributes are obtained through a linear combination of specific features, while ensuring they fall in the [0, 10] interval. Finally, they introduce two new metrics: the threat rating, defined as the sum of the motivation and intention attributes, and, the capability rating, defined as the sum of the resource and skill attributes. From these two final values falling in the range [0, 20], they plot the results in a heat map to identify where most attackers lie, and, consider only the outliers as threats.

3.3 Generalized Methodology

In our proposed generalized methodology, we add a time constraint to the attacks when grouping the logs together. Indeed, because of the dynamic assignment of IP addresses, even if two logs come from the same IP address, we cannot always be sure that they come from the same attacker. For this, we decide to add a time constraint of one hour as done in [6,17]. This means that if two logs share the same IP address and the time interval between these two logs is less than an hour, they are considered to come from the same attacker.

Also, in [11], not all equations are explicitly shown, in that the weight distributions are not specified. Therefore, in this work we explicitly calculate the added value of a specific feature for a characteristic as $added\_value = \frac{(given\_value - mean)}{std}$. Where, "mean" and "std" (i.e. standard deviation) are calculated for each feature independently, and "given_value" represents the value of the considered attacker for that feature. Therefore, the added value represents how far, in terms of standard deviation, the given value is from the mean. It is similar to having a linear combination where each feature is weighted corresponding to its distribution.

Finally, we change the way to characterize the attackers to make it easier to generalize to other protocols. Indeed, as will be seen in Sect. 4.1, the attributes used in [11] are sometimes too specific to the Cowrie honeypot. Therefore, we characterize the attackers in terms of:

- **Motivation:** the amount of effort the attacker puts into the attack,
- **Resourcefulness:** the degree of expertise and automation of an attacker,
- **Stealth:** the amount of effort the attacker puts into not getting caught,
- **Intention:** the attacker's goals and severity of the attack, and
- **Originality:** to identify "script kiddies" from legitimate malefactors.

4 Evaluation

4.1 Replication of Results

In practice, Fraunholz et al. [11] do not give the exact equations from which they derived the values of each attribute. Indeed, they mention the features they used for each attribute, however, do not show the weight associated to each feature. Therefore, without having the specifics, we use the previous equation to find the added value of each feature for an attribute. Then, for comparison purposes, we scale the obtained attribute values to the corresponding range. Also, Fraunholz et al. [11] mention that they could not find a way to express the attackers' intentions. Therefore, to find the threat rating they consider the intention score to be the same as the motivation score, which is what we are doing for this replication as well.

Motivation Ratings. To calculate the motivation ratings, three features are used: the number of commands entered, the number of sessions initiated, and the time spent in all these sessions. These are easily reproducible with the data at hand, except for session-less protocols like Modbus or Redis. For these protocols, we approximate the time spent in all sessions as the total time of the attack and the number of sessions initiated is considered to be already accounted for by the number of commands entered. Figure 1 shows the results obtained without scaling the feature. Most attackers obtain a motivation score between 0 and 20, with a few exceptions obtaining a much higher score.

Looking back at the logs, we see two trends to explain those outliers. The first one is that one of the honeypots did not implement a time-to-live, and some attackers exploited that to maintain some sessions open for a up to four months.

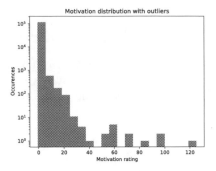

Fig. 1. Motivation ratings with outliers

The motive isn't clear but the attackers' intent could be to cause a denial of service. Therefore the "time spent in all sessions" feature is very high for those attackers, compared to the others. The second way to explain those outliers is through the "number of commands" feature. Indeed, where most attackers only sent between zero and a few hundreds of commands, some sent tens of thousands of commands and therefore, have a very high motivation score. To compare our results with the ones obtained in [11], we scale the values in the same range as they had. However, if we just scale the results as they are in Fig. 1, the resulting distribution will be skewed towards those outliers. Therefore, to get a meaningful comparison, we first remove the outliers and then scale the values. These results are shown in Fig. 2.

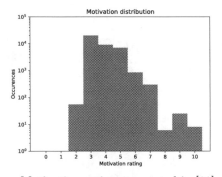 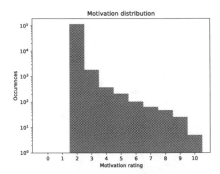

Motivation ratings presented in [11]   Reproduction of Motivation calculation

Fig. 2. Comparison of the Motivation ratings distributions

With our dataset, we obtain similar results for the motivation ratings. The major difference is that we see more attackers with a low motivation score. This is probably the result of adding the constraint on time when aggregating the logs into attacks, which gives more "small" attacks where the attackers simply send a few scans but do not act on them.

Resources Ratings. To calculate the resources ratings, only one feature can be used with the data we have. Indeed, in [11], Fraunholz et al. used the inter-arrival time of the attacker's commands as well the number of credentials tried when logging into the honeypot. However, in the honeypots we are using, the attackers do not need to log in, either because of the specification of the protocols (like Modbus) or because the login function is disabled in the honeypots. This leaves only the inter-arrival times as a suitable feature to reproduce their results. Figure 3 shows the results obtained without scaling the feature. Most attackers obtain a resources score between 0 and 2000, with a few exceptions.

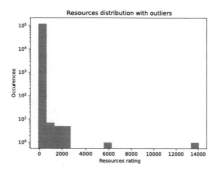

Fig. 3. Resources ratings with outliers

Looking back at the logs, we see that the resources outliers correspond to attackers for which we have several observations on a small interval, usually having one new observation every 0.1 s. For the same reason as discussed above, we remove the outliers before scaling the values for the comparison, as shown in Fig. 4. With our dataset, the results we get are a bit different, having very few attackers with a high resource rating. We presume this is because only one of the two features is usable with our data, which compromises the results.

Skill Ratings. The skill attribute is the most difficult to replicate. The features used are a list of commands entered by the attacker as well as a malware detection rate returned by VirusTotal [5] and a Threat level returned by Symantec [4]. However, to get those two last features, one needs access to the malware itself, which we do not have access to, at the time of writing. We only have the command executed by the attacker (i.e. the name of the malware) and sometimes the IP address the attacker used to obtain the malware. In the end, to approximate the malware detection rate, we use the number of times that IP address was flagged as malicious by VirusTotal. However, this feature is not easy to generalize for all protocols. Therefore, for most protocols, only the number of

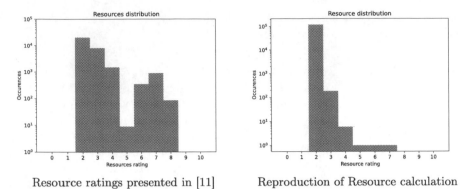

Resource ratings presented in [11]   Reproduction of Resource calculation

Fig. 4. Comparison of the Resources ratings distributions

commands entered by the attacker is used. Only for some protocols, do we also have the approached malware detection rate. Figure 5 shows the direct comparison between the results as there are no outliers for this attribute. However, for the reasons explained above, those results are difficult to compare.

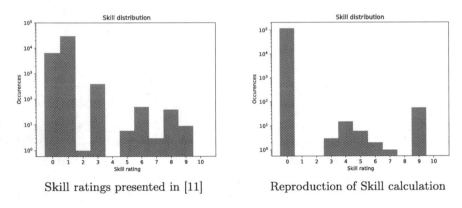

Skill ratings presented in [11]   Reproduction of Skill calculation

Fig. 5. Comparison of the Skill ratings distributions

Final Results. From the attributes defined above, we get the threat and capability ratings for each attacker. A comparison of these is shown in Fig. 6. The results are relatively similar, with most of the attackers grouped in the same place on the graph, representing the fact that most attackers are rather harmless. Here again, we see the impact of adding a time constraint when aggregating the logs with a higher density of attackers in the same group. The outliers mentioned before are also easily identified on this graph as the 21 attackers on the top left (motivation outliers) and the detached group of attackers on the right (resources outliers). However, besides the outliers that were already identified before, it is difficult to identify what characterizes the attackers in each cell of the heat map. Therefore, it is difficult to find out exactly how many attackers should be considered for a more detailed analysis. This will depend on the network administrator in charge and his or her experiences. This is an issue we address in the following.

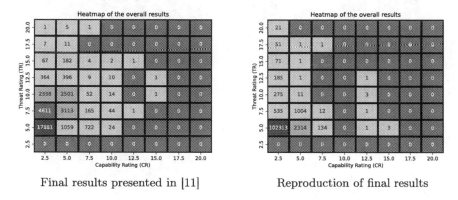

Final results presented in [11]   Reproduction of final results

Fig. 6. Comparison of the final results

4.2 Generalized Results

In this section, we present our proposed generalized methodology to characterize attackers through five attributes. We derive these attributes through features that can be extracted from many protocols. Furthermore, we include an OT protocol (i.e. Modbus) to show that the methodology is not only limited to IT protocols.

Motivation Ratings. The definition of the motivation attribute is similar to what was done in Sect. 4.1. Indeed, to determine the motivation ratings, we are using the total number of commands entered, the total time of the attack, the number of sessions initiated, and the number of protocols attacked. Results resembling the ones in Sect. 4.1 are shown on the left side of Fig. 7. There are actually a few extra outliers here from the "number of protocols" feature. Indeed, while most attackers focus on one or two protocols, some attempt to compromise up to seven different services and have, therefore, a higher motivation score. For continuity, we also show the motivation ratings scaled in the [0, 10] range after removing the outliers on the right side.

Resourcefulness Ratings. For the resourcefulness ratings, we use the inter-arrival time to capture the degree of automation of an attacker. To capture the degree of expertise and knowledge of the attacker, we use the number of

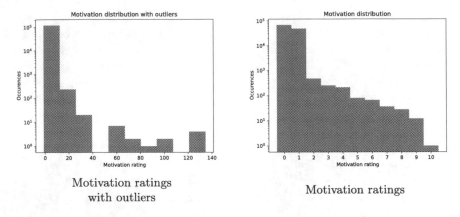

Fig. 7. Motivation results

different commands entered and the number of downloaded files. Figure 8 shows the results, which at first seem similar to the ones in Sect. 4.1. However, after removing the outliers and scaling the values, we see a different distribution. The outliers here represent attackers who sent lots of commands in a short time interval and who sent lots of different commands. Indeed, we observe that some attackers try several commands for the same goal, which would transcribe as having more expertise and knowledge in this model. The reason why most of the attackers have a medium resourcefulness score is once again because of the missing time-to-live. Indeed, the low-resourcefulness scores represent attackers who maintain a connection open for a few weeks, but only send a few commands. Therefore, the inter-arrival time is especially low for these attackers.

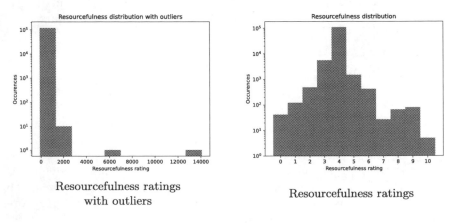

Fig. 8. Resourcefulness results

Stealth Ratings. The stealth ratings are calculated from the approached malware detection rate for the downloaded malwares, as calculated in Sect. 4.1. The idea is that if the IP address from which the malware is downloaded has been flagged as malicious by VirusTotal, then it can easily be part of a banned list. The second feature we use is the number of actions the attackers take to hide their presence. Amongst others, this includes removing written files, wiping out any written data, and resetting communication links. The last feature included in the stealth attribute is the number of scans performed by the attacker. Some observations do not explicitly contain payloads and seem to represent port scans that an attacker would do. The more scans are performed, the less stealthy the attackers are. Figure 9 shows the results with and without outliers. The single outlier, in this case, represents an attacker who takes a lot of precautions not to get caught by resetting communication links multiple times and removing any written data. On average, however, attackers do not spend much effort trying to hide themselves. The reason why the distribution of the stealth ratings is skewed on the left is that some attackers send many scans, resulting in a low stealth score. In opposition, most attackers send few scans or even no scans at all.

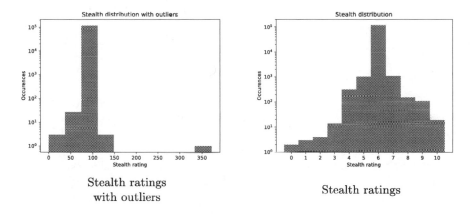

Fig. 9. Stealth results

Intention Ratings. For the intention ratings, we classify each command into one of the following actions: read, write, execute, or other. Therefore, databases are created, linking each command to the corresponding action for each protocol. For example, in SSH, changing the permissions of a file using *chmod* counts as an "other" action but running a file afterwards counts as an "execute" action. This gives, for each attack, an array describing how many times the attackers try to read data, write data, or execute some code on the system. To refine this into a 1-dimensionality characteristic we calculate $intention\_score = \alpha * execute + \beta * write + \gamma * read$. Where, α, β, and γ represent the weighting of the *execute*, *write*, and *read* values, respectively. To stay general, we evaluate each action similarly and set each weight to 0.33. Figure 10 shows the distribution of the intention ratings. The single outlier here is an attacker whose commands could all be classified as "read" and "write" actions, while targeting exclusively the Modbus protocol for more than 1500 observations. After removing the outlier and scaling the values, we see that most attackers have low intention scores, likely since most attackers perform a few scans without acting upon them.

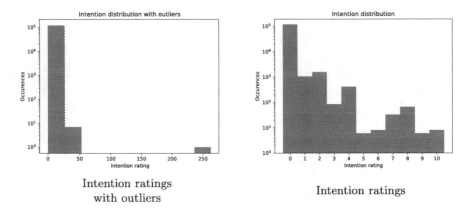

Intention ratings
with outliers

Intention ratings

Fig. 10. Intention results

Originality Ratings. The calculation of the originality ratings is done in two steps. First, a data mining algorithm is run on the attackers' commands to build a database of the most commonly used ones. This identifies 28 commands that are very frequent and used by a lot of different attackers. So far, we only use it on the SSH/Telnet observations as it yields the most promising results, but we intend to do this on the other protocols as well, as we gather more data. The originality score for each attacker starts at 28, then for each sequence used in the attackers' database we subtract 1. This means that the attackers who have an originality score of 0 enter most of the 28 commonly used commands in their attack on the SSH and Telnet protocols. Figure 11 shows the distribution of the originality ratings obtained this way. The far left side of this figure features the attackers who would be identified as "script kiddies", reusing common scripts with similar commands. The far right side of this figure features two kinds of attackers: the ones who sent only a few commands while not really performing any attack and the attackers who perform complex attacks without using common commands.

Final Results. For continuity, we can still define a threat rating and a capability rating, as shown in Fig. 12. However, we find the same problems as above; we do not know what exactly characterizes attackers in each cell and which attackers to

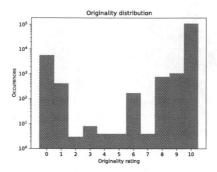

Fig. 11. Originality results

consider depends on one's experience and interpretation. Therefore, we instead propose to study the attackers with a clustering analysis. Through the use of the Elbow method applied to several metrics, we determine that the best number of clusters to split our data is 13 clusters. Figure 13 shows how many attackers each cluster contains. In the end, we have the following observations:

- The first three clusters contain more than 90% of the attackers who are identified as harmless. Indeed, these attackers usually only send a few scanning commands but do not perform any attack.
- The last cluster is the only one that contains potentially dangerous attackers. Indeed, looking back at the logs, we see that they send several hundreds or thousands of commands, which rarely use pre-built scripts. They also take several actions to hide themselves, such as removing most downloaded and written files. Finally, they try different ways to compromise the system by sending many different commands.
- The attackers who belong to the other clusters usually try a few commands like reading and writing data or exploit basic vulnerabilities such as the missing time-to-live. However, those attackers only perform basic attacks using pre-built scripts and are therefore not so alarming.

5   Discussion

As shown in Sect. 4.2, the generalized approach allows us to extend the methodology introduced by Fraunholz et al. [11] for any combination of protocols as it uses common features. Anyone who wants to analyse logs from one or several honeypots at once could therefore use this approach. Furthermore, we show that this methodology can be used on any kind of honeypot as it is shown working on low-interaction honeypots and only needs a recording of the attackers' commands. However, higher interaction honeypots will keep the attackers' interests for a longer time and might result in more attackers identified as alarming. We also propose a new way to analyse the results that returns the specific attackers that network administrators would need to consider, independently of their

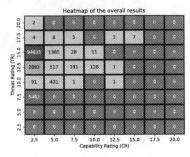

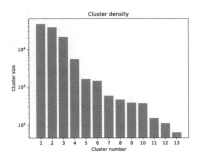

Fig. 12. Final results

Fig. 13. Cluster distribution

experience. Indeed, only the attackers who are identified as outliers through the attribute analysis and the attackers who belong to the dangerous cluster need to be considered for a more detailed analysis. This means that out of a few million logs, more than one hundred thousand attackers are identified, and out of those attackers, only 111 (49 outliers and 62 from the dangerous cluster) represent a real threat and need to be studied more thoroughly by a network administrator. However, our methodology only analyses the attackers separately and does not consider evasion techniques. Indeed, attackers who perform their attacks using multiple IP addresses are not correlated together. This is a simple evasion technique that many attackers perform and is a main limitation of the presented approach.

6   Conclusion

In this paper, we tackle the problem of cyber attacker attribution. Cyber attacker attribution tries to gain insight into attackers instead of the attacks. We expand upon an already established idea to characterize the attackers through different attributes. We generalize this approach so that it can be used on any protocol and apply it to honeypot logs collected from real attacks on several services, both IT and OT. We demonstrate that this methodology would greatly help a network administrator to identify a fixed number of attackers that need to be investigated more carefully, independently of that network administrator's experience and interpretation. Furthermore, this methodology is self-sufficient in that it does not depend on other tools and does not need human-based help to identify those attackers. In future work, our major focus will be towards considering attackers using evasion techniques. We aim to associate each attacker to a threat group as described in the MITRE ATT&CK framework [3] and link attackers who belong to the same threat group together. Finally, we will also validate this methodology on new datasets as they are gathered from the honeypots.

Acknowledgements. We would like to thank Thales Digital Solutions for their generous support to enable this work.

References

1. Cyber security breaches survey (2022). www.gov.uk/government/statistics/cyber-security-breaches-survey-2022/cyber-security-breaches-survey-2022
2. Oosterhof, M.: Cowrie (2022). www.cowrie.org
3. MITRE ATT CK, Groups (2022). www.attack.mitre.org/groups/
4. Symantec (2022). www.securitycloud.symantec.com/cc/landing
5. VirusTotal (2022). www.virustotal.com/gui/home/upload
6. Bar, A., Shapira, B., Rokach, L., Unger, M.: Identifying attack propagation patterns in honeypots using Markov chains modeling and complex networks analysis. In: 2016 IEEE International Conference on Software Science, Technology and Engineering (SWSTE 2016), pp. 28 36 (2016)
7. Buczak, A.L., Guven, E.: A survey of data mining and machine learning methods for cyber security intrusion detection. IEEE Commun. Surv. Tutorials **18**(2), 1153–1176 (2016)
8. Deshmukh, S., Rade, R., Kazi, D., et al.: Attacker behaviour profiling using stochastic ensemble of hidden Markov models. arXiv preprint arXiv:1905.11824 (2019)
9. Doynikova, E., Novikova, E., Kotenko, I.: Attacker behaviour forecasting using methods of intelligent data analysis: a comparative review and prospects. Information **11**(3), 168 (2020)
10. Fraunholz, D., Duque Anton, S., Schotten, H.D.: Introducing GAMfIS: a generic attacker model for information security. In: Begusic, D., Rozic, N., Radic, J., Saric, M. (eds.) 2017 25TH International Conference on Software, Telecommunications and Computer Networks (SOFTCOM), pp. 393–398 (2017)
11. Fraunholz, D., Krohmer, D., Anton, S.D., Schotten, H.D.: YAAS-on the attribution of honeypot data. Int. J. Cyber Situational Aware. **2**(1), 31–48 (2017)
12. Goutam, R.K.: The problem of attribution in cyber security. Int. J. Comput. Appl. **131**(7), 34–36 (2015)
13. Karafili, E., Wang, L., Lupu, E.C.: An argumentation-based reasoner to assist digital investigation and attribution of cyber-attacks. Forensic Sci. Int.-Digital Invest. **32**(S), 300925 (2020)
14. Khraisat, A., Gondal, I., Vamplew, P., Kamruzzaman, J.: Survey of intrusion detection systems: techniques, datasets and challenges. Cybersecurity **2**(1), 1–22 (2019). https://doi.org/10.1186/s42400-019-0038-7
15. Mallikarjunan, K.N., Shalinie, S.M., Preetha, G.: Real time attacker behavior pattern discovery and profiling using fuzzy rules. J. Internet Technol. **19**(5), 1567–1575 (2018)
16. Mokube, I., Adams, M.: Honeypots: concepts, approaches, and challenges. In: Proceedings of the 45th Annual Southeast Regional Conference, pp. 321–326 (2007)
17. Nawrocki, M., Wählisch, M., Schmidt, T.C., Keil, C., Schönfelder, J.: A survey on honeypot software and data analysis. arXiv preprint arXiv:1608.06249 (2016)
18. Nisioti, A., Mylonas, A., Yoo, P.D., Katos, V.: From intrusion detection to attacker attribution: a comprehensive survey of unsupervised methods. IEEE Commun. Surv. Tutorials **20**(4), 3369–3388 (2018)

Detecting Contradictions from CoAP RFC Based on Knowledge Graph

Xinguo Feng[1]([✉]), Yanjun Zhang[2], Mark Huasong Meng[3,4], and Sin G. Teo[3]

[1] The University of Queensland, St. Lucia, Australia
s.feng@uq.edu.au
[2] Cyber Security Research and Innovation (CSRI), Deakin University, Geelong, Australia
[3] Institute for Infocomm Research, A*STAR, Singapore, Singapore
[4] National University of Singapore, Singapore, Singapore

Abstract. Due to the boom of Internet of Things (IoT) in recent years, various IoT devices are connected to the internet and communicate with each other through web protocols such as the Constrained Application Protocol (CoAP). These web protocols are typically defined and described in the Request for Comments (RFC) documents, which are written in natural or semi-formal languages. Since developers largely follow the RFCs when implementing web protocols, the RFCs have become the *de facto* protocol specifications. Therefore, it is desirable to ensure that the technical details being described in the RFC are consistent, to avoid technological issues, incompatibility, security risks or even legal concerns. In this work, we propose RFCKG, a knowledge graph based contradictions detection tool for CoAP RFC. Our approach can automatically parse the RFC documents and construct knowledge graphs from them through entity extraction, relation extraction, and rule extraction. It then conducts an intra-entity and inter-entity consistency checking over the generated knowledge graph. We implement RFCKG and apply it to the main RFC (RFC7252) of CoAP, one of the most extensively used messaging protocols in IoT. Our evaluation shows that RFCKG manages to detect both direct contradiction and conditional contradictions from the RFC.

Keywords: Contradiction detection · Knowledge graph · Natural language processing · Request for comments · IoT protocols

1 Introduction

The Internet of Things (IoT) is an emerging technology in recent years. It refers to "devices and sensors" that are uniquely addressable based on their communication protocols, and are adaptable and autonomous with inherent security [5]. Its development is closely connected to many cutting-edge technologies such as blockchain [10,13], smart home [17], and machine learning [11,23,32]. During the past decade, IoT applications have experienced rapid growth and have been successfully applied on both individual (e.g., e-health, smart home) and professional levels (e.g., smart supply chain, smart city, industry IoT) [16,28]. It is estimated that there will be over 500 billion IoT devices connected to the Internet by 2030 [25].

Similar to traditional web endpoints, IoT devices communicate through the corresponding *web protocols*, which are defined by the Request for Comments (RFC) specification documents. An RFC is a specification document that describes the technical details of a web protocol. However, it is challenging to perform formal verification on an RFC because it is usually written in natural human languages. There might exist some *contradictions* and *inconsistencies* in an RFC that cannot be easily spotted. Furthermore, ambiguities might be introduced in the writing of an RFC when people have different understandings or interpretations of the protocol design. All of those issues may lead to confusion for users who want to utilise the protocol in their implementations. Take RFC7252 [24] on The Constrained Application Protocol (CoAP) as an example. Californium [12] is a significant Java implementation for CoAP. On its GitHub repository, 170 out of 2,030 issues in total (around 8%) mention the keyword RFC[1], indicating there might be discrepancies between the implementation and the description in the RFC. Those discrepancies are possibly caused by the contradictions existing in the RFC itself. Considering such contradictions may make communicating devices malfunction and introduce potential security issues, we see the need to validate if the defined technical details are consistent within the specification document.

Existing work on RFC or similar specification documents focuses on extracting finite state machines to perform security analysis dynamically [22,30]. There is limited work on detecting contradictions in natural language documents themselves, especially in specification documents like RFC. We seek a way to fill this gap. In this paper, we propose RFCKG, an approach to construct a knowledge graph from RFC documents and detect potential contradictions from the knowledge graph. We construct the knowledge graph through entity extraction, relation extraction, and rule extraction with NLP techniques, such as coreference resolution, sentence split and dependency parsing. We apply RFCKG to RFC7252 of CoAP. It manages to detect one direct contradiction and four conditional contradictions from the RFC.

We summarise our contributions as the following:

- We identify the essential components for constructing a knowledge graph from RFC documents, such as entity, relation, and rule.
- We define two types of contradictions and propose a general framework to check for them with the constructed knowledge graph.
- We propose RFCKG, a general framework to construct a knowledge graph with the extracted components of an RFC document. We demonstrate that RFCKG can successfully capture contradictions from a real-world RFC, which shows the soundness of our approach.

---

[1] Assessed on 11th August, 2022.

2   Background and Related Work

In this section, we introduce some background knowledge and related work that inspire this work.

2.1   Background

RFC. An Request for Comments (RFC) is a specification document that describes the technical details of a web protocol. It is usually written by engineers or computer scientists to describe the methods, behaviours, or innovations of the web protocol in natural human languages. Developers who wish to implement the protocol or users who wish to utilise the implementations should always refer to the RFC that defines the protocol.

Knowledge Graph. Since the technical details are all described in the specification documents, extracting the knowledge and representing it in an appropriate data structure is desired. A knowledge graph (KG) is a multi-relational graph composed of *nodes* (entities) and *edges* (relations), and each edge can be represented in a triplet (head entity, edge, tail entity).

2.2   Related Work

Knowledge Graph Representation for Documents. Li *et al.* [15] construct a knowledge graph from API documents, which can be easily accessed by developers. A knowledge graph is a multi-relational graph constructed with nodes (entities) and edges (relations), where each edge indicates the two entities are connected by a specific relation [31]. Mondal *et al.* [21] propose a way to do an end-to-end knowledge graph construction on NLP related papers to describe NLP tasks and their evaluations. Typical tasks for constructing a knowledge graph are entity extraction and relation extraction. Although there exist some tools [9, 26, 35] for these tasks, they are usually for general purposes. It is unlikely that they would work well with tasks that are domain-specific without further injecting the domain knowledge.

Rule Extraction for RFC. Rules in RFC define the functionalities and behaviours of the protocol. The natural language writing style of rules is specified in RFC 2119 [3]. In particular, it defines the modal keywords to indicate the requirement levels for rules [27]. Furthermore, RFC 8174 [14] emphasises the usage of uppercase letters for modal keywords defined in RFC 2119. Tian *et al.* [27] extract the rules with keyword matching and use dependency parsing to process the rules. Dependency parsing is also present in other work such as [33]. It works well with simple sentences but suffers with complicated sentences with multiple objects or multiple subordinate clauses.

Different Representations for Specifications. Andow *et al.* [1] construct an ontology on applications' privacy policy documents and check for logical contradictions (e.g. "Not collecting personal information" contradicts with "but collecting email address"), which is the main inspiration for this work. Wang *et al.* [30] utilise traffic, documents, and configurations of several IoT protocols and construct the finite state machines to evaluate their security. Pacheco *et al.* [22] also construct finite state machines of protocols from documents to perform attack synthesis.

Contradiction Checking for Specifications There is limited work on discovering contradictions in the text. Harabagiu *et al.* [8] propose an approach to recognise negation, contrast and contradictions for general text. Xie *et al.* [34] study the privacy policy compliance issue of virtual personal assistant apps. Wang *et al.* [29] propose a formal analysis framework to detect specification contradictions in single sign-on protocols. Mahadewa *et al.* [18] explore contradictions in privacy policy on trigger-action integration platforms. Another recent work by Meng *et al.* [19] proposes a systematic analysis methodology to scrutinize the compliance of mobile operating systems in protecting users' privacy. However, recognising contradictions in specifications documents, such as RFC, has not been well studied.

3 Problem Definition

RFCs are written in unstructured natural languages. RFCKG parses them and generates knowledge graphs that can be automatically checked for contradictions. In this section, we first define the components of the knowledge graph (Sect. 3.1), then we present the types of contradictions we target to detect in this work (Sect. 3.2).

3.1 Entity, Rule and Relation

The knowledge graph generated by RFCKG consists of three components, i.e., *entity*, *rule* and *relation*, where the *entities* and the *rules* are represented as nodes, and the *relations* are represented as edges.

Entity. We refer an entity in RFCs as an object in web protocols that has functionalities or behaviours being described. Commonly used entities include "message", "options", "token", etc. We use a single field data structure to represent an entity node in the knowledge graph: (*name*). For example, the entity "confirmable message" is represented as (*confirmable message*).

Rule. A rule node consists of a set of atomic rules appearing in a same rule statement, concatenated by logical connective "∧ (AND)", "∨ (OR)", "⊻ (XOR)" and "¬ (NEGATION)". We define an atomic rule as a four-tuple data structure:

$$(\{variable, operator, value\}, necessity),$$

in which {*variable, operator, value*} represents the rule content, and the *necessity* represents the requirement level, including "STRONG" and "WEAK", where "STRONG" indicates an absolute requirement level such as "MUST", "REQUIRED", "SHALL", "MUST NOT", and "WEAK" indicates an optional requirement such as "NOT RECOMMENDED", "MAY" and "OPTIONAL". For example, in the statement: *"Message version number MUST be set to 1 and the options of the message MUST be cached"*, the extracted rule is:

$$(\{version\_number = 1\}, STRONG) \wedge (\{cached\_options = TRUE\}, STRONG)$$

Relation. The relations RFCKG targets to extract from RFCs include (1) the relation between an entity and an entity, e.g, "A version number [entity] is a field of [relation] a message [entity]", (2) the relation between an entity and a rule, e.g., $(\{version\_number = 1\}, STRONG)$ [rule] is a rule of [relation] confirmable message [entity], and (3) the conditional relation between a rule and a rule. For example, in the statement *"If the version number of a message is not set to 1, the options of the message MUST NOT be cached"*, $(\{version\_number\ ! = 1\}, STRONG)$ [rule] is a condition of [relation] $(\{cached\_options = FALSE\}, STRONG)$ [rule]. The former is the antecedent rule and the latter is the consequent rule.

Figure 1 illustrates the KG representation of the rule statement "If the version number of a message is set to 1, the options of the message MUST NOT be cached".

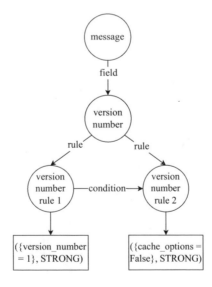

Fig. 1. RFCKG's knowledge graph representation of an example statement in RFC: "If the version number of a message is set to 1, the options of the message MUST NOT be cached."

3.2   Contradictions

The core idea of RFCKG is to represent an unstructured RFC document under analysis as a structured knowledge graph, and then to check its rules for contradiction detection. In particular, we define two types of contradictions as follows:

– **Direct contradiction.** This occurs when different rules of a same entity e - denoted as $\{r_1, ..., r_n\}_e$ contradicts with each other. That is, the conjunctions of rules is evaluated as false, i.e.,

$$\bigwedge_{i=1}^{n} \{r_i\}_e = FALSE$$

A direct contradiction is regarded as an erroneous inconsistency of an RFC which may lead to implementation issues. This contradiction captures the following three scenarios.

(1) Contradiction among plain rules. A plain rule refers to a rule that is not an antecedent rule or consequent rule. For example, consider the following rule statements *"The version number of a message MUST be set to 1"* and *"Message version number MUST be 0"*. The rules for these rule statements are $(\{version\_number = 1\}$, STRONG$)$ and $(\{version\_number = 0\}$, STRONG$)$. These are plain rules as they are not antecedent rules or consequent rules. We concatenate them and see that they evaluate as false.

$$(version\_number = 1) \wedge (version\_number = 0) = FALSE$$

(2) Contradictions between plain rule and consequent rule. It occurs when a plain rule states "A must be True", while a consequent of a conditional rule states "A is False". For example, consider the following rule statements *"The version number of a message MUST be set to 1"* and *"If the options of the message are cached, the version number of the message MUST be set to 0"*. The rule extraction and evaluation are the same as in the example above.

(3) Contradictions between the consequent of conditional rules. For example, two conditional rules state the same antecedent while implying a contradicted consequent. For example, consider the following rule statements *"If the options of the message are not cached, the version number of the message MUST be set to 1"* and *"If the options of the message are not cached, the version number of the message MUST be set to 0"*. The rule extraction and evaluation are the same as in the example above.

– **Conditional contradiction.** This occurs when the antecedent of conditional rules contradicts others. Denote c_i as an antecedent rule of a conditional proposition, RFCKG reports a conditional contradiction if

$$\bigwedge_{i=1}^{n} \{r_i, c_i\}_e = FALSE$$

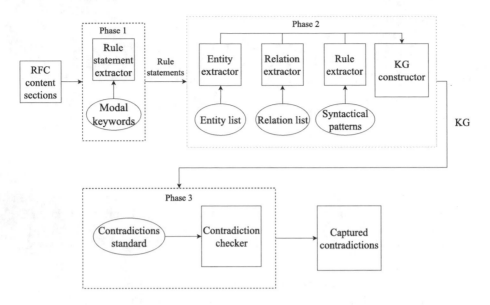

Fig. 2. Overview of approach showing three phases

For example, consider the following rule statements *"Message version number SHOULD be set to 1"* and *"If the version number of a message is not 1, the options MUST be cached"*. The rule for the first statement is ({*version_number* = 1}, STRONG), which is a plain rule. The antecedent rule for the second statement is ({*version_number* != 1}, STRONG). We concatenate them and see they evaluate as false.

$$(version\_number = 1) \wedge (version\_number\ != 1) = FALSE$$

The conditional contradictions extracted by RFCKG can highlight the instruction of error handling in RFC, which is likely ignored by the developers especially when such statements appear in different places in the document.

4   RFCKG Approach

We design RFCKG as a three-phase approach that consists of *rule statements extraction*, *knowledge graph construction* and *Contradiction detection*, as shown in Fig. 2.

4.1   Rule Statement Extraction

This phase aims to extract statements that contain rules of interest from RFCs. We first remove the irrelevant information from the document including the headers, list of content, acknowledgement, references, figures, and tables. We then use the `Natural Language Toolkit (NLTK)` [2] to split the rest of the document into sentences.

Table 1. Modal keywords for extracting rule statements

STRONG keywords	WEAK keywords
MUST, REQUIRED, SHALL, MUST NOT, SHALL NOT	SHOULD, RECOMMENDED, SHOULD NOT, NOT RECOMMENDED, MAY, OPTIONAL

Since the release of RFC2119 (which specifies the standard for keywords usage in RFCs to indicate requirement levels) in 1997 [3], RFC documents (released after 1997) enforce the use of capitalized modal verbs (such as "MUST", "MAY" and etc.) to indicate the requirement level of a rule in the specification. We therefore examine the capitalized modal verbs used in the sentences, and identify a sentence that contains those capitalized modal verbs as a rule statement. More specifically, we extract the strong statements and weak statements based on the modal keywords as shown in Table 1 following the definition of prior work [27]. Algorithm 1 in Appendix B demonstrates the details for rule statements extraction.

4.2   Knowledge Graph Construction

This phase aims to identify *entities*, *rules* and *relations* based on the extracted statements, and represent them in a knowledge graph.

4.2.1   Entity Extraction

To identify the entities, we select 56 types of common entities from summarising the terminologies from the Terminology section of RFC7252 as shown in Table 5 in Appendix A. Given a rule statement, if an entity in the predefined list appears in the statement, we add it to our extracted entity list.

4.2.2   Rule Extraction

There are seven steps for extracting rules from rule statements, which are rule context construction, rule entity determination, co-reference resolution, sentence splitting and rephrasing, conditions identifications, rule construction, and variable normalisation.

- **Context construction.** For each rule statement we extract, it is one complete sentence. To better address the later tasks, we need to construct a semantic context environment for each rule statement. For each rule statement we extract, we locate its position in the RFC document and backtrack five sentences before it. This is based on the assumption that, if a rule statement describes an entity's behaviours, the neighbouring sentences before it should also mention the same entity.
- **Rule entity determination.** When we construct the Rule nodes in a later step, we need to connect each Rule node to a corresponding Entity node. For each rule statement context, we iterate through the extracted entity list and count the occurrences of each entity. We take the entity that appears the most

as the rule entity. If there are multiple entities that have the same number of occurrences, we take the one that appears the last as the rule entity.

- **Co-reference resolution.** It is common in natural languages to use co-references to refer to words or phrases that are mentioned before. We aim to find the co-references in the rule statements and substitute them with the actual words or phrases they are referring to, so that we have complete and rich information in each rule statement for the next step. We use the co-reference resolution functionality in the spaCy [9] NLP tool to address the pronoun co-reference, such as "it", "them", etc. For other co-references that the tool cannot address, such as "this field", we use the rule entity we identify for each rule to substitute them.

- **Sentence splitting and rephrasing.** A rule statement is a sentence that describes one or several behaviours of an entity, which means the structure of the sentence can be complex. It would be easier to process the rule statement if we can split one complex sentence into multiple simple sentences but retain the semantics that describes the behaviours, so that we can process these simple sentences one at a time. To address this, we use the dependency parsing functionality in the spaCy [9] NLP tool and look for the root of the rule statement, then look for words that have a conjunction dependency relation with it. We then look for the subject of the rule statement, split the rule statement with the conjunction words, and concatenate each of the split sentences with the subject in the front. In this way, we split and rephrase the complex rule statement into multiple complete but simple rule statements. To determine the logical connective between the split sentences, we see if the keyword "and" or "or" appears in the original rule statement. If "or" appears, we determine the logical connective to be "$\lor$ (OR)". If not, we determine the logical connective to be "$\land$ (AND)".

- **Condition identification.** Recall that we define a type of contradiction as conditional contradiction in Sect. 3.2. For a rule statement, we need to know if there exists a conditional relation between different behaviours. To address this, we look for rule statements that start with the word "If", and split it at the first comma. We give the first part an *antecedent* label to indicate it is an antecedent rule, and the following part a *consequent* label to indicate it is a consequent rule. For the other situation that we describe above, we give the split sentences an *entity* label, indicating that they are plain entity rules.

- **Rule construction.** Recall that we define an atomic rule as a four-tuple data structure:

$$(\{variable, operator, value\}, necessity),$$

We construct atomic rules on a split sentence level. The rules we try to construct are operations that the entity performs to describe its behaviours. There are two main types of atomic rules. The first type specifically describes that an item is set to, equal to, larger, or smaller than a value. The other type describes an operation being performed, but does not specifically describe any value. We review part of the split sentences and define 59 syntactical patterns for spaCy [9] to extract variables for constructing the atomic rules. A syntactical pattern is a pattern that describes the dependency relations between the components we want to extract.

For example, consider the following rule statement *"Implementations of this specification MUST set the version number to 1"*. The variable we want to extract from the first example above is *"version_number"*. We look at the dependency relations of this sentence, as shown in Fig. 3. We define the pattern as *{verb, dobj, compound, prep, pobj}*, indicating that we want to extract the verb, the direct object of the verb, the compound of the direct object, the preposition of the verb, and the prepositional object of the preposition. The information we extract with this pattern from this sentence is *{set, number, version, to, 1}*. We organise the order of these words and construct the atomic rule as *({version_number, =, 1}, STRONG)*, in which the necessity "STRONG" comes from the fact that the original rule statement is a strong rule statement.

For each split sentence that belongs to a rule statement, we apply these 59 defined patterns to them and construct atomic rules accordingly. Then we apply the logical connective that we extracted above to concatenate these atomic rules to construct a Rule object that represents the original rule statement. The *entity*, *antecedent* and *consequent* rule labels are carried over to these constructed rule objects.

- **Variable normalisation.** The 59 defined syntactical patterns are applied to all split and rephrased sentences, as we want the defined syntactical patterns to be able to generalise to more sentences that have similar structures. There could be situations where variables extracted from different patterns actually mean the same thing. Also, different words might have the same or similar meanings. These different variables that actually could mean the same should be grouped as one variable as it might affect the accuracy of the contradiction checking later. To address this, for each Entity node, we gather all the variables of all the Rule nodes under it. For each variable, we use the spaCy [9] tool with its internal word embedding to get the variable's average embedding vector. Then we compute the cosine similarity between all variable pairs. If the similarity is larger than 0.9, we mark them as similar variables. After we gather all the similar variables, we substitute the variable that has the longer name with the shortest one between them.

4.2.3 Relation Extraction

For the entity-entity relation extraction, we examine each combination of the entity pair we extracted and identify the relation defined in Table 5. For the entity-rule relation extraction, recall that we already identify that each rule should belong to an entity. We simply use the "rule" relation defined in Table 5 in Appendix A. For the rule-rule relation extraction, if a rule has the *antecedent* rule label and the

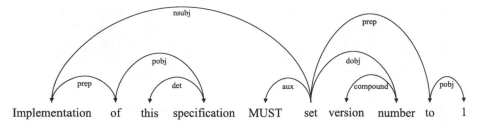

Fig. 3. Dependency relations of the example rule statement "Implementations of this specification MUST set version number to 1"

following rule from the same original rule statement has the *consequent* rule label, we use the "condition" relation defined in Table 5 in Appendix A.

4.2.4   Graph Representation

We use the open source library `NetworkX` [7] for the graph construction. We first create Entity nodes for the extracted entities and add them into the graph. We then create directed edge between Entity nodes and connect them with the corresponding relation as the edge label. For example, as a "confirmable message" [entity] is a type of [rule] a "message" [entity], the two entities are first added into the graph and an edge with the label "type" is then added which points from "message" to "confirmable message". We go through all the extracted entity pairs and their relations, and a skeleton graph (without Rule nodes) is constructed.

We then construct the Rule nodes and their corresponding entity-rule and the rule-rule edges. For each Rule node, we first add it to the graph. Then we create a directed edge with a "rule" label pointing from its possessor Entity node to itself. For example, Rule(rule={"version_number:=": 1}, necessity="STRONG") belongs to Entity(version_number). We complete the entity-rule edges construction at this state. Then we examine each Rule node and see whether it carries an *antecedent* rule label from the previous steps. If it does, we locate the corresponding Rule node that carries the *consequent* rule label and create a directed edge with a "condition" label pointing from the antecedent Rule node to the consequent Rule node.

4.3   Contradiction Detection

We now describe the contradictions detection step with the knowledge graph constructed described above. We do contradictions detection on the entity level. Recall that each atomic rule within a Rule node is constructed with the variable, the operator and the value. When checking for contradictions for an entity, we concatenate the atoms within the same Rule node with the corresponding logical operator as the Rule node's expression, then we concatenate the different Rule nodes' expressions under the same Entity node with the "∧ (AND)" operator. We then use the open source Python library `SymPy` [20] as a solver to see if it is consistent (return True of False).

To prepare for contradiction checking, we need to transform the variables and values into appropriate forms, so that the solver can construct the expressions and evaluate if they are consistent or not. For each Entity node in the graph, we traverse the graph to get all the Rule nodes that it is connected to, and separate them into entity rules, antecedent rules and consequent rules. We collect all the unique variables we extracted in the three rule sets and create a unique symbol for each of them. We also collect all the unique values for these variables. There are multiple value types for the values, such as numerical, string, and boolean. We keep the numerical values as they are and transform the other value types into unique integer values for the solver as the solver can only accept numerical values. We start by taking a seed integer, for example, 10,000, and we iterate through all the values that are not numerical. If we found a value that is not transformed yet, we assign this seed integer to it and increment the seed by 1 as the new seed, and repeat the process. To determine the appropriate value of the seed, we simply go through all the unique numerical values and pick one that does not collide with the existing values. For the operators ">", ">=", "=", "!=", "<=", and "<", we keep them and call the corresponding evaluation functions in the SymPy [20] library.

We check for direct contractions first. Recall that there are three types of direct contradictions. For the first type of contradiction, which is a contradiction between plain rules of an Entity node, we take each variable in each Rule node in the entity rules set and create an atom logical expression for it with its corresponding operator and value. We store this expression and iterate the next variable. We create another atom logical expression for the next variable and concatenate it with the previous one with the logical connective described in the Rule node. After iterating all the variables in the Rule node, we have a final expression that represents this particular Rule node. We store this final expression then iterate to the next Rule node and repeat the process. We then concatenate these two expressions that represent two different Rule nodes with "∧" as these are plain entity rules, and the variables in them should all be consistent. If it is evaluated as true, we store the concatenated expression and iterate to the next Rule node and repeat the process. If it is evaluated as false, then we find a direct contradiction. We record the contradiction and remove the second expression from the concatenated expression and iterate to the next Rule node for further contradiction checking. Algorithm 2 in Appendix B demonstrates this process.

The contradiction detection for the other two types of direct contradictions are similar. For the second type, we keep the final expression that is evaluated as true from when we check for the plain entity rules, and iterate through all the consequent Rule nodes in the same process described above. For the third type, we only iterate through the consequent Rule nodes that are pointed from the same antecedent Rule node without the final entity rules expression, in the same process described above. For any direct contradiction found, if both original rule statements have the same requirement level (both strong or weak), we cannot

Table 2. Results on knowledge graph construction from RFC7252

Rule statements			Graph nodes			Rule nodes			
Strong	Weak	Total	Entity	Rule	Total	Plain	Antecedent	Consequent	Total
136	81	217	28	319	347	220	41	58	319

recommend which one to follow. If not, we can recommend to follow the one with a strong requirement level.

We then check for conditional contradictions. The process is also similar to direct contradiction checking. We keep the final expression that is evaluated as true from when we check for the plain entity rules. We then iterate through each Rule node in the conditional rules set, construct the rule expression, concatenate the rule expression with the evaluated entity rule expression with "∧" and check if there is a contradiction between them. We do not store the concatenated expression. We iterate to the next conditional rule and repeat the process.

5   Evaluation

We implement RFCKG on RFC7252 on the CoAP protocol. In this section, we report and evaluate the results.

5.1   Knowledge Graph Construction

RFCKG extracts 217 rule statements in total on RFC7252, with 136 strong statements and 81 weak statements. From the rule statements, we extract and construct 28 Entity nodes with the predefined entity list and use two predefined relations "type" and "field" to construct the skeleton knowledge graph. From the 217 rule statements, we construct 319 Rule nodes and use the predefined relation "rule" to connect them to the corresponding Entity nodes. Out of the 319 Rule nodes, there are 220 plain entity rules, 41 antecedent rules and 58 consequent rules. RFCKG extracts the knowledge that describes the behaviours of entities in rules and represent it in a knowledge graph data structure, which can be easily accessed. Table 2 shows the results of our knowledge graph construction.

5.2   Contradiction Detection

For the contradictions checking, we captured 21 contradictions in total, with 16 direct contradictions and five conditional contradictions. Out of the 16 direct contradictions, one of them is true positive, which is a weak contradiction, and 15 of them are false positive. Out of the five conditional contradictions, four of them are true positive, and one of them is false positive. Table 3 shows the result of contradiction checking. Table 4 shows the five detected contradictions and their original rule statements.

Table 3. Results on contradiction detection from RFC7252

	True positive	False positive	Total
Direct contradiction	1	15	16
Conditional contradiction	4	1	5
Contradiction	5	16	21

Table 4. Detected contradictions and their original rule statements

	RS1	RS2	Type
C1	Implementations SHOULD also support longer length identifiers and MAY support shorter lengths	Note that the shorter lengths provide less security against attacks, and their use is NOT RECOMMENDED	Direct
C2	The Token Length field MUST be set to 0 and bytes of data MUST NOT be present after the Message ID field	If there are any bytes, they MUST be processed as a message format error	Conditional
C3	An option that is not repeatable MUST NOT be included more than once in a message	An option MAY be included one or more times in a message	Conditional
C4	Any attempt to supply a NoSec response to a DTLS request simply does not match the request and therefore MUST be rejected	Unless it does match an unrelated NoSec request	Conditional
C5	Implementations of this specification MUST set this field to 1 (01 binary)	Messages with unknown version numbers MUST be silently ignored	Conditional

5.2.1 Direct Contradiction

Refer to the two original rule statements for C1 in Table 4. The first rule statement describes shorter length identifiers MAY be supported. The second rule sentence describes that the use of shorter length identifiers is NOT RECOMMENDED. The variable extracted from both rule statements "support shorter length". The value from the first statement is True and the value from the second statement is False, hence it yields a contradiction. This contradiction might cause confusion for implementations for this functionality, e.g., one implementation supports shorter length identifiers and the others do not. Also, they are on the same requirement level, and one cannot overwrite the other.

5.2.2 Conditional Contradiction

For the four true positive conditional contradictions, all of them are to describe the handling of the situations that are different from the entity plain rules.

Refer to C5 in Table 4. The variable extracted from both rule statements is "version number", while the first rule statement states that it should be equal to 1 and the second rule statement states that it should not be equal to 1. The antecedent of the second rule statement is contradicting the first rule statement, but the consequent describes what should be done if it happens. Although these conditional contradictions are not real inconsistencies but to describe the error handling, they still deserve to be highlighted for developers to make sure the error handling practice is correctly followed.

5.2.3 False Positive Analysis

We now take a closer look at the false positive cases we found and understand why they happen. Recall that when we extract the variables from the rule statements, we defined 59 syntactical patterns for sentences with different syntactical structures and apply them to all rule statements. Then we normalise variables that have a similar meaning as one variable. The reason why these false positive contradictions are captured is that, some of the syntactical patterns are extracting irrelevant variables from some rule statements, and they are normalised as one variable, which is the same variable from other rule statements with different values. Hence a contradiction is observed. We examine all the false positive contradictions with their original rule statements, the extracted variables and the normalised variables. We find that all of them are captured due to this reason.

6 Discussion and Future Directions

We now discuss some limitations of this work and some possible future directions.

Entity and Relation Extraction. The construction of a knowledge graph is based on predefined lists of entities and relations, and it requires prior knowledge to determine the relation between the entity pairs. There exist tools for general purpose entity extraction and relation extraction. More advanced NLP tools, such as BERT [6] and GPT-3 [4], are language models pre-trained on large scale corpora and they perform well on a range of general tasks. A possible future direction is to take these existing models and further pre-train them with domain specific corpora, so that they would adapt their parameters to better relate different words within the domain specific language environment. Then we take these further pre-trained models and use them on the desired downstream tasks to construct the knowledge graph in a more automated way.

Co-reference Resolution and Sentence Simplification. Recall that when we construct the Rule nodes in Sect. 4.2.2, we introduce the co-reference resolution and spilt and rephrase techniques. Although they improve the process to construct the knowledge graph, they also input noise and errors into the graph when they cannot identify the correct co-reference or split the sentence in the wrong way. The co-reference resolution tool we use is also for general purpose. The similar idea to further pre-train an existing language model to inject domain knowledge also applies here.

Introduced Noise. In our approach, although there is some noise being introduced, we argue that it is still reasonable to do so. From our true positive direct contradiction case, the original variable being extracted are "support shorter lengths" and "use shorter lengths", and they have the value True and False respectively. If we do not normalise these two variables as one, we will not find this contradiction exists. Furthermore, our work does not target to only capture precise contradictions, but to send out warnings when we suspect that there might be a contradiction. However, a possible solution to improve this might be to split the sentences into several clusters, where each cluster contains sentences that have similar syntactical structures. We might be able to describe the syntactical structure of a sentence with features like the number of syntactical roles (verbs, subjects, etc.), positions of these roles, and so on.

Implicit Condition. Recall that when we construct the antecedent Rule nodes and the consequent Rule nodes, we identify the conditions based on the explicit use of the keyword "if". There exist some situations that the condition is expressed implicitly in the rule statements. A systematic way to identify these implicit conditional relations is worth being explored.

Reasoning Scalability. We observe that the SymPy [20] solver we use for contradictions detection is not satisfactorily efficient even on a single specification document (RFC7252), due to the large number of variables extracted and evaluated. This indicates there would be a scalability issue when we apply this approach to a broader range of documents. A recent work by Zhang *et al.* [36] inspires us that it is possible to utilise the ability of deep neural networks for more efficient reasoning.

7   Conclusion

In this work, we propose RFCKG, a knowledge graph based contradiction detection tool for RFC documents. We implement it on RFC7252 of CoAP and successfully detect five contradictions, with one direct contradiction and four conditional contradictions. We evaluate the results and propose future directions to improve our approach to be more accurate and more automated.

Appendix A Table for Predefined Entities and Relations

Table 5. Predefined entities and relations

Entities	Relations
message, empty message, version number, token length, payload, option, option number, option delta, configuration, option length, endpoint, recipient, option value, confirmable message, acknowledgement message, reset message, non-confirmable message, message id, client, get, put, delete, server, sender, response code, proxy, uri-path option, proxy-uri option, etag option, location-path option, constrained networks, datagram transport layer security, dtls, pre-shared key, psk, raw public key, x.509 certificate, certificate, application environment, post, if-match option, if-none-match option, origin server, content-format, resource discovery, intermediary, forward-proxy, reverse-proxy, coap-to-coap proxy, cross-proxy, separate response, critical option, elective option, unsafe option, safe-to-forward option	type, field, rule, condition

Appendix B Algorithms for Extracting Rule Statements and Detecting Contradictions

---

Algorithm 1. Extracting rule statements from RFC

   Input: Preprocessed RFC document $\mathcal{R}$
   Output: strong and weak rules statements sets
1: $modal\_keywords \leftarrow$ ["MUST", ... , "MAY", "OPTIONAL"]
2: $strong\_modal\_keywords \leftarrow$ ["MUST", ..., "SHALL"]
3: $strong\_rules\_statements \leftarrow [\,]$
4: $weak\_rules\_statements \leftarrow [\,]$
5: $rfc\_sentences \leftarrow NLTK.split\_sentences(\mathcal{R})$
6: **for** $i \leftarrow 0,\ length(rfc\_sentences)$ **do**
7:    $sentence \leftarrow rfc\_sentences[i]$
8:    **for** $j \leftarrow 0,\ length(modal\_keywords)$ **do**
9:      $keyword \leftarrow modal\_keywords[j]$
10:     **if** $keyword$ **in** $sentence$ **then**
11:       **if** $keyword$ **in** $strong\_modal\_keywords$ **then**
12:         $strong\_rules\_statements.append(sentence)$
13:       **else**
14:         $weak\_rules\_statements.append(sentence)$
15:       **break**
16: **return** $strong\_rules\_statements,\ weak\_rules\_statements$

Algorithm 2. Check Direct Contradictions

Input: entity_rules_set, variable_symbols_set, variable_values_set
Output: direct contradictions set, entity evaluation

1: *entity_evaluation* ← *True*
2: *entity_rules_evaluated* ← [ ]
3: *direct_contradictions* ← [ ]
4: **for** i ← 0, *length*(*entity_rules_set*) **do**
5:      *rule* ← *entity_rules_set*[i]
6:      *rule_items* ← *rule.items*
7:      *rule_necessity* ← *rule.necessity*
8:      *rule_operator* ← *rule.operator*
9:      *rule_evaluation* ← *None*
10:     **for** j ← 0, *length*(*rule_items*) **do**
11:         *variable, operator, value* ← *rule_items*[j]
12:         *variable_symbol* ← *variable_symbols_set*[*variable*]
13:         *value_integer* ← *variable_values_set*[*value*]
14:         *expression* ← *SymPy.operation*(*variable_symbol, operator, value_integer*)
15:         **if** *rule_evaluation* **is** *None* **then**
16:             *rule_evaluation* ← *expression*
17:         **else**
18:             **if** *rule_operator* **is** "AND" **then**
19:                 *rule_evaluation* ← *rule_evaluation* & *expression*
20:             **else**
21:                 *rule_evaluation* ← *rule_evaluation* | *expression*
22:     *temp_entity_evaluation* = *entity_evaluation* & *rule_evaluation*
23:     **if** *temp_entity_evaluation* **is** *False* **then**
24:         *direct_contradictions.append*((*entity_rules_evaluated, rule*))
25:     **else**
26:         *entity_evaluation* ← *temp_entity_evaluation*
27:         *entity_rules_evaluated.append*(*rule*)
28: **return** *direct_contradictions, entity_evaluation*

References

1. Andow, B., et al.: {PolicyLint}: investigating internal privacy policy contradictions on google play. In: 28th USENIX Security Symposium (USENIX security 19), pp. 585–602 (2019)
2. Bird, S., Klein, E., Loper, E.: Natural language processing with Python: analyzing text with the natural language toolkit. O'Reilly Media, Inc (2009)
3. Bradner, S.: Key words for use in RFCs to indicate requirement levels. http://datatracker.ietf.org/doc/html/rfc2119 (1997). Assessed 04 Aug 2022
4. Brown, T., et al.: Language models are few-shot learners. Adv. Neural. Inf. Process. Syst. **33**, 1877–1901 (2020)
5. Chegini, H., Naha, R.K., Mahanti, A., Thulasiraman, P.: Process automation in an IoT-fog-cloud ecosystem: a survey and taxonomy. IoT **2**(1), 92–118 (2021)
6. Devlin, J., Chang, M.W., Lee, K., Toutanova, K.: BERT: pre-training of deep bidirectional transformers for language understanding. arXiv preprint arXiv:1810.04805 (2018)
7. Hagberg, A.A., Schult, D.A., Swart, P.J.: Exploring network structure, dynamics, and function using networkx. In: Varoquaux, G., Vaught, T., Millman, J. (eds.) Proceedings of the 7th Python in Science Conference, pp. 11–15. Pasadena, CA USA (2008)

8. Harabagiu, S., Hickl, A., Lacatusu, F.: Negation, contrast and contradiction in text processing. In: AAAI, vol. 6, pp. 755–762 (2006)
9. Honnibal, M., Montani, I.: spaCy 2: Natural language understanding with Bloom embeddings, convolutional neural networks and incremental parsing (2017)
10. Huh, S., Cho, S., Kim, S.: Managing IoT devices using blockchain platform. In: 2017 19th International Conference on Advanced Communication Technology (ICACT), pp. 464–467. IEEE (2017)
11. Khan, L.U., Saad, W., Han, Z., Hossain, E., Hong, C.S.: Federated learning for internet of things: recent advances, taxonomy, and open challenges. IEEE Commun. Surv. Tutorials **PP**(99), 1 (2021)
12. Kraus, A.: californium. https://github.com/eclipse/californium (2016). Accessed 11 Aug 2022
13. Le, D.P., Meng, H., Su, L., Yeo, S.L., Thing, V.: Biff: a blockchain-based IoT forensics framework with identity privacy. In: TENCON 2018–2018 IEEE region 10 conference, pp. 2372–2377. IEEE (2018)
14. Leiba, B.: Ambiguity of uppercase vs lowercase in RFC 2119 key words. https://datatracker.ietf.org/doc/html/rfc8174 (2017). Accessed 04 Aug 2022
15. Li, H., et al.: Improving API caveats accessibility by mining API caveats knowledge graph. In: 2018 IEEE International Conference on Software Maintenance and Evolution (ICSME), pp. 183–193. IEEE (2018)
16. Lynggaard, P., Skouby, K.E.: Complex IoT systems as enablers for smart homes in a smart city vision. Sensors **16**(11), 1840 (2016)
17. Mahadewa, K., et al.: Scrutinizing implementations of smart home integrations. IEEE Trans. Softw. Eng. **47**, 2667–2683 (2019)
18. Mahadewa, K., et al.: Identifying privacy weaknesses from multi-party trigger-action integration platforms. In: Proceedings of the 30th ACM SIGSOFT International Symposium on Software Testing and Analysis, pp. 2–15 (2021)
19. Meng, M.H., et al.: Post-GDPR threat hunting on android phones: dissecting OS-level safeguards of user-unresettable identifiers. In: The Network and Distributed System Security Symposium (NDSS) (2023)
20. Meurer, A., et al.: SymPy: symbolic computing in python. Peer. J. Comput. Sci. **3**, e103 (2017)
21. Mondal, I., Hou, Y., Jochim, C.: End-to-end NLP knowledge graph construction. arXiv preprint arXiv:2106.01167 (2021)
22. Pacheco, M.L., von Hippel, M., Weintraub, B., Goldwasser, D., Nita-Rotaru, C.: Automated attack synthesis by extracting finite state machines from protocol specification documents. arXiv preprint arXiv:2202.09470 (2022)
23. Shanthamallu, U.S., Spanias, A., Tepedelenlioglu, C., Stanley, M.: A brief survey of machine learning methods and their sensor and IoT applications. In: 2017 8th International Conference on Information, Intelligence, Systems & Applications (IISA), pp. 1–8. IEEE (2017)
24. Shelby, Z., Hartke, K., Bormann, C.: The constrained application protocol (CoAP). http://datatracker.ietf.org/doc/html/rfc7252 (2014). Accessed 04 Aug 2022
25. Singh, A.K.: We will be surrounded by 500 billion connected devices by 2030, says anter virk of subcom. https://opportunityindia.franchiseindia.com/article/we-will-be-surrounded-by-500-billion-connected-devices-by-2030-says-anter-virk-of-subcom-35012 (2022). Accessed 28 Aug 2022
26. Soares, L.B., FitzGerald, N., Ling, J., Kwiatkowski, T.: Matching the blanks: distributional similarity for relation learning. arXiv preprint arXiv:1906.03158 (2019)

27. Tian, C., Chen, C., Duan, Z., Zhao, L.: Differential testing of certificate validation in SSL/TLS implementations: an RFC-guided approach. ACM. Trans. Softw. Eng. Methodol. **28**(4), 1–37 (2019).https://doi.org/10.1145/3355048

28. Uddin, H., et al.: IoT for 5g/b5g applications in smart homes, smart cities, wearables and connected cars. In: 2019 IEEE 24th International Workshop on Computer Aided Modeling and Design of Communication Links and Networks (CAMAD), pp. 1–5. IEEE (2019)

29. Wang, K., Bai, G., Dong, N., Dong, J.S.: A framework for formal analysis of privacy on SSO protocols. In: Lin, X., Ghorbani, A., Ren, K., Zhu, S., Zhang, A. (eds.) SecureComm 2017. LNICST, vol. 238, pp. 763–777. Springer, Cham (2018). https://doi.org/10.1007/978-3-319-78813-5_41

30. Wang, Q., et al.: {MPInspector}: A systematic and automatic approach for evaluating the security of {IoT} messaging protocols. In: 30th USENIX Security Symposium (USENIX Security 21), pp. 4205–4222 (2021)

31. Wang, Q., Mao, Z., Wang, B., Guo, L.: Knowledge graph embedding: a survey of approaches and applications. IEEE Trans. Knowl. Data Eng. **29**(12), 2724–2743 (2017)

32. Xiao, L., Wan, X., Lu, X., Zhang, Y., Wu, D.: IoT security techniques based on machine learning: how do IoT devices use AI to enhance security? IEEE Signal Process. Mag. **35**(5), 41–49 (2018)

33. Xie, D., et al.: DocTer: documentation-guided fuzzing for testing deep learning API functions. In: Proceedings of the 31st ACM SIGSOFT International Symposium on Software Testing and Analysis, pp. 176–188 (2022)

34. Xie, F., et al.: Scrutinizing privacy policy compliance of virtual personal assistant apps. In: Proceedings of the 37th IEEE/ACM International Conference on Automated Software Engineering (ASE) (2022)

35. Zhang, B., Xu, Y., Li, J., Wang, S., Ren, B., Gao, S.: SMDM: tackling zero shot relation extraction with semantic max-divergence metric learning. Appl. Intell. 1–16 (2022). https://doi.org/10.1007/s10489-022-03596-z

36. Zhang, C., et al.: Towards better generalization for neural network-based sat solvers. In: Gama, J., Li, T., Yu, Y., Chen, E., Zheng, Y., Teng, F. (eds) Advances in Knowledge Discovery and Data Mining. PAKDD 2022. LNCS, vol. 13281. Springer, Cham (2022). https://doi.org/10.1007/978-3-031-05936-0_16

Mobile Security

A First Look at Android Apps' Third-Party Resources Loading

Hina Qayyum[1], Muhammad Salman[1], I. Wayan Budi Sentana[1],
Duc Linh Giang Nguyen[1], Muhammad Ikram[1](✉), Gareth Tyson[2],
and Mohamed Ali Kaafar[1]

[1] Macquarie University, Sydney, NSW 2109, Australia
muhammad.ikram@mq.edu.au

[2] Hong Kong University of Science and Technology, Guangzhou, China

Abstract. Like websites, mobile apps import a range of external resources from various third-party domains. In succession, the third-party domains can further load resources hosted on other domains. For each mobile app, this creates a dependency chain underpinned by a form of implicit trust between the app and transitively connected third-parties. Hence, a such implicit trust may leave apps' developers unaware of what resources are loaded within their apps. In this work, we perform a large-scale study of dependency chains in 7,048 free Android mobile apps. We characterize the third-party resources used by apps and explore the presence of potentially malicious resources loaded via implicit trust. We find that around 94% of apps (with a number of installs greater than 500K) load resources from implicitly trusted parties. We find several different types of resources, most notably JavaScript codes, which may open the way to a range of exploits. These JavaScript codes are implicitly loaded by 92.3% of Android apps. Using VirusTotal, we classify 1.18% of third-party resources as suspicious. Our observations raise concerns for how apps are currently developed, and suggest that more rigorous vetting of in-app third-party resource loading is required.

1 Introduction

Mobile apps have become extremely popular [54], however, recently there has been a flurry of research [25,31] exposing how many of these apps carry out misleading or even malicious activities. These acts range from low-risk (*e.g.,* usage of services and inter process communication which may drain the battery, CPU or memory) to high-risk (*e.g.,* harvesting data and ex-filtrating to third-parties [31].

We are interested in understanding the root source of this suspicious (or *malicious*) activity. Past work has treated this question as trivial—naturally, the root source of suspicious activity is the app's developer [25]. However, in this paper, we counter this assumption and shed light on the true complexity of suspicious app activity. We focus on the use of dynamically loaded *third-party* resources within apps. Mobile apps often load these resources from a range of third-party domains which include, for example, ad providers, tracking services, content distribution networks (CDNs) and analytics services. Although loading

X. Yuan et al. (Eds.): NSS 2022, LNCS 13787, pp. 193–213, 2022.
https://doi.org/10.1007/978-3-031-23020-2_11

these resources is a well known design decision that establishes *explicit trust* between mobile apps and the domains providing such services, it creates complexity in terms of attribution. For example, it is not clear whether an app developer *knows* the third party resources are suspicious. This is further complicated by the fact that certain third-party code can further load resources from other domains. This creates a *dependency chain* (see Fig. 1 for example), where the first-party app might not even be aware of the resources being loaded during its execution. This results in a form of *implicit trust* between mobile apps and any domains loaded further down the chain.

Consider the example BBC News [4] Android mobile app (cf. Fig. 1) which loads JavaScript code from the widgets.com domain, which, upon execution loads additional content from another third-party, ads.com. Here, BBC News as the first-party, *explicitly* trusts widgets.com, but *implicitly* trusts ads.com. This can be represented as a simple dependency chain in which widgets.com is at level 1 and ads.com is at level 2 (see Fig. 1). Past work tends to ignore this, instead, collapsing these levels into a single set of third-parties [21,41].

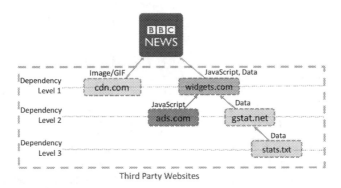

Fig. 1. Example of Android App dependency chain, including malicious third-party (in red). Here, Dependency Level 1 and Dependency Level ≥ 2 represent resources loaded from explicitly and implicitly trusted parties, respectively. (Color figure online)

This, however, overlooks a vital security aspect for resources loaded by mobile apps. For instance, it creates a significant security challenge, as mobile apps lack visibility on resources loaded further down their domain's dependency chain. The dynamic nature of the content is loaded and the wide adoption of in-path traffic alterations [16,45] further complicates the issue. The potential threat should not be underestimated as errant active content (*e.g.,* JavaScript code) opens the way to a range of further exploits, *e.g.,* Layer-7 DDoS attacks [42] or malvertising [46] and ransomware campaigns [33].

In this work, we study dependency chains in Android apps. We use static and dynamic analysis to extract the URLs requested by apps and leverage our distributed crawling framework to retrieve apps' resource dependency chains. We then use VirusTotal API [32] to augment apps' dependency chains to characterize any suspicious resource loading. By analyzing 7,048 apps, we explore their implicit dependencies on third parties; we find that over 98.2% of apps have dependency chains > 1, and therefore rely on an implicit trust model (Sect. 3). Although the majority (84.32%) of these have short chains of 4 and below levels, a notable minority (5.12%) have chains exceeding 5 levels. We also analyze different types of resource types and interestingly find JavaScript codes to be implicitly loaded by 92.3% of Android apps. This is perhaps due to app developers are unaware of the risks of implicitly trusting active content like JavaScript codes imported in WebView. Moreover, we inspect the categories of third-parties and find the predominance of the "Business" category across all dependency levels *i.e.*, 39.34% of all loaded resources at level 1, which increases to 40.54% at level 3, then to 51.4%, and so on. We also investigate the most occurring implicit third-parties and find `google-analytics.com` and `doubleclick.net` to be imported by 83.8% and 79.41%, respectively.

Although the above findings expose the analyzed Android apps to a new attack surface (as implicit trust makes it difficult for Android apps' owners or developers to vet third-parties), arguably, this alone does not create a security violation. Hence, we proceed to test whether or not these chains contain any malicious or suspicious third parties. To this end, we classify third-party domains into innocuous vs suspicious. Using several VirusTotal thresholds (which we refer to as VTscore (explained in Sect. 2.5)), we find that a considerable fraction of the third-parties involved in the dependency chains is classified as suspicious. These perform suspicious activities such as requesting sensitive resources and sending HTTP(S) requests to known malicious domains. We find that 1.18% of third-parties are suspicious with a VTscore $\geq$ 10 (i.e. at least 10 AntiVirus services flagged them as malicious domains). This fraction naturally decreases when increasing the VTscore, for example with the VTscore of $\geq$ 40 the number of suspicious websites is 0.16% only. We then further investigate JavaScript code and find that more than half of the code (51%) implicitly trusted (i.e., loaded at trust level 2 and beyond) have a VTscore $\geq$ 30 which suggests high confidence in the security assessment. Finally, to foster further research, we release the dataset and scripts used in this paper to the research community: https://mobapptrust. github.io/.

2   Background and Methodology

Figure 2 presents an overview of the steps involved in analyzing apps' resource dependency.

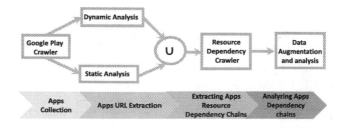

Fig. 2. Overview of our measurement methodology.

2.1   Third-Party Ecosystem

Third-parties extend an app's capabilities by providing useful content (*e.g.,* video, audio) and ways (*e.g.,* libraries and codes) to track users and deliver advertisements. Third-party services such as content delivery networks (CDNs), advertisers, and trackers have been around for years [38]. Recent years have seen apps relying on a wide range of third-party mobile ad and tracking services [31,48], typically fetched from ad aggregators such as `doubleclick.net` and AdMob through the ad libraries embedded in apps. Generally, an app developer registers with an ad aggregator, who provides the developer with a developer ID and an ad library which will be embedded in the app to fetch ads from other third-parties advertisers. The app developer is then paid by the ad provider based on the number of ad clicks or impressions, or both.

In the context of mobile advertising, the advertisers are parties who wish to advertise their products, the publishers are mobile applications (or their developers) that bring advertisements to the users. Ad networks or aggregators link the publishers to the advertisers, being paid by the latter and paying the former. Tapping on advertisements may lead users to content on Google Play or to web links. This often happens through a chain of several webpage redirections [30,40]. We generally refer to all these URLs in the webpage redirections as the redirection chain and the final webpage as the landing page. Ad networks themselves may participate in complex relationships with each other [30]. Certain parties, such as ad networks, run so-called ad exchanges where a given ad space is auctioned among several bidding ad networks so as to maximize profits for the publishers [14]. Ad networks also have syndication relationships with each other: an ad network assigned to fill a given ad space may delegate that space to another network. Such delegation can happen multiple times through a chain of ad networks and is visible in the redirection chains.

2.2   Collecting App Metadata from Google Play

It is first necessary to collect a representative sample of mobile apps. As we wish to study the infiltration by suspicious third-parties, we strive to obtain a set of 'mainstream' apps (rather than fringe or malware related apps). Thus, we implement a Google Play crawler. This first obtains the app ID (or package name) for the top 50 apps listed within 10 Google Play categories: game, entertainment, business, communication, finance, tools, productivity, personalization, news & magazines, and education. Our crawler follows a breadth-first-search approach for any other app considered as *"similar"* by Google Play and for other apps published by the same developer. For each (*free*) app, we collect its metadata and executables (apks). We collect all metadata: number of downloads, category, average rating, negative/positive reviews, and developer's website.

We collected 10,000 *free* apps from Google Play of which we successfully analyze 7,048 apps. Due to obfuscation and protection against source code our static analysis tools (further detailed below in Sect. 2.3) failed to decompile 2,469 apps. Similarly, 483 require *login* to interact with the apps' declared activities, thus our dynamic analysis tools failed to analyze them. Overall, our corpus consists of 7,048 apps distributed across 27 different categories (collected in Dec 2018). For context, Fig. 3 presents the number of apps we have with different ratings and number of downloads. Our dataset also consists of apps that receive high user ratings: 70.7% of the apps have more than 4-star ratings and 72% of them have 500K+ downloads as depicted in Fig. 3. These apps have 364,999,376 downloads (the sum of lower values of the installs). We argue this constitutes a reasonable sample of apps considered to be both mainstream and non-malicious in nature.

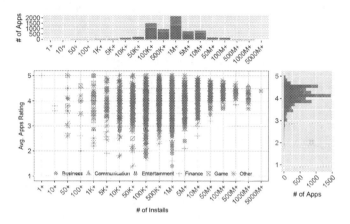

Fig. 3. An overview of analyzed apps' install and ratings on Google Play.

2.3 Extracting Apps' Resource Dependency Chains

It is next necessary to extract the third-party (web) resources utilized by each analyzed app. As depicted in Fig. 2, we extract this set of URLs/domains in two ways: *First*, for each app, we use the Google Play Unofficial Python API [9] to download each app's executable, and use `ApkTool` [3]–a static analysis tool– to decompile them. We then leverage regular expressions to comprehensively search and extract embedded URLs/domains in the decompiled source code. *Second*, we use a dedicated testbed, composed of a smartphone that connects to the Internet via a computer configured as a WiFi access point (AP) with dual-stack support. The WiFi AP runs `MITMProxy` [10] to intercept all the traffic being transmitted between the mobile device and the Internet. This allows us to observe the resources loaded (or URLs/domains requested) by each app. To automate the execution of apps in our corpus, we leverage `MonkeyRunner` [11] to launch an app in our test mobile phones and to interact with an app by emulating user interactions such as clicking and swapping on all *activities* defined in the `AndroidManifest.xml` files. We exclude 483 apps from our analysis as they have only *login* activities defined in the AndroidManifest.xml files. To complete the execution and rendering of each activity, we enforce a 20-second waiting time and 400 s runtime session per app executing, on average, 35 different activities. For each app, we combine the list of URLs/domains extracted from the app's source code and the app's network traffic. The above two techniques result in 414,387 URLs and 89,787 domains that correspond to 16,069 s-level domains.

2.4   Resource Dependency Dataset

Once we have the third-party resources for each analyzed app, we next strive to reconstruct the dependency chain. To this end, we build a crawling framework to collect apps' resource dependency chains. As mobile browsers have limited automation options and instrumentation capabilities, we modify the Chrome Headless crawler, detailed in [35], to imitate Google apps' WebViews. To ensure that we would see the correct mobile WebViews, leveraging previous work [18], our instrumentation involves: overriding the navigator object's user agent, OS platform, appVersion and appCodeName strings; and screen dimensions. Specifically, we emulate Chrome on Android, as it uses the same WebKit layout engine as the desktop Chrome used in the crawls. Recall that this covers the sequence of (JavaScript) resources that trigger further fetches.

For each of the 414,387 URLs identified, we then load and render it using our Chromium Headless crawler, detailed in [35]. This Chromium-based Headless [24] crawler renders a given URL/domain and tracks the resource dependencies by recording network requests sent to third-party domains. The requests are then used to reconstruct the dependency chain between each app and its requested URLs. Essentially, a dependency chain is constructed by analyzing each parent and child domain duple. We then extract the URL of the parent domain, the URL of the child domain, and the URL of the referrer. If the referrer differs from the parent, we add a branch from the parent to the referrer and then from the referrer to the child. Otherwise, if the parent is the referrer, we add a branch from the parent to the child. This is done for every parent and child tuple returned from our crawler. Note that each app can trigger the creation of multiple dependency chains. This process results in 414,387 dependency chains extracted (one per URL), creating a total set of 4,670,741 URLs.

Figure 1 presents an example of a dependency chain with 3 levels. *level 1* is loaded directly by the app, and is therefore explicitly trusted by it (*i.e.,* BBC News). *level 2* and *3*, however, is implicitly (or indirectly) trusted as the BBC News app may not necessarily be aware of their loading. For simplicity, we consider any domain that differs from the domain owned–obtained the domain from Google Play–by the analyzed app to be a third-party. More formally, to construct the dependency chain, we identify third-party requests by comparing the second level domain of the page (*e.g.,* bbc.com) to the domains of the requests (*e.g.,* cdn.com and ads.com via widgets.com).

Those with different second-level domains are considered third-party. We ignore the sub-domains so that a request to a domain such as player.bbc.com is not considered a third-party. Due to the lack of purely automated mechanism to disambiguate between site-specific sub-domains (*e.g.,* player.bbc.com) or country-specific sub-domains (*e.g.,* bbc.co.uk), tldextract [36] for this task. Moreover, we distinguish between first-party second-level domains, in which case the developer of an app also owns the domain, and third-party domains, which include ad networks, trackers, social networks, and any other party that an app contacts. For instance, `twitter.com` is a first-party to the Twitter App but it is a third-party to BBC News.

2.5   Meta-data Collection from VirusTotal

The above steps result in a dependency chain being created for each URL loaded by an app. As a major goal within our work is to identify potentially suspicious third-party resources, it is necessary to annotate these dependency chains with data about the potential risks. To achieve this, we leverage the VirusTotal public API to automatize our classification process. VirusTotal is an online solution that aggregates the scanning capabilities provided by 68 AV tools, scanning engines, and datasets. It has been commonly used in the academic literature to detect malicious apps, executables, software, and domains [31]. Upon submitting a URL, VirusTotal provides a list of scans from 68 anti-virus tools. We use the report API to obtain the VTscore for each third-party URL belonging to mobile apps in our dataset. Concretely, this score is the number of AV tools that flagged the website as *malicious* (max. 68). We further supplement each domain with their WebSense category provided by the VirusTotal's *record* API. During the augmentation, we eliminate invalid URLs (1.7%) in each dependency chain. Thus, we collect the above metadata for each second-level domain in our dataset. This results in a final sample of 4,675,173 URLs consisting of 89,787 unique domains from which we extract 16,699 unique second-level domains.

3   Analysis of Apps' Resource Dependency Chains

We begin by characterizing the resources imported by apps. We seek to determine if apps do, indeed, rely on implicit trust.

3.1   Characterizing Apps' Implicit Trust

We analyze the resource loaded per app (resp. per category of apps) and measure the "depth" of implicit trust, *i.e.,* how many levels in the dependency chain an app loads resources from. Collectively, the 7,048 apps in our dataset make 4,670,901 calls to 414,387 unique external resources, with a median of 509 external resources per app. To dissect this, Table 1 presents the percentage of apps that both explicitly and implicitly trust third-party resources. We separate apps into their popularity, based on their number of downloads on the Play store.

Table 1 shows that the use of third-party resources is extremely common. 98.2% of explicitly trust third-parties at least once, with 22.1% importing externally hosted JavaScript code. Moreover, around 95% of the apps do rely on *implicit* trust chains, *e.g.,* they allow third-parties to load further third-parties on their behalf. This trend is already well-known [30] in the web context; here we confirm it for mobile apps. Note, the propensity to form dependency chains (≥ 2) is marginally higher in more popular apps; for example, 94% of apps with

Table 1. Overview of the dataset for different ranges of a number of apps' install. The rows indicate the proportion of a number of app installs that explicitly and implicitly trust at least one third-party (*i*) resource (of any type); and (*ii*) JavaScript code.

	Number of Installs						
	1-5B	1-10K	10K-100K	100K-500K	500K-5M	5M-50M	50M-5B
	(7048)	(119)	(391)	(1456)	(3069)	(1588)	(425)
Apps that trust at least one third-party which loads:							
Any Resources:							
Explicitly (Lvl. 1)	98.2%	89.9%	93.6%	97.1%	98.2%	99.0%	99.3%
Implicitly (Lvl. $\geq$ 2)	95%	82%	**86%**	93%	**94%**	96%	98%
JavaScript:							
Explicitly	22.1%	26.7%	25.3	23.1%	20.6%	21.7%	18.1%
Implicitly	92.3%	65.5%	79.3%	90.9%	92.9%	94.3%	92.0%

a number of installs $\geq$ 500K have dependency chains compared to 86% of apps with a number of installs $\leq$ 100K.

We next inspect the *depth* of the dependency chain. Intuitively, long chains are undesirable as they typically have a deleterious impact on resource load times [55] and increase attacks surface, *e.g.,* drive-by downloads [17,19], malware and binary exploitation [44,47,51,52], or phishing attacks [56].

Figure 4a presents the CDF of chain level for all apps in our dataset. For context, apps are separated into their sub-categories.[1] It shows that 84.32% of the analyzed apps create chains of trust of level 4 or below. Overall, we find that all mobile apps import ≈5.12% of their external resources from level 5 and above. However, there is also a small minority that dramatically exceeds this level. In the most extreme case, we see `AntiVirus 2019` [2], having 1M+ downloads and average rating 4.2, with a chain containing 7 levels, consisting of mutual calls between `pubmatic.com` (online marketing) and `mathtag.com` (ad provider). Other notable examples include `RoboForm Password Manager` [13] (productivity app with 500K+ downloads and average rating 4.3), `Borussia Dortmund` [5] (sport, 1M+, 4.5), and `Cover art Evite: Free Online & Text Invitations` [7] (social, 1M+, 3.9) have a maximum dependency level of 7. We argue that these complex configurations make it extremely difficult to reliably audit such apps, as an app cannot be assured of which objects are later loaded. Briefly, we also note that Fig. 4b reveals subtle differences *between* different categories, according to WebSense categorization (cf. Sect. 2.5), of third-party domains. For example, those classified as Business and Adverts are most likely to be loaded at level 1; this is perhaps to be expected, as many ad brokers naturally serve and manage their own content. In contrast, Social Network third-parties (*e.g.,* Facebook plug-ins) are least likely to be loaded at level 1.

---

[1] We include the most popular categories and group subcategories (Arcade, Action, Adventure, Board, Card, Casino, Casual, Educational, Music, Puzzle, Racing, Role Playing, Simulation, Strategy, Sports, Trivia, and Word) to 'Game'.

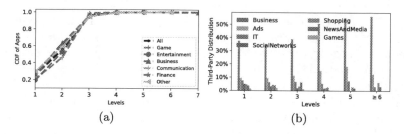

Fig. 4. (a) CDF of dependency chain levels (broken down into categories of apps); and (b) distribution of third-parties across various categories and levels.

3.2   Characterizing the Types of Resources

The previous section has confirmed that a notable fraction of apps creates dependency chains with (up to) 7 levels. Next, we inspect the types of imported resources within these dependency chains. For analyzed (categories of) apps at each level of the resource dependency chain, we classify the types of loaded resources into six main types: Data (consisting of HTML, XML, JSON, plain text, and encoded files), Image, JavaScript code, CSS/Fonts, Audio, and Video. We were unable to classify 5.28% of resources loaded by the analyzed apps. On a closer look, we find that 98% of these uncategorized resources were imported from 242 unique, static IP addresses via WebSockets while 2% of the uncategorized resources were requested from localhost (127.0.0.1).

Table 2 presents the volume of each resource type imported at each level in the trust chain. We observe that the make-up of resources varies dramatically based on the level in the dependency chain. For example, the fraction of images imported tends to increase—this is large because third-parties are in turn loading images (*e.g.,* for adverts). In contrast, the fraction of JavaScript codes decreases as the level in the dependency chain increases: 27.2% of resources at level 2 are JavaScript codes compared to just 11.92% at level 5. This trend is caused by the fact that new levels are typically created by JavaScript execution (thus, by definition, the fraction of JavaScript codes must be deplete along the chain). However, it remains at a level that should be of concern to app developers as this confirms a significant fraction of JavaScript code is loaded from potentially unknown implicitly trusted domains.

Table 2. Breakdown of resource types requested by the analyzed apps across each level in the dependency chain. The total column refers to the number of resource calls made at each level. Here *JS* represents the JavaScript code category of imported resources.

Lev.	Total	Data	Image	JS	CSS/Font	Audio	Video	Uncategorized
1	315,217	91.76%	3.74%	1.4%	0.06%	0.21%	0.07%	2.76%
2	4,040,882	10.22%	45.55%	27.2%	13.12%	0.06%	0.17%	3.53%
3	171,035	8.13%	33.11%	23.62%	5.36%	0.03%	0.01%	29.75%
4	63,179	1.6%	24.16%	14.32%	0.48%	0%	0%	59.43%
5	6,116	14.34%	18.35%	11.92%	8.19%	0%	0%	47.2%
≥ 6	383	7.31%	26.11%	1.04%	0%	0%	0.52%	65.01%

To build on this, we also inspect the *categories*, taken from WebSense (see Sect. 2.5 for details), of third-party domains hosting these resources. Figure 4b presents the make-up of third-party categories at each level in the chain. It is clear that, across all levels, Business and Advertisement domains make up the bulk of third-parties. We also notice other highly demanded third-party categories such as Business, Ads, and IT. These are led by well-known providers, *e.g.*, `google-analytics.com` (web-analytics–grouped as in business category as per VirusTotal reports) provides resources to 83.78% of the analyzed apps. This observation is in line with the fact that 81.4% of the analyzed apps embed Google ads and analytic service libraries. The figure also reveals that the distributions of categories vary slightly across each dependency level. For example, 37.7% of all loaded resources at *level 1* come from Business domains compared to 39.1% at *level 3, i.e.,* overall, the proportion increases across dependency levels. We also observe similar trends for resources loaded from Ads and IT (*e.g.*, web hosting) domains.

In contrast, social network third-parties (*e.g.*, Facebook) are mostly presented at *level 1* (4.89%) and 2 (3.26%) with a significant drop at *level 3*. The dominance of Business and Advertisements is not, however, caused by a plethora of Ads domains: there are far fewer Ads domains than Business (see Table 4). Instead, it is driven by a large number of requests for advertisements: even though Ads domains only make up 9.01% of third-parties, they generate 13.58% of resources. Naturally, these are led by major providers. Importantly, these popular providers can trigger further dependencies; for example, 79.41% of apps leverage `doubleclick.net` which imports 11% of its resources from further implicitly trusted third-party domains. This makes such third-parities means for online fraudulent activities and ideal propagator of "malicious" resources for any other domains having implicit trust in it [39].

4   Analyzing Malicious Resource Dependency Chains of Apps

The previous section has shown that the creation of dependency chains is widespread, and there is therefore extensive implicit trust within the mobile and third-party app ecosystem. This, however, does not shed light on the activity of resources within the dependency chains, nor does it mean that the implicit

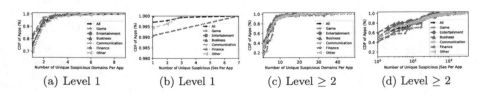

(a) Level 1   (b) Level 1   (c) Level $\geq$ 2   (d) Level $\geq$ 2

Fig. 5. CDFs of number of unique suspicious domains contacted and JavaScript codes downloaded by apps (broken down into apps' categories) at explicit level (Level = 1) and implicit level (Level $\geq$ 2).

trust is abused by third-parties. Thus, we next study the existence of *suspicious* third-parties, which could lead to abuse of the implicit trust. Within this section, we use the term *suspicious* (to be more generic than malicious) because VirusTotal covers activities ranging from low-risk (*e.g.,* sharing private data over unencrypted channels) to high-risk (malware).

4.1 Do Apps Load Suspicious Third-Parties?

First, we inspect the fraction of third-party domains that trigger a warning by VirusTotal. From our third-party domains, in Table 4, 14.95% have a VTscore of 1 or above, *i.e.,* at least one virus checker classifies the domain as suspicious. If one treats the VTscore as a ground truth, this confirms that popular websites do load content from suspicious third-parties via their chains of trust. However, we are reticent to rely on VTscore = 1, as this indicates the remaining 67 virus checkers did not flag the domain[2]

Table 4 shows the fraction of third-parties that are classified as suspicious using several VTscore thresholds. For context, we separate third-parties into their respective categories. If we classify any resource with a VTscore of ≥ 10 as suspicious, we find that 1.18% (188) of third-party domains are classified as suspicious with 1.36% of all resource calls in our dataset going to these third-parties. Notably this only drops to 0.59% with a *very* conservative VTscore of ≥ 20. We observe similar results when considering thresholds in the [5...50] range. We therefore conservatively refer to domains with a VTscore ≥ 10 as suspicious in the rest of this analysis.

4.2 Do Apps' Dependency Chains Contain Suspicious Parties?

The above has shown that apps do load suspicious resources. We next inspect where in the dependency chains these resources are loaded at. Additionally, we inspect apps that inherit suspicious JavaScript resources from the explicit and various implicit levels. We focus on JavaScript codes as active web content that poses great threats with significant attack surfaces consisting of vulnerabilities related to client-side JavaScript when executed in apps WebView mode, such as cross-site scripting (XSS) and advanced phishing [37,56].

Figure 5 depicts the cumulative distributions (CDFs) of number of unique suspicious domains and JavaScript codes per (different categories of) apps. Although we do not observe significant differences among the various apps' categories, however, from the trends in the sub-figures, interestingly, we find that the majority of (resp. JavaScript codes) resources classified as suspicious are located at level 2 in the dependency chain (*i.e.,* implicitly trusted by the app).

Overall, we find that 21.46% (1,513) of the analyzed apps import at least one resource from a suspicious domain with VTscore ≥ 10. Table 5 shows well-known apps, ranked according to the number of unique suspicious third-parties in their chain of dependency. We note that the popular (most vulnerable) apps belong

---

[2] Diversity is likely caused by the databases used by the various virus checkers [15].

to various categories such as Productivity, Finance, Education, and Communication. This indicates that there is no one category of domains that inherits suspicious JavaScript codes. However, we note that the first mobile apps categorized as "Productivity" represent the majority of most exposed domains at level ≥ 2, with 16% of the total number of apps implicitly trusting suspicious JavaScript codes belonging to the Business Category, with the distant second being the "Communication" Category and third the "Finance" category. The number of suspicious JavaScript codes loaded by these apps ranges from 3 to 25 JavaScript codes. We note the extreme case of 35% app *implicitly* importing at least 6 unique suspicious JavaScript programs from 3 unique suspicious domains. Moreover, we observe at most 7 unique third-parties (combining both explicit and implicit level) that is a cause of suspicious JavaScripts in mobile apps. This happens for Package Tracker [12], with over 1M install and 4.6 average rating on Google Play, having third-party domains such as `nrg-tk.ru`, `yw56.com.cn`, `bitrix.info`, `fundebug.com`, and `ghbtns.com`.

4.3   How Widespread Are Suspicious Parties?

We next inspect how "popular" these suspicious third-parties are at each position in the dependency chain, by inspecting how many Android apps utilize them. Figure 6 displays the CDF of resource calls to third-parties made by each app in our dataset. We decompose the third-party resources into various groups (including total *vs.* suspicious). As mentioned earlier, we take a conservative approach and consider a resource suspicious if it receives a VTscore ≥ 10.

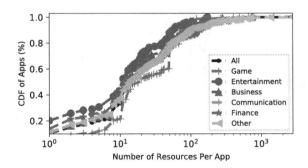

Fig. 6. CDF of resources loaded per app from various categories of third-parties.

The figure reveals that suspicious parties within the dependency chains are commonplace: 12.76% of all apps contain at least 3 third-parties classified as suspicious in their dependency chain. Remarkably, 21.48% of apps load resources from third-parties at least once. Hence, even though only 9.01% of third-party domains are classified as suspicious, their reach covers nearly one-fifth of the apps (indirectly via implicit trust).

This is a product of the power-law distribution of third-party "popularity" across Android apps: The top 20% of third-party domains cover 86% (3,650,582) of all resource calls. Closer inspection shows that it is driven by prominent third-parties: `github.io` and tapjoy.com, and `baidu.com` obtaining, during the measurement period, VTscore of 11, 18, and 21 suggesting a high degree of certainty of being suspicious. For instance, in the case of "Egypt News Moment by Moment" [6] which loaded JavaScript resources from github.io, it was actually caused by github.io loading another third-party, `ghbtn.com`, which is known to be abused by attackers for hosting malware [8] and phishing kits [22].

4.4   Which Suspicious Third-Parties Are Most Prevalent?

Next, we inspect in, Table 6, the top 10 most frequently encountered suspicious third-party domains that are providing suspicious JavaScript resources to first-parties (as opposed to the most exposed Android apps domains shown earlier in Table 5). We rank these suspicious third-party domains according to their prevalence in the Web ecosystem and further decompose our analysis at explicit and implicit levels in the table. We found `github.io` is the most called domain. Interestingly, we find several suspicious third-party domains from the Top 100 Alexa ranking. For instance, `baidu.com`, a search engine website mostly geared toward East-Asian countries has been used by 253 apps and is ranked 4 by Alexa. This domain is found to be one of the most prevalent suspicious third-party domains at both level 1 (140 apps) and levels ≥ 2 (113 apps). An obvious reason for this domain's presence is because of other infected (malware-based) apps that try to authenticate users from such domains [43]. Others such as `tapjoy.com` and `baidu.com` are also among the most prevalent third-party domains at level 1. These websites were reported to contain malware in their JavaScript codes [20] and suggest users promote [49] and install potentially unwanted programs [1].

While it is *not shown in the table*, we also note the presence of `qq.com`, a Chinese Search Engine ranked high by Alexa. This is among the top 10 most encountered suspicious third-party domains, as defined by 13 AV tools within VirusTotal. Closer inspection reveals this is likely due to repeated instances of insecure data transmission, use of `qq.com` fake accounts for malware manifestation and for data encryption Trojans [26,34,53].

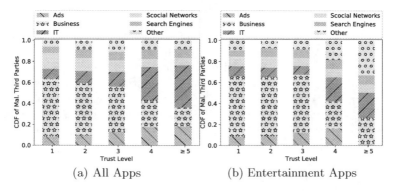

(a) All Apps   (b) Entertainment Apps

Fig. 7. Distribution of calls to suspicious third-party domains (VT score ≥ 10) per category at each level, for all (Fig. 7a) and Entertainment (Fig. 7b) apps.

4.5   At Which Level Do Suspicious Third-Parties Occur?

Next, by inspecting the location(s) in the dependency chain where the malicious third-parties are situated and the *types* of apps that load them, we analyze the impact of suspicious resources loaded on mobile apps. This is vital as implicitly trusted (level ≥ 2) resources are far more difficult for an app developer (or owner) to remove—they could, of course, remove the intermediate level 1 resource, but this may disrupt their own business activities.

Table 3 presents the proportion of apps that import at least one resource with a VTscore ≥ 10. We separate resources into their level in the dependency chain. Interestingly, the majority of resources classified as suspicious are located at level 1 in the dependency chain (*i.e.*, they are explicitly trusted by the app). 41.2% of the analyzed apps containing suspicious third-parties are "infected" via level 1. This suggests that the app developers are not entirely diligent in monitoring their third-party resources and may purposefully utilize such third-parties [28].

4.24% of the analyzed apps import at least 11 resources from suspicious via *implicit* trust (*i.e.*, level ≥ 2). In these cases, the Game developers are potentially unaware of their presence. The most vulnerable category is Games: 23.34% of Game apps import *implicitly* trusted resources from level 2 with a VTscore $\geq$ 10. Notably, among the 78 Game apps importing suspicious JavaScript resources from trust level 2 and deeper, we find 41 apps loading advertisements from `adadvisor.net`. One possible reason is that ad-networks could be infected, or victimized with malware to perform malvertising [39,50] or binary exploitation [47,51].

Table 3. Proportion of apps importing resources classified as suspicious (with VTscore ≥ 10) at each level.

Lv.	All apps		Games apps		Entert. apps		Business apps		Comm. Apps	
	All	JS	All	JS	All	JS	All	JS	All	JS
1	41.20%	37.37%	55.40%	43.43%	53.61%	47.20%	49.23%	45.38%	47.41%	45.25%
2	4.24%	1.29%	23.34%	4.53%	10.09%	3.50%	7.53%	3.21%	8.09%	3.05%
3	1.01%	0.13%	1.59%	0.40%	3.26%	0.18%	1.070%	0.29%	2.20%	0.10%
4	0.11%	$\leq 0.1\%$	0.51%	$\leq 0.1\%$	0.80%	$\leq 0.1\%$	0.60%	$\leq 0.1\%$	0.40%	$\leq 0.001\%$
≥ 5	$\leq 0.10\%$	0	$\leq 0.001\%$	$\leq 0.1\%$	$\leq 0.001\%$	$\leq 0.1\%$	$\leq 0.001\%$	$\leq 0.1\%$	$\leq 0.001\%$	0.00%

Similar, albeit less extreme, observations can be made across Entertainment (abbreviated as Entert. in Table 3) and Business apps. Briefly, Fig. 7 displays the categories of (suspicious) third-parties loaded at each level in the apps' dependency chains—it can be seen that the majority are classified as Business according to WebSense domain classification (cf. Sect. 2.5). This is, again, because of several major providers classified as suspicious such as `comeet.co` and `dominionenergy.com`. Furthermore, it can be seen that the fraction of advertisement resources also increases with the number of levels due to the loading of further resources (*e.g.*, images).

We next strive to quantify the level of suspicion raised by each of these JavaScript programs. Intuitively, those with higher VTscores represent a higher threat as defined by the 68 AV tools used by VirusTotal. Hence, Fig. 8 presents

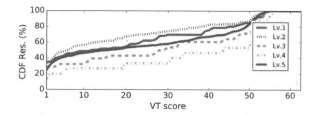

Fig. 8. CDF of suspicious JavaScripts (VTscores ≥ 1) at different levels in the chain.

the cumulative distribution of the VTscores for all JavaScript resources loaded with VTscore ≥ 1. We separate the JavaScript programs into their location in the dependency chain. A clear differences can be observed, with level 2 obtaining the highest VTscore (median 28). In fact, 51% of the suspicious JavaScript resources loaded on trust level 2 have a VTscore > 30 (indicating *very* high confidence).

Figure 9 also presents the breakdown of the domain categories specifically for suspicious JavaScript codes. Clear trends can be seen, with IT (*e.g.*, `dynaquestpc.com`), News and Media (*e.g.*, `therealnews.com`), Entertainment (*e.g.*, `youwatchfilm.net`) and Business (*e.g.*, `vindale.com`) are dominating. Clearly, suspicious JavaScripts cover a broad spectrum of activities. Interestingly, we observed that 63% and 66%, respectively, of IT and News & Media JavaScript codes, are loaded from level ≥ 2 in contrast to 17% and 25% of JavaScript code from Social Networks and Streaming loaded at *level 1*.

We next strive to quantify the level of suspicion raised by each of these JavaScript programs. Intuitively, those with higher VTscores represent a higher threat as defined by the 68 AV tools used by VirusTotal. Hence, Fig. 8 presents the cumulative distribution of the VTscores for all JavaScript resources loaded

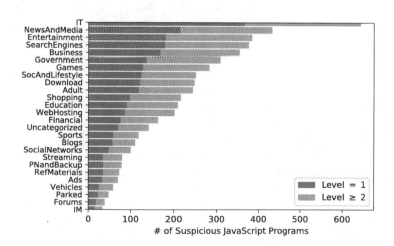

Fig. 9. Breakdown of suspicious JavaScript resources based on the category of the domain.

with VTscore ≥ 1. We separate the JavaScript programs into their location in the dependency chain. A clear difference can be observed, with level 2 obtaining the highest VTscore (median 32). In fact, 78% of the suspicious JavaScript resources loaded on trust level 2 have a VTscore > 52 (indicating *very* high confidence).

This is a critical observation since as mentioned earlier, while suspicious third-parties at level 1 can be ultimately removed by apps' developers if flagged as suspicious, this is much more difficult for *implicitly* trusted resources further along the dependency chain. If the intermediate (non-suspicious) *level 1* resource is vital for the webpage, it is likely that some operators would be unable or unwilling to perform this action. The lack of transparency and the inability to perform a vetting process on implicitly trusted loaded resources further complicates the issue. It is also worth noting that the VTscore for resources loaded further down the dependency chain is lower (*e.g., level 4*). For example, 92% of level 2 resources receive a VTscore below 3. This suggests that the activity of these resources is more contentious, with a smaller number of AV tools reaching a consensus.

5   Related Work

We examine literature that measures third-party ecosystems on the web [29,30] and mobile platforms [48]; then review the security and privacy implication of loading resources from third-parties and illuminate on the chain of resource loading. Previous works analyzed the presences of third-party JavaScript libraries and ill-maintained external web servers making exploitation via JavaScript trivial [41]. Lauinger *et al.* led a further study, classifying sensitive libraries and the vulnerabilities caused by them [37]. Gomer *et al.* analyzed users' exposure to third-party tracking in the context of search queries, showing that 99.5% of users are tracked by popular trackers within 30 clicks [23]. Hozinger *et al.* found 61 third-party JavaScript exploits and defined three main attack vectors [27]. Our work differs quite substantially from these studies in that we are not interested in the third-party JavaScript code itself, nor the simple presence of third-party tracking domains embedded in tweets or in a webpage. Instead, we are interested in *how* mobile apps' users are exposed to third-parties and the presence of third-parties in the redirect chain. In contrast to our work, these prior studies ignore the presence of chains of resource loading and treat all third-parties as "equal", regardless of where they are loaded when users click on a given URL embedded in a tweet or webpage.

Kumar *et al.* [35] characterized websites' resource dependencies on third-party services. In line with our work, they found that websites' third-party resource dependency chains are widespread. This means, for example, that 55% of websites, among Alexa top 1M, are prevented from fully migrating to HTTPS by the third-parties that provide resources to them. More related work is Ikram *et al.* [30], who perform a large-scale study of suspicious resource loading and dependency chains in the Web, and around 50% of first-party websites render content that they did not directly load. They also showed that 84.91% of websites have short dependency chains (below 3 levels). The study reported that

1.2% of these suspicious third-parties have remarkable reach into the wider Web ecosystem. To the best of our knowledge, we are the first to characterize the chains of resource loading of mobile apps. Moreover, we also characterize the role of apps' suspicious resource loading. We suggest that more rigorous vetting of in-app third-party resources is required.

Table 4. Overview of suspicious third-parties in each category. **Col.2-4:** number of third-party websites in different categories, the number of resource calls to resources, and the proportion of calls to suspicious JavaScript code. **Col.5-9:** Fraction of third-party domains classified as suspicious (*Num.*), and fraction of resource calls classified as suspicious (*Vol.*), across various VTscores (i.e., ≥ 1 and ≥ 40).

Category	Third-parties	Total calls	Suspicious JS	VTScore ≥ 1		VTScore ≥ 5		VTScore ≥ 10		VTScore ≥ 20		VTScore ≥ 40	
				Num.	Vol.	Num.	Vol.	Num.	Vol.	Num.	Vol.	Num.	Vol.
Business	5,073 (33.43%)	1,030,635	63,970 (6.21%)	14.75%	47.59%	1.70%	2.75%	1.13%	1.17%	0.61%	0.22%	0.12%	0.09%
Ads	1,367 (9.01%)	623,261	100,843 (16.18%)	24.58%	60.65%	2.93%	5.36%	1.54	5.03%	0.59%	0.08%	0.08%	0.01%
IT	1,173 (7.73%)	41,841	887 (2.12%)	13.98%	14.54%	1.62%	3.42%	0.68%	1.61%	0.26%	0.09%	0%	0%
Shopping	607 (4.0%)	137,686	990 (0.72%)	13.51%	12.01%	1.98%	0.37%	1.32%	0.17%	1.15%	0.13%	0.66%	0.12%
NewsAndMedia	549 (3.62%)	76,566	1,205 (1.57%)	15.12%	28.86%	3.28%	0.94%	2.37%	0.93%	1.09%	0.14%	0.18%	0.03%
Social Networks	246 (1.62%)	160,789	5,033 (3.13%)	19.51%	85.77%	1.63%	0.59%	0.81%	0.59%	0.81%	0.59%	0%	0%
Games	244 (1.61%)	27,419	358 (1.30%)	16.39%	16.40%	2.46%	3.11	1.64%	1.96%	1.23%	1.93%	1.23%	1.93%
Others	5,916 (38.99%)	2,656,419	213,604 (8.04%)	12.98%	89.83%	1.81%	1.066%	1.12%	0.05%	0.50%	0.60%	0.15%	0.027%
Total	15,175 (100%)	4,670,741	386,890 (8.28%)	14.95%	73.69%	1.93%	2.03%	1.18%	1.36%	0.59%	0.44%	0.16%	0.06%

Table 5. Top 5 most exposed apps (with VTscore ≥ 10) ranked by the number of unique suspicious domains.

Unique suspicious domains (and JSes) at level = 1							
#	App	Cat.	Rat.	Insta.	Dom.	JSes	Chain len.
1	Dashlane Pass. Manag.	Prod.	4.6	1M+	9	3	7
2	BPI	Fina.	4.3	1M+	7	4	5
3	Korean Dictionary	Educ.	4.2	100K+	7	5	6
4	RoboForm Pass. Manag.	Prod.	4.3	500K+	7	4	7
5	Bane Voice Changer	Enter.	3.4	1M+	6	2	4
Unique suspicious domains (and JSes) at level ≥ 2							
#	App	Cat.	Rat.	Insta.	Dom.	JSes	Chain len.
1	Package Tracker	Prod.	4.6	1M+	37	34	4
2	SGETHER Live Stream.	Vid. Play.	4.0	1M+	36	252	5
3	Opera Browser	Comm.	4.4	100M+	34	64	5
4	Adrohelm Antivirus	Comm.	4.2	1M+	34	48	7
5	NFL Game Centre	Game	4.1	50M+	31	34	3

Table 6. Top 5 most prevalent suspicious third-party domains (VTscore $\geq$ 10) on level 1 and level $\geq$ 2 providing resources to Apps. The number of apps (# Apps) having the corresponding suspicious third-party domain in their chain of dependency.

#	Third-party domain	Alexa rank	VTscore	# Apps	Category
\multicolumn{6}{l}{Prevalence of third-parties at Level = 1}
1	github.io	50	11	769	IT
2	tapjoy.com	47,720	18	199	IT
3	baidu.com	4	21	140	SearchEngine
4	oracle.com	825	10	39	IT
5	dominionenergy.com	16,757	12	31	Business
\multicolumn{6}{l}{Prevalence of third-parties at Level $\geq$ 2}
1	baidu.com	4	21	113	SearchEngine
2	sil.org	64,483	16	17	Ads
3	comeet.co	87,766	13	117	Business
4	cloudfront.net	264	11	12	WebHosting
5	amazonaws.com	1,597	10	8	WebHosting

6   Concluding Remarks

This paper explored dependency chains in Android apps. Focusing on how external resources are loaded by mobile apps, we found that over 98.2% of apps *do* rely on implicit trust. Although the majority (70.91%) of the analyzed apps have short chains, we found apps with chains up to 7 levels of dependency. Perhaps unsurprisingly, the most commonly encountered *implicitly* trusted third-parties are well-known analytics services and ad-networks domains (*e.g.,* google-analytics.com and doubleclick.net), however, we also observed various less common domains to be implicitly trusted third-parties. In our future work, we wish to perform longitudinal measurements to understand how these metrics of maliciousness evolve over time. We are particularly interested in understanding the (potentially) ephemeral nature of threats. To provide apps' users better control of their privacy and to facilitate secure resource loading, we also aim to investigate ways to automatically identify and sandbox suspicious parties in the resource dependency chains to alert users to security vulnerabilities (resp. HTTPS downgrades) of at each level of dependency chains.

References

1. Android.tapjoy — symantec (2019). https://www.symantec.com/security-center/writeup/2014-052619-4702-99
2. AntiVirus 2019 (2019). https://play.google.com/store/apps/details?id=com.androhelm.antivirus.free2

3. Apktool - a tool for reverse engineering 3rd party, closed, binary android apps (2019). https://ibotpeaches.github.io/Apktool/
4. BBC News (2019). https://play.google.com/store/apps/details?id=bbc.mobile.news.ww
5. Borussia Dortmund (2019). https://play.google.com/store/apps/details?id=de.bvb.android
6. Egypt news moment by moment (2019). https://play.google.com/store/apps/details?id=com.egy.new
7. Evite: Free Online & Text Invitations (2019). https://play.google.com/store/apps/details?id=com.evite
8. Github-hosted malware targets accountants with ransomware (2019). https://www.bleepingcomputer.com/news/security/github-hosted-malware-targets-accountants-with-ransomware/
9. Google play unofficial python 3 API library (2019). https://github.com/alessandrodd/googleplay_api
10. mitmproxy - an interactive HTTPS proxy (2019). https://mitmproxy.org
11. monkeyrunner — Android Developers (2019). https://developer.android.com/studio/test/monkeyrunner/
12. Package tracker (2019). https://play.google.com/store/apps/details?id=de.orrs.deliveries
13. RoboForm Password Manager (2019). https://play.google.com/store/apps/details?id=com.siber.roboform
14. Bashir, M.A., Arshad, S., Robertson, W., Wilson, C.: Tracing information flows between ad exchanges using retargeted ads. In: USENIX Security (2016)
15. Canto, J., Dacier, M., Kirda, E., Leita, C.: Large scale malware collection: lessons learned. In: SRDS (2008)
16. Chen, J., et al.: Forwarding-loop attacks in content delivery networks. In: NDSS (2016)
17. Cova, M., Kruegel, C., Vigna, G.: Detection and analysis of drive-by-download attacks and malicious javascript code. In: Web Conference (WWW) (2010)
18. Das, A., Acar, G., Borisov, N., Pradeep, A.: The web's sixth sense: a study of scripts accessing smartphone sensors. In: SIGSAC (2018)
19. Egele, M., Wurzinger, P., Kruegel, C., Kirda, E.: Defending browsers against drive-by downloads: mitigating heap-spraying code injection attacks. In: Flegel, U., Bruschi, D. (eds.) DIMVA 2009. LNCS, vol. 5587, pp. 88–106. Springer, Heidelberg (2009). https://doi.org/10.1007/978-3-642-02918-9_6
20. IBM X-Force Exchange: Statcounter session hijack (2005). https://exchange.xforce.ibmcloud.com/vulnerabilities/20506
21. Falahrastegar, M., Haddadi, H., Uhlig, S., Mortier, R.: Anatomy of the third-party web tracking ecosystem. In: Traffic Measurements Analysis Workshop (TMA) (2014)
22. Gatlan, S.: Github service abused by attackers to host phishing kits (2019). https://www.bleepingcomputer.com/news/security/github-service-abused-by-attackers-to-host-phishing-kits/
23. Gomer, R., Rodrigues, E.M., Milic-Fraying, N., Schrafel, M.: Network analysis of third party tracking: user exposure to tracking cookies through search. In: WI-IAT (2013)
24. Google: Headless chromium (2018). https://chromium.googlesource.com/chromium/src/+/lkgr/headless/README.md
25. Grace, M.C., Zhou, W., Jiang, X., Sadeghi, A.R.: Unsafe exposure analysis of mobile in-app advertisements. In: WISEC (2012)

26. GreenBerg, A.: Hack brief: malware hits 225,000 (jailbroken, mostly Chinese) iphones (2015). https://www.wired.com/2015/08/hack-brief-malware-hits-225000-jailbroken-mostly-chinese-iphones/

27. Holzinger, P., Triller, S., Bartel, A., Bodden, E.: An in-depth study of more than ten years of java exploitation. In: CCS (2016)

28. Ibosiola, D., Castro, I., Stringhini, G., Uhlig, S., Tyson, G.: Who watches the watchmen: exploring complaints on the web. In: Web Conference (WWW) (2019)

29. Ikram, M., Asghar, H.J., Kâafar, M.A., Mahanti, A., Krishnamurthy, B.: Towards seamless tracking-free web: improved detection of trackers via one-class learning. PoPETs (2017)

30. Ikram, M., Masood, R., Tyson, G., Kaafar, M.A., Loizon, N., Ensafi, R.: The chain of implicit trust: an analysis of the web third-party resources loading. In: WWW (2019)

31. Ikram, M., Vallina-Rodriguez, N., Seneviratne, S., Kaafar, M.A., Paxson, V.: An analysis of the privacy and security risks of android VPN permission-enabled apps. In: IMC (2016)

32. VirusTotal Inc.: Virustotal public API (2019). https://www.virustotal.com/en/documentation/public-api/

33. Janosik, J.: Russia hit by new wave of ransomware spam (2019). https://www.welivesecurity.com/2019/01/28/russia-hit-new-wave-ransomware-spam/

34. Knockel, J., Senft, A., Deibert, R.: WUP! there it is privacy and security issues in QQ browser (2016). https://citizenlab.ca/2016/03/privacy-security-issues-qq-browser/

35. Kumar, D., Ma, Z., Mirian, A., Mason, J., Halderman, J.A., Bailey, M.: Security challenges in an increasingly tangled web. In: WWW (2017)

36. Kurkowski, J.: Accurately separate the TLD from the registered domain and subdomains of a URL, using the public suffix list (2018). https://github.com/john-kurkowski/tldextract

37. Lauinger, T., Chaabane, A., Arshad, S., Robertson, W., Wilson, C., Kirda, E.: Thou shalt not depend on me: analysing the use of outdated javascript libraries on the web. In: NDSS. The Internet Society (2017)

38. Lerner, A., Simpson, A.K., Kohno, T., Roesner, F.: Internet jonesa and the raiders of the lost trackers: an archaeological study of web tracking from 1996 to 2016. In: 25th USENIX Security (2016)

39. Li, Z., Zhang, K., Xie, Y., Yu, F., Wang, X.: Knowing your enemy: understanding and detecting malicious web advertising. In: CCS (2012)

40. MalwareDontNeedCoffee: A doubleclick https open redirect used in some malvertising chain (2015). https://malware.dontneedcoffee.com/2015/10/a-doubleclick-https-open-redirect-used.html

41. Nikiforakis, N., et al.: You are what you include: large-scale evaluation of remote javascript inclusions. In: CCS (2012)

42. Pellegrino, G., Rossow, C., Ryba, F.J., Schmidt, T.C., Wählisch, M.: Cashing out the great cannon? on browser-based DDoS attacks and economics. In: USENIX Sec (2015)

43. Popa, B.: 85 infected android apps stealing social network passwords found on play store (2017). https://news.softpedia.com/news/85-infected-android-apps-stealing-social-network-passwords-found-on-play-store-518984.shtml

44. Rastogi, V., Shao, R., Chen, Y., Pan, X., Zou, S., Riley, R.: Are these ads safe: detecting hidden attacks through the mobile app-web interfaces. In: NDSS (2016)

45. Reis, C., Gribble, S.D., Kohno, T., Weaver, N.C.: Detecting in-flight page changes with web tripwires. In: NSDI (2008)

46. Sequa, J.: Large angler malvertising campaign hits top publishers (2016). https://blog.malwarebytes.com/threat-analysis/2016/03/large-angler-malvertising-campaign-hits-top-publishers/
47. Starov, O., Dahse, J., Ahmad, S.S., Holz, T., Nikiforakis, N.: No honor among thieves: a large-scale analysis of malicious web shells. In: WWW (2016)
48. Tang, Z., et al.: iOS, your OS, everybody's OS: vetting and analyzing network services of iOS applications. In: 29th USENIX Security Symposium (USENIX Security 2020), pp. 2415–2432 (2020)
49. Unuchek, R.: Leaking ads securelist (2018). https://securelist.com/leaking-ads/85239/
50. Vance, A.: Times web ads show security breach (2009). https://www.nytimes.com/2009/09/15/technology/internet/15adco.html
51. Vanrykel, E., Acar, G., Herrmann, M., Diaz, C.: Leaky birds: exploiting mobile application traffic for surveillance. In: ICFCDS (2016)
52. Vigna, G., Valeur, F., Balzarotti, D., Robertson, W., Kruegel, C., Kirda, E.: Reducing errors in the anomaly-based detection of web-based attacks through the combined analysis of web requests and SQL queries. JCS **17**(3) (2009)
53. Virus, Q.R.: How to remove nintendonx@qq.com virus completely (2017). https://quickremovevirus.com/how-to-remove-nintendonxqq-com-virus-completely7
54. Wang, H., et al.: An explorative study of the mobile app ecosystem from app developers' perspective. In: WWW (2017)
55. Wang, X.S., Balasubramanian, A., Krishnamurthy, A., Wetherall, D.: Demystify page load performance with wprof. In: USENIX NSDI (2013)
56. Whittaker, C., Ryner, B., Nazif, M.: Large-scale automatic classification of phishing pages. In: NDSS (2010)

Comprehensive Mobile Traffic Characterization Based on a Large-Scale Mobile Traffic Dataset

Shuang Zhao(ID), Jincheng Zhong(ID), Shuhui Chen$^{(\boxtimes)}$(ID), and Jianbing Liang(ID)

National University of Defense Technology, Changsha 410073, China
{zhaoshuang16,zhongjincheng14,shchen,jianbing}@nudt.edu.cn

Abstract. Mobile traffic has accounted for a principal part of network traffic with the ways of accessing the Internet shifting to mobile devices. Subsequently, mobile traffic analysis becomes the focus of research. However, there is a lack of studies on mobile traffic characterization, while the traffic characteristics are important for obtaining a clear understanding of mobile networks. To make up for this research gap, this paper provides a comprehensive overview and characterization of current mobile application traffic. The properties of mobile traffic are described from four perspectives based on a large-scale mobile traffic dataset, including basic information (the destination IP, the destination Port, and the protocol), domain name usage, HTTP/TLS protocol usage, and the traffic flow. Besides, the properties of mobile traffic shown by different application categories are also analyzed simultaneously. Finally, a discussion is provided on how the presented observations work on various traffic analysis tasks in mobile networks.

Keywords: Mobile traffic characterization · Mobile traffic properties · Mobile traffic analysis

1 Introduction

As shown in mobile application (app) analytics reports [1–3], mobile apps account for roughly 90% of smartphone usage and 56% of web page views worldwide in 2021. These indicate that the ways of accessing the Internet have turned to mobile devices, and mobile app traffic has accounted for a majority of network traffic. Accordingly, mobile traffic analysis becomes a new research hotspot [4].

To perform mobile traffic analysis tasks better, it is essential to have a clear understanding of mobile traffic. On the one hand, the measurement of mobile traffic provides the researchers with an independent view of what is happening on the mobile Internet, which forms the foundation of simulation and emulation studies. On the other hand, the traffic properties could greatly affect researchers' decision-making. However, we notice that there is a lack of a comprehensive characterization of the current mobile traffic. The answers to questions about the properties of mobile traffic are difficult to be found from a few references. For instance, "How much of mobile traffic is encrypted now?", "Are there any differences between the traffic properties of different categories of apps?", "How many

X. Yuan et al. (Eds.): NSS 2022, LNCS 13787, pp. 214–232, 2022.
https://doi.org/10.1007/978-3-031-23020-2_12

connections in mobile traffic have DNS requests in front of them?". Given the scarcity of research work that characterizes mobile traffic from multiple perspectives, interested parties usually need to go through a large number of studies and synthesize fragmented measurements of mobile traffic to gain an initial overview of mobile traffic [4].

Several possible reasons why the measurements of mobile traffic have not received sufficient attention are as follows. Firstly, most elements in mobile networks, such as protocols, communication methods, and data transmission, are similar to those of traditional desktop networks. This makes it easy to transfer the measurement of traditional networks directly to mobile networks. However, this straight migration is reckless as mobile networks grow and update rapidly. Secondly, many challenging issues arise as mobile network traffic dominates, such as mobile traffic identification, privacy protection, and user profiling. These issues have gained more attention than basic mobile network measurements. Besides, although capturing mobile traffic is not difficult, the lack of labels (e.g. app label, service label) for the traffic makes it difficult to characterize mobile traffic at such high levels. Lastly, the rapid iterations of mobile networks may introduce concerns that the measurement of current mobile networks may quickly become outdated. This may further lead many researchers to underestimate the necessity of mobile traffic characterization.

To fill this research gap, a comprehensive mobile traffic characterization is provided in this paper. In contrast to other research efforts that give fragmented descriptions of mobile traffic, our work provides interested parties with up-to-date information on the properties of mobile traffic from multiple perspectives and in multiple dimensions. Moreover, our work measures the mobile traffic at the app/app category level as the dataset that supports our work is labeled at the app level. We hope that this work could serve as a basis for helping interested parties to better conduct their research. Overall, we gain insight into the properties of mobile traffic from four perspectives based on a large-scale labeled mobile traffic dataset:

(1) The properties of mobile traffic in its basic information are analyzed. The basic information includes the protocol, the destination IP (dstIP), and the destination Port (dstPort).
(2) The properties of domain names used in mobile traffic are summarized.
(3) Two most commonly used protocols in mobile networks, namely HTTP and TLS, are investigated in detail.
(4) The properties of traffic biflows are measured. Besides, the traffic properties shown by different apps and app categories are analyzed.

The rest of this paper is organized as follows. Section 2 introduced the related work. The mobile traffic dataset is described in Sect. 3. Then, the mobile traffic is characterized from four perspectives and the detailed findings are provided in Sect. 4. Section 5 discusses how the findings assist in improving various mobile traffic analysis tasks. Finally, Sect. 6 concludes the paper.

2   Related Work

Mauro et al. [4] summarize works that investigate the network traffic generated by specific apps or a population of mobile devices. Those works generally focus on the protocol composition of the traffic, the characteristics of traffic in size and arrival time, or the traffic behavior of specific apps. The main traffic properties that emerged from those works are highlighted in [4]. However, some conclusions in those works are no longer applicable as the properties of mobile traffic have changed greatly over time. For instance, the conclusion "Android apps typically do not encrypt their network traffic" is not in conformity with the reality now.

Several studies build the temporal and spatial profile of mobile traffic based on large-scale unlabeled mobile traffic. Hoang et al. [5] provide the analysis of traffic obtained from an LTE Network. The daily and weekly throughput patterns of mobile traffic are given in their work. Besides, they summarize the traffic intensity behaviors on weekdays and weekends. Similarly, Shi et al. [6] capture the weekly, daily, and hourly temporal patterns in the mobile traffic load across base stations. Their analysis shows that there are patterns in traffic distribution across time. Moreover, the patterns are predictable. Lastly, five traffic patterns are extracted and mapped to five types of geophysical locations related to urban ecology. In addition, Fang et al. [7] measure the mobile web traffic based on a massive real commercial dataset. Several web traffic properties are extracted, such as the web parsing time and the web page size. For the above works, the analysis of traffic properties at the app level is insufficient.

Other works almost only briefly depict the traffic properties from part of the point of view when introducing their datasets. Wang et al. [8] point out that most apps transmit their data based on the HTTP protocol since they use ports 80 and 443 for communication. Aceto et al. [9] release the MIRAGE-2019 dataset and provide a description for it. Specifically, the packet length distribution of two apps (Dropbox and Slither.io) is presented. Then, they report the distribution of the packet length and inter-arrival time for three different app categories (Productivity, Sports, and Games). According to MIRAGE-2019, more than 88% of the traffic flows have volumes less than 100KB. Meanwhile, downstream traffic accounts for 65% of the volume of the whole traffic. Based on a private mobile traffic dataset, Rezaei et al. [10] conclude that the majority of the mobile traffic flows are carried by TCP. Besides, only streaming and video/voice apps contain a significant amount of UDP traffic, with their UDP flows accounting for around 10% of the whole traffic flow. Sengupta et al. [11] investigate the cipher suites used for encrypting mobile traffic. After extracting the SeverHello and ClientHello TLS handshake messages from the mobile traffic, they parse those messages to find out how the cipher suites are used by different apps. Chen et al. [12] analyze their manually collected mobile dataset. They find that around 79.9% of the traffic flows contain an X.509 certificate.

Compared with the existing studies, our work provides a more comprehensive description and measurement of mobile traffic. On the one hand, our work includes the points of interest of the existing work, and further validates and updates those points of interest with a recent mobile traffic dataset. On the other hand, our work extracts the properties of mobile traffic in higher dimensions, including the app level and the app category level.

3   Mobile Traffic Dataset

Netlog is used to collect mobile traffic and label it at the app level [13]. The core functions of Netlog are built on the VPNService (an API provided in Android SDK). Netlog would create a virtual network interface after it is installed and launched on an Android device. Then it could create a duplicate copy of the device's network traffic at the userspace without requiring the root permission. Besides, Android provides the UID, which can be used to map a traffic flow to a specific app by Android's PackageManager API. By this means Netlog could collect and label mobile traffic. Since Netlog collects the traffic before it is encapsulated and forwarded by the VPNService, hence no additional bias will be introduced into the traffic during this traffic collection process.

Based on Netlog, our traffic collection was conducted during 2020.05-2020.07 with the participation of 224 volunteers. The volunteers were asked to install and operate the designated apps on their smartphones. At last, a total of about 636 GB of traffic data is collected from 785 apps, with 611.23 GB of data labeled. There are five types of networks are found in our collection, including 2G, 3G, 4G, LTE_CA, and WIFI. Besides, the smartphones used in the collection involve at least 9 brands and 94 models. Overall, the mobile traffic is captured under diverse configurations. This dataset will be made public after anonymization in our future work [14]. After preprocessing, we found that 350 apps (quoted as head apps) account for 99.39% of the collected traffic in bytes. According to the main functionalities provided by apps, the head apps are classified into 22 categories as listed in Table 1.

It is worth mentioning that our dataset has some unavoidable limitations. Firstly, the apps we selected are all from China, which leads to some of the analysis results may not apply to other regions, such as the domain name usage.

Table 1. Categories of the head apps.

Category	# of apps	Traffic (GB)	Category	# of apps	Traffic (GB)
Tools	18	24.64	News	5	10.88
Online shopping (OShop)	34	56.41	Video	38	108.55
Social Comm (SComm)	13	25.46	Health & exercise (HE)	8	9.59
Game	17	18.82	Audio	6	4.12
Finance	48	91.68	Community platform (CPlat)	20	24.70
Browser	9	9.18	Phone beauty (Beauty)	2	4.78
Reading	25	34.24	Input method (Input)	4	2.14
Convenient life (Life)	35	66.39	File transfer (FTrans)	7	17.35
Education (Edu)	21	40.83	Business (Bus)	4	2.31
Travel & navigation (TN)	15	24.21	Children (Child)	9	12.17
Security	4	3.13	Photography (Photo)	8	14.27

Secondly, the users' individual behavioral preferences may affect the traffic properties of an app to some extent. For instance, the traffic properties of an app could be dominated by the functions executed in one path if the user over-executes a certain path. Thirdly, this dataset was collected in 2020, which does not strictly represent the latest mobile traffic. However, our subsequent analysis finds that some characteristics of mobile traffic, such as duration and flow size, are not significantly different from those of many years ago. Finally, the distribution of our app set differs from the distribution of apps present in practical mobile networks, which may introduce some noise. However, considering the scale of this dataset, we believe that the statistical results on this dataset are worthy of reference.

4   Mobile Traffic Characterization

In this section, mobile traffic is characterized from four perspectives, including basic information, domain name usage, HTTP/TLS protocols usage, and the traffic flow.

Basic information refers to the five-tuple information of packets, including Protocol, source IP (srcIP), source Port (srcPort), destination IP (dstIP), and destination Port (dstPort). The srcIPs of all packets in our dataset are set with a fixed value due to the mechanism of Netlog. In addition, most apps randomly select srcPorts to build their connections. Therefore, we analyze the properties of Protocol, dstIP, and dstPort of mobile traffic in detail.

Based on the five-tuple information, mobile traffic can be grouped into biflows, which are usually chosen as the analysis objects in the existing researches [15]. In our work, mobile traffic is characterized from the viewpoints of traffic bytes and biflows. For simplicity, flow is also used in this paper to represent biflow.

4.1   Basic Information

Protocol. Firstly, the protocols used in mobile traffic are investigated. Fig. 1 provides the distribution of mobile traffic under different protocols.

It can be seen from Fig. 1 that mobile traffic mainly relies on TCP to transmit data, and TCP traffic accounts for 97.34% and 72.13% in bytes and flows, respectively. Although UDP traffic has a ratio of 27.12% in flows, 22.08% of them are DNS. However, UDP-based DNS traffic only occupies 0.1% of mobile traffic in bytes, the majority of UDP traffic (2.64%) transmits application data. HTTP and HTTPS are the mainly used application layer protocols for TCP traffic. HTTPS traffic accounts for 46.53% and 40.88% of the total traffic in bytes and flows respectively, which is close to HTTP traffic in bytes and even exceeds HTTP traffic in flows. Therefore, encrypted traffic has become the main part of mobile traffic. In addition, a few DNS data are found to be transmitted using TCP. Lastly, there is a small amount of ICMP traffic in mobile traffic in addition to TCP and UDP.

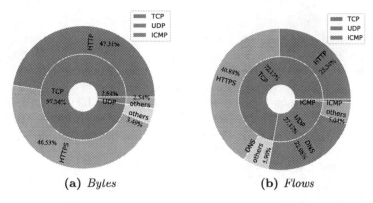

(a) *Bytes*   **(b)** *Flows*

Fig. 1. Bytes and flows distribution of mobile traffic under different protocols. (For clarity, the protocols with extremely small ratios are not displayed in the figures, such as ICMP and DNS in (a)).

In terms of IPv6, 0.5% and 2.72% of mobile traffic adopt it in bytes and flows. It seems that there is a low adoption rate of IPv6 in mobile traffic at present.

Then we investigate how apps and app categories use UDP and HTTPS to transmit their data. Figure 2 gives the number of apps under the different ratio of flows transmitting application data using HTTPS/UDP. Figure 3 provides the average ratio of flows transmitting application data using HTTPS/UDP for each app category.

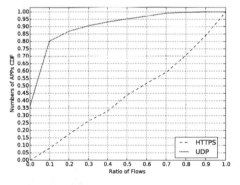

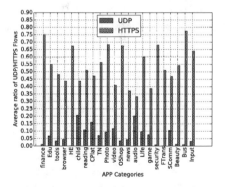

Fig. 2. The number of apps (CDF) under the different ratio of flows that transmit application data based on HTTPS/UDP.

Fig. 3. The average flow ratio that transmits application data based on HTTPS/UDP for each app category.

As Fig. 2 shows, the UDP flows generated by more than 80% of the apps account for less than 10% of their total traffic flows. Moreover, 127 apps do not adopt UDP at all. As shown in Fig. 3, children and audio apps produce the most UDP flows (about 20% of their traffic in flows). The app categories of the second echelon using UDP flows include community platform, video, and social community. The common feature between those categories is that many video and audio resources are usually provided by apps in these categories. In other words, apps that need to access a large number of audio and video resources usually generate more UDP traffic than other apps.

In terms of HTTPS, the HTTPS flows generated by 56.28% of the head apps are more than half of their total traffic flows, and 16% of the head apps are more than 90%. Besides, finance and business apps show the highest average ratios of HTTPS flows, which both are over 70%. The following six app categories, health & exercise, photography, online shopping, convenient life, security, and input method, fall into the ratio space of 60%–70%. Such results are in line with expectations, since such apps generally access the most sensitive information of users. Lastly, the average ratio of HTTPS flows of audio apps is the smallest, which is 33.3%.

Destination Port. The dstPort refers specifically to the port used by the server. Besides, we focus on how dstPorts of TCP flows distribute. A total of 7,305,801 flows are obtained and 7,762 different dstPorts are extracted after filtering the TCP flows of 350 head apps.

Four ports are used by the overwhelming majority of the flows among thousands of dstPorts, including 443, 80, 8080, and 8081. The proportion of flows using these four ports reaches 95.96%, and the proportion for each port is 58.21%, 34.71%, 1.34%, 1.70%, respectively. It is consistent with the fact that mobile traffic mainly uses HTTP/HTTPS to transmit data, as these four ports are the default ports of these two protocols. The rest ports (quoted as random ports) used by the remainder 294,859 flows fall into 7 to 65243. The number of random ports used by each head app is shown in Fig. 4. Note that five head apps are not included in Fig. 4, because the number of random ports used by these five apps far exceeds that of the other 345 apps. These five apps use 2107, 2337, 707, 1634, and 978 random ports, respectively. Compared with these five apps, 335 apps out of the rest 345 apps use no more than 30 random ports.

Then, we analyze the distribution of the random ports to find out whether apps have a preference for the selection of random ports. The value range of the dstPort (0–65535) is divided into 66 buckets equally, each with a length of 1000. The ratio of flows falling into each bucket is depicted in Fig. 5. As Fig. 5 shows, the apps are prone to choose small ports that are less than 15000 although the random ports are widely distributed. Besides, it can be observed that the ratio of flows within the bucket 8000–9000 is far larger than others. Meanwhile, there are other three small peaks in the range of 30000–31000, 33000–34000, and 55000–56000.

Destination IP. Similarly, the dstIP refers to the IP used by the server. Based on our dataset, 42,670 different dstIPs are obtained from the TCP flows of 350 head apps. Meanwhile, 111,352 $<app, dstIP>$ pairs are extracted, each pair implies that there is at least one request that exists from the app to that $dstIP$.

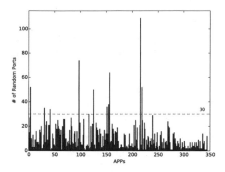

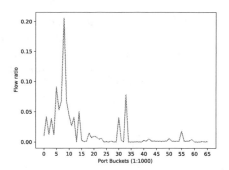

Fig. 4. The number of random ports used by 345 head apps.

Fig. 5. The ratio of flows for random port buckets.

We found that 72.34% of these dstIPs were accessed by only one app and led 42.9% of TCP flows. Therefore, the dstIP would be a valuable attribute for many traffic analysis tasks. For instance, the performance of mobile traffic identification may be improved when the dstIP is added as a feature. However, it is worth mentioning that the dstIP is unstable in some cases, especially for the mobile network. The application of Content Delivery Network (CDN) in mobile networks makes the dstIP changes frequently. For the rest of the dstIPs, we found that one dstIP is visited at most by 128 apps in our dataset. Besides, 250 different dstIPs are visited by one app on average for 340 head apps. The number of visited dstIPs of the remaining 10 apps is significantly higher than that of the other 340 apps, which are distributed between 1092–4494. The

Lastly, 41.46% of TCP flows with SYN handshake are established after a DNS request. In other words, these flows obtain their dstIPs by DNS requests. Therefore, the rich information in DNS packets is worthy of attention to assist relevant traffic analysis tasks.

4.2 Domain Name Usage

In this section, the usage of the domain name in mobile traffic is analyzed. A total of 19,538 unique domain names are found by parsing the DNS response packets in our traffic dataset.

Length of Domain Names. The maximum and minimum lengths of the found domain names are 73 and 5, with an average length of 25.3. Meanwhile, 80% of domain names have a length of less than 35. In addition, the number of domain names in the following length ranges, [0–10], [30–40], and [50–60], is smaller than that in other ranges. Overall, the majority of domain names fall into the length range of 10 to 35. As for the level deepness of domain names, we find 7 types, namely 2–8. The distribution ratios of domain names with level 2 to level 8 are around 1%, 54.76%, 34.27%, 8.26%, 1.63%, 0.01%, 0.01%. respectively.

Top 10 Domain Names. Table 2 lists the top 10 second-level domain names that provide the most services under three different standards. The three standards are the number of requests responded by the domain name, the traffic volume generated from the domain name, and the number of apps that visit the domain name. The obtained top 10 domain names are overlapped under these three ranking standards, while there are some changes.

For the top 10 domain names with the most number of requests, nine of them are registered by the five largest Internet companies in China, including Tencent, ByteDance, Baidu, Alibaba, and Kuaishou. Each company has developed multiple apps that are popular in China. Therefore, it is understandable that these domain names are frequently visited. The remaining domain name, xdrig.com, provides data analysis services, which contributes to its high access frequency.

There is an obvious change in the top 10 domain names under the standard of traffic volume. The domain name that provides audio/video resources has a higher ranking, such as ixigua.com and videocc.net. In addition, some domain names providing cloud services enter the top 10, such as bcebo.com and alicdn.com.

Lastly, new features are reflected in terms of the top 10 domain names that are visited by the maximum number of apps. For these 10 domain names, they either provide services to multiple apps that were developed by one company (e.g., qq.com provides services for dozens of apps from Tencent), or they belong to third-party service providers and provide third-party services, such as cloud services (e.g., aliyuncs.com), map services (e.g., amap.com), and data analysis services (e.g., umeng.com and getui.com), or they meet the above two cases at the same time. Such features can be beneficial to the mobile traffic analysis tasks such as discovering third-party services.

Table 2. Top 10 second-level domain names under three different standards.

Top-10 second-level domain names		
Number of requests	Traffic volume	Number of apps
qq.com	ixigua.com	qq.com
douyincdn.com	qq.com	baidu.com
yximgs.com	yximgs.com	umeng.com
pstatp.com	sm.cn	pstatp.com
xdrig.com	bcebos.com	snssdk.com
snssdk.com	pstatp.com	taobao.com
baidu.com	alicdn.com	aliyuncs.com
ixigua.com	videocc.net	ctobsnssdk.com
gtimg.cn	lianhaikeji.com	amap.com
taobao.com	baidu.com	getui.com

Domain Names, DstIPs, and Apps. Finally, we explore the domain name usage from the following two angles, the correlations between domain names and dstIPs, and the correlations between domain names and apps.

There is a many-to-many relationship between dstIPs and domain names due to the application of CDN, cloud services, load balancing, and other technologies. One dstIP could support multiple domain names. On the contrary, one domain name could associate with multiple dstIPs. In our dataset, we found that there is an average of 10.66 dstIPs behind one domain name, with a maximum of 1,014 different dstIPs for one domain name. For each dstIP, a maximum/minimum of 790/4 domain names are deployed on it, with an average of 16 domain names per dstIP.

For domain names and apps, about 72.56% of domain names are accessed by one app. It indicates that there is a strong correlation between domain names and apps. Meanwhile, this correlation is more stable than the correlation between dstIPs and apps. Therefore, the information contained in DNS can be utilized to analyze mobile traffic at the app level, if the mapping relationship between the domain names and apps can be determined.

4.3 HTTP/TLS Usage

This section examines what properties of HTTP and TLS are presented in mobile traffic since they are the mainstream protocols used by mobile networks. The following analysis is conducted on the HTTP/TLS flows with the TCP 3-way handshake.

HTTP. We focus on "Request Method" and "Host" for the fields of the HTTP request. There is a set of predefined request methods in HTTP protocol, such as GET and POST. Different request methods are usually applied in different scenarios. Five kinds of request methods are found in our dataset, including GET, POST, HEAD, OPTIONS, and PUT. The proportions of traffic using these request methods in flows and bytes are listed in Table 3.

Table 3. The usage of "Request Method" in mobile traffic.

Request method	Flows	Bytes
GET	57.142%	97.058%
POST	42.692%	2.828%
HEAD	0.157%	0.099%
OPTIONS	0.0008%	0.0001%
PUT	0.00792%	0.013%

As shown in Table 3, most of the HTTP flows use GET and POST to transfer application data. The other three methods appear occasionally. In addition, the number of HTTP flows using POST is close to that using GET. However, the HTTP flows using GET transmit 97.058% of data. Therefore, it can be inferred that the large data block is usually transmitted by the way of GET, while the HTTP flows with POST only transmit a small amount of data.

As for the field of "Host", it is found that 75.75% of HTTP flows are not empty in this field, and those flows account for 98.02% of HTTP traffic in bytes. This field could provide rich information for many mobile traffic analysis tasks. The high non-empty rate of this field implies that it could play a promising role in related analysis tasks.

TLS. The handshake phase of TLS flows is plaintext, which is often exploited by mobile traffic analysis tasks. Therefore, we further explore the properties of TLS shown in the handshake phase.

(1) Packets transmitted during the handshake

Firstly, we calculated the bytes and number of packets that are transmitted during the handshake phase. The CDF of those two statistics are shown in Fig. 6 and Fig. 7, respectively. The number of packets is calculated as the number of packets between the first packet after the TCP 3-way handshake and the first packet that transfers the application data. The size of bytes is the sum of the payload length from the L3 layer of those packets.

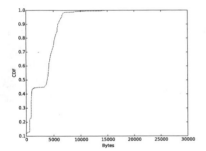 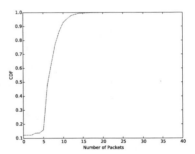

Fig. 6. The CDF of transferred bytes during the TLS handshake.

Fig. 7. The CDF of transferred number of packets during the TLS handshake.

As Fig. 6 shows, despite the long tail, the bytes transmitted during the TLS handshake are mainly distributed in two intervals: [647,1123] and [3701–6790]. These two intervals contain 28.6% and 51.12% of flows, respectively. For the tasks that need to analyze the TLS handshake, exploiting the first 6790 bytes of TLS flows would be a good choice since it already holds all the handshake information of 98.12% of TLS flows. For the number of packets transferred during the TLS handshake, at most 37 packets are found in our dataset. However, around 83.5% of flows only have 6 to 15 packets in this phase, and 99.66% of flows have less than 16 packets. Among those flows, about 12.26% of flows transfer their application data without the TLS handshake. Therefore, it is sufficient to analyze the first 15 packets for most TLS flows.

(2) Cipher Suites Usage

Secondly, we paid attention to the cipher suites supported by the client and the server. In one ClientHello packet, the client offers the server a sequence of cipher suites ordered in the preference of the client. Each cipher suite defines a set of methods, such as the encryption algorithm and pseudorandom function, that will be needed to establish a connection and transmit data using TLS.

There are 246 different cipher suites are extracted from the ClientHello packets in our dataset. The use rate of each cipher suite and the number of apps that support the cipher suite are shown in Fig. 8. It can be seen from Fig. 8 that several cipher suites appear more frequently than others. In addition, there is a positive correlation between the use rate and the number of apps. The values of cipher suites with use rates higher than 0.1 are listed in Table 4. The detailed cipher suites information corresponding to these values can be found in [16]. Appendix A also provides the corresponding cipher suites mentioned in this paper for quick looking up. In addition to the 22 cipher suites listed in Table 4, the use rates of other cipher suites are close to 0.01 or even less.

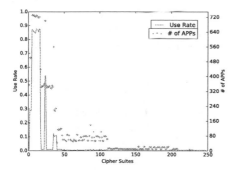

Fig. 8. The usage of each cipher suite (the client end).

Table 4. Cipher suites with use rate higher than 0.1 (the client end).

Use rate	Cipher suite	#
0.8–0.9	49171, 47, 49172, 49199, 49195, 156, 49200, 49196, 157, 52393, 52392, 53	12
0.5–0.6	49161, 49162	2
0.2–0.3	4865, 4866, 4867	3
0.1–0.2	10, 51, 57, 158, 159	5

After receiving the ClientHello packet, the server would select one cipher suite and send its choice to the client by a ServerHello packet. We found that 22 kinds of cipher suites were selected by servers after parsing the ServerHello packets. Among these 22 cipher suites, 16 of them come from Table 4. Moreover, all 12 cipher suites with a use rate between 0.8 to 0.9 had been selected by servers. On the contrary, the 3 cipher suites with a use rate between 0.2 to 0.3 had not been used by any server. Table 5 lists the usage details of cipher suites selected by servers with a frequency greater than 10^{-2}. Note that the server-side cipher suites provided by 15.86% of TLS flows were empty. It can be seen from Table 5 that the server has a strong bias towards the cipher suite. Although all of the cipher suites in Table 5 have more than 80% use rate on the client side, 49199 (TLS_ECDHE_RSA_WITH_AES_128_GCM_SHA256) is the most commonly used cipher suite, which is preferred by nearly half of the TLS flows. In addition to 49199, only cipher suites 49200 (TLS_ECDHE_RSA_WITH_AES _256_GCM_SHA384) and 52392 (TLS_ECDHE_RSA_WITH_ CHACHA20_POLY1305_SHA256) are often selected.

Table 5. The usage details of 6 kinds of cipher suites.

Cipher suite	Use rate (ServerHello)	Use rate (ClientHello)	Number of apps using it
49199	49.32%	87.11%	732
49200	20.66%	85.71%	730
Empty	15.86%	/	/
52392	6.19%	84.64%	725
49195	2.57%	86.96%	732
53	1.93%	87.48%	721
156	1.27%	86.91%	721

Lastly, we examined the extension field of Server Name Indication (SNI) in the ClientHello packets. This field plays an important role in a variety of traffic analysis tasks. We found that 81.31% and 95.35% of traffic have a non-empty SNI in flows and bytes, which means that the analysis that relies on this field could deal with the majority of the encrypted traffic.

4.4 Traffic Flow

In this section, we look into four attributes of mobile traffic from the perspective of the flow, including the flow size, the number of packets per flow, the flow duration, and the ratio of downlink traffic to uplink traffic per flow (D/U). Meanwhile, we refine the property differences in these four attributes of different

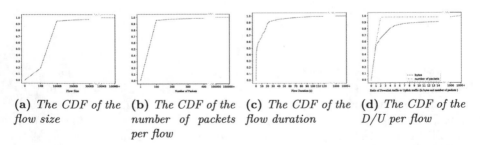

(a) *The CDF of the flow size*   **(b)** *The CDF of the number of packets per flow*   **(c)** *The CDF of the flow duration*   **(d)** *The CDF of the D/U per flow*

Fig. 9. The CDFs of mobile traffic flows in the flow size, the number of packets, the flow duration, and the D/U.

app categories. Figure 9 provides the CDFs of the above four attributes of mobile TCP flows. Several conclusions can be drawn from Fig. 9.

About one fifth of the flows have a flow size less than 1 KB as shown in Fig. 9a, and 94.79% of the flows have a flow size less than 100 KB. Although most mobile traffic flows are "mice" flows, few "elephant" flows are found in our dataset. For example, the sizes of 66 flows in our dataset are larger than 100 MB.

In terms of the number of packets per flow, 95.57% of the flows have less than 100 packets as shown in Fig. 9b. Although the number of packets usually increases with the increase of the flow size, our statistics show that the growth of the number of packets is slower than the growth of the flow size. In other words, for the flows with large sizes, they would give priority to adding the number of bytes carried by each packet, rather than using more packets.

Then, the duration of mobile traffic flows shows the characteristics of short and fast. As shown in Fig. 9c, more than half of the flows (51.22%) ended in 2 s, and 96.6% of the flows ended within 1 min. The remaining flows almost ended within 2 min.

As for the D/U per flow, we measure it from the aspects of bytes and the number of packets. In terms of bytes, the D/U of 53.67% of flows is less than 1, which indicates that there is a considerable need to upload data in mobile networks. The D/U of the remaining flows is mainly distributed between 1–30. Among them, 34.18% and 4.75% of the flows fall into the interval of 1–7 and 7–30, respectively. In terms of the number of packets, the D/U of 56.92% of the flows is less than 1, which is similar to the scenario in bytes. However, 40.67% out of the remaining 43.08% of the flows have a D/U between 1–2. This result demonstrates that the number of downlink packets is close to that of uplink packets even if the downlink bytes far exceed the uplink bytes.

We calculate the average and median values of these four attributes for apps in different categories to refine the properties differences between app categories. The results are depicted in Fig. 10. For each category, the average and median values are presented in the first column and the second column, and each point in the columns is an app that belongs to the category. Due to space limitations, we do not display the apps that are outside the set maximum value of the y-axis in the subgraphs. Note that such cases are rare.

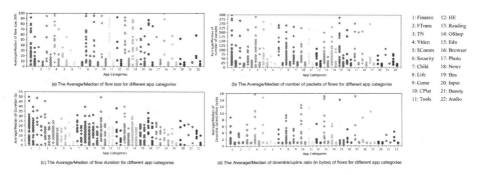

Fig. 10. The Average/Median of four attributes of flows for different app categories.

Figure 10a shows the flow size distribution for different app categories. On the whole, the average flow sizes of all categories are higher than the median flow sizes. It implies that although there is a large number of "mice" flows in mobile networks, "elephant" flows account for the main part of mobile traffic. In the same category, the average flow sizes of different apps are widely distributed, while the median flow sizes are generally small. Among different categories, the average flow sizes of Child, Reading, Photo, and Beauty are relatively larger than that of other categories, while other significant differences are not found. The distribution of the number of packets for different app categories is similar to that of the flow size.

In terms of the flow duration, it can be seen from Fig. 10c that the average values and the median values of different apps in the same category are close, and the value distributions are compact. Among these 22 categories, Security, Browser, and Beauty have large minimum average values, which are higher than 10 s. However, their maximum average values are lower than 40 s. Contrarily, business apps show small median values of flow duration.

Lastly, for the D/U (in bytes), the average values and median values of Security, Edu, Bus, and Input are very close, and both of them are about 1. It can be inferred that most flows of apps in these categories need to upload and download data to the server at the same time. For the remaining categories, their average values are generally much larger than their median values, and their median values are mainly distributed between 0–2. Besides, the apps of Video, SComm, CPlat, and Reading have relatively large average values, which indicates that these apps have the need to obtain a large number of resources from the server.

5 Discussion

This section discusses how our observations can be employed to achieve the relevant parties' goals, and several examples are provided. We believe that our work could provide more inspiration than the examples we give.

5.1 Network Operator

Based on the findings of our work, the network operator could learn the composition of mobile traffic and how network resources are used by mobile apps, so as to deploy and configure the network resource reasonably, improve the network resource utilization and the quality of user experience. In addition, some of our observations could be employed by the network operator to analyze the mobile app usage in the current network and adopt corresponding control strategies. For instance, if a large amount of UDP traffic is observed in the network, it may be an indicator that some users are accessing apps or web pages rich in audio and video resources, which should not appear in some working scenarios.

5.2   Mobile Traffic Researcher

With the surge of mobile traffic, more researchers turn their attention to mobile traffic analysis. Mauro et al. [4] investigate the mobile traffic analysis tasks and identify 13 goals, such as traffic characterization, app identification, and PII leakage detection. Our work belongs to the category of traffic characterization according to their classification. Moreover, we notice that our findings could assist the design and decision-making of other mobile traffic analysis tasks. Two examples are provided as follows.

(1) Identification Tasks

There are several identification tasks in the field of mobile traffic analysis, such as app identification, service identification, user action identification, and device identification [17]. For those identification tasks, some inspirations can be drawn from our work.

Firstly, the traffic properties found in our work could help researchers mine effective features for identifying mobile traffic. For example, the statistics such as the flow size, the flow duration, and the up/down link traffic ratio could be taken into account in the feature design. For the solution based on deep learning, it usually uses the raw packets as its input. In this case, the number of packets and the number of bytes used for input are the hyperparameters of the model for such solutions. As pointed out by Wang et al. [13], the most effective features found by deep learning models exist in the TLS handshake packets. Therefore, the first 6–15 packets and the first 647–6790 bytes of TLS flows are pretty good hyperparameters selection ranges based on our findings. Besides, considering that there is still a high proportion of HTTP and DNS traffic in the mobile network, the rich plaintext information contained in such traffic could be exploited in the identification tasks.

(2) Malware Detection

For the traffic properties of benign apps described in our work, they can be regarded as preliminary knowledge for malicious behavior detection in mobile traffic. For example, the length of the domain name is an important indicator for malicious domain name detection [18]. Another example is botnet detection. In a botnet, the command & control server will frequently change its domain name to enhance the concealment. While our statistics show that an average of 16 domain names are deployed on a dstIP. Therefore, abnormal behavior of one IP may be reflected when a large number of domain names are counted on that IP. In addition, the purpose of some malicious apps is to steal user data. Hence, they would frequently collect user information and upload it to the server. Such behaviors may result in different up/down link traffic properties from what we have observed.

6   Conclusion

Although researches on mobile traffic have become hotspots, there is still a lack of clear and comprehensive understanding of the current mobile application traffic. This paper fully describes the properties of mobile application traffic from multiple perspectives, including its basic information, domain name usage, HTTP/TLS usage, and traffic flow. In addition, based on these four perspectives, this paper gives an in-depth analysis from the viewpoints of bytes, flows, and application categories. Compared with the existing work, the measurement of mobile traffic in this work is more comprehensive and detailed. On the whole, this paper not only provides an overview of the current mobile application traffic but also could provide guidance for the research of relevant parties. For future work, more dimensions on the characterization of mobile traffic could be complemented, such as the service level. In addition, it is valuable to analyze how mobile traffic properties change in the dimension of time.

Appendix A

Table 6 provides the cipher suites mentioned in this paper.

Table 6. The cipher suites look up table.

Value	Description
10	TLS_RSA_WITH_3DES_EDE_CBC_SHA
47	TLS_RSA_WITH_AES_128_CBC_SHA
51	TLS_DHE_RSA_WITH_AES_128_CBC_SHA
53	TLS_RSA_WITH_AES_256_CBC_SHA
57	TLS_DHE_RSA_WITH_AES_256_CBC_SHA
156	TLS_RSA_WITH_AES_128_GCM_SHA256
157	TLS_RSA_WITH_AES_256_GCM_SHA384
158	TLS_DHE_RSA_WITH_AES_128_GCM_SHA256
159	TLS_DHE_RSA_WITH_AES_256_GCM_SHA384
4865	TLS_AES_128_GCM_SHA256
4866	TLS_AES_256_GCM_SHA384
4867	TLS_CHACHA20_POLY1305_SHA256
49161	TLS_ECDHE_ECDSA_WITH_AES_128_CBC_SHA
49162	TLS_ECDHE_ECDSA_WITH_AES_256_CBC_SHA
49171	TLS_ECDHE_RSA_WITH_AES_128_CBC_SHA
49172	TLS_ECDHE_RSA_WITH_AES_256_CBC_SHA
49195	TLS_ECDHE_ECDSA_WITH_AES_128_GCM_SHA256
49196	TLS_ECDHE_ECDSA_WITH_AES_256_GCM_SHA384
49199	TLS_ECDHE_RSA_WITH_AES_128_GCM_SHA256
49200	TLS_ECDHE_RSA_WITH_AES_256_GCM_SHA384
52392	TLS_ECDHE_RSA_WITH_CHACHA20_POLY1305_SHA256
52393	TLS_ECDHE_ECDSA_WITH_CHACHA20_POLY1305_SHA256

References

1. Statista Research Department. Mobile app usage - Statistics & Facts. https://www.statista.com/topics/1002/mobile-app-usage/
2. Buildfire. Mobile app Download Statistics & Usage Statistics (2021) . https://buildfire.com/app-statistics/
3. First Site Guide. Mobile Web Traffic Stats and Facts in 2021. https://firstsiteguide.com/mobile-traffic-stats/
4. Conti, M., Li, Q.Q., Maragno, A., Spolaor, R.: The dark side(-channel) of mobile devices: a survey on network traffic analysis. IEEE Commun. Surv. Tutor. **20**(4), 2658–2713 (2018). https://doi.org/10.1109/COMST.2018.2843533
5. Trinh, H.D., Bui, N., Widmer, J., Giupponi, L., Dini, P.: Analysis and modeling of mobile traffic using real traces. In: IEEE 28th Annual International Symposium on Personal, Indoor, and Mobile Radio Communications, pp. 1–6 (2017). https://doi.org/10.1109/PIMRC.2017.8292200
6. Shi, H., Li, Y.: Discovering periodic patterns for large scale mobile traffic data: method and applications. IEEE Trans. Mob. Comput. **17**(10), 2266–2278 (2018). https://doi.org/10.1109/TMC.2018.2799945
7. Fang, C., Liu, J., Lei, Z.: Fine-grained HTTP web traffic analysis based on large-scale mobile datasets. IEEE Access **4**, 4364–4373 (2016). https://doi.org/10.1109/ACCESS.2016.2597538
8. Wang, R., Liu, Z., Cai, Y., Tang, D., Yang, J., Yang, Z.: Benchmark data for mobile app traffic research. In: 15th EAI International Conference on Mobile and Ubiquitous Systems: Computing, Networking and Services, pp. 402–411 (2018). https://doi.org/10.1145/3286978.3287000
9. Aceto, G., Ciuonzo, D., Montieri, A., Persico, V., Pescape, A.: MIRAGE: mobile-app traffic capture and ground-truth creation. In: International Conference on Computing, Communications and Security, pp. 1–8 (2019). https://doi.org/10.1109/CCCS.2019.8888137
10. Rezaei, S., Kroencke, B., Liu, X.: Large-scale mobile app identification using deep learning. IEEE Access **8**, 348–362 (2019)
11. Sengupta, S., Ganguly, N., De, P., Chakraborty, S.: Exploiting diversity in android TLS implementations for mobile app traffic classification. In: World Wide Web Conference, pp. 1657–1668 (2019). https://doi.org/10.1145/3308558.3313738
12. Chen, Y., Zang, T., Zhang, Y., Zhou, Y., Wang, Y.: Rethinking encrypted traffic classification: a multi-attribute associated fingerprint approach. In: IEEE 27th International Conference on Network Protocols, pp. 1–11 (2019). https://doi.org/10.1109/ICNP.2019.8888043
13. Wang, X., Chen, S., Jinshu, S.: Real network traffic collection and deep learning for mobile app identification. Wirel. Commun. Mob. Comput. **2020**, 1–14 (2020). https://doi.org/10.1155/2020/4707909
14. NUDT_MobileTraffic. https://github.com/Abby-ZS/NUDT_MobileTraffic
15. Aceto, G., Ciuonzo, D., Montieri, A., Pescape, A.: Mobile encrypted traffic classification using deep learning: experimental evaluation, lessons learned, and challenges. IEEE Trans. Netw. Serv. Manag. **16**(2), 445–458 (2019). https://doi.org/10.1109/TNSM.2019.2899085
16. Transport Layer Security (TLS) Parameters. https://www.iana.org/assignments/tls-parameters/tls-parameters.xhtml#tls-parameters-4

17. Bub, D., Hartmann, L., Bozakov, Z., Wendzel, S.: Towards passive identification of aged android devices in the home network. In: Proceedings of the 2022 European Interdisciplinary Cybersecurity Conference, pp. 17–20 (2022). https://doi.org/10.1145/3528580.3528584
18. Almashhadani, A.O., Kaiiali, M., Carlin, D., Sezer, S.: MaldomDetection: a system for detecting algorithmically generated domain names with machine learning. Comput. Secur. **93**(2020), 1–13 (2020)

DOT-M: A Dual Offline Transaction Scheme of Central Bank Digital Currency for Trusted Mobile Devices

Bo Yang[1,2(✉)] 🆔, Yanchao Zhang[1,2], and Dong Tong[1,2]

[1] National Fintech Evaluation Center, Beijing, China
[2] Research and Development Center, Bank Card Test Center, Beijing, China
{yangbo,zhangyanchao,tongdong}@bctest.com

Abstract. In recent years, many major economies have paid close attention to central bank digital currency (CBDC). As an optional attribute of CBDC, dual offline transaction is considered to have great practical value under the circumstances for payment without network connection. However, there is no public report or paper on how to securely design or implement the dual offline transaction function specifically for CBDC. In this paper, we propose DOT-M, a practical dual offline transaction scheme designed for the mobile device user as either a payer or a payee. Precisely, adopting secure element (SE) and trusted execution environment (TEE), the architecture of trusted mobile device is constructed to protect security-sensitive keys and execution of the transaction protocol. According to the trusted architecture, the data structure for offline transaction is designed as well. On this basis, we describe the core procedures of DOT-M in detail, including registration, account synchronization, dual offline transaction, and online data updating. A prototype system is implemented and finally tested with possible parameters. The security analysis and experimental results indicate that our scheme could meet the practical requirement of CBDC offline transaction for mobile users from both aspects of security and efficiency.

Keywords: Central bank digital currency (CBDC) · Dual offline transaction · Secure element (SE) · Trusted execution environment (TEE)

1 Introduction

Currently, a number of central banks are exploring central bank digital currency (CBDC). According to the latest survey conducted by the Bank for International Settlements (BIS) [1] on central banks in 65 countries or economies, about 86% have carried out researches on digital currencies. Meanwhile, the proportion of central banks that were performing experiments or developing a proof-of-concept prototype increased from 42% in 2019 to 60% in 2020. In October 2020, the European Central Bank released the report on a digital euro [2], which analyzed the causes and potential impacts of the launch of the digital. In July 2021, the

X. Yuan et al. (Eds.): NSS 2022, LNCS 13787, pp. 233–248, 2022.
https://doi.org/10.1007/978-3-031-23020-2_13

People's Bank of China issued the Progress on Research and Development of E-CNY in China [3].

Just as its name implies, dual offline transaction means the e-payment executed between the payer and the payee, neither of whom could connect to their online bank accounts as online e-payment. There are several papers [4,5] that have given some optional solutions by using cryptographic methods or blockchain technology. Actually, to achieve the same user experience as cash used in an environment without network, CBDC is supposed to support dual offline transaction.

For the public, mobile devices are the most convenient medium to reach CBDC or other e-payment services. In recent years, some standardization organizations in payment field have been exploring secure mechanisms and services on smart mobile devices. EMVCo proposes Software-based Mobile Payments [6] that make use of commercially available software protection techniques such as white-box cryptographic, obfuscation, and binary protection. Payment Card Industry (PCI) also puts forward some similar solutions [7] that do not require the use of a hardware-based secure element, and emphasizes that they are not suitable for offline payment scenarios. The above solutions of the only software-based protection are mainly designed for online payment scenarios. They heavily depend on the back-end banking system.

1.1 Design Principles

In consideration of CBDC, there should be several specific requirements for dual offline transaction scheme. The following desired design principles are essential to achieve a practical scheme and guide our efforts going forward.

Centralized Banking System. On account of financial regulation, CBDC usually adopts the centralized banking system and related mechanism rather than peer-to-peer electronic cash transfer or distributed ledger technology.

High Security. Since it is relevant to the money topic which is concerned by any people for protecting their property, the security issue is of prime significance. The basic requirement for dual offline transaction is exactly guaranteeing the correct payer paying the correct value of effective digital currencies to the correct payee. Consequently, the secure cryptographic protocol, specialized mechanism for mobile devices and accurate key protection are necessary. Furthermore, three fundamental security properties should be satisfied for dual offline transaction.

- **Unforgeability.** Unforgeability involves two aspects: unforgeability for identity, and unforgeability for digital currency. Firstly, unforgeability for identity means that the adversary can forge neither the identity of an user nor the wallet of an user. Secondly, unforgeability for digital currency means that the adversary cannot forge the digital currency issued by the central bank and cannot forge its transaction records.
- **Preventing Double-spending.** Double-spending problem refers to the phenomenon that the same digital currency is paid for twice or more times repeatedly. The problem should be prevented.

– **Non-repudiation.** Non-repudiation means that the payer and the payee cannot deny their offline transaction behaviors. It ensures the effectiveness of a transaction.

1.2 Related Work

Digital Currency. With the continuous development of cryptography, numerous innovations have been created in the research field of electronic cash (e-cash) and e-payment. E-cash introduced by Chaum [8], allows users to withdraw digital coins from a bank and to spend them to merchants in an anonymous way, thus perfectly emulates conventional cash transactions.

Offline Electronic Payment. With regard to existing works, current offline transaction methods [4] generally fall into three categories. The first category is about the offline POS terminal transaction. However, this scenario model is limited and inapplicable for CBDC. The second category is blockchain-based offline situations. Unfortunately, blockchain-based transactions violate the design principle for centralized CBDC system. The third category is the utilization of cryptography to solve the both issues of offline transaction and preserving user privacy. Kutubi et al. [5] presented their secure offline electronic payment scheme respectively by adopting untraceable blind signature (BS). Whereas, the obviously increasing protocol and computation complexity is inadequate to guarantee the robustness and efficiency for CBDC.

Mobile Security. In this field, purely software-based secure techniques, such as software obfuscation and white-box cryptography, are more vulnerable in the face of attacks from bottom system or hardware [6]. In comparison, the technique of jointly using SE and trusted execution environment (TEE) [9,10] on mobile devices endows us with a feasible technical route. SE provides tamper-resistant mechanism to keep core assets secure. Isolated from a rich execution environment (REE), TEE aims to protect sensitive codes execution and against both OS layer attacks and other software-based attacks. In general, SE and TEE (or similar forms) are widely deployed and enabled in a great number of today's mobile devices. As a prevalent example of providing TEE for embedded devices, ARM TrustZone [11] has been used to execute security-critical services. Based on ARM TrustZone Yang et al. [12] proposed AEP-M, a practical anonymous e-payment scheme for mobile devices. In fact, applying both SE and TEE is an appropriate choice for related to the security of a country's monetary sovereignty. To the best of our knowledge, there is no dual offline transaction scheme specially designed for mobile devices using SE and TEE.

1.3 Our Contribution

Based on SE and TEE, we propose DOT-M, a practical dual offline transaction scheme for trusted mobile devices, which enables an user to pay digital currency of CBDC securely and efficiently without Internet to the other equivalent user.

This is a complete work to design an efficient dual offline transaction scheme of CBDC integrated with SE and TEE.

For device-centered design, we make following steps towards practical and secure usage:

- For the scenario of dual offline transaction of CBDC, the secure solution for trusted mobile device is specially constructed;
- DOT-M utilizes a series of secret keys, which are derived from a terminal master key reproduced in SE, to protect users' digital currency of CBDC and data;
- The sensitive codes on the user side of DOT-M are isolated and executed in TEE for the possibility that the guest OS is compromised;
- In DOT-M, users could authenticate each other's identity and wallet identity, as well as the authenticity of CBDC in the absence of a network.

We also design the data structure of CBDC in order to split the value of one integrated digital currency flexibly when dual offline transaction is executed. In the meantime, the security properties of the transaction protocol are guaranteed, which include preventing man-in-the-middle attack, preventing intruder attack, preventing malicious payer or payee, preventing double-spending, non-repudiation and unforgeability. Furthermore, we implement a prototype of DOT-M and evaluate its efficiency at the security level of 256-bit. The experimental results show that our scheme is efficient enough for practical usage, even from the perspective of mobile devices.

2   System Model and Assumptions

2.1   Notation

In the paper, we use the notation shown in Table 1.

Table 1. Notation used in this paper

Notation	Descriptions
$y := x$	y assigned as x
$x \| y$	Concatenation of x and y
$(y_1, ..., y_j) \leftarrow \mathsf{A}(x_1, ..., x_i)$	An algorithm with input $(x_1, ..., x_i)$ and output $(y_1, ..., y_j)$
$\mathsf{Sign}(k, m)$	Digital signature for a message m using a private key k

2.2   System Model

The system model of DOT-M proposed in this paper is composed of three kinds of participating entities: mobile device $\mathcal{R}$ of payee and mobile device $\mathcal{P}$ of payer, central bank $\mathcal{C}$. $\mathcal{R}$ and $\mathcal{P}$ are bound with payee and payer respectively, and the user behaviors are achieved through the mobile device. The mobile device used for the trader is equipped with security chip for SE and ARM processor chip supporting TrustZone extension technology for TEE. Both of the devices could communicate with each other through NFC or Bluetooth for dual offline transaction. In charge of providing CBDC services and CBDC wallet applications, $\mathcal{C}$ should be a central bank or a third-party agency authorized by the central bank. Generally, $\mathcal{C}$ has multiple data centers to meet the needs of powerful computing and big data storage capabilities. Figure 1 illustrates our system model.

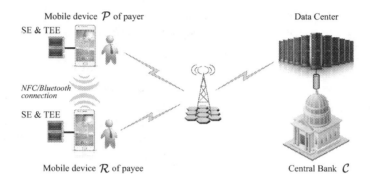

Fig. 1. System model of DOT-M.

2.3 Security Assumptions and Threat Model

We establish the scheme on the following assumptions:

Assumption 1. The various security mechanisms designed and implemented for SE and TEE by their manufacturers are correct and have not been deliberately planted backdoors.

Assumption 2. All the basically standard cryptographic algorithms are correctly applied and implemented without security risk.

Assumption 3. Mobile device manufactures correctly enable and initialize SE and TEE for each device before delivery. As a consequence, each device has its predefined unique device key with the certificate.

Assumption 4. The communications between every two entities build on secure transport protocols like TLS, which can provide protection for data transmission.

These assumptions are quite tenable because the mentioned requirements have been generally satisfied in practically industrial activity.

However, we ignore the malicious behaviors of tampering with the TrustZone hardware. Moreover, we do not cover anonymity, unlinkability and untraceability for our scheme.

3   DOT-M Scheme for Mobile Devices

In this section, we provide a security solution on mobile device for CBDC. Depending on it, the design of data structure for offline transaction and the construction of DOT-M scheme are detailed.

3.1   Security Solution on Mobile Device

The security solution is the terminal foundation for establishing reliable dual offline transaction. Three parts constitute the solution: the specific architecture of trusted mobile device, key derivation with sensitive data management and basic key system of CBDC.

3.1.1   The Architecture of Trusted Mobile Device

Leveraging SE and TEE technology, we design a trusted mobile device architecture for DOT-M. Both $\mathcal{P}$ and $\mathcal{R}$ rely on this architecture to securely execute dual offline transaction. On the basis of the software and hardware capabilities of existing mobile device, we build the security solution that targets at economy, flexibility and extensibility.

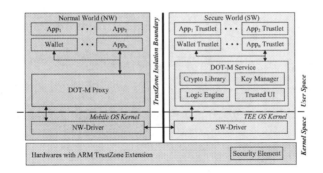

Fig. 2. Architecture of trusted mobile device for DOT-M.

Combined with SE, TEE can shield the integrity of the execution process of sensitive programs, the confidentiality and the integrity of sensitive data, which is fundamental to the security of offline transaction. Figure 2 shows the detailed architecture with the way the components interact with each other. The basic functionality of DOT-M in the architecture contains two components: untrusted DOT-M Proxy in normal world (NW) and security-sensitive DOT-M Service in secure world (SW). The different components are formally described as follows.

DOT-M Proxy. As a bridge between user space and kernel space in NW, it can directly communicate with the normal mobile applications. Waiting for their requests, the proxy handles the parameters and preprocesses them. According to the request type, the proxy would call DOT-M Service for substantive computations of the scheme and finally return the results.

DOT-M Service. It is the core component to perform DOT-M secure computations and operations. The execution of the component codes is under the well protection of TrustZone isolation mechanism. The detailed description of the subcomponents can be found in the extended version of this paper [15].

Wallet and Wallet Trustlet. For upperlevel interaction, the CBDC application released by $\mathcal{C}$ consists of two parts: an App for NW called Wallet and an App Trustlet for SW called Wallet Trustlet. Wallet provides users with the general GUI, remote service access and other basic functions, while Wallet Trustlet is securely loaded and trusted for handling security-sensitive inputs, data operations and communications with the other device through NFC or Bluetooth during dual offline transaction.

Components in Hardwares. Protected by TrustZone mechanism, SE is only accessible for SW. With a variety of hardware protection mechanisms for resisting the laboratory-level attack, SE contributes to generate the master key and act as the root of trust in DOT-M.

3.1.2 Key Derivation and Sensitive Data Management

Prior to describing the concrete construction of DOT-M, we show how to derive root keys using SE and how to protect sensitive data.

Master Key Generation. Inside SE, the terminal master key tmk is generated by the true random number generator (TRNG). When the mobile device is powered on for the first time, a fixed-length data is read from the TRNG as tmk, and then it resides in this SE. This key is unique for each SE bound with each mobile device so that it is also considered as the root.

Key Derivation. Before delivery of the mobile device, SE is customized to have the deterministic key derivation function $\mathsf{KDF}: \widetilde{\mathcal{K}} \leftarrow \widetilde{\mathcal{S}} \times \{0,1\}^*$, where $\widetilde{\mathcal{S}}$ is the key seed space, and $\widetilde{\mathcal{K}}$ is the derived key space. Using KDF, the storage root key can be derived as $srk \leftarrow \mathsf{KDF}_{tmk}(\texttt{"storage\_root"})$. srk is used by Key Manager in TEE for generating specific storage keys to preserve sensitive data. Besides, other functional root keys, such as identity root key, for building trust chain could be derived similarly by using KDF with different parameters. They are just regained via KDF in the same way when needed.

Sensitive Data Management. Utilizing the storage keys derived from srk and the generic methods for data protection by TrustZone, DOT-M Service could seal the sensitive data of the scheme as blobs to permanently store with protecting their confidentiality and integrity. When needed, these data could be recovered through unsealing operation.

3.1.3 Basic Key System of CBDC

Aside from the assumption about bottom protocols of transportation in Sect. 2.3, the entire secure foundation of CBDC for upper layer is also established through the public key certificate infrastructure (PKI). Table 2 shows the definitions of different certificates and keys in our scheme for offline transaction.

Table 2. The definitions for certificates and keys.

Symbol	Definition	Origin
pk_C	Public key for verifying digital currency of CBDC	Issued by C
(usk_i, upk_i)	Private-public key pair of user i	Generated in TEE
$ucert_i$	Certificate of user i	Issued by C
(wsk_j, wpk_j)	Private-public key pair of wallet for user j	Generated in TEE
$wcert_j$	Certificate of wallet for user j	Issued by C
pwd	Payment password of wallet	Set by user

Preset in CBDC wallet application, the unified public key pk_C is used for verifying the digital currency issued by the central bank C. When a wallet application is started on a mobile device by its user for the first time, (usk, upk) and (wsk, wpk) are generated in TEE through DOT-M Service and sent to C, then C issues $ucert$ and $wcert$ respectively for the user. For the same user, his $wcert$ is recorded and associated with his $ucert$ in C's database. Subsequently, the user is required to set a payment password pwd through TUI on his device for future transactions.

3.2   Design of Data Structure

In this section, we propose the design of data structure for DOT-M.

3.2.1   Data Structure of Currency Block

Figure 3 shows the data structure of currency block for offline transaction. The structure consists of form of presentation, offline transaction record, remaining amount of value, number of times of offline transaction. The instance of this data structure represents a certain amount of digital currency as a whole with its information. The offline transaction about this currency block is the procedure to consume the digital currency until the remaining amount of value turns into 0. During one transaction, several currency blocks would be used to pay simultaneously.

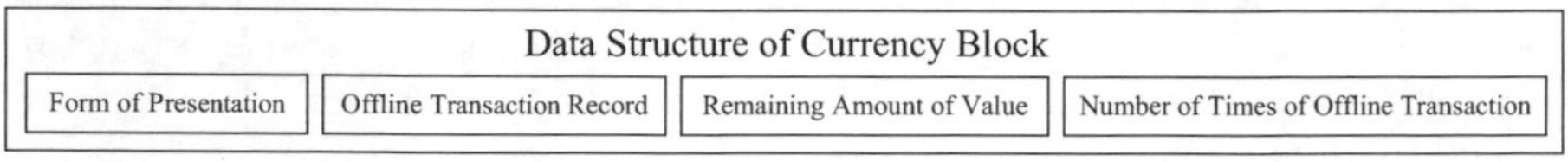

Data Structure of Currency Block			
Form of Presentation	Offline Transaction Record	Remaining Amount of Value	Number of Times of Offline Transaction

Fig. 3. Data structure of currency block for offline transaction of CBDC.

The form of presentation describes a basic piece of digital currency of CBDC that could be paid and verified. It is able to define any amount of original value of digital currency in a single string issued (i.e. signed) by the central bank $\mathcal{C}$. Its data save the original currency information that would never be changed during the offline transaction. The data structure of offline transaction record is linked list that records all the necessary contents of each offline transaction involved this currency block. Remaining amount of value represents the currently spendable amount of value of the digital currency and would be deducted after each transaction. Number of times of offline transaction increments by 1 after each transaction and is used for the maximum limit of dual offline transaction for the sack of efficiency and security.

The form of presentation is formally a string shown in Fig. 4. The form contains at least the unique serial number, amount of value, original owner and signature of $\mathcal{C}$.

Serial number	Amount of Value	Original Owner	...	Signature of Central Bank $\mathcal{C}$

Fig. 4. Form of presentation for the digital currency of CBDC.

Figure 5 shows data structure of offline transaction record which is a linked list. Recording the information of a single offline transaction, each node contains transaction amount, transaction timestamp, $\mathcal{P}$'s certificate $ucert_{\mathcal{P}}$, $\mathcal{R}$'s certificate $ucert_{\mathcal{R}}$, signature of $\mathcal{P}$.

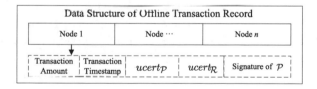

Fig. 5. Data structure of offline transaction record.

3.2.2 Data Structure of Wallet

Figure 6 shows the data structure of the wallet for mobile user, which contains data structure of currency block, wsk, $wcert$, $pk_{\mathcal{C}}$, total remaining amount of value in wallet. The key $pk_{\mathcal{C}}$ is for verifying the signature of $\mathcal{C}$ for each digital currency. In one instance of the data structure of wallet, there could be several instances of currency blocks due to how much digital currency the user has.

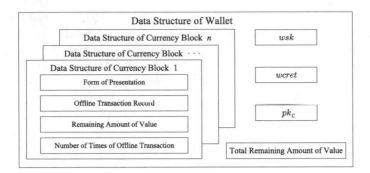

Fig. 6. Data structure of wallet.

3.2.3   Data Structure of User

This paper also defines and applies the user data structure described in Table 2, including *usk*, *ucert* and *pwd*. In our scheme, the data structure of user with its keys is used to identify the behaviors of different transaction users bound with their real back-end accounts, while the data structure of wallet with its keys is to identify the user's exact wallet for paying or receiving the digital currency during the dual offline transaction.

3.3   The Details of Dual Offline Transaction Scheme

The scheme description of this paper only considers the case in which the user has one wallet application with one instance of its data structure. In real life, an user would have several wallet applications on his device, and it is one of the reasons why there is a need to distinguish wallet keys with user keys.

The dual offline transaction scheme mainly consists of 4 procedures: registration, account synchronization, dual offline transaction and online data updating. Exception handling is also necessary for the scheme's validity and availability.

3.3.1   Registration

This procedure is specifically divided into the following parts:

1. User downloads the CBDC wallet application on the mobile device and its two parts (i.e. Wallet and Wallet Trustlet) are installed and activated.
2. User starts the application for the first time, and it connects to central bank $\mathcal{C}$, and verifies that $\mathcal{C}$ is real.
3. User sets the account and login password of the application. User's mobile device generates (usk, upk) in TEE, and sends upk to $\mathcal{C}$. $\mathcal{C}$ issues $ucert$, and sends $ucert$ to user's mobile device where $ucert$ is well protected by sealing described in Sect. 3.1.2.
4. User's mobile device generates (wsk, wpk) in TEE, and sends wpk to $\mathcal{C}$. $\mathcal{C}$ issues $wcert$, and sends $wcert$ to user's mobile device to seal.
5. User sets pwd of wallet for payment.

3.3.2   Account Synchronization

When the mobile device is connected to the Internet, the wallet application connects to $\mathcal{C}$ for account ledger synchronization. The information synchronized with the ledger mainly includes the wallet data structure so that the user gets his pre-existing digital currency from his online account and put it into the wallet application on his mobile device which is prepared for offline transaction. DOT-M Service seals and saves the synchronized data of wallet as sensitive data.

3.3.3   Dual Offline Transaction

Before the transaction starts, $\mathcal{R}$ and $\mathcal{P}$ complete the following preparations:

1. $\mathcal{R}$ requires the payee to input the payment amount on the device.
2. $\mathcal{P}$ requires the payer to input the wallet payment password pwd on the device, and validate it.
3. $\mathcal{R}$ and $\mathcal{P}$ establishes a secure channel through NFC or Bluetooth.

Next, the dual offline transaction begins, and there are 9 major steps in the protocol as shown in Fig. 7.

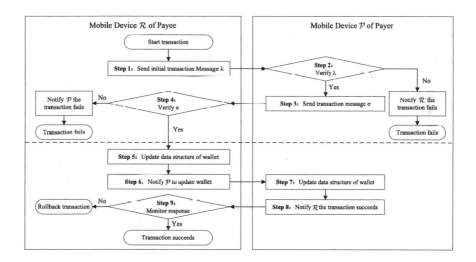

Fig. 7. Dual offline transaction protocol.

Step 1. $\mathcal{R}$ builds the initial transaction information λ, and sends it to $\mathcal{P}$.

1. Use $usk_{\mathcal{R}}$ to output a signature $\alpha \leftarrow \mathsf{Sign}(usk_{\mathcal{R}}, tsn)$, where tsn is the unique serial number of transaction.
2. Use $wsk_{\mathcal{R}}$ to output a signature $\beta \leftarrow \mathsf{Sign}(wsk_{\mathcal{R}}, v)$, where v is the amount of value for offline transaction.
3. Send $\lambda := (\ tsn\| \ v \ \| \ \alpha \ \| \ ucert_{\mathcal{R}} \ \| \ \beta \ \| \ wcert_{\mathcal{R}})$ to $\mathcal{P}$.

Step 2. $\mathcal{P}$ verifies λ through the following steps.

1. Obtain $upk_{\mathcal{R}}$ from $ucert_{\mathcal{R}}$, and verify α.
2. Obtain $wpk_{\mathcal{R}}$ from $wcert_{\mathcal{R}}$, and verify β.
3. Check whether v and payee's identity indeed accord with the payer's original intention by showing the contents for the payer.
4. Check whether the remaining amount of value of its wallet is greater than the offline transaction amount.

If the above sub-steps fail, $\mathcal{P}$ would notify $\mathcal{R}$ the transaction fails, and close the transaction.

Step 3. $\mathcal{P}$ builds the transaction message σ, and sends it to $\mathcal{R}$.

1. Choose one or a cluster of applicable currency blocks as needed, generate the transaction record nodes for the corresponding blocks, append all generated nodes to the blocks, and assemble the transaction data tsd.
2. Use $wsk_{\mathcal{P}}$ to output a signature $\gamma \leftarrow \mathsf{Sign}(wsk_{\mathcal{P}}, tsd)$.
3. Send $\sigma := (tsd \parallel \gamma \parallel wcert_{\mathcal{P}})$ to $\mathcal{R}$. More clearly, the data structures of tsd and σ are shown in Fig. 8.

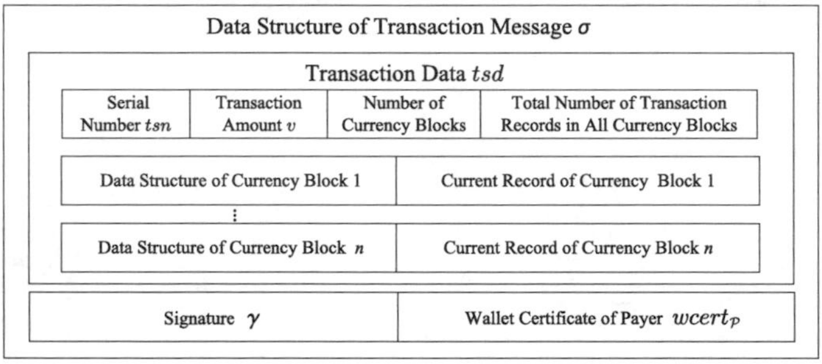

Data Structure of Transaction Message σ			
Transaction Data tsd			
Serial Number tsn	Transaction Amount v	Number of Currency Blocks	Total Number of Transaction Records in All Currency Blocks
Data Structure of Currency Block 1		Current Record of Currency Block 1	
Data Structure of Currency Block n		Current Record of Currency Block n	
Signature γ		Wallet Certificate of Payer $wcert_{\mathcal{P}}$	

Fig. 8. Data structure of transaction message.

Step 4. $\mathcal{R}$ verifies σ through the following steps.

1. Obtain $wpk_{\mathcal{P}}$ from $wcert_{\mathcal{P}}$, and verify γ.
2. Obtain $upk_{\mathcal{P}}$ from $ucert_{\mathcal{P}}$, and verify the authenticity of all current offline transaction records. Similarly, $\mathcal{R}$ can verify the authenticity of all previous transaction records via linked lists inside different currency blocks.
3. Use $pk_{\mathcal{C}}$ to verify that the digital currency of CBDC is exactly issued by $\mathcal{C}$.

If the above sub-steps fail, $\mathcal{R}$ would notify $\mathcal{P}$ the transaction fails, and close the transaction.

Step 5. $\mathcal{R}$ updates the data structure of wallet, mainly involving linking each current node to the corresponding record inside its currency block, increasing the number of times of offline transaction in each currency block, and renewing remaining offline amount of wallet.

Step 6. $\mathcal{R}$ notifies $\mathcal{P}$ to update the data structure of wallet by sending a notification message signed using $usk_{\mathcal{R}}$.

Step 7. $\mathcal{P}$ verifies the message using $upk_{\mathcal{R}}$ from **Step 2** and updates its data structure of wallet.

Step 8. $\mathcal{P}$ notifies $\mathcal{R}$ that the transaction is successful.

Step 9. $\mathcal{R}$ monitors the response from $\mathcal{P}$. If $\mathcal{R}$ receives the response from $\mathcal{P}$ within the due time, $\mathcal{R}$ closes the successful transaction and shows the message, otherwise it rollbacks transaction, and restores the data structure of wallet to the state before the start of this transaction. Only when the payee sees the success message on the screen of $\mathcal{R}$, he admits this effective transaction.

3.3.4   Online Data Updating

Whenever $\mathcal{R}$ connects to Internet, it submits the previous offline transaction data of the wallet to the CBDC system server for account ledger synchronization. Similar, $\mathcal{P}$ also does online updating for his account synchronization. However, once $\mathcal{C}$ finds the updating data from $\mathcal{R}$ are inconsistent with those from $\mathcal{P}$, $\mathcal{C}$ would give priority to $\mathcal{R}$'s data and execute corresponding exception handling.

3.3.5   Exception Handling and Security Analysis

Exceptional situations that have bad impacts may occur during the procedure of the dual offline transaction. As a consequence, the exception handling should be considered and triggered timely in case of the failure for synchronization of either critical data or the changing amount of digital currency. The part below the dotted line of Fig. 7 shows the prepared design for the exceptional situation. The whole procedure of dual offline transaction can be categorized into 6 kinds of exceptional situations. Besides, DOT-M satisfies the six security properties, three of which are described in Sect. 1.1 as the design principles. For details, the exception handling methods, security properties and the analysis can be found in the extended version of this paper [15].

4   Implementation and Evaluation

In this section, we first present the prototype of DOT-M from both aspects of hardware and software. Afterwards, we show the efficiency and performance evaluation of the proposed scheme based on our prototype system.

4.1   Implementation

For simulating the complete dual offline transaction process, we use one PC platform as the central bank server and implement the CBDC background service on this platform, which can apply two-way authentication with the wallet application, generate or destroy digital currency, and issue certificates and wallet parameters etc. Moreover, the implementation also involves the simulation of mobile device, which is described as follows.

Hardware Platform. We utilize two Hikey-960 development boards whose operating systems are Android 9.0 to simulate the mobile devices of two parties. The HiKey-960 development board is based around the Kirin-960 processor with four ARM Cortex-A73 and four Cortex-A53 cores. The board is equipped with 3 GB of LPDDR4 SDRAM memory and 32 GB of UFS 2.0 flash storage. The function of TEE is supported and enabled by the hardware on the board. In order to simulate NFC communication that conforms to the ISO14443 protocol with the maximum transmission rate of 424 kbps, we choose to use serial communication at the same rate as NFC to transmit data between devices. In addition, we adopt STM32F103 module to act as the security chip (i.e. SE).

Software Implementation. For the software implementation of DOT-M on the mobile device, we respectively develop Wallet in Android, the trusted services and Wallet Trustlet in OP-TEE which is compliant with GP's TEE Specifications [13]. For the cryptographic algorithms used in our scheme, such as the SM series algorithms, we implement them based on GmSSL 3.0 [14] static library and at the security level of 256-bit. 7053 lines of code (LOC) in C language totally comprise our components and auxiliary functions in TEE and SE. Besides, we program one test application that could execute upon DOT-M scheme. It contains 896 LOC for Wallet running in NW and 736 LOC for Wallet Trustlet in SW.

4.2 Efficiency and Performance Evaluation

We measure the performance of DOT-M on the prototype system revolving around mobile devices especially for the frequent process of dual offline transaction. In our scheme, a dual offline transaction requires the payer and payee to interact with each other twice and complete the 9 steps together. The transaction

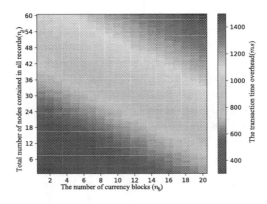

Fig. 9. The colormap of the transaction time overheads (ms).

time overhead is significantly affected by three operations: signing, verifying, and data communicating. Decided by the data length, the time overhead of communicating does not fluctuate dramatically because the speed of NFC or Bluetooth is quite enough for transferring necessary data in offline transaction. However, the number of signing and verifying operations are positively correlated with both the number n_b of currency blocks used in the transaction and the total number n_d of nodes contained in the linked lists of all the offline transaction records.

We design an experiment to evaluate our scheme's total time overheads of the whole transaction between the payer and payee under the conditions of different n_b and n_d which also decide the data length to communicate, as shown in Fig. 9. Each average experimental result is taken over 100 test-runs. In the figure, the points of time overhead located in the top right corner have more time-consuming than those in the bottom left corner. The statistical results show that as n_b and n_d increase respectively, the time overheads of completing a transaction gradually increase and n_b has more influence than n_d on transaction time. Generally, the users would be rather satisfied if the transaction time is less than 1000 ms (ms). The optional parameter combinations of (n_b, n_d) such as (6, 42), (10, 36), (16, 24) and (20, 18) all meet the requirement of normal use. In some extremely bad cases such as combination (20, 60), the time overhead is 1590 ms which is also completely acceptable for the mobile users. Furthermore, from our experiment, when the combination changes from (1, 1) to (20, 60), we find that the time overhead of data communicating just grows from 112 ms to 568 ms. It is rather stable. According to our efficiency analysis and experimental results, DOT-M can be considered as a reasonably efficient scheme for dual offline transaction on mobile devices.

5   Conclusion

In this paper, we propose DOT-M, a complete and practical dual offline transaction scheme for mobile devices using SE and TEE. DOT-M takes both security and efficiency specially for mobile users. The scheme supports transactions that can be completed when both the mobile devices of payer and payee are offline. Our implementation and evaluation convince that DOT-M is quite practical for dual offline transaction through mobile devices.

References

1. Ready, steady, go?-Results of the third BIS survey on central bank digital currency. https://www.bis.org/publ/bppdf/bispap114.htm/
2. Report on a digital euro. https://www.ecb.europa.eu/pub/pdf/other/Report_on_a_digital_euro4d7268b458.en.pdf/
3. Progress on research and development of E-CNY in China
4. Gupta, Y.K., Jeswani, G., Pinto, O.: M-Commerce offline payment. SN Comput. Sci. **3**(1), 1–11 (2022)

5. Kutubi, M.A.A.R., Alam, K.M.R., Morimoto, Y.: A simplified scheme for secure offline electronic payment systems. High-Confidence Comput. **1**(2), 100031 (2021)
6. EMV Mobile Payment software-based Mobile Payment Security Requirements version 1.4. https://www.emvco.com/
7. Payment Card Industry (PCI) software-based PIN entry on COTS (SPoC^{TM}) magnetic stripe readers annex security and test requirements version 1.1
8. Chaum, D.: Blind signatures for untraceable payments. In: Chaum, D., Rivest, R.L., Sherman, A.T. (eds.) Advances in Cryptology, pp. 199–203. Springer, Boston, MA (1983). https://doi.org/10.1007/978-1-4757-0602-4_18
9. Yang, B., Feng, D.G., Qin, Y.: A lightweight anonymous mobile shopping scheme based on DAA for trusted mobile platform. In: IEEE TrustCom 2014, pp. 9–17. IEEE (2014)
10. Yang, B., Yang, K., Qin, Yu., Zhang, Z., Feng, D.: DAA-TZ: an efficient DAA scheme for mobile devices using ARM TrustZone. In: Conti, M., Schunter, M., Askoxylakis, I. (eds.) Trust 2015. LNCS, vol. 9229, pp. 209–227. Springer, Cham (2015). https://doi.org/10.1007/978-3-319-22846-4_13
11. ARM Security Technology building a secure system using TrustZone technology. https://documentation-service.arm.com
12. Yang, B., Yang, K., Zhang, Z., Qin, Yu., Feng, D.: AEP-M: practical anonymous E-payment for mobile devices using ARM TrustZone and divisible E-cash. In: Bishop, M., Nascimento, A.C.A. (eds.) ISC 2016. LNCS, vol. 9866, pp. 130–146. Springer, Cham (2016). https://doi.org/10.1007/978-3-319-45871-7_9
13. GlobalPlatform Technology TEE system architecture version 1.2. https://globalplatform.org/specs-library/tee-system-architecture/
14. Guan, Z.: The GmSSL Project. http://gmssl.org
15. Yang, B., Zhang, Y.C., Tong, D.: DOT-M: A Dual Offline Transaction Scheme of Central Bank Digital Currency for Trusted Mobile Devices (extended version). ePrint (2022). https://eprint.iacr.org/2022/1443

A Beyond-5G Authentication and Key Agreement Protocol

Mohamed Taoufiq Damir[(✉)], Tommi Meskanen, Sara Ramezanian,
and Valtteri Niemi

Department of Computer Science, University of Helsinki,
Helsinki Institute for Information Technology (HIIT), Helsinki, Finland
{mohamed.damir,tommi.meskanen,sara.ramezanian,valtteri.niemi}@helsinki.fi

Abstract. The standardized Authentication and Key Agreement protocol for 5G networks (5G AKA) have several security and privacy vulnerabilities. In this paper, we propose a novel authentication and key agreement protocol for 5G and beyond that is compatible with the standardized 5G AKA. Our protocol has several privacy and security properties, e.g., perfect forward secrecy, resistance against linkability attacks, and protection against malicious SNs. Moreover, both the user identity protection and the perfect forward secrecy are handled using Key Encapsulation Mechanisms (KEM), which makes our protocol adaptable to the quantum-safe setting. To analyze the performance of the proposed protocol, we use the post-quantum KEM CRYSTALS-Kyber, recently chosen to be standardized by NIST, and NIST post-quantum Round 4 candidate KEMs. The results for communication and computation costs show that utilizing our protocol is feasible in practice and sometimes outperforms the public-key cryptography used in 5G AKA, i.e., ECIES. We further prove the security of our protocol by utilizing *ProVerif*.

Keywords: 6G · 5G AKA · Post-quantum cryptography · Privacy · Security

1 Introduction

The 5G technology positively impacts several industries, such as healthcare, transportation, and autonomous vehicles [12]. However, the emergence of 5G has increased the concerns about the security and privacy of mobile users [13]. A proper authentication mechanism is essential to provide many services, e.g., roaming. The 3rd Generation Partnership Project (3GPP) group, responsible for the standardization of 3G, 4G, and 5G, specified the security architecture and procedures for 5G in its technical specification [TS 33.501]. A major component of the specification is the *Authentication and Key Agreement* (AKA) protocol in 5G. Compared to previous mobile generations, the 5G specification emphasised

This work was supported by the Business Finland Consortium Project "Post-Quantum Cryptography" under Grant 754/31/2020.

more on user privacy, which is due to the importance and the high demand for privacy. We also recall that the 5G standards were developed while new privacy regulations have taken effect, for example, the European Union's General Data Protection Regulation (GDPR) [17]. Unfortunately, and shortly after standardizing the 5G AKA by 3GPP, various security and privacy issues have been discovered, for example, linkability attacks [6–8] and the lack of a full protection against compromised/impersonated SNs. The latter was identified during the 5G AKA Tamarin formal verification [3]. Moreover, passive/active attacks on 5G networks became a realistic threat [18], which is due to the gradually increasing availability of the necessary software and hardware to perform such (fake base station) attacks.

Among the new features in the 5G AKA, is the protection of the user identity using public-key cryptography, i.e., the ECIES algorithm. However, it is expected that such a solution would not last for a long period with the rise of quantum computers. A sufficiently large quantum computer can break many currently used cryptographic algorithms including the ECIES, see Sect. 2.3. Therefore, some of the mechanisms in 5G that are considered secure and private at the time of writing, such as users' identity protection, may be broken once large-scale quantum computers appear. It is unclear when such a quantum computer will be available, but it is worth mentioning that some leading companies such as Google and IBM are working on developing quantum computers and they are offering access to their computers over the cloud. Thus, the average attacker is expected to get access to quantum devices (over the cloud), while the average user is still using "classical" devices. Hence, there is interest in cryptography that works on classical devices but with the property of resisting quantum attacks, called *Post-Quantum Cryptography* (PQC).

In this context, we consider perfect forward secrecy, which is concerned with an attacker who is recording present (encrypted) sessions, with the hope of decrypting those at some future time point. The break would be possible if some long-term secrets were broken at that later time point, e.g., by using a quantum computer.

In this work, we propose a novel AKA protocol that has several security and privacy properties, while keeping in mind further practical considerations such as backward compatibility with previous mobile generations and the adaptability to quantum-resistant cryptography. Our detailed contributions and the properties of our protocol are given in Sect. 4.

2   Preliminaries

2.1   5G Terms and Acronyms

For the purposes of our discussions, we reduce the mobile network architecture to three relevant entities: (1) The *User Equipment* (UE) which further consists of the *Universal Subscriber Identity Module* (USIM) and the *Mobile Equipment* (ME), (2) the *Home Network* (HN), and (3) the *Serving Network* (SN). In 5G, the Home Network assigns to every subscriber, and a USIM, a globally unique identifier that is called the *Subscription Permanent Identifier* (SUPI). The SUPI can be used to track and locate users. For protecting user privacy, the SN assigns to the UE a *Globally Unique Temporary Identity* (GUTI), which is a temporary and frequently changing identifier. The idea is to use, as often as possible, GUTI instead of SUPI but there are also circumstances where the GUTI cannot be used as an identifier.

To avoid sending the SUPI as a plaintext, [TS 33.501] includes a mechanism to conceal the SUPI, resulting in *Subscription Concealed Identifier* (SUCI). The SUPI concealment is done by using a HN public key, pk_H, stored at the USIM with an *Elliptic Curves Integrated Encryption Scheme* (ECIES). In 5G, the UE and the HN share a long term key K, and a sequence number SQN, where K is stored at the temper-resistant part of the USIM at the UE side, while SQN is used to check synchronization and detect replay attacks. The SUPI/GUTI, K and SQN are used to establish a mutual authentication and key agreement between the UE and SN via the HN.

2.2   Key Encapsulation Mechanisms

A *key encapsulation mechanism* (KEM) is a scheme that is used in cryptographic protocols to exchange symmetric keys. A KEM is a triple of algorithms **KEM** = (**KeyGen**(), **Encaps**(), **Decaps**()) with a key space $\mathcal{K}$, where

- **KeyGen**() is a non-deterministic algorithm that generates a pair of public and secret key (pk, sk).
- **Encaps**(pk) is a non-deterministic key encapsulation algorithm. The input of **Encaps**(pk) is pk and its outputs are a ciphertext c and a key $k \in \mathcal{K}$.
- **Decaps**(sk, c) is a deterministic key decapsulation algorithm. The inputs of **Decaps**(sk, c) are sk and c, and the algorithm returns a key $k \in \mathcal{K}$ or $\perp$ denoting failure.

The three algorithms work together in a natural fashion, e.g., both **Encaps** and **Decaps** produce the same key k when the input keys pk and sk are chosen from the same pair.

2.3   Post-Quantum Cryptography

The security of the most popular practical public-key cryptography schemes is based on the hardness of integer factoring and the difficulty of calculating discrete logarithms. In [1], Shor showed that these two problems can be efficiently solved by a sufficiently large-scale quantum computer. In December 2016, the National Institute of Standards and Technology in the USA (NIST) initiated a standardization process by announcing a call for proposals for Post-Quantum (PQ) KEMs. In July 2022, NIST selected the CRYSTALS-Kyber KEM to be the primary algorithm recommended for standardization. Additionally, NIST picked four other algorithms for the next (4th) selection round. These four include BIKE, Classic McEliece, HQC, as well as the SIKE KEM. Our protocol uses "generic" KEMs, but for evaluating the protocol performance, we consider PQ KEMs. We give further details on implementing the mentioned algorithms[1] as part of our protocol in Sect. 8.

2.4   Used Symmetric Primitives

In order to be consistent with the 3GPP standardization, we use the same notations as in [3GPP TS 33.501]. In our protocol we use a *Key Derivation Function* (KDF) which is based on SHA256, and seven symmetric key algorithms that are denoted by $f_1, f_2, f_3, f_4, f_5, f_1^*$ and f_5^*. Please note that although 3GPP did not fully standardize the above functions, 3GPP requires that breaking the security of these functions should require approximately 2^{128} operations. The MILENAGE algorithm set [3GPP TS 35.205] provides examples of the functions $f_1 - f_5^*$ which utilize an AES-128 block cipher as a kernel function. Please note that the AES-256 is quantum-resistant and can be utilized as kernel function (because it has the same block size as AES-128).

3   Related Work

Various works have pointed out security and privacy issues in mobile network authentication and key agreement (AKA) protocols. One of these issues is related to linkability attacks. Such attacks consist of the attacker linking protocol executions based on the user's behavior to conclude some critical information about the user, for example, their identity or location. In [6], the authors described an attack where they exploited the failure messages in previous mobile AKA protocols to track the target user, and the authors proposed concealing the error messages using the HN public key. In [7], Fouque et al. discovered another attack that accrues despite the fix proposed in [6]. The work in [8], described a threat where the attacker can guess the pattern of the *sequence number* by exploiting the synchronization failure message sent by a target UE. In our protocol, we abandon the use of sequence numbers to avoid potential de-synchronization attacks.

The mentioned linkability attacks became a central issue in many recent works on 5G/6G AKA protocols, see for instance [2] and the references therein. In [3], the authors provided a formal verification of 5G AKA, where they pointed out further security issues in the studied protocol. They showed that if the SN is compromised, then the attacker can make the SN assign the session key to a different UE, that is because the session key and the user identifier are sent to the SN in two different messages. Moreover, the UE is unable to detect SN impersonation attacks before the key confirmation with the SN, which is not mandatory in 5G AKA. That is because there is no mechanism at the UE allowing this last to check if it is talking to the SN that has the identity that

---

[1] We discard the evaluation of SIKE as this algorithm has been shown to be insecure after it was selected.

was verified by the HN. The last issue is due to the lack of a key confirmation message from the SN to the UE.

Solutions to the SN related problems identified in [3] while considering linkability were studied in [4,5], but these works did not consider further security properties, e.g., perfect forward secrecy. In our quantum resistance context, we expect that an attacker is currently recording the (encrypted) messages sent between the UE and the SN in the hope of compromising the long-term keys of either the UE or HN by some other means, for example, a large-scale quantum computer. In the standardized 5G AKA and previous generations, compromising the long-term keys will imply compromising previous session keys. In other words, the property of perfect forward secrecy is not provided. Such an issue in mobile networks was studied in [10,11,16]. In both [10,11], the perfect forward secrecy is based on the intractability of the discrete logarithm problem. Consequently, these proposals are vulnerable to quantum attacks (Shor's algorithm). The work in [16] uses generic encryption in the protocol that we might assume to be post-quantum, but their protocol lacks protection against malicious and impersonated SNs.

The perfect forward secrecy in [10,11] follows from a Diffie-Hellman (DH) type key exchange. Thus, replacing DH in these works with a post-quantum key exchange would make them quantum resistant. However, at the time of writing no post-quantum key exchange is considered for standardization. In our work, both the SUPI protection and the perfect forward secrecy are based on KEMs which gives our protocol the possibility of implementing post-quantum KEMs in particular. Implementing post-quantum KEMs in 5G was considered in [15], but the authors only consider the identification phase of the AKA protocol. Thus, further security features, e.g., linkability, and forward secrecy were not covered.

As a side note on the work in [10], we would like to point out that the authors used ProVerif to formally verify their protocol. We remarked that the code published in [10] considers the channel between the UE and SN as secure, while the channel between the SN and the HN is insecure. It should actually be the converse. We re-implemented the authors' verification with the corrected assumptions and noted that two of the claimed properties are then false (items 4 and 9, Section 5.1, pp. 324). We applied a minor correction to the Proverif code and item 9 turns out to be true after all. However, item 4 cannot be true. More precisely, item 4 states that the SN can distinguish a legit identification message (the first message in the protocol from the UE to SN) from an identity sent by an attacker, which is not ensured by the proposed protocol. In the next section, we list our contributions in more detail.

4   Contributions

We present a novel authentication and key agreement protocol for beyond-5G, where we consider various privacy and security issues from previous mobile generations. We summarise the security properties of our protocol as follows:

Table 1. Comparison of the security and privacy properties of our protocol with the prior art.

Properties	[11]	[10]	[4]	[5]	5G AKA	[2]	[16]	Ours
Unlinkability	✗	✓	✓	✓	✗	✓	✓	✓
Perfect forward secrecy	✓	✓	✗	✗	✗	✗	✓	✓
Compromised/impersonated SN protection	✗	✓	✓	✓	✗	✗	✓	✓
Quantum-safe	✗	✗	✗	✗	✗	✗	✓	✓
Coverage over GUTI	✓	✗	✗	✓	✓	✗	✗	✓

(1) SUPI confidentiality;
(2) Mutual authentication between UE and SN via the HN;
(3) Confidentiality of the session key;
(4) Protection against the attacks in [3] (compromised/impersonated SNs);
(5) Perfect forward and backward secrecy;
(6) Unlinkability and protection against replay attacks;
(7) Compatibility with the KEM paradigm, esp. with standardized PQ KEMs.

Moreover, we use the formal verification tool ProVerif to prove some of the above claims. Furthermore, we give an overview of practical implementation of our protocol. First, we describe some backward compatibility properties of our protocol with previous mobile generations, see Sect. 5.3. Second, we discuss implementing the protocol using Kyber, the post-quantum KEM recently selected by NIST and round4 KEM NIST finalists, see Sect. 8. We show that implementing our protocol with such KEMs, and especially Kyber, outperforms the public-key cryptography used nowadays (i.e., ECIES) in 5G AKA.

Table 1 compares the security and privacy properties of our protocol with those properties of several recent works.

5   Our Protocol

The proposed protocol consists of two phases. Phase A is the identification phase, where the UE is identified by the HN. Phase B is an authentication phase, which allows the UE and the HN to securely authenticate each other.

5.1   Phase A: The Identification Phase

The identification phase consists of three steps, a message from the UE to the SN, a message from the SN the HN, and an identification confirmation/abortion at the HN.

In our protocol, and as in 5G AKA, the parameters at the UE are the SN and HN identities denoted respectively by ID_{SN} and ID_{HN}. The USIM stores also, K, a shared long term key with the HN, and the HN public key pk_H. In our protocol, pk_H is a KEM key. The communication between the UE and SN is either initiated by the UE, e.g., for outgoing call, or by the SN, e.g., for incoming call. In both cases, the UE has to send an identifier (SUCI or GUTI) to the SN. In our context, the two cases are similar. In the rest of this section, we cover the SUCI case, while the GUTI case is covered in Sect. 6. The identification procedure for the SUCI case goes as follows:

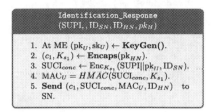

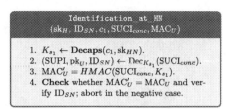

Fig. 1. Identification response from the UE to HN

Fig. 2. Identification of the UE at the HN

1. The SN sends an identification request to UE.
2. Identification response from the UE (Fig. 1):
   - The ME starts by freshly generating a pair of public/private KEM keys $(\text{pk}_U, \text{sk}_U)$.
   - The ME generates a shared KEM key K_{s_1} and a cipher text c_1 using an encapsulation algorithm and the HN public key pk_H.
   - The ME conceals the SUPI, pk_U and ID_{SN} using the key K_{s_1} and a symmetric encryption $\text{Enc}_{K_{s_1}}$. We denote such a concealment by SUCI_{conc}.
   - The ME computes a MAC tag using HMAC with $\text{SUCI}_{conc}, K_{s_1}$.
   - Finally, the UE sends $(c_1, \text{SUCI}_{conc}, \text{MAC}_U, \text{ID}_{HN})$ to SN.
3. The message from SN to HN: Once the SN receives $c_1, \text{SUCI}_{conc}, \text{MAC}_U$, and ID_{HN} from UE, the SN generates a random 256 bit string R_{SN}, and then forwards $(c_1, \text{SUCI}_{conc}, \text{MAC}_U, R_{SN})$ to the HN.
4. The UE Identification at the HN (Fig. 2): The parameters at the HN are, sk_H, the KEM secret key (bound to pk_H), and ID_{SN}. Once the HN recieves $(c_1, \text{SUCI}_{conc}, \text{MAC}_U, R_{SN})$ from the SN, the HN proceeds on identifying the UE using the algorithm in Fig. 2, where $\text{Dec}_{K_{s_1}}$ denotes a symmetric decryption using the key K_{s_1}, which is resulting from the decapsulation $\textbf{Decaps}(c_1, \text{sk}_{HN})$.

The next step consists of the generation of an authentication challenge for the UE by the HN.

5.2 Phase B: The Authentication Phase

Once the MAC check passes at the HN (Fig. 2), the HN retrieves the UE's long term key K based on SUPI, derives the key K_{s_2} and the ciphertext c_2 using the appropriate KEM encapsulation algorithm and pk_U. In more detail, we have:

1. The HN computes an authentication vector using the `Auth_Vector` algorithm depicted in Fig. 3.

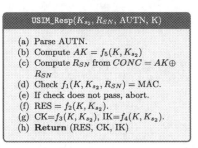

USIM_Resp(K_{s_2}, R_{SN}, AUTN, K)

(a) Parse AUTN.
(b) Compute $AK = f_5(K, K_{s_2})$
(c) Compute R_{SN} from $CONC = AK \oplus R_{SN}$
(d) Check $f_1(K, K_{s_2}, R_{SN})$ = MAC.
(e) If check does not pass, abort.
(f) RES = $f_2(K, K_{s_2})$.
(g) CK=$f_3(K, K_{s_2})$, IK=$f_4(K, K_{s_2})$.
(h) **Return** (RES, CK, IK)

Fig. 4. Challenge response at the USIM

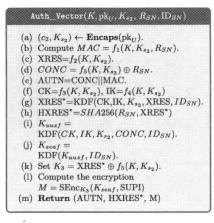

Auth_Vector(K, pk$_U$, K_{s_2}, R_{SN}, ID$_{SN}$)

(a) $(c_2, K_{s_2}) \leftarrow$ **Encaps**(pk$_U$).
(b) Compute $MAC = f_1(K, K_{s_2}, R_{SN})$.
(c) XRES=$f_2(K, K_{s_2})$.
(d) $CONC = f_5(K, K_{s_2}) \oplus R_{SN}$.
(e) AUTN=CONC||MAC.
(f) CK=$f_3(K, K_{s_2})$, IK=$f_4(K, K_{s_2})$
(g) XRES*=KDF(CK,IK, K_{s_2}, XRES, ID_{SN}).
(h) HXRES*=$SHA256(R_{SN}, $XRES*)
(i) $K_{ausf} =$ KDF($CK, IK, K_{s_2}, CONC, ID_{SN}$).
(j) $K_{seaf} =$ KDF(K_{ausf}, ID_{SN}).
(k) Set $K_3 = $XRES* $\oplus f_5(K, K_{s_2})$.
(l) Compute the encryption $M = $SEnc$_{K_3}(K_{seaf}, $SUPI)
(m) **Return** (AUTN, HXRES*, M)

Fig. 3. Challenge and key material generation at HN

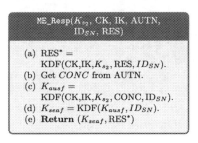

ME_Resp(K_{s_2}, CK, IK, AUTN, ID$_{SN}$, RES)

(a) RES* = KDF(CK,IK,K_{s_2}, RES, ID_{SN}).
(b) Get $CONC$ from AUTN.
(c) $K_{ausf} =$ KDF(CK,IK,K_{s_2}, CONC, ID$_{SN}$).
(d) $K_{seaf} = $KDF($K_{ausf}, ID_{SN}$).
(e) **Return** (K_{seaf}, RES*)

Fig. 5. Session key and RES* generation at the ME.

2. Next, the HN sends AUTN, M, HXRES* and c_2 to the SN.
3. The SN forwards both AUTN and c_2 to the UE.
4. At the UE side:
   - The ME first obtains the key K_{s_2} using the decapsulation algorithm with the stored secret key sk$_U$, namely $K_{s_2} \leftarrow$ **Decaps**(c_2, sk$_U$).
   - The USIM receives K_{s_2} from the ME, then proceeds on computing the response to the challenge using the `USIM_Resp` algorithm in Fig. 4.
   - The ME generates RES* and the key material using `ME_Resp` as depicted in Fig. 5.
   - The ME forwards RES* the SN.
5. The SN receives the value of RES* from the UE and then
   - compares SHA256(RES*, R_{SN}) with HXRES*. If the two values are not equal, then abort.
   - the SN uses R_{SN} to obtain $f_5(K, K_{s_2})$ from CONC.
   - computes $K_3 = $RES* $\oplus f_5(K, K_{s_2})$.
   - The SN obtains the SUPI and K_{seaf} by decrypting M using K_3.
   - The SN sends a confirmation message to the HN.

5.3   Remarks on the Enhancements Required by Our Protocol

In mobile telephony, and from a design point of view, it is desirable to implement novel protocols ensuring backward compatibility with previous mobile generations. In our protocol, the authentication response at the UE uses the same algorithms as in 5G AKA, see TS 33.501, namely, ME_Resp and USIM_Resp depicted in Figs. 5 and 4. The only difference between our proposed protocol and the UE computations in 5G AKA is the used input for such algorithms. More precisely, we use R_{SN} instead of the *sequence number* (SQN) and we use K_{s_2} instead of a random bitstring generated at the HN. Consequently, our protocol would require only minor extensions at the USIM level.

6   The Case of GUTI

In the above, we covered the case where the identification is based on the permanent identifier SUPI. However, the much more frequent case is when the *Global Unique Temporary Identifier* (GUTI) is used. The use of GUTI is favored over the use of SUPI in 5G (and also in earlier generations) because it is a frequently changing identifier that is chosen independently of SUPI. When GUTI is used as an identifier, no (asymmetric) encryption is required at the UE side. In the best case, after every successful communication, the SN assigns a new GUTI to the UE over the established secure channel.

As in the case of SUPI, the communication can be initiated either by the UE or the SN. In the rest of this section, we assume that the UE identification is based on GUTI, where the UE sends its GUTI to the SN. Next, the SN either chooses to continue using the shared session keys from the previous connection or starts a fresh authentication via the HN. Note that in both cases a new GUTI can be allocated to the UE. In the latter case, the authentication (in 5G AKA) is similar to the SUPI case. Hence, the resulting session key K_{seaf} will suffer from the mentioned security issues. In this section, we equip our protocol with a mechanism covering the GUTI case.

We recall that after a successful run of our protocol, the UE and the HN share the key K_{s_2} and the random bit string R_{SN} generated by the SN. We further require that after each successful protocol run, both the UE and the HN store a hash value

$$K_S = h(K_{s_2}, R_{SN}),$$

where h is an appropriate standard hash function. After storing K_S, both K_{s_2} and R_{SN} are deleted. Moreover, we require that with every GUTI assignment, the SN generates and sends, in addition to the GUTI, a random bitstring R'_{SN} to the UE over the established secure channel. The idea behind our solution for the GUTI case is to replace K_{s_2} with

$$K'_S = K_S \oplus R'_{SN}.$$

in our SUPI-based protocol. The procedure goes as follows:

1. In the beginning of the connection establishment, the UE identifies itself by sending GUTI.
2. The SN resolves the SUPI from GUTI and forwards the SUPI with the stored R'_{SN} and a freshly generated new random bitstring R_{SN} to the HN.
3. The HN notices that GUTI has been used as an identifier, computes K'_S based on R'_{SN} and the stored K'_S, and runs Auth_Vector with K'_S instead of K_{s_2}.
4. Similarly, the UE runs AT_ME and USIM_Resp with K'_S instead of K_{s_2}.
5. After all steps in the protocol have been completed successfully, both the UE and the HN replace K_S with $h(K'_S, R_{SN})$. Then everything is ready for another run of a GUTI-based authentication.

In the last step above, the HN may delete the old K_S because it knows that the UE has completed the protocol successfully. On the other hand, the UE has to keep also the old K_S until it gets confirmation from the SN about successful completion of the whole protocol also on the HN side. This confirmation may be given in several ways, either explicitly or implicitly, but we leave the details out of scope of this paper.

Please note that the forward security in the case of SUPI (resp., GUTI) is based on the shared K_{s_2} (resp., K_S), while the protection against compromised/impersonated SNs follows from the contribution of the SN, i.e., R_{SN} and the MAC check at the UE in both the SUPI and the GUTI case. By assumption, the parameters K_{s_2}, K_S are shared only between the UE and the HN, while R_{SN} and R'_{SN} are shared by the UE, SN and HN. Moreover, the SUPI and GUTI protocols are similar, and the only difference consists of replacing K_{s_2} by K_S. Furthermore, and thanks to the hash function h, it is practically impossible to link K_{s_2} to K_S. The same is true for R_{SN} and R'_{SN} as they are randomly and independently generated. Consequently, a SUPI based protocol execution and a subsequent GUTI based protocol execution cannot be linked to each other. Due to the similarity between the GUTI and SUPI cases, we mainly focus on the security analysis of the SUPI based protocol.

7   Security Analysis

We prove the security of our protocol by utilizing ProVerif [14], which is one of the well-known formal verification tools.

7.1   Threat Model

We assume a Dolev-Yao model for attackers. Moreover, to evaluate the forward-secrecy property, we consider a more powerful attacker, i.e., an attacker that can compromise some parties. Thus, we additionally consider the eCK model [19]. Our formal verification can be split into two parts. The first part consists of proving the security of a *clean session*. During this session, the adversary cannot control any party and does not have access to the parties' long-term or temporary keys. More precisely, we prove that after the execution of a clean session, our protocol ensures authentication and secrecy of the SUPI, long-term key K, sk_{HN}, and the session key. In the second part of our verification, we assume that the HN or UE (or both) are compromised; we then prove that our protocol satisfies the forward-secrecy property under such assumptions.

Next, we precise our assumptions on the protocol's channels and components. Our assumptions are drawn from the 5G requirements specified in TS 33.501.

Assumptions on the Channels. As in the case of 5G, our protocol uses two separate channels. The first one is the radio channel between the UE and the SN; see the 5G specification, TS 33.501. We assume the presence of a Dolev-Yao attacker who can intercept, manipulate and replay messages on this channel. The second channel is a wired channel between the SN and HN; in contrast with the above radio channel, the channel between the SN and HN is explicitly specified by TS 33.501 as a e2e core network interconnection channel. Consequently, we adopt the assumption that such a channel is secure, namely, a channel that provides both confidentiality and integrity.

Assumptions on the Components. We recall that our protocol consists of three components, the UE, the SN and the HN. Our assumptions on the protocol components are the following: (1) The UE consists of the USIM and the ME. In our protocol we assume that both the asymmetric (post-quantum) encryption and the session key K_{seaf} derivation are performed by the ME, where the ME uses parameters that are given by the USIM. In our model, we consider the UE to be one single secure entity. More precisely, the exchange between the ME and USIM is assumed to be secure and the key K_{seaf} is protected at the UE after the execution of the protocol. Moreover, the long term key K is residing at the temper-resistant part of the USIM, thus, assumed to remain protected. (2) The attacker cannot obtain the key K_{seaf} at the SN. (3) The long term parameters at the HN, i.e., K and sk_H are protected during the protocol execution. Note that in the context of forward secrecy we assume that such parameters leaked after an honest execution of the protocol.

7.2 Formal Verification

Our verification consists of four parts. The process at the UE, the process at the SN, the process at the HN, denoted by UE, SN, HN respectively, and a main process to conclude to proof. Our ProVerif code with implementation details and design choices on the chosen primitives, i.e., XOR, KEM. is available in our repository at https://github.com/Secure-6G/ProVerif-AKA-6G.

Verification Results. Our verification shows the excitability of our protocol by showing that each pair of successive messages is executed in sequence. We further prove the secrecy of the protocol long term parameters, namely, K the long term key at the UE/HN, sk_{HN}, the secret key at the HN and the long term identifier SUPI. Moreover, the authentication of the UE by the SN by the help of the HN is proved. Finally, Proverif shows that forward-secrecy holds even if the long term keys at the UE and HN have been compromised.

7.3 Further Security Features

Protection Against Compromised and Impersonated SNs. As mentioned in Sect. 3, 5G AKA suffers from two attacks identified in [3]. The first attack follows from an attacker compromising the SN and resulting in making the SN to assign the wrong SUPI to the session key. As pointed in [3], this attack is due to the fact that the SUPI and the session key are sent in two different messages (and not bound together). The second attack results from the lack of a mechanism allowing the UE to detect if the received authentication is sent by correct SN.

In our protocol, both the session key and the SUPI are sent to the SN as a single encrypted message M during authentication. At this stage, the SN is not able to obtain the key K_3 used to encrypt M, as it depends on XRES*, the expected challenge response from the UE. In fact, the SN will only receive the response from the UE after the latter has authenticating both the HN and the SN, thanks to the MAC check at the UE, which depends on R_{SN} and K. Consequently, both binding the SUPI and the session key to each other, and checking the validity of the message sent by the SN to the UE are achieved by the above procedure.

Preventing Linkability and Replay Attacks. A linkability attack is an attack where the attacker is able to distinguish if different sessions belong to the same user. Examples of linkability attacks on mobile networks protocols include failure message linkability attack [6], encrypted SUPI replay attack [7] and sequence number inference attack [8], which are all particular cases of replay attacks. Our protocol prevents such attacks by providing resistance to replay attacks. Assuming that the channel between the SN and the HN is secure, then the vulnerable message flow of our protocol reduces to the messages sent between the UE and the SN. There is only one message from the SN to the UE consisting of the ciphertext c_2 resulting from an encapsulating using the freshly generated UE public key and the quantity AUTN consisting of $f_5(K, K_{s_2}) \oplus R_{SN}$ and $MAC = f_5(K, K_{s_2}, R_{SN})$. Assume that the ciphertext c_2 is produced by a KEM ensuring the Indistinguishability under Chosen Plaintext Attack (IND-CPA), which is the case for the post-quantum KEMs used in the next section to evaluate our protocol. Then any replayed cipher c_2 in our protocol will be detected by the UE. Moreover, the MAC in AUTN depends on the freshly generated key K_{s_2} and randomness R_{SN}. We recall that K_{s_2} is protected by the freshly generated secret key sk_U of the UE, while R_{SN} is obtained using K and K_{s_2}. Consequently, replayed, handcrafted c_2, AUTN (or both) will be detected by the UE via the mentioned MAC check.

Post-Quantum Forward Secrecy. A general technique to achieve forward secrecy is to equip every protocol execution with a "fresh" authenticated Diffie-Hellman (DH) key exchange, that is to create an independence between the session key and the long term keys. This approach was used, e.g., in mobile telephony AKA protocols in [10,11]. In theory, such proposals can be modified to become quantum secure by replacing DH by a similar post-quantum key exchange. At the time of writing, PQ key exchanges are still not at the same maturity level as KEMs. Moreover, using KEMs instead of DH have been shown to be more efficient in some contexts, e.g., the TLS protocol [20]. Thus, we argue that in this direction, a novel feature of our protocol is in the use of the (post-quantum) KEM paradigm to ensure perfect forward secrecy in 5G and beyond instead of using DH type key exchange.

8   Feasibility of Our Protocol

In this section, we discuss potential implementations of our protocol. Our aim is to compare our protocol with the standardized 5G AKA. At the UE side (resp., HN side), we use the same symmetric primitives as in 5G AKA, with one hash extra hash $f_1(\text{pk}_U, K)$ (resp., one extra hash and one symmetric encryption). Hence, we will restrict our comparison to asymmetric primitives, i.e., KEMs. For the SN, our protocol is only required to perform a random number generation, a symmetric decryption and an XOR operation, as additional operations compared to 5G AKA, thus we only focus on the operations at the UE and HN.

Computational Cost. At the UE side, our protocol uses one KeyGen and one Encaps before sending the first message to the SN, then the UE decapsulates the ciphertext c_2 sent by the HN. In 5G AKA, the UE uses one ECIES KEM encapsulation for the SUPI encryption, Hence, comparing the running time of asymmetric primitives in our protocol (at the UE) with 5G AKA reduces to comparing the time of one ECIES key encapsulation with the running time of a KEM's **KeyGen + Encaps + Decaps**. For the SUPI encryption in 5G AKA, TS 33.501, gives the options of using two ECIES profiles, namely, with Curve25519 and Secp256r1. For our protocol, we use CRYSTALS-Kyber recently chosen by NIST for standardization, and the potential algorithms for further standardization: BIKE, Classic McEliece, and HQC. Moreover, and to fairly compare the mentioned algorithms, we use the KEM implementations with parameters offering the security level required by 3GPP, which is equivalent to 128-bits AES. The computational cost figures of the asymmetric primitives at the UE are depicted in Table 2. Table 2 is generated using liboqs [9], which is an open source C library for quantum-safe cryptographic algorithms, where the implementations are directly from NIST submissions. For the ECIES profiles we use OpenSSL. The computations are performed on a 3.5 GHz Core (i7-7567U).

We recall that our aim is to rank the implementations when various algorithms are used. Hence, the used device is not relevant in this context (mobile phone or workstation). Using Table 2, we remark that Kyber outperforms both ECIES profiles. The most significant computational cost comes from Classic McEliece. It is worth mentioning that the heaviest operation in Classic McEliece is the KeyGen which takes approximately 14 ms.

Next, we evaluate the operations at the HN using an approach similar to the operations at the UE. Compared to 5G AKA, which requires only one ECIES decapsulation at the HN, our protocol uses one Decaps and one Encaps at the HN (plus one hash and one symmetric encryption). Similarly to the case of UE,

Kyber outperforms both ECIES profiles, similarly to the computations at the UE, the use of Classic McEliece at the HN is faster than ECIES Secp256r1.

Communication Cost. Table 3 illustrates the (KEM) parameter sizes of the used schemes. In 5G AKA, the UE sends a SUCI, a MAC and a KEM ciphertext over the radio channel to the SN and this last forwards these parameter to the HN. Next, the HN forwards an authentication vector to the UE via the SN. Finally, the UE sends a challenge response to the HN via the SN. In our protocol, and in addition to the 5G AKA messages, the UE sends a symmetric encryption of a KEM public key, while the HN responds with an additional KEM ciphertext to the UE. From Table 3 we clearly see that ECIES provides a small communication cost compared to post-quantum KEMs, while Classic McEliece has the most significant communication cost due to the size of the public key. We note that the standardized Kyber offers the best communication cost among the studied PQ KEMs. Please note that our comparison considered that some quantum resistant scheme must replace ECIES in the near future. Hence, the focus is on determining which PQ KEM is most suitable for our scheme.

Table 2. Running time of the asymmetric primitives at the UE and HN (milliseconds).

Algorithm	At UE	At HN
ECIES Curve25519	0.040	0.040
ECIES Secp256r1	0.180	0.180
Kyber	0.026	0.019
Classic McEliece	14.047	0.047
BIKE	0.882	0.672
HQC	0.421	0.331

Table 3. Communication cost (bytes)

Algorithm	sk	pk	Cipher	key
ECIES Curve25519	32	32	32	32
ECIES Secp256r1	32	32	32	32
Kyber	1632	800	768	32
Classic McEliece	6452	261120	128	32
BIKE	5223	1541	1573	32
HQC	2289	2249	4481	64

9 Conclusion

We presented an authentication and key agreement protocol for 5G and beyond with further security and privacy features that are not offered by the standardized 5G AKA. Such features include resistance to known linkability attacks, perfect forward secrecy, and protection against compromising and impersonating the SN. Moreover, in our protocol, we abandoned the use of sequence numbers to avoid possible desynchronization attacks. Furthermore, our protocol covers the case of GUTI which is usually ignored in similar works. We used Proverif to formally verify some of our security claims. Finally, we gave an overview of potential implementations of the protocol using NIST post-quantum KEM candidates. In summary, we illustrated a theoretical and practical implementation of a (quantum) safe AKA protocol for beyond-5G and presented a supporting argument for its security features using both formal and classical methods.

As mentioned in the threat model, active attackers between the USIM and ME are omitted. While not considered in our protocol, we emphasize that our protocol does not prevent an attacker from requesting the session key from the USIM or ME, especially an attacker able to compromise the long term key K. This problem is left as future work.

References

1. Shor, P.: Algorithms for quantum computation: discrete logarithms and factoring. In: Proceedings of 35th Annual Symposium FOCS, pp. 124–134 (1994)
2. Wang, Y., Zhang, Z., Xie, Y.: Privacy-preserving and standard-CompatibleAKA protocol for 5G. In: 30th USENIX Security Symposium (USENIX Security 2021), pp. 3595–3612 (2021)
3. Basin, D., Dreier, J., Hirschi, L., Radomirovic, S., Sasse, R., Stettler, V.: A formal analysis of 5G authentication. In: Proceedings of the 2018 ACM SIGSAC Conference on Computer and Communications Security, pp. 1383–1396 (2018)
4. Braeken, A., Liyanage, M., Kumar, P., Murphy, J.: Novel 5G authentication protocol to improve the resistance against active attacks and malicious serving networks. IEEE Access **7**, 64040–64052 (2019)
5. Koutsos, A.: The 5G-AKA authentication protocol privacy. In: 2019 IEEE European Symposium on Security and Privacy (EuroS&P), pp. 464–479 (2019)
6. Arapinis, M., et al.: New privacy issues in mobile telephony: fix and verification. In: Proceedings of the 2012 ACM CCS, pp. 205–216 (2012)
7. Fouque, P., Onete, C., Richard, B.: Achieving better privacy for the 3GPP AKA protocol. In: Proceedings on Privacy Enhancing Technologies 2016, pp. 255–275 (2016)
8. Borgaonkar, R., Hirschi, L., Park, S., Shaik, A.: New privacy threat on 3G, 4G, and upcoming 5G AKA protocols. In: Proceedings on Privacy Enhancing Technologies 2019, pp. 108–127 (201)
9. Liboqs (2019). https://github.com/open-quantum-safe/liboqs
10. Liu, T., Wu, F., Li, X., Chen, C.: A new authentication and key agreement protocol for 5G wireless networks. Telecommun. Syst. **78**(3), 317–329 (2021). https://doi.org/10.1007/s11235-021-00815-9
11. Arkko, J., Norrman, K., Näslund, M., Sahlin, B.: A USIM compatible 5G AKA protocol with perfect forward secrecy. In: 2015 IEEE Trustcom/BigDataSE/ISPA, vol. 1, pp. 1205–1209 (2015)
12. Attaran, M.: The impact of 5G on the evolution of intelligent automation and industry digitization. J. Ambient Intell. Humaniz. Comput. 1–17 (2021)
13. Ahmad, I., Kumar, T., Liyanage, M., Okwuibe, J., Ylianttila, M., Gurtov, A.: 5G security: analysis of threats and solutions. In: 2017 IEEE Conference on Standards for Communications and Networking (CSCN), pp. 193–199 (2017)
14. Blanchet, B., Abadi, M., Fournet, C.: Automated verification of selected equivalences for security protocols. J. Logic Algebr. Program. **75**, 3–51 (2008)
15. Ulitzsch, V., Park, S., Marzougui, S., Seifert, J.: A post-quantum secure subscription concealed identifier for 6G. In: Proceedings of the 15th ACM Conference on Security and Privacy in Wireless and Mobile Networks, pp. 157–168 (2022)
16. Hojjati, M., Shafieinejad, A., Yanikomeroglu, H.: A blockchain-based authentication and key agreement (AKA) protocol for 5G networks. IEEE Access **8**, 216461–216476 (2020)

17. Regulation (EU) 2016/679 of the European Parliament and of the Council. Regulation (EU) 679/2016 (2016)
18. Chlosta, M., Rupprecht, D., Pöpper, C., Holz, T.: 5G SUCI-catchers: still catching them all? In: Proceedings of the 14th ACM Conference on Security and Privacy in Wireless and Mobile Networks, pp. 359–364 (2021)
19. LaMacchia, B., Lauter, K., Mityagin, A.: Stronger security of authenticated key exchange. In: International Conference on Provable Security, pp. 1–16 (2007)
20. Schwabe, P., Stebila, D., Wiggers, T.: Post-quantum TLS without handshake signatures. In: Proceedings of the 2020 ACM SIGSAC Conference on Computer and Communications Security, pp. 1461–1480 (2020)

IoT Security

A Survey on IoT Vulnerability Discovery

Xinbo Ban[1]([✉]) [ID], Ming Ding[2] [ID], Shigang Liu[1] [ID], Chao Chen[3] [ID],
and Jun Zhang[1] [ID]

[1] Swinburne University of Technology, 1 John Street, Melbourne, Australia
{XBan,ShigangLiu,JunZhang}@swin.edu.au
[2] Information Security and Privacy Group, Data61, CSIRO, Sydney, Australia
Ming.Ding@data61.csiro.au
[3] Royal Melbourne Institute of Technology, 124 La Trobe Street, Melbourne,
Australia
Chao.chen@rmit.edu.au

Abstract. The introduction of the Internet of Things (IoT) ecosystem into public and private sectors has markedly changed the way people live, work, and entertain through integrating the digital system with the physical world. However, the production of new scenarios and architectures in IoT ecosystems introduces previously unknown security threats due to the vulnerabilities in the IoT software. Since various vulnerabilities lead to unexpected consequences in different parts of the IoT ecosystem, we propose 'security domain' to categorize the origin of the threats properly, including 'physical device', 'operation rule', and 'communication'. The research community has conducted a significant amount of work in the area of vulnerability discovery by utilizing 'code intelligence', representing code analysis techniques based on different types of code. With the focus on the security domains, we review recent representative work published in the dominant time to investigate the emerging research. Also, we summarize the research methodology commonly adopted in this fast-growing area. In consonance with the phases of the research methodology, each paper that discovers IoT vulnerabilities is comprehensively studied. Challenges and future work in this area have been discussed as well.

Keywords: Security and privacy · Internet of things · Vulnerability discovery

1 Introduction

Internet of Things (IoT) is envisioned to fundamentally change our lives in every aspect because it is an emerging communication paradigm that aims at connecting all kinds of objects to the Internet and harvesting data generated by sensors. The exploitable points of most IoT attacks are related to the software vulnerabilities that exist in one or more components of the IoT ecosystems. The research on IoT security shows the advantages of accurately working out a real-world vulnerability with the development of simulation technology [2]. In addition, with the help of a physical device, recent studies show that it is practical to discover

X. Yuan et al. (Eds.): NSS 2022, LNCS 13787, pp. 267–282, 2022.
https://doi.org/10.1007/978-3-031-23020-2_15

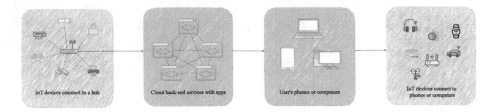

Fig. 1. Cloud-based IoT architecture for the smart world

the previously unknown vulnerabilities [8, 25, 27, 28, 30]. Since tens of thousands of new IoT devices are released every year, the research progress is always one step behind [25]. In this light, we can see the benefits of the static analysis on reused components such as [3, 11, 23].

The scope of this survey paper mainly covers revealing exploitable vulnerabilities in the IoT ecosystem with code intelligence, which is to be addressed in Sect. 2 in more detail. We suggest code intelligence as the technology is adaptive and able to manage a wide range of code types. The selection of papers focuses exclusively on English-language publications that meet the desired criteria. We search 'IoT', 'vulnerability', 'discovery' on Usenix Security Symposium (SEC), the Network and Distributed System Security (NDSS), IEEE Symposium on Security and Privacy (S&P), and ACM Computer and Communications Security (CCS), which are the top four conferences recognized by the cybersecurity community. Nevertheless, we recognize that this emphasis may lead to the overlook of the papers published at other venues. Depending on the papers collected from the top conferences, the references of them and ones that referenced them are also distilled (Fig. 1).

The main contributions of the paper include: 1) we investigate state-of-the-art IoT vulnerability discovery frameworks based on reviewed top-level papers. The research methodology, security problems, and the used datasets in IoT ecosystems have been analyzed and summarized, that highlights the existing research in this area. 2) we classify the reviewed research into three categories according to the relevant security domains: 'physical device', 'operation rule', and 'communication'. Each reference is further explained in a summary table for clarity. 3) we broadly define code intelligence as intelligent discovery methods applied such as ML, NLP, etc., and various types of code processed such as source code, binary code.

The survey is organized as below. Firstly, Sect. 2 describes the research methodology summarized from the reviewed papers. Section 3 presents a detailed review of the current research work of IoT vulnerability discovery with code intelligence in various security domains. Section 4 points out the challenges and future directions. Finally, Sect. 5 draws concluding remarks of this survey.

2   Taxonomy and Research Methodology

This section provides an understanding of the new topic on IoT vulnerability discovery through code intelligence, which is twofold: (1) a taxonomy proposed

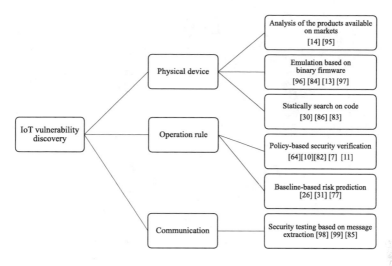

Fig. 2. IoT taxonomy

to categorize the existing technical methods with different real-world scenarios; (2) a research methodology developed to clarify the procedure of the state-of-the-art research.

2.1   Taxonomy

We propose a taxonomy for IoT vulnerability discovery with code intelligence by taking IoT architecture and security domains into consideration, as shown in Fig. 2. There are three categories of research, 'physical device', 'operation rule', and 'communication'. In the category of 'physical device', the research conducts the vulnerability analysis on the program within the firmware, which is a special-purpose operating system in a single IoT device. Analysis of physical device has three sub-classes, analysis of real-world products, emulation based on binary firmware, and static search on code. Analysis of 'operation rule' has two sub-classes, policy-based security verification, and baseline-based risk prediction. In the third research category, communication channels deliver key information in terms of IoT device authentication, verification, registration, etc. The relevant code can exist in mobile phones, physical devices, and backends.

2.2   Research Methodology

Figure 3 illustrates a research methodology that we develop to generalize the research steps shared by the existing work on IoT vulnerability discovery with code intelligence. The research methodology consists of five steps: (1) IoT threat understanding; (2) root cause analysis; (3) code acquisition and preprocessing; (4) intelligent vulnerability discovery; (5) performance evaluation.

Fig. 3. A new research methodology for IoT vulnerability discovery with code intelligence

IoT Threat Understanding. In the face of overwhelming IoT vulnerabilities, it is important for researchers to have a deep understanding of the features of IoT scenarios and the nature of cyber threats. This involves IoT ecosystems, architectures, functionalities, and potential risks. Researchers need to investigate a few key questions, what kind of IoT components are there, how they operate and communicate with each other, and where the threats come from. A full understanding of the targeted IoT scenario is fundamental to figure out the security issues in the individual component and connections among them. In summary, after this step, we obtain a basic understanding of threat type.

Root Cause Analysis. Based on the IoT threat understanding, root cause analysis is to answer a few key questions: what type of the vulnerability is, where it comes and what the consequences it would cause. For example, some experienced researchers may perform threat modeling for root cause analysis. Threat modeling is the practice of identifying and prioritizing potential threats and security mitigation. The modeling process will consider the nature of the system, the security domain, the probable attacker's profile, and the most likely attack vectors. It may address the following research questions. What is the security domain in the system? What is the most likely vulnerability to be exploited? What are the most relevant clues can be tracked?

Code Acquisition and Preprocessing. It is a crucial step to collect and process data properly. The feasibility and validity of solving the research problem depend on the quality of data is. We have witnessed a tremendous increase in both the variety and scope of code data regarding IoT security for the past few years. Generally, code acquisition starts working at gathering data from different sources depending on the scoped research problem and security domain. The code data usually need cloud storage or physical foundation as the appropriate storage services or databases [17]. In data preprocessing, the code often is required to be cleaned up for removing noisy data, merging data, and constructing the data with proper formats. In particular, supervised learning requires the labeled data for model training.

Intelligent Vulnerability Discovery. Considering code is the root cause of vulnerability, code analysis plays a critical role in uncovering vulnerabilities in a software application to prevents malicious attacks. In IoT scenarios, code can be the executable code of normal applications and the scripts for the interactions of smart devices and cloud service. Regarding IoT vulnerability discovery, static code analysis (SCA) looks at the application from the inside outperforming in a non-runtime environment without executing the program, but rather by examining the source code, binary code or other types of code for signs of security vulnerabilities [10,23]. Dynamic code analysis (DCA) looks at the application from the outside in - by examining it in its running state and trying to manipulate it Having originated and evolved separately, SCA and DCA have different strengths and weaknesses. Accordingly, a union of SCA and DCA is increasingly adopted by newly proposed researches in recent years [8]. Moreover, Machine learning (ML) Natural Language Processing (NLP) has been utilized in research of this area [1,10,22]. A few work proposed model checking [5,18] and state monitoring [8,30] for IoT code intelligence.

Performance Evaluation. The effectiveness and efficiency of the proposed code intelligence methods need to be verified, which are subject to the evaluation metrics and research objectives. When the research goal has not been reached, we should incrementally restart the circulation from research scoping to finally seek an optimal one. The effectiveness can be measured from the point of view of quality, thoroughness, consistency, and reliability. It is related to the True Positives (TP) that represents the number of correctly discovered vulnerabilities. It is also called accuracy in some existing work. The efficiency of code intelligence methods is evaluated by speed and cost in most existing work. It should be gauged based on the time that it needs to take to complete the discovery process and the cost implication of such a process. Also, some work utilize other evaluation metrics, including ROC curve, Recalls, and so on.

3   IoT Vulnerability Discovery with Code Intelligence

In this section, we review state-of-the-art IoT vulnerability discovery work by security domains as follows: (1) physical device (2) operation rule (3) communication. As shown in Fig. 2, three sub-classes including 'Analysis of the products available on markets', 'Emulation based on binary firmware' and 'Statically search on code' are reviewed under 'physical device', 'Policy-based security verification' and 'Baseline-based risk prediction' are reviewed under 'operation rule', and 'Security testing based on message extraction' are reviewed under 'communication'. In line with the methodology of IoT vulnerability discovery with code

Table 1. Overview of papers on IoT vulnerability discovery with code intelligence

Paper & Year	Vulnerability type	Security domain	Dataset
[8], 2018	Memory corruption	Physical device	17 devices; official companion mobile apps
[27], 2019	Memory corruption; command injection; cross-site scripting; information disclosure	Physical device	10 devices
[28], 2019	Memory related	Physical device	Two benchmarks; seven programs; FIRMADYNE dataset
[24], 2019	Various	Physical device	45 binary files
[7], 2016	Buffer overflow; command injection; information disclosure	Physical device	23,035 firmware images
[29], 2019	Various	Physical device	Six firmware images
[11], 2016	Various	Physical device	33,047 firmware images
[26], 2017	Various	Physical device	13 firmware images
[23], 2019	Various	Physical device; Backend; Communication	2,081 Android apps
[18], 2018	Inter-rule	Operation rule	150 SmartThings apps
[5], 2018	Inter-rule	Operation rule	65 SmartThings apps
[22], 2019	Inter-rule	Operation rule	315,393 IFTTT applets
[4], 2018	Inter-rule	Operation rule	nine system' deployments
[6], 2019	Inter-rule	Operation rule	50 SmartThings apps; 35 IFTTT applets
[10], 2018	Inter-rule	Operation rule	185 SmartThings apps
[12], 2016	Privilege design	Operation rule	132 SmartThings device handlers; 499 SmartThings apps
[21], 2017	Inter-rule	Operation rule	19,323 IFTTT recipes
[30], 2019	Communication design	Communication	11 devices
[31], 2019	Communication design	Communication	18,166 Android apps
[25], 2020	Authentication design	Communication	77 OBD-II dongles; 21 Android apps

intelligence proposed in Sect. 2, we review and summarize the critical points of each collected work in detail. Table 1 shows some important elements of overall reviewed papers. The first column is the publication year of each work. The vulnerability type addressed in every paper can be found in the second column. Besides, the security domain the paper focuses on is in the third column. The fourth column is the dataset collected in each work.

3.1   Physical Device

In this section, we review security problems in physical devices from both IoT and IIoT devices. As shown in Fig. 4, typically, the firmware is extracted from IoT devices for code analysis. Mobile companion apps can be treated as helpful related resources if the firmware is rarely acquired.

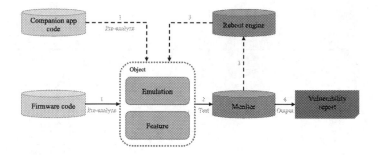

Fig. 4. Physical device. As state in Sect. 2, pre-analysis in the data prepossessing phase aims to make the code properly to run or extract the features for the following analysis. In the discovery phase, the testing could be performed based on the code emulation or feature. Then a monitor checks the status of the emulation while rebooting it if necessary. Meantime, any crash will be outputted as the result of a vulnerability report.

Analysis of Products Available on Markets. This subsection reviews some work that contributed to discovering both known and zero-day vulnerabilities from the products available on markets.

Memory-Corruption Flaws Detection in IoT Firmware: Chen et al. [8] presented an automated fuzzing framework for detection of memory corruption vulnerability, called IOTFUZZER. It is a black-box based fuzzer specifically on the IoT firmware. IoTFuzzer used the information obtained by the mobile app and dynamically ran a protocol guided-fuzzing for vulnerability discovery. This work stated that mobile apps usually had very few network activities and events, which indicates that the logic in most IoT apps was relatively simple logic. By using taint tracking, IOTFUZZER was able to find that different implementation of protocol resulted in various values for products.

Multiple Types of Vulnerabilities in Physical SOHO: Zhang et al. [27] proposed SRFuzzer to discover the multiple types of vulnerabilities in physical SOHO (small office/home office) devices. It used two models to constrain test cases to model the input semantics. The effectiveness of SRFuzzer was evaluated based on a prototype implemented by authors. Totally, 208 unique exceptional behaviors were monitored.

Emulation Based on Binary Firmware. DCA shows the advantages of discovering vulnerabilities in many ways such as fuzzing. However, it is not feasible to straightforward apply them to IoT firmware because of its heavy dependency on the actual hardware.

Correctly Execute the IoT Programs in IoT Firmware: Zheng et al. [28] presented FIRM-AFL, a high-throughput grey-box fuzzing platform for vulnerability discovery in IoT firmware. FIRM-AFL aimed to correctly execute the IoT

Table 2. Physical device

Paper	Pre-analysis	Raw feature	Method	Contribution
IOTFUZZER [8]	Mobile app analysis	Firmware	Grey-box fuzzing	15 vulnerabilities
SRFuzzer [27]	Raw request crawling	Firmware	Grey-box fuzzing	97 vulnerabilities
Firm-AFL [28]	N/A	Firmware	Grey-box fuzzing	17 vulnerabilities
AutoD [24]	Source static analysis	Firmware	White-box fuzzing	Two vulnerabilities
FIRMADYNE [7]	Binary static analysis	Firmware	PoC	14 vulnerabilities
Zheng et al. [29]	Binary static analysis	Firmware	Grey-box fuzzing	Six vulnerabilities
Genius [11]	Binary static analysis	Control flow graph	Bug search	23 vulnerabilities
VulHunter [26]	N/A	Patched difference	Bianry comparison	11 vulnerabilities
Wang et al. [23]	Mobile app analysis	Byte code text	Clustering	324 vulnerable devices

programs in user-model emulators and system-mode emulators. The proposed scheme booted up the IoT firmware up in a system-mode emulator and launched the user-level programs inside the emulator.

Improving the Efficiency and Effectiveness of Vulnerability Discovery in IoT Devices: Wang et al. [24] proposed an Automated Vulnerability Discovery (AutoD), that aimed at improving the efficiency and effectiveness of vulnerability discovery in IoT devices. Anti-Driller first generated a specific test case as input by a concolic execution engine. Then it used a fuzzer to mutate the input for fuzzing to discover the vulnerabilities.

Dynamic Analysis of Targets Linux-Based Firmware: Chen et al. [7] proposed FIRMDYNE, a dynamic vulnerability discovery system for Commercial-off-the-shelf (COTS) IoT devices, which particularly were Linux-based. FIRMDYNE acquired the firmware images as the representative dataset by employing a web crawler. In terms of evaluation, FIRMDYNE detected 14 zero-day vulnerabilities.

Greybox Fuzzing Against the Difficulties in Linux-Based Firmware: Zheng et al. [29] presented a greybox fuzzer to efficiently discover the vulnerabilities in Linux-based IoT programs. The proposed framework could generate test cases by performing binary static analysis. These test cases were useful inputs for efficient fuzzing. This efficient greybox fuzzing system contained two parts. The first part was static analysis on binary code. The second part, which was IoT program greybox fuzzing Regarding evaluation,

Statically Search on Code. Static program analysis is helpful to detect the vulnerable points without executing the code [1]. Principally, it can abstractly reason about every possible path of execution. We review a few work that collected the firmware images and search the vulnerable pattern from them [11,26]. Despite most of the images are rarely available for security testing in either format of source or binary code, the work [23] leverages the companion code for vulnerable device detection without access to the firmware.

Vulnerability Searching Based on Graphs: Feng et al. [11] proposed a bug search scheme, named Genius, based on the scalable graph. The results showed Genius significantly outperformed the baseline methods with higher recall and lower false positive rates.

Unknown Vulnerability Discovery on IIoT Devices: Xiao et al. [26] proposed VulHunter, for unknown vulnerability discovery. They evaluated the effectiveness of VulHunter. In total, 11 vulnerabilities were found in the firmware and software of the IIoT system.

Vulnerable Device Discovery Without Accessing the Physical Device: Wang et al. [23] presented a vulnerable device discovery platform with no need for accessing a physical device or its firmware code. The proposed platform utilized the analysis of mobile companion apps of the IoT devices. Additionally,

Discussion: In this section, we produce an overall description as a concluding remark in Table 2. Both [8] and [27] performed fuzzing on real physical devices. In [8], mutated messages were sent via Wi-Fi to test the device. This work was capable of discovering one type of vulnerability. But there was no limitation of the types of devices. On the other hand, web servers of devices were analyzed in [27] via cable. The authors crawled the request for further mutation. It could discover multiple types of vulnerability as long as the devices with web servers could be applied. Besides, in [29], greybox fuzzing was utilized to dynamically analyze the Linux-based IoT programs. Firm-AFL [28] proposed novel emulation for greybox fuzzer. AutoD [24] was a whitebox fuzzer, that bypassed the sanity check to address the challenges of Driller [20]. The POC method was utilized in [7]. These work leveraged the firmware as the raw feature. On the other hand, Genius [11] leveraged the ACFG, which contained the relatively rich information of code to perform bug search. Wang et al. [23] computed the particular string for an app or the entire app to perform the clustering. Furthermore, the binary SCA was performed for the further analysis in [7,11,29]. IOTFUZZER [8] and Wang et al. [23] first statically analyzed the Andriod app code. SRFuzzer [27] crawled the raw request to generate seeds for mutation.

3.2   Operation Rule

The Smart Home environment, such as SmartThings and IFTTT, [12] is mainly consisted of four main components: a hub, a companion mobile app, a cloud backend, and an IoT device. As shown in Fig. 5, the vulnerability can be found from the interactions between rules through checking these interactions.

Policy-Based Security Verification. Software model checking is a technique to check whether a pre-designed property is correct or not in a finite-state model of a system.

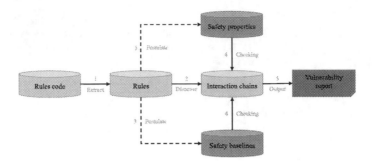

Fig. 5. Operation rule. Extraction of rules aims to model the rules since the types of rules express variously. The rules can be analyzed for interaction chain generation via the environmental channels (e.g. Temperature, humidity). The safety properties define the legal operation in an IoT ecosystem and safety baselines indicate the boundary of invulnerable rules. These can be postulated through the analysis of rules. The checking phase leverages these safety properties and baselines to check the violation of the rules.

Identifying Interaction-Level Flaws by Model Checking: Nguyen et al. [18] presented a practical system, IOTSAN, to discover 'interaction-level' vulnerabilities by using model checking as a building block.

Finding Property Violations of IoT by Model Checking: Celik et al. [5] presented a SCA system named SOTERIA to validate whether IoT apps or ecosystem adhere to conform with safety properties of the SmartThings platform. SOTERIA leveraged source code to extract intermediate representation (IR). Regarding evaluation, for market apps, nine individual apps and three multi-apps groups had more than one property violation

Identifying IoT Security Risks by Analyzing Trigger-Action Rules: Wang et al. [22] comprehensively analyzed the interactions between trigger-action (TA) rules and presented iRuler to discover inter-rule vulnerabilities within an IoT deployment.

Violation Checking by Hybrid Automated Model Checking: Bu et al. proposed an automated framework named MenSen to discover the violations in (HA-IoT). MenSen generated the LHA models based on the devices' profile documents and user-specified IFTTT rules. and checked the unwanted reachability specification created by users.

Dynamic Safety and Security Checking for IoT Devices: Celik et al. [6] proposed IoTGUARD, a dynamic IoT safety, and security checking system. IoTGUARD utilized the policy enforcement service and code instrumentation to dynamically monitor the behaviors of the devices for blocking the insecure states timely. In general, IoTGUARD checked the events and actions from apps based on a collection of policies and notified users if potential violations existed.

Table 3. Operation rule

Paper	Platform	Level	Assistance resource	Contribution
IOTSAN [18]	SmartThings	Interaction chain	System's configuration	147 vulnerabilities
SOTERIA [5]	SmartThings	Single app; interaction chain	Device capability reference file	26 vulnerable SmartApps
iRULER [22]	IFTTT	Interaction chain	Device Metadata; user's deployment configuration	66% unsafe inter-rule
MenShen [4]	IFTTT	Interaction chain	Device profile documentation	100% accuracy
IoTGUARD [6]	SmartThings; IFTTT	Single app; interaction chain	App's dynamic model	21 vulnerabilities
IOTMON [10]	SmartThings	Interaction chain	Application description	37 vulnerable chains
Fernandes et al. [12]	SmartThings	Single app	N/A	247 vulnerable SmartApps
Surbatovich et al. [21]	IFTTT	Single app; interaction chain	N/A	50% unsafe recipe

Baseline-Based Risk Prediction. For individual app and multiple apps, there are also various methods to identify the vulnerable ones. Evaluation methods are proposed to measure the risk and over-privileged level of apps. Based on the provided baseline or security issues, the measurement indicates the insecure level of the tested apps [14, 15].

Generating Physical Interaction Chains Across IoT Ecosystem: Ding and Hu [10] proposed a framework, IoTMon, that utilized the physical influence of apps to find all potentially unsafe interaction of multiple apps. They manually validated the results and found that 37 of the total (77%) were correctly identified.

Security Analysis of Smart Home Applications: Earlence et al. [12] presented an empirical and comprehensive security analysis of SmartThings. Specifically, they focused on the design vulnerabilities in SmartThings. This work explored the security-oriented aspects of SmartThings. The authors obtained a collection of 499 SmartApps were downloaded. The results showed that 276 out of 499 SmartApps (55%) were over-privileged.

Assessing the Privacy and Security Risks of IFTTT Recipes: Surbatovich et al. [21] analyzed the vulnerable IFTTT recipes that contain the potential secrecy and integrity violation by building an information flow model. In order to figure out the security and privacy threats of IFTTT recipes, the authors developed two sets of information flow labels: secrecy lattice and integrity lattice.

Discussion: Table 3 lists the papers reviewed in this section. Specifically, the platform, level, assistance resources, and contributions are summarized. Smart-Things platform was chosen to conduct the analysis in [5,10,12,18] and the IFTTT platform was analyzed by work [9,21,22]. The work [12] performed security on individual app level and the others were based on interaction level. Among

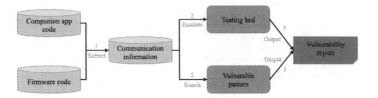

Fig. 6. Communication. As stated in Fig. 2, scenario understanding, and root cause analysis aim to ensure the necessary types of code that need to be collected for vulnerability discovery. The required data includes companion app code and firmware code. Through analyzing these code, the communication information (e.g. Pair key, UUID) can be gained. The vulnerable pattern in the code is easily searched for the identification of vulnerable points. On the other hand, a testing bed is able to be created via the collected communication information. The illegal behaviors can be outputted as vulnerable points in the vulnerability report.

these, the work [5, 6, 21] discovered the vulnerabilities on both levels. IoTGUARD [6] integrated the rule programs from both SmartThings and IFTTT to dynamically enforce the safety policy. Besides, interaction level vulnerability requires the acquisition of rule chains. Thus it is important to integrate the assistance resource for rule chain generation. IOTSAN [18] crawled the system's configuration from the web management app. SOTERIA [5] used a device capability reference file created by the authors, that included the attributes and actions. iRULER [22] took device metadata and user's deployment configuration to generate the IR. MenShen [9] required the device documentation for IoT deployment. IOTMON [10] identified the rule chain by utilizing NLP on application description.

3.3 Communication

In the IoT ecosystem, data is transmitted among devices, mobile phones, cloud backends based on several protocols as we discussed as Sect. 1. Communication is vital in the IoT ecosystem since the core functionalities of IoT are automation and data transmission. The tasks of communication include connection, pairing, bonding, and transmission. The security of key information protection in the communication channels relies on the design of tbe communication scheme. The overview of the discovery framework is illustrated in Fig. 6.

Systematically Analyzing the Security Hazards of Smart Home Platforms: Zhou et al. [30] developed a framework, that systematically understood and discovered the security issue existed in the interactions within smart home platforms. They acquired the firmware images from devices through physically dumping and created a program (phantom) that mimicked a really usable device as an assisted tool. In this work,

Automatic Fingerprinting of Vulnerable BLE IoT Devices: Zuo et al. [31] proposed an automated vulnerable device discovery tool, named BLESCOPE. In a

Table 4. Communication

Paper	Type	Technology	Protocol	Contribution
Zhou et al. [30]	Cloud-app; device-app; device-cloud	Static, dynamic analysis	TLS	N/A
BLESCOPE [31]	Device-app	Static analysis	BLE	1,757 vulnerable mobilde apps
DONGLESCOPE [25]	Device-app	Static, dynamic analysis	CAN	77 vulnerable devices

typical scenario, IoT devices need to establish a connection with their companion mobile apps. In the evaluation, BLESCOPE analyzed 18,166 apps and reported 'Just Works' pairing was adopted by 11,141 (61.3%), which indicated that the BLE channels were barely secure.

Comprehensive Vulnerability Analysis of OBD-II Dongles in IoT: Wen et al. [25] presented an analysis tool, DONGLESCOPE, that automatically and dynamically analyzed the security vulnerabilities of wireless OBD-II dongles. With the help of DONGLESCOPE, the authors found that all these dongles had at least two vulnerabilities.

Discussion: As a concluding remark for this section, an overall description is shown in Table 4. These research work analyzed the potential threats of the OTA attack or MMIM attack. Thus they performed the analysis for the message construction. BLESCOPE [31] and DONGLESCOPE [25] analyzed the code of mobilc apps. In [30], it contained not only the analysis of mobile app but also the reverse engineering of the firmware. Importantly, it also attempted to analyze the communication transmitted from the cloud.

4   Research Challenges

Although some solid research work have been published in the new area of discovering IoT vulnerabilities with code intelligence, the progress is still in its infant stage. The following subsections will discuss the crucial research challenges, which may shed light on its future paths.

Complex Domain Understanding. To achieve a general scenario understanding, some code analysts attempted to analyze the IoT ecosystem that is applied in various scenarios. The boundary of IoT security is continuously expanding. Hence, a direction of future work is to explore new IoT applications in life and work [13,19]. Looking for proper 'indirect' methods for vulnerability discovery by using relevant data is a new research interest. For example, we may build a detection system for IoT vulnerability discovery through scanning the firmware. However, owing to the difficulties of acquiring firmware, the tools can be fed by 'indirect' dataset such as codes of mobile companion apps, or the description of the devices.

Code Data Acquisition. In this survey, discovering IoT vulnerability with intelligent code analysis is modeled as a data-driven detection problem. The effectiveness of the data-driven methods depends on whether the code datasets are authentic and comprehensive. Some researchers attempted to comprehensively understand the functionalities of devices via language processing on the product description. Combining description understanding and interactions between devices to acquire the synthetic code datasets may be a new way to obtain comprehensive characteristics of the configured IoT applications. The quality of the collected code determines the performance of vulnerability prediction.

Intelligent Vulnerability Discovery. Code analysis has been applied to e.g., mobile apps and trigger-action rules for IoT vulnerability discovery. Owing to the diverse IoT programming languages used by different IoT platforms, the analysis is normally conducted on the IR code. It is challenging to convert the IR that contains sufficiently rich information and is helpful to reveal the vulnerabilities. With respect to verifying the result of vulnerability discovery, an alternative approach against passive waiting is to manually validate the output of the methodology. However, it time-consuming and unrealistic to manually check the correctness of the results in real-life implementations [16].

5   Conclusion

In this survey, we provided a roundup and a research outlook of the developing area, IoT vulnerability discovery with code intelligence. Initially, a research methodology was summarized, which is an incrementally circular process, for essentially basic phases of discovering an IoT vulnerability, consisting of IoT threat understanding, root cause analysis, code acquisition and preprocessing, intelligent vulnerability discovery, performance evaluation. On the basis of the research methodology, a comprehensive literature review of the recent research efforts was conducted on the solutions of discovering an IoT vulnerability. More specifically, since code in software plays a key role in introducing vulnerabilities and exposing security threats, the work were categorized into three groups depending on the corresponding security domains, which are 'physical device', 'operation rule', and 'communication'. Lastly, conforming to research methodology, we have discussed many of the challenges that exist in the emerging research area growing in an infant stage while elaborating on the future directions for other researchers who intend to contribute to this area. Hopefully, IoT vulnerability discovery with code intelligence can attract attention from both industry and academia. We believe this survey will be helpful towards characterizing the latency acting as a valuable guideline and reference for the future.

References

1. Ban, X., Chen, C., Liu, S., Wang, Y., Zhang, J.: Deep-learnt features for twitter spam detection. In: 2018 International Symposium on Security and Privacy in Social Networks and Big Data, pp. 208–212. IEEE (2018)

A Survey on IoT Vulnerability Discovery   281

2. Ban, X., Ding, M., Liu, S., Chen, C., Zhang, J., Xiang, Y.: TAESim: a testbed for IoT security analysis of trigger-action environment. In: Katsikas, S., et al. (eds.) European Symposium on Research in Computer Security, pp. 218–237. Springer, Cham (2021). https://doi.org/10.1007/978-3-030-95484-0_14
3. Ban, X., Liu, S., Chen, C., Chua, C.: A performance evaluation of deep-learnt features for software vulnerability detection. Concurr. Comput. Pract. Exp. **31**(19), e5103 (2019)
4. Bu, L., et al.: Systematically ensuring the confidence of real-time home automation IoT systems. ACM Trans. Cyber-Phys. Syst. **2**(3), 1–23 (2018)
5. Celik, Z.B., McDaniel, P., Tan, G.: SOTERIA: automated IoT safety and security analysis. In: USENIX, Boston, MA, USA, pp. 147–158 (2018)
6. Celik, Z.B., Tan, G., McDaniel, P.: IoTGuard: dynamic enforcement of security and safety policy in commodity IoT. In: Network and Distributed System Security Symposium, San Diego, CA, USA, pp. 1–15. The Internet Society (2019)
7. Chen, D.D., Woo, M., Brumley, D., Egele, M.: Towards automated dynamic analysis for linux-based embedded firmware. In: 23rd Annual Network and Distributed System Security Symposium, San Diego, CA, USA. The Internet Society (2016)
8. Chen, J., et al.: IoTFuzzer: discovering memory corruptions in IoT through app-based fuzzing. In: NDSS, San Diego, CA, USA. The Internet Society (2018)
9. Croft, J., Mahajan, R., Caesar, M., Musuvathi, M.: Systematically exploring the behavior of control programs. In: Proceedings of the 2015 USENIX Conference, Santa Clara, CA, USA, pp. 165–176. USENIX Association (2015)
10. Ding, W., Hu, H.: On the safety of IoT device physical interaction control. In: Proceedings of the 2018 ACM SIGSAC Conference on Computer and Communications Security, New York, NY, USA, pp. 832–846. ACM (2018)
11. Feng, Q., Zhou, R., Xu, C., Cheng, Y., Testa, B., Yin, H.: Scalable graph-based bug search for firmware images. In: 2016 ACM SIGSAC Conference on Computer and Communications Security, Vienna, Austria, pp. 480–491. ACM (2016)
12. Fernandes, E., Jung, J., Prakash, A.: Security analysis of emerging smart home applications. In: 2016 IEEE symposium on security and privacy (SP), San Jose, CA, USA, pp. 636–654. IEEE (2016)
13. Hamza, A.A., Abdel-Halim, I.T., Sobh, M.A., Bahaa-Eldin, A.M.: A survey and taxonomy of program analysis for IoT platforms. Ain Shams Eng. J. **12**(4), 3725–3736 (2021)
14. Iijima, R., Takchisa, T., Mori, T.: Cyber-physical firewall: monitoring and controlling the threats caused by malicious analog signals. In: Proceedings of the 19th ACM International Conference on Computing Frontiers, pp. 296–304 (2022)
15. Kang, H.J., Sim, S.Q., Lo, D.: Iotbox: sandbox mining to prevent interaction threats in IoT systems. In: 2021 14th IEEE Conference on Software Testing, Verification and Validation (ICST), pp. 182–193. IEEE (2021)
16. Kashaf, A., Sekar, V., Agarwal, Y.: Protecting smart homes from unintended application actions. In: 2022 ACM/IEEE 13th International Conference on Cyber-Physical Systems (ICCPS), pp. 270–281. IEEE (2022)
17. Li, J., Zhang, Y., Chen, X., Xiang, Y.: Secure attribute-based data sharing for resource-limited users in cloud computing. Comput. Secur. **72**, 1–12 (2018)
18. Nguyen, D.T., Song, C., Qian, Z., Krishnamurthy, S.V., Colbert, E.J., McDaniel, P.: IotSan: fortifying the safety of IoT systems. In: Proceedings of the 14th International Conference on Emerging Networking Experiments and Technologies, Heraklion, Greece, pp. 191–203. ACM (2018)
19. Pradeep, P., Kant, K.: Conflict detection and resolution in IoT systems: a survey. IoT **3**(1), 191–218 (2022)

20. Stephens, N., et al.: Driller: augmenting fuzzing through selective symbolic execution. In: Proceedings of 23rd Annual Network and Distributed System Security Symposium, San Diego, CA, USA. The Internet Society (2016)

21. Surbatovich, M., Aljuraidan, J., Bauer, L., Das, A., Jia, L.: Some recipes can do more than spoil your appetite: analyzing the security and privacy risks of IFTTT recipes. In: Proceedings of the 26th International Conference on World Wide Web, Perth, Australia, pp. 1501–1510 (2017)

22. Wang, Q., Datta, P., Yang, W., Liu, S., Bates, A., Gunter, C.A.: Charting the attack surface of trigger-action IoT platforms. In: Proceedings of the 2019 ACM SIGSAC Conference on Computer and Communications Security, New York, NY, USA, pp. 1439–1453. ACM (2019)

23. Wang, X., Sun, Y., Nanda, S., Wang, X.: Looking from the mirror: evaluating IoT device security through mobile companion apps. In: 28th USENIX Security Symposium, Santa Clara, CA, USA, pp. 1151–1167. USENIX Association (2019)

24. Wang, Z., et al.: Automated vulnerability discovery and exploitation in the internet of things. Sensors **19**(15), 3362 (2019)

25. Wen, H., Chen, Q.A., Lin, Z.: Plug-N-Pwned: comprehensive vulnerability analysis of OBD-II dongles as a new over-the-air attack surface in automotive IoT. In: 29th USENIX Security Symposium, Boston, MA, USA. USENIX Association (2020)

26. Xiao, F., Sha, L., Yuan, Z., Wang, R.: Vulhunter: a discovery for unknown bugs based on analysis for known patches in industry internet of things. IEEE Trans. Emerg. Top. Comput. **8**(2), 267–279 (2020)

27. Zhang, Y., et al.: SRFuzzer: an automatic fuzzing framework for physical SOHO router devices to discover multi-type vulnerabilities. In: 35th Annual Computer Security Applications Conference, San Juan, PR, USA, pp. 544–556. ACM (2019)

28. Zheng, Y., Davanian, A., Yin, H., Song, C., Zhu, H., Sun, L.: FIRM-AFL: high-throughput greybox fuzzing of IoT firmware via augmented process emulation. In: USENIX, Santa Clara, CA, USA, pp. 1099–1114. USENIX Association (2019)

29. Zheng, Y., Song, Z., Sun, Y., Cheng, K., Zhu, H., Sun, L.: An efficient greybox fuzzing scheme for linux-based IoT programs through binary static analysis. In: 38th IEEE International Performance Computing and Communications Conference, London, UK, pp. 1–8. IEEE (2019)

30. Zhou, W., et al.: Discovering and understanding the security hazards in the interactions between IoT devices, mobile apps, and clouds on smart home platforms. In: 28th USENIX Security Symposium, Santa Clara, CA, pp. 1133–1150. USENIX Association (2019)

31. Zuo, C., Wen, H., Lin, Z., Zhang, Y.: Automatic fingerprinting of vulnerable BLE IoT devices with static UUIDs from mobile apps. In: Proceedings of the 2019 ACM SIGSAC Conference on Computer and Communications Security, London, UK, pp. 1469–1483. ACM (2019)

Differentiated Security Architecture for Secure and Efficient Infotainment Data Communication in IoV Networks

Jiani Fan[1]([✉]), Lwin Khin Shar[2], Jiale Guo[1], Wenzhuo Yang[1], Dusit Niyato[1], and Kwok-Yan Lam[1]

[1] Nanyang Technological University, 50 Nanyang Avenue, Singapore, Singapore
{jiani001,jiale001,wenzhuo001}@e.ntu.edu.sg,
{DNIYATO,kwokyan.lam}@ntu.edu.sg
[2] Singapore Management University, 81 Victoria Street, Singapore, Singapore
lkshar@smu.edu.sg

Abstract. This paper aims to provide differentiated security protection for infotainment data communication in Internet-of-Vehicle (IoV) networks. The IoV is a network of vehicles that uses various sensors, software, built-in hardware, and communication technologies to enable information exchange between pedestrians, cars, and urban infrastructure. Negligence on the security of infotainment data communication in IoV networks can unintentionally open an easy access point for social engineering attacks. The attacker can spread false information about traffic conditions, mislead drivers in their directions, and interfere with traffic management. Such attacks can also cause distractions to the driver, which has a potential implication for the safety of driving. The existing literature on IoV communication and network security focuses mainly on generic solutions. In a heterogeneous communication network where different types of communication coexist, we can improve the efficiency of security solutions by considering the different security and efficiency requirements of data communications. Hence, we propose a differentiated security mechanism for protecting infotainment data communication in IoV networks. In particular, we first classify data communication in the IoV network, examine the security focus of each data communication, and then develop a differentiated security architecture to provide security protection on a file-to-file basis. Our architecture leverages Named Data Networking (NDN) so that infotainment files can be efficiently circulated throughout the network where any node can own a copy of the file, thus improving the hit ratio for user file requests. In addition, we propose a time-sensitive Key-Policy Attribute-Based Encryption (KP-ABE) scheme for sharing subscription-based infotainment data. Coupled with our NDN network, any node in the network can own the file, but only those with a valid subscription can decrypt the file, thus achieving the security of infotainment data distribution while optimizing content distribution efficiency.

This work was supported by Alibaba Group through Alibaba Innovative Research (AIR) Program and Alibaba-NTU Singapore Joint Research Institute (JRI), Nanyang Technological University, Singapore.

X. Yuan et al. (Eds.): NSS 2022, LNCS 13787, pp. 283–304, 2022.
https://doi.org/10.1007/978-3-031-23020-2_16

Keywords: Internet-of-Vehicles · Key-policy attributed-based encryption · Communication security · Cryptography · Named data networking · Blockchain

1   Introduction

The Internet-of-Vehicle (IoV) is an integration of Vehicular Ad-hoc Networks (VANET), and the Internet of Things (IoT) [10]. The IoV is a network of vehicles that uses various sensors, software, built-in hardware, and communication technologies to enable information exchange between pedestrians, cars, and urban infrastructure [14]. With seamless connectivity, IoVs can perform various functionalities, such as providing real-time navigation guidance and delivering onboard infotainment services.

IoV infotainment systems use touchscreen displays, button panels, and audio/video interfaces in the vehicle to provide information and entertainment. It is connected to onboard units via Control Area Network (CAN) to integrate various functionalities and offer a unified user interface for both entertainment (such as retrieving media content from nearby transportation infrastructure and presenting it, connecting to personal devices to enable onboard voice/video projection), and driver-assistance (such as real-time monitoring of vehicle conditions via installed cameras, receiving real-time traffic status updates, etc.). It also acts as a platform for translating input from the user into messages communicated across the IoV network via built-in Bluetooth, cellular, and Wi-Fi modules. Although there is a unanimous agreement on the importance of protecting traffic communication security [7,10,21,35], infotainment systems have not received adequate attention in their communication security. Negligence on the security of infotainment data communication in IoV networks can unintentionally open an easy access point for social engineering attacks, where attackers can influence a person psychologically to act in the interest of the attacker [23]. For example, the attacker can spread false information about traffic conditions through vehicle-to-vehicle infotainment communication, mislead drivers into crowding a particular highway and interfere with traffic management by reporting false traffic information. Furthermore, there will be distractions for drivers as they attempt to find accurate information after realizing it is incorrect, which could have a potential implication for driving safety. Hence, infotainment data communication security is important to data integrity in IoV networks and road safety.

In the literature on IoV communication and network security, most security solutions aim to provide secure communication via a single mechanism, such as user authentication using strong cryptographic operations and are growingly unfit for increasingly complicated network communication. Although these operations are required to secure crucial traffic control messages on the IoV network, they often have a high computational cost and a substantial overhead for vehicular communication. However, not all messages on the IoV network require this high level of security protection. Systems can be more efficient by reducing the complexity of the security framework and ensuring that important communications are efficiently and adequately protected by tailoring security protections according to the type and nature of data exchanged. Such an adaptation can be termed Quality-of-Security-Service (QoSS).

Similar to Quality-of-Service (QoS), Quality-of-Security-Service (QoSS) is a concept that measures the level of security in a system where there is a variable level of security services and requirements against which the system is evaluated. As a result, not all the information exchanged in the IoV ecosystem will have the same level of QoSS, and not all will require stringent authentication protection. The degree of security factors considered would subsequently be referred to as the system's level of security. By matching security requirements with security mechanisms that offer such capabilities, QoSS can enhance system performance and achieve higher user satisfaction by providing users or network tasks with a range of appropriate security choices [9].

In the case of the IoV network, due to the wide range of messages transmitted in IoV communications, different types of data can have different security and efficiency requirements, i.e. different QoSS. Depending on the nature of the infotainment content, i.e., whether the media is private or publicly available, there will be a different set of security and efficiency expectations. Public infotainment data does not require confidentiality protection, while subscription-based infotainment data needs access control based on the user's subscription status. For example, Tesla has preinstalled in-car entertainment applications, such as Netflix and Youtube, in their digital system, and users have to pay a premium subscription fee to access these entertainment applications. For infotainment services on the go, they install WiFi and cellular modems in each Tesla, and users can connect to the car, nearby WiFi networks, or personal/public hotspots, or they can pay a subscription fee and get an LTE connection with the preinstalled SIM card to enjoy infotainment services. Naturally, there will be different security expectations for such subscription services than for unpaid public services. At the same time, the same protocols that safeguard private data exchanges are not suitable for public data because public data are supposed to be accessible by all and have lower criticality for instant and long-term availability. Similarly, the communication protocol for traffic control messages has a different QoSS from public data, with top priority on maintaining the integrity and availability of the information while achieving low latency. Hence, the security design of the IoV communication network can be more effective and efficient if we consider the different QoSS of the communication to the different security mechanisms that we have in place.

This paper aims to provide differentiated security protection for infotainment data communication in IoV networks. The security mechanisms utilised to protect each communication are determined by the type of data exchanged and the security focus of such communication, i.e., the QoSS of each communication. The main contributions of this paper are summarised as follows:

- We classify data communication in the IoV network into six categories and examine its security focus. By doing so, we analyse the different QoSS of each type of data communication in terms of confidentiality, integrity, short-term availability, and long-term availability.

- We apply caching with Named Data Networking (NDN) towards infotainment data communications to improve resource distribution efficiency. Since infotainment resources such as music and films are often substantial in size, satisfying every user request by retrieving these files from the server would impose a significant communication overhead. As a result, the combination of caching and NDN network can provide an effective distribution mechanism to circulate these files throughout the network to fulfil every user request at the shortest possible hop distance.
- We develop a differentiated security architecture for securing infotainment data communication in IoV networks, leveraging the NDN technique and designing security protection on a file-to-file basis, ensuring that various types of data receive appropriate protection and eliminating the wastage of resources as in generic security solutions. By decoupling the resource's identity from the provider's identity, e.g., IP address, the data packets are self-contained and independent of where they can be retrieved and transferred. This design allows infotainment files to be easily circulated throughout the network, where any node can keep a copy of the file, thus improving the hit ratio when file requests are made.
- We propose a time-sensitive Key-Policy Attribute-Based Encryption (KP-ABE) scheme for sharing subscription-based infotainment data communication where the user can only decrypt files whose validity time falls within their subscription time. When the validity of a user's access policy expires, the user loses the ability to decrypt the files until they resubscribe from the service provider. Coupled with our NDN architecture, any node in the network can own the file, but only those with a valid subscription can decrypt the file.
- We integrate blockchain technology to manage access to subscription-based infotainment data and avoid revoked users from decrypting subscription infotainment data.

The structure of this paper is in accordance with the following: In Sect. 2, we present the related work to introduce the context of the paper. In Sect. 3, we provide an overview of the differentiated security architecture for securing infotainment data communication in the IoV network and explain our rationale and methodology. In Sect. 4, we propose a time-sensitive KP-ABE scheme for the sharing of subscription-based infotainment data communication and provide our evaluation of this scheme. In Sect. 5, we conclude our work in this paper.

2   Related Work

2.1   Internet-of-Vehicles

Given recent advancements in telecommunication technologies and more powerful computation engines, we expect our vehicles to be more intelligent and capable. IoV has come to light as a promising direction for solving the growing demand for a safer, faster, and more comfortable transportation network in cities. The IoV is a combination of Vehicular Ad-hoc Networks (VANET) and the Internet of Things (IoT). VANET is a network made up of a group of vehicles and roadside units connected by a wireless network. IoV can be seen as a superset of VANET, which has a considerable improvement over VANET. An overview of the difference between VANET and IoV can be found in [10, 24], where the authors conclude that the impediment to the commercialization of VANET is its unreliability and limited scalability to provide seamless connectivity.

The communication types in IoV include vehicle-to-vehicle (V2V) and vehicle-to-infrastructure (V2I) [1], while Vehicle-to-everything (V2X) is a combination that maximizes the advantages of both V2V and V2I [3]. To better understand the transformation of vehicle-to-everything (V2X) technology towards IoV, a survey on the challenges and opportunities arising from the evolution of V2X technology to IoV is presented in [35], where the authors also proposed an improved cloud-IoV architecture enhanced with Mobile Edge Computing (MEC) as a vision of future IoV technologies. The study of IoV covers a wide range of topics, from resource optimization for communication [16] to efficient charging systems utilizing the smart grid to optimize autonomous driving routes. Besides these topics, security and privacy challenges in IoV have attracted a lot of attention from the community because the normal operation of the IoV system is inseparable from secure, reliable, and efficient network communication and data exchange. Attackers may manipulate the real-time traffic control messages or public vehicular traffic data streams, eavesdrop on V2X private information, or intercept subscription-based infotainment data to unauthorized users, which may cause huge economic and social security damages. Therefore, it is critical to design a secure and efficient data exchange scheme using identity authentication and privacy-preserving techniques in IoV.

2.2   Caching with Named Data Networking

The efficiency of infotainment data communication in mobile networks heavily relies on data caching approaches due to the significant size of media content. Traditional communication techniques based on TCP/IP and IP will be less effective in meeting such efficiency criteria in highly dynamic mobile environments such as the IoV systems, especially as the number of devices in the network grows [4]. The IoV system often demands a higher transmission rate and more flexibility in data distribution protocols due to the continuous pursuit of better audio and video quality and the limited network bandwidth.

Named Data Networking (NDN) emerges as one of the suitable candidates for resource optimization in such networks, providing both compatibility with existing routing protocols and optimization of communication resource utilization [33]. It performs information-centric networking and can be directly applied to major IP services like Domain Name Service (DNS) and inter-domain routing policies. IP routing protocols like BGP and OSPF can be adapted to NDN with little modifications. Instead of source and destination addresses, NDN nodes send data packets by their content names. Unlike IP routers, the use of unique content identifiers for communication allows routers to keep track of packet states, allow-ing them to perform a variety of activities. The data packets are self-contained and independent of where they can be retrieved and transferred. These char-acteristics enable in-network caching of content for future requests, enhancing content mobility while eliminating the requirement for application-specific mid-dleware. Furthermore, NDN routers allow multi-path forwarding, which means they can route a user request to numerous interfaces simultaneously.

The authors in [30] first proposed to leverage NDN in the vehicular informa-tion network environment to provide efficient communication and scalable infor-mation retrieval services. Later, many works investigated NDN-based research topics in Vehicular Ad-hoc Networks (VANET) domain. In [13], the authors provided a comprehensive review of the state-of-the-art works and challenges on NDN-based VANET. The system architecture and packet forwarding phase of NDN were explained in their work. The naming schemes, routing and forwarding mechanisms, data transmission, in-network caching, mobility support solutions, security and privacy, and simulation techniques of NDN in VANET have also been surveyed in detail. After all, NDN has shown its ability to provide a safe, efficient, and infotainment-rich driving service for users. Hence, we also lever-aged NDN for data dissemination and secure and efficient subscription-based infotainment data communication in IoV.

2.3   Attribute-Based Encryption

The ability to provide infotainment services in IoV is a major commercializa-tion contributor to the continuous development of IoVs. Besides public infotain-ment services like radio channels or free media content, a significant portion of infotainment data, such as video and music files, is supported by third-party service providers and is often subscription-based. Attribute-based Encryption (ABE) [29] is a common strategy for providing access restrictions to support subscriber-only access. In IoV systems, some research works leveraged the ABE techniques for protecting data security and privacy during the data transmission and caching processes. The authors in [32] used CP-ABE to guarantee IoV data security when outsourcing and sharing IoV data in the cloud and fog. CP-ABE is also applied in [6,27,34] for secure data sharing in VANET. In addition to data confidentiality, the short-term availability of infotainment resources should also be considered to ensure secure and efficient access control of subscription-based infotainment services in IoVs. The work in [18,20] has proposed a time-based Ciphertext-Policy Attribute-Based Encryption (CP-ABE) scheme by utilizing direct revocation and maintaining a short revocation list by a secret key time validation method. The secret key time validation method can deny access to users whose access has exceeded their subscription time. They have managed to keep their revocation list short, as keys of expired users will be removed from the revocation list.

While CP-ABE encrypts messages with access policies and distributes user keys to the policies according to user attributes, KP-ABE is the exact oppo-site. In our work, we proposed a time-sensitive KP-ABE where the AES keys to decrypt files are encrypted with attributes that only privileged users' access policies can match. In this way, a user can have a broad policy tree where different combinations of keys can be used to satisfy and decrypt, allowing greater flexibility in access management. A "platinum user", for example, should be able to decrypt any content that a "gold user" can decrypt, assuming "platinum" is a higher tier subscription class than "gold". An important advantage of doing so is the relatively small amount of overhead for data protection that is being circulated in the NDN network. Unlike in CP-ABE where a large-sized access policy will be encrypted with the files to cater to potential users of varying status and characteristics, KP-ABE encrypts the files with the few attributes that a privileged user should have.

2.4   Blockchain

Blockchain has been widely used in IoV for decentralized, secure, transparent, immutable, or automatic data access control, identity management, and other applications [21]. Network nodes can audit the data access control and identity verification to avoid unauthorized access and malicious tampering [8]. Blockchain is utilized for secure and trustworthy data sharing in [11,12,22], and leveraged for identity management in [17,26,28,31] for IoV. In addition, the authors in [25] applied blockchain to protect multimedia data sharing from being tampered with or forged in IoV. A blockchain-based certificate revocation approach is proposed in [15] for reducing the communication overhead and shortening the user revocation processing time in the intelligent transportation system. To properly manage access to subscription-based infotainment data of vehicles, we also leverage blockchain in our work to verify the user's pseudo-identity, expected expiration, and transaction timestamps to avoid revoked users from decrypting subscription infotainment data.

3   Overview of System Architecture

The ability to provide infotainment services on the go is vital to the adoption of IoV systems. At the same time, the demand for a safer road environment and transportation infrastructure continues to be the main motivation for smart transportation. Furthermore, secure communication with effective and efficient privacy protection and user anonymity becomes a critical requirement due to the dynamic and open environment in which these applications operate.

Motivated by the above findings, we propose a differentiated security architecture for sharing infotainment data in IoV networks. The goal of this architecture is to provide a means for safe and efficient data exchange for public and subscription-based infotainment data, while private infotainment data should be protected using conventional authentication methods.

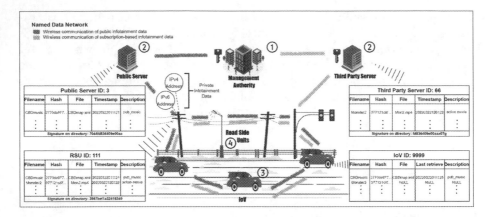

Fig. 1. Illustration of the proposed NDN-based communication security architecture.

With reference to Fig. 1, a general IoV transport system consists of four main components: (1) management authority, (2) storage servers, (3) IoVs, and (4) road-side units. The management authority (1) is the central agency that monitors the traffic status in real-time and performs traffic control operations to ease road conditions. It is also responsible for disseminating important traffic information to its subsidiary networks, such as wide-area networks consisting of roadside and traffic signalling infrastructure. Data generated here is commonly stored on central or remote cloud servers (2). Due to the high mobility of IoVs, roadside units (4) and neighbouring vehicles (3) frequently serve as data relays to support efficient traffic information communication and to provide a seamless connection to IoVs.

For the remainder of this section, we first present a classification of common data exchange in an IoV network and demonstrate the diverse security and efficiency requirements of each data type, which leads to major design considerations for security schemes in infotainment data sharing in such IoV networks that have yet to be fulfilled in many generic security schemes. Then, we introduce our model and explain how it can satisfy these requirements.

3.1   Data Classification

First of all, we classify data exchange in IoV communication and explain the security focus of data communication in each category to better illustrate the need for differentiated security schemes in such IoV networks.

1. **Vehicle-to-everything (V2X) private information exchange:** This includes any private or sensitive information about the vehicle or the user which is not meant to be shared with the public, such as electric billing messages, personalized route planning, or messages that can reveal the user's identity. Since these messages can disclose the user's private information, it is important to protect the confidentiality and integrity of these messages.

Furthermore, a heterogeneous pool of devices is integrated for communication with the vehicle, ensuring the availability of services is also vital to the IoV. environment.

2. **Traffic control messages:** These are real-time traffic control messages issued, such as traffic light messages and emergency messages (e.g. ambulance warnings and accident warnings). These messages are time-sensitive and have high requirements for message integrity and availability. Any malicious attempt that disrupts these messages can cause life-threatening consequences. Thus, communication protocols that exchange traffic control messages should implement strong security protocols against attacks on the integrity and availability of these messages.

3. **Public traffic data:** This includes publicly available information on traffic congestion status, geographic maps, infrastructure maintenance warnings, and even gas stations, fire stations, and car repair service stations. Because such information is intended for all road users, there is no requirement for confidentiality protection. On the other hand, the integrity and availability of this information are critical for road users to make informed decisions.

4. **Publicly accessible infotainment data:** This covers any publicly accessible infotainment data with no access restrictions. This category includes online websites, social media platforms, and content sharing by service providers that are publicly available for everyone to view.

5. **Subscription-based infotainment data:** This includes infotainment data provided by third-party content providers based on users' subscriptions. For such services, there is a need for authentication of the user's subscription status. Furthermore, quality of service is crucial, where availability and low latency are the top priorities, necessitating the deployment of effective caching methods.

6. **Private infotainment data:** This contains infotainment data that is restricted and not intended for the general public to view freely. For example, personal social media account content will require user identification before being accessed since such entertainment data can be private and sensitive. As a result, this type of data will need stringent security measures to ensure its confidentiality and integrity. While the availability of these data services is vital for improving customer experiences, it is less important than ensuring the availability of traffic-related information.

In Table 1, we analyze the different QoSS of each type of data communication in terms of confidentiality, integrity, long-term availability, and short-term availability for different data categories in IoV. With the finite computational resources in IoV systems, we can prioritize the security needs according to the type of data communicated and draft different security protocols to meet individual QoSS.

Table 1. Comparison among different security focuses for data categories in IoV.

Categories	Confidentiality	Integrity	Long-term Availability	Short-term Availability
V2X private information exchange	Highly critical	Highly critical	Critical	Critical
Traffic control messages	Moderate	Highly critical	Highly critical	Highly critical
Public traffic data	Not applicable	Highly critical	Critical	Moderate
Publicly accessible infotainment data	Not applicable	Highly Critical	Important for user experience	Important for user experience
Subscription-based infotainment data	Confidential against non-subscriber	Highly Critical	Important for user experience	Important for user experience
Private infotainment data	Highly Critical	Highly Critical	Important for user experience	Important for user experience

Note: We divide the availability into two categories: short-term availability (the availability of the resource when it was first requested and delivered to the intended user) and long-term availability (the availability of the resource after a significant period of time).

Private data, such as "V2X private information exchange" and "private info-tainment data," for example, should be protected by stringent authentication mechanisms to preserve its confidentiality and integrity. On the other hand, the communication protocol for "traffic control messages" has a top priority in maintaining the integrity and availability of the information while achieving low latency. The same protocols that safeguard the aforementioned data types are not suitable for public data, such as public traffic data and public infotainment data, because these public data are supposed to be accessible by all and have lower criticality for instant and long-term availability. Edge nodes in IoV networks are often desired to store this information for easy distribution. At the same time, peer-to-peer sharing will also help speed up the circulation of public information, but the integrity of the information exchanged is a concern. Similar to public information, subscription-based infotainment data provided by third-party service providers are often cached in edge nodes for fast transmission, requiring additional access restriction by subscription status.

Thus, we can observe different security and efficiency focuses among data exchanges in IoV networks. IoV network communication can be made more efficient if we provide a differentiated security implementation based on the requirements of different data categories.

3.2   Design Considerations

There are several considerations that we made in our design of the security architecture for infotainment data sharing:

Differentiated Security. Although critical information, such as traffic control messages and peer-to-peer sharing of road conditions, necessitates strict cryptographic safeguards, less sensitive public information, such as public infotainment data, has a comparatively lower demand for QoSS. Hence, we designed a differentiated security architecture where private infotainment communications are still protected using conventional authentication mechanisms. Also, files containing public infotainment data are hashed, and the directory that contains their file-names and hash values is signed using the authority's public key certificate to protect their integrity. At the same time, we proposed a time-sensitive KP-ABE scheme to facilitate the secure distribution of subscription-based infotainment data.

Minimizing IoV Network Latency. Since traffic data needs to be communicated in real-time, the IoV network can only tolerate a small level (e.g. 30–40 ms) of network latency for all network communications. However, infotainment data, like video and music files, might be several gigabytes in size. With the high mobility of IoVs, there is a need for strategic information dissemination mechanisms to enable smooth communication in such networks. Thus, we adopt NDN and cache public and subscription-based information at the RSUs to reduce the hop distance between users and data.

Re-usability of Encrypted Files. Since infotainment data files are huge, it is preferable to retrieve them from nearby devices to reduce hop distance, network overhead, and network delay. While all road users have access to public information, all encrypted subscription content in the network should be decryptable by all users whose policies meet the decryption conditions. Hence, subscription contents should not be encrypted using user-specific information but rather conform to the general conditions that privileged users have. Thus, we proposed a time-sensitive KP-ABE scheme that allows all users who have matched subscription attributes and whose subscription validity time completely covers the required time validity on files to decrypt the files. This way, the exact copy can circulate throughout the network and be decrypted by any privileged user who requests it, increasing the hit ratio.

3.3   Proposed Approach for Infotainment Data Exchange

This approach focuses on the secure and efficient transmission of infotainment data. Private data communication and traffic control messages will be protected by traditional authentication procedures [2,19], while public traffic data can be stored in files and protected in the same manner as public information files are, up to the discretion of system designers.

In our proposed architecture, illustrated in Fig. 1, **IoV users** are allowed to request files from neighbouring IoV users or any RSU that has the files, whichever is nearest to the user. If a neighbouring IoV user or RSU does not have the required file, the request is forwarded to the server, which is in charge of distributing the requested file. Aside from public information, IoV users can request any file, such as traffic-related information from the traffic authority, onboard infotainment resources from RSUs, Internet content via URLs, or user data from cloud servers. The response is parsed into NDN format and transmitted back to the IoV user by the nearest RSU that receives the request.

RSU stores a directory of resource names and file hashes. This directory is digitally signed by RSU to ensure its integrity. IoV users can obtain an update of the public directory from the RSUs and verify the digital signature of the RSU against the pre-loaded public key certificates of public infrastructures. In addition, RSUs can cache public traffic data, such as road maps and popular public infotainment data, such as public media channels, which are denoted by their resource names. Furthermore, RSU may conduct IPv4/6 operations, such as retrieving content from URLs, caching it, translating it into Named Data Network format and distributing it to requesters.

To improve the user experience, **third-party infotainment service providers** can choose to cache popular subscription content at RSUs. These files are encrypted using our time-sensitive KP-ABE on third-party servers with desirable user attributes that the service provider has distributed to its subscribed users. More details on the KP-ABE scheme can be found in the next section. The providers can choose to periodically update the stored directories in RSUs via authenticated communication between providers and RSUs. Since both the filename and the hash value of the encrypted file have been communicated to the RSUs, the encrypted file can be transmitted via untrusted channels, and its integrity can still be checked for. For the rest of this subsection, we explain our proposed interactions for the exchange of public traffic data, public infotainment data, and subscription-based data.

Exchange of Public Infotainment Data. Popular public infotainment data is cached in RSUs, and RSUs have a directory of infotainment data resource files, their hash value, last-update-timestamp and content descriptions, along with the digital certificate issued from RSU. This directory is updated with new incoming files from authorized data providers. In this directory, there are two types of files: default public infotainment files and additional public infotainment files. Once the IoV receives the directory, it verifies the digital certificate against the pre-loaded trusted certificates of public infrastructures and starts retrieving the content.

All default public infotainment information files, except those already existing in the system and have not been modified since the last retrieval, will be downloaded automatically to the IoV. In comparison, additional public infotainment files are only distributed when IoV users request them. An IoV in transit can request a new copy of the directory from the RSU or from nearby vehicles, whichever is in close proximity. Users can modify their system settings to always download the desirable media content (the next part of the movie the user is watching) when it is available. Large media files are broken down into smaller files so that the expected transmission time per file is low. Given the short amount of interaction time between fast-moving IoV and nearby RSU or neighbouring IoVs, this will lower the number of incomplete transmissions. These download requests are fulfilled by either the RSU or peers. Once the download for the entire file is complete, the IoV verifies the hash value of the file against the directory entry to check for integrity.

IoV could verify the hash value of the portion they received completely and request other portions from neighbours in proximity.

Exchange of Subscription-Based Data. Third-party content providers can cache their content in the RSU to improve the user experience or retrieve the content from their server when RSU receives the request. They encrypted the content with the user attributes such as membership status, account validity, and decryptable time period (the time period that the file can be decrypted) using the time-sensitive KP-ABE scheme. The subscription infotainment application (a user copy of the entertainment software installed) on board will have a default content directory that stores the popular content on the platform. For example, "Monster 2" is popular content among IoV users, and the service provider has included the file name of this movie and the hash value of the encrypted file in the default resource directory, which is pre-installed in the infotainment application and updated on a regular basis.

When IoV user request a particular resource, e.g. "Badguy", the IoV infotainment application can first search for the corresponding file name and hash value, i.e. "badguy.mp4" and the hash value of encrypted "badguy.mp4". If it is not present in the default list, it can request the file name and hash value of the file from the RSU. Once the IoV has the file name and hash value, it can request the file from RSU or neighbouring IoVs, and verify the hash value. Once verified, the IoV infotainment application will decrypt the file using its access policies.

The workflow of the proposed time-sensitive KP-ABE scheme for subscription-based infotainment data communication is presented in Fig. 2. The secure channel here is established using user authentication so that users can verify their accounts and make purchases for their subscriptions. Every time a user makes a new subscription, a new pseudo ID is generated based on the user's ID and the current subscription time.

Exchange of Private Infotainment Data. Private infotainment data can contain sensitive personal information. Hence it should be protected using authentication mechanisms to prevent unauthorized access to such data.

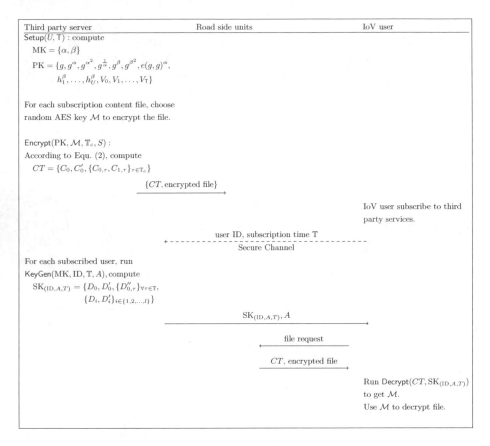

Fig. 2. Workflow of the proposed time-sensitive KP-ABE scheme for subscription-based infotainment data communication.

3.4 Subscribed User Revocation

A different pseudo-identity is generated by the service provider based on the user's identity every time they purchase their subscription. If a subscribed user decides to cancel their membership before the expiry date, the service provider can cancel the subscription and place the user's current pseudo-identity, expected expiry and transaction timestamp on the permissioned blockchain maintained by the service provider. On a daily basis, the infotainment service agent installed on IoV will query the user's current pseudo-identity to check for revocation details. If it is found, the agent will mark the user as a revoked user and stop serving the user until a new pseudo-identity is issued to the user, which also means the start of a new subscription.

When the expected expiry of the transactions stored on a permissioned blockchain is reached, those transaction records are removed from the blockchain since these pseudo-identities can no longer be used to decrypt any files from this date onwards.

4   Time-Sensitive KP-ABE Scheme

In this section, we introduce our Key-Policy Attribute-Based Encryption (KP-ABE) scheme for the secure distribution of subscription-based infotainment data in IoV networks.

Inspired by the work [18,20], we use a Hierarchical Identity-based Encryption (HIBE) based approach to control the time validity of the infotainment files. In general, the time periods are represented by a hierarchical tree which has one topmost root node and, at most three-level non-root nodes. Each node in the first level of the tree represents a year, and its child in the second level represents a month in this year. The third level nodes represent the days. Note that we also adopt the set-cover approach to select the minimum number of nodes to represent all the valid time periods. The use of HIBE in conjunction with the set cover approach can effectively reduce the number of key generations required to represent each time period. For example, if a user purchases a subscription service from 2022-JUL-01 to 2022-SEP-02, the tree of his valid time periods should contain four nodes, including 2022-JUL, 2022-AUG, 2022-SEP-01, 2022-SEP-02. Therefore, this user should obtain the corresponding attribute in their access policies for those four nodes by using HIBE in order to decrypt the ciphertext within the valid time periods. For example, the user can only decrypt files whose validity time period falls within his/her subscription time period, meaning files that have a validity time period that is equal to or is a subset of 2022-JUL-01 to 2022-SEP-02. When the validity of a user's access policy expires (after 2022-SEP-02), the user loses the ability to decrypt until they resubscribe from the service provider.

Our scheme consists of a 4-tuple of algorithms, denoted as (Setup, KeyGen, Encrypt, Decrypt), of which the construction details are shown below:

- Setup(U, T): it is a setup algorithm that takes the number of attributes U and the depth of the time tree T as input, outputs the public parameters PK and a master key MK. In specific, given the depth T, each time period is represented as a z-ary string $\{1, z\}^{\mathsf{T}-1}$, i.e., $\{2022, 09, 22\}$. The algorithm chooses a bilinear group $\mathbb{G}_1$ of prime order p with a random generator g, and randomly selects U elements from the group, i.e. $h_1, h_2, \ldots, h_U \in \mathbb{G}_1$. Besides, it also randomly chooses $\alpha, \beta \in \mathbb{Z}_p$ and $V_0, V_1, \ldots, V_{\mathsf{T}} \in \mathbb{G}_1$. Then, it outputs

$$\mathrm{MK} = \{\alpha, \beta\},$$
$$\mathrm{PK} = \{g, g^\alpha, g^{\alpha^2}, g^{\frac{1}{\alpha}}, g^\beta, g^{\beta^2}, e(g,g)^\alpha, h_1^\beta, \ldots, h_U^\beta, V_0,$$
$$V_1, \ldots, V_{\mathsf{T}}\}.$$

- KeyGen(MK, ID, $\mathbb{T}$, A): for a specific user with a pseudo-identity ID (A different pseudo-identity is generated by the service provider based on the user's identity every time that he/she purchases his/her subscription) and a set-cover of decryptable time periods, denoted as $\mathbb{T}$ that each of the elements in $\mathbb{T}$ can be represented as a z-ary representation $\tau = \{\tau_1, \tau_2, \ldots, \tau_k\} \in \{1, z\}^k$

where $k < \mathsf{T}$, give the master key MK $= \{\alpha, \beta\}$ and the LSSS access structure $A = \{M, \rho\}$, where M is an $l \times n$ matrix and ρ is a mapping function that maps each row of M into an attribute. This algorithm outputs a private key SK$_{(ID, A, T)}$ for this user according to the following operations. At first, it chooses a random masking vector $v = \{w, y_2, \ldots, y_n\} \in \mathbb{Z}_p^n$ to share the encryption exponent w. Besides, it computes $\lambda_i = v \cdot M_i$ for $\forall i \in \{1, 2, \ldots, l\}$, i.e. M_i is the i-th row vector of M. Here $\{\lambda_i\}$ are the shares of the secret w according to M. Then this algorithm can calculate

$$D_0 = e(g, g)^{\alpha w}, \ D_0' = g^{\frac{w}{\alpha}},$$

$$\left\{ D_{0,\tau}'' = \left(V_0 \prod_{j=1}^{k} V_j^{\tau_j} \right)^w \right\}_{\forall \tau \in \mathbb{T}} , \tag{1}$$

$$D_i = g^{\beta \lambda_i}, \ D_i' = \left(g h_{\rho(i)}^{\beta} \right)^{\lambda_1 ID}$$

and get the private key

$$SK_{(ID, A, T)} = \{D_0, D_0', \{D_{0,\tau}''\}_{\forall \tau \in \mathbb{T}}, \{D_i, D_i'\}_{i \in \{1, 2, \ldots, l\}}\}$$

– Encrypt(PK, $\mathcal{M}$, $\mathbb{T}_c$, S): this is the algorithm that uses the public key PK generated by the Setup algorithm to encrypt a plaintext message $\mathcal{M}$[1] associated with a set of attributes S and a set of decryptable time periods $\mathbb{T}_c$. The set S consists of attributes such as film rating and subscription tier (e.g., platinum, gold, and silver). The set $\mathbb{T}_c$ consists of some time elements $\tau = \{\tau_1', \tau_2', \ldots, \tau_{k_\tau}'\} \in \{1, z\}^{k_\tau}$ where $k_\tau < \mathsf{T}$. The set $\mathbb{T}_c$ is determined by the content provider. For example, if the provider decides that the content is valid for a particular period, $\mathbb{T}_c$ will cover that period so that only users who subscribed for this period will be able to decrypt.

The algorithm chooses a random $x \in \mathbb{Z}_p$ and for $\forall \tau \in \mathbb{T}_c$, it chooses a random $v_\tau \in \mathbb{Z}_p$. It then computes

$$C_0 = \mathcal{M} \cdot e(g, g)^{\alpha x}, \ C_0' = g^{\alpha^2 x}, \ C_{0,\tau} = g^{v_\tau},$$

$$C_{1,\tau} = g^{\alpha x} g^{\beta^2} \left(V_0 \prod_{j=1}^{k_y} V_j^{\tau_j'} \right)^{v_\tau} \tag{2}$$

where $k_y = (g^\beta h_y^\beta)^{-1}$ for $y \in S$. Finally, it outputs the ciphertext $CT = \{C_0, C_0', \{C_{0,\tau}, C_{1,\tau}\}_{\tau \in \mathbb{T}_c}\}$ along with the time periods $\mathbb{T}_c$.

– Decrypt(CT, SK$_{(ID, A, T)}$): this algorithm takes as input the ciphertext CT and a user's private key SK$_{(ID, A, T)}$, and outputs $\perp$ if any one of the following situations occurs:

1. S does not satisfy the access structure $A = \{M.\rho\}$.

---

[1] $\mathcal{M}$ is generally the 256 bits AES key used to encrypt the actual content because the size of the actual content is generally larger than the maximum size of the message that can be encrypted by ABE schemes.

2. T is not completely covered in $\mathbb{T}_c$, i.e. τ_T and all its prefixes are not in $\mathbb{T}_c$.

Otherwise, let $I = \{i : \rho(i) \in S\} \subset \{1, 2, \ldots, l\}$, there exists a set of constants $\{\omega_i \in \mathbb{Z}_p\}_{i \in I}$ satisfying that $\sum_{i \in I} \omega_i \lambda_i = w$, where λ_i are valid shares of a secret w according to M. Finally, this algorithm can decrypt CT as

$$\frac{C_0 \cdot e(D_0'', C_{0,\tau} \cdot e(C_0', D_0'))}{e(C_0', g^{1/\alpha}) \cdot \prod_{i \in I} \left(e\left(C_{1,\tau}, (D_i')^{\frac{\omega_i}{ID}} \right) \cdot e(D_i, k_{\rho(i)})^{\omega_i} \right)}.$$

The user with the appropriate access policy whose valid time period completely covers the decryption time period of the file can achieve the message decryption by solving this equation above.

The correctness of the scheme is shown below.

$$\frac{C_0 \cdot e(D_0'', C_{0,\tau} \cdot e(C_0', D_0'))}{e(C_0', g^{1/\alpha}) \cdot \prod_{i \in I} \left(e\left(C_{1,\tau}, (D_i')^{\frac{\omega_i}{ID}} \right) \cdot e(D_i, k_{\rho(i)})^{\omega_i} \right)}$$

$$= \frac{\mathcal{M} \cdot e(g,g)^{\alpha x} \cdot e\left((V_0 \prod_{j=1}^{k} V_j^{\tau j})^w, g^{v\tau} \right) \cdot e(g^{\alpha^2 x}, g^{\frac{w}{\alpha}})}{e(g^{\alpha^2 x}, g^{\frac{1}{\alpha}}) \cdot \prod_{i \in I} \left(e\left(g^{\alpha x} g^{\beta 2} \left(V_0 \prod_{j=1}^{k_y} V_j^{\tau j} \right)^{v\tau}, \left(gh_{\rho(i)}^{\beta} \right)^{\lambda_1 ID \frac{\omega_i}{ID}} \right) \cdot e\left(g^{\beta \lambda_i}, (g^{\beta} h_{h(i)}^{\beta})^{-\omega_i} \right) \right)}$$

$$= \frac{\mathcal{M} \cdot e(g,g)^{\alpha x} \cdot e\left((V_0 \prod_{j=1}^{k} V_j^{\tau j})^w, g^{v\tau} \right) \cdot e(g^{\alpha^2 x}, g^{\frac{w}{\alpha}})}{e(g^{\alpha^2 x}, g^{\frac{1}{\alpha}}) \cdot e\left(g^{\alpha x} g^{\beta 2} \left(V_0 \prod_{j=1}^{k_y} V_j^{\tau j} \right)^{v\tau}, g^w \right) \cdot e(g^{\beta w}, g^{-\beta})}$$

$$= \frac{\mathcal{M} \cdot e(g,g)^{\alpha x} \cdot e\left((V_0 \prod_{j=1}^{k} V_j^{\tau j})^w, g^{v\tau} \right) \cdot e(g^{\alpha^2 x}, g^{\frac{w}{\alpha}}) \cdot e(g,g)^{\beta^2 w}}{e(g^{\alpha^2 x}, g^{\frac{1}{\alpha}}) \cdot e\left(g^{\alpha x} g^{\beta 2} \left(V_0 \prod_{j=1}^{k_y} V_j^{\tau j} \right)^{v\tau}, g^w \right)}$$

$$= \frac{\mathcal{M} \cdot e(g,g)^{\alpha x} \cdot e(g^{\alpha^2 x}, g^{\frac{w}{\alpha}})}{e(g^{\alpha x}, g^w) \cdot e(g^{\alpha^2 x}, g^{\frac{1}{\alpha}})}$$

$$= \mathcal{M}$$

4.1   Model Evaluation

Similar to the work [18, 20] that we built upon, the security of our time-sensitive KP-ABE scheme is based on the modified decisional q-parallel-BDHE assumption. That is, as long as this assumption holds, no adversary can selectively break our time-sensitive KP-ABE scheme.

Consider a modified decisional q-parallel-BDHE game between a challenger C and the adversary H. In this game, the adversary aims to decrypt a challenge ciphertext without having the right private key.

– Initialization: the challenger C accepts an attribute set $S*$ and a decryptable time period $\mathbb{T}_c*$ from adversary H
– Setup: C runs the *Setup* algorithm and generates the public parameters PK
– Phase 1. H requests for several private keys corresponding to the identity ID, access structure $A*$, and the range of validity time periods $\mathbb{T}$ such that every returned private key satisfies at least one of the following conditions:

1. $S*$ does not satisfy the access structure $A*$
2. $\mathbb{T}_c*$ is not completely covered in $\mathbb{T}$

- Challenge. H submits two equal length message m_0 and m_1. C flips a fair coin $\beta \in \{0, 1\}$ and encrypts m_β under the attribute set $S*$ and the time $\mathbb{T}_c*$. The resulting ciphertext $CT*$ is given to H.
- Phase 2. this phase is completely the same as Phase 1.
- Guess. A outputs a guess β' of β.

In this game, adversary H is said to have a negligible advantage if the likelihood of H making a correct guess, i.e. $\beta' = \beta$, is barely more than or equal to 0.5. We can argue that our time-sensitive KP-ABE scheme is secure if all polynomial-time adversaries[2] have at most a negligible advantage in the above game. The proof of the adversary having at most a negligible advantage in such a modified decisional q-parallel-BDHE game would be very similar to the ones given in both [18,20]. This is because our construction is the same as theirs, except that in [18,20], attribute set is used in *KeyGen* algorithm and access structure is used in *Encrypt* algorithm whereas this is reversed in our scheme. However, this does not impact the security model.

We also compare the efficiency of our scheme with other revocable ABE schemes. Table 2 shows the comparison. The first row presents a revocable KPABE scheme, the second and third rows present revocable CPABE schemes, and the last row presents our scheme. We can observe that in terms of the size of the master public key (PK), ours is comparable to [18,20]. In our scheme, the size of the private key (SK) is linearly dependent on the size of the set of decryptable time periods determined by the content provider and hence our scheme may be inferior to other schemes if the content provider determines that content is to be circulated for a very long period. However, due to the volatile nature of media content, the content providers may not set the period for too long in practice. For example, if the content provider determines that a content is to be circulated for a very long period like 10 years, the maximum size would be 60 (days) +22 (months) +10($years$) − 1. In our context, the size of Ciphertext is important so that RSUs and IoVs can store and distribute them efficiently. In our scheme, the Ciphertext size is linearly dependent on $\mathbb{T}_c$, which is the decryptable period for the particular subscribed user. In comparison, in other schemes [5,18], the Ciphertext size is dependent on the size of the revocation list and the number of user attributes. Hence, the schemes may be comparable in the size of Ciphertext. On the other hand, our scheme is clearly the most efficient in decryption time. Given that short-term availability requirement is critical in our context, it is of most important to us.

---

[2] They cannot break this game in polynomial time [18].

Table 2. Efficiency comparison

Scheme	PK size	SK size	Ciphertext size	Decryption time (#pairing)
[5]	$111\mathbb{G}_1 + \mathbb{G}_2$	$(5 + 16l + 16(log^2N + logN))\mathbb{G}_1$	$(16S + 64R - 27)\mathbb{G}_1 + \mathbb{G}_2$	$16S + 37$
[18]	$(U + R + T + 3)\mathbb{G}_1 + \mathbb{G}_2$	$(S + Z + R + 1)\mathbb{G}_1$	$(l + 3)\mathbb{G}_1 + \mathbb{G}_2$	$2I + 4$
[20]	$(U + T + 3)\mathbb{G}_1 + \mathbb{G}_2$	$(S + Z + 1)\mathbb{G}_1$	$(2lR' + 1)\mathbb{G}_1 + \mathbb{G}_2$	$2IR' + 2$
Ours	$(U + T + 7)\mathbb{G}_1 + \mathbb{G}_2$	$(2l + |\mathbb{T}| + 1)\mathbb{G}_1 + \mathbb{G}_2$	$(2|\mathbb{T}_c| + 1)\mathbb{G}_1 + \mathbb{G}_2$	$2I + 3$

U: maximum number of attributes in the system, N: maximum number of users in the system, T: depth of time tree, S: number of attributes of the user, I: number of attributes used in the decryption, l: number of rows of the access structure matrix, Z: best case $Z = 2$ and worst case $Z = (T(T + 2)/2)$, R: maximum number of revoked users, R': length of the revocation list, $|\mathbb{T}|$: number of elements in the set-cover $|\mathbb{T}|$, $|\mathbb{T}_c|$: number of elements in $\mathbb{T}_c$ (best case $|\mathbb{T}|$ and $|\mathbb{T}_c| = 1$ and worst case $|\mathbb{T}|$ and $|\mathbb{T}_c| = 60$ (days) $+22$ (months) $+$(number of decryptable years-1))

5 Conclusion

In conclusion, communication security for IoV infotainment systems is essential and different types of infotainment data can have different security and efficiency requirements. Systems can be more efficient by reducing the complexity of the security framework and ensuring that important communications are adequately protected by tailoring security protections according to the type and nature of data exchanged. To achieve this, we propose a differentiated security architecture for secure and efficient infotainment data communication in IoV networks, leveraging NDN and designing security protection on a file-to-file basis, ensuring that various types of data receive appropriate protection and eliminating the wastage of resources in generic security solutions. In particular, our time-sensitive KP-ABE scheme allows content providers to set time validity on their content and protect their copyrights. In future work, we plan to investigate incentive mechanisms that encourage IoV users under our system to conduct peer-to-peer infotainment resource sharing, which is a crucial feasibility concern for improving the efficiency of resource sharing and reducing communication overheads for file retrievals.

A Summary of Math Notation and Symbols

See Table 3.

Table 3. A summary of math notation and symbols.

Symbol	Description
U	The number of attributes
T	The depth of the time tree
MK	The master key
PK	Public parameters
$\mathbb{G}_1$	A bilinear group of prime order p
g	A generator of $\mathbb{G}_1$
$h_1, h_2 \ldots h_U$	Random elements chosen from $\mathbb{G}_1$
$V_1, V_2, \ldots, V_\mathsf{T}$	Random elements chosen from $\mathbb{G}_1$
α, β	Random numbers chosen from $\mathbb{Z}_p$
ID	A user's pseudo-identity
$\mathbb{T}$	A set-cover of a user's decryptable time periods
τ	A z-ary representation of a time element
A	A LSSS access structure
M	An $l \times n$ matrix
ρ	A mapping function
$\boldsymbol{v}$	A random masking vector in $\mathcal{Z}_p^n$
ω	An encryption exponent
$\lambda_i (i = 1, 2, \ldots, l)$	The shares of ω
SK	A private key of a user
$\mathcal{M}$	A plaintext message
$\mathbb{T}_c$	A set of decryptable time periods of a message
S	A set of attributes of the message
CT	A ciphertext

References

1. Ali, I., Hassan, A., Li, F.: Authentication and privacy schemes for vehicular ad hoc networks (VANETs): a survey. Veh. Commun. **16**, 45–61 (2019)
2. Bagga, P., Das, A.K., Wazid, M., Rodrigues, J.J.P.C., Park, Y.: Authentication protocols in internet of vehicles: Taxonomy, analysis, and challenges. IEEE Access **8**, 54314–54344 (2020). https://doi.org/10.1109/ACCESS.2020.2981397
3. Barrachina, J., et al.: V2X-d: a vehicular density estimation system that combines V2V and V2I communications. In: 2013 IFIP Wireless Days (WD), pp. 1–6. IEEE (2013)
4. Chen, C., Wang, C., Qiu, T., Atiquzzaman, M., Wu, D.O.: Caching in vehicular named data networking: architecture, schemes and future directions. IEEE Commun. Surv. Tutor. **22**(4), 2378–2407 (2020)

5. Datta, P., Dutta, R., Mukhopadhyay, S.: Adaptively secure unrestricted attribute-based encryption with subset difference revocation in bilinear groups of prime order. In: Pointcheval, D., Nitaj, A., Rachidi, T. (eds.) AFRICACRYPT 2016. LNCS, vol. 9646, pp. 325–345. Springer, Cham (2016). https://doi.org/10.1007/978-3-319-31517-1_17

6. Deng, X., Gao, T., Guo, N., Xie, K.: A secure data sharing scheme based on CP-ABE in VANETs. In: Barolli, L. (ed.) Innovative Mobile and Internet Services in Ubiquitous Computing, IMIS 2022. LNNS, vol. 496, pp. 65–74. Springer, Cham (2022). https://doi.org/10.1007/978-3-031-08819-3_7

7. Fan, J., et al.: Understanding security in smart city domains from the ant-centric perspective. arXiv (2022). https://doi.org/10.48550/ARXIV.2202.05023. https://arxiv.org/abs/2202.05023

8. Guo, J., Yang, W., Lam, K.-Y., Yi, X.: Using blockchain to control access to cloud data. In: Guo, F., Huang, X., Yung, M. (eds.) Inscrypt 2018. LNCS, vol. 11449, pp. 274–288. Springer, Cham (2019). https://doi.org/10.1007/978-3-030-14234-6_15

9. Irvine, C., Levin, T.: Quality of security service. In: Proceedings of the 2000 Workshop on New Security Paradigms, February 2001. https://doi.org/10.1145/366173.366195

10. Ji, B., et al.: Survey on the internet of vehicles: network architectures and applications. IEEE Commun. Stand. Mag. **4**(1), 34–41 (2020). https://doi.org/10.1109/MCOMSTD.001.1900053

11. Kang, J., Xiong, Z., Niyato, D., Ye, D., Kim, D.I., Zhao, J.: Toward secure blockchain-enabled internet of vehicles: Optimizing consensus management using reputation and contract theory. IEEE Trans. Veh. Technol. **68**(3), 2906–2920 (2019)

12. Khelifi, H., Luo, S., Nour, B., Moungla, H., Ahmed, S.H., Guizani, M.: A blockchain-based architecture for secure vehicular named data networks. Comput. Electr. Eng. **86**, 106715 (2020)

13. Khelifi, H., et al.: Named data networking in vehicular ad hoc networks: state-of-the-art and challenges. IEEE Commun. Surv. Tutor. **22**(1), 320–351 (2019)

14. Lam, K.Y., Mitra, S., Gondesen, F., Yi, X.: Ant-centric IoT security reference architecture-security-by-design for satellite-enabled smart cities. IEEE Internet Things J. **9**(8), 5895–5908 (2022). https://doi.org/10.1109/JIOT.2021.3073734

15. Lei, A., et al.: A blockchain based certificate revocation scheme for vehicular communication systems. Futur. Gener. Comput. Syst. **110**, 892–903 (2020)

16. Li, F., Lam, K.Y., Ni, Z., Niyato, D., Liu, X., Wang, L.: Cognitive carrier resource optimization for internet-of-vehicles in 5g-enhanced smart cities. IEEE Netw., 1–7 (2021). https://doi.org/10.1109/MNET.211.2100340

17. Lin, C., He, D., Huang, X., Kumar, N., Choo, K.K.R.: BCPPA: a blockchain-based conditional privacy-preserving authentication protocol for vehicular ad hoc networks. IEEE Trans. Intell. Transp. Syst. **22**(12), 7408–7420 (2020)

18. Liu, J.K., Yuen, T.H., Zhang, P., Liang, K.: Time-based direct revocable ciphertext-policy attribute-based encryption with short revocation list. In: Preneel, B., Vercauteren, F. (eds.) ACNS 2018. LNCS, vol. 10892, pp. 516–534. Springer, Cham (2018). https://doi.org/10.1007/978-3-319-93387-0_27

19. Liu, Y., Wang, Y., Chang, G.: Efficient privacy-preserving dual authentication and key agreement scheme for secure V2V communications in an IoV paradigm. IEEE Trans. Intell. Transp. Syst. **18**(10), 2740–2749 (2017). https://doi.org/10.1109/TITS.2017.2657649

20. Liu, Z., Wang, F., Chen, K., Tang, F.: A new user revocable ciphertext-policy attribute-based encryption with ciphertext update. Secur. Commun. Netw. **2020** (2020)
21. Mollah, M.B., et al.: Blockchain for the internet of vehicles towards intelligent transportation systems: a survey. IEEE Internet Things J. **8**(6), 4157–4185 (2020)
22. Ren, Y., Zhu, F., Wang, J., Sharma, P.K., Ghosh, U.: Novel vote scheme for decision-making feedback based on blockchain in internet of vehicles. IEEE Trans. Intell. Transp. Syst. **23**(2), 1639–1648 (2021)
23. Salahdine, F., Kaabouch, N.: Social engineering attacks: a survey. Future Internet **11**(4) (2019). https://doi.org/10.3390/fi11040089. https://www.mdpi.com/1999-5903/11/4/89
24. Sharma, S., Kaushik, B.: A survey on internet of vehicles: applications, security issues & solutions. Veh. Commun. **20**, 100182 (2019). https://doi.org/10.1016/j.vehcom.2019.100182. https://www.sciencedirect.com/science/article/pii/S2214209619302293
25. Shi, K., Zhu, L., Zhang, C., Xu, L., Gao, F.: Blockchain-based multimedia sharing in vehicular social networks with privacy protection. Multimedia Tools Appl. **79**(11), 8085–8105 (2020)
26. Son, S., Lee, J., Park, Y., Park, Y., Das, A.K.: Design of blockchain-based lightweight V2I handover authentication protocol for VANET. IEEE Trans. Netw. Sci. Eng. **9**, 1346–1358 (2022)
27. Taha, M.B., Talhi, C., Ould-Slimanec, H.: A cluster of CP-ABE microservices for VANET. Procedia Comput. Sci. **155**, 441–448 (2019)
28. Tan, H., Chung, I.: Secure authentication and key management with blockchain in VANETs. IEEE Access **8**, 2482–2498 (2019)
29. Wang, X., Zhang, J., Schooler, E.M., Ion, M.: Performance evaluation of attribute-based encryption: toward data privacy in the IoT. In: 2014 IEEE International Conference on Communications (ICC), pp. 725–730 (2014). https://doi.org/10.1109/ICC.2014.6883405
30. Yan, Z., Zeadally, S., Park, Y.J.: A novel vehicular information network architecture based on named data networking (NDN). IEEE Internet Things J. **1**(6), 525–532 (2014)
31. Yang, Y., Wei, L., Wu, J., Long, C., Li, B.: A blockchain-based multidomain authentication scheme for conditional privacy preserving in vehicular ad-hoc network. IEEE Internet Things J. **9**(11), 8078–8090 (2021)
32. Zhang, J., Li, T., Obaidat, M.S., Lin, C., Ma, J.: Enabling efficient data sharing with auditable user revocation for IoV systems. IEEE Syst. J. **16**(1), 1355–1366 (2021)
33. Zhang, L., et al.: Named data networking. ACM SIGCOMM Comput. Commun. Rev. **44**(3), 66–73 (2014)
34. Zhao, Y., Zhang, X., Xie, X., Ding, Y., Kumar, S.: A verifiable hidden policy CP-ABE with decryption testing scheme and its application in VANET. Trans. Emerg. Telecommun. Technol. **33**(5), e3785 (2022)
35. Zhou, H., Xu, W., Chen, J., Wang, W.: Evolutionary V2X technologies toward the internet of vehicles: challenges and opportunities. Proc. IEEE **108**(2), 308–323 (2020). https://doi.org/10.1109/JPROC.2019.2961937

An Efficient Authenticated Group Key Agreement Protocol with Dynamic Batch Verification for Secure Distributed Networks

Tianqi Zhou[1,2,3], Wenying Zheng[3(✉)], and Haowen Tan[3]

[1] Nanjing University of Information Science and Technology, Nanjing 210044, China
[2] Kyushu University, Fukuoka 819-0395, Japan
[3] Zhejiang Sci-Tech University, Hangzhou 310018, China
zhengwy0501@126.com

Abstract. Distributed networks have attracted numerous attention since it was proposed. Most existing works mainly focus on the design and improvement of the structure of distributed networks but ignore the secure transmission of the data. In this paper, we mainly concentrate on how to securely and efficiently aggregate the data in a group manner. In particular, an authenticated group key agreement protocol is proposed for secure data transmission in distributed networks. In order to release the computational overhead of distributed nodes, a semi-trusted authority (STA) is introduced to assist the distributed nodes to do some precomputation. When introducing the STA, the collusion attack that may be derived from the STA and attackers is considered, followed by the corresponding countermeasures. Moreover, to overcome the predominantly distributed denial of service (DDoS) attack, a dynamic batch verification mechanism is devised. The presented dynamic batch verification mechanism guarantees that the proposed protocol can be run properly among legitimate nodes regardless of the existence of nodes who suffered from the DDoS attack.

Keywords: Distributed networks · Authenticated group key agreement · Secure data transmission · DDoS · Dynamic batch verification

1 Introduction

Distributed networks [12,14,18] has attracted widespread attention from industrial, academic, and governments since it was proposed. However, the existing works in distributed networks mainly focus on the design and improvement of

This work is supported by the National Natural Science Foundation of China under Grants No. 61922045, No. U21A20465, No. 62172292, No. 61877034, the China Scholarship Council under Grant No. 202109040028.

X. Yuan et al. (Eds.): NSS 2022, LNCS 13787, pp. 305–318, 2022.
https://doi.org/10.1007/978-3-031-23020-2_17

the networks structure. The security of the data transmission is usually under-estimated and ignored. To be more specific, many existing works [10] all explic-itly or implicitly assume that the raw data or local model parameters can be securely collected or assume that the transmission channel is secure without given detailed implementation. Whereas, how to guarantee the transmission security and efficiency of the raw data or local model parameters is not an easy task. That is because, the computational cost for encryption and decryp-tion can increase dramatically when the number of nodes in distributed networks becomes large. Without a well-designed and efficient encryption algorithm, the system burden can be intolerable. On the other hand, the nodes in distributed networks distribute in different geographical locations and different network envi-ronments, which are prone to suffer from the distributed denial of serves (DDoS) attack [6,8,9]. Therefore, instead of explicitly or implicitly assuming that the transmission channel is secure, it is desirable to design a secure mechanism to guarantee the transmission security in distributed networks. In this paper, we mainly concentrate on how to securely and efficiently aggregate the data in a group manner, which is a challenging issue in distributed networks.

1.1 Related Work

Distributed networks is a network structure composed of nodes distributing in different geographical locations and different network environments. In dis-tributed networks, no center nodes exists, which is a brand-new network system corresponding to the central control network system. Generally speaking, dis-tributed networks focus more on ensuring the reachability of information and less on the process of transmission. Many researches [7,11,12,14] have been pro-posed on how to architecture and management of distributed networks. How-ever, compared with the networks structure construction, methods for securing the transformation in distributed networks are relatively less.

In cryptography, the group key agreement protocol is the interactive protocol among multiple parties, by which a shared session key can only be derived among the multiple parties but no one else can learn the session key [13,19]. The group key agreement protocol is different from the two-party key agreement protocol. The latter can only support key agreement among two parties, which has been studies for a long time since it was proposed in [5]. Many mature two-party key agreement protocols have been designed and applied in various applications. In contrast, the research on group key agreement protocols is relatively few. How-ever, driven by the group-oriented applications such as video conference, online collaboration, data sharing etc., the group key agreement protocols has attracted attention in recent years. Interested readers can refer to [17] for a detailed sur-vey about well-known group key agreement protocols with constant rounds. In addition, the entity authentication technique [15] is an essential mechanism to prevent the man-in-the-middle attack in group key agreement protocols.

In this paper, in order to guarantee the transmission security in distributed networks and ensure the normal performance of the system under the DDoS attack, we present an efficient authenticated group key agreement protocol.

1.2   Main Contributions

This paper focuses on the secure data transmission and efficient data sharing in distributed networks. The main contributions of this paper are summarized as follows.

- Constructing group key agreement protocol with authentication. To support secure data transmission in distributed networks, we present a novel group key agreement protocol. The agreed session key can guarantee secure data transmission in distributed and open networks. In addition, the man-in-the-middle attack is consider which may destroy the protocol and render serious consequence. That is because the attacker who successfully performs the man-in-the-middle attack can obtain the shared session key in the name of a legal party. Then, it can learn all transmitted data between the nodes and the server without being detected. In order to resist this kind of serious attack, we introduce authentication mechanism in the group key agreement protocol, which can guarantee the security of the agreed session key and further guarantee the security of the transmitted data.
- Designing efficient batch verification mechanism. In our system model, the distributed nodes are restrained in storage and computation capability. Thus, requiring each party to perform batch verification of all group members is time-consuming which may bring latency for the system. In the real-time environment such as vehicular ad hoc networks (VANETs), the long system latency is intolerable. Thus, we design efficient batch verification mechanism for the group key agreement protocol. In particular, a semi-trusted authority (STA) is introduced to assist batch verification, who helps the resource-constrained nodes to do some precomputation. Moreover, to avoid the collusion between the STA and attackers, the concept of probabilistic random sampling is used to check the precomputation results from the STA. It is worth noting that the parameters can be selected and adjusted appropriately according to the number of group members. Consequently, the collusion attack can be checked with a desirable probability and the verification result can be convincing.
- Presenting dynamic batch verification mechanism. To overcome the predominant DDos attack in distributed networks, we present a dynamic batch verification mechanism. DDoS is easy to implement and difficult to defend, which can hinder the normal operation of the system or even paralyze the distributed system. Thus, it is desirable to consider countermeasures for DDoS when designing protocol or scheme in distributed networks. In this paper, our system model is considered under the distributed networks. Then, the authenticated group key agreement protocol is proposed to guarantee the data transmission security. In particular, members in a group agreed on a session key to encrypted the transmitted data. Without suitable countermeasures, the protocol can not be performed normally if some members undergo the DDoS attack. Therefore, we further present a dynamic batch verification mechanism to guarantee the normal performance of the protocol when facing

the DDoS attack. The main design rationales is that members who are legally and normally operating are retained, and members who do not respond or fail in verification are ignored, which is achieved through the adjustment of threshold and progressive parameters.

1.3 Organization

The reminder of this paper is organized as follows. Section 2 introduces the related techniques that will be used in the proposed protocol. Section 3 describes the system model under the distributed networks. Section 4 presents the detailed protocol, the corresponding lightweight verification with precomputation mechanism and the dynamic batch verification mechanism. Section 5 concludes this paper.

2 Preliminaries

In this section, the related techniques including group key agreement, BLS multi-signatures, and the secure transformation used in the proposed protocol are introduced. Also, some essential notations used in this paper are summarized in a table for convenient and quick reference.

2.1 Group Key Agreement Protocol

The group key agreement protocol (BD protocol) [3] proposed by Burmester and Desmedt is a well-designed group key agreement protocol, which consists of four phases and is described as follows.

- Setup: Select a multiplicative group G of order q and a generator g as the system parameters. Here, $\{G, q, g\}$ is selected such that the discrete logarithm problem in G is intractable.
- Round 1: For a group with n parties, they are organized as a ring with index i. Each party P_i selects $s_i \leftarrow\!\$\ \mathbb{Z}_p^*$ as its secret. Here, $\mathbb{Z}_p^* := \{1, 2, 3, ..., p-1\}$. Then, every party broadcasts $h_i = g^{s_i}$ as its public parameters.
- Round 2: For party P_i, it obtains the public parameters h_{i-1} and h_{i+1} from its neighbours. Then, P_i calculates as Eq. (1).

$$X_i = (h_{i+1}/h_{i-1})^{s_i} \tag{1}$$

Finally, party P_i broadcasts the calculation result among the group.
- Session key generation: After all X_is have been broadcast, each party P_i can generate the session key as Eq. (2).

$$sk_i = (h_{i-1})^{n \cdot s_i} \prod_{k=1}^{n-2} X_{i+k}^{n-(k+1)} \tag{2}$$

The design rationale of BD protocol is based on the two-party Diffie-Hellman key agreement protocol [5]. Moreover, BD protocol is proved secure under the discrete logarithm assumption and the indistinguishability technique, which implies that it is secure under the passive attack. However, BD protocol suffers from the active attack because no authentication service is offered in the original BD protocol. In the following, the man-in-the-middle attack [4] is introduced to explain why authentication service in key agreement protocol is vital.

We take the two-party Diffie-Hellman key agreement protocol as an example to demonstrate that man-in-the-middle attack will lead to serious consequence. The detailed of the attack is depicted as follows. The attack E involves in the key agreement between two honest parties A and B. E can intercept and replace the transmitted messages between A and B without being detected. Finally, A generates the session key as $sk = g^{s_e s_a}$ while B generates the session key as $sk = g^{s_e s_b}$. Moreover, both A and B think the generated session keys are shared with the intended party. However, the derived session keys from A and B are not equal. Moreover, the attacker E knows both keys make matters worse.

Thus, it can be observed that without the security guarantee under the active attacks can greatly hinder the application and deployment of the BD protocol.

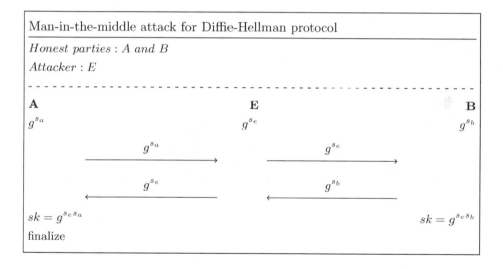

2.2 BLS Multi-Signatures

BLS multi-signatures [2] support batch verification by taking advantage of the bilinear pairing [16]. The BLS multi-signatures scheme is shown as follows.

- Setup: Generate the system parameters as $\{\hat{e}, G_0, G_1, H, \mathbb{Z}_p^*\}$. Here, $\hat{e} : G_0 \times G_1 \to G_T$ is a bilinear map and G_0, G_1 are two cyclic groups with generators g_0 and g_1, respectively. Also, $H : \mathcal{M} \to G_0$ is cryptographic hash function and $\mathbb{Z}_p^* := \{1, 2, 3, ..., p - 1\}$.
- Key generation: With the system parameters, party i selects $x_i \leftarrow_\$ \mathbb{Z}_p^*$ as its private key. Then, the corresponding public key is calculated as $pk_i = g_1^{x_i}$.
- Signature generation: To generate a signature on message $\mathcal{M}$, party i calculates $\sigma = H(\mathcal{M})^{x_i}$.
- Signature verification: To verify a signature σ on message $\mathcal{M}$ from party i, the verifier checks Eq. (3).

$$\hat{e}(g_1, \sigma) = \hat{e}(pk_1, H(\mathcal{M})) \tag{3}$$

- Signature aggregation and verification: Given n signatures from n parties on different messages, the signatures can be aggregated by Eq. (4).

$$\sigma = \sigma_1 \cdot \sigma_2 \cdot \sigma_3 \cdots \sigma_n \tag{4}$$

Then, the aggregated signature can be verifies according to Eq. (5).

$$\hat{e}(g_1, \sigma) = \hat{e}(pk_1, h_{\mathcal{M}_1}) \cdot \hat{e}(pk_2, h_{\mathcal{M}_2}) \cdot \hat{e}(pk_3, h_{\mathcal{M}_3}) \cdots \hat{e}(pk_n, h_{\mathcal{M}_n}) \tag{5}$$

In Eq. (5), $h_{\mathcal{M}_i} = H(\mathcal{M}_i)$.

2.3 Protocol Transformation

In [1], Bellare, Canetti and Krawczyk proposed a modular approach to transform a key agreement protocol step by step into an authenticated ones. In particular, based on the transformation method [1], a protocol that is secure running in the idealized authenticated communication channel can be transformed into a protocol that is still secure in the unauthenticated setting. The key point of the transformation is to introduce an authenticator. In fact, the authenticator can be implemented by a chosen message attack secure signature scheme. Then, the authenticator is used to ensure every message transmitted in the original protocol. Finally, the security of the original protocol can be guaranteed under realistic unauthenticated setting.

2.4 Notations

The primary notations appear in the paper are summarized in Table 1.

Table 1. Notations.

$\{G, G_0, G_1, G_T\}$	Cyclic groups
$\{g, g_1\}$	Generators of G and G_1
$\hat{e} : G_1 \times G_2 \rightarrow G_T$	Bilinear map
$\mathbb{Z}_p^*$	$\{1, 2, 3, ..., p-1\}$
$H : \mathcal{M} \rightarrow G_0$	Cryptographic hash function
P_i	Party in the group with index i
$s_i \in \mathbb{Z}_p^*$	Ephemeral secret of P_i
$h_i = g^{s_i}$	Public parameter of P_i
x_i	Private key of P_i
$pk_i = g_1^{x_i}$	Public key of P_i
$cert_i$	Certificate of P_i
X_i	Calculation result in round 1 of P_i
σ_i^1, σ_i^2	Signatures of P_i in round 1 and round 2, respectively
sk_i	Session key generated by P_i
ver_i	Precomputation by STA
ϵ	Progressive parameter in dynamic batch verification mechanism
λ	Threshold in dynamic batch verification mechanism

3   System Model

In this section, the system model of the proposed protocol is described under the distributed networks.

In our system, four entities are involved which are distributed servers, distributed nodes, the semi-trusted authority (STA), and the public key infrastructure (PKI). The detailed system model is illustrated in Fig. 1 and described as follows.

Distributed servers are in charge of collecting and storing data from distributed nodes. After the data are collected, the servers can train model based on the received data or just offer storage services. Finally, after the model training, the model parameters will be feedback to distributed nodes in distributed networks. Alternatively, when data are requested, servers will feedback data to distributed nodes.

Distributed nodes in the system model are resources-constrained in storage and computation capability who can only generate data but can not storage these data for a long time. It is required that nodes need to upload data periodical (e.g., 24 h) to refresh the storage space. Moreover, the computation capability of nodes is constrained thus the training task can only be outsourced to servers. Also, the verification needed the assistance from the STA.

STA is a semi-trusted authority who will assist nodes in performing authentication but may collude with attackers to run man-in-the-middle attack. In particular, in our system, the STA will help the distributed nodes to do some precomputation thereby supporting efficient batch verification between distributed

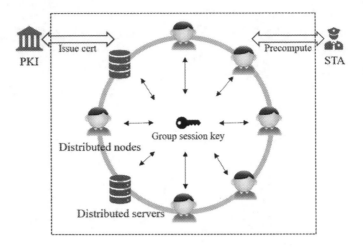

Fig. 1. The system model.

nodes. Moreover, in the dynamic batch verification phase, the STA is in charge of selecting parameters according to different authentication requirement and running the dynamic batch verification algorithm.

PKI is responsible for registering entity and issuing certificate. In our system model, entities including distributed servers, distributed nodes and STA need to register at PKI to obtain the corresponding certificates. The certificate can be used to support authentication during the group key agreement phase.

4   The Proposed Protocol

In this section, we first propose the authenticated group key agreement protocol, then introduce the STA to reduce the computational cost. Finally, the dynamic batch verification mechanism is designed to resist the DDoS attack.

4.1   Authenticated Group Key Agreement Protocol

To guarantee the transmission security in distributed networks, the authenticated group key agreement protocol is proposed. In particular, the BD protocol [3] is the basic of the proposed protocol. Then, based on the transformation method [1], the original BD protocol is transformed into an authenticated ones, which can resist the active attack. In the transformation process, the BLS multi-signatures [2] is adopted as the authenticator, which is proved to be secure under the chosen message attack.

The detailed protocol consist of 5 phases and are described as follows.

- Setup: Select key agreement parameters $\{G, q, g\}$ as the BD protocol. In order to offer authentication service during the key agreement phase, generate the BLS multi-signatures parameters as $\{\hat{e}, G_0, G_1, H, \mathbb{Z}_p^*\}$.

- Key generation: Party i selects $x_i \leftarrow_\$ \mathbb{Z}_p^*$ as its private key. Then, the corresponding public key is calculated as $pk_i = g_1^{x_i}$. Unlike the original BLS multi-signatures, to support authentication, every entity in our system need to register at the PKI with its public key and private key. Finally, PKI generates and issues the certificate $cert_i$ for the registered legal party P_i.
- Round 1: For a group with n parties, they are organized as a ring with index from 0 to $n-1$. Each party P_i selects $s_i \leftarrow_\$ \mathbb{Z}_p^*$ as its ephemeral key. Here, $\mathbb{Z}_p^* := \{1, 2, 3, ..., p-1\}$. Also, the corresponding public parameter is calculated as $h_i = g^{s_i}$. Then, to support authentication, party P_i generates signature on h_i with its private key x_i. In particular, P_i calculates $\sigma_i^1 = H(h_i)^{x_i}$. Finally, every party broadcasts $\mathcal{R}_i^1 = \{h_i, \sigma_i^1, cert_i\}$.
- Round 2: For party P_i, it obtains the messages $\mathcal{R}_{i-1}^1$ and $\mathcal{R}_{i+1}^1$ from its neighbours. Then, P_i checks Eq. (6) to verify the validity of the received messages.

$$\hat{e}(g_1, \sigma) = \hat{e}(pk_{i-1}, H(h_{i-1})) \cdot \hat{e}(pk_{i+1}, H(h_{i+1})) \qquad (6)$$

In Eq. (6), $\sigma = \sigma_{i-1}^1 \cdot \sigma_{i+1}^1$.
If Eq. (6) holds, party P_i calculates Eq. (1) to obtains X_i. Similarly, to support authentication, party P_i generates signature $\sigma_i^2 = H(X_i)^{x_i}$ on X_i with its private key x_i. Finally, party P_i broadcasts the calculation result $\mathcal{R}_i^2 = \{X_i, \sigma_i^2, cert_i\}$ among the group.
- Session key generation: After all $\mathcal{R}_i^2$ have been received, each party P_i checks Eq. (7) to verify the validity of the received messages.

$$
\begin{aligned}
\hat{e}(g_1, \sigma) &= \hat{e}(pk_0, H(X_0)) \\
&\quad \cdots \hat{e}(pk_{i-1}, H(X_{i-1})) \cdot \hat{e}(pk_{i+1}, H(X_{i+1})) \\
&\quad \cdots \hat{e}(pk_{n-1}, H(X_{n-1}))
\end{aligned}
\qquad (7)
$$

In Eq. (7), $\sigma = \sigma_0^2 \cdots \sigma_{i-1}^2 \cdot \sigma_{i+1}^2 \cdots \sigma_{n-1}^2$.
If Eq. (6) holds, party P_i can generate the session key as Eq. (2), which is shown as follows.

$$sk_i = (h_{i-1})^{n \cdot s_i} \prod_{k=1}^{n-2} X_{i+k}^{n-(k+1)}$$

In the following, the main data flow of the proposed authenticated group key agreement protocol is shown.

Authenticated Group Key Agreement Protocol

System parameters: G, q, g, g_1, $\hat{e}$, G_0, G_1, H

P_i: x_i, $pk_i = g_1^{x_i}$

P_i **The rest $n-1$ parties**

$h_i = g^{s_i}$

$\mathcal{R}_i^1 = \{h_i, \sigma_i^1\}$

$$\xrightarrow{\quad\quad\quad \mathcal{R}_i^1 \quad\quad\quad}$$

Check Eq. (6)

$X_i = (h_{i+1}/h_{i-1})^{s_i}$

$\mathcal{R}_i^2 = \{X_i, \sigma_i^2\}$

$$\xrightarrow{\quad\quad\quad \mathcal{R}_i^2 \quad\quad\quad}$$

Check Eq. (7)

Calculate Eq. (2)

finalize

Moreover, in order to show the proposed scheme clear, the interactions of the group key agreement in round 1 and round 2 are depicted in Fig. 2 and Fig. 3, respectively.

It can be observer from Fig. 2 that in the first round, each party distributes its public parameter to its neighbours. Then, in the second round as shown in Fig. 3, each party broadcasts its calculation result to all the rest $n-1$ parties. Finally, all parties in the group can generate a session key.

In order to support the proposed protocol performs in a high efficiency in distributed networks with real-time requirements, the precomputation mechanism preformed by STA is presented in the next subsection.

4.2   The Proposed Protocol with Precomputation

The STA is introduced to precompute the authentication parameters for distributed nodes. In particular, the main computational cost in the proposed protocol comes from the bilinear pairing operations in the authentication phase. That is, according to Eq. (7), each party needs to do $n-1$ bilinear pairing operations. The computational cost for bilinear pairing operations increase dramatically when the number of nodes in distributed networks becomes large, which is intolerable especially for the system with real-time requirements.

Precomputation. Note that the verification equation in the session key generation phase is the same for all n parties. Thus, it inspires us to introduce STA

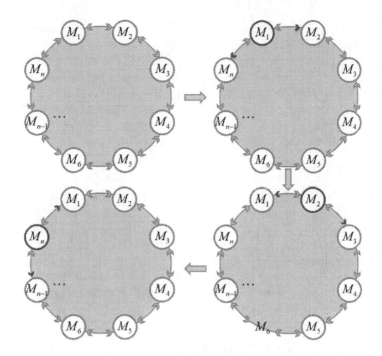

Fig. 2. Interactions in round 1.

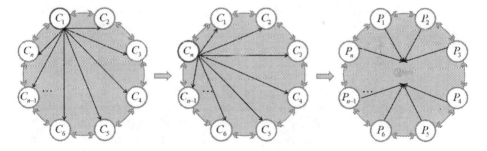

Fig. 3. Interactions in round 2.

Table 2. Precomputation from STA

Bilinear pairing operations	Precomputation
$\hat{e}(pk_0, H(X_0))$	ver_0
$\hat{e}(pk_1, H(X_1))$	ver_1
$\hat{e}(pk_2, H(X_2))$	ver_2
...	...
$\hat{e}(pk_i, H(X_i))$	ver_i
...	...
$\hat{e}(pk_{n-1}, H(X_{n-1}))$	ver_{n-1}

to assist group parties in precomputing. In particular, the precomputation from STA is shown in Table 2.

With the precomputation from STA, parties in the group can perform authentication efficiently. Whereas, it it realistic to assume that STA is semi-trusted rather than trusted. STA might collude with attackers for profit and other reasons. In particular, STA can collude with attackers by tampering with the precomputed authentication parameters to enable illegal users verified. To detect the potential misbehavior of from STA, the detection mechanism is designed as follows.

Detection. To avoid the collusion from STA and attackers, the detection mechanism is designed. In particular, the detection mechanism is performed by every party in the group based on the concept of probabilistic random sampling.

After received the precomputation result from STA, each party P_i randomly selects one samples from Table 2. Then, P_i compares the results of his calculations with the results of the sample. If the result is consistent, outputs acc_i. Otherwise, outputs ref_i and quits this session. If all parties accept, then the precomputation from STA is accepted.

4.3 Dynamic Batch Verification

In the distributed network environment, DDoS attack is an unavoidable topic. To solve this problem, we design the corresponding mechanism. In particular, we present a dynamic batch verification mechanism. Through the adjustment of threshold and progressive parameters, the designed mechanism ensures that members who are legally and normally operating are retained, and members who do not respond or fail verification are discarded. In Algorithm 1, the detailed dynamic batch verification mechanism are described.

In Algorithm 1, $\mathcal{T}$ is the precomputation results in Table 2, $\sigma_{\mathcal{T}}$ is the signatures corresponds to the authentication parameters in Table 2. In addition, the output $\mathcal{I}$ of Algorithm 1 is a list, which represents the index of the authenticated parties. Also, in Algorithm 1, ϵ is the progressive parameter. In particular, ϵ indicates the distance by which the size of $\mathcal{I}$ is reduced each time. λ denotes the threshold, which denotes the minimum size of $\mathcal{I}$. k represents the number of iterations.

Algorithm 1. Dynamic Batch Verification Mechanism

Input: $\mathcal{T}$, $\sigma_{\mathcal{T}}$

Output: $\mathcal{I}$

Detailed algorithm:

1: **Initialization:**
2: $auth\_size = \epsilon \cdot n$
3: $min\_size = \lambda \cdot n$
4: $k = iter\_num$
5: **while** $auth\_size \geq min\_size$ **do**
6:     **while** $k \geq 1$ **do**
7:         Select $auth\_size$ ver_i from Table 2 at random.
8:         Put the selected ver_i in $\mathcal{V}$.
9:         Check Eq. (7) to verify the selected ver_i.
10:        **if** Eq. (7) holds **then**
11:            $\mathcal{I} = \{i, \forall i | ver_i \in \mathcal{V}\}$
12:        **end if**
13:     **end while**
14:     **if** $\mathcal{I} \neq \mod 2 = 0$ **then**
15:         break
16:     **else**
17:         $autn\_size = \epsilon \cdot autn\_size$
18:     **end if**
19: **end while**
20: **return** $\mathcal{I}$

---

5 Conclusion

In this paper, an authenticated group key agreement protocol is proposed for secure data transmission in distributed networks. Based on the BLS multi-signatures and the transformation method, the group key agreement protocol without offering authentication service is enhanced to construct an authenticated ones. The constructed group key agreement protocol with authentication can resist both passive and active attacks. Moreover, an STA is introduced to preform auxiliary precomputation tasks. Accordingly, the potential collusion threats from STA and attackers are considered, which is prevented by the concept of probabilistic random sampling. Moreover, the dynamic batch verification mechanism is designed to resist the DDoS attack.

In our future works, performance evaluation will be conducted. Accordingly, parameters in probabilistic random sampling and dynamic batch verification mechanism can be optimized.

References

1. Bellare, M., Canetti, R., Krawczyk, H.: A modular approach to the design and analysis of authentication and key exchange protocols. In: Proceedings of the Thirtieth Annual ACM Symposium on Theory of Computing, pp. 419–428 (1998)

2. Boneh, D., Drijvers, M., Neven, G.: Compact multi-signatures for smaller blockchains. In: Peyrin, T., Galbraith, S. (eds.) ASIACRYPT 2018. LNCS, vol. 11273, pp. 435–464. Springer, Cham (2018). https://doi.org/10.1007/978-3-030-03329-3_15

3. Burmester, M., Desmedt, Y.: A secure and efficient conference key distribution system. In: De Santis, A. (ed.) EUROCRYPT 1994. LNCS, vol. 950, pp. 275–286. Springer, Heidelberg (1995). https://doi.org/10.1007/BFb0053443

4. Conti, M., Dragoni, N., Lesyk, V.: A survey of man in the middle attacks. IEEE Commun. Surv. Tutor. **18**(3), 2027–2051 (2016)

5. Diffie, W., Hellman, M.E.: New directions in cryptography. IEEE Trans. Inf. Theory **22**(6), 644–654 (1976)

6. Du, M., Wang, K.: An SDN-enabled pseudo-honeypot strategy for distributed denial of service attacks in industrial internet of things. IEEE Trans. Industr. Inf. **16**(1), 648–657 (2019)

7. Feitosa, A.E., Nascimento, V.H., Lopes, C.G.: Adaptive detection in distributed networks using maximum likelihood detector. IEEE Signal Process. Lett. **25**(7), 974–978 (2018)

8. Gavrilis, D., Dermatas, E.: Real-time detection of distributed denial-of-service attacks using RBF networks and statistical features. Comput. Netw. **48**(2), 235–245 (2005)

9. Islam, U., et al.: Detection of distributed denial of service (DDoS) attacks in IoT based monitoring system of banking sector using machine learning models. Sustainability **14**(14), 8374 (2022)

10. Jiang, Y., Zhang, K., Qian, Y., Zhou, L.: Anonymous and efficient authentication scheme for privacy-preserving distributed learning. IEEE Trans. Inf. Forensics Secur. **17**, 2227–2240 (2022). https://doi.org/10.1109/TIFS.2022.3181848

11. Liu, Z., Zhang, L., Ni, W., Collings, I.B.: Uncoordinated pseudonym changes for privacy preserving in distributed networks. IEEE Trans. Mob. Comput. **19**(6), 1465–1477 (2019)

12. Lopes, C.G., Sayed, A.H.: Incremental adaptive strategies over distributed networks. IEEE Trans. Signal Process. **55**(8), 4064–4077 (2007)

13. Shen, J., Zhou, T., He, D., Zhang, Y., Sun, X., Xiang, Y.: Block design-based key agreement for group data sharing in cloud computing. IEEE Trans. Dependable Secure Comput. **16**(6), 996–1010 (2019). https://doi.org/10.1109/TDSC.2017.2725953

14. Sun, Y., Han, Z., Liu, K.R.: Defense of trust management vulnerabilities in distributed networks. IEEE Commun. Mag. **46**(2), 112–119 (2008)

15. Wang, C., Shen, J., Lai, J.F., Liu, J.: B-TSCA: blockchain assisted trustworthiness scalable computation for V2I authentication in VANETs. IEEE Trans. Emerg. Top. Comput. **9**(3), 1386–1396 (2020)

16. Wang, C., Shen, J., Vijayakumar, P., Gupta, B.B.: Attribute-based secure data aggregation for isolated IoT-enabled maritime transportation systems. IEEE Trans. Intell. Transp. Syst. (2021). https://doi.org/10.1109/TITS20213127436

17. Xiong, H., Wu, Y., Lu, Z.: A survey of group key agreement protocols with constant rounds. ACM Comput. Surv. (CSUR) **52**(3), 1–32 (2019)

18. Zhou, T., Shen, J., He, D., Vijayakumar, P., Kumar, N.: Human-in-the-loop-aided privacy-preserving scheme for smart healthcare. IEEE Trans. Emerg. Top. Comput. Intell. **6**(1), 6–15 (2022). https://doi.org/10.1109/TETCI.2020.2993841

19. Zhou, T., Yang, H., Shen, J.: Key agreement protocol with dynamic property for VANETs. J. Cryptol. Res. **7**, 375–388 (2020)

Leveraging Frame Aggregation in Wi-Fi IoT Networks for Low-Rate DDoS Attack Detection

Bhagyashri Tushir⬮, Yuhong Liu(✉)⬮, and Behnam Dezfouli⬮

Internet of Things Research Lab, Department of Computer Science and Engineering,
Santa Clara University, Santa Clara, USA
{btushir,yhliu,bdezfouli}@scu.edu

Abstract. The proliferation of smart home Internet of Things (IoT) devices is demonstrated by their prominence in people's lives. However, the resource-constraint essence of these devices introduces various security flaws. One significant attack is the Low-rate Distributed Denial of Service (LR-DDoS) attack, which aims to disrupt the functionalities of the smart home IoT devices in a stealthy way by sending limited malicious traffic to the victim device. This paper proposes a novel set of features based on the 802.11 frame aggregation scheme to detect LR-DDoS attacks. We demonstrate that by conveying the characteristics of subframes during frame aggregation, we can uniquely embody the IoT device's benign traffic and malicious traffic in smart home networks. Compared to existing works which primarily focus on LR-DDoS attacks launched against data centers, to the best of our knowledge, this paper is the first work focusing on detecting such attacks against smart home IoT devices. We validate the effectiveness of the proposed features using the commercial off-the-shelf smart home IoT devices and by adopting various machine learning algorithms. Empirical results show that adopting the proposed features with the Random Forest achieves a 0.98 accuracy in distinguishing between benign and LR-DDoS attack traffic.

Keywords: Internet of Things (IoT) security · DDoS · Low-rate attacks · Smart home · Machine learning

1 Introduction

The number of smart home IoT devices connected to the Internet is projected to reach 75.44 billion by 2025 [1]. However, the resource-constraint essence of IoT devices makes them vulnerable to various attacks. For example, the work in [2–4] analyzed various popular consumer IoT devices and found numerous vulnerabilities. In particular, *Distributed Denial of Service (DDoS)* and energy-oriented DDoS (E-DDoS) attacks against IoT devices have attracted increasing attention since they can cause severe damage, such as high resource consumption and operational failure [3]. To exhaust the resources of victim devices promptly, DDoS adversaries often launch attacks with significantly higher rates than that

X. Yuan et al. (Eds.): NSS 2022, LNCS 13787, pp. 319–334, 2022.
https://doi.org/10.1007/978-3-031-23020-2_18

of the benign traffic. Therefore, existing studies often utilize machine learning algorithms and identify traffic with distinct statistical anomalies as malicious traffic [5–9, 17].

The idea behind *low-rate DDoS (LR-DDoS)* attacks, however, is to bypass the detection mechanisms by launching attack traffics with statistic features very similar to benign traffic. For example, the protocols used in LR-DDoS attacks are standard protocols such as TCP and UDP, which are the most common type of protocols in IoT networks [11]. Next, the LR-DDoS average flow rate is lower or similar to benign traffic. Finally, from the perspective of rate and duration, a LR-DDoS attack can have dynamic rates and duration that evolves with changes in the network environment [12]. For example, the attacks may be launched during traffic bursts to hide malicious traffic among the benign traffic. Because of such factors, detecting LR-DDoS attacks is very challenging.

Although various solutions have been proposed recently to detect LR-DDoS attacks against data centers [13–16], little effort has been made to detect LR-DDoS against smart home devices which may cause severe consequences. *Firstly,* packets (such as ICMP reply) transmitted by IoT devices in response to attack packets can be used to initiate high-rate DDoS attacks against devices outside the smart home network [4]. *Secondly,* LR-DDoS attacks can stealthily increase the power consumption of IoT devices since they process malicious packets. This could increase the consumer electricity bill. *Finally,* LR-DDoS attacks can introduce poor user experience by targeting multiple IoT devices to exhaust the home network bandwidth.

Therefore, in this work, we propose to focus on LR-DDoS attacks against smart home IoT devices. Note that due to the resource-constraint essence of IoT devices, it is possible to launch low-rate Denial of Service (LR-DoS) attacks by one machine and LR-DDoS attacks by multiple machines. For simplicity, in this work, we use the terms LR-DDoS to represent both attacks against IoT devices.

Specifically, 802.11 (WiFi), with its low-cost and wide-spreading deployment, has become an effective communication channel for IoT devices, including the smart home IoT devices [36, 37]. To reduce transmission overhead, the 802.11 standards after 802.11n adopt frame aggregation that combines multiple frames into a single frame for transmission. 802.11n describes two ways of frame aggregation, namely Aggregate MAC Protocol Service Unit (A-MSDU) and Aggregate MAC Protocol Data Unit (A-MPDU). Next, the density of frame aggregation is affected by several parameters such as the amount of data generated by the device, the interval between packet generations, and transmission rate. This means, frame aggregation, for example, is affected by the software implantation and processing resources of an IoT device, because these parameters affect packet generation rate. Building on such observations, in this work, we leverage the 802.11 data generated by smart home IoT devices and rely on *block acknowledgment (BA)* to introduce a novel set of features to detect LR-DDoS attacks in smart home networks. In particular, we explore the core mechanism of the frame aggregation scheme by exploiting characteristics such as the number of MAC protocol service unit (MPDU)s in a A-MPDU and the observed rate of the MPDUs. Since frame aggregation is affected by the network conditions such as *distance* between IoT device and Access Point (AP) and *channel utilization*, we normalize the proposed feature set by incorporating distance and channel utilization.

The primary contributions of this work are as follows:

- We propose a novel feature set that builds on the properties of 802.11 frame aggregation and is specifically suitable to be deployed on resource-constraint smart home APs for LR-DDoS detection since they are lightweight, privacy-preserving and robust under different smart home configurations. In particular, we demonstrate how 802.11 packets, specifically block acknowledgments, can be used to extract a rich set of 802.11 features. We define two essential features: aggregation intensity and MPDU rate, and show how these features can be used to distinguish between IoT devices' benign traffic and LR-DDoS attacks traffic. To the best of our knowledge this is the first work addressing LR-DDoS attack detection by characterizing frame aggregation. We further demonstrate the impact of network conditions on the proposed feature set. In particular, we show how aggregation intensity and MPDU rate of IoT network varies with changes in distance and channel utilization and later normalize the feature set.
- We validate the effectiveness of the proposed features by adopting multiple machine learning algorithms and conducting experiments on the real-world dataset collected at our lab.

The rest of the paper is organized as follows. Section 2 presents an overview of frame aggregation, the motivation behind proposed features, how features are computed, and factors influencing proposed features. We present the threat model and assumptions in Sect. 3. Next, Sect. 4 presents the machine learning-based framework and data collection setup. Section 5 validates the effectiveness of the proposed features by adopting multiple machine learning algorithms. Finally, we overview related work in Sect. 6 and conclude the paper in Sect. 7.

2   Feature Design

In this Section, we first give an overview of 802.11 frame aggregation and then discuss the motivation behind adopting frame aggregation as the primary feature used for detecting LR-DDoS attacks. Next, we show how to calculate aggregation intensity by adopting BA and finally, we normalize the proposed features by illustrating the factors affecting frame aggregation.

2.1   Frame Aggregation Overview

The underlying principle of 802.11 frame aggregation is to facilitate the accumulation of multiple MPDUs and to transmit them as one aggregated frame. Frame aggregation operates at the following two levels. (1) *A-MSDU* and (2) *A-MPDU*. A-MSDU occurs at the MAC layer, which is further aggregated into

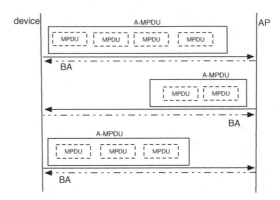

Fig. 1. Illustration of data transmission utilizing 802.11 frame aggregation.

A-MPDU when moved into the physical layer. All the MPDUs (i.e., packets)[1] in the A-MPDU have the same destination address and *traffic identifier (TID)*. Thus, the packets collected by a 802.11 sniffer are in the form of A-MPDU. Typically, an A-MPDU is followed by a BA that includes a bitmap field to report the reception status of each MPDU, as shown in Fig. 1. This work primarily focuses on leveraging A-MPDU characteristics for LR-DDoS attack detection in smart homes.

The implementation of 802.11 frame aggregation adopts the idea that traffic belonging to each TID is queued and scheduled independently. For example, the following six frames F_{a1}, F_{b1}, F_{a2}, F_{a3}, F_{b2} and F_{c1}, where F_{xi} is the ith frame with x as the TID, can be sent out as subsequent three frame (or A-MPDUs): (F_{a1}, F_{a2}, F_{a3}), (F_{b1}, F_{b2}) and (F_{c1}). The primary idea is that the transmission gap between two A-MPDUs allows assembling more packets into the TID queues except for the TID being transmitted. For instance, assume while transmitting the A-MPDU (F_{a1}, F_{a2}, F_{a3}), new MPDUs arrive with TID as b, denoted as (F_{b3}). This MPDU could be aggregated with A-MPDU (F_{b1}, F_{b2}) and sent out as (F_{b1}, F_{b2}, F_{b2}). Finally, the formation of A-MPDU is restricted by maximum A-MPDU size (65,535 B) and maximum frame transmission time (T_{max}) (e.g., 4 ms in ath9k) [27,28].

2.2   Frame Aggregation for Attack Detection

As one of the major contributions of this study is the proposal of features based on the 802.11 frame aggregation characteristics, this subsection describes the characteristics of benign traffic and the intuition behind how 802.11 frame aggregation helps to detect LR-DDoS attacks.

---

[1] The terms packet and MPDU are used interchangeably in this article.

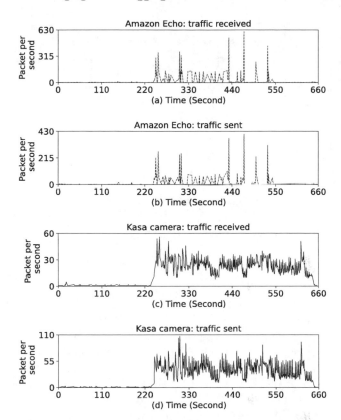

Fig. 2. Benign network traffic received/sent rates (packets per second) from Amazon Echo and Kasa camera.

IoT devices generate the following two types of traffic. (1) Standalone traffic: IoT devices have repetitive network traffic, such as regular network pings, DNS, and NTP requests, with small packets at fixed time intervals for logging purposes. (2) Active traffic: Traffic generated when users interact with the IoT devices, such as Google Home replying to the user's voice commands and Ring camera detecting activity and notifying the user phone [19]. The active traffic of IoT devices has the following characteristics. First, multiple data packets are exchanged between IoT device and the cloud server to perform one task (or request). For example, when we ask Google Home about the weather, 330710 bytes are transmitted as 325 packets, and 75208 bytes are received as 255 packets. Second, normally, the active traffic is sent in short bursts of packets. The sudden increase in the packets sent/received for a short period by Amazon Echo and Kasa represents the burst in Fig. 2.

Based on such observations, our intuition is that while transmitting active traffic associated with one request, numerous packets in the transmission queue of IoT devices are aggregated before transmission. However, in the case of LR-

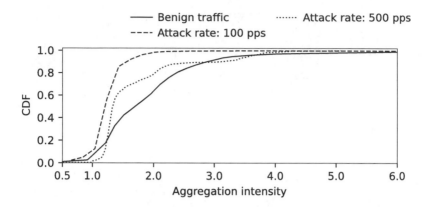

Fig. 3. 802.11 frame aggregation intensity of benign and LR-DDoS attack traffic of IoT devices.

DDoS attacks, the packets in the transmission queue would depend on the number of replies transmitted by the IoT device, which relies on the incoming attack rate. For example, IoT devices send ICMP replies, unreachable destination messages, and TCP-RSTs in response to ICMP requests, UDP, and TCP-SYN attack types, respectively. Therefore, understanding the transmission queue information, precisely length, can help detect LR-DDoS attacks. However, obtaining such details requires kernel-level access on a device, which is challenging for IoT devices, especially in the case of the passive approach. Fortunately, 802.11 frame aggregation schemes intrinsically show the property to extract transmission queue length. Hence, in this work, we adopt the characteristics of the frame aggregation schemes, such as the number of MPDUs within one A-MPDU, named *aggregation intensity*, to detect LR-DDoS attacks.

Figure 3 shows the aggregation intensity for the following two LR-DDoS attack rates, 100 and 500 packet per second (pps), and benign traffic of IoT devices used in our testbed. It is evident from Fig. 3 that for a lower incoming rate of 100 pps, the aggregation intensity is approximately 1.5; while for a higher incoming rate of 500 pps, the aggregation intensity is approximately between 1 and 4 for 90% of the outgoing traffic of IoT devices. Thus, the increase in the malicious incoming packets increases IoT devices' transmission queue length, which correlates with aggregation intensity. Further, it is observable that the aggregation intensity of benign traffic is less than 4 for 90% of benign traffic sent out by IoT devices. Based on such findings, we intend to capitalize on this variation in the aggregation intensity among benign and attack traffic to detect LR-DDoS attacks.

Aggregation intensity primarily infers an IoT device's transmission queue length while sending benign and malicious A-MPDUs. However, it does not assess how many MPDUs are sent out by IoT devices. It is noteworthy that for the exact number of A-MPDUs belonging to benign and malicious traffic sent by IoT devices, the total number of benign and malicious MPDUs might differ.

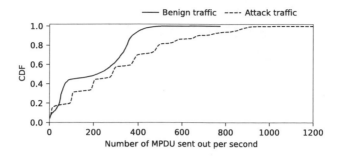

Fig. 4. Benign and malicious packets sent out per second (MPDU rate). The A-MPDUs are transmitted is between 100 to 400 per second.

The malicious traffic refers to the reply transmitted by IoT devices in response to LR-DDoS attacks. Thus, we utilize another A-MPDU metric called *MPDU rate* to count how many MPDUs are sent from the IoT device. For example, Fig. 4 shows the CDF graph for benign and malicious MPDUs sent per second (MPDU rate) by IoT devices, where the number of benign and malicious A-MPDUs transmitted is between 0 to 400 per second. The MPDU rate is 400 and 850 for 90% benign traffic and 90% malicious traffic. We rely on machine learning to leverage the difference between malicious and benign outgoing MPDU traffic rates.

2.3   A-MPDU Characteristics Extraction

This work aims to characterize 802.11 traffic, to detect LR-DDoS attacks by capturing BA to extract frame aggregation statistics. There are two primary advantages of utilizing BA over data packets. First, BAs are transmitted at a low rate compared to data packets; thus, a low-resource sniffer would be able to capture such packets. Second, one BA is generally transmitted for N number of MPDUs received. Thus, fewer BAs are sufficient to capture aggregation intensity information [34,35].

We use the bitmap and starting sequence number (SSN) fields of the BA packet to extract frame aggregation information [34,35]. The bitmap indicates the receiving status of the data packet, which is zero for failure and one for success. The SSN is the sequence number of the MPDU indicated by the first bit in the bitmap. Figure 5 shows how we compute aggregation intensity for benign and attack traffic between IoT devices and AP. Note that IoT devices use a 64-bitmap in our testbed; we identified the bitmap size from the BA packets sent/received by IoT devices. Next, Fig. 5 shows for the first A-MPDU (i.e., $A - MPDU^1$) and its corresponding BA (i.e., BA^1), the last bit of bitmap denotes MPDU with SSN as 2118. Similarly, the first bit corresponds to the 2055 SSN (2118 − 63 = 2055). 2055 is also the starting sequence number of BA. To calculate the aggregation intensity, we find the difference between two BA's SSN numbers. For example, the aggregation intensity is four (i.e., 2059 −

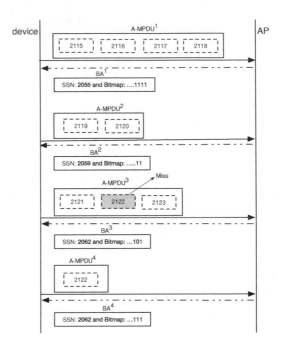

Fig. 5. Data transmission using A-MPDU frame aggregation. The sequence number (SSN) and bitmap are fields by block acknowledgment that enables aggregation intensity calculation.

$2055 = 4$) for BA^1 and BA^2. For the lost packets, for example, in $A-MPDU^4$, MPDU 2122 is lost, the BA bitmap represents the failure status by updating the received status to zero. The device then retransmits the MPDU while the BA SSN is the same (i.e., 2062). Finally, to accommodate the packet loss and increase the proposed features' effectiveness, we normalize them by understanding the influential factors.

2.4   Normalization of A-MPDU Characteristics

This work proposes the idea of adopting A-MPDU characteristics, aggregation intensity (I_a), and MPDUs rate per second (R_{nm}), into effective features that capture the various differences between LR-DDoS attacks and benign traffic. This Section discusses the influential factors and how these features are normalized.

First, we discuss the association between traffic rate and aggregation intensity. Considering there are N A-MPDUs that the device needs to transmit, and the nth A-MPDU would be sent at time t_n. The aggregation intensity (I_a^n) can be defined as the total number of MPDU belonging to TID that arrived between time t_{n-1} and t_n. As discussed in Sect. 2.2, I_a^n is affected by the traffic rate associated with a particular TID arriving between t_{n-1} and t_n. As more MPDUs

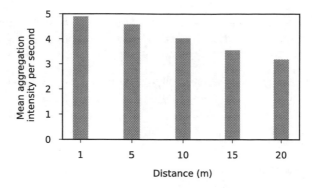

Fig. 6. Kasa camera aggregation intensity of malicious outgoing traffic versus distance shows an exponential association.

arrive at the device queue, I_a^n might increase proportionally. Figure 3 validates the association between I_a^n and traffic rate for LR-DDoS attacks. It is evident from Fig. 3 that I_a^n is higher for 500 pps attack rate compared to 100 pps rate. Thus, I_a^n increases with an increase in attack rate (or arriving traffic rate). On the other hand, benign traffic I_a^n shows no correlation with incoming packet rate since benign traffic generated by IoT devices depends on its functionality. Thus, IoT devices' I_a^n is independent of incoming traffic.

Next we show the association between IoT devices aggregation intensity and distance. Figure 6 shows the mean aggregation intensity per second versus distance for the Kasa camera for malicious outgoing traffic. It is evident from Fig. 6 that the aggregation intensity decreases with an increase in distance. Typically, the aggregation intensity decreases whenever the transmission queue has retry frames with non-consecutive sequence numbers [32]. Subsequently, the farther the IoT device from AP, the higher the number of retransmissions, decreasing the aggregation intensity. Finally, channel utilization shows linear association with aggregation intensity [33]. Thus, we normalize aggregation intensity I_a^n as follows:

$$I_a^n(N) = \frac{I_a^n * CU}{d} \qquad (1)$$

where $I_a^n(N)$ is the normalized aggregation intensity; d is the distance between the device and AP; and CU is the channel utilization. Later we standardize these features between 0 and 1. This equation holds if incoming traffic is lower or equal to 1000 pps. Beyond 1000 pps, the association might change. On this note, the following are the features proposed in this work.

- mean $I_a^n(N)$: mean of normalized aggregation intensity per second;
- std $I_a^n(N)$: standard deviation of normalized aggregation intensity per second;
- MPDU rate per second

The features are accumulated for both incoming and outgoing traffic of IoT networks.

3   Threat Model

In this Section, we discuss the assumptions and details of the threat model. We assume that the adversary has access to the local network of the smart home. The work in [4] validated this assumption. Further, we build the threat model upon the LR-DDoS attacks characteristics discussed in Sect. 1. In particular, firstly, the LR-DDoS attack rate is equivalent to the benign traffic (sent or received) by IoT devices. To achieve this goal, we analyze the benign traffic of off-the-shelf smart home IoT devices and observed the following. The rate of packets sent/received measured varies approximately from 0 to 800 pps. For example, Fig. 2(a)–(d) show the sending/receiving rates from the Amazon Echo and Kasa camera over approximately 11 min. Notably, the sending/receiving rate has peaked at time intervals when user activities are present. The maximum number of packets Amazon Echo receives and sends is 630 and 430 pps respectively, while the maximum number of packets Kasa camera receives and sends is 60 and 110 pps respectively. Thus, based on such observation, we keep the attack rate between 10 pps to 1000 pps. Secondly, we launch attacks based on IoT networks' three most common protocols: ICMP, TCP-SYN and UDP. Thirdly, in varying order, the LR-DDoS attacks are launched in bursts for 10 to 45 s. Further, the attack rate and duration vary randomly. Finally, please note that we choose the maximum attack rate as 1000 pps to show the trends of 802.11 frame aggregation among benign and LR-DDoS attack traffic. In real world settings, the adversary might increase or decrease the attack rate based on the types of IoT devices in the network.

4   Framework Overview

This Section presents a machine learning-based LR-DDoS detection framework for smart home IoT network. The proposed framework has four stages: traffic capture, grouping BAs, feature extraction, and attack detection. Next, we discuss each stage in detail.

Traffic Capture: we set up a smart IoT network testbed to collect IoT devices benign and attack data, as shown in Fig. 7. We adopted a Linksys router configured with Openwrt as a 802.11 AP to act as a smart home gateway. We connected Android phone, Amazon Echo, Google Home, Nest, Kasa and Ring cameras to the router's 802.11 network. We communicated with every IoT device for 30 min to collect and record benign data in *pcap* files. In particular, we stream

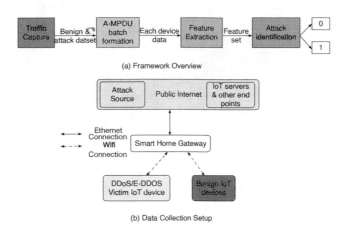

(a) Framework Overview

(b) Data Collection Setup

Fig. 7. IoT network proposed framework and corresponding data collection setup for collecting benign and attack traffic training data.

videos from the cameras to the phone while performing activities in front of cameras and ask various questions to Amazon Echo and Google Home.

Next, we collect LR-DDoS attack data. We use a `Linux` machine connected to the AP through Ethernet as an attack source. We launched ICMP, TCP-SYN, UDP LR-DDoS attacks. The attack source then targets each IoT device with each type of attack. The attacks happened in a random sequence for a random duration ranging uniformly from 1 to 60 s, with the attack rate varying between 10 pps to 1000 pps. The sniffer is kept close to AP and records pcap files of attack traffic. The sniffer collects the BA and beacon frame to compute proposed features and channel utilization. The attacks are simulated with the `hping3` utility. We collected approximately 5 min of attack traffic per device at a distance. We collect the LR-DDoS attack data at the following distances 1 m, 5 m, 10 m, 15 m, and 20 m.

BA Batch Formation: in this step, batches of BAs are formed by adopting the BA packets as discussed in Sect. 2.3 sent/received from each IoT device. The BAs are further grouped based on the MAC address for both benign and attack data. The groups are further divided into time windows (i.e., per second) by timestamps. It is interesting to note that identifying low-rate attacks on a per-device basis restricts collecting the number of flows in the smart home network. Thus, reducing the load of the AP.

Feature Extraction: from the BA groups the features discussed in Sect. 2.4 are extracted.

Attack Detection: various machine learning algorithms can distinguish benign traffic from attack traffic with high accuracy, as illustrated in Sect. 5.

Table 1. IoT devices benign and LR-DDoS attack traffic detection results

Score	k-Nearest Neighbors (KNN)	Support Vector Machine (SVM)	Decision Tree (DT)	Random Forest (RF)
Precision (Benign)	0.84	0.82	0.986	0.988
Precision (LR-DDoS)	0.81	0.87	0.979	0.989
F1 (Benign)	0.84	0.84	0.983	0.989
F1 (LR-DDoS)	0.81	0.85	0.985	0.987
Accuracy	0.82	0.84	0.982	0.988

5   Results and Discussion

This Section assesses the performance of machine learning algorithms for LR-DDoS attacks detection. We examine the effectiveness of the proposed features in terms of precision, F1 score, and accuracy. Later we discuss the importance of the features.

We use the scikit-learn Python library [24] to implement and train machine learning algorithms and validate the effectiveness of the proposed features. We tested the following machine learning algorithms for LR-DDoS detection: KNN, SVM, DT, and RF using Gini score. The hyperparameters of the machine learning algorithm are tuned. Next, we split the dataset into 75% training data and 25% testing data. Furthermore, the benign and attack traffic samples in training data are balanced to ensure strong validation results and to mitigate bias in the machine learning algorithms.

The machine learning algorithms' accuracies vary from approximately 0.82 to 0.98 shown in Table 1. Among the four algorithms, k-Nearest Neighbors (KNN) algorithm performs the worst with an accuracy of 0.82, indicating that the two different classes (benign and LR-DDoS attack) do not cluster well in feature space. Subsequently, Support Vector Machine (SVM) performs next lowest with an accuracy of 0.84. This indicates that it is difficult to cut decision regions into linear hyperplanes. Both Decision Tree (DT) and Random Forest (RF) archives accuracy approximately of 0.98 suggesting that the data is axis aligned and can be segmented in higher feature space [23].

Figure 8 illustrates the relative feature importance when the data is trained using RF algorithm. The feature importance represents the Gini score that is calculated by measuring the average decrease in the impurity score for each feature. RF is a collection of multiple DT; thus, the average over all trees in the RF builds measurement of the feature importance. We accomplish such feature importance calculation by using the scikit-learn library. Next, the MPDU rate and mean I_a contributes approximately 48% and 27% to LR-DDoS attack detection efficacy, which validate that the frame aggregation characteristics are effective for LR-DDoS detection in the smart home environment.

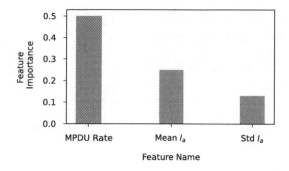

Fig. 8. The relative importance of all four features when applying RF using Gini score.

6 Related Work

Most existing works focus on defending data centers against DDoS [25, 26, 29] and LR-DDoS [13–15]. In IoT networks majority of the work focus on detecting DDoS attacks originating from IoT devices [7, 8, 30, 31], few works focus on protecting IoT devices against flood DDoS attacks [5, 6] and much less attention has been paid to protecting IoT devices from LR-DDoS attacks. Therefore, in this work, we aim to detect LR-DDoS attacks against IoT devices. To do so, we explore the properties of 802.11 frame aggregation and propose a novel, lightweight, privacy-preserving, and robust feature set that achieves 99% accuracy with machine learning algorithms.

The work in [5, 6] focuses on detecting flood attacks against IoT devices. In particular, the work in [5] proposed a feature set including packet size, inter-packet interval, and protocol type estimated for a time window to detect flood DDoS attacks on IoT devices. However, such features may not detect low-rate attacks because of two significant shortcomings. First, the authors did not consider the impact of network conditions on the proposed features. For example, an increase in the number of packet retransmission would alter (increase or decrease) the percentage of packets of a specific protocol for a time window. Second, the objective of a slow-rate attack is to approximate the benign traffic rate. Thus, the inter-packet interval may not be a significant feature for slow-rate attack detection. Next, the authors in [6] proposed an intrusion detection system to detect DDoS attacks in IoT network. The features set adopted by [6] is based on per packet characteristics such as packet length, TCP, and IP flags violating user privacy. Therefore, to overcome such challenges in this work, we consider the impact of network conditions on the proposed lightweight and privacy-preserving features and aim to detect both LR-DDoS attacks launched against smart home networks. Further, to the best of our knowledge, this is the first work detecting LR-DDoS attacks against smart home networks.

The works [20–22] use deep learning to detect DDoS attacks. Although deep learning algorithms can automatically extract high-level features from low-level ones and gain powerful representation and inference, such algorithms are associated with high computation costs. The work in [20–22] used packet-level features such as protocol, port numbers, and HTTP length. These features are fed to deep learning algorithms such as LSTM and GRU. However, such features might violate user privacy. To overcome such challenges, in this work, we engineer lightweight and privacy-preserving features that, when adopting basic machine learning algorithms such as RF achieve 0.98 accuracies in detecting LR-DDoS attacks. To the best of our knowledge, our work is the first to analyze the frame aggregation scheme among benign and attack traffic to detect low-rates attacks against IoT devices.

7   Conclusion

In this work, we showed that 802.11 frame aggregation characteristics such as aggregation intensity could accurately differentiate benign and LR-DDoS attack traffic in the smart home environments. Our selection of features is based on the hypothesis that aggregation intensity would differ among benign traffic and response sent by IoT devices to attack packets. To validate the proposed feature set, we tested four different machine learning algorithms on the real-world dataset collected at our lab using five smart home devices. We use four features to limit feature extraction's computational overhead and their real-time implementation on smart home AP. RF test set accuracy is approximately 0.99. These initial outcomes encourage further research into machine learning anomaly detection to protect smart home networks from LR-DDoS attacks.

References

1. Cvitić, I., Peraković, D., Periša, M., Botica, M.: Smart home IoT traffic characteristics as a basis for DDoS traffic detection. In: 3rd EAI International Conference on Management of Manufacturing Systems (2018)
2. Davis, B., Mason, J., Anwar, M.: Vulnerability studies and security postures of IoT devices: a smart home case study. IEEE Internet Things J. **7**, 10102–10110 (2020)
3. Tushir, B., Dalal, Y., Dezfouli, B., Liu, Y.: A quantitative study of DDoS and E-DDoS attacks on WiFi smart home devices. IEEE Internet Things J. **8**, 6282–6292 (2020)
4. Lyu, M., Sherratt, D., Sivanathan, A., Gharakheili, H., Radford, A., Sivaraman, V.: Quantifying the reflective DDoS attack capability of household IoT devices. In: Proceedings of the 10th ACM Conference on Security and Privacy in Wireless and Mobile Networks, pp. 46–51 (2017)
5. Doshi, R., Apthorpe, N., Feamster, N.: Machine learning DDoS detection for consumer internet of things devices. In: 2018 IEEE Security and Privacy Workshops (SPW), pp. 29–35 (2018)
6. Anthi, E., Williams, L., Słowińska, M., Theodorakopoulos, G., Burnap, P.: A supervised intrusion detection system for smart home IoT devices. IEEE Internet Things J. **6**, 9042–9053 (2019)
7. Jia, Y., Zhong, F., Alrawais, A., Gong, B., Cheng, X.: FlowGuard: an intelligent edge defense mechanism against IoT DDoS attacks. IEEE Internet Things J. **7**, 9552–9562 (2020)

8. Roopak, M., Tian, G., Chambers, J.: An intrusion detection system against DDoS attacks in IoT networks. In: 2020 10th Annual Computing and Communication Workshop and Conference (CCWC), pp. 0562–0567 (2020)

9. Diro, A., Chilamkurti, N.: Distributed attack detection scheme using deep learning approach for Internet of Things. Futur. Gener. Comput. Syst. **82**, 761–768 (2018)

10. Liu, Z., Yin, X., Hu, Y.: CPSS LR-DDoS detection and defense in edge computing utilizing DCNN Q-learning. IEEE Access. **8**, 42120–42130 (2020)

11. Gordon, H., Batula, C., Tushir, B., Dezfouli, B., Liu, Y.: Securing smart homes via software-defined networking and low-cost traffic classification. 2021 IEEE 45th Annual Computers, Software, and Applications Conference (COMPSAC), pp. 1049–1057 (2021)

12. Zhijun, W., Wenjing, L., Liang, L., Meng, Y.: Low-rate DoS attacks, detection, defense, and challenges: a survey. IEEE Access. **8**, 43920–43943 (2020)

13. Aiello, M., Cambiaso, E., Mongelli, M., Papaleo, G.: An on-line intrusion detection approach to identify low-rate DoS attacks. In: 2014 International Carnahan Conference on Security Technology (ICCST), pp. 1–6 (2014)

14. Zhang, N., Jaafar, F., Malik, Y.: Low-rate DoS attack detection using PSD based entropy and machine learning. In: 2019 6th IEEE International Conference on Cyber Security and Cloud Computing (CSCloud)/2019 5th IEEE International Conference on Edge Computing and Scalable Cloud (EdgeCom), pp. 59–62 (2019)

15. Zhang, X., Wu, Z., Chen, J., Yue, M.: An adaptive KPCA approach for detecting LDoS attack. Int. J. Commun Syst **30**, e2993 (2017)

16. He, Z., Zhang, T., Lee, R.: Machine learning based DDoS attack detection from source side in cloud. In: 2017 IEEE 4th International Conference on Cyber Security and Cloud Computing (CSCloud), pp. 114–120 (2017)

17. Chandola, V., Banerjee, A., Kumar, V.: Anomaly detection: a survey. ACM Comput. Surv. (CSUR) **41**, 1–58 (2009)

18. Ferrag, M., Maglaras, L., Moschoyiannis, S., Janicke, H.: Deep learning for cyber security intrusion detection: approaches, datasets, and comparative study. J. Inf. Secur. Appl. **50**, 102419 (2020)

19. Sivanathan, A., Sherratt, D., Gharakheili, H., Sivaraman, V., Vishwanath, A.: Low-cost flow-based security solutions for smart-home IoT devices. In: 2016 IEEE International Conference on Advanced Networks and Telecommunications Systems (ANTS), pp. 1–6 (2016)

20. Yuan, X., Li, C., Li, X. DeepDefense: identifying DDoS attack via deep learning. In: 2017 IEEE International Conference on Smart Computing (SMARTCOMP), pp. 1–8 (2017)

21. Yadav, S., Subramanian, S.: Detection of Application Layer DDoS attack by feature learning using Stacked AutoEncoder. In: 2016 International Conference on Computational Techniques in Information and Communication Technologies (ICCTICT), pp. 361–366 (2016)

22. Idhammad, M., Afdel, K., Belouch, M.: Detection system of HTTP DDoS attacks in a cloud environment based on information theoretic entropy and random forest. Secur. Commun. Netw. **2018** (2018)

23. Tomita, T., et al.: Sparse projection oblique randomer forests. J. Mach. Learn. Res. **21** (2020)

24. Pedregosa, F., et al.: Scikit-learn: machine learning in Python. J. Mach. Learn. Res. **12**, 2825–2830 (2011)

25. Xiao, P., Qu, W., Qi, H., Li, Z.: Detecting DDoS attacks against data center with correlation analysis. Comput. Commun. **67**, 66–74 (2015)

26. Cao, J., Yu, B., Dong, F., Zhu, X., Xu, S.: Entropy-based denial-of-service attack detection in cloud data center. Concurr. Comput. Pract. Exp. **27**, 5623–5639 (2015)
27. Erikarn How the ath9k transmit path works (2013). https://github.com/erikarn/ath9k-docs/blob/master/ath9k-xmit.txt
28. Song, L., Striegel, A.: Leveraging frame aggregation to improve access point selection. In: 2017 IEEE Conference on Computer Communications Workshops (INFOCOM WKSHPS), pp. 325–330 (2017)
29. Jiao, J., et al.: Detecting TCP-based DDoS attacks in Baidu cloud computing data centers. In: 2017 IEEE 36th Symposium on Reliable Distributed Systems (SRDS), pp. 256–258 (2017)
30. Roopak, M., Tian, G., Chambers, J.: Multi-objective-based feature selection for DDoS attack detection in IoT networks. IET Netw. **9**, 120–127 (2020)
31. Vishwakarma, R., Jain, A.: A honeypot with machine learning based detection framework for defending IoT based botnet DDoS attacks. In: 2019 3rd International Conference on Trends in Electronics and Informatics (ICOEI), pp. 1019–1024 (2019)
32. Inamullah, M., Raman, B.: 11 ac frame aggregation is bottlenecked: revisiting the block ACK. In: Proceedings of the 22nd International ACM Conference on Modeling, Analysis and Simulation of Wireless and Mobile Systems, pp. 45–49 (2019)
33. Ginzburg, B., Kesselman, A.: Performance analysis of A-MPDU and A-MSDU aggregation in IEEE 802.11 n. In: 2007 IEEE Sarnoff Symposium, pp. 1–5 (2007)
34. Saif, A., Othman, M., Subramaniam, S., Hamid, N.: An enhanced A-MSDU frame aggregation scheme for 802.11 n wireless networks. Wirel. Pers. Commun. **66**, 683–706 (2012)
35. Song, L., Striegel, A., Mohammed, A.: Sniffing only control packets: a lightweight client-side WiFi traffic characterization solution. IEEE Internet Things J. **8**, 6536–6548 (2020)
36. Ramanna, V.K., Sheth, J., Liu, S., Dezfouli, B.: IEEE Trans. Green Commun. Netw. **5**(4), 1833–1845 (2021)
37. Sheth, J., Miremadi, C., Dezfouli, A., Dezfouli, B.: EAPS: edge-assisted predictive sleep scheduling for 802.11 IoT stations. IEEE Syst. J. **16**(1), 591–602 (2021)

Supporting Cyber-Attacks and System Anomaly Detection Research with an Industry 4.0 Dataset

Lei Shi$^{(\boxtimes)}$, Shanti Krishnan, Sheng Wen, and Yang Xiang

Swinburne University of Technology, Melbourne, Australia
{lshi,Skrishnan,Swen,yxiang}@swin.edu.au

Abstract. In the era of Industry 4.0, smart devices in the manufacturing industry have become increasingly used and interconnected. However, this also increases the possibility of anomaly and cyber-attacks in the heterogeneous smart systems, resulting in failure which may have a cascading effect on different machines in the factory. Physical damage or business interruption can be caused by cyber-attacks in the manufacturing industry. Machine learning (ML) is an important enabling technology in Industry 4.0 and it can be a solution to the problem aforementioned. But there is a lack of publicly available datasets that include network and Operation technologies (OT) data containing different types of cyber-attacks in the context of Industry 4.0 manufacturing systems. Moreover, many researchers do not release the dataset they utilise which makes it difficult to benchmark or compare the work of different researchers. This paper presents a dataset which is acquired from a contemporary and realistic Industry 4.0 manufacturing system. The dataset comprises of seven different scenarios including normal operation, a range of cyber-attacks and anomalies caused by disgruntled employees as well as errors in manufacturing operations. Using the dataset, we train three machine learning models to detect attacks and anomalies, before presenting the results. We conclude that ML classifiers trained by our dataset perform well in detecting most of the attack types and anomalies. Physical and network data can be a good combination to build a robust system for detecting attacks and anomalies.

Keywords: Industry 4.0 · Anomaly detection · Cyber physical system · Machine learning · Dataset · Cyber-attacks · Intrusion detection system

1 Introduction

The manufacturing industry is undergoing the fourth industrial revolution. The Industry 4.0 market is projected to grow tremendously, and it is estimated that the market will reach USD 165.5 billion by 2026 [1]. New Industry 4.0 technologies, including the Industrial Internet of Things (IIoT), cloud computing,

X. Yuan et al. (Eds.): NSS 2022, LNCS 13787, pp. 335–353, 2022.
https://doi.org/10.1007/978-3-031-23020-2_19

data analytics, AI and machine learning have started to be implemented into production lines and throughout their processes. Machines in the factory can communicate with each other, and they can be controlled remotely. However, this synergy has made the system vulnerable to cyber-attacks such as worms, Denial of Service (DoS) and Man-in-the-middle attack (MITM) attacks [8,12,14]. At the same time, Industry 4.0 systems comprise heterogeneous smart devices and this makes it difficult to maintain and detect anomalies in an operation. In the context of Industry 4, the cyber-attacks can create physical damage to the equipment, so we can argue that cyber-attacks result in the same impact on production as an anomaly in the system. Therefore, the same method can be used to detect both equipment anomalies and cyber-attacks.

Machine learning (ML) has impacted many industries, resulting in an explosion of new smart devices and new business opportunities. According to a report by Deloitte [2] "data is the new gold", and data is at the core of machine learning. The digital innovation driven by data science will reshape how most industries function. In manufacturing, machine learning can help solve specific business problems, such as cybersecurity and predictive maintenance. With the wide adoption of smart sensors, it has never been easier to collect data and this naturally leads to the usage of data analytics and ML in the Industry 4.0 system. Models trained by the data from physical processes and networks can be used to detect cyber-attacks on critical machines or anomalies in the production process. In this way, companies are protected by being able to detect attacks and anomalies quickly and instantly trigger protective action. In this paper, we present a methodology to show that machine learning is potentially a solution to use in areas such as intrusion detection systems and anomaly detection systems.

However, because of the high cost and complexity of real industrial system, it is difficult for researchers to get opportunities to access real industrial systems and acquire data. Experimenting on real and active industrial system in the manufacturing industry is often limited due to possible disruption in production. Hence, a dataset gathered using high-fidelity testbeds is the most feasible option.

To help address this problem, this paper presents a dataset generated from an Industry 4.0 production system which uses realistic and contemporary industry devices including robot, smart sensors, conveyor belt, manufacturing execution system (MES) and Programmable Logic Controllers (PLC). Both network dataset and physical dataset including data from sensors and PLC tags are collected from the system in seven scenarios including normal operations, the system under attack and system anomaly. Finally, using the dataset, we train three machine learning models to detect the attacks and anomalies, and then demonstrate the results. The contributions of this paper can be summarised as follows:

- A dataset from a contemporary and realistic Industry 4.0 testbed includes the most commonly used devices in smart manufacturing.
- Simulated the effects of cyber-attack from worms.
- Present both physical and network data with evaluation.

- Our network data includes the traffic from three industrial communication protocols, and one of them is an encrypted protocol.

The remainder of the paper is organised as follows. Section 2 provides a literature review on existing datasets in the related fields. Section 3 describes the Industry 4.0 manufacturing testbed and network architecture. In Sect. 4, we present details of the attacks. Section 5 describes the dataset and data collection details. In Sect. 6, we describe the setup of ML metrics and the results from detecting cyber-attacks and anomalies. Finally, Sect. 7 concludes the paper.

2 Literature Review

Machine learning has been used to design intrusion detection systems (IDS) [15] and it looks to be particularly effective in recognising cyber-attacks and anomalies. It is critical to evaluate these systems so that their ability to detect attacks can be assessed. Moreover, the current smart manufacturing system is complicated and includes a system of systems. There is a necessity to create realistic data from a sufficiently complex testbed.

There are widely used datasets such as KDDCup99 [16] and CTU-13 Dataset [9], however, they present the data in a traditional network with only IT devices. As Industry 4.0 is a convergence of internet technology (IT) and operation technology (OT), it is necessary to use the testbed with OT devices to create both network data and physical data so that they can be used to explore artificial intelligence techniques and applications in the industrial control system (ICS) and cyber physical system (CPS). In recent years, some publications have presented the data in an industrial control system or cyber physical system. They focus on creating a dataset for critical infrastructures such as water distribution and smart grid. Below is a summary of the papers.

The first three publications in the Table 1 are on the application of water distribution. In [5], the authors present a simple and real set up with a PLC, two water tanks, two pumps and multiple sensors. Data in 15 situations, including normal, cyber-attack and physical attacks, were collected. The dataset consists of sensor data obtained from registers in the PLC. There is a lack of network traffic in the dataset which makes it inadequate to have a comprehensive evaluation of an IDS. By contrast, the authors in [4] present a more complex and comprehensive dataset of a real system in the Centre for Research in Cyber Security. The testbed is called Singapore University Secure Water Treatment (SWaT) and it consists of a full SCADA system with PLCs; human machine interfaces (HMIs) and multiple water tanks; sensors and actuators in six different stages. The dataset includes SWaT testbed runs without any attacks in the first 7 days, followed by launched attacks for four days. Although the system includes high-level SCADA device, the attacks were only launched against the communication between PLCs and sensors.

In [3], an ICS dataset has been generated from a hybrid system in a hardware-in-the-loop fashion. It provides both physical and network data so that the relations between cyber and physical aspects of the system can be explored. Datasets

Table 1. Datasets review

Paper	Application	Attacks	Network protocol	Real/Simulated	Physical/ Network data	ML evaluation
[3]	Water distribution	DoS, MITM, Scanning, Physical attacks	MODBUS	Hybrid	Both	Yes
[4]	Water distribution	DoS, MITM, Physical attacks	MODBUS	Real	Both	No
[5]	Water distribution	DoS, MITM	-	Real	Physical	No
[6]	Smart grid	DoS, Message suppression, Data/Control Manipulation	IEC61850	Simulated	No	No
[7]	Smart grid	Data manipulation	IEC61850	Real	Both	No
[23]	Electric traction substation	False data injection, replay, reconnaissance	S7Comm, Modbus	Real	No	Yes

from [6,7] are from smart grid systems in which different controllers and communication protocols are used compared with an ICS. Finally, the authors from [23] present two network datasets including Modbus and S7Comm, and then several ML models are trained to detect anomalies.

To the best of our knowledge, no publication has presented the dataset from a real Industry 4.0 smart factory, including both network and physical data. No publication presents complex network data including multiple industrial communication protocols with encrypted data. Instead, previous papers were mainly focused on simple protocol Modbus. Moreover, there is not much discussion on how the ML models trained by network and physical data complement each other in building a detecting system.

3   Industry 4.0 Testbed

3.1   Testbed Introduction

The testbed used in our experiment comprises 2 major subsystems: Symbiotic cell and Cyber Physical Factory (CPF). The whole system is modular and reconfigurable, and it can be used to produce customised products without needing a manual change of the system's configuration. A manufacturing execution system (MES) is used to monitor, track and control the process and order of manufacturing parts. MES sends out commands to the production line with parameters, then customised products can be manufactured with different specifications and components. In our design, the system is capable of manufacturing three different types of products: temperature meter, barometric meter and digital meter. Figure 1 is the picture of one product. The modules inside can be changed based on the type of products.

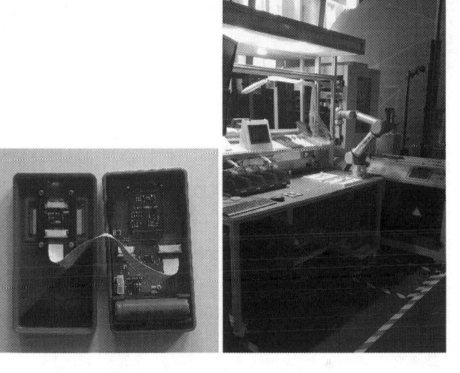

Fig. 1. Final product and symbiotic cell

3.2   Schematic and Process

Cyber Physical Factory is a learning and research platform from FESTO and it is designed for Industry 4.0 and the Industrial internet of things (IIOT). It is made of 6 modules. Starting from the storage cell, the system retrieves the back cover, assembles PCB assembly and then presents the half-finished part to the Symbiotic Cell.

As illustrated in Fig. 2, Symbiotic Cell is designed and built by the team from Swinburne Factory of the Future to integrate with CPF and form a comprehensive production line. It models the technologies of networked production and incorporates typical Industry 4.0 concepts and enabling technologies as a modular and smart factory system. It consists of a Siemens PLC, a Siemens HMI, a UR robot and a smart light system. An operator works side by side with a UR robot, which is a collaborative robot, to finish the assembly of a portable device. The dataset presented in this paper is mainly from the Symbiotic Cell.

Our testbed is a system of systems(SoS) which is a collection of dedicated and independent systems as part of a more complex system. And industrial communication protocols are used to realize machine to machine(M2M) communication. Diagram 1 shows the diagram of the testbed.

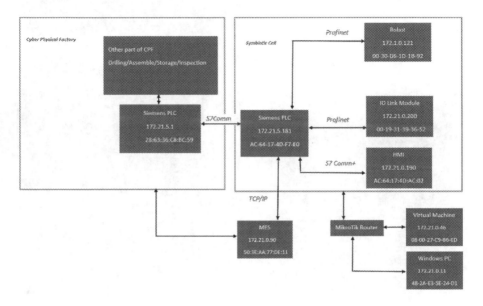

Fig. 2. Schematic of the symbiotic cell in the industry 4.0 testbed

3.3   Network Architecture

Unlike the datasets in previous papers [3,4,23] which focuses on MODBUS, our testbed is a more realistic system with a mix of widespread industrial communication protocols including Profinet, S7Comm and S7CommPlus. As shown in Diagram 1, Siemens PLC communicates with HMI using encrypted S7 Comm+ protocol and two siemens PLCs while the other systems in the Symbiotic cell use unencrypted S7Comm and Profinet protocols. Other parts of the system use the TCP/IP and some other common network protocols. Moreover, a MikroTik [11] router is connected with the Symbiotic Cell and forwards all network packets from the Symbiotic Cell to a Windows PC, and a virtual machine is used to launch cyber-attacks through the router.

Both S7 Comm and S7Comm plus are Siemens proprietary protocols and they use industrial ethernet standards and rely on ISO TCP(RFC1006). Compared with S7 Comm, S7Comm plus is a new version of communication protocol with encryption to prevent attacks such as replay attacks. In [10], the authors demonstrate the encryption algorithms of S7CommPlus and a method to break the anti-replay attack of Siemens PLC. Although packets using S7CommPlus protocol have been recorded in our datasets, the analysis of S7Comm plus is beyond the scope of this paper.

PROFINET is a leading Industrial Ethernet communication standard and it is used to exchange data between controllers and peripheral devices for an industrial control system. PROFINET is the most popular industrial ethernet protocol in factory automaton in 2022 [20]. Compared with Modbus, which keeps its simplicity, PROFINET is working towards integration with Industry 4.0. Hence, PROFINET has more features with functional safety (PROFIsafe) and allows for easier integration with machine to machine communication protocols such as OPC UA [21]. In our evaluation section, we focus on the PROFINET protocol, with an analysis based on the communication among the smart lights (IO link) module, PLC and UR robot.

4   Attacks Details

In this work, four types of attacks including Denial of Service, Man-in-the-middle attack, Malware, Disgruntled employee attack, and System malfunction were launched within the testbed. We considered the first three of these cyber-attacks.

4.1   Denial of Service (DoS)

DoS attacks were launched to disrupt the manufacturing process and they are intended to flood devices with packets. In our setup, the Internet Control Message Protocol (ICMP) and Transmission Control Protocol (TCP) were used to flood devices in the Symbiotic Cell of the testbed. ICMP is a Ping flood attack with ICMP echo requests, while the latter is a TCP SYN flood attack in which the attacker sends SYN packets as a part of a three-way handshake of TCP. Unlike the results from other testbeds [3], the operation of our devices in the symbiotic cell, including HMI, Smart lights module, PLC and Robot were not affected by the flood of TCP SYN scan and ICMP. This could be because the Profinet connected system in our setup comprises the latest Siemens PLC, HMI and their compatible peripherals. We have designed robust hardware system to showcase Industry 4.0 principles. However, as illustrated in Table 2 the cycle time of Siemens PLC in the symbiotic Cell increased when it was is under ICMP and TCP flooding attacks.

Figure 3 shows in more detail the cycle time of each time period. Data numbers 0–427 and 1811–2023 are the periods when no DoS attack happened. On the other hand, 427–1266 and 1267–1810 are when PLC is under DoS attack. From the observation from the Fig. 3, we can conclude that the average cycle time

Table 2. PLC cycle time in different senarios

Mode	Data number	Average
Normal operation	0–427	3.07 ms
ICMP	427–1266 n	3.36 ms
TCP SYN	1267–1810	3.96 ms
Normal operation	1811–2023	3.17 ms

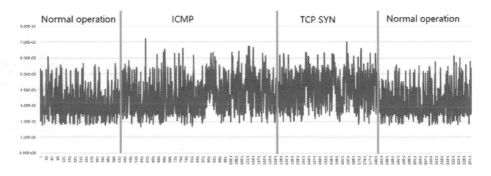

Fig. 3. PLC cycle time in different senarios

of PLC when under both ICMP and TCP SYN flooding attacks has increased. Moreover, cycle time of individual sample can be misleading, so the authors processed the data to include average cycle time in the presented dataset.

4.2   Man-in-the-middle Attack (MITM)

MITM is a cyber-attack in which the attacker intercepts and relays information between two parties. In the meantime, these two parties believe that they are directly communicating with each other. In our setup, ARP spoofing is used to intercept the real-time packets between PLC and IO devices. Address Resolution Protocol (ARP) spoofing attacks associate the victim's IP address with the attacker's MAC address in the ARP table, so that the packets are sent to attackers instead of victims. ARP attacks can easily disconnect the devices from the system. However, if a device was made inaccessible due to DoS, PLC or HMI could quickly identify the problem and indicate the disconnection status. So together with ARP attacks, we use IP forwarding to avoid malicious activities from being found.

4.3   Malware

Computer worms are developed to attack industrial devices. Instead of only affecting computers and stealing information, they also start to cause physical destruction to equipment. The most famous attack is Stuxnet, it modifies the

Siemens PLC and causes the failure of the uranium enrichment process. The whole attack process is very complicated and costly, which includes a chain of attacks to vulnerabilities in the Windows operation system, printer and TIA Portal [13]. In our experiment, we simulate the attack by using similar steps of the Stuxnet - PLC programs are modified and downloaded to PLC. The dataset can be used to validate the effectiveness of the intrusion detection system (IDS) against a modified PLC program. Hence, it is useful to the research for the purpose of defending attacks towards PLC controlled physical systems like Stuxnet.

4.4 Disgruntled Employee or System Malfunction

In a smart factory, a few employees look after the operations of the whole factory. If a disgruntled employee deliberately causes damage to production, it would be difficult for an employer to detect, which could lead to costly damages to the organisation. System malfunction can also cause a similar effect if the problem is not found quickly by the production staff. And due to the complexity of the production system in Industry 4.0, it is vital for technical staff to quickly detect and locate the anomaly in the system.

Because cyber-attacks can cause similar damage to the production as this type of problem, the dataset generated in this scenario can be adopted by research in both areas, and the developed algorithm may be shared as well. In our dataset, we create a scenario of a wrong part with an incorrect weight that has been produced in the previous manufacturing steps or manually loaded by the operator. This leads to the wrong product being assembled in production. Table 3 describes each type of attack and the respective attacking tools.

5   Data Collection

5.1 Dataset Overview

As described in Sect. 3, the data is from equipment within the Symbiotic Cell, MES and one module of CP factory. Because production is a process of manufacturing products one by one and step by step, it is a discrete process. For this reason, unlike previous papers on critical infrastructure [3,4,23] which collect data continuously and over a block of time, the authors in this paper collected data using the cycle time in product production. Both physical data and network data are collected in a scenario with different setups. For example, scenario one is a normal production of four products including two temperature meters, one barometric meter and two digital boards. The whole process is around 11 min with around 3 min per product. There are four types of attacks in Table 3 and dataset in a total of eight scenarios are presented. The details of each scenario are described in Table 4. Figure 4 plots the total number of samples for network and physical datasets.

Table 3. Attacks details

Attack	Details	Attacking tools	Expected impact or attacker intent
DoS	SYN scan and ICMP: Saturate the PLC/Robot Controller/HMI/Router /MES with malicious traffic	Scapy [17]	Make HMI/smart lights/PLC inaccessible to the whole system, Manufacturing forced to stop
MITM	Use ARP spoofing to launch MITM Attack against devices. What is more, uses IP forwarding to avoid being found	Ettercap [18]	Eavesdropping Adversary intercepts in the real-time packets
Malware	Alter PLC program with Two Scenarios: a. Robot uses the wrong part in the assembly. b. UR robot's speed is changed in the production	TIA Portal	a. Wrong part is used in the production b. Reduces robot speed which affects production speed
Disgruntled employee or System malfunction causing Production anomaly	Wrong part with incorrect weight has been produced in the previous manufacturing steps or manually loaded by the operator	Manual or System malfunction	Part with wrong weight is used in the production

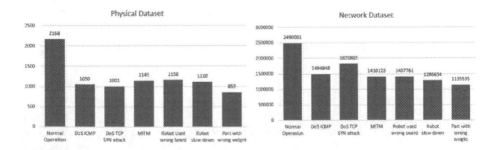

Fig. 4. Number of samples for physical and network dataset

Table 4. Datasets details

Number	Scenario	Start time	Finish time	Products
1	Normal operation	11:45:00	11:53:15	Products with one temperature meter, one barometric meter and one digital board are manufactured
2	Normal operation	3:56:58	4:06:03	Products with one temperature meter, two barometric meters and one digital board are manufactured
3	DoS ICMP attack to PLC	12:23:46	12:31:48	Products with one temperature meter, one barometric meter and one digital board are manufactured
4	DoS TCP SYN attack to PLC	12:42:06	12:50:30	Products with one temperature meter, one barometric meter and one digital board are manufactured
5	MITM	4:39.24 pm	4:48:56 pm	Products with one temperature meter, one barometric meter and one digital board are manufactured
6	Robot used wrong boards for these two products	1:03:28 pm	1:13:06 pm	Products with two temperature meters and two barometric meters
7	Slow down robot	1:54:27 pm	2:03:42 pm	One temperature meter, one barometric meter and one digital board are manufactured
8	Use part with the wrong weight	11:59:08 pm	12:06:14 pm	One temperature meter, one barometric meter and one digital board are manufactured

Physical data is collected using the logging function of Siemens PLC Tia Portal, whereas Wireshark is used to collect network data.

The data of each scenario contains the same initialisation process. This is because Wireshark needs a Profinet initialisation process to correctly dissect the packets. After data is collected, they are saved as CSV files. An extra column has been created for each set of data to characterise each record by two different labels: normal and type of attack. The final form of the dataset is in two folders, one is the original dataset and another is the processed dataset. The original data folder contains the raw physical and network data gathered in the experiment, whereas processed dataset folders contain processed datasets with labelled CSV files which can be directly fed into the ML algorithms.

Moreover, it is important to understand the distribution between normal and anomalous samples in our dataset. In Fig. 5, for the physical dataset, we summarised the proportion of labelled normal and anomalous samples in each scenario of Table 4. We can observe from Fig. 5 that there is an imbalance of sample numbers in each class. Because of a large variety of the network packets, the proportion of anomalous samples in the network dataset is much smaller. In the three scenarios of Sect. 6.2, DoS-ICMP is only 1% of the total network samples; MITM is 0.02%, and Robot-slow-down is 3.6%.

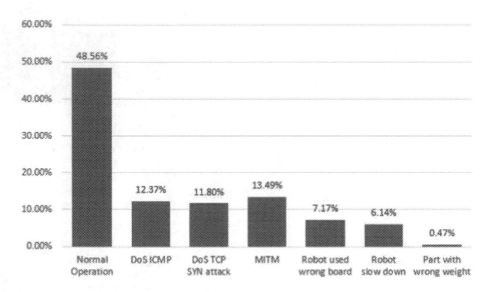

Fig. 5. Distribution between labeled normal and anomalous samples of the physical dataset

5.2   Physical Data

In our work, all the physical data was logged twice every second using Siemens PLC's internal data logging block [22] and saved into an SD card plugged into the PLC. This function allows you to store process data in CSV format. A sensor is a device to sense and measure physical values whereas actuators convert the electrical signal into physical output. In fact, the advancement of sensor technology is one of the main drivers in Industry 4.0. Table 5 below describes the physical data from different sensors and actuators. The dataset includes comprehensive data to represent the physical properties of all the devices in the Symbiotic cells.

Table 5. Physical data description

No.	Device	Name	Description
1	NA	Data	Date of acquisition
2	NA	Time	Time of acquisition
3	MES	MES_Connection	If MES has been connected to Symbiotic cell
4	Robot	Robot_Run	If Robot is in the run mode
5	Robot	Robot_Speed	Speed of Robot's moving
6	PLC	Variant number	Product variant number
7	Robot	UR_Variant_ID	ID for different products in Robot's script
8	Smart lights	Lead_op1_In	Sensor to check if Lead one light has been activated
9	Smart lights	Lead_op1_Out	Turn on Lead one light
10	Smart lights	Lead_op2_In	Sensor to check if Lead two light has been activated
11	Smart lights	Lead_op2_Out	Turn on Lead two light
12	Smart lights	Display_Light_In	Sensor to check if display module light has been activated
13	Smart lights	Display_Light_out	Turn on display module light
14	Robot	TCP_Velocity_0 TCP_Velocity_1 TCP_Velocity_2	Universal Robot Tool Center Point (TCP) Velocity
15	Robot	Joint_Velocity_0 Joint_Velocity_1 Joint_Velocity_2 Joint_Velocity_3 Joint_Velocity_4 Joint_Velocity_5	Universal Robot Joint Velocity
16	Robot	Joint_Pos_0 Joint_Pos_1 Joint_Pos_2 Joint_Pos_3 Joint_Pos_4	Universal Robot Tool joint positions
17	Robot	Joint_Current_0 Joint_Current_1 Joint_Current_2 Joint_Current_3 Joint_Current_4	Universal Robot Tool joint currents
18	Robot	TCP_Force_0 TCP_Force_1 TCP_Force_2	Universal Robot Tool Center Point (TCP) forces
19	Robot	TCP_Torque_0 TCP_Torque_1 TCP_Torque_2	Universal Robot Tool Center Point (TCP) torques

5.3   Network Data

Network traffic was captured using Wireshark software. The collection process for network traffic began when the PLC of the Symbiotic Cell is turned on. Features were extracted from the pcap file using python and saved into CSV files. As illustrated in Diagram 1, our testbed has a variety of networking devices and four different protocols that are used around Symbiotic Cell. Our dataset shows the complexity of an Industry 4.0 production line system, and each subsystem is a system itself. Both S7Comm and Profinet are proprietary industrial protocols with complicated data structure embedded in the packets. Moreover, S7CommPlus uses encryption to avoid Eavesdropping during communication, which makes it difficult to interpret the data. For this reason, in the valuation, we only take into consideration part of the information as features. Table 6 shows the parameters and formats used in the network data which we have selected for our evaluation.

Table 6. Network data description

No.	Name	Description
1	Time	Time of acquisition
2	Mac_Source	Mac address of the source
3	Mac_Destination	Mac address of the destination
4	IP_Source	IP address of the source
5	IP_Destination	IP address of the destination
6	Src_Port	Port of the source
7	Dst_Port	Port of the destination
8	Protocol	Network Protocol
9	Length	Data length

However, in the pcap files, all the data from all protocols have been presented. They can be used for future research in relation to exploring packets in a testbed with heterogeneous and encrypted protocols. It is not within the scope of this paper to dive deep into this direction.

6   Evaluation Using Machine Learning

Although machine learning has been successfully applied in areas such as computer vision and Natural Language Processing, its application in the Industry 4.0 area is still in the early stages. The dataset presented in this paper provides support to researchers in relation to the validation of machine learning algorithm. The application is mainly for intrusion and anomaly detection, but can also be extended to other areas such as predictive maintenance. In this section, we have chosen three commonly supervised learning algorithms to show the effectiveness of ML in our testbed. The three ML models we studied are: Random Forest (RF), Support Vector Machine (SVM) and Neural network (NN). Network and physical data are considered separately in our evaluation as shown in 6.1 and 6.2. Scikit-learn Python library [19] has been used to implement these models.

6.1   Evaluation Set up and Result of Physical Data

Evaluation Set up. Due to the complexity of UR robots' parameters, there are no duplicated records in the physical data. However, because manufacturing is a process of multiple steps, the anomaly only affects physical data in certain steps of the process. For example, when the cover with the wrong weight is used, it only alters the sensors' reading when the robot picks up the cover. To keep the data more accurate, when processing CSV files in this abnormal scenario, we only kept and labelled the records that have been affected by the abnormality. Furthermore, in the data gathered from DoS attacks, we applied technique to make the cycle time column of each record an average of the previous 10 readings. In this way, the readings are less affected by the noise from the system.

Because no significant numbers impact the model, no scaling has been done to the raw data. Samples for each abnormal scenario were joined with normal data to form a set of processed data. Researchers can use either the raw data or the processed dataset to validate their algorithms.

Hyper-parameters are important values that are used to control the learning process in order to obtain a model with optimal performance. Table 7 below shows the hyper-parameters in our evaluation.

Table 7. Hyperparameters

	NN	RF	SVM
Hyperparameters	Number of layers:3 Neurons per layer: 20	Number of Estimator: 20	Linear

In order to demonstrate the capacity of each algorithm, Table 8 has been defined. Because accuracy is not a good measure of evaluation for classification models, we decided to use Precision, Recall and F1-score metrics. These three metrics are used to evaluate the model's performance, and they are defined as follows:

Precision: is the fraction of the detected anomalies correctly predicted.

$$Precision = \frac{TP}{TP + FP} \tag{1}$$

Recall: is the fraction of the real anomalies are correctly detected

$$Recall = \frac{TP}{TP + FN} \tag{2}$$

where, TP = True Positive, FP = False Positive and FN = False Negative

F1-score: is the harmonic mean between recall and precision and an overall measure of a model's accuracy

$$F1\text{-}score = 2 \times \frac{Precision \times Recall}{Precision + Recall} \tag{3}$$

Result of Physical Data. Table 8 has summarised the results of Recall, Precision and F1-score for each scenario. In general, NN has the best performance of all three models; RF also shows good results except in Scenario 6; in contrast, SVM is the model that obtains the worst results.

In the scenarios on DoS attacks to PLC, all three models return better performance in Scenario 2 than 1. This fits our prediction in Sect. 3 where we show that TCP flooding affects PLC's cycle time more than ICMP attacks. Scenario 3, 4 and 5 show acceptable results for all three models. On the other hand, these algorithms do not show good result in Scenario 6. This might be because the part with the wrong weight did not create enough changes to the readings of the sensors. In fact, SVM cannot generate a result for anomaly at all and returns a value of 0 for all three metrices. Scenario 5 achieves better results as it changes the combination of some values in the PLC program which can be detected by our models.

Table 8. Physical data evaluation results

Scenarios	NN			RF			SVM		
	Recall	Precision	F1 Score	Recall	Precision	F1 Score	Recall	Precision	F1 Score
1 DoS ICMP	0.87	0.88	0.88	0.87	0.86	0.86	0.59	0.95	0.73
2 DoS TCP flooding	0.92	0.96	0.94	0.94	0.95	0.95	0.70	0.80	0.75
3 MITM	0.91	0.92	0.91	0.88	0.90	0.89	0.75	0.91	0.82
4 Slow Down Robot	0.99	1.00	1.00	1.00	1.00	1.00	0.84	0.94	0.89
5 Wrong part	0.87	0.85	0.86	0.90	1.00	0.95	0.72	0.97	0.83
6 Wrong weight	0.80	0.50	0.62	0.33	0.14	0.20	0.00	0.00	0.00

Overall, ML models applied to physical datasets in our system perform well provided that the correct physical data is collected and the anomalies are correctly labelled. Moreover, Siemens PLC has data logging capacity and all the data collected in our experiment can be conveniently set up without needing to put in additional devices. We can conclude that it is a feasible way to create tools to detect anomalies in the Industry 4.0 system using physical datasets with ML models. Our datasets will help with the validation of these techniques.

6.2   Evaluation Set Up and Result of Network Data

As discussed in Sect. 3, there are three different industrial communication protocols in our network, and one of them is encrypted. It is difficult to extract meaningful payload data because of the encryption of S7CommPlus and, what is more, the complexity and closure of proprietary communication protocols. Hence, in our evaluation, we only used some parameters and excluded payload data as described in Sect. 4. In addition, only three scenarios are selected as we believe it is enough to come to a conclusion. The same metrics and hyperparameters have been applied to each scenario at in the Table 7. Table 9 has summarised the results of network dataset.

Table 9. Network data evaluation results

Scenarios	NN			RF			SVM		
	Recall	Precision	F1 score	Recall	Precision	F1 score	Recall	Precision	F1 score
1 DoS ICMP	1.0	0.99	1.0	1.0	1.0	1.0	0.78	0.64	0.70
2 MITM	1.0	1.0	1.0	1.0	1.0	1.0	1.0	1.0	1.0
3 Slow Down Robot	0.90	0.00	0.00	0.84	0.00	0.00	0.00	0.00	0.00

We can conclude that models trained by network datasets without payload data are adequate in cyber-attack scenarios in our experiment, but they are not sufficient to identify physical anomalies. As illustrated in Table 9, the precision of all three ML models comes back to a value of Zero in scenario 3. This means no detected anomalies are correctly predicted. There are several reasons why network dataset is not fit to train machine learning models in detecting physical anomalies in an Industry 4.0 system.

1. Network dataset requires additional device to collect all the packets in the network. In our setup, a MikroTik router has been added to the system to forward all packets.
2. Although network dataset includes the current state of physical process, it is hard for the data to be extracted because of its encryption and proprietary industrial communication protocols.
3. Models that are trained by physical data perform well in predicting anomalies and cyber-attacks in our experiment. And physical dataset is easily obtained from PLC.

Moreover, in our experiment, although the models trained by network data perform well in Scenarios 1 and 2 with cyber-attacks, there are other simpler methods to detect attacks in the network traffic instead of machine learning. For example, we can defend MITM attacks by only allowing known IP addresses in the traffic. Nevertheless, our network datasets can be used as raw data to support the research of cybersecurity and anomaly detection in an Industry 4.0 system.

7   Conclusion

Industry 4.0 has already started to generate a significant impact on the current industry. The fusion of IT and OT is driving the development of smart factory, but this also makes the system more vulnerable to cyber-attacks. At the same time, this change leads to more a complicated system and it creates difficulties in detecting the anomalies in the system. We believe machine learning techniques have the potential to solve these problems. But a lack of datasets from a realistic and contemporary Industry 4.0 system is one of the main barriers to researchers. In this work, we present a dataset obtained from an Industry 4.0 system. The testbed has enough complexity to generate datasets for the purpose of cyber-security and anomaly detection research. It is comprised of a system called Symbiotic Cell and Festo Cyber Physical Factory. We created six attack scenarios and then deploy attacks to generate both network and physical datasets. In both datasets, each row has been labelled as either normal or a type of attack. Finally, experiments have been implemented to quantify the performance of three ML algorithms. Results show that ML classifiers trained by our datasets perform well in detecting all the attack types and anomalies except one scenario. On the other hand, although network data is adequate to train ML algorithms in our experiment, it is difficult to extract payload data from network data in a complicated and realistic Industry 4.0 system. In addition, cyber-attacks may not have an impact on the physical process, in which case the network dataset can complement the physical data. Hence, physical and network data can be a good combination to build a robust system in detecting attacks and anomaly.

References

1. Market and markets. https://www.marketsandmarkets.com/Market-Reports/industry-4-market-102536746.html. Accessed 4 Sep 2022
2. Deloitte. https://www2.deloitte.com/global/en/pages/real-estate/articles/future-real-estate-data-new-gold.html. Accessed 4 Sep 2022
3. Faramondi, L., Flammini, F., Guarino, S., Setola, R.: A hardware-in-the-loop water distribution testbed dataset for cyber-physical security testing. IEEE Access **9**, 122385–122396 (2021). https://doi.org/10.1109/ACCESS.2021.3109465
4. Goh, J., Adepu, S., Junejo, K., Mathur, A.: A Dataset to Support Research in the Design of Secure Water Treatment Systems (2016)
5. Laso, P., Brosset, D., Puentes, J.: Dataset of Anomalies and Malicious Acts in a Cyber-Physical Subsystem. Data in Brief, 14 (2017). https://doi.org/10.1016/j.dib.2017.07.038.

6. Biswas, P.P., Tan, H.C., Zhu, Q., Li, Y., Mashima, D., Chen, B.: A synthesized dataset for cybersecurity study of IEC 61850 based substation. In: 2019 IEEE International Conference on Communications, Control, and Computing Technologies for Smart Grids (SmartGridComm), pp. 1–7 (2019). https://doi.org/10.1109/SmartGridComm.2019.8909783

7. Ahmed, C., Kandasamy, N.K.: A Comprehensive Dataset from a Smart Grid Testbed for Machine Learning Based CPS Security Research (2021). https://doi.org/10.1007/978-3-030-69781-5_9

8. Shi, L., Chen, X., Wen, S., Xiang, Y.: Main Enabling Technologies in Industry 4.0 and Cybersecurity Threats (2020). https://doi.org/10.1007/978-3-030-37352-8_53

9. CTU-13 Dataset. https://www.stratosphereips.org/datasets-ctu13. Accessed 31 May 2022

10. Cheng, L., Donghong, L., Liang, M.: The spear to break the security wall of S7CommPlus (2017). https://media.defcon.org/DEFCON25/DEFCON25presentations/ChengLei/DEFCON-25-Cheng-Lei-The-Spear-to-Break-the-SecurityWall-of-S7CommPlus-WP.pdf. Accessed 10 Sep 2022

11. MiroTic Homepage. https://mikrotik.com/. Accessed 10 Sep 2022

12. The Real Story of Stuxnet. https://spectrum.ieee.org/the-real-story-of-stuxnet. Accessed 10 Sep 2022

13. Tia Portal: https://new.siemens.com/global/en/products/automation/industry-software/automation-software/tia-portal.html. Accessed 10 Sep 2022

14. Kumar, M.: Irongate - New Stuxnet-like Malware Targets Industrial Control Systems (2016). https://thehackernews.com/2016/06/irongate-stuxnet-malware.html. Accessed 10 Sep 2022

15. KishorWagh, S., Pachghare, V., Kolhe, S.: Survey on intrusion detection system using machine learning techniques. Int. J. Comput. App. **78**, 30–37 (2013). https://doi.org/10.5120/13608-1412

16. KDD Cup 99 Dataset. http://kdd.ics.uci.edu/databases/kddcup99/kddcup99.html. Accessed 10 Sep 2022

17. Scapy homepage. https://scapy.net/. Accessed 10 Sep 2022

18. Ettercap Scapy homepage. https://www.ettercap-project.org/. Accessed 10 Sep 2022

19. Ettercap Scapy homepage. https://scikit-learn.org/stable/. Accessed 10 Sep 2022

20. Carlsson, T.: Industrial networks keep growing despite challenging times (2022). https://www.hms-networks.com/news-and-insights/news-from-hms/2022/05/02/industrial-networks-keep-growing-despite-challenging-times. Accessed 10 Sep 2022

21. Dias, A.L., Sestito, G.S., Turcato, A.C., Brandão, D.: Panorama, challenges and opportunities in PROFINET protocol research. In: 2018 13th IEEE International Conference on Industry Applications (INDUSCON, pp. 186–193 (2018). https://doi.org/10.1109/INDUSCON.2018.8627173

22. Siemens: Recording and monitoring process data (2020). https://support.industry.siemens.com/cs/attachments/64396156/64396156_S7-1x00_DataLogging_DOC_V4.0_en.pdf. Accessed 10 Sep 2022

23. Gomez, A.L., et al.: On the generation of anomaly detection datasets in industrial control systems. IEEE Access **7**, 177460–177473 (2019). https://doi.org/10.1109/ACCESS.2019.2958284

Privacy-Preserving Machine Learning Protocols and Systems

The Force of Compensation, a Multi-stage Incentive Mechanism Model for Federated Learning

Han Xu$^{1(\boxtimes)}$ ⓘ, Priyadarsi Nanda^{1} ⓘ, Jie Liang^{1} ⓘ, and Xiangjian He^{2} ⓘ

^{1} University of Technology Sydney, 15 Broadway, Ultimo, NSW 2007, Australia
han.xu@student.uts.edu.au, {priyadarsi.nanda,jie.liang}@uts.edu.au
^{2} University of Nottingham Ningbo China, 199 Taikang East Road, Yinzhou District Ningbo 315104, Zhejiang Province, China
Sean.He@nottingham.edu.cn

Abstract. In federated learning, data owners 'provide' their local data to model owners to train a mature model in a privacy-preserving way. A critical factor in the success of a federated learning scheme is an optimal incentive mechanism that motivates all participants to fully contribute. However, the privacy protection inherent to federated learning creates a dual ethical risk problem in that there is information asymmetry between the two parties, so neither side's effort is observable. Additionally, there is often an implicit cost associated with the effort contributed to training a model, which may lead to self-interested, opportunistic behaviour on both sides. Existing incentive mechanisms have not addressed this issue. Hence, in this paper, we analyse how dual ethical risk affects the performance of federated learning schemes. We also derive an optimal multi-stage contract-theoretic incentive mechanism that minimises this risk, and experiment with calculating an optimal incentive contract for all participants. To our best knowledge, this is the first time that dual ethical risk for federated learning participants has been discussed. It is also the first time that an optimal incentive mechanism to overcome this issue has been developed.

Keywords: Federated learning · Ethical risk · Incentive mechanism

1 Introduction

In this era of AI, more and more complex applications based on machine learning are being introduced into our daily lives. It is now possible to train a highly accurate machine learning model by feeding it vast amounts of real-world data. However, we are also in an era with an emphasis on privacy protection, and various privacy protection regulations around the world, such as the GDPR in the EU [3], restrict data sharing. This creates a significant problem for machine learning where training a well-performing model invariably means accessing private data - and lots of it. In this context, federated learning, an inherently private

This research is supported by Australian Research Council's Linkage grant.

X. Yuan et al. (Eds.): NSS 2022, LNCS 13787, pp. 357–373, 2022.
https://doi.org/10.1007/978-3-031-23020-2_20

learning scheme introduced by Google in 2016 [6–8], has received much attention. With federated learning, participants train a model collaboratively without ever needing to expose their sensitive raw data. An initialised global model is distributed to the data owners (clients) via a federated learning server, and each client trains the model locally using its own private data. Only the updated parameters of the model are then uploaded to the server for aggregation. After the uploaded parameters have been integrated, the server sends the updated model back to the clients for further training. This process is repeated until the accuracy of the model reaches its target.

In the years since 2016, the concept of federated learning has been expanded to include horizontal federated learning, vertical federated learning, and federated migrated learning [13], while the participants fall into two groups: the model owners and the data owners. The architecture of a simple federated learning scheme is shown in Fig. 1. The data owners consume their resources to collect, clean and process large quantities of qualified training data. They also provide the computational and communication resources required for local training. The model owners consume resources throughout the training process for parameter integration, model tuning, optimisation, and more. Thus, an incentive mechanism is needed to compensate both parties for the resources consumed and to motivate them to collaborate. To maximise performance, both parties need to contribute their resources to the fullest degree. However, the privacy-preserving mechanisms within the federated learning paradigm creates information asymmetry between the participants causing a double ethical risk problem where neither side's effort is observable. In addition, there is often a cost associated with the effort, which may lead to self-interested, opportunistic behaviour on both sides given the disparity of interests and the information asymmetry. Consider a practical example: a medical association with several hospital members wants to work with a company that specialises in image recognition to build an automated CT image recognition model that can label suspected lung cancer nodules in CT images. The medical association cannot observe how much effort the model provider puts into the training, and nor can the model provider observe whether the healthcare association is putting enough effort into collecting and processing high-quality/quantity training data. Both parties can only directly observe the training results at particular stages. As such, there is a double ethical risk in this kind of federated learning case.

Much work has been done on different aspects of incentive mechanisms for federated learning - work that can be found in some of the recently published state-of-art surveys [16,17]. Currently, most reward-based incentive mechanisms focus on model owner-led reward schemes. These are typically designed to maximise federated learning outcomes for model owners, while minimising the incentives offered to the data owners. However, to the best of our knowledge, the issue of dual ethical risk in federated learning has not been addressed. Hence, in this paper, we propose an incentive mechanism that differs from the status quo. In our mechanism, the data owners are Stackelberg game leaders, which address the above dual ethical risk. Our focus is on the ethical risk problems with federated

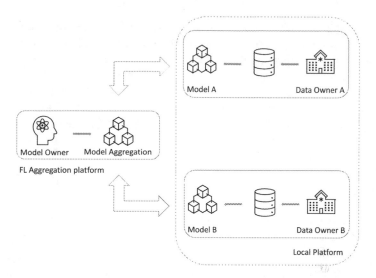

Fig. 1. Client-server architecture FL Model

learning, i.e., how to gauge the implicit efforts of both groups of participants and how this problem might be countered using multi-stage game theory. This is our focus because the implicit efforts targeted by our incentive mechanism are highly significant to the success of federated learning schemes.

To this end, our research examines the game between data owners and model owners within a federated learning process, where the efforts of neither party are directly observable. The solution involves a multi-stage incentive mechanism designed for two parties, where the incentive contract is defined before the start of training.

Our contribution to the literature is insight into an optimal multi-stage incentive contract and an endogenous optimal payoff point description. More specifically, this article shows that the optimal scheme for the data owner who leads the incentive contract should, to the extent possible, return all later stages incentive payments to the model owner.

The remainder of the paper is structured as follows. Section 2 reviews the existing incentive mechanisms for federated learning. Section 3 presents the incentive mechanism model used in our research and the results, and Sect. 4 provides a simulation example to validate the model. Finally, conclusions and future work are drawn in Sect. 5.

2   Related Works

This section positions our research within the existing literature by reviewing relevant studies on incentive mechanisms for federated learning.

When implementing federated learning, participants are often reluctant to participate in training a model unless they receive some benefit for doing so. This is because contributing to a model's training can be a highly resource-intensive undertaking. In addition, an information asymmetry exists between the data owners and the model owners. Thus, a well-designed incentive mechanism can be crucial to the success of federated learning. Such a mechanism is needed to encourage collaboration between all participants and reduces the potentially damaging effects of information asymmetry. For the best possible outcome, the incentive mechanism needs to determine the optimal level of participation and rewards for all parties to keep everyone involved motivated and engaged. Optimisation problems, such as utility maximisation, are all about deriving the best strategy.

Incentive mechanisms typically consist of two phases: contribution assessment and reward allocation. [12] The main contribution assessment strategies are:

- Self-declared contribution assessment. A self-declared contribution assessment is a direct way for data owners to report their contributions to the model owner. Data size and computational resource capacity are among the many metrics used to evaluate the self-declared contribution of a data owner [4].
- Shapley value contribution assessment. Shapley value [9] is a method of utility assessment based on marginal contributions. One of the advantages of this strategy is that it eliminates the effect of the order in which the participants joined the 'collective' in order to calculate a fairer estimate of their marginal contribution. Therefore, payoffs are calculated purely from the contributions provided regardless of sequencing for a fairer distribution of rewards. It is most common in cooperative games. Many recent studies have discussed the assessment of data owner contributions based on Shapley values and its refinement [5, 10].

After assessing the contribution of the data owners, the model owners should allocate the two types of rewards to data owners to maintain and/or increase their participation level.

- Offer rewards. Model owners can reward data owners before training. The payoffs can be determined by the quality of the resources provided [18] or the outcome of a vote [11].
- Share profits. In this scenario, the model owner shares the profits that the model has generated with the data owners after the model has been trained. In these situations, payoff delays may affect the participant's likelihood to contribute. However, a reward-sharing scheme [14, 15] allows for a given budget to be divided dynamically.

3   The Multi-stage Incentive Mechanism Model

To ensure the success in federated learning and allow for the best training result, it is crucial to implement an effective incentive mechanism that minimises the possibility of dual ethical risk. Based on the discussion in the previous section, no existing incentive mechanism has suitably addressed this issue. This section introduces a multi-stage incentive mechanism model based on contract theory. It addresses the dual ethical risks associated with federated learning while incentivising both parties to cooperate successfully. Note that, for simplicity, the game assumes one data owner and one model owner. A contract-theoretic solution for federated learning scenarios with more than one data owner is left to future work.

3.1   The Model

The two participants in our model, the data owner and the model owner, are risk-neutral. Both parties agree that the entire training process will be conducted in K stages, with both parties jointly checking the training results at the end of each stage to confirm that the training was successful. Additionally, both parties agree that the contract cannot be ended earlier than these K stages unless the training fails. We assume that the effort value committed by the data owner at stage k is De_k, and the effort value committed by the model owner at stage k is Me_k. De_k and Me_k are both uncorrelated variables. Furthermore, $De_k \geq 0, Me_k \geq 0$.

Table 1 lists the notations commonly used in this paper for ease of reference.

Table 1. Commonly used notations

Notation	Description
k	Training stages, $k = 1, \cdots K$.
Me_k	The effort committed by the model owner at stage k
De_k	The effort committed by the data owner at stage k
$P_k(Me_k, De_k)$	The probability of successful training at stage k
$C(Me_k)$	The effort cost of the model owner at stage k
$C(De_k)$	The effort cost of the data owner at stage k
V_k	The incremental value of the model after stage k
M_k	The market value of the model at stage k
I_k	The data owner's costs at stage k
DR_k	Total expected revenue of the data owner from stage k to K
MR_k	Total expected revenue of the model owner from stage k to K
R_k	The reward received by the model owner if training success at stage k
$X_k(Me_k, De_k)$	The model's performance at stage k
ϕ, ν	The weight parameters of the model at stage k

Naturally, the performance of a model, e.g., the accuracy of its inferences, will be higher if the data owner contributes more effort to providing more and higher quality data. Similarly, if the model owner puts in more effort, such as improving the algorithm, model performance will also increase. The model's performance is assumed to be

$$X_k(Me_k, De_k) = 1 - e^{-\phi(Me_k, De_k)^\nu},$$

where ϕ and ν are the weight parameters.

Figure 2 shows the relationship between the performance of a typical federation learning model and the effort values Me and De of the training participants.

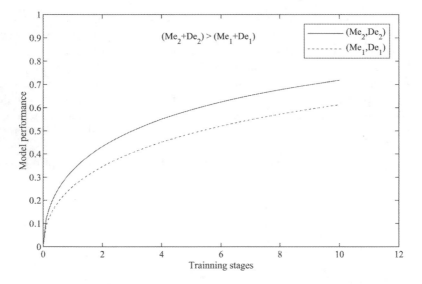

Fig. 2. Federated machine learning performance

The following assumptions are made over the probability that training at stage k will be successful:

$$P_k(Me_k, De_k),$$

and

$$1 \geq P_k(Me_k, De_k) \geq 0, \frac{\partial P_k(Me_k, De_k)}{\partial Me_k} > 0, \frac{\partial P_k(Me_k, De_k)}{\partial De_k} > 0,$$

$$\frac{\partial^2 P_k(Me_k, De_k)}{\partial Me_k{}^2} < 0, \frac{\partial^2 P_k(Me_k, De_k)}{\partial De_k{}^2} < 0, (k = 1, \cdots, K).$$

Thus, there is a positive correlation between the probability of successful training and the efforts contributed by the data and model owners. The probability of success increases as Me_k and De_k increase with diminishing marginal returns.

The cost of inputting effort by the two parties in the training stage k are $C(Me_k)$ and $C(De_k)$. Obviously, these costs increase as the effort increases, i.e., $C'(Me_k) > 0$, $C'(De_k) > 0$. Similarly, the marginal cost of effort increases as well, i.e., $C''(Me_k) > 0$, $C''(De_k) > 0$.

Suppose that federated learning is successful in stage k. In that case, the data owner receives the incremental value of the upgraded model as V_k (V_k is a constant agreed upon by both participants before the contract), and the training continues into stage $k+1$. Assuming that the model's market value at the end of stage k is M_k and the data owner's cost at stage k is I_k, we have $V_k = M_k - I_k$. After all K stages of training have been completed, the data owner receives the final value of the model as $\sum_{k=1}^{K} V_k = \sum_{k=1}^{K}(M_k - I_k)$.

DR_k and MR_k are defined as the total expected revenues of the data owner and model owner from stage k to K. Logically, the data owner will only participate in training if they believe that the total expected revenue will be positive. If the total expected revenue in stages k to K turns out to be a loss, the data owner will drop out at any stage from $k + 1$ to K and terminate the contract. Therefor, we can assume that $V_k + DR_{k+1} > 0$ and $DR_k \geq 0$. This assumption is reasonable because it assumes that the parties have some opportunity to argue success or failure at each stage. If the data owner expects a negative payoff, they will claim failure to get out of the contract. It is assumed that before a particular point in the training $V_k < 0$, i.e., the data owner's contribution is more significant than the benefit. After that point, the data owner's payoff becomes positive. This assumption ensures that the data owner agrees to cooperate with the model owner for the purposes of training the model. R_k represents the reward given by the data owner to the model owner if the training is successful at stage k. The event sequence in the contract is shown in Fig. 3.

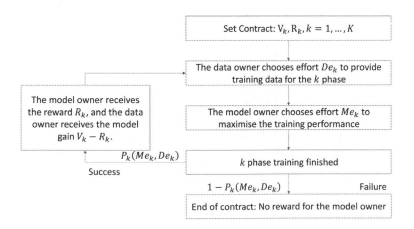

Fig. 3. Contract execution stages

Before entering the federated learning scheme, the data owner and the model owner need to agree on the reward $R_k > 0$ $(k = 1, \cdots, K)$ and set up the contract. The model owner receives R_k from the data owner after training is confirmed to be successful in stage k. According to the contract, the model owner commits the optimal level of effort $Me_k{}^*$ to maximise their expected return MR_k. At the same time, the data owner also to commit the optimal level of effort $De_k{}^*$ to maximise DR_k. If the training result is successful at the end of stage k, the value of the updated model held by the data owner increases by V_k, and the model owner receives the reward R_k from the data owner. Training then proceeds to the next stage. If stage k training fails, both the model owner and the data owner gain nothing for that stage. Note that the optimal strategy for the Stackelberg game leader is to not reward the follower for failure at each stage of the game [1,2]. Both parties will pay $C(Me_k)$ and $C(De_k)$ regardless of success or failure. Thus, the following recursive equation describes the profit of the data owner and the model owner,

$$MR_k = P_k(Me_k, De_k)[R_k + MR_{k+1}] - C(Me_k) \tag{1}$$

and

$$DR_k = P_k(Me_k, De_k)[V_k - R_k + DR_{k+1}] - C(De_k), k = 1, \cdots, K. \tag{2}$$

In our model, the contract is set before the first phase. The relevant payoffs in the first phase are DR_1 for the data owner and MR_1 for the model owner. Note that the payoff for stage k is directly effected by the payoffs for stage $k+1$. Expanding the above recursive equations, we have:

$$MR_m = \sum_{k=m}^{K} \left\{ \prod_{j=m}^{k} P_j(Me_j, De_j) R_k \right\} \\ - \sum_{k=m}^{K} \left\{ \prod_{j=m}^{k-1} P_j(Me_j, De_j) C(Me_k) \right\} \tag{3}$$

and

$$DR_m = \sum_{k=m}^{K} \left\{ \prod_{j=m}^{k} P_j(Me_j, De_j)(V_k - R_k) \right\} \\ - \sum_{k=m}^{K} \left\{ \prod_{j=m}^{k-1} P_j(Me_j, De_j) C(De_k) \right\}. \tag{4}$$

3.2   Research Findings

In this section, we outline the findings of the above model, beginning with the optimal effort $De_k{}^*$ of the data owner.

The derivative of the data owner's payoff with respect to their effort De_k from Eq. 2 is

$$\frac{dDR_k}{dDe_k} = \frac{dP_k(Me_k, De_k)}{dDe_k}(V_k - R_k + DR_{k+1}) - \frac{dC(De_k)}{dDe_k}$$

$$= 0 \quad (k = 1, \cdots, K),$$

(5)

where

$$\frac{dP_k(Me_k, De_k)}{dDe_k}(V_k - R_k + DR_{k+1}) = \frac{dC(De_k)}{dDe_k} \quad (k = 1, \cdots, K).$$

(6)

Thus, the optimal effort $De_k{}^*$ of the data owner is:

$$De_k{}^* = De_k{}^*(V_k - R_k + DR_{k+1}).$$

(7)

Corollary 1. *The optimal effort of the data owner is a function of the incremental value of the model, the reward to the model owner, and the data owner's expectation of future payoffs. Reducing the reward to the model owner and increasing the incremental value of the model and the data owner's expectations for the future should motivate the data owner to put in more effort and reduce their ethical risk.*

In the same way, we can solve the optimal effort $Me_k{}^*$ of the model owner. The derivative of the model owner's payoff with respect to it's effort Me_k from Eq. 1 is

$$\frac{dMR_k}{dMe_k} = \frac{dP_k(Me_k, De_k{}^*)}{dMe_k}(R_k + MR_{k+1}) - \frac{dC(Me_k)}{dMe_k}$$

$$= 0 \quad (k = 1, \cdots, K).$$

(8)

Thus, the optimal effort $Me_k{}^*$ of the model owner is:

$$Me_k{}^* = Me_k{}^*(R_k + MR_{k+1}).$$

(9)

Corollary 2. *The optimal effort level of the model owner is positively correlated with the reward and their expected future payoff. Higher rewards from the data owner and increasing the model owner's future expectations should motivate the model owner to work harder and reduce any ethical risks.*

Based on Corollaries 1 and 2, we have the following conditions:

$$
\begin{cases}
\frac{dP_k(Me_k, De_k)}{dDe_k}(V_k - R_k + DR_{k+1}) = \frac{dC(De_k)}{dDe_k}; \\
\frac{dP_k(Me_k, De_k)}{dMe_k}(R_k + MR_{k+1}) = \frac{dC(Me_k)}{dMe_k} \quad (k = 1, \cdots, K).
\end{cases}
\tag{10}
$$

Corollary 3. *An optimal incentive mechanism should be such that the marginal benefit of each participant's effort equals their marginal cost.*

Given the optimal level of effort $Me_k{}^*$ and $De_k{}^*$ for the model owner and data owner, MR_m in Eq. 3 satisfies the following conditions:

$$
\frac{\partial MR_m}{\partial R_k} = \prod_{j=m}^{k} P_j(Me_j{}^*, De_j{}^*) \quad (k = 1, \cdots, K; m \le k).
\tag{11}
$$

From Eq. 11,

$$
\frac{\frac{\partial MR_1}{\partial R_k}}{\frac{\partial MR_1}{\partial R_{k+1}}} = \frac{\prod_{j=1}^{k} P_j(Me_j{}^*, De_j{}^*)}{\prod_{j=1}^{k+1} P_j(Me_j{}^*, De_j{}^*)} = \frac{1}{P_{k+1}(Me_{k+1}{}^*, De_{k+1}{}^*)} > 1
\tag{12}
$$

$$
(k = 1, \cdots, K - 1).
$$

Then

$$
\left. \frac{\partial MR_1}{\partial R_k} \right|_{Me_j{}^*, De_j{}^*} > \left. \frac{\partial MR_1}{\partial R_{k+1}} \right|_{Me_j{}^*, De_j{}^*} \quad (k = 1, \cdots, K - 1).
\tag{13}
$$

Corollary 4. *The marginal utility of the rewards diminishes for the model owner over time. Therefore, to encourage the model owner to increase their effort, the rewards for the model owner in the incentive mechanism should be gradually increased as training continues. This should mean the incentive mechanism stays effective in motivating the model owner to work hard.*

The optimal incentive $R_k{}^* > 0$ $(k = 1, \cdots, K)$ for the model owner is determined before starting the first stage of training. Therefore, the optimal payoff $R_k{}^*$ of the data owner can also be solved. The first-order condition of data owner with respect to payoff R_k from Eq. 2 is

$$
\left. \frac{\partial DR_1}{\partial R_k} \right|_{R_i{}^*, i=1, \cdots, K} = \left[P_1{}'(Me_1{}^*, De_1{}^*)Me_1{}^{*\prime} \frac{\partial MR_2}{\partial R_k} \right.
$$

$$
\left. + P_1{}'(Me_1{}^*, De_1{}^*)De_1{}^{*\prime} \frac{\partial DR_2}{\partial R_k} \right] (V_1 - R_1 + DR_2)
$$

$$
+ P_1(Me_1{}^*, De_1{}^*) \frac{\partial DR_2}{\partial R_k} - C'(De_1^*)De_1^{*\prime} \frac{\partial DR_2}{\partial R_k} = 0.
\tag{14}
$$

From Corollary 4, we can derive $\frac{\partial MR_2}{\partial R_k} = \prod_{j=2}^k P_j(Me_j^*, De_j^*)$ and from Corollary 1, we can derive $P_1'(Me_1^*, De_1^*)(V_1 - R_1 + DR_2) - C'(De_1^*) = 0, V_1 - R_1 + DR_2 > 0$. Substituting both of these into Eq. 14 and rearranging the terms yield:

$$\{De_1^{*\prime}[P_1'(Me_1^*, De_1^*)(V_1 - R_1 + DR_2) - C'(De_1^*)] + P_1(Me_1^*, De_1^*)\}$$

$$\frac{\partial DR_2}{\partial R_k} + P_1'(Me_1^*, De_1^*)Me_1^* \left[\prod_{j=2}^k P_j(Me_j^*, De_j^*) \right] (V_1 - R_1 + DR_2) = 0.$$

$$(15)$$

Then,

$$\frac{\partial DR_2}{\partial R_k}\bigg|_{R_i^*, i=1,\cdots,K} = -\frac{1}{P_1(Me_1^*, De_1^*)} P_1'(Me_1^*, De_1^*)Me_1^{*\prime}$$

$$\left[\prod_{j=2}^k P_j(Me_j^*, De_j^*) \right] (V_1 - R_1 + DR_2) < 0.$$

$$(16)$$

Thus, if $R_k^* > 0$ and $R_j^* > 0, j > k$, then

$$\frac{\partial DR_2}{\partial R_j}\bigg|_{R_i^*, i=1,\cdots,K} = \left(\prod_{i=k+1}^j P_i(Me_i^*, De_i^*) \right) \frac{\partial DR_2}{\partial R_k}\bigg|_{R_i^*, i=1,\cdots,K}$$

$$> \frac{\partial DR_2}{\partial R_k}\bigg|_{R_i^*, i=1,\cdots,K}.$$

$$(17)$$

Corollary 5. *The expected payoff to the model owner increases marginal utility for the data owner over time. Intuitively, the data owner always wants to delay the reward to the model owner, while the model owner wants to receive the reward as early as possible. For the data owner, the later the reward is given to the model owner, the more likely it is for ethical risk to be avoided.*

From Corollary 5, for $k > 1$,

$$\frac{\partial DR_1}{\partial R_k} = \left[P_1(Me_1^*, De_1*)'Me_1^{*\prime}\frac{\partial MR_2}{\partial R_k} + P_1(Me_1^*, De_1*)'De_1^{*\prime}\frac{\partial DR_2}{\partial R_k} \right]$$

$$(V_1 - R_1 + DR_2) + P_1(Me_1^*, De_1*)\frac{\partial DR_2}{\partial R_k} - C(De_1^*)'De_1^{*\prime}\frac{\partial DR_2}{\partial R_k}.$$

$$(18)$$

For every $m < k$,

$$\frac{\partial DR_m}{\partial R_k} = \left[P_m(Me_m^*, De_m*)'Me_m^{*\prime}\frac{\partial MR_{m+1}}{\partial R_k} \right.$$

$$\left. + P_m(Me_m^*, De_m*)'De_m^{*\prime}\frac{\partial DR_{m+1}}{\partial R_k} \right] (V_m - R_m + DR_{m+1}) \quad (19)$$

$$+ P_m(Me_m^*, De_m*)\frac{\partial DR_{m+1}}{\partial R_k} - C(De_m^*)'De_m^{*\prime}\frac{\partial DR_{m+1}}{\partial R_k},$$

and for every k,

$$\frac{\partial DR_k}{\partial R_k} = [P_k(Me_k{}^*, De_k*)' Me_k^{*'} - P_k(Me_k{}^*, De_k*)' De_k^{*'}](V_k - R_k + DR_{k+1})$$
$$- P_k(Me_k{}^*, De_k*) + C(De_m{}^*)' De_k^{*'}. \tag{20}$$

From Corollary 1, we can derive $P_k(Me_k{}^*, De_k*)'(V_k - R_k + DR_{k+1}) - C(De_k)^{*'} = 0$, and substituting this into the three equations above, we have

$$\frac{\partial DR_1}{\partial R_k} = \left(\prod_{j=1}^{k} P_j(Me_j{}^*, De_j{}^*) \right) \sum_{i=1}^{k} \frac{1}{P_i(Me_i{}^*, De_i{}^*)}$$
$$P_i'(Me_i{}^*, De_i{}^*) Me_i{}^*[V_i - R_i + DR_{i+1}] - \prod_{j=1}^{k} P_j(Me_j{}^*, De_j{}^*), \tag{21}$$

and

$$\frac{\partial DR_1}{\partial R_{k+1}} = \frac{\partial DR_1}{\partial R_k} P_{k+1}(Me_{k+1}{}^*, De_{k+1}{}^*)$$
$$+ \left(\prod_{j=1}^{k} P_j(Me_j{}^*, De_j{}^*) \right) P_{k+1}'(Me_{k+1}{}^*, De_{k+1}{}^*) \tag{22}$$
$$Me_{k+1}^{*'}[V_{k+1} - R_{k+1} + DR_{k+2}] = 0 \quad (k = 1, \cdots, K-1).$$

Since $\frac{\partial DR_1}{\partial R_k}\big|_{R_i{}^*, i=1,\cdots,K} = 0$, from Eq. 22, we can derive $V_{k+1} - R_{k+1} + DR_{k+2} = 0$. It is known that $DR_{K+1} = 0$, so it follows that $R_K{}^* = V_K$, so $DR_K = 0$. Similarly, for any δ, there is $1 \le \delta \le K - 1$. If $Me_\delta{}^* > 0$ and $R_\delta{}^* > 0$, then:

$$\begin{cases} R_k{}^* = V_k & (k = \delta+1, \cdots, K). \\ DR_k = 0 & (k = \delta+1, \cdots, K). \end{cases} \tag{23}$$

Then,

$$DR_1 = \sum_{j=1}^{\delta-1} \left(\prod_{i=1}^{j} P_i(Me_i{}^*, De_i{}^*)(V_j - C(De_i{}^*)) \right)$$
$$+ \left(\prod_{i=1}^{\delta-1} P_i(Me_i{}^*, De_i{}^*) \right) P_\delta(Me_\delta{}^*, De_\delta{}^*)[V_\delta - R_\delta]. \tag{24}$$

Theorem 1. *The data owner can receive their optimal payoff at point δ during training such that*

$$\begin{cases} R_k{}^* = 0 & (k < \delta), \\ R_k{}^* = V_k{}^*, DR_k{}^* = 0 & (k > \delta), \end{cases} \tag{25}$$

and

$$\begin{cases} DR_1 \geq \sum_{j=1}^{\delta-1} \left(\prod_{i=1}^{j} P_i(Me_i{}^*, De_i{}^*)(V_j - C(De_j{}^*)) \right), \\ DR_1 \leq \sum_{j=1}^{\delta} \left(\prod_{i=1}^{j} P_i(Me_i{}^*, De_i{}^*)(V_j - C(De_j{}^*)) \right). \end{cases} \tag{26}$$

Theorem 1 shows an optimal payoff point for the data owner, where the data owner receives the total payoff from the federated learning process and the reward given to the model owner is zero in phases $1 - \delta$. However, after that point, the data owner does not have any profit, the expected future payoffs are zero, and the benefit goes entirely to the model owner. Thus, point δ is the optimal payoff point for the data owner. Essentially, what Theorem 1 indicates is that, for a federated learning scenario initiated by the data owner, the optimal incentive scheme is one where as much of the incremental value of the model as possible is paid to the model owner. Therefore, success in the later stages of training is based on the success in the earlier stages and, in turn, rewards in the later stages incentivise effort in the earlier stages. Overall, giving back as much of the value created by the model owner's efforts as possible in the later stages is the least costly incentive scheme for the data owner.

4   Experimental Evaluation

To complement the analytical findings and evaluate the performance of our incentive mechanism for federated learning, we create a multi-stage contract simulator for the data and model owners. The simulator evaluates the impact of different reward settings on the level of effort contributed by each participant and gives the total payoff for both parties.

4.1   Experiment Settings

Assume that the incremental model values are $V_1 = 1, V_2 = 2$ and $V_3 = 3$, where federated learning is carried out in 3 stages (i.e., $K = 3$) and the functional expression for the probability of success at each stage is $P_k(Me_k, De_k) = MIN(0.6(Me_k + De_k), 1)$. As we will see later, the equilibrium effort satisfies $0.6(Me_k{}^* + De_k{}^*) < 1$, so we can count $P_k(Me_k, De_k) = 0.6(Me_k + De_k)$. We also assume that the effort cost of the model owner's function is $C(Me_k) = Me_k{}^2$, and the effort cost of the data owner's function is $C(De_k) = De_k{}^2$, such that the utility function of the model owner is

$$mr_k = 0.6(Me_k + De_k)(R_k + mr_{k+1}) - Me_k{}^2, \quad k = 1, 2, 3,$$
$$mr_4 = 0.$$

Taking the utility function for each stage and deriving it to its effort level determines the optimal effort yield for the model owner:

$$Me_k{}^* = \frac{\partial mr_k}{\partial Me_k} = 0.3(R_k + mr_{k+1}) \quad k = 1, 2, 3.$$

Repeating the same approach, and its based on Eq. 24, we can derive the utility function of the data owner and their optimal effort:

$$dr_k = 0.6(Me_k + De_k)(V_k - R_k + dr_{k+1}) - De_k{}^2, \quad k = 1, 2, 3,$$
$$dr_3 = 0, dr_4 = 0.$$
$$De_k{}^* = \frac{\partial dr_k}{\partial De_k} = 0.3(V_k - R_k + dr_{k+1}) \quad k = 1, 2, 3,$$
$$De_3 = 0.$$

The utility functions and the optimal efforts of the two parties in different stages are listed in Table 2.

Table 2. The utility functions and the optimal efforts, $K = 3$

K	Data owner	Model owner
1	$dr_1 = 0.6(Me_1 + De_1)(V_1 - R_1 + dr_2) - De_1{}^2$ $De_1 = 0.3(V_1 - R_1 + dr_2)$	$mr_1 = 0.6(Me_1 + De_1)(R_1 + mr_2)$ $Me_1 = 0.3(R_1 + mr_2)$
2	$dr_2 = 0.6(Me_2 + De_2)(V_2 - R_2 + dr_3) - De_2{}^2$ $De_2 = 0.3(V_2 - R_2 + dr_3)$	$mr_2 = 0.6(Me_2 + De_2)(R_2 + mr_3)$ $Me_2 = 0.3(R_2 + mr_3)$
3	$dr_3 = 0$ $De_3 = 0$	$mr_3 = 0.6(Me_3 + De_3)(R_3 + mr_4)$ $mr_4 = 0, Me_3 = 0.3(R_3 + mr_3)$

4.2   Experimental Result and Discussion

Figure 4 shows the optimal rewards yielded for the model owner, calculated by recurring the above equations in Table 2 and the derivative of the data owner's payoff dr_1 with respect to the reward $R_2{}^*$:

$$R_1{}^* = 0, R_2{}^* = 0.4085, R_3{}^* = 3,$$

where the probabilities of successes are $P_1(Me_1{}^*, De_1{}^*) = 0.3707, P_2(Me_2{}^*, De_2{}^*) = 0.5058, P_3(Me_3{}^*, De_3{}^*) = 0.54$. As predicted by Theorem 1, the optimal

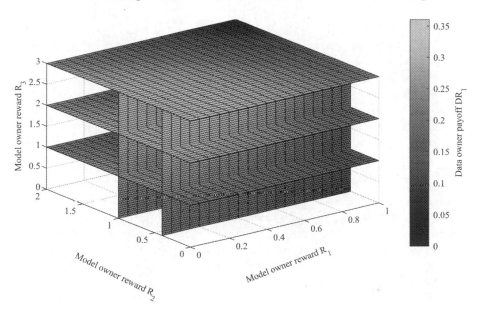

Fig. 4. The optimal rewards yielded for the model owner

payoff point for the data owner is $\delta = 2$, and $R_1{}^* = 0, R_3* = V_3$, and $0 < R_2 < V_2$. The data owner's expected payoff is $dr_1 = 0.3608$, which is consistent with Theorem 1,

$$\begin{cases} dr_1 \geq P_1(Me_1{}^*, De_1{}^*)(V_1 - De_1{}^2) = 0.2878, \\ dr_1 \leq P_1(Me_1{}^*, De_1{}^*)(V_1 - De_1{}^2) + P_2(Mc_2{}^*, De_2{}^*)(V_2 - De_2{}^2) = 1.1841. \end{cases}$$

Table 3. The reward settings vs the best efforts of each stage

Reward settings	DO expected payoff dr_1	Stg1 BEs $Me_1 + De_1$	Stg2 BEs $Me_2 + De_2$	Stg3 BEs $Me_3 + De_3$
$R_1 = 0, R_2 = 0.2, R_3 = 3$	0.3508	0.6114	0.843	0.9
$R_1{}^* = 0, R_2{}^* = 0.4085, R_3{}^* = 3$	*0.3608*	*0.6179*	*0.843*	*0.9*
$R_1 = 0, R_2 = 1, R_3 = 3$	0.3386	0.6109	0.843	0.9
$R_1 = 0.5, R_2 = 0.4085, R_3 = 3$	0.2949	0.6179	0.843	0.9

We have taken some relevant data from the simulator to make it easier to understand, as shown in Table 3. This table shows the effects of the reward value settings at different stages on the efforts of the participants and the expected payoff for the data owner in the incentive contract. Some settings around the optimal one have been selected as comparisons: $R_1{}^* = 0, R_2{}^* = 0.4085, R_3{}^* = 3$. From the results, we can see that:

1. Any deviation from the optimal value of $R_2{}^* = 0.4085$ negatively impacts the efforts of both participants and the expected training payoff for the data owner. This means that any reward setting that deviates from the optimal value $R_2{}^*$ will increase the ethical risk of the participants.
2. If the data owner keeps $R_2 = R_2{}^*$ and increases the reward R_1 for stage 1, this scenario is identical to the optimal incentive scenario in terms of the effort values at each stage. However, the data owner's expected training payoffs will be significantly lower. From a self-interested perspective by the data owner, as the leader of the incentive contract, there is no incentive to increase the reward given to the model owner at Stage 1.

Thus, we can conclude that our model is able to reduce the dual ethical risk of federated learning due to information asymmetry. It can motivate the participants to exert an optimized effort to training, confirming the intuition behind our model that the success in the later stages is based on success in the earlier stages. Thus, rewards in the later stages incentivise efforts in the earlier stages. Moreover, giving back as much of the value created by the model owner's efforts in the later stages is the least costly incentive scheme for the data owner.

5   Conclusion and Future Works

In this paper, we have used the framework of a dynamic game to investigate the dual ethical risk problem between model owners and data owners in federated learning. The model used is novel and it has derived optimal incentive payoff contracts for the data and model owners through two sets of analyses: one for a multi-stage incentive payoff game and the other for the dual ethical risk affecting the contract design. The output is an optimal payoff point for the data owners. Our approach has provided insights into the characteristics of optimal incentive contracts between data owners and model owners in federated learning schemes, including their endogenous optimality. Specifically, our study has shown that, for a federated learning scenario initiated by the data owner, the optimal incentive scheme is one where as much of the incremental value of the model as possible is paid to the model owner. There could be several possible extensions of this paper, which requires further research in this field. First, we explored the dual ethical risk problem in the data owner-led federated learning scenario using a multi-stage incentive model. Further work will extend this model in other scenarios and can be compared comprehensively with existing incentive mechanisms. Second, we negated the possibility of multiple data owners to treat them as a single entity. It would be interesting to consider multi-data owners joining the game at different stages as a possible extension to our proposed model. The third extension of this paper would be to investigate how the efforts of model and data owners with fair preferences in the later stages of cooperation (based on fair preference theory) are affected by the value of benefits and new compensation schemes.

References

1. Bergemann, D., Hege, U.: Venture capital financing, moral hazard, and learning. J. Banking Financ. **22**(6–8), 703–735 (1998)
2. Elitzur, R., Gavious, A.: A multi-period game theoretic model of venture capitalists and entrepreneurs. Eur. J. Oper. Res. **144**(2), 440–453 (2003)
3. European Parliament, C.o.t.E.U.: Guide to the general data protection regulation (2018). https://www.gov.uk/government/publications/guide-to-the-general-data-protection-regulation
4. Feng, S., Niyato, D., Wang, P., Kim, D.I., Liang, Y.C.: Joint service pricing and cooperative relay communication for federated learning. In: 2019 International Conference on Internet of Things (iThings) and IEEE Green Computing and Communications (GreenCom) and IEEE Cyber, Physical and Social Computing (CPSCom) and IEEE Smart Data (SmartData), pp. 815–820. IEEE (2019)
5. Jia, R., et al.: Towards efficient data valuation based on the Shapley value. In: The 22nd International Conference on Artificial Intelligence and Statistics, pp. 1167–1176. PMLR (2019)
6. Konečnỳ, J., McMahan, H.B., Ramage, D., Richtárik, P.: Federated optimization: Distributed machine learning for on-device intelligence. arXiv preprint arXiv:1610.02527 (2016)
7. Konečnỳ, J., McMahan, H.B., Yu, F.X., Richtárik, P., Suresh, A.T., Bacon, D.: Federated learning: Strategies for improving communication efficiency. arXiv preprint arXiv:1610.05492 (2016)
8. McMahan, H.B., Moore, E., Ramage, D., y Arcas, B.A.: Federated learning of deep networks using model averaging. arXiv preprint arXiv:1602.05629 (2016)
9. Nowak, A.S., Radzik, T.: The Shapley value for n-person games in generalized characteristic function form. Games Econom. Behav. **6**(1), 150–161 (1994)
10. Sim, R.H.L., Zhang, Y., Chan, M.C., Low, B.K.H.: Collaborative machine learning with incentive-aware model rewards. In: International Conference on Machine Learning, pp. 8927–8936. PMLR (2020)
11. Toyoda, K., Zhang, A.N.: Mechanism design for an incentive-aware blockchain-enabled federated learning platform. In: 2019 IEEE International Conference on Big Data (Big Data), pp. 395–403. IEEE (2019)
12. Tu, X., Zhu, K., Luong, N.C., Niyato, D., Zhang, Y., Li, J.: Incentive mechanisms for federated learning: From economic and game theoretic perspective. IEEE Trans. Cogn. Commun. Netw. **8**, 1566–1593 (2022)
13. Yang, Q., Liu, Y., Chen, T., Tong, Y.: Federated machine learning: concept and applications. ACM Trans. Intell. Syst. Technol. (TIST) **10**(2), 1–19 (2019)
14. Yu, H., et al.: A fairness-aware incentive scheme for federated learning. In: Proceedings of the AAAI/ACM Conference on AI, Ethics, and Society, pp. 393–399 (2020)
15. Yu, H., et al.: A sustainable incentive scheme for federated learning. IEEE Intell. Syst. **35**(4), 58–69 (2020)
16. Zeng, R., Zeng, C., Wang, X., Li, B., Chu, X.: A comprehensive survey of incentive mechanism for federated learning. arXiv preprint arXiv:2106.15406 (2021)
17. Zhan, Y., Zhang, J., Hong, Z., Wu, L., Li, P., Guo, S.: A survey of incentive mechanism design for federated learning. IEEE Trans. Emerg. Top. Comput. **10**, 1035–1044 (2021)
18. Zhang, W., et al.: Blockchain-based federated learning for device failure detection in industrial IoT. IEEE Internet Things J. **8**(7), 5926–5937 (2020)

A Privacy-Preserving Distributed Machine Learning Protocol Based on Homomorphic Hash Authentication

Yang Hong[1(✉)], Lisong Wang[1], Weizhi Meng[2], Jian Cao[3], Chunpeng Ge[1], Qin Zhang[1], and Rui Zhang[1]

[1] College of Computer Science and Technology, Nanjing University of Aeronautics and Astronautics, Nanjing 211106, China
{hongyang,wangls}@nuaa.edu.cn
[2] DTU Compute, Technical University of Denmark, Lyngby, Denmark
[3] School of Cyber Science and Engineering, SouthEast University, Nanjing, China

Abstract. Privacy-preserving machine learning is a hot topic in Artificial Intelligence (AI) area. However, there are also many security issues in all stages of privacy-oriented machine learning. This paper focuses on the dilemma that the privacy leakage of server-side parameter aggregation and external eavesdropper tampering during message transmission in the distributed machine learning framework. Combining with secret sharing techniques, we present a secure privacy-preserving distributed machine learning protocol under the double-server model based on homomorphic hash function, which enables our protocol verifiable. We also prove that our protocol can meet client semi-honest security requirements. Besides, we evaluate our protocol by comparing with other mainstream privacy preserving frameworks, in the aspects of computation, communication complexity analysis, in addition to a concrete implementation from the perspective of model convergence rate and execution time. Experimental results demonstrate that the local training model tends to converge at nearly 50 epochs where the convergence time is less than 400 s.

Keywords: Privacy-preserving · Homomorphic hash function · Distributed machine learning · Secure aggregation

1 Introduction

Machine Learning has become an indispensable supporting technology for Big Data, Internet of Things (IoT), and Cloud Computing. However, the risk of privacy leakage exists in all phases of machine learning, including data acquisition, model training, and model prediction, which poses potential challenges to the state of machine learning.

How to balance the relationship between data interaction and privacy preserving has become a crucial issue. At present, researchers often adopt obfuscation and cryptography methods to fulfill these requirements. Obfuscation operation is realized by randomization, noise addition, and other differential-privacy

X. Yuan et al. (Eds.): NSS 2022, LNCS 13787, pp. 374–386, 2022.
https://doi.org/10.1007/978-3-031-23020-2_21

technologies. Cryptography methods include Secure Multi-Party Computation (SMPC) [23], Oblivious Transfer (OT) [17], Garbled Circuit (GC) [24], Secret Sharing (SS) [20] and Homomorphic Encryption (HE) [19]. Bonawitz et al. [6] proposed a practical secure aggregation scheme in Federated Learning via masking techniques, which not only enables multiple users to aggregate without leaking their privacy to the server, but also prevents dropout and delays effectively at the same time. The overhead of secure model aggregation, however, creates a major bottleneck in scaling secure federated learning to a large number of users. Bonawitz et al. [1] further replaced the complete communication graph with a k-regular graph of logarithmic degree, which enabled the linear overheads and maintain security guarantees. To break quadratic growth of secure aggregation overhead in [6], Guler and Avestimehr [22] firstly used Turbo-aggregate to reduce the overhead of secure aggregation to $O(N \log N)$ from $O(N^2)$. Based on the model of two non-colluding cryptographic servers, Gongguang et al. [14] designed an efficient aggregation scheme with non-interactive pairwise key generation method with low communication and computation overheads. Combing with additive homomorphism technique, Mandal et al. [13] handled the training task under federated learning for linear regression and logistic regression. Apart from this, it provided prediction services.

While the existing research of privacy-preserving machine learning is more concerned about optimization of communication efficiency. Another key challenge in model aggregation is tampering with messages by external eavesdroppers. Given these constraints, we are motivated to design a protocol that can not only prevent a certain percentage of clients from colluding, but also can make itself verifiable.

1.1   Our Contributions

We present a secure aggregation of gradients in distributed machine learning framework with double servers that can prevent external eavesdroppers from tampering the information. To realize its verifiability, we encrypt the gradient information with homomorphic hash function in the transferring process. Comparing the passed hash value with clients' own generated hash value can determine whether the gradient value has been tampered with. An overview of our protocol is shown in Algorithm 1, with security proof. In terms of experiment, to evaluate the performance of our protocol, we also compare the convergence rate and execution time with other secure aggregation frameworks, including Federated Learning [15] and Practical Secure Aggregation [6]. It demonstrates that our model tends to converge at nearly 50 epochs where the convergence time is less than $400s$. In addition, we demonstrate it meets client semi-honest security from the perspective of Probability Theory. Meanwhile, based on the theoretical analysis of computation and communication complexity, experimental results shows that the execution time goes up with respect to each client and server as the dataset size increases.

2   Related Work

A potential solution for secure aggregation in privacy preserving machine learning is utilizing cryptographic approaches, including multi-party computation (MPC), homomorphic encryption, or differential privacy. MPC technique mainly adopts Garbled Circuit (GC), Secret Sharing, and Oblivious transfer [17, 20, 23]. However, the bottleneck of Garbled Circuit is the high communication overhead, and requirement of offline computation [3]. Burkhart et al. [7] focused on the optimization of MPC in terms of network security and supervision. Homomorphic encryption is one cryptographic primitive that usually applied to encrypted data aggregation [18]. However, computation complexity in encryption field is another obstacle for homomorphic encryption, and simultaneously it relies on the size of encrypted data [8]. Differential privacy mainly masks the initial data by adding noise data to protect sensitive data information, which does not affect the computation outcome significantly [9]. However, this noise insertion approach entails the trade-off between privacy and accuracy.

For the parameters, secure aggregation in distributed machine learning domain, Bonawitz et al. [5] proposed the secure aggregation method. While this functionality enabled a broad range of offline computational tasks, scaling concerns limited its scope of use. Therefore, Bell et al. [1] proposed the secure aggregation achieving polylogarithmic communication and computation per client, which improved the asymptotics for secure aggregation. To solve the problem that the overhead of secure aggregation grows quadratically with the number of users [5], So et al. [22] adopted Turbo-Aggregate method with n users which achieved a secure aggregation $O(n \log n)$, as opposed to $O(n^2)$. Different from secure centralized computation, Liu et al. [12] proposed a collaborative privacy-preserving learning system based on deep learning, which cannot share local data with the servers. Shokri and Shmatikov [21] proposed a solution by sharing the model's gradients among clients during the training process via parameter servers. Nasr et al. [16] then improved the efficiency observably, while ignoring the risk of parameter leakage poses a potential threat to the model. Therefore, comparing with the existing research work, this paper mainly focuses on how to prevent parameter leakage or being eavesdropped during transferring process. Our privacy-preserving protocol adopts secret sharing scheme and achieves the verifiable property by combining it with homomorphic hash verification function.

3   Background

3.1   Secret Sharing

Shamir's Secret Sharing [20] is a powerful cryptographic primitive that enables each participant to split a secret s into n shares, such that any t can reconstruct the s, but any set of at most $t - 1$ shares gives no information about s.

Definition 1. *Shamir's Secret Sharing is composed of a Sharing algorithm S and a Reconstruct algorithm R, where* $n \geq t$.

$$S(s, t, n) \rightarrow \{< s>_0, < s>_1, \cdots, < s>_n\} \tag{1}$$

$$R(\{< s>_0, < s>_1, \cdots, < s>_n\}, t) \rightarrow s \tag{2}$$

3.2   Secret Sharing with Homomorphic Hash Authentication

Secret Sharing Scheme is effective in the semi-honest model. Simultaneously, to resist external eavesdroppers tampering with gradient information in the message transferring process, we apply the Secret Sharing into Homomorphic Hash Authentication with a global key α. Here, we simplify the $Hash$ to H.

$$S(s, H, t, n, \alpha) \rightarrow \{(< s>_0, \cdots, < s>_n), [H(\alpha, < s>_0), \cdots, H(\alpha, < s>_n)]\} \tag{3}$$

where S holds the secret s, the $Hash$ authentication H, the threshold t, a global key α and the number of servers m as input. Meanwhile, it takes the Secrets Shares with Hash Authentication shares as the output.

$$R\{(< s>_0, \cdots, < s>_n), [H(\alpha, < s>_0), \cdots, H(\alpha, < s>_n)]\} \rightarrow s \tag{4}$$

R takes the output of S as input, and the output is the initial secret s.

3.3   Homomorphic Hash Authentication

In algebra domain, homomorphism is a mapping between two algebraic structures that keeps the structure constant [10], i.e., there is a mapping Φ: $X \rightarrow Y$ that satisfies:

$$\Phi(x * y) = \Phi(x) \oplus \Phi(y) \tag{5}$$

where $*$ is the operation in X and $\oplus$ is the operation in Y.

Homomorphic Hash Authentication was firstly proposed in [11], which aimed to verify whether the file has been manipulated in the distributed file system. Homomorphic hash function can compute the hash value of a single file block separately, and then combines all the hash values of single file to obtain that of the whole file. Therefore, to verify whether the file has been altered, we can take the partial file, compute the corresponding hash value and match the hash value of the whole file. Regarding the security of homomorphic hash function, it mainly refers to whether the adversary can find a pair of collisions of the probabilistic polynomial-time algorithm in Probabilistic Polynomial Time (PPT).

Definition 2. *The cluster of Hash is generated by probabilistic polynomial time algorithm $G = (Hgen, H)$ [2], where $Hgen$ is a Hash function generator. It outputs the description of a member of a hash function and H_K is the hash value of K. For the arbitrary cluster of Hash G, the arbitrary probability algorithm A and the security parameter $\lambda = (\lambda_p, \lambda_q)$ enables:*

$$Adv(A) = \Pr[Hgen(\lambda) \rightarrow K; A(K) \rightarrow (x_1, x_2) : H_K(x_1) = H_K(x_2) \wedge x_1 \neq x_2] \tag{6}$$

We denote G as a secure Hash function if for all the adversaries with time complexity $Adv(A) < \varepsilon(\lambda)$, where $\varepsilon(\lambda)$ is a negligible function, and $\tau(\lambda)$ is the polynomial of λ.

4   Privacy Preserving Protocol

We devise the secure aggregation protocol in distributed machine learning with two servers and n clients based on Secret Sharing techniques. The protocol's framework is shown in Fig. 1, which runs in a synchronous network, where g_i represents the gradient of the coefficient ω_i. Algorithm 1 illustrates the secure aggregation process.

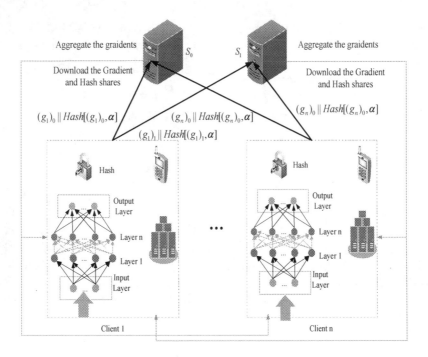

Fig. 1. The architecture of our secure aggregation protocol

4.1   Correctness Analysis

Correctness Proof of Secret Sharing Scheme. Our protocol is designed based on Shamir's Secret Sharing scheme. The parameter servers in our protocol are responsible for aggregating the gradients' shares. For instance, $(x)_i$ is the secret shares of x, $(y)_i$ is the secret shares of y, then we can argue $(z)_i = (x)_i + (y)_i$ is the secret shares of $z = x + y$. Applying into our scheme, each server S_j gets

---

Algorithm 1. Secure Aggregation Protocol for Distributed Machine Learning

---

Input:

    Preparation Phase: Global key α (α is only known to clients), n clients P_i, 2 servers S_j, where $i \in [n]$, $j \in [2]$, training model CNN $LeNet - 5$.

      Clients: Initialize gradients g_i and all hash shares to zero.

      Servers: Initialize all the servers' parameters.

Output:

    $\sum_i \sum_j Hash[(g_i)_j, \alpha]$ and $\sum_i \sum_j (g_i)_j$ when the train model is convergent.

1: **while** CNN does not converge **do**
2:     **Local Training and Uploading Phase:**
3:     $i = 1$
4:     **for** $i = 1$ to n **do**
5:       P_i trains the CNN model through a mini-batch from the local datasets.
6:       P_i computes gradient g_i and homomorphic hash $Hash[(g_i), \alpha]$.
7:       **for** $j = 0, 1$ **do**
8:         P_i generates $(g_i)_j$ by Secret Sharing and sends to server j.
9:         P_i generates hash shares $Hash[(g_i)_j, \alpha]$ and send to server j.
10:       **end for**
11:     **end for**
12:     **Gradients Aggregation and Downloading Phase:**
13:     **for** $j = 0, 1$ **do**
14:       Each Server S_j does aggregation for gradients $\sum_i (g_i)_j$ and related homomor-phic hash $\sum_i Hash[(g_i)_j, \alpha]$.
15:       **for** $i - 1$ to n **do**
16:         S_j downloads $\sum_i (g_i)_j$ and $\sum_i Hash[(g_i)_j, \alpha]$ to Client P_i.
17:       **end for**
18:     **end for**
19:     **Reconstruction and Verifying phase:**
20:     **for** $i = 1$ to n **do**
21:       P_i reconstructs the aggregated gradients $\sum_j \sum_i (g_i)_j$
22:       P_i Aggregates the downloaded hash values $\sum_j \sum_i Hash[(g_i)_j, \alpha]$
23:       P_i generates the hash of aggregated gradients and Compare it with $\sum_j \sum_i Hash[(g_i)_j, \alpha]$
24:       **if** they are not equal **then**
25:         The Gradient has been tampered.
26:       **end if**
27:     **end for**
28:     **Updating and iteration phase:**
29:       Continue to update the gradients with SGD algorithm, repeat the process until the model is convergent or abort if the Verification fails.
30: **end while**

$\sum\limits_{i=1}^{n} (g_i)_j$ theoretically, where $j \in \{1, 2, \cdots, m\}$. After downloading the gradients, each client would conduct aggregation $\sum\limits_{j}^{m} [\sum\limits_{i=1}^{n} (g_i)_j]$ theoretically since receiving sufficient gradient shares.

Suppose that in finite field F_q, we have secrets S and S', n is the number of clients and t is the threshold, where $q > n$ [4]. For $S, S' \in F_q$, we select $s_1, \cdots, s_{t-1}, s'_1, \cdots, s'_{t-1} \in F_q$ and let:

$$
\begin{aligned}
f(x) &= s + \sum_{i=1}^{t-1} s_i x^i \\
g(x) &= s' + \sum_{i=1}^{t-1} s'_i x^i
\end{aligned}
\tag{7}
$$

Meanwhile, we define Π as the secret sharing system, where $1 \le i \le n$.

$$
\begin{aligned}
\Pi(s, s_1, \cdots, s_n) &= (f(x_1), f(x_2), \cdots, f(x_n)) \\
\Pi(s', s'_1, \cdots, s'_n) &= (g(x_1), g(x_2), \cdots, g(x_n))
\end{aligned}
\tag{8}
$$

Then we distribute the secret shares to each client P_i and compute the sum of two secret shares that are denoted as $\Pi(s, s_1, \cdots, s_n) * (s', s'_1, \cdots, s'_n)$, where $*$ is the operation between secret sharing schemes.

$$
\begin{aligned}
&\Pi(s, s_1, \cdots, s_n) * (s', s'_1, \cdots, s'_n) \\
&= (f(x_1) + g(x_1), \cdots, f(x_n) + g(x_n)) \\
&= (s + \sum_{i=1}^{t-1} s_i x_1^i + s' + \sum_{i=1}^{t-1} s'_i x_1^i, \cdots, s + \sum_{i=1}^{t-1} s_i x_n^i + s' + \sum_{i=1}^{t-1} s'_i x_n^i) \\
&= (s + s' + \sum_{i=1}^{t-1} (s_i + s'_i) x_1^i, \cdots, s + s' + \sum_{i=1}^{t-1} (s_i + s'_i) x_n^i) \\
&= \Pi(s + s', s_1 + s'_1, \cdots, s_n + s'_n)
\end{aligned}
\tag{9}
$$

Correctness Proof of Homomorphic Hash Authentication. The sum of homomorphic hash values equals to the homomorphic hash of the sum [8]. In other words, if we assume that $Hash(x)$ and $Hash(y)$ are the homomorphic hash values of x and y, then $Hash(x) + Hash(y) = Hash(x + y)$.

Assume we have secrets $x_1, x_2, \cdots, x_n$ and a global key α, we can get the homomorphic hash values of x_i and their sum, where $i \in \{1, 2, \cdots, n\}$ and p is a big prime number.

$$
Hash(x_i, \alpha) \bmod p = \alpha Hash(x_i) \bmod p
\tag{10}
$$

$$
\sum_{i=1}^{n} Hash(x_i, \alpha) \bmod p = Hash(\sum_{i=1}^{n} x_i, \alpha) \bmod p = \alpha \sum_{i=1}^{n} Hash(x_i) \bmod p
\tag{11}
$$

4.2   Security Analysis

In this section, we analyze the security of our scheme in presence of semi-honest adversaries, meaning they leak no sensitive information about one honest user's dataset, as long as the adversaries corrupt no more than ε clients, where $\varepsilon < \frac{n}{2}$. Then we also analyze the external eavesdropping resistance process to reveal protocol effectiveness.

Clients Semi-honest Security. In Clients Semi-honest model, what adversary A can get about honest clients is the sum of their gradients.

$$\sum_{j \in honest} g_j = \sum_{i \in U} g_i - \sum_{a \in U \backslash j} g_a \tag{12}$$

As mentioned before, adversary A corrupts no more than ε clients, so the number of the honest clients is $|U| - \varepsilon$, where U is clients set. For simplicity, we denote $\sum_{j \in honest} g_j$ as H, H_a is the a th element of H, and $g_{j,a}$ is the a th element of g_j. It is obvious that the range of H_a is $[-(|U| - \varepsilon), (|U| - \varepsilon)]$, and if and only if $g_{j,a} = 1$ or $g_{j,a} = -1$, $\forall j \in honest$, then $|H_a| = |U| - \varepsilon$, i.e.,

$$|H_a| = |U| - \varepsilon \Leftrightarrow \begin{cases} g_{j,a} = 1, \forall j \in honest \\ or \\ g_{j,a} = -1, \forall j \in honest \end{cases} \tag{13}$$

Also, the adversary A can get the true value for a particular honest client if and only if $|H_a| = |U| - \varepsilon$. Otherwise, $H_a \in (-(|U| - \varepsilon), (|U| - \varepsilon))$, the adversary A gets no true value of gradients towards a particular client. Based on the assumption $\Pr[g_{j,a} = 1|g_j] \leq \frac{1}{p}, (p > 1)$, without losing generality, we focus on the $Event1 = \{H_a = |U| - \varepsilon\}$. As the corrupted clients are no more than ε, so the probability of Event 1 is

$$\Pr[Event1] \leq \frac{1}{p^{|U| - \varepsilon}} \tag{14}$$

So the probability of Event 1 is negligible along with the number of clients as long as $\varepsilon < \frac{|U|}{2}$,

External Eavesdropping Resistance. We assume that the global key α is only known to clients in advance. Therefore, if the external eavesdroppers tamper with the gradients, for example, they substitute $\sum_i (g_i)_j$ with $\sum_i (g_i')_j$, then client P_i can check whether $Hash(\sum_i (g_i')_j, \alpha)) = Hash(\sum_i (g_i)_j, \alpha)$. If these two hash values are not matched, the clients can argue verification fails and abort the protocol execution. Figure 2 illustrates this kind of tampering attacks vividly. Generally speaking, our protocol is verifiable when facing external tampering.

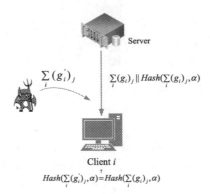

Fig. 2. A schematic of an external eavesdropper tampering with parameters

4.3 Performance Analysis

We analyse the communication and computation overhead for the clients and servers with n clients and m servers, respectively, where $m = 2$. Note that we ignore the Hash function generation time and suppose the gradient length is a constant value l.

Client computation: $O(m^2)$. Each client's computation overhead can be broken up as (1) creating Shamir Secret Shares of g_i, which is $O(m^2)$ and (2) performing $O(m)$ complexity in reconstruction process, including summation of $(g_i)_j$ ($O(m)$) and summation of Hash authentication function ($O(m)$).

Client communication: $O(n^2 + m)$. The communication cost of each client consists of two parts: (1) performing $n(n-1)/2$ negotiation times with other clients($O(n^2)$) and (2) uploading shares of gradient $(g_i)_j$ to servers ($O(m)$).

Server computation: $O(n)$. The server computation can be broken up into as aggregating the gradients of all clients $\sum_j \sum_i (g_i)_j$ and $\sum_j \sum_i Hash[(g_i)_j, \alpha]$ ($O(n)$).

Server communication: $O(n)$. Each server's communication overhead mainly exists in downloading the gradient $\sum_i (g_i)_j$ and Hash shares $\sum_i Hash[(g_i)_j, \alpha]$ to each client ($O(n)$).

5 Evaluation and Results

5.1 Experimental Setup

Our simulation experiment was implemented on the platform with an Intel(R) Core(TM) i7-9750H CPU@2.60GHz and E5-2650 V3@2.30GHz servers with 64G RAM in the LAN setting. $SHA256$ was selected as a hash authentication function. Each client established an SSL secure channel with each server sequentially. We measure the protocol performance under the deep learning framework using Pytorch 1.7.

5.2 Experimental Results and Discussion

We evaluate our approach regarding the training time and the exchanged data volume using a distributed machine learning framework to train $LeNet - 5$ on the MNIST dataset. MNIST is a dataset of handwritten digits formatted as 32 $\times$32 images.

We set the number of servers and clients to 2 and 100, respectively, then compare convergence rate and execution time with other frameworks, including Federated Learning [15] and Practical Secure Aggregation framework [6]. The results are shown in Fig. 3(a) and Fig. 3(b). In Fig. 3(a), all three different frameworks tend to be convergent after 50 epochs, up to nearly 92%. From Fig. 3(b), because of the homomorphic hash aggregation and authentication process, the execution time of the Practical Secure Aggregation framework [6] is higher than that of our protocol without clients dropout. Meanwhile, Fig. 3(b) also reflects that the execution time of the federated learning is much lower than the other two frameworks, which is less than $\frac{1}{6}$ of our protocol. The main reason is that clients do not need to negotiate with each other to generate a global model and some parameters independently in federated learning, which squeezes the time effectively.

To evaluate the protocol comprehensively, we explore the convergence rate and execution time with different scales of clients. As seen in Fig. 4(a), the number of clients has no evident effect on the convergence rate. The CNN model is still convergent after 50 epochs, not affected by the change of clients number. Figure 4(b) suggests that the protocol execution time has a positive correlation with the number of clients. The larger the number of clients, the longer the protocol execution time. This is corresponding to what we envisioned before. Simultaneously, Table 1 illustrates the execution time of each client and server. With the number of clients increasing, the execution time of each client and each server becomes longer. Finally, we illustrate the overall communication overheads of the system along with the number of clients in one training epoch in Table 2.

Table 1. Time consumption of Each Client and Each Server with 2 servers

Number	Type	
	Each client	Each server
100 clients	726 ms	1209 ms
250 clients	884 ms	1328 ms
500 clients	1023 ms	2180 ms

In Fig. 5, we measure the time needed for sharing, reconstruction, and addition operations along with the number of CNN parameters. Therefore, we change the number of CNN parameters. As illustrated in Fig. 5, for CNN parameters at 40000, our presented protocol could share them within 0.5 ms, compute the addition of two shares in about 1.2 ms, and reconstruct them in around 1.4 ms.

Table 2. Overall communication overheads along with the number of clients

Number	Type	
	Secret sharing	Homomorphic hash
100 clients	66875 kb	40909 kb
250 clients	160625 kb	109091 kb
500 clients	316875 kb	222727 kb

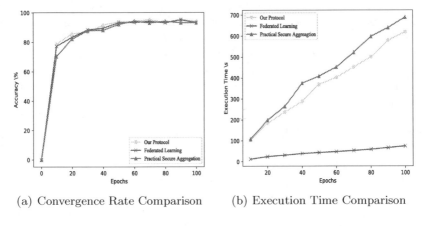

(a) Convergence Rate Comparison   (b) Execution Time Comparison

Fig. 3. Experimental results for convergence rate and protocol execution time

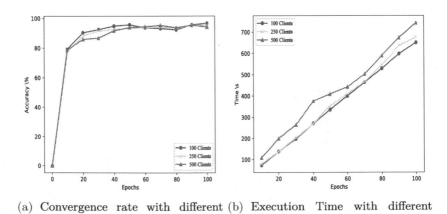

(a) Convergence rate with different   (b) Execution Time with different
clients   clients

Fig. 4. Convergence rate and protocol execution time for 100, 250, 500 clients

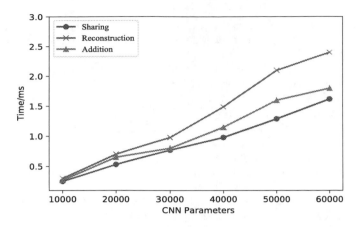

Fig. 5. Computation overhead for sharing, reconstruction and addition with one thread

6 Conclusion

We presented a privacy-preserving secure aggregation scheme for distributed machine learning. Our scheme not only prevents a certain percentage of clients or servers from colluding, but also resists external eavesdroppers from tampering with gradient information. This particularly allows our protocol to be verifiable. Simultaneously, the correctness in the clients semi-honest model scenario was proved. The further work includes an additional complementation, such as resisting Hash collisions and exploring Non-IID datasets experimental results, and performing a systematic implementation of our protocol.

References

1. Bell, J.H., Bonawitz, K.A., Gascón, A., Lepoint, T., Raykova, M.: Secure single-server aggregation with (poly) logarithmic overhead. In: Proceedings of the 2020 ACM SIGSAC Conference on Computer and Communications Security, pp. 1253–1269 (2020)
2. Bellare, M., Goldreich, O., Goldwasser, S.: Incremental cryptography: the case of hashing and signing. In: Desmedt, Y.G. (ed.) CRYPTO 1994. LNCS, vol. 839, pp. 216–233. Springer, Heidelberg (1994). https://doi.org/10.1007/3-540-48658-5_22
3. Ben-Or, M., Goldwasser, S., Wigderson, A.: Completeness theorems for non-cryptographic fault-tolerant distributed computation. In: Providing Sound Foundations for Cryptography: On the Work of Shafi Goldwasser and Silvio Micali, pp. 351–371 (2019)
4. Benaloh, J.C.: Secret sharing homomorphisms: keeping shares of a secret secret (extended abstract). In: Odlyzko, A.M. (ed.) CRYPTO 1986. LNCS, vol. 263, pp. 251–260. Springer, Heidelberg (1987). https://doi.org/10.1007/3-540-47721-7_19
5. Bonawitz, K., et al.: Practical secure aggregation for federated learning on user-held data. arXiv preprint arXiv:1611.04482 (2016)
6. Bonawitz, K., et al.: Practical secure aggregation for privacy-preserving machine learning. In: Proceedings of the 2017 ACM SIGSAC Conference on Computer and Communications Security, pp. 1175–1191 (2017)

7. Burkhart, M., Strasser, M., Many, D., Dimitropoulos, X.: Sepia: privacy-preserving aggregation of multi-domain network events and statistics. Network 1(101101), 15–32 (2010)
8. Damgård, I., Pastro, V., Smart, N., Zakarias, S.: Multiparty computation from somewhat homomorphic encryption. In: Safavi-Naini, R., Canetti, R. (eds.) CRYPTO 2012. LNCS, vol. 7417, pp. 643–662. Springer, Heidelberg (2012). https://doi.org/10.1007/978-3-642-32009-5_38
9. Geyer, R.C., Klein, T., Nabi, M.: Differentially private federated learning: a client level perspective. arXiv preprint arXiv:1712.07557 (2017)
10. Jürgen, S.: A homomorphism theorem for partial algebras. In: Colloquium Mathematicum, vol. 21, pp. 5–21. Institute of Mathematics Polish Academy of Sciences (1970)
11. Krohn, M.N., Freedman, M.J., Mazieres, D.: On-the-fly verification of rateless erasure codes for efficient content distribution. In: 2004 Proceedings of IEEE Symposium on Security and Privacy, pp. 226–240. IEEE (2004)
12. Liu, M., Jiang, H., Chen, J., Badokhon, A., Wei, X., Huang, M.C.: A collaborative privacy-preserving deep learning system in distributed mobile environment. In: 2016 International Conference on Computational Science and Computational Intelligence (CSCI), pp. 192–197. IEEE (2016)
13. Mandal, K., Gong, G.: PriVFL: practical privacy-preserving federated regressions on high-dimensional data over mobile networks. In: Proceedings of the 2019 ACM SIGSAC Conference on Cloud Computing Security Workshop, pp. 57–68 (2019)
14. Mandal, K., Gong, G., Liu, C.: Nike-based fast privacy-preserving high dimensional data aggregation for mobile devices. Technical report, CACR Technical report, CACR 2018–10, University of Waterloo, Canada (2018)
15. McMahan, B., Moore, E., Ramage, D., Hampson, S., y Arcas, B.A.: Communication-efficient learning of deep networks from decentralized data. In: Artificial Intelligence and Statistics, pp. 1273–1282. PMLR (2017)
16. Nasr, M., Shokri, R., Houmansadr, A.: Comprehensive privacy analysis of deep learning: stand-alone and federated learning under passive and active white-box inference attacks (2018)
17. Rabin, M.O.: How to exchange secrets with oblivious transfer (2005). http://eprint.iacr.org/2005/187 harvard University Technical Report 81 talr@watson.ibm.com 12955. Accessed 21 June 2005
18. Rastogi, V., Nath, S.: Differentially private aggregation of distributed time-series with transformation and encryption. In: Proceedings of the 2010 ACM SIGMOD International Conference on Management of Data, pp. 735–746 (2010)
19. Rivest, R.L., Adleman, L., Dertouzos, M.L., et al.: On data banks and privacy homomorphisms. Found. Secur. Comput. 4(11), 169–180 (1978)
20. Shamir, A.: How to share a secret. Commun. ACM 22(11), 612–613 (1979)
21. Shokri, R., Shmatikov, V.: Privacy-preserving deep learning. In: Proceedings of the 22nd ACM SIGSAC Conference on Computer and Communications Security, pp. 1310–1321 (2015)
22. So, J., Guler, B., Avestimehr, A.S.: Turbo-aggregate: breaking the quadratic aggregation barrier in secure federated learning. IEEE J. Sel. Area Inf. Theory. 2, 479–489 (2021)
23. Yao, A.C.: Protocols for secure computations. In: 23rd Annual Symposium on Foundations of Computer Science (SFCS 1982), pp. 160–164. IEEE (1982)
24. Yao, A.C.C.: How to generate and exchange secrets. In: 27th Annual Symposium on Foundations of Computer Science (SFCS 1986), pp. 162–167. IEEE (1986)

An Efficient Clustering-Based Privacy-Preserving Recommender System

Junwei Luo[1(✉)] (ID), Xun Yi[1] (ID), Fengling Han[1] (ID), Xuechao Yang[1] (ID), and Xu Yang[2]

[1] School of Computing Technologies, RMIT University, Melbourne, Australia
c.junwei.luo@gmail.com, {xun.yi,fengling.han,xuechao.yang}@rmit.edu.au
[2] School of Mathematics and Statistics, Fujian Normal University, Fuzhou, China
yangxu91@fjnu.edu.cn

Abstract. Recommender systems help online services deliver personalised content and facilitate information overload. Collaborative Filtering is a commonly used technique for building recommender systems. It analyses data collected from users in order to predict their preferences, this causes concerns over the privacy and security of the data as conventional techniques do not prioritise data privacy. Incorporating cryptography into recommender systems resolves the privacy issues, and yet it is impractical in many cases due to the computational overhead imposed by the cryptography and the sheer amount of data needed for computations. In this paper, we propose an efficient clustering-based privacy-preserving recommender system. The system employs homomorphic encryption for protecting user data while retaining the ability to generate recommendations using Collaborative Filtering. To facilitate information overload, a secure clustering technique is adopted to partition data prior to generating recommendations. The proposed system is secure under the semi-honest adversary model. Experiments show that the proposed system is efficient, scalable and produces accurate recommendations.

Keywords: Recommender system · Privacy-preserving · Collaborative filtering · Clustering

1 Introduction

Over the past decade, there has been an explosive growth of data generated from various online services such as social platforms, e-commerce and so on. As a result, finding the relevant information for users within a short time becomes critical for online service providers. Recommender systems facilitate the problem of information overload and provide a way to effectively deliver information to the users, benefiting both the users and reducing the server load. Collaborative Filtering (CF), which is one of the most commonly used techniques for implementing recommender systems, analyses feedbacks such as ratings collected from users and predicts their preferences to make decisions about what information should be delivered to different users.

While employing a recommender system to resolve information overload has become a common practice, issues related to user privacy have been raised over

X. Yuan et al. (Eds.): NSS 2022, LNCS 13787, pp. 387–405, 2022.
https://doi.org/10.1007/978-3-031-23020-2_22

the years. Recommender systems exploit user ratings, which are considered to be private, to predict the preferences of a user for generating recommendations. A study [7] shows that ratings collected by a recommender system are enough to infer data subject and their transactions. In addition, as computing power is usually sourced from a third-party domain such as the cloud, both the online service provider and cloud will have access to user data. Furthermore, as more and more countries propose various privacy laws to prevent online services from abusing user data for profits, it becomes clear that a privacy-preserving solution for recommendations is desirable.

Privacy-preserving recommender systems incorporate various security mechanisms to the data and algorithms to improve security. Crypto-based approaches [2,4,8,13] apply homomorphic encryptions to the data and compute the recommendations without decryption. Other approaches involve various data perturbation techniques such as k-anonymity [24], perturbation [21] and differential privacy [28] to protect user privacy. Data perturbation usually lowers the accuracy of the recommendation since noises are added to the data. Crypto-based approaches, on the other hand, offer stronger security compared to perturbation-based solutions, and yet these solutions suffer from performance issues as the homomorphic computations are expensive and time-consuming.

In this paper, we pay attention to the crypto-based recommender systems as they provide stronger security and better accuracy. We notice that existing works solely focus on applying different encryption schemes, such as ElGamal [12], Paillier [20] and BGV [6] to the algorithm for recommendations, they fail to realise that the sheer amount of data participated in computations also plays a role in affecting the practicability of the proposed arts. Inspired by the shortcoming, we propose an efficient privacy-preserving recommender system that further improves the performance while maintaining the same utility as other existing crypto-based works. The basic idea is that data are clustered into multiple groups to reduce computations while maintaining accuracy. When a user requests a recommendation, only the data from the group similar to the user input will be used for computation. However, as data are encrypted, clustering is done in encrypted form to guarantee data confidentiality.

This paper makes the following contributions:

1. We propose a privacy-preserving recommender system. The proposed system applies Item-based Collaborative Filtering as the recommending mechanism and utilises homomorphic encryption to enable recommendations while protecting all user data. Additionally, a secure clustering mechanism is adopted for improving recommending efficiencies.
2. We conduct a security analysis and the results show that the proposed system is secure under the semi-honest security model and does not leak any information that could be used to re-identify a data subject in storage and during the computations.
3. The proposed system is evaluated regarding its efficiency and precision. The results demonstrate that the proposed system is efficient compared to the

baseline. Two datasets are employed during the accuracy comparison and the proposed system remains accurate with an error rate of less than 1%.

The rest of the paper is organised as follows: Sect. 2 discusses the preliminaries for our model, which is presented in Sect. 3. Section 4 discusses the detail of our proposed system, followed by the security analysis in Sect. 5. The detailed evaluation is shown in Sect. 6. Section 7 presents the related work. Lastly, Sect. 8 concludes the paper.

2 Preliminaries

2.1 Collaborative Filtering

Collaborative Filtering is a technique commonly employed in recommender systems for information filtering. It analyses feedback from users and predicts how likely a user will enjoy other items based on the analysed result. Item-based Collaborative Filtering (ICF) [26] measures item-to-item similarities and gives a predicted result based on the similar items. Let $r_{m,i}$ be the rating of item i from user u_m, I_i and I_j be two items represented in vector spaces, where $I_i \leftarrow \{r_{1,i}, r_{2,i}, \cdots, r_{M_i}\}$ and $I_j \leftarrow \{r_{1,j}, r_{2,j}, \cdots, r_{M_j}\}$. The similarity $s_{i,j}$ between two items is measured using Cosine Similarity in the Eq. 1.

$$s_{i,j} = sim(I_i, I_j) = \frac{I_i \cdot I_j}{\|I_i\| \|I_j\|} = \frac{\sum_{m=1}^{M} r_{m,i} r_{m,j}}{\sqrt{\sum_{m=1}^{M} r_{m,i}^2} \sqrt{\sum_{m=1}^{M} r_{m,j}^2}} \tag{1}$$

Recommendation $P_{u,i}$ of i-th item for the user u can be predicted using the Eq. 2.

$$P_{u,i} = \frac{\sum_{k \in S_i} (s_{i,k} * r_{u,k})}{\sum_{k \in S_i} (|s_{i,k}|)} \tag{2}$$

where S_i denotes a list of most similar items to i-th item.

2.2 ElGamal

ElGamal [12] is a public key cryptography introduced in 1985. The ElGamal is an additively homomorphic encryption scheme that allows some computations without the need for decryption.

Key Generation

- Choose a cyclic group G of a prime order q with a generator g at random;
- Choose a secret key sk from $\mathbb{Z}_q^*$ at random;
- Compute the public key $pk = g^{sk}$.

The values (pk, G, q, g) are publicly known whilst the secret sk is kept private.

Encryption: To encrypt a message $m \in G$ using a public key pk, randomly select an integer $r \in (\mathbb{Z}_q^*)$ and compute the following:

$$E(m, pk) = (c_1, c_2) = (g^r \bmod p, g^m \cdot pk^r \bmod p)$$

Decryption: Given a ciphertext $E(m, pk) = (c_1, c_2)$, one might recover the message using the secret key sk and compute the following:

$$D(E(m, pk), sk) = \frac{c_2}{c_1{}^{sk}} \bmod p$$

Homomorphic Addition: Given two ciphertexts $E(m1, pk)$ and $E(m2, pk)$, summation of two ciphertexts over the ciphertext space is computed as follows:

$$E(m1 + m2, pk) = E(m_1, pk) \cdot E(m_2, pk)$$
$$= (g^{r_1 + r_2} \bmod p, g^{m_1 + m_2} \cdot pk^{r_1 + r_2} \bmod p)$$

2.3   K-means Clustering

The k-means clustering algorithm [18] was first described in 1967. It partitions a set of multi-dimensional points into k number of clusters in which each point is assigned to a cluster with the closest distance. Let x be a point and k be the number of clusters, where each cluster has a centroid $\mu_j, 1 \leq j \leq k$. During the update stage, all points $x \in X$ are assigned to their nearest cluster (see Eq. 3). The k-means is a hard clustering which means that a point can only be assigned to one cluster, if multiple clusters share the same distance, a random cluster will be chosen to assign. When clustering is done, each centroid of the cluster is updated according to the Eq. 4.

$$S_i = \left\{ x_p : \left\| x_p - \mu_i \right\|^2 \leq \left\| x_p - \mu_j \right\|^2 \ \forall j, 1 \leq j \leq k \right\} \tag{3}$$

$$\mu_i = \frac{1}{\|S_i\|} \sum_{x_j \in S_i} x_j \tag{4}$$

3   Our Model

In this section, we present the design of our model. We first give an overview of the proposed model and introduce several involved components. After that, we discuss different data structures and notations used in our model. Lastly, we define an adversary model for our proposed system Fig. 1.

3.1   Overview

Our proposed system is composed of three main components:

- **Recommender Server (RS)** is the centralised server that users interact with, it offers storage for user data and provides computing resources for generating recommendations.
- **Security Server (SS)** is a trusted curator responsible for providing security-related functionalities and participating in secure computations with the RS and users.

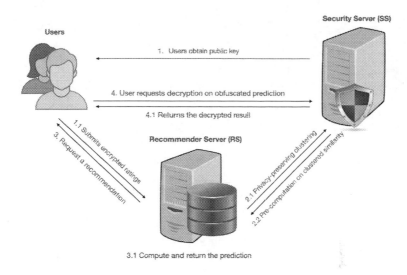

Fig. 1. An architectural overview of the proposed recommender system.

- **Users** are data owners that provide information such as ratings for the RS to generate recommendations.

The proposed system consists of two stages: an offline stage includes collecting and pre-processes data and an online stage provides the functionality of privacy-preserving recommendations.

The offline stage includes initialisation, clustering and data preprocessing. During the initialisation, the RS initialises data structures for managing user data and the SS generates public/private keys, where the private key sk is kept secret and the public key pk is shared with all participants. Users obtain the public key pk from the SS and encrypt their ratings prior to submitting to the RS for future recommendations. During clustering, both RS and SS execute privacy-preserving k-means to partition encrypted ratings into k clusters. Lastly, data pre-processing computes item-to-item similarities for the clustered dataset in preparation for the online stage.

When the preprocessing is finished, the system transitions into the online stage and is ready for recommendations. A target user submits her encrypted recommending query to the RS for a recommendation. The RS locates the nearest cluster to the target users and computes the recommendations based on the data from the closest cluster. Results are sent back to the target user, in which the user will communicate with the SS for decryption.

3.2   Data Structure

User ratings are represented as vectors, a rating is a non-negative integer given by the user about an item in the system. Let R_i be a list of ratings from user

u_i, where $R_i \leftarrow r_{i,j}$ for $1 \leq j \leq N$ and N denotes the total number of ratings.

$$R_i \leftarrow \{r_{i,1}, r_{i,2}, \cdots, r_{i,N}\}$$

The user u_i element-wise encrypts R_i, denoted as R'_i, and submits the encrypted vectors to the RS.

$$R'_i \leftarrow \{E(r_{i,1}), E(r_{i,2}), \cdots, E(r_{i,N})\}$$

For simplicity, an encrypted rating r is denoted as r'. Let I'_i be a list of ratings for i-th items given by all users, where $I'_i \leftarrow \{r'_{1,i}, r'_{2,i}, \cdots, r'_{M,i}\}$ and M denotes the number of users. As the proposed system is based on clustering for improving efficiency and accuracy, let k be the number of clusters, μ be a list of centroids for each cluster and $\mathcal{T}$ be the finalised cluster. The RS manages submitted ratings and similarities in a user-item dictionary $\mathcal{D}$ as described in the Table 1. Table 2 denotes all notations used throughout the paper.

Table 1. Data structure of dictionary $\mathcal{D}$

	I'_1	I'_2	$\cdots$	I'_N
R'_1	$\{r'_{1,1}$	$r'_{1,2}$	$\cdots$	$r'_{1,N}\}$
$\vdots$	$\vdots$	$\vdots$	$\vdots$	$\vdots$
R'_M	$\{r'_{M,1}$	$r'_{M,2}$	$\cdots$	$r'_{M,N}\}$

3.3 Adversary Model

Semi-honest adversary model is adopted similar to other existing PPCF schemes. Under the adversary model, all parties are honest but curious, meaning that they faithfully follow the designed protocol and do not deviate, while they might attempt to learn the secret from the computation and stored data. Further, all parties could potentially be malicious, while they do not collude with each other. Following such an adversary model, three different attack scenarios are defined.

Attack 1: Under this attack, the RS becomes malicious and will attempt to disclose or learn information about stored user data. Further, the RS could obverse any communication and computation between respective parties in an attempts to disclose any information.

Attack 2: Similarly, the SS becomes malicious and will try to learn private information by observing the communication and computation with different parties.

Attack 3: A malicious user who has certain background knowledge about a victim could compose queries to the RS for recommendation, in an attempt to infer a data subject from the recommended ratings.

Table 2. Notations

RS:	Recommender Server
SS:	Security Server
u_i:	User i
pk:	The public key from SI
sk:	The private key from SI
$E()$:	Encryption under the key pk
$D()$:	Decryption under the key sk
$\oplus$:	Homomorphic Addition
M:	The number of users
k:	The number of clusters
N:	The number of items
itr:	The number of clustering iterations
$r_{i,j}$:	A rating of j-th item from user u_i, $r_{i,j} \in R_i$
$r'_{i,j}$:	An encrypted rating of j-th item from user u_i, $r'_{i,j} \in R'_i$
I'_i:	A list of ratings for i-th item given by all users
$\mathcal{T}_n$:	n-th entry of the user-item matrix $\mathcal{T}$
$\mathcal{R}_{n,i}$:	i-th user rating from n-th cluster $\mathcal{T}_n$
$\mathcal{I}_{n,i}$:	i-th item from n-th cluster $\mathcal{T}_n$
$\mathcal{D}$:	A dictionary that maintains R' by the RS
μ:	A collection of encrypted centroids for each cluster, $\mu \leftarrow \mu_j$ for $1 \leq j \leq k$

4   Our Privacy-Preserving Collaborative Filtering Protocols

In this section, we present the proposed system in detail. As noted there exist two stages: the offline stage collects and pre-processes the data and the online stage provides recommending services to the users.

4.1   Offline Stage

Initialisation: In this stage, the RS initially sets up $\mathcal{D}$ for data storage and the SS generates a keypair, where pk is public and sk is securely kept by the SS. A user u_i element-wise encrypts her rating data $r_i \in R_i$ using the key pk from SS, denoted as R'_i. The user u_i submits the encrypted rating R'_i to the RS for clustering and computing similarities. All encrypted ratings from users are stored in the table $\mathcal{D}$ as shown in Table 1.

Clustering: To cluster encrypted data, our proposed system leverages a privacy-preserving k-means clustering [23]. The clustering scheme exploits several privacy-preserving protocols such as SMP for multiplication [24], decomposition (SBD) [25] and comparison (SMIN) [24] over the ciphertext space as a building block for the privacy-preserving k-means (PPKM) clustering proposed by [23].

The RS picks a value k values from $\mathcal{D}$ as the initial centroid μ for partitioning data, where $\mu \leftarrow \mu_j$ for $1 \leq j \leq k$. The PPKM takes as input $\mathcal{D}, k, \mu, itr$

and outputs a set of clustered data $\mathcal{T}$. Specifically, for each rating vector $R'_i \in \mathcal{D}$, where $R'_i \leftarrow \{r'_{i,1}, r'_{i,2}, \cdots, r'_{i,N}\}$, the PPKM mechanism first measures the distance between R'_i and k centroids stored in μ using Secure Square Euclidean Distance (SSED) [24], which results in k numbers of encrypted distance values $D_{i,j}, j \in k$. The distances are fed into the SBD protocol that decomposes the encrypted integer into a list of encrypted bits, which is used for comparison using SMIN to find the shortest distance among all $D_{i,j}$. The centroid μ_t that corresponds to the shortest distance is returned and the rating R'_i is assigned to the matrix $\mathcal{T}_t$, where $1 \leq t \leq k$.

When all items are assigned to respective clusters, the centroid of each cluster is recalculated based on the newly assigned ratings and μ is updated accordingly. The RS repeatedly executes above steps with SS to securely assign ratings into k clusters. In the end, the PPKM outputs the clustered dataset $\mathcal{T}$ that consists of k user-item matrices $\mathcal{T}_n \in \mathcal{T}$ and centroids $\mu_n \in \mu$, $1 \leq n \leq k$. It should be noted that the k-means is applied to user inputs R' for aggregating users who rated similar items into a group. In item-to-item collaborative filtering, items rated by the same group of users are deemed to be similar. During the preprocessing stage, each item $\mathcal{I}_{n,i} \in \mathcal{T}_n$ will be used for measuring similarities.

Algorithm 1: Privacy-preserving cosine similarity computation

---

    Input : $\mathcal{T}_n$
    Output: S'_n
1 $S'_n \leftarrow \emptyset$
2 **for** $i \leftarrow 1$ **to** $size(\mathcal{T}_n)$ **do**
3      $\mathcal{I}_{n,i} \leftarrow \mathcal{T}_n.get(i)$
4   **for** $j \leftarrow i+1$ **to** $size(\mathcal{T}_n)$ **do**
5         $\mathcal{I}_{n,j} \leftarrow \mathcal{T}_n.get(j)$
6         $p'_{i,j} \leftarrow sumProd(\mathcal{I}_{n,i}, \mathcal{I}_{n,j})$
7         $q'_i \leftarrow sumSqrt(\mathcal{I}_{n,i})$
8         $q'_j \leftarrow sumSqrt(\mathcal{I}_{n,j})$
9         $s'_{i,j} \leftarrow cos(p'_{i,j}, q'_i, q'_j)$
10         $S'_{n_{i,j}} \leftarrow s'_{i,j}$
11   **end**
12 **end**
13 **return** S'_n

Item Preprocessing. After obtaining $\mathcal{T}$, similarities between items are computed prior to the online stage for better efficiency. Note that similarity is computed in the same cluster as users who rated similar items are clustered into the same group. Algorithm 1 denotes the computation of similarity between two items according to the Eq. 1. For each cluster $\mathcal{T}_n \in \mathcal{T}, 1 \leq n \leq k$, the RS retrieves the i-th item $\mathcal{I}_{n,i}$ from $\mathcal{T}_n$ and computes the similarity with other items $\mathcal{I}_{n,j}$, where $1 \leq j \leq size(\mathcal{T}_n), i \neq j$. In line 6 of Algorithm 1, the RS computes the sum product of two items I'_i and I'_j as follows:

$$p'_{i,j} = sumProd(\mathcal{I}_{n,i}, \mathcal{I}_{n,j}) = \prod_{m=1}^{M} r'_{i,m} \otimes r'_{j,m}$$

where $\otimes$ denotes multiplication of two ciphertexts using the SMP protocol [24]. Similarly, line 7 computes the sum of squares of each rating for the item I'_i by multiplying the rating by itself.

$$q'_i = sumSqrt(\mathcal{I}_{n,i}) = \prod_{m=1}^{M} r'_{i,m} \otimes r'_{i,m}$$

For computing the cosine similarity between I'_i and I'_j, the RS submits $p'_{i,j}, q'_i$ and q'_j to the SS. Upon receiving the data, the SS computes the following:

$$s'_{i,j} = cos(p'_{i,j}, q'_i, q'_j) = E\left(\frac{D(p'_{i,j})}{\sqrt{D(q'_i)} \cdot \sqrt{D(q'_j)}}\right)$$

where $s'_{i,j}$ is the cosine similarity between I'_i and I'_j according to the Eq. 1. It is worth noting that ElGamal expects integers whilst the similarity $s'_{i,j}$ is likely to be a floating point number. As a result, $s'_{i,j}$ are normalised and rounded prior to encryption. Both RS and SS interactively compute the similarity for all items in a cluster and the results are stored in S'_n, where $1 \leq n \leq k$. The RS maintains all $S'_n \in S'$ for generating recommendations.

4.2   Online Stage

Recommendation. A target user u_t retrieves the public key pk from the SS and submits a recommending query to the RS. Let $R_t \leftarrow \{r_{t,1}, r_{t,2}, \cdots, r_{t,N}\}$ be the rating of user u_t. The user chooses an item i that needs to be rated, and element-wise encrypts her profile, denoted as R'_t. The user submits a tuple $\{R'_t, i\}$ to the RS for a recommendation. Upon receiving the request, the RS measures the distance between R'_t and μ using Secure Distance Measurement in Algorithm 2. Specifically, the distance between R'_t and $\mu_n \in \mu$ is measured using the SSED algorithm, which produces k intermediate distance values $D'_t \leftarrow D'_{t,j}$ for $1 \leq j \leq k$. The distance value is then used by the SBD for decomposition and the SKMIN algorithm, which is based on SMIN with support for finding the minimal value among k distances. The SKMIN outputs the centroid μ_t nearest to the user input R'_t.

After that, the recommendation of a rating for the user u_t is computed using the items from the nearest cluster as denoted in Eq. 2. Note that the similarity is divided into two parts $\mathcal{N}'_t$ and $\mathcal{D}'_t$. Specifically, let S'_t be the list of similarities closest to the centroid μ_t from the S', the similarity $s'_{i,j} \in S'_t$ between the requested item i by the user and other items j, where $1 \leq j \leq N, i \neq j$ is

---

Algorithm 2: Secure Distance Measurement (SDM)

    Input : R'_t, μ
    Output: μ_t
1 **for** $j \leftarrow 1$ **to** k **do**
2     $D_{t,j} \leftarrow \text{SSED}(R'_t, \mu_j)$
3     $\tilde{D}_{t,j} \leftarrow \text{SBD}(D_{t,j})$
4 **end**
5 $\mu_t \leftarrow \text{SKMIN}(\tilde{D}_t, \mu)$
6 **return** μ_t

---

multiplied with the rating $r'_{t,j}$ of j-th item from the user u_t. Each multiplication of the j-th ratings from user u_t and the similarity s'_i, j is summed together using homomorphic addition, N'_t denotes the summation of the above computation.

$$\mathcal{N}'_t = \prod_{s'_{i,j} \in S'_t} s'_{i,j} \otimes r'_{t,j}$$

where $\otimes$ denotes multiplication using SMP. Similarly, the second computation involves the summation of all similarities $s'_{i,j}$ from S'_t, which the result is denoted as D'_t.

$$\mathcal{D}'_t = \prod_{s'_{i,j} \in S'_t} s'_{i,j}$$

Notice that multiplication over ciphertext space is equal to addition in the plaintext space. It is obvious that when N'_t and D'_t are combined, the predicted rating for i-th item requested by user u_t is generated.

$$P'_{t,i} = \frac{\mathcal{N}'_t}{\mathcal{D}'_t} = \frac{\prod_{s'_{i,j} \in S'_t} s'_{i,j} \otimes r'_{t,j}}{\prod_{s'_{i,j} \in S'_t} s'_{i,j}}$$

However, the RS is unable to finalise the result $P'_{t,i}$ due to the difficulty of dividing two large ciphertexts. As a result, both N'_t and D'_t are returned to the target user u_t, in which the user can execute a decryption protocol with the SS to privately decrypt and get the result.

Decryption. In this stage, the RS has finished computing partial predicted ratings N'_t and D'_t for the target user u_t. As the sk is privately owned by SS, the user u_t obfuscates the partial ratings with two integers n, d chosen at random and computes $(\mathcal{N}'_t)^n$ and $(\mathcal{D}'_t)^d$, and shuffle the list at random prior to submission. Note that the ciphertext exponentiation with a plaintext exponent n is equivalent to $\mathcal{N}_t \cdot n$ after the decryption. The obfuscated partial ratings are submitted to the SS via a secure communication channel. Upon receiving the request, the SS simply decrypts and returns the values to the user, denoted as $(\mathcal{N}_t \cdot n) \leftarrow D((\mathcal{N}'_t)^n)$ and $(\mathcal{D}_t \cdot d) \leftarrow D((\mathcal{D}'_t)^d)$ respectively. Lastly, the user u_t de-obfuscates

---

Algorithm 3: Generating recommendation

Input   : R'_t, S', μ_t, i

Output: $P_{t,i}$

1 $S'_t \leftarrow S'.get(\mu_t)$

2 **while** $s'_{i,j} \in S'_t$ **do**

3      $\mathcal{N}'_t \leftarrow \mathcal{N}'_t \oplus (s'_{i,j} \otimes r'_{t,j})$

4      $\mathcal{D}'_t \leftarrow \mathcal{D}'_t \oplus s'_{i,j}$

5 **end**

6 **return** $\mathcal{N}'_t, \mathcal{D}'_t$

---

and un-scrambled the decrypted results to compute the following to reveal the predicted rating.

$$P_{t,i} = \frac{\mathcal{N}_t \cdot \frac{1}{n}}{\mathcal{D}_t \cdot \frac{1}{d}}$$

5   Security Analysis

In this section, we analyse the security of the proposed system and show that it can achieve sufficient privacy. Under the adversary model, each party faithfully follows the designated protocols and does not deviate, either party could be malicious but they do not collude with each other including users, RS and SS. The proposed system is said to be secure if, for any malicious party, no information leakage could be used to identify a data subject during both the offline and online stages.

Malicious Recommender Server: In the offline stage, user ratings are encrypted using the public key from SS before submitting to the RS for storage and computation. The cryptographic primitive ElGamal [12] is IND-CPA secure, in which the RS is unable to distinguish whether two ciphertexts are generated using the same message. Hence, all private data submitted by users are secure.

In the clustering stage, both RS and SS interactively execute the PPKM to cluster encrypted ratings. Several mechanism that serve as a building block for PPKM, which includes SSED, SMIN [24] and SBD [25], have proven to be secure under the semi-honest adversary model by respective authors. The RS learns the number of ratings assigned to each cluster in $\mathcal{T}$. In the preprocessing stage, the RS runs Algorithm 1 to compute similarities between items for each clustered in $\mathcal{T}$ using the SBD [25]. As all computations in the preprocessing stage are in ciphertext space, the RS is unable to learn anything from the computation.

In the online stage, the RS is responsible for finding the nearest cluster using Algorithm 2 that is composed of the aforementioned secure protocols such as SSED, SBD and SMIN which are secure. Lastly, the RS executes Algorithm 3 to compute the recommendation for the user using the SMP [24] and homomorphic addition. Similarly, the RS learns nothing from the computations as they are computed in the ciphertext space.

Malicious Security Server: In the offline stage, SS is responsible for generating a key pair. In the clustering stage, the SS participates in the re-calculation of the centroids as decryption is needed. As a result, the SS can learn the number rating vectors assigned to each cluster in $\mathcal{T}$, as well as the centroid μ. In preprocessing stage, the SS can learn the similarities between items as the similarities are computed on decrypted values aggregated by the RS. We stress that the leakage is benign as long as the similarities between items are not deemed to be private in many cases. In the online stage, the SS involves in the final decryption stage. However, as the partial ratings, $\mathcal{N}'$ and $\mathcal{D}'$ are obfuscated by the target user before submission, the SS can only learn the obfuscated ratings.

Malicious Users: A malicious user can submit fake ratings to the system in an attempt to reveal ratings made by other users. However, as the item-to-item similarities are securely computed prior to the recommendation, it remains to be seen if a malicious user can disclose any information from the similarity.

6   Evaluation

In this section, we assess the performance of our proposed system regarding its computational overhead and recommendation accuracy.

6.1   Experimental Settings

The proposed system is implemented in Java. For the secure k-means, we implemented the pipelined PPKM for better performance. The ElGamal cryptographic primitive is implemented using the BigInteger library. The key length (pk, sk) for the ElGamal is set to 1,024 bits in all experiments. For better efficiency, a lookup table to resolve the Discrete Logarithm problem for the ElGamal has been pre-computed. All benchmarks and evaluations are conducted on a workstation computer with an Intel Core i7-8850H and 32GB of DDR4 2400MHz RAM. We use OpenJDK 11 LTS as the Java runtime to evaluate the computational overhead of the proposed system. *MovieLens* 100k [15] is the dataset that the proposed system uses for the evaluation.

6.2   Performance of Secure Clustering

As the proposed system utilises secure clustering prior to computing item-to-item similarities, we assess the runtime for executing a round of clustering with various k and I, denoted as the number of clusters and items respectively. Figure 2a shows the computational overhead of data clustering. With a fixed item size $I = 20$ and various $k = \{2, 4, 6\}$, the clustering takes around 165, 184 and 190 s to complete, resulting in an 8% increase in the total execution time on average. Adding more items to the dataset does not alter the average time measured in a significant way. With $I = 100$, the PPKM takes 321, 340 and 345 s to finish a round of clustering.

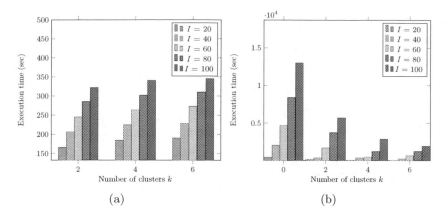

Fig. 2. Performance of clustering (a), computing item-to-item similarities (b)

While increasing the size of clusters adds an insignificant amount of performance penalty to the execution time, adding more items results in a much heavier performance penalty on the execution time. Given a fixed number of clusters $k = 2$ and various items $I = \{40, 60, 80, 100\}$, the execution time starts from 206 s when $I = 40$, to 245 s after increasing I to 60 and 321 s when the I is set to 100. As a result, we measure an increase of 20% in the total execution time for clustering data by adding more items. Similarly, with a bigger cluster value k, the total execution time increases slightly as measured above.

Overall, the experiment concludes that adding more items to the dataset will have a more significant performance penalty on the overall execution time than increasing the size of the cluster. Further, clustering is an iterative process that involves multiple rounds of updating the dataset to reach an optimal state, which adds even more complexity to the computation and the amount of time. Fortunately, as the clustering is usually done during the initialisation, any changes that occur after the initialisation will only result in updating the cluster once. Furthermore, as data are clustered into k groups, this significantly improves the performance for computing item-to-item similarities which will be discussed in the next section.

6.3 Performing Item-to-Item Similarity Computations

While the clustering indeed adds a significant amount of time to the offline stage, it grants several benefits when pre-computing item-to-item similarities. To demonstrate how the clustering affects the performance, a baseline is set up that computes the item-to-item similarities without partitioning data, whilst our proposed system only computes the similarities with items in the same group. For simplicity, we use $k = 0$ to denote the baseline. Figure 2b shows the computational time for computing item-to-item similarities. When the dataset contains a small subset of data, says $I = 20$, computing the similarities takes 505 s, whilst

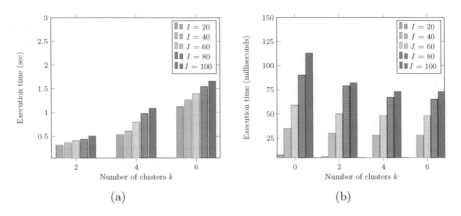

Fig. 3. finding the closest cluster (a) and computing the recommendation (b) with various I and k.

the runtime is reduced significantly after the clustering, we measure 208 s when $k = 2$, 105 and 69 s when k is increased 4 and 6 respectively. Adding more items to the dataset results in an even more significant improvement to the overall runtime, from 13,012 s when the item size is increased to 100 with no clustering, to 5,717, 2,893 and 1,988 s when the number of clusters is set to 2, 4 and 6 respectively.

The results show that the computational time is directly related to the number of clusters k, where each cluster computes the similarity independently with the items in the same group. As a result, computing the similarities in different clusters can be effectively parallel, hence further reducing the computational time. Considering that modern online services contain thousands of items in the system, we argue that data clustering is effective in relieving computational overheads while maintaining accuracy and preserving user privacy.

6.4 Generating a Recommendation

As the proposed system utilises clustering to group similar items before generating a recommendation, we first evaluate the performance of finding a suitable cluster for a target user. Figure 3a shows the computational time for measuring the distance between user input and centroids. Given that $k = 2$, the SDM algorithm finds the closest distance in less than 0.5 s regardless of the dimensions, and the time increases steadily to around 1.5 s when k is increased to 6. As can be seen that the number of clusters k determines how quickly can a cluster be securely retrieved. Recall that a large k benefits the similarity computations during the offline stage, here it adds more complexity to the distance measurement as more computations and comparisons are needed.

Lastly, to generate a recommendation, similarities between the target item and other similar items are used for the computation. Recall that there is a baseline for evaluating the execution time of computing similarities, which is denoted as $k = 0$. We use the same notation to describe the baseline that did not use clustering before computing a recommendation. Figure 3b presents the result computational time for generating a recommendation. The difference in computational time between the baseline and clustered data is insignificant, where most computations can be done within 0.1 s regardless of the size of clusters and the number of items in the system. We stress that the clustering is only beneficial to the performance when it comes to pre-computing item-to-item similarities as pipelined executions are made possible after clustering.

6.5   Analysing the Recommendation Accuracy

To measure the impact of how clustering might affect the accuracy of recommended items, a baseline is set up and compared with our proposed system. Similarly, the baseline does not employ clustering whilst the proposed system only computes the predicted score using the data from a cluster. Additionally, to better represent the accuracy, an extra dataset *Jester* [14] has been added to the evaluation. Unlike the *MovieLens* where data are sparsely distributed, the *Jester* dataset contains over 1 million ratings from 24,983 users over 100 items, which has a higher density rate of around 25% compared to 10% from the *Movie-Lens*. Each item I from the *Jester* dataset has a range from -10 to 10 and 99 indicates that the user has not rated the item. For simplicity, the scale has been adjusted from 0 to 20. During the clustering, the k initial centroids are chosen at random, and the clustering is iteratively performed between the RS and SS 10 times to reach an optimal state. The measurement for recommending accuracy is the Mean Average Error (MAE) between the baseline and proposed system. We measure the error rate of predicted ratings when comparing the baseline and the proposed system with various k and I.

$$MAE = \frac{\sum_{i=1}^{n} |y_i - x_i|}{n}$$

Figure 4a shows the result of comparing recommending accuracy between the baseline and proposed system using the *MovieLens* dataset. Under the setting $I = 200$, the baseline gets a predicted score of 2.2, whereas the proposed system returns 2.21, 2.19 and 2.2 when the number of clusters k is set to 2, 4 and 6 respectively. Adding more items to the dataset does not disrupt the pattern as can be seen that both the baseline and proposed system perform similarly regardless of the settings k and I. Replacing the dataset with *Jester*, the observed patterns are consistent as shown in Fig. 4b, where both the baseline and proposed system manage to maintain consistency across different settings k and I. One exception is that the predicted rating drops significantly when all items are present in the dataset while the proposed system reduces the rating linearly. Table 3 shows that the average error rate of the proposed system is less than 1% when compared to the baseline while improving the performance during item-to-item similarity computation by k times.

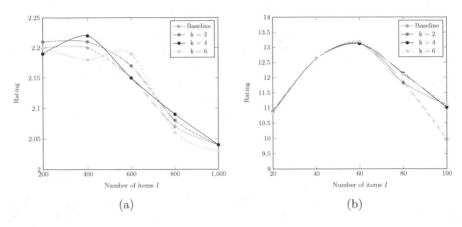

Fig. 4. Comparison of recommending accuracy between the baseline and proposed system using *MovieLens* (a) and *Jester* (b)

Table 3. Comparison of Mean Absolute Error (MAE) between the baseline and proposed system

MovieLens				Jester			
I	Baseline	Ours	MAE	I	Baseline	Ours	MAE
200	2.2	2.2	0.01	20	10.897	10.846	0.114
400	2.2	2.203	0.03	40	12.625	12.618	0.017
600	2.15	2.17	0.06	60	13.141	13.147	0.076
800	2.07	2.076	0.02	80	11.843	12.02	0.381
1000	2.04	2.03	0.01	100	9.967	11.033	2.504

7   Related Work

Privacy-preserving recommender systems can be divided into two types: crypto-based recommender systems apply cryptographic methods to protect data while perturbation-based methods introduce randomised noises into data and/or recommending mechanisms. Canny [8] proposes the first privacy-preserving recommender system using homomorphic encryption, which is a type of public key cryptography that enables computations over the ciphertext space. It applies the cryptosystem to collaborative filtering for protecting user privacy. Basu et al. [4] propose a cloud-based collaborative filtering scheme using ElGamal encryption to enable private computations. Similarly, Erkin et al. [13] propose a user-based collaborative filtering scheme using Paillier encryption, which is later extended by the author to reduce computational overhead using an optimised approach called data packing, enabling multiple encrypted values to be packed and computed once. Badsha et al. [1] propose a privacy-preserving collaborative filtering scheme using the ElGamal cryptosystem for content-based and item-based filtering. Kim et al. [16] propose a collaborative filtering system using matrix factorisation, the authors adopt fully homomorphic encryption for securing data while maintaining the functionality. Casino and Patsakis [10] propose a clustering-based recommender system using Locality-Sensitive Hashing, an algorithm that uses hashing to cluster similar items into groups. Further, to eliminate the limitations of centralised RS, the authors adopt blockchain to enable distributed recommendations. Badsha et al. [3] propose a QoS recommendations using user-based collaborative filtering to help users recommend various web services. The work exploits user location information in a private way to improve accuracy and employs Fully Homomorphic Encryption to resolve the problem of homomorphic encryption, a limitation that partially homomorphic encryption schemes such as ElGamal and Paillier has.

Perturbation-based schemes focus on adding randomised noises into the data to protect user privacy while providing a reasonable accuracy to the recommendations. Polat et al. [21] propose a perturbation-based method that perturbs two rating data in a way that when combined, cancels part of the noise. The author later applies the same method [22], along with SVD to provide better privacy for collaborative filtering. Meng et al. [19] adopt the noise randomisation technique to enable location-based recommendations for delivering POI contents. Berkovsky et al. [5] propose a distributed collaborative filtering scheme where each party owns partial of the user profile, along with applying a data obfuscation scheme to the data for stronger privacy. Casino et al. [9] incorporate k-anonymity to collaborative filtering for protecting user privacy. The idea is later refined by Wei et al. [27], where the privacy level of k-anonymity is further enhanced using l-diversity and t-closeness. Li et al. [17] propose a distributed and unsynchronised collaborative filtering method with randomised noises. Chen et al. [11] propose a distributed novel POI recommendation scheme using machine learning and employ differential privacy for data masking for protecting the model.

8 Conclusion

In this paper, we propose an efficient, clustering-based privacy-preserving recommender system. Our proposed system employs item-based collaborative filtering for generating recommendations. All user data are encrypted using ElGamal to enable computations over ciphertexts while preserving user privacy. To facilitate computational burdens imposed by the cryptosystem, a privacy-preserving clustering mechanism is introduced to boost the performance. The proposed system is secure under the semi-honest adversary model. The proposed system is implemented and experimental results show that the proposed system significantly improves performance for preprocessing encrypted data while producing an accurate rating over the clustered dataset. In the future, we plan to extend the work by incorporating different clustering approaches and evaluate their impacts in performance and precisions.

References

1. Badsha, S., Yi, X., Khalil, I.: A practical privacy-preserving recommender system. Data Sci. Eng. 1(3), 161–177 (2016)

2. Badsha, S., Yi, X., Khalil, I., Bertino, E.: Privacy preserving user-based recommender system. In: 2017 IEEE 37th International Conference on Distributed Computing Systems (ICDCS), pp. 1074–1083. IEEE (2017)
3. Badsha, S., et al.: Privacy preserving location-aware personalized web service recommendations. IEEE Trans. Serv. Comput. **14**(3), 791–804 (2018)
4. Basu, A., Vaidya, J., Kikuchi, H., Dimitrakos, T.: Privacy-preserving collaborative filtering for the cloud. In: 2011 IEEE Third International Conference on Cloud Computing Technology and Science, pp. 223–230. IEEE (2011)
5. Berkovsky, S., Eytani, Y., Kuflik, T., Ricci, F.: Enhancing privacy and preserving accuracy of a distributed collaborative filtering. In: Proceedings of the 2007 ACM Conference on Recommender Systems, pp. 9–16 (2007)
6. Brakerski, Z., Gentry, C., Vaikuntanathan, V.: (Leveled) fully homomorphic encryption without bootstrapping. ACM Trans. Comput. Theor. (TOCT) **6**(3), 1–36 (2014)
7. Calandrino, J.A., Kilzer, A., Narayanan, A., Felten, E.W., Shmatikov, V.: You might also like: privacy risks of collaborative filtering. In: 2011 IEEE Symposium on Security and Privacy, pp. 231–246. IEEE (2011)
8. Canny, J.: Collaborative filtering with privacy. In: Proceedings of 2002 IEEE Symposium on Security and Privacy, pp. 45–57. IEEE (2002)
9. Casino, F., Domingo-Ferrer, J., Patsakis, C., Puig, D., Solanas, A.: A k-anonymous approach to privacy preserving collaborative filtering. J. Comput. Syst. Sci. **81**(6), 1000–1011 (2015)
10. Casino, F., Patsakis, C.: An efficient blockchain-based privacy-preserving collaborative filtering architecture. IEEE Trans. Eng. Manage. **67**(4), 1501–1513 (2019)
11. Chen, C., Zhou, J., Wu, B., Fang, W., Wang, L., Qi, Y., Zheng, X.: Practical privacy preserving poi recommendation. ACM Trans. Intell. Syst. Technol. (TIST) **11**(5), 1–20 (2020)
12. ElGamal, T.: A public key cryptosystem and a signature scheme based on discrete logarithms. IEEE Trans. Inf. Theor. **31**(4), 469–472 (1985)
13. Erkin, Z., Veugen, T., Toft, T., Lagendijk, R.L.: Generating private recommendations efficiently using homomorphic encryption and data packing. IEEE Trans. Inf. Forensics Secur. **7**(3), 1053–1066 (2012)
14. Goldberg, K., Roeder, T., Gupta, D., Perkins, C.: Eigentaste: a constant time collaborative filtering algorithm. Inf. Retrieval **4**(2), 133–151 (2001)
15. Harper, F.M., Konstan, J.A.: The movielens datasets: history and context. ACM Trans. Interact. Intell. Syst. (TIIS) **5**(4), 1–19 (2015)
16. Kim, J., Koo, D., Kim, Y., Yoon, H., Shin, J., Kim, S.: Efficient privacy-preserving matrix factorization for recommendation via fully homomorphic encryption. ACM Trans. Priv. Secur. (TOPS) **21**(4), 1–30 (2018)
17. Li, D., et al.: An algorithm for efficient privacy-preserving item-based collaborative filtering. Future Gener. Comput. Syst. **55**, 311–320 (2016)
18. MacQueen, J.: Classification and analysis of multivariate observations. In: 5th Berkeley Symposium on Mathematical Statistics and Probability, pp. 281–297 (1967)
19. Meng, S., Qi, L., Li, Q., Lin, W., Xu, X., Wan, S.: Privacy-preserving and sparsity-aware location-based prediction method for collaborative recommender systems. Future Gener. Comput. Syst. **96**, 324–335 (2019)
20. Paillier, P.: Public-key cryptosystems based on composite degree residuosity classes. In: Stern, J. (ed.) EUROCRYPT 1999. LNCS, vol. 1592, pp. 223–238. Springer, Heidelberg (1999). https://doi.org/10.1007/3-540-48910-X_16

21. Polat, H., Du, W.: Privacy-preserving collaborative filtering using randomized perturbation techniques. In: Third IEEE International Conference on Data Mining, pp. 625–628. IEEE (2003)
22. Polat, H., Du, W.: Privacy-preserving collaborative filtering. Int. J. Electron. Commer. **9**(4), 9–35 (2005)
23. Rao, F.Y., Samanthula, B.K., Bertino, E., Yi, X., Liu, D.: Privacy-preserving and outsourced multi-user k-means clustering. In: 2015 IEEE Conference on Collaboration and Internet Computing (CIC), pp. 80–89. IEEE (2015)
24. Samanthula, B.K., Elmehdwi, Y., Jiang, W.: K-nearest neighbor classification over semantically secure encrypted relational data. IEEE Trans. Knowl. Data Eng. **27**(5), 1261–1273 (2014)
25. Samanthula, B.K., Chun, H., Jiang, W.: An efficient and probabilistic secure bit-decomposition. In: Proceedings of the 8th ACM SIGSAC Symposium on Information, Computer and Communications Security, pp. 541–546 (2013)
26. Sarwar, B., Karypis, G., Konstan, J., Riedl, J.: Item-based collaborative filtering recommendation algorithms. In: Proceedings of the 10th International Conference on World Wide Web, pp. 285–295 (2001)
27. Wei, R., Tian, H., Shen, H.: Improving k-anonymity based privacy preservation for collaborative filtering. Comput. Electr. Eng. **67**, 509–519 (2018)
28. Zhu, T., Li, G., Ren, Y., Zhou, W., Xiong, P.: Differential privacy for neighborhood-based collaborative filtering. In: Proceedings of the 2013 IEEE/ACM International Conference on Advances in Social Networks Analysis and Mining, pp. 752–759 (2013)

A Differential Privacy Mechanism for Deceiving Cyber Attacks in IoT Networks

Guizhen Yang[1], Mengmeng Ge[2], Shang Gao[1], Xuequan Lu[1], Leo Yu Zhang[1(✉)], and Robin Doss[1]

[1] Deakin University, Geelong Waurn Ponds, Australia
{guizhen.yang,shang.gao,xuequan.lu,leo.zhang,robin.doss}@deakin.edu.au
[2] University of Canterbury, Christchurch, New Zealand
mge43@uclive.ac.nz

Abstract. Protecting Internet of Things (IoT) network from private data breach is a grand challenge. Data breach may occur when networks' statistical information is disclosed due to network scanning or data stored on the IoT devices is accessed by attackers because of lack of protection on IoT devices. To protect IoT networks, effective proactive cyber defence technologies (e.g., Moving Target Defence (MTD) and deception) have been proposed. They defend against attacks by dynamically changing attack surface or hiding true network information. However, little work considered the protection of statistical information of IoT network, such as the number of VLANs or the number of devices across VLANs. This type of information may leak the network's operational information to attackers (e.g., functional information of VLANs). To address this problem, we propose a differential privacy (DP)-based defence method to mitigate its leakage. In this paper, we strategically obfuscate VLANs' statistical information by integrating DP with MTD and deception technologies. Software-defined networking technology is leveraged to manage data flows among devices and support shuffling-based MTD. Two strategies (random and intelligent) are considered for defence deployment. A greedy algorithm is designed to explore the trade-off between defence cost and privacy protection level. We theoretically prove that the proposed method meets the definition of DP, thus offering solid privacy protection to the operational information of an IoT network. Extensive experimental results further demonstrate that, for a given defence budget, there exists a trade-off between protection level and cost. Moreover, the intelligent deployment strategy is more cost-effective than the random one under the same settings.

Keywords: Differential privacy · Internet of Things · Deception · Moving target defence · Software defined networking

1 Introduction

Internet of Things (IoT) is a network of physical objects (e.g., devices, instruments, vehicles, buildings and other items) embedded with electronics, circuits,

X. Yuan et al. (Eds.): NSS 2022, LNCS 13787, pp. 406–425, 2022.
https://doi.org/10.1007/978-3-031-23020-2_23

sensors and network connections to collect and exchange data [1]. It allows these objects to communicate by wired or wireless communications (e.g., Bluetooth, ZigBee and 5G) and share data across existing network infrastructure [2]. Nowadays, IoT networks are growing rapidly and contain around 28 billion objects [3] that communicate with each other. They bring a lot of benefits to human beings but also provide opportunities for attackers to collect valuable information and launch attacks which may severely impact operations and normal functionality of IoT devices [4,5]. Thus, effective protection and defence mechanisms are needed to protect the IoT networks from potential attacks.

In an IoT network, devices are usually grouped into different VLANs according to their functions and/or locations [6]. Statistical information, such as the total or average number of devices per VLAN, or the number of VLANs, may leak the network's operational information, or expose potential attack targets. For example, a Radiology department often has a limited number of medical imaging devices due to the budget limitation. The medical imaging devices collect data from patients and upload it to the server where doctors access patients' data for diagnosis purposes. Attackers may be able to deduce the VLAN where these medical imaging devices are located based on the network statistical information (e.g., the number of user machines in a VLAN is potentially much larger than the number of critical devices, such as medical imaging devices or servers, in a separate VLAN). Once attackers identify a vulnerable Internet-of-Medical Things (IoMT) device or a vulnerable user machine, they can pivot toward the server. The consequences are expensive if patients' private information is disclosed. Therefore, it is necessary to minimise the leakage of statistical information, increasing the difficulty of deducing potential targets by the attackers, preventing them from breaking into the network and launching further attacks.

However, there is little prior work considering the security issues caused by the leakage of statistical information. The motivation of our work lies within the privacy protection of statistical information of IoT networks. We aim at developing a defence method to obfuscate the statistical information of an IoT network and mislead attackers. Figure 1 shows two examples of VLAN obfuscation. In a healthcare IoT network, we assume there is a vulnerable device t_i (in red square, belonging to a radiologist) on VLAN 3 (i.e., the staff office). It has direct access to a file server on VLAN 5 which stores medical imaging data from multiple medical devices on the network. If t_i is compromised, the attacker may pivot and compromise the server.

Intuitively, to prevent the attacker from locating the server through devices in other VLANs, we can increase the attack cost of identifying a potential target by hiding true network information. It can be done by increasing the device diversity, such as deploying decoy t_i' (Fig. 1(b) and 1(c)), or by changing the attack surface, such as shuffling t_i's IP address to make it appear on VLAN 2 but not on VLAN 3 (Fig. 1(d)). When the attackers scan the network, they may not accurately deduce the operational information of VLANs because of the obfuscated virtual location of t_i. Hence, the attack cost is increased and the operational information of the network is protected to some extent.

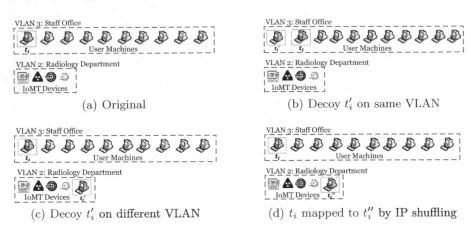

(a) Original

(b) Decoy t'_i on same VLAN

(c) Decoy t'_i on different VLAN

(d) t_i mapped to t''_i by IP shuffling

Fig. 1. Examples of VLAN obfuscation.

However, this kind of simple deception methods do not protect the operational information well against the attacker with stronger background (i.e., side channel information). For the scenario considered above, this background knowledge can be derived from the simple fact that the probability of t_i on VLAN 3 is much higher than that of the decoy t'_i on VLAN 2 (Fig. 1(c)). That said, by simply counting the number of devices on both VLANs, the attacker can distinguish real t_i and fake t'_i or t''_i, and easily workaround the aforementioned deception methods. From this view, it is necessary to also obfuscate the VLAN's statistical information (e.g., the number of devices) to offer protection against informed attackers.

In this paper, we first use differential privacy (DP) to obfuscate VLAN's statistical information. The number of devices per VLAN is strategically changed under a given privacy budget ϵ. Two defence mechanisms are then applied to achieve the obfuscation. Finally, we adopt a greedy algorithm to optimise the deployment of defence choices and find the trade-off between defence cost and privacy budget. The defence mechanisms used in this work include: (1) deception technology to deploy decoys into network [7], and (2) IP-shuffling based Moving Target Defence (MTD) technology to obfuscate the attack surface [8].

The main contributions of this paper are summarised as follows:

- We are the first to integrate DP with software-defined networking (SDN)-based MTD and deception technologies to solve the security issues caused by leakage of statistical information of IoT network. Using VLAN information as an example, we add the Laplace noise to the number of devices per VLAN and obtain the obfuscated set of VLANs, based on which, deception technologies can be further applied by the defender.

- We design a greedy algorithm to find optimal trade-offs between privacy budget and defence cost under given defence budgets.
- Extensive experimental results validate the effectiveness and scalability of the proposed method on different scaled IoT networks.

The rest of the paper is organised as follows. Section 2 introduces related work. Section 3 presents the proposed method. System model, attack model and defence model are described in Sect. 4. Experimental results and their analysis are given in Sect. 5. Section 6 discusses the limitations and future directions.

2   Related Work

MTD Technologies: Moving target defence [8–10] is one of the common proactive defence mechanisms that has emerged to deceive potential attacks [11,12]. It aims at hurdling attacks by constantly changing the attack surface. With MTD, the complexity, diversity and randomness of systems or networks are increased to disrupt attackers' actions during the reconnaissance phase of cyber kill chain. There are three common MTD techniques: shuffling, redundancy and diversity. In our case, we use IP shuffling which is a common network shuffling technique for an increased complexity of the IP address space.

Ge et al. [13] re-configured the IoT network topology to deal with non-patchable vulnerabilities. By maximising the number of patchable nodes along the route to the base station, the attack effort is increased while maintaining the average shortest path length. The work [14] considered hybrid approaches by combining different defence mechanisms. Decoys are strategically deployed into the network and a patch management solution is applied to solve unpatchable vulnerabilities under a constraint budget. Further study in [15] proposed an integrated defence technique for intrusion prevention. It explains "when to move" and "how to move". The former performs network topology shuffling with four strategies (i.e., fixed/random/adaptive/hybrid), and the latter shuffles a decoy IoT network with three strategies (i.e., genetic algorithm/decoy attack path-based optimisation/random).

The work [16] randomly shuffled communication protocols in an IoT network. It solves problems such as "what to move" by utilising moving parameters to determine shuffled protocol, "how to move" by using a discrete & uniform probability distribution to determine the next moving parameter, and "when to move" by adopting fixed or random time interval. The paper also analyses multi-criteria to find a trade-off among system performance, business impact and the success probability of a given attack.

Deception Techniques: Deception techniques aims to mislead and deceive attackers [7,17]. Honeypot [18,19] is one of the commonly exploited technologies in cyberdeception. It is created as a fake asset and shows attackers misleading information, luring them into the honeypot environments to divert them. However, how to create honeypots, how many to deploy, when and where to deploy are still unsolved problems [12].

La et al. [19] formulated a Bayesian Game model to reflect the defender's imperfect knowledge of the incoming user's type (e.g., malicious or not). It addresses the key issues of how the defender reacts different observations on the attacker and which deception strategies are optimal to both the attacker and defender. However, It does not take the false positive and false negative into account to measure the effective results. Tsemogne et al. [20] introduced a zero-sum one-sided partially observable stochastic game model to investigate cyberdeception techniques against botnets propagation in IoT networks.

Ye et al. [21] presented a differentially private game-theoretic approach for cyber deception. They use DP to dynamically change the number of systems and obfuscate their configurations in three situations: reallocating system configurations, deploying decoys and taking systems offline. However, limitations, like how to guarantee the number of systems to be taken offline fewer than that of the current live hosts, are not addressed. Additionally, taking systems offline is irrational in reality due to due to interrupting normal services from systems.

This paper focuses on solving the security issues caused by the leakage of statistical information of IoT networks. Our work is also built on top of DP, but it obfuscates IoT network's statistical information (e.g., the number of devices) to resist informed attackers through the integration of MTD and deception technologies.

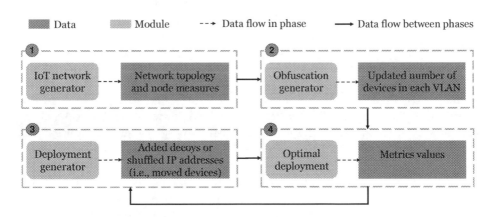

Fig. 2. Workflow of the proposed approach.

3   Proposed Approach

To effectively manage nodes (devices) and their data flows, we utilise SDN technology [22]. An SDN controller communicates with SDN switches in the IoT network. Servers, user machines and IoT devices are connected to the SDN switches. The switches transform data flows to the SDN controller for further processing. We also leverage the SDN technology to deploy shuffling-based MTD, as well as managing the communication between the SDN controller and switches via virtual-to-real or real-to-virtual IP addresses mapping.

The overall workflow of our proposed approach is shown in Fig. 2. It consists of 4 phases: IoT network model generation, information obfuscation by DP mechanism, deployment strategy generation using IP shuffling and deception, and deployment optimisation by finding the trade-off between defence cost and privacy budget.

In **Phase 1**, we generate the system model along with node measures based on the network information. In specific, the IoT network generator takes network topology as input with node connectivity information. The output is statistical information of the network (e.g., set of devices in each VLAN and set of VLANs on a given IoT network) and node measure (e.g., the betweenness centrality (BC) of each node that captures how much a given node is in-between other nodes [23]).

In **Phase 2**, we adopt DP to obfuscate the statistical information of VLANs. The obfuscation generator takes the statistical information of the network (c.g., the number of devices in each VLAN) and the node measures from **Phase 1** as input, and adds Laplace noise to the set of devices per VLAN under the DP framework. The output is the updated number of devices in each VLAN. We denote the original IoT network as N and the new obfuscated IoT network as N'. For each VLAN k, the number of devices is changed from $|N_k|$ to $|N_k'|$ after obfuscation. There is a possibility that $|N_k'| < 0$ since the Laplace noise is a random variant. It means that the devices moved out from VLAN k is large than the devices on VLAN k, which is violated in the real world. Hence, we use $\Delta N_k^* = |N_k'| - |N_k|$ as an optimal set of devices that should be moved out from or added into VLAN k to solve this problem, aiming at adapting to real-world scenarios, including guaranteeing the number of devices moved out is less than that of the current live devices. These to-be-moved devices are also candidates for IP-shuffling based MTD in **Phase 3**. Therefore, we call ΔN_k^* is an optimal set of devices after the improved obfuscation.

In **Phase 3**, we use the deployment generator to update the network information as specified by the updated set of devices for each VLAN from the output of **Phase 2** and the original set of devices per VLAN. The deployment generator deploys the defence strategies produced by the randomisation module or the optimisation module in **Phase 4**. The output is the updated IoT network after the deployment of defences. We use the MTD technology - IP address shuffling to change the attack surface and the deception technology - decoy to mislead attackers. As mentioned earlier, we leverage SDN to implement shuffling-based MTD. In our proposed approach, the SDN controller is also used to manage SDN switches. The SDN switches are used to forward packets to the SDN controller for handling the data flow and controlling packet forwarding. We assume each device has a real IP address (rIP). The rIP is mapped to one virtual IP address (vIP) which is selected from a group of randomly generated virtual IP addresses (vIPs). Only the SDN controller and the device know its rIP, while other devices in the IoT network use the mapped vIP to communicate with the device. The mapping between rIP to vIPs is managed by the SDN controller [24,25].

In **Phase 4**, we consider two strategies for defence deployment: random and intelligent strategies. The randomisation module starts by randomly selecting a VLAN k. Depending on the obfuscation outcome of **Phase 2**, it either randomly selects a device for IP shuffling or deploys a decoy on VLAN k. The intelligence module starts by selecting a VLAN k based on their criticality. Depending on the obfuscation outcome of **Phase 2**, it then selects a device for IP shuffling or deploys a decoy on VLAN k based on the devices' or decoys' criticality. In particular, if the number of devices on VLAN k increases (i.e., $\Delta N_k^* > 0$), the defender deploys ΔN_k^* number of decoys into VLAN k; If the number decreases (i.e., $\Delta N_k^* < 0$), the defender moves $|\Delta N_k^*|$ number of devices from VLAN k to another VLAN by shuffling the IP addresses of these devices to that VLAN. As discussed in **Phase 3**, the SDN controller can shuffle vIP addresses[1]. We develop a greedy algorithm (GA) to compute the optimal deployment by exploring the trade-off between defence cost and privacy protection level. GA aims to minimise the defence cost under different privacy budgets at each stage. The selection of VLAN, decoy or device can be determined by their criticality. The higher criticality the object has, the higher priority it takes.

We consider the security metric as the defender's cost. It is the total cost of deploying decoys to the IoT network and moving devices from one VLAN to another (e.g., shuffling IP addresses). The privacy protection level is determined by the privacy budget used in **Phase 2** (i.e., how much Laplace noise to add for information obfuscation).

4   System, Attack and Defence Models

This section describes the system model, attack model and defence model of our proposed approach.

4.1   System Model

We consider the internal network of a smart healthcare network as shown in Fig. 3. The internal network consists of servers, a SDN controller and SDN switches, user machines (e.g., computers) and IoT devices. Assume traditional defence techniques are in place, including intrusion detection systems (IDS) and anti-virus software. The servers, user machines and IoT devices are connected to the SDN switches.

4.2   Attack Model

In this smart healthcare network, servers are used to store patients' medical records (e.g., medical diagnosis reports and radiological images). If they are

---

[1] IP shuffling does not change the VLAN that a device resides nor affect the communications between the device and other devices; but it gives attackers a different network view in their reconnaissance phase.

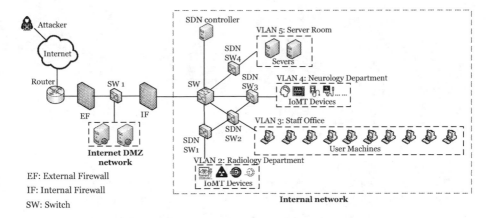

Fig. 3. Example of Software-Defined healthcare IoT network.

compromised, attackers may steal the data for economic gain [26]. The disclosure of patients' data can pose a serious threat to the health and safety of individuals. Therefore, we assume these servers could be potential attack targets.

Based on the observation of real-world scenarios, we assume the attackers have the following capabilities.

- Attackers can leverage various scanning tools to collect information about the target network (e.g., number of devices, network topology and operating system of a host) and identify weaknesses for exploitation (e.g., known and zero-day vulnerability). Attackers are able to utilise some firewall/IDS evasion techniques to avoid blocking and detection.
- Attackers may be able to identify attack targets with less time or cost by analysing the collected information. For example, the real location of one device can be deduced by comparing gathered information (e.g., counting the number of changed devices per VLAN) before an attack is launched on the device.
- It is highly unlikely for attackers to directly compromise the servers as they are assumed to be well-protected due to the traditional defence techniques placed on the network.
- Attackers lack knowledge of existence of decoy system. Once the attackers realise the device they interact with is a decoy, they terminate the interaction immediately and attempt to find a new target.
- Attackers can not compromise the SDN controller and SDN switches which are assumed to be secure.

4.3   Defence Model

The proposed defence model covers two stages: the obfuscation of VLANs through DP, and the deployment of two defence technologies for obfuscation. Table 1 lists the notations used in this work.

Table 1. Notations and definitions.

Notations	Definitions
N	Set of devices in a network
N'	Set of devices in a network after obfuscation
K	Set of VLANs
N_k	Set of devices in VLAN k
N'_k	Set of devices in VLAN k after obfuscation
ΔN_k^*	An optimal set of devices moved out from or added into VLAN k after improved obfuscation
$m1(k,j) \rightarrow 0,1$	Function to move a device from VLAN k to VLAN j with MTD
$m2(d,k) \rightarrow 0,1$	Function to deploy a decoy d into VLAN k with deception
$c1(k,j)$	Cost of moving a device from VLAN k to VLAN j when $m1(k,j) = 1$
$c2(d,k)$	Cost of deploying a decoy d into VLAN k when $m2(d,k) = 1$

Obfuscation of VLANs: Differential privacy is a framework that provides theoretical guarantee to protect any individual record in a dataset from leaking or being exploited by all possible informed attackers [27]. DP has been successfully applied to the network security field [21,28]. However, existing studies on DP-based network security solutions still have limitations. In this work, we try to address the privacy security issues caused by leakage of statistical information of IoT networks and overcome the limitations we have found in [21] when applying DP to obfuscate the statistical information of networks.

Briefly speaking, DP operates on two neighbouring datasets D and D' which differ by only one record. For a query function f that maps dataset D to an output value range $\mathbb{R}$, $f : D \rightarrow \mathbb{R}$, DP randomises this query f such that its output from D and D' cannot be distinguished by any attacker. The maximal difference of the query function f is called sensitivity ΔS ($\Delta S = \max_{D,D'} \|f(D) - f(D')\|_1$), which affects the level of noise added during randomisation. The formal definition of DP is given as follows.

Definition 1 (ϵ-*Differential Privacy* [29]). *An algorithm $\mathcal{A}$ provides ϵ-differential privacy for any pair of neighbouring datasets D and D' if the algorithm $\mathcal{A}$ satisfies:*

$$\Pr[\mathcal{A}(D) \in \Omega] \leq \exp(\epsilon) \cdot \Pr[\mathcal{A}(D') \in \Omega] \tag{1}$$

where Ω is the output of algorithm $\mathcal{A}$ performing on D (or the neighbouring D'), ϵ is the privacy budget, ranging from 0 to 1 for counting queries. It controls how much noise or randomness is added to the raw data. The higher the ϵ value, the lower the noise is; or the lower the ϵ value, the higher the noise is.

There are two most widely used mechanisms to achieve DP (i.e., Laplace and Exponential). We focus on the Laplace mechanism, which adds Laplace noise to the true query answer (i.e., the number of devices per VLAN). Denote Lap(b)

Algorithm 1. Strawman obfuscation approach of VLANs

Input: $|N_1|, \cdots, |N_k|$
Output: $|N_1'|, \cdots, |N_k'|$ and $\Delta N_1^*, \cdots, \Delta N_k^*$
1: Calculate the minimum value of set of devices on VLANs $a_{min} : |N_1|, \cdots, |N_k|$
2: **for** $k = 1 \to K$ **do**
3:     $|N_k'| \leftarrow |N_k| + \left\lceil Lap\left(\frac{\Delta \cdot K}{\epsilon}\right)\right\rceil$
4:     **if** $|N_k'| \leq 0$ **then**
5:         $|N_k'| \leftarrow a_{min}/2$
6:     **end if**
7:     $\Delta N_k^* \leftarrow |N_k'| - |N_k|$
8: **end for**
9: Obtain $|N_1'|, \cdots, |N_k'|, a_{min}, \Delta N_1^*, \cdots, \Delta N_k^*$.

---

the noise sampled from the Laplace distribution with scaling b, we have the following definition and properties.

Definition 2 (The Laplace Mechanism [29]). *Given a function $f :\to \mathbb{R}$ over a dataset D, then*

$$\tilde{f}(D) = f(D) + \text{Lap}\left(\frac{\Delta S}{\epsilon}\right) \tag{2}$$

satisfies ϵ-DP.

Theorem 1 *Sequential composition* [29]: *Suppose there are k algorithms $\mathcal{A}_1$, $\mathcal{A}_2, \cdots, \mathcal{A}_k$ that satisfy ϵ_1-DP, ϵ_2-DP, $\cdots$, ϵ_k-DP, respectively, with respect to the input dataset D. Publishing $t = (o_1, o_2, \cdots, o_k)$, which is the output value of the algorithms performing on D, satisfies $(\sum_{i=1}^{k} \epsilon_i)$-DP.*

Theorem 2 *Post-processing* [29]: *Suppose an algorithm $\mathcal{A}_1(\cdot)$ satisfies ϵ-DP, then for any algorithm $\mathcal{A}_2$, the composition of $\mathcal{A}_1$ and $\mathcal{A}_2$, i.e., $\mathcal{A}_2(\mathcal{A}_1(\cdot))$, satisfies ϵ-DP.*

Based on DP's definition and properties, we present a strawman obfuscation approach for the VLANs in Algorithm 1. In line 3, Laplace noise is added to each $|N_k|$ to obfuscate the number of devices on VLAN k. In our case, Δ is the maximum change (i.e., shuffling a device's IP address or deploying a decoy) made to VLANs. By definition, $\Delta = 1$.

However, as the Laplace noise is a random variant, there is a possibility that $|N_k'| < 0$, which means the number of devices needs to be moved out of one VLAN (i.e., by IP address shuffling) may be greater than the number of devices in that VLAN, which violates reality. Therefore, lines 4–6 are used to limit the number of devices left in VLANs (after moving devices out) to be one half of the original minimum number of devices in the VLANs. In this way, the issue of how to guarantee the number of systems to be taken offline fewer than that of the current live devices from [21], can be avoided naturally.

On the other hand, another extreme situation, where the total number of devices to-be-moved is greater than the total number of available decoys (under

---

Algorithm 2. Improved VLAN obfuscation approach

Input: $\Delta N_1^*, \cdots, \Delta N_k^*$
Output: Updated values of $\Delta N_1^*, \cdots, \Delta N_k^*$
1: **for** $k = 1 \to K$ **do**
2:    **if** $\Delta N_k^* < 0$ **then**
3:        $moveOut \leftarrow N_k^*$
4:    **else**
5:        $moveIn \leftarrow N_k^*$
6:    **end if**
7: **end for**
8: $sumOut \leftarrow \text{abs}(\text{sum}(moveOut));$
9: $sumIn \leftarrow \text{sum}(moveIn)$
10: **if** $sumOut > sumIn$ **then**
11:    **for** $i = 0 \to \text{len}(moveOut)$ **do**
12:        $temp = moveOut[i]$
13:        $moveOut[i] = (\frac{moveOut[i]}{sumOut}) * sumIn$
14:        $\Delta N_{\Delta N^*.index(temp)}^* = moveOut[i]$
15:    **end for**
16: **end if**
17: Obtain $\Delta N_1^*, \cdots, \Delta N_k^*.$

---

a certain budget), may occur. In this case, the extra devices to-be-moved need to be taken offline to ensure DP. Clearly, in our example application, it is irrational to take devices offline as this will disrupt services for patients. Therefore, we design Algorithm 2 to deal with this situation. In line 13, we regard the number of devices moved per VLAN as being proportional to the total number of fake assets added.

In this way, our approach not only ensures the satisfaction of DP but also avoids taking devices offline, which is an irrational defence method to protect devices from [21].

Proposition 1 *Both Algorithm 1 and Algorithm 2 satisfy ϵ-DP.*

Deployment of Defence Mechanisms: After obtaining the outcomes of VLAN obfuscation, the remaining task is to implement the obfuscation of VLANs to deceive attackers. As discussed earlier, we use MTD and deception technologies to achieve the obfuscation. Without loss of generality, we assume the cost of moving one device out of one VLAN to another VLAN is cheaper than adding a decoy, so the defender prefers IP-shuffling based MTD to cyber deception.

Deception: The defender utilises deception technology if the number of devices in VLAN k increases (i.e., $\Delta N_k^* > 0$). The defender deploys ΔN_k^* number of additional devices on VLAN k for deceiving possible attackers. The additional devices can be decoys or devices that are moved from other VLANs if those VLANs have a reduced number of devices after obfuscation, or a mix of decoys and devices from other VLANs.

To minimise the cost while maximising security and preserving privacy, we need to decide (1) which VLAN should be selected first for deploying decoys and (2) what decoys should be deployed. In particular, we select a VLAN based on its criticality. Take the healthcare network as an example, we consider the total cost of devices per VLAN as the VLAN's criticality because critical devices like servers and medical devices often have a higher price. We consider the cost of decoy deployment based on the license fees by decoy type [14,30]. A decoy at a lower price will have a higher priority being deployed into a VLAN.

To increase the chance of decoy interacting with attackers, the decoys should resemble the devices in the real network [14]. In our case study, we choose real OS for server decoys (i.e., full OS-based decoy) and emulator software for other device decoys (i.e., emulated decoy). Full OS-based decoys have higher interaction capability with attackers but will incur a higher cost than the emulated ones.

Shuffling: The defender resorts to MTD if the number of devices in VLAN k decreases (i.e., $\Delta N_k^* < 0$). The defender moves $|\Delta N_k^*|$ number of devices from VLAN k to another VLAN by shuffling IP addresses of these devices in that VLAN.

In particular, we select devices based on their criticality. Betwenness centrality (BC) is considered which measures the centrality of a node (device) in a graph (topology) based on the shortest path [31]. BC can be formulated as

$$BS(t_i) = \sum_{t_s \neq t_d} \frac{\sigma_{sd}(t_i)}{\sigma_{sd}}, \tag{3}$$

where σ_{sd} is the total number of shortest paths from the source nodes t_s to the destination node t_d. The $\sigma_{sd}(t_i)$ is the number of those paths that pass through the node t_i. The node/device with a higher BC plays a more important role in the network and is more likely to be an attack target. Therefore, in this work, a device with a higher BC will be shuffled first.

Motivated by the studies on IP address shuffling [24,25], we adopt this MTD technology in our work. When needed, a device's rIP can be randomly mapped to one vIP from a pool of $(|K| - 1)$ vIPs. As the noise introduced by DP is random, the device of the VLAN under study can be shuffled to any other $(|K| - 1)$ VLANs. Before shuffling, a new set of $(|K| - 1)$ vIPs for each device is randomly generated. The communication process between the source device and destination device under IP shuffling-based MTD (i.e., rIP-to-vIP mapping and vIP-to-rIP mapping) as bellow.

As we mentioned in **Phase 3** in Sect. 3, only the SDN controller and the device itself know their rIPs while other devices use vIPs to communicate with each other. When the source device sends a packet to the nearest SDN switch, the SDN switch transmits the packet to the SDN controller. The SDN controller receives the packet to map vIP to rIP from the packet header information, and updates the flow-table entry of all SDN switches (e.g., Open-Flow-Switches). Each switch uses the flow rules to convert the rIP into the vIP in the packet header. The SDN switch near the destination device convert the vIP of the destination device in a packet header to its rIP. Hence, both the source device and destination device do not know each other's rIP and the mapping is transparent to an end device with no service disruption since rIPs of devices remain unchanged [24, 25].

Optimal Defence Deployment: Deploying any defence technology can reduce the security risk of a given IoT network, but it may incur costs as well. We treat this cost-increasing problem as an optimisation problem. Due to the discrete nature of our problem formulation, we use greedy algorithm to find the trade-off between the defence cost and the privacy protection. The objective function is

$$\underset{C1(k,j),C2(d,k)}{\arg\min} \quad M1(k,j) * C1(k,j) + M2(d,k) * C2(d,k)$$

$$\text{s.t.} \quad \begin{cases} M1(k,j) \in \{0,1\}, \\ M2(d,k) \in \{0,1\}, \end{cases}$$

where $M1(k', k) * C1(k', k)$ represents the cost of moving devices from VLAN k to VLAN j, and $M2(d, k) * C2(d, k)$ is the cost of adding decoys d into VLAN k.

5   Evaluation

5.1   Simulation Setup

Figure 3 shows an example smart healthcare system where IoT technologies are heavily adopted [32, 33]. It consists of 4 VLANs, with 4 IoMT devices in VLAN2 (e.g., Ultrasound, X-Ray, MRI and CT Scanner in the Radiology Department that send images to servers), 10 user machines in VLAN3 (i.e., staff office), and 5 IoMT devices in VLAN4 (e.g., Electroencephalography Monitor and Neuron Endoscopes sensor in the Neurology Department) and 2 servers in VLAN5 (i.e., server room). VLAN5 can be accessed by other three VLANs as IoT devices need to send patients' information to the servers for storage or processing. VLAN2 and VLAN4 are connected to VLAN3 for administration purposes.

Based on the above structure, we consider 3 different scaled IoT networks (i.e., small, medium and large) in the case study. For each network scale, we run 1000 rounds of simulations to evaluate the scalability of our method. In each round of simulation, the numbers of servers and user machines are fixed, while the IoT device number varies. For small-scale, we consider 2 servers, 10 user machines, 9 IoMT devices. The network shown in Fig. 3 is of small-scale. For medium-scale, we consider 2 servers, 50 user machines, and IoMT device number ranging from 50 to 100 per VLAN with an increment of 25 in each simulation. For large-scale, we consider 2 severs, 100 user machines, and the IoMT device number ranging from 125 to 200 per VLAN with an increment of 25 in each simulation. To evaluate the adaptability of the method, we also consider 2 servers, 100 user machines, 400 IoMT devices, and increase the number of VLANs from 4 to 7 with an increment of 1 in each simulation.

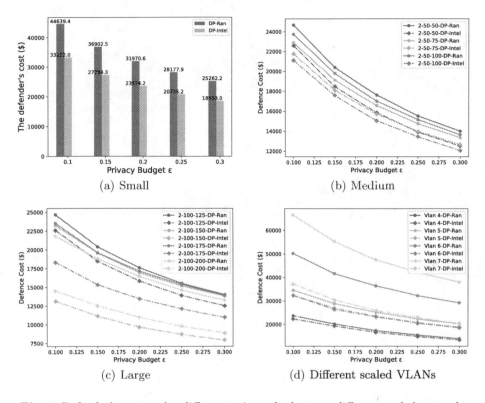

Fig. 4. Defender's cost under different privacy budgets on different scaled networks

5.2 Deception Cost

We consider the deception costs of two defence mechanisms. Each decoy is purchased individually with an annual license fee by type [34,35]. The estimated decoy prices from different manufacturers are shown in Table 2. Assume each IoT device added to VLAN is of the same type and provided by the same manufacturer. Prices for the deception products are the same as the prices shown in Table 2. In the example network, if one device is moved from one VLAN to another, it is switched off first before the move. During the moving period, there is moving cost incurred as well. For simplicity, we treat the moving cost within one hour as the cost of one shuffling operation, i.e., 150$ per hour per device.

5.3 Strategies to Deploy Defence Mechanisms

Two strategies are considered when deploying defence mechanisms based on the obfuscation results: random selection of VLAN, decoy, or device (*DP-Ran*) and intelligent selection of VLAN, decoy, or device based on their criticality as mentioned in Sect. 4.3 (*DP-Intel*). We set the privacy budget ranging from 0.1 to 0.3 with an increment of 0.05. Each simulation has 1000 rounds with random noise added.

Table 2. Annual license fees for decoys [34, 35]

Products	Types	Annual license fees ($)
Ultrasound	Emulation, Windows 8	200
X-Ray	Emulation, Windows 8	200
Magnetic Resonance Imaging (MRI)	Emulation, Windows 8	200
CT Scanner	Emulation, Windows 8	200
Electroencephalographs Monitor	Emulation, Windows 8	200
Nerve Monitor	Emulation, Windows 8	200
Neuron Endoscopes	Emulation, Windows 8	200
Spinal endoscopes	Emulation, Windows 8	200
Electromyography Monitor	Emulation, Windows 8	200
Computer	Emulation, Windows 8	300
Server	Full OS, Linux	1500

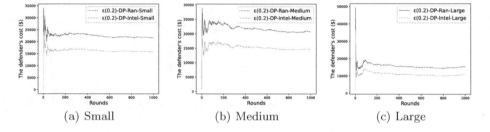

(a) Small   (b) Medium   (c) Large

Fig. 5. Defender's cost under privacy budget $\epsilon = 0.2$ on different scaled networks

Figure 4(a) shows the results of the small-scale IoT network. It can be seen that the defence costs under both strategies decrease with the increasing privacy budget. The intelligent selection strategy has a better defence performance with less defence cost under the same privacy budget. According to [30], if the healthcare provider has a defence budget of $25,000.00, the intelligent strategy with a privacy budget of 0.15–0.2 is the best defence option. By adding a small noise to the number of devices per VLAN, we obfuscate the attacker, and the defence cost is well under the budget. That suggests a smaller privacy budget provides a higher protection level.

Figure 4(b) and 4(c) show the defender's costs under different privacy budgets for medium-scale and large-scale networks. The defence cost decreases with the increasing privacy budget under *DP-Ran* and *DP-Intel*. This is because fewer devices to be moved or fewer decoys to be added into the networks for obfuscation. We can also see that the defence cost under *DP-Intel* is lower than that under *DP-Ran* with the same privacy budget. It verifies that our approach performs well on different scaled IoT networks and the defence cost decreases with the increasing privacy budget.

In Fig. 4(b), it can be seen that the *2-50-100-DP-Ran* has a higher defence cost than *2-50-75-DP-Ran* but a lower cost than *2-50-50-DP-Ran*. It is because the level of noise added to the number of devices per VLAN is random and the random strategy is used to select devices to be shuffled or decoys to be added. For the same reason, a similar case with *DP-Ran* can be seen in Fig. 4(c) where random noise has an impact on *DP-Intel* and causes varying defence costs.

Figure 4(d) shows the defender's cost under different privacy budgets and a fixed number of IoT devices in varying VLANs (from 4 to 7). When the privacy budget increases, the defence cost decreases. The reason is because small noise is added when the privacy budget is larger and fewer assets are moved or added. On the other hand, with the increase of VLAN number, the defender's cost also increases under the same privacy budget and two selection strategies *DP-Ran* and *DP-Intel*.

Particularly, in Fig. 4, for either *DP-Ran* or *DP Intel*, when the privacy budget increases, the difference between the defence costs under different sizes of networks decreases. For example, when $\epsilon = 0.3$, under each strategy, the difference between defence costs with different network sizes are minimal. It is because when the privacy budget ϵ is larger, the level of added noise is higher. It means the number of devices per VLAN can be very different with noise and without and the network's statistical information can not be obfuscated. The attacker can obtain the true operational information of IoT networks by analysing the col-located statistical information which is non-obfuscated, and then launch attack on real devices.

It can be seen in Fig. 4(a), a good trade-off is achieved between the defence cost and the privacy budget when the privacy budget is 0.2. We also conduct experiments with 1000 rounds of simulation and privacy budget being 0.2 to observe the trend of defence cost. The results are shown in Fig. 5. It is obvious that the defence costs of *DP-Intel* are lower than those of *DP-Ran*, indicating our approach performs well on protecting the IoT networks under a defence budget.

6   Conclusion

In this work, we are motivated by the attack model where attackers may exploit the statistical information of IoT networks (e.g., the number of devices per VLAN), infer the operational information of VLANs and launch attacks. To address this problem, we utilise a differential privacy mechanism to obfuscate the network information by adding Laplace noise to change the number of devices per VLAN. We then use two defence technologies to achieve the obfuscation. We evaluate our approach by considering different scaled networks to find the trade-off between defence cost and privacy budget. The simulation results show that our approach with intelligent selection strategy has a better performance compared to the random selection strategy. In our work, as we focus more on applying differential privacy mechanism to obfuscate VLANs and protect the network, the greedy strategy used for implementing MTD and deception technologies is simplified. In our future work, we will consider more sophisticated and effective strategies to select VLANs, devices and decoys for deletion or addition, as well as different MTD techniques for obfuscation. Using different privacy-preserving solutions, such as (ϵ, δ)-DP and Gaussian DP, is also worth exploring.

A   Proof of Proposition 1

Proof In the case of **Algorithm** 1, for neighbouring datasets N_k and N'_k, without loss of generality, let $\mathcal{A}$ be the step of Algorithm 1 that injects Laplace noise (i.e., Line 3 of Algorithm 1) and X be a random variable that follows $\mathrm{Lap}((\frac{|K|\cdot\Delta}{\epsilon}))$. For any output value z, we have:

$$\frac{\Pr[\mathcal{A}(N_k) = z]}{\Pr[\mathcal{A}(N'_k) = z]} \le \exp^{\frac{\epsilon}{|K|}}. \tag{4}$$

For any count function f, $A_{f(N_k)} = f(N_k) + \mathrm{Lap}(\frac{|K|\cdot\Delta}{\epsilon})$, it is easy to conclude

$$
\begin{aligned}
\frac{\Pr[\mathcal{A}_{f(N_k)} = z]}{\Pr[\mathcal{A}_{f(N'_k)} = z]} &= \frac{\Pr[f(N_k) + X = z]}{\Pr[f(N'_k) + X = z]} \\
&= \frac{\Pr[X = z - f(N_k)]}{\Pr[X = z - f(N'_k)]} \\
&= \frac{\frac{\epsilon}{2 \cdot |K| \cdot \Delta} \cdot \exp^{\frac{-\epsilon \cdot |z - f(N_k)|}{|K| \cdot \Delta}}}{\frac{\epsilon}{2 \cdot |K| \cdot \Delta} \cdot \exp^{\frac{-\epsilon \cdot |z - f(N'_k)|}{|K| \cdot \Delta}}} \\
&= \exp^{\left(\frac{-\epsilon \cdot |z - f(N_k)|}{|K| \cdot \Delta} - \frac{-\epsilon \cdot |z - f(N'_k)|}{|K| \cdot \Delta}\right)} \\
&= \exp^{\left(\epsilon \cdot \left(\frac{|z - f(N'_k)| - |z - f(N_k)|}{|K| \cdot \Delta}\right)\right)} \\
&\le \exp^{\left(\frac{\epsilon \cdot |f(N'_k) - f(N_k)|}{|K| \cdot \Delta}\right)}.
\end{aligned} \tag{5}
$$

Since the sensitivity Δ is 1 as mentioned before, and by definition of sensitivity, $\Delta = \max_{N_k, N'_k} \|f(N'_k) - f(N_k)\|_1$. Hence, Eq. (5) becomes

$$
\begin{aligned}
\frac{\Pr[\mathcal{A}_{f(N_k)} = z]}{\Pr[\mathcal{A}_{f(N'_k)} = z]} &= \frac{\Pr[f(N_k) + X = z]}{\Pr[f(N'_k) + X = z]} \\
&\le \exp^{\left(\frac{\epsilon \cdot |f(N'_k) - f(N_k)|}{|K| \cdot \Delta}\right)} \\
&\le \exp^{\left(\frac{\epsilon}{|K|}\right)}.
\end{aligned} \tag{6}
$$

Thus, each step of Algorithm 1 satisfies $\frac{\epsilon}{|K|}$-DP. As there are $|K|$ steps in Algorithm 1, based on Theorem 1, Algorithm 1 satisfies $(\sum_{i=1}^{|K|} \frac{\epsilon}{|K|})$-$DP$. Therefore, Algorithm 1 satisfies ϵ-DP.

Without loss of generality, denote Algorithm 1 as $\mathcal{A}_1$ and Algorithm 2 as $\mathcal{A}_2$. In the case of **Algorithm** 2, for neighbouring N_k and N'_k, let z be the output value of algorithm $\mathcal{A}_1$ and O be the set of output value of algorithm $\mathcal{A}_2$. According to the discussion above, we have proved $\mathcal{A}_1$ satisfies ϵ-DP, so we have

$$\frac{\Pr[\mathcal{A}_1(N_k) = z]}{\Pr[\mathcal{A}_1(N'_k) = z]} \le \exp^{\epsilon}. \tag{7}$$

For any $o \in O$, we have

$$
\begin{aligned}
\Pr[\mathcal{A}_2\left(\mathcal{A}_1(N_k)\right) = o] &= \sum_{o \in O} \Pr[\mathcal{A}_1(N_k) = z]\Pr[\mathcal{A}_2(z) = o] \\
&\leq \sum_{o \in O} \exp^{\epsilon}\Pr[\mathcal{A}_1(N_k') = z]\Pr[\mathcal{A}_2(z) = o] \\
&= \sum_{o \in O} \exp^{\epsilon}\Pr[\mathcal{A}_2\left(\mathcal{A}_1(N_k')\right) = o].
\end{aligned}
\tag{8}
$$

Hence, according to Eq. (8), we have

$$
\frac{\Pr[\mathcal{A}_2\left(\mathcal{A}_1(N_k)\right) = o]}{\Pr[\mathcal{A}_2\left(\mathcal{A}_1(N_k')\right) = o]} \leq \exp^{\epsilon},
\tag{9}
$$

Therefore, Algorithm 2 also satisfies ϵ-DP based on the Post-processing Theorem 2.   ⊓

References

1. Gokhale, P., Bhat, O., Bhat, S.: Introduction to IoT. Int. Adv. Res. J. Sci. Eng. Technol. **5**(1), 41–44 (2018)
2. Atzori, L., Iera, A., Morabito, G.: The internet of things: a survey. Comput. Netw. **54**(15), 2787–2805 (2010)
3. Help Net Security. Threat highlight: Analysis of 5+ million unmanaged, iot, and iomt devices (2020). https://www.helpnetsecurity.com/2020/07/24/analysis-of-5-million-unmanaged-iot-and-iomt-devices/
4. THALES. IoT security issues in 2022: A business perspective (2020). https://www.thalesgroup.com/en/markets/digital-identity-and security/iot/magazine/internet-threats
5. Ge, M., Kim, D.S.: A framework for modeling and assessing security of the internet of things. In: 2015 IEEE 21st International Conference on Parallel and Distributed Systems (ICPADS), pp. 776–781. IEEE (2015)
6. Nayak, A.K., Reimers, A., Feamster, N., Clark, R.: Resonance: dynamic access control for enterprise networks. In: Proceedings of the 1st ACM Workshop on Research on Enterprise Networking, pp. 11–18 (2009)
7. Almeshekah, M.H., Spafford, E.H.: Planning and integrating deception into computer security defenses. In: Proceedings of the 2014 New Security Paradigms Workshop, pp. 127–138 (2014)
8. Jajodia, S., Ghosh, A.K., Swarup, V., Wang, C., Wang, X.S.: Moving Target Defense: Creating Asymmetric Uncertainty for Cyber Threats, vol. 54. Springer, Heidelberg (2011). https://doi.org/10.1007/978-1-4614-0977-9
9. Crouse, M., Prosser, B., Fulp, E.W.: Probabilistic performance analysis of moving target and deception reconnaissance defenses. In: Proceedings of the Second ACM Workshop on Moving Target Defense, pp. 21–29 (2015)
10. Wang, C., Lu, Z.: Cyber deception: overview and the road ahead. IEEE Secur. Priv. **16**(2), 80–85 (2018)
11. Cho, J.H., et al.: Toward proactive, adaptive defense: a survey on moving target defense. IEEE Commun. Surv. Tutor. **22**(1), 709–745 (2020)

12. Ge, M., Cho, J., Ishfaq, B., Dong, S.K.: Modeling and analysis of integrated proactive defence mechanisms for internet of things. In: Modeling and Design of Secure Internet of Things (2020)
13. Ge, M., Hong, J.B., Yusuf, S.E., Kim, D.S.: Proactive defense mechanisms for the software-defined internet of things with non-patchable vulnerabilities. Future Gener. Comput. Syst. **78**, 568–582 (2018)
14. Ge, M., Cho, J.-H., Kamhoua, C.A., Kim, D.S.: Optimal deployments of defense mechanisms for the internet of things. In: 2018 International Workshop on Secure Internet of Things (SIoT), pp. 8–17. IEEE (2018)
15. Ge, M., Cho, J.-H., Kim, D.S., Dixit, G., Chen, I.-R.: Proactive defense for internet-of-things: Integrating moving target defense with cyberdeception. arXiv preprint arXiv:2005.04220 (2020)
16. Mercado-Velázquez, A.A., Escamilla-Ambrosio, P.J., Ortiz-Rodriguez, F.: A moving target defense strategy for internet of things cybersecurity. IEEE Access **9**, 118406–118418 (2021)
17. Lu, Z., Wang, C., Zhao, S.: Cyber deception for computer and network security: survey and challenges. arXiv preprint arXiv:2007.14497 (2020)
18. Juels, A., Rivest, R. L.: Honeywords: making password-cracking detectable. In: Proceedings of the 2013 ACM SIGSAC, pp. 145–160 (2013)
19. La, Q.D., Quek, T.Q., Lee, J., Jin, S., Zhu, H.: Deceptive attack and defense game in honeypot-enabled networks for the internet of things. IEEE Internet Things J. **3**(6), 1025–1035 (2016)
20. Tsemogne, O., Hayel, Y., Kamhoua, C., Deougoué, G.: Game theoretic modeling of cyber deception against epidemic botnets in internet of things. IEEE Internet Things J. **9**, 2678–2687 (2021)
21. Ye, D., Zhu, T., Shen, S., Zhou, W.: A differentially private game theoretic approach for deceiving cyber adversaries. IEEE TIFS **16**, 569–584 (2020)
22. ONF. Openflow switch specification (2017). https://opennetworking.org/sdn-resources/openflow-switch-specification/
23. Cadini, F., Zio, E., Petrescu, C.-A.: Using centrality measures to rank the importance of the components of a complex network infrastructure. In: Setola, R., Geretshuber, S. (eds.) CRITIS 2008. LNCS, vol. 5508, pp. 155–167. Springer, Heidelberg (2009). https://doi.org/10.1007/978-3-642-03552-4_14
24. Yoon, S., Cho, J.-H., Kim, D.S., Moore, T.J., Free-Nelson, F., Lim, H.: Attack graph-based moving target defense in software-defined networks. IEEE Trans. Netw. Serv. Manag. **17**(3), 1653–1668 (2020)
25. Sharma, D.P., Kim, D.S., Yoon, S., Lim, H., Cho, J.-H., Moore, T.J.: Frvm: flexible random virtual ip multiplexing in software-defined networks. In: 12th IEEE International Conference On Big Data Science and Engineering (TrustCom/BigDataSE), pp. 579–587. IEEE (2018)
26. TrapX. Security's deception grid (2017). https://www.scmagazine.com/trapx-security-deceptiongrid/article/681820
27. Dwork, C.: Differential privacy: a survey of results. In: Agrawal, M., Du, D., Duan, Z., Li, A. (eds.) TAMC 2008. LNCS, vol. 4978, pp. 1–19. Springer, Heidelberg (2008). https://doi.org/10.1007/978-3-540-79228-4_1
28. Zhu, T., Xiong, P., Li, G., Zhou, W., Philip, S.Y.: Differentially private model publishing in cyber physical systems. Future Gener. Comput. Syst. **108**, 1297–1306 (2020)
29. Li, N., Lyu, M., Su, D., Yang, W.: Differential privacy: from theory to practice. Synth. Lect. Inf. Secur. Priv. Trust **8**(4), 1–138 (2016)

30. Attivo Networks. Attivo botsink deception platform (2016). https://www.scmagazine.com/product-test/-/attivo-botsink-deception-platform
31. Alavizadeh, H., Hong, J.B., Kim, D.S., Jang-Jaccard, J.: Evaluating the effectiveness of shuffle and redundancy mtd techniques in the cloud. Comput. Secur. **102**, 102091 (2021)
32. James, A., Simon, M.B.: Medjack. 3 medical device hijack cyber attacks evolve. In: Proceedings of RSA Conference, San Francisco, CA, USA (2017)
33. Meggitt, S.: Medjack attacks: the scariest part of the hospital (2018)
34. Medical Equipment Leasing Cost. Medical equipment leasing cost (2020). https://costhack.com/medical-equipment-leasing-cost/
35. Computer. How much does it cost to lease it equipment? (2022). https://www.costowl.com/rental/equipment-leasing/equipment-leasing-computer-cost/

Privacy-Preserving Networked Systems and Protocols

Privacy-Preserving Online Ride-Hailing Matching System with an Untrusted Server

Hongcheng Xie[1]([⊠]), Zizhuo Chen[1], Yu Guo[2], Qin Liu[3], and Xiaohua Jia[1]

[1] City University of Hong Kong, Hong Kong, China
{hongcheng.xie,zizhuo.chen}@my.cityu.edu.hk, csjia@cityu.edu.hk
[2] Beijing Normal University, Beijing, China
yuguo@bnu.edu.cn
[3] Wuhan University, Hubei, China
qinliu@whu.edu.cn

Abstract. With the popularity of Online Ride-Hailing (ORH) service, there are growing concerns about location privacy because the taxis and passengers need to upload their locations to the service provider. These locations can be used to infer the users' personal information. In this paper, we propose a privacy-preserving online ride-hailing matching system, which allows an untrusted service provider to calculate the distances between the taxis and one passenger and find the nearest taxi by itself while protecting the users' location privacy. To calculate the distances in road networks, we leverage Road Network Embedding (RNE) in our proposed system. We propose a secure distance calculation scheme to conduct RNE distance calculation securely. In this scheme, we redesign Property-Preserving Hash (PPH) with Pseudo-Random Functions (PRF) and use PRF-based PPH to calculate the distance between two RNE location vectors securely. To enhance security, we embed the partition ID and generation time in PRF-based PPH ciphertext to limit the ciphertext match-ability. Our security analysis and experimental evaluation show that our proposed system is secure and efficient.

1 Introduction

The vigorous development of Online Ride-Hailing (ORH) services has greatly facilitated people's daily travel. Unlike traditional taxi cabs that require passengers to hail a car on the street, ORH allows passengers to request a ride using their mobile phones. The service provider can then match them with the nearest taxi based on their location information. According to Uber's latest financial report [16], there are about 109 million monthly active platform consumers in Uber.

However, with the growing popularity of ORH services, our society has also raised strong concerns about the privacy and security of location data. Passengers and taxis must upload their locations to the untrusted service provider.

The service provider can infer their private information, such as driving paths or daily activities, based on their uploaded locations.

To address the security issue, a line of papers [3,9,11,12,18,20] have been proposed to provide ORH services while ensuring location privacy. The works [3,12] were proposed to protect data privacy by cloaking the locations. Since cloaking may result in a loss of matching accuracy, ORide [11] leveraged the cryptographic primitives to encrypt the precise locations and matched the nearest taxi based on Euclidean distances. However, Euclidean distance cannot accurately describe the distances in the road network. In [9], Luo *et al.* proposed a design that uses Road Network Embedding (RNE) [13] as the distance metric instead of Euclidean distance. The authors leveraged Homomorphic Encryption and Garbled Circuits to protect the RNE locations. However, it needs another non-colluded crypto provider to assist the service provider, which leads to high bandwidth overhead and multiple communication rounds. Recently, the authors [20] devised an ORH scheme that allows a service provider to perform privacy-preserving ride-hailing services without involving a third server. Nevertheless, recent work shows that the service provider can infer the underlying plaintext under some scenarios [17].

In this paper, we propose a privacy-preserving ORH scheme that allows an untrusted service provider to find the nearest taxi for a passenger by itself while protecting location privacy. Our design leverages RNE [13] to transform the locations in the road network and calculate the distance between two locations. To conduct the secure ride-matching, we redesign Privacy-Preserving Hash (PPH) with Pseudo-Random Functions (PRFs) and propose a secure difference calculation with PRF-based PPH. With PRF-based PPH, the component in RNE vectors will be divided and encrypted into several bit-block ciphertexts. Each block ciphertext corresponds to a mask weighted difference. Using the binary comparison between the PRF values, the service provider can calculate the RNE distances from the ciphertexts and find the nearest taxi for one passenger. To enhance security, we divide the map into several partitions. The partition ID and ciphertext generation time will be embedded into the block ciphertext. Given a passenger ciphertext, it ensures that only the taxi ciphertexts from the same partition and generated at the same time can be used to calculate the distances. It reduces the number of candidate taxi ciphertexts cryptographically to improve the system security. The efficient primitive PRF also improves the PPH's performance significantly. Besides, we design a tagging scheme to further reduce the computation overhead in PPH. The service provider can compare the PRF values with the same tag. Security analysis and experimental evaluation demonstrate that our proposed system is secure and efficient.

2   Related Works

Some studies proposed some non-cryptographic solutions to hide the exact locations. PrivateRide [12] hides the pick-up and drop-off locations via cloaking. In [22], the authors proposed a cloaking scheme to match the passenger and taxi based on their grid IDs. In [4], the authors proposed a cloaking algorithm based on Hilbert Curve. However, such solutions cannot provide accurate service as they use imprecise locations.

Cryptography techniques, such as secure range query [2,7,19] and homomorphic encryption [6], can be used to address this issue. In [1], the authors proposed a privacy-preserving scheme that determines the meeting point based on Private Set Intersection. The authors in [14] leveraged secure kNN to calculate the trip similarity. Pham *et al.* [11] proposed a scheme that encrypts the exact locations of passengers and taxis and finds the nearest taxi based on homomorphic encryption and their Euclidean distances. However, Euclidean distances cannot represent the distances in road network. To better represent the distances in the road network, some works used different kinds of transformation methods to represent the road distances. Yu *et al.* [21] proposed a privacy-preserving ride matching system that utilized Hypercube embedding to transform the locations. They used Somewhat Homomorphic Encryption to calculate the Hamming distance between two transformed locations in the ciphertext domain. Luo *et al.* [9] utilized Road Network Embedding (RNE) to transform the locations. They leveraged homomorphic encryption and Garbled Circuit to calculate the distances and find the nearest taxi in a privacy-preserving manner. However, it needs another server to help the service provider in ride-matching. In [20], the authors proposed a PPH-based scheme that allows the cloud server to provide the privacy-preserving ORH service by itself. However, the server can infer the plaintexts under some scenarios in this system [17].

3   Preliminaries

3.1   Road Network Embedding

Road Network Embedding (RNE) [13] is a technique that transforms a road network into a high dimensional space to calculate the approximate distance between two points. In this scheme, every point in the road network can be assigned a vector. The distance between two points can be estimated by using their given vectors. The road network can be defined as a weighted graph $G = (V, E)$, where V is the set of road intersections, and E is the set of roads. We assume that G is an undirected graph. Let n denote the size of V, and $d(a, b)$ denote the length of minimum weighted path between a and b. A point u can be transformed into an $O(log^2 n)$-dimension vector as follows.

Let $\beta = O(logn)$ and $\kappa = O(logn)$. We define R as a set which consists of $\beta \cdot \kappa$ subsets of V, i.e., $R = \{S_{1,1}, ..., S_{1,\kappa}, ..., S_{\beta,1}, ..., S_{\beta,\kappa}\}$. Each subset $S_{i,j}$ is a random subset of V with 2^i nodes. For example, the subsets $S_{1,1}, ..., S_{\beta,1}$ have 2 nodes each. The subsets $S_{\beta,1}, ..., S_{\beta,\kappa}$ have 2^β nodes each. Let $D(u, S_{i,j})$ denote the minimum distance between u and the nodes in $S_{i,j}$, i.e., $D(u, S_{i,j}) = \min_{u' \in S_{i,j}} d(u, u')$. Thus, the embedded vector $E(u)$ of node u can be defined as:

$$E(u) = (E_{1,1}(u), ..., E_{1,\kappa}(u), ..., E_{\beta,1}(u), ..., E_{\beta,\kappa}(u)) \tag{1}$$

where $E_{i,j}(u) = D(u, S_{i,j})$.

Now we consider a moving object o which is moving on the edge between node u and node v. The component $E_{i,j}(o)$ of its embedded vector $E(o)$ can be defined as Eq. 2.

$$E_{i,j}(o) = \min\{d(o, u) + D(u, S_{i,j}), d(o, v) + D(v, S_{i,j})\} \qquad (2)$$

Given the embedded vectors $E(u)$ and $E(v)$ of two points u and v, the shortest distance $\delta(u, v)$ between u and v can be estimated by calculating the chessboard distance between $E(u)$ and $E(v)$, as shown in Eq. 3.

$$\delta(u, v) = \max_{i,j}(|E_{i,j}(u) - E_{i,j}(v)|) \qquad (3)$$

3.2   Pseudo-Random Function

A Pseudo-Random Function (PRF) is a function $f : \{0,1\}^n \times \{0,1\}^s \rightarrow \{0,1\}^m$ where its output is computationally indistinguishable from the output of a random oracle. Formally, a function $f : \{0,1\}^n \times \{0,1\}^s \rightarrow \{0,1\}^m$ is a (t, ϵ, q)-PRF if given $k \in \{0,1\}^s$ and $x \in \{0,1\}^n$, it is efficient to calculate $f_k(x) = f(x, k)$, and for any t-time oracle algorithm A, we have $|Pr_{\in\{0,1\}^s}[A^{f_k}] - Pr_{f\in\mathcal{F}}[A^f]| < \epsilon$ where $\mathcal{F} = \{f : \{0,1\}^n \rightarrow \{0,1\}^m\}$ and A makes at most q queries to the oracle.

3.3   Property-Preserving Hash

Property-Preserving Hash (PPH) [2] allows an entity to reveal the order of ciphertexts. Given the PPH ciphertexts $\hat{x}$ and $\hat{x'}$ of two bits x and x', we define the property P as Eq. 4.

$$P(\hat{x}, \hat{x'}) = \begin{cases} 1 & x = x' + 1 \\ 0 & \text{otherwise} \end{cases} \qquad (4)$$

In particular, the PPH ciphertext $\hat{x}$ includes two matchable ciphertexts of x and $x + 1$. Thus, given $\hat{x}$ and $\hat{x'}$, $P(\hat{x}, \hat{x'}) = 1$ if the matchable ciphertext of x in $\hat{x}$ matches the ciphertext of $x' + 1$ in $\hat{x'}$. With property P, the order between two ciphertexts can be determined.

4   Problem Statements

4.1   System Model

Our system model considers a ride-hailing system that helps a passenger find the nearest taxi in the road network. As shown in Fig. 1, our system consists of three entities, i.e., *service provider*, *taxis*, and *passengers*. *Service provider* is the entity that performs taxi-passenger matching based on their encrypted locations. It calculates the approximate distances between each taxi and an incoming passenger based on their ciphertexts and matches them by selecting the nearest taxi. *Taxis* are entities waiting for passengers. They encrypt their locations and upload the ciphertexts to Service Provider periodically to find the matched passenger. *Passengers* are the entities who want to hail the nearest taxi to start their trips. They encrypt their locations and upload the ciphertexts to Service Provider to find the nearest taxi.

According to Eq. 3, to calculate the distance and select the nearest taxi securely, our design should be able to calculate the comparable difference from the vector ciphertexts.

4.2 Threat Model

We assume that the service provider is *honest-but-curious*. It honestly follows our proposed design, but is curious to learn the private information about the locations of the taxis and passengers from the ciphertexts and results. In practice, ride-hailing service provider are usually large reputable companies. Active attacks can be detected easily. We also assume that the passengers and the taxis are *fully trusted* so that they can keep their secret keys secure. The road data that is used to generate the location vectors is assumed to be public.

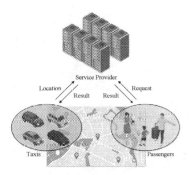

Fig. 1. System Structure.

5 Proposed System

5.1 Secure Distance Calculation from PRF-based PPH

In this section, we discuss about how to encrypt the RNE vectors and calculate the distances between two vectors. Let $E_i(u)$ denote the i-th component of the RNE vector $E(u)$, and z denote the ID of the partition in the map. Suppose that there is one passenger u_p and one taxi u_t in the road network. Their RNE vectors are $E(u_p)$ and $E(u_t)$. They are in the partition z and the vectors are generated at time slot s. To securely calculate the distance between u_p and u_t in the RNE context, we need to securely calculate the difference between the i-th pair of components first, i.e., $E_i(u_p) - E_i(u_t)$.

To encrypt the components $E_i(u_p)$ from the passenger, the passenger first divides the binary representation of $E_i(u_p)$ into m bit-blocks with the same block size l. We denote by $[E_i(u_p)]_j$ the j-th bit-block of $E_i(u_p)$, where j counts from 0 and is indexed from the least significant bit. For instance, we suppose that $E_i(u_p)$ is 41 ("101001" in binary) and it will be divided into 3 bit-blocks with block size 2. $[E_i(u_p)]_2$ is "10", $[E_i(u_p)]_1$ is "10" and $[E_i(u_p)]_0$ is "01". The component $E_i(u_t)$ from the taxi is also divided into m bit-blocks as above.

We discuss about how to encrypt $[E_i(u_p)]_j$ first. As the block size is l, there are 2^l possible values for one block, i.e., from 0 to $2^l - 1$. Let q denote the possible value, i.e., $q \in [0..2^l - 1]$. For each $q \in [0..2^l - 1]$, we calculate the difference between it and $[E_i(u_p)]_j$. Note that we need to multiply the difference by a block weight instead of calculating it directly. Each block $[E_i(u_p)]_j$ has its position-related block weight, similar to bit weight. We denote by w_j the block weight for the j-th block and define $w_j = (2^l)^j$. In the aforementioned example, the weight of $[E_i(u_p)]_2$ is $(2^2)^2 = 16$. The weight represents the contribution of the difference in one block. Let $[E_i(u_p)]_{j,q}$ denote the tuple of the possible value q and the weighted difference between $[E_i(u_p)]_j$ and q. To encrypt one block $[E_i(u_p)]_j$, we encrypt all the possible values q to the matchable ciphertexts in PPH together with their corresponding weighted differences. To protect the weighted difference, it should be masked by a token so that it can be unmasked if and only if there is a correct token from the block ciphertext of the taxi. We will discuss the details later.

The set that needs to be encrypted for $[E_i(u_p)]_j$ is defined as shown in Eq. 5, including all possible values with their weighted differences.

$$\{[E_i(u_p)]_{j,q} = (q, (q - [E_i(u_p)]_j) * w_j)|q \in [0..2^l - 1]\} \tag{5}$$

To encrypt the block $[E_i(u_t)]_j$ from the taxi, we generate the matchable ciphertext for $[E_i(u_t)]_j$ itself instead of all the possible values on the passenger's side. Our basic idea is to ensure that the matchable ciphertext of $[E_i(u_t)]_j$ matches the ciphertext of q if and only if $[E_i(u_t)]_j = q$. Thus, the weighted difference between q and $[E_i(u_p)]_j$ is that between $[E_i(u_t)]_j$ and $[E_i(u_p)]_j$ so that the difference is revealed correctly.

Now we focus on how to encrypt one possible tuple $[E_i(u_p)]_{j,q}$ based on PPH. We leverage PRF as the matching cryptographic primitive. Let $[E_i(\hat{u}_p)]_{j,q}$ denote the ciphertext of $[E_i(u_p)]_{j,q}$. It is defined as

$$\begin{aligned} (tag_{i,j,q}, F(H(k_1, q||i||j||z||s), \gamma_j), \\ F(H(k_2, q||i||j||z||s), \gamma_j) \oplus ((q - [E_i(u_p)]_j) * w_j)) \end{aligned} \tag{6}$$

where $||$ is the string concatenation operator, $\oplus$ is the XOR operator, H and F are PRFs, γ_j is a random number shared among all the ciphertexts for block $[E_i(u_p)]_j$, and k_1 and k_2 are two secret keys shared among the passengers and taxis. They are distributed by a key manager, an independent admittance control entity that is not involved in taxi matching. $tag_{i,j,q}$ is a tag used to improve the query efficiency, which is defined as

$$tag_{i,j,q} = F(H(k_1, q||i||j||z||s), \gamma_j) \& (2^\theta - 1) \tag{7}$$

where $\&$ is bit-wise AND operator, and θ is a pre-defined value which is smaller than l. That means we use the last θ bits as the tag of this ciphertext. The ciphertexts with the same tag can be grouped together. The ciphertext order in one group can be shuffled. We will discuss about how to use it to improve the query efficiency later.

We denote by $[E_i(\hat{u}_p)])_j$ the ciphertext of block $[E_i(u_p)]_j$. $[E_i(\hat{u}_p)]_j$ includes the ciphertexts of all possible tuples $[E_i(u_p)]_{j,q}$ and the random nunce γ_j, as shown in Eq. 8.

$$[E_i(\hat{u}_p)]_j = \{\gamma_j, [E_i(\hat{u}_p)]_{j,q} | q \in [0..2^l - 1]\} \tag{8}$$

In the above discussion, we have discussed that we generate the matchable ciphertext for $[E_i(u_t)]_j$ itself for the taxi block. In particular, the ciphertext $[E_i(\hat{u}_t)]_j$ is defined as Eq. 9.

$$(H(k_1, [E_i(u_t)]_j||i||j||z||s), H(k_2, [E_i(u_t)]_j||i||j||z||s)) \tag{9}$$

The ciphertexts of $E_i(u_p)$ and $E_i(u_t)$ consists of the ciphertexts of all the blocks respectively, as shown in Eq. 10 and Eq. 11.

$$E_i(\hat{u}_p) = \{[E_i(\hat{u}_p)]_j | j \in [0..2^l - 1]\} \tag{10}$$

$$E_i(\hat{u}_t) = \{[E_i(\hat{u}_t)]_j | j \in [0..2^l - 1]\} \tag{11}$$

Thus, given two block ciphertexts $[E_i(\hat{u}_p)]_j$ and $[E_i(\hat{u}_t)]_j$, the service provider can scan the possible ciphertexts in $[E_i(\hat{u}_p)]_j$. The block ciphertext $[E_i(\hat{u}_t)]_j$ matches one possible ciphertext $[E_i(\hat{u}_p)]_{j,q}$ if and only if Eq. 12 holds, which the left side is from $[E_i(\hat{u}_p)]_{j,q}$ and the right side is the PRF value with the ciphertext from $[E_i(\hat{u}_t)]_j$ and γ_j from $[E_i(\hat{u}_p)]_j$.

$$F(H(k_1, q||i||j||z||s), \gamma_j) \overset{?}{=} F(H(k_1, [E_i(u_t)]_j||i||j||z||s), \gamma_j) \tag{12}$$

According to Eq. 12, we can find that Eq. 12 holds if and only if $q = [E_i(u_t)]$. The other parameters in PRF also ensures that they are from the j-th block in the i-th components, from the same zone z, and generated at the same time slot s.

To improve query efficiency, we can extract the last θ bits of the right side in Eq. 12, as shown in Eq. 13. We can only test the possible ciphertexts $[E_i(\hat{u}_p)]_{j,q}$ with the same tag, i.e., $tag' = tag_{i,j,q}$, to reduce the number of matching tests.

$$tag' = F(H(k_1, [E_i(u_t)]_j||i||j||z||s), \gamma_j)\&(2^\theta - 1) \tag{13}$$

Once $[E_i(\hat{u}_t)]_j$ matches one $[E_i(\hat{u}_p)]_{j,q}$, we can generate the mask $mask_j$ with $H(k_2, [E_i(u_t)]_j||i||j||z||s)$ from $[E_i(\hat{u}_t)]_j$ and γ_j from $[E_i(\hat{u}_p)]_j$, as shown in Eq. 14. According to Eq. 6, we can find that $mask_j$ is equal to the mask of weighted difference $(q - [E_i(u_p)]_j) * w_j$ if $[E_i(u_t)]_j = q$, i.e., they are matched.

Thus, by using XOR operation, we can reveal the weighted difference $([E_i(u_t)]_j - [E_i(u_p)]_j) * w_j$ from the block ciphertext.

$$mask_j = F(H(k_2, [E_i(u_t)]_j||i||j||z||s), \gamma_j) \tag{14}$$

After revealing $([E_i(u_t)]_j - [E_i(u_p)]_j) * w_j$ for all $j \in [0..m]$, the absolute difference between the i-th components $|E_i(u_t) - E_i(u_p)|$ can be calculated as Eq. 15.

$$|E_i(u_t) - E_i(u_p)| = |\sum_{j \in [0..m]} (([E_i(u_t)]_j - [E_i(u_p)]_j) * w_j)| \tag{15}$$

Let $E(\hat{u}_t)$ and $E(\hat{u}_p)$ denote the ciphertexts of RNE vectors $E(u_t)$ and $E(u_p)$ respectively. The ciphertext $E(\hat{u}_t)$ for the taxi is defined as Eq. 16. It consists of the ciphertexts of all the components, the time slot and the partition ID.

$$E(\hat{u}_t) = \{s, z, E_i(\hat{u}_t)|i \in [0..\beta \cdot \kappa]\} \tag{16}$$

The ciphertext $E(\hat{u}_p)$ for the passenger is defined as Eq. 17.

$$E(\hat{u}_p) = \{s, z, E_i(\hat{u}_p)|i \in [0..\beta \cdot \kappa]\} \tag{17}$$

As we can calculate the absolute differences for one pair of components, given the ciphertexts of two RNE vectors, the distance between one passenger and one taxi can be calculated according to Eq. 3.

In summary, the service provider can calculate the RNE distance between a passenger and a taxi securely if they are from the same partition and their ciphertexts are generated in the same time slot.

5.2 Passenger-Driver Matching

In Sect. 5.1, we discussed about how to calculate the distance between a passenger and a taxi. Let U_t denote the set of all taxis, and $E(\hat{U}_t)_{z,s}$ denote the ciphertexts of the taxis with partition ID z and time slot s. Given a passenger's ciphertext $E(\hat{u}_p)$ with partition ID z and time slot s, as the partition ID and time slot are included explicitly, the service provider can select the taxis with the same partition ID and time slot to calculate the distances, i.e., between $E(\hat{u}_p)$ and the ciphertexts in $E(\hat{U}_t)_{z,s}$. It can reduce the number of candidate taxis to improve the query efficiency. These two values that are embedded in PRFs also ensures that the service provider cannot calculate the distance between two ciphertexts if their partition IDs or time slots are different. After calculating all the distances between $E(\hat{u}_p)$ and the ciphertexts in $E(\hat{U}_t)_{z,s}$, the service provider selects the taxi with minimum distance as the nearest taxi. The distance does not leak the location information of both passenger and taxi.

In the above design, only the passenger and taxi in the same partition can be matched. However, the nearest taxi in one partition may not be the nearest one in the global map. To improve the accuracy, we let the taxi in the partition z generate the another extra 8 ciphertexts of its current RNE vectors with z', which is the adjacent partition of z. Thus, a taxi will participate the matching procedure for its partition and its neighbor partitions. Relatively, one hailing request from a passenger will be served by the taxis from its partition and its neighbor partitions. This design can improve the query accuracy of our proposed system.

5.3   Early Stopping in Distance Calculation

In the above discussion, we calculate the absolute differences for all the components and select the maximum as the distance between the passenger and one taxi. The taxi with smallest distance will be selected as the nearest taxi. As the service provider needs to calculate the distances between the passenger and taxis one by one, we denote by min as the current smallest distance when the service provider is calculating the distance between the passenger u_p and one taxi u_t. We have one observation.

Observation: We suppose that the service provider is calculating the absolute difference between the i-th pair of components, i.e., $|E_i(u_t) - E_i(u_p)|$. u_t is not the nearest taxi if $|E_i(u_t) - E_i(u_p)| > min$, as the distance between u_p and u_t is impossible to be smaller than $|E_i(u_t) - E_i(u_p)|$ according to Eq. 3. The distance must be larger than the current smallest distance min if $|E_i(u_t) - E_i(u_p)| > min$.

According to the above *Observation*, the distance calculation between u_p and u_t can be terminated if the service provider finds that $|E_i(u_t) - E_i(u_p)| > min$. Thus, the unneccessary calculation can be avoided.

6   Security Analysis

6.1   Leakage Definition

As the difference between two components are calculated from the revealed weighted differences in plaintext, our security analysis will focus on the secure block weighted difference calculation. First we define the following leakage functions:

Leakage Function $\mathcal{L}_1(u)$: Let $(tag_{i,j,q}, CT_1, CT_2)$ denote the ciphertext in Eq. 6. Given a block value u from one passenger, the leakage function for passengers is defined as $\mathcal{L}_1(u) = (\langle |tag_{i,j,q}|, |CT_1|, |CT_2| \rangle, l, |\gamma|)$, where l is the block size, and $|tag_{i,j,q}|, |CT_1|, |CT_2|$, and $|\gamma|$ are the bit lengths.

Leakage Function $\mathcal{L}_2(u^*)$: Let (CT_1', CT_2') denote the ciphertext in Eq. 9. Given a block value u^* from one taxi, the leakage function for taxis is defined as $\mathcal{L}_2(u^*) = (|CT_1'|, |CT_2'|)$.

Leakage Function $\mathcal{L}_3(\hat{u}, \hat{u}^*)$: Given two block ciphertexts from a passenger and a taxi, the leakage function for the comparison is defined as $\mathcal{L}_3(\hat{u}, \hat{u}^*) = (MP, dif, N_{t \times t})$, where MP is the matched possible ciphertext, dif is the revealed weighted difference, and $N_{t \times t}$ is a symmetric binary matrix that records the repeated comparisons.

Based on the simulation-based security definition in [5], the security definition of our system is defined as follows.

Definition 1. *Let $\Omega = \{$EncPassBlock, EncTaxiBlock, BlockDiff$\}$ be the secure block weighted difference calculation scheme, $\mathcal{A}$ be a probabilistic polynomial time (PPT) adversary, $\mathcal{S}$ be a PPT simulator, and λ be the security parameter. The probabilistic experiments $\textbf{Real}_{\Omega,\mathcal{A}}(1^\lambda)$ and $\textbf{Ideal}_{\Omega,\mathcal{A},\mathcal{S}}(1^\lambda)$ are defined as:*

$\textbf{Real}_{\Omega,\mathcal{A}}(1^\lambda)$: *$\mathcal{A}$ selects a block value u and lets a passenger generate a ciphertext via EncPassBlock. Then $\mathcal{A}$ launches a polynomial number of comparisons, which lets a taxi generate the ciphertext via EncTaxiBlock, and gets the result via BlockDiff. Finally, $\mathcal{A}$ outputs a bit as the output.*

$\textbf{Ideal}_{\Omega,\mathcal{A},\mathcal{S}}(1^\lambda)$: *$\mathcal{A}$ selects the block value u. $\mathcal{S}$ simulates the ciphertext for $\mathcal{A}$ based on $\mathcal{L}_1$. Then $\mathcal{A}$ launches a polynomial number of comparisons adaptively, which lets $\mathcal{S}$ simulate the ciphertexts based on $\mathcal{L}_2$ and the comparisons based on $\mathcal{L}_3$. Finally, $\mathcal{A}$ outputs a bit as the output.*

Definition 2. *Ω is $(\mathcal{L}_1, \mathcal{L}_2, \mathcal{L}_3)$-secure if for any PPT adversary $\mathcal{A}$, there exists a PPT simulator $\mathcal{S}$ such that $|Pr[\textbf{Real}_{\Omega,\mathcal{A}}(1^\lambda) = 1] - Pr[\textbf{Ideal}_{\Omega,\mathcal{A},\mathcal{S}}(1^\lambda) = 1]| \leq neg(\lambda)$, where $neg(\lambda)$ is a negligible function for λ.*

6.2 Analysis

Theorem 1. *Ω is $(\mathcal{L}_1, \mathcal{L}_2, \mathcal{L}_3)$-secure if F and H are PRFs.*

Proof. We first define a sequence of hybrid experiments.

$\mathcal{H}_0$: It is the same as the experiment $\textbf{Real}_{\Omega,\mathcal{A}}(1^\lambda)$.

$\mathcal{H}_1$: It is the same as $\mathcal{H}_0$, except that $\mathcal{S}$ picks random strings as the passenger's ciphertext using $\mathcal{L}_1$ instead of calling F.

$\mathcal{H}_2$: It is the same as $\mathcal{H}_1$, except that $\mathcal{S}$ picks random strings as the taxi's ciphertext using $\mathcal{L}_2$ instead of calling H.

$\mathcal{H}_3$: it is the same as $\mathcal{H}_2$, except that $\mathcal{S}$ simulates the comparison result using $\mathcal{L}_3$ adaptively, which is $\textbf{Ideal}_{\Omega,\mathcal{A},\mathcal{S}}(1^\lambda)$.

First, due to the pseudo-randomness of PRF, $\mathcal{A}$ cannot distinguish between a PRF string and a random string computationally. Thus, $\mathcal{H}_0$ and $\mathcal{H}_1$ is computationally indistinguishable to $\mathcal{A}$. Due to the same reason, $\mathcal{H}_1$ and $\mathcal{H}_2$ is also computationally indistinguishable to $\mathcal{A}$. In $\mathcal{H}_3$, $\mathcal{S}$ generates the random strings if one taxi's block value is not requested before. Otherwise, it returns the same ciphertext. As discussed before, $\mathcal{A}$ cannot distinguish between the random string and the ciphertexts generated by PRF computationally. Thus, $\mathcal{H}_2$ and $\mathcal{H}_3$ are computationally indistinguishable. In summary, $\textbf{Real}_{\Omega,\mathcal{A}}(1^\lambda)$ and $\textbf{Ideal}_{\Omega,\mathcal{A},\mathcal{S}}(1^\lambda)$ are computationally indistinguishable to $\mathcal{A}$. This completes the proof.

6.3 Discussion About the Difference Leakage

In the comparison, weighted differences for matched possible ciphertexts will be leaked to the service provider. One ciphertext for a passenger's block includes

2^l possible ciphertexts with different weighted differences. An attack against PPH shows that a passenger's block value can be revealed if the service provider collects block ciphertexts from 2^l taxis, each of which leaks a different weighted difference from this passenger's block ciphertext [17]. However, in our proposed system, the attack is difficult to be achieved under real-world conditions. For example, according to the statistics [15] from Uber, there are about 14,000 taxis in Hong Kong. We suppose that taxis are distributed uniformly. If we set the partition scheme to 20×20 and set the block size l to 12, there are about 315 taxis in a 3×3 area, which can participate in one passenger's comparison, but the number of needed taxis is at least 4096. It is difficult to be achieved.

7 Experimental Evaluation

7.1 Experiment Setup

The prototypes of our proposed system and the baseline [20] are implemented by C. The evaluations were conducted on a computer equipped with Intel i7-10700 and 64 GB memory. The binary length of one component in a vector is set as 24. Our proposed system uses HMAC-SHA256 as the PRF and uses the first 128 bits. We compare with the baseline [20], a privacy-preserving ride-hailing system based on RNE and PPH with bilinear maps. It is implemented by Pairing-Based Cryptography library [10] with Type A, where r is 160 bits and q is 512 bits. The block size l in the baseline is set as 2. We use a real-world dataset [8] which includes road information of 21048 nodes and 21693 edges. The passengers and taxis are generated randomly on the edges. The results is the mean of 10 trials.

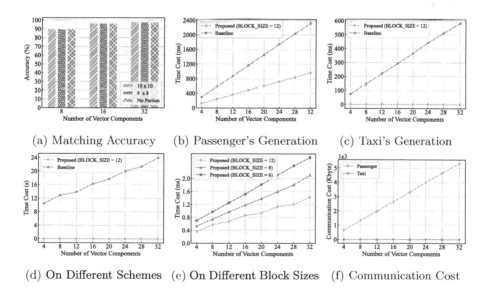

(a) Matching Accuracy   (b) Passenger's Generation   (c) Taxi's Generation

(d) **On Different Schemes**   (e) **On Different Block Sizes**   (f) Communication Cost

Fig. 2. System evaluation

7.2   Performance

Accuracy: Since RNE estimates the distances in the road network, it may incur inaccurate result. Moreover, we use partition to reduce the number of candidate taxis. We evaluate the accuracy of our system and the influence of partition granularity on accuracy. We generate 100 passengers randomly and count the number of passengers whose matched taxis from RNE are the same as the ground truths. From Fig. 2a, the accuracy raises as the component raises. The accuracy is 98% when the component is 32. Our partition scheme is not influence on the accuracy.

The Performance of Generation: Figure 2b shows that the passenger's time cost of ciphertext generation increases when the number of components increases. Figure 2c illustrates that taxi's also increases as the number of components increases. The taxi's time cost is smaller than the passenger's, although the taxi needs to encrypt 9 vector ciphertexts for different partition IDs. That is because the passenger needs to encrypt several possible values for each block encryption, while the taxi only needs to encrypt one value. According to Fig. 2f, as the same reason, the taxi's cost is smaller than the passenger's. It is reasonable because taxis need to upload their tokens frequently to wait for the passenger.

The Performance of Taxi-Passenger Matching: Our evaluation is conducted under 800 taxis and the partition scheme 10×10. According to Fig. 2d, we can find that the time cost of our scheme is significantly better than the baseline. From Fig. 2e, the time costs of all the three block settings raise linearly as the number of components increases. We can find that the time cost decreases as the block size increases, as the increase of the block size leads to the decrease of the number of blocks in one vector component. Although the number of the ciphertexts for the possible values is exponential to the block size in one block, the service provider needs to compare only a small part of them by using our tag optimization scheme. The comparison costs in one block with different block size are close. Thus, less blocks result in less time cost. PRFs provide efficient ciphertext matching, and our partition design and tagging scheme reduce the number of ciphertext matching operations.

8   Conclusion

In this work, we proposed a privacy-preserving online ride-hailing system with an untrusted server. The service provider can find the nearest taxi for one passenger by itself. We used RNE to transform the road location to a vector. To calculate the distance securely, we redesigned PPH using PRF as its matching primitive, and used PRF-based PPH to propose a secure distance calculation scheme. To enhance security, we divided the map into several partitions and embedded the information about partition and generation time into PPH ciphertexts. The efficient PRFs and our tag scheme improve the efficiency. We provided the security analysis, and evaluation results showed that our system is accurate and efficient.

Acknowledgement. This work is financially supported by NSFC under Grant No. 62102035, and HKRGC under Grant No. CityU 11213920.

References

1. Aïvodji, U.M., Gambs, S., Huguet, M.J., Killijian, M.O.: Meeting points in ridesharing: a privacy-preserving approach. Transp. Res Part C: Emerging Technol. **72**, 239–253 (2016)
2. Cash, D., Liu, F.-H., O'Neill, A., Zhandry, M., Zhang, C.: Parameter-hiding order revealing encryption. In: Peyrin, T., Galbraith, S. (eds.) ASIACRYPT 2018. LNCS, vol. 11272, pp. 181–210. Springer, Cham (2018). https://doi.org/10.1007/978-3-030-03326-2_7
3. Chow, C.Y., Mokbel, M.F., Liu, X.: A peer-to-peer spatial cloaking algorithm for anonymous location-based service. In: Proceedings of the 14th ACM GIS, pp. 171–178 (2006)
4. Cui, N., Yang, X., Wang, B.: A novel spatial cloaking scheme using hierarchical hilbert curve for location-based services. In: Cui, B., Zhang, N., Xu, J., Lian, X., Liu, D. (eds.) WAIM 2016. LNCS, vol. 9659, pp. 15–27. Springer, Cham (2016). https://doi.org/10.1007/978-3-319-39958-4_2
5. Curtmola, R., Garay, J., Kamara, S., Ostrovsky, R.: Searchable symmetric encryption: improved definitions and efficient constructions. J. Comput. Secur. **19**(5), 895–934 (2011)
6. Fan, J., Vercauteren, F.: Somewhat practical fully homomorphic encryption. Cryptology ePrint Archive (2012)
7. Guo, Y., Xie, H., Wang, M., Jia, X.: Privacy-preserving multi-range queries for secure data outsourcing services. IEEE TCC (2022)
8. Li, F., Cheng, D., Hadjieleftheriou, M., Kollios, G., Teng, S.-H.: On trip planning queries in spatial databases. In: Bauzer Medeiros, C., Egenhofer, M.J., Bertino, E. (eds.) SSTD 2005. LNCS, vol. 3633, pp. 273–290. Springer, Heidelberg (2005). https://doi.org/10.1007/11535331_16
9. Luo, Y., Jia, X., Fu, S., Xu, M.: pride: privacy-preserving ride matching over road networks for online ride-hailing service. IEEE TIFS **14**(7), 1791–1802 (2018)
10. Lynn, B.: On the implementation of pairing-based cryptosystems. Ph.D. thesis, Stanford University Stanford, California (2007)
11. Pham, A., Dacosta, I., Endignoux, G., Pastoriza, J.R.T., Huguenin, K., Hubaux, J.P.: Oride: a privacy-preserving yet accountable ride-hailing service. In: 26th {USENIX} Security 17), pp. 1235–1252 (2017)
12. Pham, A., et al.: Privateride: a privacy-enhanced ride-hailing service. PoPETs **2017**(2), 38–56 (2017)
13. Shahabi, C., Kolahdouzan, M.R., Sharifzadeh, M.: A road network embedding technique for k-nearest neighbor search in moving object databases. GeoInformatica **7**(3), 255–273 (2003)
14. Sherif, A.B., Rabieh, K., Mahmoud, M.M., Liang, X.: Privacy-preserving ride sharing scheme for autonomous vehicles in big data era. IEEE IoTJ **4**(2), 611–618 (2016)
15. Uber: Uber marks 6 years in Hong Kong (2020). https://www.uber.com/en-HK/newsroom/uber-marks-6-years-in-hong-kong/
16. Uber: Uber announces results for third quarter 2021 (2021). https://investor.uber.com/news-events/news/press-release-details/2021/Uber-Announces-Results-for-Third-Quarter-2021/

17. Vivek, S.: Comments on" a privacy-preserving online ride-hailing system without involving a third trusted server. arXiv preprint arXiv:2112.06449 (2021)
18. Wang, F., et al.: Efficient and privacy-preserving dynamic spatial query scheme for ride-hailing services. IEEE TVT **67**(11), 11084–11097 (2018)
19. Wong, W.K., Cheung, D.W.l., Kao, B., Mamoulis, N.: Secure KNN computation on encrypted databases. In: Proceedings of the 2009 ACM SIGMOD International Conference on Management of Data, pp. 139–152 (2009)
20. Xie, H., Guo, Y., Jia, X.: A privacy-preserving online ride-hailing system without involving a third trusted server. IEEE TIFS **16**, 3068–3081 (2021)
21. Yu, H., Jia, X., Zhang, H., Shu, J.: Efficient and privacy-preserving ride matching using exact road distance in online ride hailing services. IEEE TSC **15**, 1841–1854 (2020)
22. Zhu, L., Li, M., Zhang, Z., Qin, Z.: Asap: an anonymous smart-parking and payment scheme in vehicular networks. IEEE TDSC **17**(4), 703–715 (2018)

Efficient and Fine-Grained Sharing of Signed Healthcare Data in Smart Healthcare

Jianghua Liu[1], Lei Xu[1(✉)], Bruce Gu[2], Lei Cui[3], and Fei Zhu[4]

[1] Nanjing University of Science and Technology, Nanjing, China
xuleicrypto@gmail.com
[2] Victoria University, Footscray, Australia
Bruce.gu@vu.edu.au
[3] Shandong Computer Science Center (National Supercomputer Center in Jinan),
Jinan, China
[4] RMIT University, Melbourne, Australia

Abstract. Smart healthcare, as an examplar domain, is empowered by the remarkable miniaturization of sensors and the proliferation of smart devices, which lead to the production of massive amounts of healthcare data. Smart healthcare in the future is expected as a health service system that uses wearable devices, IoT, and mobile internet to dynamically collect and deliver healthcare data and then intelligently provide healthcare services. However, security is increasingly being challenged due to the highly valuable data transformed in such a healthcare network that might be tampered with by malicious users or disclosed without considering the privacy of patients. These pose new challenges for improving healthcare services' safety, quality, and efficiency. In this paper, we propose a redactable signature scheme (RSS) with a short signature and fine-grained sharing control for authenticating the integrity and authenticity of healthcare data while preserving the privacy of patients in the smart healthcare system. The security analysis of our construction shows that it achieves unforgeability and unlinkability. Finally, the efficiency comparison with other related solutions indicates that our scheme could solve the security issues for healthcare data sharing in the smart healthcare system with less computational and communication overhead.

Keywords: Smart healthcare · Authentication · Fine-grained · Privacy-preserving · Unlinkability

1 Introduction

The Internet of Things (IoT) offers a significant and beneficial impact on integrating existing and new technologies. Different from the traditional internet, IoT connects all sorts of connected "Things" (interrelated and intelligence computing devices) into a comprehensive network to exchange data with others over the

X. Yuan et al. (Eds.): NSS 2022, LNCS 13787, pp. 443–458, 2022.
https://doi.org/10.1007/978-3-031-23020-2_25

Internet. Smart community, an IoT application, refers to some concrete examples such as smart homes, smart healthcare, and smart grids enabling a variety of monitoring and control applications. Smart healthcare is an appealing practice of smart community which is a healthcare service system that uses the new generation of information technologies, such as artificial intelligence, 5G, cloud computing, big data, and IoT to transform the traditional medical system in an all-round way. This healthcare network enables to dynamically access information, connect people, materials, and institutions related to healthcare, and then actively manage and respond to medical ecosystem needs in an intelligent manner, which makes healthcare more personalized, more convenient, and more efficient. However, given the sensitive nature and high value of healthcare data delivered among multi participants in such a system, the issues of patients data privacy and data security remain a sore point for the sound development of smart healthcare.

Security and privacy issues are crucial in smart healthcare system due to the direct involvement of sensitive patients' health data. The threats exist during the transformation of physiological information from sensors to the end-users who need to leverage the validity and value of the data to provide appropriate service. For example, if the information is tampered with halfway by an attacker, the data users (professionals or related practitioners) would be misleading to make the wrong decision or obtain inaccurate analysis results. This might cause an extremely dangerous effect on the human's life. A malicious attacks could happen during every transformation stage in this scenario. Therefore, to ensure the validity of disseminated medical data, it is quite necessary to have a complete set of authentication and confidentiality protection mechanisms that prevent attackers from obtaining and modifying such sensitive information. A digital signature-based authentication mechanism provides both data integrity verification and data source identification, which is desired for authentication in the healthcare service system. Under the current digital signature definition, the entire data is signed, thereby forcing the data holder to disclose the whole signed data to a third party for the signature to be verifiable. Appropriate alteration of signed data, however, should be allowed in some scenarios for privacy-preserving requirements other than that for integrity.

One suitable cryptographic approach to solve the above incompatibility is redactable signature scheme (RSS) in which certain changes to signed data are authorized such that the resulting changed data's authenticity is still verifiable while preserving the confidentiality of some sensitive data. Let $M = \{m_1, m_2, \ldots, m_n\}$ be a message with n blocks, σ be a valid signature of M. The message blocks m_i in RSS are allowed to be removed publicly without invaliding the signature. In particular, a valid signature σ' for message M' can be derived without interacting with the original signer, where M' is the remaining message after deleting m_i from M. It is obvious that all approved changes from the signer should be verifiable in this notion. Thus, RSS is helpful in the implementation of privacy-preserving handling of document disclosure, anonymous credentials, social networks, and smart grid.

1.1   Related Work

Since the introduction of redactable signature [1,2], it has been deployed in a number of practical scenarios, such as smart grid systems, government documents release, health data sharing [3,4], smart grid systems [5,6] and social networks [7], etc. However, the signature length in the construction of linear documents increases linearly with the number of message blocks. Most redactable signature schemes with sets or lists seem hard to solve this problem. Aiming to solve this issue, Sanders [8] proposed a very efficient redactable signature scheme for anonymous credentials. The signature is with a constant size including only 4 elements and can be verified with k exponentiations, where k is the size of signed document. However, the construction suffers from a large public key, quadratic in n. In the following work, Sanders [9] put forward an improved version of the construction of [8] for improving the revocation for group signature, which retains all the nice features of the latter but with a public key only linear in n. Simultaneously, Yang et al. [10] proposed a redactable signature scheme with designated redactors based on the ring trapdoor preimage sampleable functions.

Redactable signatures could satisfy the demand for sharing parts of the signed healthcare data to third parties who can still verify its authenticity and integrity. Bauer et al. [11] proposed a hash tree-based redactable signature scheme to solve the disclosure dependencies control issue. However, it lacks the unforgeability and privacy proofs. Then, Slamanig et al. [12] proposed a general construction of RSS for XML documents by replacing the binary tree with a general tree resembling the natural structure of electronic healthcare documents. Nevertheless, neither the general construction nor the extension is implemented to evaluate the performance in storage and computational overhead. Subsequently, to guarantee the authenticity and integrity of clinical document architecture (CDA) documents while supporting to concealment of some private personal information, Wu et al. [13] proposed to implement an applicable and compact redactable signature scheme for the clinical document by using the existing web technologies. But the size of resulting document increases remarkably if a user redacts more information. Moreover, the security of implemented RSS is not analyzed. To provide redactable and verifiable Continuity of Care Documents (CCDs) in a distributed health IT service system, Brown et al. [14] introduced a redactable signature scheme based on Merkle Hash Tree. However, this construction is insufficient in the security analysis, and the medical providers have no control over the data blocks that have dependent constraints. In recent years, featured with different security properties and application scenarios, Liu et al. introduced several redactable signature schemes [15,16] to eliminate the redaction control issues in RSS. To improve the efficiency and security of most RSS, Liu et al. introduced some advanced constructions [17,18]. Recently, Yan et al. [19] combined redactable signature with private hash function to achieve the source reliability verification of sensing data without revealing the privacy of participants for mobile crowdsensing. At present, although some attention have been paied to the privacy and transparency of RSS, they only achieved partial information hiding instand of unlinkability.

1.2   Contribution

Under the deployment of RSS in smart healthcare system, apparently, the data owner could hide the sensitive information in sharing of healthcare data meanwhile any end-user can still verify the data authenticity. Even through RSS could realize show-or-hide operations over signed healthcare data, the revealed data is vulnerable to the additional redaction attack. Moreover, the linkability of redacted signature with the original signature would invalid the privacy protection feature of RSS. It is therefore a necessary to eliminate the additional redaction attack and linkability of RSS in practical applications. Another challenge of RSS is that the signature length, signature computation and verification time should satisfy the high efficiency requirement in smart healthcare system. Aiming to address the security and efficiency issues while deploying RSS in smart healthcare system, our contributions in this paper can be summarized as follows.

- We propose a concrete redactable signature scheme based on bilinear pairings, LSSS, and MSP for secure and efficient sharing of healthcare data in smart healthcare system. Our proposed solution solves the integrity and origin authentication of shared healthcare data with privacy preservation.
- In our design, data blocks are associated with a fine-grained access control policy such that only those blocks satisfying the policy could be shared. This property not only improves the flexibility of data access but also enhances the security of shared healthcare data by prohibiting the additional redaction.
- We formally define and prove the security properties of our proposed scheme in unforgeability and unlinkability. The analysis results indicate our scheme satisfies the security requirements for healthcare data sharing.
- We conduct an efficiency evaluation of our RSS by comparing it with other related works. The analysis results show that our scheme is more practical for the secure sharing of healthcare data with fine-grained control.

1.3   Paper Organization

The rest of this paper is organized as follows. Section 2 is devoted to the preliminaries required by this paper. The definitions of RSS is described in Sect. 3. Section 4 describes our proposed construction. Section 5 gives the analysis of proposed scheme. Section 6 concludes this paper.

2   Preliminaries

This section firstly provides some general notations over all this paper. Then, several relative cryptographic primitives are provided, including the access structure, monotone span program, linear secret sharing scheme, and bilinear pairings.

2.1 General Notations

In this paper, we consider the healthcare data M in smart healthcare system as a set of message blocks $\{m_i\}_{i=1}^{l}$. The minimum redactable unit are blocks $m_i \in \{0,1\}^*$. The number of blocks in M is denoted with $|M|$, i.e., $|M| = l$. The security level of a cryptographic scheme is controlled by the secret key size which depends on an integer $\lambda \in \mathbb{N}$ called security parameter. Let $s \xleftarrow{R} S$ denote the assignment of a uniformly and independently distributed random element from the set S to the variable s. For all $j > 0$ and $\lambda > \lambda_0$, if there exists λ_0 such that $\epsilon(\lambda) < \frac{1}{\lambda^j}$ then a function $\epsilon(\lambda)$ is called negligible. An exception or error output of an algorithm is represented with the symbol $\perp \notin \{0,1\}^*$. The probability of an event Event in experiment exp is denoted with symbol $\mathrm{Adv}_{\mathsf{exp}}^{\mathsf{Event}}(\lambda)$.

2.2 Access Structure

Let $\mathcal{U}$ be a set of parties. An access structure [20] on $\mathcal{U}$ is a collection $\mathbb{A}$ of non-empty sets of parties, i.e., $\mathbb{A} \subseteq 2^{\mathcal{U}} \backslash \{\emptyset\}$. The sets in $\mathbb{A}$ are called the authorized sets and the sets not in $\mathbb{A}$ are called unauthorized sets with respect to $\mathbb{A}$. An access structure $\mathbb{A}$ is called monotone access structure if $\forall B, C \in \mathbb{A}$: if $B \in \mathbb{A}$ and $B \subseteq C$, then $C \in \mathbb{A}$. A set B satisfies $\mathbb{A}$ (in other words, $\mathbb{A}$ accept B) if and only if B is an authorized set in $\mathbb{A}$, i.e., $B \in \mathbb{A}$. In the context of this paper, the role of parties is played by message block, and $\mathbb{A}$ contains the authorized subsets of message blocks that are not redactable. We restrict our attention to monotone access structure.

2.3 Monotone Span Program

Monotone span program (MSP), a linear algebraic model of computation, constitutes a significant component in realizing our fine-grained redaction control policy. In order to represent the monotone boolean formula using monotone span program, the monotone boolean formula is first converted into an access tree with the method introduced in [21]. Then, an access tree can be converted into an equivalent matrix $\mathbf{E}$ [3]. After the above changes, all leaf nodes are labeled with vectors which form the rows of a linear secret-sharing matrix. Let $\mathcal{P} : \{0,1\}^n \to \{0,1\}$ denote an access policy [21]. A MSP for $\mathcal{P}$ is an $\ell \times t$ matrix $\mathbf{E}$ over a finite field $\mathbb{F}$. Please refer to [15] for more detail about MSP.

2.4 Linear Secret Sharing Scheme

A Linear Secret-Sharing Scheme (LSSS) [20] $\Pi_{\mathbb{A}}$ for the access structure $\mathbb{A}$ over a set $\mathcal{S}$ is called linear (over $\mathbb{Z}_p$) if 1) The shares of a secret $s \in \mathbb{Z}_p$ for each party form a vector over $\mathbb{Z}_p$; and 2) For each access structure $\mathbb{A}$ on $\mathcal{S}$, there exists a matrix $\mathbf{E}$ with n rows and c columns called the sharing-generating matrix for Π. A function ρ defines each row number i of matrix $\mathbf{E}$ as $\rho(i)$, that labels the rows of $\mathbf{E}$ with elements from $\mathcal{S}$. Let vector $\vec{\omega} = (s, y_2, \ldots, y_c)^T$, where s is the secret will be shared into n parts, and $y_2, \ldots, y_c$ are chosen in $\mathbb{Z}_p$ randomly.

$\mathbf{E}\vec{\omega}$ is the vector of n shares of s and each share in $\mathbf{E}\vec{\omega}$ "belongs" to the party $\rho(i)$. We refer to the pair $(\mathbf{E}, \rho)$ as the policy of the access structure $\mathbb{A}$. An LSSS also enjoys the linear reconstruction property and security requirement. Unauthorized sets reveal no information about the secret. For more detail about the secret reconstruction, please refer to [20].

2.5   Bilinear Pairings

Let $\mathbb{G}_1$ and $\mathbb{G}_2$ be two multiplicative cyclic groups of the same prime order p along with a computable map, called pairing, $e : \mathbb{G}_1 \times \mathbb{G}_2 \to \mathbb{G}_T$ satisfying the following properties:

-   Non-degenerate: Let $1_{\mathbb{G}_T}$ denote the identity of $\mathbb{G}_T$ and then $e(g_1, g_2) \neq 1_{\mathbb{G}_T}$;
-   Bilinear: $e(u^a, v^b) = e(u, v)^{ab}$ for $a, b \in \mathbb{Z}_p$, $\forall u \in \mathbb{G}_1$, and $\forall v \in \mathbb{G}_2$; and
-   Computability: For all $g_1 \in \mathbb{G}_1$ and $g_2 \in \mathbb{G}_2$, $e(g_1, g_2)$ can be computed efficiently.

The general case $\mathbb{G}_1 \neq \mathbb{G}_2$ with type 3 pairings in [22] is considered throughout the paper. This is not a significant restriction since this type of pairings has been broadly used for efficiency and security reasons. It is also stressed that type 1 and type 2 pairings in [22] should be strictly prohibited for causing our signature scheme totally insecure.

Definition 1 (Assumption 1 [23]). *Let $(p, \mathbb{G}_1, \mathbb{G}_2, e)$ be a type 3 bilinear group setting, with g and $\tilde{g}$ a generator of $\mathbb{G}_1$ and $\mathbb{G}_2$, respectively. On input an arbitrary length m, we define an oracle $\mathcal{O}(m)$ by choosing a random element $\sigma_1 \in \mathbb{G}_1$ and outputting a pair $(\sigma_1, \sigma_1^{x+H(m)y})$, where x and y are randomly chosen in $\mathbb{Z}_p$. No PPT adversary can efficiently generate such a pair for a new message m^* without enquiring $\mathcal{O}(m)$ even given an unlimited access to $\mathcal{O}(m)$ and $(\tilde{g}, \mathbb{G}_1, \mathbb{G}_2)$, where $\sigma_1 \neq 1_{\mathbb{G}_1}$.*

3   Redactable Signature Scheme

Given a valid signature σ on a message block set $\{m_i\}_{i=1}^l$, it is redactable if a new valid signature $\sigma_{\mathcal{I}}$ on a subset $\{m_i\}_{i \in \mathcal{I}}$ is derivable, where $\mathcal{I} \in [1, l]$. The key feature of RSS is that the message blocks $\{m_i\}_{i \in \overline{\mathcal{I}}}$ are no longer an essential for the verification of $\sigma_{\mathcal{I}}$, where $\overline{\mathcal{I}} = [1, l] \backslash \mathcal{I}$. The syntax of redactable signature scheme and its security are formally defined in this section.

3.1   Syntax

There are three entities in the framework of RSS, namely the signer, redactor, and verifier. The implementation of this framework consists of four polynomial time algorithms (KeyGen, Sign, Verify, Redact) defined as follows:

KeyGen(1^λ): This algorithm takes as input a security parameter 1^λ. It outputs a key pair (pk, sk), where pk is a public key for signature verification, and sk is a secret key for signing: $(pk, sk) \leftarrow$ KeyGen(1^λ).

Sign(sk, M): On input sk and a message M with n message blocks $\{m_i\}_{i=1}^n$, this algorithm outputs a signature σ for M: $(M, \sigma) \leftarrow$ Sign(sk, M).

Verify($pk, M_{\mathcal{I}}, \sigma_{\mathcal{I}}$): This algorithm takes as input pk, a message $M_{\mathcal{I}}$ and a signature $\sigma_{\mathcal{I}}$. It outputs a bit $b \in \{0, 1\}$ or $\perp$ otherwise, where $b = 1$ means valid: $b \leftarrow$ Verify($pk, M_{\mathcal{I}}, \sigma_{\mathcal{I}}$).

Redact($pk, M, \mathcal{I}, \sigma$): This algorithm takes as input pk, a message M, a subset $\mathcal{I} \subset [1, n]$, and a signature σ. It executes redaction operation and outputs a signature $\sigma_{\mathcal{I}}$ on $\{m_i\}_{i \in \mathcal{I}}$: $(M_{\mathcal{I}}, \sigma_{\mathcal{I}}) \leftarrow$ Redact($pk, M, \mathcal{I}, \sigma$).

3.2   Security Notion

A secure RSS should satisfy correctness, unforgeability, and unlinkability.

Correctness. An RSS satisfies the correctness if the output bit b of Vreify algorithm is always 1 for every genuinely generated keys, signed message and redaction manipulation.

Signing Correctness. If the origin signature passes the verification equation Verify(pk, M, σ) = 1 for any $\lambda \in \mathbb{N}$, any key pair $(pk, sk) \leftarrow$ KeyGen(1^λ), and any message-signature pair $(M, \sigma) \leftarrow$ Sign(sk, M), then an RSS satisfies the signing correctness.

Redaction Correctness. If Verify($pk, M_{\mathcal{I}}, \sigma_{\mathcal{I}}$) = 1 holds for any $\lambda \in \mathbb{N}$, any key pair $(pk, sk) \leftarrow$ KeyGen(1^λ), any pair (M, σ) with Verify(pk, M, σ) = 1, any set $\mathcal{I}$ with redacted message-signature pair $(M_{\mathcal{I}}, \sigma_{\mathcal{I}}) \leftarrow$ Redact($pk, M, \sigma, \mathcal{I}$), then an RSS satisfies the redaction correctness.

Unforgeability. An RSS satisfies the unforgeability if without having access to sk, the probability is negligible for any PPT attacker to output a pair (M^*, σ^*), such that: *(i)* the pair (M^*, σ^*) passes the verification test, and *(ii)* M^* is either *(A)* not a redaction of any message queried to the signing oracle (i.e. $M^* \not\subseteq M_j$), or *(B)* Is an unauthorized redaction of a message queried to the signing oracle, where (M^*, σ^*) represents the M_j query from adversary $\mathcal{A}$ to the signing oracle.

Definition 2 (Unforgeability). *An RSS := (KeyGen, Sign, Verify, Redact) is EUF-CMA (existentially unforgeable under adaptive chosen-message attacks) if the probability for any PPT adversary $\mathcal{A}$ in winning the following game is $\epsilon(\lambda)$.*

Game 1 : Unforgeability$_{\mathcal{A}}^{RSS}(1^\lambda, n)$

- **Setup:** *To obtain a private key (sk, pk), the challenger runs KeyGen and resets $c \leftarrow 0$ and $Q_1 \leftarrow \emptyset$. Then adversary $\mathcal{A}$ receives pk.*
- **Query Phase:** *Adversary $\mathcal{A}$ executes signature queries to challenger with pk by adaptively choosing at most $|Q_1|$ message $M_1, \cdots, M_{|Q_1|}$. For each query, the challenger runs $(M_j, \sigma_j) \leftarrow$ Sign(sk, M_j) and forwards (M_j, σ_j) to $\mathcal{A}$, stores $Q_1[c] = (M_j, \sigma_j)$ and updates $c \leftarrow c + 1$.*
- **Output:** *After queries, $\mathcal{A}$ outputs a pair (M^*, σ^*) and wins the above game if $M^* \neq \emptyset$ and (1) $\forall j < c, \exists m_k \in M^* : m_k \notin M_j$ and (2) Verify(pk, M^*, σ^*) = 1.*

An RSS is *unforgeable* if $\text{Adv}_{\mathcal{A}}^{\text{Unforgeability}}(\lambda)$ is negligible in **Game 1** for any PPT adversary $\mathcal{A}$ even it has access to signatures on messages of its choice, where $\text{Adv}_{\mathcal{A}}^{\text{Privacy}}(\lambda) = \left| \Pr[b' = b] - \frac{1}{2} \right|$ is defined as the advantage that $\mathcal{A}$ has in the above game.

Unlinkability. In this paper, we adopt unlinkability instead of the transparency and privacy [24] to state the information hiding property for the redaction operation since the definition of unlinkability implies both transparency and privacy. Unlinkability requires that it should be hard for any PPT adversary to link a redacted signature $\sigma_{\mathcal{I}}$ to its origin signature σ unless the corresponding revealed set $\{m_i\}_{i \in \mathcal{I}}$ trivially allows to do so. This also implies that no information of the hidden set $\{m_i\}_{i \in \overline{\mathcal{I}}}$ is leaked by $\sigma_{\mathcal{I}}$. The following experiment formally defines this property.

Definition 3 (Unlinkability). *An RSS* := (KeyGen, Sign, Verify, Redact) *is unlinkability if the advantage in wining the following game is a negligible function of the security parameter* λ *for any PPT adversary* $\mathcal{A}$.

Game 2 : $\text{Unlinkability}_{\mathcal{A}}^{RSS}(1^{\lambda}, n)$

- **Setup:** *To obtain a public key pk and a private key sk, the challenger runs* KeyGen *and forwards pk to adversary* $\mathcal{A}$.
- **Phase 1:** *The adversary* $\mathcal{A}$ *adaptively chooses* $|Q_2|$ *message* $(M_1, M_2, \cdots, M_{Q_2})$ *and requests signature with pk on them. The challenger runs* $(M_i, \sigma_i) \leftarrow$ Sign(sk, M_i) *and sends* (M_i, σ_i) *to* $\mathcal{A}$ *for every query.*
- **Challenge:**
  1. *After* **Phase 1**, *adversary* $\mathcal{A}$ *outputs two messages* $M^0 = \{m_j^{(0)}\}_{j=1}^n$ *and* $M^1 = \{m_j^{(1)}\}_{j=1}^n$ *satisfies* $m_j^{(0)} = m_j^{(1)}$ *for* $j \in \mathcal{I}$. *Then,* $\mathcal{A}$ *sends* M^0, M^1 *and* $\mathcal{I}$ *to the challenger.*
  2. *The challenger randomly chooses a bit* $b \in \{0, 1\}$ *and generates signature* $\sigma^b \leftarrow$ Sign(sk, M^b). *Then a redacted signature for* $M_{\mathcal{I}}^b$ *is computed* $\sigma_{\mathcal{I}}^b \leftarrow$ Redact$(pk, M^b, \sigma^b, \mathcal{I})$.
- **Phase 2:** *As in* **Phase 1**, $\mathcal{A}$ *can proceed signing oracle queries again.*
- **Guess:** *Eventually,* $\mathcal{A}$ *wins the above game if* $b' = b$, *where* b' *is a guess of* b *that* $\mathcal{A}$ *exported in this.*

A redactable signature scheme satisfies the *unlinkability* if $\text{Adv}_{\mathcal{A}}^{\text{Unlinkability}}(\lambda)$ is negligible for any PPT adversary $\mathcal{A}$ in **Game 2**, where the advantage of $\mathcal{A}$ is defined as $\text{Adv}_{\mathcal{A}}^{\text{Unlinkability}}(\lambda) = \left| \Pr[b' = b] - \frac{1}{2} \right|$.

4   Our Construction

In this section, we introduce our main construction, an efficient redactable signature scheme with fine-grained redaction control for the secure sharing of healthcare data in smart healthcare systems. This construction not only achieves the security and efficiency of basic authentication requirements but also realizes fine-grained sharing control. The fine-grained sharing control is implemented by introducing a linear secret sharing scheme into the construction of redactable signature scheme. Concretely, to sharing a signed healthcare data, the signer chooses a secret and generates n secret shares by deploying the monotone span program and linear secret sharing scheme [20], and each share is associated to a data block. The secret is embedded in the original signature which could be be recovered if the shared data blocks satisfy the monotone span program defined access control policy. The deployment of this construction in smart healthcare system is shown in Fig. 1. A large number of healthcare data are constantly collected and transmitted to the gateway devices. The gateway devices run the signing algorithm and upload the signed data and its corresponding signature to the cloud. Then, the data owner accesses the cloud and generates a redacted version of data and its corresponding signature by calling the redaction algorithm while receiving a request from end-users. Any end-user could verify the authenticity of the receiving data. The concret construction of this scheme consists of four algorithms: KeyGen, Sign, Verify and Redact.

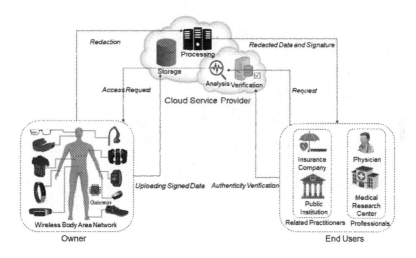

Fig. 1. The framework of deploying our RSS in smart healthcare system.

KeyGen($1^\lambda, n$): This algorithm takes as input a security parameter 1^λ and an integer n, where n is the universal number of data block. Then, it generates $(g, \widetilde{g}) \xleftarrow{\$} (\mathbb{G}_1^*, \mathbb{G}_2^*)$ along with $(x, y_1, \ldots, y_n) \xleftarrow{\$} \mathbb{Z}_p$ and computes the public key parameters $(\widetilde{X}, \widetilde{Y}_1, \ldots, \widetilde{Y}_n) \leftarrow (\widetilde{g}^x, \widetilde{g}^{y_1}, \ldots, \widetilde{g}^{y_n})$. These bilinear groups must be of type 3, where $\mathbb{G}_1^* = \mathbb{G}_1 \backslash \{1_{\mathbb{G}_1}\}$ and $\mathbb{G}_2^* = \mathbb{G}_2 \backslash \{1_{\mathbb{G}_2}\}$. A fine-grained redaction control policy $\mathcal{P}$ is depicted by the monotone boolean formula. The inputs of this formula are associated with the healthcare data block in a healthcare document. This policy can be converted into a monotone span program which is a $n \times t$

matrix $\mathbf{M}$. Then, a secret $s \xleftarrow{R} \mathbb{Z}_p$ value is chosen and a vector $\vec{\omega} = (s, y_2, \ldots, y_t)^T$ in which $y_i \xleftarrow{R} \mathbb{Z}_p$ is constructed, where s is the secret to be divided into n shares. For $1 \leq i \leq n$, it calculates $s_i = \mathbf{M} \cdot \vec{\omega}$, and each share "belongs" to $\rho(i)$, where ρ defines each row number i of matrix $\mathbf{M}$ as $\rho(i)$ that labels the rows of $\mathbf{M}$ with healthcare data block. Then, it computes $(\widetilde{Z}_1, \ldots, \widetilde{Z}_n) \leftarrow (\widetilde{g}^{s_1}, \ldots, \widetilde{g}^{s_n})$. Finally, this algorithm outputs $(\widetilde{X}, \widetilde{Z}_1, \ldots, \widetilde{Z}_n, \widetilde{Y}_1, \ldots, \widetilde{Y}_n)$ as a public key pk for verification and then $(s, x, y_1, \ldots, y_n)$ as a secret key sk for signing.

$\mathsf{Sign}(sk, M)$: This algorithm takes as inputs a secret key sk and a set of healthcare data M with l blocks $\{m_i\}_{i=1}^l$. It selects a random $\sigma_1 \xleftarrow{\$} \mathbb{G}_1^*$ and computes $\sigma_2 \leftarrow \sigma_1^{x+s+\sum_{i=1}^l y_i H(m_i)}$. The output of this algorithm is a signature $\sigma = (\widetilde{\sigma}_1, \sigma_1, \sigma_2)$, where H is a collision resistant hash function and $\widetilde{\sigma}_1$ is set as $1_{\mathbb{G}_2}$.

$\mathsf{Verify}(pk, M_\mathcal{I}, \sigma)$: This algorithm takes as input a public key pk, a set of healthcare data $M_\mathcal{I}$ with a set of blocks $\{m_i\}_{i \in \mathcal{I}}$ and a signature σ (redacted or not). It checks whether the following equality is satisfied:

$$\prod_{i \in \mathcal{I}} e(\sigma_1, \widetilde{Z}_i)^{\omega_i} e(\sigma_1, \widetilde{X} \cdot \widetilde{\sigma}_1 \prod_{i \in \mathcal{I}} \widetilde{Y}_i^{H(m_i)}) = e(\sigma_2, \widetilde{g}), \qquad (1)$$

where ω_i is defined as the constants $\{\omega_i \in \mathbb{Z}_p\}_{i \in \mathcal{I}}$ such that if the shared healthcare data blocks satisfies the fine-grained redaction policy then $s = \sum_{i \in I} \omega_i s_i$. It outputs 1 if the equality holds.

$\mathsf{Redact}(pk, M, \sigma, \mathcal{I})$: This algorithm takes as input a public key pk, a set of healthcare data M, the corresponding signature σ, and a subset $\mathcal{I} \subset [1, l]$. It generates 2 random scalars $w, r \xleftarrow{\$} \mathbb{Z}_p$ and computes $\sigma_1' \leftarrow \sigma_1^r$, $\sigma_2' \leftarrow \sigma_2^r \cdot \sigma_1'^w$, $\widetilde{\sigma}_1' \leftarrow \widetilde{g}^w \prod_{i \in \overline{\mathcal{I}}} \widetilde{Y}_i^{H(m_i)}$, where $\overline{\mathcal{I}} = [1, l] \backslash \mathcal{I}$. If $\mathcal{I} = \emptyset$ then $\widetilde{\sigma}_1' = \widetilde{g}^w$. In all cases, the redactor returns the derived signature $\sigma_\mathcal{I} = (\widetilde{\sigma}_1', \sigma_1', \sigma_2')$ on $M_\mathcal{I}$. $(pk, M_\mathcal{I}, \sigma_\mathcal{I})$

Correctness. Let $(\widetilde{\sigma}_1', \sigma_1', \sigma_2')$ be a redacted signature on $M_\mathcal{I}$ output by the Redact algorithm. Then we have:

$$
\begin{aligned}
&\prod_{i \in \mathcal{I}} e(\sigma_1', \widetilde{Z}_i)^{\omega_i} e(\sigma_1', \widetilde{X} \cdot \widetilde{\sigma}_1' \prod_{i \in \mathcal{I}} \widetilde{Y}_i^{H(m_i)}) \\
&= \prod_{i \in \mathcal{I}} e(\sigma_1^r, \widetilde{g}^{s_i})^{\omega_i} e(\sigma_1^r, \widetilde{g}^x \cdot \widetilde{g}^w \prod_{i \in \mathcal{I}} \widetilde{Y}_i^{H(m_i)} \cdot \prod_{i \in \overline{\mathcal{I}}} \widetilde{Y}_i^{H(m_i)}) \\
&= e(\sigma_1^r, \widetilde{g})^{\sum_{i \in \mathcal{I}} s_i \cdot \omega_i} e(\sigma_1^r, \widetilde{g}^{x+w+\sum_{i=1}^l y_i H(m_i)}) \\
&= e(\sigma_1^{r \cdot s}, \widetilde{g}) e(\sigma_1^{r(x+w+\sum_{i=1}^l y_i H(m_i))}, \widetilde{g}) \\
&= e(\sigma_1^{rw} \cdot \sigma_1^{r(x+s+\sum_{i=1}^l y_i H(m_i))}, \widetilde{g}) = e(\sigma_1'^w \cdot \sigma_2^r, \widetilde{g}) = e(\sigma_2', \widetilde{g}),
\end{aligned}
\qquad (2)
$$

which shows the correctness of our scheme.

5 Analysis of Our Construction

5.1 Security Analysis

The unforgeability of our redactable signature scheme relies on *Assumption 1* and the collision resistance property of H. We prove the unforgeability follows the *Definition 2*, where H is assumed to be collision resistance secure and modeled as a random oracle that maps its inputs uniformly onto $\mathbb{Z}_p$. Thus, we only prove that our scheme is EUF-CMA security if the *Assumption 1* holds. As for the unlinkability, we prove the information of not be shared data blocks and the original signatures are perfectly hidden by the randomness inserted in redacted signature.

Theorem 1. *Our redactable signature scheme achieves EUF-CMA security under* Assumption 1. *Explicitly, if the advantage of an adversary has in breaking the EUF-CMA is ε, then there exists an adversary against the* Assumption 1 *with probability over $\varepsilon - \frac{Q}{q}$.*

Proof. Let $\Sigma = $ (KeyGen, Sign, Verify, Redact) denote our construction, and $\mathcal{A}$ be a PPT adversary against the EUF-CMA security. We construct an efficient algorithm $\mathcal{B}$ using $\mathcal{A}$ to against *Assumption 1*. Let $\mathcal{C}$ be the challenger in the following game. Without loss of generality, it is assumed that once $\mathcal{A}$ requests a signature on M or outputs a forgery (M, σ), then M has previously queried to H.

Setup. The public key pk that $\mathcal{B}$ receives from $\mathcal{C}$ contains the public parameters $(p, \mathbb{G}_1, \mathbb{G}_2, \mathbb{G}_T, e)$ along with $(\widetilde{g}, \widetilde{X}, \widetilde{Y})$ are set as in *Assumption 1*. Then, algorithm $\mathcal{B}$ chooses $\{\alpha_j, \beta_j\}_{j=1}^{j=n} \overset{\$}{\leftarrow} \mathbb{Z}_p$ and sets $\widetilde{Y}_j \leftarrow \widetilde{Y}^{\beta_j} \widetilde{g}^{\alpha_j}$. Additionally, a random function $H : \{0, 1\}^* \rightarrow \mathbb{Z}_p$ is chosen. It outputs $pk \leftarrow (\widetilde{g}, \widetilde{X}, \widetilde{Y}_j)$ and forwards it to $\mathcal{A}$.

Queries. In this phase, the adversary $\mathcal{A}$ has access to make polynomial-time limited queries to H as well as signing oracle $\mathsf{Sign}_{pk}(\cdot)$. When $\mathcal{B}$ receives a signature generation query on a healthcare document $M_i = \{m_{i,1}, \ldots, m_{i,l}\}$ from adversary $\mathcal{A}$, it first answers the random-oracle queries of $\mathcal{A}$ with uniform elements of $\mathbb{Z}_p$, and then requests a signature on $m_i = \sum \beta_j H(m_{i,j})$ to the signing oracle and so receives $\sigma = (\sigma_1, \sigma_2)$. The signature σ satisfies $e(\sigma_2, \widetilde{g}) = e(\sigma_1, \widetilde{X} \cdot \widetilde{Y}^{\sum \beta_j H(m_{i,j})})$. Finally, $\mathcal{B}$ computes $\sigma_2' \leftarrow \sigma_1^{\sum \alpha_j H(m_{i,j})} \cdot \sigma_2$ and returns $\sigma' = (\sigma_1, \sigma_2')$ to $\mathcal{A}$. The output is a valid signature on M_i from the view of $\mathcal{A}$ since:

$$e(\sigma_2', \widetilde{g})$$
$$= e(\sigma_1^{\sum \alpha_j H(m_{i,j})} \cdot \sigma_2, \widetilde{g})$$
$$= e(\sigma_1^{\sum \alpha_j H(m_{i,j})}, \widetilde{g}) \cdot e(\sigma_2, \widetilde{g})$$
$$= e(\sigma_1, \widetilde{g}^{\sum \alpha_j H(m_{i,j})}) \cdot e(\sigma_1, \widetilde{X} \cdot \widetilde{Y}^{\sum \beta_j H(m_{i,j})}) \tag{3}$$
$$= e(\sigma_1, \widetilde{X} \cdot \prod \widetilde{g}^{\alpha_j H(m_{i,j})} \widetilde{Y}^{\beta_j H(m_{i,j})})$$
$$= e(\sigma_1, \widetilde{X} \cdot \prod (\widetilde{g}^{\alpha_j} \widetilde{Y}^{\beta_j})^{H(m_{i,j})}) = e(\sigma_1, \widetilde{X} \cdot \prod \widetilde{Y}_j^{H(m_{i,j})}).$$

Output. Finally, the adversary $\mathcal{A}$ outputs a signature $\sigma = (\sigma_1, \sigma_2)$ on a healthcare document M^* after making Q queries. It is a valid forgery if M^* has never been queried to the signing oracle, and σ passes the following verification formulas:

1. $e(\sigma_2, \widetilde{g}) = e(\sigma_1, \widetilde{X} \cdot \prod \widetilde{Y}_j^{H(m_j^*)})$;
2. $M^* \neq M_i$.

If $\exists i \in \{1, \ldots, Q\}$ such that $\sum \beta_j H(m_{i,j}^*) = \sum \beta_j H(m_j^*)$, then $\mathcal{B}$ aborts. Otherwise, it outputs $\sigma^* = (\sigma_1^*, \sigma_2^*)$, where $\sigma_1^* \leftarrow \sigma_1$ and $\sigma_2^* \leftarrow \sigma_2 \cdot \sigma_1^{-\sum \alpha_j \cdot H(m_j^*)}$, together with $m^* \leftarrow \sum \beta_j H(m_j^*)$:

$$e(\sigma_2^*, \widetilde{g})$$
$$= e(\sigma_1^{-\sum \alpha_j H(m_j^*)} \cdot \sigma_2, \widetilde{g})$$
$$= e(\sigma_1^{-\sum \alpha_j H(m_j^*)}, \widetilde{g}) \cdot e(\sigma_2, \widetilde{g})$$
$$= e(\sigma_1, \widetilde{g}^{-\sum \alpha_j H(m_j^*)}) \cdot e(\sigma_1, \widetilde{X} \cdot \prod \widetilde{Y}_j^{H(m_j^*)}) \tag{4}$$
$$= e(\sigma_1, \widetilde{g}^{-\sum \alpha_j H(m_j^*)}) \cdot e(\sigma_1, \widetilde{X} \cdot \prod (\widetilde{Y}^{\beta_j} \widetilde{g}^{\alpha_j})^{H(m_j^*)})$$
$$= e(\sigma_1, \widetilde{X} \cdot \prod \widetilde{Y}^{\beta_j H(m_j^*)}) = e(\sigma_1, \widetilde{X} \cdot \widetilde{Y}^{\sum \beta_j H(m_j^*)}) = e(\sigma_1, \widetilde{X} \cdot \widetilde{Y}^{m^*}).$$

Under the *Assumption 1*, this is a valid forgery with respect to public key pk^* if m^* has never been queried to the signing oracle. Let $\{\gamma_j\}_{j=1}^l \overset{\$}{\leftarrow} \mathbb{Z}_p$, and set $\beta_j' \leftarrow \beta_j - \gamma_j$ and $\alpha_j' \leftarrow \alpha_j + y\gamma_j$. The public parameter $\widetilde{Y}$ is generated by choosing $y \overset{\$}{\leftarrow} \mathbb{Z}_p$ such that $\widetilde{Y} = \widetilde{g}^y$. Then one can have $\widetilde{g}^{\alpha_j'} \widetilde{Y}^{\beta_j'} = \widetilde{g}^{\alpha_j + y\gamma_j} \widetilde{Y}^{\beta_j - \gamma_j} = \widetilde{g}^{\alpha_j} \widetilde{Y}^{\beta_j} = \widetilde{Y}_j$. Therefore, from $\mathcal{A}$'s point of view, all its signature queries are answered with the signing oracle from challenger rather than a revised version from $\mathcal{B}$. Moreover, it is totally independent of the β_j in the complete view of the adversary. Hence, $\mathcal{B}$ aborts with a probability upper-bounded by $\frac{Q}{q}$.

Theorem 2. *Our construction achieves unlinkability in the information-theoretical sense as defined in Definition 3.*

Proof. In the sense of information-theoretical, the signatures generated in our redactable signature scheme are unlinkability, i.e., the bit b secretly chosen in the unlinkability experiment is hidden perfectly. Let κ be a random element of $\mathbb{Z}_p$ and τ be an element randomly chosen in $\mathbb{G}_1$. For a signature $\sigma = (\widetilde{\sigma}_1, \sigma_1, \sigma_2)$ on healthcare document M with n blocks $\{m_i\}_{i=1}^l$ and any subset $\mathcal{I} \subset [1, l]$, it is defined $w = \kappa - \sum_{i \in \overline{\mathcal{I}}} y_i H(m_i)$ and $r = \frac{v}{\iota}$, where v and ι are such that $\tau = g^v$ and $\sigma_1 = g^\iota$. Since both κ and τ are chosen randomly, w and r are also randomly distributed so as the distributions containing them in the Redact algorithm. Deploying the above parameters, the Redact algorithm outputs a redacted signature $\sigma_{\mathcal{I}} = (\widetilde{\sigma}_1', \sigma_1', \sigma_2')$ on $\{m_i\}_{i=1}^l$ with: $\sigma_1' \leftarrow \sigma_1^r = \tau$, $\sigma_2' \leftarrow \sigma_2^r \cdot \sigma_1'^w = \tau^{x+s+\sum_{i \in \mathcal{I}} y_i H(m_i)} \cdot \tau^\kappa$, $\widetilde{\sigma}_1' \leftarrow \widetilde{g}^w \prod_{i \in \overline{\mathcal{I}}} \widetilde{Y}_i^{H(m_i)} = \widetilde{g}^\kappa$. Apparently, this signature satisfies the verification equality. The randomness of τ and κ implies the distribution of redacted signature $\sigma_{\mathcal{I}}$ is clearly independent of the hidden blocks $\{m_i\}_{i \in \overline{\mathcal{I}}}$ and the original signature. Therefore, it is infeasible to output a guess of the bit b with non-negligible advertage even for an unbounded adversary.

5.2   Efficiency Analysis

We analyze the complexity of our construction by comparing our scheme with the most relevant systems in communication and computational complexity. The comparison of our scheme with the most relevant systems [8, 25, 26] are presented in Table 1. Table 1 provides some important figures in communication. For clarity, we only take some key expensive operations such as exponentiations, hash function, and pairings into consideration during signature generation and verification. Although the pk's size of [25] is constant and the shortest, the number of data block causes the signatures' size increases linearly. On the contrary, compared with the signatures' size of [25], our scheme has a constant and shorter length than [8, 26].

As shown in Table 2, it is obvious that the computational cost of Redact in [25] is negligible. It's execution of Sign and Verify algorithms, however, is realized by consuming a large number of computing resources while comparing with others. The computation cost of our scheme is similar with [8] which is much lower than [26] when omitting the negligible evaluation of hash function. As for the security, [25] only achieves additional redaction control but no unlinkability. This is just the opposite of [8, 26] which only reaches unlinkability. Overall, our scheme is the first lightweight one realizes coarse-grained additional redaction control and unlinkability with constant signature size.

Table 1. Communication cost

Schemes	pk	σ	$\sigma_{\mathcal{I}}$
[25]	$1\mathbb{G}_2$	$(l+1)\mathbb{G}_1$	$(|\mathcal{I}|+1)\mathbb{G}_1$
[8]	$\frac{n^2+n+2}{2}\mathbb{G}_1 + n\mathbb{G}_2$	$2(\mathbb{G}_1 + \mathbb{G}_2)$	$2(\mathbb{G}_1 + \mathbb{G}_2)$
[26]	$(2n+1)\mathbb{G}_1 + (n+1)\mathbb{G}_2$	$3\mathbb{G}_1 + 1\mathbb{G}_2$	$3\mathbb{G}_1 + 1\mathbb{G}_2$
Ours	$(2n+1)\mathbb{G}_2$	$2\mathbb{G}_1 + 1\mathbb{G}_2$	$2\mathbb{G}_1 + 1\mathbb{G}_2$

Table 2. Computation cost

Schemes	Sign	Redact	Verify
[25]	$l(e_1 + H)$	–	$p_{(l+1)} + |\mathcal{I}|(H + p_2)$
[8]	$1r_2 + 1e_2$	$2(|\overline{\mathcal{I}}| + 1)e_1 + 3e_2$	$2p_2 + |\mathcal{I}|e_1$
[26]	$1r_1 + 1e_1$	$2(l + 1)e_1 + (|\overline{\mathcal{I}}| + 1)e_2 + |\mathcal{I}|H$	$|\mathcal{I}|(e_1 + e_2 + H) + 2p_2$
Ours	$1r_1 + 1e_1 + lH$	$3e_1 + (|\overline{\mathcal{I}}| + 1)e_2 + |\overline{\mathcal{I}}|H$	$1p_3 + (|\mathcal{I}| + |\mathcal{S}|)e_2 + |\mathcal{I}|H$

The costs of **Redact** and **Verify** consider for a set $\{m_i\}_{\mathcal{I}}$ with $|\mathcal{I}|$ blocks, where $|\overline{\mathcal{I}}|$ denotes the hidden set from $\{m_i\}_l$ in **Sign**. Here, r_i denotes the generation of a random element in $\mathbb{G}_i$, e_i denotes an exponentiation in $\mathbb{G}_i$, for $i \in \{1, 2\}$, H denotes the evaluation of a hash function, and p_i denotes an equation involving i pairings.

6   Conclusion

The efficient sharing of signed healthcare data with privacy preservation issues in smart healthcare systems are explored. To overcome the security flaws, we presented an RSS with short signature and fine-grained sharing control, which realized shared data authentication, privacy protection, unlinkability, and fine-grained additional redaction control. The security analysis of our RSS indicates this construction achieves unlinkability and unforgeability which satisfy the security demands in sharing of healthcare data in smart healthcare systems. Furthermore, we conducted extensive efficiency analyses of the proposed scheme by comparing with other related works. The results imply our scheme is sound in guarding the privacy and authenticity of shared healthcare data with lightweight resource expense. In our future work, we plan to further design some more lightweighted implementation, multi-redactor accountability and signer anonymous fully unlinkability RSS to improve the security and efficiency for sharing of healthcare data in smart healthcare systems.

Acknowledgment. This work is supported by National Natural Science Foundation of China (62202226, 62202228), Natural Science Foundation of Jiangsu Province (BK20220935, BK20210330) and Fundamental Research Funds for the Central Universities (30922010917).

References

1. Johnson, R., Molnar, D., Song, D., Wagner, D.: Homomorphic signature schemes. In: Preneel, B. (ed.) CT-RSA 2002. LNCS, vol. 2271, pp. 244–262. Springer, Heidelberg (2002). https://doi.org/10.1007/3-540-45760-7_17
2. Steinfeld, R., Bull, L., Zheng, Y.: Content extraction signatures. In: Kim, K. (ed.) ICISC 2001. LNCS, vol. 2288, pp. 285–304. Springer, Heidelberg (2002). https://doi.org/10.1007/3-540-45861-1_22
3. Liu, J., Huang, X., Liu, J.K.: Secure sharing of personal health records in cloud computing: ciphertext-policy attribute-based signcryption. Futur. Gener. Comput. Syst. **52**, 67–76 (2015)
4. Liu, J., Ma, J., Wu, W., Chen, X., Huang, X., Xu, L.: Protecting mobile health records in cloud computing: A secure, efficient, and anonymous design. ACM Trans. Embedded Comput. Syst. (TECS) **16**(2), 1–20 (2017)

5. Pöhls, H.C., Karwe, M.: Redactable signatures to control the maximum noise for differential privacy in the smart grid. In: Cuellar, J. (ed.) SmartGridSec 2014. LNCS, vol. 8448, pp. 79–93. Springer, Cham (2014). https://doi.org/10.1007/978-3-319-10329-7_6
6. Lahoti, G., Mashima, D., Chen, W.-P.: Customer-centric energy usage data management and sharing in smart grid systems. In: Proceedings of the first ACM Workshop on Smart Energy Grid Security, pp. 53–64 (2013)
7. Pöhls, H.C., Bilzhause, A., Samelin, K., Posegga, J.: Sanitizable signed privacy preferences for social networks. In: GI-Jahrestagung, p. 409. Citeseer (2011)
8. Sanders, O.: Efficient redactable signature and application to anonymous credentials. In: Kiayias, A., Kohlweiss, M., Wallden, P., Zikas, V. (eds.) PKC 2020. LNCS, vol. 12111, pp. 628–656. Springer, Cham (2020). https://doi.org/10.1007/978-3-030-45388-6_22
9. Sanders, O.: Improving revocation for group signature with redactable signature. In: Garay, J.A. (ed.) PKC 2021. LNCS, vol. 12710, pp. 301–330. Springer, Cham (2021). https://doi.org/10.1007/978-3-030-75245-3_12
10. Yang, S., Huang, X., Zheng, M., Ma, J.: Ring trapdoor redactable signatures from lattice. In: Deng, R., et al. (eds.) ISPEC 2021. LNCS, vol. 13107, pp. 190–208. Springer, Cham (2021). https://doi.org/10.1007/978-3-030-93206-0_12
11. Bauer, D., Blough, D.M., Mohan, A.: Redactable signatures on data with dependencies and their application to personal health records. In: Proceedings of the 8th ACM Workshop on Privacy in the Electronic Society, pp. 91–100 (2009)
12. Slamanig, D., Rass, S.: Generalizations and extensions of redactable signatures with applications to electronic healthcare. In: De Decker, B., Schaumüller-Bichl, I. (eds.) CMS 2010. LNCS, vol. 6109, pp. 201–213. Springer, Heidelberg (2010). https://doi.org/10.1007/978-3-642-13241-4_19
13. Wu, Z., Hsueh, C., Tsai, C., Lai, F., Lee, H., Chung, Y.: Redactable signatures for signed CDA documents. J. Med. Syst. **36**(3), 1795–1808 (2012)
14. Brown, J., Blough, D.M.: Verifiable and redactable medical documents. In: AMIA Annual Symposium Proceedings, vol. 2012, p. 1148. American Medical Informatics Association (2012)
15. Liu, J., Ma, J., Zhou, W., Xiang, Y., Huang, X.: Dissemination of authenticated tree-structured data with privacy protection and fine-grained control in outsourced databases. In: Lopez, J., Zhou, J., Soriano, M. (eds.) ESORICS 2018. LNCS, vol. 11099, pp. 167–186. Springer, Cham (2018). https://doi.org/10.1007/978-3-319-98989-1_9
16. Liu, J., Ma, J., Xiang, Y., Zhou, W., Huang, X.: Authenticated medical documents releasing with privacy protection and release control. IEEE Trans. Dependable Secure Comput. **18**(1), 448–459 (2019)
17. Liu, J., Hou, J., Huang, X., Xiang, Y., Zhu, T.: Secure and efficient sharing of authenticated energy usage data with privacy preservation. Comput. Secur. **92**, 101756 (2020)
18. Liu, J., et al.: Leakage-free dissemination of authenticated tree-structured data with multi-party control. IEEE Trans. Comput. **70**(7), 1120–1131 (2020)
19. Yan, X., Ng, W.W., Zeng, B., Zhao, B., Luo, F, Gao, Y.: P2sim: privacy-preserving and source-reliable incentive mechanism for mobile crowdsensing. IEEE Internet Things J. (2022)
20. Beimel, A., et al.: Secure schemes for secret sharing and key distribution (1996)
21. Goyal, V., Pandey, O., Sahai, A., Waters, B.: Attribute-based encryption for fine-grained access control of encrypted data. In: Proceedings of the 13th ACM Conference on Computer and Communications Security, pp. 89–98 (2006)

22. Galbraith, S.D., Paterson, K.G., Smart, N.P.: Pairings for cryptographers. Discret. Appl. Math. **156**(16), 3113–3121 (2008)
23. Pointcheval, D., Sanders, O.: Short randomizable signatures. In: Sako, K. (ed.) CT-RSA 2016. LNCS, vol. 9610, pp. 111–126. Springer, Cham (2016). https://doi.org/10.1007/978-3-319-29485-8_7
24. Derler, D., Pöhls, H.C., Samelin, K., Slamanig, D.: A general framework for redactable signatures and new constructions. In: Kwon, S., Yun, A. (eds.) ICISC 2015. LNCS, vol. 9558, pp. 3–19. Springer, Cham (2016). https://doi.org/10.1007/978-3-319-30840-1_1
25. Miyazaki, K., Hanaoka, G., Imai, H.: Digitally signed document sanitizing scheme based on bilinear maps. In: Proceedings of the 2006 ACM Symposium on Information, Computer and Communications Security, pp. 343–354 (2006)
26. Sanders, O.: Improving revocation for group signature with redactable signature. IACR Cryptol. ePrint Arch. 2020, 856 (2020)

Enabling Secure Deduplication in Encrypted Decentralized Storage

Bo Zhang[1], Helei Cui[1]([✉])(iD), Yaxing Chen[1], Xiaoning Liu[2], Zhiwen Yu[1], and Bin Guo[1]

[1] School of Computer Science, Northwestern Polytechnical University, Xi'an, Shaanxi, China
bo.zhang@mail.nwpu.edu.cn,{chl,yxchen,zhiwenyu,guob}@nwpu.edu.cn
[2] School of Computing Technologies, RMIT, Melbourne, Victoria, Australia
xiaoning.liu@rmit.edu.au

Abstract. With the rapid development of blockchain technology, decentralized cloud storage services are emerging and have been a storage new option in this era. They aim to leverage the unused storage resources across the network to build a more economical and reliable distributed storage network and thus eliminate the trust in the centralized storage providers via matured blockchain consensus mechanisms. However, current solutions either lack the protection of user data privacy or apply conventional encryption methods that cannot support cross-user deduplication over encrypted data. These limitations make them struggle to balance the need for optimized storage space utilization and encrypted data protection, especially in the scenario where the user's files are geographically distributed in different nodes around the world. In this paper, we propose a secure deduplication system in the context of encrypted decentralized cloud storage. It utilizes smart contract to incorporate the message-locked encryption (MLE) scheme, the most prominent cryptographic primitive in secure data deduplication. With a carefully tailored design, our proposed scheme can be seamlessly deployed to the public blockchain with transparency. Together, our design enables secure data deduplication over decentralized storage, while providing stringent cryptographic data privacy guarantees. In particular, our proposed design has a natural benefit to prevent potential malicious attacks such as file ownership cheating and file ciphertext poisoning. We implement a prototype of our system and deploy it to Ethereum. Comprehensive performance evaluations are conducted with real datasets to demonstrate the effectiveness and efficiency of our design.

Keywords: Decentralized storage · Secure deduplication · Smart contract

X. Yuan et al. (Eds.): NSS 2022, LNCS 13787, pp. 459–475, 2022.
https://doi.org/10.1007/978-3-031-23020-2_26

1   Introduction

With the advancement of blockchain, decentralized applications have vigorously evolved [34–36,48]. Among them, Decentralized Cloud Storage (DCS) acts as a new storage option (e.g., Storj [16], Sia [14], Filecoin [7]), whose core idea is to incentivize users to share idle storage and hence build a more economical and reliable distributed storage network. The outsourced data may indicate the users' private information,e.g., geographical location, password, and health status. Meanwhile, data breaches exist widely [3,17] and threaten the users' personal privacy. Thus, data privacy protection becomes particularly important.

Data in DCS can be repeatedly stored, making the storage across the network overwhelmed, which increases the demand for data deduplication. Unfortunately, existing DCS designs hardly achieve the demand for optimized storage space utilization and encrypted data protection at the same time. The representative ones like Storj [16] and Sia [14], ensure data security by involving standard encryption. Data in such systems is first encrypted, and the ciphertext is split via erasure code [28], then distributed around the network. This strategy ensures data reliability at the expense of multiple storage of original files. This leads to the expanded storage of files, which increases the storage overhead of the system in general. Meanwhile, cross-user data deduplication is omitted since the user individually encrypt the files. Sharing a common key across users can mitigate such issue, but inevitably involve the threat of single client compromise [20,22,27]. The other ones, like Filecoin together with InterPlanetary File System (IPFS) [9], implement deduplication within a single user. Concerning data security, the data is only protected during transmission in fundamental design, to keep the system lightweight and free of vendor lock-in [9].

The smart contract [49] is a natural fit for the new DCS scenario, which is an auto-executed decentralized computing program on the blockchain. Each smart contract contains storage, script code and is identified by its address. Smart contract are executed by sending public transactions and are permanently recorded, making it transparent and immutable. Therefore, we consider placing the essential metadata on blockchain and enable cross-user deduplication in DCS. Yet due to the openness of the blockchain, one can download the block and analysis its content [2,6], which incur the risk that users cheating the system and illegally obtaining the outsourced data. Such features disable the conventional encryption workflow [20,23,27,33] in which store the metadata in plaintext. We take this into account and encrypt the metadata before storing it on the blockchain. Meanwhile, it is unreasonable to set huge data on-chain since the storage on smart contract has actual cost [49].

We leverage Message-Locked Encryption (MLE) [23] to protect the data privacy, which enables secure deduplication over encrypted data. But such scheme still face the client-side short information (e.g., file hash, file tag) attacks like file ownership cheating [33] and file ciphertext poisoning [50]. Concretely, the former attack refers to the users who use short information (e.g., illegal acquisition from another channel) to trick the system into adding them to the owner list and further obtain the file. The latter attack indicates the users uploading ciphertext inconsistent with file tag, thus to deceive the subsequent users.

In this paper, we propose a system built upon smart contract, that enables cross-user secure deduplication service over encrypted data for DCS. First, to accomplish optimized storage space utilization and encrypted data protection concurrently, we propose an encryption workflow on top of Convergent Encryption (CE) [29], the most prominent MLE scheme. We involve the ciphertext in major steps, user without the entire file cannot pass the verification, hence prevent short information attacks. Second, to address the information leakage caused by the openness of the public blockchain, we encrypt the metadata with a scheme built upon CE before updating it to smart contract. Through that, attackers knowing the encrypted metadata can not directly obtain the file address since the decryption requires the whole file, thus preventing the illegal analysis from the public. Third, as for storage cost, we only store the minimal necessary metadata like other designs [34,48], e.g., file index, user index. Our contributions are summarized as follows:

- We propose a system architecture that enables optimized storage space utilization and encrypted data protection simultaneously. To the best of our knowledge, our proposed system is the early one enables a blockchain-based cross-user secure deduplication on encrypted decentralized storage.
- We carefully devise the index structures and operating functions in smart contract to fit the transparent feature of the public blockchain, which minimizes on-chain storage while enhancing security against potential attacks.
- We implement a full-fledged prototype on Ethereum. We conduct extensive evaluation on real datasets to show its effectiveness and efficiency in simulate network *Ganache* and official test network *Rinkeby*.

2   Background and Preliminaries

Smart contract is first proposed by Nick Szabo in 1994 [46], described as computing programs that can automatically execute, control and record relevant events. In Ethereum [49], smart contracts consist of status, script content, address, storage space, and are stored in the Ethereum network. A smart contract can be triggered by transactions, and then executes the corresponding functions depending on the input values. Operations on the contract is irreversible and publicly recorded in the blockchain.

Gas System in Ethereum: Since the smart contract is executed without supervision, one may initiate Denial-of-Service (DoS) attacks, which invalidates the contract. Gas system is devised to resist such attacks, any transaction or operation of contract costs a certain amount *gas* [49]. User determines a pre-computed parameter *gaslimit* before deploy a contract, limiting the execution of the contract, thus prevents DoS attacks.

Message-locked encryption (MLE) [23] is a cryptographic primitive for deduplication over encrypted data. Formally, the MLE scheme is denoted as

$(\mathcal{P}, \mathcal{K}, \mathcal{E}, \mathcal{D}, \mathcal{T})$, where $\mathcal{P}$ denotes parameter generation $P \xleftarrow{\$} \mathcal{P}$, which determines the system settings. Say M is the input file, to encrypt M, the key is generated from $K \leftarrow \mathcal{K}_P(M)$. Then the ciphertext is derived from $C \leftarrow \mathcal{E}_P(K, M)$ and decrypted by $M \leftarrow \mathcal{D}_P(K, C)$, and the file tag (work as fingerprint) is generated through $T \leftarrow \mathcal{T}_P(C)$. In such a scheme, as it is called, K is derived from M itself. Thus, data owners encrypt the same file resulting in the same ciphertext without an additional server. In this work, we implement Convergent Encryption (CE) [29] as the base of our encryption workflow. Concretely, P is set to random 128-bit strings and used in the latter procedure, we use SHA256 for $\mathcal{K}/\mathcal{T}$, and $\mathcal{E}/\mathcal{D}$ is set to AES-256-CTR with a fixed IV. In the following of this paper, we use r to denote P in CE, more details refer to Sect. 4.3.

Proof-of-ownership, introduced by Halevi et al. [33], is an essential challenge-response protocol in client-side deduplication schemes [20,27,50]. It assists the server to verify whether a user indeed holds a claimed file without receiving the file, thereby solving the leakage of entire file through file hash (i.e., short information attack). Initial proof-of-ownership scheme is implemented through Merkle tree [41] and erasure code [28]. File is first encoded by erasure code and outputs several chunks. User then conducts a Merkle tree based on the these chunks and sends the root hash to server. Afterwards, server asks the user to give the sibling path of random picked leaves. Such path can be securely verified with root hash [33]. In this work, we adopt and integrate such idea into the user upload process (more details refer to Sect. 4.3), ensuring that the subsequent uploader can obtain the previous file address if and only if the user has the entire file.

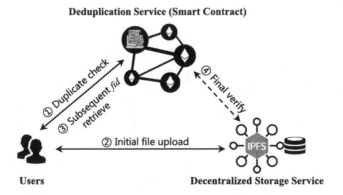

Fig. 1. Overview of our proposed design.

3 System Overview

3.1 System Model

Our design in the target DCS scenario consists of three entities, as shown in Fig. 1: backend storage service (SS), users (U), and secure deduplication service (DS). Specifically, U uses a client (e.g., a desktop or web app) to encrypt and upload files to SS for long-term storage. SS holds the ciphertext uploaded from U, which is maintained by an emerging decentralized storage provider like IPFS [9] (as used in our experiment in Sect. 5.1). DS interacts with U and SS to jointly conduct secure deduplication procedures, to significantly improve the utilization of the storage space while preventing potential attacks on cheating ownership of a specific file [33] and poisoning stored ciphertext [50]. Different from traditional centralized cloud-based schemes [43, 44], DS in our design is instantiated by the smart contract on Ethereum, which guarantees the consensus and correctness of stored metadata.

3.2 Threat Model and Assumptions

We consider a *malicious user* can utilize pieces of short information about a file (e.g., file hash tags) to cheat ownership of that file, i.e., ownership cheating attacks [27] (a.k.a., hash-only attacks [43]). This setting is consistent with the prior work in the standard cloud-based client-side deduplication scenario [43, 44]. Such short information could be obtained via certain public channels [33]. Meanwhile, the attacker can also launch poison attacks [50] (a.k.a., duplicate faking attacks [23]), i.e., uploading fake ciphertext that is inconsistent with the deduplication tag to compromise the integrity of other users' files.

In addition, consistent with existing designs on top of the blockchain [25, 34, 48], our deduplication service (i.e., smart contract) on-chain is assumed trusted, i.e., the system availability and the correctness of transaction execution can be guaranteed because of the distributed consensus protocol (e.g., Proof-of-Work and Proof-of-Stake). However, we assume that everyone can access and analyze the stored information on the chain in our target public blockchain environment.

Lastly, we assume that the encrypted file stored on backend storage, like the decentralized storage service IPFS [9], is always correct and protected. Other possible attacks to steal or tamper with these encrypted files are considered out of scope.

4 Our Proposed Design

4.1 Design Intuition

To enable efficient deduplication over encrypted files in our target public DCS scenario, directly applying MLE can not address the potential threats of malicious users. As mentioned in the Sect. 3.2, when adopting the client-side deduplication strategy, an attacker could use a short information (e.g., a file hash) to defraud the ownership or poison the ciphertext to break the integrity of other users' files. The ownership cheating attack can be addressed in the literature by running additional ownership checking steps (a.k.a., proof-of-ownership) before announcing the deduplication result [20,51]. Particularly, we involve the entire file ciphertext in the major deduplication steps, hence strengthening our design. As for poison attacks, the existing solution is to verify whether the uploaded ciphertext and the tag are consistent [50]. So here, by leveraging the tag consistency [23] property of CE, DS is able to verify if the user obeys the promise and records the malicious behavior on the blockchain.

Apart from these attacks, another challenge is that an attacker can illegally access the on-chain data via downloading and analyzing the block content [2,6]. Therefore, file address fid^1 shared by its owners cannot be stored in the plaintext as in the case of conventional cloud-based DS [43,44]. Otherwise, the attacker can bypass the normal procedure and obtain the corresponding fid directly through a specific file tag fT, and further access the ciphertext. To tackle this challenge, we introduce additional protection on fid. fid is encrypted before stored on the blockchain, and can be decrypted only if the user owns the whole file.

Additionally, we provide a fair charging model by maintaining a user index on the smart contract. Such index records the system's deduplication pattern [20], which refers to the duplicate users storing the same file. The system charges the user according to the user index, and due to the publicity of the blockchain, the system cannot deceive the user to charge additional fees. Moreover, in order to securely add uid to the index, we need to ensure that the user indeed hold the file and the user is corresponding to the uid. For the former concern, we involve proof-of-ownership [33] to verify the user. As for the latter issue, we leverage Lamport scheme [37] to generate a key pair. Communication between U and DS is signed with the user's private key, DS can verify the signature using the user's public key. Such an approach is proved secure and can not be denied by users [37]. Furthermore, to resist man-in-the-middle attacks [21], our design is implemented based on the *https* protocol.

Lastly, considering the expensive storage cost of smart contract, we are consistent with other blockchain application [34], only storing the index metadata for deduplication on the blockchain.

4.2 Data Structures and Functions

As shown in Fig. 1, our design consists of three entities, together with their functions and data structures are described as follows.

Storage Service (SS). In our design, any DCS backend can serve as SS. We leverage IPFS as our backend storage, which provides integrated APIs in file system [9], both U and DS can invoke these APIs. We stress that upload/retrieve files in IPFS are mainly used functionalities, other these two APIs are introduced as follows.

---

[1] For ease of presentation, we use fid to denote the address of the corresponding file on DCS, e.g., the content identifier (CID) for IPFS.

- $fid \leftarrow$ **IPFSAdd**(f): uploads f to the IPFS network and returns a constant file address fid (i.e., CIDs in IPFS, a 272-bits base58 encoded string). The address is obtained from the content of the file through a one-way function, each file uniquely corresponds to an address.
- $f \leftarrow$ **IPFSCat**(fid): receives fid and returns the corresponding f. The original design of IPFS does not consider cross-user deduplication, the same file in different users returns distinct fid. Therefore, we use a constant service that provides a global gateway, through which all uploads and restores are requested.

User (U). The user first signs in through a client, and then operates files in system. When uploading files, notably, if certain file U has not been stored in SS, U is called initial uploader. Otherwise, U is a subsequent uploader. Meanwhile, before upload the metadata to blockchain, one needs to encrypt fid, which is described in EncAddr. And together with other basic functions in user side are described as follows.

- $(pk, sk) \leftarrow$ **genUID**(): generates a key pair as a system account. We use ECDSA-secp256k1 as public-key encryption, the private key is 256-bits, and we let the compressed public key (256-bits) work as uid.
- $\{fK, fC, fT\} \leftarrow$ **Enc**(f): encrypts f with standard CE scheme, and outputs file key fK, ciphertext fC and file tag fT. The key and tag generations are SHA256, encryption is AES-256-CTR with a fixed IV.
- $\{aK, [fid]\} \leftarrow$ **EncAddr**(fC, r, fid): is used to encrypt file address fid. User first generates a random value r, then derives address key aK through SHA256$(r||fC)$. Here, "$||$" means string contact operation. Then, user encrypts fid via aK and obtains encrypted address $[fid]$.
- $response \leftarrow$ **dupCheck**(fT, sk, uid): user first generates fT via the above functions, and signs the message with sk through Lamport scheme, then send fT to DS for deduplicate check. If $respone = \perp$, which means the file does not exist in the current system. Otherwise if $response = \{r, [fid]\}$ means the file is uploaded before and returns the metadata corresponding to fT. (See Sect. 4.3 for detail).

Deduplication Service (DS). We utilize Ethereum as DS and design basic data structures and function calls. Figure 2 shows our metadata structure located on the blockchain, namely **FIndex** and **UIndex**. Claiming transactions in smart contracts requires the address and interface (namely ABI [49]) derived from the contract. Concretely, functions in Solidity have two categories: *view* and *pure*, the former one does not modify the contract's status, while the latter one neither modifies nor reads the status. These two kinds of functions do not consume *gas* (and are invoked by Call), while the rest of the functions cost *gas* depending on their complexity (invoked by Send). Solidity provides integrated data types (e.g., mapping, list), our data structure and functions are defined below.

- **FIndex**: $<fT : (r, [fid])>$, which is a key-value mapping from the file tag fT to the random challenge value r (i.e., public parameter P in MLE) and encrypted address $[fid]$.

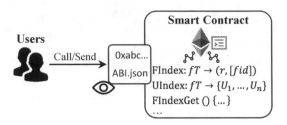

Fig. 2. An illustration of data structures and functions, where "0xabc..." denotes the contract address, "ABI.json" specifies the actual function in the contract to invoke, and "Call/Send" means different invoke methods.

- **FIndexGet**(fT): a *view* function returns the metadata of fT. If fT exists, means the file has been uploaded, function returns $(r, [fid])$, otherwise returns $\perp$.
- **FIndexPut**($fT, r, [fid]$): pushes $\{fT : (r, [fid])\}$ to FIndex, which means a new file is uploaded to system. Since the function modifies the stored data, it consumes *gas*.
- **UIndex**: $<fT : \{U_1, ..., U_k\}>$, denotes a key-value mapping from fT to the array of users that own f. Where U_i denotes user's identifier (i.e., user's public key).
  - **UIndexGet**(fT): a *view* function returns the owners of the file corresponding to fT. Returns $\perp$ if file is not uploaded, returns owner list $\{U_1, ..., U_k\}$.
  - **UIndexPut**(fT, U): adds U to the owner list of fT, the function modify the data thus costs *gas*.

4.3   Secure Deduplication in Public Blockchain

We emphasis the two main operations in our design are **Upload** and **Retrieve**. Figure 1 shows the procedures of upload request, as for the retrieve, user can directly download the file from *SS* with the local stored data. Other operations can be realized with minor revision, we omit them for the sake of brevity. We now describe above two commands in detail.

Upload Request: Depending on whether the file is uploaded, the user has two different behaviors. The process is described as follows:

- **File encryption & Tag generation**:
  U runs $\{fK, fC, fT\} \leftarrow \text{Enc}(f)$ to encrypt file and generate tag.
- **Deduplicate Check**:
  U invokes $response \leftarrow \text{dupCheck}(fT, sk)$, which sends fT to *DS*. *DS* performs $res_1 \leftarrow \text{FIndexGet}(fT)$ and $res_2 \leftarrow \text{UIndexGet}(fT)$ concurrently. If $res_1 = \perp$, *DS* sends back $\perp$. Else if $res_2 = \perp$, *DS* returns res_1. Otherwise, *DS* sends *Repeat* to user.
- **Initial Upload** ($response = \perp$):

- U calls $fid \leftarrow$ IPFSAdd(fC) to upload file and gains address.
- U executes $\{aK, r, [fid]\} \leftarrow$ EncAddr(fC, fid) to generated aK and $[fid]$, then sends $(r, fid, [fid])$ to DS. **Remark.** To ensure the data integrity, DS retrieves stored ciphertext fC_S with fid and derives stored file tag fT_S. If $fT = fT_S$, DS sends back *Succeed*, otherwise sends back *Failed*, upload finished.
- **Subsequent Upload** ($response = \{r, [fid]\}$):
  - U derives address key $aK \leftarrow$SHA256($r\|fC$), and uses aK to decrypt $[fid]$ to get fid, then save (fK, fid), upload finished.
- **Repeat Upload** ($response = Repeat$):
  We consider U has uploaded before, thus upload finished.

Retrieve Request: Since user stores the (fK, fid) locally, user can directly access fC_S from SS by invoking IPFSCat(fid), then obtains f by decrypting the ciphertext with fK.

4.4   Security Analysis

In our design, the data encryption and tag generation are based on the standard MLE [23], which is proven to achieve PRV\$-CDA security, such that any unpredictable message is indistinguishable compared to a random string with the same length. Besides, we protect the confidentiality of the file ID, i.e., fid, which indicates the actual location of outsourced data and enables data owner to fetch it. In this subsequent section, we analyze the security guarantees of our proposed design against the threats from a malicious user, that is, file ownership cheating attacks, poison attacks and brute-force attacks.

Security Against a Malicious User. A malicious user U might use a hash tag fT to cheat the DS to add him to the owner list so he could fetch the corresponding ciphertext fC from SS. The U could either send a deduplication request to the DS or directly access the data structure stored on the chain. However, given a fT, the U can only get a random challenge value r together with the encrypted file id $[fid]$. Without holding the actual file f or file ciphertext fC, the U is unable to compute the address key aK (i.e., $aK \leftarrow$SHA256(r, fC)) and return the file address fid to DS. Therefore, the final verification conducted by DS will fail and the U will not be added to the owner list.

A malicious user U might also use a correct tag for secure deduplication but upload a fake ciphertext (or a dummy fid) to compromise the integrity of other users' files [50]. However, this kind of attack will be found during the final verification step thanks to the tag consistency feature of the underlying CE scheme [23].

Further Enhancement When Facing Predictable Data. In the traditional cloud deduplication scenario, a compromised storage server might launch offline/online brute-force attacks to identify the stored ciphertext when facing predictable data [22]. This could be happened in our target DCS scenario because the key and tag for data encryption and deduplication are also deterministically

B. Zhang et al.

computed from the file itself [23]. To mitigate the offline brute-force attacks, we can either involve an additional independent third-party to obliviously embed a secret key during the key generation step [22,45] or leverage a number of online users to securely obtain a random key for a specific file [40]. Moreover, to mitigate the online brute-force attacks, we can bring the standard rate-limiting strategies as adopted in [22] and [40] into our design. Here, for easy presentation, we focus on our main design in the current version and we are aware that the data in our target public DCS scenario is often hard to predict.

5 Experimental Evaluation

5.1 Setup

We implement a prototype of our system in JavaScript and the smart contract is deployed in Solidity [15]. To evaluate its performance, we realize U and DS on Alibaba Cloud [1] with an ECS [5] instance ("ecs.c7.2xlarge" in Ubuntu Server 20.04 LTS). We conduct an IPFS network on the instance of DS as SS. Specifically, we use Javascript libraries crypto to implement AES-256-CTR and SHA256. The system uses a single thread and provides a command line interface. In terms of smart contracts, since the operations cost real tokens, it is too expensive to deploy evaluation in the main network. And the operations need a long latency of mining to be confirmed, which is inconvenient for evaluation. Therefore, we first consider evaluating our scheme on a simulated network. We use Ganache [8] to build a simulated network. Such a network has a same environment and the mining time is single CPU cycle, which allows us to focus on the performance of our encryption scheme. We use Solidity based on 0.8.16+commit.07a7930e, which is the latest version. Then, to evaluate the real-world performance, we also test our system on the test network Rinkeby [13].

To reach a better evaluation and comparison between our design and others, we choose three other deduplicate schemes at *file-level* build on IPFS APIs as our baseline.

Plaintext + IPFS APIs. The most straightforward and naive way of data deduplication, in such a scheme, files are not encrypted. We assume it as client-side deduplication, that the user computes and sends the file tag fT (i.e., hash value of file) to the server S, then S compares fT and determines whether to deduplicate the file.

MLE + IPFS APIs. We choose the most common MLE scheme, namely convergent encryption (CE) [29], in which files are encrypted. As a MLE scheme, it can be expressed as $\mathrm{CE} = (\mathcal{P}, \mathcal{K}, \mathcal{E}, \mathcal{D}, \mathcal{T})$ (see Sect. 2). To encrypt the file f, $\mathcal{P}$ generates a 128-bits random sequence P, $\mathcal{K}$ is set to SHA256($P\|f$) and returns fK, f is encrypted and decrypted with fK through AES-CTR with fixed IV, $\mathcal{T}$ takes ciphertext and outputs fT as SHA256(fC). Similarly, the user sends fT to S for deduplication check and decides whether to upload data.

DupLESS + IPFS APIs. Bellare et al. proposed DupLESS [22] to further resist brute-force attacks in predictable file sets. Compared with MLE, it involves an additional key server KS. When encrypting f, the user first interacts with KS

and blind-signs fK with a secret key fK_S through OPRF [42] protocol. In this way, any user needs to interact with the KS when obtaining the ciphertext, thus brute-force attacks can be mitigated by adding a rate limiting strategy [22]. In our implementation, elliptic-curve OPRF (EC-OPRF) [24] is used, which requires smaller key length and less computation than RSA-OPRF.

5.2 Datasets and Test Setting

Synthetic Datasets. To measure the performance in files of different sizes, we generated some dummy files of 2^i KB, $i \in \{0, 1, ..., 15\}$, i.e., from 1 KB to 32 MB. We use the Date module of JavaScript to measure the time, specific measurements are described in Sect. 5.3.

Real-World Datasets. To verify the deduplication effect of our design, we selected four public snapshots: Linux kernel, Node, MySQL and GoLang. Table 1 shows the important characteristics of the datasets.

- *Linux kernel.* A commonly used datasets for deduplication [32,39,47] We selected partial Linux kernel source code from 5.0.1 to 5.19.1 [10].
- *Node.* Partial snapshots of nodejs [12] from 17.0.0 to 18.7.0, consist of versions in different systems (e.g., Linux, x64, arm).
- *MySQL.* Partial snapshots of MySQL Server [11] from 5.0 to 5.7, snapshots contain the variants in a different system.
- *GoLang.* These snapshots are collected from the source code of Go language [4] from go1.2 to go1.19.

Table 1. Summary of tested datasets, the snapshots are originally in tar.gz format, the size and number of files represent the unzipped files, the Dedup-ratio means the deduplication ratio.

Snapshots	Total size (GB)	Total files (10^3)	Average size (MB)	Dedup-ratio
Kernel	72.62	5650.64	906.86	0.8965
Node	33.83	1304.77	183.27	0.5401
MySQL	108.34	902.68	909.33	0.1408
GoLang	74.89	1977.84	329.12	0.2267

Table 2. (**Left**) shows the theoretical storage cost for an n-byte file. (**Right**) illustrates the metadata size and percentage of tested datasets.

Scheme	Storage cost (byte)	Snapshots	Metadata (MB)	Percentage (%)
Plaintext+IPFS	$n + 66$	Kernel	441.89	0.5942
MLE+IPFS	$n + 82$	Node	102.03	0.2945
DupLESS+IPFS	$n + 98$	MySQL	70.59	0.0636
Our design	$n + 82$	GoLang	158.44	0.2017

5.3   Evaluation Results

Deduplication Effect. To validate the effect of deduplication, the *deduplication ratio* [30] (dedup-ratio for short) is proposed, which describes the reduced percentage of the original data size after deduplication. Table 1 shows the dedup-ratio of our datasets. Since all these scheme uses accurate deduplication, they have the same ratio, which means that our design achieves the optimal deduplication effect at the file level.

Storage Cost. Table 2-(Left) illustrates the file storage cost for an n-byte file of the four schemes, the cost of our owner list is described later. Our system stores encrypted system metadata (i.e., FIndex and UIndex) on the blockchain, thus we only keep the least data on-chain. Here, we briefly explain the results of the schemes.

- **In plaintext case**, the user accesses the file through fT directly, thus we need to store fT (32 bytes) and fid (34 bytes), which is $n + 66$ bytes.
- **In MLE case**, we need to store P (16 bytes random string) to retrieve the file, together with fT and fid, that is $n + 82$ bytes in total.
- **In DupLESS case**, each file needs to maintain a blind-signed key fK_S (32 bytes), fT, and fid, which is $n + 98$ bytes.
- **In our design**, the cost comes from P, fT, and fid, which sums up with $n + 82$ bytes. Particularly, as for UIndex, the uid in our design is 32 bytes, thus we have fT and several uid to maintain within UIndex. Say m is the number of uploaded files, k is the average owners each file has, and the storage of UIndex is approximately $64mk$ byte.

More comprehensively, we evaluate the metadata in our design over *Kernel*. As shown in Table 2-(Right), the metadata only takes less than 1% of datasets storage, which can be considered a small amount of overhead.

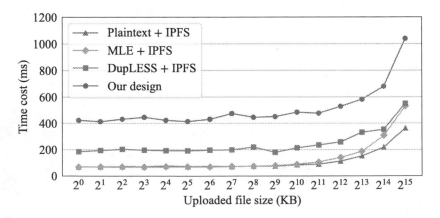

Fig. 3. Average latency of store requests in tested schemes with different file size ranging from 1 KB to 32 MB.

Time Cost. To explore the latency of upload/retrieve request in different file sizes, we tested the dummy files in Sect. 5.2. Each file is uploaded and retrieved for 100 times. Figure 3 shows the performance of the four models under different file sizes. Notably, interact with smart contract is the major latency of our design, which is 411 ms in average, takes more than 84.76% latency for files less than 1 MB. In the terms of retrieve, four schemes have the barely same performance. Instead, we measure the processing speed for different calculations, which shown in Table 3-(Left).

Table 3. (**Left**) illustrates the processing speed of different computations. (**Right**) shows the latency and gas cost of functions in *Ganche*.

Name	Speed (MBps)
Hash	264.50
Encrypt	542.05
Decrypt	618.25
IPFSAdd	190.57
IPFSCat	111.19

Name	Latency (ms)	Gas cost
FIndexGet	104.55	–
FIndexPut	306.70	24188
UIndexGet	434.45	–
UIndexPut	281.90	49428

Overhead from Smart Contract. We first evaluate the functions in *Ganache* [8] for 100 times each. Table 3-(Right) gives the latency and gas cost of four functions in *Ganache*. Then we evaluate our system in the official test network *Rinkeby* [13], the average mining time is 8.71 s, the actual gas cost is 0.00016767 ETH for both FIndexPut and UIndexPut. Concurrently, each ETH is 1709.71 USD, thus above cost is 0.287 USD.

6 Related Work

Commercial Decentralized Storage Services. There are many emerging DCS products today, i.e., Storj [16], Sia [14], and IPFS [9]. Such products can be roughly divided into two categories. The first kind, taking Storj and Sia as an example, ensures data security via some conventional encryption schemes, but does not consider data deduplication. In Storj, the file is first encrypted via AES-256, then encoded with erasure codes (the file is split into 80 pieces, and retrieving the file requires 29 pieces), and then distributed globally [16]. In Sia, similar to Storj, files are first divided into pieces in the size of 40 MB (the smaller files will be padded to 40 MB), then encrypted via Threefish [31] and split into 30 pieces at the size of 4 MB (retrieve requires 10 pieces) before distributed. Both products use erasure codes to ensure data reliability, thus the files are certainly stored as 2.76^2 times the original size in Storj (3 times in Sia). Moreover, both

---

[2] In Storj, for erasure code with the factor $k = 29$ and $n = 80$, the total storage is roughly $80/29 \approx 2.76$ times, similarly, Sia will store 3 times.

products do not consider deduplication, the same file will be redundantly stored, making the situation worse. Another type, represented by IPFS, ensures single-user deduplication but can hardly guarantee data security. Concretely, in IPFS, within a certain user, the application uses Merkle DAG [9] (i.e., an improved data structure based on the Merkle tree) to perform deduplicate check and version control, and ensure that the same content is only stored once. But the same content from several users outputs distinct DAGs and returns different fid, thus preventing the cross-user deduplication. More importantly, data in IPFS is only encrypted during transmission and finally stored in plaintext, which is an intentional decision to prevent *vendor lock-in* [9].

Secure Deduplication Over Encrypted Data. To get rid of the constraints of the server, realize cross-user data deduplication, and protect data privacy, Douceur et al. [29] proposed CE, in which the key is derived from the message to be encrypted, thus users holding the same file result in the same cipher-text without additional server. Meanwhile, many other secure deduplication schemes are proposed, e.g., [18,19]. Afterward, Bellare et al. normalized CE to MLE [23] and proposed privacy, and formalized the security notion of PRV-CDA and stronger PRV\$-CDA. They compared the various encryption schemes with different privacy strengths (e.g., CE, HCE1, HCE2). Consequentially, some schemes [20,22,27,51] realize the secure deduplication over encrypted data based on MLE. Such a scheme prevented offline brute-force attacks on *unpredictable* files but is vulnerable to *predictable* files. To further mitigate such shortcomings, Bellare et al. enhanced MLE by involving an additional key server [22]. To store the files, a client first generates the file key through MLE, then it needs to request the key server to blind-sign the file key through OPRF protocol. Thus, all store requests interact with the key server, where a rate-limiting strategy can be adopted to block the brute-force attack on predictable files. Moreover, there is also a line of work that targets block-level settings for a higher deduplication ratio. For example, BL-MLE [26] designs a dual-level scheme that combines the block keys and tags together to reduce the metadata size. UWare [27] leverages the similarity of file blocks to balance the deduplication effectiveness and system efficiency.

Blockchain-Based Deduplicate Schemes. Li et al. [38] leverage secret sharing scheme with smart contract to realize the deduplication in distributed scenario. File is split into blocks and distributed in several store service providers (SSPs). Such scheme mitigates the single point of failure in the distributed scenario but suffers from latency and overheads. Furthermore, Tian et al. [48] proposed a double-server deduplicate model and shared auditing scheme over encrypted data. In which stores the data index and system logs in blockchain, and proposed a lightweight authenticator generation algorithm with update protocol.

7 Conclusion

In this paper, we design and implement a blockchain-based cross-user secure deduplication on encrypted data. Our enhanced encryption involving the entire file during the major steps, thus ensures data security when facing public blockchain and prevents the ownership cheating attacks and duplicate poisoning attacks. We overcome the challenges come from the transparency feature of public blockchain, store the encrypted metadata on-chain and let the decryption requires the entire file thus prevents the public illegal analysis. Moreover, subsequent users do not need to upload files, which saves bandwidth as well. Evaluation results show that our design achieves decentralized secure deduplication with practical on-chain storage and computation cost.

Acknowledgements. This work was supported in part by the National Key R&D Program of China (No. 2019YFB2102200), the National Science Fund for Distinguished Young Scholars (No. 61725205), the National Natural Science Foundation of China (No. 62002294, 62202379), and the Fundamental Research Funds for the Central Universities (No. 3102019QD1001, D5000220127).

References

1. Alibaba cloud official website (2022). https://www.alibabacloud.com/
2. The blockchain data platform - Chainalysis (2022). https://chainalysis.com/
3. Data breach: Latest news & videos, photos about data breach. The Economic Times (2022). https://economictimes.indiatimes.com/topic/data-breach
4. Downloads - the go programming language (2022). https://go.dev/dl/
5. Elastic compute service (ECS): Elastic & secure cloud servers - Alibaba Cloud (2022). https://www.alibabacloud.com/product/ecs
6. Ethereum (eth) blockchain explorer (2022). https://etherscan.io/
7. Filecoin: a decentralized storage network (2022). https://filecoin.io/
8. Ganache - truffle suite (2022). https://trufflesuite.com/ganache/
9. IPFS powers the distributed web (2022). https://ipfs.io/
10. Linux kernel source code (2022). https://www.kernel.org/
11. MySQL: Download mysql community server (archived versions) (2022). https://downloads.mysql.com/archives/community/
12. Previous releases | node.js (2022). https://nodejs.org/download/release/
13. Rinkeby: Network dashboard (2022). https://www.rinkeby.io/
14. Sia - decentralized data storage (2022). https://sia.tech/
15. Solidity programming language (2022). https://soliditylang.org/
16. Storj: Decentralized cloud storage (2022). https://www.storj.io/
17. World's biggest data breaches & hacks - information is beautiful (2022). https://informationisbeautiful.net/visualizations/worlds-biggest-data-breaches-hacks/
18. Adya, A., et al.: FARSITE: federated, available, and reliable storage for an incompletely trusted environment. In: Proceedings of the 5th Symposium on Operating Systems Design and Implementation, pp. 1–14. USENIX Association (2002)
19. Anderson, P., Zhang, L.: Fast and secure laptop backups with encrypted deduplication. In: Proceedings of the LISA 2010, pp. 29–40. USENIX Association (2010)

20. Armknecht, F., Bohli, J.M., Karame, G.O., Youssef, F.: Transparent data deduplication in the cloud. In: Proceedings of the ACM CCS (2015)
21. Asokan, N., Niemi, V., Nyberg, K.: Man-in-the-middle in tunnelled authentication protocols. In: Security Protocols (2005)
22. Bellare, M., Keelveedhi, S., Ristenpart, T.: DupLESS: server-aided encryption for deduplicated storage. In: Proceedings of the USENIX Security (2013)
23. Bellare, M., Keelveedhi, S., Ristenpart, T.: Message-locked encryption and secure deduplication. In: Proceedings of the EUROCRYPT (2013)
24. Burns, J., Moore, D., Ray, K., Speers, R., Vohaska, B.: EC-OPRF: oblivious pseudorandom functions using elliptic curves. IACR Cryptology ePrint Archive, p. 111 (2017)
25. Cai, C., Xu, L., Zhou, A., Wang, C.: Toward a secure, rich, and fair query service for light clients on public blockchains. IEEE Trans. Dependable Secure Comput. **19**, 3640–3655 (2021)
26. Chen, R., Mu, Y., Yang, G., Guo, F.: BL-MLE: Block-level message-locked encryption for secure large file deduplication. IEEE Trans. Inf. Forensics Secur. **10**(12), 2643–2652 (2015)
27. Cui, H., Wang, C., Hua, Y., Du, Y., Yuan, X.: A bandwidth-efficient middleware for encrypted deduplication. In: Proceedings of IEEE DSC (2018)
28. Dimakis, A., Prabhakaran, V., Ramchandran, K.: Decentralized erasure codes for distributed networked storage. IEEE Trans. Inf. Theor. **52**(6), 2809–2816 (2006)
29. Douceur, J.R., Adya, A., Bolosky, W.J., Simon, D., Theimer, M.: Reclaiming space from duplicate files in a serverless distributed file system. In: Proceedings of the IEEE ICDCS (2002)
30. Dutch, M.: Understanding data deduplication ratios. In: SNIA Data Management Forum, vol. 7 (2008)
31. Ferguson, N., et al.: The skein hash function family. Submission to NIST (round 3), vol. 7, no. 7.5, p. 3 (2010)
32. Fu, M., et al.: Accelerating restore and garbage collection in deduplication-based backup systems via exploiting historical information. In: USENIX ATC 2014, pp. 181–192 (2014)
33. Halevi, S., Harnik, D., Pinkas, B., Shulman-Peleg, A.: Proofs of ownership in remote storage systems. In: Proceedings of the ACM CCS (2011)
34. Hu, S., Cai, C., Wang, Q., Wang, C., Wang, Z., Ye, D.: Augmenting encrypted search: a decentralized service realization with enforced execution. IEEE Trans. Dependable Secure Comput. **18**(6), 2569–2581 (2021)
35. Ivanov, N., Lou, J., Chen, T., Li, J., Yan, Q.: Targeting the weakest link: social engineering attacks in Ethereum smart contracts. In: Proceedings of the 2021 ACM Asia Conference on Computer and Communications Security, pp. 787–801 (2021)
36. Kushwah, S., Desai, A., Subramanyan, P., Seshia, S.A.: PSec: programming secure distributed systems using enclaves. In: Proceedings of the 2021 ACM Asia Conference on Computer and Communications Security, pp. 802–816 (2021)
37. Lamport, L.: Constructing digital signatures from a one way function. Technical report, CSL-98, SRI International (1979)
38. Li, J., Wu, J., Chen, L., Li, J.: Deduplication with blockchain for secure cloud storage. In: Xu, Z., Gao, X., Miao, Q., Zhang, Y., Bu, J. (eds.) Big Data, pp. 558–570 (2018)
39. Li, M., Qin, C., Lee, P.P.C.: CDStore: toward reliable, secure, and cost-efficient cloud storage via convergent dispersal. In: USENIX ATC 2015, pp. 111–124 (2015)
40. Liu, J., Duan, L., Li, Y., Asokan, N.: Secure deduplication of encrypted data: refined model and new constructions. In: Proceedings of the CT-RSA (2018)

41. Merkle, R.C.: A digital signature based on a conventional encryption function. In: Pomerance, C. (ed.) CRYPTO 1987. LNCS, vol. 293, pp. 369–378. Springer, Heidelberg (1988). https://doi.org/10.1007/3-540-48184-2_32
42. Naor, M., Reingold, O.: Number-theoretic constructions of efficient pseudo-random functions. J. ACM **51**, 231–262 (2004)
43. Rabotka, V., Mannan, M.: An evaluation of recent secure deduplication proposals. J. Inf. Secur. Appl. (JISA) **27**, 3–18 (2016)
44. Shin, Y., Koo, D., Hur, J.: A survey of secure data deduplication schemes for cloud storage systems. ACM Comput. Surv. (CSUR) **49**(4), 74 (2017)
45. Shin, Y., Koo, D., Yun, J., Hur, J.: Decentralized server-aided encryption for secure deduplication in cloud storage. IEEE Trans. Dependable Secure Comput. **13**(6), 1021–1033 (2020)
46. Szabo, N.: Formalizing and securing relationships on public networks. First Monday (1997)
47. Tarasov, V., Mudrankit, A., Buik, W., Shilane, P., Kuenning, G., Zadok, E.: Generating realistic datasets for deduplication analysis. In: USENIX ATC 2012, pp. 261–272 (2012)
48. Tian, G., et al.: Blockchain-based secure deduplication and shared auditing in decentralized storage. IEEE Trans. Dependable Secure Comput. **19**(6), 3941–3954 (2022)
49. Tikhomirov, S.: Ethereum: state of knowledge and research perspectives. In: Proceedings of the Foundations and Practice of Security (2017)
50. Xu, J., Chang, E.C., Zhou, J.: Weak leakage-resilient client-side deduplication of encrypted data in cloud storage. In: Proceedings of ACM ASIACCS (2013)
51. Zheng, Y., Yuan, X., Wang, X., Jiang, J., Wang, C., Gui, X.: Toward encrypted cloud media center with secure deduplication. IEEE Trans. Multimedia **19**(2), 251–265 (2016)

Geometric Range Searchable Encryption with Forward and Backward Security

Mengwei Yang, Chungen Xu$^{(\boxtimes)}$, and Pan Zhang

Nanjing University of Science and Technology, Nanjing 210094, Jiangsu, China
{yangmengwei,xuchung,panzhang}@njust.edu.cn

Abstract. Geometric range query is a general query algorithm over spatial data and applies to many real-world applications, such as location-based services. Considering the sensitivity of location information, how to guarantee the confidentiality of the location information while providing efficient query service becomes a big concern. Several cryptographic solutions are proposed to solve this problem, particularly those dynamic searchable encryption schemes with forward and backward privacy that provides strong security guarantees for encrypted spatial databases that support data deletion and addition. Despite the increasing efforts, recent studies show that existing solutions with these two securities either use less secure property-preserving encryption for efficiency and flexibility or intuitively build a binary tree for each dimension, which leads to poor scalability. This paper proposes a novel forward and backward secure geometric range searchable encryption scheme on encrypted spatial data. Specifically, we build a two-level index for first-step rough navigation and second-step precise testing to get accurate search results. Detailed theoretical analysis and experimental evaluation demonstrate that compared with related work, our scheme achieves strong security and sub-linear search efficiency while boosting the average update time by 70 times.

Keywords: Dynamic searchable encryption · Forward security · Backward security · Spatial data · Geometric range queries

1 Introduction

A geometric range query [1] is to retrieve spatial data records within a given shape range, such as a circle, rectangle, and polygon. And it has a wide range of applications in modern life, such as location-based service [25], urban planning [24], and location-based alert systems [10]. For example, users on social media can perform a circular range search to find nearby people by the location-based service.

This work was supported by the National Natural Science Foundation of China (No: 62072240), the National Key Research and Development Program of China (No. 2020YFB1804604), and the Natural Science Foundation of Jiangsu Province (No. BK20210330).

X. Yuan et al. (Eds.): NSS 2022, LNCS 13787, pp. 476–495, 2022.
https://doi.org/10.1007/978-3-031-23020-2_27

With the continuous growth of spatial data scale, companies and organizations tend to outsource their spatial datasets to the public cloud server to alleviate local storage and management costs. However, internal and external threats in cloud services may compromise data privacy. Encryption-before-outsourcing is an effective way to protect data confidentiality, but it will lose data availability. Searchable Symmetric Encryption (SSE) [9] is a promising cryptographic primitive which enables the search of encrypted data. Dynamic SSE (DSSE) [15] further supports dynamic updates while preserving data confidentiality and searchability. However, previous SSE schemes mainly focused on non-numerical keyword queries, for which a simple equality checking is sufficient. The geometric range queries considered in this paper typically require more complex evaluations. For example, a circular range query needs to calculate the distance between the target data and the circle's center and then compare it with the query radius. Therefore, this compute-then-compare operation makes it difficult to design an efficient geometric range searchable encryption scheme.

Nowadays, different cryptographic primitives and tools have been proposed to support geometric range queries on spatial data, such as Order-Preserving Encryption (OPE) [27], Predicate Encryption [28], secure k-nearest neighbor (kNN) computation [38], and so on [16,17,34,37,39]. On the one hand, the schemes taking these methods as building blocks cannot provide a good balance between security and efficiency. For instance, the order leakage of OPE can be used to infer the plaintext values by inference attacks [26]. Predicate Encryption can enhance security, but expensive pairing operations limit performance in practice. On the other hand, some schemes support dynamic updates due to location relocation or facility addition of spatial data, but little consideration is given to forward and backward security, which is necessary for any newly designed dynamic schemes. Recently, Wang et al. [37] proposed a forward secure spatial DSSE scheme based on Order-Revealing Encryption (ORE) [18] and Quadtree data structure, but the order leakage still exists after comparison in ORE [12]. Besides, the ORE-encrypted index tree will leak the order and distribution of the entire database before any query. Kermanshahi et al. [17] also considered forward/backward security, but their two schemes have poor scalability and low update efficiency with search content disclosure.

In light of the above discussions, we motivate the study of designing a general forward and backward secure dynamic scheme that supports geometric range queries on encrypted spatial data with better security. In particular, our scheme protects the privacy of stored data and search queries without leaking the order of data. And at a high level, the core idea of our design is to build a two-level index as distilling from previous solutions [22,34]. Specifically, the first level index involves decomposing a spatial space into a conceptual hierarchical structure, transforming a geometric range query into multiple single-keyword queries. The second level index involves judging whether spatial data is within a query range by another data structure.

Finally, our contributions to this paper are summarized as follows:

- We propose a new forward and backward secure DSSE scheme for geometric range queries on encrypted spatial data. It effectively converts comparison evaluations in range queries into simple equality-checking evaluations.
- By giving detailed leakage functions during the update and search operations, we rigorously prove the security of our scheme.
- Compared with the prior art [17], the experimental results show that our construction has better update performance and comparable search performance on average. For example, for fixed dimension size 2^{18} and update size 100, the update time of our scheme is approximately 288× shorter than [17].

Organization. The remainder of this paper is organized as follows. In Sect. 2, we introduce the related work. Section 3 presents preliminaries, and Sect. 4 describes the definition of DSSE and some security definitions. Then, in Sect. 5, we provide the details of our proposed scheme and give its leakage function and security analysis. Section 6 presents the experimental evaluation. Finally, a conclusion is given in Sect. 7.

2   Related Work

Dynamic Searchable Symmetric Encryption. In 2000, Song et al. [29] proposed the first practical Searchable Encryption (SE) scheme that realized keyword queries in a ciphertext environment. Then many kinds of literature have carried out further research on security, efficiency, and functionality [7,9,15,40,41]. Kamara et al. [15] extended traditional static SSE to dynamic SSE. However, new features will introduce novel security risks, and the file injection attack [42] exploits the leakage during dynamic updates to launch the attack. This attack emphasizes the importance of forward security in a dynamic setting. Forward security was first introduced by Stefanov et al. [30] and formally defined by Bost [4]. Bost [5] also defined the concept of backward security in DSSE and gave three types of backward security from strongest to weakest. And these two kinds of security gradually become essential requirements for any newly designed DSSE scheme.

Geometric Range Query. Much literature has proposed encrypted geometric range searchable schemes based on cryptographic primitives. For example, Ghinita and Rughinis [10] utilized Hidden Vector Encryption [2] to design a location-based alert system, in which if the current location of a mobile user satisfies a range search predicate, an alarm can be sent to him immediately. Wang et al. [33] and Zhu et al. [43] separately proposed circular-specific range searchable schemes. Unfortunately, none of the schemes mentioned above supports range queries with arbitrary geometric shapes. Then, Wang et al. proposed several schemes [32,34] to support arbitrary range queries on spatial data based on pairing-based Shen-Shi-Waters (SSW) Encryption [28]. The main idea of their schemes is to encrypt the spatial data and query range in an equality-vector form and then evaluate the inner product to check whether the point meets

Table 1. Comprehensive comparison

Scheme	Type	Dynamism	Forward security	Backward security	Cryptographic tools[†]
CRSE [33]	Circle	✗	–	–	Pairing-based SSW encryption
EPQ [43]	Circle	✗	–	–	Improved homomorphic encryption
SQ-tree [37]	Rectangle	✓	✗	✗	ORE
SQ-tree$_{FS}$ [37]	Rectangle	✓	✓	✗	ORE & CPRF
Construction I [17]	Rectangle	✓	✗	Type-II	SKE/ASHE
Construction II [17]	Rectangle	✓	✓	Type-II	ASHE
FastGeo [34]	Arbitrary	✓	✗	✗	Pairing-based SSW encryption
EGRQ [39]	Arbitrary	✓	✗	✗	kNN
Ours	Rectangle[‡]	✓	✓	Type-II	SC-PRF

[†] SKE is symmetric key encryption, CPRF is constrained pseudo-random function, SC-PRF is set-constrained PRF, and ASHE is additive symmetric homomorphic encryption.

[‡] Note that our scheme can also support arbitrary shapes range queries by enumerating all possible data points within the query range in the plaintext domain, as used in [34].

the query condition. And some follow-up works [13,14,22] have improved Wang et al.'s work, but these works still rely on SSW encryption, so expensive pairing operations limit performance in practice.

Other works used kNN as building blocks [19,23,39]. Luo et al. [23] used secure kNN computation with a geometric transformation to enable a generalized geometric range search on encrypted spatial data. Later, Li et al. [19] broke Luo's scheme through an effective attack method and provided an enhanced solution for multi-dimensional range queries. Xu et al. [39] used secure kNN computation and the polynomial fitting technique to search encrypted spatial data with additional access control. In addition, OPE and tree structures (e.g., R-tree) are often combined to reduce the search time [16,39].

Taking forward and backward security into account in the dynamic scheme, recently, Wang et al. [37] proposed an efficient and forward-secure spatial DSSE scheme based on ORE and Quadtree data structure. But ORE-derived search tokens are long-term valid, so the server can reuse these tokens without the client's permission to test subsequent unmasked data, which reveals more information during search operations. Kermanshahi et al. [17] also considered forward/backward security and proposed two concrete schemes. However, the essence of their idea is to perform two one-dimensional range queries, so its scalability is poor. And the use of binary tree and additive symmetric homomorphic encryption (ASHE) results in high update cost and search query leakage.

Finally, Table 1 presents a comprehensive comparison between our scheme and existing schemes.

3   Preliminaries

In this section, we describe the necessary cryptographic primitives and building blocks used in our scheme. Let λ be the security parameter, $negl(\lambda)$ be a negligible function in λ. The symbol $x \xleftarrow{\$} \mathcal{X}$ denotes x is sampled uniformly random from a finite set $\mathcal{X}$; $|\cdot|$ denotes the number of elements in a set; a$\|$b denotes the concatenation of a and b; $\cap$ denotes the relative position of a point or range in a specific area.

3.1   Set-Constrained Pseudorandom Function (SC-PRF)

We recall the syntax of SC-PRFs here. SC-PRFs is a specific class of constrained PRFs [3]. Let $F : \mathcal{K} \times \mathcal{X} \rightarrow \mathcal{Y}$ be a PRF that can be computed by a deterministic polynomial time algorithm: on input $(k, x) \in \mathcal{K} \times \mathcal{X}$, the algorithm outputs $F(k, x) \in \mathcal{Y}$.

A PRF $F : \mathcal{K} \times \mathcal{X} \rightarrow \mathcal{Y}$ is a set-constrained PRF if there exists an additional key space $\mathcal{K}_c$ and two additional algorithms F.Cons and F.Eval such that:

- F.Cons(k, S) is a PPT algorithm that takes as input a PRF key $k \in \mathcal{K}$ and the description of a set $S \subseteq \mathcal{X}$. It outputs a set-constrained key $k_S \in \mathcal{K}_c$. This constrained key k_S enables the evaluation of $F(k, x)$ for all $x \in S$ and no other x.
- F.Eval(k_S, x) is a deterministic polynomial-time algorithm that takes as input a constrained key $k_S \in \mathcal{K}_c$ for set $S \subseteq \mathcal{X}$ and an element $x \in \mathcal{X}$, it outputs $y \in \mathcal{Y}$.

Correctness. It is required that for all k, x and $S \subseteq \mathcal{X}$, we have

$$F.\text{Eval}(k_S, x) = \begin{cases} F(k, x), & \text{if } x \in S \\ \bot, & \text{otherwise} \end{cases}$$

where $k_S = F.\text{Cons}(k, S)$.

3.2   Hierarchical Encoding

We introduce a hierarchical encoding technique [10] that divides the data space into multiple hierarchical grids indexed by a binary form and organized into a quadtree-like spatial structure. More specifically, to encode a two-dimensional dataset for given data space, we first define a level-0 grid that is identical to it and represents the root. Then the level-0 grid is divided into four equal-size grids, and each of these will have a 2-bit binary index: 00 for the bottom left, 01 for the top left, 10 for the bottom right, and 11 for the top right [10]. Next, divide each level-i grid into four equal-size sub-grids at level $i+1$, and concatenate the newly obtained 2-bit indexes to the end of the previous step index. This partitioning continues until the side length is smaller than a predetermined threshold.

Figure 1 gives an example of Hierarchical Encoding with three levels. For simplicity, we assume that the data space is a square and the dimension range is a power of 4, but by using padding, the model can be adapted to any size. We use a hierarchical structure because it can reduce the size of the search token. For example, if a level-i grid is fully covered by the query range, you can skip all children of this grid to make the token generation process more efficient.

3.3   Hilbert Curve

The Hilbert curve is a space-filling curve. Due to the good locality-preserving properties, it is often used in schemes that support geometric range queries

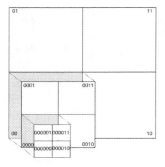

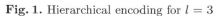

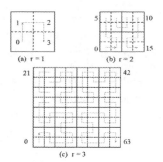

Fig. 1. Hierarchical encoding for $l = 3$

Fig. 2. Examples of $r = 1, 2$ and 3 Hilbert curves

[22,36]. It can run through the entire space and index each discrete unit as an ordered number. In this way, two adjacent points in a two-dimensional space are also close after being mapped to a one-dimensional space. Specifically, each dimension of the two-dimensional spatial space is divided into 2^r regions evenly, and the entire space can then be divided into 2^{2r} regions evenly. And each region can be regarded as a continuous $2r$-bits value, where r is the order of the Hilbert curve. Figure 2 shows three Hilbert curves of order $r = 1, 2$ and 3. In this paper, we adopt the method in [21] to convert two-dimensional spatial data into a one-dimensional value on the Hilbert curve.

3.4 Prefix Member Verification

We recall the prefix membership verification scheme [20] here. The prefix family of a w-bits data item $x = b_1 b_2 \cdots b_w$ (prepending 0s if needed) is a set of $w + 1$ elements and denoted as $\mathcal{F}(x) = \{b_1 b_2 \cdots b_w, b_1 b_2 \cdots b_{w-1}*, \cdots, b_1 * \cdots *, * * \cdots *\}$, where each element (i.e., prefix) denotes a range and symbol $*$ indicates a wildcard of 0 or 1. Let $S([a, b])$ be a set of minimum number of prefixes that cover exactly the given range $[a, b]$, where each prefix and a, b are also represented by a w-bits binary form. Then there is a conclude that for any number x and query range $[a, b]$, $x \in [a, b]$ if and only if $\mathcal{F}(x) \cap S([a, b]) \neq 0$. For example, the prefix family of a 3-bits data item 4 is $\mathcal{F}(4) = \{100, 10*, 1**, ***\}$. To query all data items in range $[2, 7]$, we generate the search query as $S([2, 7]) = \{01*, 1**\}$, then $\mathcal{F}(4) \cap S([2, 7]) = 1 ** \neq \emptyset$, thus $4 \in [2, 7]$.

4 DSSE Definition And Security Definitions

Let the spatial database be DB $= \{(p_i, ind_i)\}_{i=1}^N$, where (p_i, ind_i) is the coordinate and identifier pair of the i-th data point, and N is the number of spatial data in the spatial space Δ_T^2. In this paper, we only consider a two-dimensional data space, and T is the range of each dimension. For simplicity, we assume each dimension has the same size. That is, for any spatial data $p = (x, y)$, where x and y are the coordinate value of p in x- and y-dimension, we have $x, y \in [0, T - 1]$. At last, let q be a search query, and $\text{DB}(q)$ denotes the set of data identifiers that match q.

We will organize spatial data into a hierarchical storage structure, and because the number of levels in the hierarchy is denoted by l, thus each spatial data in DB belongs to l girds from level-l to level-1. Then we can associate every data point with l "keywords", where "keywords" refer to an artifact representing the hierarchical grids for search and update operations. Thus to update a data point, we have to update all "keywords" that contain it. And for a search query, we can reduce a geometric range query to multiple single-keyword queries.

4.1   Dynamic Searchable Symmetric Encryption

Definition 1 (DSSE [5]). *A DSSE scheme consists of a PPT algorithm* **Setup** *and two protocols* **Search**, **Update** *executed between a client and a server:*

- **Setup**$(1^\lambda, \text{DB}) \rightarrow (\text{EDB}, sk, \sigma)$: *Given the security parameter λ and the database DB, the algorithm outputs the encrypted database EDB, the master secret key sk, and the client's internal state σ. And EDB is sent to the server, sk and σ are secretly stored by the client.*
- **Search**$(sk, \sigma, q; \text{EDB}) \rightarrow (\sigma', \text{DB}(q); \text{EDB}')$: *This is a protocol between the client whose inputs are a key sk, a state σ, and a query q; and the server whose input is an encrypted database EDB. At the end of the protocol, the protocol outputs a new state σ' with a set of matching results $\text{DB}(q)$ for the client; and a (possibly) updated database EDB' for the server. In this paper, we conduct multiple single-keyword queries as a geometric range query.*
- **Update**$(sk, \sigma, op, in; \text{EDB}) \rightarrow (\sigma'; \text{EDB}')$: *This is a protocol between the client whose inputs are sk and σ, and an operation $op \in \{add, del\}$ with its input $in = (w, ind)$, where in is parsed as a keyword-identifier pair; and the server with input EDB. The protocol returns an updated state σ' to the client and an updated encrypted database EDB' to the server. In our scheme, to update a data point, we need to update all "keywords" containing it.*

A DSSE scheme is correct if the search protocol returns the correct responses for each query except with negligible probability. See [6] for more details.

4.2   Security Model

Formally, the security of a DSSE scheme is captured by a real-world versus ideal-world formalization with a stateful leakage function $\mathcal{L}$ for simulation. Each component of $\mathcal{L} = \{\mathcal{L}^{Stp}, \mathcal{L}^{Srch}, \mathcal{L}^{Updt}\}$ is the information that can be learned by the adversary during **Setup**, **Search**, and **Update** operations respectively. The security game is given below, and adversary $\mathcal{A}$ would distinguish which game he interacts with during the experiment.

- **Real**$_\mathcal{A}(1^\lambda)$: on inputting a database DB chosen by $\mathcal{A}$, the challenger runs **Setup**$(1^\lambda, \text{DB})$ and sends generated EDB to $\mathcal{A}$. For a polynomial number of search queries and update queries adaptively asked by $\mathcal{A}$, the challenger runs the corresponding **Search** and **Update** protocol and sends generated transcripts to $\mathcal{A}$. Finally, $\mathcal{A}$ returns a bit b.
- **Ideal**$_{\mathcal{A},\mathcal{S}}(1^\lambda)$: on inputting a database DB chosen by $\mathcal{A}$, the simulator $\mathcal{S}$ returns EDB using $\mathcal{L}^{Stp}(1^\lambda, \text{DB})$. $\mathcal{A}$ adaptively makes a polynomial number of queries. For a search query q, $\mathcal{S}$ returns the transcripts generated with $\mathcal{L}^{Srch}(q)$. For an update query (op, in), $\mathcal{S}$ returns the transcripts generated with $\mathcal{L}^{Updt}(op, in)$. Finally, $\mathcal{A}$ returns a bit b.

Definition 2 (Adaptive security). *A DSSE = (Setup, Search, Update) scheme is $\mathcal{L}$-adaptively-secure, if for all PPT adversary $\mathcal{A}$, there exists a PPT simulator $\mathcal{S}$ such that:*

$$|\Pr[\textbf{Real}_\mathcal{A}(1^\lambda) = 1] - \Pr[\textbf{Idea}_{\mathcal{A},\mathcal{S}}(1^\lambda) = 1]| \leq \text{negl}(\lambda)$$

Search Pattern [4]. The leakage function $\mathcal{L}$ takes a query list Q as implicit input, Q records all queries issued so far. And each entry of Q is (u, w) for a search query on keyword w, or (u, op, in) for an op update query with input in. The integer u is a timestamp initially set to 0 and incremented at each query. Then the search pattern (sp) for a keyword w is defined as $sp(w) = \{u|(u, w) \in Q\}$ (only matches search queries).

4.3 Forward Privacy

Forward and backward privacy capture the leakage of a DSSE scheme during the update and search operations. Informally, forward privacy requires that old search tokens cannot match newly updated data.

Definition 3 (Forward Privacy [4]). *A $\mathcal{L}$-adaptively-secure DSSE scheme is forward-private iff the update leakage function $\mathcal{L}^{Updt}$ can be written as $\mathcal{L}^{Updt}(op, w, ind) = \mathcal{L}'(op, ind)$, where $op \in \{add, del\}$ is an update operation, (w, id) is a related keyword and file identifier pair, and $\mathcal{L}'$ is a stateless function.*

Remark. For our geometric range queries, we parse an update as a point-identifier pair (p, ind) and the leakage function of it will be $\mathcal{L}^{Updt}(op, p, ind) = \mathcal{L}'(op, ind, l)$, where l is the number of levels in hierarchy.

4.4 Backward Privacy

Backward privacy (BP) requires that previously added and later deleted data cannot be found between two consecutive identical searches. Bost et al. [5] formalized three types of backward privacy from strongest to weakest (Type-I to Type-III). Here, we only aim for Type-II and extend the original single-keyword query setting to a geometric range query setting, similar to the one-dimensional range DSSE scheme [35]. And before presenting the definition, we

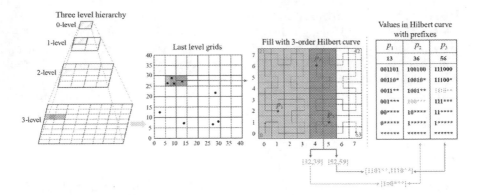

Fig. 3. A description of the second level index

first define several additional functions on the query list Q. **TimeDB**$(w) =$ $\{(u, ind)|(u, add, (w, ind)) \in Q \land \forall u', (u', del, (w, ind)) \notin Q\}$ is the function that returns files currently matching w and when they are inserted. **Updates**$(w) =$ $\{u|(u, add, (w, ind)) \in Q \lor (u, del, (w, ind)) \in Q\}$ is the function that returns the timestamp of all update operations on w.

Suppose $KSet_q$ is the "keyword" (i.e., grid) set involved in the range query q, and our extended backward privacy definition of Type-II is given below.

Definition 4 (Backward Privacy [5,35]). *An $\mathcal{L}$-adaptively-secure geometric range DSSE scheme is Type-II backward-private: iff $\mathcal{L}^{Updt}(op, p, ind) = \mathcal{L}'(op, p)$, $\mathcal{L}^{Srch}(q) = \mathcal{L}''((\textbf{TimeDB}(w), \textbf{Updates}(w))_{w \in KSet_q})$, where $\mathcal{L}'$ and $\mathcal{L}''$ are stateless functions.*

5   Construction

5.1   Overview

As mentioned before, the core idea of our design is to build a secure two-level index, in which the first level is used for navigation and the second for further filtering. And the first level index is naturally formed by a keyword-based DSSE scheme (recall Sect. 4). For the second-level index, only the bottommost grid in the hierarchy will intersect with the query range, requiring further filtering. So to obtain accurate search results, we fill every level-l grid with the Hilbert curve[1]. Then each data point in DB is ordered by the Hilbert curve and further represented by a prefix family. Inspired by the 'XSet' data structure of Oblivious Cross-Tags (OXT) protocol [7], which is used to determine if a keyword-file pair is in an encrypted database, we build a similar comparison set from each prefix family, named 'CSet' as the second level index to judge the relationship between spatial data and range query. Figure 3 illustrates the construction and search of the second-level index, the colored area is searched by the server, but the blue area is the actual query range.

---

[1] Each data point is kept with n digital after decimal point, so if the side length of the level-l grid is d, we can adopt an r-order Hilbert curve to fill it, where $10^n d \leq 2^r$.

5.2 Description

Let $F_1, F_2 : \{0,1\}^\lambda \times \{0,1\}^* \rightarrow \{0,1\}^\lambda$ be two PRFs, $\widetilde{F}_1, \widetilde{F}_2 : \{0,1\}^\lambda \times \mathbb{N} \rightarrow \{0,1\}^\lambda$ be two SC-PRFs, $H_1, H_2 : \{0,1\}^* \rightarrow \{0,1\}^\lambda$ be two cryptographic hash functions, (Enc, Dec) be the encryption and decryption algorithms of a secure symmetric key encryption (SKE) scheme. In this paper, we assume that updates come in batches. For example, the client makes batch updates once a day. Algorithm 1 formally describes our scheme with the **Setup** algorithm, **Update** and **Search** protocols.

Setup. Given the security parameter λ, the client first generates two λ-bits keys: k_s for SKE and k_e for SKE. Then, he initializes a global counter gc and sets these two keys k_s and k_e, the number of levels in the hierarchy l, the order of adopted Hilbert curve r and gc as internal state σ. Finally, the client sends an initially empty encrypted database EDB and CSet to the server.

Before describing **Update** and **Search** protocols, we define two functions: **mapPoint** and **mapRange** (see Algorithm 2). These functions will be used in **Update** and **Search** respectively. Briefly, **mapPoint** is a function for the client to compute the index of the level-l grid to which the data point belongs via the before-mentioned hierarchical encoding technique. Then the ancestral $l - 1$ grids indexes can be fetched by truncating the last two digits of the level-l index iteratively. And **mapRange** is a function for the client to decompose the query range q in a hierarchical structure into two collections: the grids that are fully/partially covered by q, and denoted as $FCSet/PCSet$ respectively.

Update. To update a set of data points D into the encrypted database, the client will generate update tokens in the counter model for D. In specific, for each update tuple $(op, p, ind) \in D$, the grid index (also known as a keyword w) is first generated by calling **mapPoint** function. Then for all grids containing p, the client fetches the state pair (T_w^{gc}, c) from 'W', where T_w^{gc} is the search token generated by SC-PRF $\widetilde{F}_1$ with keyword token k_w as key and current global counter gc as input, and c is the local update counter initialized to 0. Finally, the update token tuple $(addr, val)$ is generated by H_1 and SKE respectively.

The above is only the processing of the first level index, and the second level index CSet also needed to be updated for an accurate search result (lines 16–24). To this end, the client computes the relative position of p in a level-l grid, then computes its corresponding Hilbert curve value and outputs the prefix family of it (i.e., $\mathcal{F}(\mathcal{H}(p \cap w))$). Then for each prefix $\tau_j \in \mathcal{F}(\mathcal{H}(p \cap w))$, the client generates second-level search token T_{w,τ_j}^{gc} by SC-PRF $\widetilde{F}_2$ just as he does for T_w^{gc}. Additionally, the element of CSet (i.e., ctag) is generated based on the hash of T_{w,τ_j}^{gc} and the local counter c. And at the end of the protocol, the global counter is increased by 1.

Search. To search all data points within a geometric range q, the client first calls **mapRange** to get two grid collections $FCSet$ and $PCSet$. Then for each keyword $w \in FCSet$, the client generates a forward secure key ST_w as a first level search token, which allows only the evaluation of $\widetilde{F}_1$ on $[0, gc-1]$. While for each

Algorithm 1. FBDSSE-GRQ

Setup(λ, l, r)

1: $k_s, k_e \xleftarrow{\$} \{0,1\}^{\lambda}$
2: global counter $gc \leftarrow 0$
3: Set $\sigma \leftarrow (k_s, k_e, l, r, gc)$
4: EDB $\leftarrow \emptyset$, CSet $\leftarrow \emptyset$
5: Send EDB and CSet to the Server.

Update(σ, D; EDB, CSet)

Client:
1: Parse σ as (k_s, k_e, l, r, gc)
2: W, AddEDB, AddCSet $\leftarrow \emptyset$
3: **for** each $d = (op, p, ind) \in D$ **do** $\triangleright$ $p = (x, y)$
4:     $x_1 y_1 x_2 y_2 \cdots x_l y_l \leftarrow$ mapPoint(p)
5:     **for** $i = l : 1$ **do**
6:         Let $w = x_1 y_1 x_2 y_2 \cdots x_i y_i$
7:         $(T_w^{gc}, c) \leftarrow$ W[w]
8:         **if** $(T_w^{gc}, c) = \perp$ **then**
9:             $k_w \leftarrow F_1(k_s, w)$
10:            $T_w^{gc} \leftarrow \widetilde{F}_1(k_w, gc)$, $c \leftarrow 0$
11:        **end if**
12:        W[w] $\leftarrow (T_w^{gc}, c + 1)$
13:        $addr \leftarrow H_1(T_w^{gc} || c)$
14:        $val \leftarrow$ SKE.Enc($k_e, op || ind$)
15:        AddEDB $\leftarrow$ AddEDB $\cup \{(addr, val)\}$
16:        **if** $i = l$ **then**
17:            $\{\tau_1, \tau_2, ..., \tau_{2r+1}\} \leftarrow \mathcal{F}(\mathcal{H}(p \cap w))$
18:            **for** $j = 1 : 2r + 1$ **do**
19:                $k_{w, \tau_j} \leftarrow F_2(k_s, w || \tau_j)$
20:                $T_{w, \tau_j}^{gc} \leftarrow \widetilde{F}_2(k_{w, \tau_j}, gc)$
21:                $ctag \leftarrow H_2(T_{w, \tau_j} || c)$
22:                AddCSet $\leftarrow$ AddCSet $\cup$ $ctag$
23:            **end for**
24:        **end if**
25:    **end for**
26: **end for**
27: $\sigma \leftarrow ((k_s, k_e, l, r, gc + 1))$
28: Send AddEDB, AddCSet to the Server.

Server:
29: **for** each $(addr, val) \in$ AddEDB **do**
30:     EDB[$addr$] $\leftarrow val$
31: **end for**
32: CSet $\leftarrow$ CSet $\cup$ AddCSet

Search(σ, q)

Client:
1: Parse σ as (k_s, k_e, l, r, gc)
2: $tk_1, tk_2 \leftarrow \emptyset$, $tk \leftarrow \{\}$
3: $\{FCSet, PCSet\} \leftarrow$ mapRange(q)
4: **for** each $w \in FCSet$ **do**
5:     $k_w \leftarrow F_1(k_s, w)$
6:     $ST_w \leftarrow \widetilde{F}_1.Cons(k_w, [0, gc - 1])$
7:     $tk_1 \leftarrow tk_1 \cup ST_w$
8: **end for**

9: **for** each $w \in PCSet$ **do**
10:     $k_w \leftarrow F_1(k_s, w)$
11:     $ST_w \leftarrow \widetilde{F}_1(k_w, [0, gc - 1])$
12:     $ctoken_w \leftarrow \emptyset$
13:     $\{\tau_1, ..., \tau_{|w \cap q|}\} \leftarrow S(\mathcal{H}(w \cap q))$
14:     **for** $j = 1 : |w \cap q|$ **do**
15:         $k_{w, \tau_j} \leftarrow F_2(k_s, w || \tau_j)$
16:         $ST_{w, \tau_j} \leftarrow \widetilde{F}_2.Cons(k_{w_i, \tau_j}, [0, gc - 1])$
17:         $ctoken_w[j] \leftarrow ST_{w, \tau_j}$
18:     **end for**
19:     $tk_2 \leftarrow tk_2 \cup \{(ST_w, ctoken_w)\}$
20: **end for**
21: $tk \leftarrow \{gc - 1, tk_1, tk_2\}$
22: Send tk to the Server

Server:
23: Parse tk as $\{ctr, tk_1, tk_2\}$, Res $\leftarrow \emptyset$
24: **for** each $ST \in tk_1$ **do**
25:     **for** $j = ctr : 0$ **do**
26:         $T_j \leftarrow \widetilde{F}_1.Eval(ST, j)$
27:         $c \leftarrow 0$, $addr \leftarrow H_1(T_j || c)$
28:         **while** $addr \in$ EDB **do**
29:             $val \leftarrow$ EDB[$addr$]
30:             Res $\leftarrow$ Res $\cup \{val\}$
31:             $c \leftarrow c + 1$, $addr \leftarrow H_1(T_j || c)$
32:         **end while**
33:     **end for**
34: **end for**
35: **for** each $(ST, ctoken) \in tk_2$ **do**
36:     **for** $j = ctr : 0$ **do**
37:         $T_j \leftarrow \widetilde{F}_1.Eval(ST, j)$
38:         $c \leftarrow 0$, $addr \leftarrow H_1(T_j || c)$
39:         **while** $addr \in EDB$ **do**
40:             $val \leftarrow$ EDB[$addr$]
41:             $flag \leftarrow false$
42:             **for** $k = 1 : ctoken.size$ **do**
43:                 $T_{j,k} \leftarrow \widetilde{F}_2.Eval(ctoken[k], j)$
44:                 **if** $H_2(T_{j,k} || c) \in CSet$ **then**
45:                     $flag \leftarrow true$
46:                     break;
47:                 **end if**
48:             **end for**
49:             **if** $flag = true$ **then**
50:                 Res $\leftarrow$ Res $\cup \{val\}$
51:             **end if**
52:             $c \leftarrow c + 1; addr \leftarrow H_1(T_j || c)$
53:         **end while**
54:     **end for**
55: **end for**
56: Send Res to the Client

Client:
57: Decrypt RES with k_e, and return points identifiers that has not been deleted

keyword $w \in PCSet$, the client does similarly as in $FCSet$, except that he needs to generate second-level search tokens $ctoken$ to filter out matched data points. Specifically, the client computes the relative range of q on w and then transforms it into multiple one-dimensional ranges on the Hilbert curve [8]. Note that for

Algorithm 2.

mapPoint

Input: the data point $p = (x, y)$, the number of levels in the hierarchy l, and the range of spatial space in x- and y-dimension, denoted as T_x and T_y

Output: a level-l grid $x_1 y_1 \ldots x_l y_l$ to which p belongs

1: $x_1 \ldots x_l \leftarrow \mathbf{Map}(x, T_x, l)$
2: $y_1 \ldots y_l \leftarrow \mathbf{Map}(y, T_y, l)$
3: **return** $x_1 y_1 \ldots x_l y_l$
1: **function** $\mathbf{Map}(d, T, l)$
2:    $min = 0, max = T$
3:    $mid = (min + max)/2$
4:    **for** $i = 1 : l$ **do**
5:      **if** $d < mid$ **then**
6:        $d_i \leftarrow 0, max = mid$
7:      **else**
8:        $d_i \leftarrow 1, min = mid$
9:      **end if**
10:     $mid = (min + max)/2$
11:    **end for**

12:    **return** $d_1 \ldots d_l$
13: **end function**

mapRange

Input: the query range q, the number of levels in the hierarchy l

Output: the grid collection $FCSet$ and $PCSet$ that is fully or partially covered by q

1: $FCSet, PCSet \leftarrow \emptyset$
2: **for** each gird w in level-l **do**
3:    **if** $w \cap q \neq null$ and $w \notin q$ **then**
4:      $PCSet \leftarrow PCSet \cup w$
5:      $q \leftarrow q \setminus w$
6:    **end if**
7: **end for**   ▷ Lines 2-7 are stripping the surrounding grids from q to get a specific range that is fully covered by q in hierarchy
8: Decompose q into fewest girds that exactly covers q by hierarchical structure, i.e., $FCSet$ ▷ We leverage the method in [31] to decompose q
9: **return** $\{FCSet, PCSet\}$

Table 2. Comparison with prior work.

Scheme	Server computation		Client computation		Communication	
	Search	Update	Search	Update	Search	Update
FastGeo [34]	$O(\tau)(2m+2) \cdot t_p$	$O(1)$	$O(q_1)(t_F + 8m \cdot t_e)$	$O(1)((6m+2) \cdot t_e + t_F)$	$O(|\mathrm{DB}(q)|)$	$O(1)$
SQ-tree$_{FS}$ [37]	$O(n_{new})(t_{\tilde{F}.Eval} + t_H + t_{XOR}) + (\log_4 N + M) \cdot t_{ORE.Comp}$	$O(1)$	$O(1)(t_{\tilde{F}.Cons} + 4 \cdot t_{ORE.ENC_L})$	$O(1)(t_{\tilde{F}} + 2 \cdot t_{ORE.Enc_R} + t_H + t_{XOR})$	$O(|\mathrm{DB}(q)|)$	$O(1)$
Construction-II [17]	$O(\log q_1 + \log q_2)$	$O(2^{t+2} - 2) \cdot t_{XOR}$	$O(\log q_1 + \log q_2)$	$O(2^{t+1}) \cdot (t_F + t_{SKE.Enc})$	$O(1)$	$O(2^{t+1})$
Ours	$O(n_q + n_{max})(t_{\tilde{F}.Eval} + t_H) + O(n_{q'} \alpha)(t_{\tilde{F}.Eval} + t_H)$	$O(l + (2r + 1))$	$O(P_1 + P_2)(t_F + t_{\tilde{F}.Cons}) + O(P_2 \alpha)(t_F + t_{\tilde{F}.Cons})$	$O(l + (2r + 1))(t_F + t_{\tilde{F}} + t_H) + O(l) \cdot t_{SKE.Enc}$	$O((P_1 + P_2) \log n_{gc} + P_2 \cdot \alpha \log n_{gc} + n_q)$	$O(l + (2r + 1))$

m is the length of the vector, τ is the number of instances the server needs to evaluate; n_{new} is the number of newly inserted data points, M is the maximum capacity of children in the deepest non-leaf node, N is the dataset size; t is the bit length of coordinates (x and y); n_q is the total number of updates related to the data involved in q, n_{max} is the maximum number of entries supported by set-constrained PRF $\tilde{F}$, $n_{q'}$ is the number of data the server needs to further evaluate, α is the average number of query prefixes for each grid in $PCSet$, P_1 and P_2 is the size of $FCSet$ and $PCSet$, n_{gc} is current global counter value; t_p is the time cost for a pairing operation, t_e is the time cost for a exponentiation operation, $t_{ORE.Enc_L}$, $t_{ORE.Enc_R}$ and $t_{ORE.Comp}$ are the time cost for left/right encryption and comparison algorithm of ORE, t_F is the time cost for PRF, t_H is the time cost for Hash function, t_{XOR} is the time cost for a XOR operation, $t_{SKE.Enc}$ is the time cost for a encryption operation of SKE.

each prefix τ_j in query prefix family $S(\mathcal{H}(q \cap w_i))$, the client should generates another constrained key ST_{w,τ_j} as second level search token, which also allows only the evaluation of $\widetilde{F}_2$ on $[0, gc - 1]$. After receiving search tokens from the client, the server will traverse an implicit search chain in EDB from the latest node (corresponding to global counter $gc - 1$) to the oldest node (corresponding to 0) to retrieve all matched (encrypted) point identifiers. Particularly, for each search token tuple $(ST, ctoken)$ in tk_2, when a valid val is retrieved from EDB, the server should check if there exists a search token $T_{j,k} = \widetilde{F}_2.Eval(ctoken[k], j)$ such that the hash value $H_2(T_{j,k}\|c)$ belongs to CSet.

5.3   Comparison

Table 2 gives the complex comparison of the schemes that also build a two-level index but do not consider forward/backward security and the schemes that provide forward/backward security but use different approaches from ours. In comparison, we set a $q_1 \times q_2$ rectangle as the query range q, where q_1 and q_2 is the range of q in x-dimension and y-dimension, respectively. Compared to the previous solutions, our scheme sacrifice just a little search efficiency for strong security combined with Table 1.

5.4   Security Analysis

In this subsection, we first argue that our scheme satisfies forward and backward security and then describe the leakage function $\mathcal{L}$. Finally, we prove that our scheme is $\mathcal{L}$-adaptively-secure.

Intuitively, on the one hand, the constrained key generated by SC-PRF allows only the evaluation on a counter set corresponding to the inserted data, and the server cannot predict the value of SC-PRF for inputs outside of that set, so our scheme satisfies forward security. On the other hand, we achieve backward security by encrypting the identifier and operation of data through a two-round trip general transformation of Bost et al. [5]. This method is extensively used in existing solutions to provide Type-II backward security at the cost that the client needs to decrypt all received results, remove the deleted item locally, and return the non-deleted identifiers to the server to get actual matched data.

The detailed leakage function $\mathcal{L} = (\mathcal{L}^{Stp}, \mathcal{L}^{Srch}, \mathcal{L}^{Updt})$ of our scheme is given below:

- $\mathcal{L}^{Stp}(\lambda, l, r) = \bot;$
- $\mathcal{L}^{Updt}(D = \{(op, P, ind)\}) = (|D| \cdot l, |D| \cdot (2r + 1));$
- $\mathcal{L}^{Srch}(q) = (\mathcal{L}'_1(q), \mathcal{L}'_2(q)),$ where

$$\mathcal{L}'_1(q) = ((sp(w), \mathbf{TimeDB}(w), \mathbf{Updates}(w))_{w \in FCSet})$$

$$\mathcal{L}'_2(q) = ((((sp(w\|\tau), \mathbf{TimeDB}(w\|\tau), \mathbf{Updates}(w\|\tau))_{\tau \in S(\mathcal{H}(q \cap w))}),$$
$$sp(w), \mathbf{TimeDB}(w), \mathbf{Updates}(w))_{w \in PCSet})$$

Then, we prove that our scheme achieves $\mathcal{L}$-adaptively-security.

Theorem 1. *Let F_1 and F_2 be two pseudorandom functions, $\widetilde{F}_1$ and $\widetilde{F}_2$ be two set-constrained pseudorandom functions, SKE be a secure symmetric encryption scheme, H_1 and H_2 be two hash functions modeled as random oracles. Our scheme is $\mathcal{L}$-adaptively-secure for $\mathcal{L} = \{\mathcal{L}^{Stp}, \mathcal{L}^{Srch}, \mathcal{L}^{Updt}\}$ as above.*

Proof. The proof is given in Appendix.

6   Performance Evaluation

This section presents the performance evaluation of our proposed construction over encrypted spatial data. The experiment was conducted on a desktop computer with Windows 10 Intel (R) Core (TM) i5-10400F CPU @ 2.90 GHz and 16 GB RAM in Java Programming Language. The security parameter λ is set to 256 bits, and for cryptographic functions, we instantiate PRFs and hash functions via SM3, where $PRF(key, data) = Hash(key||data)$. In addition, SC-PRFs are instantiated with the tree-based GGM PRF [11]. We set the height of the tree to 10, which means that if a batch update is carried out once a day, it can last more than two years in total. Then the data owner can download the entire database to clean up the deleted entries and re-encrypt the database to restart the system. In addition, SM4 in the CBC model is used to instantiate SKE. And in the following experiments, we set the query range to be squared to facilitate control over the range size. Each experimental result is an average of 10 trials.

6.1   Comparison with Previous Solutions

We compare our scheme with Construction II [17] because it provides both forward and backward security in existing solutions. Note that the bitmap string is used in Construction II to denote the points identifiers, and in our experiment, the length of the string (i.e., the predefined size of the database) is set to 1000. For our scheme, we adopt the 3-order and 5-order Hilbert curve to fill the last level grid for comparison, where "$r = 3$" corresponds to the optimal search case (i.e., the range query is exactly decomposed into several hierarchical grids), and "$r = 5$" corresponds to the general search case. In the following experiments, the update time includes the token generation time of the client and server update time. And the search time consists of the client search token generation time, the server search time, and the client decryption time.

Firstly, we evaluate the effect of different spatial dimension sizes and batch update sizes on update time. As shown in Fig. 4(a), when the batch update size is set to 100, the update time of Construction II is greatly affected by the dimension size compared with ours. For example, when the dimension size is 2^{18}, the update time of Construction II is approximately 288× higher than both our $r = 3$ and $r = 5$ settings. The reasons are that in Construction II, the client needs to update all leaf nodes in two binary trees to achieve forward security, and the server then needs to update all nodes in two binary trees. As for changing the batch update size, when the dimension size is set to 2^{10}, Fig. 4(b) shows that the update time of our scheme increases with the batch update size, whereas Construction II does not change much since the point identifiers are denoted by a bitmap string. In summary, the update performance of our scheme is better than Construction II.

Next, we vary the query range size ($[0, 200] \times [0, 200], [0, 400] \times [0, 400], [0, 600] \times [0, 600], [0, 800] \times [0, 800], [0, 1000] \times [0, 1000]$) to evaluate the search performance, where the dimension size is fixed to 2^{10}, and the database size is 100. As shown in Fig. 5(a), both schemes' search time increases with the

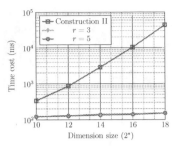
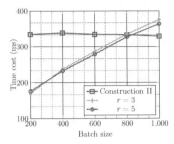

(a) Update time vs. dimension size

(b) Update time vs. batch size

Fig. 4. Update comparison

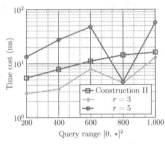
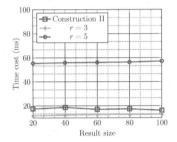

(a) Search time vs. query range

(b) Search time vs. result size

Fig. 5. Comparison

query range, and Construction II is better than our $r = 5$ setting but worse than our $r = 3$ setting at the same time. Note that the reasons for the exceptions at $[0,800] \times [0,800]$ are that the query range is exactly decomposed to hierarchal grids that are fully covered by it in the $r = 5$ setting, so it corresponds to the fewest query prefixes than other ranges. While in the $r = 3$ setting, it decomposes into fewer query prefixes than adjacent ranges by **mapRange** function. Finally, we fix the query range size and vary the search result size, and Fig. 5(b) shows that the search time of Construction II is shorter than our $r = 5$ setting, which corresponds to the general search case. The search time of Construction II is slightly longer than our $r = 3$ setting because the client needs to generate multiple keys to decrypt the result set due to the use of ASHE. What's more, although the search performance of Construction II is better than ours in general, it uses the label of the index tree node as the search token, which directly leaks the range query to the server, resulting in query privacy disclosure.

7   Conclusion

In this paper, we propose a forward and backward private DSSE scheme that supports geometric range queries over encrypted spatial data. Specifically, we transform a range query into multiple single-keyword queries through a hierarchical storage structure. Then, we leverage the Hilbert curve and prefix member verification scheme to further judge the relationship between the spatial data and query range. We can see from the theoretical and experimental analysis that our scheme is secure and efficient compared with existing works. In future work, we will consider extending our construction to support multi-dimensional encrypted data search.

A   Appendix

Similar to the proofs in [5,35], we derive a series of games from $\mathbf{Real}_{\mathcal{A}}(1^{\lambda})$ to $\mathbf{Ideal}_{\mathcal{A},\mathcal{S}}(1^{\lambda})$. By showing that every two consecutive games are indistinguishable, we argue that the adversary cannot distinguish $\mathbf{Real}_{\mathcal{A}}(1^{\lambda})$ from $\mathbf{Ideal}_{\mathcal{A},\mathcal{S}}(1^{\lambda})$ except with negligible probability. We assume the adversary $\mathcal{A}$ makes at most q_1 and q_2 polynomial-size queries to the H_1 oracle and H_2 oracle, respectively.

Game G_0: G_0 is exactly the real-world game. Therefore, we have

$$|\Pr[\mathbf{Real}_{\mathcal{A}}(1^{\lambda}) = 1] - \Pr[G_0 = 1]| = 0$$

Game G_1: G_1 is the same as G_0, except that G_1 maintains two maps: MF_1 and MF_2, instead of calling the PRF F_1 and F_2 for the keyword token queries. Take MF_1 for example, MF_1 stores (w, k_w) pairs. When a new keyword w is queried, G_1 returns a random string from $\{0,1\}^{\lambda}$ as k_w and stores it in $MF_1[w]$ for subsequent queries. The processing of MF_2 is similar to that of MF_1. Thus G_0 is indistinguishable from G_1, otherwise, we can distinguish between the pseudorandom function and a truly random function.

Game G_2: In this game, we model the hash function H_1 as a random oracle. That is, instead of querying H_1 to generate $addr$, G_2 picks a random string from $\{0,1\}^{\mu_1}$ and stores it in a map MH_1: $addr \xleftarrow{\$} \{0,1\}^{\mu_1}$, $MH_1[w, gc\|c] = addr$. Then, during the search protocol, we update the reference table H_1 for the random oracle H_1 by setting $H_1(T_w^{gc}\|c) = MH_1[w, gc\|c]$. However, if $(T_w^{gc}\|c)$ is already in table H_1, i.e., the adversary queries H_1 on $(T_w^{gc}\|c)$ before the search, then inequality $H_1(T_w^{gc}\|c) \neq MH_1[w, gc\|c]$ arises with non-negligible probability (call it a **bad** event), the adversary realizes the game is G_2. Next, we show that the possibility of the **bad** happening is negligible.

    If the adversary can set **bad** to true, it can break the security of SC-PRF $\widetilde{F}_1$ by constructing a reduction $\mathcal{B}_1$ from a distinguisher $\mathcal{A}$ inserting $l \cdot N$ $addr$-val pairs in the database [5]. Since $\mathcal{A}$ makes at most q_1 queries to the random oracle H_1, and T_w^{gc} is uniformly random by the security definition of SC-PRF, the probability of **bad** being set to true is

$$\Pr[\mathbf{bad}\ is\ set\ to\ \mathbf{true}] \leq \mathbf{Adv}_{\widetilde{F}_1,\mathcal{B}_1}^{SC-PRF}(1^{\lambda}) + \frac{q_1}{2^{\lambda}}$$

Besides, inserting $l \cdot N$ *addr-val* pairs in DB implies an $l \cdot N$ loss in the distinguishing advantage between G_1 and G_2 to the event of setting **bad** to **true**, we have

$$|\Pr[G_1] - \Pr[G_2]| \leq l \cdot N \cdot \mathbf{Adv}_{\widetilde{F}_1, \mathcal{B}_1}^{\text{SC-PRF}} + \frac{lNq_1}{2^\lambda}.$$

Game G_3: In G_3, we do similarly as in G_2, but for H_2. The distinguishing advantage between G_2 and G_3 consists of: the advantage of a reduction $\mathcal{B}_2$ breaking the security of SC-PRF $\widetilde{F}_2$ from a distinguisher $\mathcal{A}$ inserting $N(2r+1)$ *ctags* in DB, and the probability H_2 was queried on T_{w,τ_j}^{gc}. Thus, we have

$$|\Pr[G_2] - \Pr[G_3]| \leq N(2r+1) \cdot \left(\mathbf{Adv}_{\widetilde{F}_2, \mathcal{B}_2}^{\text{SC-PRF}} + \frac{q_2}{2^\lambda} \right).$$

Game G_4: Compared to G_3, we replace the encryption of (op, ind) with the encryption of a random string in G_4. The security of SKE guarantees that the ciphertext *val* in G_3 and G_4 is indistinguishable, otherwise, we can construct a reduction $\mathcal{B}_3$ to break the security of SKE. So we have

$$|\Pr[G_3 = 1] - \Pr[G_3 = 1]| \leq \mathbf{Adv}_{\mathcal{B}_3}^{\text{SKE}}(1^\lambda)$$

Game G_5: It is the last ideal-world game, where the simulator $\mathcal{S}$ generates a view only based on the leakage function $\mathcal{L}$. Let $\underline{w} \leftarrow sp(w).min$, $\underline{w||\tau} \leftarrow sp(w||\tau).min$ be the timestamp when w and $w||\tau$ are retrieved for the first time after **Setup**, then $\underline{w}$ and $\underline{w||\tau}$ are used to uniquely identify the items related to unknown w and $w||\tau$ in $\overline{\text{MF}}_1$ and MF_2, and keyword tokens k_w and $k_{w,\tau}$ are sampled on the fly during the search. In addition, instead of directly mapping $(T_w^{gc}||c)$ and $(T_{w,\tau_j}^{gc}||c)$ to the random values picked for MH_1 and MH_2, we implicitly map $(T_w^{gc}||c)$ to the global update counter, and $(T_{w,\tau_j}^{gc}||c)$ to a pair of a global counter and a local counter, and program the random oracles H_1 and H_2 accordingly with **Updates**(w) and **Updates**$(w||\tau)$ during the search, where **Updates**$(w||\tau)$ was slightly modified to additionally include the order of *ctag* corresponding to τ in its adjacent $2r+1$ *ctags* for simulation.

The update protocol in both games outputs uniformly random values with the same distribution, and the client output of **Search** is the same, so G_4 and G_5 are indistinguishable. Thus we have

$$\Pr[G_4 = 1] = \Pr[G_5 = 1]$$

In summary, we have

$$|\Pr[\mathbf{Real}_{\mathcal{A}}(1^\lambda) = 1] - \Pr[\mathbf{Ideal}_{\mathcal{A},\mathcal{S}}(1^\lambda) = 1]| \leq \text{negl}(\lambda)$$

References

1. Agarwal, P.K., Erickson, J., et al.: Geometric range searching and its relatives. Contemp. Math. **223**, 1–56 (1999)

2. Boneh, D., Waters, B.: Conjunctive, subset, and range queries on encrypted data. In: Vadhan, S.P. (ed.) TCC 2007. LNCS, vol. 4392, pp. 535–554. Springer, Heidelberg (2007). https://doi.org/10.1007/978-3-540-70936-7_29

3. Boneh, D., Waters, B.: Constrained pseudorandom functions and their applications. In: Sako, K., Sarkar, P. (eds.) ASIACRYPT 2013. LNCS, vol. 8270, pp. 280–300. Springer, Heidelberg (2013). https://doi.org/10.1007/978-3-642-42045-0_15

4. Bost, R.: οφος: forward secure searchable encryption. In: Proceedings of the 2016 ACM SIGSAC Conference on Computer and Communications Security, pp. 1143–1154 (2016)

5. Bost, R., Minaud, B., Ohrimenko, O.: Forward and backward private searchable encryption from constrained cryptographic primitives. In: Proceedings of the 2017 ACM SIGSAC Conference on Computer and Communications Security, pp. 1465–1482 (2017)

6. Cash, D., et al.: Dynamic searchable encryption in very-large databases: data structures and implementation. Cryptology ePrint Archive (2014). https://eprint.iacr.org/2014/853

7. Cash, D., Jarecki, S., Jutla, C., Krawczyk, H., Roşu, M.-C., Steiner, M.: Highly-scalable searchable symmetric encryption with support for Boolean queries. In: Canetti, R., Garay, J.A. (eds.) CRYPTO 2013. LNCS, vol. 8042, pp. 353–373. Springer, Heidelberg (2013). https://doi.org/10.1007/978-3-642-40041-4_20

8. Chung, K.L., Tsai, Y.H., Hu, F.C.: Space-filling approach for fast window query on compressed images. IEEE Trans. Image Process. 9(12), 2109–2116 (2000)

9. Curtmola, R., Garay, J., Kamara, S., Ostrovsky, R.: Searchable symmetric encryption: improved definitions and efficient constructions. J. Comput. Secur. 19(5), 895–934 (2011)

10. Ghinita, G., Rughinis, R.: An efficient privacy-preserving system for monitoring mobile users: making searchable encryption practical. In: Proceedings of the 4th ACM Conference on Data and Application Security and Privacy, pp. 321–332 (2014)

11. Goldreich, O., Goldwasser, S., Micali, S.: How to construct random functions. J. ACM (JACM) 33(4), 792–807 (1986)

12. Grubbs, P., Sekniqi, K., Bindschaedler, V., Naveed, M., Ristenpart, T.: Leakage-abuse attacks against order-revealing encryption. In: 2017 IEEE Symposium on Security and Privacy (SP), pp. 655–672. IEEE (2017)

13. Guo, R., Qin, B., Wu, Y., Liu, R., Chen, H., Li, C.: MixGeo: efficient secure range queries on encrypted dense spatial data in the cloud. In: Proceedings of the International Symposium on Quality of Service, pp. 1–10 (2019)

14. Guo, R., Qin, B., Wu, Y., Liu, R., Chen, H., Li, C.: LuxGeo: efficient and secure enhanced geometric range queries. IEEE Trans. Knowl. Data Eng. (2021). https://doi.org/10.1109/TKDE.2021.3093909

15. Kamara, S., Papamanthou, C., Roeder, T.: Dynamic searchable symmetric encryption. In: Proceedings of the 2012 ACM Conference on Computer and Communications Security, pp. 965–976 (2012)

16. Kamel, I., Talha, A.M., Aghbari, Z.A.: Dynamic spatial index for efficient query processing on the cloud. J. Cloud Comput. 6(1), 1–16 (2017). https://doi.org/10.1186/s13677-017-0077-0

17. Kermanshahi, S.K., et al.: Geometric range search on encrypted data with forward/backward security. IEEE Trans. Dependable Secure Comput. 19(1), 698–716 (2020)

18. Lewi, K., Wu, D.J.: Order-revealing encryption: new constructions, applications, and lower bounds. In: Proceedings of the 2016 ACM SIGSAC Conference on Computer and Communications Security, pp. 1167–1178 (2016)
19. Li, X., Zhu, Y., Wang, J., Zhang, J.: Efficient and secure multi-dimensional geometric range query over encrypted data in cloud. J. Parallel Distrib. Comput. **131**, 44–54 (2019)
20. Liu, A.X., Chen, F.: Privacy preserving collaborative enforcement of firewall policies in virtual private networks. IEEE Trans. Parallel Distrib. Syst. **22**(5), 887–895 (2010)
21. Liu, X., Schrack, G.: Encoding and decoding the Hilbert order. Softw.: Pract. Exp. **26**(12), 1335–1346 (1996)
22. Liu, Z., Wu, L., Meng, W., Wang, H., Wang, W.: Accurate range query with privacy preservation for outsourced location-based service in IOT. IEEE Internet Things J. **8**(18), 14322–14337 (2021)
23. Luo, Y., Fu, S., Wang, D., Xu, M., Jia, X.: Efficient and generalized geometric range search on encrypted spatial data in the cloud. In: 2017 IEEE/ACM 25th International Symposium on Quality of Service (IWQoS), pp. 1–10. IEEE (2017)
24. Mark, D.B., Otfried, C., Marc, V.K., Mark, O.: Computational Geometry Algorithms and Applications. Springer, Berlin (2008). https://doi.org/10.1007/978-3-540-77974-2
25. Narayanan, A., Thiagarajan, N., Lakhani, M., Hamburg, M., Boneh, D., et al.: Location privacy via private proximity testing. In: NDSS, vol. 11 (2011)
26. Naveed, M., Kamara, S., Wright, C.V.: Inference attacks on property-preserving encrypted databases. In: Proceedings of the 22nd ACM SIGSAC Conference on Computer and Communications Security, pp. 644–655 (2015)
27. Popa, R.A., Li, F.H., Zeldovich, N.: An ideal-security protocol for order-preserving encoding. In: 2013 IEEE Symposium on Security and Privacy, pp. 463–477. IEEE (2013)
28. Shen, E., Shi, E., Waters, B.: Predicate privacy in encryption systems. In: Reingold, O. (ed.) TCC 2009. LNCS, vol. 5444, pp. 457–473. Springer, Heidelberg (2009). https://doi.org/10.1007/978-3-642-00457-5_27
29. Song, D.X., Wagner, D., Perrig, A.: Practical techniques for searches on encrypted data. In: Proceeding 2000 IEEE Symposium on Security and Privacy. S&P 2000, pp. 44–55. IEEE (2000)
30. Stefanov, E., Papamanthou, C., Shi, E.: Practical dynamic searchable encryption with small leakage. Cryptology ePrint Archive (2013). https://eprint.iacr.org/2013/832
31. Tsai, Y.H., Chung, K.L., Chen, W.Y.: A strip-splitting-based optimal algorithm for decomposing a query window into maximal quadtree blocks. IEEE Trans. Knowl. Data Eng. **16**(4), 519–523 (2004)
32. Wang, B., Li, M., Wang, H.: Geometric range search on encrypted spatial data. IEEE Trans. Inf. Forensics Secur. **11**(4), 704–719 (2015)
33. Wang, B., Li, M., Wang, H., Li, H.: Circular range search on encrypted spatial data. In: 2015 IEEE Conference on Communications and Network Security (CNS), pp. 182–190. IEEE (2015)
34. Wang, B., Li, M., Xiong, L.: FastGeo: efficient geometric range queries on encrypted spatial data. IEEE Trans. Dependable Secure Comput. **16**(2), 245–258 (2017)
35. Wang, J., Chow, S.S.: Forward and backward-secure range-searchable symmetric encryption. Proc. Priv. Enhancing Technol. **1**, 28–48 (2022)

36. Wang, X., Ma, J., Li, F., Liu, X., Miao, Y., Deng, R.H.: Enabling efficient spatial keyword queries on encrypted data with strong security guarantees. IEEE Trans. Inf. Forensics Secur. **16**, 4909–4923 (2021)
37. Wang, X., Ma, J., Liu, X., Miao, Y., Zhu, D.: Spatial dynamic searchable encryption with forward security. In: Nah, Y., Cui, B., Lee, S.-W., Yu, J.X., Moon, Y.-S., Whang, S.E. (eds.) DASFAA 2020. LNCS, vol. 12113, pp. 746–762. Springer, Cham (2020). https://doi.org/10.1007/978-3-030-59416-9_48
38. Wong, W.K., Cheung, D.W.L., Kao, B., Mamoulis, N.: Secure KNN computation on encrypted databases. In: Proceedings of the 2009 ACM SIGMOD International Conference on Management of Data, pp. 139–152 (2009)
39. Xu, G., Li, H., Dai, Y., Yang, K., Lin, X.: Enabling efficient and geometric range query with access control over encrypted spatial data. IEEE Trans. Inf. Forensics Secur. **14**(4), 870–885 (2018)
40. Xu, L., Sun, S., Yuan, X., Liu, J.K., Zuo, C., Xu, C.: Enabling authorized encrypted search for multi-authority medical databases. IEEE Trans. Emerg. Top. Comput. **9**(1), 534–546 (2019)
41. Xu, L., Yuan, X., Zhou, Z., Wang, C., Xu, C.: Towards efficient cryptographic data validation service in edge computing. IEEE Trans. Serv. Comput. (2021). https://doi.org/10.1109/TSC.2021.3111208
42. Zhang, Y., Katz, J., Papamanthou, C.: All your queries are belong to us: the power of {File-Injection} attacks on searchable encryption. In: 25th USENIX Security Symposium (USENIX Security 16), pp. 707–720 (2016)
43. Zhu, H., Lu, R., Huang, C., Chen, L., Li, H.: An efficient privacy-preserving location-based services query scheme in outsourced cloud. IEEE Trans. Veh. Technol. **65**(9), 7729–7739 (2015)

Blockchain Security

Towards Secure and Trustworthy Flash Loans: A Blockchain-Based Trust Management Approach

Yining Xie, Xin Kang(✉) , Tieyan Li , Cheng-Kang Chu ,
and Haiguang Wang

Digital Identity and Trustworthiness Laboratory, Huawei Singapore Research Center,
Singapore, Singapore
kang.xin@huawei.com

Abstract. Flash loan has become one of the most creative tools in DeFi industry. The explosive development of flash loan is due to its circumvention to borrower default risk and platform liquidity risk. But it also greatly reduces the cost required by the attacker to execute an attack. Hackers can use flash loans to obtain a large amount of disposable funds in a very short period of time, and then exploit the vulnerabilities in smart contracts to carry out attacks and steal a large amount of wealth. Therefore, a trustworthy framework has become one of the security measures that flash loan platforms must take. This paper makes a comprehensive study on flash loan, especially flash loan attack. Firstly, we briefly introduce the basic concept, platforms and application scenarios of flash loan, summarize the existing flash loan attack events and classify them. After that, we compare the existing credit scoring agencies. Then, we introduce the RFM model in marketing and improve it by combining the on-chain and off-chain behaviors of users. Finally, we propose a trustworthy architecture combining the improved RFM model with the role-based trust assessment model and periodic node behavior trust evaluation model. The future development of DeFi and Flash Loan is also analyzed.

Keywords: DeFi · Flash loan · Trust · Trustworthiness

1 Introduction

1.1 Background and Motivation

In recent years, DeFi platform loans have exploded. The extended portfolio is becoming more diversified, and hidden financial risks are emerging. Flash loan was born and became one of the most creative and disruptive DeFi tools. It differs from traditional loans in an important feature that it does not need any collateral and credit approval process, greatly reducing the loan threshold for both borrowers and lenders. Flash loans themselves rely on smart contracts, and the lending process is instantaneous, meaning the entire loan process may only take a few seconds. If the borrower does not repay the money in a single blockchain transaction, the loan process will be reversed as if it never happened. This key difference is why borrowers are able to get a loan quickly without any collateral or credit checks because it removes the risks of default. The existence of flash loan itself has no vulnerability, but it enables attackers to leverage a huge amount of funds at a very low cost in an extremely short period of time, and carry out price manipulation or arbitrage among multiple protocols, resulting in a large number of fund losses of DeFi platforms.

To solve this problem, credit models that collect both on-chain and off-chain information and transform it into intuitive credit scores have been proposed as a promising solution. Ideally, a well-developed credit model is an industry-recognized and decentralized measure of credit. Specific individual risks are standardized while avoiding errors caused by single-dimensional strong rejection rules and solving the problem of how to integrate fragmented and unstructured information into a scientific accounting system. To achieve this, we investigated and analyzed the two most important steps in credit evaluation, data collection and user behavior quantification, and proposed an improved method to identify trusted users and grant them discriminated rank of authority.

1.2   Related Works

As an emerging tool in DeFi industry, there is not much research on flash loans. Most of the existing works simply introduce and explore DeFi as a whole industry, and identify it as one of the successful use cases of smart contracts, aiming to categorize the differences and advantages of DeFi from traditional financial services [1]. Reference [2] proposed that arbitrage trades can be automatically made on the DeFi platform. A comprehensive measurement study [3] of the actual deployment of DeFi price oracles found that the price reported often deviated from the current exchange rate. Reference [4] measured the various risks faced by liquidation participants and quantified the instability of existing lending protocols.

Generally, the existing research defends DeFi attacks from two aspects: transaction detection and vulnerability mining. Reference [5] explored the design flaws of DeFi protocols and gave a novel strategy that allows governance attacks. Reference [6] categorized DeFi security issues in a hierarchical manner by classifying different attacks into respective DeFi architecture layers. A real-time attack detection system, which can identify potentially vulnerable DeFi projects based on an automatic security analysis process was proposed in [7]. Reference [8] found a framework based on logic-driven and graph-driven transaction analysis. In [9], an attack parameter optimization framework was proposed to expand and quantify the possible losses. Reference [10] designed three patterns to identify flash Loan transactions. A decentralized debt derivative called Atomic Bond Cross-chain Debt (ABCD) was introduced to bridge the gap between the growth of flash loan protocols [11]. A multi-block MEV (MMEV) type attack was described in which the attacker colludes with a miner/proposer who can mine/propose two blocks in a row [12].

1.3 Contribution and Novelty

There are few existing studies on flash loan, and most security schemes focus on transaction detection and vulnerability mining, ignoring the importance of user credibility. Therefore, from the perspective of trustworthiness, it is necessary to further study how to use user on-and-off-chain information to analyze user behavior. In order to fill the gap in this field, this paper makes contributions in the following aspects:

1. We give a comprehensive overview of flash loan and flash loan attacks, classify and summarize the application scenarios and attack events, and prospect and analyze them from the perspective of trustworthiness.
2. We reconstruct the traditional RFM model to make it more in line with the usage scenarios in the DeFi field, calculate the corresponding variables of each user in a standardized way, solve the problem that unstructured information is difficult to integrate, and quantified the on-chain and off-chain behavior of users.
3. We propose a trustworthy architecture for identifying abnormal users. The reconstructed RFM model is combined with the permission control model and periodic node credit evaluation model to generate dynamic and sustainable user credit scores, and give different loan permissions to users with different ranks.

The remainder of this paper is organized as follows. In Sects. 2 and 3, we summarize the platform, process, and usage scenarios of flash loan. In Sect. 4, we analyze and classify flash loan attacks. In Sect. 5, we introduce existing trustworthy architectures and their design mechanisms. In Sects. 6, 7, and 8, we propose a new trustworthy architecture and look forward to its future development.

2 Preliminary of Flash Loan

2.1 Flash Loan Platforms on Ethereum

There are three major flash loan platforms on Ethereum, including Aave, dYdX, and Uniswap.

As an integrated loan agreement, Aave is more similar to the traditional loan logically, and the loan parameters can be directly executed on the Ethereum blockchain. They also have a user-friendly loan contract template for users to create their own flash loan conveniently and quickly. The disadvantage is that Aave has to charge a 0.09% fee, which will reduce the user's profit margin [13].

When a user makes a flash loan through the dYdX, it essentially executes multiple transactions in a single meta-transaction, such as loan, repayment and the user's execution strategy, etc. Only one entry is needed to interact with the smart contract, which can save transaction fees. And dYdX has a huge advantage, that is, there is no handling fee [14].

Uniswap V2 is essentially flash Swap rather than flash Loan. The advantage of Uniswap V2 is that it is more flexible than the previous platforms whose loan currency and repayment currency must be the same, allowing users to make payments in other tokens. But Uniswap V2 still charges a 0.3% handling fee, resulting in a sharp drop in profits [15].

2.2 Flash Loan Platforms on Binance Smart Chain

In addition to Ethereum, flash loan platforms have also started to appear on Binance Smart Chain. Taking C.R.E.A.M. for example, C.R.E.A.M [16]. It is the first money market to offer flash loans on Binance Smart Chain, C.R.E.A.M. will provide the widest range of assets and the service charge of C.R.E.A.M. is very low at 0.03%, only the second dYdX. Compared to the regular flash loan program, V-Cred [17] is more of a personal project than a real public flash loan platform which has not been deployed to the main network. So the next steps for V-Cred would be to deploy it on main-net to open up for cross decentralised exchange arbitrage.

2.3 Atomicity of Flash Loan

A trade can fall back because of its atomicity. Atomic exchange is a kind of support two running on the different blockchain network encryption currency rapid exchange of technology, the condition to realize the exchange of atoms using hash time locking contracts, creating automatic self-execution of the contract, once meet some predetermined rules, this contract will perform a particular operation, complete the transaction, the spending of the transaction cost is very low or don't need to charge [18].

3 Application of Flash Loan in DeFi

The main applications of flash loans are arbitrage, liquidation, collateral swapping, and refinancing.

Arbitrage refers to making profits by taking advantage of the price difference of a certain currency on different platforms [19]. The three elements enable arbitrage include large amounts of capital to take advantage of these tiny point spreads, automated trading strategies with continuous discovery of inefficiencies, and low-latency code to connect and deploy strategies.

If the value of the user's collateral falls sharply, the collateral may be liquidated by the lending platform at a very low price. When users do not want their collateral to be liquidated, they can self-liquidate using flash loan before liquidation occurs, thus avoiding paying the liquidation fee as high as 13%. The purpose of self-liquidation is not to make profits, but to reduce losses.

Assuming that users borrow from the platform with a certain token as collateral, and then want to change the collateral into another token, they can use flash Loan to repay the loan first, then swap the collateral to another one and apply for a new loan, finally then repay the flash loan with the loan, so as to realize the collateral swapping. Finally refinancing allows users to successfully obtain a lower interest rate loan without any external funding.

4   Flash Loan Attacks

A flash loan attack is a DeFi attack in which a loan was obtained from a flash loan platform and used in combination with various types of operations to manipulate market prices for a profit. Flash loan attack is now the most common type of DeFi attack because such attacks are the cheapest to carry out and the easiest to escape. It can be roughly divided into four types: Bidding Up Arbitrage, Manipulating Oracle Machine, Reentrant Attack, and Technical Vulnerability.

4.1   Bidding up Arbitrage

Bidding Up Arbitrage and Manipulating Oracle Machine attack modes are essentially the use and manipulation of net worth calculation. In fact, they want to raise the price of their own assets with the help of other people's capital and then sell at a high price for profit. The targets here can be machine gun pools, lending platforms, leveraged trading platforms, and other DeFi modules.

On February 16,2020, bZx was attacked and lost 360,000 dollars in 15 s [21]. The attacker first borrowed 10,000 ETH from dYdX, then used it to hoard wBTC, and then used bZx margin trading to transfer orders to KyberSwap, which basically tripled the price of wBTC. However, when the attack occurred, the built-in integrity checks were not started. Finally the attacker got a 71% arbitrage profit and the flowchart is shown in Fig. 1.

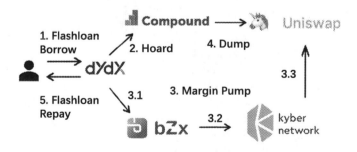

Fig. 1. Bidding Up Arbitrage on bZx

4.2   Manipulating Oracle Machine

Oracle Machine mainly obtains price information in two ways. One is to simply take existing off-chain price data from a price API or exchange. Another way is to calculate the immediate price by querying the chain of decentralized exchanges.

Off-chain data are generally slow responding to price fluctuations. It usually requires a small number of privileged users with absolute trust to push the data on the chain. On-chain data is always up to date, but it can be easily manipulated by attackers, which can cause catastrophic losses [3].

On July 25, 2020, yEarn's new contract yVault was discovered having manipulating oracle machine vulnerability [22]. The value of a single yVault token is determined by the ratio of minted tokens to deposited tokensy. In this case, a user who swaps between USDC and MUSD will not receive a 1:1 exchange rate. This means that the value of BPT can temporarily inflate, which allows an attacker to manipulate the price at will and subsequently deplete the vault. The flowchart is shown in Fig. 2.

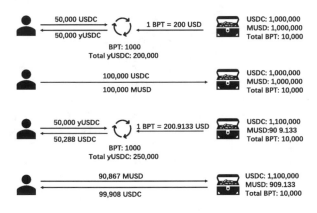

Fig. 2. Manipulating Oracle Machine on yVault

4.3   Reentrant Attack

Reentrant vulnerability exists in the interaction process between contracts. The potential risk point is that an external contract can take over the flow of control and modify data that is not expected in the contract, forcing it to perform unexpected actions. When attackers call the vulnerability function in the victim's contract many times, they can achieve the purpose of repeatedly adding tokens to their account [20].

On April 19, 2020, Lendf.me suffered from a reentrant attack [23] and cumulative losses are about $24,696,616. The attacker used the vulnerability to cover his fund balance and continuously double the amount of cash that could be withdrawn, and transferred to imBTC in multiple amounts, each of which doubled the last amount. The flowchart is shown in Fig. 3.

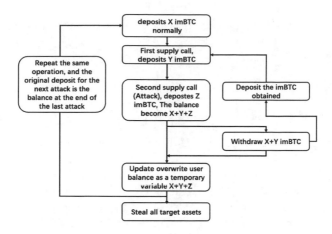

Fig. 3. Reentrance vulnerability on Lendf.me

4.4   Technical Vulnerability and Sociology Vulnerability

Some contracts may contain vulnerable functions that allows an attacker to withdraw deposit balances without specifying withdrawals internally [24]. This led attacker to be able to withdraw not only his own deposits but also the entire balance of the same amount as in the previous vault.

5   The Existing Credit Scoring Systems

On November 21, 2020, TrustToken launched TrueFi, an unsecured loan agreement. TrueFi combines CeFi and DeFi's on-chain contract credit rating system to enable unsecured lending. The credit assessment model is managed by holders of TRU tokens, which are used to vote on whether or not to approve a loan. TrueFi V3 has launched a credit scoring model. The model provides an objective TrueFi credit score for borrowers by combining a number of on-chain and off-chain factors. Ratings range from 0 to 255 [25].

ARCx issues DeFi Passport to quantify the credibility of each DeFi Passport holder based on their credit score. The credit score, which will be determined by analyzing the holder's Ethereum address history activity, is set to a range of 0 to 999 points, which determines the rate of collateral offered by the agreement to the user [26]. The advanced factors include the maturity of the loan from the mainstream decentralized lending platform and whether the collateral is cleared. The scoring system is designed to assess users' loyalty to the protocol, their enthusiasm for on-chain governance, and whether they are genuine traders.

CreDA is built on Ethereum Layer2, it will span multiple chains such as BSC, Polkadot, and HECO. The CreDA protocol uses data from all public chains for deep mining. The credit predictor models participants' public history cross-chain data by building a network of predictor and trusted computing elements through the W3C compliant DID protocol. In this way, the credit predictor provides users with comprehensive, dynamic credit ratings through decentralized technology [27].

6   Relevant Models

6.1   Role-Based Trust Assessment Model

In traditional Role-based Access Control (RBAC) model, the association between users and roles and between roles and permissions can realize the association between users and permissions. However, RBAC model is not suitable for the environment that requires dynamic control of user permission mapping or dynamic granularity control. It is easy to encounter some security risks in the authorization process and has low flexibility. Attribute-based Access Control (ABAC) uses attributes of users, resources, and environment as the basis for authorization and Access judgment. Therefore, the combination of RBAC and ABAC is more suitable for assigning roles with different levels of trust to users.

Trust management can be used to assess user credibility. It mainly evaluates the trust of users by calculating the trust value. The comprehensive trust value of a user is calculated based on user attributes, user behavior feedback, and user reputation. User attributes include the IP address, access times, access time, access duration, access status, transaction times, transaction amount, and held assets of a user on each platform. The user attribute trust value is calculated by quantifying the user attribute factor and assigning the corresponding weight. Then, the relationship between the comprehensive trust value and the set threshold is used to judge whether the user is trustworthy, decide whether to accept the user's request for resource access and assign roles to the user. On this basis, RBAC and ABAC models are combined to further implement the access control mechanism.

6.2   Periodic Node Behavior Trust Evaluation Model

The heart of the bayesian network inference prediction is the reliability of the prior probability and conditional probability and the rationality of the prior probability which is obtained by statistical analysis and expert advice mainly. This part needs to be combined with the user's real identity and the third party credit platforms by assigning different reliability to multiple off-chain agencies. Thus, a trust evaluation model and abnormal behavior detection algorithm can be implemented based on node behavior detection. The direct trust value, statistical trust value, and recommended trust value are taken as the input of the abnormal behavior detection algorithm to calculate the comprehensive trust value of node behavior and judge whether there are malicious attacks on the network. Bayes network has great advantages in predicting trend changes under the action of multiple factors, as it can be combined with many advantages of Bayes network for the trust evaluation of user nodes on trading platforms.

6.3   RFM Model

RFM model is widely used in many analysis models of customer relationship management, which plays an important role in measuring customer value and customer profitability. The model can integrate three indexes of customers' recent transaction behavior, total transaction frequency, and transaction amount, and distinguish customers through the data feedback of the three indexes.

R (Recency): The Latest Consumption. The amount of time elapsed since a user's last purchase. The larger R-value is, the longer it has been since the last consumption. R index reflects the user's familiarity with the brand and the frequency of repurchase.

F (Frequency): Consumption Frequency. The number of purchases made by a user over a period of time. The higher the value of F is, the more transactions a customer has made in the recent period. F index reflects users' loyalty to the brand and whether buying habits are formed.

M (Monetary): Amount of Consumption. The amount spent by a user over a period of time. A larger value of M indicates a larger customer's consumption power. M index reflects user value and product recognition.

7   On Building Trustworthy System for Flash Loan

7.1   The Improved RFM Model Based on User On-Chain Behavior

In general, users' on-chain and off-chain behaviors are very diverse, so how to select the available behaviors and how to apply these behaviors to credit evaluation becomes a problem. A user usually corresponds to multiple behavior relationships, which can be classified into different types of transactions. For each type of behavior, variables corresponding to each person need to be calculated in a standardized way to measure the characteristics of people corresponding to a series of behaviors. Therefore, we introduce the RFM model which is often used in marketing and reconstruct it to make a better qualitative and quantitative analysis of user behavior [28].

According to the characteristic data on the chain, the elements in the RFM model can be given new meanings. R can refer to the amount of a recent successful flash loan. F represents the number of lightning loan execution failures within a certain period, that is, the number of repayment failures, which represents whether the user has sufficient ability to use flash loan; M represents the customer's account balance at a given time. The larger the balance, the higher the customer's ability and likelihood to repay. Through the new RFM model, the features screened out by RFM model are applied to the analysis of flash loan users again. However using these three indicators alone is not enough, combined with on-chain scenarios, it can be modified into the following categories:

1. Mining: describe the transaction behavior of users participating in liquidity mining. Different users have different habits, and annual returns and interest rates are also different.

2. Transaction: depict the historical transaction records of the user's wallet. Depending on the amount and frequency of daily transactions, users' repayment ability may vary.

3. Credit: describe the user's previous loan behavior. If users have other consumer loan behaviors before, they may be used to consumer loans and thus have better credit status. Describes user transactions using DeFi or Flash loan. Different users have different habits, and lending platforms, mortgages, and loan amounts are also different. It includes the length of borrowing on mainstream decentralized loan platforms, whether the collateral is cleared, whether a large number of collateral positions can be maintained while maintaining a high mortgage rate, and how willing and able to repay under high volatility [25].

4. Other categories: describe users' highly entertaining behaviors such as buying lottery tickets and non-homogeneity tokens, which can not only separate users but also effectively identify non-malicious accounts.

5. Evaluation classification: such as profit cultivation score, airdrop score, governance score, trader score, etc. Consider the loyalty of users to the agreement, the initiative of on-chain governance, and determine whether they are real traders.

The five user characteristics mentioned above can be applied to the basic indicators of RFM, so that each behavior type corresponds to one indicator, which makes our data richer and more meaningful. To a certain extent, the shortcoming of hysteresis in RFM model is alleviated. In addition, due to the instability of on-chain transactions and the volatility of virtual currency prices, these five indicators alone are not a good measure of user value. Therefore, we added an indicator V (Volatility) on the basis of the original RFM model to reflect the standard deviation of each transaction amount. For example, when a user makes a flash loan transaction, V is the standard deviation of each loan amount within a limited time.

Now our RFM model has six dimensions. To categorize users, we need to divide each dimension again with a gradient. As the values of the six dimensions differ greatly, each indicator is generally divided into 3–4 layers by the labeling method. The first level is the last user with the most recent transaction time and the fourth level is the last user with the most recent transaction time. In this way, each user will have six tags. Obviously, users with all six dimensions in tier1 are the most valuable and trustworthy, because they have the most recent transaction time, the largest transaction frequency and number, the largest transaction volume, and the most stable transaction amount. In addition, we can also use methods such as K Means clustering analysis to mark customers with more homogeneous characteristics and compare the results with the marking method to achieve better customer segmentation.

7.2   The Improved RFM Model Combined with Role-Based Trust Assessment Model

For some platforms with less stringent credit requirements, the improved RFM model can be directly combined with the role-based trust assessment model. Depending on the granularity, the number of dimensions and gradients can be controlled. Because the results of RFM model are flexible and dynamic, this scheme solves the problem that RBAC model is difficult to dynamically control user permission mapping or realize a dynamic granular control environment, to some extent, increases the flexibility of RBAC model, and avoids the security risks that are easily encountered in the process of partial authorization. According to the generation of new transactions on the chain, the labels of the corresponding RFM model will also change, and the user will be given new roles and teammate privileges. If the user has not transacted on the chain for a long time, the user can also recover the permissions granted from the role as needed. When DeFi loans and flash loans are conducted by different roles, their approval time, loan ceiling, repayment date, loan interest rate, and collateral are all different, thus reducing the possibility of flash loan attacks and alleviating the possible harm caused by flash loans [29].

7.3   The Improved RFM Model Combined with Periodic Node Behavior Trust Evaluation Model

However, for some platforms that require strict credit evaluation, just relying on the above labeling and role management is not enough. We can combine the on-chain behavior and off-chain behavior for analysis. As mentioned in the previous chapter, some on-chain credit evaluation platforms and lending platforms have started to cooperate with off-chain credit evaluation agencies to realize KYC and better evaluate whether users are trustworthy. In addition, we can also combine the improved RFM model with the periodic node behavior trust evaluation model. Instead of using labelling method, each indicator of the RFM model can be quantitatively analyzed. Through normalization and standardization algorithms, the serval dimensions of each type of transaction are calculated as specific values, and the same or different weights are given to the four dimensions in combination with different application scenarios. The schematic diagram is shown in Fig. 4.

1. Direct trust value
   The direct trust value can be combined with the off-chain credit agency to help the community judge new users by referring to the credit score already issued. To bring the chain information as reliably as possible, for individual users, it is necessary to consider the user's effective identity, loan repayment history, income, personal financial assets such as bank deposits, bonds, funds, and other certificates, personal property ownership certificate; In view of the company, also need to consider the company background, including health, compliance, legal, accounting and regulatory and company structure, payment history, operation, and trading history, at the same time considering

encryption and traditional financial assets under management experience, at the same time considering asset types and their hosting, including asset coverage, leverage, liquidity and risk exposure.

2. Recommended trust value.
   It is not reasonable to measure the trustworthiness of users on the chain only by the direct trust value obtained off the chain, so it is necessary to refer to the observed value of other nodes to evaluate nodes more objectively. Lending platforms usually invite trusted users as the first batch of test users during the test phase. The feature extraction is carried out for whitelist users, and the trust model is constructed according to the user portrait. The similarity between whitelist users and ordinary users is compared, and their cosine similarity, Jaccard similarity, and Euclidean distance are calculated as the recommended trust value.

3. Trust value of historical statistics
   Too much subjectivity will affect the credibility of trust evaluation. Therefore, the subjectivity and objectivity of trust must be considered in the trust evaluation of node behavior, and a large number of long-term statistical data of node behavior can be evaluated objectively with stability and representativeness. RFM model quantification index can be calculated in this part, so the user's transaction history can be used as one of the important indicators for anomaly detection. Whether malicious users brush credit scores is also a problem. Malicious users should be avoided from obtaining credit scores through a large number of ordinary transactions.

4. Timeliness Factor and Penalty Factor
   These factors mainly avoid carrying out malicious recommendations for malicious users in the network, and the trust degree is punished in the case of malicious deception, and the trust value of malicious nodes is rapidly reduced. The larger the value is, the faster the trust degree decreases; otherwise, the slower the trust degree decreases. The timeliness factor quantifies the timeliness of data from multiple dimensions such as frequency, earliest transaction, and latest transaction.

The data mentioned above are weighted according to the proportion to get the final trust value of the user, and compared with the minimum trust value of the system to analyze whether the user is an abnormal user. For users with different registration time, different weights are given. For example, the trust value of new users accounts for a higher weight in the calculation process of off-chain information and guarantee information, which falls down over time. For users with a long registration time, the proportion of historical things will become higher and higher until reaching the threshold.

There are two ways to calculate the minimum trust value. One is to calculate the trust value of the known malicious users and take their maximum value as the minimum trust value. The second is to take the minimum value of each step of weighting operation in theory, there is subjective judgment; Third, each step of the weighted calculation takes the maximum value of different malicious users and combines the maximum value of all malicious users into a threshold value.

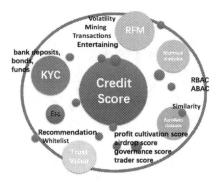

Fig. 4. Trust modeling

At the same time, this model aims to pursue the lowest false positive value and higher recall rate as possible. We can create an intermediate state between malicious users and ordinary users to maximize the experience of normal users who are misjudged as malicious users. To a certain extent, the permissions of this type of user are restricted, such as reducing the loan amount, and the permissions of the users as normal users are dynamically restored with the growth of the user's usage time.

8   The Future of Flash Loan

After experiencing a rapid development stage, decentralized finance has shown a certain degree of decline. How to release the value of pledged funds, avoid the risks, and volatile losses brought by smart contracts, and realize automatic repayment has become the concern of the industry. For the rest of the problems, the fundamental solution is to establish a reliable credit system and the mechanism of execution of punishment. The biggest difficulty in solving the credit mechanism problem by mapping information from off-chain to on-chain is that it cannot be decentralized and anonymized. But as flash loan attacks become more rampant, the mapping of reality to the crypto world is inevitable.

Flash loan, as an innovative financial instrument, can efficiently provide a large amount of funds and promote the circulation of value. At the same time, attackers certainly use it to steal assets. According to most of the existing attacks, we know that the manipulation methods of the attackers are not complicated, but the defense means at the present stage are not comprehensive enough, so it is difficult to respond and counter in time. After suffering a lot of painful costs, the weaknesses of oracle machines and protocol code logic loopholes were exposed. For the ecological security of blockchain, in addition to strengthening the verification and testing of a variety of technologies, the research and development of a reliable trusted system are imperative.

9   Conclusion

In recent years, security problems in the field of decentralized finance, especially those related to flash loan, have become increasingly serious. In addition to code audit and transaction detection, building a secure and reliable trustworthy system is one of the solutions. This paper introduces the basic concepts and functions of flash loan, and generalizes and analyzes the categories and specific attack events of flash loan attacks. Furthermore, the existing credit platforms have been introduced, and an improved RFM model based on users' on-chain and off-chain behaviors has been proposed. Finally, A potential overall Trust architecture is proposed by combining role-based trust assessment model and periodic node behavior trust evaluation model with the improved RFM model.

References

1. Amler, H., Eckey, L., Faust, S., Kaiser, M., Sandner, P., Schlosser, B.: DeFi-ning DeFi: challenges & pathway. In: 2021 3rd Conference on Blockchain Research & Applications for Innovative Networks and Services (BRAINS), pp. 181–184(2021). https://doi.org/10.1109/BRAINS52497.2021.9569795
2. Zhou, L., Qin, K., Cully, A., Livshits, B., Gervais, A.: On the just-in-time discovery of profit-generating transactions in DeFi protocols. In: 2021 IEEE Symposium on Security and Privacy (SP), pp. 919–936(2021). https://doi.org/10.1109/SP40001.2021.00113
3. Liu, B., Szalachowski, P., Zhou, J.: A first look into DeFi Oracles. In: 2021 IEEE International Conference on Decentralized Applications and Infrastructures (DAPPS), pp. 39–48 (2021). https://doi.org/10.1109/DAPPS52256.2021.00010
4. Qin, K., Zhou, L., Gamito, P., Jovanovic, P., Gervais, A.: An empirical study of DeFi liquidations: incentives, risks, and instabilities. In: The 21st ACM Internet Measurement Conference, IMC 2021, New York, NY, USA, pp. 336–350 (2021). https://doi.org/10.1145/3487552.3487811
5. Gudgeon, L., Perez, D., Harz, D., Livshits, B., Gervais, A.: The decentralized financial crisis. In: 2020 Crypto Valley Conference on Blockchain Technology (CVCBT), pp. 1–15(2020). https://doi.org/10.1109/CVCBT50464.2020.00005
6. Luo, R., et al.: DeFi security: a preliminary exploration of attacks, detection and defense. J. Guangzhou Univ. Nat. Sci. Ed., 1–15 (2022)
7. Wang, B., et al.: BLOCKEYE: hunting for DeFi attacks on blockchain. In: 2021 IEEE/ACM 43rd International Conference on Software Engineering: Companion Proceedings (ICSE-Companion), pp. 17–20 (2021). https://doi.org/10.1109/ICSE-Companion52605.2021.00025
8. Ferreira Torres, C., Iannillo, A.K., Gervais, A., State, R.: The eye of horus: spotting and analyzing attacks on Ethereum smart contracts. In: Borisov, N., Diaz, C. (eds.) FC 2021. LNCS, vol. 12674, pp. 33–52. Springer, Heidelberg (2021). https://doi.org/10.1007/978-3-662-64322-8_2
9. Qin, K., Zhou, L., Livshits, B., Gervais, A.: Attacking the DeFi ecosystem with flash loans for fun and profit. In: Borisov, N., Diaz, C. (eds.) FC 2021. LNCS, vol. 12674, pp. 3–32. Springer, Heidelberg (2021). https://doi.org/10.1007/978-3-662-64322-8_1

10. Wang, D., Wu, S., Lin, Z.: Towards a first step to understand flash loan and its applications in DeFi ecosystem. In: Proceedings of the 9th International Workshop on Security in Blockchain and Cloud Computing, SBC 2021, pp. 23–28 (2021). https://doi.org/10.1145/3457977.3460301

11. Tefagh, M., Bagheri, F., Khajehpour, A., Abdi, M.: Atomic bonded cross-chain debt. In: 2020 the 3rd International Conference on Blockchain Technology and Applications, ICBTA 2020, New York, NY, USA, pp. 50–54 (2020). https://doi.org/10.1145/3446983.3446987

12. Mackinga, T., Nadahalli, T., Wattenhofer, R.: TWAP Oracle attacks: easier done than said? In: 2022 IEEE International Conference on Blockchain and Cryptocurrency (ICBC), pp. 1–8 (2022). https://doi.org/10.1109/ICBC54727.2022.9805499

13. Aave homepage. https://aave.com/. Accessed 01 Aug 2022

14. dYdX homepage. https://dydx.exchange/. Accessed 05 Aug 2022

15. UNISWAP homepage. https://uniswap.org/. Accessed 05 Aug 2022

16. Cream homepage. https://app.cream.finance/. Accessed 06 Aug 2022

17. V-CRED homepage. http://www.v-cred.trade/. Accessed 10 Aug 2022

18. Xu, J., Ackerer, D., Dubovitskaya, A.: A game-theoretic analysis of cross-chain atomic swaps with HTLCs. In: 2021 IEEE 41st International Conference on Distributed Computing Systems (ICDCS), pp. 584–594 (2021). https://doi.org/10.1109/ICDCS51616.2021.00062

19. Boonpeam, N., Werapun, W., Karode, T.: The arbitrage system on decentralized exchanges. In: 2021 18th International Conference on Electrical Engineering/Electronics, Computer, Telecommunications and Information Technology (ECTI-CON), pp. 768–771 (2021). https://doi.org/10.1109/ECTI-CON51831.2021.9454673

20. Cecchetti, E., Yao, S., Ni, H., Myers, A.C.: Compositional security for reentrant applications. In: 2021 IEEE Symposium on Security and Privacy (SP), pp. 1249–1267 (2021). https://doi.org/10.1109/SP40001.2021.00084

21. bZx homepage. https://bzx.network/. Accessed 05 Aug 2022

22. Yearn homepage. https://yearn.finance/. Accessed 05 Aug 2022

23. Lendf.me homepage. https://cryptobonuses.com/. Accessed 05 Aug 2022

24. Eleven.Finance homepage. https://eleven.finance/. Accessed 05 Aug 2022

25. TrueFi homepage. https://truefi.io/. Accessed 11 Aug 2022

26. ARCx homepage. https://arcx.game/passport. Accessed 10 Aug 2022

27. CreDA homepage. https://www1.creda.app/home. Accessed 08 Aug 2022

28. Parikh, Y., Abdelfattah, E.: Clustering algorithms and RFM analysis performed on retail transactions. In: 2020 11th IEEE Annual Ubiquitous Computing, Electronics & Mobile Communication Conference (UEMCON), pp. 0506–0511 (2020). https://doi.org/10.1109/UEMCON51285.2020.9298123

29. Shahen, J., Niu, J., Tripunitara, M.: Cree: a performant tool for safety analysis of administrative temporal role-based access control (ATRBAC) policies. In: IEEE Transactions on Dependable and Secure Computing, vol. 18, no. 5, pp. 2349–2364 (2021). https://doi.org/10.1109/TDSC.2019.2949410

Forward Traceability for Product Authenticity Using Ethereum Smart Contracts

Fokke Heikamp[1,4](✉) ⓘ, Lei Pan[1,4] ⓘ, Rolando Trujillo-Rasua[3,4] ⓘ,
Sushmita Ruj[2,4] ⓘ, and Robin Doss[1,4] ⓘ

[1] Centre for Cyber Security Research and Innovation (CSRI), Deakin University,
Geelong, Australia
folmer.heikamp@research.deakin.edu.au, {l.pan,robin.doss}@deakin.edu.au
[2] University of New South Wales, Sydney, Australia
sushmita.ruj@unsw.edu.au
[3] Universitat Rovira i Virgili, Tarragona, Spain
rolando.trujillo@urv.cat
[4] Cyber Security Cooperative Research Centre, Perth, Australia

Abstract. One of the most sought-after properties in supply chains is traceability. Traceability involves knowing where a product has been and what happened to it, helping to establish product authenticity. Current traceability solutions focus on generating and storing data but do not verify whether the stored data is correct. In this short paper, we address such a limitation. We do so by introducing forward traceability: an extension of standard traceability definitions with correctness as an additional feature, making forward traceability well-suited for real-time counterfeit detection. We also provide an implementation of forward traceability in a decentralised system in the Solidity language, which we tested on the Ethereum platform. Our proof-of-concept is available on GitHub.

Keywords: Forward traceability · Supply chain security · Blockchain · Authentication

1 Introduction

Counterfeiting is a significant problem in supply chains. A prominent attack pattern counterfeiters use is the infiltration of fake products within a legitimate supply chain [15], making fake products to be sold as legit by the supply chain retailers themselves. Assume a scenario where a manufacturer of counterfeit Ray-Ban sunglasses wants to sell fake products as authentic. A way to do this, without causing alarm, is by selling them through a legitimate supply chain. A case in point: in 2012 the United States bought counterfeits of the drug Avastin sold by legitimate retailers [15].

Counterfeiting is a lucrative criminal activity. Lou et al. [11] estimate the global counterfeit market value at 400 billion dollars. Counterfeit products are not bound to regulations and are usually of lesser quality. This situation can have a severe impact, especially in the pharmaceutical supply chain where fake medicine impacts the patient's life [19]. Counterfeits also cause reputational and financial damage to the owner of the original product [15].

There are numerous articles on countering counterfeiting in supply chains [8, 15,17–19]. A key idea in this direction is traceability, whereby a product is traced from its origin to its destination. Products whose trace is incomplete or lost are thus regarded as potentially fake. We observe, however, that most traceability solutions in the literature [2,18] do not verify trace correctness as products move throughout the supply chain, limiting themselves to storing traceability data. This makes those solutions unsuited for real-time counterfeit detection.

Contributions. In this short paper, we introduce the notion of forward traceability as the capacity of supply chain participants to verify each step taken by a product under the assumption that the product's path has been established at its origin. We make this notion formal within a formalism based on Labelled Transition Systems. To our knowledge, ours is the first definition of supply chain traceability that allows supply chain participants to verify the authenticity (trace correctness) of the products they handle. To illustrate the practicality of forward traceability, we design and implement a technical proof-of-concept of forward traceability in Ethereum.

Organisation. The paper is organized as follows. In the next section, we give an overview of related research. Section 3 formally defines forward traceability. Section 4 shows our proof of concept in Solidity of a system satisfying forward traceability. In Sect. 5, we evaluate the costs of our implementation. Lastly, we conclude our work in Sect. 6.

2   Related Work

Our work is influenced by path authentication protocols, such as Pathchecker [12], Tracker [1], Checker [3], and StepAuth [2]. Like in path authentication protocols, a product in a forward traceability system is expected to go through a pre-established path. Path authentication protocols, however, do not satisfy traceability, because supply chain participants cannot tell, for example, the origin of a product.

Lately, blockchain has been introduced in traceability solutions [6,7,11,14, 19]. For example, Salah et al. [14] provide a proof-of-concept traceability framework for soybeans in the agricultural supply chain using smart contracts. Sunny et al. [16] use Microsoft Azure Blockchain Workbench instead. Their approach is inflexible, as it assumes a fixed supply chain topology. Westerkamp et al. [20] provide a traceability solution using non-fungible tokens. Their method tokenizes every physical object to an NFT. Their protocol allows products to be split and combined into new products. Munoz et al. [4] present an NFT-based traceability solution specific to the logging industry.

Even though blockchain-based solutions may suffer from scalability issues [13], they have the attractive feature of making data immutable. Commercial traceability providers like EverLedger and TradeLens use blockchain technology, indicating its relevancy. However, none of the solutions above defines trace correctness, making them unsuitable for applications where a product's path has to be verified. Others, like [5,10,18], are either based on a custom-made blockchain or restricted to specific supply chain domains, such as copyright of digital pictures and provenance.

We further observe that several approaches use a fixed supply chain topology for their traceability solution. If the supply chain changes, the whole solution has to be rewritten. Our solution is not bound by such restrictions.

We provide a comparison table (Table 1) to show the difference between the various blockchain-based traceability solutions mentioned earlier. Observe that most of them are specific to a supply chain type.

Table 1. Comparison of similar traceability solutions

TD: Traceability definition, **F**: Flexible, **AV**: Auto verification

✓: yes, **O**: partial, **X**: no

Author	Building blocks	Supply chain	TD	F	AV
Salah et al. [14]	Smart contract	Agricultural	O	O	O
Sunny et al. [16]	Smart contract	Pharmaceutical	X	X	X
Westerkamp et al. [20]	Smart contract, NFT	Product assembly	X	✓	X
Kumar et al. [10]	Smart contract	Textile	X	X	O
Toyoda et al. [18]	Smart contract	Post-supply chain	X	✓	O
Munoz et al. [4]	Smart contract, NFT	Logging	X	O	O
Igarashi et al. [5]	Smart contract	Digital pictures	X	✓	X
Kuhn et al. [9]	Smart contract, NFT	Product assembly	O	✓	X
Our work	Smart contract	Generic	✓	O	✓

3   Forward Traceability

We define a forward traceability system as a system that can reconstruct and verify past events and is also able to determine future steps that a product has to take.

Forward traceability works as follows: we have a supply chain producing products. We also have actions that are applied to products. An event is an action applied to a product at a time and location. The state of a supply chain describes which events have been applied to the product. We call this state a *trace* because it documents the history of the product. This is the first half of forward traceability. The second half is about how we verify a product. The verification is built around the `valid` predicate. If the valid predicate holds for a product, then we know the product is authentic. The benefit of using a valid predicate is that it allows for multiple solutions. If a predicate does not perform well we can try another interpretation without changing the definition of forward traceability. In our interpretation, we build the valid predicate that states that a product has to follow a specific path to be authentic. This approach has been used before in the context of path authentication [1,2,12].

Definition 1 (Path). *Let X be the universe of products moving throughout the supply chain and P the universe of supply chain participants. A path for a product $x \in X$ is a sequence of participants $path(x) = (p_1, \ldots, p_n)$, where $p_i \in P$, for all $i \in \{1 \ldots n\}$.*

We let supply chain participants store information about the product they handle in the form of events.

Definition 2 (Event). *Let A be the set of actions supply chain participants perform on products. An event is a tuple $(x, action, actor, timestamp, data)$, where $x \in X$ is a product, $action \in A$ an action, $actor \in P$ a supply chain participant, timestamp is the date and time, and data is auxiliary data. We use E to denote the set of all events and e^{actor} to denote an event e executed by an actor a.*

A supply chain traceability system tracks a product through the supply chain.

Definition 3 (Supply chain traceability system). *A supply chain traceability system is a transition system $(S, \rightarrow)$ where:*

- *S is a set of states. Each state s is a partial mapping from X to E^*, where E^* denotes the set of sequences formed with elements from E. Intuitively, $s(x) = e_1, \ldots, e_n$ means that a series of actions, $a_1, \ldots, a_n$, have been applied to the product x.*
- *$\rightarrow$ is a partial order on states representing how the system makes progress. We require $\rightarrow$ to be increasing in steps of one. That is, $s \rightarrow s'$ implies that if $s(x) = e_1, \ldots, e_n$, then $s'(x) = e_1, \ldots, e_{n+1}$. In words, traces always iterate forward.*

A supply chain traceability system only collects data. To validate the trace, we need to determine product correctness. We anchor our product correctness on a valid predicate. The main reason is that there are alternatives to validate a product trace. If we use a valid predicate that is always true, our system is simplified into a traditional traceability system to provide backward compatibility.

Definition 4 (Product correctness). *Let valid be a predicate on traces. A product x is said to be correct in a supply chain system $(S, \rightarrow)$ if for every state $s, x \in domain(s) \implies valid(s(x))$.*

Supply chain correctness is a generalization of product correctness. If every product in the supply chain is valid, then the whole supply chain is correct.

Definition 5 (Supply chain correctness). *A supply chain traceability system $(S, \rightarrow)$ is said to be correct if every product $x \in X$ is correct in $(S, \rightarrow)$.*

Most traceability solutions only implement Definition 3, but not Definitions 4 and 5. That is, they provide a way to generate and store events but do not tell whether those traces are valid (correct). By creating a system that satisfies all three definitions, we focus on real-time detection. This feature allows for real-time error detection, which is particularly useful for counterfeit detection and food recall.

For our purposes, we use the following interpretation of the valid predicate.

$$valid(x) \iff \forall_{i \in 1...|s(x)|} \left(s(x)_i^{actor} = path(x)_i \right) \tag{1}$$

Note that in the definition above we are assuming a universal definition of $path(x)$. If needed, this could be made of the system itself. Further note that our interpretation of the valid predicate has been already used within the domain of path authentication protocols [1,2].

4   A Proof of Concept Implementation

We made a proof-of-concept of a forward traceability system in Ethereum using Truffle, Ganache, and MetaMask.

4.1   Requirements

For our solution, we see a path as a sequence of checkpoints a product has to go through to be validated. We call these checkpoints, readers. Every reader creates an event describing what happened to the product at that point. This event includes product ID, reader ID, timestamp, and data. For our design, we use one kind of event, describing that the reader has processed the product. We show this setup in Fig. 1. Our system has the following requirements:

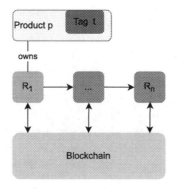

Fig. 1. Our scenario

1. Given a product x and a set of events E, a reader should be able to construct its trace $s(x)$.
2. Given a product x, a path p, and a set of events E, a reader should be able to verify the path according to the provided valid predicate.
3. Given a product x, a path p, and a set of events E, a reader should be able to construct the future steps of the product.

4.2 Design

In our implementation, we distinguish three different actions: "register participant", "register product", and "update product". We model these actions using three smart contracts. The essential one is the *product* smart contract. Every physical product is an instance of this contract. The other two contracts are lookup tables for products and participants. These smart contracts list all users and products and provide address-to-name translations. Our implementation is available on GitHub[1].

After a product is registered, the product is updated sequentially by the addresses specified in the path. The updating participant has to prove two things: it is the next step in the path and it possesses the secret key obtained from the previous step. If the participant is the next step, a new event is generated and added to the *Product* smart contract. After that, the verify function is executed on the latest event. The verify function checks if the data signature matches the data and if the *hmac* of the previous event is correct. It can check the last part because the message sender should have the right key to verify the *hmac*. The message sender cannot prove ownership if the key is unavailable. We assume that the participant has some means to transport the shared secret key securely to the next owner. If the verify function returns false, the transaction is reverted, and the smart contract is restored. The sequence diagram for the update phase is seen in Fig. 2.

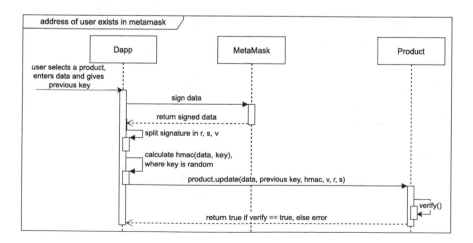

Fig. 2. Product update sequence diagram

---
[1] https://github.com/mr-torgue/Forward-Trace-Explorer.

4.3   Informal Security Argument

In line with previous work, we rely on the fact that data in the blockchain is immutable, i.e. an adversary cannot change or delete traceability data. Furthermore, using a shared key between participants, we do not solely rely on blockchain security. An adversary would need to obtain both the private key and shared key to update the trace of a product. In future work, we would like to include a more thorough security analysis. This security analysis should formally prove that our system is secure under a given threat model.

5   Evaluation

Our protocol is evaluated on cost. Our evaluation on cost is in line with current research on traceability systems [4, 20].

5.1   Setup

Our experiment runs on an Ubuntu 22.04 VirtualBox VM with two virtual CPU cores and 8 GB of memory. Testing is done using the truffle/mocha testing suite. The experiment is constructed so that everything except for the path length changes. We calculated the cost of an operation by taking the balance difference before and after the operation. We use the `web3.eth.getBalance` call to enquire about the balance in wei.

For our experiment, we initialized 256 products and 10 participants. The path length for the products ranges from 1 to 256. The maximum path length is set to 256 because a single product will rarely be read more than 256 times.

5.2   Results

Figure 3 shows the total GAS cost plotted against path length. Table 2 shows the costs for various path lengths (between 1 and 256) in GAS, Eth, and A\$. Our primary unit for costs is gas because they remain fixed. For simplicity, we assume that the gas cost is 10Gwei and an Eth to A\$ rate of A\$2300.

Figure 3 shows that total costs scale linearly with path length. This is in line with results from other research [4, 20]. The "add product to lookup table" step remains constant because it is independent of path length. Create scales linearly because it has to allocate more bytes to store a larger path. The update function scales linearly because it has to be executed $|path|$ times.

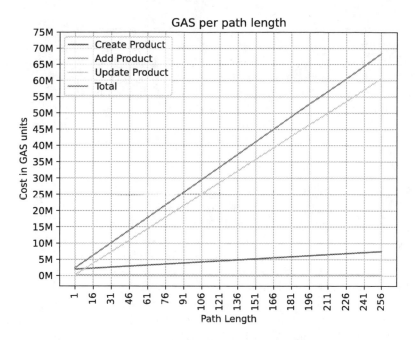

Fig. 3. Costs in GAS per path length

Table 2. Costs for path length 1, 16, and 256

	Length	GAS	Gwei	A$
Create	1	2.12M	21.20M	48.87
	16	2.30M	23.00M	52.82
	256	7.48M	74.80M	171.94
Add	1	0.19M	1.90M	4.47
	16	0.18M	1.80M	4.12
	256	0.18M	1.80M	4.12
Update	1	0.24M	2.40M	5.56
	16	3.80M	38.00M	87.36
	256	60.70M	607.00M	1,396.06
Total	1	2.56M	25.60M	58.90
	16	6.27M	62.70M	144.30
	256	68.35M	683.50M	1572.12

The costs can be significantly reduced with some optimizations. Each participant is represented using an unsigned integer (uint32) instead of an address to reduce the required storage for a path by a factor of 8. It can be further optimized by moving all data to off-chain storage and only keeping references on-chain. Also, note that costs can be divided among participants. In that case, the update costs for 256 can be divided by 256, which is about 5 dollars each. Tracking individual items might be too expensive. Batching is an often employed mechanism to save costs. It will decrease the granularity but will decrease costs as well. For example, if one ship is in batches of 100, they could use one tag for one batch, so the costs per unit are the total cost divided by 100.

It is important to note that traceability always comes at a cost, even in traditional settings. A traceability solution should be cheap enough so that the benefits outweigh the costs.

6   Conclusion

In this paper, we introduce the notion of forward traceability. A forward traceability system is stricter than a traditional traceability system because it has two additional requirements. It needs to automatically verify traceability data and know the future steps a product is expected to take in the supply chain. Our concept offers a new way of determining product authenticity, which is especially useful when real-time detection is required.

We define traceability using a transition system and introduce trace correctness as the expectation that a product has been going through a pre-defined path. We argue that our definition is flexible enough to accommodate other interpretations of a valid trace. We provided a proof of concept using Ethereum smart contracts, demonstrating that forward traceability is feasible.

For future work, we plan to perform a formal security analysis of our system design. We also plan to include privacy requirements, allowing participants to limit the information they share. Because our preliminary experiments show that the costs of our forward traceability are not low, we will explore more efficient implementations. The code and data for our work are available on GitHub.

Acknowledgements. The work has been supported by the Cyber Security Research Centre Limited whose activities are partially funded by the Australian Government's Cooperative Research Centres Programme.

References

1. Blass, E.o., Elkhiyaoui, K., Molva, R., Antipolis, E.S.: Tracker: security and privacy for RFID-based supply chains. In: In NDSS 2011, 18th Annual Network and Distributed System Security Symposium, 6–9 February 2011, p. 2011 (2011)
2. Bu, K., Li, Y.: Every step you take, I'll be watching you: practical StepAuthEntication of RFID paths. IEEE Trans. Inf. Foren. Secur. **13**(4), 834–849 (2018). https://doi.org/10.1109/TIFS.2017.2768022
3. Elkhiyaoui, K., Blass, E.o., Molva, R.: Checker: on-site checking in RFID-based supply chains. In: In Proceedings of the Fifth ACM Conference on Security and Privacy in Wireless and Mobile Networks, WISEC 2012, pp. 173–184. ACM (2012)
4. Felipe Munoz, M., Zhang, K., Shahzad, A., Ouhimmou, M.: LogLog: a blockchain solution for tracking and certifying wood volumes. In: 2021 IEEE International Conference on Blockchain and Cryptocurrency (ICBC), pp. 1–9 (2021). https://doi.org/10.1109/ICBC51069.2021.9461153

5. Igarashi, T., Kazuhiko, T., Kobayashi, Y., Kuno, H., Diehl, E.: Photrace: A blockchain-based traceability system for photographs on the internet. In: 2021 IEEE International Conference on Blockchain (Blockchain), pp. 590–596 (2021). https://doi.org/10.1109/Blockchain53845.2021.00089

6. Islam, M.D., Shen, H., Badsha, S.: Integrating blockchain into supply chain safeguarded by PUF-enabled RFID. Internet Things 18, 100505 (2022). https://doi.org/10.1016/j.iot.2022.100505

7. Jing, Z., Hu, N., Song, Y., Song, B., Gu, C., Pan, L.: On the design and implementation of a blockchain-based data management system for ETO manufacturing. Appl. Sci. 12(18), 9184 (2022)

8. Khalil, G., Doss, R., Chowdhury, M.: A novel RFID-based anti-counterfeiting scheme for retail environments. IEEE Access 8, 47952–47962 (2020). https://doi.org/10.1109/ACCESS.2020.2979264

9. Kuhn, M., Funk, F., Franke, J.: Blockchain architecture for automotive traceability. Procedia CIRP 97, 390–395 (2021). https://doi.org/10.1016/j.procir.2020.05.256

10. Kumar, V., Agrawal, T.K., Wang, L., Chen, Y.: Contribution of traceability towards attaining sustainability in the textile sector. Text. Clothing Sustain. 3(1), 1–10 (2017). https://doi.org/10.1186/s40689-017-0027-8

11. Lou, M., Dong, X., Cao, Z., Shen, J., He, D.: SESCF: a secure and efficient supply chain framework via blockchain-based smart contracts. Sec. and Commun. Netw. 2021 (2021). https://doi.org/10.1155/2021/8884478

12. Ouafi, K., Vaudenay, S.: Pathchecker: an RFID application for tracing products in suply-chains. In: In Workshop on RFID Security – RFIDSec 2009, pp. 1–14 (2009)

13. Pearson, S., et al.: Are distributed ledger technologies the panacea for food traceability? Glob. Food Secur. 20, 145–149 (2019). https://doi.org/10.1016/j.gfs.2019.02.002

14. Salah, K., Nizamuddin, N., Jayaraman, R., Omar, M.: Blockchain-based soybean traceability in agricultural supply chain. IEEE Access Pract. Innov. Open Solut. 7, 73295–73305 (2019). https://doi.org/10.1109/ACCESS.2019.2918000

15. Soon, J.M., Manning, L.: Developing anti-counterfeiting measures: the role of smart packaging. Food Res. Int. 123, 135–143 (2019). https://doi.org/10.1016/j.foodres.2019.04.049

16. Sunny, J., Undralla, N., Madhusudanan Pillai, V.: Supply chain transparency through blockchain-based traceability: an overview with demonstration. Comput. Ind. Eng. 150, 106895 (2020). https://doi.org/10.1016/j.cie.2020.106895

17. Syed, N.F., Shah, S.W., Trujillo-Rasua, R., Doss, R.: Traceability in supply chains: a Cyber security analysis. Comput. Secur. 112, 102536 (2022). https://doi.org/10.1016/j.cose.2021.102536

18. Toyoda, K., Mathiopoulos, P.T., Sasase, I., Ohtsuki, T.: A novel blockchain-based product ownership management system (POMS) for anti-counterfeits in the post supply chain. IEEE Access Pract. Innov. Open Solut. 5, 17465–17477 (2017). https://doi.org/10.1109/ACCESS.2017.2720760

19. Uddin, M.: Blockchain medledger: hyperledger fabric enabled drug traceability system for counterfeit drugs in pharmaceutical industry. Int. J. Pharm. 597, 120235 (2021). https://doi.org/10.1016/j.ijpharm.2021.120235

20. Westerkamp, M., Victor, F., Küpper, A.: Tracing manufacturing processes using blockchain-based token compositions. Digit. Commun. Netw. 6(2), 167–176 (2020). https://doi.org/10.1016/j.dcan.2019.01.007

BSB: Bringing Safe Browsing
to Blockchain Platform

Zhuang Zhou[1], Cheng Tan[1,2]($\boxtimes$)(iD), Shiyun Liu[1], Rongwei Yu[3], Siwei Wu[4](iD),
and Shengwu Xiong[2](iD)

[1] School of Computer Science and Artificial Intelligence,
Wuhan University of Technology, Wuhan 430070, China
{305271,cheng_tan,liushiyun}@whut.edu.cn
[2] Sanya Science and Education Innovation Park, Wuhan University of Technology,
Sanya 572000, China
xiongsw@whut.edu.cn
[3] School of Cyber Science and Engineering, Wuhan University, Wuhan 430072, China
roewe.yu@whu.edu.cn
[4] College of Computer Science and Technology, Zhejiang University, Hangzhou
310007, China
wusw1020@zju.edu.cn

Abstract. Programmable Blockchain brings a new type of decentralized applications (Dapps) that facilitate transfer of assets across users without a third party. The popularity of Ethereum Dapps brings themselves great security risks: they have been under various kinds of attacks from cybercriminals to gain profit. As the back-end of Dapps, smart contracts have been exploited their programming errors to steal cryptocurrency or tokens. Multiple approaches have been proposed to detect unsafe contracts. This paper presents a Blockchain Safe Browsing (BSB) platform to effectively disseminate smart contract detection results to contract users, and vulnerable contract owners. Based on those results, contract blacklist can be generated to provide user warning service, which is used to warn users before making transactions with unsafe contracts. Meanwhile, a contract owner notify mechanism is developed to help contract owners study the vulnerability details of their contract so that they can patch the vulnerabilities in time. Among the mechanism, the researchers will gain profits from shared data, which in turn inspire them keep uploading their research results. Moreover, as the most valuable asset for the researchers, vulnerability exploit details will be encrypted before uploading, and can only be decrypted by contract owners, which prevent the details being leaked and utilized by cybercriminals. Extensive evaluations using real datasets (with 2,880 unsafe contracts) demonstrate that our prototype can function as intended without sacrificing user experience, and warn users at the millisecond level.

Keywords: Blockchain · Safe browsing · Contract blacklist · User warning · Contract owner notify

X. Yuan et al. (Eds.): NSS 2022, LNCS 13787, pp. 524–543, 2022.
https://doi.org/10.1007/978-3-031-23020-2_30

1 Introduction

Blockchain platform achieves trusted asset transfer across users without a third party. Smart contracts which are executed on top of Blockchain platform have been used as the back-end of Dapps for payments, crowd funding, voting, or governance [33]. Among them, Blockchain-asset-enabled finance ecosystem (DeFi) have attracted a recent surge in popularity with millions of daily transaction volume, billions of locked up United States dollar (USD), as well as a plethora of newly emerging protocols (for lending, staking, and exchanges) [44]. The great profits attracted cybercriminals to fix their gaze on those Dapps and exploit their Blockchain back-end, smart contracts. Code-based vulnerabilities in smart contracts were usually exploited through attack transactions to steal cryptocurrency or tokens [23], which loss was over billions of USD [6].

In recent years, the security issues on smart contracts attract increasing attentions from researchers. By analyzing contract code and checking for known vulnerable patterns, static analysis [10,14,15,19,24,27,31,34,36] can be used to detect vulnerabilities in a deployed contract. Dynamic analysis [12,13,18,29] is to detect vulnerabilities by executing the deployed contracts. Recent works [4,42,43] also replay history transactions and record EVM bytecode-level traces to detect predefined attacks. With the rapid growth of the DeFi ecosystem, security issues were also reported [37,38,41,44].

Aside from vulnerability assessment, studies on real-world Dapp attacks and frauds are also conducted to detect the contracts deployed by cybercriminal, such as phishing [40], Ponzi [5], and honeypot [35]. Blockchain platform urgently needs an effective method to help users stay away from unsafe contracts in order to create an enticing investment environment [8]. In this paper, unsafe contracts include those contracts which are vulnerable, phishing, Ponzi, and honeypot.

However, there is a gap between users, owners, and security researchers of smart contract. Contract vulnerability exploit details were usually published through academic papers, chart rooms, and blogs. Such negative methods cannot guarantee that contract owners or users can get the details in time [16], while the details may be utilized by cybercriminals. To avoid such consequences, some authors refrained from mentioning any particular smart contract [18], which in turn affect users and owners to learn about the vulnerabilities. Meanwhile, to accept responsible disclosure, some Dapp owners have to leave contact information on their front-end, which are conflict with the anonymous feature of Blockchain platform. After responsible disclosure, contract owners may still have no intention to patch the vulnerabilities until attack incidents happen [25], as it is quite cumbersome to deal with a vulnerable contract and restore a safe state. Users may not verify the safety of smart contract before making transactions, which make them suffer unnecessary loss.

In summary, a bridge is needed to effectively disseminate detection results from security researchers to users and owners of smart contract. Safe Browsing (SB) is a popular security service to protect web users by showing warnings to them when they attempt to navigate to dangerous sites or download dangerous files. SB also notifies webmasters when their websites are compromised by malicious actors and helps them diagnose and resolve the problem so that their visitors stay safe [11]. Inspired by SB, we wish to take advantage of existing security analysis results to prevent users making transactions with unsafe contracts, and motivate contract owners patching the vulnerabilities in time.

Our work: In this paper, we design a Blockchain Safe Browsing (BSB) platform, and implement it on Ethereum Blockchain, which is the most prominent framework for Dapps [39], with over 15 million contracts deployed [26].

We integrate BSB with Ethereum wallet to provide two functionalities: user warning, and contract owner notify. Based on the shared results from security researchers, contract blacklist can be generated to provide user warning service. Users can query whether target contracts are unsafe before making transactions with them. Similar to SB, the general detection procedure of user warning is to check if the target contract is present on a list of unsafe contracts, collected and maintained by a remote server [2]. We will reserve a local filter that contains the blacklist on the client side to circumvent heavy communication overhead. We hope that such warnings can avoid users making transactions with unsafe contracts, as their assets maybe stolen by cybercriminals. No matter vulnerable contracts are exploited or not, such warnings will motivate contract owners patching the vulnerabilities as quickly as possible, otherwise users may have no willing to make transactions with their contracts.

From another perspective, an integrated contract blacklist, whose contents are contributed by different security researchers, would certainly improve user experience as each researcher is likely to hold a list of unsafe contracts that others do not possess [10,13,15,18,19,24,36,42]. We name those contract security researchers who share their results as blacklist providers.

User warning service shall be free to the users, otherwise they have no need to use it. To ensure user experience and against the latest threats, contract blacklist shall be updated continuously, which is not easy for blacklist providers. Breidenbach [3] uses bug bounties to incentivize security analyses of smart contracts, which bridges the bounty payer and the bug finder. Profits will bring blacklist providers the motivation to keep updating. We develop an incentive method in contract owner notify mechanism to help blacklist providers gain profits from shared results. Contract owners will pay a little for the vulnerability exploit details of their contracts, which are the most valuable assets of blacklist providers. To prevent vulnerability exploit details from being leaked to the adversaries, the public key of contract owners will be recovered and utilized to encrypt the vulnerability exploit details, so that only the private key of contract owners can decrypt them. To directly notify contract owners about contract vulnerabilities, BSB platform will verify the identities of the users, and vulnerable contract owners will be notified that there are vulnerabilities in their contracts, and they can purchase related vulnerability reports to study vulnerability exploit details.

To the best of our knowledge, BSB is the first design that enables *safe browsing on Blockchain platform*. Our contributions are as follows:

1) We propose the first BSB platform which attracts researchers sharing their research results to support user warning service and contract owner notify mechanism. The former warns users before they make transactions with unsafe contracts, while the latter notifies contract owners that vulnerabilities are in their contracts, and helps them obtain vulnerability exploit details.
2) To prevent vulnerability exploit details from being leaked, an encryption mechanism is developed based on the public key cryptography of Blockchain platform. Such a mechanism guarantee that only contract owners can decrypt the encrypted data.
3) We implement a full-fledged BSB prototype, consisting of a client for users, a handler for blacklist providers, and a server for data management. The evaluation with real datasets shows the efficiency of our design.

2 Preliminaries

2.1 Ethereum and Smart Contract

Ethereum is a public Blockchain-based distributed computing platform to allow users to run smart contracts which can implement a set of rules for managing digital assets. There are two types of Ethereum accounts: Externally Owned Accounts (EOAs) controlled by private keys (owned by users), and Contract Accounts controlled by code (known as smart contracts). During its operations, the Ethereum Blockchain tracks the change of every account's state through recording transactions. The recorded transactions are also called external transactions, as it is a signed data package storing a message to be sent from an EOA to another account. Contract accounts also have the capability to transfer Ether, call another contract, or create new contract. Such actions are called internal transactions (or messages), as they are not signed by the private key, and internal transactions are triggered by an external or internal one.

Due to the immutability nature, the deployed contracts are unpatchable. Contract owner shall warn users to deprecate the vulnerable contract, move its all funds to a safely EOA, patch the contract code and deploy it, move the funds to the new one and notify all users. The community explored the proxy pattern to allow upgradable smart contracts [30]. One contract is split into: i) an immutable proxy one which holds all funds and all internal state, but does not implement any business logic; ii) a logic one which implements all the business logic, but is completely stateless. The users just make an external transaction to proxy contract, an internal transaction will automatically generated to call the corresponding function in logic contract.

2.2 Dapp and Wallet

Dapps utilizes a set of smart contracts as its on-chain back-ends, for the purposes such as encoding task logic and maintaining persistent storage of its consensus-critical states [18], while also contains offchain components such as its front-end (e.g., a website) for communicating with users. For example, Fomo3D [42], is powered by 5 smart contracts that handles the transactions for different actions, like buying keys, withdrawing from vault, picking a vanity name, etc.

As famous Dapps, DeFi supports a multitude of different financial applications [38], such as List of Booking, Automated Market Maker (AMM), Stablecoin, Flash Loans, etc. Uniswap is an AMM Dapp which provides the cryptocurrency exchange service. Liquidity providers need to deposit a pre-determined amount of cryptocurrencies to the pool in the AMM. In return for providing liquidity to the protocol, they can earn fees from trades in their pool.

A wallet is a software application that serves as the primary user interface to Ethereum [1]. The wallet controls access to a user's money, managing keys and addresses, tracking the balance, and creating and signing transactions. In addition, some Ethereum wallets can also interact with contracts, such as ERC20 tokens. Wallets don't have custody of users' funds, they are just tools for managing EOAs, which means that users can swap wallet providers at any time.

2.3   Elliptic Curve Cryptography

Elliptic Curve Cryptography (ECC) is a type of asymmetric or public key cryptography based on the discrete logarithm problem as expressed by addition and multiplication on the points of an elliptic curve [28]. Ethereum uses a specific elliptic curve called secp256k1. The digital signature algorithm used in Ethereum is the Elliptic Curve Digital Signature Algorithm (ECDSA). After the creation of raw transaction, it shall be signed by a private key. Three components of an ECDSA digital signature will be made: r, s, and v, which can be used to derive EOA's public key [1].

In this paper, we want to encrypt target report with ECC public key, and decrypt it with the corresponding private one. Elliptic Curve Integrated Encryption Scheme (ECIES) combines ECC-based asymmetric cryptography with symmetric ciphers to provide data encryption by recipient's public key and decryption by its private key [22]. The ECIES encryption scheme uses ECC cryptography, key-derivation function, symmetric encryption algorithm, and Message authentication codes (MAC) algorithm combined together. In our work, the secp256k1 elliptic curve is used for the public-key calculations.

3   System Overview

BSB platform bridges three different entities: the user, who wants to make transactions with smart contracts; the contract owner, who deploys the vulnerable contracts; and the blacklist provider, who has expertise and capabilities to collect, verify and update a list of unsafe contracts.

As shown in Fig. 1, Blacklist providers rely on the handlers to upload research results to the server. They shall encrypt the reports which contains the exploit details of contract vulnerabilities before uploading. The server is responsible for generating contract blacklist for local enquiry, and responding report request

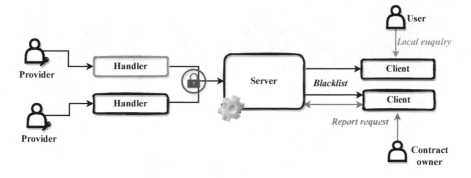

Fig. 1. The overview of BSB platform. (Color figure online)

from the clients. The clients automatically download the latest contract black-list from the server to provide two functionalities. The users rely on the client for checking whether target contract is known to be unsafe(the blue line). The own-ers of known vulnerable contracts will be notified that there are vulnerabilities in their contracts, and they can apply for those vulnerability exploit details(the red line).

Threat Model and Assumptions. To ensure the correctness of uploaded research results, we ensure that blacklist providers are contract security researchers as well, who have the incentive to study and detect unsafe contracts. During registration process, a manual verification is set up to verify the identi-ties of blacklist providers as security researchers of smart contract. In this work, blacklist providers can gain profits from shared research results, which attract them willingly and periodically upload data to the platform. We assume those blacklist providers are semi-trusted. They faithfully share their research results, as fake results will seriously affect their reputations.

Meanwhile, we consider that users are semi-trusted as well. They may be masqueraded by adversaries. However, they should be unable to obtain the vul-nerability exploit reports by using the client, as those can only be decrypted by the private key of contract owners.

4   Design

To improve the practicality of BSB, we wish to generate an integrated con-tract blacklist whose contents are contributed by different blacklist providers. Shared research results will be standardized and authorized, while the vulnera-bility exploit reports will be priced and encrypted. The public key of contract owners will be recovered and used to encrypt the reports of their contracts to avoid the details being leaked. The reports will be traded to contract owners to gain profits for security researchers, which inspires them to periodically upload their research results to the platform. Based on contract blacklist, user warning service can avoid users making transactions with unsafe contracts, which moti-vate contract owners to patch their contracts in time. To achieve contract owner notify mechanism, BSB will confirm the EOAs of contract owners and push related vulnerable contract lists to them. The users can purchase the reports and decrypt them by the private key to obtain the details.

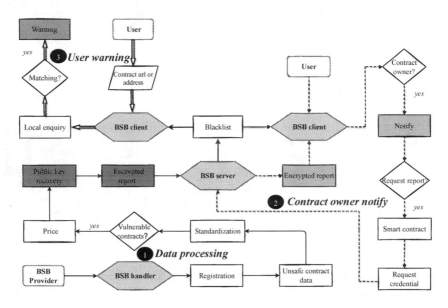

Fig. 2. Flowchart of our BSB platform: 1) the arrow ⟶ shows the routine of data processing initiated by blacklist provider; 2) the arrow --→ shows the process of contract owner notify and report request; 3) the arrow ⇒ shows the complete detection routine when there is a match in local enquiry.

4.1   Data Processing

The first step of BSB platform is to generate contract blacklist, which work-flow is shown as data processing phase of Fig. 2. To authorize and price shared data, we implemented registration function. Each blacklist provider shall provide its personal information to verify its identity as a security researcher of smart contract. The account information of verified provider will be recorded in authentication table of BSB server. Through BSB handler, blacklist providers upload their unsafe contract information, encrypted reports and their price to BSB server, which will be stored in data table with the account information.

To standardize different formats of data from different blacklist providers, we predefined the format of data table in BSB server: unique identity (UID), threat type, contract address, contract URL, contract type, contract owner, price, and GridFS ID of encrypted vulnerability reports. UID is to distinguish multi-vulnerabilities of one contract. The uploaded unsafe contract information include threat type, contract address, contract URL, contract type, and contract owner. Threat type describes the label of unsafe contract. Contract type is to describe whether it is proxy contract. The reports which contain vulnerability exploit details shall be encrypted and priced before uploading. To achieve contract owner notify mechanism, we define contract owner as the sender's EOA in external transaction which directly create contract or trigger an internal transaction to create contract. In data table, GridFS ID is utilized to locate encrypted vulnerability reports. With data table, a contract blacklist will be generated to support the functionalities of BSB client.

Algorithm 1. Ethereum Public Key Recover.

Input: CA: Vulnerable contract address; G: The generator of secp256k1;
Output: pk: The public key of contract owner;
1: $txhash \leftarrow$ request(CA);
2: $(r, s, v, chainID) \leftarrow$ request($txhash$);
3: $recovery =$ calculateSigRecovery(v ,$chainID$);
4: $prefix = recovery$ & 1 ? 03 : 02 ;
5: $R =$ Point.fromHex($prefix\|$ numTo32bStr(r));
6: $n = CURVE$, $h = HASH(M)$; // M is message
7: $u_1 = -h * r^{-1} \bmod n$;
8: $u_2 = s * r^{-1} \bmod n$;
9: $Q = u_1 * G + u_2 * R$;
10: $(x, y) = Q$;
11: $pk = 04\|x\|y$;

Unsafe contract information is public to all the users, while the reports of vulnerability exploit details are only available to contract owners. To prevent the details being leaked, BSB handler encrypts the vulnerability reports locally before sending to BSB server. ECC is utilized by Ethereum to achieve EOA generation and transaction verification. Each contract owner holds its private key. We recover the public key of contract owner to encrypt the report so that none can decrypt it except the owner of the private key.

Algorithm 1 illustrates the detailed procedure for Ethereum public key recovery. With the recovered public key and the report as the input, we utilize the ECIES encryption algorithm locally to calculate ciphertext public key, ciphertext, symmetric algorithm parameters, and MAC code. Those output will be stored in a file called encrypted report which will be uploaded to BSB server.

4.2   Contract Owner Notify

Figure 3 is a deep description to contract owner notify phase in Fig. 2. To start contract owner notify mechanism, BSB client shall verify their identities first. We integrate wallet function into BSB client so that users need to log into their wallets before operating. Based on the EOA, BSB client will determine whether it is a vulnerable contract owner, and if so, it will traverse contract blacklist and push a list of related vulnerable contract addresses to remind the user that there are vulnerabilities in their contracts. If they wish to obtain an exploit detail, a request transaction shall be made.

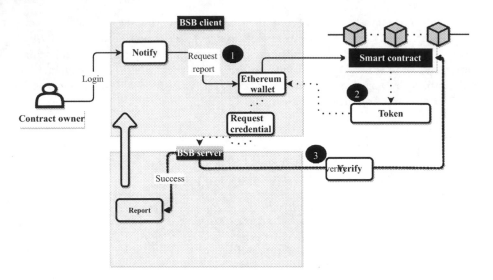

Fig. 3. Contract owner notify process.

We deployed a smart contract to response report request. Two external functions can be called: request function which is to store the UID of target report into contract storage and store ethers in contract balance, and transfer function which is to transfer ethers from contract balance to target EOA.

Request transaction is to transfer enough ethers to our contract to purchase target report. After its successful execution, a token will return to BSB client, which will be sent to BSB server as request credential. Through the credential, BSB server will determine which report the owner wants to purchase, and whether the owner pays enough ethers for it. If yes, BSB client can request to download the report. With the encrypted report and the private key held by contract owner as input, the ECIES decryption algorithm is utilized to produce the original plaintext report, which will be stored locally for the user to study.

After contract owner deploys a new contract to patch the vulnerability, it shall make a specific transaction to transfer ethers from our contract to the EOA of blacklist provider. After its successful execution, a token will be sent from BSB client to BSB server. With the token, BSB server will confirm that the vulnerability has been patched, and blacklist provider have obtained the profits. The proxy contract which is confirmed to be patched will be removed from contract blacklist, while the others will be kept.

4.3 User Warning

User warning service is to serve the users who want to make transactions with smart contracts. The workflow of user warning is shown in Fig. 2, the enquiry is to determine whether target contract is unsafe. BSB client supports both URL query and address query. Considering the growth of contract blacklist, to enhance the query performance, BSB client maintains an additional filter to efficiently prove the non-existence of contracts. When receiving an input from the user, BSB client firstly calculates the contract address, then the local filter is used to query if the address is in the blacklist. If miss, the contract address is definitely not existed in contract blacklist, BSB client will display a safe dialog to the user. If hit, the contract address may exist in contract blacklist, BSB client further query contract blacklist to determine whether the contract is unsafe. If hit, the contract is unsafe ,and a dialog with its threat type will be showed to warn the user not to make a transaction with target contract.

5   Implementation

We implemented three major components of BSB platform: BSB handler, BSB server, and BSB client. Next, we will describe their implementation in detail.

5.1   BSB Handler

BSB handler is a website implemented in Javascript, which consists of two functions: registration and data processing. Registration interface is provided to help blacklist providers register accounts. Before uploading research results, blacklist providers shall log in their accounts first to achieve the binding between uploaded data and their account information.

According to predefined formats of data table, BSB handler helps each blacklist provider standardize its data locally to support further database storage and blacklist generation. Blacklist providers input unsafe contract address or URL, threat type, and contract type in the interface. Infura API, ethjs-ens and ethjs-provider-http libraries are utilized to resolve a valid ENS name to a contract address, or look up a valid ENS name based on a contract address. Meanwhile, Infura API and JSON-RPC methods have been utilized to obtain contract creation transaction fields, which include the EOA of contract owner.

The report of contract vulnerability exploit detail shall be encrypted locally before sending to BSB server. With the fields of contract creation transaction, EthereumJS VM repository Monorepo has been utilized to return the public key of contract owner. Through eccrypto library, ECIES encryption algorithm has been achieved to encrypt vulnerability report with generated public key.

5.2   BSB Server

BSB server consists of three functions: data storage, blacklist generation, and report request processing. To facilitate contract blacklist generation and report request processing, BSB server provides a centralized storage. An authentication table is created to record the account information of verified blacklist providers. A data table is created to store all the data of unsafe contracts, including UID, threat type, contract address, contract URL, contract type, contract owner, price, and GridFS ID of encrypted vulnerability reports. For each entry, two extra

Boolean states are predefined. The purchase state is to support multi-download, while the patch state is to remove patched proxy contract from contract blacklist.

To against the latest threats, contract blacklist requires immediate generation once blacklist provider uploads a new version. To support the functionalities of BSB client, contract blacklist includes UID, provider name, provider EOA, threat type, contract URL, contract address, contract owner, and price.

After receiving the request credentials, BSB server will determine which report the owner wants to purchase, and whether the owner pays enough ethers for it. If enough, it will set the purchase state of target item as true, and return an OK tag to BSB client. After receiving report download request, BSB server checks if purchase state is true, and if so, it will send target report to BSB client. After receiving the transfer token, BSB server will set the patch state of target report as true. The proxy contract which is confirmed to be patched will be removed from contract blacklist, while the others will be kept.

We use Java to implement the functions of data storage, blacklist generation, and report request processing. Specifically, MongoDB is utilized to establish authentication table and data table, while GridFS is utilized to manage encrypted reports. In the future, we may decouple database from BSB server, which will be quite difficult using LFS. We utilize GridFS to manage encrypted reports as it is easier to extend or implement distributed processing.

5.3   BSB Client

To make BSB platform easy to use, we build our client application in the form of website. BSB client aims to warn users before they make transactions with unsafe contracts, and help contract owners obtain vulnerability reports to support them patching their contracts in time. BSB client includes three functions: blacklist query, report request, and Ethereum wallet.

We integrate an Ethereum wallet into BSB client so that each user has to log in an EOA before using the functionalities provided by BSB client. We choose to integrate MetaMask extension because it implements a light crypto wallet and a gateway to Blockchain apps [20]. MetaMask is a software cryptocurrency wallet used to interact with the Ethereum Blockchain. It allows users to access their Ethereum wallet through a browser extension or mobile app, which can then be used to interact with Dapps. MetaMask is commonly used, as its browser extension had over 30 million monthly active users in June 2022.

After logged in, BSB client automatically downloads the latest contract blacklist from BSB server. Similar to SB, BSB client also requires local storage for data to circumvent heavy communication overhead. A local copy of contract blacklist is loaded in the memory to speed query operations. Yet its implementation is rather straightforward. All data with respect to contract blacklist is fetched from BSB server updated by blacklist providers. Our implementation carries through the principle of accelerating the client-side operations as much as possible, achieving a rather low-level runtime memory cost in the meanwhile. We will discuss the local overhead of BSB client in Sect. 6.

Considering the growth of contract blacklist, to enhance the query performance, BSB client maintains an additional local filter to efficiently prove the non-existence of the objects. The filter helps BSB client providing both user warning service and contract owner notify mechanism. Following a similar approach adopted in PPSB service [7], we apply Bloom filter technique to quickly detect the vast majority of normal users or safe contracts, which consequentially decrease response time dramatically. After local contract blacklist is updated, BSB client creates a Bloom filter in the memory that contains all the addresses of unsafe contracts and vulnerable contract owners in blacklist.

According to the EOA that logged in, BSB client will firstly determine whether the user is a vulnerable contract owner. If hit, it will traverse contract blacklist and push a list of related vulnerable contract addresses to remind that the user can obtain the reports about exploit details. Report request function will be activated if contract owner wishes to obtain those reports. It will help create request transaction and send request credential to BSB server. After receiving OK tag from BSB server, report request function will request to download target report. After download, it will require the user to input its private key to decrypt target report through ECIES decryption algorithm. Similar to BSB handler, we implemented BSB client in Javascript and utilize Elliptic curve cryptography library eccrypto for decrypting the reports. The decrypted report will be downloaded locally for further study.

To confirm whether a contract is safe, the user only needs to input an address or URL in the corresponding query interface, blacklist query function will calculate contract address and perform quick query in Bloom filter. If miss, the contract is definitely not in contract blacklist, and BSB client will return a safe tag to the user. If hit, blacklist query function will query contract blacklist to determine whether the contract is unsafe. If so, it will show warnings to the user to avoid it making transactions with unsafe contracts.

In summary, Bloom filter helps to facilitate the testing of non-existing objects, thus achieving better query performance. On the other hand, due to the additional query of the Bloom filter, the query of contract owner and unsafe contract has a slightly higher cost. We will evaluate the cost of Bloom filter in Sect. 6.

To against the latest threats, local contract blacklist requires regular updates once BSB client starts. Note that every update comprises not only the add operation associated with recently incorporated unsafe contracts, but also the delete operation accountable for the removal of patched entries. It is necessary that obsolete information in local contract blacklist is removed timely in order to optimize client-side storage. Besides, we use the standard Bloom filter in our current prototype, which does not support the "delete" operation and requires a full update. This is sufficiently efficient as the size of Bloom filter is relatively small, say 64 kB for 40,000 entries with false positive rates less than 5%. We are aware that the partial update mode can also be made available by using some "dynamic" Bloom filter at the cost of additional overhead [9].

6   Evaluation

We evaluate the overhead imposed by BSB components on each party, and the end-to-end throughput and latency of the application using BSB platform. We deploy our BSB server on the AWS EC2 instance "t2.micro" (1 vCPU with 1 GB RAM) in Linux (Ubuntu server 20.04 LTS), which is deployed in Tokyo, Asia. We recorded the storage consume of uploaded data, and evaluated the memory overhead and the time consume of contract blacklist generation. We evaluated the usage of BSB handler and BSB client on the following three devices: (i) laptop: MacBook Pro equipped with 2.4 GHz Intel Core i5 CPU, 16 GiB RAM, (ii) laptop: with 2.7 GHz Intel i7, 16 GiB RAM, Windows, (iii) desktops: with 2.9 GHz Intel i7, 4 GB RAM, Linux. We evaluated the encryption time and upload time of BSB handler. As for BSB client, the overhead of user warning service and contract owner notify mechanism were evaluated seriously.

Two real datasets are used respectively in our instance: D1 - 104 contracts which contain vulnerabilities like reentrancy, access control, arithmetic, bad randomness, etc. D2 - 2880 contracts which are recognized as phishing, Ponzi, or honeypot. Among 104 vulnerability exploit reports for D1 dataset, 46 txt format reports are from 1 KB to 10 KB, 10 doc format reports are from 10 KB to 1 MB, and 48 pdf format reports are from 1 MB to 10 MB.

6.1   BSB Handler

BSB handler is responsible for registration and data processing. The time consume of registration is hard to evaluate as it is seriously affected by manual verification. After inputting unsafe contract address or URL, threat type, and contract type through the interface, BSB handler will automatically calculate contract owner and its public key. We recorded the time consume of 10 times of repeat work on three devices, and the average time consume is 935.67 ms. Then we evaluated the time consume to encrypt and upload reports of different sizes. To facilitate quantitative comparison, we choose 5 reports of representative size: 1 KB, 10 KB, 100 KB, 1MB, and 10 MB. On three devices, we tested 10 sets for each size of reports and took the average. As shown in Table 1, we can conclude that the size of Ciphertext report is over 3.5 times larger than Plaintext one. The EncryptTime is acceptable as it is less than 3 s for encrypting 10 MB size of report. Due to the network latency, the time consume of BSB handler to upload the data fluctuate a lot.

6.2   BSB Server

We firstly evaluated the storage overhead of authentication table, data table, and encrypted reports. Authentication table records the account information of the user, which are just 0.2 kB storage overhead for each entry of account information. Data table stores all the information of unsafe contracts, we uploaded 2,984 entries of unsafe contract, and the storage overhead of each entry is less than 0.4 kB. We also uploaded 104 encrypted reports to BSB sever. The encrypted

Table 1. Average encryption and upload overhead.

Plaintext Size (kB)	Ciphertext Size (kB)	EncryptTime (ms)	UploadTime (ms)
1	4	11.49	216.26
10	35	25.39	292.58
100	380	40.56	805.33
1,000	3,500	387.44	6,053.42
10,000	35,000	2,866.22	50,774.31

reports are small in number but great in storage overhead. The average storage overhead of each encrypted report is over 13,157 kB. Considering the great storage overhead of encrypted reports, we may decouple GridFS database from BSB server to extend or implement distributed processing in the future.

After data table has been updated by blacklist providers, BSB server automatically generates a contract blacklist to support the functionalities of BSB client. We further estimated the average time consume and storage overhead to create contract blacklist. To facilitate quantitative comparison, we generated simulation data to populate data table. As shown in Table 2, the storage overhead increases linearly as the entries increase. The time consume grows slowly with the increase of entries. When the number of entries increases to 40,000, the time consume skyrockets due to the memory swap of the node.

Table 2. Average time consume and storage overhead for creating contract blacklist.

Count	Time (ms)	Storage (kB)
2,500	104.12	985
5,000	163.94	1,971
10,000	245.62	3,942
20,000	430	7,884
40,000	1,581.67	15,770

6.3   BSB Client

Firstly, we calculate the overhead of BSB client to download contract blacklist and load it into the memory. We populate data table with simulation data to facilitate quantitative comparison. As shown in Table 3, the local storage and the memory occupy of contract blacklist increase linearly as the entries increase. The average time consume to download contract blacklist and load it into the memory increases as the entries increase, and are seriously affected by the network latency and the device configuration. In summary, the overall time consume of blacklist download and memory upload is less than 2 s, and the memory occupy is less than 20 MB, which will not seriously affect the daily usage of web browsers.

Table 3. Average overhead to download contract blacklist and load it into the memory.

Count	Storage (kB)	GetTime (ms)	LoadTime (ms)	MemOccupy (kB)
2,500	929.89	389.58	11.49	875.86
5,000	1863.68	455.67	15.56	1751.04
10,000	3727.36	564.53	23.93	3512.32
20,000	7454.72	1013.08	39.29	7024.64
40,000	14919.68	1687.71	73.88	14059.52

Compared with over 15 million of deployed smart contracts on Ethereum Mainnet [26], verified unsafe contracts are just a small amount. The owners of vulnerable contract are too little proportion in over 100 million EOAs [32]. Thus, we apply Bloom filter technique [21] to quickly filter the vast majority of normal users or safe contracts, which consequentially decrease response time dramatically. In our work, we set false positive rate less than 5%, as it is enough small for user's daily usage, and memory usage is minimal. We evaluated the overhead of Bloom filter generation. As shown in Fig. 4, even the number of blacklist entries are 40,000, it takes only 1 s and 64 kB to generate a Bloom filter which contains all the addresses of unsafe contracts and vulnerable contract owners.

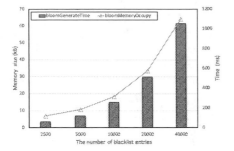

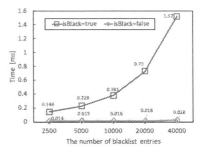

Fig. 4. Evaluation of memory usage and time consume for bloom filter.

Fig. 5. Average time consume of vulnerable contract owner authentication.

Next, we evaluated the efficiency of Bloom filter. It will be firstly used to determine whether the user is a vulnerable contract owner. The time consume of such authentication is shown in Fig. 5, we can see that if the EOA is not a contract owner, time consume is from 0.014 ms to 0.028 ms. After that, the user can only utilize user warning service. If the EOA may be a vulnerable contract owner, contract owner notify mechanism will take extra time to traverse contract blacklist and push a list of related vulnerable contract addresses to the user. However, such work will not affect the daily usage of the users, as it exhibits authentication speed at the millisecond level in the course of our experiments.

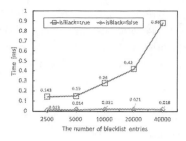

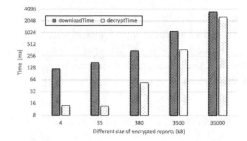

Fig. 6. Average time consume of unsafe contract judgement.

Fig. 7. Average time consume of report download and decrypt.

We further evaluated the time consume of BSB client to determine whether the smart contract is unsafe. Local enquiry to a target contract will be firstly executed in Bloom filter. If hit, contract blacklist will be further queried to determine whether the contract is unsafe. The time consume of local enquiry is shown in Fig. 6. We can see that if target contract is definitely not in the blacklist, time consume of local enquiry is from 0.013 ms to 0.021 ms. Blacklist query has to take extra time consume if target contract may be existed in the blacklist, as the blacklist has to be queried to determine whether the contract is unsafe. However, local enquiry to a target contract will not let users wait too long, as it takes less than 0.88 ms in average to query an unsafe contract from the blacklist with 40,000 entries.

Finally, we evaluated the overhead of contract owner notify mechanism. We evaluated the download time and the decryption time of the encrypted report, because the time consume of report request in the mechanism is affected by the network speed and the mining speed of Ethereum Blockchain. The request transaction may wait in the memory pool of miners if the user does not set high gas price. We utilized 5 encrypted reports of representative size which are calculated in §6.1 to facilitate quantitative comparison. The average time consume of BSB client to download and decrypt report is shown in Fig. 7. In theory, the increase of download time and decrypt time is proportional to the size of the encrypted report. In practical, they are affected by the network latency and the device configuration. After tests, the time consume of BSB client to decrypt the encrypted report is close to the time consume of BSB handler to encrypt the original report, as the ECIES algorithm uses a shared secret key for symmetric data encryption and decryption, which is derived from secp256k1 elliptic curve and ECDH key exchange scheme.

7   Discussion

Discussion on (Malicious) Blacklist Providers. As a safe browsing platform, the malicious party might leverage BSB as an attack vector against smart contracts/Dapps. They may insert a number of fake reports about safe contracts, so that they can obtain illegal profits from ransom or promotion. In the future, some review-based management mechanisms (e.g., reputation-based ranking) may be developed to help us distinguish those blacklist providers who are confirmed to upload fake reports. Nevertheless, how to make the review system more robust is an open question, and the progress in this field could be borrowed by our system in the future.

Privacy Concerns. When enabling SB services, users do have privacy concerns that their visited URLs (i.e., browsing history) could be collected and further abused, thus various researches have been studied to protect the users' privacy [7] [17]. In Blockchain platform, transaction data are exposed to all participants, which will expose the contract address as well. BSB does not have privacy concerns about browsing history yet, but with the development of privacy technologies in Blockchain systems, we shall consider privacy concerns in our works in the future.

Decentralized Implementation. Refer to SB, we designed a BSB server for centralized data storage and management. BSB server is used for blacklist generation, and responsible for report request processing. We plan to develop some review-based management mechanisms in BSB server to detect and prevent fake reports. In the future, we may change the centralized implementation of BSB server to decentralized one. Each blacklist provider shall deploy a server to safely manage and disseminate their research results, while vulnerable contract owners can make direct communication for bargaining the price. However, without data management right, review-based management mechanisms can hardly be implemented. We may achieve a mechanism for users to add or remove blacklist providers, so that they can choose the ones with good reputations.

Safe Browsing in Other Programming Blockchain Platforms. We propose a method to mitigate the problem that users suffer from untimely dissemination of contract vulnerability information. Our work establishes a safe browsing framework on Ethereum Platform to support user warning service and contract owner notify mechanism, but the same method can be applied to other popular Blockchain platforms which also support the running of smart contracts and have their unique features. There are a lot of security researches detecting contract vulnerabilities on those platforms, too.

8   Conclusion

In this paper, we propose a BSB platform which is able to disseminate smart contract detection results to smart contract users and vulnerable contract owners. Based on shared results, contract blacklist can be generated to provide user warning service, which is able to warn users before they make transactions with unsafe contracts. A contract owner notify mechanism is developed to push vulnerability exploit details to contract owners to help vulnerabilities being patched in time, and no detail leak will happened during its operation. Among the mechanism, the researchers will gain profits from shared data, which in turn inspire them keep uploading their research results. Our evaluation shows the efficiency of BSB platform. In the future, we would like to migrate to our safe browsing framework to other popular Blockchain platforms.

Acknowledgments. The authors would like to thank the anonymous reviewers of NSS 2022 for their helpful comments and this research was supported by the Fundamental Research Funds for the Central Universities (213110001), in part by Sanya Science and Education Innovation Park of Wuhan University of Technology under Grant (2020KF0059), in part by the National Key Research and Development Program of China (No. 2020YFB1805400, 2020YFB4500800), in part by the National Natural Science Foundation of China (No. 42071431, 62176194), in part by the Provincial Key Research and Development Program of Hubei, China (No. 2020BAB101), in part by the Major project of IoV (No. 2020AAA001), and in part by Project of Sanya Yazhou Bay Science and Technology City (No. SKJC 2022 PTDX 031).

References

1. Antonopoulos, A.M., Wood, G.: Mastering Ethereum: Building Smart Contracts and DApps. O'Reilly Media, Sebastopol (2018)
2. Bell, S., Komisarczuk, P.: An analysis of phishing blacklists: Google safe browsing, OpenPhish, and PhishTank. In: Proceedings of the Australasian Computer Science Week Multiconference, pp. 1–11 (2020)
3. Breidenbach, L., Daian, P., Tramèr, F., Juels, A.: Enter the hydra: towards principled bug bounties and Exploit-Resistant smart contracts. In: 27th USENIX Security Symposium (USENIX Security 18), pp. 1335–1352 (2018)
4. Chen, T., et al.: SODA: a generic online detection framework for smart contracts. In: Proceedings of the 27th Network and Distributed System Security Symposium. (NDSS) (2020)
5. Chen, W., Zheng, Z., Cui, J., Ngai, E., Zheng, P., Zhou, Y.: Detecting ponzi schemes on ethereum: towards healthier blockchain technology. In: Proceedings of the 2018 World Wide Web Conference, pp. 1409–1418 (2018)
6. Coghlan, J.: More than $1.6 billion exploited from defi so far in 2022. https://cointelegraph.com/news/more-than-1-6-billion-exploited-from-defi-so-far-in-2022 (2022)
7. Cui, H., Zhou, Y., Wang, C., Wang, X., Du, Y., Wang, Q.: PPSB: an open and flexible platform for privacy-preserving safe browsing. IEEE Trans. Dependable Secure Comput. **18**(4), 1762–1778 (2019)
8. Du, Y., Zhou, A., Wang, C.: Enhancing cryptocurrency blocklisting: a secure, trustless, and effective realization. In: 2022 IEEE 42nd International Conference on Distributed Computing Systems (ICDCS), pp. 1133–1143. IEEE (2022)
9. Fan, B., Andersen, D.G., Kaminsky, M., Mitzenmacher, M.D.: Cuckoo filter: practically better than bloom. In: Proceedings of the 10th ACM International on Conference on emerging Networking Experiments and Technologies, pp. 75–88 (2014)
10. Frank, J., Aschermann, C., Holz, T.: ETHBMC: a bounded model checker for smart contracts. In: 29th USENIX Security Symposium (USENIX Security 20), pp. 2757–2774 (2020)
11. Google: Google safe browsing (2022). https://safebrowsing.google.com/

12. He, J., Balunović, M., Ambroladze, N., Tsankov, P., Vechev, M.: Learning to fuzz from symbolic execution with application to smart contracts. In: Proceedings of the 2019 ACM SIGSAC Conference on Computer and Communications Security, pp. 531–548 (2019)

13. Jiang, B., Liu, Y., Chan, W.: ContractFuzzer: fuzzing smart contracts for vulnerability detection. In: 2018 33rd IEEE/ACM International Conference on Automated Software Engineering (ASE), pp. 259–269. IEEE (2018)

14. Jiao, J., Kan, S., Lin, S.W., Sanan, D., Liu, Y., Sun, J.: Semantic understanding of smart contracts: executable operational semantics of solidity. In: 2020 IEEE Symposium on Security and Privacy (SP), pp. 1695–1712. IEEE (2020)

15. Kalra, S., Goel, S., Dhawan, M., Sharma, S.: ZEUS: analyzing safety of smart contracts. In: Network and Distributed System Security Symposium (NDSS), pp. 1–12 (2018)

16. Karalabe: How to pwn fomo3d, a beginners guid (2018). https://www.reddit.com/r/ethereum/comments/916xni/how_to_pwn_fomo3d_a_beginners_guide/

17. Kogan, D., Corrigan-Gibbs, H.: Private blocklist lookups with checklist. In: 30th USENIX Security Symposium (USENIX Security 21), pp. 875–892 (2021)

18. Krupp, J., Rossow, C.: teEther: Gnawing at ethereum to automatically exploit smart contracts. In: 27th USENIX Security Symposium (USENIX Security 18), pp. 1317–1333 (2018)

19. Luu, L., Chu, D.H., Olickel, H., Saxena, P., Hobor, A.: Making smart contracts smarter. In: Proceedings of the 2016 ACM SIGSAC Conference on Computer and Communications Security, pp. 254–269 (2016)

20. MetaMask: The crypto wallet for Defi, Web3 Dapps and NFTs | metamask (2022). https://metamask.io/

21. Minier, T.: bloom-filters - v3.0.0 (2022). https://callidon.github.io/bloom-filters/

22. Nakov, S.: Practical cryptography for developers book (2022). https://cryptobook.nakov.com/

23. Nguyen, T.D., Pham, L.H., Sun, J.: sGUARD: towards fixing vulnerable smart contracts automatically. In: 2021 IEEE Symposium on Security and Privacy (SP), pp. 1215–1229. IEEE (2021)

24. Nikolić, I., Kolluri, A., Sergey, I., Saxena, P., Hobor, A.: Finding the greedy, prodigal, and suicidal contracts at scale. In: Proceedings of the 34th Annual Computer Security Applications Conference, pp. 653–663 (2018)

25. OpenZeppelin: Exploiting an erc777-token uniswap exchange (2019). https://github.com/OpenZeppelin/exploit-uniswap#exploit-details

26. Perez, D., Livshits, B.: Smart contract vulnerabilities: vulnerable does not imply exploited. In: 30th USENIX Security Symposium (USENIX Security 21), pp. 1325–1341 (2021)

27. Permenev, A., Dimitrov, D., Tsankov, P., Drachsler-Cohen, D., Vechev, M.: VerX: safety verification of smart contracts. In: 2020 IEEE Symposium on Security and Privacy (SP), pp. 1661–1677. IEEE (2020)

28. Rezai, A., Keshavarzi, P., Moravej, Z.: Secure scada communication by using a modified key management scheme. ISA Trans. **52**(4), 517–524 (2013)

29. Rodler, M., Li, W., Karame, G.O., Davi, L.: Sereum: protecting existing smart contracts against re-entrancy attacks. In: Network and Distributed System Security Symposium. (NDSS) (2019)

30. Rodler, M., Li, W., Karame, G.O., Davi, L.: EVMPatch: timely and automated patching of ethereum smart contracts. In: 30th USENIX Security Symposium (USENIX Security 21), pp. 1289–1306 (2021)

31. So, S., Lee, M., Park, J., Lee, H., Oh, H.: VERISMART: a highly precise safety verifier for ethereum smart contracts. In: 2020 IEEE Symposium on Security and Privacy (SP), pp. 1678–1694. IEEE (2020)
32. Studio, G.: Ethereum: number of active addresses (2022). https://studio.glassnode.com/metrics?a=ETH&m=addresses.ActiveCount
33. Su, L., et al.: Evil under the sun: understanding and discovering attacks on ethereum decentralized applications. In: 30th USENIX Security Symposium (USENIX Security 21), pp. 1307–1324 (2021)
34. Torres, C.F., Schütte, J., State, R.: Osiris: hunting for integer bugs in ethereum smart contracts. In: Proceedings of the 34th Annual Computer Security Applications Conference, pp. 664–676 (2018)
35. Torres, C.F., Steichen, M., et al.: The art of the scam: demystifying honeypots in ethereum smart contracts. In: 28th USENIX Security Symposium (USENIX Security 19), pp. 1591–1607 (2019)
36. Tsankov, P., Dan, A., Drachsler-Cohen, D., Gervais, A., Buenzli, F., Vechev, M.: Securify: practical security analysis of smart contracts. In: Proceedings of the 2018 ACM SIGSAC Conference on Computer and Communications Security, pp. 67–82 (2018)
37. Wang, D., Feng, H., Wu, S., Zhou, Y., Wu, L., Yuan, X.: Penny wise and pound foolish: quantifying the risk of unlimited approval of ECR20 tokens on ethereum. In: 25th International Symposium on Research in Attacks, Intrusions and Defenses (RAID 2022) (2022)
38. Wang, D., et al.: Towards understanding flash loan and its applications in Defi ecosystem (2020). arXiv preprint arXiv:2010.12252
39. Wood, G., et al.: Ethereum: a secure decentralised generalised transaction ledger. Ethereum Project Yellow Pap. **151**(2014), 1–32 (2014)
40. Wu, J., et al.: Who are the phishers? Phishing scam detection on ethereum via network embedding. IEEE Trans. Syst. Man Cybern. Syst. **PP**, 1–11 (2020)
41. Wu, S., et al.: DeFiRANGER: detecting price manipulation attacks on DeFi applications (2021). arXiv preprint arXiv:2104.15068
42. Wu, S., et al.: Time-travel investigation: toward building a scalable attack detection framework on ethereum. ACM Trans. Softw. Eng. Methodol. (TOSEM) **31**(3), 1–33 (2022)
43. Zhang, M., Zhang, X., Zhang, Y., Lin, Z.: TXSPECTOR: uncovering attacks in ethereum from transactions. In: 29th USENIX Security Symposium (USENIX Security 20), pp. 2775–2792 (2020)
44. Zhou, L., Qin, K., Cully, A., Livshits, B., Gervais, A.: On the just-in-time discovery of profit-generating transactions in DeFi protocols. In: 2021 IEEE Symposium on Security and Privacy (SP), pp. 919–936. IEEE (2021)

Blockchain-Powered Systems

Practical Anonymous Multi-hop Locks for Lightning Network Compatible Payment Channel Networks

Mengling Liu$^{(\boxtimes)}$ [iD] and Man Ho Au [iD]

The University of Hong Kong, Pokfulam, Hong Kong
mengling@connect.hku.hk

Abstract. Bitcoin, among other blockchain-based cryptocurrencies, has become increasingly popular. The expensive consensus process, however, severely limits the throughput of these systems. Allowing majority of the payment transactions to be settled off-chain, Payment channels (PC) have become a promising approach to address the scalability problem. Payment channel network (PCN) enables the payment between two users who do not have a direct PC through multi-hop payment across several payment channels. Lightning Network (LN), which handles around one trillion transactions per day, is the most well-known PCN deployed in practice. Improving the security and privacy of payment via PCN is an active research area. Recently, Malavolta et al. formalised a new cryptographic primitive known as anonymous multi-hop locks (AMHL) and demonstrated how it can be used to build a secure and privacy-preserving PCN. In this paper, we give a new construction of AMHL with the following features: (1) LN compatible, i.e., it can be deployed into LN seamlessly; (2) secure in the universal composable framework; (3) highly efficient. Using our AMHL, a multi-hop payment with 5 users requires only 1458 bytes of off-chain communication. It compares favorably to state-of-the-art LN-compatible solutions, e.g., Fulgor and AMHL based on ECDSA, which requires 5 MB and 1.8 MB respectively. Furthermore, our solution is round-efficient. Specifically, the sender only needs to send one message to each node along the payment route.

Keywords: Bitcoin · Lightning network · Privacy · Security · Efficiency

1 Introduction

Bitcoin has established itself as an alternative global payment system. Instead of managing transactions in a ledger controlled by a (trusted) centralized institute, Bitcoin records transactions in the Bitcoin blockchain, a public ledger maintained by a set of mutually distrusted nodes. These nodes, often known as miners, ensure the ledger's consistency through a robust consensus process based on proof-of-work. While the process makes Bitcoin decentralised and permissionless, this rather expensive consensus process limits the Bitcoin transaction rate to at most

© The Author(s), under exclusive license to Springer Nature Switzerland AG 2022
X. Yuan et al. (Eds.): NSS 2022, LNCS 13787, pp. 547–560, 2022.
https://doi.org/10.1007/978-3-031-23020-2_31

ten transactions per second. In contrast, mainstream global payment systems such as Visa can confirm up to 56000 transactions per second.

While alternative cryptocurrencies aiming to address scalability issues have been proposed, Bitcoin still dominates the market in terms of number of users and market capitalisation. As such, various proposals from the academia and the industry have been developed to overcome Bitcoin's scalability issue [5,18]. The Bitcoin community also regard this as an important concern.

A promising approach to address the scalability problem is to move the majority of transactions off-chain. The payment channel is the leading proposal of this approach. Specifically, two users, say, Alice and Bob, who need to transact regularly publish only two on-chain transactions. The first one, namely, open channel, deposit bitcoins into a multi-signature address controlled by Alice and Bob. The second one, namely, close channel, sends bitcoins to Alice and Bob according to their final balances in the channel. As Alice and Bob can perform multiple payments by updating the channel balance locally without broadcasting additional transactions into Bitcoin Network, the demand for recording transactions on the Blockchain can be greatly reduced.

Payment Channel Network (PCN), which combines payment across several payment channels, supports payment between users who have no direct payment channel with each other. Among different proposals of fully-fledged PCN for Bitcoin, the most prominent PCN is Lightning Network (LN) [17] which handles about one trillion transactions per day. It has attracted numerous research on PCNs for Bitcoin [11–14,18,21,24,25]. Current LN compatible PCN proposals are, however, inefficient or fall short of providing adequate and rigorous privacy and security gaurantee.

Similar to a typical payment channel, LN employs Hash Time Lock Contract (HTLC) to ensure atomicity, i.e., either all parties along the payment route receive their agreed share of coins or none of them receive anything. To ensure this, a multi-hop payment requires that a common hash value is included in transactions along the payment route. Using the same hash value in all HTLC along the payment route, however, causes privacy concern. In particular, an observer can link all intermediate payments into one specific payment if they use the same hash value in their HTLCs. Furthermore, it also leads to security issues. Specifically, [13] proposed wormhole attack, which allows two colluding users along the payment route to skip nodes between them and steal transaction fees of the skipped intermediaries nodes. Existing solutions [1,2,10,15,16,19,22] of PCN does not adequately considers these security and privacy issues.

Malavolta et al. [12] initiated the rigorous treatment on the privacy of PCN by presenting the first formal definition in the universal composability framework [4]. They also present Fulgor, a secure solution (in the random oracle model) based on HTLC. Subsequently, Malavolta et al. [13] presented wormhole attack, introduced a cryptographic primitive called anonymous multi-hop lock (AMHL), gave a UC definition of secure AMHL, and showed that AMHL suffices in the construction of PCN. They present two provably secure constructions of AMHL. The first one is based on homomorphic one-way functions, and the second one is based on script-less locking mechanism (ECDSA-based AMHL). Since Bitcoin's scripting language does not support homomorphic one-way function evaluations, the former construction is not compatible with LN. In this paper, therefore, when we refer to the AMHL construction of [13], we are referring to the ECDSA-based AMHL (referred to as MMSKM19 hereafter). We would like to remark that while Fulgor is not proven secure explicitly against wormhole attack, [13] implied that fulgor is secure against such an attack. In terms of practicality, the sender needs to transmit approximately 5MB of data to each intermediary node in Fulgor. For MMSKM19, the communication cost is 1.8 MB at the cost of an increased number of communication rounds (4 rounds are needed between each pair of neighbour nodes).

Privacy issues are also investigated in hub-based proposals such as BOLT [6], Tumblebit [7], and A2L [23]. However, all of them focus on a single-hop payment channel (sender-hub, hub-receiver). Extension of these hub-based solutions to support multi-hop payment remains an open issue.

1.1 Our Contributions

In this paper, we present a practical construction of AMHL. The practicality of our construction can be illustrated in the following aspects.

Compatibility. We give a construction that is fully compatible with LN. Specifically, the on-chain portion of our construction relies only on time-lock and evaluation of hash functions and can thus be used in major cryptocurrencies such as Bitcoin and is thus fully compatible with LN.

Security. We proved that our AMHL construction is UC-secure. In particular, our security analysis does not rely on the random oracle model.

Performance. Our construction compares favourably to the state-of-the-art solutions, namely, Fulgor and MMSKM19. For a payment route with 5 nodes, the communication cost of our solution is 1458 bytes. The corresponding numbers are 5MB and 1.8MB respectively for Fulgor and MMSKM19. In terms of round complexity, our solution and Fulgor require the sender to send a single message to each node along the payment route, while MMSKM19 requires each node to conduct 4 communication rounds with its neighbours.

2 Preliminaries

2.1 Anonymous Multi-hop Lock (AMHL)

We recall the definition of AMHL from [13]. Here U_i denotes the i-th participant of the multi-hop payment, with U_0 being the sender, and U_n being the receiver.

Definition 1 (AMHL). *An AMHL is a tuple of five algorithms/protocols, namely, (KGen, Setup, Lock, Rel, Vf), described as follows.*

- $\{(sk_i, pk), (sk_j, pk)\} \leftarrow (KGen_{U_i}(1^\lambda), KGen_{U_j}(1^\lambda))$: *On input security parameter 1^λ, the key generation protocol returns a shared public key and a secret key sk_i (sk_j, respectively) to U_i and U_j. This protocol is cryptocurrency and payment channel specific. For example, it involves the creation of a multi-sig address for payment channel in Bitcoin.*

– $\{s_0^I, ..., (s_n^I, k_n)\} \leftarrow (Setup_{U_0}(1^\lambda, U_1, ..., U_n), Setup_{U_1}(1^\lambda), ..., Setup_{U_n}(1^\lambda))$: On input a vector of identities $(U_1, ..., U_n)$ and the security parameter 1^λ, the setup protocol returns s_i^I to user U_i where $i \in [0, n]$ and returns a additionally key k_n to U_n. This protocol allows the sender, U_0, to create payment route with U_n being the receiver. The states $s_0^I, ..., s_n^I$ allows the users along the payment route to setup the locks, and k_n allows the receiver to open the last lock.

– $\{(\ell_{i+1}, s_i^R), (\ell_{i+1}, s_{i+1}^L)\} \leftarrow (Lock_{U_i}(s_i^I, sk_i, pk), Lock_{U_{i+1}}(s_{i+1}^I, sk_{i+1}, pk))$: the locking protocol allows U_i (with state s_i^I) and U_{i+1} (with state s_{i+1}^I) to setup a lock. The lock protocol returns a lock, denoted as ℓ_{i+1}, a right state s_i^R to U_i, and a left state s_i^L to U_{i+1}.

– $\{0, 1\} \leftarrow Vf(\ell, k)$: On input a lock ℓ, and a key k, this algorithm outputs a bit $b \in \{0, 1\}$. If $Vf(\ell, j) = 1$, we say k is an opening key of lock ℓ.

– $k' \leftarrow Rel(k, (s_i^I, s_i^R, s_i^L))$: On input an opening key k and a triple of states (s_i^I, s_i^R, s_i^L), the release algorithm returns a new key k'. Looking ahead, this algorithm is used by user i to obtain an opening key for its left lock given the opening key of its right lock. That is, if k is an opening key of the lock between user U_i and U_{i+1} (i.e., lock ℓ_{i+1}), this algorithm outputs k' which is an opening key of the lock between s and U_i (i.e., lock ℓ_i).

AMHL Implies PCN. We now explain how these algorithms are used to support multi-hop payment for any cryptocurrency supporting conditional payment where condition can be represented as locks and opening keys.

1. First, each pair of participants along the route create the link with each other by invoking KGen algorithm that simulates the opening of payment channels and the creating of an address controlled by both parties in the channel.
2. The sender invokes the Setup protocol and inputs the users' identities along the payment route he has picked. Upon completion of this protocol, each user along the route obtains its secret state, and the receiver (i.e., U_n) additionally receives a key k_n.
3. In the locking phase, each pair of users along the route cooperate to generate a lock ℓ. The successful lock generation represents that U_i has committed that if U_{i+1} can "open" the lock, U_i will execute the specific and application-dependent action (e.g., transfer bitcoins to U_{i+1}). We say U_{i+1} successfully opens lock ℓ_i if it reveals key k_i such that $Vf(\ell_i, k_i)$ returns 1.
4. After finishing the locking phase, the receiver U_n can immediately release its left lock (i.e., ℓ_n) with the key k_n. U_{n-1} can then make use of k_n and the Rel algorithm to obtain a key for ℓ_{n-1}. In other words, each intermediary can recover a valid key for its left lock with the valid key of its right lock by calling the Rel algorithm.

2.2   Non-interactive Zero-Knowledge

A non-interactive zero-knowledge proof system (NIZKs) [3] allows a prover to convince a verifier that some statement is true without revealing any additional information. We consider the common reference string (CRS) model and assume all parties have access to the same string (generated by a trusted party according to some distribution). Specifically, an NIZKs in the CRS model consists of three efficient algorithms, namely, nizk.$\mathcal{G}$, nizk.$\mathcal{P}$, nizk.$\mathcal{V}$. Common reference string crs is generated by algorithm nizk.$\mathcal{G}(\lambda)$. Algorithm $\pi \leftarrow$ nizk.$\mathcal{P}(\text{crs}, w, x)$ is used by the prover to generate the proof and algorithm $\{0, 1\} \leftarrow$ nizk.$\mathcal{V}(\text{crs}, x, \pi)$ is used by the verifier to verify the proof, where x and w denotes the statement and its witness respectively.

Efficient (in terms of proof size and verification time) construction of UC-secure NIZK exists (in the common reference string model). We use the basic lifting technique of C∅C∅ framework [8] on ZK-SNARKs to instantiate the UC-secure NIZK[1]. The formal definition can be found in [8].

3 Security Model

Security of AMHL is formally defined by [13] in the universal composability framework [4]. Informally speaking, security is established when the behavior of all parties in the real-world is indistinguishable to an ideal world where all computational are conducted through a trusted party (aka ideal functionality). The following definition formally capture this requirement.

Attacker Model. We model the users along the payment route as Turing machines that interact with ideal functionality $\mathcal{F}$ through secure and authenticated channels. We model the adversary $\mathcal{A}$ as a PPT machine that is given access to the interface $corrupt(\cdot)$ which takes the user identifier U as the input and responds with the secret state of U. After being corrupted, the user U's incoming and outgoing communications are routed through $\mathcal{A}$. We consider the static corruption model that requires the adversary to invoke $corrupt(\cdot)$ and input user identifiers ahead of time.

Communication Model. We assume participants can communicate securely in a synchronous network. We regard privacy leak due to observation of the communication to be out of scope of this work.

Universal Composability. We use $EXEC_{\Pi,\mathcal{A},\mathcal{E}}$ to denote the ensemble of the outputs of environment $\mathcal{E}$ when interacting with the attacker $\mathcal{A}$ and honest users running protocol Π.

---

[1] We only require the NIZK to be weak UC-secure. A weak UC-secure NIZK allows an adversary to maul an existing proof to a new proof for the same statement. Looking ahead, it suffices for our construction since we merely require witness to be extracted in the UC setting. Thus we use the basic lifting technique of [8] which only achieve this weak version of UC security.

Definition 2 (Universal Composability). *A protocol Π UC-realizes an ideal functionality $\mathcal{F}$ if for any PPT adversary $\mathcal{A}$ there exists a simulator $\mathcal{S}$ such that for any environment $\mathcal{E}$ the ensembles $EXEC_{\Pi,\mathcal{A},\mathcal{E}}$ and $EXEC_{\mathcal{F},\mathcal{S},\mathcal{E}}$ are computationally indistinguishable.*

Ideal Functionality. We recall the ideal functionality for the AMHLs here. Instead of modelling the overall characterization of PCNs, ideal functionality $\mathcal{F}_{amhl}$ only model the functionality of locks. Specifically, each pair of users needs to create a link with each other, which is similar to the opening of the channel in PCNs. We recall notations of $\mathcal{F}_{amhl}$ first. U and L denote sets of users and locks, respectively, which are used to keep track of users and locks. The entry $(lid_i, U_i, U_{i+1}, f, lid_{i+1})$ will be stored where lid is the unique lock identifier along the route in L, U_i and U_{i+1} are users linked by the lock lid. The status of locks is represented by the flag $\in \{Init, Lock, Rel\}$. The next lock identifier lid_{i+1} is also in the entry. The function $(getStatus(\cdot))$ is used to extract lock information when taking the lock identifier as the input, and $updateStatus(\cdot, \cdot)$ function is used to change the status of the lock. The definition of the ideal functionality is given as follows.

Ideal Functionality $\mathcal{F}_{amhl}$

- **KeyGen**: Upon receiving $(sid, U_j, \{L, R\})$ from U_i, it receives (sid, b) from U_j by sending $(sid, U_i, \{L, R\})$ to U_j. If $b = \bot$, it sends $\bot$ to U_i and then abort the process.
- **Setup**: Upon receiving $(sid, U_0, ..., U_n)$ from U_0,
  - if $\forall i \in [0, n-1] : (U_i, U_{i+1}) \notin \mathcal{U}$, it will abort the process.
  - It samples $lid_i \leftarrow \{0, 1\}^{\lambda}$ for $\forall i \in [0, n-1]$.
  - It inserts $(lid_0, U_0, U_1, Init, lid_1)$ into $\mathcal{L}$ and sends the tuple $(sid, \bot, lid_0, \bot, U_1, Init)$ to U_0.
  - It inserts $(lid_{n-1}, U_{n-1}, U_n, Init, \bot)$ into $\mathcal{L}$ and sends the tuple $(sid, lid_{n-1}, \bot, U_{n-1}, \bot, Init)$ to U_n. The information is also sent to U_0.
  - For all $i \in [0, n-1]$, it inserts $(lid_i, U_i, U_{i+1}, Init, lid_{i+1})$ into $\mathcal{L}$ and sends the tuple $(sid, lid_{i-1}, lid_i, U_{i-1}, U_{i+1}, Init)$ to U_i. The information is also sent to U_0.
- **Lock**: Upon receiving (sid, lid) from U_i,
  - if $getStatus(lid) \neq Init$ or $getLeft(lid) \neq Ui$, it will abort the process.
  - It receives (sid, b) from $getRight(lid)$ by sending the tuple $(sid, lid, Lock)$ to $getRight(lid)$.
  - If $b = \bot$, it sends $\bot$ to U_i and then abort the process.
  - It calls updateStatus(lid, Lock) to change the status of the lock and sends the tuple $(sid, lid, Lock)$ to U_i.
- **Release**: Upon receiving (sid, lid) from U_i,
  - $getStatus(lid) \neq Lock$, abort.

- if $getRight(lid) \neq U_i$ or $getStatus(getNextLock(lid)) \neq Rel$ and $getNextLock(lid) \neq \perp$ then sends $(sid, lid, \texttt{ForceUnlock})$ to U_0. If U_0 replies 0 or does not reply, abort. Else, continue. Note that an honest U_0 will always reply 0 for $(\cdot, \cdot, \texttt{ForceUnlock})$.
- It calls $updateStatus(lid, Rel)$ to change the status of the lock and sends the tuple (sid, lid, Rel) to $getLeft(lid)$.
- **GetStatus**: Upon receiving (sid, lid) from U_i, it returns $(sid, lid, getStatus(lid))$ to U_i.

Each pair of users along the route can use the KeyGen algorithm to create the link with each other. The Setup interface allows user U_0 (i.e., sender) to set up a path starting from U_0 along the route. The Lock interface provides a user with a way to promise a lock with its right neighbor. The Release algorithm provides the user with an interface to release the lock with its left neighbor if the user is either the receiver or its right lock has been released before. Finally, the GetStatus interface allows one to extract the current information of the lock.

Discussion. As discussed in [13], AMHL give a useful abstraction for the construction of PCN. We briefly discuss the intuitive requirements of an AMHL, including correctness, atomicity, consistency and relationship anonymity, and how the above ideal functionality captures these requirements.

- **Correctness** the AMHL is correct if the verification algorithm Vf returns 1 for an honestly generated lock and key pair.
- **Atomicity** An AMHL is atomic if each participant of the multi-hop payment can release their left lock when their right lock has been released. This is guaranteed by the $\mathcal{F}_{amhl}$ as (1) the locks in the payment path and their status are tracked by $\mathcal{F}_{amhl}$. (2) the releasing operation in $\mathcal{F}_{amhl}$ allows the user to release a lock when the follow-up lock has been released or the user is the receiver.
- **Consistency** Consistency means that no adversary in the payment path can release its left lock before his right lock being released. This captures wormhole attack when colluding participants can bypass some intermediaries and steal their transaction fees. The release interface of $\mathcal{F}_{amhl}$ guaranteed this: one participant can release the key of his left lock only if he is the receiver or his right lock has been unlocked. The adversary cannot skip any intermediate nodes in the path in this situation, so the wormhole attack is impossible.
- **Relationship Anonymity** Relationship Anonymity means that except the sender and the receiver, all participants can only know the left and right neighbors along the payment route. $\mathcal{F}_{amhl}$ captures this property by sampling lock identifiers independently and preventing intermediaries from knowing additional lock identifiers except for their left and right lock.

– **On Malicious Sender** Our definition of ideal functionality explicitly gives
the sender the power to release a lock that an intermediary node should
not be able to open. Roughly speaking, atomicity is still guaranteed even
if the sender is malicious. However, consistency and relationship anonymity
does not hold when the sender is dishonest. Note that since the keys for all
locks are generated by the sender, a malicious sender can always help an
intermediary node to open a lock before his/her right lock has been released.
One could argue that a rationale sender will not do this, since due to atomicity,
when the right lock in the middle is released, the left neighbor can release its
lock which eventually will charge back to the sender. Nonetheless, we would
like to allow the sender to be malicious in the security analysis and thus
need to explicitly give this power to U_0 in the ideal functionality. This is the
main difference between our model and the model in [13]. Consequently, their
analysis assumes the sender is honest.

We further note that in the ideal functionality, setup is invoked by the sender
and thus the sender knows the route. The implication of the modelling choice
is that the sender always know the payment path, which, as stated in [13], is
necessary.

4   Construction

Let $\lambda = (\lambda_1, \lambda_2)$ with $\lambda_2 \leq \lambda_1$ be a security parameter[2]. Let $H : \{0,1\}^* \rightarrow \{0,1\}^{\lambda_1}$ be a cryptographic hash function[3]. Let $G : \{0,1\}^{\lambda_2} \rightarrow \{0,1\}^{\lambda_1}$ be a
pseudorandom generator.

Let $\mathsf{nizk}.\mathcal{G}, \mathsf{nizk}.\mathcal{P}, \mathsf{nizk}.\mathcal{V}$ be an NIZK proof system for binary relation R_{crs} :
$(\{0,1\}^{\lambda_1}, \{0,1\}^{\lambda_1}, \{0,1\}^{\lambda_2}) \times \{0,1\}^{\lambda_1} \rightarrow \{0,1\}$ such that $R_{\mathsf{crs}}((x_1, x_2, x_3), w) = 1$
if and only if $x_2 = H(w)$ and $x_1 = H(w \oplus G(x_3))$. Here, we assume $crs = \mathsf{nizk}.\mathcal{G}$
is computed by a trusted party.

In the setup phase, U_0 is in charge of generating indistinguishable locks along
the route and sending the specific lock and the corresponding partial key to each
intermediate U_i except that only U_n will know the entire key. Besides, to prove
the validity of the values sent to each node, the sender also should provide zero-
knowledge proof. If the proof is not valid, any node along the route will abort
the protocol. During the locking phase, the adjacent nodes will establish the
lock together. Once the last lock has been generated successfully, U_n can open
it immediately, while each intermediate node can open its left lock only when
receiving the key of its right lock. The setup protocol is shown in Fig. 1. The
lock protocol, release and verification algorithm are shown in Fig. 2.

Note that KeyGen represent the opening of the payment channel (which is
payment channel dependent) and is thus omitted.

---

[2] We recommend $\lambda_1 = 256$ and $\lambda_2 = 168$ for 128-bit security.

[3] In our implementation, we use SHA256. In the security analysis, we require that H
is collision-resistant.

$\underline{Setup_{U_i}(1^\lambda)}$ $\qquad\qquad$ $\underline{Setup_{U_0}(U_1, ..., U_n)}$ $\qquad\qquad$ $\underline{Setup_{U_n}(1^\lambda)}$

$$s_n \leftarrow \{1,0\}^{\lambda_2}$$
$$k_n = G(s_n)$$
$$\ell_n = H(k_n)$$
$$\forall i \in [n-1, 1] : s_i \leftarrow \{1,0\}^{\lambda_2}$$
$$k_i = k_{i+1} \oplus G(s_i)$$
$$\ell_i = H(k_i)$$

compute the statement $x_i = (\ell_i, \ell_{i+1}, s_i, \cdot)$ and

the witness $w_i = (k_{i+1}, \cdot)$ s.t $(x_i, w_i) \in R_{crs}$

$$\pi_i \leftarrow \mathsf{nizk}.\mathcal{P}(\mathsf{crs}, x_i, w_i)$$

$\xleftarrow{\quad x_i, \pi_i \quad}$ $\qquad$ $\xrightarrow{\quad \ell_n, s_n \quad}$

$b \leftarrow \mathsf{nizk}.\mathcal{V}(\mathsf{crs}, x_i, \pi_i)$
if $b = 0$ then abort
return $(\ell_i, \ell_{i+1}, s_i)$ $\qquad\qquad$ return $(0, \ell_1, 0)$ $\qquad\qquad$ return $((\ell_n, 0, 0), s_n)$

Fig. 1. The setup protocol between the sender and other participants.

$\underline{Lock_{U_i}(s_i^I, sk_i, pk)}$ $\qquad\qquad\qquad\qquad\qquad$ $\underline{Lock_{U_{i+1}}(s_{i+1}^I, sk_{i+1}, pk)}$
parse s_i^I as $(\ell_i, \ell_{i+1}, s_i)$ $\qquad\qquad\qquad\qquad\qquad$ parse s_{i+1}^I as $(\ell'_{i+1}, \ell_{i+2}, s_{i+1})$

$\xrightarrow{\quad \ell_{i+1} \quad}$

If $\ell_{i+1} \neq \ell'_{i+1}$ then abort

return $(\ell_{i+1}, \bot)$ $\qquad\qquad\qquad\qquad\qquad\qquad$ return $((\ell'_{i+1}, \bot)$

$\underline{Rel(k, (s^I, s^R, s^L))}$
parse s_i^I as (ℓ, ℓ', s)
return $k \oplus G(s)$

$\underline{Vf(\ell, k)}$
return 1 if $H(k) = \ell$ and 0 otherwise

Fig. 2. The lock protocol is executed between U_i and U_{i+1} for $i = 0$ to n. The rel protocol is executed by participant U_i when it receive the key from U_{i+1}. Tthe verification algorithm is used to check the validity of the key.

Informal Discussion on the Security of Our Construction. In the setup phase, the AMHL is initialized by sender U_0. U_0 samples n random values $(s_1, s_2, \ldots, s_n)$ to generates n locks. Note that the lock is simply a hash lock. That is, lock ℓ_i can be opened by key k_i such that $\ell_i = H(k_i)$. These keys are generated iteratively such that $k_i = k_{i+1} \oplus G(s_i)$. Due to the pseudorandom property of G, and that each s_i are generated uniformly at random, the keys are computationally indistinguishable from uniformly random. Thus, our construction guarantees relationship anonymity.

The zero-knowledge proof π_i is used to assure intermediary node U_i that if ℓ_{i+1} is released, i.e., someone reveal k_{i+1} such that $\ell_{i+1} = H(k_{i+1})$, U_i will be able to compute k_i (by $k_i = k_{i+1} \oplus G(s_i)$) s.t. $\ell_i = H(k_i)$. In other words, U_i will be able to release lock ℓ_i (i.e., the left lock) if someone release lock ℓ_{i+1} (i.e., the right lock). Specifically, π_i guarantees that the provers knows[4] a certain value k_{i+1} such that:

$$\ell_{i+1} = H(k_{i+1}) \wedge \ell_i = H(k_{i+1} \oplus G(s_i)).$$

In other words, the zero-knowledge proof is crucial in ensuring atomicity.

Security Analysis. Theorem 1 states the security of our construction. Its proof will be available in the full version of this paper.

Theorem 1 (UC-Security). *Our construction UC-realizes the ideal functionality $\mathcal{F}_{amhl}$ assuming H is collision-resistant, G is pseudorandom, (nizk.$\mathcal{G}$, nizk.$\mathcal{P}$, nizk.$\mathcal{V}$) is a weak UC-secure NIZK proof system.*

Choice of Security Parameters. Base on the security proof, H is required to be collision-resistant. Due to the birthday paradox, finding a collision in H takes approximately $O(2^{\lambda_1/2})$ time. For 128-bit security, we thus recommend setting λ_1 to be 256. For G, we require that its output is computationally indistinguishable to a uniform λ_1-bit string. Assume that a polynomial-time attacker sees 2^{40} outputs of G (each of which uses an uniformly independent seed of length λ_2), and we require that each of them to be indistinguishable from a λ_1-bit uniform strings, we recommend setting λ_2 to be 168 for 128-bit security.

5   Performance Evaluation

We instantiated hash function H with SHA-256 that is compatible with Bitcoin and the LN[5]. We use the basic lifting in C∅C∅ framework [8] to instantiate our weak UC-secure NIZK from RSA-OAEP encryption with 2048-bit modulus,

---

[4] Looking ahead, existence of such k_{i+1} is not sufficient. We must ensure that the simulator is able to extract the witness. This, in combination with the collision-resistance property of H, ensures U_i that if the right lock is released, he/she will be able to release its left lock.

[5] For simplicity, the off-chain pseodrandom generator G is also instantiated using SHA-256.

ECDSA digital signatures and zk-SNARKs as the underlying NIZK. We conducted our experiments on a Tencent cloud service with an Intel(R) Xeon(R) Gold 6133 CPU@2.50 GHz, and 8 GB RAM, running OS Ubuntu 20.04 LTS (Focal Fossa). Note that as for the computational cost, we only focus on the generation and verification of zero-knowledge proof, the most expensive part of the protocol. The comparison of the computation, and communication overhead is shown in Table 1.

In terms of the communication overhead, each zero-knowledge proof size is 383 bytes. Since we need three zero-knowledge proofs (recall that zero-knowledge proofs are needed for each intermediary node except the sender and receiver) for the payment with 5 users, the total size of the zero-knowledge proofs is 1149 bytes. Besides, the sender needs to transmit the locks and their opening keys to each user. Except for the receiver, each intermediary node receives two locks while the receiver only receives one lock. Since the size per lock is 32 bytes, the total communication cost is 224 bytes. Each node also receives one secret value which is 21 bytes in size. The total transmission cost of secret values is 84 bytes. Thus, the sender needs to transmit 1458 bytes. As for the computation overhead, even though the proof generation time is non-negligible, the sender is in charge of generating the proof which can be done in parallel to decrease the time significantly.

Remarks. We have a few remarks regarding the comparison, practicality and security analysis.

- The comparison condition favours Fulgor: our parameters are chosen with 128-bit security while Fuglor uses a security parameter of 80-bit security for their zero-knowledge proof system.
- Since the zero-knowledge proof is independent of the identity of the nodes along the payment path, the sender can pre-compute these proofs in advance before knowing the payment path in our scheme. This further improves the practicality.
- While our security proof does not make explicit use of the random oracle (RO), our instantiation requires RO. Specifically, our pseudorandom function G is instantiated using SHA-256 (whose pseudorandomness is trivial assuming RO), and the security of RSA-OAEP and ECDSA also relies on the random oracle model.

Table 1. Comparison table of the computation, and communication overhead for a 4-hop payment between Fulgor [12], MMSKM19 [13], and our construction where "B" presents byte, "ms" presents millisecond, and "s" presents second.

	Size	Rounds	ZKGen.time	ZKVer.time
Fulgor	5 MB	1 per hop	684 ms	546 ms
MMSKM19	1.8 MB	4 per hop	141 ms	76 ms
Our solution	1458 B	1 per hop	33 s	16 ms

6   Conclusion

We construct an efficient version of LN-compatible AMHL, and prove that our construction is UC-secure assuming the hash function is collision-resistant, the zero-knowledge proof system is weak UC-secure, and the existence of an efficient pseudorandom generator. We instantiate the LN-compatible AMHL based on the efficient weak-UC secure zero-knowledge proof system from CØCØ framework [8] and SHA256. Furthermore, our construction can be deployed directly to LN. Performance evaluation illustrates that the our construction is practical: for a payment with 4 hops, the total communication cost is merely 1458 bytes.

References

1. Androulaki, E., Karame, G.O., Roeschlin, M., Scherer, T., Capkun, S.: Evaluating user privacy in bitcoin. In: Sadeghi, A.-R. (ed.) FC 2013. LNCS, vol. 7859, pp. 34–51. Springer, Heidelberg (2013). https://doi.org/10.1007/978-3-642-39884-1_4
2. Barber, S., Boyen, X., Shi, E., Uzun, E.: Bitter to better—how to make bitcoin a better currency. In: Keromytis, A.D. (ed.) FC 2012. LNCS, vol. 7397, pp. 399–414. Springer, Heidelberg (2012). https://doi.org/10.1007/978-3-642-32946-3_29
3. Blum, M., Feldman, P., Micali, S.: Non-interactive zero-knowledge and its applications (extended abstract). In: Simon, J. (ed.) Proceedings of the 20th Annual ACM Symposium on Theory of Computing, 2–4 May 1988, Chicago, Illinois, USA, pp. 103–112. ACM (1988). https://doi.org/10.1145/62212.62222
4. Canetti, R.: Universally composable security: a new paradigm for cryptographic protocols. In: 42nd Annual Symposium on Foundations of Computer Science, FOCS 2001, 14–17 October 2001, Las Vegas, Nevada, USA, pp. 136–145. IEEE Computer Society (2001). https://doi.org/10.1109/SFCS.2001.959888
5. Decker, C., Wattenhofer, R.: A fast and scalable payment network with bitcoin duplex micropayment channels. In: Pelc, A., Schwarzmann, A.A. (eds.) SSS 2015. LNCS, vol. 9212, pp. 3–18. Springer, Cham (2015). https://doi.org/10.1007/978-3-319-21741-3_1
6. Green, M., Miers, I.: Bolt: anonymous payment channels for decentralized currencies. In: Thuraisingham, B.M., Evans, D., Malkin, T., Xu, D. (eds.) Proceedings of the 2017 ACM SIGSAC Conference on Computer and Communications Security, CCS 2017, Dallas, TX, USA, 30 October–03 November 2017, pp. 473–489. ACM (2017). https://doi.org/10.1145/3133956.3134093
7. Heilman, E., Alshenibr, L., Baldimtsi, F., Scafuro, A., Goldberg, S.: TumbleBit: an untrusted bitcoin-compatible anonymous payment hub. In: 24th Annual Network and Distributed System Security Symposium, NDSS 2017, San Diego, California, USA, 26 February–1 March 2017. The Internet Society (2017). https://www.ndss-symposium.org/ndss2017/ndss-2017-programme/tumblebit-untrusted-bitcoin-compatible-anonymous-payment-hub/
8. Kosba, A., et al.: C0C0: a framework for building composable zero-knowledge proofs. Cryptology ePrint Archive (2015)
9. Kosba, A.E., Papamanthou, C., Shi, E.: xJsnark: a framework for efficient verifiable computation. In: Proceedings of the 2018 IEEE Symposium on Security and Privacy, SP 2018, 21–23 May 2018, San Francisco, California, USA, pp. 944–961. IEEE Computer Society (2018). https://doi.org/10.1109/SP.2018.00018

10. Koshy, P., Koshy, D., McDaniel, P.: An analysis of anonymity in bitcoin using P2P network traffic. In: Christin, N., Safavi-Naini, R. (eds.) FC 2014. LNCS, vol. 8437, pp. 469–485. Springer, Heidelberg (2014). https://doi.org/10.1007/978-3-662-45472-5_30

11. Li, P., Miyazaki, T., Zhou, W.: Secure balance planning of off-blockchain payment channel networks. In: 39th IEEE Conference on Computer Communications, INFO-COM 2020, Toronto, ON, Canada, 6–9 July 2020, pp. 1728–1737. IEEE (2020). https://doi.org/10.1109/INFOCOM41043.2020.9155375

12. Malavolta, G., Moreno-Sanchez, P., Kate, A., Maffei, M., Ravi, S.: Concurrency and privacy with payment-channel networks. In: Thuraisingham, B.M., Evans, D., Malkin, T., Xu, D. (eds.) Proceedings of the 2017 ACM SIGSAC Conference on Computer and Communications Security, CCS 2017, Dallas, TX, USA, 30 October–03 November 2017, pp. 455–471. ACM (2017). https://doi.org/10.1145/3133956.3134096

13. Malavolta, G., Moreno-Sanchez, P., Schneidewind, C., Kate, A., Maffei, M.: Anonymous multi-hop locks for blockchain scalability and interoperability. In: 26th Annual Network and Distributed System Security Symposium, NDSS 2019, San Diego, California, USA, 24–27 February 2019. The Internet Society (2019). https://www.ndss-symposium.org/ndss-paper/anonymous-multi-hop-locks-for-blockchain-scalability-and-interoperability/

14. McCorry, P., Möser, M., Shahandasti, S.F., Hao, F.: Towards bitcoin payment networks. In: Liu, J.K., Steinfeld, R. (eds.) ACISP 2016. LNCS, vol. 9722, pp. 57–76. Springer, Cham (2016). https://doi.org/10.1007/978-3-319-40253-6_4

15. Meiklejohn, S., Orlandi, C.: Privacy-enhancing overlays in bitcoin. In: Brenner, M., Christin, N., Johnson, B., Rohloff, K. (eds.) FC 2015. LNCS, vol. 8976, pp. 127–141. Springer, Heidelberg (2015). https://doi.org/10.1007/978-3-662-48051-9_10

16. Meiklejohn, S., et al.: A fistful of bitcoins: characterizing payments among men with no names. In: Papagiannaki, K., Gummadi, P.K., Partridge, C. (eds.) Proceedings of the 2013 Internet Measurement Conference, IMC 2013, Barcelona, Spain, 23–25 October 2013, pp. 127–140. ACM (2013). https://doi.org/10.1145/2504730.2504747

17. Poon, J., Dryja, T.: The bitcoin lightning network: scalable off-chain instant payments (2016)

18. Prihodko, P., Zhigulin, S., Sahno, M., Ostrovskiy, A., Osuntokun, O.: Flare: an approach to routing in lightning network. White Paper, 144 (2016)

19. Reid, F., Harrigan, M.: An analysis of anonymity in the bitcoin system. In: 2011 IEEE 3rd International Conference on Privacy, Security, Risk and Trust (PAS-SAT), PASSAT/SocialCom 2011, and 2011 IEEE 3rd International Conference on Social Computing (SocialCom), Boston, MA, USA, 9–11 October 2011, pp. 1318–1326. IEEE Computer Society (2011). https://doi.org/10.1109/PASSAT/SocialCom.2011.79

20. Rivest, R.L., Shamir, A., Adleman, L.M.: A method for obtaining digital signatures and public-key cryptosystems (reprint). Commun. ACM **26**(1), 96–99 (1983). https://doi.org/10.1145/357980.358017

21. Sivaraman, V., et al.: High throughput cryptocurrency routing in payment channel networks. In: Bhagwan, R., Porter, G. (eds.) 17th USENIX Symposium on Networked Systems Design and Implementation, NSDI 2020, Santa Clara, CA, USA, 25–27 February 2020, pp. 777–796. USENIX Association (2020). https://www.usenix.org/conference/nsdi20/presentation/sivaraman

22. Spagnuolo, M., Maggi, F., Zanero, S.: BitIodine: extracting intelligence from the bitcoin network. In: Christin, N., Safavi-Naini, R. (eds.) FC 2014. LNCS, vol. 8437, pp. 457–468. Springer, Heidelberg (2014). https://doi.org/10.1007/978-3-662-45472-5_29

23. Tairi, E., Moreno-Sanchez, P., Maffei, M.: A^2l: anonymous atomic locks for scalability in payment channel hubs. In: 42nd IEEE Symposium on Security and Privacy, SP 2021, San Francisco, CA, USA, 24–27 May 2021, pp. 1834–1851. IEEE (2021). https://doi.org/10.1109/SP40001.2021.00111

24. Tang, W., Wang, W., Fanti, G.C., Oh, S.: Privacy-utility tradeoffs in routing cryptocurrency over payment channel networks. Proc. ACM Meas. Anal. Comput. Syst. 4(2), 29:1–29:39 (2020). https://doi.org/10.1145/3392147

25. Tripathy, S., Mohanty, S.K.: MAPPCN: multi-hop anonymous and privacy-preserving payment channel network. In: Bernhard, M., et al. (eds.) FC 2020. LNCS, vol. 12063, pp. 481–495. Springer, Cham (2020). https://doi.org/10.1007/978-3-030-54455-3_34

Blockchain Based Regulatory Technology Deployment for Real Estate Transaction

Ru Ray Raymond Chao$^{(\boxtimes)}$, Joseph K. Liu, and Kai Su

Monash University, Melbourne, Australia
rrchao@gmail.com, {joseph.liu,christopher.su}@monash.edu

Abstract. This research investigates opportunities for deploying blockchain-based regulatory technology (RegTech) in the real estate industry, particularly the mortgage application process in real estate transactions. The real estate industry entails a broad range of regulatory requirements. Processes to fulfil these requirements are primarily inefficient and costly. Blockchain features many characteristics that can effectively deploy RegTech to make real estate transactions more efficient, accurate, faster and at a lower cost. This paper conducts a literature review and semi-structured interviews with a range of industry stakeholders to reveal four main categories of problems in the sector, examine five use cases of blockchain deployments, study in-depth the mortgage process as the primary target area for blockchain-based RegTech deployment, propose six desired attributes of an ideal mortgage process and offer a solution framework to encompass these attributes. The study also considers the limitations of blockchain-based RegTech solutions and suggests future considerations for such development.

Keywords: Real Estate Transaction · RegTech · Regulatory compliance · Permissionless blockchain · Mortgage · Smart contract · Tokenisation

1 Introduction

The inauguration of bitcoin in 2008 [1] has brought a great deal of public attention to the potential of blockchain and the disruptive effect this technology can instigate in different areas such as finance and supply chain [2]. It occurred the same year as the "subprime" financial crisis that spurred a wave of new regulations to tighten the scrutinisation of financial institutions and their products. The crisis was predominantly caused by complex mortgage-backed securities (MBS), leading to the concealment of systematic and underlying risks by sophisticated mathematical models [3]. New regulations aiming to improve transparency, and the disclosure of organisational governance and risks, inevitably lead to higher reporting and compliance costs. Financial institutions spend over US$214 billion annually to meet compliance requirements [4]. Regulatory technology (RegTech) has since been introduced to relieve the growing burden of regulatory compliance.

Global real estate represents the single largest asset class, with a total value estimated at US$326.5 trillion in 2020 [5]. It is more than the value of the global equity and debt

© The Author(s), under exclusive license to Springer Nature Switzerland AG 2022
X. Yuan et al. (Eds.): NSS 2022, LNCS 13787, pp. 561–579, 2022.
https://doi.org/10.1007/978-3-031-23020-2_32

market combined [6, 7]. The real estate industry is also heavily regulated. Despite its stake, it still relies profoundly on manual and inefficient processes to fulfil regulatory requirements, causing problems such as high transaction costs, long settlement periods, and low liquidity [8]. This research conducts a literature review and semi-structured interviews with industry stakeholders to analyse how RegTech can be deployed via blockchain technology to tackle the existing challenges faced by the real estate industry. Current studies and use cases in blockchain-based solutions for the real estate industry can be broadly categorised into two groups. One group utilises tokenisation to represent shares of a legal entity that holds the title to a property [9–11]. This initiative explores possibilities to improve liquidity and fractionalise ownership. Another group deploys permissioned blockchains as an alternative to the existing centralised land registry system [12, 13]. Both groups, however, offer limited insights to resolve the issues faced by the real estate industry fundamentally. This research, therefore, aims to fill these gaps by exploring blockchain-based RegTech deployment opportunities that can considerably improve processes related to property transactions and satisfy regulatory requirements. This paper makes the following contributions:

We concluded that an enhanced process that can efficiently fulfil regulatory requirements could resolve a significant portion of the challenges faced by the real estate industry. The remainder of this paper is organised as follows: Sect. 2 describes the existing problems in the real estate industry and reviews current use cases of adopting blockchain technology for this industry. Section 3 explains the research methodology and the rationale behind it. Section 4 illustrates and analyses the survey results and performs an in-depth study of the mortgage process as the foremost opportunity to deploy blockchain-based RegTech. The ideal attributes of a real estate transaction are presented, followed by a discussion of the features of blockchain technology that support these attributes. Section 5 provides a detailed solution architecture for the mortgage process. Section 6 discusses the limitations of such blockchain-based RegTech deployment. Finally, Sect. 7 concludes the research and explores the implications for future development.

2 Background

This section provides an overview of the real estate industry's challenges, blockchain use cases, and the rationale behind this research.

2.1 Four Categories of Challenges in the Real Estate Industry

The real estate industry is heavily regulated and has made modest improvements in its processes and systems. Studies revealed it has been difficult to introduce new technology as many stakeholders are involved, often with conflicting interests [9]. The fear of job loss due to automated workflow and disintermediation also leads to resistance to change [14]. The challenges can be summarised into four categories:

- Process inefficiencies: Real estate transactions still rely on an extensive range of intermediaries and processes to fulfil regulatory requirements. The processes, including mortgage applications, are often complex, manual-based, and repetitive causing transactions to be slow, expensive, and prone to error and fraud [15–18].
- Information irregularities: Property-related information is often managed by different organisations at different sites with varying data formats [19]. These problems lead to a lack of information transparency, data error and fraud [20]. The principle of caveat emptor also renders home buyers the sole responsibility of conducting necessary due diligence about the properties they want to invest in [21]. Often during a transaction, only minimum information is disclosed, and a considerable amount of data is misplaced [10].
- High capital requirements: Properties, unlike equity or bonds, are inherently illiquid [10]. The investment cannot be readily fractionalised, resulting in an extensive amount of capital required. Transactions typically take months to settle, compared to days in the case of equity trading. Inefficient processes and lengthy settlements make it challenging to trade frequently, unnecessarily locking up large amounts of capital.
- Single point of failure: A land registry is a centralised authority that records various property rights and ownership changes [22]. Land registration can be complicated when multiple rights and claims are held by different parties, such as financial institutions, tenants, owners, and developers [24]. As a centralised body, the land registry lacks adequate checks and balances and verification mechanisms for record accuracy. It also encourages corruption and fraud [22]. An estimated 80% of those who interacted with the Land Administration Department in India claimed to pay bribes [26]. A centralised system can also be vulnerable to cyber-attacks and data breaches, raising integrity concerns [22]. The Indian state of Karnataka's land registry was compromised three times in 2018, where land records were altered [26].

2.2 Current State-of-the-Art Blockchain Deployments

Multiple pieces of literature and industry use cases have been exploring blockchain deployment in the real estate industry. These initiatives can be broadly categorised into five groups:

- Tokenisation of indirect ownership can be achieved through non-fungible tokens (NFTs) representing the shares of a legal entity, often known as a special purpose vehicle (SPV) [10], that holds the title to a property. This indirect ownership structure provides a quick and easy workaround to digitise the ownership [11]. It supports the fractionalised title, improves liquidity, and reduces the capital requirement of property investment.
- Tokenisation of direct ownership uses NFT as "a digital representation of the economic value and ownership of property, by which they can be traded" [27]. A permissionless blockchain platform becomes the registry system [28]. Owners prove their ownership and execute transactions directly using private keys [29].
- Smart contracts to streamline and automate the conveyancing and registration processes are considered a natural extension of property ownership digitisation [30]. Processes, including bidding, contract execution, payment transfer, title registration,

notarisation, identity, and legitimacy verification, are deemed executable by smart contracts without a trusted third party (TTP) [31]. A standardised, streamlined, and automated process can significantly reduce cost, settlement time, and processing error while efficiently meeting regulatory requirements [31].

- Consolidation of property data can be achieved using blockchain technology to establish a clear trace of records [11]. It allows participants to review and update information in a structured and transparent manner to prevent "shadow transactions" from occurring [21]. Building Information Model (BIM) can become the basis of a standardised property information source [31]. Other information may include transaction and maintenance ledgers, taxation, valuations, insurance claims, and owners association archives. Blockchain can significantly improve transparency, information parity, fraud resilience and data accuracy, which is fundamental to property transactions [21].
- Land registry on blockchain attempts to establish a distributed and more secure land registry system [13]. A blockchain solution may benefit countries where the integrity of enforcing authority can be questionable [23] due to fraud, corruption, or a lack of quality [24]. It can prevent fraudulent documents, listings [31] and illegal ownership changes [23]. It also facilitates efficient title search and document retrieval, reducing bureaucracy and waiting time for participants [26]. The use cases include implementations in The Republic of Georgia [14], Sweden [12] and the Indian State of Andhra Pradesh [26].

2.3 Concerns About Current Blockchain Deployments

An in-depth review identifies the following drawbacks of current blockchain research and implementations in the real estate industry:

- Tokenisation through indirect property ownership using securitised SPV is a temporary solution for digitising property ownership. It partially resolves the liquidity concerns of real estate but generates issues about the title to the property. It may lead to agency problems, such as fraudulent sales of underlying assets without agreement from token owners [10]. Since it is complex and costly to go through a tedious due diligence and securitisation process, widespread adoption of such a technique is not likely to occur.
- Tokenisation through direct ownership by NFTs, on the other hand, requires a significant overhaul of the current legal system to enforce land registration on blockchain and resolve corresponding legal disputes. Particular protocols may also be required for the tokens to represent various rights and claims over the property held by different parties, such as financial institutions, tenants, owners, and developers [24].
- Smart contracts to automate conveyancing processes imply significant disintermediation in the sector, requiring a shift of government and other industry stakeholders' roles and practices. The social and legal challenges of implementing such practices in an industry known for resistance are enormous [19].
- Similarly, the consolidation of property data on the blockchain requires all industry stakeholders to participate in sharing and maintaining property data. As discussed in Sect. 2.1, there is a substantial barrier to sharing property information within the

sector. There is also no detailed framework that describes how to implement data consolidation on the blockchain.

- Land registry on blockchains has been put into practice [12, 14, 26]. Nevertheless, all use cases utilise permissioned blockchain. Transactions are validated and recorded only by the land authority and some authorised third parties, such as banks and real estate agents [31]. The public is not allowed to participate. Besides, in jurisdictions where people do not generally trust the land registry, the authorities have little incentive to transform the land registry into a transparent system. They also perceive blockchain as a tool to undermine their control [32].

2.4 Importance of the Research

This research presents significant opportunities to deploy Regtech in a heavily regulated real estate industry.

- Real estate is the largest asset class globally, valued at US$326.5 trillion in 2020 [5], more than the value of the global equity market of US$120.4 trillion [6] and the debt market of US$119 trillion combined [7].
- The challenges described in Sect. 2.1 are mainly attributed to complex systems and processes involving human intervention in fulfilling the regulatory requirements at different phases of a property transaction.
- Regulations, however, are not intended to reduce efficiency and complicate processes. They help organisations and individuals engage in business activities fairly and securely. If appropriately implemented, regulatory compliance should improve results for all stakeholders creating better product value, providing consumer protection, managing systematic risks, ensuring economic stability, and promoting efficiency, competitiveness, and a satisfying experience.
- As explained in Sect. 2.3, the current research and use cases for blockchain deployment in the real estate industry are not addressing its fundamental challenges [9, 26, 30].
- Moreover, there has not been an industry-wide survey to understand the actual problems this industry is facing and to design the most relevant possible solution for such issues.
- The real estate industry is ideal for studying how RegTech can resolve regulatory compliance challenges, improve process efficiency, and minimise risks. Blockchain exhibits an astounding number of characteristics that can deploy RegTech effectively.

Therefore, a study to understand the challenges, identify a significant opportunity, and subsequently design an effective blockchain-based RegTech solution is paramount to the real estate industry.

3 Research Methodology

The research takes a phased approach by defining the main research question and guiding questions based on findings from the literature review. Semi-structured interviews are conducted with twenty-one industry stakeholders to uncover the sector's main problems. The research analyses findings from the survey and identifies the most profound issue. A blockchain-based RegTech solution is devised and re-evaluated with selected participants. Evaluation feedback is further analysed and presented in the paper.

4 Findings and Analysis

The survey uncovered various issues, categorised and analysed in this section. Figure 1 illustrates the number of times issues were raised and the severity of each category of challenges outlined in Sect. 2.1 by mortgage and by all the problems within the category. The severity of the category is calculated as the average of the impact rating of issues in that category, with '5' being the most severe.

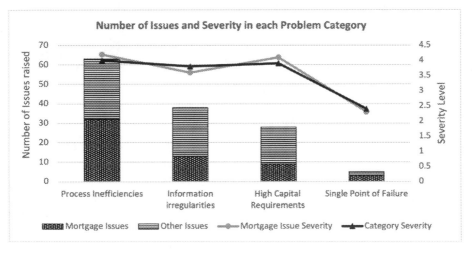

Fig. 1. Distribution of Issues and Severity in each Problem Category.

The process inefficiencies category receives the most grievances (63 instances), followed by information irregularities (38) and high capital requirements (28). The severity of these categories is similar within the range of 3.8–4.2, except for the "single point of failure" category, which records 2.4. The number of issues raised with the "single point of failure" category is also low at only five instances. A remarkable discovery is that mortgage-related problems account for 43% of all the issues raised and appear in every category of challenges. One may attribute the high percentage to 48% of interviewees being homeowners or property investors. Nonetheless, the in-depth study in Sect. 4.1 strongly indicates that the mortgage application process represents a significant opportunity for RegTech deployment using Blockchain technology.

Despite the issues raised, participants were generally satisfied with real estate transactions in Australia. The conveyance process has improved and streamlined gradually over the years. Participants have not identified any significant flaws in the process. The calibre of solicitors and conveyancers in Australia is considered high. Some functions have been digitised, including signing contracts on a tablet and on-site deposit transfers. These digitised processes help provide a smoother experience for buyers and vendors.

4.1 In-Depth Study of Mortgage-Related Issues

The mortgage process has been identified as the most significant opportunity for in-depth study for the following reasons:

- Mortgage-related issues account for 43% of all the issues raised in the survey.
- Although the mortgage application process is a financial servicing process, it is a crucial part of most real estate transactions [33]. It also likely represents the most significant share of property investment and the borrower's financial debt.
- From lenders' perspective, mortgage comprises a significant portion of the lending business. The global mortgage market revenue is estimated to be US$11.5 trillion in 2021 [34], 51% of the total financial services market of US$22.5 trillion [35].
- As a result of the 2008 mortgage-backed securities financial crisis, compliance costs for financial institutions have increased dramatically to a staggering US$214 billion in 2021 [4].
- The introduction of RegTech in the mortgage process can represent considerable benefits for lenders regarding compliance costs, operational efficiency, risk mitigation and competitiveness. It also presents enormous value to borrowers in controlling their data, obtaining better mortgage products and overall user experience.
- Unlike current blockchain initiatives described in Sect. 2.2, blockchain-based RegTech deployment in the mortgage process does not require substantial disintermediation nor a significant overhaul of the existing legal system. It is, therefore, likely to encounter the least social and political barrier.
- In addition, a thorough search for related research in the First Quartile (Q1) journal has not returned tangible results.

Hence, despite the original intention to identify opportunities in real estate transactions, we have focussed on the mortgage process for an in-depth study to propose an appropriate blockchain-based RegTech deployment solution. The research has further investigated, in addition to borrowers, the pain points of lenders and regulators, who are the other two critical stakeholders in the mortgage process.

Borrowers' Pain Points

- **Lack of control:** Borrowers generally feel the mortgage requirement is rigid, providing limited product variety. The mortgage business is highly protected, with little competition and motivation for product innovation. As interest rates rise, borrowers are eager to see more innovative and competitive mortgage products. Borrowers also criticise a lack of measures to control their data and high-quality advisory support to strengthen their financial positions over time to help them obtain a better rate in a mortgage application.
- **Lack of efficiency:** Mortgage application is tedious, manual-driven, time-consuming and repetitive.
- **Lack of transparency:** The application process is opaque regarding evaluation criteria, processing lead time, status updates and access to competitive products. Lead time is long (30–60 days), uncertain and varies largely by cases and lenders.

- **Maintain privacy:** While evaluating the solution proposed in Sect. 6, the interviewees specifically raised concerns about privacy protection measures on the blockchain.

Lenders' Pain Points

- **Inefficiency in application data consolidation.** Each application collects data from different sources of different formats, quality, and accuracy. The process needs to consolidate a considerable amount of data, which is time-consuming and costly. Many borrowers are not competent in maintaining financial records leading to missing, inconsistent, or incomplete documents. The survey shows that lenders tend to manage the application process hastily and do not attempt to understand the customers well about their objectives and financial situations.
- **Difficulty in verification.** On the other hand, lenders invest many resources in verifying customer documents and information. There is a general lack of trust between borrowers and lenders due to the limited inquiry time. Data verification is difficult as it also requires highly skilled staff to detect signs of fraudulent and inaccurate representations [16].
- **Changes in practices and demographics affect assessment effectiveness.** COVID-19 has a lasting effect on the mortgage process. For instance, most applications have switched to contactless submission, although personal interviews are important for assessment [36]. The workforce demographics have also shifted from fixed positions to a more free-lance manner with fluctuating income. An adaptive assessment model is considered necessary.
- **Inefficiency in regulatory reporting.** Regulatory reporting requires extensive staffing by lenders to process, consolidate and submit. Different regulators require different documentation and reporting [3]. These obligations are primarily principle-based, with grey areas, and do not provide a definitive guideline. Every lending organisation, and even the same lender at different times, may have different interpretations of the regulatory requirements [36].
- **High capital requirements.** Lastly, as the cost of capital and operations continues to rise, lenders are eager to improve efficiency and reduce overall costs in processing mortgage applications and fulfilling compliance requirements.

Regulators

- The high entry barrier for new players. In addition to ensuring compliance, regulators understand the cost of regulatory compliance that raises the entry barrier restricting competition [3].
- Multiple regulators with different requirements lead to complex and inefficient compliance processes. In Australia, the primary regulators for mortgage compliance include the following:
  - Australian Securities & Investments Commission (ASIC) ensures responsible lending conduct [16, 17].
  - Australian Prudential Regulation Authority (ARPA) licenses and regulates financial institutions and receives mortgage lending reports [37].

- The Reserve Bank of Australia (RBA) requires mortgage-backed securities reports [38].
- Inefficiency in the reporting verification. When regulators receive reporting data from lenders, they will reconcile and validate it. When errors are detected, they need to manually inquire and await responses from corresponding lenders as original data are stored in respective lenders' systems [36].
- Data irregularities and lack of transparency. Reporting process receives data from different systems with different data schema. There are often problems associated with data consistency and provenance. Data conversion to meet reporting requirements and different interpretations of rules by lenders also lead to errors [3]. In addition, a lack of data transparency leads to a poor understanding of systematic risks, especially those associated with MBSs [3].

4.2   Desired Attributes of Ideal Mortgage Process

We decoded the pain points into six desired attributes that constitute an ideal mortgage process. Table 1 explains in detail the six attributes. The same table also describes how the characteristics of permissionless blockchain can support each attribute. The control and efficiency attributes are essential throughout the mortgage process. Control attribute enables stakeholders to interact directly with processes and data without relying on unnecessary intervention. Efficiency attribute concerns both functions and data. It is enhanced by the transparency and immutability of processes and data, ensuring verifiability. Lastly, a transparent system such as the blockchain must embed effective privacy measures to protect data owners.

Table 1. Six desired attributes of an ideal mortgage process and the supporting blockchain characteristics.

Attributes to Ideal Mortgage Process	Blockchain Characteristics supporting the Attributes
Control. Mortgage-related processes should enable all borrowers, lenders, and regulators to interact directly with the corresponding functions and data without unnecessary intervention and hindrance from TTP	A permissionless blockchain is decentralised and open. Any participant can read and write to the network [23]. This openness allows all parties to interact directly with the processes and data facilitated by the blockchain platform
Efficiency. Data needs to be standardised and consistent. Processes need to be smooth, intuitive, automated, and free of manual intervention	Smart contracts automate processes and interact directly with users. It can execute the conditions agreed upon by participants without manual intervention by intermediaries or TTP [39]

(continued)

Table 1. (*continued*)

Attributes to Ideal Mortgage Process	Blockchain Characteristics supporting the Attributes
Transparency. Transparency of data, marketing information and processes allows participants to take part comfortably, monitor risks, and make appropriate decisions	On a permissionless blockchain, transactions and smart contracts are transparent and can be examined by all users
Verifiability. Data traceability and provenance to enable practical verification by participants. Verifiability ensures data integrity and accuracy	The public can verify that each data update follows the consensus protocol without going through a TPP [23]
Immutability. A function that further enhances data integrity by preventing improper manipulation of data	Blockchain networks' decentralised and redundancy nature prevents information tampering. Ethereum has over 300,000 nodes, and it is almost impossible to launch a cyber attack against a network of this scale [40]
Privacy. Transparency should not compromise privacy. Personal data recorded should be kept private unless explicitly shared by the owner	Cryptography can achieve platform transparency while preserving the privacy of individual participants [23]

5 Blockchain-Based RegTech Solution

This section proposes a solution architect for blockchain-based RegTech implementation in the mortgage process. The solution is designed by incorporating the analysis outlined in Sect. 4 into the conceptual regulatory framework of Australia's mortgage process explained in Sect. 5.1.

5.1 Regulatory Framework for Mortgage Process

Figure 2 summarises Australia's mortgage process, broadly divided into four main stages: Inquire, Verify, Assess and Contract Management [15–17].

- RF.1 During the Inquire stage, regulations require lenders to perform adequate inquiries to borrowers concerning their requirements, objectives, and financial situations.
- RF.2 In the Verify stage, regulations require lenders to prove adequate verification of information obtained to ensure accuracy and reliability. Verification is usually done manually and is laborious, requiring experienced and skilled staff to uncover errors and fraud.
- RF.3 The Assess stage requires lenders to perform an adequate assessment to ensure the product offer is not "unsuitable" for the borrower.
- RF.4 Contract management contains four stages:
- RF.4.1 Mortgage advertisements must include comparison rates and fees.

- RF.4.2 Before entering a contract, lenders must provide a summary of contract details and the borrower's statutory rights & obligations.
- RF.4.3 When entering a contract, lenders must provide the borrower with a written agreement.
- RF.4.4 During the contract term, the lender must provide a periodical account statement to the borrower.

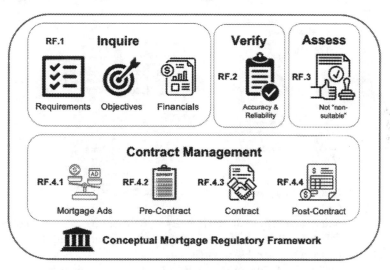

Fig. 2. Australia Mortgage Process Regulatory Framework.

5.2   Solution Phase 1: Pre-mortgage Inquiry Phase

The proposed solution contains two phases. The first phase is the Pre-Mortgage Inquiry phase, which corresponds to the Inquiry stage (RF.1). This stage is often treated hastily in real life, and borrowers usually need to provide only two months of financial information. Contrary to current practice, our solution emphasises the importance of the Inquiry stage to understand the customer well and verify data at the source. We recommend that the inquiry process begins sufficiently before the mortgage application process. Government and financial institutions should invest in the necessary infrastructure to understand the customers in depth, provide financial advisory services and strengthen consumers' data control, as summarised in Fig. 3.

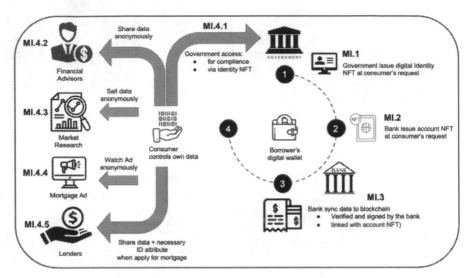

Fig. 3. Solution Architect for the Pre-Mortgage Inquiry Phase.

The Pre-Mortgage Inquiry phase contains four main steps.

- MI.1 Borrower first establishes a digital identity verified and signed by the government in the form of NFT. It will be stored in the borrower's digital wallet, recorded on the blockchain and is not transferable to other parties.
- MI. 2 Borrower then links this digital identity NFT with their bank account. The corresponding bank would issue an NFT representing the borrower's account, also stored in the borrower's digital wallet. The digital wallet allows the borrower to share data, sign-off transactions and interact with smart contracts.
- MI. 3 At the borrower's consensus, the bank will synchronise data associated with the borrower's bank account to the blockchain. The introduction of consumer data rights legislation [18] in 2020 enables individuals to authorise financial institutions to share their data with third parties. The data recorded onto the blockchain is similar to how blockchain platforms currently record cryptocurrency transactions. The blockchain is a distributed ledger technology to record transactions and is well-positioned to support this task. It provides a complete picture of the borrower's income, investment portfolio and expenses. The data is linked directly with the bank account NFT.
- MI.4 Borrowers take control of their data and share it with suitable financial service providers for different purposes.
  - MI.4.1 Government access for compliance requirements can be made via the identity NFT. Due to system transparency, regulators can tailor the reporting requirements without the involvement of financial service providers.
  - MI.4.2 Borrowers can choose to share data anonymously for financial advisory services. As described in Sect. 4.1, it takes time for individuals to establish a credible and traceable record, improve their financial position, and determine their financial objectives and requirements.

- MI.4.3 Consumers can also monetise their data for market research, advertisements, or other commercial purposes, without disclosing their identity. Consumers control data sharing through the access control functions of digital wallets.
- MI.4.4 Mortgage advertisements can tailor their offers to match borrowers' needs and automatically display other comparative rates and fees (RF.4.1).
- MI.4.5 Borrowers can apply for a mortgage by sharing only necessary data and identity attributes, such as age and citizenship, to prove their eligibility. The application can be done once and submitted seamlessly to various vendors without repetitive and manual processes.

Phase 1 provides a non-intrusive way to inquire about the borrowers and assists in building an appealing personal credit portfolio that lenders would welcome. Lenders who understand better a customer's financial situation and payback ability can minimise the mortgage risk and provide a more competitive mortgage product to the customer. There are two requirements for the proposed inquiry process framework:

- An open data format standard guarantees interoperability with different systems and high efficiency in the data processing.
- Identity and data written to the blockchain must be verified and signed by the sources, such as the government and banks. Third parties can verify the data's authenticity through these sources' public keys. This requirement ensures data integrity and prevents time-consuming but often fruitless verification.

5.3 Solution Phase 2: Mortgage Phase

Successful implementation of the Pre-Mortgage Inquiry phase would simplify the Mortgage phase in multiple folds. As presented in Fig. 4, the proposed Mortgage phase contains 15 steps shown below, amongst which 12 steps can benefit from the blockchain-based RegTech deployment.

1. A borrower can initiate a mortgage application request through different mediums, such as mobile apps or financial service providers.
2. The borrower's property purchase and mortgage eligibility can be confirmed through their digital wallet sharing the necessary identity attributes, such as age and citizenship.
3. After confirmation, the medium can broadcast the request to registered lenders.
4. Interested lenders can accept the request and create a mortgage case NFT linked with the borrower's digital wallet. All actions, events, processed data, and involved parties will generate logs on the blockchain throughout the mortgage process. The NFT links all these logs to provide the basis for compliance and reporting needs.
5. The lenders can consolidate the borrower's data on the blockchain with the borrower's consensus.

6. Lenders can use smart contracts to instantly verify (RF.2) the borrower's data using the public keys of data sources (MI.2). Manual verification for error or fraud detection is no longer necessary. Transparency (A.3) allows regulators to inspect the smart contracts' logic, the corresponding process executed, events and data retrieved directly to confirm compliance.

7. Smart contracts can also automate the mortgage assessment process (RF.3). A borrower can instantly review the progress status, evaluation criteria and results.

8. A pre-approval is confirmed with initial conditions lodged into smart contracts for the borrower's review (RF.4.2). This enables the borrower to search for properties that meet the mortgage contract requirements.

9. Lenders can carry out property valuation off-chain based on the borrower's selection and update the state of smart contracts accordingly.

10. Through smart contracts, a borrower can review the terms and conditions of the mortgage contract in addition to the written document (RF.4.3). The blockchain will also record corresponding activity logs and make them available for reporting or spot check by the regulator.

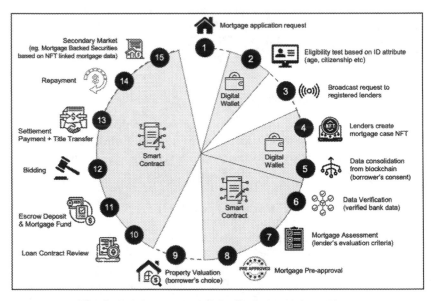

Fig. 4. Solution Framework for Phase 2: Mortgage Phase.

11. Smart contracts can also manage the escrow account for the borrower's property deposit fund and the lender's mortgage fund. The funds can be processed based on the terms and conditions pre-determined by the borrower and lender in the mortgage contract.

12. Smart contracts can also facilitate the bidding process, replacing the role of auctioneer. Prospective buyers link their escrow account with the blockchain-enabled

bidding process and bid online. The property is sold to the highest bidder at the vendor's will. Every bid detail is recorded on the blockchain, allowing follow-up review by regulators or the public.

13. Smart contracts can complete settlement by transferring allocated funds in the facilitated escrow account according to a pre-defined schedule. Smart contracts can also facilitate ownership tokenisation, real estate transactions, conveyance process, and land registration, as described in Sect. 2.2.

14. During the mortgage term (RF.4.4), smart contracts can facilitate repayment with monthly statements and balance updates available to borrowers and regulators.

15. The entire mortgage data and documents are linked with the case NFT. All mortgage-associated information is transparent, verifiable, and immutable. The NFT, with its associated data and smart contracts, fully represent the originated mortgage's ownership and economic value. These features allow the NFT to be traded easily in a secondary market. Lenders, regulators, and investors can assess the risk as a standalone item or a part of a more extensive portfolio for systematic risk review.

5.4 Discussion

The design of the blockchain-based RegTech mortgage process solution is first based on analysing the survey results from interviewing real estate industry stakeholders, focusing on the pain points raised by borrowers, lenders and regulators. These pain points are further decoded into six attributes essential for an ideal mortgage process. The design incorporates the six attributes into a conceptual model for Australia's mortgage regulatory framework to form the solution architecture. The solution emphasises the importance of the pre-mortgage inquiry stage for regulators and lenders:

- Standardise the data format to avoid system interoperability issues and other inefficiencies in the data processing.
- Verify and sign the data by trusted sources, such as the government, banks, and lenders.
- Adapting to the decentralisation of permissionless blockchain allows all stakeholders complete control of their data.

Figure 5 demonstrates how the design correlates with Australia's mortgage regulatory framework. Phase 1, the Pre-Mortgage Inquiry phase, focuses on meeting the needs of borrowers. It provides them with the necessary infrastructure to control their data, access services and manage privacy directly. Contrary to current practice, nearly half of the solution architecture is geared towards the inquiry stage to ensure the necessary information that is accurate, verified and immutable.

Phase 2, the Mortgage phase, builds on the Phase 1 infrastructure to equip lenders and regulators with the efficiency enabled by blockchain. Smart contracts can automate data consolidation, verification, assessment, pre-approval, contract review, fund and transfer management, bidding, settlement, and post-mortgage repayment. The bank account and mortgage NFT links with the entire process event log and corresponding data, allowing regulators to examine it flexibly and conveniently.

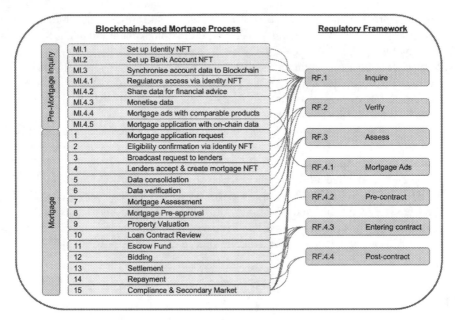

Fig. 5. Linkage tree analysis of Blockchain-based RegTech Mortgage Process in addressing Mortgage Regulatory Framework.

6 Limitations

Despite its potential to significantly improve the efficiency of regulatory compliance and resolve the existing real estate industry challenges, blockchain-based RegTech deployment in real estate transactions is still in its early stage. Evaluation of the proposed solution with industry stakeholders has incorporated several improvements into the solution in Sect. 5. The review also identifies various limitations listed below that could impede its adoption in the real world. It is also important to point out that the proposed solution is a high-level design that demonstrates how to solve the problems identified in the mortgage process and create value for primary stakeholders. It does not contain implementation details specifying data formats, system components or codes. The research recommends a future study to put forth a detailed implementation plan.

- **Lack of Digital Identity Infrastructure.** Many major blockchain networks like Ethereum do not verify participants' identities. Nevertheless, a verified digital identity is necessary to execute mortgage applications or real estate transactions to fulfil legal obligations, such as age and citizenship requirements [41]. Creating national or international e-ID via blockchain is key to the wide application of blockchain deployment in the real estate sector [41].
- **Privacy Protection.** Data on a permissionless blockchain is accessible by anyone, and this transparency attribute inevitably brings up privacy concerns, especially for property buyers and mortgage applicants. Other participants can obtain personal data from

real estate transactions or associated mortgage approval. The privacy and data security mechanisms must be defined and confirmed at the beginning stage of blockchain solution development [32]. Privacy can be attained by cryptography computation. The case of Zerocash illustrates the possibility of providing transparency for verifying the system's state while preserving the complete anonymity of investors using sophisticated cryptography [42].

- **Legal Enforceability of Smart Contracts.** Smart contracts are versatile in automating all main processes of real estate transactions, including token ownership transfer, mortgage application and approval, fund transfer, mortgage repayment, and default handling. Conditions and logic depicted in a traditional contract can be executed on the blockchain with minimal manual intervention. The current legal system, however, has not been positioned to support the practice of smart contracts. Court challenges may arise to overturn the action taken by smart contracts.

7 Conclusion

Real estate is the largest asset class in the world, and property transactions are high-stake and highly regulated activities. Nevertheless, existing property transaction processes are complex, manual-driven, error-prone, time-consuming, and costly. Effective RegTech deployment can considerably enhance property transaction processes to fulfil regulatory requirements. We outlined the challenges faced by the real estate industry, many of which are related to inefficiencies in fulfilling regulatory requirements. We proposed the desired attributes of ideal mortgage transactions for regulatory compliance and illustrated how blockchain properties could effectively empower these attributes. The research presented opportunities to deploy blockchain-based RegTech in real estate transactions and detailed such implementation for the scenario of the mortgage application process.

Permissionless blockchain, a decentralised platform, is transparent and open for all stakeholders to participate directly. Transactions and data on the network are verifiable, immutable, and secure. Smart contracts can automate these processes and minimise manual intervention while seamlessly fulfilling regulatory requirements. We conclude that permissionless blockchain can support RegTech deployment in real estate transactions. This study identified three main limitations that could hinder the widespread adoption of blockchain-based RegTech deployment, i.e., digital identity infrastructure, privacy on blockchain and legal enforceability of smart contracts. The expansion of the current study would be: (i) to investigate the framework for e-ID on the permissionless blockchain; (ii) to define a comprehensive privacy protection measure in a transparent and open blockchain platform; and (iii) to adapt the legal system to enforce smart contracts so that they can effectively automate processes in fulfilling associated regulatory requirements. It is reasonable to believe a blockchain-based RegTech implementation will hold numerous promises for the real estate industry, where efficiency, trust and security elements are imperative to the stakeholders.

References

1. Nakamoto, S.: Bitcoin: A Peer-to-Peer Electronic Cash System (2008). https://doi.org/10.1007/s10838-008-9062-0
2. Malhotra, D., Saini, P., Singh, A.K.: How blockchain can automate KYC: systematic review. Wireless Pers. Commun. **122**(2), 1987–2021 (2021). https://doi.org/10.1007/s11277-021-08977-0
3. Gozman, D., Liebenau, J., Aste, T.: A case study of using blockchain technology in regulatory technology. MIS Q. Exec. **19**(1), 19–37 (2020)
4. Counting the cost (Cost of compliance vs Cost of Non-compliance) (2021). https://1rs.io/2021/10/11/counting-the-cost-cost-of-compliance/
5. Savills. The total value of global real estate. Report, Savills Research (2021). https://www.savills.com/impacts/Impacts3_pdfs/The_total_value_of_global_real_estate.pdf
6. Research Quarterly: Fixed Income - Issuance and Trading (2021). SIFMA. https://web.archive.org/web/20210513170717/https://www.sifma.org/wp-content/uploads/2021/01/US-Research-Quarterly-Fixed-Income-Issuance-Trading-2021-04-13-SIFMA.pdf
7. Global Equity Markets Primer. SIFMA (2021). https://www.sifma.org/wp-content/uploads/2021/11/SIFMA-Insights-Global-Equity-Markets-Primer-FINAL-FOR-WEB.pdf
8. Dijkstra, M.: Blockchain: Towards Disruption in the Real Estate Sector: An exploration on the impact of blockchain technology in the real estate management process. Delft University of Technology, Delft (2017)
9. Baum, A.: Tokenization - the future of real estate investment? J. Portfolio Manage. **47**(10), 41–61 (2021)
10. Gupta, A., Rathod, J., Patel, D., Bothra, J., Shanbhag, S., Bhalerao, T.: Tokenization of real estate using blockchain technology. In: Zhou, J., et al. (eds.) ACNS 2020. LNCS, vol. 12418, pp. 77–90. Springer, Cham (2020). https://doi.org/10.1007/978-3-030-61638-0_5
11. Smith, J., Vora, M., Benedetti, D.H., Yoshida, K., Vogel, Z.: Tokenized Securities & Commercial Real Estate. MIT Management Sloan School (2019)
12. Rizzo, P.: Sweden's blockchain land registry to begin testing in March. CoinDesk (2017). https://www.coindesk.com/markets/2017/01/10/swedens-blockchain-land-registry-to-begin-testing-in-march/
13. Shuaib, M., Daud, S.M., Alam, S., Khan, W.Z.: Blockchain-based framework for secure and reliable land registry system. Telkomnika **18**(5), 2560–2571 (2020)
14. Manski, S.: Building the blockchain world: Technological commonwealth or just more of the same? Strateg. Chang. **26**(5), 511–522 (2017)
15. National Consumer Credit Protection Act 2009. https://www.legislation.gov.au/Details/C2020C00215
16. Regulatory Guide 273 Mortgage brokers: Best interests duty. https://asic.gov.au/media/5641325/rg273-published-24-june-2020.pdf
17. Schedule 1 to the National Consumer Credit Protection Regulations 2010. https://www.legislation.gov.au/Details/F2022C00106
18. Consumer Data Right. https://www.oaic.gov.au/consumer-data-right/cdr-legislation
19. Spielman, A.: Blockchain: digitally rebuilding the real estate industry. Doctoral dissertation, Massachusetts Institute of Technology (2016)
20. Saull, A., Baum, A., Braesemann, F.: Can digital technologies speed up real estate transactions? J. Property Invest. Finan. **38**(4), 349–361 (2020)
21. Veuger, J.: Trust in a viable real estate economy with disruption and blockchain. Facilities (Bradford, West Yorkshire, England) **36**(1/2), 103–120 (2018)
22. Shuaib, M., et al.: Identity model for blockchain-based land registry system: a comparison. Wireless Commun. Mob. Comput. (2022)

23. Wüst, K., Gervais, A.: Do you need a blockchain? (2017). https://eprint.iacr.org/2017/375. pdf
24. Vos, J., Lemmen, C., Beentjes, B.: Blockchain based land administration: feasible, Illusory or a Panacea. In: Paper prepared for presentation at the 2017 world bank conference on land and poverty (2017)
25. Pankratov, E., Grigoryev, V., Pankratov, O.: The blockchain technology in real estate sector: experience and prospects. In: IOP Conference Series: Materials Science and Engineering, vol. 869, no. 6, p. 062010 (2020)
26. Kshetri, N.: Blockchain as a tool to facilitate property rights protection in the Global South: lessons from India's Andhra Pradesh state. Third World Quart. **43**(2), 371–392 (2022)
27. Wouda, H.P., Opdenakker, R.: Blockchain technology in commercial real estate transactions. J. Property Invest. Finan. (2019)
28. Konashevych, O.: General concept of real estate tokenization on blockchain. Eur. Property Law J. **9**(1), 21–66 (2020)
29. Konashevych, O.: Constraints and benefits of the blockchain use for real estate and property rights. J. Prop. Plan. Environ. Law (2020)
30. Garcia-Teruel, R.M.: Legal challenges and opportunities of blockchain technology in the real estate sector. J. Prop. Plan. Environ. Law **12**(2), 129–145 (2020)
31. Schneider, J., Blostein, A., Lee, B., Kent, S., Groer, I., Beardsley, E.: "Goldman Sachs equity research profiles in innovation", Blockchain Putting Theory into Practice, Goldman Sachs, New York, NY (2016)
32. Monrat, A.A., Schelén, O., Andersson, K.: A survey of blockchain from the perspectives of applications, challenges, and opportunities. IEEE Access **7**, 117134–117151 (2019)
33. Financial Times: Banks adopt blockchain for mortgage valuation system (2016). www.ft. com/content/c856787c-9523-11e6-a1dc-bdf38d484582
34. Mortgage Lending Market Research, 2031 (2022). https://www.alliedmarketresearch.com/ mortgage-lending-market-A17282
35. Financial Services: Sizing the Sector in the Global Economy. (2021). https://www.invest opedia.com/ask/answers/030515/what-percentage-global-economy-comprised-financial-ser vices-sector.asp
36. Regtech responsible lending webinar. https://asic.gov.au/for-business/innovation-hub/asic-and-regtech/asic-regtech-initiative-series-2019-20/regtech-responsible-lending-webinar// event-details
37. Reporting Practice Guide - ARPA (2020). https://www.apra.gov.au/sites/default/files/RPG% 20223.0%20January%202018.pdf
38. Data to be Reported - RBA (2020). https://www.rba.gov.au/securitisations/data-to-be-rep orted/
39. Bandyopadhyay, R.: Land system in India: A historical review. Economic and Political Weekly, A149-A155 (1993)
40. Maeng, S.H., Essaid, M., Ju, H.T.: Analysis of ethereum network properties and behaviour of influential nodes. In: 2020 21st Asia-Pacific Network Operations and Management Symposium (APNOMS), pp. 203–207. IEEE, September 2020
41. Sullivan, C., Burger, E.: E-residency and blockchain. Comput. Law Secur. Rev. **33**(4), 470–481 (2017)
42. Sasson, E.B., et al.: Zerocash: decentralised anonymous payments from bitcoin. In: 2014 IEEE Symposium on Security and Privacy, pp. 459–474(2014)

CVallet: A Blockchain-Oriented Application Development for Education and Recruitment

Zoey Ziyi Li[1]([⊠]) [iD], Joseph K. Liu[1] [iD], Jiangshan Yu[1] [iD], Dragan Gasevic[2] [iD], and Wayne Yang[1]

[1] Department of Software System and Cybersecurity, Monash University, Melbourne, Australia
`zoey.li@monash.edu`
[2] Department of Human Centred Computing, Monash University, Melbourne, Australia

Abstract. The application of blockchain technology in education has gained increased attention from researchers and practitioners in the past few years. However, most pilots are stuck in the prototype stage and meet industrial adoption barriers. In this study, targeting the identified hindering factors, we develop an education credentials management and verification DApp to improve the adoption potentiality of blockchain through methodological, social and industrial aspects. Firstly, we innovatively incorporate a co-design method based on blockchain-oriented software engineering (BOSE), which may bring new implications for future studies of user-centred DApp development methods. Through intensive research of user experiences, not only do we improve the social awareness and knowledge of this new technology but we also develop more precise functional goals that can solve actual industrial pain points. Finally, our proposed prototype makes improvements in terms of architecture modular design, selection of blockchain, and leverage of interoperability-supported tools with the expectation to improve the application adoption further, particularly in the education and recruitment sectors.

Keywords: Blockchain adoption · DApp development · Education credentials · Co-design · Blockchain-oriented software engineering

1 Introduction

Education credentials, such as certificates, qualifications, transcripts and other proofs of educational achievements, have been widely accepted as "employability currency" in labour markets all over the world [14]. On the one hand, individual learners invest a significant amount of time and money to accumulate their "employability currency" in exchange for better-paid positions when negotiating with their future employers. In 2020–21, the average tuition fees for a full-time undergraduate student (attending 4-year programs) ranged from US$14,200

Supported by Algorand Foundation.

to US$23,200 in total according to U.S. national education statistics of the 50 states [6]. On the other hand, recruiters, either from industries or institutions, regard education credentials as important criteria to assess applicants' relevant skills and knowledge that match their recruiting positions [7]. In general recruitment descriptions, education and employment backgrounds are linked directly or indirectly to the position's salary package and payment rate, especially for professional positions.

1.1 Motivations

The close relationship between education credentials and potentially higher-paid job positions leads to attractive incentives that drive people's fraudulent intentions and behaviours of credential counterfeits and theft. In the past decade, the production of forged credentials has become a global issue, with numerous credential factories selling fake diplomas, degrees, and transcripts [2]. A simple google search of "buy fake certificates" can return pages of credentialing fraudsters. Not only can these fraudsters make forged certificates look authentic with institutions' stamps, signatures and seals, some of them even promise to insert the fake learning record into a targeted institution's internal database and fool the national education authority's verification website [3]. It would appear that anything can be faked as long as the purchasers are ready to pay a high price, which seriously undermines the value of credentials and educational equity. As a result, to prevent employment fraud, hiring companies have to face rising costs on recruitment verification and lean on screening services [9]. According to a recent industry outlook, the global market of employment screening services reached US$4,957 million in 2020 and is expected to double in 2028 [21]. This phenomenon is deteriorating under the global epidemic of COVID-19, where national or regional lockdowns drive more online education programs that generate various types and vast amounts of credentials. Despite the fact that countries around the world have issued rigorous regulations and laws to protect education credentials' quality and authenticity, there is an unstoppable trend that trust between stakeholders is eroding [2].

Alternatively, blockchain technology promises to offer an effective complement for traditional regulations and management to fix the trust issue. One successful practical case of blockchain is Bitcoin, a digital alternative of fiat currency that replaces the traditional trust model with the use of cryptographic proof and distributed network. In the education credentialing scenario, agreed by numerous studies [8,9,11], blockchain technology can benefit education with the following attributes: 1) decentralization can reduce the risks of centralized management of learning records and prevent single-point attacks; 2) immutability can prevent credentials from being maliciously modified by any party; 3) transparency can rebuild trust between stakeholders and guarantee the authenticity of credentials, declared achievements and skills; and 4) self-sovereignty authorize students to take full control over their credentials in a privacy-preserving way. One recent survey study[11] has categorized the blockchain applications into five areas after examining all the papers published after 2016: degree verification (28.75%), educational record management (22.5%), students' professional ability evaluation

(18.75%), institute systems (15%), and online learning environments (15%). All of these practices indicate promising potentials of blockchain applications in the education field.

1.2   Low-Adoption Factors

However, similar to blockchain applications in other industries, a majority of educational proposals are stuck at the prototype design stage with low industrial adoption rate, mostly due to the following hindering factors:

– Short of DApp development guidelines: the blockchain wave has driven the fast development of applications with various functions, but there is no standardized and complete method to guide developers' practices [12]. This leads to such problems as ambiguous product positioning, designed functions that can not directly solve users' pain points, overly redundant and complex architecture, and some hidden security risks [12].
– Lack of collaboration between DApp clusters: most of the current DApps fall into solo development that does not extend and support each other's existing functions, leading to a waste of resources and a less collaborative development community [9].
– Legal and regulation issue: decentralisation, as the distinctive benefit of blockchain, eliminates single authority and centralised operation. However, it may also violate some national or regional authorities' interests and local data protection regulations [11];
– Social' awareness and user-acceptance issue: the public has insufficient experience and awareness of blockchain technology. Besides, the previous application designs lack systematic users involvement strategies, which may also lead to low user acceptance of the DApp [9];
– Blockchain-related issue: there always exist trade-off considerations when choosing a suitable blockchain that best matches the business requirements. Different blockchain types come along with different consensus mechanisms that can affect blockchain transaction speed and workload threshold [9,11], which in turn affect DApp performance and user experiences. Additionally, blockchain technology is evolving, and how it can integrate and interoperate with established systems and what roles it plays within the whole ecosystem lacks enough empirical practice [25].

1.3   Contribution

This study, in an effort to increase blockchain adoption rate in industries, makes the following contributions through three aspects: methodological, social and industrial.

1. Methodologically, we innovatively integrate a co-design method with BOSE, and propose an adapted method with three development stages. Since the exploration of systematic DApp engineering approaches is still in its very

early stage, this adapted approach and practical case validation can provide implications for future research in user-centred blockchain software engineering.

2. Socially, we involve 97 learners and 12 recruiters from 9 industries to join the DApp development, which process can increase not only social awareness of this new technology but also user-acceptance of the DApp. More importantly, we carefully examine the learners' interactions with education credentials and learn from recruiters' empirical verification methods. This effort differentiates our prototype from previous studies since it is developed upon authentic social analysis instead of laboratory assumptions. Therefore, the prototype functionality can better anchor the stakeholders' pain points and solve existing social problems.

3. Industrially, we develop a blockchain-based educational achievements management and verification system, named CVallet (stem from CV + Wallet), that provides stakeholders with practical tools to improve their work efficiency. The enterprise dashboard can reduce recruiters' workload in the current recruitment procedure with one-stop verification. The lifelong learners dashboard is a digital wallet to store, manage and share individuals' learning credentials in a secure and verifiable manner. In addition, the system is developed in a modular manner with higher extensible potentialities. It supports functional extensions based on business development and user requirements changes in the future. Besides, the proof-of-concept application is based on the Algorand blockchain with lower running costs and faster performance.

The rest of the paper is structured as follows: Sect. 2 summarises relevant projects and compares our work with them. Section 3 describes the methodology theories that support our prototype development. Section 4 presents the detailed development procedure, proposed architecture and implementation. In the last section, we conclude the paper and suggest future work.

2 Background

In this section, we first review some related blockchain solutions of education credentialing, and then compare our proposed system with them based on a layered comparison framework developed especially for educational DApps [9].

2.1 Related Work

Blockcerts [22] is the first and most widespread credentialing system, focused on issuance and verification of credentials, developed by MIT Media Lab since 2016. It supports education providers to create and issue cryptographically-signed academic credentials through transactions on either Bitcoin or Ethereum blockchain with their learners. The signed credentials includes some metadata to support later verification such as blockchain receipt (contains transaction ID), recipient's profile, issuer's ID and url, public key, and signature. The verification steps include fetching and comparing these metadata (e.g. hash of the certificate and the Merkle root) that stored on blockchain are aligned with the values on the credentials. Therefore, it can support any party to verify the authenticity and integrity of the credentials through its verification portal. In other words, any modification or fraudulence can be detected if this information is not matched with each other. However, authors in [1] tested the security of Blockcerts by using a fabricated issuer profile with a valid key pair to issue fake credentials that can slip through all the validation steps.

QualiChain [4,13] is a Pan-European decentralised platform, funded by the European Union, for storing, sharing and verifying both educational and employment certificates. Compared to Blockcerts, Qualichain aims to cover a lot more comprehensive application scenarios: (i) supporting lifelong learning; (ii) supporting smart curriculum design; (iii) staffing the public sector; and (iv) providing HR consultancy and competency management services. This leads to very complex architecture design of the system and confusion of the system's goals. Even though the project team runs a number of workshops to engage users and promote QualiChain products, some users reflected that the purposes of the application "need to be made clearer" in their recent deployment report [13]. Besides, the user interfaces are not intuitive and concise for users to interact with according to its official pilot evaluation report [16]. These users' feedback may indicate the ambiguity of the product positioning of each pilot and the complex functional architecture of the system design.

Another education-employment focused proposal is called E^{2}C-Chain [10]. Besides of comparing hashes and signatures, it innovatively introduces an incentive mechanism to involve participating nodes (users) to verify the authenticity of educational and employment information. Firstly, employees choose a set of credentials or skills that should be verified by the system. Then, the system-selected verifiers will act as endorsers for each credential or skill. Every endorser has a particular weight score that represent the verification weight. When the total weight scores reach to a valid threshold, the credential or skill is verified successfully and can be added to a new block. The good aspect of this mechanism is the authenticity of credentials and previous working experiences do not rely on the issuers any more, but instead they rely on the public recognition through endorsement. But the negative side is the verification has to wait for a few rounds of endorsement, and if the verify weight cannot reach the qualifying score, the skill or certificate cannot finish the verification. As such, it may not be more efficient than the traditional reference check in current recruitment practices.

A few other projects, though not focused on recruitment verification, are closely related to secure education records transferring. BOLL [17] supports learning records transferring between different institutions by defining three types of smart contracts. However, since every learning activity will trigger different smart contracts that update the learning logs on the chain, the BOLL system's execution requires different gas fees. Moreover, its performance depends on the amount of computational resource and power that leads to a long waiting period (the tested average waiting time is 14 min per transaction). Comparatively, Mishra et al. [15]'s proposed system's performance and scalability improve greatly (15 s per block) by moving some implementations off-chain. It also adds up a privacy-preserving mechanism for sharing students' credentials. However, since it was also built on Ethereum blockchain, the PoW consensus limits performance improvements.

2.2 Comparison Framework

Regards of the prototype improvements, we use a layered comparison framework [9] as a guideline to compare CVallet with previous studies (see Fig. 1). Briefly, we design and conduct intensive user involvement studies to promote user acceptance and adoption of the DApp at the prerequisites layer. At the application layer, the prototype is designed and developed in a modular manner for extensible and flexible development in the future. In the implementation, CVallet is built on Algorand blockchain (PoS) to enable the application with faster performance, combine on-chain and off-chain data storage to improve economic efficiency, and adopt interoperability-supported tools to achieve a higher interoperability goal.

Comparison of CVallet with Other Related Works								
Info	Prerequisite Layer			Application Layer			Blockchain	
Project name	Landscape Analysis	User Study	Co-design	Main functions	Check Validity of issuers	Modularity	Consensus	Data Storage
Blockcerts	NA	NA	No	Credentials Issuing and Verification	No	No	Pow	on-chain only
E2C-Chain	Yes	No	No	Education and employmentl certification system	Yes	No	Pow	on-chain only
QualiChain	Yes	Yes	No	Support lifelong learning, curriculum design, staffing the public sector, HR	NA	Yes	PoW	on-chain + Qualichain DB
BOLL	Yes	No	No	Learning records transfer between institutions	Yes	No	PoW	on-chain + MongoDB
CVallet*	Yes	Yes	Yes	Credentials management and recruitment verification	Yes	Yes	PoS	on-chain + MongoDB/IPFS

Fig. 1. A layered comparison between current applications and our proposed prototype.

3 Methodology

Aiming to improve the DApp adoption in education and recruitment settings, we use the Blockchain-Oriented Software Engineering (BOSE) and a co-design approach as two facilitators of the prototype design. We use BOSE as a guideline to support blockchain-oriented software development, and adopt the co-design method to increase user-acceptance of a system. In this section, we briefly review the two facilitating methods, propose our adapted approach and then demonstrate it by developing a proof of concept prototype in the following Section.

3.1 BOSE

BOSE is an emerging term in recent years that refers to software engineering practices to facilitate DApp development and was firstly proposed by Porru et al. [18] in 2017. Marchesi et al. [12] developed BOSE into a nine-step engineering approach named ABCDE, which can support the complete development life-cycle, from designing, developing, and deploying the application and ongoing maintenance including 1) set the goals of the system; 2) find the actors who interact with the DApp; 3) define user stories; 4) divide the system into two subsystems; 5) design the smart contracts; 6) code and test the smart contracts; 7) design user interfaces; 8) code and test the interfaces; and 9) integrate, test and deploy the DApp system [12]. It is noticeable that this method sets system goals as the starting point to lead the following steps, which may mislead the system design directions due to insufficient user study and ambiguous under-standings of requirements. Besides, the method is based on the adaptation of Agile methods, the original goal of which is to obtain timely market feedback and user requirements changes. This may indicate that researchers have been implicitly aware of the importance and difficulty of understanding multiple user needs beforehand. But they did not propose a specific strategy to solve this dif-ficulty. Therefore, co-design seems to be a promising approach to address this problem for the following reasons.

3.2 Co-design

Co-design approaches have gained increasing recognition for establishing a shared vision between application developers and industrial stakeholders. They have been proven to offer systematic strategies to ensure the implemented sys-tems meet stakeholders' desired needs and the designed functions rely on the evidence collected through co-design processes [24]. The benefits of co-design include [23]: 1) benefit the designed project with better-defined services, more efficient design process and more loyalty of users; 2) benefit users with a better fit of their requirements and higher satisfaction; and 3) benefit the organization with better relations between customers and service provider and more successful innovations.

In education settings, there is a trend to involve educational stakeholders to join a co-design approach underpinning the development of education technology tools in order to increase users' acceptance and adoption of new technologies. For example, Tsai et al. [24] highlight the value of co-design in learning analytics tools development, identify the design needs and elicit users' requirements through several stages of user participatory processes and analysis. Pozdniakov et al. [19] adopt co-design methods to design and deploy a real-time monitoring tool used in classrooms. It has split the design into two parts: co-design study in close collaboration with teachers and validation study of an authentically designed interface. Both studies start with users' investigation through interviews, ana-lyzing their pain points, and using collected data to support decision-making in application design. The attributes of co-design approaches may overcome the limits of BOSE and empower DApps with higher user acceptance.

3.3   Our Adapted Approach

Inspired by BOSE and co-design approaches and based on the genuine development experiences, our refined approach comprises three stages. Figure 2 illustrates the interactions and relationships between the three stages.

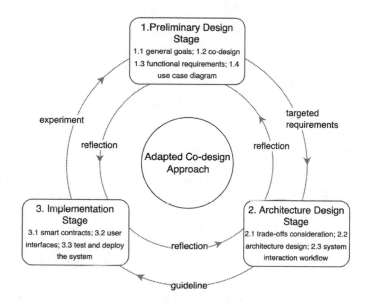

Fig. 2. Adapted DApp development approach

- The preliminary design stage aims to narrow a large industry scope down to a few most desired and feasible points, define the targeted user groups and collect essential information for the next development stage. It includes four steps: 1) set general goals through industry analysis; 2) engage users through co-design; 3) elicit functional requirements of the system based on the evidence collected from the last step; and 4) develop use cases diagram to present interactions between actors and the system.
- The architecture design stage makes decisions about what functionality should be allocated to what components within the system, and how components constructed into a whole system. It includes: 1) trade-off considerations that may affect cost efficiency (type of blockchain), performance (on-chain & off-chain data storage), and security (consensus protocol) et.[25]; and 2) architectural illustration to demonstrate the system structure, which presents what roles the blockchain is playing and how it interacts with other components. The decision-makings of this stage should reflect on the results of the preliminary design stage.
- The implementation stage includes: smart contract development, user interface development, test and deploy the combined DApp system, reassess the

development goals, and adjust the design of previous steps. Noticeably, the whole design procedure is not a linear process but a dynamic and reciprocating process where each stage lays a foundation for the next stage and the results of each stage act as reflections of previous stages' revisions and improvements.

4   CVallet Development

This section describes the design and development of the CVallet system using the proposed DApp development methodology.

4.1   Preliminary Design Stage

Set General Goals. The emerging problems, mentioned in the Introduction section, in the current education credentialing system call for an innovative system that can rebuild the trust infrastructure to sort out the social and industrial order. Therefore, similar to relevant precursors, our first goal is to establish a secure, reliable, and tamper-proof credentialing system underpinned by blockchain. In addition, we expect to increase the industry adoption rate, so the second goal is to develop a convenient and handy gadget that can solve industry practitioners' pain points and improve industry workflow efficiency.

Co-design with Users. We developed a two-phases co-design approach to understand users' pain points in daily practices and to elicit requirements for the application:

- Phase 1 aims to understand how learners interact with their education credentials in practices. This phase involves two steps. In step one, we involved 97 learners to collect their real-life experiences of managing, sharing and certifying credentials (the survey is accessible at: learners survey). Based on the findings of step one, we developed more targeted interview questions in step two. We invited six participants to join the interview game with seven scenarios (the interview is accessible at: learners interview).
- Phase 2 aims to find out 1) the concurrent verification procedure, 2) verification criteria and methods, and 3) verification challenges in industries, therefore we invited 12 senior recruiters to join the consultation interview phase (A sample of interview questions is accessible at: Recruiters interview). All of the participants have more than five years of working experience in verifying educational and employment credentials. Their working background can cover nine industries: headhunters, tertiary institutions, digital media, investment consulting, oil and mining, consumer goods, non-for-profits, and real estate and information technology.

After the data collection of the two phases, two coders conducted three rounds of thematic coding supported by NVivo and reached a Cohen' kappa score of 0.93 in the last round (The full coding scheme accessible at: complete codebook). The data analysis leads to the following remarkable **findings**:

- *Top 5 credentials management methods:* 1) scan and save digital copies on personal computers (22.48%, 67 out of 97 participants vote for this option); 2) save on a hard drive or USB (17.11%, 51 votes); 3) use cloud storage (15.44%, 46 votes); 4) save on smart phones (12.75%, 38 votes); 5) send copies to email box and print several copies for physical storage (both share 11.74%, 35 votes). We find that almost every learner chooses more than one method to store credentials to prevent lost or damage. In fact, 63.22% of them agree on their worries about losing or damaging important credentials. In addition, 36.78% of them do not know where and how to get damaged or lost credentials recovered.
- *Top 5 verification methods:* 1) resume screening – recruiters verify CVs and resumes through checking conformity between each experience and each corresponding timelines; 2) interview screening – recruiters conduct several rounds of interviews to check conformity and consistency throughout; 3) reference check – recruiters call back candidates' previous managers or supervisors to collect evidence to prove experiences authenticity; 4) rely on third party – recruiters approach to either authorities' verification channels or the screening service companies.
- *Top 5 verification challenges (Table 1):* 1) the current verification method cannot guarantee authenticity and recruiters complain that there is no effective tool to verify credentials; 2) the recruiter has spotted intentions of fraudulent behaviours or encountered fraudulent credentials; 3) the whole procedure is time-consuming involving many back-and-forth steps; 4) recruitment and verification results are largely depending on recruiters' professional judgement and working experiences; 5) subjective evidence: the verifying documents are provided by candidates and the proofs are provided by the candidate's preferred referees.
- *Shared concerns (Appendix Fig. 5):* There are some joined codes indicate shared concerns of both learners and recruiters: 1) time-consuming – both learners and recruiters spend lots of times and go through back-and-forth procedures; 2) relevant credentials – learners tend to choose credentials that can improve their employability and recruiters look for relevant studying and working experience that match with their listed positions; 3) lack of trust – recruiters and learners do not trust one another completely. 4) privacy concerns: Learners are worry about privacy leakage even though they were asked for permission of background check. Some recruiters also indicate they have to check candidates' personal information even though they do not want to suspect and pry.

Table 1. Top five verification challenges.

Code	Description	freq
No Effective Method	The recruiter complains the current methods turn out to be difficult to verify the authenticity	12
Fraudulent Intention	The recruiter has spotted intentions of fraudulent behaviours; the recruiter has encountered fraudulent credentials	12
Time Consuming	The current working is mainly depends on human power with numerous of back-and-forth steps, which are time consuming	10
Personal Judgment	The verification result is based on the recruiter's professional but personal experiences and judgment	10
Subjective Evidence	Recruiters have to accept what the person says, the evidence and proof is provided by a candidate's preferred referees	8

Functional Requirements and Use Cases. Based on the above findings, we extract users' requirements and the corresponding functional requirements presented in Table 2 that supports self-explaining considering the limited space. Subsequently, since UML diagrams are frequently recommended by a few studies [12,25], we translate Table 2 requirements into UML user cases diagram to present interactions between classes of users and the subsystems (see Appendix Figure 6). In short description, learners can upload, receive, manage and share credentials securely in learning portfolio management system, and recruiters can request and verify various credentials efficiently in credential verification system.

Table 2. Elicited requirements

User requirements	Corresponding functional requirements
Learners need:	The system can:
- a secure place to store and manage various credentials;	- support various credentials management and categorization at one place;
- a privacy-preserving method of sharing their credentials;	- support encryption of data and self-sovereign over data and accessibility
- a time-efficient way to convince relying parties about their previous study or working experiences	- support verification of credentials or can be certified automatically by the system
Recruiters need:	The system can:
- a more objective way than traditional reference check to verify various credentials	- support the verification of credentials from the recruitment checklist
- transparent information about candidates' authentic experiences without peeping into individuals' privacy	- return an instructional value without revealing individuals' private information
- a time-efficient tool due to release the heavy workload	- cut down existing recruitment screening procedure into fewer steps

4.2 Architecture Design Stage

Considerations. We take the following considerations while developing the system architecture. Firstly, one of the desired attributes is to comply with W3C standards, such as Verifiable Credentials(VCs) and Decentralized Identifiers (DIDs), to maximize interoperability, encourage interested parties to make collaborative contributions, ensure tamper resistance of the data, and simplify the prototype implementation [5, 20]. VCs consist three parts to facilitate verification: metadata (credential type, issuance date and a public key for verification purposes), claims (the learner and the graduated institution) and proofs (the issuer's digital signature) [5]. DIDs represent a novel class of globally unique identifiers where each entity can have as many DIDs as required to preserve the appropriate separation of identities, personas, and interactions since the production and assertion of Decentralized Identifiers are entity-controlled [20]. Secondly, we chose Algorand blockchain to build the prototype over Bitcoin and Ethereum because it is more computational efficient with faster transaction speed and is less likely to fork. These features are significantly essential to maintain learning records' continuity and integrity and deliver a better application performance. The third consideration is on-chain vs. off-chain data storage. Since blockchain is not suitable for big data storage but is essential for trust proofs [25], we decided to store issuers' public keys, fileID, and signatures on-chain, while the complete records would be stored in selected databases (e.g. MongoDB and IPFS).

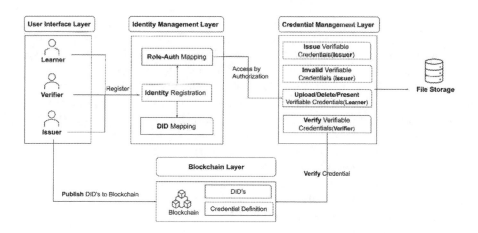

Fig. 3. Architecture of CVallet

CVallet Architecture. Our proposed CVallet (as seen in Fig. 3) has four layers: User Interface Layer, Identity Management Layer, Credential Management Layer and Blockchain Layer, and each layer contains multiple components and functional modules (only the main components and modules are displayed). The whole system is developed in an extensible manner with plugin function modules considering that future extensions may be required when business requirements change or expand.

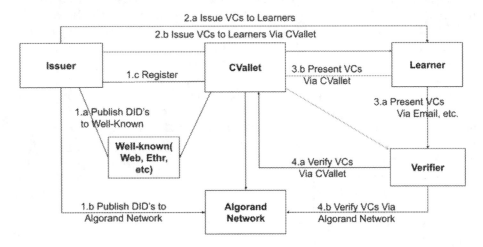

Fig. 4. Workflow demonstration. Note: numbers 1 to 4 denote the order from VC's generation to verification, and a, b, and c indicate three ways are available to perform the process.

We interpret the interactions between different components and modules in Fig. 4. To begin, the issuer can publish a DID document either to a well-known address (1.a) (e.g. https://www.issuer-domain/.well-known/did.json), or to a blockchain wallet address (1.b). Alternatively, issuers can register their details with a public key in CVallet System (1.c). CVallet will handle the identity registration and DID mapping process (as shown in Fig. 3). Then, when the issuer digitally signs the certificate, VCs could be issued to Learners either directly (2.a) or via CVallet (2.b). In step three, learners could share their VCs with a verifier (3.a) or present VCs via CVallet. Finally, the verifier can instantly verify whether the certificate is valid or not using the digital signature verification method by the details in DID document retrieved from either CVallet (4.a) or Blockchain network (4.b). Any manipulation with the credential will lead to the failure of digital signature verification.

4.3 CVallet Prototype Implementation

To demonstrate the deployment of the CVallet in a real-world setting, we built a proof-of-concept prototype of the back-end server and front-end interfaces. The back-end server comprises the following modules: identity management, credentials management, and credential verification. We produce a universal unique identifier (UUID) for each registered user in the identity management module.

Multiple DIDs are associated with the user's UUID. We provide both on-chain and off-chain credential verification options; credentials can be verified either through a smart contract or registration information in CVallet. As for the front-end interfaces, we developed different dashboards for different user groups.

Implementation Settings. We implemented our code in Python for the back-end server, JavaScript for the front-end interface and MongoDB for the off-chain data storage. We created a smart contract for on-chain verification and deployed it on the Algorand Testnet. The following are the main tools and frameworks used in CVallet:

- FastAPI (Python based Framework) https://fastapi.tiangolo.com/
- Nodejs Express Framework https://expressjs.com/
- MongoDB https://www.mongodb.com/
- Algorand Testnet Dispenser https://bank.testnet.algorand.network/
- Algorand Testnet Explorer https://testnet.algoexplorer.io/
- Algorand Sandbox https://github.com/algorand/sandbox

Deployment Settings. We use all free tier server instances that Heroku provides to deploy our back-end server and front-end interface in the US region. The free server RAM is 512 MB in size, and the network bandwidth is soft limited at 2 TB per app per month (around 800 bits per second). MongoDB free version single cluster is used for the off-chain data storage. The original credential file with a 1-page pdf can be up to 1 MB. The size of a verifiable credential is much smaller because it only contains metadata. It varies from 1 KB to 2 KB with the W3C data model. In the CVallet system, we support both ways above.

Time. The request-response time or execution time requirements vary amongst industries in different sectors. For example, those dot-com companies that do most of their internet business require a response time of a half second. In comparison, 5 s for the response time is enough for manufacturing industries. To evaluate the performance of the CVallet, firstly, we tested the first packet arrival took around 240 ms and the internet latency around 1 s. Then we test the two primary functions: credential uploading and verification. These two functions are relatively time-consuming compared with others. For each of the 10 trials, we choose a smaller file of 4 KB and a larger one of 663 KB. The smaller sized file results average execution times of 1.29 s and 1.21 s for credential uploading and verification respectively. While the comparable time expenses for the larger file are 1.912 and 1.843 s in corresponding tasks. In addition, the average execution time heavily depends on many factors, such as internet speed, server configuration, server bandwidth, database performance, etc. We use free version servers and database tiers in our settings. It is accessible with an uploading time within 2 s and a verification time within 1.5 s in the credential uploading and verification scenario. In the future, we plan to deploy the CVallet system in an enterprise configuration and evaluate its performance.

5   Conclusion and Future Directions

In this study, we first explore a human-centred DApp engineering approach by integrating one BOSE approach with a co-design method. Then, we developed a prototype of blockchain-oriented education credentials management and verification system established on Algorand blockchain as a proof-of-concept, supported by intensive user experiences research to increase the user-acceptance potentiality. The *reflections* and *future directions* are elaborated as follows:

Methodology Aspect: The DApp development method presented in this paper is the first study to integrate a co-design method with a BOSE approach. It inherited the advantages of BOSE and co-design, complementing a reflective and iterative development procedure to increase the DApp user acceptance. This methodological proposal calls for a human-centred design need to connect the DApp development with business settings and corresponding stakeholders (hereby refers to learners and recruiters and scenarios of their interactions with credentials), aiming to promote blockchain adoption in the education and recruitment industry. However, since this method is a new attempt to combine an engineering approach with a human-centred method in the blockchain application field, it does not have enough experimental results to prove its overall validity. Although we test this method to develop CVallet prototype, the limited empirical tests cannot prove it to be a solid software engineering approach. Instead, we tend to bring valuable inspirations to BOSE development through this methodological proposal from an interdisciplinary perspective. The future work may include: 1) refining the method with more development experiments; 2) detailing the smart contracts development; and 3) developing design principles of connecting blockchain with traditional systems.

Social and Industrial Aspects: Socially, this study adds values on: 1) social awareness and knowledge of blockchain technology; 2) increased mutual understanding between educational and industrial stakeholders and blockchain practitioners; and 3) blockchain exploration and application for social goods. From industrial perspective, this study has: 1) spotted practical challenges in industries' recruitment sector; 2) eliminated misalignment between designing assumptions and authentic industrial requirements; 3) developed a blockchain solution to improve work efficiency and reduce cost of traditional verification workflow; and 4) designed and implemented the prototype to test the technical and economic feasibility of the blockchain solution. However, since the product development is still in the initial prototype stage and has not yet been tested within industrial companies, it lacks sufficient user testing to support the practicality of the application. Furthermore, since user involvement is essential throughout the product development cycle when industrial requirements change and blockchain solution evolves, we expect to launch regular workshops to re-involve users in future development stages.

Appendix

Shared Concerns

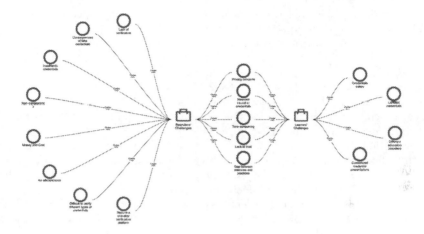

Fig. 5. Shared concerns between learners and recruiters

User Stories

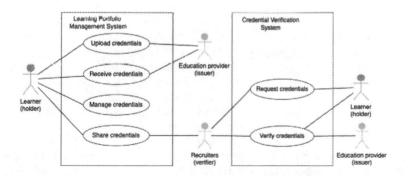

Fig. 6. Use case diagram Note: actors on the left side of the system boxes are initiators, while right-side actors are responders. The same-coloured actors indicate the same user group.

References

1. Baldi, M., Chiaraluce, F., Kodra, M., Spalazzi, L.: Security analysis of a blockchain-based protocol for the certification of academic credentials. arXiv preprint arXiv:1910.04622 (2019)
2. Caldarelli, G., Ellul, J.: Trusted academic transcripts on the blockchain: a systematic literature review. Appl. Sci. **11**(4), 1842 (2021)
3. Chung, F.: The great Aussie degree scam: forgers raking in thousands selling bogus qualifications (2015). https://www.news.com.au/finance/work/careers/the-great-aussie-degree-scam-forgers-raking-in-thousands-selling-bogus-qualifications/news-story/37a95801652821f9357ba94c20bbf29a
4. Consortium, Q.: Decentralised qualifications' verification and management for learner empowerment, education reengineering and public sector transformation. https://cordis.europa.eu/project/id/822404
5. Consortium, W.W.W., et al.: Verifiable credentials data model 1.1: expressing verifiable information on the web (2022). https://www.w3.org/TR/vc-data-model/
6. National Center for Education Statistics: Price of attending an undergraduate institution. The Condition of Education (2020)
7. Gallagher, S.R.: Educational credentials come of age: a survey on the use and value of educational credentials in hiring. Center for the Future of Higher Education & Talent Strategy (2018)
8. Grech, A., Camilleri, A.F.: Blockchain in education. Publications Office of the European Union, Luxembourg (2017)
9. Li, Z.Z., Liu, J.K., Yu, J., Gasevic, D.: Blockchain-based solutions for education credentialing system: Comparison and implications for future development. In: 2022 IEEE International Conference on Blockchain (Blockchain), pp. 79–86 (2022). https://doi.org/10.1109/Blockchain55522.2022.00021
10. Liyuan, L., Meng, H., Yiyun, Z., Reza, P.: E2̂ c-chain: a two-stage incentive education employment and skill certification blockchain. In: 2019 IEEE International Conference on Blockchain, pp. 140–147. IEEE (2019)
11. Loukil, F., Abed, M., Boukadi, K.: Blockchain adoption in education: a systematic literature review. Educ. Inf. Technol. **26**(5), 5779–5797 (2021)
12. Marchesi, L., Marchesi, M., Tonelli, R.: ABCDE-agile block chain DApp engineering. Blockchain Res. Appl. **1**(1–2), 100002 (2020)
13. Mikroyannidis, A.: Work-in-progress: piloting smart blockchain badges for lifelong learning. In: Auer, M.E., Hortsch, H., Michler, O., Köhler, T. (eds.) Mobility for Smart Cities and Regional Development - Challenges for Higher Education. ICL 2021. Lecture Notes in Networks and Systems, vol. 389. Springer, Cham (2022). https://doi.org/10.1007/978-3-030-93904-5_74
14. Milligan, S., Kennedy, G.: To what degree? alternative micro-credentialing in a digital age. In: Visions for Australian Tertiary Education, pp. 41–54 (2017)
15. Mishra, R.A., Kalla, A., Braeken, A., Liyanage, M.: Privacy protected blockchain based architecture and implementation for sharing of students' credentials. Inf. Process. Manage. **58**(3), 102512 (2021)
16. Nadia Politou (ATOS), Ingo Keck (TIB), Panagiotis Kokkinakos, Christos Botsikas(NTUA): Qualichain pilot evaluation and lessons learnt. Technical report (2022). https://alfresco.epu.ntua.gr/share/s/-eTjAueIQ5-9mH_G2Om0nQ
17. Ocheja, P., Flanagan, B., Ueda, H., Ogata, H.: Managing lifelong learning records through blockchain. Res. Pract. Technol. Enhanced Learn. **14**(1), 4 (2019). https://doi.org/10.1186/s41039-019-0097-0

18. Porru, S., Pinna, A., Marchesi, M., Tonelli, R.: Blockchain-oriented software engineering: challenges and new directions. In: 2017 IEEE/ACM 39th International Conference on Software Engineering Companion. IEEE (2017)
19. Pozdniakov, S., et al.: The question-driven dashboard: How can we design analytics interfaces aligned to teachers' inquiry? In: 12th International Learning Analytics and Knowledge Conference (LAK22) (2022)
20. Reed, D., et al.: Decentralized identifiers (DIDs) v1. 0: core architecture, data model, and representations. W3C Working Draft 8 (2022)
21. Research, A.M.: Employment screening services market outlook 2028 (2021). https://www.researchandmarkets.com/reports/5031500/employment-screening-services-market-by-service?utm_source=BW&utm_medium=PressRelease&utm_code=f5px fl&utm_campaign=1571725+-+Global+Employment+Screening+Services+Market +(2021+to+2028)+-+by+Service%2c+Application+and+Geography&utm_exec=ja mu273prd
22. Ronning, A., Chung, W.W.: Blockcerts v3 proposal (2019)
23. Steen, M., Manschot, M., De Koning, N.: Benefits of co-design in service design projects. Int. J. Des. **5**(2), 53–60 (2011)
24. Tsai, Y.S., Singh, S., Rakovic, M., Lim, L.A., Roychoudhury, A., Gasevic, D.: Charting design needs and strategic approaches for academic analytics systems through co-design. In: 12th International Learning Analytics and Knowledge Conference (LAK22) (2022)
25. Xu, X., Weber, I., Staples, M.: Architecture for Blockchain Applications. Springer, Cham (2019). https://doi.org/10.1007/978-3-030-03035-3

Decentralized Access Control for Secure Microservices Cooperation with Blockchain

Ning Xi, Yajie Li, and Jin Liu[✉]

School of Cyber Engineering, Xidian University, Xi'an, China
nxi@xidian.edu.cn, jiinl@stu.xidian.edu.cn

Abstract. The wide-spread cloud-native technologies have accelerated the flourish of large-scale and high-concurrency microservices today. However, due to the flexibility and complexity of cooperation procedure, it is difficult to realize high-efficient security management on these mircoservices. Traditional centralized access control has flaws of relying on a centralized third-party manager and single-point failure while decentralized mechanisms are suffering from the inconsistency of policies defined by different participants. This paper firstly proposes a practical decentralized access control framework and scheme for secure microservices cooperation based on the blockchain. In our scheme, we realize the separate management on the individualized access policy by vendors instead of a central authority. Secondly, we build a permission blockchain to maintain the consistency and integrity of the policies. Through the analysis and experiments, it shows that our solution gracefully eliminates policy differences while the update cost achieves nearly constant.

Keywords: Microservices · Service cooperation · Access control · Permission management · Blockchain

1 Introduction

Cloud-native technology greatly improves the quality of various modern IT applications, such as smart transportation [5], smart home [17], and smart healthcare [2]. Microservices are the core of cloud-native application architecture. Built as a distributed set of small, independent services that interact through a shared fabric, microservices enable a highly efficient and flexible approach to delivery the large, complex cloud-native applications by cooperation [3]. Each microservice is encapsulated with a specific business capability and its data. Heterogeneous services can cooperate centered around APIs provided by cloud-native architectures, such as REST, gRPC, and NATS protocols.

However, loosely coupled services pose a great security challenge to application security during their cooperation, i.e., unauthorized access to cross-service

Supported by the Major Research plan of the National Natural Science Foundation of China (Grant No. 92167203), the National Key R&D Program of China (Grant No. 2018YFE0207600), Natural Science Basis Research Plan in Shaanxi Province of China (Grant No. 2022JM-338).

data and service. Adversaries could access sensitive data or services by calling the exposed cross-service API instead of calling the target service directly. Access control provides a basic and effective way to protect individual service and their data [6,9]. [24] proposed a key management scheme based on hierarchical access control. [13] is dedicated to solving the adaptive scheduling scheme based on data flow management policy. Remote control communication is implemented based on authentication in [19].

Above access control policies rely on a central authority for management. The centralized framework is suffering from a single point of failure. Besides, it is difficult to realize individualized access control due to the high cost of the management of complex policies. Therefore, [21] proposed a decentralized access control scheme for service access. Each Manufacturer can define and manage its policies. The decentralized way simplifies the management, significantly improves the QoS, and overcomes the bottleneck of the single point of failure. This method simplifies the management overhead of complex policies and overcomes the problems caused by centralization, but it also introduces new problems. [14] has proposed the first decentralized access control scheme for microservices in the cloud. It realizes a high-efficient and secure microservice management. However, decentralized approaches also arise some serious security issues in mircoservices cooperation. On the one hand, different microservices may define conflict policies. On the other hand, some malicious vendors could use their privileges to deliver the microservice to illegal users by encapsulating the original one as a new microservice. So the consistency of policies has become a major challenge in those decentralized schemes.

Given the challenges existing in the above approaches, we propose a novel decentralized access control scheme for secure microservices cooperation based on the blockchain. Firstly, we provide a decentralized access control framework for loosely coupled services. Service vendors can define the individualized access policies by themselves instead of a central authority, which is more practical in the distributed cloud-native system. Secondly, we build a permission blockchain to maintain the consistency of the access control policies. Each policy on the blockchain cannot be directly tampered with by cloud platform managers. Therefore, we can overcome the security threats caused by illegal access policies. The contributions of this paper are as follows:

(1) For service calls between microservices, combined with the immutability of blockchain, an access control model based on a permission graph is designed to reduce policy storage overhead, realizing safe and efficient distributed access control.
(2) We design a permission extraction scheme based on static analysis, which can accurately extract the calling relationship between microservices before the service is deployed and run on the cloud platform.
(3) We design a blockchain-based permission decision-making scheme, which implements a decision-making management mechanism based on consensus among multiple manufacturers, ensures immutability and consistency, and effectively avoids unauthorized access and cross-service unauthorized access.

(4) We implement our scheme based on Kubernetes and Hyperledger Fabric, and compare it with other traditional access control scheme. The evaluation results show that our scheme realize a high-efficient decentralized access control with affordable cost.

The rest of this paper is organized as follows. In Sect. 2, we focus on a survey of related work. Section 3 describes motivations and requirements. Section 4 describes the proposed solution in more detail. The experimental design and discuss the experimental results are provided in Sect. 5, and we finally present the conclusions and future works in Sect. 6.

2   Related Work

To solve the problem of cross-service unauthorized access in microservices, we summarize the current related methods, including the following four categories.

Automatic Generation of Policies. The traditional centralized access control mechanism requires unified policy management by security managers, which is difficult to meet the security sharing requirements of distributed big data. In particular, security managers may be untrustworthy and risk policy leakage. Documentation can better express the developer's intent, but such documentation does not always exist [16,23]. At the same time, these methods are often coarse-grained and incomplete due to the limitations of Natural Language Processing(NLP). Generally, we infer rule criteria and policy structure from traffic through collected traces or historical data. The effectiveness of this scheme depends on the granularity and completeness of the tracking [22]. In addition, applications run ahead of time to collect data, which can lead to an attack on Windows.

Secure Communication Between Microservices. Reference [8] Adjust the interconnection between microservices through the aggregation and distribution functions of the gateway. When registering a microservice, the microservice itself creates uniquely identified endpoints bound to event channels or methods. Reference [12] presented a graph-based access control that automatically creates a model of legitimate communication relationships, with interactive updates through an easy-to-understand interface. This solution implements a self-learning IoT firewall. But there is a lack of filtering of traffic on the first boot.

Attribute-Based Access Control. The literature [10] implemented attribute-based access control (ABAC) and proposes AoT. AoT is an authentication and access control scheme for IoT device lifecycle, that facilitates secure (in terms of stronger authentication) wireless interoperability of new and guest devices in a seamless manner. Based on the non-interactive multi-authority ABE (NI-MA-ABE) scheme. [25] proposed a completely decentralized outsourced ABE scheme (FDO-ABE) as the access control architecture of MEC. However, the downside of this approach is that the modeling process is time-consuming and error-prone, making them unsuitable for flexible microservice applications.

Blockchain-Based Access Control. Reference [18] designed an attribute-based encryption scheme to ensure the privacy and security of medical data. In this system, all the health care information of the users is grouped into a block, which makes the amount of stored data too large, and further leads to the poor performance of the blockchain. Literature [11] proposed a completely decentralized authorization management framework for pseudonyms and privacy protection, enabling users to own and control their data. Based on the key of authorized access to resources, [20] designed OSCAR, a method of access control of the Internet of things using object security.

For the above problems, we design an automatic generation method for the inter-service access control policy of microservices using blockchain. On the one hand, we use source code static analysis technology and taint tracking technology to generate a request relationship diagram for microservices. This can effectively reduce permission blockchain and platform data storage scale, and improve the overall operating performance to a certain extent. On the other hand, we store the service permission determination and service permission whitelist in the blockchain to ensure the immutability and confidentiality of service permissions. The decision-making mechanism and the service management platform are separated, which effectively avoids the risks brought by the platform and management personnel.

3   Motivation and Requirements

3.1   System Model

Microservices architecture is an evolution of the traditional service-oriented architecture, which emphasizes the splitting of systems into small and lightweight architectures designed to perform very cohesive business functions. Container technology provides convenience for lightweight independent deployment of services. At present, the mainstream microservice management framework includes Swarm, Kubernetes, Mesos, AWS ECS, and so on. On this basis, the microservice permission management system framework we designed includes three core elements, microservices, cloud platforms, and users, as shown in Fig. 1.

The cloud platform relies on the open source cloud computing technology Kubernetes, which is an open architecture that facilitates the integration of various cluster management functions, making the one-stop container cloud platform a mainstream application.

Users are divided into microservice manufacturers, platform managers, and application developers. Microservice manufacturers provide basic microservices and whitelists. Based on management requirements, the platform managers complete the cloud platform environment preparation, dependency check, and deployment and operation of service components. Application developers implement their applications by calling the underlying microservices.

The entire application process is executed on the cloud platform. The microservice manufacturers build initial microservice whitelists and determine the callable relationship among microservices. When a user develops and deploys

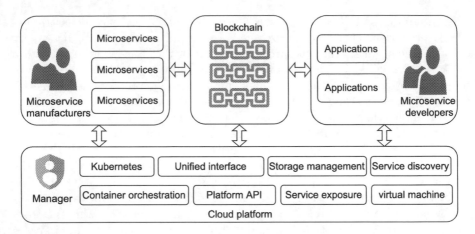

Fig. 1. System model.

an application, the platform sends a microservice request to the blockchain, obtains the permission relationship diagram of the microservice whitelist, performs collaborative combination and use of services, and finally obtains the request result. In particular, collaborative calls can be made between microservices to facilitate request fulfillment.

3.2   Threat Model

In order to ensure the security of service calls between microservices and prevent malicious attacks and tampering by attackers, the security model of this paper involves the security requirements of three roles.

(1) Microservice manufacturers do not provide microservices to unauthorized users. To ensure the confidentiality of service data, the microservice manufacturers upload the whitelists to the blockchain. Based on security, platform managers are not allowed to make policies. In addition, microservice components are heterogeneous, and it is necessary to prevent cross-microservice calls from occurring in the collaboration of a large number of microservices.
(2) Malicious platform managers try to obtain the white list of microservice manufacturers for illegal purposes. Therefore, platform managers are untrustworthy. Allowing him/her to manage the policy may tamper with or compromise the service.
(3) The attacker masquerades as a microservice developer. He attempted unauthorized access and cross service unauthorized access. This is fatal for microservices.

4   Decentralized Access Control for Secure Microservices Cooperation with Blockchain

Based on the system model and threat model, we design an automatic generation scheme for inter-service access control policies for microservices using blockchain. Its overall framework is shown in Fig. 2.

The flow is shown as follows. It is divided into the permission extraction phase and the permission decision-making phase. In the permission extraction phase, static analysis and taint tracking technology are used to obtain the request permission graph of microservices accessing other services through the network, and the calling relationship between microservices can be accurately extracted before the service is deployed and run on the cloud platform. In the decision-making phase, based on the blockchain, we generate the permission decision relationship graph of microservices to determine whether the request relationship can be authorized. Through the Microservice manufacturers uploading the basic service call list, we realize the decision management mechanism based on multi-manufacturer consensus.

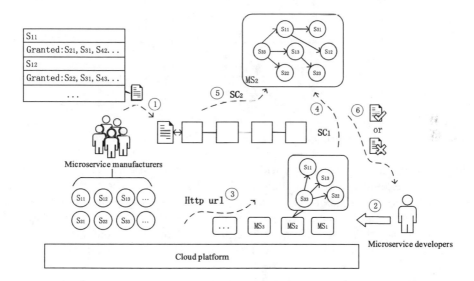

Fig. 2. Graph-based access between microservices.

4.1   Permission Extraction

Microservices architecture achieves decomposing what was originally a huge monolithic application into a series of services. The dynamics and complexity among microservices make microservice management difficult. In order to more intuitively represent the microservice call relationship, we abstract the microservice call relationship in the application into a graph model. According to the typical characteristics of the small scale of the microservice design architecture and the consistency of the service invocation mechanism in the same type of applications, in the permission extraction phase, we use static analysis-based request extraction to identify the request service relationship in the microservice source code. It includes processes such as semantic identification, reverse tracking, program slicing, generating a request list, and generating a request topology graph, as shown in Fig. 3.

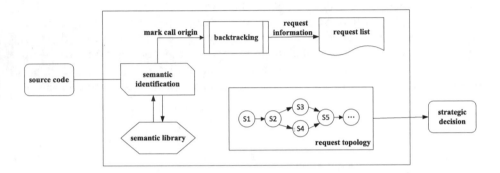

Fig. 3. Permission extraction

Semantic Identification. To determine the relevant service invocation request statements in the application source code, we formulate different semantic libraries according to the particularity of dynamic and static languages. Semantic recognition is used for identification, as the support link of the reverse tracking technology in the later phase. Because of the feature of adopting multiple programming languages in the process of microservices development, a semantic recognition model is constructed by using different language semantic libraries. The statements in the source code with service calls are identified as the starting point of the next phase.

Note that functions are called differently in programming languages. Take Java and Python as examples. The former method is bound to the corresponding class object, and the Java package name and function method name should be included when building the semantic library. The latter uses the method call of *package name.function name* when using functions. Table 1 summarizes the semantic libraries of common service calls in microservices in Java and Python.

Next enter the recognition process when the language semantic library is established. Specifically, judging whether the code refers to the function package name in the semantic library can determine whether there is an external service call.

Table 1. Java and Python semantic libraries for common service calls in microservices.

Language	Library name	Function name
Java	javax.ws.rs.client	get, post, put, delete, head, method, invoke
	org.springframework.web.client	execute, exchange, getForObject, getForEntity, postForObject, put, postForEntity, delete
	org.apache.solr.client.solrj	query, request, ping
Python	requests	requests.get

Case 1: When there is a corresponding package name in the source code, first start to traverse each line of code, extract the function name in the code through regular expressions and match the function name in the semantic library, then record the number of lines of code segments that satisfy the representation, and finally output this line of code.

Case 2: If the function package name is not referenced in the source code, we consider that there is no external service call request.

Reverse Tracking. Statements with service calls are identified in the source code, then uses as starting points to perform backward taint propagation on the control flow graphs. By doing so, we can get the program fragments associated with each call. Finally, traverse the slice to obtain the complete call path information.

More specifically, the source code of the identification is input into the direction tracking algorithm, which is used as the starting point for pollution transmission, and the program slices related to the stain are output. After obtaining the identification code, the variable name extraction and function parameter extraction are carried out on this line of code. After obtaining the parameter data of the pollution source, iterative traversal propagation is generally divided into three cases: assignment, path splicing, and function call. The tainted parameters are extracted for the statements in these three cases respectively, and then the parameters are added to the tainted list for the next iterative traversal tracking.

Request List Generation. Performing reverse traversal to generate complete calling information after obtaining the relevant program slice files of each calling program. The specific function information to be called can be located by generating a list of request lists in JSON format. We use source_svc to represent the source service. Additionally, the request list contains the request type, domain name, and port number.

Request Topology Graph Generation. The microservice request relationship topology graph is based on the microservice request list. The request list is generated based on the request list and static analysis results.

The input to the graph we are concerned with is a list of requests in JSON format. The nodes represent services, and the directed edges represent the calling relationship between services.

Nodes collection: focus on two types of services. A node represents the current microservice node that needs to be deployed when its in-degree is zero. Other nodes represent the basic service being invoked. The data comes from the value of source_svc and the name field in the list of related services in the microservice.

Edges collection: focus on calling the relationship between services. Specifically, the source service source_svc in each manifest list points to the service name. Details are presented in Algorithm 1.

Algorithm 1. topo( )

Require: $RequesSvc\_Json$
Ensure: $G_{Request}$(request relationship topology graph)
1: **for** i in $RequesSvc\_Json$ **do**
2:     $nodes.append(svc\_dict[$"source_svc"$])$
3:     $nodes.append(svc\_dict[$"name"$])$
4:     $edges.append((svc\_dict[$"source_svc"$], svc\_dict[$"name"$]))$
5:     // remove duplicates
6:     $G = nx.Graph()$
7:     $nx.draw(G, with\_labels = True, node\_color =' y',)$
8:     $plt.show()$
9: **end for**

4.2   Decision-Making Phase

In this section, we explain more details of the permission decision-making phase. Blockchain is used to achieve policy generation, storage, and decision-making. By storing the service permission determination and a whitelist of permissions services in the blockchain, immutability, and confidentiality are guaranteed. In addition, the use of graph storage policy and permission determination can effectively reduce the storage size of permission blockchain and improve the efficiency of permission determination. This means improved overall operational performance. As shown in Fig. 4, this phase mainly includes the stored procedure of service whitelist, stored procedure of permission graph, and permission determination process.

Microservice owners: Microservice owners include microservice platforms and microservice manufacturers. Microservice manufacturers can control microservices to generate personalized policies. The microservice platform holds the microservices provided by the microservice developers to facilitate the generation of permission graph for later access control.

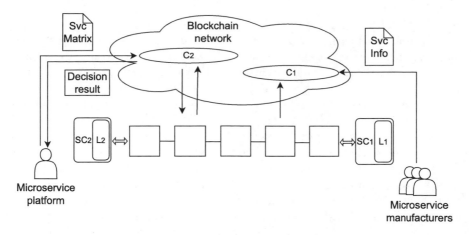

Fig. 4. Architecture of the permission decision-making phase.

Channels: We design two channels, C1 and C2, each responsible for the communication between different data owners and the blockchain. They provide a completely independent communication mechanism. When a chain code definition is submitted to a channel, the smart contract in the chain code are available to applications on that channel. It is essential for data and communications to maintain privacy. The independence of C1 and C2 is of sufficiency to help organizations separate them from the workflows of different counterparties. More importantly, it is sufficient to enable them to coordinate independent activities when necessary.

Smart contracts: We design two smart contracts, SC1 and SC2, each responsible for the communication to generate access control policies for microservices. They read and write ledger data in the corresponding channel and application code.

The above design is mainly applied to the microservice permission generation phase and the permission decision-making phase.

Permission Generation Phase. At this phase, the microservice owners is microservice manufacturers. Manufacturers upload the encrypted whitelist of service calls on the blockchain network channel C1 according to the smart contract SC1. Transactions are recorded in ledger L1.

Decision-Making Phase. At this phase, we need to design the application code for the interaction between the micro service platform and blockchain. The core task of this phase is to submit the service request relationship graph obtained in the permission extraction phase to the blockchain network channel C2, and perform permission determination according to the smart contract SC2. Specifically, there are two cases: (1) Perform permission determination according to the corresponding permission graph in the ledger L2 if the service exists in the ledger L2. (2) According to the service list, the data is taken from the ledger L1 to generate the permission graph and uploaded to the ledger L2 to determine when the microservice does not have a permission graph in the ledger L2. If the request graph in the application is a subset of the permission graph, it is considered that the call can be authorized, otherwise the authorization is denied.

The representation method of the relevant graphs in this design are all presented in the data structure of the adjacency list. In the AccessMatrix field of SvcMatrix, it is composed of an array of type SvcInfo in L1.

We perform the following steps when the request relationship graph uploaded by the service platform already exists in the ledger L2. First, read the corresponding permission graph, and traverse the list of security access services involved in the service. Then it is determined whether the list in the request graph is a subset of the security list in the permission graph. If it is a subset, it means that the request path where the service is located in the request graph can be authorized. At this point, the next service path determination can be performed. If the subset condition is not met, the authorization is denied. The result is returned to the service platform. The specific algorithm is shown in Algorithm 2.

Algorithm 2. DecisionMaking( )

Require: $G_{Request}$ (microservice permission request graph) and $S_{Ledger2}$ (the ledger L2 corresponding to SC2)

Ensure: decision-making result

1: get microservice $ID, G_{Request}.SvcID$

2: **if** $G_{Request}.SvcID$ exists in ledger L2 **then**

3:     obtain the permission graph $G_{Permission}$ of the microservice from the ledger L2
    $G_{Permission} = S._{Ledger2}.ReadAsset(Ledge2, G_{Request}.SvcID)$

4:     **if** every term $SaveSvc$ in $G_{Request}.AccessMatrix$ is not a subset of $G_{Permission}.AccessMatrix$ **then**

5:         Permission Dined

6:         Permission Granted

7:     **else**

8:         Connect Ledger1 create new Matrix: Svc2Matrix()

9:         DecisionMaking()

10:     **end if**

11: **end if**

The request is sent to the smart contract SC2 if the upload request graph is not recorded in L2. SC2 queries the ledger L1 according to the service ID involved in the request graph to obtain the security access service list corresponding to the service ID and returns the data to SC2. SC2 encapsulates the data in SvcMatrix format. Finally, the permission decision-making is executed. Algorithm 3 shows the specifics.

Algorithm 3. Svc2Matrix( )

Require: $G_{Request}$ (microservice permission request graph)
Ensure: $G_{Permission}$ (permission graph corresponding to microservice)
1: $G_{Permission} = G_{Request}.SvcID, G_{Request}.SvcName, AccessMatrix$
2: channel2 post $G_{Request}$ to channel1
3: Channel1:
4: **for** $SvcID$ in $G_{Request}$ **do**
5:     Get $SvcInfo$ from Ledger1
6:     $append(G_{Permission}.AccessMatrix, SvcInfo)$
7:     channel1 post $G_{Permission}$ to channel2
8:     channel2 update Ledger2 with $G_{Permission}$ and $CreateAsset()$
9: **end for**

---

5 Experiments

In this section, we explore the capabilities and security of the blockchain-based inter-microservice access control policy automatic generation method described above. Our evaluation aims to answer the following three questions:

Q1: What are the advantages of our proposed scheme over other advanced methods?

Q2: How efficient is the microservice when it updates the calling relationship (add microservice calls and delete microservice calls)?

Q3: How does the access control mechanism affect the performance of the application itself?

5.1 Experiment Platform

We explain the simulation setup in more detail. During the experiment, the host CPU used is the 10th generation CPU of the Intel I5 series, and the main frequency of the CPU is 3.40 GHz. The main memory is 12 G. The operating system used is the Centos7 system based on the Linux kernel. The microservice platform used is the cluster management platform built by Kubernetes v1.20.4. The blockchain system used is HyperLedger Fabric 2.2. The code is written in Python and Golang.

The method we designed is practiced with the open-source microservice BookInfo as an example. BookInfo is a heterogeneous microservice application consisting of four separate microservices. This app mimics an online bookstore and can display information about the books in the bookstore. The main programming languages of this application are Java and Python.

5.2 Security

Based on the characteristics of blockchain, such as centerless, transparent, and distributed, we verify the security improvements brought by the proposed approach to microservice applications. In Table 2 we analyze the security differences between several common access control policy schemes and our design

Table 2. Method comparison.

Policy	MC/AC[1]	D/C[2]	Controllability	Integrity	Non-repudiation
Token [15]	MC	C	✔	✔	–
Documents [22]	MC	C	✔	✔	–
Model [12]	AC	D	✔	–	–
Documents+Model [1]	AC	D	✔	–	–
Blockchain+Model [4]	AC	D	✔	–	✔
Graph [7]	AC	D	✔	✔	✔
Graph+Blockchain [Our scheme]	AC	D	✔	✔	✔

[1]MC means managers configuration and AC means automatic configuration.
[2]D means distributed management and C means concentrated management.

scheme. The focus of our solution is that the access control mechanism relies on the whitelist provided by the microservice manufacturers, and based on the blockchain, multi-manufacturer consensus decision-making is realized.

5.3 Efficiency

The feature of the method we propose is that when the calling policies between microservices changes, new microservices are called and deleted according to the whitelist provided by the microservice manufacturers, without rebuilding the generated graph. Therefore, the purpose of this experiment is to evaluate microservices deployment, add new microservice calls, and reduce access control processing time in the case of microservice calls. Specifically, we mainly focus on three situations:

(1) Deploy the microservice application into the microservice platform.
(2) Add policy calls based on the original microservices.
(3) Delete the policies call based on the original microservices.

We compare access control methods based on graphs and decision trees [7], and the experimental results are shown in Fig. 5.

It can be seen from Fig. 5(a) that when new policies are added, adding new callings relationship to the existing policies can effectively reduce policy redundancy. For example, when adding 540 strategies, the running time of [7] is 1952 ms, while ours is around 715 ms. The running time is reduced by at least half.

As can be seen from Fig. 5(b), when a microservice is deleted, the call relationship diagram of the microservice is always smaller than the permission policy diagram composed of the whitelist provided by the microservice manufacturer. Therefore, there is no need to regenerate new policies, reducing the overhead of uploading policies to the blockchain and improving performance. Experimental results show that our running time is within half of the running time of [7].

We counted the time required to make a decision when adding a service call and deleting a service call in the microservice, as shown in Fig. 6.

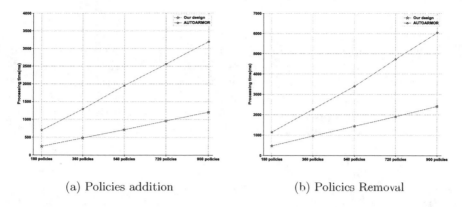

(a) Policies addition   (b) Policies Removal

Fig. 5. Comparison of the running time of (a) Policies addition and (b) Policies Removal.

It takes about 6 ms to add a new microservice call, and about 5 ms to add two new microservice calls. It takes about 5 ms to add 120 microservice calls. There is a similar situation for deleting microservice calls. Therefore, according to the overall statistical trend in Fig. 6, we find that the decision time required for adding microservice calls and deleting microservice calls is roughly the same, and most of the time required is between 4 and 7 ms. This is gratifying, which means that the solution we designed is stable and feasible, and the decision time is within the acceptable range.

Figure 7 counts the time overhead of microservices performing access control for the first time, including the permission extraction phase and the permission decision-making phase. It takes about 204 s when 100 microservices first perform access control. Since two data upload operations are required during the policy generation process, the policy generation time is increased.

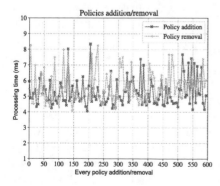

Fig. 6. Time distribution of decision-making for adding and deleting microservice calls.

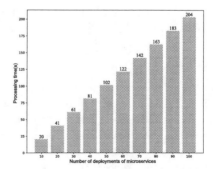

Fig. 7. Time of initial deployment of microservices.

5.4   Performance

To evaluate the impact of the implementation of this scheme, access performance was measured using the evaluation application in two scenarios, with and without the use of this method. We take the case of no access control policy installed as the baseline and use Jmeter to develop a load generator to record the specific conditions of the applications service performance with and without this solution, including end-to-end latency (Fig. 8), throughput (Fig. 9), and CPU usage (Fig. 10).

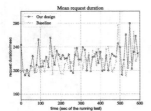
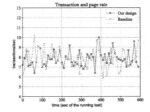
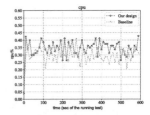

Fig. 8. End-to-end latency.   **Fig. 9.** Throughput.   **Fig. 10.** CPU usage.

As we can see, in Fig. 8, the access control mechanism is separated from the platform, and the impact on the requested traffic time of the application is negligible. Figure 9 reflects a similar situation. Specifically, when using an access control mechanism, it does not affect the performance of the application.

Figure 10 reflects the use of CPU. When using the access control mechanism in this article, the CPU is slightly higher because we store the access decision part in the block chain. However, it can be observed that the difference in CPU is between 0.2%, which is acceptable.

To sum up, this experiment shows that our access control policy mechanism can not only ensure security but also has almost no impact on the performance of the application itself.

6   Conclusion

To solve the security flaws on centralized access control, we propose a practical decentralized access control method for microservices cooperation. Firstly, we generate the permission graph based on individual access policies for the following inter-service access during the mircroservice cooperation. During access, we can extract the inter-service invocation logic of the cooperation application by using static analysis technology. Secondly, the block chain is adopted to realize the decentralized policy management mechanism based on the consensus of multi-manufacturer, while it can also ensure the policy consistency and integrity. Experimental results show that our solution can eliminate the policy difference in access control among microservices. Besides, the complexity microservice update is nearly constant. In future, we will improve the performance policy generation while ensuring security.

References

1. Alohaly, M., Takabi, H., Blanco, E.: A deep learning approach for extracting attributes of ABAC policies. In: Proceedings of the 23nd ACM on Symposium on Access Control Models and Technologies, pp. 137–148 (2018)
2. Baker, S.B., Xiang, W., Atkinson, I.: Internet of things for smart healthcare: technologies, challenges, and opportunities. IEEE Access **5**, 26521–26544 (2017)
3. Gannon, D., Barga, R., Sundaresan, N.: Cloud-native applications. IEEE Cloud Comput. **4**(5), 16–21 (2017)
4. Islam, M.A., Madria, S.: A permissioned blockchain based access control system for IoT. In: 2019 IEEE International Conference on Blockchain (Blockchain), pp. 469–476. IEEE (2019)
5. Jan, B., Farman, H., Khan, M., Talha, M., Din, I.U.: Designing a smart transportation system: an internet of things and big data approach. IEEE Wirel. Commun. **26**(4), 73–79 (2019). https://doi.org/10.1109/MWC.2019.1800512
6. Keller, A., Ludwig, H.: The WSLA framework: specifying and monitoring service level agreements for web services. J. Netw. Syst. Manage. **11**(1), 57–81 (2003)
7. Li, X., Chen, Y., Lin, Z., Wang, X., Chen, J.H.: Automatic policy generation for {Inter-Service} access control of microservices. In: 30th USENIX Security Symposium (USENIX Security 21), pp. 3971–3988 (2021)
8. Lu, D., Huang, D., Walenstein, A., Medhi, D.: A secure microservice framework for IoT. In: 2017 IEEE Symposium on Service-Oriented System Engineering (SOSE), pp. 9–18. IEEE (2017)
9. Lu, L., Li, Z., Wu, Z., Lee, W., Jiang, G.: CHEX: statically vetting android apps for component hijacking vulnerabilities. In: Proceedings of the 2012 ACM Conference on Computer and Communications Security, pp. 229–240 (2012)
10. Neto, A.L.M., et al.: AoT: authentication and access control for the entire IoT device life-cycle. In: Proceedings of the 14th ACM Conference on Embedded Network Sensor Systems CD-ROM, pp. 1–15 (2016)
11. Ouaddah, A., Abou Elkalam, A., Ait Ouahman, A.: FairAccess: a new blockchain-based access control framework for the internet of things. Secur. Commun. Netw. **9**(18), 5943–5964 (2016)
12. Pahl, M.O., Aubet, F.X., Liebald, S.: Graph-based IoT microservice security. In: NOMS 2018–2018 IEEE/IFIP Network Operations and Management Symposium, pp. 1–3. IEEE (2018)
13. Panno, D., Riolo, S.: A new centralized access control scheme for D2D-enabled mmWave networks. IEEE Access **7**, 80697–80716 (2019)
14. Preuveneers, D., Joosen, W.: Access control with delegated authorization policy evaluation for data-driven microservice workflows. Future Internet **9**(4), 58 (2017)
15. Preuveneers, D., Joosen, W.: Towards multi-party policy-based access control in federations of cloud and edge microservices. In: 2019 IEEE European Symposium on Security and Privacy Workshops (EuroS&PW), pp. 29–38. IEEE (2019)
16. Saadaoui, A., Scott, L.S.: Web services policy generation based on SLA requirements. In: 2017 IEEE 3rd International Conference on Collaboration and Internet Computing (CIC), pp. 146–154. IEEE (2017)

17. Solaimani, S., Keijzer-Broers, W., Bouwman, H.: What we do - and don't - know about the smart home: an analysis of the smart home literature. Indoor Built Environ. **24**(3), 370–383 (2015)
18. Thwin, T.T., Vasupongayya, S.: Blockchain-based access control model to preserve privacy for personal health record systems. Secur. Commun. Netw. **2019**, 1–15 (2019)
19. Vince, T., Slavko, O.: Enhanced centralized access control system. In: 2019 IEEE International Conference on Modern Electrical and Energy Systems (MEES), pp. 474–477 (2019)
20. Vučinić, M., Tourancheau, B., Rousseau, F., Duda, A., Damon, L., Guizzetti, R.: OSCAR: object security architecture for the internet of things. Ad Hoc Netw. **32**, 3–16 (2015)
21. Wang, S., Zhang, Y., Zhang, Y.: A blockchain-based framework for data sharing with fine-grained access control in decentralized storage systems. IEEE Access **6**, 38437–38450 (2018)
22. Xiang, C., et al.: Towards continuous access control validation and forensics. In: Proceedings of the 2019 ACM SIGSAC Conference on Computer and Communications Security, pp. 113–129 (2019)
23. Yu, L., Zhang, T., Luo, X., Xue, L., Chang, H.: Toward automatically generating privacy policy for Android apps. IEEE Trans. Inf. Forensics Secur. **12**(4), 865–880 (2016)
24. Zhang, Q., Wang, Y.: A centralized key management scheme for hierarchical access control, vol. 4, pp. 2067–2071 (2004)
25. Zhang, Z., Huang, G., Hu, S., Zhang, W., Wu, Y., Qin, Z.: FDO-ABE: a fully decentralized lightweight access control architecture for mobile edge computing. In: 2021 IEEE 6th International Conference on Computer and Communication Systems (ICCCS), pp. 193–198. IEEE (2021)

Blockchain-Based Access Control for Secure Smart Industry Management Systems

Aditya Pribadi Kalapaaking[1]($\boxtimes$)(ID), Ibrahim Khalil[1](ID),
Mohammad Saidur Rahman[1](ID), and Abdelaziz Bouras[2](ID)

[1] School of Computing Technologies, RMIT University, Melbourne, VIC, Australia
aditya.pribadi.kalapaaking@student.rmit.edu.au
[2] College of Engineering, Qatar University, Doha, Qatar
abdelaziz.bouras@qu.edu.qa

Abstract. Smart manufacturing systems involve a large number of interconnected devices resulting in massive data generation. Cloud computing technology has recently gained increasing attention in smart manufacturing systems for facilitating cost-effective service provisioning and massive data management. In a cloud-based manufacturing system, ensuring authorized access to the data is crucial. A cloud platform is operated under a single authority. Hence, a cloud platform is prone to a single point of failure and vulnerable to adversaries. An internal or external adversary can easily modify users' access to allow unauthorized users to access the data. This paper proposes a role-based access control to prevent modification attacks by leveraging blockchain and smart contracts in a cloud-based smart manufacturing system. The role-based access control is developed to determine users' roles and rights in smart contracts. The smart contracts are then deployed to the private blockchain network. We evaluate our solution by utilizing Ethereum private blockchain network to deploy the smart contract. The experimental results demonstrate the feasibility and evaluation of the proposed framework's performance.

Keywords: Blockchain · Smart contract · Access control · Smart manufacturing · Industry 4.0

1 Introduction

The advancement of communication and Internet-of-Things (IoT) technologies has pushed the rapid development of smart industries or industry 4.0 to allow more efficient and customizable production and logistic operations. However, IoT devices collect a massive amount of data associated with their surroundings and influence cloud computing resources for storing and examining data to extract valuable insights.

Cloud technologies [4] is a superior technology that solves the problems in smart manufacturing systems. By offering the necessary platforms and infrastructure, cloud computing technology ensures efficient data management at a

X. Yuan et al. (Eds.): NSS 2022, LNCS 13787, pp. 615–630, 2022.
https://doi.org/10.1007/978-3-031-23020-2_35

reasonable price. As a result, cloud service providers may manage data from smart manufacturing service providers effectively and affordably.

However, cloud-based smart manufacturing systems bring up some security and trust issues. The centralized nature of cloud-based data storage enables a single authority to oversee the management of cloud-based data storage. As a result, the cloud service provider is susceptible to a single point of failure for the smart manufacturing services and stored transaction data. However, most cloud service providers employ advanced security measures to thwart outside cyber-attacks. For example, an untrustworthy employee of the cloud service provider could alter or tamper with customer data or transactions. Therefore, internal cyberattacks against the cloud platform are not secure.

Blockchain is a distributed system that links data structure for data storage, ensuring the data is resistant to modification. Initially, blockchain applications were limited to cryptocurrencies and financial transactions. The invention of smart contracts oversees the development of more diverse application scenarios such as healthcare [11] and supply chains [12]. Since blockchain is a decentralized system, it can solve a single point of failure from the cloud. To prevent resources stored in the cloud from being accessed or stolen by illegal users, access control is required for supplementary solutions.

Therefore, a trustworthy smart manufacturing system is needed to guarantee the integrity of stored data and maintain the proper accessibility of the users' data in smart manufacturing management systems. The contributions of our work are summarized as follows:

- provisioning of cloud-based search to aid in timely retrieval of end-user data
- blockchain-based storage to provide strong immutability for data provided by IoT devices
- access control powered by smart contracts to protect the ability of users to modify, view or delete the data

2   Related Work

Azaria et al. [17] proposed a decentralized management system, creating a prototype that showed an immutable database that provided access to their data via the facilities acting as miners in a blockchain network. These projects rely on proof-of-work (PoW) consensus processes, which demand a lot of processing power.

Although data retrieval is still computationally intensive, Wang et al. [1] developed the blockchain-based Data Gateway to encourage end-users to own, monitor, and exchange their data. Measa et al. [8] also proposed using blockchain to publish and transfer resource usage rights regulations between users. However, they only used a hypothetical proof-of-concept Bitcoin implementation.

[16] employed a blockchain-based framework to transmit data between institutions in the cloud, employing access protocols and smart contracts to track data movement and spot breaches. The lengthy response time of requests, which might take up to twenty minutes, is still a significant issue.

The issue of data protection on blockchain has been addressed. Zyskind et al. [18] established a decentralized management system that uses a multi-party protocol for automatic access control to ensure users own their data.

The Ethereum ledger and attribute-based encryption technologies are combined in a decentralized storage architecture that Wang et al. [14] characterised as a blockchain-based data exchange architecture. Using the smart contracts on Ethereum.

A multi-authority attribute-based access management system was proposed by Guo et al. [3].

The FairAccess system was proposed by Ouaddah et al. [10], and it uses a local ledger that is implemented on a Raspberry Pi computer to allow transactions to grant, obtain, delegate, and revoke access.

Table 1. Overview of related work

Model	Description	Remarks
[1]	Provide a decentralised management system for Health record, using permission management instead of access control	each node store specific information, however in the blockchain each node should have same record, permission management system consume huge computation resource
[8]	Provide a blockchain-based mechanism to published access rights	The access control still vulnerable to tampering attack, there are no experiment or evaluation set up for this concept in the paper
[17]	Proposed a healthcare framework with utilising blockchain for the storage system	Change the traditional database into the blockchain. However, the access control is placed on the end-user gateway which is not effective
[16]	Proposed a blockchain-based framework using a smart contract to authenticate the access for every query	In this paper, all the data still stored in a traditional database. They rely on the smart contract as an access control since in the architecture there is not any access control layer is used

Based on the current works, none of these earlier publications discuss the use of smart contracts with role-based access control systems, particularly with smart manufacturing based on the Internet of Things. In Table 1, summarize the key point from our proposed method from the previous work.

3   Proposed Framework

This section presents our proposed blockchain-based access control. First, we present an overview of the system architecture. Next, we discuss the various components of our proposed framework in detail.

3.1   Overview of the Proposed Framework

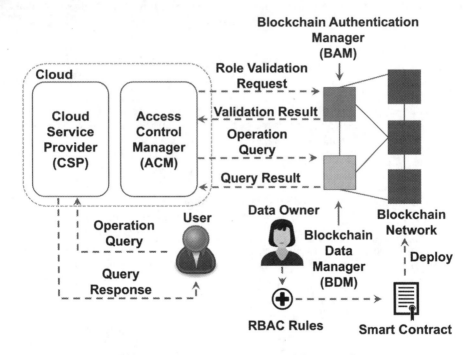

Fig. 1. Overview of the proposed framework

The framework integrates blockchain and smart contract in cloud-based smart manufacturing management systems for tamper proof access control. There are two types of participants in the system: *data owner* and *users*. Data owners are the smart manufacturer (e.g., Administrator), whilst a user can be a engineer, product quality assurance, courier, supply-chain manager or even the customer itself. A large amount of data is generated by the various smart manufacturer sensors and devices, which authorised users gain access to for review or update.

Thus, it is paramount that user roles are verified given the sensitive nature of the data. However, role specifications themselves may be tampered and so, to ensure trustworthy definition and verification of roles, smart contracts are used.

Here, we integrate blockchain into the system, with smart contracts being deployed to all blockchain nodes. User authentication details (e.g., user id and roles) are stored within the blockchain to harden against modification attacks. Moreover, customers' transaction data is stored distributively amongst the blockchain nodes. Overview of the proposed framework is illustrated in Fig. 1.

To ease explanation in later sections, we break down the components of the proposed framework as follows:

- **Cloud Service Provider (CSP)** acts as the interface between users and data, allowing direct communication and acting as an intermediary by answering user requests with results contained within. The actual query operation itself is performed by the ACM.
- **Access Control Manager (ACM)** only allows authorised access to data by users via requests. This involves user registration, role validation, and the retrieval of user rights. To ensure trustworthiness, it communicates with the blockchain network for user role validation.
- **Blockchain Authentication Manager (BAM)** communicates with the ACM on behalf of the blockchain. It receives a user-role validation task as a transaction, communicating with other nodes to validate and retrieves the correct role with the help of smart contracts.
- **Blockchain Database Manager (BDM)** is another node in the blockchain network. Generally, it is responsible for executing transactions in the blockchain network, performing operations on blockchain data, and producing authenticated results.

3.2   System Model

Assume that a set of transaction records is stored as a blockchain in a blockchain network BCN. In the blockchain, U be the set of n types of *users* that is denoted as $U = \{u_1, u_2, \ldots, u_n\}$. R be the set of m *roles* and denoted as $R = \{r_1, r_2, \ldots, r_m\}$.

R_{u_i} is the set of roles that is assigned to the user u_i. A role r_i is associated with one or more *rights*. The set G of k rights is denoted as $G = \{g_1, g_2, \ldots, g_k\}$. Let, Att be the set of l attributes in the transaction records that is denoted as: $Att = \{att_1, att_2, \ldots, att_l\}$. A right g_i is the set of l boolean values indicating the accessibility on l different attributes of a transaction record.

The formal definition of the Roles-based access control (RBAC) model is defined as follows:

Definition 3.1. The RBAC model ($RBAC_M$) is a tuple:

$$RBAC_M = <A_{U,R}, A_{R,G}, G>\qquad(1)$$

where:

- $A_{U,R} = U \times R$, is the set of all possible *role assignment relations* between users and roles. A user type $u_i \in U$ can be assigned to roles $\{r' | r' \subseteq R\}$, then the role assignment can be denoted as $A_{u_i,r'} \subseteq A_{U,R}$.
- $A_{R,G} = R \times G$, is the set of all possible *right association relations* between roles and rights. A role $r_i \in R$ is associated with rights $\{g' | g' \subseteq G\}$, then the right association can be denoted as $A_{r_i,g'} \subseteq A_{R,G}$.
- $g_i \in G$ can be denoted as $g_i = \{b_1, b_2, \ldots, b_l\}$ where b_j is the accessibility indicator on the jth attribute $(1 \leq j \leq l)$ and $b_j = true$ or $false$. The value $b_j = true$ indicates that the jth attribute $att_j \in Att$ is accessible and $b_j = false$ indicates otherwise.

The accessibility of a particular type of user is verified based on the $RBAC_M$. To obtain the accessibility, a user needs to send a data access request. The *data access request* can be formally defined as follows:

Definition 3.2. A data access request is a function $req(p, param)$, where p is the unique user ID with a user type $p.type$, and $param$ is the list of query parameters containing q attribute (att) and value (val) pairs. $param$ can be represented as: $param = \{(att_1, val_1), (att_2, val_2), \ldots, (att_q, val_q)\}$.

Definition 3.3. An *Accessibility Rule* is a set AR of semantics that must be satisfied to verify the accessibility of the user p while sending a request $req(p, param)$. AR comprises of the following semantics:

$$p.type \subseteq U, \tag{2}$$

$$p.role \subseteq A_{U,R} \text{ and } p.role = A_{u_p,r_p}. \tag{3}$$

$$p.rights \subseteq A_{R,G} \text{ and } p.rights = A_{r_i,g'}. \tag{4}$$

$$\forall att_i \in param.Att', param.Att' \subseteq Att \land att_i \in g'. \tag{5}$$

The $RBAC_M$ model is defined in a *smart contract* (SC) to ensure the trustworthy validation of accessibility based on the semantics AR. The formal definition of the smart contract can be provided as below:

Definition 3.4. A smart contract (SC) is a tuple:

$$SC = < Op, AR >, \tag{6}$$

where Op is set of operations in SC and AR is the set of accessibility rules.

3.3 Role-Based Access Control Using Smart Contract

This section describes the proposed role-based access control using smart contracts. The proposed role-based access control mechanism involves several steps. Each step is described below:

Step-1: *Initialization*. The data owner, the access control layer (ACM), the blockchain authentication manager (BAM), and the blockchain data manager (BDM) all generate keys as part of the initialization process. Assume that $KeyGen()$ is a key generation algorithm based on public-key cryptography that generates a public-key (PK) and private-key (PR) pair. Using $KeyGen()$, the data owner creates a key pair made up of a public key (PK_{DO}) and a private key (PR_{DO}). The data owner will use this key pair to deploy the smart contract and carry out its activities. The data owner preserves PR_{DO} as a secret and shares PK_{DO} with the cloud's ACM and the blockchain network's BAM. Using $KeyGen()$, ACM also creates a key pair, including a public key (PK_{ACM}) and a private key (PR_{ACM}). The key-pairs for BAM and BDM are generated similarly as follows: PK_{BAM}, PR_{BAM}, and PK_{BDM}, PR_{BDM}.

Step-2: *Generation and Deployment of Smart Contracts*. In this stage, the data owner establishes roles for various user types and sets the access control rules (AR) depending on those user types. The data owner then uses AR as described in Definition 3.4 to create a smart contract (SC). In order to deploy SC in the blockchain network, the data owner sends a transaction to the BAM called Tx_{SC}. Formally, Tx_{SC} can be written as follows:

$$Tx_{SC} = \{ID_{DO}, ID_{BAM}, cost_{SC}, Sign(SC, PR_{DO})\}, \qquad (7)$$

where:

- ID_{BAM} is the unique ID of the blockchain authentication manager (BAM).
- ID_{DO} is the unique ID of the data owner representing the transaction generator.
- $cost_{SC}$ is the price of running the transaction TX_{SC}.
- $Sign(SC, PR_{DO})$ is the signed smart contract SC that is constructed using a digital signature technique with the data owner's private key PR_{DO}.

A smart contract scripting language for the blockchain platform can be used to create SC. The blockchain platform for this study is Ethereum, and SC is created using the Solidity programming language. Section 4.1 discusses the implementation specifics. Figure 2 shows the SC creation and deployment operations.

Step-3: *User Registration*. By giving each user one or more roles in this stage, the data owner creates new users and registers them. When a user is created, roles are assigned, and the user roles are stored on the blockchain. The data owner issues a blockchain transaction called Tx_{UR}. The Blockchain Data Manager (BDM) receives Tx_{UR} from the data owner, which is forwarded to the blockchain network for inclusion in the blockchain. The following is a formal representation of Tx_{UR}:

$$Tx_{UR} = \{ID_{DO}, ID_{BDM}, cost_{UR}, Sign(U_{pro}, PR_{DO})\}, \qquad (8)$$

where:

- ID_{BDM} is the unique ID of the blockchain data manager (BDM).
- ID_{DO} is the unique ID of the data owner representing the transaction generator.

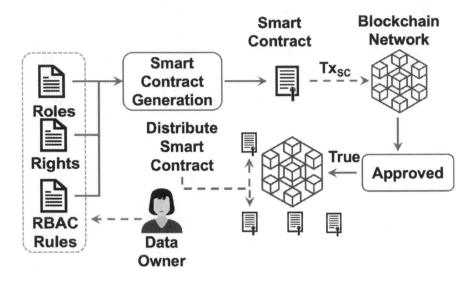

Fig. 2. Generation and deployment of Smart Contract

- $cost_{UR}$ is the price of running the transaction TX_{UR}.
- $Sign(U_{pro}, PR_{DO})$ is the signed user data U_{pro} that is produced using a digital signature schemes with data owner's private-key PR_{DO}. U_{pro} is the digitally signed user data U_{pro} that was created using the private key of the data owner PR_{DO}. The list of user data known as U_{pro} is denoted as $U_{pro} = \{p, R'_p\}$, where p is the user's unique ID and R'_p is the set of user roles such that $R'_p \subseteq R$.

The only transactions Tx_{UR} that the data owner can create are those for adding users and assigning roles. Before storing Tx_{UR} into the blockchain, the network verifies it. As a result, malicious users cannot create fake user roles or alter those that already exist.

Step-4: *User Role Validation and Granting Access.* In this stage, a user role is verified, and access is granted to a system-authorized user. After signing up for the system, a user can send a data access request to the cloud service provider (CSP) using the syntax $req(p, param)$. The access control layer (ACM) receives $req(p, param)$ from the cloud service provider. The user role validation transaction Tx_V is then created by ACM and sent to BAM for user role validation. The following is a representation of Tx_V:

$$Tx_V = \{ID_{ACM}, ID_{BAM}, cost_V, \\ ID_{SC}, Sign(p.role, PR_{ACM})\}, \tag{9}$$

where:

- ID_{ACM} is the unique ID of ACM denoting the transaction generator.
- ID_{BAM} is the unique ID of the blockchain authentication manager (BAM).
- $cost_V$ is the cost of executing the transaction TX_V.
- ID_{SC} is the smart contract's unique ID.
- $Sign(p.role, PR_{ACM})$ is the signed user role that is produced using a digital signature schemes with ACM's private-key PR_{ACM}.

In the blockchain network, BAM propagates Tx_V to verify user roles. Using the smart contract SC, the user role is verified. The matching rights ($p.rights$) of the user are then returned to BAM, signed by BAM, and sent to ACM. $Sign(p.rights, PR_{BAM})$ can be used to represent the signed rights. ACM then gives the user p the rights. The user role validation procedure based on smart contracts is represented by the Algorithm 1.

Algorithm 1: Smart Contract based user role validation process

---

Input:
        $p.type$, type of current user p

Output:
        $p.rights$, rights of current user p

1   **while** CSP **do**
2   **if** $p.type \subseteq U$ **then**
3   **if** $p.role \subseteq A_{U,R} \wedge p.role = A_{u_p,r_p}$ **then**
4         $SendTx_V =$
           $ID_{ACM}, ID_{BAM}, cost_V, ID_{SC}, Sign(p.role, PR_{ACM}) to SC$ **if** Tx_V
           is valid **then**
5   **return** $p.rights$ **return** $p.rights = $ NULL **if** $p.rights \neq NULL$
           then
6   ACM grants access to user p with $p.rights$
7   **end**
8   **else**
9         $p.rights \neq valid$
10   **end**
11   **else**
12   Invalid User
13   **end**
14   **else**
15   Invalid User
16   **end**
17 **endWhile**

Step-5: *Accessibility Based Operation.* The user does the action in this stage in accordance with the responsibilities and rights granted to the user. The sequence diagram for the entire accessibility-based operation is shown in Fig. 3. An end user is initially authenticated by the CSP. The end user then issues an ACM inquiry request. The ACM retrieves the rights for the user and confirms the roles with BAM. After then, the ACM sends the query request to the BDM for processing. For the request, the BDM creates a query result and transmits it to the CSP. The end-user receives the result from CSP.

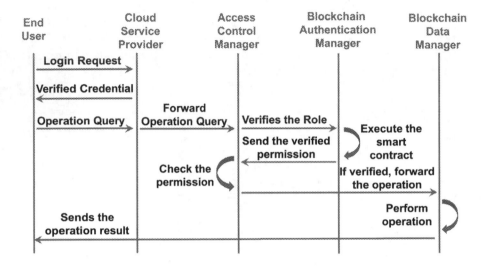

Fig. 3. Accessibility based operation

4   Experimental Results

In this section, we show several experiments conducted to evaluate the performance of our proposed framework and discuss the results.

4.1   Experimental Setup

In our experiments, we run the experiments with the AWS EC2 cloud. We use *T2.XLarge* instance and it has 4 vCPU and 1 GB of RAM that simulate medium size smart manufacturer server.

The implementation of the prototype comprises of the *core framework* and the *blockchain*. The core framework is developed as a Java server-side application, which is then interfaced with an Ethereum blockchain emulated in Ganache [7], which includes ten accounts as default with 100 ethers. Accounts and held Ethereum sums may be changed as needed.

Each account can send and receive Ethereum transfers, or engage in smart contract activities. By forming a block for each operation, the Ganache blockchain also provides miner consent. Therefore, it is not required to wait for the transfers to be approved in the virtual environment [5]. We develop and communicate smart contracts using both Solidity [9] and the Truffle [15] framework. NodeJS [13] is used to communicate between servers and Ethereum nodes. To enable communication between the Java-based core framework and the Ethereum blockchain environment, Web3j [6] is used.

4.2 Results and Performance Evaluation

To begin, we examine the cost to generate the smart contracts. Cost here is computed in terms of *Gas*, the unit used in the Ethereum network. For comparison, the deployment cost of the systems proposed by Cruz *et al.* in [2] is shown in Fig. 4 alongside the costs incurred by the proposed approach. As seen, results indicate that our generation costs consistently track 50% lower across a similar number of roles. This bodes well for the cost-effectiveness of our approach.

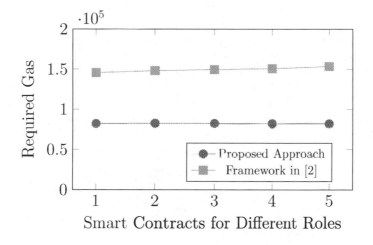

Fig. 4. Required Gas to generate smart contracts

Next, we examine at the time cost to produce the query results in Fig. 5 where several concurrent query operations are performed and then transmitted to the ACM to be processed. The goal is to imitate concurrent consumers querying the blockchain for particular sets of data. All queries are forwarded via the ACM to the BDM, which controls network-wide query activities. The timings displayed reflect projected peaks and troughs within operational times for different simultaneous query requests of 100 to 300. According to the results, execution times rise linearly as the number of requests increases. Even at the upper end, we saw responses in 86 s for 300 simultaneous requests, which would serve all users in a typical mid-size smart manufacturing. Please note that when the system is implemented on more potent machines, these timings will dramatically improve.

Figure 6 shows the execution times for the deployment $(\text{---}\bullet\text{---})$ and verification $(\text{------}\times\text{------})$ of smart contracts in our framework. In this experiment, blockchain-deployed smart contracts are made for various permissions within certain positions. We also confirm their rights in order to be thorough. Giving the admin permission to complete the order after carefully reviewing the quality and quantity is one example. Therefore, the client can inform the manufacturer if there is an issue with the products (such as a wrong amount or a damaged item).

The deployment phase, which demands around 115 to 130 ms over the 20 usage rights we defined, is more time-consuming, as was to be expected. With a speed range of 5 to 15 ms, the verification phase is quicker. Both phases have a slight rising trend, with the time taken growing as more rights are added. With the manager, accountant, technician, and administrative personnel all having distinct and purposeful usage rights within their responsibilities, it is envisaged that the chosen number of 20 will more than satisfy standard smart manufacturer requirements.

In Fig. 7 we analyze the time needed to generate the blockchain for the smart manufacturer data across various amounts of records $(\text{---}\times\text{---})$ and nodes $(\text{---}\bullet\text{---})$. The objective is to monitor performance as we scale up the number of participating nodes and records in the network. We scale the number of records from 10,000 to 50,000 after limiting the number of blockchain nodes to 4. As a result, we observe a rising linear trend, with 10K records starting at 1.069 s and 50K records ending at 2.155 s. This indicates the potential of incorporating a substantial amount of manufacturer-provided IoT data into the system, such as access control and consumer transactions. The processing time will be shortened by using a full server with greater power.

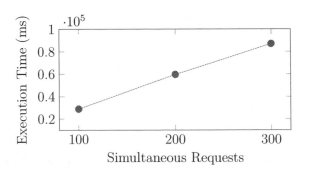

Fig. 5. Execution time for query requests

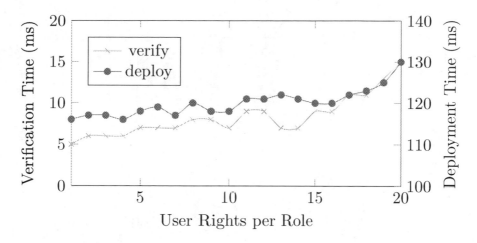

Fig. 6. Deployment and verification times of specific usage rights within user roles

Finally, in the same Fig. 7, we observe the impact of including more blockchain nodes in the system. In this instance, we set the record count at 10K and test against 2 to 20 nodes. Once more, we observe a linear growth from two nodes at 112 ms to twenty nodes at 2231 ms. These results indicate the viability of the strategy if scaling up to a more extensive blockchain is necessary, keeping in mind the hardware limits once more.

4.3 Discussion

The proposed framework integrates blockchain and smart contract technology. This ameliorates some of the known issues with centralized cloud platforms as we seek to decentralize important access-control mechanisms and thus harden them against attacks. The immutability afforded by the blockchain is a crucial pillar of this framework, with malicious actors facing an uphill task if they wish to tamper with actual data. Further, as the roles and rights of system users are defined in smart contracts, which in turn are also replicated to all nodes in the blockchain, attacks such as privilege escalations or false authorizations are minimized.

Each data request is submitted as a blockchain transaction in the suggested architecture. These transactions comprise the creation of smart contracts (Tx_{SC}), registration of users (Tx_{UR}), and validation of user roles (Tx_V). The associated transaction generator uses public-key cryptography to sign each of the transactions above digitally. The signature will be secure if the correct key settings are applied. Using the aggregated key, users can confirm the search result. Because of this, even a 51% attack cannot change the query result. Hence, the proposed framework guarantees the verifiability of the query result.

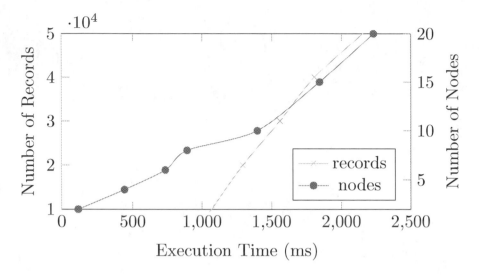

Fig. 7. Generation times across number of records and nodes

Results presented in Sect. 4, highlight the efficacy and performance of the proposed blockchain-enabled role-based access control (RBAC). The experiments show that execution times for most operations (i.e., generation and verification of user roles) follow a linear trend without spikes as we increase the number of records and nodes within the network. With the limited source in mind, we postulate that a larger variant of the proposed approach would perform better in an environment with more powerful machines. It is reasonable to expect that significant smart manufacturing would be able to accommodate the computational requirements.

5   Conclusion

In this paper, a blockchain-based access control framework is proposed to ensure the integrity of the data and transaction within the context of a smart manufacturing. First, a decentralized data storage model is introduced that stores the transactions records in the blockchain. The blockchain of records are replicated across multiple nodes to ensure integrity and to protect against tampering. Second, a smart contract-based access control mechanism is proposed to define the roles of different system users. Different roles and their corresponding rights can be created and stored in multiple smart contracts to be deployed in the blockchain network. The smart contracts are replicated amongst nodes in the network, with user role creation and validation tasks generated only via valid blockchain transactions. Accordingly, false user roles cannot be created and none of the existing user roles can be modified by an attacker. As seen in the experimental results, the proposed role-based access control (RBAC) using smart contracts is cost-effective. Moreover, execution times for smart contract generation and verification tasks showed linear characteristics, which points both to the efficiency and scalability of the approach. The hierarchy of roles necessary for the beneficial role and proper management is not taken into account by the current approach. Our future goal is to include a hierarchical model for roles and rights management.

Acknowledgement. This work is part of the NPRP11S-1227-170135 project. The authors would like to express their gratitude to the QNRF (Qatar Foundation) for its support and funding for the project activities.

References

1. Azaria, A., Ekblaw, A., Vieira, T., Lippman, A.: MedRec: using blockchain for medical data access and permission management. In: 2016 2nd International Conference on Open and Big Data (OBD), pp. 25–30. IEEE (2016)
2. Cruz, J.P., Kaji, Y., Yanai, N.: RBAC-SC: role-based access control using smart contract. IEEE Access **6**, 12240–12251 (2018)
3. Guo, H., Meamari, E., Shen, C.C.: Multi-authority attribute-based access control with smart contract. In: Proceedings of the 2019 International Conference on Blockchain Technology, pp. 6–11 (2019)
4. Hayes, B.: Cloud computing (2008)
5. Karatas, E.: Developing Ethereum blockchain-based document verification smart contract for Moodle learning management system. Online Submission **11**(4), 399–406 (2018)
6. Labs, W.: Web3j. https://docs.web3j.io/
7. Lee, W.-M.: Testing smart contracts using ganache. In: Beginning Ethereum Smart Contracts Programming, pp. 147–167. Apress, Berkeley, CA (2019). https://doi.org/10.1007/978-1-4842-5086-0_7
8. Di Francesco Maesa, D., Mori, P., Ricci, L.: Blockchain based access control. In: Chen, L.Y., Reiser, H.P. (eds.) DAIS 2017. LNCS, vol. 10320, pp. 206–220. Springer, Cham (2017). https://doi.org/10.1007/978-3-319-59665-5_15
9. Mukhopadhyay, M.: Ethereum Smart Contract Development: Build Blockchain-Based Decentralized Applications Using Solidity. Packt Publishing Ltd (2018)
10. Ouaddah, A., Abou Elkalam, A., Ait Ouahman, A.: FairAccess: a new blockchain-based access control framework for the internet of things. Secur. Commun. Netw. **9**(18), 5943–5964 (2016)
11. Rahman, M.S., Khalil, I., Bouras, A.: Formalizing dynamic behaviors of smart contract workflow in smart healthcare supply chain. In: Park, N., Sun, K., Foresti, S., Butler, K., Saxena, N. (eds.) SecureComm 2020. LNICST, vol. 336, pp. 391–402. Springer, Cham (2020). https://doi.org/10.1007/978-3-030-63095-9_25
12. Rahman, M.S., Khalil, I., Bouras, A.: A framework for modelling blockchain based supply chain management system to ensure soundness of smart contract workflow. In: HICSS, pp. 1–10 (2021)
13. Tilkov, S., Vinoski, S.: Node. js: using javascript to build high-performance network programs. IEEE Internet Comput. **14**(6), 80–83 (2010)
14. Wang, S., Zhang, Y., Zhang, Y.: A blockchain-based framework for data sharing with fine-grained access control in decentralized storage systems. IEEE Access **6**, 38437–38450 (2018)

15. Wimmer, C., Würthinger, T.: Truffle: a self-optimizing runtime system. In: Proceedings of the 3rd Annual Conference on Systems, Programming, and Applications: Software for Humanity, pp. 13–14 (2012)
16. Xia, Q., Sifah, E.B., Asamoah, K.O., Gao, J., Du, X., Guizani, M.: MedShare: trust-less medical data sharing among cloud service providers via blockchain. IEEE Access **5**, 14757–14767 (2017)
17. Yue, X., Wang, H., Jin, D., Li, M., Jiang, W.: Healthcare data gateways: found healthcare intelligence on blockchain with novel privacy risk control. J. Med. Syst. **40**(10), 218 (2016)
18. Zyskind, G., Nathan, O., et al.: Decentralizing privacy: using blockchain to protect personal data. In: 2015 IEEE Security and Privacy Workshops, pp. 180–184. IEEE (2015)

Attacks

Driver Locations Harvesting Attack
on pRide

Shyam Murthy$^{(\boxtimes)}$ and Srinivas Vivek

International Institute of Information Technology Bangalore, Bengaluru, India
{shyam.sm,srinivas.vivek}@iiitb.ac.in

Abstract. Privacy preservation in Ride-Hailing Services (RHS) is intended to protect privacy of drivers and riders. pRide, published in IEEE Trans. Vehicular Technology 2021, is a prediction based privacy-preserving RHS protocol to match riders with an optimum driver. In the protocol, the Service Provider (SP) homomorphically computes Euclidean distances between encrypted locations of drivers and rider. Rider selects an optimum driver using decrypted distances augmented by a new-ride-emergence prediction. To improve the effectiveness of driver selection, the paper proposes an enhanced version where each driver gives encrypted distances to each corner of her grid. To thwart a rider from using these distances to launch an inference attack, the SP blinds these distances before sharing them with the rider.

In this work, we propose a passive attack where an honest-but-curious adversary rider who makes a single ride request and receives the blinded distances from SP can recover the constants used to blind the distances. Using the unblinded distances, rider to driver distance and Google Nearest Road API, the adversary can obtain the precise locations of responding drivers. We conduct experiments with random on-road driver locations for four different cities. Our experiments show that we can determine the precise locations of at least 80% of the drivers participating in the enhanced pRide protocol.

Keywords: Ride-hailing services · Privacy and censorship · Attacks

1 Introduction

According to a recent research by MordorIntelligence [8], the global Ride-Hailing Services (RHS) market, valued at USD 113 billion in 2020, is expected to reach USD 230 billion by 2026. With such a huge reach, individual privacy and security issues are always of primary concern. Ride-Hailing Service Providers (SP) like Uber, Lyft, Ola provide services in many parts of the world. Among other features, the SP facilitates ride booking and fare payment options for their customers, namely riders who subscribe with the SP for RHS. Drivers of vehicles such as cars and motorcycles sign-up with the SP in order to offer rides. At the time of subscription, the SP collects private information of riders and drivers in order to provide services effectively as well as required by local governance laws. In addition, the SP collects statistics of riders and drivers for every ride that is offered in its network. This naturally brings up the topic of individual data privacy concerns from both riders as well as drivers over their data held by the SP. Also, curious or malicious drivers or riders might be interested in learning more about the other parties. There are a number of works and their analysis in the literature that look at privacy-preserving RHS, we list some of them in Sect. 5.

Huang *et al.* proposed *pRide* [4], a privacy-preserving online RHS protocol that aims to provide the optimum driver in a global perspective thereby minimizing the unnecessary travel distance to pick the rider. The protocol makes use of a deep learning model to predict emergence of new ride requests in a ride-hailing region to enable the SP to make use of such prediction while matching optimum drivers to ride requests. They show that by using such a prediction model in a global perspective, the overall distance travelled by a matching driver is minimized compared with matching a nearest driver in the local region. The protocol proposes to use a Somewhat Homomorphic Encryption (SHE) scheme to encrypt rider and driver locations. The advantage of using a homomorphic encryption scheme is that it allows computations on ciphertexts so that the result of computation is available only after decryption. Fully Homomorphic Encryption (FHE) schemes that support potentially any number of homomorphic operations have high cost in terms of large ciphertexts and high computation latency. Hence, many practical applications that know, a priori, the bound on the number of homomorphic operations, prefer to use SHE schemes. In the pRide paper, the authors use the FV cryptosystem [1] in the implementation of their scheme. Even though applications make use of semantically secure cryptosystems, careful analysis is required to make sure no unintended security holes are introduced while adapting the cryptosystem to their applications.

The pRide protocol, described in more detail in Sect. 2, has two parts, the basic protocol and an enhanced version. We discuss the basic protocol in this paragraph. In the initialization phase, SP divides the area of its operation into grids, the details of which are made available to all parties. SP keeps a record of ride requests emanating from each grid over specific time epochs and trains a prediction model using this information. It then uses this information to predict the grid-based distribution of requests for the next period, denoted by $PR(g)$, namely the prediction result for grid id g. Drivers, registered with the SP, submit their current grid id to the SP so that the SP can maintain the driver distribution map. A rider who wishes to hail a ride, picks a (public key, secret key) pair, encrypts her coordinates and sends the ciphertext and public key to SP along with the ride request. When SP receives the ride request, it performs a search for a suitable driver in a preset order of grids around the rider's grid and obtains a list of candidate drivers using the driver distribution map. SP then forwards the ride request to all candidate drivers. To offer their ride, drivers respond to SP by encrypting their location using the rider's public key. SP then homomorphically computes the square of the Euclidean distance between rider and drivers' encrypted locations and forwards the same to the rider along with $PR(g)$ where g is the driver's grid id. Rider decrypts the distances[1] and picks the shortest distance D_0. It then performs two checks over the list of sorted distances. First, is $D_i - D_0 < D_0 - D_{diag}$?, where D_i is the distance for i^{th} driver and D_{diag} is the length of the diagonal of the grid, and second, does the model predict *no* new ride request emerging in the driver's grid within a short time period? When both these conditions are satisfied, the rider informs SP about the selected index i after which the SP facilitates secure ride establishment with the rider and selected driver.

In order to optimize their ride matching, the paper proposes *enhanced pRide* built on top of the basic pRide protocol, but having a different method to pick the optimum driver. They show that they get better results when a driver *also* provides her encrypted distance to the farthest corner of her grid. This way the rider can use that distance, instead of D_{diag} in the aforementioned check to select the optimum driver. However, the authors notice that if such a distance is decrypted by an adversarial rider, she can launch an inference attack to obtain driver's locations. In order to thwart such an attack, the paper proposes a novel method where the driver provides SP with her encrypted distances to the four corners of her grid. SP then picks random integers to homomorphically blind the distances before sharing the same with the rider. Rider then decrypts the blinded distances and applies a *private comparison algorithm* which determines the result of the inequality $D_i - D_0 < D_0 - D_{maxdist}$, where $D_{maxdist}$ is the distance between the driver and the farthest corner of her grid g. Finally, using this inequality and $PR(g)$, it outputs the optimum selected driver.

As described earlier, in the enhanced pRide protocol, the SP homomorphically blinds the encrypted distances with random integers before sharing them with the rider. In this paper, we show that such a blinding scheme is insecure, whence an adversary rider can recover the underlying distances and then deduce the locations of at least 80% of the drivers responding to a single ride request of the rider when using the enhanced pRide protocol.

1.1 Comparison with ORide [12] Protocol

The pRide paper shows that their enhanced scheme is more effective with the same level of security as that of the basic version with only a small compromise in its efficiency. In addition, by way of experiments, they show their computation cost is significantly better compared to a state-of-the-art protocol named ORide [12]. We note here that the method in the basic pRide protocol where the SP employs the homomorphic property of SHE to compute the Euclidean distance between driver and rider to share the encrypted distances with rider is identical to what is described in the ORide paper. The part that is different is that in the ORide paper to pick the nearest driver, only drivers inside the rider's grid are

---

[1] Henceforth in the paper, we use the term distance to mean squared Euclidean distance.

chosen as candidate drivers, whereas in the pRide protocol, only drivers outside the rider's grid are candidate drivers so as to optimize in a global perspective.

In [5], Kumaraswamy *et al.* demonstrated a driver locations harvesting attack by honest-but-curious riders on the ORide protocol, where they determine the exact locations of 40% of drivers participating in the ORide protocol. In the same paper, the authors also provide a mitigation solution wherein a driver gives her perturbed location instead of her actual location. The aforementioned attack on the ORide protocol and the mitigating solution are both applicable to the basic pRide protocol.

In [10], Murthy *et al.* demonstrated a driver locations harvesting attack, again by honest-but-curious adversary riders, using triangulation on the ORide protocol, where they show that they can determine the exact locations of all participating drivers in the ORide protocol. Further, they extend their method onto the mitigation solution suggested by [5] and show that they can determine locations of between 25% to 50% of the participating drivers.

As mentioned earlier, in the pRide protocol, the method where the rider obtains encrypted driver distances is identical to that in the ORide protocol. Due to this, any location harvesting attack on ORide, like in the cases of [5] and [10], are also directly applicable to the basic pRide protocol.

1.2   Our Contribution

We present a passive driver location harvesting attack on the *enhanced* pRide protocol. The honest-but-curious adversary rider issues a single ride request with a search radius $(SR) = 1$, such that grids adjacent to the rider's grid are searched (as explained in the pRide paper, Section V-B-4, pp. 6). In our attack, the adversary rider receives, per driver, a set of encrypted blinded distances between the driver's location and each corner of the driver's grid. One would expect that such a blinding process would make it hard for the rider to deduce anything about the underlying distances.

Rider decrypts the ciphertexts received from SP to obtain blinded distances. Next, by computing the Greatest Common Divisor (GCD) of the blinded distances and eliminating common factors, the rider recovers the blinding values after which the distances are easily obtained. Rider now has the four distances from driver to each corner of the driver's grid. Using these distances, the rider computes four equiprobable driver locations in each of the four grids adjacent to the rider's grid. This is due to the fact that the distances are in random order and, so, there is no correlation between each corner of the grid and its distance to the driver. Rider knows the distance between herself and each responding driver. Now, using the distance between herself and a particular responding driver (say, δ), the rider draws a rider-circle with center as her location and radius $= \delta$. Probable driver locations that lie on the rider-circle are filtered in and in case multiple such locations are obtained, Google Nearest Roads API [2] is used to output one location that is closest to a motorable road. We conduct our experiments using rectangular grids on four different cities around the world and the results are summarized in Table 1. We show that we can obtain exact driver locations of up to 80% of drivers who respond to a rider's request.

Our attack invalidates Theorem 4, pp. 9, of the pRide paper [4], which states that pRide is adaptively $\mathcal{L}_{access}$ semantically secure against semi-honest adversaries, where $\mathcal{L}_{access}$ gives the access pattern of the SP and rider, which is simply the list of drivers that respond to a specific ride request. Hence, when our attack is combined with that in [10], the driver location security of the pRide paper is fully compromised, and so is the mitigation solution of [5] if applied to the basic pRide protocol. We stress that the attack from [10] is not directly applicable to the pRide protocol, but works only in combination with our attack.

The rest of the paper is organized as follows. Section 2 describes the pRide protocol. Section 3 describes our attack. Section 4 gives details about our experiments and results. Section 5 gives some of the recent works in privacy-preserving RHS, followed by conclusions.

2   Overview of pRide Protocol

In this section, we provide an overview of the pRide protocol followed by a description of the threat model adopted therein. For more details, the interested reader is referred to the original paper [4].

Remark: Unless qualified as enhanced or basic, we will use the term *pRide protocol* to refer to the complete pRide protocol, consisting of both the basic and enhanced parts.

2.1   pRide Protocol

pRide is a privacy-preserving online ride-hailing protocol augmented with a grid-based rider emergence prediction. The key objective of the protocol is to achieve optimum driver selection in a global perspective instead of picking the nearest driver as done in other works [12,13]. Selecting such a driver might be a better choice in order to minimize the overall empty travel distance traversed by drivers to pick up riders in the whole system. The prediction of requests based on deep learning plays an important role in driver selection.

The protocol has two parts, the basic protocol and an enhancement, built on top of the basic protocol, are summarized in the following steps. Steps 1 to 10 constitute the basic pRide protocol, followed by steps of the enhanced pRide protocol.

1. The three parties involved in the pRide protocol are: driver, rider and service provider (SP). The SP does not collude with either rider or drivers. The SP as well as the users, namely, drivers and riders, are honest-but-curious entities who execute the protocol correctly, but are keen on knowing about each other's sensitive information. The protocol aims to protect all users' privacy from other riders and drivers, such that the precise location of one party is not learnt by the other party during the ride matching process. However, only after a driver is matched with a rider, they start to communicate through a secure channel.

2. During system initialization, the SP divides its area of its operation into rectangular grids of suitable sizes (size is based on sufficient ride density so as to maintain rider anonymity) and publishes the same. For example, a city like New York City together with its surrounding boroughs, where the SP is allowed to provide rides as permitted by local authorities, can be termed as the SP's area of operation.

3. Drivers, available to offer rides, submit their real-time grid id to the SP to enable it to maintain a driver distribution map.

4. Rider, wishing to hail a ride, generates a key pair (public key p_k, private key s_k) from the FV SHE scheme [1], encrypts her location using p_k, and submits a ride-request along with her location ciphertext, her current grid id and p_k to the SP. The FV SHE scheme works on integers, hence, the coordinates of users are encoded as integers using UTM format[2].

5. SP keeps a record of ride requests in each grid and maintains a real-time ride request distribution map in every time period. It makes use of Convolutional long short-term memory (Convolutional LSTM [15]) to train a prediction model with the ride request distribution information. Based on a temporal sequence of grid information, SP obtains prediction result $PR(g)$, a non-negative integer which predicts the number of requests in the next time period for grid id g.

6. As soon as SP receives the ride request, it performs a driver search with a search radius (SR) in a preset order of grids starting with the grid nearest to rider. The rider's grid is not searched so as to avoid the nearest driver who would always be found in the rider's grid. When $SR = 1$, only grids adjacent to the rider are searched. Using the driver distribution map, SP creates a list of candidate drivers and forwards the ride-request to all such drivers.

7. When the ith driver d_i receives the ride-request, she encrypts her location using p_k and forwards it to SP.

8. SP homomorphically computes the square of the Euclidean distance between the rider and drivers' locations. It then forwards these distances to rider along with driver id i and $PR(g_i)$, g_i is i's grid id.

9. Rider uses s_k to decrypt the distances and sorts them to obtain the smallest distance D_0. For each distance in the sorted list, she runs the following two checks to pick the optimum driver:
   (a) $2D_0 - D_i > D_{diag}$, where D_i is the distance for i^{th} driver and D_{diag} is the length of the diagonal of the grid.
   (b) $PR(g_i)$, where g_i is the driver's grid id, which checks if no new ride request is emerging in a short time in grid g_i.

10. As soon as both the aforementioned conditions are satisfied, rider determines the optimum driver and informs the same to SP to continue with secure ride establishment between rider and selected driver.

11. In order to improve the effectiveness of driver selection, the authors notice that they can minimize the empty distance travelled by the driver by using

---

[2] Universal Transverse Mercator: a map-projection system for geographical locations [19].

$D_{maxdist}$ instead of D_{diag} in the ride selection check (Step 9), where $D_{maxdist}$ is the distance between the driver and the farthest corner in her grid. However, the authors realize that an adversary rider, after decryption, can use $D_{maxdist}$ to launch an inference attack to obtain driver's precise location. They, therefore, propose *enhanced pRide* to thwart such an attack.

12. In the enhanced pRide protocol, each driver, in addition to sending encryptions of her coordinates, also sends the encryptions of distances to each corner of her grid to the SP.

13. To pick the optimum driver, rider now needs to perform the check $2D_0 - D_i > D_{maxdist}$, for each driver i, using a *private comparison algorithm*, as explained below (Steps 15, 16 and 17).

14. As in the earlier basic pRide protocol, rider receives a list of distances to each of the candidate drivers, decrypts them and selects the smallest D_0.

15. In order to find the optimum driver, for each D_i, $i > 0$, rider sets $D' = 2D_0 - D_i$, encrypts D' as $\widetilde{D'}$ and sends $\widetilde{D'}$ and i to SP.

16. SP receives encrypted distances to each of the four corners of the ith driver's grid as $(\widetilde{D_{ll}}, \widetilde{D_{lu}}, \widetilde{D_{rl}}, \widetilde{D_{ru}})$. SP generates random positive blinding integers e and r, and homomorphically blinds each of the ciphertexts as

$$\widetilde{V'} = e \cdot \widetilde{D'} + \tilde{r}$$
$$\widetilde{V_{ll}} = e \cdot \widetilde{D_{ll}} + \tilde{r}$$
$$\widetilde{V_{lu}} = e \cdot \widetilde{D_{lu}} + \tilde{r} \qquad (1)$$
$$\widetilde{V_{rl}} = e \cdot \widetilde{D_{rl}} + \tilde{r}$$
$$\widetilde{V_{ru}} = e \cdot \widetilde{D_{ru}} + \tilde{r}.$$

It then sends each of these blinded values to rider.

Remark: Homomorphic addition of two ciphertexts, and homomorphic multiplication of ciphertext with plaintext can be done very efficiently in SHE.

17. Rider decrypts each of these blinded values and compares V' with each of $(V_{ll}, V_{lu}, V_{rl}, V_{ru})$. If V' is greater than all the four values, then it implies that $D' > D_{maxdist}$.

18. Rider then uses this comparison result and $PR(g)$ value as in the basic pRide protocol to select the optimum driver and informs the same to SP. If these checks fail, then the Steps 15 through 18 are repeated until an optimum driver is obtained by walking through each entry in the candidate driver list.

The authors evaluate the performance of their enhanced pRide protocol over real-world datasets. Their results show that their protocol is effective in saving empty distance as well as in maintaining drivers' privacy during the ride matching process. Finally, they compare the basic and enhanced versions of pRide and prove that the latter is more effective in choosing the optimum driver with the same level of privacy. The security of their protocol is based on the apparent hardness of retrieving the blinding parameters when given only the blinded values.

In our attack described in Sect. 3, we show that we can determine the underlying distance values when given only their blinded values, where blinding is done as described in Step 16. We then go on to use the distances to get the precise coordinates of responding drivers.

2.2   Threat Model

We consider the same threat model considered in the pRide protocol, where all parties, namely the SP, drivers and riders, are honest in executing the protocol. Riders submit valid requests by encrypting their correct coordinates to the SP, and the drivers also submit the encryptions of their current coordinates to the SP. SP does not collude with either drivers or riders. Drivers do not collude with riders.

All parties are honest-but-curious in the protocol. Thus, each party is curious to know more about the sensitive information of the other party. In particular, riders are curious to know about drivers' locations and vice-versa. pRide also considers the case of an adversary rider who follows the protocol correctly but launches an inference attack by performing private computations on received driver coordinates to infer drivers' precise locations, and so the authors propose enhanced pRide to thwart such an attack. Their paper aims to preserve driver and rider location information from SP, and to preserve driver location information from rider.

In this paper, we consider the same threat model to model the adversaries. The ride request issued by an honest-but-curious adversary rider is indistinguishable from a ride request issued by any other legitimate rider in the protocol. In a real-life scenario, a competitor SP with the intention of harvesting driver information of another SP, can mount such an attack without being detected by the target SP.

3   Our Attack

In this section, we present our driver location harvesting attack on the enhanced pRide protocol by a honest-but-curious adversary rider (R). R issues a single ride request as per the pRide protocol. SP will not be able to distinguish between a ride request issued by an adversary rider versus another by a legitimate rider. In this section, for ease of exposition, we explain the recovery of location of one particular driver D_p, who has responded to ride request by R, shown in Fig. 1. D_p is located at distance δ from R. Our attack extends easily to all responding drivers, since each response is handled independently by the SP.

3.1   Retrieving Distances

R issues a ride request as per the pRide protocol with search radius $SR = 1$. By this, only the grids adjacent to the rider's grid are searched by SP for candidate drivers.

We recall here the steps of pRide and enhanced pRide protocols from Sect. 2.1. In Step 14, the rider R obtains the distances between herself and all the responding drivers in the clear (distance between R and D_p is δ). In addition, from Step 16, R receives the ciphertexts $(\widetilde{V'}, \widetilde{V_{ll}}, \widetilde{V_{lu}}, \widetilde{V_{rl}}, \widetilde{V_{ru}})$, which after decryption gives $(V', V_{ll}, V_{lu}, V_{rl}, V_{ru})$. We know that $\widetilde{D'}$ is the encryption of $2D_0 - \delta$, and

$$
\begin{aligned}
V' &= e \cdot \widetilde{D'} + \tilde{r} \\
V_{ll} &= e \cdot \widetilde{D_{ll}} + \tilde{r} \\
V_{lu} &= e \cdot \widetilde{D_{lu}} + \tilde{r} \\
V_{rl} &= e \cdot \widetilde{D_{rl}} + \tilde{r} \\
V_{ru} &= e \cdot \widetilde{D_{ru}} + \tilde{r},
\end{aligned}
\tag{2}
$$

where e and r are the blinding integers chosen by SP.

R then computes the difference of every pair from $(V_{ll}, V_{lu}, V_{rl}, V_{ru})$, decrypts them using her secret key and stores them as (P, Q, R, S, T, U), in no particular order.

The differences, thus obtained, are

$$
\begin{aligned}
P &= V_{ll} - V_{lu} = e \cdot (D_{ll} - D_{lu}) \\
Q &= V_{ll} - V_{rl} = e \cdot (D_{ll} - D_{rl}) \\
R &= V_{ll} - V_{ru} = e \cdot (D_{ll} - D_{ru}) \\
S &= V_{lu} - V_{rl} = e \cdot (D_{lu} - D_{rl}) \\
T &= V_{lu} - V_{ru} = e \cdot (D_{lu} - D_{ru}) \\
U &= V_{rl} - V_{ru} = e \cdot (D_{rl} - D_{ru}).
\end{aligned}
\tag{3}
$$

It can be easily seen that the GCD of any two of (P, Q, R, S, T), say P and Q, will give either e or its multiple. The latter case will occur when $(D_{ll} - D_{lu})$ and $(D_{ll} - D_{rl})$ are not relatively prime, and by eliminating any common factors between them, we can hope to retrieve the exact value of e with a high probability.

Remark: The probability of n randomly chosen integers being coprime is $\frac{1}{\zeta(n)}$, where ζ is the Riemann Zeta function [20], and for two such integers the probability is $\frac{6}{\pi^2}$. This means in about 60% of cases we can find the value of e straightaway, and in rest of the cases we can try to eliminate common factors.

Notice that each of the D_{xy} values are squares of the Euclidean distance between the driver's location and each corner of her grid. Let the driver's coordinates (to be determined) be (x, y) and the known corners of her grid be (x_1, y_1), (x_2, y_2), (x_3, y_3) and (x_4, y_4). W.l.o.g,

$$
D_{ll} = (x_1 - x)^2 + (y_1 - y)^2
\tag{4}
$$

$$
D_{lu} = (x_2 - x)^2 + (y_2 - y)^2.
\tag{5}
$$

Hence, $P = e \cdot \left(\left((x_1 - x)^2 + (y_1 - y)^2 \right) - \left((x_2 - x)^2 + (y_2 - y)^2 \right) \right)$, which simplifies to

$$P = e \cdot \left((x_1 - x_2)(x_1 + x_2 - 2x) + (y_1 - y_2)(y_1 + y_2 - 2y) \right). \tag{6}$$

By eliminating common factors, if any, we obtain

$$P' = e \cdot P / (\mathrm{GCD}(x_1 - x_2, y_1 - y_2) * \mathrm{GCD}(2, x_1 + x_2, y_1 + y_2)). \tag{7}$$

And similarly, we get Q', R', S', T', U'. Finally, $\mathrm{GCD}(P', Q', R', S', T', U')$ gives the value of e.

Remark: The coordinates of each of the grids are known at system initialization time. Hence, any common factors between the coordinates can be computed offline.

In Step 15, rider has the value of $\widetilde{D'}$, using which the value of $\widetilde{r}$ is obtained from $V' = e \cdot \widetilde{D'} + \widetilde{r}$. And, finally, using e and $\widetilde{r}$, $(\widetilde{D_{ll}}, \widetilde{D_{lu}}, \widetilde{D_{rl}}, \widetilde{D_{ru}})$, and, hence, $(D_{ll}, D_{lu}, D_{rl}, D_{ru})$ are obtained.

Remark: In case we obtain a negative value for $\widetilde{r}$, it implies that our recovery of e is in error.

3.2 Retrieving Driver Locations

R does not know the correlation between the D_{xy} distances and the corners of the grid as they are distances given in random order. In addition, since the search radius $SR = 1$, any of the four grids adjacent to the rider's grid can be a potential grid of driver D_p.

Using the four distance values $(D_{ll}, D_{lu}, D_{rl}, D_{ru})$ as radii and each of the respective grid corners as center of circles, rider obtains four points in each grid where all the four circles intersect. These points, in their respective grids, represent the equiprobable locations of driver D_p. Figure 1 gives a pictorial view of our attack. Adversary rider R is located in grid g. Driver D_p is located in grid g_4, at a distance δ from R. Each of the four probable driver locations in each adjacent grids g_1 through g_4 are shown as small blue dots in each grid.

Using the distance between R and D_p, namely δ, R draws a rider-circle of radius $= \delta$ around herself. As long as the driver has reported her correct coordinates, it is guaranteed that at least one of the 16 equiprobable driver locations will lie on the circumference of the rider-circle. If more than one such location is obtained, then the rider makes use of Google Nearest Road API [2] to find the nearest road to each of such locations. Since we assume that the driver is located on a motorable road, the adversary algorithm will output the location closest to the nearest road.

3.3 Analysis of Our Attack

As described in Sect. 2.1, the pRide protocol makes use of a semantically secure cryptosystem, namely the FV SHE scheme [1], to encrypt the locations of drivers

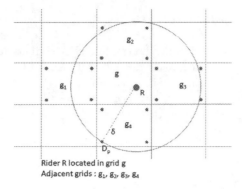

Rider R located in grid g
Adjacent grids : g_1, g_2, g_3, g_4

Fig. 1. Recovered driver locations shown as small dots each in grid g_1 through g_4.

and rider, using which driver distances are computed homomorphically. In order to pick the closest driver, the distances need to be sorted which will need a high-depth circuit resulting in an inefficient implementation with SHE. Hence, the rider, in the basic pRide protocol, receives all encrypted distances, decrypts and sorts them to pick the closest driver efficiently. Using the distances to all drivers, the rider is able to perform the attacks described in [5] and [10], on the basic pRide protocol.

As described in Section of 2.1, the enhanced pRide protocol, SP homomorphically blinds the distances to the four corners of drivers' grid, using random positive integers (Eq. 1). However, as we show in Sect. 3.1, this blinding method is insecure.

The mitigation solution of [5], where the locations are perturbed, can be applied to the pRide protocol. While the attack of [10] is still applicable on the basic pRide protocol, we look at our attack on its enhanced version, when the mitigation solution is applied to the pRide protocol. In that case, in response to a ride request, the driver would pick a uniform random location inside a circle of radius τ around her original location. She then sends the encryption of that random location to the SP, as well as the encrypted distances from the random location to each of the corners of her grid. We note that τ should not be too large, as that would have an adverse effect on driver selection by rider. Our attack, where we retrieve the distances to grid corners, described in Sect. 3.1, would be applicable without any change. However, one of the retrieved location(s), in this case, would be the random location picked by the driver instead of her actual location. The adversary could then apply the attack of [10] to uncover the actual driver locations, with a high probability. Since the retrieved locations might not be on a motorable road due to perturbation, the effectiveness of being able to use Google Nearest Road API to retrieve driver locations need to studied.

4   Experiments and Results

We use Sagemath 8.6 [16] to implement our attack described in Sect. 3.1 where we retrieve driver distances. The attack, described in Sect. 3.2, where we retrieve the driver locations, was implemented in Python and used the Google Nearest Road APIs for Python [3]. Both parts of the attack were executed on a commodity laptop with 512 GB SSD and AMD Ryzen 5 processor. Our Sagemath and Python programs are available at:
https://github.com/shyamsmurthy/nss2022.

4.1   Experiment Details

Our experiments were run on grids of size about $4\,\text{km}^2$ superimposed on maps of 4 large cities around the world, namely, Los Angeles, London, New York City and Paris. The size of the grid is comparable to what is reported in the pRide paper. We have done experiments with the number of drivers as 5, 15 and 25 per grid, in each case distributed randomly throughout each grid but located on motorable areas. We note here that the number of drivers does not have a bearing on our attack since the SP encrypts and blinds each driver's distances independent of one other.

In each of the maps, we picked random driver locations situated on motorable roads. Next, a rider location was picked from a random grid in the map. As explained in Sect. 3.1, grids adjacent to the rider's grid was examined and distances between drivers in those grids and the rider were made available to the rider. Except for the predicted result (PR) values, this is same as what is available to the rider in the pRide protocol. The PR values do not have any bearing on our attack since they do not have any effect on either blinding or encryption of distances.

Next, from each of the adjacent grids and for each driver in such grid, the distances from each such driver to her respective grid corners were computed, and blinded using random integers picked from the range $[1, 2^{24}]$, as the maximum UTM (northing) value of 10^7 can be represented using 24 bits. In addition, a distance value known to the adversary is also blinded using the same random integers. These blinded distances were made available to the adversary rider. Again, this exactly mimics the behaviour of the enhanced pRide protocol.

Finally, we run the attack described in Sect. 3 to retrieve the distances followed by retrieving the driver locations.

Remark 1: It is claimed that the security of the pRide protocol relies on the hardness of obtaining the blinding parameters when given only the blinded values. We show in our attack that the adversary can recover the blinding parameters with a high probability.

Remark 2: In our experiments, we have used a search radius $SR = 1$. Our attack methodology can be easily extended to higher values of search radius. Since the order of grid traversal is known a priori, the new attack has to compute equiprobable locations in each of the possible grids and continue with our driver retrieval attack, as described in Sect. 3.2.

4.2   Results

The results of our experiments are tabulated in Table 1. The pRide paper uses a 64×64 grid over the city of Chengdu, China, and mentions a maximum of 16000 drivers in their experiments, which translates to about 4 drivers per grid on average. As it can be much larger in high density areas in the city, we run our experiments with 5, 15 and 25 drivers per grid. It takes less than 1 s to recover the locations of 25 drivers.

In order to retrieve the distances, we first recover the blinding integers e and r as described in Sect. 3.1. As shown in Table 1, we can retrieve at least 80% of the distances successfully, averaged from 10 runs of the experiments for each driver count over each city. In the unsuccessful cases, we find that the value of the blinding value e retrieved by our algorithm is a multiple of the actual value of e, and we report this as a failure.

Next, we use the successfully retrieved distances to obtain the precise driver locations. Here, we use our attack described in Sect. 3.2. We see that this part correctly retrieves close to 99% of the driver locations. Hence, our overall driver location harvesting algorithm retrieves at least 80% of the drivers participating in the enhanced pRide protocol.

Table 1. Percentage of driver locations recovered for multiple cities.

City	Number of participating drivers (per grid)	%age of driver coordinates correctly recovered
Los Angeles	5	80
	15	95
	25	89
London	5	85
	15	81
	25	86
New York City	5	90
	15	95
	25	93
Paris	5	85
	15	93
	25	88

5   Related Works

There is a large body of work on privacy-preserving RHS which consider preserving privacy of drivers and riders. ORide [12] and PrivateRide [13], both proposed by Pham *et al.*, were some of the early works that aimed to preserve rider privacy against SP and drivers. While PrivateRide makes use of a cloaking region to maintain privacy, ORide scheme is based on SHE to encrypt driver and rider locations so as to make use of homomorphic properties of SHE to select nearest driver. Kumaraswamy *et al.* [5] proposed an attack that aims to determine locations of drivers participating in the ORide protocol. In their attack, an adversary rider can reveal locations of up to 40% of drivers who respond to a single ride request. They provide a countermeasure to thwart the attack while preserving sufficient anonymity. Murthy *et al.* [10] proposed an attack that uses triangulation by four colluding adversaries to obtain locations of all drivers participating in the ORide protocol.

Luo *et al.* [7] proposed a privacy-preserving ride-matching service also named *pRide*. Their protocol involves using two non-colluding servers: SP and CP (a third-party crypto server), and uses Road Network Embedding (RNE) [14] such that the road network is transformed to a higher dimension space to enable efficient distance computation between the network entities. However, the disadvantage of their scheme is the use of two non-colluding servers which incurs inter-server communication costs. Yu *et al.* [22] proposed lpRide protocol which also uses RNE but uses a modified version of Paillier encryption scheme [11] to preserve privacy of participating entities. Vivek [17] demonstrated an attack on the lpRide protocol where they show that any rider or driver can learn the coordinates of other participating riders. TRACE [18] is a privacy-preserving dynamic spatial query RHS scheme proposed by Wang *et al.*, that uses a quadtree structure and provides high-efficiency in terms of complexity and communication overhead. Kumaraswamy *et al.* [6] demonstrated an attack on the TRACE protocol where the SP can identify the exact locations of riders and drivers. Xie *et al.* [21] proposed a protocol that also uses RNE to efficiently compute shortest distances. Their scheme makes use of property-preserving hash functions where the SP can not only compute the rider to driver distances, but also pick the nearest driver. This way they eliminate the need for an auxiliary crypto server. All the works listed earlier picks the nearest driver to fulfil a ride request. pRide [4], proposed by Huang *et al.*, does not match the nearest driver but considers a global matching strategy with the aim of reducing the empty distance travelled by driver to pick the rider. Murthy *et al.* [10] gave an attack on the ORide protocol, using triangulation, where they recover locations of all participating drivers. In addition, by using more number of colluding adversaries, they show they can recover locations of up to 50% of drivers participating in the variant of ORide protocol that uses the mitigation solution of [5].

6   Conclusions

In this paper, we presented an attack on enhanced pRide [4] protocol, a privacy-preserving RHS. We show that an honest-but-curious adversary rider can determine the coordinates of about 80% of drivers responding to the rider's ride request as per the pRide protocol.

From Sect. 1.1, we see that locations of all drivers participating in the basic pRide protocol can be recovered by one or more adversary riders. As per the protocol, the rider chooses the optimum driver when given the plaintext distances to all drivers, and this fact is exploited by the adversary. Alternatively, the SP can select the optimum driver homomorphically. Since sorting and searching are high-depth circuits, it is not efficient to perform these operations using SHE schemes. However, FHE schemes can be explored to evaluate their suitability for practical RHS solutions.

The enhanced pRide protocol needs to perform comparisons and in order to preserve privacy, the values are blinded. However, since the order needs to be preserved, the blinding values are the same for all the comparands, which leads to the attack. Other secure order-preserving techniques need to be explored. However, as shown in [9], careful analysis is needed which would otherwise lead to further attacks.

In summary, we show that although protocols may seem secure in theory, a thorough analysis should be done which otherwise would expose severe vulnerabilities and security holes, as demonstrated by our attack in this paper.

Acknowledgements. We thank the anonymous reviewers for their review comments. This work was partly funded by the Infosys Foundation Career Development Chair Professorship grant for Srinivas Vivek.

References

1. Fan, J., Vercauteren, F.: Somewhat practical fully homomorphic encryption. Cryptology ePrint Archive (2012). http://eprint.iacr.org/2012/144
2. Google: Google Maps Platform (2019). https://developers.google.com/maps/documentation/roads/intro/. Accessed 01 Aug 2022
3. Google: Google Maps Platform, client libraries for google maps web services (2019). https://developers.google.com/maps/web-services/client-library. Accessed 01 Aug 2022
4. Huang, J., Luo, Y., Fu, S., Xu, M., Hu, B.: pRide: privacy-preserving online ride hailing matching system with prediction. IEEE Trans. Veh. Technol. **70**(8), 7413–7425 (2021). https://doi.org/10.1109/TVT.2021.3090042
5. Kumaraswamy, D., Murthy, S., Vivek, S.: Revisiting driver anonymity in ORide. In: AlTawy, R., Hülsing, A. (eds.) SAC 2021. LNCS, vol. 13203, pp. 25–46. Springer, Cham (2022). https://doi.org/10.1007/978-3-030-99277-4_2
6. Kumaraswamy, D., Vivek, S.: Cryptanalysis of the privacy-preserving ride-hailing service TRACE. In: Adhikari, A., Küsters, R., Preneel, B. (eds.) INDOCRYPT 2021. LNCS, vol. 13143, pp. 462–484. Springer, Cham (2021). https://doi.org/10.1007/978-3-030-92518-5_21

7. Luo, Y., Jia, X., Fu, S., Xu, M.: pRide: privacy-preserving ride matching over road networks for online ride-hailing service. IEEE Trans. Inf. Forensics Secur. **14**(7), 1791–1802 (2019)
8. Mordor Intelligence: Ride-Hailing Market - Growth, Trends, Covid-19 Impact, And Forecasts (2022–2027) (2020). https://www.mordorintelligence.com/industry-reports/ride-hailing-market. Accessed 23 July 2022
9. Murthy, S., Vivek, S.: Cryptanalysis of a protocol for efficient sorting on SHE encrypted data. In: Albrecht, M. (ed.) IMACC 2019. LNCS, vol. 11929, pp. 278–294. Springer, Cham (2019). https://doi.org/10.1007/978-3-030-35199-1_14
10. Murthy, S., Vivek, S.: Passive triangulation attack on oRide (2022). https://doi.org/10.48550/ARXIV.2208.12216. https://arxiv.org/abs/2208.12216
11. Nabeel, M., Appel, S., Bertino, E., Buchmann, A.: Privacy preserving context aware publish subscribe systems. In: Lopez, J., Huang, X., Sandhu, R. (eds.) NSS 2013. LNCS, vol. 7873, pp. 465–478. Springer, Heidelberg (2013). https://doi.org/10.1007/978-3-642-38631-2_34
12. Pham, A., Dacosta, I., Endignoux, G., Troncoso-Pastoriza, J.R., Huguenin, K., Hubaux, J.: ORide: a privacy-preserving yet accountable ride-hailing service. In: Kirda, E., Ristenpart, T. (eds.) 26th USENIX Security Symposium, USENIX Security 2017, Vancouver, BC, Canada, 16–18 August 2017, pp. 1235–1252. USENIX Association (2017)
13. Pham, A., et al.: PrivateRide: a privacy-enhanced ride-hailing service. PoPETs **2017**(2), 38–56 (2017). https://doi.org/10.1515/popets-2017-0015
14. Shahabi, C., Kolahdouzan, M.R., Sharifzadeh, M.: A road network embedding technique for k-nearest neighbor search in moving object databases. In: Voisard, A., Chen, S. (eds.) ACM-GIS 2002, Proceedings of the Tenth ACM International Symposium on Advances in Geographic Information Systems, McLean, VA (near Washington, DC), USA, USA, 8–9 November 2002, pp. 94–10. ACM (2002)
15. Shi, X., Chen, Z., Wang, H., Yeung, D.Y., Wong, W.K., Woo, W.C.: Convolutional LSTM network: a machine learning approach for precipitation nowcasting. In: Proceedings of the 28th International Conference on Neural Information Processing Systems - Volume 1, NIPS 2015, pp. 802–810. MIT Press, Cambridge (2015)
16. Stein, W., et al.: Sage Mathematics Software (Version 8.6). The Sage Development Team (2019). http://www.sagemath.org
17. Vivek, S.: Attacks on a privacy-preserving publish-subscribe system and a ride-hailing service. In: Paterson, M.B. (ed.) IMACC 2021. LNCS, vol. 13129, pp. 59–71. Springer, Cham (2021). https://doi.org/10.1007/978-3-030-92641-0_4
18. Wang, F., et al.: Efficient and privacy-preserving dynamic spatial query scheme for ride-hailing services. IEEE Trans. Veh. Technol. **67**(11), 11084–11097 (2018)
19. Wikipedia contributors: Universal Transverse Mercator coordinate system (2020). https://en.wikipedia.org/wiki/Universal_Transverse_Mercator_coordinate_system. Accessed 01 Aug 2022
20. Wikipedia contributors: Coprime Integers (2022). https://en.wikipedia.org/wiki/Coprime_integers. Accessed 09 Aug 2022
21. Xie, H., Guo, Y., Jia, X.: A privacy-preserving online ride-hailing system without involving a third trusted server. IEEE Trans. Inf. Forensics Secur. **16**, 3068–3081 (2021)
22. Yu, H., Shu, J., Jia, X., Zhang, H., Yu, X.: lpRide: lightweight and privacy-preserving ride matching over road networks in online ride hailing systems. IEEE Trans. Veh. Technol. **68**(11), 10418–10428 (2019)

Rebound Attacks on **SKINNY** Hashing with Automatic Tools

Shun Li, Guozhen Liu(✉), and Phuong Pham

School of Physical and Mathematical Sciences, Nanyang Technological University,
Singapore, Singapore
{shun.li,guozhen.liu}@ntu.edu.sg, pham0079@e.ntu.edu.sg

Abstract. In ToSC'20, a new approach combining Mix-Integer Linear Programming (MILP) tool and Constraint Programming (CP) tool to search for boomerang distinguishers is proposed and later used for rebound attack in ASIACRYPT'21 and CRYPTO'22. In this work, we extend these techniques to mount collision attacks on SKINNY-128-256 MMO hashing mode in classical and quantum settings. The first results of 17-round (and 15-round) free-start collision attack on this variant of SKINNY hashing mode are presented. Moreover, one more round of the inbound phase is covered leading to the best existing classical free-start collision attack of 19-round on the SKINNY-128-384 MMO hashing.

Keywords: Collision attacks · Rebound attacks · Quantum computation · Constraint programming · SKINNY

1 Introduction

In this work, we focus on the security analysis of SKINNY [1] family of lightweight block ciphers on Matyas-Meyer-Oseas (MMO) hashing mode [13]. Since introduced in CRYPTO'16, SKINNY attracts great attention from the community. It not only has competitive performance but also provides strong security guarantees in both single key as well as related key settings. A great amount of work ranging from standard cryptanalysis of the block cipher to constructing other cryptographic structures such as hash functions and the Authenticated Encryption with Associated Data (AEAD) schemes based on the block cipher has been published since it's proposed.

Two block sizes, *i.e.*, 64-bit and 128-bit are specified for the SKINNY family. For each block size n, the tweakey size t is defined as n, $2n$ and $3n$ for different variants which are denoted by SKINNY-n-t. For example, if $n = 128$, $t = 384$, we have the variant SKINNY-128-384. As there are too many works published on SKINNY, to explain our work in a neat and concise way only the related works are briefly introduced.

© The Author(s), under exclusive license to Springer Nature Switzerland AG 2022
X. Yuan et al. (Eds.): NSS 2022, LNCS 13787, pp. 649–666, 2022.
https://doi.org/10.1007/978-3-031-23020-2_37

Related Work. In ToSC'20, Delaune *et al.* [6] proposed a new approach which combines the Mix-Integer Linear Programming (MILP) tool and the Constraint Programming (CP) tool to search for boomerang distinguishers on SKINNY. In this work, we extend their work to design advanced automatic models to search truncated differential trails of the SKINNY variants. In ASIACRYPT'21, Dong *et al.* [8] presented a MILP-based technique to mount quantum rebound attacks on the SKINNY-128-384 MMO hashing. Later in CRYPTO'22, Dong *et al.* [7] combine triangulation and rebound attack to further increase the attacked rounds of SKINNY-128-384 MMO in both classical and quantum settings.

Our Contribution. The results of our work are summarized in Table 1. We mainly focus on rebound attacks on SKINNY-128-256 MMO hashing mode in classical and quantum settings. As far as we know, this is the first result on this SKINNY variant. In this work, the differential trails of SKINNY variants that are generated with the MILP-CP based automatic tools are widely employed to serve the cryptanalytic purpose. Moreover, we extend the 5-round trail of the inbound phase of the SKINNY-128-384 MMO to 6-round which gives the best attacking result.

Organization. This article is organized as follows. In Sect. 2, we give a brief description of SKINNY and introduce some basic notions as well as algorithms used in quantum computation. We revise the primary techniques that are broadly utilized in our work in Sect. 3. Section 4 and Sect. 5 are the demonstration of several attacks on SKINNY MMO hashing. Section 6 concludes the paper.

2 Preliminaries

2.1 SKINNY MMO Hashing

SKINNY is a family of lightweight tweakable block ciphers that follow the classical substitution-permutaion network (SPN) and the TWEAKEY framework [11]. There are 6 variants in the SKINNY family each of which is denoted by SKINNY-n-t, where n (resp. t) denotes the block size (resp. tweakey size). Specifically, the block size $n \in \{64, 128\}$ and the tweakey size $t = z \cdot n$ with $z \in \{1, 2, 3\}$. The number of rounds of SKINNY-64-64/128/192 and SKINNY-128-128/256/384 are 32/36/40 and 40/48/56 respectively. The internal states of both the 64-bit and 128-bit versions are represented with 4×4 array of cells with each cell being a nibble in case of $n = 64$ and a byte in case of $n = 128$. The tweakey which can contain both key and tweak material are essentially a group of z 4×4 arrays

Table 1. A summary of the results

SKINNY-128-256-MMO

Target	Attack	Rounds	Time	C-Mem	qRAM	Setting	Ref
Compression	Free-start	15/48	$2^{55.8}$	–		Classical	Sect. 5.2
Function		17/48	$2^{49.5}$	–		Quantum	Sect. 5.1
	any	Any	2^{64}	–		any	[2, 10, 18]
	any	any	$2^{42.7}$	–	$2^{42.7}$	Quantum	[3]
	any	any	$2^{51.2}$	$2^{25.6}$	–	Quantum	[4]

SKINNY-128-384-MMO

Target	Attack	Rounds	Time	C-Mem	qRAM	Setting	Ref
Compression	Free-start	19/56	$2^{51.2}$	–		Classical	[7]
Function		21/56	$2^{46.2}$	–		Quantum	[7]
		19/56	2^{35}	–		Classical	Sect. 4

where $z \in \{1, 2, 3\}$. For all the SKINNY variants, the cells of state and tweakey are numbered row-wise. The round operations are described in the following and illustrated with Fig. 1.

1. *SubCells* (SC) - The non-linear substitution layer that adopts 4-bit (resp. 8-bit) S-box for $n = 64$ (resp. $n = 128$) variants.
2. *AddConstants* (AC) - Xoring round constants to the first three cells of the first column of the internal state.
3. *AddRoundTweakey* (ART) - Adding tweakey (denoted by tk_i) to the internal state. Namely, the first two rows of tk_i are xor'ed. The round tweakey is computed with
   - $z = 1$: $tk_i = (TK_1)_i$
   - $z = 2$: $tk_i = (TK_1)_i \oplus (TK_2)_i$
   - $z = 3$: $tk_i = (TK_1)_i \oplus (TK_2)_i \oplus (TK_3)_i$
   where $(TK_1)_i$, $(TK_2)_i$ and $(TK_3)_i$ of the i-th round are generated with the *tweakey scheduling algorithm*.
4. *ShiftRows* (SR) - Circular right shift on each row of the internal state. The number of shifts in each row j is j for $0 \leq j \leq 3$.
5. *MixColumns* (MC) - Multiplying each column of the internal state by a 4×4 binary matrix which is non-MDS, i.e.,

$$\text{MC} \begin{pmatrix} a \\ b \\ c \\ d \end{pmatrix} = \begin{pmatrix} 1\,0\,1\,1 \\ 1\,0\,0\,0 \\ 0\,1\,1\,0 \\ 1\,0\,1\,0 \end{pmatrix} \times \begin{pmatrix} a \\ b \\ c \\ d \end{pmatrix} \text{ and } \text{MC}^{-1} \begin{pmatrix} a \\ b \\ c \\ d \end{pmatrix} = \begin{pmatrix} 0\,1\,0\,0 \\ 0\,1\,1\,1 \\ 0\,1\,0\,1 \\ 1\,0\,0\,1 \end{pmatrix} \times \begin{pmatrix} a \\ b \\ c \\ d \end{pmatrix}. \quad (1)$$

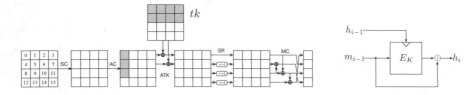

Fig. 1. Round function of SKINNY   **Fig. 2.** MMO mode

Tweakey Scheduling Algorithm (TSA). A linear tweakey scheduling algorithm is taken. The tweakey input is first loaded with a n, $2n$ or $3n$-bit tweakey input, *i.e.*, TK_1 with $z = 1$, (TK_1, TK_2) with $z = 2$, and (TK_1, TK_2, TK_3) with $z = 3$. The round tweakeys are generated as follows:

1. *Cell Permutation*: a permutation P defined as

$$P = [9, 15, 8, 13, 10, 14, 12, 11, 0, 1, 2, 3, 4, 5, 6, 7]$$

   is applied to each of the TK_m arrays, namely, $TK_m[i] \leftarrow TK_m[P[i]]$ for all $0 \leq i \leq 15$ and $m \in 1, \cdots, z$.
2. *LFSR Update*: cells in the first two rows of TK_2 / (TK_2, TK_3) for $z = 2$ / 3 are individually updated using a 4-bit (if the cell is a nibble) or a 8-bit (if the cell is a byte) LFSR. Note that TK_1 is not updated in this phase.

SKINNY Hashing in MMO Mode. A great category of cryptographic hash functions are based on one-way compression functions which are generally built from block ciphers. The Matyas-Meyer-Oseas (MMO) is one of the most extensively used method to transform any normal block cipher into a one-way compression function [13,15]. As illustrated in Fig. 2, by applying (keyed) permutations with SKINNY round functions in MMO hashing mode, compression functions (denoted as f) are constructed. The SKINNY hashing H in MMO mode is therefore defined following the Merkle-Damgård construction [5,16], *i.e.*, $H(m) = h_n$ with

$$h_0 = IV$$
$$h_i = f(m_{i-1}, h_{i-1}) \oplus m_{i-1}, \text{ where } i \in \{1, \cdots, n\}.$$

Here m denotes the message which is spilt into n message blocks m_i, h_i are the intermediate variables or chaining values, and IV is the abbreviation for initial value or initial vector.

2.2   The Rebound Attack

The rebound attack was introduced by Mendel et al. in [14] to mount collision attacks on hash functions that are constructed from block ciphers and permutations. As illustrated in Fig. 3, there is an inbound phase and two outbound phases in the rebound attack where the targeted block cipher or permutation F is split into three subparts, namely, $F = F_{fw} \circ F_{in} \circ F_{bw}$.

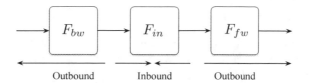

Fig. 3. The rebound attack

In the inbound phase, the meet-in-the-middle technique is exploited to search truncated differential trails of low probability. For example, given the patterns of both input and output differences of the inbound trails, the whole truncated trails are determined with the meet-in-the-middle method. Afterwards, state pairs (named as starting points for the outbound phase) that conform to the inbound trails are generated. The number of starting points is called the degree of freedom in the inbound phase. In the outbound phase, the starting points are propagated backward and forward through F_{bw} and F_{fw} to obtain pairs that fulfill the outbound trails as well as other extra constraints in a brute-force fashion.

In essence, the rebound attack is a technique to efficiently generate message pairs that satisfy the inbound phase while only exhaustive search is involved in the outbound phase. Assuming the probability of outbound trail is p, $1/p$ starting points must be prepared in the inbound phase to expect one pair following the outbound trail. Hence, the degree of freedom should be larger than $1/p$.

2.3 Collision Attacks and Its Variants

In regards to the cryptanalysis of a hash function H, a *collision attack* generates a message pair (m, m') such that $H(IV, m) = H(IV, m')$. Except for the standard collision, other well-accepted variants include *semi-free-start collision* and *free-start collision*. The goal of a *semi-free-start collision attack* is to find a pair (u, m) and (u, m') such that $H(u, m) = H(u, m')(u \neq IV)$ while the goal of a *free-start collision attack* is to find a pair (v, m) and (v', m') so that $H(v, m) = H(v', m')(v \neq v')$.

The semi-free-start collision and free-start collision attack on compression functions are defined in similar way if the hash function H is constructed by iterating the compression function with Merkle-Damgård construction. For example, both the semi-free-start and free-start collision attack on the MMO hashing mode shown in Fig. 2 could take the advantage of the degrees of freedom from the chaining value h_{i-1} through the key schedule algorithm. In effect, better attacks such as [12,17] were presented with this consideration. The significance of semi-free-start and free-start collision attacks should not be overlooked in security evaluation of Merkle-Damgård construction cause any kind of collision resistance including semi-free-start and free-start collisions is defined in its design principle.

2.4 Quantum Computing

Grover's Algorithm. Grover's algorithm [9] is a quantum algorithm to solve the searching problem in a database which was later proved being optimal [19]. The database search problem is described in the following.

Problem 1. Let $F : \{0,1\}^n \to \{0,1\}$ be a boolean function. Supposing there is only one x such that $F(x) = 1$ and a quantum oracle access to F is given, find the x.

It approximately requires 2^n queries before finding the x in the classical setting. In comparison, the x is found with only $O(\sqrt{2^n} = 2^{n/2})$ queries with Grover's algorithm. Alternatively, the time complexity of the database search problem in the quantum setting is quadratic faster than that of the classical ones. In the general case of Problem 1 where $|\{x : F(x) = 1\}| = 2^t$, the Grover's algorithm returns x after making $O(\sqrt{2^n/2^t})$ quantum queries to F with high probability. As summarized in Table 1 the $2^{n/2}$ complexity is actually a tight bound of preimage attacks on hash functions in the quantum setting thanks to the optimality of the algorithm.

Except for the Grover's algorithm, there are other quantum collision finding aogirthm with better bounds. The BHT algorithm is introduced to generate collisions for a random function in $O(2^{n/3})$ time and $O(2^{n/3})$ quantum queries under the assumption that quantum random access memory (qRAM) is available [3]. The quantum algorithm is subsequently extended to any random function [20]. If qRAM is not available the BHT algorithm become less efficient, *e.g.*, even slower than the birthday attack. To overcome the flaw, Chailloux et al. [4] proposed an efficient algorithm (called CNS) to efficiently generate a collision in time $\tilde{O}(2^{2n/5})$ with a quantum computer of $O(n)$ qubits. In that case, a large classical memory of size $\tilde{O}(2^{n/5})$ is required.

The bounds of quantum collision on hash functions based on SKINNY variants of 128-bit block size with the general quantum search algorithms are summarized in Table 1. That is, the quantum collision bound with Grover's algorithm is 2^{64} time complexity while the bound with BHT (or CNS) algorithm is $2^{42.7}$ (or $2^{51.2}$) time complexity but qRAM (or classical memory) is required.

3 Merging Multiple Inbound Phase

In this section, the *multiple inbound* technique that concatenates several 1-round inbound phases is proposed to extend the rounds covered in the inbound phase. Essentially, those 1-round inbound phases are connected by free bytes of the corresponding tweakeys. Therefore, it must be ensured that the value assignments to the related tweakeys of different rounds are not over-defined through the tweakey scheduling algorithm.

An example of a 3-round inbound phase (as depicted in Fig. 4) that merges two 1-round inbound phases is described to explain the multiple inbound phases. Note that the AC operation is omitted in the round function as it doesn't change the difference. The SC operation is relabelled as SB for the rest of the paper. The ART operation (resp. the subtweakey tk) is relabelled as AK (resp. the subkey k) as the tweakey is treated the same as a normal round key in the cryptanalysis.

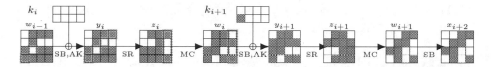

Fig. 4. The 3-round multiple inbound phases[1] (The gray boxes represent the active cells. The green and red boxes indicate the values are concerned.) (Color figure online)

In the multiple inbound phase, given the differential trail generated by the MILP-CP based automatic tools, the goal is to find state and key pairs that conform to the selected inbound phase. By taking advantage of the degrees of freedom from the subkeys k_i and k_{i+1} which can be efficiently calculated from tweakeys, the inbound phase is implemented with low memory. In specific,

- valid values of involved bytes in round states $w_{i-1}, x_i, w_i, x_{i+1}, w_{i+1}, x_{i+2}$ are first computed according to the (differential distribution table) DDT of the S-box where the input/output values satisfying input/output differences are stored. Note that x_i, *i.e.*, the intermediate state after SB and before AK operations, is not reflected in Fig. 4 considering that it shares the same difference pattern with w_{i-1}.
- valid values for pair of x_j, w_j can be further eliminated according to the inner operations of round function such as SB, SR, and MC. For example, green cells in Fig. 4 are traced in the following way,
  - $x_i[9, 12]$ pass AK without change;
  - $y_i[3, 6, 9, 12]$ pass to $z_i[3, 7, 11, 15]$;
  - and $w_i[3, 7, 11, 15] = \mathrm{MC}(z_i[3, 7, 11, 15])$.
  Similar treatments apply to those red cells. As a consequence, $w_i[15]$ is related with both w_{i-1} and x_{i+2} which can be utilized as an effective filter for pairs.

When all valid values in $w_j[12, 13, 14, 15](j \in \{0, 1, \ldots, r-1\})$ are determined, we merge them to find a valid pair of state and subkeys. For instance, if we randomly pick a value for $w_{i-1}[12]$ and $w_i[15]$, the value of $w_i[3]$ can be easily obtained as $w_i[3] = \mathrm{SB}(w_{i-1}[12]) \oplus w_i[15]$ according to the MixColumn operation (1). By randomly picking another value for $x_{i+2}[7]$, $w_{i+1}[7]$ is computed from $w_{i+1}[7] = \text{SB}^{-1}(x_{i+2}[7])$. Likewise, $z_{i+1}[3]$ is equal to $w_{i+1}[7]$ in accordance with the MixColumn operation (1), and $y_{i+1}[3] = z_{i+1}[3]$ due to the ShiftRow operation. Hence, subkey value $k_{i+1}[3] = \text{SB}(w_i[3]) \oplus y_{i+1}[3]$.

In a nutshell, with this multiple inbound technique, the pairs of states as well as subkeys that follow the sophisticated inbound differential trail of longer rounds are effortlessly generated.

4   Improved Free-Start Collision Attack on **SKINNY**-128-384 **MMO** in Classical Setting

In this section, we introduce an improved 19-round free-start collision attack on SKINNY-128-384 MMO hashing mode in classical setting. Aided by the technique developed in the last section, compared with the previously best result of the 5-round inbound phase given in [7], we obtain the first 6-round inbound phase. It's worth noticing that 6-round is the longest rounds covered by the inbound phase due to the constraint on the degree of freedom of the tweakeys. In total, an improved 19-round classical free-start collision attack with significantly reduced complexity is mounted given that one round of the exhaustive outbound phase is moved to the inbound phase.

In regards to the 19-round SKINNY-128-384 MMO hashing mode, the differential trail shown in Fig. 8 in Appendix A which contains a 6-round inbound phase and a 13-round outbound phase is employed to derive the free-start collision attack in classical setting. We'd like to emphasize that the 19-round differential trial is generated with the automatic tools based on the model published in [6]. The 6-round multiple inbound phase covers from state w_7 to x_{13}. The outbound phase happens with probability 2^{-35}.

The effort of the 19-round rebound (or collision) attack is devoted to the 6-round multiple inbound phase as only exhaustive search involved in the outbound phase. Hence, as illustrated in Fig. 5, only the inbound phase of the whole 19-round differential trails (which is shown in Fig. 8) is elaborated in this section. To launch the rebound attack, a multi-step *precomputation* method is performed to collect a number of pairs (*i.e.*, starting points) satisfying the 6-round inbound trail as shown in Fig. 5. Thanks to the great degree of freedom of the tweakey, enough starting points are prepared by changing the exact value of the 384-bit tweakey.

Precomputation in the Multiple Inbound Phase. The multi-step precomputation of the inbound phase that construct the conforming data pairs is explained with Fig. 5.

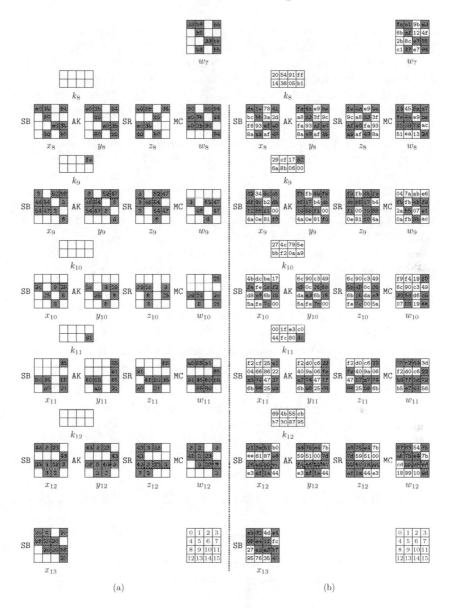

Fig. 5. The 6-round multiple inbound phase of SKINNY-128-384: (a) The value of differences are given; (b) The value of state and subkey of one of the pair are given. And the values of k_i are the XOR of subkeys and constants of AC operator.

1. Let's first consider the states from z_{10} to x_{11} in Fig. 5(a). According to the definition of SKINNY round function, we have $z_{10}[9, 11, 13] = \text{SR}(x_{10}[11, 9, 14])$ and all active bytes of w_{10} can be deduced by assessing DDT with fixed value of differences specified in Fig. 5(a). In the second column of z_{10} and w_{10}, we have conditions "$w_{10}[5] \oplus w_{10}[13] = z_{10}[9]$" and "$w_{10}[1] \oplus w_{10}[13] = z_{10}[13]$" corresponding to Equation (1), both of which provide a filter of 2^{-8}. As the differences of the inbound trail are dedicatedly determined in advance, there are enough pairs to verify the filters derived from a given differences. For example, if $(w_{10}[5], w_{10}[13], z_{10}[9]) \in (\text{DDT}[00_x][00_x] \times \text{DDT}[8_x][a0_x] \times \text{DDT}[47_x][8_x])$ are assigned for the condition "$w_{10}[5] \oplus w_{10}[13] = z_{10}[9]$", where $\text{DDT}[00_x][00_x]$ represents a full set containing $\{00_x, 01_x, \ldots \ldots, ff_x\}$, and $\text{DDT}[8_x][a0_x]$ is the subset of DDT with input-output differences $(8_x, a0_x)$, the size of all combinations of pairs is therefore $|\text{DDT}[00_x][00_x] \times \text{DDT}[8_x][a0_x] \times \text{DDT}[47_x][8_x]| = 256 \cdot 2^4 \cdot 2^3 > 2^8$.

2. When the value of $w_{10}[13]$ is chosen in the last step, $z_{11}[12]$ is determined with the related round operations as well. In addition, with all active bytes of w_{11} deduced through the DDT of round 12, state values of $z_{11}[8, 9, 10, 11]$ are computed with Eq. (1) accordingly. The condition $w_{11}[0] \oplus w_{11}[12] = z_{11}[12]$ in the first column of z_{11} and w_{11} is deduced in the same way, which acts as another filter of 2^{-8}.

3. Perform similar steps from z_8 to w_{12}, we get a data and key pair as shown in Fig. 5(b) conforming to the whole 6-round inbound trail.

The starting points collected in the multiple inbound phase are exhaustively checked in the outbound phase to search at least one pair that fulfill the outbound trail at the same time. In this work, a 19-round free-start collision attack on the SKINNY-128-384 MMO hashing mode with complexity 2^{35} is successfully obtained. Note that it's a practical free-start collision attack.

5   Free-Start Collision Attack on **SKINNY**-128-256 MMO

In this section, we further introduce classical and quantum rebound attack on SKINNY-128-256 MMO hashing mode. In comparison with Sect. 4, less degree of freedom is provided from the tweakey of the SKINNY-128-256 MMO. Thus, less rounds is covered in the inbound phase, *i.e.*, a 3-round inbound phase is generated.

5.1   17-Round Quantum Free-Start Collision Attack

In quantum setting, we derive the free-start collision attack on MMO hashing mode with 17-round SKINNY-128-256 using the differential characteristic shown in Fig. 9 in Appendix A. The 3-round multiple inbound phase starts from state w_7 to x_{10}. The outbound phase happens with probability 2^{-99}.

The identical cryptanalytic strategy described in Sect. 4 is applied to this 17-round attack. A similar precomputation process illustrated in Fig. 6 is performed in the 3-round multiple inbound phase to generate starting points that are exhaustive searched in the outbound phase.

Overall, we obtain a 17-round free-start collision attack on SKINNY-128-256 MMO hashing in quantum setting of time complexity $2^{49.5}$ with the Grover's algorithm.

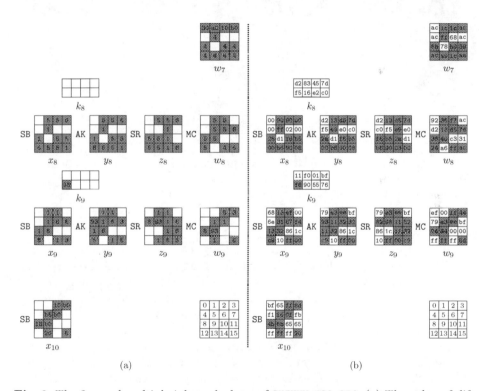

Fig. 6. The 3-round multiple inbound phase of SKINNY-128-256: (a) The value of differences are given; (b) The value of state and subkey of one of the pair are given. And the values of k_i are the XOR of subkeys and constants of AC operator.

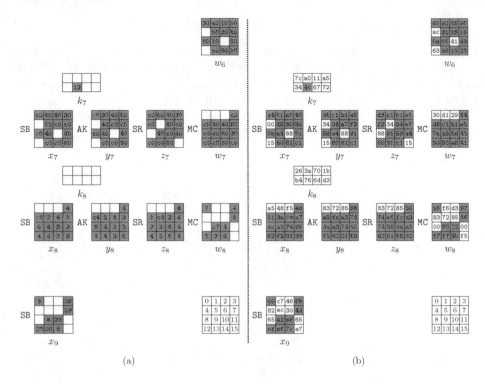

Fig. 7. The 3-round multiple inbound phase of `SKINNY-128-256`: (a) The value of differences are given; (b) The value of state and subkey of one of the pair are given. And the values of k_i are the `XOR` of subkeys and constants of `AC` operator.

5.2   15-Round Classical Free-Start Collision Attack

The differential trail of the first classical free-start collision attack on 15-round SKINNY-128-256 MMO hashing mode is given in Fig. 10 in Appendix A. The multiple inbound phase includes 3 rounds starting from round 7 to round 9. The way to find starting points in the inbound phase is exactly the same as the 17-round attack in Sect. 5.1.

An example of the precomputed starting point shown in Fig. 7 also satisfies the differential of the last two rows of w_5 to x_6. Since the outbound phase that excludes the S-boxes in the last two rows of x_6 happens with probability $2^{-55.8}$, the final time complexity of the 15-round free-start collision attack is $2^{55.8}$ in classical setting.

6   Conclusions

In this paper, we investigate the security of the SKINNY MMO hashings in quantum and classical settings with respect to collision attacks. Typically, the rebound method is used to achieve the collision attacks on SKINNY-128-256 and SKINNY-128-384 MMO hashings. We develop the MILP-CP based automatic tools to search truncated differential trails of longer rounds for the SKINNY variants. The multiple inbound phase technique is also proposed to cover more rounds. Totally, we present a practical 19-round free-start collision attack on SKINNY-128-384 MMO in classical setting, a 17-round (resp. 15-round) free-start collision attack on SKINNY-128-256 MMO in quantum (resp. classical) setting. As far as we know, all those attacks are the currently best results of collision attacks on those SKINNY hashings. These results serve as an indication that, to achieve long-term security to the post-quantum era, current symmetric-key crypto-systems require careful security re-evaluation or even re-design before being adopted by post-quantum cryptography schemes.

Acknowlegements. This research is partially supported by Nanyang Technological University in Singapore under Start-up Grant 04INS000397C230, and Ministry of Education in Singapore under Grants RG91/20 and MOE2019-T2-1-060.

A   Figures on the Quantum and Classical Collision Attack on SKINNY MMO Hashing

The 19-round SKINNY-128-384 using the differential characteristic shown in Fig. 8 in quantum setting.

The quantum 17-round and classical 15-round free-start collision attack on SKINNY-128-256 MMO hashing mode which are shown in Fig. 9 and Fig. 10 respectively.

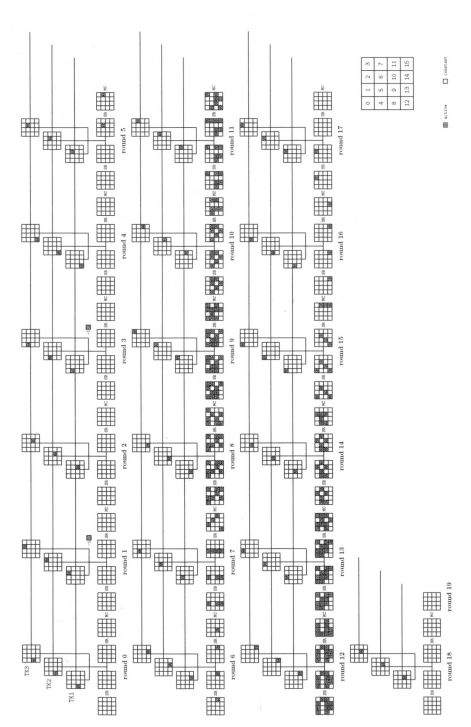

Fig. 8. Free-start collision attack on 19-round SKINNY-128-384

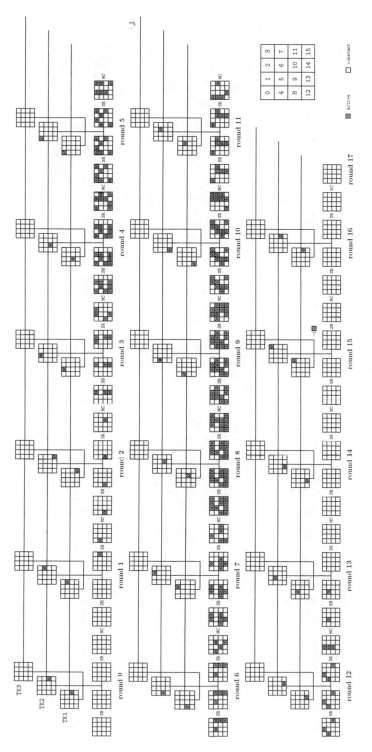

Fig. 9. Free-start collision attack on 17-round SKINNY-128–256

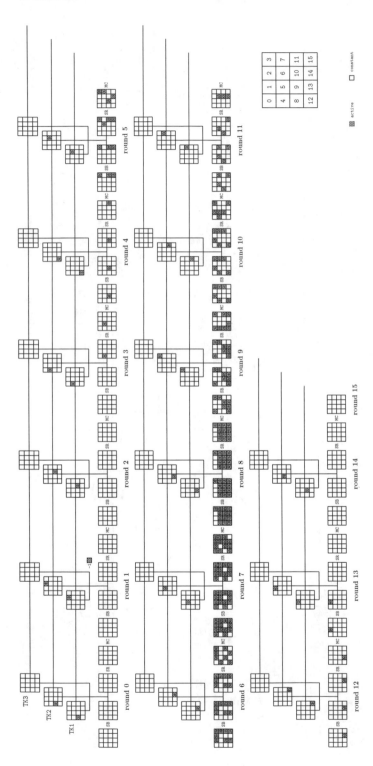

Fig. 10. Free-start collision attack on 15-round SKINNY-128-256

References

1. Beierle, C., et al.: The SKINNY family of block ciphers and its low-latency variant MANTIS. In: Robshaw, M., Katz, J. (eds.) CRYPTO 2016. LNCS, vol. 9815, pp. 123–153. Springer, Heidelberg (2016). https://doi.org/10.1007/978-3-662-53008-5_5
2. Bernstein, D.J.: Cost analysis of hash collisions: will quantum computers make SHARCS obsolete. SHARCS **9**, 105 (2009)
3. Brassard, G., HØyer, P., Tapp, A.: Quantum cryptanalysis of hash and claw-free functions. In: Lucchesi, C.L., Moura, A.V. (eds.) LATIN 1998. LNCS, vol. 1380, pp. 163–169. Springer, Heidelberg (1998). https://doi.org/10.1007/BFb0054319
4. Chailloux, A., Naya-Plasencia, M., Schrottenloher, A.: An efficient quantum collision search algorithm and implications on symmetric cryptography. In: Takagi, T., Peyrin, T. (eds.) ASIACRYPT 2017. LNCS, vol. 10625, pp. 211–240. Springer, Cham (2017). https://doi.org/10.1007/978-3-319-70697-9_8
5. Damgård, I.B.: A design principle for hash functions. In: Brassard, G. (ed.) CRYPTO 1989. LNCS, vol. 435, pp. 416–427. Springer, New York (1990). https://doi.org/10.1007/0-387-34805-0_39
6. Delaune, S., Derbez, P., Vavrille, M.: Catching the fastest boomerangs application to SKINNY. IACR Trans. Symmetric Cryptol. **2020**(4), 104–129 (2020). https://doi.org/10.46586/tosc.v2020.i4.104-129
7. Dong, X., Guo, J., Li, S., Pham, P.: Triangulating rebound attack on AES-like hashing. Cryptology ePrint Archive (2022)
8. Dong, X., Zhang, Z., Sun, S., Wei, C., Wang, X., Hu, L.: Automatic classical and quantum rebound attacks on AES-like hashing by exploiting related-key differentials. In: Tibouchi, M., Wang, H. (eds.) ASIACRYPT 2021. LNCS, vol. 13090, pp. 241–271. Springer, Cham (2021). https://doi.org/10.1007/978-3-030-92062-3_9
9. Grover, L.K.: A fast quantum mechanical algorithm for database search. In: Proceedings of the Twenty-Eighth Annual ACM Symposium on Theory of Computing, pp. 212–219 (1996)
10. Hosoyamada, A., Sasaki, Yu.: Finding hash collisions with quantum computers by using differential trails with smaller probability than birthday bound. In: Canteaut, A., Ishai, Y. (eds.) EUROCRYPT 2020. LNCS, vol. 12106, pp. 249–279. Springer, Cham (2020). https://doi.org/10.1007/978-3-030-45724-2_9
11. Jean, J., Nikolić, I., Peyrin, T.: Tweaks and keys for block ciphers: the TWEAKEY framework. In: Sarkar, P., Iwata, T. (eds.) ASIACRYPT 2014. LNCS, vol. 8874, pp. 274–288. Springer, Heidelberg (2014). https://doi.org/10.1007/978-3-662-45608-8_15
12. Lamberger, M., Mendel, F., Rechberger, C., Rijmen, V., Schläffer, M.: Rebound distinguishers: results on the full whirlpool compression function. In: Matsui, M. (ed.) ASIACRYPT 2009. LNCS, vol. 5912, pp. 126–143. Springer, Heidelberg (2009). https://doi.org/10.1007/978-3-642-10366-7_8
13. Matyas, S.M.: Generating strong one-way functions with cryptographic algorithm. IBM Tech. Discl. Bull. **27**, 5658–5659 (1985)
14. Mendel, F., Rechberger, C., Schläffer, M., Thomsen, S.S.: The rebound attack: cryptanalysis of reduced whirlpool and. In: Dunkelman, O. (ed.) FSE 2009. LNCS, vol. 5665, pp. 260–276. Springer, Heidelberg (2009). https://doi.org/10.1007/978-3-642-03317-9_16
15. Menezes, A.J., van Oorschot, P.C., Vanstone, S.A.: Handbook of Applied Cryptography. Instructor 202101 (2021)

16. Merkle, R.C.: One way hash functions and DES. In: Brassard, G. (ed.) CRYPTO 1989. LNCS, vol. 435, pp. 428–446. Springer, New York (1990). https://doi.org/ 10.1007/0-387-34805-0_40

17. Sasaki, Yu., Wang, L., Wu, S., Wu, W.: Investigating fundamental security require- ments on whirlpool: improved preimage and collision attacks. In: Wang, X., Sako, K. (eds.) ASIACRYPT 2012. LNCS, vol. 7658, pp. 562–579. Springer, Heidelberg (2012). https://doi.org/10.1007/978-3-642-34961-4_34

18. van Oorschot, P.C., Wiener, M.J.: Parallel collision search with cryptanalytic appli- cations. J. Cryptol. **12**(1), 1–28 (1999)

19. Zalka, C.: Grover's quantum searching algorithm is optimal. Phys. Rev. A **60**(4), 2746 (1999)

20. Zhandry, M.: A note on the quantum collision and set equality problems. arXiv preprint arXiv:1312.1027 (2013)

A Combination Reduction Algorithm and Its Application

Wei Yang[1], Shaojun Yang[1,2]($\boxtimes$), Wei Wu[1], and Yong Zhao[3]

[1] School of Mathematics and Statistics, Fujian Normal University,
Fuzhou 350117, China
shaojunyang@outlook.com
[2] State Key Laboratory of Cryptology, Beijing 100878, China
[3] College of Computer and Cyber Security, Fujian Normal University,
Fuzhou 350117, China

Abstract. After the Snowden incident, cryptographic subversion attack has attracted widespread attentions. Subversion attack is an unconventional attack inside machines, which has strong concealment. It will threaten the security of existing cryptography systems and seriously damage the confidentiality and integrity of communication. In this paper, we construct a subversion attack scheme on the multi-bit version of the learning with errors (LWE) encryption scheme proposed by Peikert, Vaikuntanathan and Waters, which is similar to the construction over the single-bit LWE encryption scheme. During the construction, the NTRU encryption scheme proposed by Zhang et al., is used to encrypt and decrypt the underlying message. In addition, the process of embedding underlying message into LWE ciphertext can be transformed into solving the ISIS problem. Therefore, a subversion attack scheme on the multi-bit version of LWE encryption scheme can be constructed by solving the ISIS problem successfully. With proper parameters selection, we use BKZ algorithm, BKZ algorithm and segment-LLL combined reduction algorithm to solve the ISIS problem, respectively. Finally, our experiments show that the combination reduction algorithm can improve the success rate of solving ISIS problem, and then promote the attack effect of subversion attack.

Keywords: Lattice reduction algorithm · Subversion attack · Lattice · ISIS

1 Introduction

Subversion attack (SA) refers to an attack method in which an attacker tampers with the internal operation process of some cryptosystems, and embeds a backdoor to steal user's information or private keys. It is difficult for users to detect whether the internal algorithm of the cryptosystem has been tampered with. Therefore, SA exists inside machines with strong invisibility. Besides, SA can be applied to many fields, such as public key encryption, digital signature, and will pose a serious threat to the security of the existing cryptosystems.

X. Yuan et al. (Eds.): NSS 2022, LNCS 13787, pp. 667–683, 2022.
https://doi.org/10.1007/978-3-031-23020-2_38

The research on the subversive attack technology can be traced back to the concept of subliminal channels proposed by Simmons [1] in 1984. The subliminal channel technology is the prototype of SA, and can transmit messages for designated receivers and senders. In addition, they took "criminal problems" as an example, and constructed the subliminal channel technology by using digital signatures. In 1996, Young and Yung [2] studied the SETUP (secretly embedded trapdoor under protection) attack, and given generalized and standardized definition. This attack could embed backdoors into black-box cryptosystems. In 2013, Snowden et al. [3] exposed the United States Project Prism, and showed that U.S. government agencies spy on users by embedding backdoors in widely used cryptosystems. Backdoors could make systems far less reliable as thought. The Snowden incident has aroused scholars' interest in SA. Subsequently, researching the subversive attack technology in the existing cryptosystems has become a hot topic.

In a cryptosystem, by combining the concept of black-box cryptography and the SETUP attack, Bellare, Paterson and Rogaway [4] proposed an algorithm substitution attack (ASA) that can replace the encryption algorithm. The security of this attack is non-adaptive and non-continuous. In 2015, Mironov and Stephens-Davidowitz [5] proposed "Cryptographic Reverse Firewall" (CRF) via imitating the real firewall in the traditional network security system. CRF prevents message leakage by modifying the messages sent and received in protocols. Thus, CRF effectively resists the attack behavior existing inside machines. In the same year, Atensive, Magri and Venturi [6] proposed a symmetric subversion attack model over digital signature schemes. Particularly, when an attacker attacks with an adaptive and continuous manner, the signature scheme should remain unforgeable. But the attack only satisfies weak undetectability. In 2017, Liu et al. [7] proposed a more general asymmetric subversion attack model with strong undetectability and signature key recoverability.

With the rapid development of quantum technology, public-key cryptosystems rely on difficult problems in traditional number theory, will be insecure any more. Therefore, public-key cryptosystems that can resist quantum attacks have received lots of attentions. Lattice-based cryptography can resist quantum attacks, and is the most promising candidate among post-quantum cryptography algorithms because of its simple operations and strong security guarantee. There are many public-key encryption schemes in lattices. In 1998, Silverman, Hoffstein and Pipher [8] designed a public-key encryption scheme in NTRU lattices. In 2005, the LWE encryption scheme was introduced by Regev [9] for encrypting the single-bit message, and its security relies on the LWE problem. In 2008, Peikert, Vaikuntanathan and Waters [10] given a multi-bit version of the LWE-based encryption scheme in [9]. They have the same public key size. However, the amortized running time of each message bit is only $\tilde{O}(n)$, and the ciphertext extension length is small. In 2010, Lyubashevsky, Peikert and Regev [11] proposed a public-key cryptosystem from ring-LWE, which reduced the size of public keys using ring structures and improved the efficiency.

According to the idea of Young and Yung [12,13] about backdoors for RSA and discrete logarithms, in 2017, Kwant et al. [14] used the ECC backdoor to attack NTRU encryption scheme. In this attack, attackers can recover the underlying message efficiently from some ciphertext. In 2018, Xiao and Yu [15] showed how to subvert the ring-LWE encryption scheme, which embed ring-LWE backdoors by encoding techniques. As the security of the attack also depends on the ring-LWE problem, the whole scheme is post-quantum secure. In 2019, by embedding the NTRU ciphertext in the encryption scheme [9], Yang et al. [16] successfully constructed a backdoor for the LWE-based encryption scheme designed by Regev. Moreover, the attacker recovered the underlying message, only using the private key of NTRU. And the core problem of this construction is to solve the Inhomogeneous Small Integer Solution problem (ISIS).

In this paper, we similarly construct a subversion attack on the multi-bit version of the LWE scheme proposed by Vaikuntanathan and Waters [10]. To embed the underlying message into the ciphertext, the key problem of the construction can still be transformed into solving the ISIS problem. Therefore, the success rate of solving the ISIS problem will directly affect the attack effect of the SA. Then, we combine basic reduction algorithms, and form a new reduction algorithm, to improve the success rate of solving this problem. This algorithm calls combination reduction algorithm to reduce the lattice, and obtains a better lattice reduction basis. Furthermore, we improve the success rate of solving the ISIS problem, that is, the attack effect of subversion attack.

1.1 Lattice Reduction Algorithm

In 1982, Lenstra, Lenstra and Lovász [17] pioneered the LLL reduction basis and the LLL algorithm. This algorithm outputs a non-zero short vector about an approximate factor $((1+\epsilon)\sqrt{4/3})^{(n-1)/2}$ in polynomial time, where ϵ is a constant greater than 0. Many scholars have improved the LLL algorithm from the aspect of optimizing the reduction effect or its running time. In 1988, Schnorr [18] used floating-point operations to reduce the running time of the LLL algorithm. In 1994, Schnorr and Euchner [19] proposed the concept of the BKZ reduction basis and given the BKZ algorithm. The BKZ algorithm has an additional input parameter, that is, a blocksize β. Though these algorithms can improve the LLL algorithm from different angles, the reduced basis obtained is not ideal when the lattice dimension is high. In 2001, Koy and Schnorr [20] proposed the Segment-LLL algorithm, which can effectively reduce lattice basis with dimension $n < 1000$. In 2011, Chen and Nguyen [21] used the extreme pruning technique to reduce the running time of the enumeration subroutine, and obtained the BKZ 2.0 algorithm. In 2016, Aono et al. [22] analyzed the selection of the blocksize β in the BKZ algorithm, and proposed a progressive BKZ (progressive-BKZ) algorithm, which reduced the time complexity. In 2016, Lu, Liu and Li [23] adopted greedy algorithm and partial column vector reduction, to decrease the number of basis vector swaps and size reductions in the process of LLL algorithm, as well as the computational complexity of LLL algorithm. The summary of LLL algorithm, BKZ algorithm and Segment-LLL algorithm is as follows

Table 1. Summary of lattice reduction algorithms.

Reduction algorithm	Time	Hermite factor	Approximation factor
LLL	$n^5 A$	$(4/3)^{\frac{n-1}{4}}$	$(4/3)^{\frac{n-1}{2}}$
BKZ	$\mathrm{poly}(n) \cdot T_{\mathrm{SVP}}(\beta)$	$\sqrt{\alpha_\beta}^{1+\frac{(n-1)}{2(\beta-1)}}$	$\alpha_\beta^{\frac{(n-1)}{2(\beta-1)}}$
Segment-LLL	$n^3 (\log n) A$	$(4/3+\varepsilon)^{\frac{n-1}{4}}$	$(4/3+\varepsilon)^{\frac{n-1}{2}}$

Notes: n: lattice dimension; A: computing the number of bit operations required for $O(n^2)$ bit integer arithmetic; $T_{\mathrm{SVP}}(\beta)$: the running time of calling the enumeration algorithm on the β dimension lattice base; $\alpha_\beta := \|\mathbf{b}_1\|/\|\tilde{\mathbf{b}}_\beta\|$.

2   Preliminaries

2.1   Lattice and Discrete Gaussian Distribution

Given n linearly independent vectors $\mathbf{b}_1, \ldots, \mathbf{b}_n \in \mathbb{R}^m$, $\Lambda(\mathbf{B}) = \{\sum_{i=1}^{n} x_i b_i, x_i \in \mathbb{Z}\}$ is called a lattice generated by $\mathbf{b}_1, \ldots, \mathbf{b}_n$, where $\mathbf{B} = (\mathbf{b}_1, \ldots, \mathbf{b}_n)$ is a basis.

For any $\mathbf{x} \in \mathbb{R}^n$ and $\alpha \in \mathbb{R}^+$, $\rho_\alpha(\mathbf{x}) := \exp(\dfrac{-\pi \|\mathbf{x}\|^2}{\alpha^2})$ is called an n-dimensional Gaussian function. In particular, for any n-dimensional lattice Λ,

$$D_{\Lambda,\alpha}(\mathbf{x}) := \frac{\rho_\alpha(\mathbf{x})}{\rho_\alpha(\Lambda)}, \mathbf{x} \in \Lambda$$

is named the discrete Gaussian distribution over Λ.

Lemma 1 ([24]). *For any discrete Gaussian distribution $D_{\mathbb{Z}^n,\alpha}$,*

$$\Pr[\mathbf{x} \leftarrow D_{\mathbb{Z}^n,\alpha} : \|\mathbf{x}\| > \alpha\sqrt{n}] \leq 2^{-n+1}.$$

2.2   NTRU Public Key Encryption Scheme

In 1998, Silverman, Hoffstein and Pipher [8] designed the NTRU-based encryption scheme over polynomial rings. Since only limited modular multiplication operations are used in the process of encryption and decryption algorithms, the scheme operates efficiently. But it lacks a strict security proof. By now, people have proposed various attacks to analyse its security. Since then, to resist attacks, scholars have optimized the NTRU encryption scheme by selecting appropriate parameters [25] and plaintext padding schemes [26]. In 2016, National Institute of Standards and Technology (NIST) launched worldwide call for Post-Quantum Cryptography Standards. Chen et al. [27] submitted the NTRU encryption scheme in the first round of candidate algorithm solicitation. The algorithm has successfully entered the third round and is possible to become a public standard algorithm in NTRU lattices for key encryption scheme.

Given security parameter λ, integer $q' = q'(\lambda)$, and the degree of cyclotomic polynomial ring R is $N = N(\lambda)$. One set $T_N = \{a_{N-1}x^{N-1} + \ldots + a_0 | a_i \in \{-1, 0, 1\}, 0 \leqslant i \leqslant N-1\}$, $T_N(r, s)$ contains polynomials in T_N with r ones and

s minus ones. We assume that the message space is $\mathcal{M} = R_2 =: \mathbb{Z}_2[x]/(x^N - 1)$, integers q' and p' satisfy: $q' > p'$ and $\gcd(p', q') = 1$. There are three probabilistic time algorithms in the NTRU public key encryption scheme which satisfy the following:

- Input the security parameter λ. One selects two polynomials $g \in T_N$ and $f \in T_N(d+1, d)$ at random. If $f \in R_{q'}$ is irreversible, reselects f until $f \in R_{q'}$ is invertible, and then outputs a public key pk $:= h \equiv g/(p'f + 1) \mod q'$, and the private key sk $:= (p'f, g)$.
- To encrypt a message $m \in \mathcal{M}$ with the public key h, one selects polynomial $\zeta \in T_N$ from a seed rseed $= H(m, h)$, and computes $t = \zeta * h$. Then, he samples $m_{mask} \in T_N$ based on tseed $= H(t)$ and computes $m' = m - m_{mask} \mod p'$. Finally, output a ciphertext $e = t + m' \in \mathbb{Z}_{q'}^N$.
- To decrypt the ciphertext e using the private key f, one recovers m' by $m' = f * e \mod p'$ and gets $t = e - m'$. One recovers $m_{mask} \in T_N$ from tseed $= H(t)$, $m = m' + m_{mask} \mod p'$, and gets $\zeta \in T_N$ by rseed $= H(m, h)$. If the equation $p'\zeta * h = t$ holds, then outputs the message m, otherwise outputs $\perp$.

Remark 1. (Security) In 2011, Stehlé and Steinfeld [28] given a reduction from the worst case problem on an ideal lattice to a certain NTRU problem. Precisely, on the circular polynomial ring $R = \mathbb{Z}[x]/(x^N + 1)$, $N = 2^r, r \in \mathbb{Z}^+$, the NTRU cryptosystem is IND-CPA secure, if the γ-Ideal-SVP problem over ideal lattice is hard. Recently, Yu et al. [29] generalized the provable security of the prime number N. In our work, the parameters of NTRU scheme is based on [29]. Moreover, we assume NTRU scheme satisfies IND\$-CPA security [16]. IND\$-CPA security is a little different from the IND-CPA security. In the game used to define IND\$-CPA security, when the adversary chooses plaintext to challenge the encryption oracle, if $b = 1$, oracle returns ciphertext, and if $b = 0$, the oracle returns a random vector in $\mathbb{Z}_{q'}^N$.

2.3 LWE Public Key Cryptosystem

The LWE problem was first proposed by Regev [9] in 2005. He proved that by choosing appropriate parameters, there is a quantum reduction from the LWE problem to the worst-case GapSVP or SIVP problem on lattices. So the LWE-based cryptographic schemes have a strict security proof. The positive integer n, prime integer $q > 2$, and error distribution $\chi = \bar{\Psi}_\alpha$ ($\bar{\Psi}_\alpha$ is the discrete Gaussian distribution with mean 0 as well as standard deviation $\alpha q/\sqrt{2\pi}$ on $\mathbb{Z}_q$) are parameters icluded in LWE.

Definition 1 (LWE Distribution, [9]). *For a secret vector $\mathbf{s} \in \mathbb{Z}_q^n$, the LWE distribution $A_{\mathbf{s},\chi}$ over $\mathbb{Z}_q^n \times \mathbb{Z}_q$ as the one obtain by: sampling $\mathbf{a} \leftarrow U(\mathbb{Z}_q^n)$, $x \leftarrow \chi$ (χ is a discrete Gaussian distribution), and returning $(\mathbf{a}, b = \langle \mathbf{s}, \mathbf{a} \rangle + x \mod q)$.*

Definition 2 (Decision-LWE, [9]). *The Decision-LWE problem is to distinguish between the distribution $A_{\mathbf{s},\chi}$ and the uniform distribution on $U(\mathbb{Z}_q^n \times \mathbb{Z}_q)$.*

Definition 3 (Search-LWE, [9]). *Given m independent samples from the LWE distribution $A_{\mathbf{s},\chi}$, calculate the secret vector $\mathbf{s}$.*

Given integer $p = \text{poly}(n) \geq 2$, integer $\ell = \text{poly(n)} \geq 1$ and prime $q = \text{poly(n)} > \text{p}$. In addition, all operations are performed in the ring $\mathbb{Z}_q$. The multi-bit LWE public key encryption scheme [16] is described as follows:

- **LWEKeyGen** (1^n): Choose $\mathbf{S} \leftarrow \mathbb{Z}_q^{n \times \ell}$, $\mathbf{A} \leftarrow \mathbb{Z}_q^{n \times m}$ uniformly and $x_{i,j} \leftarrow \chi(1 \leq i \leq \ell, 1 \leq j \leq m)$. Let $\mathbf{X} = (x_{ij})$ and $\mathbf{P} = \mathbf{S}^T \mathbf{A} + \mathbf{X} \in \mathbb{Z}_q^{\ell \times m}$. Finally, one returns pk $= (\mathbf{A}, \mathbf{P})$ and sk $= \mathbf{S}$.
- **LWEEnc** (pk $= (\mathbf{A}, \mathbf{P}), \mathbf{v}$): To encrypt a message $\mathbf{v} \in \mathbb{Z}_p^\ell$, one chooses a vector $\mathbf{e} \leftarrow \{0,1\}^m \subset \mathbb{Z}_q^m$ uniformly and calculates $\mathbf{t} = \lfloor \mathbf{v} \cdot \frac{q}{p} \rceil \in \mathbb{Z}_q^\ell$. Finally, output a ciphertext pair $(\mathbf{u}, \mathbf{c}) = (\mathbf{A}\mathbf{e}, \mathbf{P}\mathbf{e} + \mathbf{t}) \in \mathbb{Z}_q^n \times \mathbb{Z}_q^\ell$.
- **LWEDec** (sk $= \mathbf{S}, (\mathbf{u}, \mathbf{c})$): To obtain the plaintext $\mathbf{v} \in \mathbb{Z}_p^\ell$, one needs to compute $\mathbf{d} = \mathbf{c} - \mathbf{S}^T \mathbf{u} \in \mathbb{Z}_q^\ell$ and recovers $v_i (1 \leq i \leq \ell)$ satisfies $d_i - \lfloor v_i \cdot \frac{q}{p} \rceil$ mod q is the closest to 0.

Lemma 2 (Correctness, [16]). *For a given prime $q \geq 4pm$, real $\alpha \leq 1/(p \cdot \sqrt{m} \cdot \omega(\sqrt{\lg n}))$, the algorithm **LWEDec** decrypts correctly with overwhelming probability, over the matrix $\mathbf{X}$ is randomly selected from the error distribution χ.*

Lemma 3 (Security, [16]). *For a given prime $q \geq 4pm$, real $\alpha \leq 1/(p \cdot \sqrt{m} \cdot \omega(\sqrt{\lg n}))$, and $m \geq 3(n + \ell) \lg q$, the LWE cryptosystem is IND-CPA secure, assuming that Decision-LWE is hard.*

2.4   Subversion Attack

Given a public key cryptosystem $\Pi = (\textbf{KGen}, \textbf{Enc}, \textbf{Dec})$, the subversion attack (i.e. password backdoor attack) [10] on Π includes three algorithms: $\widetilde{\textbf{KGen}}$, $\widetilde{\textbf{Enc}}$ and **Recv**. All algorithms are executed by the attacker and performed as follows.

- $\widetilde{\textbf{KGen}}(1^n)$: The attacker obtains subversion key pair.
- $\widetilde{\textbf{Enc}}(\text{pk}, \text{spk}, \mathbf{m}, \mathbf{m}')$: To attack on Π, the attacker replaces **Enc** with $\widetilde{\textbf{Enc}}$. $\widetilde{\textbf{Enc}}$ takes public key pk, subversion public key spk, message $\mathbf{m}$ and underlying message $\mathbf{m}'$ as input, outputs a modified ciphertext. The user can recover the message by $\mathbf{m} = \textbf{Dec}(\mathbf{c}, \text{sk})$.
- **Recv**(ssk, $\mathbf{c}$): The attacker uses subversion private key ssk to recover underlying messages $\mathbf{m}'$.

Subversion attack has two important properties: post-quantum secret undetectability and arbitrary message recovery.

Post-Quantum Secret Undetectability (PQSU). In this paper, we assume that the receiver does not know the subversion private key. Given a ciphertext, the receiver uses the detector $\mathcal{D}$ to judge whether the algorithm **Enc** is replaced by the algorithm $\widehat{\textbf{Enc}}$. If $\mathcal{D}$ has quantum computing ability, this process is called quantum detection. The security of detection is defined by the adversary game in Table 2. In the game, $\mathcal{D}$ selects the message $\mathbf{m}$ and $\mathbf{m}'$ randomly, and sends them to the challenge encryption oracle $\overline{\textbf{Enc}}$. The advantage of $\mathcal{D}$ detecting subversion is given by $\mathbf{Adv}_{\Pi,\widetilde{\Pi}}^{det}(\mathcal{D}) = |2\mathrm{Pr}[b = b'] - 1|$.

Definition 4 ([10]). *SA on Π is ϵ-PQSU under the chosen-plaintext attack if* $\mathrm{Pr}[b = b'] \leq \dfrac{1}{2} + \dfrac{\epsilon}{2}$ *for any detector $\mathcal{D}$ with quantum computing capability, i.e.,* $\mathbf{Adv}_{\Pi,\widetilde{\Pi}}^{det}(\mathcal{D}) \leq \epsilon$. *In addition, if $\epsilon = \mathrm{negl}(n)$, SA satisfies PQSU.*

Table 2. Game used to define security.

Game DETECT$_{\Pi,\widetilde{\Pi}}^{\mathcal{D}}$	$\overline{\textbf{Enc}}(\mathrm{pk}, \mathrm{spk}, \mathbf{m}, \mathbf{m}')$
$(\mathrm{ssk}, \mathrm{spk}) \leftarrow_\$ \mathbf{KGen}(1^n)$	$b \leftarrow_\$ \{0,1\}$
$(\mathrm{sk}, \mathrm{pk}) \leftarrow_\$ \mathbf{KGen}(1^n)$	if (b=1) then
Choose $\mathbf{m}, \mathbf{m}'$ randomly	$\mathbf{c} \leftarrow_\$ \mathbf{Enc}(\mathbf{m}, \mathrm{pk})$
Send $(\mathrm{pk}, \mathrm{spk}, \mathbf{m}, \mathbf{m}')$ to $\overline{\textbf{Enc}}$	else
$b' \leftarrow_\$ \mathcal{D}(\mathrm{spk}, \mathrm{pk}, \mathrm{sk}, \mathbf{c})$	$\mathbf{c} \leftarrow_\$ \widehat{\textbf{Enc}}(\mathbf{m}, \mathbf{m}', \mathrm{spk}, \mathrm{pk})$
return b'	return $\mathbf{c}$ to $\mathcal{D}$

Arbitrary Message Recovery (AMR). Arbitrary message recovery security is defined by a game in Table 3. $\mathcal{M}$ represents the plaintext space and $\mathbf{m}'$ is a underlying message. If the adversary $\mathcal{A}$ successfully recovers the underlying message $\mathbf{m}'$ from the ciphertext $\mathbf{c} \leftarrow_\$ \widehat{\textbf{Enc}}(\mathbf{m}, \mathbf{m}', \mathrm{spk}, \mathrm{pk})$, the attacker wins the game. The advantage of $\mathcal{A}$ recovers the underlying message $\mathbf{m}'$ is measured by $\mathbf{Adv}_{\Pi,\widetilde{\Pi}}^{mr}(\mathcal{A}) = \mathrm{Pr}[\mathrm{AMR}_{\Pi,\widetilde{\Pi}}^{\mathcal{A}} = 1]$.

Table 3. Game used to define arbitrary message recovery security.

Game AMR$_{\Pi,\widetilde{\Pi}}^{\mathcal{A}}$	$\widehat{\textbf{Enc}}(\mathbf{m}', \mathrm{pk}, \mathrm{spk})$
$(\mathrm{ssk}, \mathrm{spk}) \leftarrow_\$ \mathbf{KGen}(1^n)$	$\mathbf{m} \leftarrow_\$ \mathcal{M}$
$(\mathrm{sk}, \mathrm{pk}) \leftarrow_\$ \mathbf{KGen}(1^n)$	$\mathbf{c} \leftarrow_\$ \widehat{\textbf{Enc}}(\mathbf{m}, \mathbf{m}', \mathrm{spk}, \mathrm{pk})$
$\mathbf{m}'' \leftarrow_\$ \mathcal{A}^{\widehat{\textbf{Enc}}}(\mathrm{spk}, \mathrm{ssk}, \mathrm{pk})$	return $\mathbf{c}$
return $\mathbf{m}'' = \mathbf{m}'$	

Definition 5 ([10]). *SA on Π is called $(1 - \epsilon)$ recoverable if $\mathbf{Adv}_{\Pi,\widetilde{\Pi}}^{mr}(\mathcal{A}) \geq (1 - \epsilon)$ for an arbitrary message and any PPT subversion attack adversary $\mathcal{A}$. In addition, when $\epsilon = \mathrm{negl}(n)$, SA on Π is named arbitrary message recoverable.*

2.5   Lattice Reduction Algorithms

For $1 \leq i \leq n+1$, π_i denotes the orthogonal projection over $(\mathbf{b}_1, ..., \mathbf{b}_{i-1})^{\perp}$. For $1 \leq i \leq j \leq n$, we denote the local projected block $(\pi_i(\mathbf{b}_i), \pi_i(\mathbf{b}_{i+1}), ..., \pi_i(\mathbf{b}_j))$ as $\mathbf{B}_{[i,j]}$, and the lattice $\mathcal{L}_{[i,j]}$ is spanned by $\mathbf{B}_{[i,j]}$.

Definition 6 (BKZ reduced bases, [19]). *An ordered basis* $\mathbf{B} = (\mathbf{b}_1, ..., \mathbf{b}_n)$ *of the lattice is BKZ reduced with blocksize* β *if it has properties 1.2.:*

1. $|\mu_{j,i}| \leq \dfrac{1}{2}, 1 \leq i < j \leq n;$
2. $\pi_i(\mathbf{b}_i) = \lambda_1(\mathcal{L}_{[i,j]}), 1 \leq i \leq n, j = \min(i + \beta - 1, n).$

The first component of the output of the Block Korkin-Zolotarev (BKZ) algorithm satisfies: $\|\mathbf{b}_1\|/\mathrm{vol}(\mathcal{L})^{1/n} \leq \sqrt{\gamma_\beta}^{1+(n-1)/(\beta-1)}$, and the running time of the algorithm is related to ENUM. BKZ performs ENUM to find a non-zero vector $\mathbf{x}$ satisfying $\pi_i(\mathbf{x}) = \lambda_1(\mathcal{L}_{[i,j]})$. We describe this in Algorithm 1.

Algorithm 1. The BKZ Algorithm

Input: A basis $\mathbf{B} = (\mathbf{b}_1, ..., \mathbf{b}_n)$, blocksize $\beta \in \{2, ..., n\}$, Gram-Schmidt triangular matrix μ, and $\mathbf{B}^* = (\mathbf{b}_1^*, ..., \mathbf{b}_n^*)$
Output: The basis $(\mathbf{b}_1, ..., \mathbf{b}_n)$ is $\beta - \text{BKZ}$ reduced
1: $z \leftarrow 0$; $i \leftarrow 1$; $\text{LLL}(\mathbf{b}_1, ..., \mathbf{b}_n, \mu)$
2: **while** $z < n - 1$ **do**
3:     $i \leftarrow (i \mod (n-1)) + 1$; $j \leftarrow \min(i + \beta + 1, n)$; $h \leftarrow \min(j + 1, n)$
4:     $\mathbf{x} \leftarrow \text{ENUM}(\|\mathbf{b}_i^*\|^2, ..., \|\mathbf{b}_j^*\|^2, \mu_{[i,j]})$
5:     **if** $\mathbf{x} \neq (1, 0, ..., 0)$ **then**
6:         $z \leftarrow 0$; $\text{LLL}(\mathbf{b}_1, ..., \mathbf{b}_{i-1}, \sum_{s=i}^{j} \mathbf{b}_s x_s, \mathbf{b}_i, ..., \mathbf{b}_h, \mu)$
7:     **else**
8:         $z \leftarrow z + 1$; $\text{LLL}(\mathbf{b}_1, ..., \mathbf{b}_h, \mu)$
9:     **end if**
10: **end while**
11: **return** β-BKZ reduced basis $\mathbf{B}$

In 2001, Koy and Schnorr presented an efficient variant of LLL reduction algorithm, which is called k-Segment-LLL algorithm. We divide the matrix $\mathbf{B} = (\mathbf{b}_1, ..., \mathbf{b}_n)$ into m segments $\mathbf{B}_l = (\mathbf{b}_{k(l-1)+1}, ..., \mathbf{b}_{kl})$ for $l = 1, ..., m$, and let $D(l) = \|\mathbf{b}_{k(l-1)+1}^*\|^2 \cdots \|\mathbf{b}_{kl}^*\|^2$.

Definition 7 (Segment-LLL reduced bases, [20]). *We call an basis* $\mathbf{B} = (\mathbf{b}_1, ..., \mathbf{b}_n)$, $n = km$, k-Segment-LLL reduced with $\delta \in (\dfrac{1}{4}, 1]$ *if it satisfies for* $\alpha = 1/(\delta - \dfrac{1}{4})$:

1. $|\mu_{j,i}| \leq \dfrac{1}{2}, 1 \leq i < j \leq n,$
2. $\delta \|\mathbf{b}_i^*\|^2 \leq \|\mathbf{b}_{i+1}^*\|^2 + \mu_{i+1,i}^2 \|\mathbf{b}_i^*\|^2, i \neq 0 \mod k,$

3. $D(l) \leq (\alpha/\delta)^{k^2} D(l+1)$, $l = 1, ..., m$,
4. $\delta^{k^2} \|\mathbf{b}_{kl}^*\|^2 \leq \alpha \|\mathbf{b}_{kl+1}^*\|^2$, $l = 1, ..., m$.

The first component of the output of the Segment-LLL algorithm satisfies: $\delta^{2k^2+n-1} \|\mathbf{b}_1\|^2 \leq \alpha^{n-1} \lambda_1^2$, and it speeds up the reduction time of lattices of dimension n by a factor $O(n)$. loc-LLL(l) of segments is done using local coordinates of size k. Here gives segment-LLL reduction algorithm.

Algorithm 2. Segment-LLL Algorithm
___
Input: A basis $\mathbf{b}_1, ..., \mathbf{b}_n$, δ, k, m and $n = km$
Output: k-Segment LLL reduced basis of $\mathcal{L}(\mathbf{B})$
1: $l = 1$
2: **while** $l \leq m - 1$ **do**
3: loc-LLL(l)
4:   **if** $D(l-1) > (\alpha/\delta)^{k^2} D(l)$ or $\delta^{k^2} \|\mathbf{b}_{k(l-1)}^*\|^2 > \alpha \|\mathbf{b}_{k(l-1)+1}^*\|^2$ **then**
5:    $l \neq 1$ then $l = l - 1$
6:   **else**
7:    $l = l + 1$
8:   **end if**
9: **end while**
10: **return** k-Segment-LLL reduced basis $\mathbf{b}_1, ..., \mathbf{b}_n$

---

3 Combination Reduction Algorithm

3.1 ISIS Problem And Solutions

The ISIS problem [30] is described as: given parameters (n, m, q, ε), random matrix $\mathbf{A} \in \mathbb{Z}_q^{n \times m}$ and a fixed vector $\mathbf{y} \in \mathbb{Z}^n$, find a non-zero vector $\mathbf{e} \in \mathbb{Z}^m$ such that $\mathbf{Ae} = \mathbf{y} \mod q$ and $\|\mathbf{e}\| \leq \varepsilon$. When $\varepsilon = \mathrm{poly}(n)$ and $q \geq \varepsilon \cdot w(n \log n)$, there exists a reduction from certain ISIS problem to a worst-case lattice SIVP$_\gamma$ problem with $\gamma = \varepsilon \cdot \tilde{O}(\sqrt{n})$.

The basic idea of solving the ISIS problem is to transform ISIS into hard problem in a specific lattice. Then, by using LLL, BKZ, Segment-LLL and other lattice basis reduction algorithms on this lattice to solve hard problems, we obtain the solution of ISIS. For a given ISIS problem, consider the $(m + n + 1)$-dimensional full-rank lattice basis $\mathbf{C}$:

$$\begin{pmatrix} \mathbf{I}_{m \times m} & \mathbf{0}_{m \times 1} & \mathbf{A}_{n \times m}^T \\ \mathbf{0}_{1 \times m} & 1 & \mathbf{y}_{n \times 1}^T \\ \mathbf{0}_{n \times m} & \mathbf{0}_{n \times 1} & q\mathbf{I}_{n \times n} \end{pmatrix} \in \mathbb{Z}^{(m+n+1) \times (m+n+1)},$$

and the lattice Λ' generated by $\mathbf{C}$. If $\mathbf{e}$ is a solution of the ISIS problem, $\pm \mathbf{v} = (\mathbf{e}, -1, \mathbf{0})^T \in \Lambda'$. The norm of $\mathbf{v}$ satisfies $\|\mathbf{v}\| = \sqrt{\|\mathbf{e}\|^2 + 1} \leq \sqrt{\varepsilon^2 + 1}$. Therefore, $\pm \mathbf{v}$ is the shorter vector in the lattice Λ', and one can transform the ISIS problem into an approximate shortest vector problem on lattice Λ'.

3.2   Combination Reduction Algorithm

Theoretically, with respect to improving the conditions of the lattice reduction algorithm, since the input basis will directly affect the quality of the output basis, the lattice reduction algorithm can be improved from the perspective of optimizing the input basis. This provides new idea for constructing a more effective lattice reduction algorithm. In practice, Bai, Liu and Li [31] used the joint Gauss-LLL algorithm, and pointed out through simulation that after $\lfloor n/2 \rfloor$ times Gauss reduction, and then LLL reduction for the lattice basis, the eventual lattice basis is better than the basis outputted by the LLL algorithm. Moreover, the combination algorithm is more efficient. In 2014, Peng et al. [32] showed that the combination of LLL algorithm and BKZ algorithm is more efficient in solving the knapsack problem, and the running time is greatly improved. Therefore, the combined reduction algorithm is better than a single lattice basis reduction algorithm in practice. In this paper, we combine the Segment-LLL algorithm and the BKZ algorithm to get a better basis. The combination reduction algorithm is described as follows.

Algorithm 3. Combination Reduction Algorithm

Input: A basis $\mathbf{B} = (\mathbf{b}_1, \ldots, \mathbf{b}_n) \in \mathbb{Z}^m$, integer k and $k|n$, a blocksize β and the upper
    limit of the number of loops num.
Output: The basis $\mathbf{B} = (\mathbf{b}_1, \ldots, \mathbf{b}_n)$ is reduced
 1: **for** $c = 1$; $c \leq num$; $c++$ **do**
 2:    Segment-LLL($\mathbf{B}$, k)
 3:    BKZ($\mathbf{B}$, β)
 4: **end for**
 5: **return B**

---

4   Subversion Attack on LWE Encryption Scheme

Through the construction of SA in [10], we propose a subversion attack scheme on the multi-bit LWE encryption scheme [16] in this section. To embed the underlying message over the LWE ciphertext, we need to solve the ISIS problem $\mathbf{A}\mathbf{e}' \equiv \mathbf{c}' \pmod q$. Subversion attack can be successfully constructed when the ISIS problem has a solution. In practical, obtaining $\mathbf{e}'$ is very difficult when n is large. By dividing the temporary ciphertext $\mathbf{c}'$ into blocks, we can reduce the difficulty of the ISIS problem and make it easier to get a solution.

Positive integer n, message space modulus p, integer q, sample number m, and error rate α are parameters involved in the LWE encryption scheme. N, p', $q' = q$ are parameters included in the NTRU encryption scheme.

Let $\mathbf{A} = (\mathbf{A}_{l \times m}, \mathbf{A}_{(n-l) \times m}) \in \mathbb{Z}_q^{n \times m}$, $\mathbf{c}' = (\mathbf{c}'_l, \mathbf{c}'_{n-l}) \in \mathbb{Z}^n$, and integer $l < n$. The subversion attack on the multi-bit LWE encryption scheme consists of three steps - $\widetilde{\mathbf{KGen}}$, $\widetilde{\mathbf{Enc}}$ and $\widetilde{\mathbf{Recv}}$.

- $\widetilde{\mathbf{KGen}}(1^n, 1^\lambda)$ contains two sub-algorithms:

- A sender runs $\mathbf{LWEKeyGen}(1^n)$ algorithm and gets the public/private key pair of the LWE public key encryption scheme

$$(\bar{\mathbf{A}} = (\mathbf{A}, \mathbf{P}), \mathbf{S}) \leftarrow_{\$} \mathbf{LWEKeyGen}(1^n).$$

- An attacker runs $\mathbf{KGen}_{\mathrm{ntru}}(1^\lambda)$ algorithm and generates the subversion keys as

$$(h, (f, g)) \leftarrow_{\$} \mathbf{KGen}_{\mathrm{ntru}}(1^\lambda).$$

- $\widetilde{\mathbf{Enc}}(\mathrm{pk}, \mathrm{spk}, \mathbf{m}, \mathbf{m}')$: Assume $\mathbf{m}' \in R_2$. The subversion encryption algorithm contains three sub-algorithms $\mathbf{Enc}_{\mathrm{ntru}}$, $\mathbf{LatticeSolve}$ and $\mathbf{LWEEnc}'$.

- $\mathbf{Enc}_{\mathrm{ntru}}(\mathbf{m}', \mathrm{spk})$: Given the underlying message $\mathbf{m}' \in R_2$ and NTRU public key h, outputs the temper ciphertext $\mathbf{c}'$ by

$$\mathbf{c}' \leftarrow_{\$} \mathbf{Enc}_{\mathrm{ntru}}(\mathbf{m}', h).$$

Let $N = lt$, then $\mathbf{c}'$ can be rewrote as $\mathbf{c}' = (\mathbf{c}'_1, \ldots, \mathbf{c}'_t)$, where $\mathbf{c}'_i \in \mathbb{Z}_q^l$.
- $\mathbf{LatticeSolve}(\mathbf{A}_{l \times m}, \mathbf{c}'_i)$: Input matrix $\mathbf{A}_{l \times m}$ and vector $\mathbf{c}'_i$, the output vector $\mathbf{e}'_i$ satisfies

$$\mathbf{A}_{l \times m} \mathbf{e}'_i \equiv \mathbf{c}'_i \pmod{q},$$

where q is the modulo parameter of NTRU and $\mathbf{e}'_i \in \mathbb{Z}^m$.
- $\mathbf{LWEEnc}'(\mathbf{m}_i, \mathrm{pk}, \mathbf{e}'_i)$: Input message $\mathbf{m}_i \in \mathbb{Z}_p^\ell$, public key $\bar{\mathbf{A}}$ and $\mathbf{e}'_i$, calculate

$$(\mathbf{u}_i, \mathbf{c}_i) = \mathbf{LWEEnc}'(\mathbf{m}_i, \bar{\mathbf{A}}, \mathbf{e}'_i),$$

and output ciphertext pair $(\mathbf{u}_i, \mathbf{c}_i) \in \mathbb{Z}_q^n \times \mathbb{Z}_q^\ell$.

- $\mathbf{Recv}(\mathbf{c}', \mathrm{ssk})$: The attacker can collect t pieces of $\mathbf{u}_i$, and ciphertext $\mathbf{c}'$ is formed by the first l rows of each $\mathbf{u}_i$. Then, the underlying message $\mathbf{m}' \in R_2$ can be recovered through the NTRU decryption algorithm

$$\mathbf{m}' = \mathbf{Dec}_{\mathrm{ntru}}(\mathbf{c}', f).$$

4.1   Application of Combination Algorithm in Subversion Attack

The core of the subversion attack is the ISIS problem: $\mathbf{e}^T \mathbf{A}_{l \times m}^T = \mathbf{c}_{l \times 1}^T \mod q$. In general, the selected l will lead a higher rank of the corresponding lattice basis $\mathbf{C}$, and get the solution of the ISIS problem directly through the lattice reduction algorithm is difficult. In 1993, Cohen [33] used the intersection lattice method to reduce the dimension of the embedded lattice basis.

The details are as follows: Consider the full-rank lattice $\mathbf{M}_i$ $(1 \le i \le l)$ of dimension $(m + 2)$:

$$\begin{pmatrix} \mathbf{I}_{m \times m} & \mathbf{0}_{m \times 1} & \mathbf{a}_i^T \\ \mathbf{0}_{1 \times m} & 1 & \mathbf{e}_i \\ \mathbf{0}_{1 \times m} & 0 & q \end{pmatrix} \in \mathbb{Z}^{(m+2) \times (m+2)}, \tag{1}$$

where $\mathbf{a}_i$ represents row i of matrix $\mathbf{A}$. Lattice basis $\mathbf{M}_i$ generates lattice $\mathcal{L}_i$ $(1 \leq i \leq l)$, and the intersection of lattice $\mathcal{L}_i$ is noted as $\mathcal{L}$:

$$\mathcal{L} = \bigcap_{i=1}^{l} \mathcal{L}_i. \tag{2}$$

If the intersection $\mathcal{L}$ contains the short vector $\pm\mathbf{v} = (\mathbf{e}, -1, 0)^T$, then $\mathbf{e}$ can be obtained through lattice reduction algorithm by Algorithm 2.

Algorithm 4. LatticeSolve

Input: A basis $\mathbf{A}^T \in \mathbb{Z}_q^{m \times n}$, integer k with $k|n$, the blocksize β and the upper limit of the number of loops num.

Output: Vector $\pm\mathbf{v}$

1: For $1 \leq i \leq n$, construct matrix $\mathbf{M}_i$ from Eq (1)
2: Set $\mathcal{L}_i = \mathcal{L}(\mathbf{M}_i)$
3: Calculate basis $\mathbf{B}$ of intersection lattice $\mathcal{L}$ by Eq (2)
4: **for** $c = 1; c \leq num; c++$ **do**
5:    Segment-LLL($\mathbf{B}$, k)
6:    BKZ($\mathbf{B}$, β)
7:    **if** $\pm\mathbf{v}$ belong to the reduced matrix $\mathbf{B}$, **then**
8:       **return v**
9:       **break**
10:   **end if**
11: **end for**
12: **return** $\perp$

4.2 The Property of Subversion Attack

Arbitrary Message Recovery. The difference between **LWEEnc$'$** and **LWEEnc** is the $\mathbf{e} \leftarrow \{0,1\}^m$ in **LWEEnc**, while $\mathbf{e}'$ of **LWEEnc$'$** satisfies $\mathbf{Ae}' \equiv \mathbf{c}' \pmod{q}$.

In the subversion encryption algorithm $\widetilde{\mathbf{Enc}}$, compute:

$$(\mathbf{u}, \mathbf{c}) = (\mathbf{Ae}', \mathbf{Pe}' + \mathbf{t}) \pmod{q}$$
$$= (\mathbf{Ae}', \mathbf{S}^T\mathbf{Ae}' + \mathbf{Xe}' + t(\mathbf{m}')) \pmod{q}.$$

Since $\mathbf{Ae}' \equiv \mathbf{c}' \pmod{q}$, the ciphertext pair can be expressed as:

$$(\mathbf{u}, \mathbf{c}) = (\mathbf{c}', \mathbf{S}^T\mathbf{Ae}' + \mathbf{Xe}' + t(\mathbf{m}')).$$

Since $\mathbf{c}' = \mathbf{c}_1$, the NTRU decryption algorithm can directly recover $\mathbf{m}'$. In addition, we have $\langle \mathbf{X}, \mathbf{e}' \rangle < q/4$. So the recipient can successfully get the message $\mathbf{m}$ by **LWEDec**.

Post-Quantum Secret Undetectability. The subversion attack scheme on the multi-bit version LWE encryption scheme meets the post-quantum secret undetectability, which is based on NTRU encryption scheme satisfying IND$ − CPA.

Theorem 1. *Let* Π *denotes the public key encryption scheme, and the subversion attack scheme is* $\Pi' = (\widetilde{\mathbf{KGen}}, \widetilde{\mathbf{Enc}}, \mathbf{Recv})$. *If* $\mathcal{D}$ *is a* PQSU *adversary on* Π' *that can query the oracle of* $\mathbf{Enc}$ *at most* k *times, then*

$$\mathbf{Adv}_{\Pi,\widetilde{\Pi}}(\mathcal{D}) \leq \epsilon.$$

Proof. The proof of the theorem is referred to Appendix A.

5 Experiment Analysis

The experimental platform we use is that, PC with Intel® Core(TM) i7-10700 @ 2.90 GHz×16. The parameters of the LWE scheme are set to $(n, q, m) = (65, 521, 182)$. This parameter setting satisfies the security conditions. In the experiment, the random matrix $\mathbf{A} \in \mathbb{Z}_q^{n \times m}$ and the random vector $\mathbf{c} \in \mathbb{Z}_q^l$ are generated using the NTL library [34]. In addition, we combine the BKZ and Segment-LLL algorithm, and use the results as the experimental group, the result obtained by the BKZ algorithm as the control group. The value range of the block size β in the BKZ algorithm is $\{10, 14, 18, 22\}$, The upper limit of the combinatorial reduction algorithm is 5. For each parameter set (l, β), we conduct 50 groups of examples in experiments. The experimental data are in Table 4, Table 5 and figures:

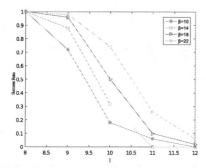

Fig. 1. The success rate of combinatorial reduction algorithm.

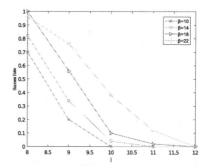

Fig. 2. The success rate of BKZ algorithm.

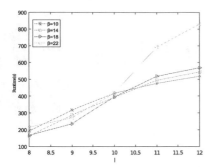

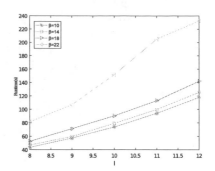

Fig. 3. The running time of the combinatorial reduction algorithm.

Fig. 4. The running time of the BKZ
algorithm.

In Figs. 1 and 2, we can see that the success rate of the combined reduction algorithm in solving the ISIS problem is higher than that of using only the BKZ algorithm. Moreover, in Figs. 3 and 4, we can see that our scheme takes a long time to run the combined reduction algorithm. But when $l \geq 12$, both reduction algorithms are difficult to obtain the solution of the ISIS problem.

Table 4. The success rate of BKZ
reduction algorithm.

success rate \ β / l	10	14	18	22
8	0.7	0.82	1	0.96
9	0.2	0.34	0.56	0.76
10	0	0.04	0.1	0.38
11	0	0	0.02	0.12
12	0	0	0	0

Table 5. The success rate of combinatorial reduction algorithm.

success rate \ β / l	10	14	18	22
8	1	1	1	1
9	0.72	0.88	0.96	0.98
10	0.18	0.32	0.5	0.74
11	0.06	0	0.1	0.26
12	0	0	0.02	0.06

6   Conclusion

In this paper, we construct a subversive attack on the multi-bit version of the LWE public key encryption scheme. Moreover, our experiments show that the combined reduction algorithm can increase the success rate of solving the ISIS problem, and improve the effect of the subversion attack.

Acknowledgements. The authors would like to thank anonymous reviewers for their helpful comments. This work is supported by National Natural Science Foundation of China (62032005, 62172096), Natural Science Foundation of Fujian Province (2019J01428, 2020J02016) and Open Fund of State Key Laboratory of Cryptology (MMKFKT202008).

A   Appendix

Proof. In game G_i, S_i denotes $b = b'$, $\mathcal{A}$ is an adversary, the game is described in Table 6.

Game G_1 and G_2 differ only in the encryption stage: In game G_1, the vector $\mathbf{c_1} \leftarrow_\$ \mathbf{Enc_{ntru}}(\mathbf{m}', \mathrm{spk})$, while in game G_2, $\mathbf{c_1} \leftarrow_\$ \mathbb{Z}_q^N$. $\epsilon_1 = |\Pr[S_2] - \Pr[S_1]|$ is negligible, since the $\mathrm{IND\$ - CPA}$ security of NTRU encryption scheme.

Game G_2 and G_3 differ only in the **LatticeSolve** stage: In game G_2, the vector $\mathbf{e_1} \leftarrow_\$ \mathbf{LatticeSolve}(\mathbf{A}, \mathbf{c_1})$, while in Game G_3, $\mathbf{e_1} \leftarrow_\$ \mathbb{Z}^m$. In game G_2, $\mathbf{c_1}$ is sampled from $\mathbb{Z}_q^N$ randomly, and $\mathbf{A} \mathbf{e_1} \equiv \mathbf{c_1} \pmod{q'}$. When matrix $\mathbf{A}$ is fixed, it is hard to distinguish between $\mathbf{e_1} \leftarrow_\$ \mathbf{LatticeSolve}(\mathbf{A}, \mathbf{c_1})$ and $\mathbf{e_1} \leftarrow_\$ \mathbb{Z}^m$. Thus $\epsilon_2 = |\Pr[S_3] - \Pr[S_2]|$ is negligible.

In game G_3, the vector $\mathbf{e_1}$ is sampled from $\mathbb{Z}^m$ randomly and the algorithm $\widetilde{\mathbf{Enc}}$ is consistent with the algorithm in the original LWE encryption scheme. Therefore,

$$\epsilon_3 = |2\Pr[S_3] - 1| = 0.$$

Let $\epsilon = 2\epsilon_1 + 2\epsilon_2 + \epsilon_3$, the advantage of $\mathcal{D}$ to detect SA satifies:

$$\begin{aligned}
\mathbf{Adv}_{\Pi,\widetilde{\Pi}}(\mathcal{D}) &= |2\Pr[S_1] - 1| \\
&= |2\Pr[S_1] - 2\Pr[S_2] + 2\Pr[S_2] - 2\Pr[S_3] + 2\Pr[S_3] - 1| \\
&\leq |2\Pr[S_1] - 2\Pr[S_2]| + |2\Pr[S_2] - 2\Pr[S_3]| + |2\Pr[S_3] - 1| \\
&= 2\epsilon_1 + 2\epsilon_2 + \epsilon_3 \\
&= \epsilon.
\end{aligned}$$

Because NTRU and LWE encryption scheme are both post-quantum cryptograph, this conclusion still holds even though adversy has quantum computing capabilities.

Table 6. The description of game $G_1 - G_3$.

Game$_1(n)$	Game$_2(n)$	Game$_3(n)$
$b \leftarrow_\$ \{0, 1\}$	$b \leftarrow_\$ \{0, 1\}$	$b \leftarrow_\$ \{0, 1\}$
$(\mathrm{ssk}, \mathrm{spk}) \leftarrow_\$ \widetilde{\mathbf{KGen}}(1^n)$	$(\mathrm{ssk}, \mathrm{spk}) \leftarrow_\$ \widetilde{\mathbf{KGen}}(1^n)$	$(\mathrm{ssk}, \mathrm{spk}) \leftarrow_\$ \widetilde{\mathbf{KGen}}(1^n)$
$(\mathrm{sk}, \mathrm{pk}) \leftarrow_\$ \mathbf{KGen}(1^n)$	$(\mathrm{sk}, \mathrm{pk}) \leftarrow_\$ \mathbf{KGen}(1^n)$	$(\mathrm{sk}, \mathrm{pk}) \leftarrow_\$ \mathbf{KGen}(1^n)$
$b' \leftarrow_\$ \mathcal{D}^{\overline{\mathbf{Enc}}}$	$b' \leftarrow_\$ \mathcal{D}^{\overline{\mathbf{Enc}}}$	$b' \leftarrow_\$ \mathcal{D}^{\overline{\mathbf{Enc}}}$
return $b = b'$	**return** $b = b'$	**return** $b = b'$
$\overline{\mathbf{Enc}}(\mathbf{m}, \mathrm{pk}, \mathrm{spk})$	$\overline{\mathbf{Enc}}(\mathbf{m}, \mathrm{pk}, \mathrm{spk})$	$\overline{\mathbf{Enc}}(\mathbf{m}, \mathrm{pk}, \mathrm{spk})$
if $(b = 1)$ then	if $(b = 1)$ then	if $(b = 1)$ then
$c \leftarrow_\$ \mathbf{Enc}(\mathbf{m}, \mathrm{pk})$	$c \leftarrow_\$ \mathbf{Enc}(\mathbf{m}, \mathrm{pk})$	$c \leftarrow_\$ \mathbf{Enc}(\mathbf{m}, \mathrm{pk})$
else	else	else
$c \leftarrow_\$ \widetilde{\mathbf{Enc}}(\mathbf{m}, \mathrm{pk}, \mathrm{spk})$	$c \leftarrow_\$ \widetilde{\mathbf{Enc}}(\mathbf{m}, \mathrm{pk}, \mathrm{spk})$	$c \leftarrow_\$ \widetilde{\mathbf{Enc}}(\mathbf{m}, \mathrm{pk}, \mathrm{spk})$
return c	**return** c	**return** c
$\widetilde{\mathbf{Enc}}(\mathbf{m}, \mathrm{pk}, \mathrm{spk})$	$\widetilde{\mathbf{Enc}}(\mathbf{m}, \mathrm{pk}, \mathrm{spk})$	$\widetilde{\mathbf{Enc}}(\mathbf{m}, \mathrm{pk}, \mathrm{spk})$
$\mathbf{c_1} \leftarrow_\$ \mathbf{Enc_{ntru}}(\mathbf{m}', \mathrm{spk})$	$\mathbf{c_1} \leftarrow_\$ \mathbb{Z}_q^N$	$\mathbf{c_1} \leftarrow_\$ \mathbb{Z}_q^N$
$\mathbf{e_1} \leftarrow_\$ \mathbf{LatticeSolve}(\mathbf{A}, \mathbf{c_1})$	$\mathbf{e_1} \leftarrow_\$ \mathbf{LatticeSolve}(\mathbf{A}, \mathbf{c_1})$	$\mathbf{e_1} \leftarrow_\$ \mathbb{Z}^m$
$c \leftarrow_\$ \mathbf{Enc}'(\mathbf{m}, \mathrm{pk}, \bar{\mathbf{A}}, \mathbf{e_1})$	$c \leftarrow_\$ \mathbf{Enc}'(\mathbf{m}, \mathrm{pk}, \bar{\mathbf{A}}, \mathbf{e_1})$	$c \leftarrow_\$ \mathbf{Enc}'(\mathbf{m}, \mathrm{pk}, \bar{\mathbf{A}}, \mathbf{e_1})$

References

1. Simmons, G.J.: The prisoners' problem and the subliminal channel. In: Chaum, D. (ed.) Advances in Cryptology 1983, pp. 51–67. Springer, MA (1984). https://doi.org/10.1007/978-1-4684-4730-9_5

2. Young, A., Yung, M.: The dark side of Black-Box cryptography or: should we trust capstone? In: Koblitz, N. (ed.) CRYPTO 1996. LNCS, vol. 1109, pp. 89–103. Springer, Heidelberg (1996). https://doi.org/10.1007/3-540-68697-5_8

3. Ball, J., Borger, J., Greenwald, G., et al.: Revealed: how US and UK spy agencies defeat internet privacy and security. Know Your Neighborhood 6, 1–10 (2013)

4. Bellare, M., Paterson, K.G., Rogaway, P.: Security of symmetric encryption against mass surveillance. In: Garay, J.A., Gennaro, R. (eds.) CRYPTO 2014. LNCS, vol. 8616, pp. 1–19. Springer, Heidelberg (2014). https://doi.org/10.1007/978-3-662-44371-2_1

5. Mironov, I., Stephens-Davidowitz, N.: Cryptographic reverse firewalls. In: Oswald, E., Fischlin, M. (eds.) EUROCRYPT 2015. LNCS, vol. 9057, pp. 657–686. Springer, Heidelberg (2015). https://doi.org/10.1007/978-3-662-46803-6_22

6. Ateniese, G., Magri, B., Venturi, D.: Subversion-resilient signature schemes. In: Ray, I., Li, N., Kruegel, C. (eds.) CCS 2015, pp. 364–375. New York, NY, USA (2015). https://doi.org/10.1145/2810103.2813635

7. Liu, C., Chen, R., Wang, Y., Wang, Y.: Asymmetric Subversion Attacks on Signature Schemes. In: Susilo, W., Yang, G. (eds.) ACISP 2018. LNCS, vol. 10946, pp. 376–395. Springer, Cham (2018). https://doi.org/10.1007/978-3-319-93638-3_22

8. Hoffstein, J., Pipher, J., Silverman, J.H.: NTRU: a ring-based public key cryptosystem. In: Buhler, J.P. (ed.) ANTS 1998. LNCS, vol. 1423, pp. 267–288. Springer, Heidelberg (1998). https://doi.org/10.1007/BFb0054868

9. Regev, Oded.: On lattices, learning with errors, random linear codes, and cryptography. J. ACM. 56(6), 1–40 (2009)

10. Peikert, C., Vaikuntanathan, V., Waters, B.: A framework for efficient and composable oblivious transfer. In: Wagner, D. (ed.) CRYPTO 2008. LNCS, vol. 5157, pp. 554–571. Springer, Heidelberg (2008). https://doi.org/10.1007/978-3-540-85174-5_31

11. Lyubashevsky, V., Peikert, C., Regev, O.: On ideal lattices and learning with errors over rings. In: Gilbert, H. (ed.) EUROCRYPT 2010. LNCS, vol. 6110, pp. 1–23. Springer, Heidelberg (2010). https://doi.org/10.1007/978-3-642-13190-5_1

12. Young, A., Yung, M.: Kleptography: using cryptography against cryptography. In: Fumy, W. (ed.) EUROCRYPT 1997. LNCS, vol. 1233, pp. 62–74. Springer, Heidelberg (1997). https://doi.org/10.1007/3-540-69053-0_6

13. Young, A., Yung, M.: Malicious cryptography: Exposing Cryptovirology. Wiley, J., and Sons, Indiana (2004)

14. Kwant, R., Lange, T., Thissen, K.: Lattice klepto. In: Adams, C., Camenisch, J. (eds.) SAC 2017. LNCS, vol. 10719, pp. 336–354. Springer, Cham (2018). https://doi.org/10.1007/978-3-319-72565-9_17

15. Xiao, D., Yu, Y.: Klepto for ring-LWE encryption. Comput. J. 61(8), 1228–1239 (2018)

16. Yang, Z., Chen, R., Li, C., et al.: On the security of LWE cryptosystem against subversion attacks. Comput. J. 63(4), 495–507 (2020)

17. Lenstra, A.K., Lenstra, H.W.,Lovász, L.: Factoring polynomials with rational coefficients. Mathematische Annalen. 261, 515–534 (1982)

18. Schnorr, C.P.: A more efficient algorithm for lattice basis reduction. J. Algor. **9**(1), 47–62 (1988)
19. Schnorr, C.P., Euchner, M.: Lattice basis reduction: improved practical algorithms and solving subset sum problems. Math. Program. **66**(1), 181–199 (1994)
20. Koy, H., Schnorr, C.P.: Segment LLL-reduction of lattice bases. In: Silverman, J.H. (ed.) CaLC 2001. LNCS, vol. 2146, pp. 67–80. Springer, Heidelberg (2001). https://doi.org/10.1007/3-540-44670-2_7
21. Chen, Y., Nguyen, P.Q.: BKZ 2.0: better lattice security estimates. In: Lee, D.H., Wang, X. (eds.) ASIACRYPT 2011. LNCS, vol. 7073, pp. 1–20. Springer, Heidelberg (2011). https://doi.org/10.1007/978-3-642-25385-0_1
22. Aono, Y., Wang, Y., Hayashi, T., Takagi, T.: Improved progressive BKZ algorithms and their precise cost estimation by sharp simulator. In: Fischlin, M., Coron, J.-S. (eds.) EUROCRYPT 2016. LNCS, vol. 9665, pp. 789–819. Springer, Heidelberg (2016). https://doi.org/10.1007/978-3-662-49890-3_30
23. Lu, L., Liu, W., Li, J.: An effective LLL reduction algorithm. J. Wuhan Univ. Natl. Sci. Ed. **41**(8), 1118–1124 (2016)
24. Micciancio, D., Regev, O.: Worst-case to average-case reductions based on gaussian measures. In: Proceedings of the 45th Symposium on Foundations of Computer Science. (eds.) FOCS 2004, pp. 372–381. IEEE (2004). https://doi.org/10.1109/FOCS.2004.72
25. Howgrave-Graham, N., Silverman, J.H., Whyte, W.: Choosing parameter sets for NTRUEncrypt with NAEP and SVES-3. In: Menezes, A. (ed.) CT-RSA 2005. LNCS, vol. 3376, pp. 118–135. Springer, Heidelberg (2005). https://doi.org/10.1007/978-3-540-30574-3_10
26. Howgrave-Graham, N., et al.: The impact of decryption failures on the security of NTRU encryption. In: Boneh, D. (ed.) CRYPTO 2003. LNCS, vol. 2729, pp. 226–246. Springer, Heidelberg (2003). https://doi.org/10.1007/978-3-540-45146-4_14
27. Chen, C., Hoffstein, J., Whyte, W., et al.: NIST PQ Submission: NTRUEncrypt A lattice based encryption algorithm. https://csrc.nist.gov/Projects/PostQuantum-Cryptography/Round-1-Submissions. Accessed 23 Jan 2018
28. Stehlé, D., Steinfeld, R.: Making NTRU as Secure as Worst-Case Problems over Ideal Lattices. In: Paterson, K.G. (ed.) EUROCRYPT 2011. LNCS, vol. 6632, pp. 27–47. Springer, Heidelberg (2011). https://doi.org/10.1007/978-3-642-20465-4_4
29. Yu, Y., Xu, G., Wang, X.: Provably secure NTRU instances over prime cyclotomic rings. In: Fehr, S. (ed.) PKC 2017. LNCS, vol. 10174, pp. 409–434. Springer, Heidelberg (2017). https://doi.org/10.1007/978-3-662-54365-8_17
30. Gentry, C., Peikert, C., Vaikuntanathan, V.: Trapdoors for hard lattices and new cryptographic constructions. In: Ladner, R., Chair, P. (eds.) STOC 2008, pp. 197–206. New York, NY, USA (2008). https://doi.org/10.1145/1374376.1374407
31. Bai, J., Liu, N., Li, Z.: New lattice reduction algorithm based on Gauss and LLL reduction. J. Comput. Eng. **39**(11), 147–149 (2013)
32. Peng, L., Hu, L., Huang, Z., et al.: Actual complexity of modular knapsack vector problem and practical security of a lattice based public key cryptosystem. J. Cryptol. Res. **1**(3), 225–234 (2014)
33. Cohen, H.: A Course in Computational Algebraic Number Theory. Springer-Verlag, Berlin (1993)
34. Shoup, V.: N.T.L A library for doing number theory. http://www.shoup.net/ntl/ 26-8-2018. Accessed 23 Jun 2021

Cryptographic Algorithms
and Protocols

Evaluating the Security of Merkle-Damgård Hash Functions and Combiners in Quantum Settings

Zhenzhen Bao[1,3]($\boxtimes$)(iD), Jian Guo[1]($\boxtimes$)(iD), Shun Li[1,2]($\boxtimes$)(iD),
and Phuong Pham[1]($\boxtimes$)(iD)

[1] School Of Physical And Mathematical Sciences, Nanyang Technological University,
Singapore, Singapore
{guojian,shun.li}@ntu.edu.sg, zzbao@tsinghua.edu.cn,
pham0079@e.ntu.edu.sg
[2] Department of Computer Science and Engineering, Shanghai Jiao Tong University,
Shanghai, China
[3] Institute for Network Sciences and Cyberspace, Tsinghua University, Beijing, China

Abstract. In this work, we evaluate the security of Merkle-Damgård (MD) hash functions and their combiners (XOR and concatenation combiners) in quantum settings. Two main quantum scenarios are considered, including the scenario where a substantial amount of cheap quantum random access memory (qRAM) is available and where qRAM is limited and expensive to access. We first convert a rich set of known tools invented for generic attacks in the classical setting to quantum versions. That includes Joux's multi-collision, expandable message, diamond structure, and interchange structure. With these basic tools in hand, we then present generic quantum attacks on the MD hash functions and hash combiners, and carefully analyze the complexities under both quantum scenarios. The considered securities are fundamental requirements for hash functions, including the resistance against collision, (second-)preimage, and herding attacks. The results are consistent with the conclusions in the classical setting, that is, the considered resistances of the MD hash functions and their combiners are far less than ideal, despite the significant differences in the expected security bounds between the classical and quantum settings. Particularly, the generic attacks can be improved significantly using quantum computers under both scenarios. These results serve as an indication that classical hash constructions require careful security re-evaluation before being deployed to the post-quantum cryptography schemes.

Keywords: Merkle-damgård · Hash combiner · XOR · Concatenation · Quantum · Generic attack

1 Introduction

In light of recent and projected progress in building quantum computers [18,21], more and more quantum algorithms have recently been applied to cryptanalysis

X. Yuan et al. (Eds.): NSS 2022, LNCS 13787, pp. 687–711, 2022.
https://doi.org/10.1007/978-3-031-23020-2_39

against classical cryptography systems to assess their security strength against quantum computers. In the past, most if not all crypto-systems were designed to resist attacks by conventional computers taking advantage of the limited computation power the real world may possess in the classical setting. In other words, these crypto-systems are only computationally secure, not information theoretically secure, under conventional computers. However, quantum computers have significant advantage of speedup computing (a.k.a. quantum supremacy) over conventional ones, which results in completely broken of some crypto-systems, and others with security strength weakened. For instance, Shor's factoring algorithm [31] is a powerful quantum algorithm to factorize an integer M in polynomial time with respect to the bit length of M, which can be used to break all current RSA standards and many other public-key crypto-systems. Therefrom, public-key crypto-systems have attracted a lot of attention from the research community and government agencies, e.g., the ongoing effort by NIST on postquantum cryptography standardization [30]. On the other hand for symmetric-key cryptography, Grover's search algorithm [19] is able to find a marked data in an unstructured database of size N in just $O(\sqrt{N})$ time, vs. $O(N)$ for brute-force search in classical setting. This generally reduces the security strength in bits by half of most keyed symmetric-key crypto-systems, e.g., the secret key of AES-128 can be recovered within a complexity of roughly 2^{64} vs. 2^{128} in the classical setting by brute-force search.

In this paper, we re-assess the fundamental security properties, i.e., collision, preimage, and second-preimage resistance, of some hash constructions that have existed for long in the classical setting of the real world, under some quantum settings. We focus on *iterated* hash functions, in particular those following the Merkle-Damgård construction (MD) [12,29], where a single compression function is called iteratively in order to extend the input domain from a fixed length to arbitrary length and the digest length is the same as that of internal state as for most of the standards like MD5, SHA-1, and SHA-2.

The security of hash constructions has been well studied in the classical setting in the past few decades. For Merkle-Damgård construction, it is known that the collision resistance of the hash function can be reduced to that of the underlying compression function [12,29]. The existence of multi-collisions was formally introduced by Joux [24] in 2004, and the first generic second-preimage was found by Kelsey and Schneier [26] in 2005 and later improved by Andreeva *et al.* [3,5]. Herding attack was introduced first by Kelsey and Kohno [25] in 2006 and was later improved by Andreeva *et al.* [4]. It is noted that second-preimage attacks and herding attacks are all utilizing collisions and hence complexities are well above birthday bound.

In the quantum setting, the security of these hash constructions has also received some investigations. In [34], Zhandry proved that the Merkle-Damgård construction with ideal (cannot be distinguished from a random oracle) underlying compression function cannot be distinguished from a random oracle with more than negligible advantage. In [20], Hosoyamada and Yasuda proved that Merkle-Damgård construction with Davies-Meyer (DM-mode) compression function is quantum one-way function, and the lower bound of the number of queries required by preimage attacks is $O(2^{n/2})$—that given by the generic Grover's search algorithm. It is reckoned in [10] that similar proof to that in [20] could be done also with the Matyas-Meyer-Oseas (MMO) mode compression function. These works provide provable security lower bound for the Merkle-Damgård constructions in quantum settings. Yet, the rich set of tools invented in previous work to do generic attacks, which provide security upper bound, on Merkle-Damgård hash constructions in classical settings still remain to be fully exploited in quantum settings.

Besides the single hash functions, we also re-evaluate the security of hash combiners in quantum settings. We focus on two typical hash combiners, *i.e.*, the concatenation combiner and the exclusive-or (XOR) combiner. Given two (independent) hash functions $\mathcal{H}_1$ and $\mathcal{H}_2$, the concatenation combiner returns $\mathcal{H}_1(M)\|\mathcal{H}_2(M)$, and the XOR combiner returns $\mathcal{H}_1(M) \oplus \mathcal{H}_2(M)$. In practice, people may wonder whether we can combine existing hash functions to achieve long term security instead of replacing existing infrastructure to new ones (in SSL v3 [17] and TLS 1.0/1.1 [13,14], MD5 and SHA-1 were combined in various ways, including concatenation combiner and XOR combiner [16]). The main purpose of hash combiners might be to achieve *security amplification*, *i.e.*, the hash combiner offers higher security strength than its component hash functions, or to achieve *security robustness*, *i.e.*, the hash combiner remains secure as long as at least one of its component hash functions is secure. We know from the results of previous cryptanalyses that in the classical setting, the hash combiners are not as secure as expected (e.g., guarantee its security if either underlying hash function remains secure, or as secure as a single ideal hash function). Concretely, the attacks on XOR combiners by Leurent and Wang [28] in 2015 and on concatenation combiners by Dinur [15] in 2016 showed surprising weaknesses, which either contradicts the intended purposes of security robustness or security amplification. These results were then improved and summarized by Bao *et al.* in [6,7]. However, some techniques used in previous cryptanalyses of hash combiners in the classical setting cannot be directly accelerated using quantum computers (e.g., those attacks on combiners exploiting properties of random functional graphs). Whereas generic attack is accelerated in the quantum setting, that is, the security upper bound of an ideal hash function is lower. Thus, the broken primitives (e.g., the investigated hash combiners) in the classical setting might be unbroken (no better attacks than the most generic attack) in the quantum setting. So, we investigate this question and aim to provide references.

1.1   Our Contributions

In this paper, we port most of the important and generic attacks in the classical settings against Merkle-Damgård construction and hash combiners, make adjustments of the attack algorithms whenever necessary, and carefully evaluate the complexities in the quantum setting. Table 1 summarizes detailed complexities. Surprisingly, most of the (second-)preimage attacks and herding attacks in the classical setting still constitute valid attacks in the quantum setting.

Table 1. Security status of Merkle-Damgård hash functions and hash combiners (polynomial factors are ignored for exponential complexities)

Target	Property	CS		Scenario $\mathcal{R}_1$		Scenario $\mathcal{R}_2$			Reference
		CTime	CMem	QTime	QMem	QTime	QMem	CMem	
$\mathcal{H}$	Collision	$2^{n/2}$	$O(1)$	$2^{n/3}$	$2^{n/3}$	$2^{2n/5}$	$O(n)$	$2^{n/5}$	[9,11]
	Preimage	2^n	$O(1)$	$2^{n/2}$	$O(n)$	$2^{n/2}$	$O(n)$	$O(1)$	[19]
	2nd Preimage	$2^{n/2}$ [26]	$2^{n/2}$	$2^{n/3}$	$2^{n/3}$	$2^{3n/7}$	$O(n)$	$2^{3n/7}$	Sect. 4.2
	Herding	$2^{2n/3}$ [25]	$2^{n/3}$	$2^{3n/7}$	$2^{3n/7}$	$2^{11n/23}$	$O(n)$	$2^{7n/23}$	Sect. 4.3
$\mathcal{H}_1 \oplus \mathcal{H}_2$	Collision	$2^{n/2}$	$O(1)$	$2^{n/3}$	$2^{n/3}$	$2^{2n/5}$	$O(n)$	$2^{n/5}$	[9,11]
	Preimage	$2^{11n/18}$ [6]	$2^{11n/18}$	$2^{10n/21}$	$2^{n/3}$	$2^{52n/105}$	$2^{n/7}$	$2^{n/5}$	Sect. 5.1
	2nd Preimage	$2^{11n/18}$ [6]	$2^{11n/18}$	$2^{10n/21}$	$2^{n/3}$	$2^{52n/105}$	$2^{n/7}$	$2^{n/5}$	Sect. 5.1
	Herding	$2^{2n/3}$ [4]	$2^{n/3}$	$2^{4n/9}$	$2^{n/3}$	$2^{24n/49}$	$2^{n/7}$	$2^{n/5}$	Sect. 5.3
$\mathcal{H}_1 \| \mathcal{H}_2$	Collision	$2^{n/2}$ [24]	$O(n)$	$2^{n/3}$	$2^{n/3}$	$2^{3n/7}$	$2^{n/7}$	$2^{n/5}$	Sect. 5.2
	Preimage	2^n [24]	$O(n)$	$2^{n/2}$	$2^{n/3}$	$2^{n/2}$	$O(n)$	$2^{n/5}$	Sect. 5.2
	2nd Preimage	$2^{25n/34}$ [6]	$2^{25n/34}$	$2^{n/2}$	$2^{n/3}$	$2^{n/2}$	$O(n)$	$2^{n/5}$	Sect. 5.2
	Herding	$2^{2n/3}$ [4]	$2^{n/3}$	$2^{4n/9}$	$2^{n/3}$	$2^{24n/49}$	$2^{n/7}$	$2^{n/5}$	Sect. 5.3

CS: Classical Setting   QTime: Quantum Time
QMem: Quantum Memory   CMem: Classical Memory

The attacks in quantum settings are divided into two scenarios, depending on whether cheaply accessible quantum random access memory is available or not, and they are named Scenario $\mathcal{R}_1$ and Scenario $\mathcal{R}_2$. Scenario $\mathcal{R}_1$ refers qRAM supporting access in constant time regardless of the size of the memory, while it costs $O(R)$ time for each access to quantum memory of size $O(R)$ and also linear time for each access to classical memory in Scenario $\mathcal{R}_2$.

This article is organized as follows. In the next Sect. 2, we introduces some basic notions and algorithms used in quantum computation. Section 4 and 5 are the demonstration of several attacks on Merkle-Damgård structures and hash combiners. Section 6 concludes the results and presents some open problems. We revise some important techniques for our attack belong with the quantum version of these techniques in Sect. 3.

2   Basic Quantum Algorithms for Collision and Search

In this section, we briefly introduce hash functions, hash combiners, qRAM, and quantum algorithms used throughout this paper.

2.1   Merkle-Damgård Hash Construction

Define $\mathcal{H}$ for a cryptographic hash function that maps arbitrarily long messages to an n bit digest, i.e., $\mathcal{H} : \{0,1\}^* \to \{0,1\}^n$. Like most iterated hash functions, to hash a message M, the Merkle-Damgård (MD) construction first pads and splits the message bits into message blocks of fixed length (e.g., b bits), i.e., $M = m_1 \| m_2 \| \cdots \| m_L$, where the last message block m_L comprises the bit encoding of the original message length. Then, starting from a public initial value $IV = x_0$, the message block with the intermediate state is hashed by the same compression function H iteratively, i.e., $x_i = h(x_{i-1}, m_i)$ for $i = 1, \ldots, L$ (see Fig. 1). In the quantum setting, the MD hash functions are proven to be quantum one-way functions [20], while other security properties remain largely un-exploited in the quantum setting.

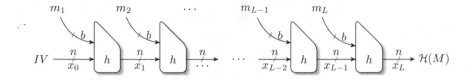

Fig. 1. Merkle-Damgård hash function

The XOR combiner and concatenation combiner based hash functions following MD structure are demonstrated in the following figures.

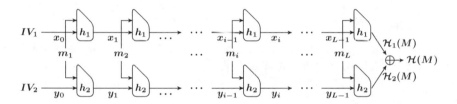

Fig. 2. The XOR combiner

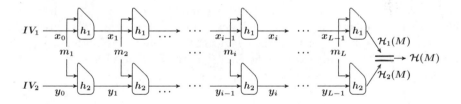

Fig. 3. The concatenation combiner

2.2 QRAM

Quantum random access memory (qRAM) can be considered as a quantum counterpart of random access memory (RAM) from the classical setting, which allows accessing (read or write) the elements in memory with constant time regardless of storage size. There are two types of qRAM: *quantum-accessible classical memory* (QRACM), which allows to access the classical data in quantum superpositions, and *quantum-accessible quantum memory* (QRAQM), where the data is stored in quantum memory. Suppose that we want to store a list of data (classical or quantum) $D = (x_0, x_1, \cdots, x_{2^k-1})$, where x_i is an n-bit data. Then the $qRAM$ for accessing data D is constructed as a quantum gate and defined via a unitary operator $U_{\text{qRAM}}(D)$ by

$$U_{\text{qRAM}}(D) : |i\rangle|y\rangle \mapsto |i\rangle|y \oplus x_i\rangle$$

where $i \approx \{0,1\}^k$ and y is an n-bit value. Since qRAM is a powerful model with requirement of specific physical architecture, many quantum algorithms take advantage of it to reduce time complexity, such as the algorithm for collision search [9] requires QRACM and element distinctness [2] requires QRAQM. Though qRAM is still a controversial issue, it is essential to evaluate the cryptography systems in the scenario that qRAM is big and cheap to access (we will call this quantum model as Scenario $\mathcal{R}_1$). On the other hand, a relatively more realistic model is to assume that qRAM is costly and accessing to R quantum qubit memory costs $O(R)$ time as in [11,22] (we will call this quantum model as Scenario $\mathcal{R}_2$). We will analyze the complexities of our attacks in both Scenario $\mathcal{R}_1$ and Scenario $\mathcal{R}_2$ with respective optimal choices of attack parameters.

2.3 Grover's Search Algorithm

The quantum algorithm for searching a marked point in a database is firstly introduced by Grover in [19]. In 1999, Zalka [32] proved that Grover's algorithm is optimal for the searching problem. It considers the following problem.

Problem 1. Let F be a Boolean function, $F : \{0,1\}^n \rightarrow \{0,1\}$. Suppose that there is only one x such that $F(x) = 1$. Then, find x.

In the classical setting, the number of queries to find x is approximately 2^n, while Grover's algorithm can find x by making only $O(\sqrt{2^n} = 2^{n/2})$ queries. That is, in the quantum setting, the time complexity for the database search problem is quadratic faster than the classical ones. Due to the optimality of the algorithm, the $2^{n/2}$ complexity is the tight security level of preimage resistance of hash functions in quantum setting, as summarized in Table 2.

Table 2. Comparison of security upper bounds of ideal hash functions in classical and quantum settings (polynomial factors are ignored for exponential complexities).

Property	Classical setting		quantum setting				
	CTime	CMem	QTime	qRAM	CMem	Optimal	reference
Collision	$2^{n/2}$	$O(1)$	$2^{n/3}$	$2^{n/3}$	–	YES	Scenario $\mathcal{R}_1$ [9,33]
			$2^{2n/5}$	$O(n)$	$2^{n/5}$	unknown	Scenario $\mathcal{R}_2$ [11]
Preimage	2^n	$O(1)$	$2^{n/2}$	$O(n)$	$O(1)$	YES	Scenario $\mathcal{R}_2$ [19,32]

Some variants of Problem 1 involve the general case with $|\{x : F(x) = 1\}| = 2^t$. Then, with high probability, Grover's algorithm returns x after making $O(\sqrt{2^n/2^t})$ quantum queries to F.

2.4   Quantum Collision Finding Algorithms

Brassard, Høyer, and Tapp in [9] first introduced a quantum algorithm (so-called BHT algorithm) to find a collision for a (2-to-1) random function in time $O(2^{n/3})$ and $O(2^{n/3})$ quantum queries, with an additional assumption that quantum random access memory (qRAM) is available. Subsequently, Zhandry in [33] extended this result to any random function with the size of the domain at least the square root of the size of the codomain, which is more relevant for hash functions or permutations in cryptographic settings. It considers the following problem.

Problem 2. Let $H : \{0,1\}^n \to \{0,1\}^n$ be a random function. Find x and x' such that $H(x) = H(x')$.

In the classical setting, finding collisions of a random function in range $\{0,1\}^n$ can be done after making $O(2^{n/2})$ queries, following the Birthday Paradox. While the BHT algorithm makes use of Grover's algorithm to find a collision in $O(2^{n/3})$ queries. Due to the optimality of the algorithm, $2^{n/3}$ is also the tight security level of the collision resistance of hash functions, in Scenario $\mathcal{R}_1$. In this paper, we consider the situation where qRAM is available, and the BHT algorithm can be applied efficiently for the collision finding problem of hash functions.

SCENARIO $\mathcal{R}_2$. In this situation, each lookup operation within the memory of size $O(2^{n/3})$ costs $O(2^{n/3})$ time, hence resulting in an inefficient algorithm even slower than the birthday attack. Chailloux et al. [11] proposed an efficient algorithm (denoted by CNS) to find a collision of hash function in time $\tilde{O}(2^{2n/5})$ with a quantum computer of $O(n)$ qubits, but large classical memory of size $\tilde{O}(2^{n/5})$.

2.5   Quantum Walk Algorithm For The Element Distinctness Problem

In the quantum setting, it is proven in [1] that the number of quantum queries for solving this problem is at least $O(N^{2/3})$. Up to now, only one algorithm, named as the *quantum walk algorithm* proposed in [2] reaches this bound. Recall this quantum walk algorithm for the following problem.

Problem 3. Given a set $S = \{x_1, x_2, ..., x_N\}$, does it exist i, j such that $1 \leq i < j \leq N$ and $x_i = x_j$? If yes, return i, j.

The element distinctness problem cannot be solved by an algorithm more efficiently than a brute force approach in the classical setting. This is because, only after $O(N)$ queries and sorting can one find two elements of the same value in a set of N elements. The Ambainis's quantum walk algorithm makes $O(N^{2/3})$ queries and requires $O(N^{2/3} \log N)$ qubits memory.

SCENARIO $\mathcal{R}_2$. The Ambainis's quantum walk algorithm for element distinctness problem can work efficiently and better than other algorithms in the scenario where the qRAM is available and it costs constant time to access qRAM gates (*i.e.*, Scenario $\mathcal{R}_1$). Very recently, to tackle with the situation that qRAM is not cheap and accessing R qubits quantum memory costs $O(R)$ operators or quantum gates, Jaques and Schrottenloher in [22] improved the quantum walk algorithm for golden collision problem (a more general case of the element distinctness problem), there the new algorithm requires $O(N^{6/7})$ computations and $O(N^{2/7})$ quantum memory, without using the qRAM. More explicitly, the assumption on the memory model in the quantum walk algorithm in [22] is that quantum memory is costly to access but free to maintain, which seems more realistic than Scenario $\mathcal{R}_1$. Thus, in this paper, when discussing the complexities of the presented attacks that calling a quantum walk algorithm in Scenario $\mathcal{R}_2$, we follow this assumption.

3   Collision-Search-Based Tools And Their Quantum Versions

In this section, we introduce several collision-search-based tools commonly used in generic attacks in classical settings. For each of them, we discuss how to transform it into a tool in quantum settings and re-evaluate the complexity. In the sequel, we denote by $\mathcal{H}$ an MD hash function, h for its compression function, and h^* for arbitrary times of iteration on h.

3.1   Multi-Collision (MC [24]).

Joux in [24] proposes an efficient way to obtain a large set of messages mapping a starting state to a common ending state on iterated hash functions, which is known as Joux's multi-collisions.

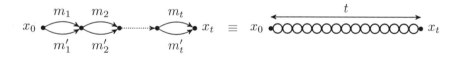

Fig. 4. Multi-collision and its condensed representation in R.H.S. [23]

Multi-Collision (MC) in Quantum Settings. In Scenario $\mathcal{R}_1$, the t birthday attacks for finding t collisions to build a 2^t-$\mathcal{M}_{\mathsf{MC}}$ can be done by calling t times of BHT algorithm. As a result, the total complexity, which is $t \cdot 2^{n/2}$ in the classical setting, is $t \cdot 2^{n/3}$ in the quantum setting. The quantum counterpart of building a 2^t-$\mathcal{M}_{\mathsf{MC}}$ is given in Algorithm 1.

The complexity of Algorithm 1 is dominated by calling the BHT algorithm t times; hence, it requires $O(t \cdot 2^{n/3})$ quantum queries, $O(t \cdot 2^{n/3})$ computations, and $O(2^{n/3})$ qRAM.

Algorithm 1: Building a 2^t-Joux's MC in Quantum Settings

Require: Given an oracle of the compression hash function h, an initial value x_0 and qRAM.

1. Initialize the data structure $\mathcal{M}_{\text{MC}}$ to store pairs of message blocks.
2. For $i = 1, ..., t$:
   (a) Start a BHT algorithm by querying $2^{n/3}$ message blocks m'_j to the oracle of h, sort according to the second entry and store all the pairs in list L, if L contains a collision, output the collision immediately.
   Store all pairs $(m'_j, h(x_{i-1}, m'_j))$ in L to qRAM.
   Construct the oracle: $F : \{0,1\}^n \rightarrow \{0,1\}$ by defining $F(m) = 1$ if and only if there exist $(m'_j, h(x_{i-1}, m'_j))$ in qRAM such that $h(x_{i-1}, m'_j) = h(x_{i-1}, m)$ and $m'_j \neq m$.
   (b) In the BHT algorithm, apply the Grover's search algorithm using oracle F:
      i. Initialize the state of the Grover's search to be the uniform superposition of 2^n messages;
      ii. After running about $\frac{\pi}{4} \cdot 2^{n/3}$ Grover steps, measure the state and return a pair of message blocks (m_i, m'_i) such that $h(x_{i-1}, m_i) = h(x_{i-1}, m'_i)$.
   (c) Obtain $x_i = h(x_{i-1}, m_i)$, append (m_i, m'_i) to $\mathcal{M}_{\text{MC}}$.
3. Output $(x_t, \mathcal{M}_{\text{MC}})$.

In Scenario $\mathcal{R}_2$, we can replace the BHT algorithm with the algorithm in [11], which requires $O(2^{2n/5})$ computations and $O(2^{n/5})$ classical memory. Then, the resulted quantum algorithm 1 requires $O\left(t \cdot 2^{2n/5}\right)$ quantum queries and $O(2^{n/5})$ classical memory.

Note that this quantum version of the Joux's multi-collision will be used in building more complex structures (interchange structure in Sect. 3.4), and in the presented preimage attacks (Sect. 5.1 and 5.2).

3.2 Expandable Message (EM [26]).

Kelsey and Schneier in [26] invented the *expandable message*, which is similar to Joux's multi-collision. By generating t collisions with pairs of message fragments of length $(1, 2^i + 1)$ for $i \approx \{0, 1, ..., t - 1\}$, one can get 2^t colliding messages whose lengths cover the range of $[t, t + 2^t - 1]$ (see Fig. 5). The complexity is of $2^t + t \cdot 2^{n/2}$ computations. This expandable message can be used to bypass the Merkle-Damgård strengthening and carry out a long message second-preimage attack on MD with roughly $2^n / L$ computations for a given challenge of L blocks.

Expandable Message (EM) in Quantum Settings. Since the main idea of building a 2^t-expandable message is finding the collision between a message of a single block and a message of length $2^i + 1$ for $0 \leq i \leq t - 1$, this step can be done by applying the BHT algorithm in quantum setting. Similar to finding collisions in quantum setting for building Joux's multi-collision, for each i, we calculate

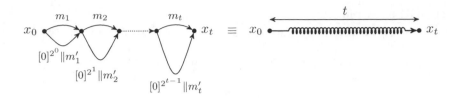

Fig. 5. Expandable message and its condensed representation in R.H.S. [23]

the hash value x_{i-1}^* of message $[0]^{2^i}$ from the hash value x_{i-1} , and find a pair of message blocks (m_i, m_i') such that $h(x_{i-1}, m_i) = h(x_{i-1}^*, m_i') = x_i$. Then the constructing a message of length $s \in [t, t + 2^t - 1]$ step is proceeded in the same way as in the classical setting, as we look at the decomposition of $s - t$ in t-bit binary base. We select the long message $[0]^{2^i} \| m_i'$ in the iteration i if the i-th LSB of $s - t$ is equal to 1, otherwise, we select the single block message m_i instead. The complexity of this quantum algorithm is different from classical expandable message algorithm just by the collision search step; hence, it is of $2^t + t \cdot 2^{n/3}$ quantum computations in Scenario $\mathcal{R}_1$, or of $2^t + t \cdot 2^{2n/5}$ quantum computations using CNS algorithm in Scenario $\mathcal{R}_2$.

This quantum version of the expandable message will be used in the presented quantum second-preimage attack on the MD hash function (Sect. 4.2).

3.3 Diamond Structure (DS [25]).

Kelsey and Kohno in [25] invented the diamond structure. Similar to Joux's multi-collisions and Kelsey and Schneier's expandable message, diamond is also a kind of multi-collision. The difference is that, instead of mapping a single starting state to a final state in the form of sequential chain, a 2^t-diamond maps a set of 2^t starting states to a common final state in the form of a complete binary tree (see Fig. 6). Blackburn in [8] pointed out that the construction method and its complexity provided in [25] have a flaw, and offered a more rigorous analysis and construction method. The method in [8] requires $O(\sqrt{t} \cdot 2^{\frac{(n+t)}{2}})$ message blocks and $n \cdot \sqrt{t} \cdot 2^{\frac{(n+t)}{2}}$ computations, and will be converted into quantum method later in this section. Kortelainen and Kortelainen in [27] presented another method for constructing the diamond structure. The new method could reduce the message requirement to $O(2^{\frac{(n+t)}{2}})$. However, it becomes more intricate by separating the procedure into jumps, phases, and steps. During different phases and steps, different number of new messages are added and old messages are recycled, which makes the phases and steps more dynamic and the workloads are not balanced compared with previous methods.

Diamond is originally used in herding attacks on hash functions [25]. In [3–5], Andreeva *et al.* exploited the diamond structure to develop generic second-preimage attacks on Dithered hash function and Hash-Twice. Besides, the diamond structure was also used to device a second-preimage attack on Merkle-

Damgård hash function with shorter messages than that in the long-message second-preimage attack in [26].

Diamond Structure (DS) in Quantum Settings. We adapt the construction method in [8] to build the diamond in the quantum setting. The framework is to build the complete binary tree of the diamond with given 2^t states as the leaves, layer by layer. The following description in Algorithm 2 focuses on the construction from one layer to the next, and takes the first two layers for example.

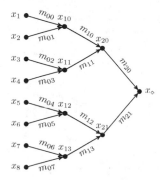

Fig. 6. A 2^3-diamond

In Algorithm 2, according to [8], to find a perfect matching[1] in $\mathcal{G}$, the probability p for each pair of vertices being connected by an edge should be no less than $(\ln 2^t)/2^t \approx t \cdot 2^{-t}$. So, for each state x_i, the required number of other states that can lead to a collision with x_i is t. At this condition, we repeat Grover's algorithm t times for each state in Step 2. Then, the probability for each pair of (x_i, x_j) being mapped to a collision is $p \approx (t \cdot (L \cdot S))/2^n$. That requires $p \approx (t \cdot (L \cdot S))/2^n = (t \cdot 2^{n-t})/2^n$. That is, $L \cdot S \approx 2^{n-t}$. Let
$$\begin{cases} L = t^{d_1} \cdot 2^\ell, \\ S = t^{d_2} \cdot 2^s, \end{cases} \text{then} \quad \begin{cases} d_1 + d_2 = 0, \\ \ell + s = n - t. \end{cases} \quad \text{To balance the complexity of Step 1}$$
and Step 2, we set $2^t \cdot t \cdot \sqrt{S} = 2^t \cdot L$, that is, $\begin{cases} 2 + d_2 = 2d_1, \\ s = 2\ell. \end{cases}$ Accordingly, we
have $\begin{cases} d_1 = 2/3, \ \ell = (n-t)/3 \\ d_2 = -2/3, \ s = 2(n-t)/3. \end{cases}$ Therefore, $\begin{cases} L = t^{2/3} \cdot 2^{(n-t)/3} \\ S = t^{-2/3} \cdot 2^{2(n-t)/3}. \end{cases}$ As a
conclusion, using the above method in Scenario $\mathcal{R}_1$, the total time complexity for

---

[1] In graph $\mathcal{G}$, if there exists a set of edges, no two of which share a vertex, then the set of edges is called a matching. M is a maximum matching in $\mathcal{G}$ if no matching in $\mathcal{G}$ contains more edges than M does. If matching M in $\mathcal{G}$ contains every vertex, then M is called a perfect matching. Our goal here, is to find a perfect matching in $\mathcal{G} = (\mathcal{V}, \mathcal{E})$, of which the vertex set is $\mathcal{V} = \{x_1, \ldots, x_{2^t}\}$ and $(x_i, x_j) \approx \mathcal{E}$ if x_i and x_j generate an obtained collision.

building t layers of a 2^t-diamond is $O(t^{2/3} \cdot 2^{(n+2t)/3})$, and memory complexity is $O(t^{2/3} \cdot 2^{(n+2t)/3})$ qRAM.

Algorithm 2: Building One Layer of Diamond in Quantum Settings

Denote by $X = \{x_1, \ldots, x_{2^t}\}$ the set of states at the first layer of the diamond.

Let $M = \{m_1, \ldots, m_L\}$ be a space of L message blocks.

1. For each $x_i \in X$, compute a table $T_i = \{(h(x_i, m_j), (x_i \| m_j)) \mid m_j \in M\}$ with the hash values as the index and the concatenation of x_i and m_j as the contents of entries. Combine all 2^t tables into a single table without merging and store in the qRAM.

2. For each $x_i \in X$, repeat the following t times:
   (a) Let $M' = \{m'_1, \ldots, m'_S\}$ be a new space of S message blocks.
   (b) Initialize the uniform superposition state of message blocks in space M'.
   (c) Use Grover's algorithm to search for a collision between the set of hash values $\{h(x_i, m'_j) \mid m'_j \in M'\}$ and the set of $2^t \cdot L$ values store in the qRAM. Each step in Grover's algorithm, after accessing qRAM, it returns $|b \oplus 1\rangle$ if $h(x_i, m)$ collides with some element in qRAM, otherwise, it returns $|b\rangle$.

   With the collisions obtained by the quantum computation, construct the associated graph $\mathcal{G} = (\mathcal{V}, \mathcal{E})$, of which the vertex set is $\mathcal{V} = \{x_1, \ldots, x_{2^t}\}$ and $(x_i, x_j) \in \mathcal{E}$ if x_i and x_j generate an obtained collision. This is same as did in the last part of Step 2 of the method in the classical setting (see [8]).

3. Find the perfect matching contained in $\mathcal{G}$ same as Step 3 of the method in the classical setting (see [8]).

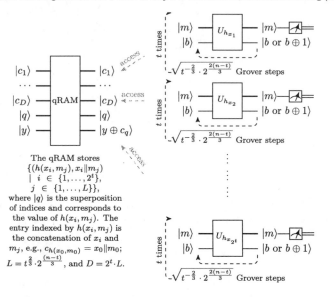

In Scenario $\mathcal{R}_2$, the time complexity to find a collision is of $(2^{n-t})^{2/5}$ computations. Therefore, building a 2^t-diamond structure requires $O(t^{2/3} \cdot 2^t \cdot 2^{2(n-t)/5}) = O(t^{2/3} \cdot 2^{(2n+3t)/5})$ computations, with $O(t^{2/3} \cdot 2^t \cdot 2^{(n-t)/5}) = O(t^{2/3} \cdot 2^{(n+4t)/5})$ classical memory.

This quantum version of the diamond structure will be used in the presented quantum herding attack on the MD hash function (Sect. 4.3) and the quantum herding attack on combiners (Sect. 5.3).

3.4 Interchange Structure (IS [28])

Leurent and Wang in [28] invented the interchange structure, which is used to devise a preimage attack on the XOR combiner. The interchange structure contains a set of messages $\mathcal{M}_{\mathrm{IS}}$ and two sets of states $\mathcal{A}$ and $\mathcal{B}$, such that for any pair of states $(A_i, B_j \mid A_i \in \mathcal{A}, B_j \in \mathcal{B})$, one can pick a message M from $\mathcal{M}_{\mathrm{IS}}$ such that $A_i = \mathcal{H}_1(IV_1, M)$ and $B_i = \mathcal{H}_2(IV_2, M)$. To build a 2^t-interchange structure (with 2^t states for each hash function), one can cascade $2^{2t} - 1$ building modules named switches. The effect of a switch is that a state in one computation chain of one hash function can make pair with two states in two computation chains of the other hash function. A switch can be built using multi-collisions and the birthday attack (see Fig. 7a). The total complexity to build a 2^t-interchange structure is of $\tilde{O}(2^{2t+n/2})$ computations.

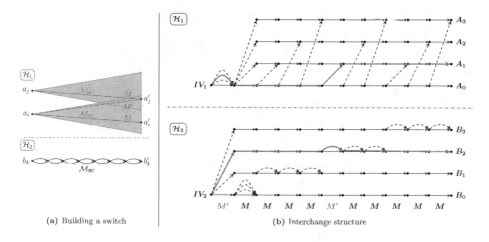

(a) Building a switch   (b) Interchange structure

Fig. 7. Interchange structure and its building block

Algorithm 3: Building a Single Switch in Quantum Settings

1. Use the quantum Joux's multi-collision algorithm to build a set $\mathcal{M}_{\mathrm{MC}}$ of $2^{n/2}$ messages for h_2^* that link the starting state b_k to the same state b_k', i.e., $\forall M \approx \mathcal{M}_{\mathrm{MC}}$, $h_2^*(b_k, M) = b_k'$.
2. Use a quantum walk algorithm to find a collision in the set of $2^{n/2+1}$ elements which are $h_1^*(a_i, M)$ and $h_1^*(a_j, M)$ for all the messages M in $\mathcal{M}_{\mathrm{MC}}$. With high probability (constant), the algorithm return a pair of messages denoted as (M_i, M_i') that $h_1^*(a_i, M_i) = h_1^*(a_j, M_i')$.
3. Use the message M_i to compute the missing chains: $b_j' = h_2^*(b_j, M_i)$, $a_j' = h_1^*(a_j, M_i)$. With high probability, all the chains reach distinct values; if not, restart the algorithm with a new multi-collision.

Interchange Structure (IS) in Quantum Settings. The interchange structure starts with building a single switch, which is constructed by building a $2^{n/2}$-Joux's multi-collision for the hash function $\mathcal{H}_2$ and finding a collision between the hash value of $\mathcal{H}_1$ from different states (a_i, a_j) and some pair of message $(\hat{M}, \hat{M}')$. These two steps can be replaced by the quantum algorithm for building Joux's multi-collisions and the quantum walk algorithm for the element distinctness problem. The quantum algorithm for building a single switch is described as follows in Algorithm 3.

In Scenario $\mathcal{R}_1$, the complexity of Algorithm 3 is dominated by the building a multi-collision in Step 1, since Step 2 requires $O((2^{n/2+1})^{2/3}) = O(2^{n/3})$ quantum computations and $O(2^{n/3})$ quantum memory. Hence, Algorithm 3 requires $O\left(\frac{n}{2} \cdot 2^{n/3}\right)$ quantum queries to the compression functions, $O\left(\frac{n}{2} \cdot 2^{n/3}\right)$ quantum time and $O(2^{n/3})$ quantum memory.

In Scenario $\mathcal{R}_2$, Step 1 needs $O\left(\frac{n}{2} \cdot 2^{2n/5}\right)$ quantum computations and $O(2^{n/5})$ classical memory, but when it comes to Step 2, the number of computations is higher, that is, $O((2^{n/2+1})^{6/7} = O(2^{3n/7})$ quantum computations and $O((2^{n/2})^{2/7}) = O(2^{n/7})$ quantum memory. Therefore, in this model, the time complexity for Algorithm 3 to build a single switch is of $O(2^{3n/7})$.

The framework for building a 2^t-interchange structure in quantum setting is the same as in the classical setting. One builds the required $2^{2t} - 1$ switches as the following: first, build a single switch from (a_0, b_0) to each of (a_0, b_k); then, for each k, build switches from (a_0, b_k) to all (a_j, b_k) for all $j = 0, ..., 2^t - 1$. To reach the chain (a_j, b_k) from (a_0, b_0), we first find the switch to jump from (a_0, b_0) to (a_0, b_k) in the first step, then find the switch to jump from (a_0, b_k) to (a_j, b_k) in the second step. Then the complexity to build an interchange structure is $O\left(\frac{n}{2} \cdot 2^{2t+n/3}\right)$ for both quantum queries and time and $O(2^{n/3})$ quantum memory in Scenario $\mathcal{R}_1$, or $O(2^{2t+3n/7})$ and $O(2^{n/5})$ classical memory, $O(2^{n/7})$ quantum memory in Scenario $\mathcal{R}_2$.

This quantum version of the interchange structure will be used in the presented quantum preimage attack on the XOR-combiners (Sect. 5.1).

4   Security Of Merkle-Damgård Structure in Quantum Settings

In this section, we explicate baselines for the security of Merkle-Damgård hash functions with respect to basic requirements in quantum settings, considering both Scenario $\mathcal{R}_1$ and Scenario $\mathcal{R}_2$. That includes the resistance against multi-collision, preimage, second-preimage attacks, and herding attacks.

4.1   Multi-Collision Attack

For the multi-collision attack on the Merkle-Damgård structure, as has been introduced in Sect. 3, following Joux's method and using BHT algorithm for each collision search, finding 2^t-collisions requires $O(t \cdot 2^{n/3})$ quantum computations and $O(2^{n/3})$ qRAM in Scenario $\mathcal{R}_1$. Since the time complexity to find a collision of any hash function is $O(2^{n/3})$ in Scenario $\mathcal{R}_1$, we can see that, same as in the classical setting, the quantum security of MD structure against multi-collision attack is only polynomial higher than the collision resistance of its compression function. In Scenario $\mathcal{R}_2$, 2^t-collisions of an MD hash function can be obtained by combining Joux's method and CNS algorithm with time complexity $O(t \cdot 2^{2n/5})$ and requires $O(2^{n/5})$ classical memory.

4.2   Preimage And Second-Preimage Attack

For an n-bit hash function, a security upper bound with respect to (second-) preimage attack in the quantum setting is directly provided by a plain Grover's algorithm, that is $O(2^{n/2})$ quantum computations. Thus, only attacks with complexity lower than the Grover's search algorithm can be seen as successful attacks. For the preimage resistance of MD hash construction, we cannot achieve better attacks than a plain Grover's search on an ideal hash. For the second-preimage resistance of MD hash construction, basing on the long-message second-preimage attack in [26], one can launch a quantum attack with the complexity lower than the generic Grover's attack.

Given message M_{target} of length $2^k + k + 1$, the goal is to find a second-preimage whose hash value is equal to that of the M_{target}. The quantum attack is described in Algorithm 4.

Algorithm 4: Second-Preimage Attack on MD Hash in Quantum Settings

1. Build a set of expandable messages to cover the whole range of $[k, k + 2^k - 1]$ using the quantum algorithm as described in Sect. 3.2. Denote this set by $\mathcal{M}_{EM}$, and the hash value after processing expandable message in $\mathcal{M}_{EM}$ by $\bar{x}$.

2. Let $x_0 = IV$, $M_{target} = m_1 \| m_2 \| \cdots \| m_{2^k+k+1}$.
   Compute $x_i = h(x_{i-1}, m_i)$ for i from 1 to $2^k + k + 1$.
   This step is to compute 2^k intermediate hash values of M_{target} and store results $x_{k+1} \ldots x_{2^k+k+1}$ to qRAM.

3. Use Grover's algorithm to find a message block to link the iterated hash value of expandable message to one of the intermediate hash values of M_{target}, i.e. find M_{link} such that $h(\bar{x}, M_{link}) = x_j$ for some j. Since the probability of the appearance of M_{link} is 2^{k-n}, we proceed $\pi/4 \cdot 2^{(n-k)/2}$ Grover steps before measure the superposition state to get M_{link}.

4. Find a message M^* of length $j - 1$ in $\mathcal{M}_{EM}$.

5. Return the second-preimage $M^* \| M_{link} \| m_{j+1} \| \cdots \| m_{2^k+k+1}$

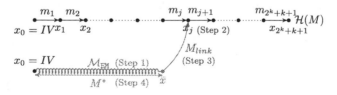

Attack in Scenario $\mathcal{R}_1$. The total complexity includes the complexity to build the expandable message with $2^k + k \cdot 2^{n/3}$ computations, $O(2^k)$ evaluations of compression function to compute the intermediate hash values of M_{target} and $\pi/4 \cdot 2^{(n-k)/2}$ evaluations to find M_{link}. Therefore, the total workload to find a second-preimage for a given message of length $2^k + k + 1$ is $2^{k+1} + k \cdot 2^{n/3} + \pi/4 \cdot 2^{(n-k)/2}$ quantum computations. Since the complexity of this attack in the classical setting is about $k \cdot 2^{n/2+1} + 2^k + 2^{n-k+1}$, the quantum version speeds up the attacks in classical setting when the given message is of length less than $2^{n/2}$.

THE BEST-CASE COMPLEXITY. The minimum attack complexity is achieved when $\dfrac{n}{3} = \dfrac{n-k}{2}$, i.e., $k = \dfrac{n}{3}$. Therefore, the second-preimage attack for a long message of length $O(2^{n/3})$ requires $O(n \cdot 2^{n/3})$ quantum computations and $O(2^{n/3})$ quantum memory. This complexity is only higher than that of the collision attack by BHT algorithm by a polynomial factor.

Attack in Scenario $\mathcal{R}_2$. The set of expandable messages can be built with $2^k + k \cdot 2^{2n/5}$ quantum computations, using $O(2^{n/5})$ classical memory. In Step 2, we store 2^k intermediate hash values of M_{target} to classical memory. In Step 3, different from using the Grover's algorithm as in Scenario $\mathcal{R}_1$, we apply the multi-target preimage search algorithm in [11] to search for message block M_{link}. The other steps do not change in this model, then the total work can be done in time $2^{k+1} + k \cdot 2^{2n/5} + 2^{n/2-k/6} + 2^k$.

THE BEST-CASE COMPLEXITY. The best-case complexity of this attack in Scenario $\mathcal{R}_2$ is achieved when $k = \dfrac{n}{2} - \dfrac{k}{6}$, i.e., $k = \dfrac{3n}{7}$. The optimal time complexity is $O(2^{3n/7})$, with classical memory of size $O(2^{3n/7})$.

4.3   Herding Attack

The herding attack on Merkle-Damgård constructions is first introduced in [25], which is a special form of chosen-target preimage attack. In this attack, an adversary chooses a public hash value h_T, and then, she is challenged with a prefix P. Her goal is to find a suffix S such that $h_T = H(P\|S)$. Since h_T is chosen by the adversary, she can specifically choose it after some pre-computations, such as the root value of a diamond structure built on the compression function h.

In the following, we extend the classical herding attack to its quantum version, which uses the diamond structure and Grover's search algorithm. The attacker first builds the diamond structure by a quantum computer. In this diamond structure, from any of the intermediate hash values, she can produce a message which leads to the same final hash value h_T. She then publicizes h_T to commit. After receiving the challenged message P, the attacker applies Grover's algorithm to find a suffix message block S. The detailed attack is described in Algorithm 5.

Attack in Scenario $\mathcal{R}_1$**.** The total complexity of the herding attack is $k^{2/3} \cdot 2^{(n+2k)/3} + 2^{(n-k)/2}$ quantum computations, with $O(k^{2/3} \cdot 2^{(n+2k)/3})$ quantum memory.

THE BEST-CASE COMPLEXITY. The best complexity is achieved when $\frac{n+2k}{3} = \frac{n-k}{2}$, *i.e.* $k = \frac{n}{7}$, which results in the optimal $\tilde{O}(2^{3n/7})$ quantum computations.

Attack in Scenario $\mathcal{R}_2$**.** In this model, the 2^k-diamond structure can be built with time complexity of $O(k^{2/3} \cdot 2^{(2n+3k)/5})$; and the search of M_{link} can be done by using multi-target preimage algorithm with time complexity of $O(2^{n/2-k/6})$. Then the total complexity is $O(k^{2/3} \cdot 2^{(2n+3k)/5} + 2^{n/2-k/6})$ quantum computations, with $O(k^{2/3} \cdot 2^{(n+4k)/5})$ classical memory.

Algorithm 5: Herding Attack on MD Hash in Quantum Settings

1. Build the diamond structure using the quantum algorithm describe in Sect. 3.3: from 2^k starting hash values $D - \{x_i\}_{i=1}^{2^k}$ to the root value h_T. This step can be done in $O(k^{2/3} \cdot 2^{(n+2k)/3})$ computations. Commit h_T and publicize it.
2. Receive the challenged prefix: P.
3. Find a linking message: apply Grover's algorithm to search for a single block message M_{link} such that the value $h(P\|M_{link})$ collides with some value x_j in D. This step can be done in $O(2^{(n-k)/2})$ quantum queries and returns M_{link}.
4. Produce the message: $M = P\|M_{link}\|M_j$ where M_j is a sequence of message blocks linking x_j to h_T following the diamond structure built before.

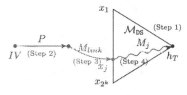

THE BEST-CASE COMPLEXITY. The optimal time complexity is achieved when $\frac{2n+3k}{5} = \frac{n}{2} - \frac{k}{6}$, *i.e.*, $k = \frac{3n}{23}$, which results in $\tilde{O}(2^{11n/23})$ time and $\tilde{O}(2^{7n/23})$ classical memory.

5 Security of Hash Combiners in Quantum Settings

In this section, we present quantum attacks on hash combiners. For preimage, second-preimage, and herding attacks, the ideal quantum security are all $2^{n/2}$ (resp. 2^n) for XOR (resp. concatenation) combiners, which are bounded by attacks directly using Grover's search algorithm. For collision attack, the ideal quantum security bound is $2^{n/3}$ (resp. $2^{2n/3}$) for XOR (resp. concatenation) combiners, which is provided by the BHT's algorithm.

In the following, we present a quantum preimage attack on XOR combiners, which provides updated security upper bound in quantum settings for its resistance against (second-) preimage attack. We then present quantum collision, (second-) preimage attacks, and herding attacks on concatenation combiners. We note that, the presented herding attack on concatenation combiners applies to XOR combiners as well.

In the sequel, we denote by $\mathcal{H}_1$ and $\mathcal{H}_2$ the underlying hash functions, h_1 and h_2 their compression functions, and h_1^* and h_2^* the arbitrary times of iterations of h_1 and h_2, respectively.

5.1   Preimage Attack on XOR Combiners in Quantum Settings

In this section, we extend the preimage attack on XOR combiners in [28] to its quantum version. Let V denote the target value. The goal is to find a message M such that $\mathcal{H}_1(M) \bigoplus \mathcal{H}_2(M) = V$. The framework of the attack in the quantum setting is the same as that in the classical setting, which can be described as follows, and also detailed in Algorithm 6.

1. Build an interchange structure starting from the initialization vectors (IV_1, IV_2) and ending up with two sets of terminal states $\mathcal{A} = \{A_j \mid j = 1, \ldots, 2^k\}$ and $\mathcal{B} = \{B_i \mid i = 1, \ldots, 2^k\}$.
2. Launch a meet-in-the-middle procedure between the two sets $\mathcal{A}$ and $\mathcal{B}$, to find a message block m, and a state $A_{j^*} \in \mathcal{A}$ and a state $B_{i^*} \in \mathcal{B}$, such that $h_1(A_{j^*}, m) = V \bigoplus h_2(B_{i^*}, m)$.

   This procedure contains two levels of iteration. The outer level of iteration is on the message block m, and the inner level of iteration is on the pairs of states $(A_i, B_j) \in \mathcal{A} \times \mathcal{B}$ under a fixed value of m. In the quantum version, the inner lever of iteration is implemented using a quantum walk algorithm, and the outer level of iteration is implemented using Grover's search algorithm.

The details of the quantum algorithm is described in Algorithm 6.

Algorithm 6: Preimage attack on XOR combiners in Quantum Settings

1. Build a 2^k-interchange structure using the quantum algorithm described in Sect. 3.4. This structure starts with IV_1 and IV_2 and ends with two ending point sets $\{A_j | j = 1 \cdots 2^k\}$ and $\{B_i | i = 1 \cdots 2^k\}$, so that for any state pair (A_j, B_i), we can easily find a message linking from starting points to it.
2. For each message block m, let $F(m)$ be the indicator function that $F(m) = 1$ if there exist a pair (A_{j^*}, B_{i^*}) in the two sets of ending points such that $h_1(A_{j^*}, m) = V \oplus h_2(B_{i^*}, m)$, and $F(m) = 0$ otherwise. To calculate $F(m)$, we use the quantum walk algorithm to find a collision between the two sets $\{A_j' = h_1(A_j, m) | j = 1 \cdots 2^k\}$ and $\{B_i' = V \oplus h_2(B_i, m) | i = 1 \cdots 2^k\}$. Denote this step by $U_{\text{QW-test}}$ and the ancillary qubit to indicate the value of F by $|b\rangle$.
3. Use Grover's algorithm to find a message block m^* satisfying $F(m^*) = 1$ in the space of 2^{n-2k} message blocks. Since the probability of finding a match between the above two sets is 2^{2k-n}, it requires performing about $\frac{\pi}{4} \cdot 2^{(n-2k)/2}$ Grover's steps.
4. Return $M = M^* \| m^*$ where M^* is the message mapping (IV_1, IV_2) to (A_{j^*}, B_{i^*}) corresponding to the hash values of $\mathcal{H}_1$ and $\mathcal{H}_2$.

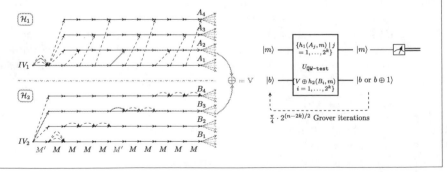

Attack in Scenario $\mathcal{R}_1$. Since the evaluation of $F(m)$ is performed during Grover's algorithm, the total computational complexity is the multiplication of the complexity of evaluating $F(m)$ and the total number of Grover's steps plus the complexity of building the interchange structure. It requires approximately $\frac{n}{2} \cdot 2^{2k+n/3}$ quantum computations to build a 2^k-interchange structure, $(2 \cdot 2^k)^{2/3}$ quantum computations to find a collision between the two sets of 2^{k+1} elements, and $\frac{\pi}{4} \cdot 2^{n-2k}$ iterations in Grover's algorithm. Then, the total workload required is

$$\frac{n}{2} \cdot 2^{2k+n/3} + 2^{2(k+1)/3} \cdot \frac{\pi}{4} \cdot 2^{(n-2k)/2} \approx \frac{n}{2} \cdot 2^{2k+n/3} + 2^{n/2-k/3}.$$

THE BEST-CASE COMPLEXITY. The minimum complexity of the quantum preimage attack on XOR combiners based on the interchange structure can be achieved by selecting a message block that makes two parts of the complexity equal. When n is large enough that $\frac{n}{2}$ is negligible compared to $2^{n/3}$, we select the parameter k such that

$$2k + \frac{n}{3} = \frac{n}{2} - \frac{k}{3},$$

i.e., $k = \frac{n}{14}$. This results in a total complexity $O(2^{10n/21})$, which is slightly faster than Grover's algorithm. When n is small, we choose the value of k such that

$$\log_2 n - 1 + 2k + \frac{n}{3} = \frac{n}{2} - \frac{k}{3},$$

i.e., $k = \frac{3}{7} \cdot \left(\frac{n}{6} + 1 - \log n \right)$. For the attack to be faster than Grover's, it requires $k > 0$ and the value of n should be large enough to satisfy $\frac{n}{6} + 1 - \log_2 n > 0$, e.g., $n \geq 20$.

Attack in Scenario $\mathcal{R}_2$. As analyzed in Sect. 3.4, the complexity of building a 2^k-interchange structure in this situation is $O(2^{2k+3n/7})$ time, $O(2^{n/5})$ classical memory and $O(2^{n/7})$ quantum memory. Step 3 of Algorithm 6 can be done after $O\left(2^{6(k+1)/7} \cdot \frac{\pi}{4} \cdot 2^{(n-2k)/2} \right) = O(2^{n/2-k/7})$ evaluations, since the quantum walk to search a collision in a set of 2^{k+1} elements requires $O(2^{6(k+1)/7})$ computations and $O(2^{k/7})$ quantum memory. Combined with the complexity of Step 1, the total computational complexity is $O(2^{2k+3n/7} + 2^{n/2-k/7})$.

THE BEST-CASE COMPLEXITY. Choosing k such that $2k + \frac{3n}{7} = \frac{n}{2} - \frac{k}{7}$, i.e., $k = \frac{n}{30}$ can minimize the time complexity of the preimage attack on XOR combiners to $2^{52n/105}$.

5.2 Collision Attack, Preimage Attack, and Second-Preimage attack on Concatenation Combiners in Quantum Settings

In this section, we present the collision attack and preimage attack on concatenation combiners in the quantum setting, which are directly converted from the classical attacks in [24]. Both quantum attacks use the quantum algorithm for building the Joux's multi-collision (refer to Sect. 3.1) and the quantum walk algorithm (refer to Sect. 2.5) for finding a collision from a set, which is different from the classical method by brute-force search.

Collision Attack. Here we introduce the quantum collision attack, which aims to find a pair of message blocks (M, M') such that $\mathcal{H}_1(M) \| \mathcal{H}_2(M) = \mathcal{H}_1(M') \| \mathcal{H}_2(M')$. The collision attack follows two steps:

Step 1: Apply Algorithm 1 to build $2^{n/2}$-Joux's multi-collision for the first compression hash function. Denote this set by $\mathcal{M}_{\text{MC}}$. This step can be done in $O\left(\frac{n}{2} \cdot 2^{n/3}\right)$ time complexity.

Step 2: Apply quantum walk algorithm to find a collision of the second hash function in a set of $2^{n/2}$ message blocks constructed from $\mathcal{M}_{\text{MC}}$. This step can be done in $O\left((2^{n/2})^{2/3}\right) = O(2^{n/3})$ time.

The time complexities of the two steps are balanced at $\tilde{O}(2^{n/3})$, using $O(2^{n/3})$ quantum memory. In Scenario $\mathcal{R}_2$, Step 1 can be done in $O\left(\frac{n}{2} \cdot 2^{2n/5}\right)$ time, using $O(2^{n/5})$ classical memory; Step 2 can be done in $O\left((2^{n/2})^{6/7}\right) = O(2^{3n/7})$ time, using $O(2^{n/7})$ memory. The total time and classical memory complexities under this scenario are $O(2^{3n/7})$ and $O(2^{n/5})$, respectively.

Preimage Attack. Let $V_1 \| V_2$ be a prefix of $2n$ bits. The goal of a preimage attack is to find a message M such that the concatenation of the outputs of the hash functions, $\mathcal{H}_1$ and $\mathcal{H}_2$ acting on M, is equal to V, i.e., $\mathcal{H}_1(M) \| \mathcal{H}_2(M) = V_1 \| V_2$. We can directly generate a quantum attack based on Grover's algorithm to search for M in a space of 2^{2n} message blocks. With high probability, there exists one message M that satisfies the above condition; this attack require approximately $\pi/4 \cdot 2^n$ Grover steps to find M. This attack is considered as a generic quantum attack on any ideal hash construction of $2n$ output bits.

To devise a more efficient attack on concatenation combiners of MD hashes than the above most generic attack, we extend the attack in [24] to its quantum version. That is, we first build a 2^n-Joux's multi-collision for the first hash function $\mathcal{H}_1$ by Algorithm 1, and denote this set by $\mathcal{M}_{\text{MC}}$. All messages in $\mathcal{M}_{\text{MC}}$ have the same hash value as x. From the hash value x, we find a message block m among 2^n message blocks so that $h(x, m) = V_1$. This step can be done by Grover's algorithm in $O(2^{n/2})$ time. For the hash function $\mathcal{H}_2$, search M_1 from the set $\mathcal{M}_{\text{MC}}$ such that $\mathcal{H}_2(M_1 \| m) = V_2$. Since the cardinality of $\mathcal{M}_{\text{MC}}$ is 2^n, it is expected there is at least one such message M_1. This step can be done by Grover's algorithm searching in the space of messages in $\mathcal{M}_{\text{MC}}$ with time complexity $O(2^{n/2})$. Therefore, the total workload required is $O(n \cdot 2^{n/3} + 2^{n/2}) = O(2^{n/2})$, using $O(2^{n/3})$ quantum memory in Scenario $\mathcal{R}_1$. In Scenario $\mathcal{R}_2$, the time complexity of a quantum attack does not change so much, which is $O(n \cdot 2^{2n/5} + 2^{n/2}) = O(2^{n/2})$;

because it is dominated by the searching step, in which we can simply replace the quantum memory by a classical memory of size $O(2^{n/5})$. This attack exponentially speeds up the plain quantum attack using Grover's search, and also exponentially improves the classical attack, of which the time complexity is $O(2^n)$.

Compared to the quantum preimage attack on one MD hash function of n bits, the attack on concatenated combiners only require a constant factor of more evaluations.

Second-Preimage Attack. Since the second-preimage attack can be implied from the preimage attack, the complexity is similar to the preimage attack.

5.3 Herding Attack on Concatenation Combiners in Quantum Settings

The quantum herding attack on a single MD hash function has been introduced in Sect. 4.3. In this section, we adapt the quantum herding attack to concatenation of two MD hashes. The framework of the attack follows that of the classical attack in [4], in which the main idea is that by constructing a multi-collision $\mathcal{M}_{MC}$ for $\mathcal{H}_1$ one can use the messages in $\mathcal{M}_{MC}$ to builds a diamond structure for $\mathcal{H}_2$. The high level description of the attack is as follows, which is also illustrated by the figure in Algorithm 7.

1. **Phase 1 - off-line precomputation.**
   (a) Build a succeeding of three structures for $\mathcal{H}_1$: a diamond structure $\mathcal{M}_{DS1}$, a Joux's multi-collision $\mathcal{M}_{MCs}$, and a Joux's multi-collision $\mathcal{M}_{MC\ell}$. Terminate at a state T_1.
   (b) Build one structure for $\mathcal{H}_2$: a diamond structure $\mathcal{M}_{DS2}$ using the messages in $\mathcal{M}_{MC\ell}$. Terminate at a state T_2.
   (c) Commit $T_1 \| T_2$ to the public.
2. **Phase 2 - on-line.**
   (a) Being challenged by a prefix P, compute the two intermediate states $x_P = h_1^*(IV_1, P)$ and $y_P = h_2^*(IV_2, P)$.
   (b) For $\mathcal{H}_1$, find a message block m^* mapping x_P to one of the leaf states x_j of $\mathcal{M}_{DS1}$, retrieve the message fragment S_1 mapping x_j to the root of $\mathcal{M}_{DS1}$. For $\mathcal{H}_2$, compute $y_T = h_2^*(IV_2, P\|m^*\|S_1)$
   (c) For $\mathcal{H}_2$, find a message fragment S_2 in $\mathcal{M}_{MCs}$ mapping y_T to one of the leaf states y_i of $\mathcal{M}_{DS2}$. Retrieve the message fragment S_3 mapping y_i to the root of $\mathcal{M}_{DS2}$, which is T_2.
   (d) Response with $M = P\|m^*\|S_1\|S_2\|S_3$.

Attack in Scenario $\mathcal{R}_1$. The details of the quantum herding attack is presented in Algorithm 7.

Algorithm 7: Herding Attack on Concatenation Combiners in Quantum Settings

Phase 1 - off-line precomputation.

(a) Build a diamond $\mathcal{M}_{DS1}$ for $\mathcal{H}_1$, which starts from 2^k states $D_1 = \{x_i\}_1^{2^k}$ and are all mapped to the root value x_T. That can be done using the quantum algorithm in Sect. 3.3. From the hash value x_T, build a 2^{n-k}-Joux's multi-collision $\mathcal{M}_{MCs}$, in which all messages map x_T to a state x_{M_0}. Continue to build a $2^{nk/2}$-Joux's multi-collision (consists of k fragments and each fragment is of length $n/2$) on $\mathcal{H}_1$ from the starting state x_{M_0} and mapping to the state T_1, and denote it by $\mathcal{M}_{MC\ell}$. Denote the terminal states of each of the k fragments of $\mathcal{M}_{MC\ell}$ by x_{M_i} for i from 1 to k (note that $x_{M_k} = T_1$).

(b) Build a diamond $\mathcal{M}_{DS2}$ for $\mathcal{H}_2$, which starts from 2^k states $D_2 = \{y_i\}_1^{2^k}$. The messages used to building $\mathcal{M}_{DS2}$ are all chosen from the set $\mathcal{M}_{MC\ell}$. For example, the messages mapping the first layer of 2^k states to the 2^{k-1} states in $\mathcal{M}_{DS2}$ are chosen from the set of $2^{n/2}$ messages in the first fragment of $\mathcal{M}_{MC\ell}$ mapping x_{M_0} to x_{M_1}. To build the next layer from D_2, use the quantum walk algorithm to find a collision in the set of $2^{n/2}$ messages for pairs of states in D_2, with $O(2^{n/3})$ quantum computations. Repeats this step until reaching a root T_2 for $\mathcal{M}_{DS2}$. Note that, the building method for $\mathcal{M}_{DS2}$ is different from the quantum algorithm describe in Sect. 3.3. That is because, the messages should be selected from the set $\mathcal{M}_{MC\ell}$, which is limited. Therefore, building the diamond structure $\mathcal{M}_{DS2}$ costs $O(2^k \cdot 2^{n/3}) = O(2^{(n+3k)/3})$ computations.

(c) Commit $T_1 \| T_2$ to the public.

Phase 2 - on-line. Being challenged with a prefix P, proceed as follows.

(a) Compute the two intermediate states $x_P = h_1^*(IV_1, P)$ and $y_P = h_2^*(IV_2, P)$.

(b) Search for a message block m^* that maps x_P to one of the leaf states x_j of $\mathcal{M}_{DS1}$. This is done by using Grover's algorithm, which accesses the quantum oracle of h_1 to find m^* in $O(2^{(n-k)/2})$ steps.

(c) Retrieve the message S_1 in $\mathcal{M}_{DS1}$ that maps x_j to the root. Compute $y_T = h_2^*(IV_2, P \| m^* \| S_1)$.

(d) Search for a message fragment S_2 among $\mathcal{M}_{MCs}$ that maps y_T to one of the leaf states y_i of $\mathcal{M}_{DS2}$. This is done by using Grover's algorithm again.

(e) Retrieve the message fragment S_3 in $\mathcal{M}_{DS2}$ that maps y_i to the root, which is T_2. Due to the way of construction of $\mathcal{M}_{DS2}$ in Phase 1, for $\mathcal{H}_1$, the message fragment S_3 also maps the starting state of $\mathcal{M}_{MC\ell}$ to T_1.

(f) Response with $M = P \| m^* \| S_1 \| S_2 \| S_3$.

The time complexity of the precomputation phase includes that of building $n - k + nk/2$ Joux's-multicollision and that of building the two diamond structures $\mathcal{M}_{DS1}$ and $\mathcal{M}_{DS2}$. Therefore, the total time complexity is $O\left((n - k + (nk)/2) \cdot 2^{n/3} + 2^{(n+3k)/3}\right) = O(2^{(n+3k)/3})$. The online phase is done in time complexity $O(2^{(n-k)/2})$. Therefore, the total work is done in $O(2^{(n+3k)/3} + 2^{(n-k)/2})$ quantum time, with $O(2^{n/3})$ quantum memory since the quantum memory can be re-used after each iteration.

THE BEST-CASE COMPLEXITY. To minimize the time complexity of the herding attack on concatenated hashes, we choose the length of the message which balances the time complexity of two phases, i.e., $(n + 3k)/3 = (n - k)/2$. Then with the value $k = n/9$, the attack is optimized with $O(2^{4n/9})$ time, while a naive quantum herding attack using Grover's algorithm requires about $O(2^n)$ quantum computations to search for the suffix S.

Attack in Scenario $\mathcal{R}_2$. The difference in this model lies in the complexity of building $n - k + (nk)/2$ Joux's multi-collisions, building the diamonds, and finding message fragments linking from collision values to one of starting points of diamonds. To build $\mathcal{M}_{DS2}$, we need 2^k iterations to merge pairs of hash values into one. This step costs $O(2^k \cdot (2^{n/2})^{6/7}) = O(2^{3n/7+k})$ computations and $O(2^{n/7})$ quantum memory size. Then, the precomputation phase is of $O\left((n - k + (nk)/2) \cdot 2^{2n/5} + 2^{3n/7+k}\right) = O(2^{3n/7+k})$ time complexity, using $O(2^{n/5})$ classical memory, and $O(2^{n/7})$ quantum memory size.

THE BEST-CASE COMPLEXITY. The best attack is achieved when k satisfies $3n/7+k = n/2-k/6$, i.e., $k = 3n/49$. It gives the time complexity of $O(2^{24n/49})$.

6   Conclusions

In this paper, we studied the security of various constructions of hash functions in quantum settings with respect to important attacks: collision attacks, (second-) preimage attacks, and herding attacks. We analyzed the complexities of these attacks under different quantum memory models. The results show that our attacks in both models have better time complexity than that of the generic attacks by directly applying Grover's algorithm, and exponentially reduce both time and memory complexities compared to the classical attacks. The cryptanalysis results of hash combiners in quantum settings is consistent with that in the classical setting, that is, the security of most hash combiners are not as high as commonly expected, and can be even lower than that of a single underlying hash function. These results serve as an indication that, to achieve long-term security to the post quantum era, current symmetric-key crypto-systems require careful security re-evaluation or even re-design before being adopted by post-quantum cryptography schemes.

References

1. Aaronson, S., Shi, Y.: Quantum lower bounds for the collision and the element distinctness problems. J. ACM (JACM) **51**(4), 595–605 (2004)
2. Ambainis, A.: Quantum walk algorithm for element distinctness. SIAM J. Comput. **37**(1), 210–239 (2007)
3. Andreeva, E., et al.: New second-preimage attacks on hash functions. J. Cryptol. **29**(4), 657–696 (2016)
4. Andreeva, E., Bouillaguet, C., Dunkelman, O., Kelsey, J.: Herding, second preimage and trojan message attacks beyond Merkle-Damgård. In: Jacobson, M.J., Rijmen, V., Safavi-Naini, R. (eds.) SAC 2009. LNCS, vol. 5867, pp. 393–414. Springer, Heidelberg (2009). https://doi.org/10.1007/978-3-642-05445-7_25
5. Andreeva, E., Bouillaguet, C., Fouque, P.-A., Hoch, J.J., Kelsey, J., Shamir, A., Zimmer, S.: Second preimage attacks on dithered hash functions. In: Smart, N. (ed.) EUROCRYPT 2008. LNCS, vol. 4965, pp. 270–288. Springer, Heidelberg (2008). https://doi.org/10.1007/978-3-540-78967-3_16
6. Bao, Z., Dinur, I., Guo, J., Leurent, G., Wang, L.: Generic attacks on hash combiners. J. Cryptol. 1–82 (2019)

710   Z. Bao et al.

7. Bao, Z., Wang, L., Guo, J., Gu, D.: Functional graph revisited: updates on (second) preimage attacks on hash combiners. In: Katz, J., Shacham, H. (eds.) CRYPTO 2017. LNCS, vol. 10402, pp. 404–427. Springer, Cham (2017). https://doi.org/10.1007/978-3-319-63715-0_14
8. Blackburn, S.R., Stinson, D.R., Upadhyay, J.: On the Complexity of the Herding Attack and Some Related Attacks on Hash Functions. Cryptology ePrint Archive, Report 2010/030 (2010). http://eprint.iacr.org/2010/030
9. Brassard, G., HØyer, P., Tapp, A.: Quantum cryptanalysis of hash and claw-free functions. In: Lucchesi, C.L., Moura, A.V. (eds.) LATIN 1998. LNCS, vol. 1380, pp. 163–169. Springer, Heidelberg (1998). https://doi.org/10.1007/BFb0054319
10. Canteaut, A., et al.: Saturnin: a suite of lightweight symmetric algorithms for post-quantum security. IACR Trans. Symmetric Cryptol. 2020(S1), 160–207 (2020). https://doi.org/10.13154/tosc.v2020.iS1.160-207
11. Chailloux, A., Naya-Plasencia, M., Schrottenloher, A.: An efficient quantum collision search algorithm and implications on symmetric cryptography. In: Takagi, T., Peyrin, T. (eds.) ASIACRYPT 2017. LNCS, vol. 10625, pp. 211–240. Springer, Cham (2017). https://doi.org/10.1007/978-3-319-70697-9_8
12. Damgård, I.: A design principle for hash functions. In: Brassard, G. (ed.) Advances in Cryptology - CRYPTO'89. LNCS, vol. 435, pp. 416–427. Springer, Heidelberg, Germany, Santa Barbara, CA, USA (Aug 20–24, 1990)
13. Dierks, T., Allen, C.: The TLS protocol version 1.0. RFC 2246, 1–80 (1999). https://doi.org/10.17487/RFC2246
14. Dierks, T., Rescorla, E.: The transport layer security (TLS) protocol version 1.1. RFC 4346, 1–87 (2006). https://doi.org/10.17487/RFC4346
15. Dinur, I.: New attacks on the concatenation and XOR hash combiners. In: Fischlin, M., Coron, J.-S. (eds.) EUROCRYPT 2016. LNCS, vol. 9665, pp. 484–508. Springer, Heidelberg (2016). https://doi.org/10.1007/978-3-662-49890-3_19
16. Fischlin, M., Lehmann, A., Wagner, D.: Hash function combiners in TLS and SSL. In: Pieprzyk, J. (ed.) CT-RSA 2010. LNCS, vol. 5985, pp. 268–283. Springer, Heidelberg (2010). https://doi.org/10.1007/978-3-642-11925-5_19
17. Freier, A.O., Karlton, P., Kocher, P.C.: The secure sockets layer (SSL) protocol version 3.0. RFC 6101, 1–67 (2011). https://doi.org/10.17487/RFC6101
18. Google: Google Quantum Computing. https://research.google/teams/applied-science/quantum/
19. Grover, L.K.: A fast quantum mechanical algorithm for database search. In: Proceedings of the Twenty-eighth Annual ACM Symposium on Theory of Computing, pp. 212–219 (1996)
20. Hosoyamada, A., Yasuda, K.: Building quantum-one-way functions from block ciphers: davies-meyer and merkle-damgård constructions. In: Peyrin, T., Galbraith, S. (eds.) ASIACRYPT 2018. LNCS, vol. 11272, pp. 275–304. Springer, Cham (2018). https://doi.org/10.1007/978-3-030-03326-2_10
21. IBM: IBM Quantum Computing. https://www.ibm.com/quantum-computing/
22. Jaques, S., Schrottenloher, A.: Low-gate quantum golden collision finding. Cryptology ePrint Archive, Report 2020/424 (2020). https://eprint.iacr.org/2020/424
23. Jha, A., Nandi, M.: Some Cryptanalytic Results on Zipper Hash and Concatenated Hash. Cryptology ePrint Archive, Report 2015/973 (2015). http://eprint.iacr.org/2015/973
24. Joux, A.: Multicollisions in iterated hash functions. application to cascaded constructions. In: Franklin, M. (ed.) CRYPTO 2004. LNCS, vol. 3152, pp. 306–316. Springer, Heidelberg (2004). https://doi.org/10.1007/978-3-540-28628-8_19

25. Kelsey, J., Kohno, T.: Herding hash functions and the nostradamus attack. In: Vaudenay, S. (ed.) EUROCRYPT 2006. LNCS, vol. 4004, pp. 183–200. Springer, Heidelberg (2006). https://doi.org/10.1007/11761679_12

26. Kelsey, J., Schneier, B.: Second Preimages on n-Bit Hash Functions for Much Less than 2^n Work. In: Cramer, R. (ed.) EUROCRYPT 2005. LNCS, vol. 3494, pp. 474–490. Springer, Heidelberg (2005). https://doi.org/10.1007/11426639_28

27. Kortelainen, T., Kortelainen, J.: On diamond structures and trojan message attacks. In: Sako, K., Sarkar, P. (eds.) ASIACRYPT 2013. LNCS, vol. 8270, pp. 524–539. Springer, Heidelberg (2013). https://doi.org/10.1007/978-3-642-42045-0_27

28. Leurent, G., Wang, L.: The sum can be weaker than each part. In: Oswald, E., Fischlin, M. (eds.) EUROCRYPT 2015. LNCS, vol. 9056, pp. 345–367. Springer, Heidelberg (2015). https://doi.org/10.1007/978-3-662-46800-5_14

29. Merkle, R.C.: One way hash functions and DES. In: Brassard, G. (ed.) CRYPTO 1989. LNCS, vol. 435, pp. 428–446. Springer, New York (1990). https://doi.org/10.1007/0-387-34805-0_40

30. National Institute for Standards and Technology, USA: Post-Quantum Cryptography Standardization (2017). https://csrc.nist.gov/projects/post-quantum-cryptography

31. Shor, P.W.: Algorithms for quantum computation: discrete logarithms and factoring. In: 35th Annual Symposium on Foundations of Computer Science, Santa Fe, New Mexico, USA, 20–22 November 1994, pp. 124–134. IEEE Computer Society (1994). https://doi.org/10.1109/SFCS.1994.365700

32. Zalka, C.: Grover's quantum searching algorithm is optimal. Phys. Rev. **60**(4), 2746 (1999)

33. Zhandry, M.: A note on the quantum collision and set equality problems. arXiv preprint arXiv:1312.1027 (2013)

34. Zhandry, M.: How to record quantum queries, and applications to quantum indifferentiability. In: Boldyreva, A., Micciancio, D. (eds.) CRYPTO 2019. LNCS, vol. 11693, pp. 239–268. Springer, Cham (2019). https://doi.org/10.1007/978-3-030-26951-7_9

An Efficient Lattice-Based Encrypted Search Scheme with Forward Security

Xiaoling Yu[1], Lei Xu[2(✉)], Xin Huang[1], and Chungen Xu[2]

[1] College of Data Science, Taiyuan University of Technology, Taiyuan, China
`huangxin@tyut.edu.cn`
[2] School of Mathematics and Statistics, Nanjing University of Science and Technology, Nanjing, China
`xuleicrypto@gmail.com, xuchung@njust.edu.cn`

Abstract. Public-key encryption with keywords search (PEKS) can realize the retrieval of ciphertext data, which is a vital cryptographic primitive in the field of cloud storage. However, in practical applications, the secret keys of users are often exposed due to careless store or computer attacks, which causes privacy disclosure. Furthermore, considering the attack from quantum computers, this paper designs a lattice-based PEKS scheme with forward security which can reduce the damage from key exposure. Different from previous schemes, this scheme combines the binary tree structure and lattice basis extension algorithm to achieve the one-way key evolution mechanism which allows data users to update their secret keys periodically. Thus, the security of the scheme can be still guaranteed when the secret keys are exposed. Moreover, with the update of secret keys, data users' public keys in our construction are fixed, which helps to save storage cost further, while public key in other existing scheme changes along with the update. Theoretic analysis shows that our scheme is more efficient when compared with the previous scheme.

Keywords: Public-key encryption with keywords search · Lattice · Forward security · Key exposure · Post-quantum security

1 Introduction

Public-key encryption with keywords search (PEKS) allows conducting retrieval over the encrypted database, which protects data privacy and keeps data searchability. Classical PEKS schemes include three parties, data owner, receiver who has a pair of public key and secret key, and a server. Generally, the data owner encrypts data using the receiver's public key and then uploads the encrypted data to the (cloud) server. To perform the retrieval of encrypted data, the receiver computes a search token using his own secret key and sends it to the server as a search request. Except supporting secure storage, the server also conducts a match (test) between the encrypted data and the given token, and returns the corresponding retrieval results if the match succeeds.

However, as data user, the receivers' secret keys are often exposed because of careless store or network attacks. In PEKS schemes, an adversary can compute search tokens of any keywords based on the exposed secret key. Considering practical applications, searchable encryption systems often support dynamically adding files under the cloud storage. The combination of the exposed tokens and the newly added files will lead to the leakage of data privacy. Forward security provides one of the solutions to minimize the damage resulting from the exposure of secret keys.

Contributions and Technique Roadmaps: In this work, we show a lattice-based PEKS scheme with forward security, considering the attack from quantum computers. Different from previous schemes, this scheme combines the binary tree structure and lattice basis extension algorithm to achieve a one-way key evolution mechanism. This mechanism supports that the receiver's secret keys are updated with the change of time periods, to achieve forward security. Such a one-wayness guarantees that even though a current key is compromised, an adversary can not generate a valid search token of past time to search cipher-text. Then this scheme further employs the minimal cover set to achieve the update of the receiver's secret keys with time periods, based on the key evolution mechanism. Compared with the previous scheme, our scheme is more efficient. Moreover, during the process of secret key update, the public key in our scheme is fixed, which saves unnecessary storage overhead.

Inspired by the works [1,10,15], most specifically, we use the leaf nodes of a binary tree structure of the depth l to discretize the time into 2^l segments. The lattice trapdoor generation algorithm is used to obtain a matrix A_0 as the public key and the lattice basis T_0 as the initial secret key of the receiver, which is also used to represent the **root** node of the binary tree. Then we choose $2l$ randomly uniform matrices $A_i^{(b_i)}$ of the size as A_0 for $i \in \{1, 2, \ldots, l\}$ and $b_i \in \{0, 1\}$. For each node $\Theta^{(i)} = (\theta_1, \ldots, \theta_i)$ with $\theta_i \in \{0, 1\}$ and $i \in \{1, 2, \ldots, l\}$, we set the corresponding matrix $F_{\Theta^{(i)}} = [A_0 || A_1^{(\theta_1)} || \ldots || A_i^{(\theta_i)}]$. Then we can employ the lattice basis extension algorithm to compute the trapdoor of any node, inputting the corresponding matrix and the trapdoor of the **root** node (or the trapdoor of its ancestor node). According to the property of the basis extension algorithm, the computation of lattice trapdoors can not be operated inversely, which realizes a one-way key evolution. After arranging the trapdoor of each node, we apply the minimal cover set to guarantee the secret key sk_t in time period t includes the ancestor trapdoor for time periods t' ($t' \geq t$) and does not include any trapdoor for time periods t'' ($t'' < t$).

1.1   Related Works

Lattice-Based PEKS: In 2004, Boneh et al. [7] proposed the first public-key encryption with keywords search scheme which is constructed by transforming an identity-based encryption (IBE) scheme based on bilinear maps. Considering the attack from quantum computers, Gu et al. [13] showed the first lattice-based PEKS scheme based on LWE hardness assumption in 2015. Then, Zhang et al.

[25] constructed a lattice-based PEKS scheme with a designated cloud server to resist keyword guessing attacks. Yang et al. [22] showed a lattice-based PEKS scheme supporting fuzzy keywords search, under the multimedia cloud. Zhang et al. [24] designed a proxy identity-based searchable encryption scheme in lattices, which allows authorizing the operation authority of data encryption to other users. Mao et al. [18] showed a lattice-based encryption scheme with conjunctive keywords search. Kuchta et al. [14] gave an attribute-based searchable encryption scheme from lattices. Xu et al. [20] constructed a lattice-based PEKS with multi-writer scheme, which is also an identity-based design to save the cost of key management. Focusing mainly on the experimental analysis of efficiency and parameters of lattice-based schemes, Behnia et al. [6] showed two constructions based on the hardness of the LWE problem and NTRU structure, respectively. These two schemes realize the security under the standard model by processing the keywords bit by bit. Xu et al. [21] designed an identity-based searchable public-key encryption scheme from ideal lattices, which has achieved considerable performance improvement in communication and computation through a large number of experiments.

Forward Security: The exposure of the user's secret key is undoubtedly a great threat for many cryptographic primitives, and it is easy to occur in the real scene. To this end, Anderson [4] first introduced forward security to minimize the damage from exposure of secret keys. Then, some forward secure cryptosystems were proposed, such as forward secure signatures [15–17] and public-key encryption schemes [5,9,11]. Bost [8] firstly designed the forward secure searchable encryption of symmetric cryptography, in response to possible attacks on dynamic searchable encryption. Accordingly, under the public key encryption system, Zeng et al. [23] introduced the definition of forward security for PEKS and showed a construction based on bilinear maps, where the search token is bound with its generation time period to achieve the forward security. Zhang et al. [26] showed the first forward secure PEKS construction from lattices, where this scheme used lattice basis delegation technique to achieve the key evolution.

1.2   Organization

The rest of this paper is organized as follows. Section 2 shows preliminaries on lattice, hardness assumptions and related algorithms. Then we introduce the syntax of PEKS with forward security as Sect. 3. In Sect. 4, the specific construction in lattices is given. Finally, we give a conclusion in Sect. 5.

2   Preliminaries

2.1   Notations

$\|A\|$ is the norm of a matrix A, which can be computed as the maximum l_2 norm of the column vectors of A. Without special description, bold lower-case letters denote column vectors. A function $negl(n)$ is negligible if for any $c > 0$

and all suffieient large n, $negl(n) < \dfrac{1}{n^c}$ holds. $\|\widetilde{A}\|$ means the Gram-Schmidt norm of the matrix A, where $\widetilde{A}$ is the Gram-Schmidt orthogonalization of A. $\mathbf{s} \xleftarrow{\$} S$ represents that an element $\mathbf{s}$ is chosen uniformly at random from a set S. Given two random variables X and Y over a countable domain S, a function $\Delta(X,Y) = \dfrac{1}{2}\sum_{s \in S}|X(s) - Y(s)|$ is defined to be statistical distance. If the distance $\Delta(X,Y)$ is negligible, we say X and Y are statistically close. $f(x) = O(g(x))$ means there exist positives c and m such that for any $x > m$, $f(x) \leqslant c \cdot g(x)$. $f(x) = \omega(g(x))$ means $\lim\limits_{x \to \infty} \dfrac{f(x)}{g(x)} = \infty$.

2.2 Lattice

Definition 1 (Lattice). *Given positive integers n, m and some linearly independent vectors $\boldsymbol{b}_i \in \mathbb{R}^m$ for $i \in \{1, 2, \ldots, n\}$, the set generated by the above vectors $L(\boldsymbol{b}_1, \boldsymbol{b}_2, \ldots, \boldsymbol{b}_n) = \{\sum_{i=1}^{n} x_i \boldsymbol{b}_i | x_i \in \mathbb{Z}\}$ is a lattice.*

From the above definition, the set $\{\mathbf{b}_1, \mathbf{b}_2, \ldots, \mathbf{b}_n\}$ is a lattice basis. We say m is the dimension and n is the rank. A lattice is full-rank if its dimension equals to rank, namely, $m = n$.

Definition 2. *For positive integers n, m and a prime q, a matrix $A \in \mathbb{Z}_q^{n \times m}$ and a vector $\boldsymbol{u} \in \mathbb{Z}_q^n$, define:*

$$\Lambda_q^{\perp}(A) := \{\boldsymbol{e} \in \mathbb{Z}^m | A\boldsymbol{e} = 0 \mod q\}.$$
$$\Lambda_q(\Lambda) := \{\boldsymbol{e} \in \mathbb{Z}^m | \exists \boldsymbol{s} \subset \mathbb{Z}_q^n, A^T\boldsymbol{s} = \boldsymbol{e} \mod q\}.$$
$$\Lambda_q^{\boldsymbol{u}}(A) := \{\boldsymbol{e} \in \mathbb{Z}^m | A\boldsymbol{e} = \boldsymbol{u} \mod q\}.$$

We can note that $\Lambda_q^{\boldsymbol{u}}(A)$ isn't a lattice but a shift of lattice $\Lambda_q^{\perp}(A)$, where $\Lambda_q^{\boldsymbol{u}}(A) = \Lambda_q^{\perp}(A) + \mathbf{t}$ for a vector $\mathbf{t} \in \Lambda_q^{\boldsymbol{u}}(A)$. Assuming that $T \in \mathbb{Z}^{m \times m}$ is a basis of $\Lambda_q^{\perp}(A)$, T is a basis of $\Lambda_q^{\perp}(BA)$ for a full-rank $B \in \mathbb{Z}_q^{n \times n}$.

2.3 Hardness Assumption

Definition 3. *[1] For $\alpha \in (0,1)$ and a prime q, let Ψ_α denote a probability distribution over $\mathbb{Z}_q$ by choosing $x \in \mathbb{R}$ from the normal distribution with mean 0 and standard deviation $\alpha/\sqrt{2\pi}$, outputs $\lfloor qx \rceil$.*

Definition 4 (Learning with errors, LWE). *[19] For a positive integer n, set $m = m(n)$ and $\alpha \in (0,1)$ such that a prime $q = q(n) > 2$ and $\alpha q > 2\sqrt{n}$, a secret $\boldsymbol{s} \xleftarrow{\$} \mathbb{Z}_q^n$, define the following distributions over $\mathbb{Z}_q^{n \times m} \times \mathbb{Z}_q^m$:*

- *LWE distribution: choose uniformly a matrix $A \xleftarrow{\$} \mathbb{Z}_q^{n \times m}$, and sample $\boldsymbol{e} \leftarrow \Psi_\alpha^m$, output $(A, A^T\boldsymbol{s} + \boldsymbol{e}) \in \mathbb{Z}_q^{n \times m} \times \mathbb{Z}_q^m$;*

– *Uniform distribution: choose uniformly a matrix* $A \xleftarrow{\$} \mathbb{Z}_q^{n \times m}$ *and a vector* $\boldsymbol{x} \xleftarrow{\$} \mathbb{Z}_q^m$, *output* $(A, \boldsymbol{x}) \in \mathbb{Z}_q^{n \times m} \times \mathbb{Z}_q^m$.

The decisional LWE problem is to distinguish between the above distributions. The $(\mathbb{Z}_q, n, \Psi_\alpha)-LWE$ *problem is hard, if for any probability polynomial time (PPT) adversary* $\mathscr{A}$, $|Pr[\mathscr{A}(A, A^T\boldsymbol{s} + \boldsymbol{e}) = 1] - Pr[\mathscr{A}(A, \boldsymbol{x}) = 1]|$ *is negligible on* n.

The LWE problem has been proved as hard as approximating the worst-case Gap-SVP and SIVP with certain factors [19].

2.4   Lattice Algorithms

Definition 5 (Gaussian distribution). *Given parameter* $\sigma \in \mathbb{R}^+$, *a vector* $\boldsymbol{c} \in \mathbb{R}^m$ *and a lattice* Λ, $\mathbf{D}_{\Lambda,\sigma,\boldsymbol{c}}$ *is a discrete gaussian distribution over* Λ *with a center* $\boldsymbol{c}$ *and a parameter* σ, *denoted by* $\mathbf{D}_{\Lambda,\sigma,\boldsymbol{c}} = \dfrac{\rho_{\sigma,\boldsymbol{c}}(x)}{\rho_{\sigma,\boldsymbol{c}}(\Lambda)}$ *for* $\forall x \in \Lambda$, *where* $\rho_{\sigma,\boldsymbol{c}}(\Lambda) = \sum_{x \in \Lambda} \rho_{\sigma,\boldsymbol{c}}(x)$ *and* $\rho_{\sigma,\boldsymbol{c}}(x) = \exp(-\pi \dfrac{\|x - \boldsymbol{c}\|^2}{\sigma^2})$. *When* $\boldsymbol{c} = 0$, *we abbreviate* $\mathbf{D}_{\Lambda,\sigma,0}$ *as* $\mathbf{D}_{\Lambda,\sigma}$.

Here we introduce some lattice algorithms. In the proposed scheme, the *TrapGen* algorithm will be used for generating the original keys of receiver. And the preimage sample algorithm *SamplePre* is for computing the search token. The lattice basis extension algorithm *ExtBasis* is used to update secret keys.

Lemma 1 (TrapGen algorithm). *[2, 3, 12] Given integers* n, m, q *with* $q > 2$ *and* $m \geqslant 6n \log q$ *as the input, there is a PPT algorithm TrapGen, outputs a matrix* $A \in \mathbb{Z}_q^{n \times m}$ *along with a basis* T_A *of lattice* $\Lambda^\perp(A)$, *namely,* $A \cdot T_A = 0 \bmod q$, *where the distribution of* A *is statistically close to uniform on* $\mathbb{Z}_q^{n \times m}$, *and* $\|\widetilde{T_A}\| \leqslant O(\sqrt{n \log q})$. *This algorithm can be denoted by* $(A, T_A) \leftarrow TrapGen(n, m, q)$.

Lemma 2 (Preimage sample algorithm). *Given a matrix* $A \in \mathbb{Z}_q^{n \times m}$ *with a basis* $T_A \in \mathbb{Z}_q^{m \times m}$, *a vector* $\boldsymbol{u} \in \mathbb{Z}_q^n$, *and a parameter* $\sigma \geqslant \|\widetilde{T_A}\| \cdot \omega(\sqrt{\log m})$ *as the input, where* $m \geqslant 2n\lceil \log q \rceil$, *there is a PPT algorithm SamplePre, outputs a sample* $\boldsymbol{e} \in \mathbb{Z}_q^m$ *distributed in* $\mathbf{D}_{\Lambda_q^u(A),\sigma}$, *such that* $A\boldsymbol{e} = \boldsymbol{u} \bmod q$. *We denote this algorithm by* $\boldsymbol{e} \leftarrow SamplePre(T_A, \boldsymbol{u}, \sigma)$.

Lemma 3 (ExtBasis algorithm). *Given an arbitrary* $A \in \mathbb{Z}_q^{n \times m}$ *whose columns generate the group* $\mathbb{Z}_q^n$, *an arbitrary basis* $S \in \mathbb{Z}^{m \times m}$ *of* $\Lambda^\perp(A)$, *and an arbitrary matrix* $A' \in \mathbb{Z}_q^{n \times m'}$, *there is a deterministic ploynomial-time algorithm ExtBasis which can output a basis* S'' *of* $\Lambda^\perp(A'') \subseteq \mathbb{Z}^{m \times m''}$ *such that* $\|\widetilde{S}\| = \|\widetilde{S''}\|$, *where* $A'' = A\|A'$, $m'' = m + m'$. *Moreover, the above results can be applied to the situation that the columns of* A' *are prepended to* A. *We denote this algorithm by* $S'' \leftarrow ExtBasis(A'', S)$.

3 Syntax of Forward Secure Public-Key Encryption with Keywords Search

This section introduces syntax and security model of forward secure PEKS. The forward security in public-key searchable encryption schemes can not allow the token to be used to search the ciphertext generated at the time periods after the time for generating this token, i.e., the token at the time period t_1 can not be used to search the ciphertext at the time period t_2, where $t_1 < t_2$.

3.1 System Model

One forward secure PEKS scheme consists of five algorithms, $\varPi$ =(**Setup, KeyUpdate, Enc, Token, Test**).

- $(pp, pk, sk_0) \leftarrow$ **Setup**(λ): Given the security parameter λ as input, this algorithm outputs system public parameter pp, the receiver's public key pk and the initial secret key sk_0.
- $sk_{t+1} \leftarrow$ **KeyUpdate**(pp, pk, sk_t, t): Given the public parameter pp, the receiver's public key pk and secret key sk_t with the time period t as the input, the key update algorithm generates the receiver's secret key sk_{t+1} with the time period $t+1$. Furthermore, the previous secret key sk_t is deleted.
- $C_{w,t} \leftarrow$ **Enc**(w, pk, t): Given a keyword w, the receiver's public key pk and the time period t as input, the encryption algorithm returns the ciphertext $C_{w,t}$ of the keyword w at the time period t.
- $T_{w',t} \leftarrow$ **Token**(sk_t, w'): Given a keyword w', the receiver's secret key sk_t at period time t as input, the token generation algorithm outputs a search token $T_{w',t}$.
- **Test**$(T_{w',t}, C_{w,t}, pk)$: Given the token $T_{w',t}$, the ciphertext $C_{w,t}$, as well as the public key pk as input, the test algorithm outputs 1 if and only if the ciphertext and the token contain the same keyword and the token is generated after the time periods that the keywords were encrypted, otherwise outputs 0.

3.2 Security Model

Here we define ciphertext indistinguishability of forward secure PEKS under chosen keywords attack. The security model requires that there is no PPT adversary who can distinguish a ciphertext with a random element chosen from the ciphertext space. We introduce the following security game $Exp_{\mathscr{A}}$ to define the above model. Given security parameter λ, an adversary $\mathscr{A}$ and a challenger $\mathscr{C}$ carry out this game.

The adversary can query adaptively oracles for polynomial times. To move to the next time period, the adversary can query key update oracle to obtain the secret key sk_{t+1} for the time period $t+1$. To realize forward security, the adversary selects a target time period t^*, and the oracle queries require that the query time periods $t > t^*$. Once the adversary queries the key update oracle, then he cannot issue the token query for the past time periods.

- **Setup:** The challenger $\mathscr{C}$ generates the public parameter pp and outputs the receiver's public-secret key pair (pk, sk_0) by running setup algorithm of the proposal. Then $\mathscr{C}$ sends pp and pk to the adversary $\mathscr{A}$, and keeps the initial key sk_0 secret.
- **Query 1:** The adversary $\mathscr{A}$ can perform some oracle queries, the details of challenger's responses are give below.
    - **Key Update query:** When the time period $t < T - 1$, the challenger updates the secret key sk_t to sk_{t+1} and updates the time period t to $t+1$. If $t = T - 1$, $\mathscr{C}$ will return an empty string as sk_T.
    - **Token query:** The adversary queries token for any keyword in the time periods t he chooses. The query requires that the time period $t > t^*$, where t^* is the target time period.
- **Challenge:** $\mathscr{A}$ chooses two keywords w_0^*, w_1^* as the challenged keywords in time period t^* which have not been queried for token oracle. Then $\mathscr{A}$ submits them to $\mathscr{C}$. $\mathscr{C}$ chooses a single bit $b \in \{0,1\}$ at random, and computes the ciphertext $C^* \leftarrow \mathbf{Enc}(w_b^*, pk, t^*)$ to return to $\mathscr{A}$.
- **Query 2:** $\mathscr{A}$ is allowed to issue the above queries for any keywords except w_0^*, w_1^*.
- **Guess:** From the above queries, $\mathscr{A}$ outputs a guess $b' \in \{0,1\}$ about b. If $b' = b$, we say $\mathscr{A}$ wins this game.

The advantage of $\mathscr{A}$ wins the above game is defined by $\boldsymbol{Adv}_{Exp_{\mathscr{A}}}(\lambda) = |Pr[b' = b] - \dfrac{1}{2}|$.

Definition 6. *We say a PEKS scheme satisfies forward secure ciphertext indistinguishability under chosen keywords attack, if the advantage $\boldsymbol{Adv}_{Exp_{\mathscr{A}}}(\lambda)$ on the security parameter λ is negligible.*

4   PEKS Scheme from Lattice

This section shows the specific construction of a lattice-based forward secure searchable encryption scheme.

4.1   Binary Tree for time Periods Enroll and Update

To realize forward security, our construction employs binary tree encryption structure [9] and lattice basis extension technique for the time period update and the setting of lattice trapdoor for each node. The details are described as follows.

- We assign the time periods $t \in \{0, 1, \ldots, 2^l - 1\}$ to the leaf nodes of the binary tree with depth l from leaf to right. Here we show an example as Fig. 1, where the depth of the tree is $l = 3$ and the number of time intervals is 8.

- On each time period t, there is an unique path from the **root** node to leaf node $t = (t_1, \ldots, t_l)$, where for the ith level, $t_i = 0$ if the node in this path is left node and $t_i = 1$ if the node in this path is right node. Similarly, for the ith level node ($i \neq l$, namely, the none-leaf node), its path from the **root** node to this node is denoted uniquely by $\Theta^{(i)} = (\theta_1, \ldots, \theta_i)$, where $\theta_i \in \{0, 1\}$ is defined as same as t_i.
- We run *TrapGen* algorithm and obtain a random matrix $A_0 \in \mathbb{Z}_q^{n \times m}$ and the lattice basis T_{A_0} for lattice $\Lambda^\perp(A_0)$. Then we set that A_0 is the corresponding matrix for **root** node and T_{A_0} is the lattice trapdoor for **root** node.
- We define the corresponding matrix $F_{\Theta^{(i)}} = [A_0||A_1^{(\theta_1)}||\ldots||A_i^{(\theta_i)}]$ for $\Theta^{(i)}$, and the matrix $F_t = [A_0||A_1^{(t_1)}||\ldots||A_l^{(t_l)}]$ for the time period t, respectively. $A_i^{(b)}$ are random matrices for $i \in \{1, 2, \ldots, l\}$ and $b \in \{0, 1\}$.
- There is a corresponding lattice trapdoor $T_{\Theta^{(i)}}$ for each node $\Theta^{(i)}$ of the binary tree. We employs lattice basis extension technique *ExtBasis* to achieve the lattice trapdoor update.
  - Given the original lattice trapdoor T_{A_0}, the trapdoor $T_{\Theta^{(i)}}$ can be computed as follows.

$$T_{\Theta^{(i)}} \leftarrow ExtBasis(F_{\Theta^{(i)}}, T_{A_0}),$$

  where $F_{\Theta^{(i)}} = [A_0||A_1^{(\theta_1)}||\ldots||A_i^{(\theta_i)}]$.
  - The trapdoor can also be computed easily from its any ancestor's trapdoor. For example, given $T_{\Theta^{(k)}}$,

$$T_{\Theta^{(i)}} \leftarrow ExtBasis(F_{\Theta^{(i)}}, T_{\Theta^{(k)}}),$$

  where $F_{\Theta^{(i)}} = [A_0||A_1^{(\theta_1)}||\ldots||A_i^{(\theta_i)}]$ and $\Theta^{(i)} = (\theta_1, \ldots, \theta_k, \theta_{k+1}, \ldots, \theta_i)$ for $k < i$.
- Similarly, the above methods are suitable for computing the lattice trapdoor for the time period (i.e., a leaf node) if its ancestor's lattice trapdoor is know.

4.2 Our Construction

The proposed construction is described below.

- **Setup(λ, l):** Given security parameter λ and the depth of a binary tree l, set $T = 2^l$ is the number of time periods, system parameters n, m, q, σ, α, where q is prime, σ is the parameter of preimage sample algorithm, α is the parameter of Gaussian distribution, the setup algorithm performs the following operations:
  - Set a hash function $H : \{0, 1\}^* \to \mathbb{Z}_q^n$.
  - Choose random matrices $A_1^{(0)}, A_1^{(1)}, \ldots, A_l^{(0)}, A_l^{(1)} \in \mathbb{Z}_q^{n \times m}$.
  - Run *TrapGen(n, m, q)* algorithm to obtain a random matrix A_0 and a basis T_{A_0} of lattice $\Lambda^\perp(A_0)$ as the receiver's public key and the initial secret key, respectively.

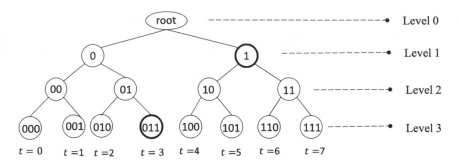

Fig. 1. Binary tree of depth $l = 3$, here each node is denoted by a binary representation.

- Output the public parameter $pp = (q, n, m, \sigma, \alpha, H, A_1^{(0)}, A_1^{(1)}, \ldots, A_l^{(0)}, A_l^{(1)})$.

– **KeyUpdate**(pp, sk_t, pk, t)**:** Given a public parameter pp, the secret key sk_t with time t and public key pk as input, the key evolution mechanism is need to achieve the secret key update as follows.

- For any leaf node t of the binary tree, a minimal cover $Node(t)$ represents the smallest set that contains an ancestor of all leaves after (and including) time t, namely, $\{t, t+1, \ldots, T-1\}$. For example as Fig. 1, $Node(0) = \{root\}$, $Node(1) = \{001, 01, 1\}$, $Node(2) = \{01, 1\}$, $Node(3) = \{011, 1\}$, $Node(4) = \{1\}$, $Node(5) = \{101, 11\}$, $Node(6) = \{11\}$, $Node(7) = \{111\}$.
- Each node of the binary tree owns the corresponding secret key, for example, in the node "01" in Level 1, its secret key is T_{01} which is the basis for lattice $\Lambda^{\perp}(F_{01})$ and $F_{01} = [A_0 || A_1^{(0)} || A_2^{(1)}]$. Then the secret key sk_t at time t consists of the secret keys of all of the nodes in the set $Node(t)$.
- Based on the above rules on secret keys, we have $sk_0 = \{T_{A_0}\}$, $sk_1 = \{T_{001}, T_{01}, T_1\}$, where T_{001}, T_{01}, T_1 are the corresponding trapdoor (basis) for $F_{001} = [A_0 || A_1^{(0)} || A_2^{(0)} || A_3^{(1)}]$, $F_{01} = [A_0 || A_1^{(0)} || A_2^{(1)}]$, $F_1 = [A_0 || A_1^{(1)}]$, respectively.
- To realize the key update from sk_t to sk_{t+1}, the receiver need to determine the minimal cover $Node(t+1)$ firstly, then compute all trapdoors of nodes which are in $Node(t+1) \backslash Node(t)$ by using the methods introduced in Sect. 4.1, and delete the trapdoors of nodes in $Node(t) \backslash Node(t+1)$. Finally, the receiver can determine the secret key sk_{t+1}. Here we show an example, given $sk_1 = \{T_{001}, T_{01}, T_1\}$, then $sk_2 = \{T_{01}, T_1\}$, where $Node(2) \backslash Node(1) = \{01, 1\}$ and $Node(1) \backslash Node(2) = \{001\}$.

– **Enc**(w, pk, t)**:** Given keyword w, the receiver's public key $pk = A_0$, and the time t as the input,

- Select a random vector $\mathbf{s}$ from a uniform distribution over $\mathbb{Z}_q^n$,
- Choose a noise vector $\mathbf{y} \leftarrow \Psi_\alpha^{(l+1)m}$ and $x \leftarrow \Psi_\alpha$, where Ψ_α is a distribution over $\mathbb{Z}_q$ as Definition 3.
- Compute $c_1 = H(w)^T \mathbf{s} + x \in \mathbb{Z}_q$,
- Compute $\mathbf{c}_2 = F_t^T \mathbf{s} + \mathbf{y} \in \mathbb{Z}_q^{(l+1)m}$, where $F_t = [A_0 || A_1^{(t_1)} || \ldots || A_l^{(t_l)}]$.
- Return the ciphertext $C_w = (c_1, \mathbf{c}_2)$.
- **Token**(w, sk_t): For the keyword w, the receiver's secret key sk_t with the time period t,
    - Check if sk_t does not contain the lattice basis $T_{\Theta^{(t)}}$, run $ExtBasis(F_{\Theta^{(t)}}, T_{\Theta^{(k)}})$ to output $T_{\Theta^{(t)}}$, where $T_{\Theta^{(k)}}$ is an ancestor basis of $T_{\Theta^{(t)}}$ in the secret key sk_t.
    - Run $SamplePre(T_{\Theta^{(t)}}, H(w), \sigma)$ and returns $\mathbf{e} \in \mathbb{Z}_q^{(l+1)m}$ which satisfies $F_t \cdot \mathbf{e} = H(w)$.
    - Return $T_w = \mathbf{e}$ as the token.
- **Test**(T_w, C_w, pp): The server performs the test as follows:
    - Compute $r = c_1 - \mathbf{e}^T \mathbf{c}_2$.
    - If $|r| \leq \lfloor \frac{q}{4} \rfloor$, return 1, which implies this test succeeds. Otherwise, return 0.

4.3 Correctness and Parameters

For the **Test** algorithm, we have the following result:

$$
\begin{aligned}
r &= c_1 - \mathbf{e}^T \cdot \mathbf{c}_2 \\
&- H(w)^T \mathbf{s} + x - \mathbf{e}^T \cdot (F_t^T \mathbf{s} + \mathbf{y}) \\
&= H(w)^T \mathbf{s} + x - \mathbf{e}^T \cdot F_t^T \mathbf{s} - \mathbf{e}^T \cdot \mathbf{y} \\
&= x - \mathbf{e}^T \cdot \mathbf{y},
\end{aligned}
$$

where $x - \mathbf{e}^T \cdot \mathbf{y}$ is error term. To decrypt correctly, we need to make sure that these error terms are less than $\frac{q}{4}$. Moreover, some parameters should satisfy the following conditions to guarantee the related algorithms work:

- The algorithm $TrapGen$ can be able to operate, then $m \geqslant 6n \log q$.
- The algorithm $SamplePre$ can be able to operate, then $m \geqslant 2n\lceil \log q \rceil$ and $\sigma \geq \|\tilde{T}\| \cdot \omega(\sqrt{\log m})$, where T is a lattice basis.
- The LWE reduction can be able to operate, then $q > 2\sqrt{n}/\alpha$.

4.4 Security Analysis

Theorem 1. *The proposed forward secure PEKS scheme is ciphertext indistinguishability under chosen keywords attack, if $(\mathbb{Z}_q, n, \Psi_\alpha) - LWE$ problem is intractable.*

Proof. Assume that there exists an adversary $\mathscr{A}$ who can break the cipher-text indistinguishability under chosen keywords attack of our scheme with non-negligible probability ϵ. According to the adversary, we construct a challenger $\mathscr{C}$ to solve the LWE problem with a probability of at least ϵ' and in polynomial time for a target time period $t^* = (t_1^*, t_2^*, \ldots, t_l^*)$.

$\mathscr{C}$ firstly obtains some samples $(\mathbf{u}_i, v_i) \in \mathbb{Z}_q^n \times \mathbb{Z}_q$ from the LWE oracles, where $i = 1, \ldots, \overline{m}$ and $\overline{m} = (l+1)m$. All of $\mathbf{u}_i$ are chosen randomly, and either all of v_i are randomly selected or equal to $\mathbf{u}_i^T \mathbf{s} + y_i$, where $\mathbf{s}$ is a uniform secret, and y_i is the independent Gaussian noise distributed from Ψ_α. Let $\mathbf{v} = (v_1, v_2, \ldots, v_{\overline{m}})^T$.

Setup: $\mathscr{C}$ sets the public key pk and public parameters pp according to the following steps:

- Assemble F_{t^*} by the $\overline{m}$ samples above, i.e., set $F_{t^*} = (\mathbf{u}_1, \mathbf{u}_2, \ldots, \mathbf{u}_{\overline{m}})$.
- $\mathscr{C}$ invokes the *TrapGen* to generate $A_0 \in \mathbb{Z}_q^{n \times m}$ with a short basis T_0 of $\Lambda^\perp(A_0)$.
- For node $t_k = t_k^*$, set $A_k^{(t_k)} = [\mathbf{u}_{km+1}, \ldots, \mathbf{u}_{(k+1)m}]$ for $k \in \{1, 2, \ldots, l\}$. For other nodes $t_k \neq t_k^*$ and $k \in \{1, 2, \ldots, l\}$, select randomly l matrices $A_1^{(t_1)}, \ldots, A_l^{(t_l)}$ from the uniform distribution over $\mathbb{Z}_q^{n \times m}$.
- $\mathscr{C}$ sends $pk = A_0$ and $pp = (A_1^{(0)}, A_1^{(1)}, \ldots, A_l^{(0)}, A_l^{(1)})$ to $\mathscr{A}$, and keeps T_0 secret.

Query 1: The adversary $\mathscr{A}$ is allowed queried the following oracles in polynomial times. And the challenger $\mathscr{C}$ returns the corresponding responses as follows.

- **Key Update Query:** If $t \leq t^*$, where $t = (t_1, \ldots, t_l)$, $\mathscr{C}$ aborts the query. Otherwise, set $k \leq l$ be the minimum index such that $t_k \neq t_k^*$. Then, $\mathscr{C}$ uses the trapdoor $T_{A_k^{(t_k)}}$ to compute the key T_{t_k} for the node t_k

$$T_{t_k} \leftarrow ExtBasis(E || A_k^{(t_k)}, T_{A_k^{(t_k)}}),$$

where $E = [A_0 || A_1^{(t_1)} || \ldots || A_{k-1}^{(t_{k-1})}]$ from which $\mathscr{C}$ computes all keys in sk_t as in the real key update algorithm.
- **Token Query:** $\mathscr{A}$ makes token queries for keyword w at time period t. If $H(w) = 0$, the game aborts and returns a random bit $b' \in \{0, 1\}$. Otherwise, $\mathscr{C}$ replies as follows:
  - $\mathscr{C}$ checks if sk_t does not contain the lattice basis $T_{\Theta^{(t)}}$, run $ExtBasis$ $(F_{\Theta^{(t)}}, T_{\Theta^{(k)}})$ to output $T_{\Theta^{(t)}}$, where $T_{\Theta^{(k)}}$ is an ancestor basis of $T_{\Theta^{(t)}}$ in the secret key sk_t.
  - $\mathscr{C}$ computes $H(w)$ and runs $SamplePre(T_{\Theta^{(t)}}, H(w), \sigma)$ to get a sample $\mathbf{e} \in \mathbb{Z}_q^{(l+1)m}$.
  - $\mathscr{C}$ returns $\mathbf{e}$ to the adversary $\mathscr{A}$.

Challenge: $\mathscr{A}$ chooses two keywords w_0^*, w_1^* and sends them to $\mathscr{C}$. $\mathscr{C}$ checks firstly if $H(w^*) = 0$, $\mathscr{C}$ aborts the game and outputs a random bit $b' \in \{0, 1\}$. Otherwise, $\mathscr{C}$ generates the ciphertext for the target time period t^* as follows:

- $\mathscr{C}$ chooses randomly $w^* \in \{w_0^*, w_1^*\}$ prompted by the adversary as the challenged ciphertext, and sets $c_1^* = H(w^*)^T \mathbf{s} + x \in \mathbb{Z}_q$ for $x \leftarrow \Psi_\alpha$ as in the real scheme.
- $\mathscr{C}$ computes $c_2^* = F_{t^*}^T \mathbf{s} + \mathbf{y}$ for $\mathbf{y} \leftarrow \Psi_\alpha^{(l+1)m}$.
- $\mathscr{C}$ chooses a random bit $b \in \{0, 1\}$. If $b = 0$, $\mathscr{C}$ sends (c_1^*, c_2^*) generated from the above methods. Otherwise, $\mathscr{C}$ chooses randomly $(c_1, c_2) \in \mathbb{Z}_q \times \mathbb{Z}_q^{(l+1)m}$ and sends it to the adversary.

Query 2: The adversary $\mathscr{A}$ can continue the queries as in the Query phase 1 with the restriction that $\mathscr{A}$ cannot query for the challenge keywords w_0^*, w_1^*.

Guess: Based on the above queries, the adversary outputs a guess b' of b by executing the following steps:

If the LWE oracle is pseudorandom, for $F_{t^*} = (\mathbf{u}_1, \mathbf{u}_2, \ldots, \mathbf{u}_{\overline{m}})$ and the random noise vector $\mathbf{y} \in \mathbb{Z}_q^{(l+1)m}$ distributed as Ψ_α. Then we have $c_2^* = F_{t^*}^T \mathbf{s} + \mathbf{y} = (\mathbf{u}_1, \mathbf{u}_2, \ldots, \mathbf{u}_{\overline{m}})^T \mathbf{s} + \mathbf{y}$ is a valid part of the challenged ciphertext. Moreover, $c_1^* = H(w^*)^T \mathbf{s} + x$ is also a valid part of the challenged ciphertext which is statistically close to the uniform in $\mathbb{Z}_q$, since $\mathbf{s}$ is a uniform secret and x is the independent Gaussian noise distributed from Ψ_α. If LWE oracle is random, $\mathbf{v}$ is uniform in $\mathbb{Z}_q^{(l+1)m}$. Then, the challenged ciphertext is uniform in $\mathbb{Z}_q \times \mathbb{Z}_q^{(l+1)m}$. We assume a case that $\mathscr{A}$ guesses successfully the keyword w_1^* is used in the part of challenged ciphertext and the time period t^*, then this case occurs with probability $1/q_t T$, where q_t is the number of token queries. Thus, if $\mathscr{A}$ can break the ciphertext indistinguishability under chosen keywords attack of our scheme with non negligible probability ϵ, then $\mathscr{C}$ has the advantage $\epsilon' = \epsilon/q_t T$ to solve the LWE problem. The proof is completed.

4.5   Performance Comparison

Here we compare with the other PEKS scheme [26] on the performance of the computational cost, the ciphertext size and token size. There are some notations in Table 1, H: hash operation, M: modular multiplication, I: matrix inversion operation; m: the dimension of matrix, τ: security level of testing in the scheme of [26]; l_q: the size of element in $\mathbb{Z}_q$; T_{BD}: *BasisDel* operation; T_{SL}: *SampleLeft* operation which is a sample algorithm found in [26], T_{SP}: *SamplePre* operation; T_{EB}: *ExtBasis* algorithm.

We can note that the sizes of ciphertext and token in our scheme are more longer than that in the scheme of [26], especially for the size of token. On the other hand, our scheme is more efficient than the scheme of [26]. Moreover, in our scheme, the public key is fixed, which can save the unnecessary storage overhead.

Table 1. The comparison with other scheme

Schemes	[26]	Ours
Ciphertext size	$(m+1)\tau \cdot l_q$	$(m(l+1)+1)l_q$
Token size	ml_q	$(l+1)m \cdot l_q$
Enc cost	$3M + I + H$	$2M + H$
Token cost	$H + M + I + T_{BD} + T_{SP}$	$T_{SP} + H + T_{EB}$
Test cost	$M + H$	M
Fixed public key	No	Yes

5   Conclusion

In this paper, we show a forward secure searchable encryption scheme. This scheme is designed based on the integer lattice which can realize the post-quantum security. Combining with the binary tree encryption and lattice basis extension algorithm, we achieve the update of secret keys with the change of time periods. The research on the related constructions from some special lattices, such as ideal lattice, module lattice will be an interesting point for improving the efficiency and setting of parameters.

Acknowledgment. The authors would like to thank the support from Fundamental Research Program of Shanxi Province (No. 20210302124273, No. 20210302123130), Scientific and Technological Innovation Programs of Higher Education Institutions in Shanxi (No. 2021L038), Shanxi Scholarship Council of China 2021-038, National Natural Science Foundation of China (No. 62072240, No. 62202228), Natural Science Foundation of Jiangsu Province under Grant (BK20210330), China. The authors also gratefully acknowledge the helpful comments and suggestions of other researchers, which has improved the presentation.

References

1. Agrawal, S., Boneh, D., Boyen, X.: Lattice basis delegation in fixed dimension and shorter-ciphertext hierarchical IBE. In: Rabin, T. (ed.) CRYPTO 2010. LNCS, vol. 6223, pp. 98–115. Springer, Heidelberg (2010). https://doi.org/10.1007/978-3-642-14623-7_6
2. Ajtai, M.: Generating hard instances of the short basis problem. In: Wiedermann, J., van Emde Boas, P., Nielsen, M. (eds.) ICALP 1999. LNCS, vol. 1644, pp. 1–9. Springer, Heidelberg (1999). https://doi.org/10.1007/3-540-48523-6_1
3. Alwen, J., Peikert, C.: Generating shorter bases for hard random lattices. In: 26th International Symposium on Theoretical Aspects of Computer Science, STACS, Freiburg, Germany, vol. 3, pp. 75–86 (2009)
4. Anderson, R.: Two remarks on public key cryptology. Technical report, Computer Laboratory, University of Cambridge (2002)
5. Baek, J., Vu, Q.H., Shoufan, A., Jones, A., Wong, D.S.: Stateful public-key encryption schemes forward-secure against state exposure. Comput. J. **56**(4), 497–507 (2013)

6. Behnia, R., Ozmen, M.O., Yavuz, A.A.: Lattice-based public key searchable encryption from experimental perspectives. IEEE Trans. Depend. Secur. Comput. **17**(6), 1269–1282 (2020)
7. Boneh, D., Di Crescenzo, G., Ostrovsky, R., Persiano, G.: Public key encryption with keyword search. In: Cachin, C., Camenisch, J.L. (eds.) EUROCRYPT 2004. LNCS, vol. 3027, pp. 506–522. Springer, Heidelberg (2004). https://doi.org/10.1007/978-3-540-24676-3_30
8. Bost, R.: Σοφος: forward secure searchable encryption. In: Proceedings of the ACM SIGSAC Conference on Computer and Communications Security, Vienna, Austria, pp. 1143–1154 (2016)
9. Canetti, R., Halevi, S., Katz, J.: A forward-secure public-key encryption scheme. In: Biham, E. (ed.) EUROCRYPT 2003. LNCS, vol. 2656, pp. 255–271. Springer, Heidelberg (2003). https://doi.org/10.1007/3-540-39200-9_16
10. Cash, D., Hofheinz, D., Kiltz, E., Peikert, C.: Bonsai trees, or how to delegate a lattice basis. In: Gilbert, H. (ed.) EUROCRYPT 2010. LNCS, vol. 6110, pp. 523–552. Springer, Heidelberg (2010). https://doi.org/10.1007/978-3-642-13190-5_27
11. Dodis, Y., Katz, J., Xu, S., Yung, M.: Key-insulated public key cryptosystems. In: Knudsen, L.R. (ed.) EUROCRYPT 2002. LNCS, vol. 2332, pp. 65–82. Springer, Heidelberg (2002). https://doi.org/10.1007/3-540-46035-7_5
12. Gentry, C., Peikert, C., Vaikuntanathan, V.: Trapdoors for hard lattices and new cryptographic constructions. In: Proceedings of the 40th Annual ACM Symposium on Theory of Computing, Victoria, British Columbia, Canada, pp. 197–206 (2008)
13. Gu, C., Zheng, Y., Kang, F., Xin, D.: Keyword search over encrypted data in cloud computing from lattices in the standard model. In: Qiang, W., Zheng, X., Hsu, C.-H. (eds.) CloudCom-Asia 2015. LNCS, vol. 9106, pp. 335–343. Springer, Cham (2015). https://doi.org/10.1007/978-3-319-28430-9_25
14. Kuchta, V., Markowitch, O.: Multi-authority distributed attribute-based encryption with application to searchable encryption on lattices. In: Phan, R.C.-W., Yung, M. (eds.) Mycrypt 2016. LNCS, vol. 10311, pp. 409–435. Springer, Cham (2017). https://doi.org/10.1007/978-3-319-61273-7_20
15. Le, H.Q., et al.: Lattice blind signatures with forward security. In: Liu, J.K., Cui, H. (eds.) ACISP 2020. LNCS, vol. 12248, pp. 3–22. Springer, Cham (2020). https://doi.org/10.1007/978-3-030-55304-3_1
16. Ling, S., Nguyen, K., Wang, H., Xu, Y.: Forward-secure group signatures from lattices. In: Ding, J., Steinwandt, R. (eds.) PQCrypto 2019. LNCS, vol. 11505, pp. 44–64. Springer, Cham (2019). https://doi.org/10.1007/978-3-030-25510-7_3
17. Liu, J.K., Yuen, T.H., Zhou, J.: Forward secure ring signature without random oracles. In: Qing, S., Susilo, W., Wang, G., Liu, D. (eds.) ICICS 2011. LNCS, vol. 7043, pp. 1–14. Springer, Heidelberg (2011). https://doi.org/10.1007/978-3-642-25243-3_1
18. Mao, Y., Fu, X., Guo, C., Wu, G.: Public key encryption with conjunctive keyword search secure against keyword guessing attack from lattices. Trans. Emerg. Telecommun. Technol. **30**, 1–14 (2018)
19. Regev, O.: On lattices, learning with errors, random linear codes, and cryptography. J. ACM **56**(6), 34:1–34:40 (2009)
20. Xu, L., Yuan, X., Steinfeld, R., Wang, C., Xu, C.: Multi-writer searchable encryption: an LWE-based realization and implementation. In: Asia Conference on Computer and Communications Security, AsiaCCS, Auckland, New Zealand, pp. 122–133 (2019)

21. Xu, L., Yuan, X., Zhou, Z., Wang, C., Xu, C.: Towards efficient cryptographic data validation service in edge computing. In: IEEE World Congress on Services, SERVICES, Barcelona, Spain, 10–16 July 2022, p. 14 (2022)
22. Yang, Y., Zheng, X., Chang, V., Ye, S., Tang, C.: Lattice assumption based fuzzy information retrieval scheme support multi-user for secure multimedia cloud. Multimedia Tools Appl. **77**, 9927–9941 (2018). https://doi.org/10.1007/s11042-017-4560-x
23. Zeng, M., Qian, H., Chen, J., Zhang, K.: Forward secure public key encryption with keyword search for outsourced cloud storage. IEEE Trans. Cloud Comput. **10**(1), 426–438 (2022)
24. Zhang, X., Tang, Y., Wang, H., Xu, C., Miao, Y., Cheng, H.: Lattice-based proxy-oriented identity-based encryption with keyword search for cloud storage. Inf. Sci. **494**, 193–207 (2019)
25. Zhang, X., Xu, C.: Trapdoor security lattice-based public-key searchable encryption with a designated cloud server. Wirel. Pers. Commun. **100**(3), 907–921 (2018)
26. Zhang, X., Xu, C., Wang, H., Zhang, Y., Wang, S.: FS-PEKS: lattice-based forward secure public-key encryption with keyword search for cloud-assisted industrial internet of things. IEEE Trans. Depend. Secur. Comput. **18**(3), 1019–1032 (2021)

Strengthening the Security of AES Against Differential Fault Attack

Anit Kumar Ghosal$^{(\boxtimes)}$ and Dipanwita Roychowdhury

Department of Computer Science and Engineering, IIT Kharagpur, Kharagpur, India
anit.ghosal@gmail.com

Abstract. AES, the NIST standard block cipher, is most widely used for cryptographic applications. Till date, AES is secured against all types of cryptographic attacks like algebraic or statistical attacks. Unfortunately, AES is vulnerable against side channel attacks. Differential Fault Attack is a powerful cryptanalytic technique against AES. The most successful fault attacks on AES form linear equations with a number of faulty and fault free ciphertexts to find out the key. Our proposal to protect AES from Differential Fault Attack is to add a new diffusion layer in each round to enlarge the exhaustive key-search space by generating a minimum number of equations. The existing result on AES key recovery using this kind of fault attack is 2^{32}, which is further improved to 2^8. With our approach, the security is enhanced by increasing key-search space to 2^{84}.

Keywords: AES Rijndael · Differential Fault Attack · Diffusion layer · SPN cipher

1 Introduction

Block ciphers are the modern workhorse of cryptography. Advanced Encryption Standard (AES) [4] is the current standard block cipher which is known to be secured till date against cryptanalytic attacks that exploit the algebraic analysis or algorithmic properties. Unfortunately, AES is vulnerable against side channel attacks or implementation attacks. Fault attack is the most devastating implementation attack against block cipher. The first use of fault attack has been conceived by Boneh et al. [2], where the idea is to intentionally inject a fault in an intermediate state of the algorithm and then study the disturbed execution, i.e., faulty output and fault free output. One of the most popular targets of fault attacks has been the Advanced Encryption Standard (AES). In literature, several approaches of Differential Fault Analysis (DFA) attacks on AES have been reported so far [2,4–6,8–10]. Optical fault induction [5] is one of the techniques in the fault-based side channel cryptanalysis of AES and has gained considerable attention. The most successful fault analysis attack on AES is presented in [10]. Here, a fault is induced in the 9th round of AES that requires 250 faulty ciphertexts to recover the key. The same idea has been extended in [8] and an attacker can retrieve the whole AES-128 key using 128 faulty ciphertexts. Further improvement is proposed in [9] and it is shown that fault induced between

© The Author(s), under exclusive license to Springer Nature Switzerland AG 2022
X. Yuan et al. (Eds.): NSS 2022, LNCS 13787, pp. 727–744, 2022.
https://doi.org/10.1007/978-3-031-23020-2_41

8th or 9th round of the MixColumns operation requires 40 faulty ciphertexts to retrieve the desired key. Piret et al. [6] show that if a byte level fault is induced at the input of 8th or 9th round of AES-128 algorithm, an attacker can retrieve the whole AES-128 key with two faulty ciphertexts. Moradi et al. [11] extend the idea to show a more general fault model with greater fault coverage rate. Recently, Murdock et al. [33] use the differential fault analysis technique of [21] in AES-NI as implemented by Jovanovi[1]. As a consequence of their work, Intel has removed the support for Software Guard Extension (SGX) in 12th generation Intel Core 11000 and 12000 processors. This motivates us to strengthen AES against Differential Fault Attack [16,21].

Usually, fault attacks are not prevented at the cipher design level. So, the cipher designer has to rely on the person who is actually implementing the circuit or the software developer or the network administrator to get the assurance that an adequate countermeasure is taken. Hence, countermeasures are designed and analysed separately for AES [24,27,32,34]. In literature, the countermeasures are divided broadly into two categories. Firstly, the countermeasures try to prevent the fault happening in the first place. On the other side, the countermeasures try to eliminate the fault either by means of redundancy [13,26] or protocol level. The countermeasures that use redundant computations are *detection* [29], *infection* [23,25,31] etc. The protocol level countermeasures are generally *re-keying* [18], *masking plaintext* etc. In [12,14], authors show how to protect an AES implementation against Power Analysis Attacks using masking. Apart from this, there are efficient exploitation of simple encodings such as additive masking (e.g., Boolean ones in [20]) or multiplicative ones [7,14]. The main advantage of these simple schemes is that they enable efficient implementations in software platform [30]. In case of *detection-based* countermeasures, execution of algorithm is doubled and both the results are compared to detect faults. By injecting the same faults in both paths, an attacker can bypass the comparison. Moreover, the comparison itself also offers possible attacks. Since such detection countermeasure does not give satisfactory answer [22], later *infective* computation is proposed. The idea is to modify the ciphertext in such a random manner so that an attacker fails to guess the key from ciphertext. This idea also has some drawbacks as identified in [25]. Another new approach can be stronger confusion and diffusion layer by adding some functionalities in the diffusion layer or making S-box more secure to protect the cipher from DFA attacks. One of the most popular attacks in AES is to form a system of equations by analysing faulty and fault free ciphertexts to discover the key [16]. Block ciphers like AES, Khazad [3], Midori [28] use Maximum Distance Separable (MDS) matrix or near-MDS matrix in diffusion layer along with some kind of permutation and cipher like Present [15] uses only random permutation due to lightweight applications. To strengthen the security of AES against DFA, we use the first countermeasure, i.e., restriction of the fault propagation at the initial level. An *extra diffusion layer in each round* of AES is proposed to enlarge the exhaustive key-search space by restricting the formation of system of linear equations.

---

[1] https://github.com/Daeinar/dfa-aes.

Our Contribution. In this work, an additional diffusion layer to the AES block cipher, *MixColumn-Plus*, is proposed to make the cipher less susceptible against differential fault attacks. Here, the main idea is to enlarge the exhaustive key-search space by reducing the number of linear equations so that the differential fault attacks become much more costlier to the attacker. The end complexity is around 2^{84} compared to only 2^8, for original AES. Introduction of the proposed layer at each round reduces DFA vulnerabilities in the practical implementation (i.e., *hardware* or *software*) of AES. Further, the proposed *MixColumn-Plus* (or *InvMixColumn-Plus*) matrix can be broken into a binary matrix followed by InvMixColumns (or MixColumns) matrix which is efficient for the practical implementation.

Organization. The paper is organized as follows. Section 2 describes the background of AES and the existing attack strategy whereas Sect. 3 illustrates the operation of MixColumn-Plus layer. Detailed analysis, results and applications are given in Sect. 4, while Sect. 5 focuses on security analysis. Finally, we conclude the paper in Sect. 6.

2   Background

AES-Rijndael. The description of AES-Rijndael algorithm is mentioned in [4]. We consider the AES algorithm with both key and message size of 128 bit. Input block is arranged as a 4×4 bytes fashion called state matrix. The algorithm is composed of ten rounds and the key is generated from the KeySchedule algorithm. Encryption process of AES in each round uses the following steps:

- **SubBytes.** SubBytes is the only non-linear step of the block cipher. Each input byte x is transformed by affine transformation to the output byte as $y = Ax^{-1} + B$, where A and B both are constant matrices.
- **ShiftRows.** Every row of the state matrix is cyclically rotated by a certain number of byte positions.
- **MixColumns.** Each column of the state matrix is linearly transformed. Every column is considered as a 4-dimensional vector where each element belongs to $F(2^8)$. A 4×4 matrix M whose elements are also in $F(2^8)$ is used to map this column into a new vector. This operation is applied on all the 4 columns of the state matrix. Here, M and its inverse M^{-1} are defined as follows:

$$M = \begin{pmatrix} 02\ 03\ 01\ 01 \\ 01\ 02\ 03\ 01 \\ 01\ 01\ 02\ 03 \\ 03\ 01\ 01\ 02 \end{pmatrix} \quad M^{-1} = \begin{pmatrix} 0e\ 0b\ 0d\ 09 \\ 09\ 0e\ 0b\ 0d \\ 0d\ 09\ 0e\ 0b \\ 0b\ 0d\ 09\ 0e \end{pmatrix}.$$

- **AddRoundKey.** The subkey generated from the KeySchedule algorithm is a bitwise XOR operation with the state matrix.

Similarly, decryption process of AES in each round consists of InvShiftRows, InvSubBytes, AddRoundKey, InvMixColumns. First 9 rounds of AES-Rijndael encryption are identical except the last round where the MixColumns operation does not exist.

Fault Model of the Existing Attack. We consider single byte fault model where only one byte b_{ij} is assumed to be faulty with a byte fault of f_{ij}, where i and j refers to the row and column indices of the state matrix ($0 \leq i, j \leq 3$). The number of faulty bits in a byte is denoted by $w(f_{ij})$ ($1 \leq w(f_{ij}) \leq 8$). The fault value should be non-zero and an attacker has the ability to target with precision one byte of the AES state, at the time of their choice, without any side effect. It should be assumed that the fault injection is transient, has no permanent effect, and is always effective. Any hardware failure should be discarded (i.e., there is no fault induced by the electronic device in itself).

2.1   Existing Related Research

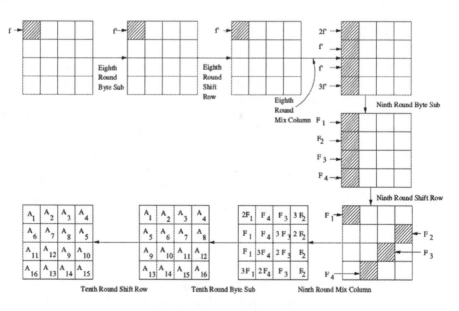

Fig. 1. Fault propagation process induced in the input of 8th round [16]

Differential Fault Analysis (DFA) [1] is a type of side channel attack where an attacker disturbs cryptographic computations by injecting faults in the intermediate state of cipher. The ultimate goal of the attacker is to recover the secret key by exploiting the erroneous results. Differential Fault Attack on AES shows that using a single byte fault [16] secret key can be retrieved with an exhaustive search of 2^{32}. We are restricting ourselves to AES-128 only. Let P be the 128 bit plaintext matrix, K be the 128 bit key matrix which produces fault free ciphertext CT and faulty ciphertext CT'. All matrices are arranged in the following fashion:

$$P = \begin{pmatrix} p_1 & p_5 & p_9 & p_{13} \\ p_2 & p_6 & p_{10} & p_{14} \\ p_3 & p_7 & p_{11} & p_{15} \\ p_4 & p_8 & p_{12} & p_{16} \end{pmatrix} \quad K = \begin{pmatrix} k_1 & k_5 & k_9 & k_{13} \\ k_2 & k_6 & k_{10} & k_{14} \\ k_3 & k_7 & k_{11} & k_{15} \\ k_4 & k_8 & k_{12} & k_{16} \end{pmatrix}$$

$$CT = \begin{pmatrix} x_1 & x_5 & x_9 & x_{13} \\ x_2 & x_6 & x_{10} & x_{14} \\ x_3 & x_7 & x_{11} & x_{15} \\ x_4 & x_8 & x_{12} & x_{16} \end{pmatrix} \quad CT' = \begin{pmatrix} x_1' & x_5' & x_9' & x_{13}' \\ x_2' & x_6' & x_{10}' & x_{14}' \\ x_3' & x_7' & x_{11}' & x_{15}' \\ x_4' & x_8' & x_{12}' & x_{16}' \end{pmatrix},$$

where each byte p_i, k_i, x_i, x_i' takes value from $\{0,...,255\}$, $\forall i \in \{1, ..., 16\}$.

Working strategy of the attack is described as follows. When a single byte fault $\boldsymbol{F}$ (or $\boldsymbol{f}$) is injected at the start of 8th round in $(0,0)^{th}$ byte position, the MixColumns operation propagates this fault into entire column of the state matrix at the round end. At the start of 9th round, ShiftRow spreads the fault into one byte at each column of the entire state matrix as $\boldsymbol{F_1}$, $\boldsymbol{F_2}$, $\boldsymbol{F_3}$ and $\boldsymbol{F_4}$ respectively. Here, $\boldsymbol{F_1}$, $\boldsymbol{F_2}$, $\boldsymbol{F_3}$ and $\boldsymbol{F_4}$ denote the fault at $(0,0)^{th}$, $(1,3)^{th}$, $(2,2)^{th}$ and $(3,1)^{th}$ positions respectively. The next MixColumns step propagates the fault to the remaining twelve bytes. At the end of 9th round these faults lead to some byte inter-relationship as mentioned in Fig. 1.

Algorithm 1. AES-Encrypt with MixColumn-Plus Layer	**Algorithm 2.** AES-Decrypt with MixColumn-Plus Layer
Input: Plaintext P and Key K	**Input: Ciphertext C and Key K**
Output: Ciphertext C	**Output: Plaintext P**
1: $RoundNo = 1$;	1: $RoundNo = 10$;
2: $AddRoundKey()$;	2: $AddRoundKey()$;
3: **while** $RoundNo \leq 9$ **do**	3: **while** $RoundNo \neq 1$ **do**
4: $SubBytes()$;	4: $InvShiftRows()$;
5: $ShiftRows()$;	5: $InvSubBytes()$;
6: $MixColumns()$;	6: $AddRoundKey()$;
7: $MixColumn\text{-}Plus()$;	7: $InvMixColumns()$;
8: $AddRoundKey()$;	8: $InvMixColumn\text{-}Plus()$;
9: $RoundNo = RoundNo + 1$;	9: $RoundNo = RoundNo - 1$;
10: **end while**	10: **end while**
11: **if** $RoundNo \leq 10$ **then**	11: **if** $RoundNo \leq 1$ **then**
12: $SubBytes()$;	12: $InvShiftRows()$;
13: $ShiftRows()$;	13: $InvSubBytes()$;
14: $AddRoundKey()$;	14: $AddRoundKey()$;
15: **end if**	15: **end if**
16: **end Function**	16: **end Function**

The attacker obtains a pair of ciphertext CT and CT'. These ciphertexts are used to form a set of linear equations [16,17]. Considering the byte inter-relationship after 9th round using $Inverse\ SubBytes\ (ISB)$ with key matrix values (k_1, k_{14}), fault value at $(0,0)^{th}$ position ($\boldsymbol{F_1}$) can be equated with fault value at $(1,3)^{th}$ position $(\boldsymbol{F_2})$ by multiplying with the corresponding MixColumns matrix coefficients. Similarly, the other two equations can be formed with the byte inter-relationship of $\boldsymbol{F_2}$ and $\boldsymbol{F_3}$ at positions $[(1,3)$ and $(2,2)]$ and that of $\boldsymbol{F_4}$ and $\boldsymbol{F_2}$ at positions $[(3,1)$ and $(1,3)]$ (Fig. 1). Thus, the system of equations can be deduced as follows:

$$1 \times [ISB(x_1 + k_1) + ISB(x_1' + k_1)] = 2 \times [ISB(x_{14} + k_{14}) + ISB(x_{14}' + k_{14})].$$

$$1 \times [ISB(x_{14} + k_{14}) + ISB(x_{14}' + k_{14})] = 1 \times [ISB(x_{11} + k_{11}) + ISB(x_{11}' + k_{11})].$$

$$1 \times [ISB(x_8 + k_8) + ISB(x_8' + k_8)] = 3 \times [ISB(x_{14} + k_{14}) + ISB(x_{14}' + k_{14})].$$

Here, $+$ denotes *exclusive-or* operation of two bytes. These equations are used to reduce the exhaustive key-search space of 32 bits out of the key. Initially, an attacker removes all such key pairs that do not satisfy the first equation and the next remaining candidates are used to find k_{11} and k_8 respectively. Average number of candidate keys from the above system of equations are 2^8. In similar way, three different system of equations are formed as described in [16]. Combining all the equations, in total $2^{8*4} = 2^{32}$ candidate keys need to be explored. Here, the assumption is that an attacker has to induce the fault at a known byte position (i.e., $(0,0)^{th}$ byte position of the state matrix). However, the idea of attack can be easily extended when the fault location is completely unknown. Since there are 16 possible positions in AES state matrix, fault can be induced at any of these 16 positions. Thus, total $16*2^{32} = 2^{36}$ keybits have to be exhaustively searched, which can be computed in a modern processor easily. It increases the chance of performing fault attack using less costly methods, like voltage fluctuations and clock glitches.

3 MixColumn-Plus: An Additional Diffusion Layer to AES

Our aim is to strengthen the security of AES against single byte fault attack. As mentioned in the previous section, AES is vulnerable against byte fault attack where a single byte fault in start of 8th round affecting four bytes in a column at the round end. Focusing on the property of byte inter-relationship, we propose a new layer called MixColumn-Plus after AES MixColumns operation without hampering the original AES steps (Fig. 2). Algorithm 1 and Algorithm 2 illustrates the AES algorithm for encryption and decryption with MixColumn-Plus layer. The operation of MixColumn-Plus on the state matrix Y is same as that of the MixColumns operation of AES that is multiplication of MixColumn-Plus matrix X_{enc} with the state matrix Y. Similarly, X_{dec} represents InvMixColumn-Plus matrix for decryption. X_{enc} and X_{dec} matrices are defined as follows:

$$X_{enc} = \begin{pmatrix} 0c & 08 & 0f & 0a \\ 0a & 0c & 08 & 0f \\ 0f & 0a & 0c & 08 \\ 08 & 0f & 0a & 0c \end{pmatrix} \quad X_{dec} = \begin{pmatrix} 00 & 00 & 03 & 02 \\ 02 & 00 & 00 & 03 \\ 03 & 02 & 00 & 00 \\ 00 & 03 & 02 & 00 \end{pmatrix}.$$

Further, the X_{enc} matrix can be broken as follows:

$$X_{enc} = \begin{pmatrix} 01\ 01\ 00\ 01 \\ 01\ 01\ 01\ 00 \\ 00\ 01\ 01\ 01 \\ 01\ 00\ 01\ 01 \end{pmatrix} \times \begin{pmatrix} 02\ 03\ 01\ 01 \\ 01\ 02\ 03\ 01 \\ 01\ 01\ 02\ 03 \\ 03\ 01\ 01\ 02 \end{pmatrix} \times \begin{pmatrix} 05\ 00\ 04\ 00 \\ 00\ 05\ 00\ 04 \\ 04\ 00\ 05\ 00 \\ 00\ 04\ 00\ 05 \end{pmatrix}.$$

$$\implies X_{enc} = \begin{pmatrix} 01\ 01\ 00\ 01 \\ 01\ 01\ 01\ 00 \\ 00\ 01\ 01\ 01 \\ 01\ 00\ 01\ 01 \end{pmatrix} \times \begin{pmatrix} 0e\ 0b\ 0d\ 09 \\ 09\ 0e\ 0b\ 0d \\ 0d\ 09\ 0e\ 0b \\ 0b\ 0d\ 09\ 0e \end{pmatrix}.$$

In similar way, the X_{dec} matrix can be broken as follows:

$$\implies X_{dec} = \begin{pmatrix} 01\ 01\ 00\ 01 \\ 01\ 01\ 01\ 00 \\ 00\ 01\ 01\ 01 \\ 01\ 00\ 01\ 01 \end{pmatrix} \times \begin{pmatrix} 02\ 03\ 01\ 01 \\ 01\ 02\ 03\ 01 \\ 01\ 01\ 02\ 03 \\ 03\ 01\ 01\ 02 \end{pmatrix}.$$

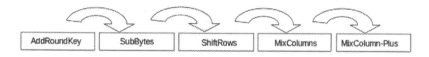

AddRoundKey   SubBytes   ShiftRows   MixColumns   MixColumn-Plus

Fig. 2. MixColumn-Plus layer added in AES-128 round

The consequence is that MixColumn-Plus and InvMixColumn-Plus both operations can be implemented as a series of simple matrix multiplication steps as shown earlier in X_{enc} and X_{dec}. Also, coefficients of the two matrices in both equations are same as the *MixColumns* and *InvMixColumns* matrix. Now, we analyze the security of AES against single byte fault attack with the introduction of MixColumn-Plus layer. Let the single byte fault, denoted as $\boldsymbol{F}$, in the $(i, j)^{th}$ byte of state matrix be introduced (where $i = 0$ and $j = 0$) at the start of 8th round MixColumns. Due to the MixColumns matrix multiplication, fault spreads into the entire i^{th} column of the matrix (where $i = 0$), as shown below:

MixColumns $\rightarrow$

$$\begin{pmatrix} 02\ 03\ 01\ 01 \\ 01\ 02\ 03\ 01 \\ 01\ 01\ 02\ 03 \\ 03\ 01\ 01\ 02 \end{pmatrix} \times \begin{pmatrix} F\ x_5\ x_9\ x_{13} \\ x_2\ x_6\ x_{10}\ x_{14} \\ x_3\ x_7\ x_{11}\ x_{15} \\ x_4\ x_8\ x_{12}\ x_{16} \end{pmatrix} = \begin{pmatrix} 2 \times F_1\ x_5''\ x_9''\ x_{13}'' \\ F_2\ x_6''\ x''_{10}\ x_{14}'' \\ F_3\ x_7''\ x_{11}''\ x_{15}'' \\ 3 \times F_4\ x_8''\ x_{12}''\ x_{16}'' \end{pmatrix}.$$

One step of multiplication is written as follows:

$$\implies (02\ 03\ 01\ 01) \times \begin{pmatrix} F \\ x_2 \\ x_3 \\ x_4 \end{pmatrix} = \left(2 \times F_1 + 3 \times x_2 + x_3 + x_4\right) = \left(2 \times F_1 + x_1''\right).$$

As expression $\left(2 \times F_1 + x_1''\right)$ contains a faulty byte with some value x_1'', we denote the whole thing as faulty byte $2 \times F_1$. Similar convention is used for the other faulty bytes.

The MixColumn-Plus matrix X_{enc} is multiplied with the state matrix Y which nullifies the fault in the $(i,j)^{th}$ byte (where $i = 2$ and $j = 0$), i.e., x_3'. So, i^{th} column of the state matrix (where $i = 0$) contains only three faults:

MixColumn-Plus $\rightarrow$

$$\begin{pmatrix} 0c\ 08\ 0f\ 0a \\ 0a\ 0c\ 08\ 0f \\ 0f\ 0a\ 0c\ 08 \\ 08\ 0f\ 0a\ 0c \end{pmatrix} \times \begin{pmatrix} 2 \times F_1 & x_5'' & x_9'' & x_{13}'' \\ F_2 & x_6'' & x_{10}'' & x_{14}'' \\ F_3 & x_7'' & x_{11}'' & x_{15}'' \\ 3 \times F_4 & x_8'' & x_{12}'' & x_{16}'' \end{pmatrix} = \begin{pmatrix} F_1 & x_5' & x_9' & x_{13}' \\ F_2 & x_6' & x_{10}' & x_{14}' \\ x_3' & x_7' & x_{11}' & x_{15}' \\ F_4 & x_8' & x_{12}' & x_{16}' \end{pmatrix}.$$

Let us assume that F_1 denotes the fault in $(0,0)^{th}$ position of resultant state matrix, F_2 denotes the fault in $(1,0)^{th}$ position of resultant state matrix and F_4 denotes the fault in $(3,0)^{th}$ position of resultant state matrix and NF denotes no fault, i.e., fault is not present into that cell. Now, after AddRoundKey, Sub-Bytes, and ShiftRows of the 9th round, the resultant state matrix contains fault F_1, F_2, and F_4 at $(0,0)^{th}$, $(1,3)^{th}$ and $(3,2)^{th}$ locations respectively. The next MixColumns along with MixColumn-Plus operation spreads the fault into six bytes instead of remaining twelve bytes in the earlier case. Byte inter-relationship of the state matrix is defined below:

$$\begin{pmatrix} F_1 & x_5' & x_9' & x_{13}' \\ x_6' & x_{10}' & x_{14}' & F_2 \\ x_{11}' & x_{15}' & x_3' & x_7' \\ x_{16}' & F_4 & x_8' & x_{12}' \end{pmatrix} \implies \begin{pmatrix} F_1 & F_4 & NF & F_2 \\ F_1 & NF & NF & F_2 \\ NF & F_4 & NF & F_2 \\ F_1 & F_1 & NF & NF \end{pmatrix}.$$

Here, 1st, 2nd and 4th columns of the state matrix contain the fault only. So, combining the MixColumns and MixColumn-Plus layer, faults are confined to present in three columns only. Internal working strategy of the 8th round MixColumns and MixColumn-Plus operations are described below:

$$\begin{pmatrix} 0c\ 08\ 0f\ 0a \\ 0a\ 0c\ 08\ 0f \\ 0f\ 0a\ 0c\ 08 \\ 08\ 0f\ 0a\ 0c \end{pmatrix} \times \begin{pmatrix} 02\ 03\ 01\ 01 \\ 01\ 02\ 03\ 01 \\ 01\ 01\ 02\ 03 \\ 03\ 01\ 01\ 02 \end{pmatrix} \times \begin{pmatrix} F & x_5 & x_9 & x_{13} \\ x_2 & x_6 & x_{10} & x_{14} \\ x_3 & x_7 & x_{11} & x_{15} \\ x_4 & x_8 & x_{12} & x_{16} \end{pmatrix} = \begin{pmatrix} F_1 & x_5' & x_9' & x_{13}' \\ F_2 & x_6' & x_{10}' & x_{14}' \\ x_3' & x_7' & x_{11}' & x_{15}' \\ F_4 & x_8' & x_{12}' & x_{16}' \end{pmatrix}.$$

$$\implies \begin{pmatrix} 01\ 01\ 00\ 01 \\ 01\ 01\ 01\ 00 \\ 00\ 01\ 01\ 01 \\ 01\ 00\ 01\ 01 \end{pmatrix} \times \begin{pmatrix} F & x_5 & x_9 & x_{13} \\ x_2 & x_6 & x_{10} & x_{14} \\ x_3 & x_7 & x_{11} & x_{15} \\ x_4 & x_8 & x_{12} & x_{16} \end{pmatrix} = \begin{pmatrix} F_1 & x_5' & x_9' & x_{13}' \\ F_2 & x_6' & x_{10}' & x_{14}' \\ x_3' & x_7' & x_{11}' & x_{15}' \\ F_4 & x_8' & x_{12}' & x_{16}' \end{pmatrix}.$$

In the below matrix, 01 implies $0x01$, i.e., 1 in binary, 00 implies $0x00$, i.e., 0 in binary. It is assumed that

$$M3 = \begin{pmatrix} 01 \ 01 \ 00 \ 01 \\ 01 \ 01 \ 01 \ 00 \\ 00 \ 01 \ 01 \ 01 \\ 01 \ 00 \ 01 \ 01 \end{pmatrix}.$$

It is evident from the above analysis that combination of the MixColumns and MixColumn-Plus can be treated as same operation if it would be operated by $M3$. So, instead of introducing MixColumn-Plus, replacing the MixColumns transformation of AES and multiplying state matrix with $M3$ can also strengthen against single byte fault attack. Presence of 0 in each column of $M3$ prevents fault propagation in one byte out of four in a column. Here, $M3$ is a circulant, involutive binary matrix with branch number 4. Such binary involutive matrix helps to achieve InvMixColumn-Plus lightweight.

4 Strengthening AES with MixColumn-Plus

This section analyses the strength of AES after addition of MixColumn-plus. Let us consider the 8th round of original AES in Fig. 1. A single byte fault is injected in the 1st byte of state matrix. During the MixColumns, fault spreads into the entire 1st column of the state matrix and ShiftRow propagates the fault into every column [16]. Now, if we consider the byte inter-relationship after 9th round using *Inverse SubBytes* (ISB) with fault value F_1 at $(0,0)^{th}$ position, key matrix values (k_1, k_{14}) can be equated with fault value F_2 at $(1,3)^{th}$ position by multiplying with the corresponding MixColumns matrix coefficients. In similar way, using byte inter-relationship of F_2 ($(1,3)^{th}$ position) and F_3 ($(2,2)^{th}$ position), an equation can be formed and same for F_4 ($(3,1)^{th}$ position) and F_2 ($(1,3)^{th}$ position) as illustrated in Fig. 1. So, the system of equations can be deduced as follows:

$$1 \times [ISB(x_1 + k_1) + ISB(x_1' + k_1)] = 2 \times [ISB(x_{14} + k_{14}) + ISB(x_{14}' + k_{14})].$$

$$1 \times [ISB(x_{14} + k_{14}) + ISB(x_{14}' + k_{14})] = 1 \times [ISB(x_{11} + k_{11}) + ISB(x_{11}' + k_{11})].$$

$$1 \times [ISB(x_8 + k_8) + ISB(x_8' + k_8)] = 3 \times [ISB(x_{14} + k_{14}) + ISB(x_{14}' + k_{14})].$$

An attacker uses above system of equations to reduce the solution space for the key bytes $(k_1, k_{14}, k_{11}, k_8)$. Initially, the key values that do not satisfy the first equation are removed, and the remaining values are used to find k_{11} and k_8 respectively. The average size of the reduced key space per 32 bits is 2^8. Similarly, three different system of equations are formed for the remaining 96 bits. After analysing the four different system of equations [16], an attacker ends up with exhaustive search space of 2^{32}.

Adding a new layer in AES reduces the number of linear equations. As the less number of equations are formed, the attack complexity of [16] is increased. In the subsequent section, we analyze the same equation formation by combining the MixColumns and MixColumn-Plus layer.

4.1   Analysis of MixColumn-Plus

With MixColumn-Plus layer, three faults F_1, F_2 and F_4 are present in $(0,0)^{th}$, $(1,3)^{th}$, $(3,1)^{th}$ locations (i.e., unlike the four faulty bytes in the MixColumns layer). So, an attacker fails to form one linear equation to find out the keys $(k_1, k_{14}, k_{11}, k_8)$:

$$1 \times [ISB(x_1 + k_1) + ISB(x_1' + k_1)] = 1 \times [ISB(x_{14} + k_{14}) + ISB(x_{14}' + k_{14})].$$

$$1 \times [ISB(x_{14} + k_{14}) + ISB(x_{14}' + k_{14})] = \boldsymbol{NF} \times [ISB(x_{11} + k_{11}) + ISB(x_{11}' + k_{11})].$$

$$1 \times [ISB(x_8 + k_8) + ISB(x_8' + k_8)] = 1 \times [ISB(x_{14} + k_{14}) + ISB(x_{14}' + k_{14})].$$

$\boldsymbol{NF}$ denotes no-fault into the cell. In the above system of equations, 2nd equation formation is impossible since fault propagation is not present. Hence, an attacker uses brute-force search to get the key byte k_{11}. So, the remaining two equations generate 160 keys approximately after pruning, i.e., $\approx 2^8$. In total, $2^8 \times 2^8 \approx 2^{16}$ candidate keys are generated.

To find the keys (k_9, k_6, k_3, k_{16}), an attacker needs to apply brute-force technique due to no fault propagation into 2nd column as defined in the earlier section. Hence, no key inter-relationships are formed. So, an attacker ends up with 2^{32} candidate keys:

$$\boldsymbol{NF} \times [(ISB(x_3 + k_3) + ISB(x_3' + k_3)] = \boldsymbol{NF} \times [ISB(x_9 + k_9) + ISB(x_9' + k_9)].$$

$$\boldsymbol{NF} \times [(ISB(x_9 + k_9) + ISB(x_9' + k_9)] = \boldsymbol{NF} \times [ISB(x_{16} + k_{16}) + ISB(x_{16}' + k_{16})].$$

$$\boldsymbol{NF} \times [ISB(x_6 + k_6) + ISB(x_6' + k_6)] = \boldsymbol{NF} \times [ISB(x_9 + k_9) + ISB(x_9' + k_9)].$$

Out of the six equations, only four are possible due to the presence of zero in the internally generated matrix for which fault spreads only in three bytes out of four bytes in a column. Now in order to obtain $(k_5, k_2, k_{15}, k_{12})$, an attacker uses the following equations:

$$1 \times [ISB(x_{12} + k_{12}) + ISB(x_{12}' + k_{12})] = 1 \times [ISB(x_5 + k_5) + ISB(x_5' + k_5)].$$

$$1 \times [ISB(x_5 + k_5) + ISB(x_5' + k_5)] = \boldsymbol{NF} \times [ISB(x_2 + k_2) + ISB(x_2' + k_2)].$$

$$1 \times [ISB(x_{15} + k_{15}) + ISB(x_{15}' + k_{15})] = 1 \times [ISB(x_5 + k_5) + ISB(x_5' + k_5)].$$

In order to obtain $(k_{13}, k_{10}, k_7, k_4)$, an attacker uses the following equations:

$$1 \times [ISB(x_{10} + k_{10}) + ISB(x_{10}' + k_{10})] = 1 \times [ISB(x_7 + k_7) + ISB(x_7' + k_7)].$$

$$1 \times [ISB(x_7 + k_7) + ISB(x_7' + k_7)] = \boldsymbol{NF} \times [ISB(x_4 + k_4) + ISB(x_4' + k_4)].$$

$$1 \times [ISB(x_{13} + k_{13}) + ISB(x_{13}' + k_{13})] = 1 \times [ISB(x_7 + k_7) + ISB(x_7' + k_7)].$$

From above six equations 2^{32} possible keys are generated. In the next section, we show that how MixColumn-Plus reduces DFA attack by increasing the exhaustive key-search space.

4.2   Results

As an attacker is able to form less number of equations, some candidate keys are impossible to generate. In that case, brute-force technique has to use with no other option. Let us consider the keys (k_9, k_6, k_3, k_{16}). In the above analysis, NF is present in their coefficient. Hence, 32 bits of the AES key has to be found with 2^{32} possible ways. Now, for the keys $(k_1, k_{14}, k_{11}, k_8)$, $(k_5, k_2, k_{15}, k_{12})$ and $(k_{13}, k_{10}, k_7, k_4)$ six equations are possible in total compared to nine as described in the original work. Since, one equation is absent from each of the three key sets, brute-force search is required for the 8 bits out 32 keybits. The remaining 24 bits of $(k_1, k_{14}, k_{11}, k_8)$ can be found out from the above two equations with an exhaustive search of 2^8. Thus, 2^{16} candidate keys are generated for $(k_1, k_{14}, k_{11}, k_8)$ in total and such three key sets are present. Combining three different key sets $(k_1, k_{14}, k_{11}, k_8)$, $(k_5, k_2, k_{15}, k_{12})$ and $(k_{13}, k_{10}, k_7, k_4)$, an attacker has to search $2^{16} \times 2^{16} \times 2^{16} \approx 2^{48}$ candidate keys exhaustively. For 128 bit AES key, the attacker has to perform exhaustive search of $2^{48} \times 2^{32} \approx 2^{80}$ if fault location is known earlier. When the exact fault location is not known to the attacker, all 16 possible positions of the state matrix has to be explored. In this scenario, an attacker has to search $16 \times 2^{80} \approx 2^{84}$ candidate keys exhaustively.

Security Against other DFA Attacks. With MixColumn-Plus layer, an attacker has to search 2^{82} candidate keys compared to 2^{34} in earlier case [17]. Similarly, complexity of the attack [21] is increased to 2^{84} from 2^8 as no inter-key relations are formed between 8th and 9th round of the MixColumns. Piret et al. [6] show that with an exhaustive search of 2^{40} candidate keys, AES-128 cryptosystem can be broken easily by inducing a single fault. Their attack is strengthened to 2^{72} after applying MixColumn-Plus. The first DFA attack on AES is shown by Giraud et al. [10] by which the secret key can be retrieved with less than 250 ciphertexts. Now, with MixColumn-Plus layer, an attacker needs more than 250 ciphertexts to carry out the previous attack [10]. Our approach is also applicable in case of AES-192 and AES-256. Such layer helps to increase the exhaustive search space to 2^{72} or more to find the desired key. In Table 1a, we give a comparison of the various DFA attacks on AES with MixColumn-Plus layer.

Avalanche Effect. In Table 1b and Table 1c, we give the results of avalanche effect in original AES and AES with MixColumn-Plus layer. For a single bit change in the plaintext, almost 53 to 72 bits are changed in the ciphertext in case of AES with MixColumn-Plus whereas in the original AES 60 or more bits are changed for the same input and key (Table 1b and Table 1c). Three different plaintexts are taken and a single bit is changed at a time of these plaintexts. Corresponding ciphertexts are given in the next column for a fixed key $K=$ {0f 15 71 c9 47 d9 e8 59 0c b7 ad d6 af 7f 67 98}.

Applications in Practical Scenario. Unfortunately, security does not come for free and even considering state-of-the-art various AES countermeasures incur additional expenses. The proposed MixColumn-Plus layer can be broken into a binary matrix followed by AES InvMixColumns matrix. Since the hardware implementation of AES InvMixColumns is already available in the market, we need to estimate the extra cost of adding the binary matrix with that. Similarly, InvMixColumn-Plus matrix can be broken into a binary matrix followed by AES MixColumns matrix. With this extra cost of adding a binary matrix with AES, the effort of an adversary to perform DFA attack increases 2^{76} *times*, i.e., 2^8 to 2^{84}. By deploying such diffusion layer in Internet of things (IoT) and embedded system, the security of the system against DFA is increased. In software platforms like OpenSSL crypto library (libcrypto), Libgcrypt, Crypto++, cryptlib etc., such additional layer can be incorporated to make the cipher less susceptible against DFA attacks. Our further research work is to analyze the energy costs, delays in hardware platform due to additional overhead of an extra diffusion layer.

5 Security Analysis

To analyze the security of our method, we refer to the classical IND-CPA game. First, we compare ciphertext produced by our algorithm (with MixColumn-Plus layer) with respect to *pseudorandom permutation* (PRP) and secondly, referring to the classical IND-CPA security, we introduce a term called $\boldsymbol{IND_{sf}}$-$\boldsymbol{CPA}$ security to take into account that an adversary can inject a single byte fault. The idea behind $\boldsymbol{IND_{sf}}$-$\boldsymbol{CPA}$ security is to restrict fault propagation by some randomized function.

Let $Perm(D)$ denotes the set of all permutations on D. Let $F : K \times D \to R$ be a family of functions from D to R indexed by key K. We use $F(K, D)$ as a family of functions, i.e., block cipher. If $D = R$ then $F_k(.)$ is a permutation on D for each $k \in K$. Suppose $E : K \times D \to D$ is a family of functions. If A is a computationally bounded adversary with oracle access, we denote the PRP advantage of A in attacking $E_k(.)$ as follows:

$$Adv_{E_k}^{prp}(A) = Pr[k \xleftarrow{\$} K : A^{E_k(.)} = 1] - Pr[g \xleftarrow{\$} Perm(D) : A^{g(.)} = 1].$$

Now, if an adversary A makes query at most q number of times to its encryption oracle with maximum time t then

$$Adv_{E_k}^{prp}(q, t) = \max_{A}\{Adv_{E_k}^{prp}(A)\}.$$

Ciphertext produced by original AES is a PRP and above advantage denote maximum PRP security of AES with respect to the adversary A. Addition of a new layer in AES reduces branch number to 4. So, we denote ciphertext produced by our algorithm as *little weak pseudorandom permutation* (*lwprp*). In our case, if A is a computationally bounded adversary with oracle access, we denote the *lwprp* advantage of A in attacking $E_k^{sf}(.,.)$ as follows:

$$Adv_{E_k^{sf}}^{lwprp}(A) = Pr[k \xleftarrow{\$} K : A^{E_k^{sf}(.,.)} = 1] - Pr[g \xleftarrow{\$} Perm(D) : A^{g(.)} = 1].$$

Table 1. Comparison of AES with MixColumn-Plus and traditional AES against DFA and Avalanche Effect.

Fault Attack Type	AES version	Fault Model	Fault Injection Round	Traditional AES Candidate keys	AES with MixColumn-Plus Candidate keys
Single byte without improvement [16]	AES-128	1 byte fault	Before 8th or 9th MixColumns	2^{80}	2^{101}
Single byte with improvement [16]	AES-128	1 byte fault	Before 8th or 9th MixColumns	2^{36}	2^{84}
Diagonal attack [17]	AES-128	1 random faulty diagonal	Before 8th SubBytes	2^{34}	2^{82}
DFA Against SPN as application to AES [6]	AES-128	Byte fault	Before 8th SubBytes or 9th SubBytes	2^{40}	2^{72} or more
DFA on AES using a single fault [21]	AES-128	1 byte fault	Before 8th or 9th MixColumns	2^{8}	2^{84}
DFA against AES-192 and AES-256 with minimal faults [19]	AES-192	Byte fault	Before 8th or 9th MixColumns	2^{32}, 2^{8}	2^{72}, 2^{72} or more
DFA against AES-192 and AES-256 with minimal faults [19]	AES-256	Byte fault	Before 8th or 9th MixColumns	2^{32}	2^{72} or more

(a) Comparison of AES with MixColumn-Plus and traditional AES against DFA

128 bit plaintext	Affected bit position in ciphertext	128 bit ciphertext
01 23 45 67 99 ab cd ef fe dc ba 98 76 54 32 10	Original plaintext	97 bf 59 02 88 da ba e0 a3 b8 3a 01 31 88 31 eb
02 23 45 67 99 ab cd ef fe dc ba 98 76 54 32 10	8th bit from MSB	fa af 79 1a 6b ba 7c 57 19 41 b6 05 06 56 7a b3
01 23 45 66 99 ab cd ef fe dc ba 98 76 54 32 10	32th bit from MSB	a3 1b d1 3d 0f 93 b3 97 ca f6 48 79 4b 38 cc 38
01 23 45 67 95 ab cd ef fe dc ba 98 76 54 32 10	40th bit from MSB	31 35 1f 02 2a 3b 8c 20 4b 82 58 96 51 e6 24 fd
01 00 00 00 00 03 00 00 00 00 05 00 00 00 00 07	Original plaintext	7d cb 63 11 8f 38 8a 59 6f 50 a0 f9 2e 17 1c c6
01 00 01 00 00 03 00 00 00 00 05 00 00 00 00 07	24th bit from MSB	bd 01 78 f7 cb 92 80 01 ef 7e be 2b 3d bc 3f df
01 02 11 44 06 87 21 00 42 00 05 48 98 22 90 07	Original plaintext	bb d1 b9 1c af ca 1e f4 08 c9 c7 f1 32 ac 57 43
01 03 11 44 06 87 21 00 42 00 05 48 98 22 90 07	16th bit from MSB	72 7e 0f fc ce 05 f5 5c 65 3e 3e db 52 ce a6 a2

(b) Avalanche Effect on AES with MixColumn-Plus layer

128 bit plaintext	Affected bit position in ciphertext	128 bit ciphertext
01 23 45 67 99 ab cd ef fe dc ba 98 76 54 32 10	Original plaintext	1b d6 c2 f8 aa b0 6c 72 ae b5 8a b6 a9 d7 c9 1f
02 23 45 67 99 ab cd ef fe dc ba 98 76 54 32 10	8th bit from MSB	b4 1a 80 bf 98 6b 7a a6 59 0b c9 66 81 dc 20 88
01 23 45 66 99 ab cd ef fe dc ba 98 76 54 32 10	32th bit from MSB	c2 b1 15 66 09 e1 35 c0 c2 92 9b 91 48 82 74 86
01 23 45 67 95 ab cd ef fe dc ba 98 76 54 32 10	40th bit from MSB	7c 79 ea 3f e5 12 25 eb e6 ec 3f c8 54 20 6d 2c
01 00 00 00 00 03 00 00 00 00 05 00 00 00 00 07	Original plaintext	42 21 24 a0 98 c6 f5 dc e6 2d 08 cf b1 c3 9b 73
01 00 01 00 00 03 00 00 00 00 05 00 00 00 00 07	24th bit from MSB	0f 12 92 ee 33 e2 e1 3f c4 32 f6 01 b5 a1 00 2b
01 02 11 44 06 87 21 00 42 00 05 48 98 22 90 07	Original plaintext	d9 89 85 18 13 6a e6 05 34 22 88 dd 12 cf 68 92
01 03 11 44 06 87 21 00 42 00 05 48 98 22 90 07	16th bit from MSB	8d 98 b5 fc 42 b9 17 a2 f9 89 62 be cd 09 5b b6

(c) Avalanche Effect on original AES

The above advantage is same as PRP except that our encryption scheme $E_k^{sf}(.,.)$ is a little weak due to the reduction of branch number. If an adversary A makes query at most q number of times to its encryption oracle with maximum time t then

$$Adv_{E_k^{sf}}^{lwprp}(q,t) = \max_A \{Adv_{E_k^{sf}}^{lwprp}(A)\}.$$

Let $\Pi = (K, E, D)$ be an $IND\text{-}CPA$ secure symmetric encryption scheme $(\pi = AES)$ with key space K, message space P, ciphertext space CT and security parameter n. The encryption oracle $E_k(.)$ on input $p \in P$, $k \in K$ returns $E_k(p) \in CT$. The faulty encryption oracle $E_k^{sf}(.,.)$ takes input $p \in P$, $k \in K$ and $f \in F$, where f is the fault parameter determined by fault model and it returns $E_k^{sf}(p, f) \in CT$ and $f \in F$ (i.e., $E_k^{sf}(.,.)$ denotes the encryption scheme with new functional layer where a single byte fault is present). We now formally define $IND_{sf}\text{-}CPA$ as follows:

Game 1. $IND_{sf}\text{-}CPA(A, \Pi)$

procedure Initialization()
$\quad k \xleftarrow{\$} K \qquad\qquad\qquad\qquad \Rightarrow$ chosen by encryption oracle
$\quad \{p^0, p^1\} \xleftarrow{\$} P \qquad\qquad\qquad \Rightarrow$ chosen by an adversary
$\quad b \xleftarrow{\$} \{0, 1\} \qquad\qquad\qquad\quad \Rightarrow$ chosen by encryption oracle
$\quad x = E_k(p^b)$
$\quad success = 0$
end procedure

procedure $Adv(x, E_k(.), E_k^{sf}(.,.))$
$\quad$ **for** $i = 1$ to $q \qquad\qquad\qquad \Rightarrow q$ no of oracle queries by A
$\qquad x_i^{0'} \leftarrow E_k^{sf}(p^0, f)$
$\qquad x_i^{1'} \leftarrow E_k^{sf}(p^1, f)$
$\quad$ **end for**
$\quad$ **return** $b' \xleftarrow{\$} \{0, 1\} \quad \Rightarrow$ using $(x, x_i^{0'}, x_i^{1'})$ an adversary guesses b'
end procedure

procedure Finalize()
$\quad$ **if** $b' = b$ **then**
$\qquad success = 1$
$\quad$ **endif**
$\quad$ **return** $success$
end procedure

With respect to $IND_{sf}\text{-}CPA$ game, an adversary wins the game if he correctly guesses the value of b. Let A be the computationally bounded adversary who can query at most q number of times with maximum time t.

$$Adv_{\Pi}^{IND_{sf}-CPA}(A) = [Pr[A^{E_k(p^0),E_k^{sf}(.,.)} = 1] - Pr[A^{E_k(p^1),E_k^{sf}(.,.)} = 1]].$$

$$Adv_{\Pi}^{IND_{sf}-CPA}(q,t) = \max_{A}\{Adv_{\Pi}^{IND_{sf}-CPA}(A)\}.$$

Thus, for a symmetric encryption scheme Π to be $IND_{sf}\text{-}CPA$ secure $Adv_{\Pi}^{IND_{sf}\ CPA}(A)$ must be upper bounded by a negligible function ϵ of security parameter n.

Definition 1. *A Symmetric Encryption scheme Π is said to be $IND_{sf}\text{-}CPA$ secure if there exists a computationally bounded adversary A who have capability to induce a single byte fault in $E_k^{sf}(.,.)$ and observe the outputs, there exists a negligible function ϵ such that*
$$\max_{A} [\ Pr[A^{E_k(p^0),E_k^{sf}(.,.)} = 1]\ -\ Pr[A^{E_k(p^1),E_k^{sf}(.,.)} = 1]] \le \epsilon(n).$$

From definition it is clear that $IND_{sf}\text{-}CPA \Rightarrow IND\text{-}CPA$ but converse may not be true. Next, we achieve $IND_{sf}\text{-}CPA$ from $IND\text{-}CPA$ by reducing $Adv_{\Pi}^{IND_{sf}-CPA}(A)$ to $Adv_{\Pi}^{IND-CPA}(A)$, i.e., $IND\text{-}CPA \Rightarrow IND_{sf}\text{-}CPA$.

Theorem 1. *An $IND\text{-}CPA$ secure symmetric encryption scheme π is also $IND_{sf}\text{-}CPA$ secure if there exists a randomized transformation function $\mathcal{N}$ such that $E_k^{sf}(.,.) \xrightarrow{\mathcal{N}} \mathcal{PR}(.,.)$, where oracle $\mathcal{PR}(.,.)$ returns $|E_k^{sf}(.,.)|$ random bits.*

Proof. Let A be a computationally bounded adversary and it is shown that how we reduce $Adv_{\Pi}^{IND_{sf}-CPA}(A)$ to $Adv_{\Pi}^{IND-CPA}(A)$ to achieve $IND_{sf}\text{-}CPA$ security from $IND\text{-}CPA$ security using $\mathcal{N}$.

$Adv_{\Pi}^{IND_{sf}-CPA}(A)$
$= [\ Pr[A^{E_k(p^0),E_k^{sf}(.,.)} = 1] - Pr[A^{E_k(p^1),E_k^{sf}(.,.)} = 1]]$
$= [\ Pr[A^{E_k(p^0),\mathcal{PR}(.,.)} = 1] - Pr[A^{E_k(p^1),\mathcal{PR}(.,.)} = 1]]$
- $E_k^{sf}(.,.)$ transforms to $\mathcal{PR}(.,.)$ through $\mathcal{N}$, i.e., $E_k^{sf}(.,.) \xrightarrow{\mathcal{N}} \mathcal{PR}(.,.)$ since $E_k^{sf}(.,.)$ returns pseudorandom bits $\mathcal{PR}(.,.)$ through $\mathcal{N}$
$= [\ Pr[A^{E_k(p^0)} = 1] - Pr[A^{E_k(p^1)} = 1]]$
- $A^{E_k(.),\mathcal{PR}(.,.)} \Longleftrightarrow A^{E_k(.)}$
$= Adv_{\Pi}^{IND-CPA}(A) \le \epsilon(n).$

With a new transformation function $\mathcal{N}$ added in AES called MixColumn-Plus layer, algorithm still achieves $IND\text{-}CPA$ security. Applicability of our theorem is that if an attacker injects a single byte fault in $E_k^{sf}(.,.)$, security against the attack is actually strengthened by MixColumn-Plus layer.

6   Conclusion

In this work, we enhance the security of AES against single byte fault attack by adding an extra diffusion layer. It increases the effort of an attacker that has to spend to retrieve a key by leveraging on single byte differential fault attack. Exhaustive key-search space is increased to 2^{84} compared to the earlier case of 2^8. Keeping original AES subfunctions intact in each round, an additional Mix-Columns transformation layer is added, namely the MixColumn-Plus, with the aim of reducing the number of equations an adversary can write observing a faulty plaintext and its correct counterpart. Such layer makes fault attack too expensive to carry out in hardware or software platforms. Many other block ciphers are not secured against fault attacks based on algebraic equation formation. Further research can be pursued on the applicability of our approach to enhance the security of those ciphers.

References

1. Biham, E., Shamir, A.: Differential fault analysis of secret key cryptosystems. In: Kaliski, B.S. (ed.) CRYPTO 1997. LNCS, vol. 1294, pp. 513–525. Springer, Heidelberg (1997). https://doi.org/10.1007/BFb0052259
2. Boneh, D., DeMillo, R.A., Lipton, R.J.: On the importance of checking cryptographic protocols for faults. In: Fumy, W. (ed.) EUROCRYPT 1997. LNCS, vol. 1233, pp. 37–51. Springer, Heidelberg (1997). https://doi.org/10.1007/3-540-69053-0_4
3. Barreto, P.S.L.M., Rijmen, V.: The Khazad legacy-level block cipher. Primitive submitted to NESSIE, September 2000
4. Joan, D., Vincent, R.: The Design of Rijndael. Springer, Heidelberg (2002). https://doi.org/10.1007/978-3-662-04722-4
5. Skorobogatov, S.P., Anderson, R.J.: Optical fault induction attacks. In: Kaliski, B.S., Koç, K., Paar, C. (eds.) CHES 2002. LNCS, vol. 2523, pp. 2–12. Springer, Heidelberg (2003). https://doi.org/10.1007/3-540-36400-5_2
6. Piret, G., Quisquater, J.-J.: A differential fault attack technique against SPN structures, with application to the AES and KHAZAD. In: Walter, C.D., Koç, Ç.K., Paar, C. (eds.) CHES 2003. LNCS, vol. 2779, pp. 77–88. Springer, Heidelberg (2003). https://doi.org/10.1007/978-3-540-45238-6_7
7. Golić, J.D., Tymen, C.: Multiplicative masking and power analysis of AES. In: Kaliski, B.S., Koç, K., Paar, C. (eds.) CHES 2002. LNCS, vol. 2523, pp. 198–212. Springer, Heidelberg (2003). https://doi.org/10.1007/3-540-36400-5_16
8. Blömer, J., Seifert, J.-P.: Fault based cryptanalysis of the advanced encryption standard (AES). In: Wright, R.N. (ed.) FC 2003. LNCS, vol. 2742, pp. 162–181. Springer, Heidelberg (2003). https://doi.org/10.1007/978-3-540-45126-6_12
9. Dusart, P., Letourneux, G., Vivolo, O.: Differential fault analysis on A.E.S. In: Zhou, J., Yung, M., Han, Y. (eds.) ACNS 2003. LNCS, vol. 2846, pp. 293–306. Springer, Heidelberg (2003). https://doi.org/10.1007/978-3-540-45203-4_23
10. Giraud, C.: DFA on AES. In: Dobbertin, H., Rijmen, V., Sowa, A. (eds.) AES 2004. LNCS, vol. 3373, pp. 27–41. Springer, Heidelberg (2005). https://doi.org/10.1007/11506447_4

11. Moradi, A., Shalmani, M.T.M., Salmasizadeh, M.: A generalized method of differential fault attack against AES cryptosystem. In: Goubin, L., Matsui, M. (eds.) CHES 2006. LNCS, vol. 4249, pp. 91–100. Springer, Heidelberg (2006). https://doi.org/10.1007/11894063_8

12. Herbst, C., Oswald, E., Mangard, S.: An AES smart card implementation resistant to power analysis attacks. In: Zhou, J., Yung, M., Bao, F. (eds.) ACNS 2006. LNCS, vol. 3989, pp. 239–252. Springer, Heidelberg (2006). https://doi.org/10.1007/11767480_16

13. Bar-El, H., Choukri, H., Naccache, D., Tunstall, M., Whelan, C.: The sorcerer's apprentice guide to fault attacks. Proc. IEEE **94**(2), 370–382 (2006)

14. Schramm, K., Paar, C.: Higher order masking of the AES. In: Pointcheval, D. (ed.) CT-RSA 2006. LNCS, vol. 3860, pp. 208–225. Springer, Heidelberg (2006). https://doi.org/10.1007/11605805_14

15. Bogdanov, A., et al.: PRESENT: an ultra-lightweight block cipher. In: Paillier, P., Verbauwhede, I. (eds.) CHES 2007. LNCS, vol. 4727, pp. 450–466. Springer, Heidelberg (2007). https://doi.org/10.1007/978-3-540-74735-2_31

16. Mukhopadhyay, D.: An improved fault based attack of the advanced encryption standard. In: Preneel, B. (ed.) AFRICACRYPT 2009. LNCS, vol. 5580, pp. 421–434. Springer, Heidelberg (2009). https://doi.org/10.1007/978-3-642-02384-2_26

17. Saha, D., Mukhopadhyay, D., RoyChowdhury, D.: A diagonal fault attack on the advanced encryption standard. Cryptology ePrint Archive, Report 2009/581 (2009)

18. Medwed, M., Standaert, F.-X., Großschädl, J., Regazzoni, F.: Fresh re-keying: security against side-channel and fault attacks for low-cost devices. In: Bernstein, D.J., Lange, T. (eds.) AFRICACRYPT 2010. LNCS, vol. 6055, pp. 279–296. Springer, Heidelberg (2010). https://doi.org/10.1007/978-3-642-12678-9_17

19. Kim, C.H.: Differential fault analysis against AES-192 and AES-256 with minimal faults. In: 2010 Workshop on Fault Diagnosis and Tolerance in Cryptography (FDTC), pp. 3–9. IEEE (2010)

20. Rivain, M., Prouff, E.: Provably secure higher-order masking of AES. In: Mangard, S., Standaert, F.-X. (eds.) CHES 2010. LNCS, vol. 6225, pp. 413–427. Springer, Heidelberg (2010). https://doi.org/10.1007/978-3-642-15031-9_28

21. Tunstall, M., Mukhopadhyay, D., Ali, S.: Differential fault analysis of the advanced encryption standard using a single fault. In: Ardagna, C.A., Zhou, J. (eds.) WISTP 2011. LNCS, vol. 6633, pp. 224–233. Springer, Heidelberg (2011). https://doi.org/10.1007/978-3-642-21040-2_15

22. Van Woudenberg, J., Witteman, M., Menarini, F.: Practical optical fault injection on secure microcontrollers. In: 2011 Workshop on Fault Diagnosis and Tolerance in Cryptography (FDTC), pp. 91–99, September 2011

23. Gierlichs, B., Schmidt, J.-M., Tunstall, M.: Infective computation and dummy rounds: fault protection for block ciphers without check-before-output. In: Hevia, A., Neven, G. (eds.) LATINCRYPT 2012. LNCS, vol. 7533, pp. 305–321. Springer, Heidelberg (2012). https://doi.org/10.1007/978-3-642-33481-8_17

24. Lomné, V., Roche, T., Thillard, A.: On the need of randomness in fault attack countermeasures - application to AES. In: Bertoni, G., Gierlichs, B. (eds.) Fault Diagnosis and Tolerance in Cryptography, FDTC 2012, pp. 85–94. IEEE Computer Society (2012)

25. Battistello, A., Giraud, C.: Fault analysis of infective AES computations. In: 2013 Workshop on Fault Diagnosis and Tolerance in Cryptography (FDTC), pp. 101–107, August 2013

26. Moro, N., Heydemann, K., Encrenaz, E., Robisson, B.: Formal verification of a software countermeasure against instruction skip attacks. J. Cryptogr. Eng. **4**(3), 145–156 (2014). https://doi.org/10.1007/s13389-014-0077-7

27. Tupsamudre, H., Bisht, S., Mukhopadhyay, D.: Destroying fault invariant with randomization. In: Batina, L., Robshaw, M. (eds.) CHES 2014. LNCS, vol. 8731, pp. 93–111. Springer, Heidelberg (2014). https://doi.org/10.1007/978-3-662-44709-3_6

28. Banik, S., et al.: Midori: a block cipher for low energy. In: Iwata, T., Cheon, J.H. (eds.) ASIACRYPT 2015. LNCS, vol. 9453, pp. 411–436. Springer, Heidelberg (2015). https://doi.org/10.1007/978-3-662-48800-3_17

29. Breier, J., Jap, D. Bhasin, S.: The other side of the coin: analyzing software encoding schemes against fault injection attacks. In: 2016 IEEE International Symposium on Hardware Oriented Security and Trust, HOST 2016, McLean, VA, USA, 3–5 May 2016, pp. 209–216 (2016)

30. Goudarzi, D., Rivain, M.: How fast can higher-order masking be in software? In: Coron, J.-S., Nielsen, J.B. (eds.) EUROCRYPT 2017. LNCS, vol. 10210, pp. 567–597. Springer, Cham (2017). https://doi.org/10.1007/978-3-319-56620-7_20

31. Patranabis, S., Chakraborty, A., Mukhopadhyay, D.: Fault tolerant infective countermeasure for AES. J. Hardw. Syst. Secur. **1**(1), 3–17 (2017)

32. Zhang, J., Wu, N., Zhou, F., Ge, F., Zhang, X.: Securing the AES cryptographic circuit against both power and fault attacks. J. Electr. Eng. Technol. **14**(5), 2171–2180 (2019). https://doi.org/10.1007/s42835-019-00226-6

33. Murdock, K., Oswald, D., Garcia, F.D., Van Bulck, J., Gruss, D., Piessens, F.: Plundervolt: software-based fault injection attacks against Intel SGX. In: 41st IEEE Symposium on Security and Privacy (2020)

34. Gruber, M., et al.: DOMREP-an orthogonal countermeasure for arbitrary order side-channel and fault attack protection. IEEE Trans. Inf. Forensics Secur. **16**, 4321–4335 (2021)

Author Index

Printed in the United States
by Baker & Taylor Publisher Services